KU-499-844

LONGMAN

TOP POCKET ENGLISH DICTIONARY

Longman 

Longman Group UK Limited,
*Longman House, Burnt Mill,
Harlow, Essex CM20 2JE,
England
and Associated Companies
throughout the world*

© Longman Group UK
Limited 1989, 1990
All rights reserved; no part of this publication may be reproduced, stored in a retrieval system, or transmitted in any form, or by any means, electronic, mechanical, photocopying, recording, or otherwise, without the prior written permission of the Publishers.

*Set in Monophoto Nimrod
Printed in Great Britain
By Wm. Collins & Sons Ltd.,
Glasgow*

First published 1989
Expanded edition 1990
Second impression 1990

British Library Cataloguing in Publication Data
Longman top pocket English dictionary, – New ed –
1. English language – Dictionaries
423

ISBN 0–582–07637–4

Dictionary manager
Penny Stock

Lexicographers
John Ayto
Steve Curtis
Susan Engineer

Editors
Stephen Crowdy
Elizabeth Walter

Production and Design
Ken Brooks
Giles Davies
Clive McKeough
Geoff Sida

Guide to the Dictionary

main entries (words, abbreviations, prefixes and suffixes) in a single alphabetical list	**abeyance** *n fml* cessation of use **-able** *suffix* that can have the stated thing done to it: ***washable*** **ABM** *abbrev. for* antiballistic missile
alternative spellings and forms	**ageism, agism** *n* discrimination on grounds of age **antechamber** also **anteroom** *n* small room leading to a larger one
pronunciations shown when difficult or confusing	**aileron** /ˌaylərɔn/ *n* movable edge of an aircraft wing, giving control
part of speech	**Airedale** *n* large terrier with wiry black and tan coat
label showing when, where, or how a word is used	**airplane** *n AmE* aeroplane **albeit** /awlˈbee·it/ *conj fml* even though
irregular plurals of nouns and forms of verbs and adjectives	**alight**[1] *vi* **alighted** *or* **alit** get down; come down **alkali** *n* **-lis** *or* **-lies** substance that forms a chemical salt when combined with an acid **–line** *adj*
example phrases to illustrate usage or make meanings clearer	**allow for** *phr vt* to take into consideration: *We must allow for the train being late.*
lozenge symbol marking a different part of speech for the same word	**anger** *n* fierce displeasure ♦ *vt* make angry
word formed by adding an ending to a headword	**annex** *vt* take control of (esp. land) **~ation** *n*
word formed by changing the ending of a headword	**annihilate** /əˈnie·əˌlayt/ *vt* destroy completely **–lation** *n*

Pronunciation Guide

symbol	*pronounced as in*
a	bad
ah	father
aw	saw
ay	make
e	bed
ee	sheep
eə	hair
i	ship
ie	bite
ie-ə	fire
iə	here
o	pot
oh	note
onh	restaurant
oo	put
ooh	boot
ooə	cure
ow	now
owə	power
oy	boy
oyə	employer
u	cut
uh	bird
ə	about
ch	cheer
dh	they
g	gone
j	jump
kh	loch
ng	sing
s	soon
sh	fish
th	thing
y	yet
z	zero
zh	pleasure

b, d, f, h, k, l, m, n, p, r, t, v, w are pronounced as usual.

The mark ˈ goes before the syllable on which main stress falls: the mark ˌ goes before a syllable carrying minor stress.

Abbreviations Used in the Dictionary

abbrev.	abbreviation
adj	adjective
adv	adverb
AmE	American English
arch.	archaic
AustrE	Australian English
aux	auxiliary
BrE	British English
CanE	Canadian English
cap.	capital
conj	conjunction
derog	derogatory
e.g.	for example
esp.	especially
etc.	etcetera
euph	euphemistic
fml	formal
IndE	Indian English
infml	informal
interj	interjection
lit	literary
med	medical
n	noun
NZE	New Zealand English
p.	participle
phr v	phrasal verb
pl.	plural
prep	preposition
pres.	present
pron	pronoun
SAfrE	South African English
sing.	singular
sl	slang
t.	tense
tdmk	trademark
tech	technical
US	United States
usu.	usually
v	verb
vi	intransitive verb
vt	transitive verb
vi/t	intransitive/transitive verb

A

A, a the 1st letter of the English alphabet

a also (*before a vowel sound*) **an** *indefinite article, determiner* **1** one: *a doctor* **2** (before some words of quantity): *a few weeks* **3** for each: *6 times a day*

A1 *adj* **1** (of a ship) completely seaworthy **2** first-rate

AA *abbrev. for:* **1** Alcoholics Anonymous **2** Automobile Association

AAA *abbrev. for:* **1** *BrE* Amateur Athletics Association **2** *AmE* Automobile Association of America

aardvark *n* African mammal that feeds on ants and termites

AB *abbrev. for:* **1** able seaman **2** *AmE* Bachelor of Arts

aback *adv* **be taken aback** be suddenly shocked

abacus *n* frame with sliding balls on wires, used for counting

abaft *adv* towards or at the stern of a ship ♦ *prep* to the rear of; nearer to the stern than

abandon *vt* **1** leave completely **2** give up: *to abandon our search* **3** give (oneself) up completely to a feeling: *He abandoned himself to grief.* ♦ *n* freedom from inhibition **~ment** *n* **~ed** *adj* free from all restraint

abase *vt* make (esp. oneself) lose self-respect **~ment** *n*

abashed *adj* uncomfortable and ashamed

abate *vi/t* (cause to) become less fierce **~ment** *n*

abattoir *n BrE* slaughterhouse

abbess *n* woman who is the head of a convent

abbey *n* monastery or convent

abbot *n* man who is the head of a monastery

abbreviate *vt* make shorter **-ation** *n* short form of a word

ABC *n* **1** the alphabet as taught to children **2** the rudiments of a subject

ABC *abbrev. for:* **1** American Broadcasting Company **2** Australian Broadcasting Commission

abdicate *vi/t* give up (a position or right) officially **-cation** *n*

abdomen *n* part of the body containing the stomach **abdominal** *adj*

abduct *vt* take (a person) away illegally **~ion** *n*

abeam *adv, adj* at right angles to the length of a ship or aircraft

abecedarian *adj* **1** alphabetical **2** rudimentary ♦ *n* person learning the alphabet, or the rudiments of something

abed *adj, adv arch* in bed

aberration *n* change from a usual state **~ant** *adj*

abet *vt* **-tt-** *law* give help to (a crime or criminal) **~tor** *n*

abeyance *n fml* cessation of use

abhor *vt fml* hate very much **~rent** *adj* deeply disliked **~rence** *n*

abide *v* **abided** *or* **abode, abode 1** *vt* bear; tolerate: *I can't abide rudeness.* **2** *vi lit* remain; dwell **abide by** *phr vt* obey (laws, etc.)

abiding *adj* without end: *an abiding love*

ability *n* power; skill

-ability *suffix* capacity to act or be acted on in the stated way: *excitability*

abject *adj* **1** deserving great pity: *abject poverty* **2** without self-respect: *an abject apology* **~ly** *adv*

abjure *vt* renounce on oath

ablaze *adj* **1** on fire; burning **2** shining brightly

able *adj* **1** having the power to do something: *Will you be able to come?* **2** clever; skilled

-able *suffix* that can have the stated thing done to it: *washable*

able-bodied *adj* strong and healthy

able seaman *n* trained sailor in the British navy

ablutions *pl n fml* washing oneself

ably *adv* skilfully

ABM *abbrev. for:* antiballistic missile

abnegate *vt fml* surrender; renounce **-ation** *n*

abnormal *adj* not ordinary; unusual **~ly** *adv* **~ity** *n*

abo *n* **abos** *AustrE taboo* aborigine

aboard *adv, prep* on or onto (a ship, plane, etc.)

abode[1] *n* home

abode[2] *past t. and p. of* abide

abolish *vt* bring to an end by law **-ition** *n*

abominable *adj* hateful; very bad **-bly** *adv*

abominable snowman *n* yeti

abominate *vt* hate intensely **-ation** *n*

aboriginal *adj* (of people and living things) having lived in a place from the earliest times **aboriginal** *n*

aborigine /ˌabəˈrijinee/ *n* an aboriginal, esp. in Australia

abort *v* **1** *vt* cause (a child) to be born too soon for it to live **2** *vi/t* end before the expected time: *abort the space flight* **~ive** *adj* unsuccessful **~ion** *n* medical operation to abort a child **~ionist** *n* person who performs abortions

abound *vi* **1** exist in great quantity **2** be amply supplied

about-turn *n esp. BrE* change to the opposite position or opinion.
the streets **3** concerning: *She told us all about the stars.* **4** busy or concerned with: *While you're about it, make me a cup of tea too.* ♦ *adv* **1** around: *papers lying about* **2** somewhere near: *Is there anyone about?* **3** a little more or less than: *about 5 miles* **4** so as to face the other way **5 be about to** be going to: *We're about to leave.*

about-turn *n esp. BrE* change to the opposite position or opinion

above *prep* **1** higher than; over: *fly above the clouds* **2** more than **3** too good for: *He's not above stealing.* ♦ *adv* **1** higher: *the clouds above* **2** more: *aged 20 and above* **3** earlier in a book: *the facts mentioned above*

aboveboard *adj* without any attempt to deceive

above-mentioned *adj* referred to previously

abracadabra *interj* exclamation or magic word accompanying a conjuring trick

abrade *vt* rub away

abrasive *adj* **1** causing the rubbing away of a surface **2** rough and annoying: *an abrasive personality* ♦ *n* substance used to rub things smooth **-sion** *n* **1** rubbing away **2** grazed patch of skin

abreast *adv* **1** side by side **2 keep/be abreast of** know the most recent facts about

abridge *vt* make (a book, etc.) shorter

abridgment *n* something abridged: *an abridgment of the play for radio*

abroad *adv* to or in another country

abrogate *vt* put an end to officially **-tion** *n*

abrupt *adj* **1** sudden and unexpected **2** rough and impolite **~ly** *adv* **~ness** *n*

abscess *n* swelling on or in the body, containing pus

abscond *vi* go away suddenly because one has done something wrong

abseil /ˈapsiel/ *vi* descend a steep slope using a rope

absence *n* **1** (period of) being away: *absence from work* **2** non-existence: *the absence of information*

absent *adj* **1** not present **2** showing lack of attention: *an absent look* ♦ *vt* keep (oneself) away

absentee *n* person who is absent **absentee** *adj* **~ism** *n* absence from work

absentia *n* **in absentia** in a person's absence

absent-minded *adj* too concerned with one's thoughts to be aware of one's actions or surroundings **~ly** *adv* **~ness** *n*

absinthe *n* green liqueur with a bitter taste

absolute *adj* **1** complete; undoubted:

absolute nonsense **2** having unlimited power: *an absolute ruler* **3** not measured by comparison with other things **~ly** *adv* **1** completely **2** (used to express agreement) certainly

absolution *n* act of absolving, esp. declaration of forgiveness by a priest

absolutism *n* government by an absolute ruler

absolve *vt* free (someone) from fulfilling a promise, or from punishment

absorb *vt* **1** take in (esp. liquids, heat, or sound) **2** fill the attention of: *I was absorbed in a book.* **~ent** *adj* able to absorb e.g. liquids **~ing** *adj* interesting **absorption** *n*

abstain *vi* **1** refrain from (esp. drinking) **2** withhold one's vote **~er** *n*

abstemious /əbˈsteemi·əs/ *adj* not allowing oneself much food or drink

abstention *n* act of abstaining, esp. from voting

abstinence *n* abstaining, esp. from alcoholic drink

abstract *adj* **1** existing as a quality or concept rather than as something real or solid: *Beauty is abstract but a house is not.* **2** general rather than particular: *an abstract discussion of crime, without reference to actual cases* **3** (in art) not realistic ♦ *n* **1** abstract work of art **2** short form of a document ♦ *vt* **1** remove **2** summarize **~ed** *adj* absent-minded **~ion** *n*

abstruse *adj* difficult to understand

absurd *adj* unreasonable; (funny because) false or foolish **~ly** *adv* **~ity** *n*

abundant *adj* more than enough **~ly** *adv* **-dance** *n*

abuse *vt* **1** say bad things to or about **2** use badly: *abuse one's power* ♦ *n* **1** cruel or rude words **2** wrong use: *the abuse of drugs* **abusive** *adj* using cruel or rude words

abutment *n* support on which a bridge or arch rests

abut on *phr vt* **-tt-** lie next to

abysmal /əˈbizməl/ *adj* very bad **~ly** *adv*

abyss *n* great hole that seems bottomless

AC *abbrev. for:* alternating current

a/c *abbrev. for:* account

acacia *n* **-cias** *or* **-cia** tropical tree from which gum is obtained

academic *adj* **1** about schools and education **2** not related to practical situations: *a purely academic question* ♦ *n* **1** university teacher **2** someone who values skills of the mind more than practical ones **~ally** *adv*

academician *n* member of an academy

academy *n* **1** society of people interested in the advancement of art, science, or literature **2** school for training in a special skill: *a military academy*

Academy Award *n* Oscar

acanthus *n* **1** Mediterranean ornamental shrub **2** ornamental carving in the shape of acanthus leaves

accede *vi fml* **1** agree to a demand, etc. **2** enter high office

accelerate *vi/t* (cause to) move faster **-ration** *n*

accelerator *n* **1** instrument in a car, etc., that is used to increase its speed **2** device that makes subatomic particles move at a very high speed

accent *n* **1** particular way of speaking, usu. connected with a place or a social class **2** mark written over or under a letter, such as that on the 'e' of 'café' **3** stress placed on a word, syllable, or note of music ♦ *vt* pronounce with added force

accentuate *vt* direct attention to; give importance to

accept *v* **1** *vi/t* receive (something offered), esp. willingly **2** *vt* believe or agree to: *Did she accept your reasons for being late?* **~able** *adj* good enough; worth accepting: *an acceptable gift* **~ance** *n*

access *n* **1** way in; entrance **2** means of using or getting something: *Students need access to books.* ♦ *vt* obtain (stored information) from a computer's memory **~ible** *adj* easy to get or get to **~ibility** *n*

accession *n* coming to a high position: *the Queen's accession to the throne*
accessory *n* **1** thing that is added but is not a necessary part: *car accessories such as a radio* **2** also **accessary** *law* person who is not present at a crime but who helps in doing it **accessory** *adj*
access time *n* time taken by a computer to find and use a piece of information in its memory
accidence *n* part of grammar dealing with inflections
accident *n* **1** something, (esp. unpleasant)that happens unexpectedly **2** chance: *more by accident than design* **~al** *adj* **~ally** *adv*
accidental *n* a sharp or flat occurring in a piece of music which is not provided for in the key signature
accident-prone *adj* more liable to have accidents than most people
acclaim *vt* greet with public approval **acclaim** *n* **acclamation** *n* expressions of approval
acclimatize *vi/t* make or get used to the weather in a new place **-tization** *n*
acclivity *n* ascending slope
accolade *n* strong praise
accommodate *vt fml* **1** provide with a place to live in **2** help by making changes: *to accommodate your wishes* **-dating** *adj* helpful **-dation** *n* place to live; room, house, etc.
accompaniment *n* **1** something which is used or provided with something else **2** music played at the same time as singing or another instrument
accompanist *n* player of a musical accompaniment
accompany *vt* **1** go with, as on a journey **2** happen at the same time as: *Lightning usually accompanies thunder.* **3** play a musical accompaniment to
accomplice *n* person who helps someone to do wrong
accomplish *vt* succeed in doing **~ed** *adj* skilled **~ment** *n* **1** something one is skilled at **2** act of accomplishing something
accord *v* **1** *vi* agree: *That does not accord with your previous statement.* **2** *vt* grant ♦ *n* **1** agreement; harmony **2 of one's own accord** without being asked; willingly
accordance *n* **in accordance with** in a way that agrees with
according as *conj fml* depending on whether
accordingly *adv* **1** appropriately **2** therefore
according to *prep* **1** as declared by: *According to my watch, it's 4 o'clock.* **2** in a way that agrees with: *paid according to the amount of work done*
accordion *n* musical instrument played by compressing the middle part to force air through holes controlled by keys worked by the fingers
accost *vt* go up and speak to (esp. a stranger), often threateningly
account *n* **1** report; description: *give an account of what happened* **2** record of money received and paid out **3** money kept in a bank or building society **4** arrangement of credit **5** advantage; profit: *He turned his knowledge to good account.* **6 on account of** because of **7 on no account/not on any account** not for any reason **8 take into account/take account of** give thought to; consider
account for *phr vt* **1** give or be an explanation for **2** give a statement showing how money has been spent
accountable *adj* responsible **-bility** *n*
accountancy, accounting *n* work of an accountant
accountant *n* person who controls and examines money accounts
accoutrements /əˈkoohtrəməntz/ *pl n* also *AmE* **accouterment** equipment, esp. for a soldier
accredited *adj* **1** officially representing one's government in a foreign country **2** having the power to act for an organization **3** officially recognized as reaching a certain standard or quality **accreditation** *n*
accretion *n* **1** increase in size **2** something added **3** growth of separate parts

(e.g. of a plant) into one **accrete** *v*
accrue *vi* come as an increase or advantage
accumulate *vi/t* make or become greater; collect into a mass **–lation** *n* **–lative** *adj*
accumulator *n* **1** part of a computer where numbers are stored **2** rechargeable battery **3** series of racing bets in which any winnings are staked on the next race
accuracy *n* being accurate; exactness
accurate *adj* exactly correct **~ly** *adv*
accursed *adj* **1** *lit* under a curse **2** (used for expressing one's annoyance with something)
accusation *n* (statement) accusing someone of something
accusative *adj, n* (being) the form of a noun, pronoun or adjective which shows that it is used as, or with, the direct object of a sentence
accuse *vt* charge (someone) with doing wrong **accuser** *n* **accusingly** *adv*
accustom *vt* make used (to) **accustomed** *adj* **1** usual **2** in the habit of
AC/DC *adj sl* bisexual
ace *n* **1** playing card with one mark or spot on it **2** person of the highest skill **3** (in tennis) very fast and strong serve that the opponent cannot hit back ♦ *adj infml* very good or very skilled ♦ *vt* score an ace against
acerbic /əˈsuhbik/ *adj* **1** sour in taste **2** (of a person or manner) clever in a rather cruel way **–ity** *n*
acetate *n* chemical made from acetic acid
acetic *adj* of or producing acetic acid or vinegar
acetic acid *n* major acid in vinegar
acetylene /əˈsetileen/ *n* gas used esp. as fuel
ache *vi* have a continuous dull pain **ache** *n*
achieve *vt* **1** finish successfully **2** get by effort: *achieve results* **~ment** *n* **1** successful finishing of something **2** something achieved
Achilles' heel /əˈkileez/ *n* small but important weakness
Achilles tendon *n* tendon joining the calf muscles to the heelbone
acid *adj* sour; bitter ♦ *n* **1** chemical substance containing hydrogen **2** *sl* the drug LSD **~ic** *adj* **1** acid **2** acid-forming **~ity** *vt* make or convert into acid **~ity** *n* acid taste or quality
acid rain *n* rain containing harmful quantities of acid as a result of industrial pollution
acid test *n* test of the value of something
acidulous *adj lit* caustic (2)
ack-ack *adj, n* antiaircraft (fire)
acknowledge *vt* **1** admit; recognize as a fact **2** show one is grateful for **3** state that one has received: *acknowledge a letter* **4** show that one recognizes (someone) **–edgment, -edgement** *n*
acme /ˈakmi/ *n* highest point; best example
acne *n* skin disorder common among young people, in which spots appear on the face and neck
acolyte *n* **1** assistant of a priest **2** follower
acorn *n* nut of the oak tree
acoustics *pl n* **1** scientific study of sound **2** qualities that make a place good or bad for hearing in **acoustic** *adj*
acquaint *vt* **1 acquaint someone with** tell; make known to **2 be acquainted (with)** have met socially; know **~ance** *n* **1** person whom one knows slightly **2** knowledge gained through experience
acquiesce *vi* agree, often unwillingly **–escent** *adj* **–escence** *n*
acquire *vt* gain; come to possess
acquisition *n* **1** act of acquiring **2** something acquired **–tive** *adj* in the habit of acquiring things **–tively** *adv* **–tiveness** *n*
acquit *vt* **-tt- 1** decide that (someone) is not guilty: *The jury acquitted him (of murder).* **2** conduct (oneself) in the stated way: *He acquitted himself rather badly.* **~tal** *n* release from a criminal charge
acre *n* a measure of land equal to 4,840 square yards

acreage *n* area measured in acres
acrid *adj* (of taste or smell) bitter; stinging
acrimony *n* bitterness of manner or language **–nious** *adj* **–niously** *adv*
acrobat *n* person who performs skilled gymnastic feats **~ic** *adj* **~ics** *n*
acronym *n* word made from the first letters of a name, such as NATO
across *adv, prep* from one side to the other; on or to the other side (of)
across-the-board *adj* influencing or having effects on people or things of all types or at every level **across-the-board** *adv*
acrylic *n* chemical used in making paints and synthetic fibre
act *v* **1** *vi* do something: *She acted on my suggestion.* **2** *vi/t* perform in a play or film **3** *vi* produce an effect: *Does the drug take long to act?* **act up** *phr vi* behave badly **act out** *phr vt* express (e.g. feelings) in behaviour ♦ *n* **1** something that one has done; an action of a particular kind: *an act of terrorism* **2** law made by parliament **3** main division of a stage play **4** short event in a stage or circus performance **5** example of insincere behaviour used for effect: *She was just putting on an act.*
acting *adj* appointed to do the duties of a position for a short time ♦ *n* art of performing in a play
action *n* **1** process of doing something **2** something done: *Her prompt action saved his life.* **3** way something works **4** effect: *the action of light on photographic film* **5** military fighting or a fight **6** main events in a book or play: *The action takes place in Italy.* **7** *law* legal charge of guilt: *bring an action against him* ♦ *vt* take action on **~able** *adj* giving grounds for legal action
action painting *n* (product of) a form of painting in which the artist applies his colours by e.g. dribbling, smearing or throwing them onto the canvas
action stations *interj* (an order to soldiers, sailors etc. to get ready for battle)
activate *vt* make active **–ation** *n*
active *adj* **1** doing things; able to take action **2** marked by vigorous activity **~ly** *adv*
activist *n* person taking an active part in politics **~ism** *n* belief in vigorous political activity
activity *n* **1** movement or action: *political activity* **2** something done, esp. for interest or pleasure: *leisure activities*
act of God *n* an unpredictable and unpreventable event, esp. a natural catastrophe
actor *n* person who acts in a play or film
actress *n* female actor
actual *adj* existing as a fact; real **~ly** *adv* **1** in fact; really **2** (showing surprise): *He actually offered me a drink!* **~ity** *n* real fact
actuary *n* statistician who calculates insurance risks **-rial** *adj*
actuate *vt* **1** put into action **2** rouse to action
acuity /ə'kyooh·əti/ *n* keenness of perception
acumen /'akyoomən/ *n* ability to judge quickly
acupuncture *n* method of curing diseases by putting special needles into certain parts of the body
acute *adj* **1** severe; very great: *acute shortage of water* **2** (of the mind or senses) working very well **3** (of an angle) less than 90° **4** (of a mark) put above a letter, e.g. é, to show pronunciation **~ly** *adv* **~ness** *n*
ad *n infml* advertisement
AD (in the year) since the birth of Christ: *in 1066 AD*
adage /'adij/ *n* proverb
adagio , **-ios** *n, adj, adv* (piece of music) in a slow, graceful manner
adamant *adj* refusing to change one's mind ♦ *n* a very hard stone **~ly** *adv*
Adam's apple *n* lump at the front of the throat that moves when one talks or swallows
adapt *vt* make suitable for new conditions **~able** *adj* able to change

~ability *n* **~ation** *n* act of adapting: *an adaptation of the play for radio*
adapter **, -or** *n* **1** person who adapts **2** electrical plug allowing more than one piece of equipment to run from the same socket
ADC *abbrev. for:* **1** aide-de-camp **2** analogue-digital converter
add *v* **1** *vt* put with something else: *add a name to the list* **2** *vi/t* join (numbers) together **3** *vt* say also **add up** *phr vi* make sense; seem likely: *The facts just don't add up.*
addendum *n* **-da** addition to a book
adder *n* small poisonous snake
addict *n* person who cannot stop a harmful habit **~ion** *n* **~ive** *adj* habit forming
addicted *adj* dependent on something, esp. a drug
addition *n* **1** act of adding **2** something added **3 in addition (to)** as well (as) **~al** *adj* as well; added **~ally** *adv* also
additive *n* substance, esp. a chemical one, added to something else
addled *adj* **1** (of someone's brain) confused **2** (of an egg) rotten
add-on *n* piece of equipment connected to a computer that increases its usefulness
address *n* **1** identification of the place where someone lives **2** speech made to a group of people ♦ *vt* **1** write a name and address on **2** direct a speech to: *She addressed the crowd.*
adduce *vt* provide by way of explanation, illustration etc.
adenoids *pl n* mass of tissue between the back of the nose and the throat **–oidal** *adj* of (swollen) adenoids
adept *adj* highly skilled ♦ *n* person who is adept at something
adequate *adj* enough; good enough **~ly** *adv* **–quacy** *n*
adhere *vi* stick firmly, as with glue **adhere to** *phr vt* remain loyal to **adherence** *n* **adherent** *n* loyal supporter of something
adhesive *n, adj* (a substance such as glue) that can stick **–sion** *n*
ad hoc *adj* made to fill an immediate need
adieu *n* **–s** *or* **–x** *lit* farewell
ad infinitum *adv, adj* without end
adipose *adj* fatty **–sity** *n*
adj *abbrev. for:* adjective
adjacent *adj* very close
adjective *n* word which describes a noun, such as *black* in *a black hat* **–tival** *adj*
adjoin *vi/t* be next to (one another) **~ing** *adj*
adjourn *vi/t* stop (e.g. a meeting) for a while **~ment** *n*
adjudge *vt* **1** pronounce (2) **2** deem
adjudicate *vi/t* act as a judge; decide about **–cator** *n* **–cation** *n* **–cative** *adj*
adjunct *n* something added without being a necessary part
adjust *vi/t* change slightly so as to make right **~able** *adj* **~ment** *n*
adjutant *n* officer who assists a commanding officer
ad lib *adv* without preparation **ad-lib** *vi* **-bb-** invent and say without preparation **ad-lib** *adj*
adman *n infml* person who works in advertising
administer *vt* **1** manage **2** give: *administer medicine*
administration *n* **1** management or direction of the affairs esp. of a business or government **2** *esp. AmE* national government: *the Reagan Administration* **3** act of administering **–trative** *adj* **–trator** *n* **–trate** *vi/t*
admirable *adj* very good **–bly** *adv*
admiral *n* naval officer of high rank **~ty** *n*
admire *vt* regard with pleasure; have a good opinion of **admiring** *adj* **admirer** *n* **admiration** *n* feeling of pleasure and respect
admissible *adj* that can be accepted or considered
admission *n* **1** being allowed to enter a building, join a club, etc. **2** cost of entrance: *Admission £1* **3** statement admitting something
admit *vt* **-tt- 1** allow to enter; let in **2**

agree to the truth of (esp. reluctantly) **~tance** *n* right to enter **~tedly** *adv* it must be agreed that
admixture *n* (mixing in of) an ingredient
admonish *vt* scold gently; warn **-ition** *n* **-itory** *adj*
ad nauseam *adv* repeatedly and to an annoying degree
ado *n* fuss
adobe /əˈdohbi/ *n* (brick made of) heavy clay
adolescent *adj, n* (of) a boy or girl who is growing up **-cence** *n*
adopt *vt* **1** take (someone else's child) into one's family for ever **2** take and use **3** vote to accept **~ive** *adj* having adopted a child **~ion** *n*
adore *vt* **1** love and respect deeply; worship **2** like very much **adorable** very lovable **adoring** *adj* loving **adoration** *n*
adorn *vt* add beauty to; decorate **~ment** *n*
adrenalin *n* stimulating hormone released during anger, excitement, or fright
adrift *adv, adj* (of boats) floating loose; not fastened
adroit *adj* quick and skilful **~ly** *adv* **~ness** *n*
adulation *n* excessive praise or admiration
adult *adj, n* (of) a fully grown person or animal **~hood** *n*
adulterate *vt* make impure by adding something of lower quality **-ant** *n* **-ation** *n*
adultery *n* sexual relations between a married person and someone outside the marriage **adulterer, adulteress** *n* **-terous** *adj*
adumbrate *vt* foreshadow
adv *abbrev. for:* adverb
advance *vi/t* go or bring forward in position, development, etc. ♦ *n* **1** forward movement or development **2** money provided before the proper time **3** **in advance** beforehand ♦ *adj* coming before the usual time **~s** *pl n* efforts to become friends with someone **advanced** *adj* **1** far on in development **2** modern **~ment** *n* promotion
Advanced level *n* higher examination in secondary education
advantage *n* **1** something that may help one to be successful **2** profit; gain **3** **take advantage of: a** make use of somebody, as by deceiving them **b** profit from **~ous** *adj* **~ously** *adv*
advent *n* **1** coming **2** (*cap.*) the four weeks before Christmas
Advent calendar *n* large card, usu. depicting a winter or Christmas scene, in which there are little numbered windows to be opened successively on the days of Advent, or from December 1st, each window disclosing a figure or scene connected with Christmas
adventitious *adj* occurring by chance **~ly** *adv*
adventure *n* **1** exciting and perhaps dangerous experience **2** excitement; risk ♦ *vi/t* risk (one's safety) **-turer** *n* **1** person who has or looks for adventures **2** person who hopes to make a profit by taking risks **-turous** *adj* **1** also *AmE* **adventuresome** fond of adventure 2 exciting **-turously** *adv*
adverb *n* word which adds to the meaning of a verb, an adjective, another adverb, or a sentence, for example *slowly, tomorrow*, and *here* **~ial** *n, adj*
adversary *n* opponent **-sarial** *adj*
adverse *adj* unfavourable **~ly** *adv*
adversity *n* trouble
advertise *vi/t* make (something for sale) known to people, e.g. in a newspaper **-tiser** *n* **-tising** *n* business of doing this **~ment** also *infml* **ad, advert** *n* notice of something for sale
advert to *phr vt fml* mention
advice *n* opinion given to someone about what to do
advise *vt* **1** give advice to **2** *fml* inform: *Please advise me of the cost.* **3** **well-advised/ill-advised** wise/unwise **advisory** giving advice **adviser** also *AmE* **advisor** *n* **advisable** *adj* sensible; wise **advisedly** *adv* **1** wisely; after careful thought **2** purposely

advocate *n* person, esp. lawyer, who speaks in defence of a person or idea **advocate** *vt* **-cacy** *n*
adze also *AmE* **adz** *n* tool for shaping wood
aegis /ˈeejis/ *n* protection or support
aeon /ˈee·ən/ *n* **1** immeasurably long time **2** 1000 million years
aerate *vt* add gas to
aerial *n* receiver for radio or television signals ♦ *adj* in or from the air: *aerial photography*
aerobatics *n* acrobatic tricks done in an aircraft **aerobatic** *adj*
aerobics *n* active physical exercise done to strengthen the heart and lungs
aerodrome *n esp. BrE* small airport
aerodynamics *n* science of movement through the air **aerodynamic** *adj* **1** concerning aerodynamics **2** using the principles of aerodynamics
aerogramme *n* air letter
aeronautics *n* science of the flight of aircraft
aeroplane *n AmE* **airplane** *n* flying vehicle with wings and one or more engines
aerosol *n* pressurized container for dispersing liquid in a fine mist
aerospace *n* (science or industry concerned with) the air around the Earth and space beyond it **aerospace** *adj*
aesthetics, also *AmE* **es-** *n* science of beauty, esp. in art **aesthetic** *adj* **-ically** *adv* **aesthete** *n* person who professes concern with beauty and art
aetiology, also *AmE* **et-** *n* (study of) the causes of something, esp. a disease
afar *adv, n* (at) a great distance
affable *adj* friendly and pleasant **-bly** *adv* **-bility** *n*
affair *n* **1** event; set of events **2** something to be done; business **3** sexual relationship outside marriage
affect *vt* **1** cause a change in; influence: *Smoking affects your health.* **2** feign: *She affected boredom.* **~ed** *adj* not natural; pretended **~edly** *adv* **~ation** *n* unnatural behaviour
affection *n* gentle, lasting fondness **~ate** *adj* **~ately** *adv*
affiance *vt* betroth
affidavit *n law* written statement for use as proof
affiliate *vi/t* (esp. of a group) join to a larger group **-ation** *n*
affinity *n* **1** close connection or liking **2** chemical attraction
affirm *vt* declare; state **~ative** *n, adj* (statement) meaning 'yes' **~ation** *n*
affirmative action *n* positive discrimination
affix *vt* fix; fasten ♦ *n* group of letters added to the beginning or end of a word to change its meaning or use (as in '*un*tie', 'kind*ness*')
afflict *vt* cause to suffer; trouble **~ion** *n fml*
affluent *adj* wealthy; rich **-ence** *n*
afford *vt* **1** be able to pay for **2** be able to risk: *I can't afford to neglect my health.*
afforest *vt* plant with trees **~ation** *n*
affray *n* brawl
affront *vt* be rude to; offend **affront** *n*
Afghan *n* **1** (language of) an inhabitant of Afghanistan **2** knitted or crocheted shawl **3** tall slim hunting dog **Afghan** *adj*
aficionado /əˌfishyəˈnahdoh/ *n* **-dos** someone who is keenly interested in a particular activity or subject
afield *adv* **far afield** far away
AFL-CIO *n* American Federation of Labor and Congress of Industrial Organizations; an association of American trade unions
afloat *adv, adj* **1** floating **2** on a ship **3** out of debt
afoot *adv, adj* being prepared; happening
aforesaid *adj* said or named before
afraid *adj* **1** frightened: *afraid of the dark* **2** sorry (used to apologize) *'Are we late?' 'I'm afraid so.'*
afresh *adv* again
African *n, adj* (inhabitant) of Africa
African violet *n* small houseplant with hairy leaves and purple, white or pink flowers

Afrikaaner , **Afrikaner** *n* white South African of Dutch descent
Afrikaans *n* language of South Africa derived from Dutch
Afro *adj, n* (in or for) a bushy, curly hairstyle
Afro- *prefix* **1** of Africa: *Afro-American* **2** African and: *Afro-Asian*
aft *adv* near, towards, or in the back of a ship or aircraft
after *prep, conj* **1** later than: *after breakfast* **2** following: *Your name comes after mine in the list.* **3** because of: *After what he did I don't want to see him.* **4** in spite of: *After I packed it so carefully, the clock arrived broken.* **5** looking for: *The police are after him.* **6** *fml* in the style of: *a painting after Rembrandt* **7 after all** in spite of everything ♦ *adv* later; afterwards
afterbirth *n* placenta and foetal membranes discharged from the womb after birth
afterburner *n* **1** device for giving extra thrust in a jet engine **2** device for removing dangerous gases from vehicle exhaust fumes
aftercare *n* **1** treatment given to a patient after a serious illness or operation **2** welfare services for people discharged from hospital, prison, etc.
aftereffect *n* effect (usu. unpleasant) that follows some time after the cause
afterglow *n* **1** light remaining e.g. in the sky after sunset **2** pleasant feeling left by a happy event
afterlife *n* existence after death
aftermath *n* period following a bad event: *the aftermath of the war*
afternoon *n* time between midday and sunset
afters *pl n BrE infml* dessert
aftershave *n* usu. scented lotion to put on the face after shaving
aftertaste *n* (unpleasant) taste left behind after eating or drinking something
afterthought *n* idea that comes later; something added later
afterwards *adv* later; after that
again *adv* **1** once more; another time: *Say it again.* **2** back to the original place or condition: *He's home again now.* **3** besides; further: *I could eat as much again.*
against *prep* **1** in the direction of and meeting or touching: *The rain beat against the windows.* **2** in opposition to: *Stealing is against the law.* *3* as a protection from: *They were vaccinated against cholera.* **4** having as a background: *The picture looks good against that red wall.* ♦ *adj* **1** opposed **2** (esp. of odds in betting) unfavourable
agape[1] *adj* gaping
agape[2] *n* **1** Christian love **2** communal meal shared by early Christians
agar , **agar-agar** *n* gelatinous extract of seaweed used as a culture for bacteria, a laxative or a thickening agent
agate *n* coloured quartz gemstone
age *n* **1** length of time someone has lived or something has existed **2** one of the periods of human life: *old age* **3** period of history: *This is the nuclear age.* **4** long time: *We haven't met for ages.* **5 of age** old enough (usu. at 18 or 21) to be responsible in law for one's own actions ♦ *vi/t* make or become old **aged** *adj* **1** of the stated number of years: *a boy aged 10* **2** very old: *an aged man* **ageless** *adj* **1** eternal **2** showing no signs of age
-age *suffix* **1** action or result of doing the stated thing: *shrinkage* **2** cost of doing the stated thing: *postage* **3** state or rank of: *peerage*
ageism , **agism** *n* discrimination on grounds of age **ageist** *adj, n*
agency *n* **1** work or business of an agent: *an employment agency* **2** *fml* power that achieves a result: *a supernatural agency*
agenda *n* **-das** list of things to be talked about at a meeting
agent *n* **1** person who does business for other people: *An estate agent sells houses.* **2** person or thing that produces a result: *Soap is a cleansing agent.*
agent provocateur *n* **agents**

provocateurs person planted by the authorities amongst e.g. revolutionaries or criminals to incite them to take illegal action which will lead to their arrest

agglomerate *n* **1** irregular mass **2** rock made up of volcanic fragments ♦ *vi/t* (cause to) form a mass ♦ *adj* gathered into a mass

agglutinate *vt* stick together **–ation** *n*

aggrandizement, –disement /əˈgrandizmənt/ *n* increase size, power, or rank **aggrandize, –ise** *v*

aggravate *vt* **1** make worse **2** annoy: *an aggravating delay* **–vation** *n*

aggregate *n* **1** total **2** rock composed of crystals **3** sand or gravel for making concrete ♦ *vt* bring together into a whole ♦ *adj* formed of units making a whole

aggression *n* starting a quarrel or war without just cause **–sor** *n* person or country that does this

aggressive *adj* **1** always ready to attack **2** brave and determined

aggrieved *adj* showing hurt feelings

aggro *n esp. BrE infml* aggression; violence

aghast *adj* surprised and shocked

agile *adj* able to move quickly **agility** *n*

agitate *v* **1** *vt* shake (a liquid) **2** *vt* make anxious; worry **3** *vi* argue strongly in public **–tator** *n* person who agitates for political or social change **–tation** *n*

aglow *adj* bright with colour or excitement

AGM *abbrev. for:* annual general meeting; meeting of an organization held once a year to elect officials and report on the year's business.

agnostic *n, adj* (person) believing that nothing can be known about God **~ism** *n*

Agnus Dei *n* liturgical prayer (O lamb of God) often set to music

ago *adj, adv* back in time from now: *a week ago*

agog *adj* excited and eager

agonize , -ise *vi* **1** make a long and anxious effort **2** feel distress **–nized** *adj* expressing great pain **–nizing** *adj* causing great pain

agony *n* great suffering

agony aunt *n BrE* woman who gives advice on personal problems of readers in a part of a newspaper or magazine (an **agony column**)

agoraphobia *n* fear of open spaces **–phobic** *adj*

AGR *abbrev. for:* advanced gas-cooled reactor

agrarian *adj* of land, esp. farmland

agree *v* **1** *vi/t* share the same opinion; say 'yes': *I agree with you.* **2** *vi* (of statements, etc.) be the same; match **agree with** *phr vt* **1** suit the health of **2** be in accordance with **~able** *adj* pleasant **~ably** *adv* **~ment** *n* **1** state of agreeing: *The two sides reached agreement.* **2** arrangement between people or groups: *to break an agreement*

agriculture *n* farming **–tural** *adj*

agronomy *n* science of managing soil and growing crops **–mic** *adj* **–mist** *n*

aground *adv, adj* (of a ship) on or onto the shore or bottom of a body of water

ague *n lit* fever

ahead *adv, adj* **1** in front **2** into the future: *to plan ahead* **3** in advance: *to get ahead of our rivals*

ahoy *interj* (shout of greeting between sailors or from one ship to another)

AI *n* artificial intelligence

aid *n* **1** help: *She came to my aid at once.* **2** person or thing that helps: *an aid in learning a language* ♦ *vt* help

aide *n* person who helps

aide-de-camp *n* assistant of senior military officer

aide-mémoire *n* **aides-mémoire** something serving as a reminder

AIDS, Aids *n* Acquired Immune Deficiency Syndrome; very serious disease caused by a virus which breaks down the body's natural defences against infection

ail *v* **1** *vt* give pain to **2** *vi* be ill: *an ailing child* **~ment** *n* illness

aileron /ˌaylərɒn/ *n* movable edge of an

aircraft wing, giving control

aim *v* **1** *vi/t* point (esp. a weapon) towards **2** *vi* direct one's efforts; intend: *I aim to be a writer.* ♦ *n* **1** act of directing a shot **2** desired result; purpose: *What is your aim in life?* **~less** *adj* without purpose

ain't *short for:* am not, is not, are not, has not, or have not

air *n* **1** mixture of gases that we breathe **2** space above the ground: *travel by air* **3** general character of a person or place: *an air of excitement at the meeting* **4** tune **5 in the air: a** (of talk) being passed on from one person to another **b** uncertain **6 on/off the air** broadcasting/not broadcasting ♦ *v* **1** *vi/t* dry (clothes) in a warm place **2** *vi/t* make or become fresh by letting in air: *to air the room* **3** *vt* let people know: *He's always airing his opinions.* **4** *vt* broadcast **airing** *n*

airs *pl n* conceited behaviour

airbase *n* military airport

airborne *adj* **1** carried by the air **2** (of aircraft) flying

air brake *n* **1** brake worked by compressed air **2** drag for slowing an aircraft

airbrush *vt, n* (paint using) a fine spray driven by compressed air

airbus *n* aircraft carrying many passengers on short flights

air-conditioning *n* system using machines (**air-conditioners**) to control the indoor air temperature **-tioned** *adj*

air-cool *vt* cool (the cylinders of an internal-combustion engine) by the flow of air

aircraft *n* **-craft** flying machine

aircraft carrier *n* warship that carries aircraft

Airedale *n* large terrier with wiry black and tan coat

airfield *n* place where aircraft can land

airforce *n* branch of a country's military forces that fights in the air

airframe *n* body of an aircraft excluding its engines

air gun *n* gun or hand tool using power of compressed air

airhostess *n* woman who looks after passengers in an aircraft

airily *adv* in a light airy manner

airlane *n* route regularly followed by aircraft

air letter *n* prestamped sheet of thin paper which, when written on, is folded, sealed and sent by airmail

airlift *n* transport of people or supplies by aircraft, esp. to a place that is difficult to get to **airlift** *vt*

airline *n* business that carries passengers and goods by air

airliner *n* large passenger aircraft

airlock *n* **1** bubble (e.g. in a tube) that prevents the flow of liquid **2** airtight space or room

airmail *n* system of sending letters, etc., by air

airplane *n AmE* aeroplane

air pocket *n* area of low-density or descending air which causes an aircraft to drop suddenly

airport *n* place where aircraft regularly land

air raid *n* attack by military aircraft

airship *n* lighter-than-air aircraft with an engine but no wings

airsick *adj* feeling nauseous because of the motion of an aircraft

airspace *n* sky above a country, regarded as that country's property

airstrip *n* piece of ground where aircraft can land if necessary

airtight *adj* not letting air in or out

air-to-air *adj* to be fired from one aircraft to another

airway *n* airline

airworthy *adj* (of an aircraft) in safe working condition **-thiness** *n*

airy *adj* **1** open to the fresh air **2** not practical: *airy notions* **3** cheerful and careless

aisle *n* passage between seats in a public building

ajar *adv, adj* (of a door) slightly open

aka *abbrev. for:* also known as

akimbo *adj, adv* (of the arms) bent at the elbows and with the hands on the hips

akin *adj* like; similar
-al *suffix* **1** connected with: *autumnal* **2** (an) act of doing something: *arrival*
à la *prep* in the manner of; like: *à la James Bond*
alabaster *adj, n* (of or like) a fine usu. white translucent stone
à la carte *adj, adv* according to a menu that prices each item separately
alack *interj arch* alas
alacrity *n fml* quick and willing readiness
à la mode *adv* **1** in the latest fashion **2** *AmE* served with ice cream
alarm *n* **1** warning of danger **2** sudden fear **3** apparatus that gives a warning: *a burglar alarm* **4** clock that gives a time signal ♦ *vt* frighten: *alarming news* **~ist** *n* person who arouses unnecessary fear **~ist** *adj*
alas *interj* (cry expressing sorrow)
Albanian *n, adj* (inhabitant or language) of Albania
albatross *n* large, powerful sea bird
albeit /awlˈbee·it/ *conj fml* even though
albino *n* person or animal with white skin, very light hair, and pink eyes
album *n* **1** book for holding a collection (e.g. of photographs) **2** long-playing record
albumen *n* white of egg
alchemy *n* former science concerned with turning metals into gold **–mist** *n* **–mical** *adj*
alcohol *n* (drinks containing) the liquid that makes one drunk **~ism** *n* diseased condition caused by the continued drinking of too much alcohol **~ic** *adj* **~ic** *n* person addicted to alcohol
alcove *n* small partly enclosed space in a room
al dente *adj* (of pasta and vegetables) cooked just enough to be still firm when bitten
alder *n* tree of the birch family
alderman *n* (formerly) a senior member of a county or borough council
ale *n* kind of beer
alert *adj* quick to see and ask; watchful ♦ *n* **1** warning of danger **2 on the alert** ready to deal with danger ♦ *vt* warn
A level *abbrev. for:* Advanced level
alexandrine *n* line of verse consisting of six iambic feet
alfalfa *n AmE* lucerne
alfresco *adj, adv* in the open air
algae /ˈalji/ *pl n* very small plants that live in or near water **algal** *adj*
algebra *n* branch of mathematics using letters to represent values **–braic** *adj*
Algerian *n, adj* (inhabitant) of Algeria
algorithm *n* step-by-step procedure for solving a problem **~ic** *adj*
alias *n* **-ases** false name used esp. by a criminal ♦ *adv* also called: *Edward Ball, alias John Smith*
alibi *n* proof that a person charged with a crime was somewhere else when it happened
alien *n* **1** foreigner who has not become a citizen of the country where he lives **2** (in films and stories) a creature from another world ♦ *adj* **1** foreign **2** different and strange
alienate *vt* make unfriendly **–ation** *n* **–able** *adj* transferable
alienist *n AmE* psychiatrist specializing in the legal aspects of mental illness
alight[1] *vi* **alighted** *or* **alit** *fml* get down; come down
alight[2] *adj* on fire; burning
align *vi/t* **1** come or put into a line **2** come or put into agreement: *They aligned themselves with the army.* **~ment** *n*
alike *adj, adv* like one another; the same
alimentary *adj* concerning nutrition
alimentary canal *n* tubelike passage leading from the mouth to the stomach
alimony *n* money that one must pay regularly to a former wife or husband
alive *adj* **1** living; in existence **2** full of life; active **3 alive to** aware of **4 alive with** swarming with
alkali *n* **-lis** *or* **-lies** substance that forms a chemical salt when combined with an acid **–line** *adj*
alkaloid *n* organic chemical compound used as a drug
all *determiner* the whole of; every one

of: *all the bread* ♦ *adv* **1** completely: *He's all alone.* **2** for each side: *The score was 3 all.* **3 all along** from the beginning **4 all in: a** very tired **b** with everything included: *It cost £2000 all in.* **5 all out** using all possible strength and effort **6 all over** everywhere **7 all right: a** safe or satisfactory **b** I agree; yes **8 all there** having a good quick mind **9 all told** all together **10 all up** at an end; ruined ♦ *pron* **1** everyone or everything: *This is all I have.* **2 all in all** considering everything **3 (not) at all** (not) in any way: *I don't agree at all.* **4 in all** counting everyone or everything

Allah *n* (the Muslim name for) God

all-American *adj* typically or quintessentially American

allay *vt* make less

all clear *n* **1** signal that danger is past **2** go-ahead

allege *vt* declare without proof: *an alleged thief* **allegedly** *adv* **allegation** *n* unproved statement

allegiance *n* loyalty to a leader, country, etc.

allegory *n* (style of) story, poem, etc., in which the characters represent ideas and qualities **–rical** *adj*

allegretto *n, adj* (music to be played) fairly briskly and quickly

allegro *n, adj, adv* **-os** (music to be played) in a brisk lively manner

alleluia *interj, n* hallelujah

allergy *n* condition of being made ill by a particular food, drug, etc. **–gic** *adj*

alleviate *vt* make (pain or distress) less **–ation** *n*

alley *n* **1** narrow street or path **2** track along which balls are rolled in bowling or skittles

alliance *n* **1** close connections made between countries or groups for a shared purpose **2** act of forming an alliance or state of being in an alliance

alligator *n* animal like a crocodile

alliteration *n* repeating of initial consonant sounds in consecutive words **–tive** *adj*

allocate *vt* give as a share **–cation** *n*

allot *vt* **-tt-** allocate

allotment *n* **1** allocation **2** (in Britain) small piece of land rented to grow vegetables on

allow *vt* **1** let (someone) do something without opposing them; permit: *They allowed him to come.* **2** provide (esp. money or time) ♦ **allow for** *phr vt* take into consideration: *We must allow for the train being late.* **~able** *adj* **~ance** *n* **1** money provided regularly **2 make allowances** take something into consideration

alloy *n* mixture of metals

all-purpose *adj* suitable for a variety of uses

all right *adj, adv* **1** safe, unharmed, or healthy **2** acceptable **3** I/we agree **4** *infml* beyond doubt

all-round *adj* having ability in many things, esp. in various sports **~er** *n*

all-singing all-dancing *adj infml* using every possible means to attract attention

allspice *n* (spice made by grinding the berries of) a tropical American tree

all-star *adj* including many famous actors

all-time *adj* exceeding or surpassing all that have been before (or since)

allude to *phr vt* speak about indirectly **allusion** *n* **allusive** *adj*

allure *vt* attract or charm ♦ *n* power of attraction **~ment** *n* alluring thing or quality

alluvium *n* soil deposited by running water **–ial** *adj*

ally *n* person or country that helps one or agrees to help ♦ *vt* **1** unite by agreement or marriage **2 allied (to)** related or connected (to)

alma mater /ˈalmə ˈmahtə/ *n* school or college which one attended

almanac *n* book giving information about the sun, moon, and tides

almighty *adj* **1** having absolute power **2** very great

almond *n* (tree bearing) a sweet oval nut

almoner *n* (formerly) a hospital social worker

almost *adv* very nearly
alms *pl n* money or food given to poor people
almshouse *n* small house provided for the poor or aged by a private benefactor
aloft *adv* high up
alone *adv, adj* **1** without others: *He lives alone.* **2** only: *You alone can do it.* **3** free from interference: *Let him alone.*
along *adv* **1** forward; on: *Come along!* **2** with others: *Bring your sister along.* ♦ *prep* **1** from end to end of: *walk along the road* **2** somewhere on the length of
alongside *adv, prep* close to the side (of)
aloof *adj, adv* distant in feeling; not friendly **~ness** *n*
aloud *adv* in a voice that can be heard
alpaca *n* (wool from) a Peruvian llama
alpenstock *n* stick with iron point used in mountain walking
alpha *n* **1** first letter of the Greek alphabet **2** *BrE* highest mark or grade **3 alpha and omega** the beginning and the end
alphabet letters used in writing **~ical** *adj* in the order of the alphabet **~ically** *adv*
alphanumeric *adj* consisting of both letters and numbers
alpine *adj* **1** of the Alps or other high mountains **2** (of plants) growing high on mountains ♦ *n* alpine plant
already *adv* **1** by or before an expected time: *Are you leaving already?* **2** before now: *I've seen the film twice already.*
alright *adj, adv* all right
Alsatian *n* large wolf-like dog
also *adv* as well; besides
also-ran *n* person who has failed to win at a sport or in an election
altar *n* table used in a religious ceremony
altarpiece *n* painting or carving above an altar
alter *vi/t* make or become different **~ation** *n* **~able** *adj*
altercation *n* noisy argument or quarrel
alter ego *n* **alter egos** very close and trusted friend
alternate *adj* **1** happening by turns **2** every other: *He works on alternate days.* ♦ *vi/t* happen or follow by turns **~ly** *adv* **–nation** *n*
alternative *adj* **1** to be done or used instead; other **2** not conventional: *alternative medicine* **3** flouting established standards: *alternative theatre* ♦ *n* something that can be done or used instead **~ly** *adv*
although *conj* though
altitude *n* height above sea level
alto *n* **-tos** (person with) a singing voice between soprano and tenor
altogether *adv* **1** completely: *altogether different* **2** considering everything together: *Altogether, it was a good trip.* ♦ *n* **in the altogether** nude
altruism *n* unselfishness **–ist** *n* **–istic** *adj*
aluminium, *AmE* **aluminum** *n* light silver-white metal
alumna *n* **-nae** female alumnus
alumnus *n* **-ni** *esp. AmE* former student of a college
always *adv* **1** at all times: *The sun always rises in the east.* **2** for ever: *I'll always love you.* **3** very often: *He's always complaining.*
am *1st person sing. present tense of* be
am, AM *abbrev. for:* ante meridiem; before midday (used after numbers expressing time)
AM *n* amplitude modulation; a system of broadcasting in which the strength of the sound waves varies
amalgam *n* **1** mixture or combination **2** alloy of mercury and another metal used for dental fillings
amalgamate *vi/t* unite; combine **–ation** *n*
amanuensis *n* **-ses** secretary
amass *vt* gather or collect in great amounts
amateur *n* person who does something for enjoyment and without being paid **amateur** *adj* **~ish** *adj* lacking skill **~ism** *n*
amatory *adj* of or expressing love
amaze *vt* fill with great surprise

~ment *n* **amazing** *adj* **amazingly** *adv*
amazon *n* tall, strong woman **-zonian** *adj*
ambassador *n* minister of high rank representing his/her own country in another country **~ial** *adj*
ambassadress *n* **1** female ambassador **2** wife of an ambassador
amber *n* (yellow colour of) a fossil resin used for jewels **amber** *adj*
ambergris *n* waxy substance from the intestines of the sperm whale used in making perfumes
ambidextrous *adj* able to use both hands equally well
ambience /ˈambi·əns/ *n* feeling of a place **ambient** *adj* surrounding
ambiguous *adj* having more than one meaning; not clear **-uity** *n*
ambit *n* scope
ambition *n* **1** strong desire for success **2** whatever is desired in this way **-tious** *adj* **-tiously** *adv*
ambivalent *adj* having opposing feelings about something **-lence** *n*
amble *vi* walk at an easy gentle rate **amble** *n*
ambrosia *n* **1** food of Greek and Roman gods **2** wonderful food or drink **-ial** *adj*
ambulance *n* motor vehicle for carrying sick people
ambush *n* surprise attack from a place of hiding **ambush** *vt*
ameba *n AmE* amoeba
ameliorate *vt* improve **-ration** *n*
amen *interj* (at the end of a prayer) may this be true
amenable *adj* willing to be influenced
amend *vt* change and improve **~ment** *n*
amends *pl n* recompense
amenity *n* something (e.g. a park or swimming pool) that makes life pleasant
American *n, adj* (inhabitant) of North or South America, esp. the US
American football *n BrE* game played between two teams of 11 players using an oval ball that can be handled or kicked
americanize, **-ise** *vi/t* make or become American in character **-ization** *n*
amethyst *n* (purple colour of) a stone used in jewellery
amiable *adj* good tempered; friendly **-bly** *adv* **-bility** *n*
amicable *adj* done in a friendly way: *reach an amicable agreement* **-bly** *adv*
amid also **amidst** *prep* among
amidships *adv* in the middle (of a ship)
amino acid *n* any of several organic acids of which proteins are chiefly composed
amiss *adj, adv fml* **1** wrong(ly) or imperfect(ly) **2 take something amiss** be offended
amity *n fml* friendship
ammo *n infml* ammunition
ammonia *n* gas with a strong smell, used in explosives and chemicals
ammonite *n* spiral fossil of a mollusc
ammunition *n* bullets, bombs, etc.
amnesia *n* loss of memory
amnesty *n* general act of forgiveness, esp. by a state to people guilty of political offences
amoeba, *AmE* **ameba** /əˈmeebə/ *n* **-bas** *or* **-bae** living creature that consists of only one cell **-bic** *adj*
amok also **amuck** *adv* **run amok** run wild, esp. in a murderous rage
among also **amongst** *prep* **1** in the middle of: *a house among the trees* **2** in the group of; one of: *He's among the best of our students.* **3** to each of (more than two): *Divide it among the five of you.*
amontillado *n* medium-dry sherry
amoral *adj* having no understanding of right or wrong **~ity** *n*
amorous *adj* feeling or expressing love, esp. sexual love **~ly** *adv*
amorphous *adj* having no fixed form or shape
amortize *vt* pay off (a debt), or write off (a declining asset), by regularly transferring money to a sinking fund **-ization** *n*
amount *n* quantity; total ♦ *v* **amount to** *phr vt* be equal to

amour *n lit* love affair
amp also **ampere** *n* standard measure of the quantity of electricity
amperage *n* strength of an electric current measured in amps
ampersand *n* the sign & standing for 'and'
amphetamine *n* stimulating drug used esp. illegally
amphibian *n* **1** animal, such as a frog, that can live both on land and in water **2** aeroplane or motor vehicle that can operate in or from water **amphibian, -ious** *adj*
amphitheatre , *AmE* **-ter** *n* open building with rows of seats round a central space
amphora *n* ancient Greek or Roman jar with two handles and a long narrow neck
ample *adj* enough; plenty **amply** *adv* **amplitude** *n*
amplify *vi/t* **1** explain in more detail **2** make (esp. sound) stronger **–fier** *n* instrument for making sound louder **–fication** *n*
ampoule *n* small hermetically sealed glass vessel usu. containing a fluid to be injected
amputate *vi/t* cut off (part of the body) for medical reasons **–tation** *n* **amputee** *n* person who has had a limb amputated
amuck *adv* amok
amulet *n* object worn as a charm against evil
amuse *vt* **1** cause to laugh: *an amusing story* **2** cause to spend time pleasantly **~ment** *n* **1** state of being amused **2** something that passes the time pleasantly
an *indefinite article, determiner* (used before a vowel sound) a: *an elephant*
-an *suffix* **-ian**
anachronism /əˈnakrəˌniz(ə)m/ *n* person, thing, or idea placed in the wrong period of time, or seeming to belong to another age **–nistic** *adj*
anaconda *n* large S American snake
anaemia, *AmE* **anemia** *n* lack of enough red blood cells **–mic** *adj*
anaesthesia, *AmE* **anes-** /ˌanəsˈtheezh(y)ə/ *n* state of being unable to feel esp. pain
anaesthetic, *AmE* **anes-** *n* substance that stops one from feeling pain, either in a part of the body (a **local anaesthetic**) or by making one unconscious (a **general anaesthetic**) **–thetist** *n* **–thetize** *vt*
anagram *n* word made by changing the order of the letters in another word
anal *adj* of or concerning the anus
analgesic *n, adj* (substance) which makes one unable to feel pain **–getic** *n, adj*
analogy *n* **1** degree of likeness **2** explaining one thing by comparing it to something else **–gous** *adj* alike in some ways **–gue** *n* something in some ways like something else
analyse, *AmE* **-lyze** *vt* examine carefully, often by dividing something into parts
analysis *n* **1** examination of something; analysing **2** psychoanalysis **analyst** *n* **analytic** *adj* **analytically** *adv*
anapaest *n* measure of poetry consisting of two short syllables followed by one long one
anarchy *n* **1** absence of government **2** social disorder **–chism** *n* **–chist** *n* person who wishes for anarchy **–chic** *adj*
anathema *n* something hated
anatomy *n* **1** scientific study of living bodies **2** analysis: *an anatomy of modern society* **3** structure, esp. of a living organism **–mical** *adj* **–mist** *n*
ANC *abbrev. for:* African National Congress
-ance *suffix* action, state, or quality of doing or being the stated thing: *appearance/brilliance*
ancestor *n* person from whom one is descended **–tral** *adj*
ancestry *n* all one's ancestors
anchor *n* **1** device dropped into the water to stop a ship from moving **2** something that makes one feel safe ♦ *v*

1 *vi* lower the anchor 2 *vt* fix firmly in position **~age** *n* place where ships may anchor

anchorite *n* hermit

anchorperson also **-man** *or* **-woman** *n esp. AmE* broadcaster providing continuity in a news broadcast

anchovy *n* **-vies** *or* **-vy** small strong-tasting fish

ancient *adj* 1 of times long ago: *ancient Rome* 2 very old ♦ *n* person who lived long ago

ancillary *adj* providing additional help ♦ *n* helper

and *conj* 1 (joining two things) as well as: *John and Sally* 2 then; therefore: *Water the seeds and they will grow.* 3 (showing that something continues): *We ran and ran.* 4 (used instead of **to** after **come, go, try**): *Try and open it.*

andante *n, adv, adj* (music to be played) moderately slow

andiron *n* metal support for a burning log in a fireplace

androgynous /an'drojənəs/ *adj* having both male and female characteristics **-gyny** *n*

android *n* (in stories) robot in human form

anecdote *n* short interesting story that is true **-dotal** *adj* containing or telling anecdotes

anemia *n AmE* anaemia

anemometer *n* instrument for measuring wind speed

anemone *n* 1 large-flowered plant of the buttercup family 2 sea anemone

anesthesia *n AmE* anaesthesia

anew *adv* again

angel *n* 1 messenger of God 2 very kind person **~ic** *adj*

angelica *n* candied stalks used as a cake decoration and in cookery

Angelus *n* a bell rung three times in Roman Catholic countries to mark the times for the saying of a special prayer

anger *n* fierce displeasure and annoyance ♦ *vt* make angry

angina pectoris also **angina** *n* heart disorder causing sharp pain in the chest

angle[1] *n* 1 space between two lines that meet, measured in degrees 2 corner 3 point of view 4 **at an angle** not upright or straight ♦ *vt* 1 turn or move at an angle 2 represent (something) from a particular point of view

angle[2] *vi* catch fish with a hook and line **angle for** *phr vt* try to get, by indirect means: *to angle for an invitation* **angler** *n*

Anglican *n, adj* (member) of the Church of England

anglicize *vt* make English

Anglo- *prefix* 1 of England or Britain: *Anglophobe* 2 English or British and: *Anglo-Japanese*

anglophile *n, adj* (person) who likes and admires England, the English, English ways etc. **-philia** *n*

anglophobe *n, adj* (person) who dislikes and despises England, the English, English ways etc. **-phobia** *n*

Anglo-Saxon *n* (language of) a member of the Germanic peoples dominant in England from the fifth to the tenth century AD **Anglo-Saxon** *adj*

angora *n* 1 (*cap.*) type of goat or rabbit with long silky hair 2 wool made with the hair of the angora rabbit

angostura *n* bitter flavouring added to alcoholic drinks

angry *adj* 1 full of anger 2 (of the sky or clouds) stormy **angrily** *adv*

angst *n* anxiety and anguish caused esp. by considering the sad state of the world

anguish *n* great suffering, esp. of the mind **~ed** *adj*

angular *adj* 1 having sharp corners 2 (of a person) thin

anhydrous *adj* containing no water

animadvert on *phr vt fml* comment (censoriously) on **-version** *n*

animal *n* 1 living creature that is not a plant 2 all animals except human beings 3 mammal 4 person who seems to live without human thought or feeling ♦ *adj* 1 of animals 2 of the body

animate *adj* alive ♦ *vt* give life or excite-

ment to **–mated** *adj* cheerful and excited **–matedly** *adv* **–mation** *n* **1** cheerful excitement **2** process of making film cartoons
animism *n* religion according to which animals, plants, etc., are believed to have souls
animosity *n* powerful hatred
animus *n* hatred; hostility
aniseed *n* aromatic seed of the **anise** plant, used as flavouring
ankle *n* thin part of the leg, above the foot
anklet *n* ring or chain worn around the ankle
annals *pl n* history or record of events, etc., produced every year **annalist** *n*
anneal *vt* toughen (steel or glass) by heating and gradually cooling
annex *vt* take control of (esp. land) **~ation** *n*
annexe *n* building added to a larger one
annihilate /əˈnie·əˌlayt/ *vt* destroy completely **–lation** *n*
anniversary *n* day that is an exact number of years after something happened
anno Domini *adv* AD
annotate *vt* add notes to (a book) **–tation** *n*
announce *vt* state loudly or publicly **~ment** *n* public statement
announcer *n* person who reads news and introduces programmes on radio or television
annoy *vt* make a little angry **~ance** *n*
annual *adj* **1** happening once every year **2** for one year; *my annual salary* ♦ *n* **1** plant that lives for one year **2** book produced each year with the same name but new contents **~ly** *adv*
annuity *n* fixed sum of money paid each year
annul *vt* **-ll-** cause (esp. a marriage) to stop existing **~ment** *n*
annular *adj* ring-shaped
Annunciation *n* the angel Gabriel's announcement to the Virgin Mary that she would be the mother of Jesus
anode *n* part of an electrical instrument which collects electrons
anodyne *adj* **1** unlikely to offend or annoy anyone **2** easing pain ♦ *n* drug that eases pain
anoint *vt* put oil on, esp. in a ceremony
anomaly *n* something different from the usual type **–lous** *adj*
anon[1] *adv lit* soon
anon[2] *abbrev. for:* anonymous
anonymous *adj* **1** without a name **2** by an unknown author **~ly** *adv* **–mity** *n*
anopheles *n* type of mosquito that spreads malaria
anorak *n* jacket with a hood
anorexia *n* dangerous condition in which there is a loss of desire to eat **–ic** *adj*
another *determiner, pron* **1** one more: *Have another drink.* **2** a different one: *I'll do it another time.* **3** more; in addition: *It'll cost you another $20.*
answer *n* **1** what is said or written when someone asks a question or sends a letter **2** solution to a problem ♦ *v* **1** *vi/t* give an answer (to): *She answered with a smile.* **2** *vi/t* attend or act in response to: *Answer the phone!* **3** *vi/t* be as described in: *He answers to the description you gave.* **4** *vt* be satisfactory for **answer back** *phr vi/t* reply rudely (to) **answer for** *phr vt* **1** be responsible for **2** pay or suffer for **~able** *adj* **1** able to be answered **2** responsible
ant *n* insect living in a large and complex social group
-ant *suffix* (*in adjectives and nouns*) (person or thing) that does the stated thing: *disinfectant*
antagonize, –nise *vt* make into an enemy **–nism** *n* hatred; opposition **–nist** *n* opponent
Antarctic *adj, n* (of or concerning) the very cold most southern part of the world
ante- *prefix* before: *antenatal*
antecedent *n* something coming before something else, esp. **a** a noun referred to by a pronoun **b** a model for later developments **antecedent** *adj* **~s** *pl n* past family or past history
antechamber also **anteroom** *n* small

room leading to a larger one
antedate *vt* precede in time
antediluvian *adj* very old-fashioned
antelope *n* **-lopes** *or* **lope** graceful animal like a deer
antenatal *adj* existing or happening before birth
antenna *n* **1 -nae** insect's feeler **2** aerial
anterior *adj* **1** previous **2** at the head or front
anthem *n* religious song of praise
anther *n* part of the stamen which contains pollen
anthology *n* collection of poems or other writings
anthracite *n* hard, slow-burning coal
anthrax *n* often fatal disease of warm-blooded animals, e.g. sheep
anthropoid *adj* like a person
anthropology *n* scientific study of the human race **–gist** *n*
anthropomorphic *adj* regarding esp. a god or animal as having human qualities
anti- *prefix* against; opposite to: *anti-cancer/anticlockwise*
antiaircraft *adj* (of weapons) used for defence against air attack
antiballistic *adj* for use against ballistic missiles
antibiotic *n* medical substance, such as penicillin, that can kill bacteria
antibody *n* substance produced in the body which fights disease
Antichrist *n* enemy of Christ and Christianity
anticipate *vt* **1** expect: *We anticipate trouble.* **2** do something before (someone else) **3** guess (what will happen) and act as necessary **–pation** *n*
anticlerical *adj* hostile to the clergy
anticlimax *n* unexciting end to something exciting
anticlockwise *adv* in the opposite direction to the movement of a clock
antics *pl n* strange, amusing movements or behaviour
anticyclone *n* area of high air pressure, causing settled weather
antidote *n* something that prevents the effects of a poison or disease
antifreeze *n* chemical put in water to stop it freezing, esp. in car engines
antigen *n* substance that sets off the production of an antibody
antihero *n* main character in e.g. a novel or play who has none of the qualities conventionally associated with a hero
antihistamine *n* chemical substance used to treat allergies
antimacassar *n* cloth placed on the back of a chair to protect it against hair oil
antipathy *n* fixed strong dislike; hatred **–thetic** *adj*
antipersonnel *adj* (of weapons) designed to kill or injure people rather than destroy equipment
antiphon *n* **1** verse said or sung before or after part of the liturgy **2** psalm, hymn, etc. chanted or sung in alternate parts **~al** *adj*
antipodes /anˈtipəˌdeez/ *pl n* opposite side of the earth **–dean** *adj*
antiquarian *adj* of or concerned with antiques ♦ *n* student or collector of antiques
antiquated *adj* old-fashioned
antique *adj* old and therefore valuable ♦ *n* valuable old object
antiquity *n* **1** great age **2** ancient times **3** something remaining from ancient times
antirrhinum *n* snapdragon
anti-Semitism *n* hatred of Jews **–Semitic** *adj*
antiseptic *n, adj* (chemical substance) preventing disease by killing bacteria
antisocial *adj* **1** harmful to society **2** not liking to mix with people
antithesis *n* **–ses** direct opposite **–thetical** *adj*
antitoxin *n* (serum containing) an antibody which neutralizes a body toxin
antler *n* horn of a deer
antonym *n* word opposite in meaning to another word **–mous** *adj*
anus *n* hole through which solid waste leaves the bowels

anvil *n* iron block on which metals are hammered to the shape wanted

anxiety *n* **1** fear and worry **2** strong wish

anxious *adj* **1** worried and frightened **2** causing worry **3** wishing strongly: *anxious to please them* **~ly** *adv*

any *determiner, pron* **1** no matter which: *Take any you like.* **2** some; even the smallest number or amount: *Are there any letters for me?* ♦ *adv* at all: *I can't stay any longer.*

anybody *pron* anyone

anyhow *adv* **1** carelessly **2** in spite of everything

anyone *pron* **1** all people; no matter who: *Anyone can cook.* **2** even one person: *Is anyone listening?*

anyplace *adv AmE* anywhere

anything *pron* **1** any thing: no matter what: *He'll do anything for a quiet life.* **2** even one thing: *Can you see anything?* **3 anything but** not at all **4 anything like** at all like

anyway *adv* in spite of everything; anyhow

anywhere *adv* **1** at or to any place **2 anywhere near** at all near or nearly

Anzac *n* (member of) the Australian and New Zealand Army Corps in World War I

aob *abbrev. for:* any other business

aorta *n* largest artery in the body

apace *adv* quickly

apart *adv* **1** distant; separated: *villages 3 miles apart* **2** into parts: *to take a clock apart* **3 apart from: a** except for **b** as well as

apartheid /əˈpahtayt, -iet/ *n* (in South Africa) the system established by government of keeping different races separate

apartment *n* **1** room **2** *AmE* flat (5)

apathy *n* lack of interest in things **–thetic** *adj*

ape *n* large monkey with no tail ♦ *vt* copy (behaviour) stupidly

aperient *n, adj* laxative

aperitif *n* alcoholic drink before a meal

aperture *n* hole; opening

apex *n* **–es** *or* **apices** /ˈaypiseez/ highest point

APEX *adj* Advance Purchase Excursion; cheaper (esp. of air travel) because paid for well in advance of departure

aphasia *n* dumbness caused by a nervous disorder

aphid *n* small insect that sucks plant juices

aphorism /ˈafərɪz(ə)m/ *n* short wise saying

aphrodisiac *n, adj* (substance) causing sexual excitement

apiary *n* place where bees are kept **–rist** *n* bee-keeper **apiculture** *n* bee-keeping

apiece *adv* each

aplomb *n* calm self-control

apocalypse *n* (writing about) the end of the world **–lyptic** *adj* prophesying great misfortunes

apocryphal *adj* (of a story) probably untrue

apogee *n* **1** point farthest from a planet in a satellite's orbit **2** highest point

apologetic *adj* making an apology **~ally** *adv* **–tics** *pl n* argument in defence

apologia /ˌapəˈlohjyə/ *n* formal defence or explanation

apologist *n* person who strongly defends a particular belief

apologize *vi* say one is sorry for a fault **–gy** *n* **1** statement of sorrow for a fault **2 an apology for** a very poor example of (something)

apophthegm *n fml* maxim, pithy saying

apoplexy *n* stroke[1] (5) **–plectic** *adj* **1** of or concerning apoplexy **2** violently excited and angry

apostate *n* person who renounces a belief, esp. a religious faith **–asy** *n*

a posteriori *adj, adv* on the basis of observed facts

apostle *n* **1** one of the 12 first followers of Christ **2** leader of a new faith **–stolic** *adj* of or derived from the Christian apostles

apostrophe *n* the sign ('), as in *I'm*

apostrophize *vt* address (an absent person or thing) rhetorically
apothecary *n arch* pharmacist
apotheosis *n* **-ses 1** highest possible honour and glory **2** perfect example
appal, *AmE* **appall** *vt* **-ll-** shock deeply **~ling** (*AmE* **~ing**) *adj* **1** shocking **2** of very bad quality **~lingly** *adv*
apparatchik *n* bureaucrat, esp. of a Communist party
apparatus *n* **1** equipment needed for a purpose **2** bureaucracy
apparel *n fml* clothes ♦ *vt fml* dress
apparent *adj* **1** easily seen: *The reason became apparent.* **2** not necessarily real; seeming: *her apparent lack of concern* **~ly** *adv* it seems that
apparition *n* **1** ghost **2** appearance
appeal *n* **1** strong request for something: *an appeal for forgiveness* **2** attraction; interest: *He hasn't much sex appeal.* **3** formal request for a new decision ♦ *vi* **1** make a strong request: *to appeal for money* **2** please; attract: *Does the job appeal to you?* **3** ask for a new decision **~ing** *adj* attractive
appear *vi* **1** come into sight: *Spots appeared on my skin.* **2** come in view of the public: *He's appearing at the Theatre Royal.* **3** seem: *He appears to be angry.* **4** be present officially, as in a court of law **~ance** *n* **1** (an example of) the act of appearing **2** way a person or thing looks: *He changed his appearance by growing a beard.* **3 put in/make an appearance (at)** attend, esp. for a short time only
appease *vt* satisfy, esp. by agreeing to demands **~ment** *n*
appellant *n* person making an appeal **appellate** *adj* dealing with appeals
appellation *n fml* name; title
append *vt* add (esp. something written onto the end of a letter) **~age** *n* something added to, or hanging from, something else
appendectomy *n* operation to remove the appendix
appendicitis *n* disease of the appendix
appendix *n* **-dixes** *or* **-dices 1** small organ leading off the bowel **2** something added at the end of a book
appertain to *phr vt fml* belong to
appetite *n* desire, esp. for food
appetizer *n* something eaten to increase the appetite **-tizing** *adj* causing appetite
applaud *vi/t* **1** clap **2** approve strongly **applause** *n* loud praise
apple *n* kind of hard round juicy fruit
applejack *n AmE* apple brandy
apple-pie order *n* perfect order
appliance *n* apparatus; machine
applicable *adj* valid or suitable when applied: *The rule is applicable only to UK citizens.*
applicant *n* person who applies for something
application *n* **1** request: *to write applications for jobs* **2** act of putting something to use **3** particular practical use: *the industrial applications of this discovery* **4** putting something on a surface **5** careful effort
appliqué *n* decorative work in dressmaking made by sewing or sticking a piece or pieces of different material onto a larger piece
apply *v* **1** *vt* request officially: *apply for a job* **2** *vt* use for a purpose: *apply the brakes* **3** *vt* put onto a surface: *apply ointment to your skin* **4** *vi/t* give or have an effect: *Does the rule apply to me?* **5** *vt* cause to work hard: *apply oneself to the task* **applied** *adj* practical: *applied physics*
appoint *vt* **1** choose for a job **2** fix; decide: *the appointed time* **~ment** *n* **1** arrangement for a meeting **2** job: *a teaching appointment*
apportion *vt* divide and share out **~ment** *n*
apposite /ˈapəzit/ *adj* exactly suitable
apposition *n* (in grammar) a construction in which two or more usu. adjacent nouns or noun phrases refer to the same thing and perform the same function in the sentence, as in *the dog, an Alsation, was barking loudly* where 'the dog' and 'an Alsatian' are in

apposition

appraise *vt* judge the value of **appraisal** *n*

appreciable *adj* noticeable: *an appreciable difference* **–bly** *adv*

appreciate *v* **1** *vt* be thankful for **2** *vt* understand and enjoy the good qualities of: *She appreciates good wine.* **3** *vt* understand fully: *I appreciate your difficulties.* **4** *vi* (of property) increase in value **–ciative adj** **–ciation** *n*

apprehend *vt* **1** arrest **2** understand

apprehension *n* **1** anxiety; fear **2** arrest **3** understanding **–sive** *adj* worried

apprentice *n* person learning a skilled trade ♦ *vt* send as an apprentice **~ship** *n*

apprise *vt fml* tell

approach *v* **1** *vi/t* come near **2** *vt* make an offer or request to: *approach him about borrowing the money* **3** *vt* begin to consider or deal with ♦ *n* **1** act of approaching **2** way of getting in **3** method of doing something **4** speaking to someone for the first time **~able** *adj* easy to speak to or deal with

approbation *n* official approval

appropriate *adj* correct; suitable ♦ *vt* **1** set aside for a purpose **2** take for oneself **–ation** *n* **~ly** *adv*

approval *n* **1** favourable opinion **2** official permission **3 on approval** (of goods from a shop) to be returned without payment if unsatisfactory

approve *v* **1** *vi* have a favourable opinion **2** *vt* agree officially to **approvingly** *adv*

approximate *adj* nearly correct but not exact **~ly** *adv* ♦ *vi* come near **–mation** *n*

apricot *n* (colour of) a round orange fruit with a stone

April *n* **1** the 4th month of the year **2 April fool** *n* victim of a trick played on the morning of April 1st

a priori *adj, adv* on the basis of general principles or received wisdom

apron *n* garment worn to protect the front of one's clothes

apropos /ˌaprəˈpoh/ *adj* relevant

apropos, apropos of *prep* with regard to

apse *n* rounded projecting part of the East end of a church

apt *adj* **1** likely: *apt to slip* **2** exactly suitable: *an apt remark* **3** quick to learn **~ly** *adv* **~ness** *n*

aptitude *n* natural ability

aqualung *n* apparatus for breathing under water

aquamarine *n* (blue-green colour of) a transparent gemstone

aquaplane *n* board on which a person is towed behind a fast motorboat ♦ *vi* **1** ride on an aquaplane **2** *BrE* (of a car) lose grip on a wet road and slide forward out of control

aquarium *n* **-iums** *or* **-ia** glass container for live fish

aquatic *adj* living or happening in water

aquatint *n* (print made by) a method of etching a copper plate to obtain effects similar to water colour

aqueduct *n* bridge that carries water across a valley

aqueous *adj* of or resembling water

aquiline *adj* **1** of or like an eagle **2** shaped like an eagle's beak

-ar *suffix* **1** (*in adjectives*) of or being: *Polar* **2** (*in nouns*) person or thing that does the stated thing: *liar*

Arab *n* member of the Semitic people originating in Arabia **Arab** *adj*

arabesque *n* **1** intricate and graceful design **2** position in ballet ♦ *adj*

Arabian *n, adj* (inhabitant) of Arabia

Arabic *n, adj* (main language) of North Africa and the Middle East

arable *adj* (of land) used for growing crops

arachnid /əˈraknid/ *n* one of a class of creatures with eight legs, including mites and spiders

arak *n* arrack

arbiter *n* someone who is in a position to make influential judgments or to settle an argument

arbitrage *n* process of buying something (esp. a currency or commodity) in

one place and selling it at another in order to profit from differences in price
arbitrary *adj* **1** based on chance rather than reason **2** typical of uncontrolled power **–rily** *adv* **–riness** *n*
arbitrate *vi/t* act as judge in an argument **–trator** *n* **–tration** *n* settlement of an argument by the decision of a person or group chosen by both sides
arboreal *adj* of trees
arbour, arbor *n* shelter among or decorated with plants
arc *n* **1** part of the curve of a circle **2** luminous discharge of electricity passing across a gap between two electrodes
arcade *n* **1** covered passage with shops **2** row of arches
arcane *adj* mysterious and secret
arch- *prefix* chief: *archpriest*
arch[1] *n* curved part over a doorway or under a bridge ♦ *vi/t* make an arch
arch[2] *adj* **1** chief **2** sly **3** playful
archaeology *n* study of ancient remains **–gist** *n* **–gical** *adj*
archaic *adj* no longer used; old **–ism** *n*
archangel *n* chief angel
archbishop *n* chief bishop
archdeacon *n* senior clergyman who assists a bishop
archduke *n* royal prince, esp. in Austrian history
archer *n* person who shoots with a bow **~y** *n*
archetype /ˈahkiˌtiep/ *n* **1** original of which others are copies **2** perfect example **-typal, -typical** *adj*
archiepiscopal *adj* of an archbishop
archipelago /ˌahkiˈpeləgoh/ *n* area with many small islands
architect *n* person who plans buildings **~ure** *n* art of building; way of building
architrave *n* **1** part of a raised wall which rests directly on the tops of its supporting columns **2** moulding around a door or window
archives *pl n* **1** historical records **2** place where these are kept **–vist** *adj* keeper of archives
arc lamp *n* lamp producing light from an electrical arc
Arctic *n, adj* **1** (*cap.*) (of or concerning) the very cold most northern part of the world **2** very cold
arc welding *n* welding by means of an electrical arc
ardent *adj* very eager **~ly** *adv*
ardour, *AmE* **ardor** *n* strong excitement
arduous *adj* needing effort; difficult **~ly** *adv*
are *present tense pl of* be
area *n* **1** size of a surface **2** part of the world's surface: *a parking area behind the cinema* **3** subject of activity: *the area of language teaching*
arena *n* **1** enclosed space used for sports **2** sphere of activity: *the political arena*
aren't *short for:* **1** are not **2** (in questions) am not
argent *n, adj* (in heraldry and poetry) silver
Argentinian *n, adj* (inhabitant) of Argentina
argon *n* inert gas found in the air
argot /ˈahgoh/ *n* speech spoken and understood by only a small group of people
argue *v* **1** *vi* express disagreement; quarrel **2** *vi/t* give reasons for or against something **arguable** *adj* perhaps true, but not certain **arguably** *adv*
argument *n* **1** quarrel **2** reason given for or against; use of reason **~ative** *adj* quarrelsome
argy-bargy *n, esp. BrE* lively dispute
aria *n* **-as** melody for a single voice
-arian *suffix* (*in nouns*) person who supports and believes in: *libertarian*
arid *adj* **1** (of land) very dry **2** uninteresting; dull
aright *adv* rightly
arise *vi* **arose, arisen** happen; appear
aristocracy *n* (government by) the highest social class **–rat** *n* member of this class **–ratic** *adj*
arithmetic *n* calculation by numbers **~al** *adj* **~ian** *n*
arithmetic progression , **arithmetical**

progression *n* sequence of numbers, e.g. *2, 4, 6, 8, 10,* extended by adding a fixed amount to the preceding figure
ark *n* large ship, esp. the one described in the Bible
arm[1] *n* **1** upper limb **2** something shaped like this: *the arm of a chair* **3** part of a garment that covers the arm **4** part or division of the armed forces **5** **arm in arm** (of two people) with arms joined
arm[2] *vi/t* supply with weapons
armada *n* collection of armed ships
armadillo *n* **-os** South American mammal with armour of small bony plates
Armageddon *n* (esp. in the Bible) great battle or war causing terrible destruction and bringing the end of the world
armament *n* **1** weapons and other fighting equipment **2** act of preparing for war
armature *n* central rotating component of an electric motor or generator
armchair *n* chair with supports for the arms ♦ *adj* not taking an active part
armistice *n* agreement to stop fighting for a time
armour, *AmE* **armor** *n* **1** protective covering for the body in battle **2** protective metal covering on military vehicles **~y** *n* place where weapons are stored **~er** *n* person who looks after arms
armpit *n* hollow place under one's arm
arms *pl n* **1** weapons **2** coat of arms **3 up in arms** very angry and ready to argue
army *n* **1** military forces that fight on land **2** large group: *an army of ants*
arnica *n* flower from which a tincture is made which is used in the treatment of bruises
aroma *n* pleasant smell **~tic** *adj*
arose *past t. of* arise
around *adv, prep* **1 a** in various places; round: *I'll show you around (the house).* **b** somewhere near: *Is there anyone around?* **2** a little more or less than; about: *around 10 o'clock* **3 a** moving in a circle; measured in a circle: *turn around and around|three metres around* **b** on all sides: *The children gathered around.*
arouse *vt* **1** *fml* cause to wake **2** make active; excite **arousal** *n*
arpeggio *n* **-os** notes of a chord played in succession
arrack *n* alcoholic spirit made of fermented rice
arraign *vt* accuse **~ment** *n*
arrange *v* **1** *vt* put in order: *arrange flowers* **2** *vi/t* plan: *arrange to meet her* **3** *vt* set out (music) for different instruments **~ment** *n* **1** (act of making) an agreement or plan: *I have an arrangement with the bank.* **2** something that has been put in order: *a beautiful flower arrangement* **3** (example of) the setting out of a piece of music in a certain way
arrant *adj* extreme; absolute
arras *n* **arras** tapestry wall-hanging
array *n* fine show, collection, or ordered group ♦ *vt* decorate or place in order
arrears *pl n* **1** money owed from the past **2** work waiting to be done **3 in arrears** late in fulfilling obligations
arrest *vt* **1** seize by the power of the law **2** stop (a process) **3** attract (attention) ♦ *n* act of arresting
arrival *n* **1** act of arriving **2** person or thing that has arrived: *to welcome the new arrivals*
arrive *vi* **1** reach a place: *arrive home* **2** happen; come: *The day arrived.* **3** win success **arrive at** *phr vt* reach; come to: *arrive at a decision*
arrogant *adj* proud in a rude way **~ly** *adv* **-gance** *n*
arrogate *vt* claim or seize without justification
arrow *n* **1** pointed stick to be shot from a bow **2** sign (→) used to show direction
arrowroot *n* edible starch from the root of a tropical plant
arse *n BrE taboo sl* **1** also *AmE* **ass** bottom **2** also **arsehole,** *AmE* **asshole**: **a** the anus **b** stupid annoying person ♦ *v* **arse about/around** *phr vi BrE sl* waste time
arsenal *n* place where weapons are stored

arsenic *n* very poisonous substance

arson *n* crime of setting fire to property **~ist** *n*

art *n* **1** the making or expression of what is beautiful, e.g. in music, literature, or esp. painting **2** things produced by art, esp. paintings: *an art gallery* **3** skill in doing anything: *the art of conversation* **arts** *pl n* subjects of study that are not part of science

art deco *adj, n* (in) a style of geometrical and streamlined interior design which flourished esp. in the 1930s

artefact /ˈahtifakt/ *n* artifact

arteriosclerosis *n* thickening and hardening of the walls of arteries

artery *n* **1** tube that carries blood from the heart **2** main road, railway, etc. **-rial** *adv*

artesian well *n* well by which water reaches the surface under natural pressure

Artex *n tdmk* textured plaster-like covering for ceilings

artful *adj* **1** cleverly deceitful **2** skilfully put together **~ly** *adv*

arthritis *n* painful disease of the joints **-tic** *adj*

artic *n BrE sl* articulated lorry

artichoke *n* **1** also **globe artichoke** plant whose leafy flower is eaten **2** also **Jerusalem artichoke** plant whose potato-like root is eaten

article *n* **1** thing; object: *an article of clothing* **2** piece of writing in a newspaper **3** complete or separate part in a written law agreement **4** word used with nouns, such as *a, an,* and *the* in English ♦ *vt* bind by an agreement

articulate *adj* **1** (of people) able to express thoughts and feelings clearly in words **2** (of speech) having clear separate sounds and words ♦ *v* **1** *vi/t* speak or say clearly **2** *vt* unite by joints: *an articulated lorry* **-lation** **~ly** *adv*

artifact *n* something made by people

artifice *n* **1** clever trick **2** cunning

artificer *n* **1** skilled craftsman **2** military or naval mechanic

artificial *adj* **1** made by people; not natural **2** not sincere **~ly** *adv* **~ity** *n*

artificial insemination *n* introduction of sperm into the uterus by means other than intercourse

artificial intelligence *n* branch of computer science which aims to produce machines capable of imitating human intelligence

artificial respiration *n* making someone breathe again by forcing air in and out of the lungs

artillery *n* (part of the army that uses) large guns

artisan *n* craftsman

artist *n* **1** person who works in one of the arts, esp. painting **2** inventive and skilled worker **3** also **artiste** professional singer or dancer who performs in a show **~ry** *n* inventive imagination and ability **~ic** *adj* **1** of art or artists **2** showing skill in art **~ically** *adv*

artless *adj* simple and natural; almost foolish **~ly** *adv*

art nouveau *adj, n* (in) a decorative style of late 19th century origin characterized by curved lines and plant motifs

arty *adj infml* (affectedly) interested in the arts

arty-crafty *adj infml* **1** affectedly simple or rustic in design **2** arty

arvo *n AustrE infml* afternoon

-ary *suffix* (*in adjectives*) being: *legendary*

as *adv, prep* **1** (used in comparisons and examples) equally; like: *He's as old as me.* **2** when considered as being: *As a writer, she's wonderful.* ♦ *conj* **1** (used in comparisons): *He's as old as I am.* **2** in the way that: *Leave it as it is.* **3** because: *As I have no car, I can't go.* **4** when; while: *He saw her as she was getting off the bus.* **5** though: *Tired as I was, I tried to help.* **6 as it is** in reality **7 as it were** as one might say

asap *abbrev. for:* as soon as possible

asbestos *n* soft grey material that protects against fire or heat

ascend *vi/t fml* **1** go up **2** **ascend the throne** become king or queen **~ancy,**

~ency *n* controlling influence; power **~ant, -ent** *n* **in the ascendant** having or nearly having a controlling power or influence

ascent *n* act or process of ascending; way up

ascertain *vt fml* discover; make certain **~able** *adj*

ascetic /əˈsetik/ *n, adj* (a person) avoiding physical pleasures and comforts, esp. for religious reasons **~ism** *n*

ASCII *n* American Standard Code for Information Interchange; a set of 128 symbols used for easy exchange of information between a computer and other data processing machinery

ascribe to *phr vt* believe to be the work of: *He ascribes his success to luck* **ascription** *n*

aseptic *adj* without bacteria; clean **asepsis** *n*

asexual *adj* **1** without sex **2** not interested in sex **~ly** *adv*

ash *n* also **ashes** *pl* powder left when something has been burnt **~en** *adj* pale grey **ashes** *pl n* remains of a dead body after burning

ashamed *adj* feeling shame

ash can *n AmE* dustbin

Ashkenazi *n* **-zim** Jew of German or East European origin

ashlar *n* shaped stone used for facing a building

ashore *adv* on or to the shore

ashtray *n* dish for tobacco ash

Asian *n, adj* (inhabitant) of the continent of Asia

Asiatic *n, adj* Asian

aside *adv* to the side: *She stepped aside to let them pass.* ♦ *n* remark not intended to be heard by everyone present

asinine *adj* stupid

ask *v* **1** *vi/t* say a question: *'Where is it?' she asked.* **2** *vi/t* make a request for: *She asked him to wake her at 6.00.* **3** *vt* invite: *Ask them to tea.* **ask after** *phr vt* ask for news of

askance /əˈskahns/ *adv* with disapproval or distrust: *look askance*

askew *adv* not properly straight

asking price *n* price the seller puts on an item

aslant *adv* at a slant ♦ *prep* slanting over or across

asleep *adj* **1** sleeping **2** (of an arm or leg) unable to feel

asp *n* small poisonous snake

asparagus *n* plant whose stems are eaten as a vegetable

aspect *n* **1** particular side of a plan or problem **2** direction in which a room or building faces

aspen *n* poplar with quivering leaves

asperity *n* roughness

aspersion *n* **1** unkind or harmful remark: *They cast aspersions on my new book.* **2** ritual sprinkling with water

asphalt /ˈasfalt/ *n* black material used for road surfaces

asphyxiate /əˈsfiksiayt/ *vt* kill by lack of air **-ation** *n*

aspic *n* clear savoury jelly

aspirate *vt, n* (pronounce with) the sound 'h'

aspire *vi* direct one's hopes and efforts **aspiration** *n* strong desire

aspirin *n* **-rin** *or* **-rins** (tablet of) medicine that lessens pain and fever

ass *n* **1** donkey **2** foolish person **3** *AmE* arse

assail *vt* attack **~ant** *n fml* attacker

assassin *n* person who assassinates

assassinate *vt* murder (esp. a ruler or politician) **-ation** *n*

assault *n* sudden violent attack **assault** *vt*

assault course *n* area of land on which soldiers train by climbing or jumping over obstacles

assay *n* analysis of a substance ♦ *vt* **1** analyse **2** judge the quality of **3** *fml* attempt

assegai *n* native spear of southern Africa

assemble *vi/t* gather or put together: *to assemble radios|A crowd assembled.*

assembly *n* **1** group of people gathered together for a purpose **2** assembling of machine parts

assembly line *n* arrangement of workers and machines in which a product is put through various operations until complete
assent *vi fml* agree ♦ *n* agreement
assert *vt* **1** declare forcefully **2** make a strong claim to: *He asserted his authority.* **3 assert oneself** act in a way that shows one's power **~ive** *adj* forceful; showing confidence **~ion** *n* forceful statement or claim
assess *vt* judge the value or amount of **~ment** *n* **~or** *n*
asset *n* **1** property that has value and may be sold **2** valuable quality or skill
asset-stripping *n* practice of buying a company cheaply, selling all its assets to make a profit, and closing it down
asseverate *vt* solemnly affirm
asshole *n AmE* arse¹ (2)
assiduous *adj* with careful attention **~ly** *adv* **–uity** *n*
assign *vt* **1** give as a share or duty **2** decide on; name: *assign a day for the meeting* **~ment** *n* **1** duty or piece of work **2** act of assigning **~ee** *n* person to whom something is assigned
assignation *n* (secret) meeting
assimilate *vi/t* take in and accept (food, ideas, foreign people) **–lation** *n*
assist *vi/t* help **~ance** *n* **~ant** *n* person who helps
Assizes *pl n* court sessions formerly held in county towns at regular intervals
associate *v* **1** *vi/t* join as friends or partners **2** *vt* connect in the mind ♦ *n* friend or colleague ♦ *adj* of secondary status
association *n* **1** society of people joined together **2** act of joining together **3** connecting things in the mind
Association football *BrE* soccer
assonance *n* repetition of sounds, e.g. in poetry **–ant** *adj*
assorted *adj* of various types; mixed
assortment *n* mixture
assuage *vt fml* reduce (suffering)
assume *vt* **1** believe without proof: *Let's assume he isn't coming.* **2** begin to use or perform: *to assume control* **3** pretend to have: *an assumed name*
assumption *n* **1** something believed without proof **2** act of assuming
assure *vt* **1** tell firmly; promise **2** make (oneself) sure or certain **3** *BrE* insure, esp. against death **assurance** *n* **1** belief in one's own powers **2** firm promise **3** *BrE* insurance **assured** *adj* certain, esp. of one's own powers
aster *n* daisy-like flower
asterisk *n* star-like mark (*)
astern *adv* **1** in or at the back part of a ship **2** behind the stern of a ship **3** (of a ship) backwards
asteroid *n* very small planet
asthma *n* disease that causes difficulty in breathing **~tic** *adj*
astigmatism *n* inability of the eye to focus properly **–atic** *adj*
astir *adj* **1** busy and/or excited **2** out of bed
astonish *vt* surprise greatly **~ment** *n*
astound *vt* shock with surprise
astrakhan *n* (fabric resembling) the curly black fleece of lambs from the Astrakhan region of the USSR
astral *adj* of, from, or concerning stars
astray *adj, adv* off the right path
astride *adv, prep* with a leg on each side (of)
astringent *adj* **1** able to tighten the skin and stop bleeding **2** bitter; severe
astro- *prefix* of or about the stars: *astrophysics*
astrolabe *n* early instrument used to measure the altitude of stars above the horizon
astrology *n* study of the supposed influence of the stars on events and character **–ger** *n* **–gical** *adj*
astronaut *n* traveller in a spacecraft **~ics** *pl n* science of designing spacecraft
astronomy *n* scientific study of the solar system and stars **–mer** *n* **–mical** *adj* **1** of astronomy **2** very large: *astronomical sums of money*
astrophysics *n* science of the nature of the stars and the forces that influence

them **–ical** *adj*
Astroturf *n tdmk* artificial turf
astute *adj* shrewd **~ly** *adv* **~ness** *n*
asunder *adv, adj* apart
asylum *n* **1** protection and shelter **2** *becoming rare* mental hospital
asymmetric also **-rical** *adj* not symmetrical
at *prep* **1** (showing where): *at the airport* **2** (showing when): *at Christmas* **3** towards: *Look at me.* **4** by: *surprised at the news* **5** (showing how someone does something): *good at games* **6** (showing a state or continued activity): *at war* **7** (showing price, level or age): *sold at 10 cents each*
atavism *n* recurrence of a trait found in ancestors **–istic** *adj*
ataxia *n* lack of muscular coordination
ate *past t. of* eat
-ate *suffix* **1** (cause to) become or have: *hyphenate* **2** having: *fortunate*
atelier *n* artist's studio or workshop
atheism *n* belief that there is no God **–ist** *n*
athlete *n* person who practises athletics
athletics *n* physical exercises such as running and jumping **athletic** *adj* **1** of athletics **2** physically strong and active
-ation *suffix* act or result of doing the stated thing: *continuation*
-ative *suffix* **1** liking or tending to have or do: *argumentative* **2** for the purpose of: *consultative*
atlas *n* book of maps
atmosphere *n* **1** gases surrounding a heavenly body, esp. the Earth **2** air **3** general feeling of a place **–spheric** *adj* **1** of or concerning the Earth's atmosphere **2** mysteriously beautiful and strange: *atmospheric music* **–spherics** *pl n* (electrical phenomena causing) radio interference
atoll *n* ring-shaped coral island
atom *n* smallest unit of an element **~ic** *adj* **1** of atoms **2** using the power that comes from splitting atoms
atom bomb also **atomic bomb** *n* bomb that uses the explosive power of nuclear energy
atomic number *n* number of protons in the nucleus of an element
atomize, –ise *vt* make into small particles or fine spray **atomizer** *n*
atonal *adj* (of music) composed without using the key system **~ity** *n*
atone *vi* make amends (for wrongdoing) **~ment** *n*
-ator *suffix* -er[2]
atrium *n* **-ia** *or* **-iums** **1** inner courtyard in a building **2** chamber of the heart
atrocious *adj* very cruel or bad **~ly** *adv*
atrocity *n* **1** very cruel act **2** something very ugly
atrophy /ˈatrəfi/ *vi/t* (cause to) lose flesh and muscle; weaken **atrophy** *n*
atropine *n* poisonous natural substance used in medicine
attach *vt* **1** fasten **2** cause to join: *He attached himself to another group of tourists.* **3** regard as having (special meaning or importance) **4 be attached to** be fond of **~ment** *n*
attaché *n* person who helps an ambassador
attaché case *n* thin hard case with a handle, for carrying papers
attack *n* **1** (act of) violence **2** words intended to hurt **3** sudden illness ♦ *vt* **1** make an attack **2** begin (something) with eagerness and interest **~er** *n*
attain *vt* succeed in; reach **~able** *adj* **~ment** *n* **1** act of attaining **2** a skill
attainder *n* (formerly) loss of property and rights
attempt *vt* try ♦ *n* **1** effort made to do something **2 attempt on someone's life** effort to murder someone
attend *v* **1** *vt* be present at: *attend the meeting* **2** *vi* give attention **3** *vi* look after **~ance** *n* **1** act of being present **2** number of people present: *a large attendance* **~ant** *n* person who looks after a place or people **~ant** *adj*
attention *n* **1** careful thought: *pay attention to the teacher* **2** particular care or consideration: *Old cars need lots of attention.*
attentive *adj* **1** listening carefully **2** politely helpful **~ly** *adv* **~ness** *n*

attenuate *vi/t* (cause to) diminish in force, value, or severity
attest *vt* **1** declare to be true **2** be proof of: *His success attests (to) his ability.* **~ation** *n*
attic *n* room below the roof of a house
Attic *adj* of Athens or Attica
attire *n* clothes ♦ *vt* put on clothes
attitude *n* **1** way of feeling and behaving **2** position of the body **–dinal** *adj*
attorney /ə'tuhni/ *n* **1** *AmE* lawyer **2** someone with legal power to act for another
attorney general *n* **attorneys general** or **attorney generals** chief law officer of a state
attract *vt* **1** excite the admiration or interest of: *He was attracted by her smile.* **2** draw towards: *Flowers attract bees.* **~ive** *adj* interesting, pleasing **~ively** *adv* **~iveness** *n* state of being attractive **~ion** *n* **1** power of attracting **2** something attractive
attribute *n* **1** quality that belongs to a person or thing **2** something regarded as a sign of a person or position
attribute to *phr vt* ascribe to: *He attributes his success to hard work.* **–tive** *adj* **–tion** *n*
attrition *n* process of tiring, weakening, or destroying by continual worry, hardship, or repeated attacks: *a war of attrition*
attune to *phr vt* make used to or ready for
atypical *adj* not typical **~ly** *adv*
aubergine *n esp. BrE* eggplant
aubretia *n* trailing rock plant with small flowers
auburn *adj, n* (esp. of hair) reddish brown
au courant *adj* up to date
auction *n* public meeting to sell goods to whoever offers the most money ♦ *vt* sell by auction
auctioneer *n* person in charge of an auction, who calls out the prices
audacious *adj* **1** (foolishly) daring **2** disrespectful **~ly** *adv* **–city** *n*
audible *adj* able to be heard **–bly** *adv*
audience *n* **1** people listening to or watching a performance **2** formal meeting with someone important: *have an audience with the Pope*
audio *adj* of sound radio signals **audio** *n*
audio- *prefix* of, for, or using sound
audio-visual *adj* of both sight and hearing
audit *vt* examine (business accounts) officially **audit** *n* **~or** *n*
audition *n* test performance given by an entertainer ♦ *v* **1** *vi* give a test performance **2** *vt* judge in a test performance
auditorium *n* space where an audience sits
auditory *adj* of or experienced through hearing
au fait *adj* fully informed
auger *n* tool for boring holes
aught *n arch.* anything
augment *vi/t* increase
augur *v* **1** *vt* foretell **2** *vt* presage: *This rain augurs well for farmers.* **3** *vi* predict ♦ *n* soothsayer **~y** *n* **1** divining the future **2** omen
august /əw'gust/ *adj* noble and grand
August *n* the 8th month of the year
auld lang syne *n Scots* the good times past
aunt *n* sister of one's father or mother, or wife of one's uncle
Aunt Sally *n* **1** (figure of a woman used as a target in) a fairground sideshow **2** *BrE* easy target for criticism
au pair *n* young foreigner who lives with a family and helps with housework
aura *n* effect or feeling produced by a person or place
aural *adj* of or related to the sense of hearing
aureole /'awriohl/ *n* halo
aurora *n* atmospheric phenomenon consisting of bands and streamers of light seen esp. in polar skies, called the **aurora australis** in the southern hemisphere and the **aurora borealis** in the northern
auscultation *n* listening to the heart and

lungs usu. with a stethoscope
auspices *pl n fml* **under the auspices of** helped by
auspicious *adj* showing signs of future success **~ly** *adv*
Aussie *n, adj infml* Australian
austere *adj* **1** without comfort; hard: *an austere life* **2** without decoration; plain **~ly** *adv* **-terity** *n*
Australasian *n, adj* (inhabitant) of Australasia, the islands of the south and central Pacific
Australian *n, adj* (inhabitant) of Australia
Austrian *n, adj* (inhabitant) of Austria
Austro- *prefix* **1** Australian and: *Austro-Malaysian* **2** Austrian and: *Austro-Italian*
aut-, auto- *prefix* of or by oneself or itself: *autoerotic*|*automobile*
autarchy *n* absolute sovereignty
authentic *adj* known to be real; genuine **~ally** *adv* **~ate** *vt* prove to be authentic **~ation** *n* **~ity** *n* quality of being authentic
author *n* **1** writer **2** person who thinks of an idea or plan **~ship** *n*
authoress *n* female author
authoritarian *n, adj* (person) demanding total obedience to rules **~ism** *n*
authoritative *adj* deserving respect; able to be trusted **~ly** *adv*
authority *n* **1** power to command: *Who is in authority here?* **2** person or group with this power **3** authoritative person, book, etc.: *He's an authority on plants.*
authorize, -ise *vt* give formal permission for **-ization, -isation** *n*
Authorized Version *n* standard English translation of the Bible published in 1611
autism *n* disorder of childhood development marked by inability to form relationships **-istic** *adj*
autobahn *n* German motorway
autobiography *n* written account of one's own life **-phical** *adj*
autocrat *n* **1** ruler with unlimited power **2** dictatorial person **~ic** *adj* **-cracy** *n* government by an autocrat
Autocue *n tdmk* continuous prompting device, in the form of a screen display-ing text, which enables a speaker to address a usu. television audience without using notes
auto-da-fé *n* **autos-da-fé** ceremonial burning of those declared heretics by the Spanish Inquisition
autoeroticism, -erotism *n* self-induced sexual arousal **-erotic** *adj*
autograph *n* signature of someone famous ♦ *vt* sign one's name on
automate *vt* change (a process) to automation
automatic *adj* **1** (esp. of a machine) able to work by itself **2** done without thought **3** certain to happen ♦ *n* (automatic) gun **~ally** *adv*
automatic pilot *n* device that automatically steers an aircraft, ship etc.
automation *n* use of machines that need no human control
automaton /awˈtomət(ə)n/ *n* **-ta** *or* **-tons** **1** thing or machine that works by itself **2** person who acts without thought or feeling
automobile *n AmE* car
autonomous *adj* governing itself
autonomy *n* self-government
autopsy *n* postmortem
autoroute *n* French motorway
autostrada *n* **-das** or **-de** Italian motorway
autosuggestion *n* effect of a person's own ideas on their physical or mental state, behaviour, etc.
autumn *n* season between summer and winter **~al** *adj*
auxiliary *adj* helping; adding support ♦ *n* **1** helper **2** foreign soldier in the service of a country at war **3** an auxiliary verb, e.g. be, do, and may
AV *abbrev. for:* Authorized Version
avail *vi* **1** be of use **2 avail oneself of** make use of ♦ *n* **of/to no avail** of no use; without success
available *adj* obtainable **-bility** *n*
avalanche *n* mass of snow crashing down a mountain

avant-garde *adj, n* (of) people who produce the newest ideas, esp. in the arts

avarice *n* greed for wealth **avaricious** *adj*

avatar *n* **1** appearance of a Hindu god in human form **2** person who seems to embody a quality or idea

avenge *vt* revenge

avenue *n* **1** road between two rows of trees **2** way to a result

aver *vt* **-rr-** state forcefully

average *n* **1** amount found by adding quantities together and then dividing by the number of quantities **2** level regarded as usual ♦ *adj* **1** equal to the average amount **2** ordinary ♦ *vt* **1** calculate the average of **2** be or do as an average: *I average eight hours work a day.*

averse *adj* feeling dislike

aversion *n* **1** strong dislike **2** hated person or thing

avert *vt* **1** prevent from happening: *avert accidents* **2** turn away (one's eyes)

aviary *n* cage for keeping birds in

aviation *n* flying in aircraft **–tor** *n*

avid *adj* extremely keen **~ly** *adv*

avionics *pl n* development of electronics for aviation and space flight

avocado *n* **-dos** *or* **-does** green tropical fruit

avocation *n lit* **1** occupation **2** hobby

avocet *n* black and white wading bird

avoid *vt* keep away from, esp. on purpose **~able** *adj* **~ance** *n*

avoirdupois /ˌavwahdoohˈpwah/ *adj, n* (of the) system of weights in which the standard measures are the ounce, pound, and ton

avowed *adj* openly admitted

avuncular *adj* of or like an uncle

AWACS *n* Airborne Warning and Control System; an aircraft fitted with sophisticated radar equipment which provides early warning of air attack and coordinates defensive measures

await *vt* wait for

awake *adj* not asleep ♦ *vi/t* also **awaken,awoke** *or* **awakened, awoken** *or* **awaked** wake

awakening *n* **1** act of waking from sleep **2 rude awakening** sudden consciousness of an unpleasant state of affairs

award *vt* give officially: *award prizes* ♦ *n* something awarded

aware *adj* having knowledge or understanding **~ness** *n*

awash *adj* covered with water

away *adv* **1** to or at another place: *Go away!* **2** so as to be gone: *The sounds died away.* **3** continuously: *He's hammering away.* ♦ *adj* (of a sports match) played at the place of one's opponent

awe *n* respect mixed with fear

awe-inspiring *adj* causing feelings of awe

awesome *adj* causing feelings of awe

awestruck *adj* filled with awe

awful *adj* **1** very bad: *awful weather* **2** very great: *an awful lot of work* **~ly** *adv* very

awkward *adj* **1** clumsy **2** difficult to handle **3** inconvenient: *They came at an awkward time.* **4** embarrassing: *an awkward silence* **~ly** *adv* **~ness** *n*

awl *n* pointed tool for making small holes in e.g. leather

awning *n* movable cloth roof put up as a protection against sun or rain

awoke *past t. of* awake

awoken *past p. of* awake

AWOL *adj* absent without leave

awry /əˈrie/ *adj, adv* **1** not in the planned way **2** twisted or bent

axe *n* **1** tool for cutting down trees **2 have an axe to grind** have a selfish reason for one's actions ♦ *vt* put a sudden end to (jobs, plans, etc.)

axiom *n* principle accepted as true **~atic** *adj* not needing proof

axis *n* **axes** **1** line round which something spins: *the Earth's axis* **2** fixed line against which positions are measured on a graph

axle *n* bar on which a wheel turns

ayatollah *n* Shiite Muslim religious leader

aye[1] *n, adv* (person who votes) yes

aye² *adv arch.* ever
azalea *n* type of rhododendron with trumpet-shaped flowers
azure *adj, n* bright blue

B

B, b the 2nd letter of the English alphabet
b *abbrev. for:* born
BA *abbrev. for:* Bachelor of Arts
baa *vi, n* (make) the sound a sheep makes
babble *vi/t* talk quickly and foolishly **babble** *n*
babe *n* baby
babel *n* confusion of sounds or voices
baboon *n* kind of large monkey
baby *n* **1** very young child: **2** very young animal or bird: *a baby monkey* **3** *AmE infml* person, esp. a girl or woman **4** *infml* one's special responsibility ♦ *vt* treat (a person) with too much care **~ish** *adj* like a baby
baby-sitter *n* person who looks after children while their parents are out **baby-sit** *vi* **-sat**; *pres. p.* **-sitting**
baccarat *n* card game involving betting
bacchanalia *n* drunken feast; orgy **–lian** *adj*
bachelor *n* unmarried man
bacillus *n* **-lli** rod-shaped bacterium
back *n* **1** the part of one's body opposite the chest, from the neck to the bottom of the spine **2** the part furthest from the direction that something moves in or faces: *the back of the aircraft* **3** the less important side of something **4** the part of a chair that one leans against **5** the end of a book or newspaper **6 behind someone's back** without their knowledge **7 break the back of** do most or the worst part of (something) **8 have/with one's back to the wall** (be) in the greatest difficulties **9 put someone's back up** annoy someone ♦ *adv* **1** in or into an earlier place: *Put the book back on the shelf.* **2** towards the back: *Lean well back.* **3** away from the speaker: *Stand back!* **4** in reply: *Phone me back.* **5** in an earlier time: *back in 1983* ♦ *v* **1** *vi/t* move backwards: *back the car down the road* **2** *vt* support and encourage **3** *vt* bet money on **4** *vt* be or make the back of: *curtains backed with satin* **back down** *phr vi* give up an argument **back onto** *phr vt* (of a place) have at the back: *a house backing onto the river* **back out** *phr vi* not fulfil a promise **back up** *phr vt* support in an argument ♦ *adj* **1** at or in the back **2** owing from before: *back pay* **3** not current **~er** *n* **1** someone who supports a plan with money **2** someone who bets on a horse **~less** *adj*
backache *n* pain in the back
backbench *n* any of the seats in the British parliament on which rank and file members may sit **backbencher** *n*
backbiting *n* unkind talk about someone who is absent
back boiler *n* water-heating system behind a fireplace
backbone *n* **1** spine (1) **2** strongest part of something **3** strength of character
backbreaking *adj* (of work) very hard
backchat *n* answering back
backcloth *n* backdrop of painted cloth, used on a stage
backcomb *vt* comb (hair) back towards the roots, to make it look thick
backdate *vt* make effective from an earlier date
backdrop *n* background
backfire *vi* **1** (of a car engine) make a noise because the gas explodes too soon **2** have the opposite effect to that intended
backgammon *n* board game played with counters
background *n* **1** scenery behind the main object **2** (information about) conditions existing when something hap-

pens or happened **3** person's family, experience and education

backhand *n* stroke (e.g. in tennis) with the back of the hand turned in the direction of movement **~ed** *adj* **1** using or made with a backhand **2** (of a remark) indirect, esp. sarcastic **~er** *n* **1** backhand **2** bribe

backing *n* **1** help; support **2** something that makes the back of an object

backlash *n* sudden violent reaction, esp. against a political or social movement

backlog *n* things (esp. work) remaining to be done

back number *n* old issue of a newspaper or magazine

back of beyond *n infml* a very distant place, difficult to get to

backpack *n esp. AmE* rucksack ♦ *vi* go hiking with a backpack **~er** *n*

back passage *n* rectum

backpedal *vi* **-ll-** (*AmE* **-l-**) **1** pedal backwards **2** take back a statement; change an earlier opinion

back projection *n* (method of projecting) a picture on a translucent screen used in film-making usu. to provide a moving backdrop to action taking place in the foreground

backroom boy *n* person doing important but secret work

back seat *n* **1** seat at the back of a car **2** less important position

back-seat driver *n* person who gives unwanted advice to a driver or person in control

backside *n* bottom[1] (2)

backslapping *adj* (of behaviour) too friendly and noisy

backslide *vi* go back to a worse condition **–slider** *n*

backspace *vi, n* (operate) the key which moves a typewriter carriage backwards

backstage *adv, adj* **1** behind a theatre stage **2** in private

backstairs *adj* **1** secret **2** sordid

backstreet *n* street away from the main streets, esp. in a poor area of town

backstroke *n* way of swimming on one's back

back-to-backs *pl n BrE* rows of terraced houses separated only by narrow alleyways at the rear

backtrack *vi* **1** go back over the same path **2** backpedal (2)

backup *n* **1** thing or person ready to be used in place of or to help another **2** support

backward *adj* **1** towards the back **2** late in development: *a backward child* **~ness** *n*

backwards *adv* **1** towards the back, the beginning, or the past: *say the alphabet backwards* **2** with the back part in front: *put one's hat on backwards* **3 know something backwards** know something perfectly

backwash *n* backward movement in air or water caused by something moving through it

backwater *n* **1** part of a river outside the current **2** place not influenced by outside events

backwoods *pl n* remote or culturally backward area **~man** *n*

backyard *n* **1** yard behind a house **2** area under one's personal control

bacon *n* salted or smoked pig meat

bacteria *pl n sing.* **-rium** microscopic organisms many of which cause disease

bacteriology *n* (science that deals with) the life of bacteria **–gist** *n* **–gical** *adj*

bad *adj* **worse, worst 1** unpleasant: *bad news* **2** morally wrong **3** unhealthy: *Smoking is bad for you.* **4** not of acceptable quality **5** severe: *a bad cold* **6** rotten: *The apples went bad.* **7** disobedient: *a bad boy* **8 have/get a bad name** lose or have lost people's respect ♦ *n* a bad state **~ly** *adv* **1** in a bad way: *We played badly.* **2** seriously: *We were badly beaten.* **3** a great deal: *He needs help badly.*

bad blood *n* angry or bitter feeling

bad debt *n* debt that is unlikely to be paid

baddy *n infml* bad person

bade *past t. and p. of* bid[2]
badge *n* something worn to show one's rank, membership, etc.
badger *n* black and white nocturnal burrowing mammal ♦ *vt* pester
badinage /ˈbadiˌnazh/ *n* playful joking talk
badly-off *adj* **1** poor **2** lacking
badminton *n* court game played with a shuttlecock over a high net
bad-mouth *vt sl esp. AmE* speak badly of
baffle *vt* be too difficult for (someone): *a baffling question* ♦ *n* device that regulates or checks a flow
bag *n* **1** soft container that opens at the top: *a shopping bag* **2 bags of** *esp. BrE* plenty of **3 in the bag** certain to be gained♦ *v* **-gg- 1** *vt* put into a bag **2** *vt* kill (animals or birds) **3** *vt* take possession of **4** *vi* be baggy
bagatelle *n* **1** trifle (2) **2** game of hitting small balls into holes on a board
baggage *n* **1** luggage **2** *infml* flirtatious woman
baggy *adj* hanging in loose folds: *baggy jeans*
bag lady *n* homeless old woman who carries her possessions around in a bag
bagpipes *pl n* musical instrument with pipes and a bag of air
bail[1] *n* money paid so that a prisoner may be set free until tried ♦ *v* **bail out** *phr v* **1** *vt* pay bail for someone **2** *vt* help someone with money **3** *vi/t* remove water from a boat **4** *AmE* bale out (1)
bail[2] *n* piece of wood laid on top of stumps in cricket
bailey *n* outer wall of a castle
Bailey bridge *n* prefabricated bridge
bailiff *n BrE* **1** law official who takes possession of goods when money is owed **2** farm manager
bairn *n esp. Scots* child
bait *n* food used to attract esp. fish to be caught ♦ *vt* **1** put bait on (e.g. a hook) **2** make (an animal or a person) angry intentionally
baize *n* thick woollen cloth used for covering billiard tables
bake 1 *vi/t* (cause to) cook in an oven **2** *vi/t* (cause to) become hard by heating **3** *vi* become hot: *I'm baking!* **baker** *n* person who bakes bread for sale **bakery** *n* place where bread is baked (and sold)
Bakelite *n tdmk* early type of hard plastic
baker's dozen *n* thirteen
baking powder *n* powder used to make bread and cakes rise
bakkie *n SAfrE* pick-up (2)
baksheesh *n* money given as a tip
balaclava *n* knitted hood that covers the ears and neck
balalaika *n* stringed instrument with a triangular body
balance *n* **1** state in which weight is evenly spread: *It was difficult to keep my balance on the icy path.* **2** instrument for weighing **3** amount remaining somewhere: *my bank balance* **4 in the balance** uncertain(ly) **5 on balance** considering everything ♦ *v* **1** *vi/t* keep steady **2** *vi* (of two things, esp. debts) be equal **3** *vt* compare (two things): *balance the advantages against the disadvantages*
balance of payments *n* the difference between the amount of money coming into a country and the amount going out, including trade in insurance and banking
balance of power *n* situation in which the states or power blocs in a given area are of roughly equal strength and peace is thereby preserved
balance of trade *n* the difference in value between a country's imports and exports
balance sheet *n* statement of financial position
balcony *n* **1** piece of floor that sticks out from an upstairs wall **2** upstairs seats in a theatre
bald *adj* **1** with no hair on the head **2** plain: *a bald statement* **~ing** *adj* becoming bald **~ness** *n*
balderdash *n infml* nonsense
baldric *n* sword belt worn diagonally across the body

bale *n* large tightly tied mass of esp. soft material: *a bale of cotton*

baleen *n* whalebone

baleful *n* threatening **–fully** *adv*

bale out *phr v* **1** *vi BrE* escape from an aircraft **2** *vi/t* remove water from a boat

balk *v* **1** *vi* be unwilling to agree: *I balked at the price.* **2** hinder ♦ *n* rough wooden beam

ball¹ *n* **1** round object used in games **2** round mass: *a ball of string/clay* **3** round part of the body: *eyeballs* **4 on the ball** showing up-to-date knowledge and readiness to act **5 play ball** cooperate **balls** *pl n taboo sl* **1** testicles **2** nonsense

ball² *n* **1** formal occasion for dancing **2 have a ball** have a very good time

ballad *n* **1** poem that tells a story **2** popular love song

ballast *n* heavy material carried to keep a ship steady, or to be thrown from a balloon to make it rise higher ♦ *vt* fill or supply with ballast

ball bearing *n* (one of) a collection of small metal balls placed around a machine part so that it moves easily

ballcock *n* hollow floating ball that opens and closes a hole through which water flows

ballerina *n* female ballet dancer

ballet *n* **1** dance with music in which a story is told **2** music for such a dance **3** art of doing such a dance **4** group of ballet dancers

ball game *n infml* state of affairs

ballistic missile *n* missile that is guided as it rises into the air but then falls freely

ballistics *n* science of the movement of objects, such as bullets fired from a gun **ballistic** *adj*

balloon *n* **1** bag filled with gas or air so that it can float **2** small rubber bag that can be blown up and used as a toy **3 when the balloon goes up** when the action starts or the moment of danger arrives ♦ *vi* swell up like a balloon **~ing** *n* sport of riding in a balloon

ballot *n* **1** (paper used in a) secret vote **2** number of votes recorded ♦ **1** *vi* vote or decide by secret ballot **2** *vt* find out the views of (a group) by holding a vote

ballot box *n* box in which voters put their ballots

ball park *n infml* range of numbers, prices, etc., within which the correct figure is likely to be

ballpoint *n* pen with a ball at the end that rolls thick ink onto the paper

ballroom *n* large room suitable for a ball

balls up *phr vt BrE taboo sl* spoil **balls-up** *n*

ballyhoo *n* publicity-seeking activities

balm *n* **1** oily liquid used to lessen pain **2** aromatic plant **3** something that soothes

balmy *adj* (of air) soft and warm

baloney *n* nonsense

balsa *n* (light wood of) a tropical tree

balsam *n* **1** (tree that yields) balm **2** flowering plant with translucent, watery stems

balustrade /ˌbaləˈstrayd/ *n* upright posts with a bar along the top, guarding an edge where people might fall

bamboo *n* **-boos** (hollow jointed stems of) a tropical plant of the grass family

bamboozle *vt sl* deceive

ban *vt* **-nn-** forbid ♦ *n* order forbidding something

banal *adj* uninteresting because ordinary **~ity** *n*

banana *n* long yellow tropical fruit

banana skin *n BrE infml* event or situation likely to cause difficulty or embarrassment

band¹ *n* **1** narrow piece of material for fastening, or putting round something: *a rubber band* **2** stripe (1) **3** area between measurable limits: *the £10,000-£30,000 income band* **band together** *phr vi* unite for a purpose

band² *n* group of people, esp. musicians playing popular music

bandage *n* narrow piece of cloth for tying round a wound ♦ *vt* tie up with a bandage

Band Aid *n tdmk for* plaster (2)
bandanna *n* large handkerchief
b and b *abbrev. for:* (small hotel providing) bed and breakfast
bandbox *n* light cardboard or wooden box for hats
bandeau *n* **-eaux** band of material to keep the hair in place
bandicoot *n* ratlike Australasian marsupial
bandit *n* armed robber **~ry** *n*
bandolier *n* belt worn across the chest with loops for cartridges
bandstand *n* raised open-air place for a band to play
bandwagon *n* **jump on a bandwagon** join something that is popular, for personal gain
bandy[1] *vt* **bandy words** quarrel
bandy[2] *adj* (of legs) curved outwards at the knees
bane *n* cause of trouble **~ful** *adj* harmful
bang *vi/t* hit violently and noisily: *I banged my head against the ceiling.* ♦ *adv* exactly: *bang in the middle* **bang** *n*
banger *n BrE* **1** *infml* sausage **2** old car **3** noisy firework
bangle *n* band worn on the wrist as decoration
bang-on *adj, adv BrE infml* **1** completely accurate(ly); just what/as is needed **2** first-rate
banish *vt* **1** send away as a punishment **2** stop thinking about **~ment** *n*
banister *n* also **banisters** *pl n* upright posts with a bar along the top, beside a staircase
banjo *n* **-jos** *or* **-joes** stringed instrument used esp. to play popular music
bank[1] *n* **1** land beside a river or lake **2** raised heap (e.g. of earth) **3** mass of clouds **4** set of things arranged in a row: *a bank of oars* ♦ *vi* (of an aircraft) raise one side while turning
bank[2] *n* **1** place where money is kept and paid out on demand **2** place where something is kept for use: *a blood bank* ♦ *vi/t* keep (money) in a bank **bank on** *phr vt* depend on **~er** *n* person who owns, works in, or controls a bank
bank card *n* cheque card
bank holiday *n BrE* official public holiday on a weekday
banking *n* financial business of a bank
bank note *n* piece of paper money
bank rate *n* the rate of interest fixed by a central bank
bankroll *n AmE* supply of money ♦ *vt AmE infml* supply money for or pay the cost of an enterprise
bankrupt *adj* unable to pay one's debts ♦ *n* person who is bankrupt ♦ *vt* make bankrupt or very poor **~cy** *n* state of being bankrupt
banner *n* **1** *lit* flag **2** piece of cloth or board with a political message on it, carried by marchers
bannock *n* flat Scottish cake usu. made of oatmeal
banns *pl n* public declaration of an intended marriage
banquet *n* formal dinner **banquet** *vi*
banshee *n* spirit that wails to warn of approaching death
bantam *n* small chicken
bantamweight *n* boxer weighing less than 53.5 kg
banter *n* light joking talk **banter** *vi*
Bantu *n* **1** family of Southern African languages **2 -tu** or **-tus** *usu. derog* black South African
Bantustan *n derog* homeland (2)
banyan *n* Indian tree whose branches grow new trunks and roots
baobab *n* African tree with a very thick trunk
baptism *n* **1** Christian religious ceremony of touching or covering a person with water **2 baptism of fire: a** soldier's first experience of war **b** any unpleasant first experience **–tize, -tise** *vt* perform baptism on
Baptist *n* member of a Protestant church which baptizes full˚ believers **Baptist** *adj*
bar[1] *n* **1** long narrow piece of solid material: *a bar of chocolate* **2** length of wood or metal **3** group of musical notes **4** place where drinks are served **5**

bank of sand or stones under water **6** barrier **7** (*cap.*) the legal profession, esp. barristers **8 behind bars** in prison **9 prisoner at the bar** person being tried in a court of law ♦ *vt* **-rr- 1** close with a bar: *They barred themselves in.* **2** forbid; prevent: *He was barred from playing football.* ♦ *prep* **1** except **2 bar none** with no exception

bar[2] *n* unit of atmospheric pressure

barb *n* sharp point with a curved shape **~ed** *adj* **1** with short sharp points **2** (of speech) sharply unkind

barbarian *n* wild uncivilized person

barbaric *adj* **1** very cruel **2** like a barbarian **–barism** *n* condition of being a barbarian **–barous** *adj* **–ity** *n* great cruelty

barbecue *n* **1** metal frame for cooking meat outdoors **2** party where this is done ♦ *vt* cook on a barbecue

barbel *n* **1** spine projecting from the lips of some fish **2** type of fish with four barbels on its upper jaw

barber *n* person who cuts men's hair

barbiturate sleep-inducing drug

bard *n* **1** poet **2 the Bard** Shakespeare

bare *adj* **1** without clothes or covering **2** with nothing added: *the bare facts* **3** empty: *a room bare of furniture* ♦ *vt* bring to view; expose **~ly** *adv* hardly

bareback *adj, adv* riding, esp. a horse, without a saddle

bare bones *pl n* simplest but most important parts or facts

barefaced *adj* shameless

barefoot *adv* without shoes

bareheaded *adj* with the head uncovered

bargain *n* **1** agreement to do something in return for something else **2** something sold cheap **3 into the bargain** besides everything else ♦*vi* talk about the conditions of a sale **bargain for/on** *phr vt* take into account; expect

barge *n* flat-bottomed boat ♦ *vi* move heavily and rudely **barge in** *phr vi* rush in rudely; interrupt

baritone *n* (man with) a singing voice between tenor and bass

barium *n* soft metallic element

barium meal *n* solution of barium phosphate which, when swallowed, enables X-rays of the stomach and intestines to be taken

bark[1] *v* **1** *vi* make the noise dogs make **2** *vt* say in a fierce voice **3 bark up the wrong tree** have a mistaken idea ♦ *n* **1** sharp loud noise made by a dog **2 his bark is worse than his bite** he is not as bad-tempered as he appears

bark[2] *n* outer covering of a tree

barley *n* grasslike grain plant grown as a food crop

barley sugar *n* type of boiled sweet

barmaid *n* woman who serves drinks in a bar

barman *n* **-men** man who serves drinks in a bar

bar mitzvah *n* (ceremony held for) a Jewish boy of 13, assuming adult religious duties

barmy *adj sl* foolish; mad

barn *n* farm building for storing things in

barnacle *n* small shellfish that collects on rocks and ships

barney *n infml* fight, quarrel

barnstorm *vi* go on tour esp. in rural districts with e.g. a theatrical performance or a flying show

barnyard *n* farmyard

barometer *n* instrument for measuring air pressure so as to judge what weather is coming

baron *n* **1** British noble of the lowest rank **2** powerful businessman

baroness *n* **1** woman with the rank of a baron **2** wife of a baron

baronet *n* British knight, below a baron in rank **~cy** *n* rank of baronet

baronial *adj* **1** of a baron **2** imposing

baroque *adj* **1** in a decorated style fashionable in 17th-century Europe **2** (too) greatly ornamented

barque *n* type of sailing ship

barrack *vi/t BrE* interrupt by shouting

barracks *pl n* building where soldiers live

barracuda *n* large predatory fish

barrage *n* **1** heavy gunfire **2** rapid series (e.g. of questions) **3** dam built across a river **barrage** *vt*

barrel *n* **1** round wooden container **2** long tube-shaped part of a gun, pen, or camera **3 over a barrel** in a difficult position

barrel organ *n* musical instrument on wheels, played by turning a handle

barren *adj* **1** infertile **2** useless; empty: *a barren discussion* **~ness** *n*

barricade *n* something quickly built to block a street ♦ *vt* close or defend with a barricade

barrier *n* something placed in the way to prevent movement

barring *prep* except for

barrister *n* (esp. in England) lawyer who has the right to speak in the highest courts

barrow[1] *n* **1** small cart to be pushed **2** wheelbarrow

barrow[2] *n* large mound of earth over a grave

bar sinister *n* (imaginary heraldic device representing) illegitimacy

bartender *n AmE* barman

barter *vi/t* exchange goods for other goods **barter** *n*

basalt *n* greenish-black rock

bascule *n* (bridge with) a span which opens by pivoting upwards on one or both ends

base[1] *n* **1** part of a thing on which a thing stands **2** origin from which something develops or is made **3** centre from which something is controlled **4** centre for military operations **5** main part or substance of a mixture: *a vegetable base* **6** point which a player must touch in baseball to make a run **7 not get to first base (with)** not even begin to succeed (with) ♦ *vt* provide with a centre: *a company based in Paris* **base on/upon** *phr vt* form by using something else as a starting point: *a film based on a novel* **~less** *adj* without good reason **basal** *adj*

base[2] *adj* **1** *esp. lit* dishonourable **2** (of metal) not regarded as precious **~ly** *adv* **~ness** *n*

baseball *n* **1** American national team game **2** ball used in this game

baseline *n* line at the end of a court, e.g. in tennis

basement *n* room in a house below street level

base rate *n* standard rate of interest on which a bank bases its charges for lending and interest on borrowing

bases *n pl of* basis

bash *vt* hit hard ♦ *n* **1** hard blow **2 have a bash** *infml* make an attempt

bashful *adj* shy **~ly** *adv*

basic *adj* most necessary; fundamental: *basic principles* **~ally** *adv* in spite of surface behaviour or details; in reality **basics** *pl n* basic parts or principles

BASIC, Basic *n* high-level computer language

basil *n* plant of the mint family

basilica *n* **1** Roman law-court **2** large church

basilisk *n* mythical reptile whose look could kill

basin *n* **1** round container for liquids; bowl **2** washbasin **3** hollow place where water collects **4** large valley

basis *n* **bases 1** the facts, principles, etc., from which something is formed, started, or developed: *the basis of an opinion* **2** the stated way of carrying out an action, process, etc.: *working on a part-time basis*

bask *vi* lie in enjoyable warmth

basket *n* light woven container

basketball *n* **1** indoor game in which players try to throw a ball into a basket **2** large ball used in this game

basket case *n sl* very severely injured or handicapped person

Basque *n, adj* (language or inhabitant) of a region straddling the border between SW France and NE Spain

bas-relief *n* sculpture in which the design stands out slightly from the surrounding surface

bass[1] *n* **1** (man with) the lowest human singing voice **2** instrument with a low range of notes: *a bass guitar* **3** double bass

bass² *n* kind of fish that can be eaten

basset also **basset hound** *n* dog with short legs and long ears

bassinet *n* wickerwork cradle or pram

bassoon *n* large woodwind musical instrument

bastard *n* **1** child of unmarried parents **2** *sl* unpleasant person **3** *sl* man of the stated kind: *You lucky bastard!* ♦ *adj* **1** illegitimate **2** false **~y** *n* **~ize** *vt* debase

baste *vt* **1** pour fat over (meat) during cooking **2** tack (1)

bastion *n* **1** part of a castle wall that sticks out **2** place where a principle is defended: *a bastion of freedom*

bat¹ *n* **1** stick for hitting the ball in a game **2 off one's own bat** without being told to do something ♦ *vi/t* **1** strike or hit (as if) with a bat **2** *vt* **not bat an eyelid** show no sign of shock

bat² *n* mouselike animal that flies at night

batch *n* group; set

bated *adj* **with bated breath** too frightened or excited to breathe

bath *n* **1** container in which one sits to wash the whole body **2** act of washing one's whole body at one time **3** liquid in a container used for some special purpose: *an eyebath* **4** place with a swimming pool or baths for public use ♦ *v* **1** *vi* have a bath **2** *vt* give a bath to

Bath chair *n* (hooded) wheelchair

bathe *v* **1** *vi esp. BrE* swim in the sea, etc. **2** *vi AmE* have a bath **3** *vt* put in liquid: *bathe your eyes* ♦ *n* a swim **bather** *n* swimmer

bathing suit *n BrE* swimming costume

bathos /ˈbaythos/ *n* sudden change from beautiful ideas to ordinary foolish ones

bathrobe *n esp. AmE* dressing gown worn before or after bathing

bathroom *n* **1** room with a bath **2** *AmE* toilet

bathtub *n esp. AmE* bath (1)

bathysphere *n* diving chamber for deep sea observations

batik *n* (fabric printed by) a method of hand printing using dye and wax

batiste *n* fine sheer fabric

batman *n* **-men** British officer's servant

baton *n* **1** short stick used to conduct an orchestra **2** truncheon **3** stick passed on by members of a relay team

batsman *n* **-men** player in cricket who tries to hit the ball with a bat

battalion *n* army unit of 500-1,000 soldiers

batten *n* thin strip esp. of wood **batten down** *phr vt* fasten with boards

batten on *phr vi* live at the expense of

batter¹ *vi/t* **1** beat hard and repeatedly **2** cause to lose shape by continual use

batter² *n* mixture of flour, eggs, and milk esp. for making pancakes

batter³ *n* person who bats

battering ram *n* (in former times) heavy log used for breaking down castle doors

battery *n* **1** apparatus for producing electricity **2** army unit of big guns **3** line of boxes in which hens are kept **4** set of things used together: *a battery of tests* **5** unlawful use of force

battle *n* short fight between enemies or opposing groups ♦ *vi* fight; struggle

battleaxe, *Ame* **-ax** *n* **1** heavy axe for fighting **2** fierce woman

battle cruiser *n* warship slightly smaller than a battleship but faster

battlefield *n* place where a battle is fought

battlements *pl n* wall round a castle roof, with spaces to shoot through

battleship *n* large warship with big guns

batty *adj sl* slightly mad

bauble *n* cheap jewel

baulk *v BrE* balk

bauxite /ˈbawksiet/ *n* ore from which aluminium is obtained

bawd *n* woman in charge of prostitutes

bawdy *adj* about sex in a rude, funny way **-ily** *adv* **-iness** *n*

bawl *vi/t* shout loudly

bay¹ *n* **1** wide opening along a coast **2** division of a large room or building, separated by partitions

bay² *vi* make the deep cry of a large hunting dog
bay³ *n* **hold/keep at bay** keep (an enemy) away
bay⁴ *n, adj* (a horse whose colour is) reddish brown
bay⁵ also **bay tree** *n* tree with sweet-smelling leaves used in cooking
bayonet *n* knife on the end of a rifle ♦ *vt* drive a bayonet into
bayou *n* (in southern US) marshy creek or lake
bay rum *n* aromatic liquid used in cosmetics and medicines
bay window *n* three-sided window sticking out from a wall
bazaar *n* **1** sale to get money for some good purpose **2** market in an Eastern town
bazooka *n* long gun that rests on the shoulder and fires rockets
BB *abbrev. for:* **1** Boy's Brigade **2** double black (pencil)
BBC *abbrev. for:* British Broadcasting Corporation
BC *abbrev. for:* before (the birth of) Christ
BCG *abbrev. for:* Bacillus Calmette-Guérin; antituberculosis vaccine
be *v aux pres. t. sing. I* **am,** *you* **are,** *he/she/it* **is;** *pres. t. pl. we/you/they* **are;** *past t. sing. I* **was,** *you* **were,** *he/she/it* **was;** *past t. pl. we/you/they* **were;** *past p.* **been;** *pres. p.* **being** **1** (forms continuous tenses with **-ing**): *I am/was reading.* **2** (forms passives with **-ed**): *We are/were invited.* **3** (used with **to**) **a** must: *You are not to smoke.* **b** (shows future plans): *They are to be married soon.* ♦ *vi* **1** (shows that something is the same as the subject): *Today is Tuesday.* **2** (shows where or when): *He's upstairs.* **3** (shows a group or quality): *She's a doctor.* **4** (shows that something exists): *There's a hole in your sock.*
be- *prefix* cause to be or have: *bewigged/befriend*
beach *n* sandy or stony shore ♦ *vt* move (a boat) onto a beach
beach ball *n* large light ball to play with on the beach
beach buggy *n* motor vehicle for use on sandy beaches
beachcomber *n* person who searches a beach for useful things to sell
beachhead *n* area on an enemy's shore that has been captured
beachwear *n* clothing for the beach
beacon *n* fire or flashing light that gives warning
bead *n* **1** small ball with a hole through it, for threading on string **2** drop of liquid: *beads of sweat* **~ed** *adj*
beading *n* narrow ornamental moulding used e.g. on furniture and walls
beadle *n* (formerly) a minor parish church official
beady *adj* (of eyes) small and bright
beagle *n* short-legged hunting dog
beak *n* bird's hard horny mouth
beaker *n* **1** drinking cup **2** glass cup used in chemistry
be-all and end-all *n* most important thing; main purpose
beam *n* **1** long heavy piece of wood, esp. used to support a building **2** line of light from some bright object **3** radio waves sent out to guide aircraft, etc. **4** bright look or smile ♦ *v* **1** *vi* send out light **2** *vt* send out (esp. radio or television signals) in a certain direction **3** *vi* smile brightly
bean *n* **1** seed or pod of any of various plants, esp. used as food **2** **not have a bean** have no money at all
beanbag *n* **1** large bag, usu. filled with plastic pellets, used as a seat **2** small bag filled with beans or pellets used in throwing games
bear¹ *n* **1** large, heavy furry animal that eats meat, fruit, and insects **2** someone who sells shares, expecting their price to fall
bear² *v* **bore, borne** **1** *vt* carry **2** *vt* support (a weight) **3** *vt* have; show: *The letter bore no signature.* **4** *vt* suffer or accept (something unpleasant) without complaining **5** *vt* give birth to **6** *vi/t* produce (a crop or fruit) **7** *vi* move in the stated direction: *Cross the field,*

bear left, and you'll see the house. **8** *vt* be suitable for: *His words don't bear repeating.* **9** *vt* keep (a feeling toward someone) in one's mind: *I don't bear him a grudge.* **10 bear in mind** remember to consider **bear down** *phr v* **1** *vt fml* defeat **2** *vi* use all one's strength and effort **bear down on/upon** *phr vt* come towards forcefully and threateningly, esp. at high speed **bear on/upon** *phr vt* relate to **bear out** *phr vt* support the truth of **bear up** *phr vi* show courage or strength in spite of difficulties **bear with** *phr vt* show patience towards **~able** *adj* tolerable **~ably** *adv*

beard *n* hair on the face below the mouth ♦ *vt* confront **~ed** *adj*

bearer *n* **1** person who brings or carries something, e.g. the body at a funeral **2** person to whom a cheque is to be paid

bearing *n* **1** way of behaving **2** connection; relevance: *This has no bearing on the subject.* **3** direction shown by a compass **4** understanding of one's position: *get/lose one's bearings* **5** support esp. for a rotating mechanical part

bearskin *n* tall black fur cap worn by certain British soldiers

beast *n* **1** four-footed animal **2** person or thing one does not like **~ly** *adj* bad; nasty

beat *v* **beat, beaten** *or* **beat 1** *vt* hit again and again, esp. with a stick: *beat a drum* **2** *vt* mix with a fork or whisk: *beat the eggs* **3** *vi* move regularly: *I could hear his heart beating.* **4** *vt* defeat: *I beat him at tennis.* **5 beat about the bush** talk indirectly about something **6 Beat it!** *infml* Go away! **7 beat time** make regular movements to measure the speed of music ♦ *n* **1** single stroke or blow: *the beat of the drum* **2** regular stress in music or poetry **3** usual path followed by someone on duty **~er** *n* tool for beating things **~ing** *n* **1** act of giving repeated blows, usu. as punishment **2** defeat

beatific /ˌbeeəˈtifik/ *adj* showing joy and peace

beatify *vt* (in the Roman Catholic Church) declare as holy

beatitude *n* state of blessedness

beatnik *n* (in the late 1950s and early 1960s) person who rejected the usual standards of society

beau *n* **beaux, beaus 1** lover **2** *lit* dandy

Beaufort scale *n* scale for measuring wind strength

Beaujolais *n* French red wine

beaut *adj, n AustrE* marvellous (person or thing)

beauteous *adj lit* beautiful

beautician *n* person who gives beauty treatments

beautiful *adj* giving pleasure to the mind or senses **~ly** *adv* **–tify** *vt* make beautiful

beauty *n* **1** quality of being beautiful **2** someone or something beautiful

beauty spot *n* **1** place of great scenic beauty **2** black spot worn on the face

beaver *n* big rodent that builds dams across streams ♦ *vi* work hard

bebop *n* bop[3]

becalmed *adj* (of a sailing ship) unable to move because there is no wind

became *past t. of* become

because *conj* **1** for the reason that: *I do it because I like it.* **2 because of** as a result of: *I came back because of the rain.*

beck[1] *n* mountain stream

beck[2] *n* **at one's beck and call** always ready to do what one asks

beckon *vi/t* call with a movement of the finger

become *v* **became, become 1** begin to be: *become warmer* **2** *vt* be suitable for: *Such behaviour hardly becomes someone in your position.* **becoming** *adj* **1** attractive **2** suitable

becquerel *n* unit for measuring levels of radioactivity

bed *n* **1** piece of furniture to sleep on **2** bottom or base: *bed of a river* **3** piece of ground for plants **4** love-making; sex ♦ *vt* **-dd- 1** put in or on a bed: *a machine bedded in cement* **2** plant **3** have sex with **bed down** *phr v* **1** *vt* make (a person or animal) comfortable for the

night **2** *vi* make oneself comfortable for the night
bed bug *n* wingless blood-sucking insect
bedclothes *pl n* sheets, etc., on a bed
bedding *n* materials for a person or animal to sleep on
bedeck *vt lit* deck[2]
bedevil *vt* **-ll-** (*AmE* **-l-**) cause continual trouble for
bedfellow *n* **1** person who shares a bed **2** close companion; partner
bedlam *n* place of wild noisy activity
bedlinen *n* sheets and pillowcases
bed of roses *n* happy comfortable state
bedpan *n* container for a sick person's body waste
bedraggled *adj* wet, limp, and muddy
bedridden *adj* too ill or old to get out of bed
bedrock *n* **1** solid underlying rock **2** basic facts, principles, etc.
bedroom *n* room for sleeping in
bedside *n* **1** side of a bed: *bedside lamp* **2 bedside manner** way in which a doctor behaves when visiting a sick person
bed-sitter *n BrE* room for both living and sleeping in
bedsore *n* sore place on the skin, caused by lying too long in bed
bedspread *n* decorative cover for a bed
bedstead *n* main framework of a bed
bedtime *n* time for going to bed
bed-wetting *n* urinating in bed
bee *n* **1** stinging insect that makes honey **2 a bee in one's bonnet** fixed idea; obsession **3 the bee's knees** *infml* the best person or thing
beech *n* large forest tree with green or copper-brown leaves
beef *n* meat of farm cattle ♦ *vi* complain **~y** *adj* (of a person) big and strong
beefcake *n* photographs of muscular men
beefeater *n* yeoman of the guard
beehive *n* hive
beeline *n* **make a beeline for** go straight towards
been *n* **1** *past participle of* be **2** gone and come back: *Have you ever been to India?*
beep *vi, n* (make) the noise of a car horn
beer *n* alcoholic drink made from malt **~y** *adj*
beer belly, beer gut *n infml* paunch
beeswax *n* substance secreted by bees to make honeycomb and used in polishes
beet *n* **1** root from which sugar is made **2** beetroot
beetle[1] *n* insect with hard wing coverings ♦ *vi infml* move quickly
beetle[2] *n* mallet
beetling *adj* overhanging
beetroot *n* **-roots** *or* **-root** *BrE* large red root vegetable
befall *vi/t* **befell, befallen** *fml* happen (to)
befit *vt* **-tt-** *fml* be suitable for
before *prep* **1** earlier than **2** ahead of; in front of ♦ *adv* already; formerly: *I've seen you before.* ♦ *conj* **1** before the time when **2** rather than
beforehand *adv* before something else happens
befriend *vt* be a friend to
befuddle *vt* **1** make confused **2** perplex
beg *v* **-gg- 1** *vi/t* ask for (as help) **2** *vt* request politely: *I beg to differ.* **3 beg the question** to take as true something that is not yet proved **4 going begging** not wanted by anyone
beget *v* **begot, begotten** *lit* become the father of; produce
beggar *n* person who lives by begging **~ly** *adj* much too little **~y** *n* poverty
begin *vi/t* **began, begun 1** start; take the first step **2 to begin with** as the first reason **~ner** *n* person starting to learn **~ning** *n* starting point
begonia *n* tropical flowering plant
begrudge *vt* to grudge
beguile /bɪˈgaɪl/ *vt* **1** charm **2** deceive; cheat
behalf *n* **on behalf of** for; in the interests of
behave *vi* **1** (of people or things) act in a particular way **2** show good manners
behaviour, *AmE* **-ior** *n* way of behaving
behaviourism *n* system of psychology concerned with the analysis of

behaviour
behead *vt* cut off the head of
behest *n fml* **at someone's behest** by someone's command
behind *prep* **1** at or to the back of: *hide behind the door* **2** less good than: *He's behind the others in mathematics.* **3** in support of ♦ *adv* **1** behind something **2** where something was before: *I've left the key behind!* **3** late; slow: *We're behind with the rent.* ♦ *n infml* buttocks
behindhand *adv* late; slow
behold *vt* **beheld** *lit* see
beholden *adj* **be beholden to** have to feel grateful to
behove also *AmE* **behoove** *vt fml* **it behoves one to** it is right to
beige *adj, n* pale brown
being *n* **1** existence: *When did the club come into being?* **2** living thing, esp. a person ♦ *v present participle of* be
belabour *vt* **1** work too hard on: *belabour the point* **2** *arch.* beat
belated *adj* delayed; too late **~ly** *adv*
belch *v* **1** *vi* pass gas up from the stomach **2** *vt* send out (large amounts of smoke, etc.) **belch** *n*
beleaguer /bɪˈleegə/ *vt fml* **1** surround with an army **2** worry continuously
belfry *n* tower for bells
Belgian *n, adj* (inhabitant) of Belgium
belie *vt* give a false idea of
belief *n* **1** feeling that something is true, or can be trusted **2** idea that is believed: *religious beliefs*
believe *v* **1** *vt* consider to be true **2** *vi* have religious faith **believe in** *phr vt* **1** think that (something exists): *believe in fairies* **2** feel sure of the value of: *believe in lots of exercise* **believable** *adj* that can be believed **believer** *n*
Belisha beacon *n* flashing light in a yellow globe on top of a black and white pole marking a pedestrian crossing
belittle *vt* cause to seem unimportant
bell *n* **1** metal object that makes a ringing sound **2** cup-shaped object: *the bell of a flower* **3 ring a bell** remind one of something
belladonna *n* (drug obtained from) deadly nightshade
bell-bottoms *pl n* trousers with legs that are wider at the bottom
belle *n* **1** popular and attractive girl **2 belle of the ball** prettiest girl at a dance
bellicose *adj* quarrelsome **-sity** *n*
belligerent *n, adj* **1** (country that is) at war **2** (person who is) ready to fight **~ly** *adv* **-ence** *n*
bellow *vi/t* shout in a deep voice
bellows *pl n* instrument for blowing air e.g. into a fire
belly *n* **1** *infml* the part of the human body between the chest and legs **2** curved surface like this: *the belly of a plane* **~ful** *n infml* too much
bellyache *vi* complain repeatedly
belly button *n infml* navel
belly dance *n* Middle-Eastern dance by a solo female performer who jiggles, gyrates and undulates her abdomen **~r** *n*
belong *vi* be in the right place **belong to** *phr vt* **1** be the property of **2** be a member of **~ings** *pl n* one's property
beloved *n, adj* (person who is) dearly loved
below *adv, prep* in a lower place (than); under
belt *n* **1** band worn round the waist **2** circular piece of material that drives a machine **3** area with a particular quality **4 below the belt** *infml* unfair or unfairly ♦ *v* **1** *vt* fasten with a belt **2** *vt infml* hit hard **3** *vi sl, esp. BrE* travel fast **belt out** *phr vt infml* sing loudly **belt up** *phr vi sl* be quiet
beltway *n AmE* ring road
beluga *n* **1** large white sturgeon **2** white whale
BEM *abbrev. for:* British Empire Medal
bemoan *vt* express sorrow for
bemused *adj* confused
bench *n* **1** long seat **2** long worktable: *a carpenter's bench* **3 a** place where a judge sits in court **b** judges as a group
benchmark *n* **1** point of reference used in surveying land **2** something which serves as a standard
bend *vi/t* **bent** (cause to) move into a

curve or move away from an upright position ♦ *n* **1** curve **2 round the bend** *infml* mad **bends** *pl n* pain suffered by divers who come to the surface too quickly.

beneath *adv, prep* **1** below; under **2** not worthy of: *beneath contempt*

benediction *n* religious blessing

benefactor *n* person who gives money or help **–tion** *n* **1** giving of money **2** money given

benefactress *n* female benefactor

beneficent /biˈnefis(ə)nt/ *adj* doing good **–cence** *n*

beneficial *adj* (of things) helpful; useful

beneficiary *n* receiver of a benefit

benefit *n* **1** advantage; profit: *She's had the benefit of a very good education.* **2** money paid by the government to people who need it: *unemployment benefit* **3** event to raise money for some person or special purpose **4 the benefit of the doubt** favourable consideration given because there is no proof of guilt ♦ *v* **1** *vt* be helpful to **2** *vi* gain advantage

benevolent *adj* wishing to do good; kind **–lence** *n* **~ly** *adv*

benighted *adj* ignorant

benign *adj* kind and harmless

bent[1] *v* **1** *past t. and p. of* bend **2 bent on** determined on: *She's bent on winning.* ♦ *adj BrE sl* **1** dishonest **2** homosexual

bent[2] *n* special natural skill: *a natural bent for languages*

benzene also **benzol** *n* inflammable liquid used as a solvent

bequeath *vt* give to others after death

bequest *n* something bequeathed

berate *vt* speak angrily to

bereaved *adj* having lost someone by death **bereavement** *n*

bereft *adj* completely without: *bereft of hope*

beret *n* round soft flat cap

berg *n* **1** iceberg **2** *SAfrE* mountain (region)

bergamot *n* **1** type of pear **2** (fragrant oil from) the pear-shaped fruit of a small Asian tree

beriberi *n* disease caused by lack of vitamin B

berk *BrE sl* fool

berry *n* small soft fruit with seeds

berserk /bəˈzuhk/ *adj* violently angry

berth *n* **1** sleeping place in a ship or train **2** place where a ship can be tied up in harbour **3 give someone a wide berth** avoid someone ♦ *vi/t* tie up (a ship)

beryl *n* gemstone, usually green

beseech *vt* **besought** *or* **beseeched** *fml* ask eagerly

beset *vt* **beset,** *present participle* **besetting** attack continuously

beside *prep* **1** at the side of **2** in comparison with **3 beside oneself** very excited **4 beside the point** having nothing to do with the main question

besides *adv* also ♦ *prep* in addition to

besiege *vt* surround (a place) with armed forces

besmirch *vt* sully

besom *n* broom esp. of twigs

besotted *adj* **1** made foolish **2** drunk

bespatter *vt* spatter

bespeak *vt* **-spoke, -spoken 1** *lit* be an indication of **2** *arch.* order in advance

bespectacled *adj* wearing spectacles

bespoke *adj* (of clothes) made to someone's measurements

best *adj* (*superlative of* good) **1** the highest in quality or skill: *the best tennis player in America* **2 the best part of** most of ♦ *adv* (*superlative of* well) **1** in the best way: *She did best.* **2** to the greatest degree; most: *He thinks he knows best.* **3 as best one can** as well as one can ♦ *n* **1** the greatest degree of good: *She wants the best for her children.* **2** one's best effort: *I did my best.* **3 at (the) best** if the best happens **4 make the best of** do as well as one can with (something unsatisfactory) ♦ *vt* outdo

bestial /ˈbesti·əl/ *adj* **1** of or like an animal **2** (of human behaviour) very cruel **~ity** *n* **1** animal-like behaviour **2** sexual relations between a person and an animal

best man *n* man attending the

bridegroom at a wedding
bestow *vt* give
bestride *vt* straddle
best-seller *n* book, etc., that sells in very large numbers
bet *n* **1** agreement to risk money on a future event **2** sum of money risked in this way ♦ *vi/t* **bet** *or* **betted**; *pres. p.* **betting 1** risk (money) e.g. on a race **2** be sure: *I bet he's angry!*
betake *vt* **-took, -taken betake oneself** *lit* go
betel *n* fresh-tasting leaf chewed with pieces of bitter nut (**betel nut**)
bête-noire *n* **bêtes-noires** most hated person or thing
bethink *vt* **-thought bethink oneself** *arch.* **a** reconsider; think again **b** remember
betide *vt lit* **1 woe betide you** you will be in trouble **2** happen
betoken *fml* indicate
betray *vt* **1** be unfaithful to **2** make known (a secret) **~er** *n* **~al** *n*
betroth *vt* promise in marriage **~al** *n* engagement
better *adj* **1** higher in quality; more good: *a better way to do it* **2** well again after illness ♦ *adv* **1** in a better way: *It works better now.* **2 had better** ought to; should: *I'd better not tell him.* ♦ *n* **get the better of** defeat ♦ *vi/t* **1** improve **2 better oneself: a** earn more **b** educate oneself **~ment** *n* improvement **betters** *pl n* people better than oneself
between *prep* **1** in the space or time that separates: *Stand between Sue and Brian.* **2** (shows connection): *an air service between London and Paris* **3** (shows division or sharing): *The difference between spaghetti and noodles.* ♦ *adv* **1** in the space or time between things **2 few and far between** very rare
betwixt *adv, prep, arch* between
bevel *vt* **-ll-** (*AmE* **-l-**) make a sloping edge on **bevel** *n*
beverage *n* liquid for drinking, esp. one that is not water or medicine
bevy *n* large group
bewail *vt* express sorrow for
beware *vi/t* (used in giving orders) be careful!
bewilder *vt* confuse
bewitch *vt* **1** use magic on **2** charm: *a bewitching smile*
beyond *prep* **1** on the further side of: *beyond the mountains* **2** outside the limits of; more than: *beyond belief* **3 beyond me** too hard for me to understand ♦ *adv* further: *fly to Cairo and beyond*
bi- *prefix* two; twice: *biannual*
bias *n* **1** diagonal **2** tendency to deviate **3** prejudice: ♦ *vt* **-s-** *or* **-ss-** prejudice: *a biased judgment*
bias binding *n* fabric strip used in sewing curved edges or corners
bib *n* **1** piece of cloth or plastic tied under a child's chin **2** top part of an apron
Bible *n* **1** holy book of the Christians and Jews **2** (*not cap.*) authoritative book **biblical** *adj*
bibliography *n* list of writings on a subject **-pher** *n* person who writes such a list
bibliophile *n* lover of books
bibulous *adj* tending to get drunk
bicameral *adj* (of a parliament) having two chambers
bicarbonate *n* chemical used in baking and as a medicine
bicentenary also *esp. AmE* **bicentennial** *n* 200th anniversary **bicentenary** *adj*
biceps *n* **biceps** muscle of the upper arm
bicker *vi* quarrel about small matters
bicycle *n* two-wheeled vehicle ridden by pushing its pedals **bicycle** *vi*
bid *vi/t* **bid 1** offer (a price) at a sale **2** (in card games) declare what one intends to win ♦ *n* **1** amount that is bid **2** attempt: *a rescue bid* ♦ *vt* **bade** *or* **bid**, **bidden** *or* **bid**; *pres. p.* **bidding** *lit* order: *She bade him come.* **~ding** *n* **~dable** *adj* docile **~der** *n*
bide *vt* **bide one's time** wait till the right moment
bidet /ˈbeeday/ *n* low washbasin for washing the genitals and anus

biennial *adj* happening once every two years

bier *n* movable table for a coffin

biff *vt, n* (strike with) a light blow

bifocals *pl n* glasses made in two parts, suitable both for looking at distant objects and for reading **bifocal** *adj*

bifurcate *vi* divide into two branches

big *adj* **-gg- 1** of more than average size or importance **2** generous: *big hearted* **3** *infml* very popular ♦ *adv* on a grand scale

bigamy *n* being married to two people at the same time **–mist** *n* **–mous** *adj*

big bang *n* **1** cosmic explosion which brought the universe into being, according to the **big-bang theory 2** (*caps.*) deregulation and reorganization of the London Stock Exchange in October 1986

big dipper *n* **1** *BrE* roller coaster **2** (*caps.*) *AmE* the constellation of the Plough

big end *n* larger end of a connecting rod in an internal-combustion engine

big game *n* large animals hunted for sport

bighead *n infml* conceited person

bight *n* **1** loop in a rope **2** curve of a river or coast

bigot *n* person who will not change an unreasonable opinion **~ed** *adj* of or like a bigot **~ry** *n* behaviour typical of a bigot

big shot also **big noise** *n* person of great importance or influence

big time *n infml* upper echelons esp. of the entertainment industry

big top *n* circus tent

bigwig *n infml* important person

bijou /ˈbeeˌzhooh/ *adj* (esp. of a building) small and pretty

bike *n, vi* bicycle

bikini *n* woman's small two-piece swimming costume

bilateral *adj* with two sides or between two groups: *a bilateral agreement*

bilberry *n* (fruit of) a low bushy moorland plant

bile *n* **1** liquid formed in the liver **2** bad temper

bilge *n* **1** ship's bottom where water collects **2** *infml* foolish talk

bilingual *adj* using two languages

bilious *adj* **1** sick because food is not digested properly **2** peevish

bill[1] *n* **1** list of things that must be paid for **2** plan for a future law **3** *AmE* piece of paper money **4** printed notice **5 foot the bill** pay and take responsibility (for) ♦ *vt* **1** send a bill to **2** advertise in printed notices

bill[2] *n* bird's beak ♦ *v* **bill and coo** (of lovers) kiss and speak softly to each other

billabong *n AustrE* **1 a** blind channel off a river **b** dry stream bed filled seasonally **2** backwater forming a stagnant pool

billet *n* private home where soldiers are put to live ♦ *vt* put in billets

billet-doux *n* **billets-doux** love letter

billfold *n AmE* wallet

billhook *n* cutting tool with blade and hooked point, used for pruning

billiards *n* game played on a table, with balls and long sticks

billion *determiner, n* **billion** *or* **billions 1** one thousand million **2** *BrE* one million million **~th** *determiner, n, adv*

billow *n* rolling mass of smoke, etc., like a large wave **billow** *vi*

billy also **billy can** *esp. AustrE* metal can for outdoor cooking

billy goat *n* male goat

biltong *n SAfrE* strips of dried meat

bin *n* large container for storing things, or for waste ♦ *vt* store in a bin

binary *adj* **1** double **2** using only 0 and 1 as a base: *the binary scale*

bind *v* **bound 1** *vt* tie up **2** *vt* fasten (a book) into its cover **3** *vi/t* (cause to) stick together in a mass **4** *vt* cause to obey, esp. by a law or a promise: *a binding agreement* **bind over** *phr vt* (law) order **~er** *n* **1** person or thing that binds books **2** removable cover for holding papers **~ing** *n* **1** book cover **2** narrow strip of cloth

binge *n infml* period of drinking and

wild behaviour
bingo *n* **1** game played for money, by covering numbered squares on a card **2** *infml* (used to express pleased surprise)
binnacle *n* stand holding a ship's compass
binocular *adj* of both eyes
binoculars *pl n* pair of glasses like short telescopes for both eyes
binomial *n, adj* (mathematical expression) consisting of two terms connected by a plus or minus sign
bio- *prefix* connected with (the study of) living things: *biochemistry*
biochemistry *n* chemistry of living things
biodata *n AmE* curriculum vitae
biodegradable *adj* able to be broken down by the chemical action of bacteria, etc.
biography *n* written account of someone's life **–pher** *n* a person who writes this **–phical** *adj*
biology *n* scientific study of living things **–gist** *n* **–gical** *adj*
bionic *adj* **1** involving bionics **2** having more than human power
bionics *pl n* **1** study of biological systems to help development of electronics **2** use of mechanical parts to replace damaged parts of a living thing
biopic *n* biographical film
biopsy *n* removal of material from a living body to test it for possible disease
biotechnology *n* use of living cells or bacteria in industry
biped *n* two-footed creature
biplane *n* aircraft with two pairs of wings
birch *n* **1** tree with smooth wood and thin branches **2** rod made from this wood, used for flogging ♦ *vt* whip (as if) with a birch
bird *n* **1** creature with wings and feathers that can fly **2** *sl* woman **3** rude noise made as sign of disapproval **4** *BrE sl* period of time spent in prison
birdbrain *n* stupid person **~ed** *adj*
birdie *vt, n* (achieve) a score of one under par for a hole in golf
bird of paradise *n* brilliantly coloured bird of the New Guinea area
bird's-eye view *n* view seen from above, like a map
biretta *n* square cap worn by Roman Catholic clergy
Biro *n* **Biros** *tdmk for* ballpoint
birth *n* **1** act, time, or process of being born: *She gave birth to a fine baby.* **2** family origin: *French by birth*
birth control *n* contraception
birthday *n* anniversary of the day one was born
birthmark *n* mark on the skin since birth
birthrate *n* number of births during a particular time
birthright *n* something that belongs to someone because of the family or nation they were born into
birth sign *n* sign of the zodiac under which one was born
biscuit *n* **1** flat thin dry cake **2** *AmE* scone
bisect *vt* divide into two
bisexual *adj* sexually attracted to people of both sexes
bishop *n* **1** Christian priest of high rank **2** piece in chess that moves diagonally **~ric** *n* diocese
bismuth *n* heavy metallic element
bison *n* **bisons** *or* **bison** large wild hairy cowlike animal
bisque *n* thick cream soup
bistro *n* small bar or restaurant
bit[1] *v past t. of* bite
bit[2] *n* **1** small piece: *bits of paper* **2** a short time: *We walked around for a bit.* **3 a bit** rather: *I'm a bit tired.* **4 bit by bit** gradually
bit[3] *n* single unit of computer information
bit[4] *n* **1** part of a bridle that goes inside the horse's mouth **2** part of a drill that cuts
bitch *n* **1** female dog **2** *derog* unpleasant woman ♦ *vi sl* **1** complain continually **2** make nasty or hurtful remarks about others **~y** *adj* making nasty remarks

about people

bite *v* **bit, bitten 1** *vi/t* cut with the teeth **2** *vi/t* (of snakes and insects) sting **3** *vi* (of fish) accept food on a hook **4** *vi* take firm hold: *The wheels won't bite on the ice.* **5** have or show an effect: *The new taxes are beginning to bite.* **6 bite off more than one can chew** attempt too much **7 bite the bullet** suffer bravely **8 bite the dust** *infml* be killed or defeated ♦ *n* **1** piece removed by biting **2** wound made by biting **3** something to eat **4** sharpness; bitterness **biting** *adj* painful; cruel: *biting remarks*

bit part *n* small speaking part in a play, film, etc.

bitter *adj* **1** not sweet; tasting like beer or black coffee **2** very cold: *a bitter wind* **3** causing grief: *bitter disappointment* **4** full of hate: *bitter enemies* ♦ *n BrE* bitter beer **~ly** *adv* **~ness** *n* **~s** *pl n* bitter flavouring for cocktails

bittern *n* small heron

bittersweet *adj* pleasant, but mixed with sadness

bitty *adj* **1** disjointed **2** containing bits or sediment

bitumen /ˈbityoomin/ *n* sticky black substance used esp. in road-making **-minous** *adj*

bivalve *n, adj* (mollusc) with two shells jointed together

bivouac *n* camp without tents ♦ *vi* **-ck-** spend the night in a bivouac

bizarre *adj* very strange **~ly** *adv*

blab *vi* **-bb-** *sl* tell a secret

blabber *vi/t* prattle

blabbermouth *n infml* person who talks too much, esp. one who gives away secrets

black *adj* **1** of the colour of night **2** of a dark-skinned race, esp. of the Negro race **3** (of coffee) without milk **4** very bad; hopeless **5** very angry: *a black look* **6** (of humour) funny about unpleasant or dangerous people or events: *black comedy* ♦ *n* **1** black colour **2** black person ♦ *vt* **1** make black **2** (of a trade union) refuse to work with: *Black their cargo.* **~ly** *adv* **1** angrily **2** sadly **~ness** *n*

blackball *vt* vote against (someone who wants to join a club)

black belt *n* (person who holds) a high rank in judo or karate

blackberry *n* fruit of the bramble

blackbird *n* type of thrush of which the male is black

blackboard *n* board used in schools for writing on

black box *n* apparatus fitted to an aircraft to record information about an accident

blackcurrant *n* garden bush with small blue-black berries

Black Death *n* plague which ravaged Europe and Asia in the 14th century

black economy *n* business activity carried on unofficially, esp. to avoid taxation

blacken *vi/t* **1** make or become black **2** defame

black eye *n* dark skin round the eye, from being hit

blackguard *n* scoundrel

blackhead *n* spot on the skin with a black top

black hole *n* area in outer space into which everything is pulled, even light itself

black ice *n* ice that cannot be seen, on a road

blackjack *n* **1** pontoon[2] **2** *esp. AmE* cosh ♦ *vt esp. AmE* cosh

blackleg *n BrE* person who works when others are on strike

blacklist *n* list of people to be avoided or punished **blacklist** *vt*

black magic *n* magic used for evil purposes

blackmail *n* **1** getting money by threatening to make known unpleasant facts **2** influencing someone's actions by threats **blackmail** *vt* **~er** *n*

Black Maria *n* police van to carry prisoners

black market *n* unlawful buying and selling **~eer** *n*

Black Mass *n* travesty of the Christian Mass in worship of the Devil

blackout *n* **1** time of darkness enforced during wartime or caused by electrical failure **2** short loss of consciousness **3** intentional prevention of reporting: *a news blackout* **black out** *phr vi/t*
black power *n* movement for the political and economic power of black people
black pudding *n* large dark sausage made from suet and pigs' blood
black sheep *n* person in a family who brings shame on it
blacksmith *n* metalworker who makes iron things
black spot *n* part of a road where many accidents have happened
blackthorn *n* spiny shrub with small white flowers
black-tie *adj* requiring semiformal evening dress
black widow *n* highly poisonous type of spider
bladder *n* **1** sac inside the body, where waste liquid collects **2** any bag that can be filled with air or liquid
bladderwrack *n* seaweed with air bladders in its fronds
blade *n* **1** sharp cutting part of a knife **2** flat part of an oar, propeller, or bat **3** long narrow leaf: *blades of grass*
blame *vt* **1** consider responsible for something bad **2 be to blame** be guilty ♦ *n* responsibility for something bad **~less** *adj* free from guilt **~worthy** *adj* guilty
blanch *vi/t* make or become white
blancmange /blǝˈmonj/ *n* sweet dish made of milk and starch
bland *adj* **1** (of food) without much taste **2** (of people or their behaviour) showing no strong feelings or opinions **~ly** *adv* **~ness** *n*
blandishments *pl n* flattery
blank *adj* **1** without writing **2** empty or expressionless: *My mind went blank.* ♦ *n* **1** empty space **2** cartridge with no bullet in it **3 draw a blank** be unsuccessful **~ly** *adv* **~ness** *n*
blank cheque, *AmE* **blank check** *n* **1** cheque that is signed, but with the amount left blank **2** complete freedom to do what one wants
blanket *n* thick bed covering ♦ *vt* cover as if with a blanket ♦ *adj* including all cases: *a blanket rule*
blanket bath *n* all-over wash given to a person confined to bed
blankety blank *adj euph* (used in place of swear words)
blank verse *n* poetry that does not rhyme
blare *vi/t* make the loud noise of a horn **blare** *n*
blarney *n* **1** wheedling talk **2** nonsense
blasé *adj* seeming not to be concerned or excited
blasphemy *n* bad language about God and holy things **–mous** *adj* **blaspheme** *vi*
blast *n* **1** strong air movement **2** rush of air from an explosion **3** sound of a brass wind instrument **4 at full blast** as hard as possible ♦ *v* **1** *vi/t* break up (rock, etc.) with explosives **2** *vt* damn **blast off** *phr vi* (of a spacecraft) leave the ground **blast-off** *n*
blasted *adj* **1** damaged (as if) by fire or wind **2** *infml* damned
blast furnace *n* furnace for separating iron from the rock in which it is found
blatant *adj* too noticeable; shameless **~ly** *adv* **–tancy** *n*
blather *vi, n* blether
blaze *n* **1** bright flame **2** big dangerous fire **3** white mark ♦ *vi* **1** burn or shine brightly **2** spread news about: *The news was blazed across the front page.* **3 blaze a trail** lead the way
blazer *n* loose-fitting jacket
blazon *n* coat of arms ♦ *vt* proclaim
bleach *vi/t* make or become white or pale ♦ *n* chemical used for bleaching cloth
bleachers *pl n AmE* cheap unroofed seats for watching a baseball game
bleak *adj* cold and cheerless: *bleak weather* **~ly** *adv* **~ness** *n*
bleary *adj* (of eyes) red and tired **–ily** *adv* **–iness** *n*
bleat *vi, n* (make) the sound of a sheep or goat

bleed *v* **bled** /bled/ **1** *vi* lose blood **2** *vt* draw blood from, as doctors once did **3** *vt* draw off liquid or air from **4 bleed someone dry/white** take all someone's money, esp. gradually

bleep *n* repeated high sound made by a machine (a **bleeper**) to attract attention ♦ *vi/t* make, or call someone with, this sound

blemish *n* fault that spoils perfection **blemish** *vt*

blench *vi* recoil

blend *vi/t* mix together **blend in** *phr vi* go together well ♦ *n* mixture **~er** *n* kitchen mixing machine

bless *vt* **blessed** *or* **blest 1** ask God's favour for **2** make holy **3 be blessed with** be lucky enough to have **~ed** *adj* **1** holy **2** desirable **3** *infml* (used to give force to expressions of annoyance)

blessing *n* **1** God's favour **2** something one is glad of **3** approval

blether *vi* chatter foolishly **blether** *n*

blew *past t. of* blow[1]

blight *n* **1** disease of plants **2** something that spoils **3** condition of ugliness, disorder, and decay **blight** *vt*

blighter *n BrE sl* bastard (2,3): *You lucky blighter!*

blimey *interj BrE infml* (used to express surprise)

blimp *n* **1** small airship **2** *cap.* Colonel Blimp

blind *adj* **1** unable to see **2** unwilling to recognize: *blind to her faults* **3** without reason or purpose: *blind panic* **4** slightest: *He didn't take a blind bit of notice.* **5 turn a blind eye (to)** pretend not to see or notice (something, esp. something illegal) ♦ *vt* **1** make unable to see or understand **2 blind with science** confuse or fill with admiration by a show of detailed or specialist knowledge ♦ *n* **1** window covering that can be raised and lowered **2** false story that conceals the truth **3** *esp. AmE* hide for shooting game **~ly** *adv* **~ness** *n*

blind alley *n* narrow street with no way out

blind date *n* social meeting between two people, usu. a man and a woman, who have never met before

blind drunk *adj* extremely drunk

blinders *pl n AmE* blinkers

blindfold *vt* cover (the eyes) with a piece of cloth ♦ *n* piece of material to cover the eyes ♦ *adv* with the eyes covered

blind man's buff *n* game in which a blindfolded player tries to catch the others

blind spot *n* **1** part of an area that cannot easily be seen **2** something one is never able to understand

blink *v* **1** *vi/t* shut and open (the eyes) quickly **2** *vi* shine intermittently **blink** *n* **1** act of blinking **2 on the blink** not working properly

blinkers *pl n* **1** flaps that prevent a horse from seeing sideways **2** inability to see or understand **blinkered** *adj*

blip *n* **1** short sound made by a machine **2** image on a radar screen

bliss *n* complete happiness **~ful** *adj* **~fully** *adv*

blister *n* **1** watery swelling under the skin **2** swelling like this on a surface, e.g. paint ♦ *vi/t* form blisters **~ing** *adj* **1** very hot **2** very intense: *a blistering attack*

blithe *adj* free from care **~ly** *adv*

blitz *n* **1** sudden violent attack, esp. from the air **2** period of great activity for some special purpose: *an advertising blitz* ♦ *vt* attack suddenly and intensively

blizzard *n* severe snowstorm

bloated *adj* unpleasantly swollen

bloater *n* salted smoked herring

blob *n* drop of liquid or small round mass

bloc *n* group acting as a unit

block *n* **1** solid piece of material: *a block of wood* **2** large building divided into parts: *an office block* **3** distance between one street and the next: *The shop is four blocks away.* **4** group of things considered together: *a block of theatre seats* **5** blockage ♦ *vt* **1** prevent movement through **2** shut off from view **3**

prevent the success of: *to block legislation*

blockade *n* surrounding of a place, by ships or soldiers, to stop people or goods from going in or out ♦ *vt* surround in this way

blockage *n* obstruction

block and tackle *n* a pulley and rope arrangement for hoisting

blockbuster *n* something very big, effective, or successful

blockhead *n* stupid person

block letters *n* capitals

block vote *n* single vote made by a representative of a large group, e.g. a trade union, and regarded as representing all the group members

bloke *n BrE infml* man

blond *adj* **1** (of hair) light-coloured; yellow **2** also **blonde** having blond hair

blonde *n* blonde woman

blood *n* **1** red liquid that circulates through the body **2** family relationship: *people of noble blood* **3** fashionable young man **4 in cold blood** cruelly and on purpose **~less** *adj* without fighting **~y** *adj* **1** bleeding **2** (used for giving force to a remark): *You bloody fool!* **~ily** *adv*

blood-and-thunder *adj* (of a film or story) full of exciting action and meaningless violence

blood bank *n* place for storing blood or plasma for use in transfusions

bloodbath *n* massacre

blood brother *n* one of two or more men who have promised complete loyalty to one another

blood count *n* (examination of) the number of cells in a volume of blood

bloodcurdling *adj* very frightening

blood donor *n* person who gives blood for use in transfusions

blood feud *n* feud between two clans or families, involving murder

blood group *n* class of human blood

bloodhound *n* large dog that tracks people and animals

bloodletting *n* **1** killing **2** (formerly) drawing off blood as a medical treatment

blood money *n* money paid to an assassin or to the family of a murdered person

blood poisoning *n* condition in which an infection spreads from a part of the body through the bloodstream

blood pressure *n* measurable force with which blood flows through the bloodstream

bloodshed *n* killing, usu. in fighting

bloodshot *adj* (of the eyes) red

blood sport *n* killing of birds and animals for pleasure

bloodstain *n* spot of blood **~ed** *adj*

bloodstock *n* thoroughbred horses

bloodstream *n* flow of blood round the body

bloodsucker *n* **1** creature that bites and then sucks blood from the wound **2** person who tries to get as much money as possible from other people

bloodthirsty *adj* eager to kill; too interested in violence

Bloody Mary *n* cocktail of vodka and tomato juice

bloody-minded *adj* unhelpful; unreasonable **~ness** *n*

bloom *n* **1** flower **2 in the bloom of** at the best time of/for **3** powdery coating ♦ *vi* **1** produce flowers **2** show a healthy colour **3** blossom (2)

bloomer *n BrE infml* a big mistake

bloomers *pl n* women's short loose trousers gathered at the knee

blossom *n* **1** flower of a tree or bush **2 in blossom** bearing flowers ♦ *vi* **1** produce blossoms **2** develop favourably

blot *n* **1** spot, esp. of ink **2** shameful fault: *a blot on her character* **3** something ugly: *a blot on the landscape* ♦ *vt* **-tt- 1** make blots on **2** dry up (ink) **3 blot one's copybook** spoil one's good record **blot out** *phr vt* cover; hide: *Clouds blotted out the sun.*

blotch *n* large spot or mark **~y** *adj*

blotter *n* large piece of blotting paper

blotting paper *n* thick soft paper used to dry wet ink after writing

blotto *adj BrE infml* very drunk
blouse *n* woman's shirt
blow[1] *v* **blew, blown 1** *vi/t* send out air; move by the force of air: *The wind blew the tree down.* **2** *vi/t* sound made by blowing: *to blow a trumpet* **3** *vt* clean (one's nose) by blowing through it **4** *vi/t* melt (an electrical fuse) **5** *vt sl* lose (a favourable chance) as the result of foolishness **6** *vt infml* spend (money) freely **7** *vi sl* leave quickly **8** *vt infml* damn: *Well, I'm blowed!* **9 blow hot and cold (about)** be alternately favourable and unfavourable (to) **10 blow one's own trumpet/horn** *infml* praise oneself **11 blow one's top/stack** *sl* explode with anger **12 blow someone's mind** *sl* fill someone with wonder **13 blow the whistle on** *sl* cause something undesirable to stop by bringing it into the open **blow over** *phr vi* **1** (of a storm) stop blowing **2** be forgotten **blow up** *phr v* **1** *vi/t* explode **2** *vt* fill with air: *blow up the tyres* **3** enlarge (a photograph) **4** (of bad weather) start blowing: *There's a storm blowing up.* ♦ *n* act of blowing: *Give your nose a good blow.*
blow[2] *n* **1** hard stroke with the hand or a weapon **2** sudden misfortune **3 come to blows** start to fight
blow-by-blow *adj* with full details, given in the order in which they happened
blow-dry *vt* style the hair while drying it with a hand-dryer **blow-dry** *n*
blower *n* **1** apparatus for producing a current of air or gas **2** *BrE infml* telephone
blowfly *n* large fly that lays its eggs on meat
blowhole *n* **1** hole in the ice in which animals surface to breathe **2** nostril in the top of a whale's head
blowlamp *n* also **blowtorch** lamp that blows a flame (e.g. for burning off paint)
blown *past p. of* blow[1]
blowout *n* **1** very big meal **2** bursting of a container (esp. a tyre) **3** breaking out of oil or gas from a well
blowpipe *n* **1** tube for blowing air e.g. into a flame **2** tube from which a small dart is blown as a weapon
blowzy also **blowsy** *adj* (of a woman) fat, red-faced, and untidy
blubber[1] *n* fat of sea mammals, esp. whales
blubber[2] *vi* weep noisily
bludgeon *vt* **1** hit with something heavy **2** force to do something, by threats ♦ *n* club
blue *adj* **1** of the colour of the clear sky **2** sad **3** concerned with sex; improper: *blue films* ♦ *n* **1** blue colour **2 out of the blue** unexpectedly **blues** *n* **1** slow sad song or music from the southern US **2** sadness
blue baby *n* baby born with a bluish skin colour because of a heart defect
bluebell *n* woodland plant with a cluster of blue bell-shaped flowers
bluebird *n* N American songbird with blue feathers
blueblooded *adj* of noble birth
bluebottle *n* large blue-green fly
blue chip *n, adj* (an industrial share) that is expensive and in which people have confidence
blue-collar *adj* of or concerning workers who do hard or dirty work with their hands
blue-eyed boy *n infml, esp. BrE* someone's favourite (male) person
bluegrass *n* **1** bluish-green N American grass **2** country music originating from Kentucky
blue moon *n* **once in a blue moon** *infml* almost never
blue murder *n* **scream/shout blue murder** *infml* complain very loudly
blue peter *n* flag signalling that a ship is ready to leave harbour
blueprint *n* **1** copy of a plan for making or building something **2** plan of action
blue-sky *adj* done in order to test ideas, rather than for any particular practical purpose
bluestocking *n* woman thought to be too highly educated
bluetit *n* small European bird with a

yellow breast and a blue cap and tail

bluff[1] *vi* **1** deceive someone by pretending to be stronger or cleverer than one is: *They say they'll blow up the place, but they're only bluffing.* **2 bluff it out** escape trouble by continuing a deception ♦ *n* **1** action of bluffing **2 call someone's bluff** tell someone to do what they threaten to do **~er** *n*

bluff[2] *adj* **1** (of land) rising steeply **2** (of a person) rough and cheerful ♦ *n* high steep bank

bluish *adj* slightly blue

blunder *n* stupid mistake ♦ *vi* **1** make a blunder **2** move awkwardly **~er** *n*

blunderbuss *n* short thick gun with a wide muzzle

blunt *adj* **1** not sharp: *a blunt pencil* **2** not trying to be polite ♦ *vt* make less sharp **~ly** *adv* roughly and plainly **~ness** *n*

blur *n* something whose shape is not clearly seen ♦ *vt* **-rr-** make hard to see

blurb *n* short description of the contents of a book

blurt out *phr vt* say suddenly without thinking

blush *vi* become red in the face, from shame **blush** *n* **~ingly** *adv* **~er** *n* rouge

bluster *vi* **1** speak roughly and noisily **2** (of wind) blow roughly **bluster** *n* **~y** *adj* windy

BM *abbrev. for:* **1** Bachelor of Medicine **2** British Museum

BMA *abbrev for:* British Medical Association

B-movie *n* cheaply made cinema film not considered to be of very good quality

BMX *n* bicycle with a strong frame and small wheels designed esp. for cross-country or stunt riding

BO *n* body odour; unpleasant smell from a person's body

boa *n* **1** large snake that crushes its prey **2** long fluffy scarf

boar *n* **1** male pig **2** wild pig

board *n* **1** flat piece of wood **2** blackboard **3** (cost of) meals: *board and lodging* **4** committee of people controlling something **5 above board** completely open and honest **6 across the board** including all groups or members, as in an industry: *a wage increase of £10 a week across the board* **7 go by the board** (of plans) come to no result **8 on board** on a ship or public vehicle **9 sweep the board** win nearly everything ♦ *v* **1** *vt* cover with boards **2** *vt* go on board a ship, aircraft, train, etc. **3** *vi/t* get or supply meals and lodging for payment: *to board with a friend* **~er** *n* person who pays to live and receive meals somewhere

boarding card *n* official card to be given up when one boards an aircraft or ship

boardinghouse *n* private lodging house that supplies meals

boarding school *n* school at which children live instead of going there daily from home

boardroom *n* room where board meetings are held

boardwalk *n esp. AmE* walk made of planks, usu. by the sea

boast *v* **1** *vi* talk too proudly **2** *vt* have (a cause for pride): *This computer boasts many ingenious features.* ♦ *n* **1** act of boasting **2** cause for pride **~ful** *adj* full of self-praise **~fully** *adv*

boat *n* **1** water vehicle, esp. smaller than a ship ♦ *vi* go in a boat, esp. for pleasure

boater *n* stiff hat made of straw

boathook *n* pole with a hook at one end, used for holding or fending off boats

boatswain /ˈbohs(ə)n/ *n* chief seaman on a ship

boattrain *n* train that takes people to or from ships in port

bob[1] *vi* **-bb-** move quickly up and down: *a boat bobbing on the water*

bob[2] *vt* cut (a woman's hair) to shoulder-length or shorter ♦ *n* a bobbed haircut

bob[3] *n BrE infml* shilling

bobbin *n* small reel for thread

bobble *n* small fluffy ball of wool for decoration

bobby *n BrE infml* policeman
bobby socks, bobby sox *pl n AmE* girl's socks reaching above the ankle
bobcat *n* North American lynx
bobsleigh also **bobsled** *vi, n* (ride in) a sledge for two or four people, used in racing
bode *vi* **bode well/ill** be a good/bad sign for the future
bodice *n* top part of a woman's dress
bodice ripper *n* romantic usu. historical novel replete with sex and melodrama
bodily *adj* of the human body ♦ *adv* taking hold of the whole body
bodkin *n* thick blunt needle with a large eye
body *n* **1** person or animal's whole physical structure, alive or dead **2** this without the head or limbs **3** main part of something: *The important news comes in the body of the letter.* **4** group of people: *an elected body* **5** object; piece of matter: *The sun is a heavenly body.* **6** large amount: *a body of water such as a lake*
body blow *n* **1** (in boxing) blow that falls below the breast and above the waist **2** a serious setback
bodyguard *n* man or group of men guarding someone important
body language *n* physical gestures, positions, movements, etc. seen as indicators of a person's wishes, intentions or state of mind
body politic *n* nation considered as a political unit
body popping *n* solo dance form of the 1980s involving jerky robotlike body movements
body snatcher *n* person who formerly dug up corpses for sale to dissectionists
body stocking *n* close fitting garment that covers the body and often the arms and legs
body warmer *n* quilted waistcoat
bodywork *n* outside parts of a motor vehicle
Boer *n* South African of Dutch descent **Boer** *adj*
boffin *n infml* scientific expert
bog *n* **1** area of soft wet ground **2** *BrE sl* lavatory ♦ *v* **bog down** *phr vi/t* **-gg-** sink into a bog; be stuck **~gy** *adj*
bogey *n* **1** imaginary evil spirit **2** thing that is feared
boggle *vi* pause in shocked surprise
bogus *adj* pretended; false
bohemian *n, adj* (person) not following accepted social customs
boil[1] *vi/t* **1** bring or come to the temperature at which a liquid changes to gas **2** cook at this temperature: *to boil eggs* **3 boil dry** boil till no water remains **boil down to** *phr vt* be no more than: *It all boils down to a question of money.* **boil over** *phr vi* **1** (of a boiling liquid) flow over the sides of the container **2** get out of control: *The conflict boiled over into war.* **boil up** *phr v* **1** *vt* make hot and cook **2** *vi* reach a dangerous level ♦ *n* boiling point: *bring to the boil*
boil[2] *n* painful infected swelling under the skin
boiler *n* large container for boiling or heating water
boiler suit *n* overalls
boisterous *adj* noisily cheerful **~ly** *adv*
bold *adj* **1** daring; courageous **2** without respect or shame **3** clearly marked: *a bold drawing* **~ly** *adv* **~ness** *n*
bole *n* trunk of a tree
bolero /bəˈleəroh/ *n* **-os 1** lively Spanish dance **2** short sleeveless jacket
boll *n* seed pod of a cotton plant
bollard *n* short thick post, in the street or for tying boats to
bollocks *pl n BrE sl* **1** testicles **2** nonsense
Bolshevik *n, adj derog* communist
bolshy *adj infml* (of a person or their behaviour) uncooperative and argumentative
bolster *n* long pillow ♦ *v* **bolster up** *phr vt* encourage; support
bolt *n* **1** bar that fastens a door or window **2** screw used with a nut to hold things together **3** thunderbolt **4** roll of

cloth or wallpaper **5 a bolt from the blue** something unexpected and unpleasant ♦ *v* **1** *vt* fasten with a bolt **2** *vi* run away suddenly **3** *vt* swallow (food) hastily ♦ *n* act of running ♦ *adv* **bolt upright** straight and stiff

bolthole *n* place one can escape to

bomb *n* **1** container filled with explosive **2** the nuclear bomb **3 (go) like a bomb** (go) very well **4 spend/cost a bomb** spend/cost a lot of money ♦ **1** *vt* attack with bombs **2** *vi infml* move quickly **3** *vi AmE infml* fail **~er** *n* **1** aircraft that drops bombs **2** person who throws bombs

bombard *vt* **1** attack heavily with gunfire **2** attack (e.g. with questions) **3** *physics* attack with rays or particles **~ment** *n*

bombastic *adj* using high-sounding meaningless words **~ically** *adj*

bombshell *n* great shock

bona fide /ˌbohnə ˈfiedi/ *adj* real **bona fides** *n* (evidence of) honesty

bonanza *n* something very profitable

bonbon *n* sweet

bond *n* **1** something that unites: *a bond of friendship* **2** written promise, esp. to pay back money with interest **3** state of being stuck together ♦ *vt* unite; stick **bonds** *pl n* chains or ropes for tying someone up

bondage *n lit* slavery

bone *n* **1** any of the various hard parts of the body which are surrounded by flesh and skin **2 cut to the bone** reduce as much as possible **3 feel in one's bones** believe strongly though without proof **4 have a bone to pick with someone** have something to complain about ♦ *vt* take bones out of **bone up** *phr vi infml* try to learn about something quickly **~less** *adj* **bony** *adj* **1** very thin, showing the bones **2** (of food) full of bones

bone-dry *adj* perfectly dry

bonehead *n* stupid person

bone-idle *adj* very lazy

bonfire *n* large outdoor fire

bongo *n* **-os, -oes** one of a pair of small drums played with the hands

bonhomie *n* cheerful friendliness

bonk *v* **1** *infml* hit, usu. not very hard **2** *vi/t sl* have sex (with) ♦ *n* **1** *infml* hit **2** *sl* act of having sex

bonkers *adj sl* crazy

bon mot *n* **bons mots** witty and apposite remark

bonnet *n* **1** round hat tied under the chin **2** *BrE* covering over the engine of a car

bonny *adj* pretty and healthy

bonsai *n* **-ai** (art of growing) a dwarf plant, esp. a tree

bonus *n* **1** additional payment beyond what is usual **2** anything pleasant in addition to what is expected

boo *interj, n* **boos** shout of disapproval ♦ *vi/t* shout 'boo'

boob[1] *vi, n infml* (make) a stupid mistake

boob[2] *n sl* woman's breast

booby *n* fool

booby prize *n* prize given for the worst performance in a competition

booby trap *n* harmless-looking thing used for surprising people unpleasantly, such as a hidden bomb ♦ **booby-trap** *vt* **-pp-**

book *n* **1** set of sheets of paper fastened together, to be read or written in **2** collection of matches, tickets, etc., fastened like a book **3** main division of the Bible or of a long poem **4 a closed book** subject about which one knows very little **5 by the book** according to the rules **6 throw the book at** (esp. of the police) make all possible charges against ♦ *v* **1** *vi/t* order (tickets, etc.) in advance: *to book a seat* **2** *vt* write down a legal charge against: *booked for speeding* **book up** *phr vt* reserve completely **~able** *adj* **~ish** *adj* learned or literary **~s** *pl n* business accounts

bookcase *n* piece of furniture to hold books

book club *n* club that offers books cheaply to its members

bookend *n* support for a row of books

booking office *n* office where tickets are

sold and bookings made
bookkeeping *n* keeping business accounts **–er** *n*
booklet *n* small thin book
bookmaker also *infml* **bookie** *n* person who takes bets on races
bookmark *n* something put in a book to keep one's place
bookstall *n* stall where books and magazines are sold
book token *n* gift token exchangeable for a book
bookworm *n* person who loves reading
boom[1] *vi* **1** make a deep hollow sound **2** grow rapidly: *Business is booming.* ♦ *n* **1** rapid growth **2** intense business activity
boom[2] *n* **1** long pole to which a sail is attached **2** barrier across a river **3** long pole on the end of which a camera or microphone can be moved about
boomerang *n* curved stick which makes a circle and comes back when thrown ♦ *vi* have the opposite effect to that intended
boon *n fml* comfort; help
boondocks *pl n AmE infml* rough country area where few people live
boor *n* rude person **~ish** *adj* **~ishly** *adv*
boost *vt* raise; increase **boost** *n* **~er** *n* **1** something that boosts **2** additional amount of a drug
boot[1] *n* **1** heavy shoe that comes up over the ankle **2** *BrE* space at the back of a car for boxes, etc. **3 put the boot in** *sl* kick someone ♦ *vt infml* kick **boot out** *phr vt infml* send away rudely and sometimes with force
boot[2] *n* **to boot** in addition
bootee *n* child's soft or knitted shoe
booth *n* **1** tent or hut where goods are sold **2** small enclosed space: *a telephone booth*
bootleg *vi/t* **-gg-** make, carry or sell (alcoholic drink) illegally ♦ *adj* illegally produced or smuggled **~ger** *n*
bootless *adj arch.* useless, vain
booze *vi sl* drink alcohol ♦ *n sl* alcoholic drink **boozer** *sl* **1** person who boozes **2** *BrE* pub **boozy** *adj sl* showing signs of heavy drinking
booze-up *n BrE sl* party with a lot of drinking
bop *vi* dance as in a discotheque **bop** *n*
borage *n* hairy, blue-flowered herb
borax *n* white soluble boron compound
bordello *n* brothel
border *n* **1** edge **2** line between two countries ♦ *vt* put or be a border to **border on** *phr vt* be very much like: *Your remarks border on rudeness!*
borderline *adj* possibly, but not definitely, in a certain state ♦ *n* (line marking) a border
bore[1] *v past t. of* bear[2]
bore[2] *n* dull person or activity ♦ *vt* make (someone) tired or uninterested: *a boring job* **~dom** *n* state of being bored
bore[3] *vi/t* make a round hole (in) ♦ *n* **1** hole made by boring **2** measurement of the hole inside a gun or pipe
bore[4] *n* swift tidal flood
born *adj* **1 be born** come into existence by birth **2** being something by nature: *a born leader*
born-again *adj* having accepted a particular religion, esp. evangelical Christianity, esp. through a deep spiritual experience
borne *past p. of* bear[2]
boron *n* metalloid element used in hardening steel
borough *n* town, or division of a large town
borrow *v* **1** *vi/t* receive something that is lent, and will be returned **2** *vt* copy (ideas, words, etc.) **~er** *n*
borscht *n* beetroot soup
borstal *n BrE* prison school for young offenders
borzoi *n* large long-haired dog
bosh *n, interj* nonsense
bosom *n lit* **1** the front of the human chest, esp. the female breasts **2** place where one feels love, sorrow, etc. **3 a bosom friend** a very close friend **4 in the bosom of** in a close relationship with

boss[1] *n infml* person who controls others at work ♦ *vt* give orders to **~y** *adj* too fond of giving orders
boss[2] *n* round decoration sticking out from a surface
bosun *n* boatswain
botany *n* scientific study of plants **–nist** *n* **–nical** *adj*
botch *vt* make or repair (something) badly ♦ *n* bad piece of work
both *determiner, pron* this one and that one
bother *v* **1** *vt* cause inconvenience to; annoy in little ways: *Does the noise bother you?* **2** *vi* trouble oneself: *Don't bother to lock the door.* ♦ *n* trouble; inconvenience **~some** *adj* causing bother
bottle *n* **1** narrow-necked container for liquids **2** container for holding a baby's milk **3** *BrE sl* courage **4 the bottle** alcoholic drink, esp. when drunk too much: *He's on/hitting the bottle again.* ♦ *vt* put into bottles **bottle out** *phr vi BrE sl* lose one's courage **bottle up** *phr vt* control (feelings) unhealthily
bottle-feed *vi/t* **-fed** feed (a baby) from a bottle
bottle green *n, adj* very dark green
bottleneck *n* **1** narrow part of a road which slows down traffic **2** point at which progress is held up
bottom *n* **1** base; lowest part or level **2** part of the body that one sits on **3** ground under a body of water **4** far end: *the bottom of the garden* **5** cause: *get to the bottom of the trouble* **6 at bottom** really ♦ *v* **bottom out** *phr vi* reach the lowest point before rising again **~less** *adj* very deep
bottom line *n* **1** the amount of money shown (as profit or loss) at the bottom of a set of accounts **2** the most important result or consideration
botulism *n* form of food poisoning
boudoir /ˈboohdwah/ *n lit* woman's private room
bouffant /ˈboohfonh/ *adj* puffed out
bougainvillaea /ˌboohgənˈvilyə/ *n* tropical climbing plant with red or purple flowers
bough *n* large branch of a tree
bought *past t. and p. of* buy
bouillabaisse *n* sharp-tasting fish stew
bouillon *n* clear soup
boulder *n* large rock
boulevard *n* wide avenue
bounce *v* **1** *vi* (of a ball) spring back again **2** *vi/t* move up and down quickly: *She bounced into the room.* **3** *vi* (of a cheque) be returned by the bank as worthless ♦ *n* **1** act of bouncing **2** behaviour which is full of life **bouncer** *n* strong person employed (esp. at a club) to throw out unwelcome visitors
bouncing *adj* (esp. of babies) strong and healthy
-bound *suffix* (in adjectives) limited, kept in, or controlled in the stated way: *fog-bound*
bound[1] *v past t. and p. of* bind ♦ *adj* **1 bound to** sure to: *It's bound to rain* **2 bound up in** busy with
bound[2] *vi* jump **bound** *n*
bound[3] *adj* going to (a place): *bound for home*
boundary *n* outer limit; border
bounden *adj arch.* obligatory
boundless *adj* unlimited
bounds *pl n* **1** furthest limits **2 out of bounds** forbidden to be visited
bounty *n* **1** something given out of kindness, or offered as a reward **2** *fml* generosity **-tiful, -teous** *adj fml* generous
bouquet *n* **1** bunch of flowers **2** smell of a wine
bouquet garni *n* small bunch of herbs used as flavouring for stews
bourbon *n* type of American whisky
bourgeois /ˈbooəzhwah, ˈbaw-/ *n, adj* **1** (person) of the middle class **2** (person) too interested in material possessions **~ie** *n* the middle class
bourne *n arch.* limit
bout *n* short period of activity or illness
boutique *n* small fashionable shop, esp. for clothes
bovine *adj* slow and dull, like a cow
bovver *BrE sl* aggression

bow[1] *vi/t* bend forward, to show respect **bow out** *phr vi* give up a position or stop taking part in something **bow to** *phr vt* obey; accept: *I bow to your judgment.* **bow** *n*

bow[2] *n* **1** piece of curved wood with a string, for shooting arrows **2** similar piece of wood for playing stringed musical instruments **3** knot formed by doubling a string into two curved pieces ♦ *vi/t* **1** bend; curve **2** play (music) with a bow

bow[3] *n* front of a ship

bowdlerize, -ise /ˈbowdləriez/ *vt* remove unacceptable parts from (a book)

bowels *pl n* **1** pipe that carries waste matter from the stomach **2** inside part: *the bowels of the earth*

bower *n* garden shelter made with or among vines and branches

bowl[1] *n* **1** deep round container **2** anything in the shape of a bowl

bowl[2] *v* **1** *vi/t* throw or roll (a ball) in a sport **2** *vt* (in cricket) force a player out of the game by doing this **3** *vi* play bowls or bowling **bowl over** *phr vt* **1** knock down **2** surprise greatly

bow-legged *adj* having legs curving outwards at the knees

bowler[1] *n* person who bowls

bowler[2] *n BrE* man's round hard hat

bowling *n* indoor game in which a big ball is rolled along a track (a **bowling alley**)

bowls *n* outdoor game in which a big ball (a **bowl**) is rolled on grass (a **bowling green**)

bowman *n* archer

bowsprit *n* spar projecting forwards from the bow of a ship

bow tie *n* tie fastened at the front with a bow

bow window *n* curved window

bowwow *n* (used by or to children) (barking of a) dog

box[1] *n* **1** stiff container for solids **2** small enclosed space: *a telephone box* **3** *BrE sl* television: *What's on the box?* ♦ *vt* put in boxes **box in** *phr vt* enclose in a small space

box[2] *vi/t* fight with the fists, for sport: *a boxing match* **~er** *n* **~ing** *n*

box[3] evergreen tree or shrub with small leaves

Boxing Day *n* British public holiday on the first weekday after Christmas

box number *n* number used as a mailing address, esp. in replying to newspaper advertisements

box office *n* place where tickets are sold in a cinema or theatre

box room *n* small room in a house used for storage

boy *n* young male person **~hood** *n* time of being a boy **~ish** *adj* like a boy

boycott *vt* refuse to trade with or take part in **boycott** *n*

boyfriend *n* woman's male companion

bozo *n AmE sl* stupid person

bra *n* woman's undergarment supporting the breasts

braai /brie/ *v, n SAfrE* barbecue

brace *n* **1** something that stiffens or supports **2** wire worn to straighten the teeth **3** pair **4** device for turning a drilling bit **braces** *pl n* bands over the shoulders to keep trousers up ♦ *vt* **1** support **2** prepare (oneself) **bracing** *adj* health-giving

bracelet *n* decoration for the wrist

bracken *n* tall fern which grows in woodland

bracket *n* **1** support (e.g. for a shelf) jutting out below **2** either of various pairs of signs used for enclosing a piece of information, for example ( ) or [ ] **3** group of people: *the 16-25 age bracket* ♦ *vt* **1** put in brackets **2** put together

brackish *adj* (of water) not pure; a little salty **~ness** *n*

bract *n* small leaf close to a flower

brad *n* small nail

bradawl *n* tool for making holes

brag *vi* boast

braggadoccio *n lit* boastfulness

braggart *n* boastful person

Brahman, -min *n* **1** member of the highest Hindu caste **2** humped breed of cattle

braid **1** *n, vt AmE* plait **2** *n* ornamental threads twisted together to make edging for material: *gold braid*

braille *n* type of raised printing that blind people can read

brain *n* **1** the organ in the head that controls thought **2** mind; intelligence **3** *infml* clever person **4 have something on the brain** think about something continually, or too much ♦ *vt infml* hit on the head **brains** *n* **1** material of which the brain consists **2** ability to think **~less** *adj* stupid **~y** *adj* clever

brainchild *n* someone's successful idea

brain drain *n* movement of skilled people to other countries

brainpower *n* ability to reason

brainstorm *n* **1** *BrE* sudden short madness **2** *AmE* brainwave **~ing** *n* rapid exchange of ideas among a group to find answers to problems

brainwash *vt* force someone to change their beliefs **~ing** *n*

brainwave *n BrE* sudden clever idea

braise *vt* cook (meat or vegetables) slowly in a covered dish

brake[1] *n* apparatus for slowing or stopping a vehicle **brake** *vi/t*

brake[2] *n* thicket

bramble *n* common wild prickly bush

bran *n* crushed husk of grain

branch *n* **1** stem growing from the trunk of a tree **2** division; part: *branch of a railway* ♦ *vi* form branches **branch out** *phr vi* add to one's range

brand *n* **1** product of a particular producer: *my favourite brand of soup* **2** mark made, esp. by burning, to show ownership ♦ *vt* **1** give a lasting bad name to: *He was branded as a liar.* **2** mark with a brand **3** have a lasting effect on: *the experience branded her for life*

brandish *vt* wave (e.g. a weapon) about

brand-new *adj* completely unused

brandy *n* strong alcoholic drink made from wine

brandy snap *n* crisp sweet biscuit rolled into a cylinder

brash *adj* bold and disrespectful **~ly** *adv* **~ness** *n*

brass *n* **1** bright yellow metal **2** musical instruments made of this: *a brass band* **3** *BrE sl* money **~y** *adj* **1** of or like brass **2** brazen

brassed off *adj BrE sl* fed up

brasserie *n* restaurant

brass hat *n sl* senior officer

brassiere /ˈbrazi·ə/ *n* bra

brass tacks *pl n* **get down to brass tacks** *infml* discuss the really important issues or business

brat *n derog* child, esp. a bad-mannered one

bravado /brəˈvahdoh/ *n* unnecessary show of boldness

brave *adj* ready to meet pain or danger; fearless ♦ *vt* meet (danger, etc.) without fear ♦ *n* young American Indian warrior **~ly** *adv* **~ry** *n*

bravo *interj, n* **-vos** (shout of) well done!

bravura /brəˈv(y)ooərə/ *n* **1** brilliant style **2** music that is difficult to play **3** show of daring or brilliance

brawl *n* noisy quarrel **brawl** *vi*

brawn *n* **1** human muscle **2** meat from the head of a pig **~y** *adj* strong

bray *vi* make the sound a donkey makes **bray** *n*

brazen *adj* without shame **~ly** *adv*

brazier *n* container for burning coals

breach *n* **1** act of breaking e.g. a law or promise *breach of contract* **2** hole (in a wall, etc.) **3 breach of the peace** *law* fighting in public ♦ *vt* break through

bread *n* **1** food made of baked flour **2** food as a means of staying alive: *earn one's daily bread* **3** *sl* money **4 bread and butter** one's way of earning money to live on

bread-and-butter *adj* basic

breadbasket *n* **1** major grain-producing region **2** *sl* stomach

breadcrumb *n* very small bit of bread

breadfruit *n* large starchy tropical fruit

breadline *n* **on the breadline** very poor

breadth *n* **1** width **2** scope

breadwinner *n* person whose wages support a family

break *v* **broke, broken 1** *vi/t* separate

suddenly into parts: *to break a window* **2** *vi/t* make or become by breaking: *The box broke open.* **3** *vi/t* make or become useless due to damage: *a broken watch* **4** *vt* disobey; not keep: *break a promise* **5** *vi/t* interrupt; stop: *break one's journey* **6** *vi/t* (cause to) fail or be destroyed: *The scandal could break him politically.* **7** *vi/t* bring or come into notice: *The news broke.* **8** *vt* do better than (a record) **9** *vi* (of a voice) change suddenly **10** *vt* discover the secret of (a code) **11 break new/fresh ground** do something new and different **12 break the back of** finish the main or worst part of **13 break the ice** begin to be friendly with people one did not know before **14 break wind** let out gases from the bowels **break down** *phr v* **1** *vi/t* destroy; be reduced to pieces **2** *vi* (of machinery) stop working **3** *vi* fail: *The peace talks have broken down.* **4** *vi* (of a person) lose control of one's feelings **5** *vi/t* separate into kinds; divide: *break the figures down into several lists* **break even** *phr vi* make neither a loss nor a profit **break in** *phr v* **1** *vi* enter a building by force **2** *vi* interrupt **3** *vt* make (a person or animal) accustomed to something new **break into** *phr vt* **1** enter by force **2** begin suddenly: *to break into song* **3** interrupt **4** use part of, esp. unwillingly: *We'll have to break into our savings.* **break of** *phr vt* cure (someone) of (a bad habit) **break off** *phr vi/t* **1** stop; end **2** separate from the main part: *A branch broke off.* **break out** *phr vi* **1** (of something bad) start suddenly: *War broke out.* **2** show or express something suddenly: *He broke out in a rash.* **3** escape **break through** *phr vi/t* **1** force a way through **2** make a new advance **break up** *phr v* **1** *vi/t* divide into small pieces; separate **2** *vi/t* bring or come to an end: *Their marriage broke up.* **3** *vi/t* (cause to) suffer greatly **4** *vi* (of a crowd) cease to be together **5** *vi BrE* begin the school holidays **6** *AmE* amuse greatly ♦ *n* **1** act of breaking or a condition produced (as if) by breaking: *a break in the clouds* **2** pause for rest: *a coffee break* **3** change from the usual pattern or custom: *a break in the weather* **4** *infml* chance (esp. to make things better); piece of good luck

breakable *n, adj* (something) easily broken

breakage *n* **1** example of breaking **2** something broken

breakaway *n* person or thing that splits off from the main body: *a breakaway group*

breakdance *vi, n* (perform) acrobatic dancing to rock music

breakdown *n* **1** sudden failure in operation: *a breakdown in the peace talks* **2** sudden weakness or loss of power in body or mind: *a nervous breakdown* **3** division into kinds; detailed explanation

breaker *n* **1** large wave rolling onto the shore **2** person or thing that breaks something: *an ice-breaker*

break-even *adj, n* (at) the point where profit and loss are equal

breakfast *n* first meal of the day **breakfast** *vi*

break-in *n* entering of a building illegally and by force

breakneck *adj* very fast and dangerous

breakout *n* violent or forceful escape, esp. from prison

breakthrough *n* important advance or discovery

breakup *n* **1** coming to an end **2** division into parts

breakwater *n* structure protecting a harbour or beach from the force of waves

bream *n* freshwater fish related to carp

breast *n* **1** milk-producing part of a woman's body: *a breast-fed baby* **2** upper front part of the body: *his breast pocket* **3 make a clean breast of** tell the whole truth about ♦ *vt* push aside with one's chest

breast-feed *vi/t* **-fed** suckle

breastplate *n* piece of armour to protect the chest

breaststroke *n* swimming stroke in-

volving a sideways sweep of the arms
breath *n* **1** air taken into and breathed out of the lungs **2** single act of breathing air in and out once **3** sign or slight movement (of something): *There's a breath of spring in the air.* **4** moment: *In one breath he said he loved me, in the next that he didn't.* **5 out of breath** breathing very fast, as after running **6 take one's breath away** surprise one greatly **7 under one's breath** in a whisper **~less** *adj* **~lessly** *adv*
breathalyser, -lyzer *n* apparatus used by the police to measure the amount of alcohol a driver has drunk **breathalyse, -lyze** *vt*
breathe *v* **1** *vi/t* take (air, etc.) into the lungs and send it out again **2** *vt* say softly; whisper **3 breathe down someone's neck** *infml* keep too close a watch on someone **4 breathe one's last** *fml* die **~r** *n* short rest
breathtaking *adj* very exciting or unusual
breech *n* **1** buttocks **2** part of a firearm behind the barrel into which the cartridge is loaded for firing
breech delivery *n* birth in which the baby's feet or buttocks emerge first
breeches *pl n* short trousers fastened at or below the knee
breeches buoy *n* device consisting of a life buoy and canvas sling for transferring people from ship to ship along a rope
breed *v* **bred 1** *vi* (of animals) produce young **2** *vt* keep (animals, etc.) for the purpose of producing young ones **3** *vt* produce; cause: *Flies breed disease.* ♦ *n* kind of animal or plant: *a new breed of rose* **~er** *n* person who breeds animals or plants **~ing** *n* **1** business of breeding animals, etc. **2** polite manners
breeding-ground *n* **1** place where the young, esp. of wild creatures, are produced **2** place or point of origin: *a breeding-ground for disease*
breeze *n* **1** light gentle wind **2** *sl, esp. AmE* something easily done ♦ *vi* come and go quickly and unceremoniously
breezy *adj* **1** rather windy **2** cheerful in manner
breeze-block *n* light brick made of sand, cement, and coke cinders
Bren gun *n* light machine gun
brethren *pl n* (used esp. in church) brothers
Breton *n, adj* (inhabitant or language) of Brittany
breve *n* musical note equal to four minims
breviary *n* book containing prayers to be said daily by Roman Catholic priests
brevity *n* shortness
brew *v* **1** *vt* prepare (beer, tea, coffee) **2** *vi* make beer **3** *vi* gather strength: *Trouble is brewing.* ♦ *n* result of brewing: *a strong brew* **~er** *n* person who makes beer **~ery** *n* place where beer is made
briar *n* brier
bribe *vt* influence unfairly by gifts ♦ *n* something offered in this way: *judges who take bribes* **~ry** *n* giving or taking bribes
bric-a-brac *n* small decorations in a house
brick *n* **1** (piece of) baked clay for building: *brick walls* **2** something shaped like a brick **brick in/up** *phr vt* fill or enclose with bricks
brickbat *n* **1** a thrown stone **2** verbal attack
bricklayer *n* workman who puts bricks in place **–ing** *n*
brickwork *n* (part of) a structure built of bricks
bridal *adj* of a bride or wedding
bride *n* woman about to be married, or just married
bridegroom *n* man about to be married, or just married
bridesmaid *n* girl attending the bride at a wedding
bridge[1] *n* **1** structure carrying a road or railway e.g. over a river **2** raised part of a ship where the captain and officers stand **3** upper part of the nose **4** part of a musical instrument over which the

strings are stretched **5** piece of metal that keeps false teeth in place ♦ *vt* build a bridge across

bridge² *n* card game for four players

bridgehead *n* position far forward in enemy territory

bridgework *n* dental bridge

bridle *n* leather bands round a horse's head to control its movements ♦ *v* **1** *vt* put a bridle on **2** *vt* control **3** *vi* show displeasure

bridle path *n* path for horse riding

Brie *n* type of soft cheese

brief¹ *adj* **1** short: *a brief visit* **2 in brief** in as few words as possible **~ly** *adv*

brief² *n* **1** short statement of facts or instructions **2** *BrE* set of instructions setting limits to someone's powers or duties ♦ *vt* give necessary instructions or information

briefcase *n* flat leather case for papers

briefs *pl n* short underpants

brier¹ *n* straggling thorny shrub

brier² *n* (tobacco pipe made from the root of) a type of heather

brigade *n* **1** army unit of about 5000 soldiers **2** organization with certain duties: *the Fire Brigade*

brigadier *n* officer commanding a brigade

brigand *n* bandit

brigantine *n* two-masted, square-rigged sailing vessel

bright *adj* **1** giving out light; shining **2** (of a colour) strong:*bright red* **3** cheerful; happy **4** clever **5** showing hope or signs of future success: *a bright future* **~en** *vi/t* make or become bright **~ly** *adv* **~ness** *n*

bright spark *n BrE infml* clever or cheerful person

brill *adj BrE sl* very good; brilliant

brilliant *adj* **1** very bright: *brilliant blue* **2** very clever: *a brilliant idea* **3** very hopeful; successful: *a brilliant career* ♦ *n* diamond **~ly** *adv* **–liance, -liancy** *n*

brilliantine *n* oil to make men's hair look glossy

brim *n* **1** edge of a cup, etc. **2** bottom part of a hat ♦ *vi* **-mm-** be full of liquid

brimstone *n* sulphur

brindled *adj* streaked

brine *n* salt water **~y** *adj*

bring *vt* **brought 1** carry or lead towards someone: *Bring him to the party.* **2** cause to come: *His letter brought many offers of help.* **3** be sold for **4** *law* make (a charge) officially **bring about** *phr vt* cause **bring around/over/round** *phr vt* persuade into a change of opinion **bring down** *phr vt* **1** cause to fall or come down: *bring down prices* **2** reduce or lower: *to bring someone down to your own level* **bring down on** *phr vt* cause (something bad) to happen: *bring trouble down on the family* **bring forward** *phr vt* **1** introduce; suggest: *bring forward a plan* **2** schedule for an earlier time: *bring forward the meeting* **bring in** *phr vt* **1** cause to come; introduce **2** produce as profit; earn **bring off** *phr vt* succeed in doing **bring on** *phr vt* **1** cause to happen: *bring on a fever* **2** help to develop **bring out** *phr vt* **1** produce; cause to appear: *Responsibility brings out the best in her.* **2** cause (workers) to strike **3** encourage, esp. to talk **bring round/to** *phr vt* cause to regain consciousness **bring up** *phr vt* **1** educate and care for (children) **2** mention a subject **3** *esp. BrE* vomit (food)

brink *n* verge: *on the brink of disaster*

brinkmanship *n infml* art of going to the limit of safety, esp. in international politics, before stopping

brioche *n* small round bun made of light sweet dough

briquette *n* small compressed block of coal dust

brisk *adj* quick and active: *a brisk walk* **~ly** *adv* **~ness** *n*

brisket *n* meat from the breast

bristle *n* short stiff hair ♦ *vi* **1** (of hair) stand up stiffly **2** react fiercely: *bristling with anger* **bristle with** *phr vt* have plenty of: *streets bristling with armed guards* **–tly** *adj*

Brit *n infml* British person

britches *pl n* breeches

British *adj* of Britain
Briton *n* British person
brittle *adj* **1** hard but easily broken **2** lacking warmth or depth of feeling
broach *vt* **1** open (a cask or bottle) **2** introduce (a subject) for conversation
broad *adj* **1** large when measured from side to side; wide **2** not limited; respecting the ideas of others: *broad opinions* **3** not detailed: *in broad outline* **4** full; clear: *in broad daylight* **5** (of speech) showing clearly where the speaker comes from: *a broad Scots accent* **6** not acceptable in polite society: *broad humour* **~en** *vi/t* make or become broader: *Travel broadens the mind.* **~ly** *adv* more or less; mostly **~ness** *n*
broad bean *n* (plant which bears) a broad flat edible bean
broadcast *n* radio or television presentation ♦ *v* **1** *vi/t* send out (broadcasts) **2** *vt* make widely known: *He broadcast the news to his friends.* ♦ *adv* over a wide area **~er** *n* **~ing** *n*
Broad Church *n* party, esp. within the Anglican Church, which favours a tolerant and liberal approach in doctrinal matters
broadcloth *n* thick strong woollen cloth
broad jump *n AmE* long jump
broadsheet *n* something printed on a large piece of paper
broadside *n* **1** forceful spoken or written attack **2** firing of all the guns on one side of a ship
broadsword *n* sword with a broad blade for cutting rather than thrusting
brocade /brəˈkayd/ *n* decorative cloth with a raised pattern
broccoli *n* vegetable similar to a cauliflower
brochure /ˈbrohshə, -shooə/ *n* small book of instructions, or giving details of a service offered
brogue[1] /brohg/ *n* strong thick shoe
brogue[2] *n* Irish accent
broil *vt* **1** cook e.g. over a fire **2** *AmE* grill
broke[1] *past t. of* break[1]
broke[2] *adj infml* completely without money
broken *v past p. of* break[1] ♦ *adj* **1** violently separated; damaged: *a broken window* **2** not kept to; destroyed: *a broken promise* **3** imperfectly spoken or written: *broken English*
brokenhearted *adj* filled with grief
broker *n* person who buys and sells shares for others
brokerage *n* **1** (place of) business of a broker **2** fee charged by a broker
brolly *n BrE infml* umbrella
bromide *n* **1** chemical used as a sedative **2** platitude
bronchial *adj* of the branches of the windpipe
bronchitis *n* inflammation of the bronchial tubes
bronco *n* untamed horse of the western US
brontosaurus *n* large dinosaur
bronze *n* **1** (the reddish-brown colour of) a metal that is a mixture of copper and tin **2** medal made of bronze **3** sculpture made of bronze ♦ *vt* give this colour to: *bronzed by the sun*
Bronze Age *n* prehistoric age characterized by the use of bronze for making weapons and tools
brooch *n* decoration pinned to a dress
brood *n* family of birds, etc. ♦ *vi* think long and sadly about something ♦ *adj* kept for breeding **~y** **1** (of a hen) wanting to sit on eggs **2** sad and silent **~ily** *adv* **~iness** *n*
brook[1] *n* small stream
brook[2] *vt fml* allow or accept without complaining
broom *n* **1** sweeping brush with a long handle **2** shrub with long thin branches
broth *n* thin soup
brothel *n* house of prostitutes
brother *n* **1** male relative with the same parents **2** male member of the same profession or religious group **~hood** *n* **1** condition or feeling of friendliness and companionship **2** all the people in a group **~ly** *adj* **1** like a brother **2** friendly

brother-in-law *n* **brothers-in-law** brother of one's husband or wife; one's sister's husband
brought *past t. and p. of* bring
brouhaha *n* uproar
brow *n* **1** eyebrow **2** forehead **3** top of a hill
browbeat *vt* **-beat, -beaten** frighten into doing something
brown *adj, n* (of) the colour of earth or coffee ♦ *vi/t* make or become brown
browned-off *adj BrE infml* annoyed and discouraged
brownie *n* **1** good-natured goblin **2** (usu. cap.) junior Guide **3** *esp. AmE* small square of rich chocolate cake
Brownie point *n* mark of notice and approval for something good that one has done
brownstone *n AmE* (building constructed of) brown sandstone
brown study *n* reverie; pensive mood
browse *vi* **1** read without clear purpose **2** feed on young plants and grass **browse** *n*
bruise *n* discoloured place where the skin has been hurt ♦ *v* **1** *vt* cause a bruise on **2** *vi* show a bruise
brunch *n* late breakfast or early lunch
brunette also *AmE* **brunet** *n* woman of a fair-skinned race with dark hair
brunt *n* **bear the brunt of** suffer the heaviest part of (an attack)
brush *n* **1** instrument e.g. for sweeping or painting made of fibres **2** act of brushing **3** short unpleasant meeting: *a brush with the police* **4** (land covered by) small rough trees and bushes **5** tail of a fox ♦ *v* **1** *vt* clean with a brush **2** *vi/t* touch or move lightly **brush aside/away** *phr vt* refuse to pay attention to **brush off** *phr vt* refuse to pay attention to **brush up** *phr vt* refresh one's memory of: *I must brush up my French.*
brush-off *n* clear refusal to be friendly: *She gave me the brush-off.*
brushwood *n* brush (4)
brushwork *n* technique used by an artist in applying paint
brusque /brusk, broosk/ *adj* quick and rather impolite **~ly** *adv* **~ness** *n*
brussels sprout *n* vegetable like a very small cabbage
brutal *adj* without tender feeling; cruel **~ly** *adv* **~ity** *n* **~ize, ~ise** *vt* **1** make brutal **2** treat brutally
brute *n* **1** rough cruel person **2** animal ♦ like (that of) an animal in being cruel or very strong: *brute force* **brutish** *adj* like animals rather than people
BS *abbrev. for:* British Standard
BSc *abbrev. for:* Bachelor of Science
B-side *n* flip side
BST *abbrev. for:* British Summer Time
Bt *abbrev. for:* Baronet
BT *abbrev. for:* British Telecom
bubble *n* hollow ball of liquid containing air or gas ♦ *vi* **1** form, produce, or rise as bubbles **2** make the sound of bubbles rising in liquid **3** be excited **bubbly** *adj* **1** full of bubbles **2** showing happy feelings freely
bubbly *n infml* champagne
bubonic plague *n* highly infectious disease characterized by swellings (**buboes**) and fever
buccaneer *n* pirate
buck *n* **1** male of certain animals, esp. the deer, rat, and rabbit **2** *sl, esp. AmE* American dollar **3** responsibility: *to pass the buck* ♦ *v* **1** *vi* (of a horse) jump up with all four feet off the ground **2** *vt* throw off (a rider) by doing this **3** *esp. AmE* oppose: *buck the system* **buck up** *phr vt* **1** try to improve **2** make happier **~ed** *adj infml* pleased.
bucket *n* **1** (contents of) an open container with a handle, for liquids **2** large quantity: *The rain came down in buckets.* ♦ *vi* **1** *BrE infml* rain very hard **2** move jerkily or recklessly **~ful** *n* contents of a bucket
bucket shop *n infml, esp. BrE* business that obtains large quantities of tickets for air travel and sells them to the public at a low price
buckle *n* metal fastener for a belt or strap ♦ *vi/t* **1** fasten with a buckle **2** bend; twist: *a buckled wheel* **3** begin to yield: *Her knees buckled.* **buckle down**

phr vi begin to work seriously
buckram *n* stiff cotton or linen fabric
buckshee *adj, adv BrE sl* free; for nothing
buckshot *n* medium-sized lead shot used for hunting
buckwheat *n* black seed used as a cereal grain
bucolic /byooh'kolik/ *adj* of country life
bud *n* **1** flower or leaf before it opens **2 nip something in the bud** prevent (something), from succeeding ♦ *vi* **-dd-** produce buds **~ding** *adj* beginning to develop
Buddhism *n* eastern religion taught by Buddha **Buddhist** *n, adj*
buddleia *n* bush with long spikes of flowers which attract butterflies
buddy *n* **1** *infml* companion; friend **2** *AmE sl* (used as a form of address to a man)
budge *vi/t* move a little
budgerigar also *infml* **budgie** *n* small brightly coloured Australian bird
budget *n* **1** plan of how to spend money, esp. public money taken in by taxation **2** amount of money stated in this ♦ *vi* plan one's spending ♦ *adj* cheap: *budget prices*
buff *adj, n* (of) a faded yellow colour ♦ *vt* polish (metal) with something soft ♦ *n* person interested in a subject: *a film buff*
buffalo *n* **1** large African and Asian animal resembling a cow **2** bison
buffer *n* **1** spring on a railway vehicle that takes the shock when it hits anything **2** something that lessens the effect of shock
buffer zone *n* neutral area separating opposing forces or groups
buffet[1] *n* table or counter where one can get food to be eaten nearby
buffet[2] *vt* hit sharply: *buffeted by the wind* ♦ *n* sharp blow
buffoon *n* noisy fool
bug *n* **1** *AmE* any insect **2** germ **3** apparatus for secret listening **4** eager interest in something: *the travel bug* **5** fault in a machine, esp. a computer ♦ *vt* **-gg- 1** fit with a bug or eavesdrop on through a bug **2** trouble (someone) continually
bugbear *n* something feared
bugger *n sl, esp. BrE* **1** unpleasant person or thing **2** person of the stated kind: *You lucky bugger!* ♦ *interj* (used for adding force to expressions of displeasure) ♦ *vt* **1** commit sodomy with **2** spoil **~y** *n* sodomy
bugger all *n BrE taboo* nothing
buggy *n* **1** light carriage **2** pushchair
bugle *n* brass wind instrument **bugler** *n*
build *vi/t* **built** make by putting pieces together **build on** *phr vt* **1** base on **2** depend on **build up** *phr v* **1** *vt* increase; develop: *build up a business* **2** *vi* praise (something or someone) so as to influence the opinion of others ♦ *n* shape and size of one's body **~er** *n* **~ing** *n* **1** structure with a roof and walls; house, etc. **2** work of a builder
building society *n BrE* business organization in which people invest money and which lends money to people who want to buy houses
built-in *adj* **1** inherent **2** forming an integral part of (a structure): *built-in cupboards*
built-up *adj* having many buildings
bulb *n* **1** round root of certain plants **2** glass part of an electric lamp **~ous** *adj* fat and round
bulge *n* **1** swelling on a surface **2** sudden increase ♦ *vi* swell
bulk *n* **1** great size or quantity **2 in bulk** in large quantities **3 the bulk of** most of ♦ *v* **bulk large** play an important part **~y** *adj* large and fat
bulkhead *n* dividing wall in a ship
bull *n* **1** male of cattle and some other large animals **2 bull in a china shop** person who is rough where care is needed
bulldog *n* strong, sturdy dog with a broad muzzle
bulldoze *vt* move (earth, etc.) with a powerful machine (a **bulldozer**)
bullet *n* piece of shot fired from a

small gun
bulletin *n* short official report
bullfight *n* elaborately staged contest, in Hispanic countries, in which a matador baits and usu. kills a bull **~er** *n*
bullfinch *n* finch, the male of which has a pink breast
bullfrog *n* large frog which croaks loudly
bullheaded *adj* stupidly obstinate
bullion *n* bars of gold or silver
bullish *adj* marked by, tending to cause, or hopeful of rising prices (as in a stock exchange)
bullock *n* castrated bull
bullring *n* arena where bullfights take place
bull's-eye *n* centre of a target
bullshit *n sl* nonsense ♦ *vi/t* **-tt-** *sl* talk nonsense, esp. in order to persuade
bully *n* person who is cruel to people **bully** *vt*
bully beef *n* corned beef
bully boy *n* (hired) thug
bulrush *n* tall grasslike waterside plant
bulwark /ˈboolək/ *n* wall built for defence
bum¹ *n BrE sl* buttocks
bum² *n AmE sl* tramp (1) ♦ *vt* **-mm-** *sl* ask for; beg
bumble *vi* **1** speak hesitantly **2** move unsteadily
bumble bee *n* large hairy bee
bump *v* **1** *vi/t* knock violently **2** *vi* move along in an uneven way **bump into** *phr vt* meet by chance **bump off** *phr vt infml* kill **bump up** *phr vt* increase ♦ *n* **1** (sound of) a sudden blow **2** swelling **~y** *adj* uneven
bumper *n* protective bar on the front or back of a car ♦ *adj* very large: *a bumper harvest*
bumph, **bumf** *n BrE infml* useless papers or paperwork
bumpkin *n* awkward and ignorant country person
bumptious *adj* conceited **~ly** *adv* **~ness** *n*
bun *n* **1** small round sweet cake **2** hair twisted into a tight shape
bunch *n* **1** number of small things fastened together: **2** group: *a bunch of girls* ♦ *vi/t* form into a bunch
bundle *n* **1** number of articles fastened together: *a bundle of sticks* **2** a mass: *a bundle of nerves* ♦ *v* **1** *vi/t* hurry roughly **2** *vt* make into a bundle
bung *n* round piece of material to close the hole in a container ♦ *vt BrE infml* throw roughly **bung up** *phr vt* block up (a hole)
bungalow *n* house all on one level
bungle *vt* do (work) badly **–gler** *n*
bunion *n* swelling on the outer side of the big toe
bunk¹ *n* bed fixed to a wall, often above or below another
bunk² *n* **do a bunk** *BrE sl* run away ♦ *vi* run away
bunker *n* **1** place to store coal **2** shelter for soldiers **3** (in golf) sandy place from which it is difficult to hit the ball
bunkum *n* nonsense
bunny *n* (child's word for) a rabbit
Bunsen burner *n* gas burner used esp. in chemical experiments
bunting *n* decorative flags
buoy /boy/ *n* floating object fastened to the bed of the sea to show a danger ♦ *v* **buoy up** *phr vt* **1** keep floating **2** keep high
buoyancy /ˈboyənsi/ *n* **1** tendency to float **2** cheerfulness **3** ability, e.g. of prices or business activity, to remain at or return quickly to a high level **–ant** *adj* showing buoyancy **–antly** *adv*
burden *n* heavy load or duty ♦ *vt* load; trouble
burdensome *adj* being a burden: *a burdensome task*
burdock *n* weed with prickly purple flowerheads
bureau *n* **bureaus** *or* **bureaux** **1** *BrE* writing desk with a lid **2** *AmE* chest of drawers **3** government department **4** business office
bureaucracy /byooəˈrokrəsi/ *n* **1** group of government officials who are appointed, not elected **2** government by such

a group, esp. when full of unnecessary rules **–rat** *n* appointed official **–ratic** *adj* **–ratically** *adv*
burgeon *vi fml* grow; develop
burgh *n* borough
burgher *n* inhabitant of a borough or town
burglar *n* thief who breaks into buildings **–gle**, *AmE* **-glarize** *vt* break into (a building) to steal **~y** *n* (example of) the crime of being a burglar
burial *n* (ceremony of) burying
burlap *n* sackcloth
burlesque *n* **1** (writing or drama containing) mockery by imitation and exaggeration **2** variety (4) ♦ *vt* mock by imitating
burly *adj* (of a person) strong and heavy
burn[1] *v* **burnt** *or* **burned 1** *vi* be on fire: *a burning house* **2** *vt* damage or destroy by fire or acid: *burn old letters* **3** *vt* use for heating or lighting: *a wood-burning stove* **4** *vi* be very hot: *burning sands* **5** *vi* feel or wish very strongly;: *She's burning to tell you.* **6 burn one's boats/bridges** destroy all means of going back, so that one must go forward **7 burn the candle at both ends** work or be active from very early until very late; use up all one's strength by doing too many different things **burn out** *phr v* **1** *vt* make (a building) hollow by fire **2** *vi* stop burning because there is nothing left to burn **3** *vi/t* stop working through damage caused by heat **4** *vi/t* stop working because of physical or mental exhaustion ♦ *n* mark or hurt place made by burning **~ing** *adj* **1** on fire **2** very strong and urgent **~er** *n* part of a cooker, etc. that produces flames
burn[2] *n* Scottish stream
burnish *vt* polish by rubbing
burnous *n* traditional hooded cloak worn by Arabs
burnout *n* moment when the engine of a rocket or jet uses up all its fuel and stops operating
burn-up *n sl* piece of reckless high-speed driving
burp *v, n* belch
burr *n* prickly covering of a seed
burrito *n* tortilla baked with a filling
burro *n* **burros** *esp. AmE* small donkey used as a pack animal
burrow *n* hole where an animal lives ♦ *vi/t* make a hole; dig
bursar *n* person in a college who has charge of financial affairs
bursary *n* scholarship (1)
burst *vi/t* **burst 1** break suddenly by pressure from inside: *a burst tyre* **2** (cause to) come into the stated condition suddenly, often with force: *They burst open the door.* **3** be filled to breaking point (with a substance or usu. pleasant feeling): *I'm bursting to tell someone the news.* **burst into** *phr vt* **1** enter hurriedly **2** break into (2) **burst out** *phr v* **1** *vi* begin suddenly (to use the voice without speaking): *They burst out laughing.* **2** say suddenly ♦ *n* sudden outbreak or effort: *a burst of speed*
bury *vt* **1** put into a grave **2** hide away: *buried treasure*
bus *n* **1** large passenger-carrying motor vehicle **2** also **busbar** electrical connection for transferring information between parts of a computer ♦ *vt* **-ss-**, **-s-** take by bus
busby *n* bearskin
bush *n* **1** low woody plant: *rose bush* **2** wild land in Australia **~y** *adj* (of hair) growing thickly
bushbaby *n* small furry agile African mammal with large eyes
bushed *adj infml* exhausted
bushel *n* unit of capacity
Bushido *n* feudal code of the Japanese samurai
bush jacket *n* lightweight jacket with patch pockets
bush telegraph *n* grapevine
bushwhack *v AmE* **1** *vi* clear a path through undergrowth **2** *vi* camp in the woods **3** *vt* ambush
business *n* **1** trade; the getting of money **2** money-earning activity; shop, etc. **3** one's employment; duty: *A teacher's business is to teach.* **4** affair; matter **5**

like nobody's business very fast or well **~like** *adj* doing things calmly and effectively
businessman *n* **-men** man in a business firm
businesswoman *n* woman in a business firm
busk *vi BrE* play music in the street to earn money **busker** *n*
busman's holiday *n* holiday spent doing one's usual work
bus stop *n* place where buses stop for passengers
bust[1] *vt* **busted** *or* **bust** *infml* **1** break, esp. with force **2** *sl* (of the police) take to a police station **3** *sl* (of the police) enter without warning to look for something illegal **4** **-buster** *infml* person who destroys or breaks up the stated thing: *a crimebuster* ♦ *adj infml* **1** broken **2 go bust** (of a business) fail
bust[2] *n* **1** human head and shoulders as shown in a sculpture **2** woman's breasts
bustard *n* large game bird
buster *n AmE infml* (way of addressing a man)
bustle[1] *vi* be busy, often noisily **bustle** *n*
bustle[2] *n* framework that makes the back of a skirt stick out
bust-up *n sl* **1** noisy quarrel **2** a coming to an end of a relationship or partnership
busy *adj* **1** working; not free **2** full of work: *a busy morning* **3** *esp. AmE* (of telephones) in use ♦ *vt* keep (oneself) busy **busily** *adv*
busybody *n* nosy or officious person
busy lizzie *n* garden or house plant with many small white, pink or purple flowers
but *conj* **1** rather; instead: *not one, but two* **2** yet at the same time; however: *I want to go, but I can't.* **3** (shows disagreement or surprise): *But I don't want to!* ♦ *prep* **1** except: *nobody but me* **2 but for** except for; without ♦ *adv lit* **1** only: *You can but try.* **2 all but** almost ♦ *n* unwanted argument: *No buts! You're going!*
butane *n* gas used as a fuel
butch *adj infml* (of a woman) looking and acting like a man
butcher *n* **1** person who kills animals for food, or sells meat **2** cruel killer ♦ *vt* kill and prepare for food **2** kill bloodily **~y** *n* cruel needless killing
butler *n* chief male servant
butt[1] *vi/t* push with the head or horns **butt in** *phr vi* interrupt
butt[2] *n* **1** person that people make fun of **2** end of something: *cigarette butt* **3** *esp. AmE infml* bottom[1] (2) **4** large barrel
butt[3] *vt* place end to end without overlapping
butter *n* yellow fat made from cream ♦ *vt* spread butter on **butter up** *phr vt sl* flatter
buttercup *n* yellow wild flower
butterfingers *n* person likely to drop things
butterfly *n* **1** insect with large coloured wings **2** person who spends all his/her time running after pleasure: *a social butterfly* **3 butterflies in one's stomach** nervousness before doing something
buttermilk *n* liquid left after butter is made from milk
butterscotch *n* sweet made from sugar and butter boiled together
buttery *n* storeroom for food and drink, e.g. in a college
buttock *n* either of the two fleshy parts on which a person sits
button *n* **1** small round object passed through a hole to fasten a garment **2** button-like object pressed to start a machine ♦ *vi/t* fasten with a button
buttonhole *n* **1** hole for a button **2** *BrE* flower to wear on one's coat or dress ♦ *vt* stop and force to listen
buttress *n* support for a wall ♦ *vt* support; strengthen
buxom *adj* (of a woman) fat and healthy, esp. having large breasts
buy *vi/t* **bought 1** obtain by paying money **2** *infml* accept; believe ♦ *n* something bought **~er** *n* person who buys, esp. professionally for a firm

buyer's market *n* situation in which supply exceeds demand and prices are low

buyout *n* situation in which a person or group gains control of a company by buying all or most of its shares

buzz *v* **1** *vi* make the noise that bees make **2** *vi/t* call someone with an electrical signalling apparatus (a **buzzer**) **3** fly low and fast over: *Planes buzzed the crowd.* **buzz off** *phr vi infml* go away ♦ *n* **1** noise of buzzing **2** *infml* telephone call: *Give me a buzz.* **3** *sl* pleasant feeling as if from a drug

buzzard *n* **1** large hawk **2** *esp. AmE* type of vulture

buzzword *n* fashionable jargon word or phrase

BVM *abbrev. for:* Blessed Virgin Mary

by *prep, adv* **1** beside; near: *Sit by me.* **2** through; using: *enter by the door|travel by car* **3** past: *He walked by (me) without speaking.* **4** before: *Do it by tomorrow.* **5** (shows who or what does something): *a play by Shakespeare* **6** (shows amounts and measurements): *They overcharged me by £3|a room 5 metres by 4* **7** (shows how or with what): *hold it by the handle* **8** (in promises, etc.): *By God, he's done it!* **9** (shows the size of groups following each other): *The animals went in two by two.* **10** during: *to sleep by day* **11 by and by** before long **12 by and large** on the whole; usually

bye[1] also **bye-bye** *interj infml* goodbye

bye[2] *n* **1** free passage to the next round of a competition **2** (in cricket) run scored off a ball which the batsman does not hit

by-election, bye-election *n* election held between regular elections, in only one place

bygone *adj* past: *in bygone days* ♦ *pl n* **let bygones be bygones** forgive past quarrels

bylaw *n* law made by a local council

bypass *n* road that goes round a busy town ♦ *vt* avoid by going round

byplay *n* action of less importance going on at the same time as the main action

by-product *n* something produced while making something else

byre *n BrE* cowshed

bystander *n* person who watches without taking part

byte *n* unit of computer information equal to eight bits

byway *n* smaller road or path which is not much used or known

byword *n* (name of a) person, place, or thing thought to represent some (usu. bad) quality: *a byword for cruelty*

byzantine /bi'zantien/ *adj* secret, indirect, and difficult to understand

C

C, c the 3rd letter of the English alphabet

c *abbrev. for:* **1** cent(s) **2** circa **3** cubic **4** centimetre(s) **5** copyright

C *abbrev. for:* **1** Celsius **2** century

cab *n* **1** taxi **2** the part of a bus, railway engine, etc., where the driver sits

cabal *n* small group of political intriguers

cabaret /'kabəray/ *n* performance of music and dancing in a restaurant, nightclub, etc.

cabbage *n* **1** round vegetable with thick green leaves **2** *infml* **a** inactive person who takes no interest in anything **b** someone who has lost the ability to think, move, etc., as a result of illness

cabbage white *n* common large white butterfly whose larvae feed on cabbages and similar plants

cabby *n infml* taxi driver

caber *n* large heavy pole used in the Highland sport of **tossing the caber**

cabin *n* **1** small room on a ship **2** small roughly built house

cabin boy *n* boy formerly employed as a

servant on board ship
cabin cruiser *n* large motorboat with a cabin or cabins
cabinet *n* **1** piece of furniture with shelves and drawers **2** chief ministers of a government
cable *n* **1** thick heavy rope **2** wire carrying electricity, telephone messages, etc. **3** telegram ♦ *vi/t* send or tell by telegram
cable car *n* car supported in the air by a cable, for crossing valleys, going up mountains, etc.
cable television *n* system of broadcasting television by cable
caboodle *n* **the whole (kit and) caboodle** the whole lot, everything
caboose *n* **1** galley (2) **2** *AmE* guard's van
cacao *n* **-caos** (S American tree with) a fatty seed used in making cocoa and chocolate
cache *n* secret store of things
cachet /ˈkashay/ *n* **1** official stamp or seal **2** prestige; snob value
cack-handed *adj BrE* unskilful; clumsy
cackle *vi* **1** make the noise a hen makes **2** laugh unpleasantly **cackle** *n*
cacophony *n* unpleasant mixture of loud noises **–nous** *adj*
cactus *n* **-tuses** *or* **-ti** fleshy desert plant with prickles
cad *n* unscrupulous or dishonourable man **~dish** *adj*
CAD *abbrev. for:* computer-aided design
cadaver *n* corpse **~ous** *adj* **1** gaunt; emaciated **2** sickly pale
caddie *n* assistant to a golfer who carries his/her clubs
caddy *n* box or tin for tea
cadence *n* **1** intonation **2** concluding chord sequence
cadenza *n* showy solo passage in concerto movement
cadet *n* young person training in the armed forces or police
cadge *vi/t derog* get or try to get by asking; borrow
cadmium *n* soft white metallic element
cadre *n* (member of) an inner group of trained people
caesarean /siˈzeəri·ən/ *n* operation to deliver a baby through an incision in the abdomen
caesura *n* **-ras** or **-rae** break in the middle of a line of verse
cafe *n* small restaurant serving light meals and drinks
cafeteria *n* self-service restaurant or canteen
caffeine *n* stimulant found esp. in tea and coffee
caftan *n* long, loose robe traditionally worn by Arabs
cage *n* container with bars, for keeping birds or animals in ♦ *vt* put in a cage
cagey *adj* secretive
cagoule *n* lightweight anorak
cahoots *pl n* **in cahoots with** in league with for a dishonest purpose
cairn *n* pile of stones made as a memorial or landmark
caisson *n* watertight chamber used for underwater construction work or as a foundation
cajole *vt* persuade by praise or false promises **–lery** *n* persuasion by flattery
cake *n* **1** soft sweet food baked with flour, etc. **2** flat piece of something **3 (sell) like hot cakes** (sell) very quickly **4 have one's cake and eat it too** have the advantages of something without the disadvantages that go with it ♦ *vt* cover thickly: *shoes caked with mud*
CAL, Cal *abbrev. for:* computer-assisted learning
calamine *n* pink powder of zinc oxide or carbonate used in soothing lotions
calamity *n* terrible misfortune **–tous** *adj*
calcify *vi/t* (cause to) become hard as a result of deposits of lime
calcium *n* metal substance found in bones and chalk
calculate *vt* **1** find out by using numbers **2** plan, intend: *take a calculated risk* **-lable** *adj* able to be measured **–lating** *adj* coldly shrewd **–lator** *n* small machine that calculates

–**lation** *n*

calculus *n* **1** branch of mathematics for calculating continually changing quantities **2** stone (5)

calendar *n* **1** list of the days and months of the year **2** system of naming and dividing up the year.

calf[1] *n* **calves 1** young of cattle and some other large animals **2** its leather

calf[2] *n* **calves** back of the human leg, between knee and ankle

calf love *n* short-lived romantic attachment in adolescence

calibre, also *AmE* **-ber** *n* **1** quality **2** inside size of a tube or gun; bullet size

calico *n* heavy cotton cloth

caliph *n* Muslim ruler **~ate** *n* area ruled by a caliph

call *v* **1** *vi/t* speak or say loudly **2** *vt* name **3** *vt* tell to come **4** *vi* **a** make a short visit **b** make regular visits **5** *vi/t* telephone **6** *vt* say publicly that something is to happen: *call a meeting/an election/a strike* **7** *vt* consider to be: *She called me a coward.* **8** *vt* waken **call by** *phr vi* visit when passing **call for** *phr vt* **1** demand **2** need; deserve **3** collect **call off** *phr vt* **1** decide not to have (a planned event) **2** tell to keep away **call on/upon** *phr vt* **1** visit **2** ask to do something **call out** *phr vt* **1** order officially to help: *Call out the army!* **2** order to strike **call up** *phr vt* **1** telephone **2** *BrE* order to join the armed forces ♦ *n* **1** shout; cry **2** telephone conversation **3** short visit **4** demand; need: *There's no call for rudeness.* **5** command to meet, come, or do something **6 on call** ready to work if needed

call box *n* public telephone booth

caller *n* person who visits or makes a telephone call

call girl *n* woman prostitute who makes her arrangements by telephone

calligraphy *n* (art of) beautiful handwriting

calling *n* profession; trade

callipers *pl n* **1** instrument for measuring distance between surfaces **2** leg supports to help someone to walk

callisthenics *n* rhythmic bodily exercises

callous *adj* unkind; without sympathy **~ly** *adv* **~ness** *n*

callow *adj* young and inexperienced

call-up *n* order to serve in the armed forces

callus *n* an area of hard skin

calm *adj* **1** not excited; quiet **2** (of weather) not windy **3** (of the sea) smooth **calm** *n* **calm** *vi/t* make or become calm **~ly** *adv* **~ness** *n*

calorie *n* unit of heat, or of energy produced by a food

calumny *n fml* slander; false charge –**niate** *vt* slander

calve *vi* give birth to a calf

calves *pl of* calf

calypso *n* kind of West Indian song

cam *n* device to change rotary to backwards and forwards motion

CAM *abbrev. for:* computer-aided manufacture

camaraderie *n* comradely feeling

camber *n* convexity of a road surface

cambric *n* fine linen or cotton fabric

camcorder *n* combined video camera and recorder

came *past t. of* come

camel *n* large long-necked animal with one or two large humps on its back

camellia *n* ornamental shrub with roselike flowers

cameo *n* **-os 1** piece of jewellery consisting of a raised shape on a darker background **2** short piece of fine writing or acting which shows the character of a person, place or event

camera *n* **1** apparatus for taking photographs or moving pictures **2 in camera** in secret

cameraman *n* person who operates a television or film camera

camera-shy *adj* unwilling to be photographed

camiknickers *pl n* woman's undergarment combining a camisole and knickers

camisole *n* loose sleeveless underbodice

camomile *n* small, sweet-smelling plant with medicinal properties
camouflage *n* use of colour, shape, etc. to hide an object **camouflage** *vt*
camp[1] *n* **1** place where people live in tents or huts for a short time **2** group of people with the same esp. political ideas ♦ *vi* set up or live in a camp **~er** *n* **1** person who camps **2** vehicle with built-in living accommodation
camp[2] *adj infml* **1** exaggeratedly effeminate **2** so unreal, unnatural, etc., as to be amusing
campaign *n* connected set of military, political, or business actions intended to obtain a particular result ♦ *vi* lead, take part in or go on a campaign
campanile *n* bell tower
campanology *n* bell-ringing
camp bed *n* light collapsible bed
camp follower *n* **1** non-combatant, e.g. servant or prostitute, who follows an army on campaign **2** *derog.* person who, though not a member of an esp. political group, attaches himself to it usu. for personal gain
campus *n* grounds of a university, college or school
can[1] *v aux* **1** be able to **2** be allowed to; may **3** (shows what is possible): *He can be very annoying.*
can[2] *n* **1** metal container for foods or liquids **2 carry the can** *esp. BrE* take the blame ♦ *vt* **-nn-** preserve (food) in a can
Canadian *n, adj* (inhabitant) of Canada
canal *n* watercourse dug for boats to travel along or to bring water
canapé *n* savoury appetizer on morsel of toast or small biscuit
canard *n* false report; hoax
canary *n* small yellow songbird
canasta *n* card game similar to rummy
cancan *n* high-kicking dance
cancel *vt* **-ll-** (*AmE* **-l-**) **1** decide not to have (a planned event) **2** destroy the value of (a cheque, etc.) by drawing a line through it **cancel out** *phr vi/t* balance; equal: *The 2 debts cancel each other out.* **~lation** *n*
cancer *n* diseased growth in the body **~ous** *adj*
candelabrum *n* **-bra** or **-brums** decorative holder for candles or lamps, with many branches
candid *adj* honest; sincere **~ly** *adv*
candidate *n* **1** person to be chosen or elected for a position **2** person taking an examination **–dature** *n* being a candidate
candied *adj* covered with shiny sugar
candle *n* wax stick with a wick inside, which gives light when it burns
candlepower *n* measure of the intensity of light
candlestick *n* holder for a candle
candour, *AmE* **–dor** *n* being candid
candy *n esp. AmE* sweets, chocolate, etc.
candy floss *n* fluffy mass of spun sugar on a stick
cane *n* **1** stem of certain tall plants, used for making furniture, for punishing children, etc. **2 the cane** punishment with this ♦ *vt* hit with a cane
canine *adj, n* (of, for, typical of) a dog
canister *n* metal box for holding a dry substance or a gas
canker *n* disease of trees, and of animal and human flesh
cannabis *n* drug produced from hemp, smoked in cigarettes
cannelloni *n* large pasta tubes
cannery *n* factory where food is put in cans
cannibal *n* **1** person who eats human flesh **2** animal that eats its own kind **~ism** *n*
cannibalize, **–ise** *vt* use parts (of a broken machine) to repair another machine of the same kind **–istic** *adj*
cannon[1] *n* **cannons** *or* **cannon** big gun, fixed to a carriage or used on military aircraft
cannon[2] *vi* hit or knock forcefully, esp. by accident
cannon fodder *n* ordinary soldiers thought of as nothing but military material without regard for their lives
cannot *v* can not
canny *adj* clever; not easily deceived **–nily** *adv*

canoe *n* light boat moved by a paddle
canon[1] *n* **1** religious law **2** accepted standard of behaviour or thought **3** body of books accepted as genuine **~ize, ~ise** *vt* declare to be a saint **~ical** *adj* according to religious law
canon[2] *n* priest who is a member of a cathedral chapter
canoodle *vi infml* caress or cuddle
canopy *n* **1** covering, usu. of cloth, suspended over something **2** cover over the front of a plane
can't *v abbrev. for:* can not
cant[1] *n* insincere talk
cant[2] *vi/t* slope; lean
cantaloupe *n* type of melon
cantankerous *adj* quarrelsome **~ly** *adv*
cantata *n* usu. religious choral composition of medium length
canteen *n* **1** restaurant in a factory, office, etc. **2** *BrE* set of knives, forks, and spoons **3** usu. cloth-covered flask
canter *n* horse's movement, slower than a gallop **canter** *vi/t*
canticle *n* liturgical song with words taken from the Bible
cantilever *n* armlike beam sticking out from an upright support, esp. for a bridge
canto *n* **-tos** major division of a long poem
canton *n* state of the Swiss confederation
cantonment *n* quarters for troops, esp. in British India
cantor *n* singer who leads the congregation in a synagogue
canvas *n* **1** strong cloth used for tents, paintings, etc. **2** oil painting on canvas
canvass *vi/t* go through (a place) or to (people) to ask for votes or find out opinions **~er** *n*
canyon *n* deep narrow valley
cap *n* **1** soft flat hat **2** protective top of a bottle, tube, etc. ♦ *vt* **-pp- 1** cover the top of **2** do or say better than: *He capped my joke with a funnier one.* **3** give a cap to (someone) as a sign of honour, esp. for playing in a national team
capable *adj* **1** clever; skilful **2** able to do or be: *That remark is capable of being misunderstood.* **–bly** *adv* **–bility** *n* **1** having skills and apparatus necessary for the stated type of activity **2** undeveloped qualities and abilities
capacity *n* **1** amount that something can hold **2** ability; power **3** position: *speaking in my capacity as minister* **4 filled to capacity** completely full **–cious** *adj* able to hold a great deal **–itor** *n* component that stores an electrical charge
caparison *n* ornamental clothing or covering esp. for a warhorse ♦ *vt lit* adorn
cape[1] *n* loose outer garment without sleeves
cape[2] *n* piece of land sticking out into the sea
capercaillie, –cailzie *n* large grouse
capillary *n* very thin tube, esp. a blood vessel
capital[1] *n* **1** town where the centre of government is **2** wealth, esp. when used to produce more wealth or start a business **3** capital letter **4 make capital of** use to one's advantage ♦ *adj* **1** punishable by death; very serious **2** relating to financial capital **3** *infml* excellent
capital[2] *n* top part of a column
capitalism *n* system based on the private ownership of wealth **–ist** *n* person who owns capital
capitalize, –ise *vt* **1** write with a capital letter **2** supply money to (a firm) **capitalize on** *phr vt* use to one's advantage
capital letter *n* letter in its large form
capital punishment *n* punishment by death according to law
capitation *n* fixed-rate charge or payment per person
capitulate *vi* accept defeat; stop opposing **–lation** *n*
capon *n* castrated male chicken
caprice /kəˈprees/ *n* sudden foolish change of behaviour **–pricious** *adj* changing; untrustworthy **–priciously**

adv

capsicum *n* pepper (2)

capsize *vi/t* (cause a boat to) turn over

capstan *n* **1** drum-shaped cable-winding device turned e.g. to raise a ship's anchor **2** shaft that drives the tape in a tape recorder

capsule *n* **1** tiny container of medicine to be swallowed whole **2** part of a spacecraft where the pilots live

captain *n* **1** leader of a team **2** person in command of a ship or aircraft **3** officer of middle rank in the armed forces ♦ *vt* be the captain of

caption *n* words written above or below a picture or newspaper article

captious /ˈkapshəs/ *adj* peevishly critical **~ly** *adv*

captivate *vt* charm; attract

captive *n* prisoner, esp. taken in war ♦ *adj* **1** held prisoner **2** firmly anchored **–tivity** *n* state or condition of being a captive

captor *n* person who captures someone

capture *vt* **1** make a prisoner of; take control of by force **2** preserve on film, in words, etc. ♦ *n* **1** capturing; being captured **2** person or thing captured

capybara *n* very large S American rodent

car *n* **1** vehicle with wheels and a motor, used for carrying people **2** railway carriage

carafe *n* (quantity held by) a wide-necked decanter

caramel *n* **1** burnt sugar **2** sweet made of boiled sugar

carapace *n* shell (of crab, tortoise, etc.)

carat *n* unit expressing the purity of gold, or the weight of a jewel

caravan *n* **1** *BrE* small home to be pulled by a car **2** *BrE* covered cart for living in **3** group of people with vehicles or animals crossing e.g. a desert

caraway *n* plant whose strong-tasting seeds are used to give a special taste in food

carbine *n* short rifle

carbohydrate *n* food such as sugar which provides heat and energy

carbon *n* **1** substance found in diamonds, coal, etc. **2 a** coated paper used for making copies **b** copy made with this

carbonate *vt* impregnate with carbon dioxide

carbon dioxide *n* heavy gas breathed out by animals

carbon monoxide *n* poisonous gas found in e.g. motor vehicle exhaust fumes

Carborundum *n tdmk for* hard stone used as a sharpener

carboy *n* large spherical bottle for esp. corrosive liquids

carbuncle *n* **1** large painful swelling **2** red gemstone

carburettor, *AmE* **–retor** *n* apparatus that mixes the air and petrol in a car engine

carcass *n* dead body, esp. of an animal

carcinogen *n* substance causing cancer **–genic** *adj*

carcinoma *n* malignant tumour

card *n* **1** one of 52 bits of stiff paper used for various games **2** bit of stiff paper with various uses: *a membership card|a birthday card* **3** cardboard **4 get one's cards** *BrE* be dismissed from one's job **5 lay/put one's cards on the table** say what one intends to do **6 on the cards** probable **7 play one's cards right** act in the most effective manner to get what one wants **~s** *pl n* games played with cards

cardamom *n* (Indian plant with) seeds used as a spice

cardboard *n* thick stiff paper

card-carrying *adj* being a fully committed member esp. of the Communist party

cardiac *adj* of the heart

cardigan *n* short knitted coat with sleeves, usu. fastened at the front

cardinal *n* priest of the highest rank in the Roman Catholic church ♦ *adj* most important; main

cardinal number *n* 1, 2, 3, etc.

card index *n BrE* filing system using a

separate card for each item

care *n* **1** worry; anxiety **2** protection; charge **3** serious attention: *Take care not to drop it.* **4 care of** also *AmE* **in care of** at the address of **5 take care of** be responsible for **6 take into care** put (esp. a child) into a home controlled by the state to make sure of proper treatment ♦ *vi* **1** be worried; mind **2 care to** like to; want **care for** *phr vt* **1** look after; nurse **2** like to have **~ful** *adj* attentive; cautious **~fully** *adv* **~less** *adj* **1** not taking care; inattentive **2** free from care; not worried **~lessly** *adv* **~lessness** *n*

careen *vi/t* lean over on one side

career *n* **1** profession **2** general course of a person's life ♦ *vi* rush wildly **~ist** *n* very ambitious person

carefree *adj* free from anxiety

caress *n* light loving touch ♦ *vt* give a caress to

caret *n* omission mark (∧)

caretaker *n* person employed to look after a building

cargo *n* **-goes** *or* **-gos** goods carried by a ship, plane, or vehicle

caribou *n* large N American deer

caricature *n* funny drawing (or written description) of someone to make them seem silly ♦ *vt* make a caricature of

caries *n* (tooth) decay **–ious** *adj*

carillon *n* set of bells played from a keyboard

carmine *n, adj* deep red

carnage *n* killing of many people

carnal *adj* physical, of the flesh, or esp. sexual

carnation *n* sweet-smelling white, pink or red flower

carnival *n* period of public rejoicing

carnivore *n* flesh-eating animal **–vorous** *adj*

carob *n* beanlike fruit used as a chocolate substitute

carol *n* religious song of joy, esp. sung at Christmas

carousal /kəˈrowzl/ *n lit* drinking and making merry **carouse** *vi* drink and make merry

carousel *n* **1** *AmE* merry-go-round **2** rotating delivery system

carp[1] *n* **carp** *or* **carps** large freshwater fish

carp[2] *vi* complain unnecessarily

car park *n* place where cars and other vehicles may be left

carpenter *n* person who makes wooden objects **–try** *n* work of a carpenter

carpet *n* cloth for covering floors ♦ *vt* cover (as if) with a carpet

carpetbagger *n* political opportunist esp. one seeking office in an area with which he or she has no previous connection

car pool *n* **1** agreement made by people to take turns driving each other to work, etc. **2** *BrE* number of cars owned by a company for the use of its employees

carport *n* open-sided shelter for a car

carriage *n* **1** vehicle, esp. horse-drawn **2** *BrE* railway passenger vehicle **3** (cost of) moving goods **4** movable part of a machine: *the carriage of a typewriter* **5** *fml* way of walking

carriageway *n BrE* division of a road on which traffic goes

carrier *n* **1** person or business that carries goods **2** person or animal that passes diseases to others without catching them **3** aircraft carrier

carrier bag *n esp. BrE* cheap strong paper or plastic bag, esp. with handles

carrier pigeon *n* homing pigeon used to carry messages

carrion *n* dead or decaying flesh

carrot *n* **1** long orange root vegetable **2** promised reward

carry *v* **1** *vt* move while supporting; have with one: *carry a child on one's back* **2** *vt* take from one place to another **3** *vt* bear the weight of: *This beam carries the whole roof.* **4** *vt* have as a usual or necessary result: *Such a crime carries a serious punishment.* **5** *vt* contain; have: *All the newspapers carried the story.* **6** *vt* win by voting: *The motion was carried.* **7** *vi* reach a distance: *Her voice doesn't carry very far.* **8**

be carried away get excited **carry off** *phr vt* perform successfully **carry on** *phr vi* **1** continue: *carry on talking* **2** behave in a foolish excited manner **carry on with** *phr vt* **1** have a love affair with (someone) **2 to carry/be carrying on with** for the present time **carry out** *phr vt* fulfil; complete **carry through** *phr vt* **1** help to continue: *Her courage carried her through.* **2** fulfil; complete

carrycot *n esp. BrE* box-like portable bed for a baby

carry-on *n* fuss

carsick *adj* suffering from motion sickness through being in a car

cart *n* **1** wheeled vehicle pulled by an animal, or pulled or pushed by hand **2 put the cart before the horse** do things in the wrong order ♦ *vt* **1** carry in a cart **2** carry; take

carte blanche /ˌkaht ˈblonh·sh/ *n* full freedom

cartel *n* combination of independent firms, to limit competition

carthorse *n* heavy powerful horse, used for heavy work

cartilage *n* elastic substance found round the joints in animals

cartography *n* map-making **–grapher** *n*

carton *n* cardboard or plastic box

cartoon *n* **1** humorous drawing of something interesting in the news **2** film made by photographing a set of drawings **~ist** *n*

cartridge *n* **1** tube containing explosive and a bullet for a gun **2** part of a record player that holds the needle **3** container of magnetic tape

cartridge paper *n* strong thick paper esp. for drawing

cartwheel *n* gymnastic movement in which a person turns over by putting their hands on the ground and waving their legs sideways in the air

carve *v* **1** *vt* make by cutting wood, stone, etc. **2** make or acquire by one's own efforts **3** *vi/t* cut (cooked meat) into pieces **carve up** *phr vt* **1** divide into sections **2** *sl* wound with a knife **3** *BrE sl* cut in just in front of (another motorist) **carver** *n* **1** person who carves **2** knife for carving meat **3** *BrE* dining-room chair with arms **carving** *n* something carved e.g. from wood

caryatid *n* pillar in the shape of a draped female figure

Casanova *n* a man reputed to have had many love affairs

cascade *n* waterfall ♦ *vi* pour like a waterfall

case[1] *n* **1** example; situation: *I'll make an exception in your case* **2** legal question to be decided; arguments supporting one side of a question **3** form of word showing the part it plays in a sentence **4** person having medical treatment **5 in any case** whatever happens **6 in case of: a** because of anxiety about: *insure the house in case of fire* **b** if (something) happens: *In case of fire, ring the bell.* **7 (just) in case** so as to be safe (if)

case[2] *n* large box or container

casebook *n* reference book containing records of cases

case-harden *vt* give (steel) an extra hard surface

case history *n* record of patient's previous illnesses, background, etc.

casein *n* protein found in milk

casement *n* window that opens like a door

casework *n* social work involving study and usu. supervision of specific individuals or families

cash *n* **1** money in coins or notes **2** money in any form ♦ *vt* exchange (a cheque, etc.) for cash **cash in on** *phr vt* take advantage from

cash-and-carry *n, adj* (shop) where goods must be paid for and taken away by the purchaser

cash card *n* plastic card used for obtaining one's money from a cash dispenser outside a bank, at any time of day

cash crop *n* crop grown for sale

cashew *n* (tropical American tree with) a small curved nut

cashier[1] *n* person who receives and pays out money in a bank, shop, etc.

cashier[2] *vt* dismiss with dishonour from service in the armed forces
cashmere *n* fine soft wool
cash register *n* machine for recording the amount of sales
casing *n* protective covering, as on a tyre
casino *n* **-nos** building where people play gambling games
cask *n* barrel for liquids
casket *n* **1** box for jewels, letters, etc. **2** *AmE* coffin
cassata *n* ice cream containing fruit and nuts
cassava *n* (starchy edible root of) a tropical plant
casserole *n* **1** deep dish for cooking and serving meat **2** food cooked in a casserole
cassette *n* container of magnetic tape, or of photographic film
cassock *n* priest's long usu. black garment
cassowary *n* large flightless Australasian bird
cast *vt* **cast 1** *fml* throw; direct **2** give (a vote) **3** make by pouring hot metal **4** choose as an actor; choose actors for (a play) **cast about/around** *phr vi* search; look around **cast aside** *phr vt* get rid of **cast away** *phr vt* leave (someone) somewhere as the result of a shipwreck **cast down** *phr vt* make sad **cast off** *phr vi/t* unloose (a boat) ♦ *n* **1** actors in a play, film, etc. **2** act of throwing a fishing line, etc. **3** hard covering to protect a broken bone **4** object made by casting metal **5** general shape or quality: *an inquiring cast of mind* **6** slight squint **~ing** *n* thing made by pouring metal
castanets *pl n* musical instrument made of two hollow shells to be knocked together
castaway *n* shipwrecked person
caste *n* Hindu social class
castellated *adj* having battlements
caster *n* **1** small wheel on e.g. a chair **2** container with holes for salt or sugar
caster sugar *n* finely granulated sugar
castigate *vt fml* punish severely; criticize
casting vote *n* deciding vote when both sides have an equal number of votes
cast iron *n* hard but easily breakable type of iron **cast-iron** *adj* **1** made of cast iron **2** very strong; unbreakable: *a cast-iron stomach*
castle *n* **1** large building that can be defended against attack **2** chess piece shaped like a small tower
cast-off *n, adj* (piece of clothing) thrown away by the original owner
castor oil *n* thick vegetable oil used as a laxative
castrate *vt* remove the sex organs of (a male) **-tration** *n*
casual *adj* **1** informal **2** resulting from chance **3** employed for a short time **4** not serious or thorough **~ly** *adv*
casualty *n* person killed or hurt in an accident or battle
casuistry /ˈkazh(y)ooˌistri/ *n* clever but false reasoning esp. about morals **casuist** *n*
cat *n* **1** small furry animal often kept as a pet **2** animal related to this; lion, tiger, etc. **3 let the cat out of the bag** tell a secret (usu. unintentionally)
cataclysm *n fml* violent event, such as an earthquake **~ic** *adj*
catacomb /ˈkatəˌkoohm/ *n* underground burial place with many rooms
catafalque *n* ornamental structure supporting a coffin
catalepsy *n* trancelike state in which the body remains rigid and immobile **-eptic** *adj*
catalogue, *AmE* **-log** *n* list of places, goods for sale, etc., in order ♦ *vt* make a list of
catalyst *n* something that quickens activity without itself changing
catamaran *n* twin-hulled yacht
catamite *n lit* boy kept as a homosexual lover
cat-and-mouse *adj* involving patient observation and stealth to catch an opponent off guard
catapult *n BrE* Y-shaped stick with a rubber band, for shooting small stones

♦ *vt* fire (as if) from a catapult

cataract *n* **1** large waterfall **2** eye disease causing blindness

catarrh *n* disease of the nose and throat, causing a flow of mucus

catastrophe /kəˈtastrəfi/ *n* sudden terrible misfortune **–phic** *adj* **–phically** *adv*

cat burglar *n* thief who enters buildings by climbing walls, pipes, etc.

catcall *v, n* (make) a loud whistle or cry expressing disapproval, esp. at the theatre

catch *v* **caught 1** *vt* get hold of (a moving object) and stop it **2** *vt* make prisoner; trap **3** *vt* discover doing something: *I caught him reading my diary.* **4** *vt* be in time for **5** *vt* get (an illness) **6** *vi/t* get hooked or stuck: *My skirt caught in the door.* **7** *vt* hear; understand **8** *vt* to hit (a person or animal) **9 catch fire** start to burn **10 catch it** *infml* be in trouble for doing something wrong **11 catch one's breath: a** stop breathing for a moment because of surprise or shock **b** rest for a short while after hard work **12 catch sight of** see for a moment **13 catch someone's eye** attract someone's attention by looking at them **catch on** *phr vi* **1** become popular **2** understand **catch out** *phr vt* discover doing something wrong **catch up** *phr vi/t* **1** come up from behind; draw level **2 caught up in** completely interested or involved in ♦ *n* **1** getting and holding a ball **2** (amount of) something caught **3** hook, etc. for fastening something **4** hidden difficulty; snag

catch-22 *n* situation from which one is prevented from escaping by something that is part of the situation itself: *I can't get a job unless I belong to the union, and I can't join the union until I've got a job — it's a catch-22 situation!*

catch-all *adj* taking account of a wide variety of possibilities

catching *adj* infectious

catchment area *n* **1** area from which rainwater drains into a lake, reservoir, etc. **2** area from which a school gets its pupils, a hospital gets its patients, etc.

catchpenny *adj* made, written, etc. with an eye to quick sales rather than quality

catchphrase *n* fashionable phrase that everyone uses

catchword *n* often-repeated word which becomes a slogan

catchy *adj* (of a tune, etc.) easy to remember

catechism /ˈkatəˌkiz(ə)m/ *n* summary of religious doctrine in question and answer form **–chize, -chise** *vt* teach (religious doctrine) by question and answer

categorical *adj* (of a statement) unconditional; made without doubt **~ly** *adv*

category *n* division in a system; class **–gorize, -gorise** *vt* put in a category

cater *vi* provide food and drinks at a party **cater for** *phr vt BrE* provide what is necessary: *magazines catering for all opinions* **~er** *n*

caterpillar *n* **1** wormlike larva of butterfly or moth **2** endless chain of plates on the wheels of e.g. a tractor

caterwaul *vi* cry noisily

catgut *n* cord used for the strings of musical instruments

catharsis *n* **-ses** getting rid of bad feelings by expressing them through art or by reliving them **cathartic** *adj*

cathedral *n* chief church of a diocese

catheter *n* tube for insertion into a hollow body part

cathode *n* electrode by which electrons leave a circuit

cathode-ray tube *n* vacuum tube in which a beam of electrons provides a visual display (e.g. a television picture) on a fluorescent screen

catholic *adj* **1** *fml* general; broad **2** (*cap.*) Roman Catholic ♦ *n* (*cap.*) a Roman Catholic

Catholicism *n* teachings of the Roman Catholic church

catkin *n* drooping spike of small furry flowers on e.g. a willow

catnap *n* short light sleep

cat's paw *n* person used by another as a

tool or dupe
catsuit *n* woman's close-fitting all-over garment
catsup *n AmE* ketchup
cattery *n* place where cats are bred or looked after
cattle *pl n* cows and bulls
catty *adj* indirectly spiteful
catwalk *n* narrow raised platform
Caucasian *adj* white (3)
caucus *n* political meeting to decide future plans
caught *past t. and p. of* catch
cauldron *n lit* large pot for boiling things
cauliflower *n* green vegetable with a large white head
caulk *vt* stop up and make watertight
cause *n* **1** thing that produces a result: *the cause of the accident* **2** reason: *no cause for complaint* **3** purpose strongly supported: *good causes such as famine relief* ♦ *vt* be the cause of **causal** *adj* indicating a relationship of cause and effect **causative** *adj* acting as a cause
cause célèbre *n* famous lawsuit, trial or controversy
causeway *n* raised road across water, swamp, etc.
caustic /ˈkostik, ˈkaw-/ *adj* **1** able to burn by chemical action **2** (of remarks) bitter; nasty
cauterize *vt* burn (a wound) to destroy infection
caution *n* **1** great care **2** spoken warning by a policeman, magistrate, etc. ♦ *vt* warn **~ary** *adj* giving a warning
cautious *adj* with caution; careful **~ly** *adv* **~ness** *n*
cavalcade *n* procession of riders, vehicles, etc.
cavalier *adj* thoughtless; offhand
Cavalier *n* follower of King Charles in the English Civil War
cavalry *n* soldiers on horseback, or (now) with armoured vehicles
cave *n* underground hollow place
cave in *phr vi* **1** (of a roof) fall down **2** give up opposition; yield
caveat *n law* warning
cavern *n* large cave **~ous** *adj* (of a hole) very large
caviar *n* salted roe of sturgeon
cavil *vi* **-ll-** (*AmE* **-l-**) find fault unnecessarily
cavity *n fml* hole in a solid mass, such as a tooth
cavort *vi infml* (esp. of a person) jump or dance about noisily
CB *n* Citizens' Band; radio by which people can speak to each other privately
CBE *abbrev. for:* Commander of the British Empire
CBI *abbrev. for:* Confederation of British Industry
cc *abbrev. for:* cubic centimetre
CD *n* compact disc
CD-ROM *n* compact disc on which very large quantities of information can be stored for use by a computer
cease *vi/t fml* stop (an activity) **~less** *adj* unending; continuous **~lessly** *adv*
cease-fire *n* agreement to stop fighting; truce
cedar *n* (wood of) a tall evergreen tree
cede *vt fml* give (esp. land, after losing a war)
cedilla *n* hooked mark placed under c to indicate a change in pronunciation
Ceefax *n tdmk* BBC teletext service
ceiling *n* **1** upper surface of a room **2** official upper limit on e.g. prices.
celebrate *v* **1** *vt/i* mark (an event) by enjoying oneself **2** *vt* praise; honour **–brant** *n* priest who officiates at the Eucharist **–brated** *adj* famous **–bration** *n*
celebrity *n* **1** famous person **2** fame
celerity *n fml* rapidity of action
celery *n* plant whose greenish-white stems are eaten as a vegetable
celestial *adj* of the sky or heaven
celibate *n, adj* (person who is) unmarried and not sexually active, esp. for religious reasons **–bacy** *n*
cell *n* **1** small room esp. in a prison or monastery **2** small unit of living matter **3** apparatus for making electricity chemically **4** single group of people in a

secret organization
cellar *n* underground room for storing things
cello *n* **-los** large instrument of the violin family, held between the knees **cellist** *n* person who plays a cello
cellophane *n* thin transparent cellulose used esp. for wrapping
cellular *adj* **1** having many holes; porous **2** consisting of living cells
celluloid *n tdmk* **1** strong plastic formerly used for making photographic film **2 on celluloid** on cinema film
cellulose *n* main substance in plant cell walls, used in making paper, plastics, etc.
Celsius *adj, n* (in) the temperature scale in which water freezes at 0° and boils at 100°
Celtic *adj* of the **Celts**, a European people who include the Welsh and Bretons
cement *n* **1** grey powder that becomes hard like stone when mixed with water, and is used in building **2** any thick sticky glue used for filling holes or joining things ♦ *vt* join with cement; make fixed and firm
cemetery *n* burial ground
cenotaph *n* monument in memory of people killed in war
censor *n* official who examines books, films, etc., to remove anything offensive ♦ *vt* examine as a censor **~ship** *n* work of a censor; censoring
censorious *adj* always looking for mistakes and faults; severely critical
censure *n* blame; disapproval ♦ *vt* express disapproval of
census *n* official counting, esp. of a country's population
cent *n* (coin equal to) 0.01 of any of certain units of money, e.g. the dollar
centaur *n* imaginary creature, half man and half horse
centenarian *n* person aged (over) 100
centenary *n* 100th anniversary
centennial *n AmE* centenary
center *n, v AmE* centre
centi- *prefix* hundredth part: *centimetre*
centigrade *adj, n* Celsius
centime *n* coin of a value of one hundredth of a franc
centimetre, *AmE* **-ter** *n* (unit of length equal to) 1/100 of a metre
centipede *n* wormlike creature with many legs
central *adj* **1** at the centre **2** most important; main **~ly** *adv* **~ize, ~ise** *vt* bring under central control **~ization** *n* **~ism** *n* concentration of power in a central authority **~ist** *adj, n*
central heating *n* heating buildings by pipes from a single point
central processing unit *n* the most important controlling part of a computer system
central reservation *n BrE* dividing strip down the middle of a road
centre, *AmE* **-ter** *n* **1** middle point **2** place for a particular activity: *a shopping centre* **3** a middle position, in politics, not supporting extreme ideas ♦ *vi/t* gather to a centre: *His interests are centred on/round his family.*
centreboard *n* retractable keel in a small yacht
centrefold *n* (picture covering) the two middle pages of a magazine
centre of gravity *n* point in any object on which it may balance
centrepiece *n* thing in the central or most important position
centrifugal *adj* tending to move out from the centre
centrifuge *n* machine using centrifugal force to separate substances of different densities
centripetal *adj* tending to move towards the centre
centrist *n, adj* (of) a person who supports the centre in politics
centurion *n* Roman officer commanding 100 men
century *n* **1** 100 years **2** 100-year period counted forwards or backwards from Christ's birth **3** (in cricket) 100 runs made by one player
ceramics *pl n* (making of) pots, bricks, etc. **ceramic** *adj*

cereal *n* **1** food grain **2** breakfast food such as cornflakes
cerebral /ˈserəbrəl/ *adj* **1** of or connected with the brain **2** showing too much serious thinking
ceremonial *adj* for a ceremony ♦ *n* ceremony
ceremonious *adj* formally polite **~ly** *adv*
ceremony *n* **1** set of solemn actions to mark an important event **2** formal behaviour
cerise *n, adj* pinkish red
cert *abbrev. for:* **1** certainty (3) **2** certificate
certain[1] *adj* **1** sure; without doubt **2** sure to happen: *facing certain death* **3** **make certain** do something to be sure **~ly** *adv* of course
certain[2] *determiner, pron* **1** some, not named: *There are certain reasons against it.* **2** some, not a lot: *a certain amount of profit*
certainty *n* **1** established fact **2** freedom from doubt **3** something certain to be true or to happen
certificate *n* official paper stating facts **-cation** *n*
certify *vt* declare officially that something is true **-fiable** *adj BrE infml* mad
certitude *n fml* state of being or feeling certain
cerulean *adj, n* sky-blue
cervelat *n* smoked pork sausage for slicing
cervical *adj* of the narrow opening (**cervix**) of the womb
cesarean *n* caesarean
cessation *n fml* short pause or stop
cesspit *n* underground hole where a house's sewage is gathered
cf *abbrev. for:* compare
ch *abbrev. for:* chapter
chafe *v* **1** *vt* rub; make sore by rubbing **2** *vi* become impatient
chaff *n* **1** outer covers of seeds, separated from the grain **2** banter; light talk ♦ *vi/t* tease; banter
chagrin /ˈshagrin/ *n lit* annoyance and disappointment
chain *n* **1** length of metal rings joined together **2** set of connected things: *chain of mountains/of events* ♦ *vt* fasten with a chain
chain gang *n* working party of convicts all chained to one another
chain letter *n* letter, usu. requesting or promising money, which the recipient is supposed to copy and send on to other people
chain mail *n* flexible armour made of links
chain reaction *n* set of events so related that each causes the next
chain saw *n* portable power saw with a cutting edge in the form of a continuous chain
chain-smoke *vi/t* smoke (cigarettes) continually **-smoker** *n*
chain store *n* group of shops under one ownership
chair *n* **1** movable seat for one person **2** position of a chairperson **3** position of a professor ♦ *vt* **1** be chairperson of **2** *BrE* lift and carry (someone) as a sign of admiration
chairlift *n* mountain lift with seats
chairman *n* **-men** (male) chairperson
chairperson *n* person in charge of a meeting, or directing the work of a group
chairwoman *n* **-women** female chairperson
chaise longue *n* **chaise longues** or **chaises longues** sofa for reclining on, with a backrest at one end and usu. an armrest along one side
chalet *n* **1** Swiss wooden house **2** small house or hut for holidays
chalice *n* metal goblet used esp. in the Communion service
chalk *n* **1** kind of soft white rock **2** this material used for writing or drawing ♦ *vt* write with chalk **chalk up** *phr vt* succeed in getting **~y** *adj*
chalkboard *n AmE* blackboard
challenge *vt* **1** invite to a fight, match, etc. **2** question the loyalty or rightness of ♦ *n* **1** invitation to compete **2** something exciting that needs a lot of

effort –**lenging** *adj* difficult but exciting –**lenger** *n*

chamber *n* **1** *lit* bedroom **2 a** law-making body **b** room where it meets **3** enclosed space: *the four chambers of the heart*

chambermaid *n* woman who cleans hotel bedrooms

chamber music *n* music for a small group e.g. a string quartet

chamber pot *n* receptacle for urine and faeces usu. kept in the bedroom

chameleon /shəˈmeelyən, kə-/ *n* small lizard that changes colour to match its surroundings

chamois /ˈshamwah/ *n* **chamois 1** small goatlike European antelope **2** *also* **chammy** soft pliant leather used esp. for polishing and glass-cleaning

chamomile *n* camomile

champ[1] *vi* **1** (of a horse) bite noisily **2** be impatient **3 champ at the bit** be restless and difficult to control because of being impatient to do something

champ[2] *n infml* champion (1)

champagne *n* expensive sparkling white wine

champion *n* **1** person or animal that wins a competition **2** person who defends a principle or another person ♦ *vt* defend; support **~ship** *n* **1** competition to find the champion **2** position of being the champion **3** act of championing

chance *n* **1** good or bad luck **2** likelihood **3** favourable occasion; opportunity **4** risk **5 by chance** by accident ♦ *v* **1** *vt* take a risk **2** *vi fml* happen accidentally: *We chanced to meet.* ♦ *adj* accidental **~y** *adj* risky

chancel *n* eastern part of a church

chancellor *n* (*often cap.*) **1** state or legal official of high rank **2** chief minister **3** official head of a university

Chancery *n* division of the British High Court

chandelier *n* branched hanging holder for lights

chandler *n* dealer esp. in ship's supplies

change *v* **1** *vi/t* make or become different **2** *vt* give and receive in return: *change pounds into dollars* **3** *vi/t* put different clothes on **4** *vi/t* leave and enter (different vehicles) ♦ *n* **1** changing; something new: *a change of clothes* | *Let's have fish for a change.* **2 a** money returned when something bought costs less than the amount paid **b** low-value coins or notes **~able** *adj* often changing

change of life *n* menopause

channel *n* **1** narrow sea passage **2** passage for liquids **3** television station **4** way along which information passes: *go through the official channels* ♦ *vt* **-ll-** (*AmE* **-l-**) send through channels; direct

chant *vi/t* sing (words) on one note **chant** *n* **~er** *n* pipe on which the melody is played in a bagpipe

chaos *n* complete confusion **–otic** *adj* **–otically** *adv*

chap[1] *n esp. BrE* man

chap[2] *vi/t* **-pp-** (cause to) become sore, rough and cracked

chapel *n* small Christian church

chaperon , -one /ˈshapəˌrohn/ *n* older person who goes with a younger person and is responsible for their behaviour **chaperon, -one** *vt*

chaplain *n* priest in the armed forces, a hospital, etc.

chaplet *n lit* wreath worn on the head

chaps *pl n* cowboy's leather leggings

chapter *n* **1** main division of a book, usu. numbered **2** special period of history **3** (regular meeting of) a bishop's council

chapter and verse *n* the exact details of where to find a piece of information

chapter of accidents *n BrE* series of misfortunes

char[1] *vi/t* **-rr-** blacken by burning

char[2] *n BrE* **1** charwoman **2** *infml* tea

char[3] *n* small fish resembling a trout

charabanc *n BrE* old-fashioned motor coach

character *n* **1** qualities that make a person or thing different from others **2** moral strength, honesty, etc. **3** person in a book, play, etc. **4** person, esp. an odd one **5** written letter or sign: *Chinese characters* **~less** *adj* ordinary; dull

characteristic *adj* typical ♦ *n* special quality **~ally** *adv*

characterize, -ise *vt* **1** be typical of **2** describe the character of

charade *n* foolish unnecessary action **~s** *pl n* game in which words are acted by players until guessed by other players

charcoal *n* burnt wood, used for drawing with, as fuel, etc.

charge *n* **1** *vt/i* ask in payment **2** *vt* record (something) to someone's debt **3** *vi/t* rush as if to attack **4** *vt* accuse of a crime **5** *vt fml* command; give as a duty **6** *vt/i* (cause to) take in electricity: *charge a battery* **7** fill with emotion, tension etc.: *a highly charged political question* ♦ *n* **1** price asked or paid **2** control; responsibility **3** statement accusing a person of wrongdoing **4** rushing attack by soldiers, animals, etc. **5** electricity put into a battery **6 in charge (of)** responsible (for)

charge card *n* plastic card which allows one to obtain goods at a particular shop and pay later

chargé d'affaires *n* official who represents his/her government where there is no ambassador

charge hand *n BrE* worker with supervisory duties below those of a foreman

charger *n* horse for battle or parade

charge sheet *n BrE* police record of the charges brought against a prisoner

chariot *n* ancient two-wheeled horse-drawn vehicle **~eer** *n* driver of a chariot

charisma /kə'rizmə/ *n* great charm; power to win public admiration **~tic** *adj*

charity *n* **1** generosity and help to the poor, etc. **2** kindness shown in judging others **3** organization for helping people **-table** *adj* **-tably** *adv*

charlady *n* charwoman

charlatan /'shahlət(ə)n/ *n* person who falsely claims a special skill

charleston *n* 1920s ballroom dance

charlie *n BrE infml* fool

charm *n* **1** power to delight people **2** magic words; spell **3** object worn to bring good luck ♦ *vt* **1** please; delight **2** control by magic **~er** *n* person who charms **~ing** *adj* very pleasing **~ingly** *adv*

charnel house *n* repository for bones of the dead

chart *n* **1** information in the form of a picture or graph **2** map, esp. of the sea ♦ *vt* make a chart of

charter *n* **1** official statement of rights and freedoms **2** hiring of buses, planes, etc. ♦ *vt* hire (a bus, etc.) **~ed** *adj* officially allowed to practise a profession: *a chartered accountant*

Chartreuse *n tdmk* aromatic green or yellow liqueur

charwoman *n BrE* woman who works as a cleaner

chary *adj* cautious; wary **-rily** *adv*

chase[1] *vi/t* follow rapidly, in order to catch or drive away ♦ *n* **1** chasing something or someone **2 give chase** chase someone

chase[2] *vt* decorate (metal) with designs made with a tool without a cutting edge

chasm *n* very deep crack in the earth

chassé *vi, n* (perform) a gliding dance step

chassis *n* **chassis** frame on which a vehicle is built

chaste *adj* sexually pure and blameless; virtuous

chasten *vt* improve by punishment or suffering

chastise *vt fml* punish severely **~ment** *n*

chastity *n* being chaste

chasuble *n* priest's sleeveless outer vestment

chat *vt* **-tt-** talk informally **chat up** *phr vt BrE infml* talk to someone (esp. of the opposite sex) in a friendly way in order to begin a relationship, persuade them to do something, etc. **chat** *n* **~ty** *adj* **1** fond of chatting **2** having the style of informal talk

château *n* **-teaus** *or* **-teaux** French castle
chat show *n* radio or TV programme in which the host has discussions with guests
chattel *n lit* item of property
chatter *vi* **1** talk rapidly about small things **2** (of the teeth) knock together from cold or fear ♦ *n* **1** chattering talk **2** rapid speechlike sounds **~er** *n*
chatterbox *n* person who chatters
chauffeur /ˌshohˈfuh/ *n* paid driver of a private car **chauffeur** *vi/t*
chauffeuse *n* a female chauffeur
chauvinism /ˈshohvəˌniz(ə)m/ *n* proud belief that one's own country, or one's own sex, is the best **–ist** *n, adj*
cheap *adj* **1** low in price **2 a** of poor quality **b** low or offensively unpleasant **3** without serious feeling **4** needing little effort: *a cheap victory* **5** *AmE infml* stingy **6 feel cheap** feel ashamed ♦ *adv* at a low price **~en** *vi/t* make or become cheaper **~ly** *adv* **~ness** *n*
cheap-jack *adj* inferior; shoddy
cheapskate *n* stingy person
cheat *vi/t* **1** act dishonestly; treat someone deceitfully **2** avoid or escape as if by deception **cheat** *or* **cheater** *n* person who cheats
check *n* **1** examination to make sure something is correct **2** stop; control: *keep the disease in check* **3** pattern of squares **4** *AmE* restaurant bill **5** *AmE* cheque **6** *AmE* tick[1] (2) **7** (in chess) position of the king when under direct attack ♦ *v* **1** *vi/t* examine; make sure **2** *vt* hold back; control **3** *vt AmE* put somewhere to be looked after: *check one's coat at the theatre* **4** *vt AmE* tick[2] (2) **check in** *phr vi* report one's arrival at an airport, hotel, etc. **check out** *phr v* **1** *vi* leave a hotel after paying the bill **2** *vt* find out if something is true by making inquiries **3** *vi* be found to be true after inquiries have been made **check up on** *phr vt* inquire thoroughly about
checkered *adj AmE* chequered
checkers *n AmE* draughts
check-in *n* place where one goes to check in
checklist *n* complete list; inventory
checkmate *n* **1** (in chess) position of a king when under direct attack so that escape is impossible **2** complete defeat ♦ *vt* **1** (in chess) win the game with a checkmate **2** stop; completely defeat
checkout *n* pay desk in a self-service shop
checkpoint *n* place where people, vehicles, etc. are inspected or logged
checkup *n* general medical examination
Cheddar *n* smooth hard cheese
cheek *n* **1** either side of the face below the eye **2** rude behaviour ♦ *vt esp. BrE* speak rudely to **~y** *adj* rude
cheer *n* **1** shout of praise or joy **2** happiness; good spirits ♦ *vi/t* **1** make or become happy **2** shout in approval; encourage by shouting **~ful** *adj* happy **~fully** *adv* **~less** *adj* saddening **~y** *adj* merry
cheerio *interj BrE* goodbye
cheerleader *n* person who directs and leads cheering e.g. at a sports match
cheese *n* solid food made from milk
cheesecake *n* **1** dessert with a soft filling usu. containing cheese in a flan case **2** photographs of scantily-clad women
cheesecloth *n* very light, loosely woven cotton cloth
cheesed off *adj BrE sl* fed up
cheeseparing *adj, n* miserly or petty (economizing)
cheetah *n* spotted African animal of the cat family, able to run very fast
chef *n* chief cook in a restaurant, etc.
chef d'oeuvre *n* **chefs d'oeuvre** masterpiece
chemical *adj* of chemistry ♦ *n* chemical substance
chemise *n* women's undergarment
chemist *n* **1** scientist specializing in chemistry **2** *BrE* person who sells medicines, soap, etc.
chemistry *n* science of natural substances and how they combine and behave
chemotherapy *n* use of chemical sub-

stances to treat and control diseases

chenille *n* (fabric made of) yarn with a protruding pile

cheongsam *n* straight dress with a slit skirt

cheque, *AmE* **check** *n* written order to a bank to pay money

cheque card *n BrE* card given to people by a bank, promising to honour their cheques up to a certain amount

chequered *adj BrE* **1** patterned with squares in alternating colours **2** partly bad and partly good: *his chequered career*

cherish *vt fml* **1** care for; love **2** keep (hope, etc.) in one's mind: *cherish a memory*

cheroot *n* cigar with both ends cut square

cherry *n* small round fruit with a stone

cherub *n* **1** pretty child, esp. one with wings in a painting **2** (*pl* **-ubim**) kind of angel **~ic** *adj*

chess *n* board game for two players

chessman *n* **-men** piece used in chess

chest *n* **1** upper front part of the body **2** large strong box **3 get (something) off one's chest** bring (a worry) out into the open by talking

chesterfield *n* padded and buttoned sofa with arms and back of equal height

chestnut *n* **1** kind of smooth reddish-brown nut **2** chestnut-coloured horse **3** joke or story so old and well-known that it is no longer funny or interesting ♦ *adj* reddish-brown

chest of drawers *n* piece of furniture with drawers

cheval glass *n* free-standing full-length swivelling mirror

chevron *n* (inverted) V shape, esp. as used as a badge of rank

chew *vi/t* crush (food, etc.) with the teeth **chew over** *phr vt infml* think about (a question, problem, etc.)

chewing gum *n* sweet sticky substance to be chewed but not swallowed

chiack *vi AustrE* make derisive remarks (about)

Chianti *n* Italian red wine

chic *adj, n* (with) good style

chicanery /shiˈkayn(ə)ri/ *n* sharp practice

Chicano *n AmE* Mexican

chichi *adj* over-elaborate; affected

chick *n* baby bird

chicken *n* **1** common farmyard bird, esp. a young one **2** its meat ♦ *adj sl* cowardly **chicken out** *phr vi sl* decide not to do something because one is frightened

chickenfeed *n infml* insignificant amount (of money)

chicken-hearted, **-livered** *adj* cowardly

chicken pox *n* infectious disease that causes spots

chickpea *n* (edible pealike seed of) an Asiatic plant

chicory *n* **1** plant whose leaves are eaten as a vegetable **2** powder made from its roots, added to coffee

chide *vi/t* **chided** *or* **chid, chid** *or* **chidden** *fml or lit* speak to (someone) angrily; rebuke

chief *n* leader; head of something: *the chief of police* ♦ *adj* **1** highest in rank **2** main **3 -in-chief** of the highest rank: *commander-in-chief* **~ly** *adv* mainly; specially

chieftain *n* leader of a tribe, etc.

chiffon *n* sheer (silk) fabric

chignon /shiˈnyon, ˈshee-/ *n* knot of hair worn at the nape of the neck

chihuahua /chiˈwah·wə/ *n* (breed of) tiny dog of Mexican origin

chilblain *n* sore caused by exposure to cold

child *n* **children 1** young human being **2** son or daughter **3** someone who behaves like a child **~hood** *n* time of being a child **~ish** *adj* unsuitable for a grown person **~less** *adj* having no children **~like** *adj* simple; lovable

childbearing *n* process of having children

child benefit *n* allowance paid by the UK government to parent(s) in respect of each child

childminder *n esp. BrE* someone who looks after other people's children, esp.

when the parents are at work
child's play *n* something very easy to do
Chilean *n, adj* (inhabitant) of Chile
chill *vi/t* **1** make or become cold **2** (cause to) have a feeling of cold as from fear ♦ *n* **1** illness with coldness and shaking **2** unpleasant coldness **~y** *adj* **1** rather cold **2** unfriendly
chilli *n* (powder made from) the red pod of a hot pepper
chime *n* sound of a set of bells ♦ *vi/t* **1** make this sound **2** *infml* be in agreement
chimera *n* illusion
chimney *n* hollow passage to let out smoke from a fire
chimneypot *n* pipe fixed on top of a chimney
chimneystack *n* **1** tall chimney of a building such as a factory **2** *BrE* group of small chimneys
chimneysweep *n* person who cleans the insides of chimneys
chimpanzee also **chimp** *n* kind of African ape
chin *n* the part of the face below the mouth
china *n* **1** baked clay **2** plates, cups, etc., made from this
Chinatown *n* part of a city where there are Chinese restaurants, shops, etc.
chinchilla *n* **1** (soft pearly-grey fur of) a S American squirrel-like rodent **2** breed of rabbit or cat with similar fur
Chinese *n, adj* (inhabitant) of China
chink¹ *n* narrow crack
chink² *n, v* clink
chinless *BrE derog* ineffectual
chip *n* **1** small piece broken off **2** place from which this was broken **3** thin piece of potato cooked in fat **4** small piece of material on which an integrated circuit is formed **5** counter used to represent money in certain games **6 a chip off the old block** a person very like their father or mother in character **7 have a chip on one's shoulder** be quarrelsome or easily offended, as a result of feeling badly treated **8 when the chips are down** when a very important point is reached ♦ *vi/t* **-pp-** (cause to) lose a small piece from the edge **chip in** *phr v infml* **1** *vi* interrupt a conversation **2** *vi/t* add (one's share of money)
chipmunk *n* small striped American squirrel
chipolata *n* small thin sausage
chipper *adj esp. AmE* cheerful; lively
chippy *n infml* **1** carpenter **2** *BrE* chip shop
chiropodist /kiˈropədist/ *n* person who treats the human foot **-dy** *n*
chiropractor /ˈkirəˌpraktə/ *n* person who treats ailments by manipulating bones, massage, etc.
chirp *vi* make the short sharp sound of small birds **chirp** *n* **~y** *adj* (of people) cheerful
chisel *n* metal tool for shaping wood or stone ♦ *vt/i* **-ll-**(*AmE* **-l-**) **1** cut with a chisel **2** cheat
chit¹ *n* signed note showing sum of money owed (for drinks, etc.)
chit² *n* pert or self-confident girl esp. of slight build
chit-chat *n* informal light conversation; gossip
chivalry *n* **1** beliefs and practices of knights in the Middle Ages **2** good manners shown by a man towards women **-rous** *adj*
chive *n* herb with long thin leaves and a mild onion taste
chivvy *vt infml* rouse to activity
chlorine *n* greenish yellow, strong-smelling substance used to disinfect places, esp. swimming baths
chloroform *n* chemical used as an anaesthetic
chock *n* wedge placed under a wheel, barrel, etc. to stop it moving
chock-a-block *adj infml* very crowded
chock-full *adj infml* completely full
chocolate *n* **1** solid brown substance eaten as a sweet **2** small sweet covered with this **3** hot drink made from this ♦ *adj* dark brown
choice *n* **1** act of choosing **2** power of choosing: *have no choice but to obey* **3**

variety to choose from: *a big choice of shops* ♦ *adj* **1** of high quality **2** well chosen

choir *n* **1** group of singers **2** part of a church where they sit

choke *v* **1** *vt/i* stop breathing because the breathing passage is blocked **2** *vt* fill (a passage) completely ♦ *n* apparatus that controls air going into a petrol engine **choke back** *phr vt* control (esp. violent or sad feelings) as if by holding in the throat

choler *n lit* anger; irascibility **~ic** *adj*

cholera *n* serious tropical disease of the stomach and bowels

cholesterol *n* substance found in all cells of the body, which helps to carry fats

chomp *vi/t* champ[1] (1)

chook *n AustrE* chicken

choose *vi/t* **chose, chosen 1** pick out from many **2** decide

choosy *adj* fastidiously selective

chop *vt* **-pp-** cut with a sharp tool ♦ *n* **1** quick cutting blow **2** piece of lamb or pork with a bone in it

chopper *n* **1** heavy tool for chopping **2** *infml* helicopter

choppy *adj* (of water) with short rough waves

chopsticks *pl n* pair of thin sticks used in East Asia for lifting food to the mouth

chop suey *n* Chinese stew of vegetables and shredded meat

choral *adj* of a choir

chorale *n* **1** solemn piece of music based on a psalm or hymn tune **2** choir

chord *n* **1** two or more musical notes sounded together **2** straight line joining two points on a curve

chore *n* bit of regular or dull work

choreography *n* arranging dances for the stage **–pher** *n* **choreograph** *vt*

chorister *n* singer in a choir

chortle *vi* give several laughs of pleasure and satisfaction **chortle** *n*

chorus *n* **1** group of singers **2** part of a song repeated after each verse **3** something said by many people together: *a chorus of groans* ♦ *vt* sing or say together

chose *past t. of* choose

chosen *past p. of* choose

choux pastry *n* very light pastry made with egg

chow[1] *n* breed of dog with a very thick coat

chow[2] *n sl* food

chowder *n AmE* thick (seafood) soup

Christ *n* man on whose teaching Christianity is based; Jesus

christen *vt* **1** make into a member of the Christian church by baptism and giving of a name **2** name (esp. a ship) at an official ceremony **3** use for the first time **~ing** *n* ceremony of baptism

Christendom *n lit* all Christian people or countries

Christian *n* person who believes in the teachings of Christ ♦ *adj* **1** of Christianity **2** having qualities such as kindness, generosity, etc.

Christianity *n* the religion based on the life and teachings of Christ

Christian name *n* (esp. in Christian countries) a person's first name

Christian Science *n* branch of Christianity which places great emphasis on spiritual healing **Christian Scientist** *n*

Christmas *n* **1** also **Christmas Day** holy day in honour of Christ's birth; December 25th **2** period before and after this

chromatic *adj* **1** of colour **2** (of a musical scale) proceeding by semitones

chrome *n* hard metal used esp. as a shiny covering on car parts, etc.

chromosome *n* tiny thread in every living cell that controls the nature of a young animal or plant

chronic *adj* **1** (of a disease) lasting a long time **2** *infml* very bad

chronicle *n* record of historical events ♦ *vt* make a chronicle of

chronology *n* **1** science that gives dates to events **2** list of events in order **–ogical** *adj* arranged in order of time **–ogically** *adv*

chronometer /krəˈnɒmɪtə/ *n* very exact clock

chrysalis *n* shell-like form of an insect that will become a moth or butterfly
chrysanthemum *n* garden plant with large brightly-coloured flowers
chub *n* fish of the carp family
chubby *adj* pleasantly fat
chuck[1] *vt* **1** *infml* throw **2** *sl* give up; leave: *chuck (in) his job* **3** pat under the chin
chuck[2] *n* **1** cut of beef from neck area **2** adjustable device for gripping e.g. a drill bit
chuckle *vi* laugh quietly **chuckle** *n*
chuffed *adj BrE infml* pleased
chug *vi, n* (move slowly or steadily with) the sound of an old engine
chukka, **-ker** *n* period of play in polo
chum *n* friend **~my** *adj* friendly
chump *n* **1** *sl* fool **2** thick piece of meat
chunk *n* thick lump **~y** *adj* thick: *chunky sweater*
church *n* **1** building for public Christian worship **2** profession of priests and ministers **3** (*usu. cap.*) branch of Christianity: *the Catholic Church*
churchwarden *n* **1** lay parish officer in an Anglican church **2** long-stemmed clay pipe
churchyard *n* church burial ground
churlish *adj* bad-tempered; rude **~ly** *adv* **~ness** *n*
churn *n* container in which cream is shaken to make butter ♦ *vi/t* shake about violently **churn out** *phr vt* produce a large quantity of
chute *n* sloped passage for something to slide down
chutney *n* thick relish made of fruits, sugar, vinegar and spices
chutzpah *n infml* brazen audacity
CIA *n* Central Intelligence Agency; US government department that collects information, esp. secretly
cicada /siˈkahdə/ *n* insect whose males produce a shrill noise
cicatrix *n* **-trices** scar
cicerone *n* **-roni** guide esp. to the sights of a foreign town
CID *n* Criminal Investigation Department; branch of the UK police force made up of detectives
cider *n* alcoholic drink made from apples
cigar *n* roll of tobacco leaves for smoking
cigarette *n* paper tube of cut tobacco for smoking
CinC *n* commander-in-chief
cinch *n infml* **1** certainty **2** easy task
cinder *n* bit of burnt coal
cinecamera *also infml* **cine** *n* hand-held camera for taking moving pictures
cinema *n* **1** theatre where films are shown **2** films as an art or industry
cinnamon *n* yellowish-brown spice used in cooking
cipher *n* **1** system of secret writing **2** unimportant person
circa *prep fml* (used with dates) about: *circa 1000 AD*
circadian *adj* occurring in day-long periods or cycles
circle *n* **1** curved line on which every point is equally distant from the centre **2** ring **3** group of people **4** upper floor in a theatre ♦ *vi/t* **1** move round in a circle **2** draw a circle round
circlet *n* small circle, esp. a small circular ornament
circuit *n* **1** circular journey round an area **2** circular path of an electric current **~ous** *adj* going a long way round
circuit breaker *n* device that automatically cuts off electric current e.g. in the event of a short circuit
circular *adj* **1** shaped like a circle **2** moving in a circle **3** not direct ♦ *n* printed notice given to many people **~ize**, **-ise** *vt* send circulars to
circulate *vi/t* **1** move along a closed path **2** spread widely **3** move about freely **-tion** *n* **1** flow round a closed system: *the circulation of the blood* **2** passing of money among people: *the number of £5 notes in circulation* **3** number of copies of a newspaper sold
circumcise *vt* cut off the male foreskin or the female clitoris **-cision** *n*
circumference *n* distance round: *the Earth's circumference*

circumflex *n* accent mark (∧) over a vowel
circumlocution *n* evasive speech –**cutory** *adj*
circumnavigate *vt fml* sail right round
circumscribe *vt fml* limit
circumspect *adj fml* careful
circumstance *n* **1** (*usu. pl*) conditions that influence a person or event **2 in/ under no circumstances** never **3 in/ under the circumstances** because of the conditions
circumstantial *adj fml* **1** (of a description) detailed **2 circumstantial evidence** information worth knowing but not directly important
circumvent *vt* avoid by cleverness: *circumvent the tax laws*
circus *n* **1** performance of skill and daring by a group of people and animals **2** *BrE* place where several streets join **3** noisy badly behaved meeting or other such activity: *the media circus travelling with the President*
cirrhosis /si'rohsis/ *n* serious liver disease
cirrus *n* **-ri** high wispy cloud
cissy *n, adj BrE* sissy
cistern *n* container for storing water, esp. for a toilet
citadel *n* fortress; stronghold
cite *vt* **1** *fml* mention as an example **2** *law* call to appear in court **citation** *n*
citizen *n* **1** person living in a city or town **2** person with full membership of a country **~ship** *n*
Citizens' Band *n* CB
citric acid *n* weak acid from fruit juice
citron *n* (tree bearing) a fruit resembling a lemon
citrus *adj* (of fruit) of the orange family
city *n* **1** large important town **2** its citizens **3** (*cap.*) the centre for money matters in London
city hall *n* **1** town hall **2** *AmE* city government or bureaucracy
city-state *n* state, esp. in ancient Greece, consisting of a city and its surrounding territory
civet *n* **1** also **civet cat** catlike African mammal **2** substance obtained from the glands of the civet used in making perfume
civic *adj* of a city or its citizens **civics** *n* study of a citizen's rights and duties
civil *adj* **1** not military or religious **2** polite **~ly** *adv* politely **~ity** *n* politeness
civil defence *n* measures to protect civilians against enemy attack or natural disasters
civil disobedience *n* refusal to obey government demands as a form of protest
civil engineering *n* building of public roads, bridges, etc.
civilian *n, adj* (person) not of the armed forces
civilization, -isation *n* **1** high level of human development and social organization **2** particular civilized society
civilize, -ise *vt* **1** bring to civilization **2** improve in manners
civil rights *pl n* a citizen's rights to freedom and equality
civil servant *n* person employed in the civil service
civil service *n* **1** government departments, except the armed forces and law courts **2** people employed in this
civil war *n* war between people from the same country
civvies *pl n sl* civilian clothes, as opposed to military uniform
cl *abbrev. for:* centilitre
clad *adj lit* clothed; covered
cladding *n* facing (1)
claim *v* **1** *vt/i* demand (something) as one's right: *claim on the insurance* **2** *vt* declare to be true: *He claims to be rich.* ♦ *n* **1** demand for something as one's right; right to something **2** something claimed, esp. money under an insurance agreement **3** statement; declaration
claimant *n* person who claims something
clairvoyant *adj, n* (of a) person who can

see what will happen in the future **-ance** *n*

clam *n* large shellfish **clam up** *phr vi* become silent

clambake *n AmE* **1** outdoor party esp. on the beach **2** noisy sociable gathering

clamber *vi* climb with effort

clammy *adj* unpleasantly wet and sticky

clamour, *AmE* **-mor** *n* loud confused noise, esp. of complaint ♦ *vi* demand noisily: *a baby clamouring to be fed*

clamp *n* apparatus with a screw, for fastening things together ♦ *vt* fasten with a clamp **clamp down on** *phr vt* limit; prevent: *clamp down on drunken driving*

clampdown *n* imposition of restrictions

clan *n* Scottish family group

clandestine *adj* secret **~ly** *adv*

clang *vi/t* make a loud ringing sound **clang** *n*

clanger *n infml* very noticeable mistake or unfortunate remark

clangor *n* continuous clanging noise

clank *vi/t* make a sound like a heavy metal chain **clank** *n*

clap *v* **-pp- 1** *vi/t* strike (one's hands) together **2** *vt* strike lightly with the open hand: *clap him on the back* **3** *vt infml* put quickly: *clapped her in jail* **4 clap eyes on** *infml* see (someone or something) ♦ *n* **1** loud explosive noise, esp. of thunder **2** clapping **3** *sl* gonorrhea

clapboard *n AmE* weatherboard

clapped-out *adj esp. BrE* **1** (of a person) tired **2** (of a thing) old and worn out

clapper *n* **1** tongue of a bell **2 like the clappers** *BrE infml* as fast as possible

clapper-board *n* hinged board held in front of a cinema camera and banged at the start of each new take

claptrap *n* nonsense

claque *n* group hired to applaud

claret *n* red wine from Bordeaux ♦ *adj* deep red

clarify *vt fml* make more easily understood **-fication** *n*

clarinet *n* kind of woodwind musical instrument **~tist** *n* person who plays the clarinet

clarion *n* (sound of) a medieval trumpet

clarity *n* clearness

clash *v* **1** *vi* come into opposition **2** *vi* (of colours) look wrong together **3** *vi* (of events) be planned for the same time **4** *vi/t* make a loud metallic noise ♦ *n* **1** disagreement **2** metallic noise

clasp *n* **1** metal fastener **2** firm hold ♦ *vt* **1** seize firmly **2** fasten with a clasp

clasp knife *n* large single-bladed folding knife

class *n* **1** social group of a particular rank **2** system of dividing society into such groups **3 a** group of students taught together **b** period of time they are taught for **4** division; level: *a first-class carriage* **5** high quality; elegance ♦ *vt* put into a class; consider **~y** *adj* fashionable and of high class

class-conscious *adj* conscious of one's social position **~ness** *n*

classic *adj* **1** of the highest rank **2** typical: *classic example* **3** having a long history; traditional ♦ *n* piece of literature or art, a writer or artist, of lasting importance **classics** *pl n* ancient Greek and Roman literature

classical *adj* **1** following ancient Greek or Roman models **2** (of music) with serious artistic intentions **3** traditional

classify *vt* arrange into classes **-fied** *adj* **1** divided into classes **2** officially secret **-fication** *n*

classroom *n* room in a school, etc., in which a class meets for a lesson

clatter *n* noise of hard objects hitting each other ♦ *vi/t* make a clatter

clause *n* **1** group of words containing a subject and verb **2** *law* separate division of a piece of legal writing

claustrophobia *n* fear of being shut in **-bic** *adj*

clavichord *n* early keyboard instrument

clavicle *n* collarbone

claw *n* **1** sharp nail on an animal's or bird's toe **2** limb of e.g. a crab **3** curved end of some tools ♦ *vi/t* tear or pull with claws **claw back** *phr vt* take back by taxation

clay *n* earth from which bricks, pots, etc., are made

claymore *n* large sword formerly used by Scottish highlanders

clay pigeon *n* saucer-shaped object used as a target for shotguns

clean *adj* **1** not dirty **2** not yet used **3** morally pure **4** smooth; regular **5 come clean** tell the unpleasant truth ♦ *n* act of cleaning ♦ *adv* completely: *I clean forgot.* ♦ *vt* make clean **clean out** *phr vt* **1** make (the inside of a room, drawer, etc.) clean and tidy **2** take all someone's money **clean up** *phr vi/t* **1** clean thoroughly **2** *sl* make a very large sum of money **~er** *n* person or thing that cleans **~er's** *n* **1** shop where clothes, etc., are cleaned with chemicals **2 take someone to the cleaner's** cause someone to lose all their money

clean-cut *adj* **1** well-shaped **2** neat and clean in appearance

cleanly *adv* in a clean way ♦ *adj fml* always clean **-liness** *n*

cleanse *vt* make pure **cleanser** *n* chemical, etc., used for cleaning

clean-shaven *adj* with no beard

clean sweep *n* **1** complete change **2** complete victory

clear *adj* **1** easy to see through **2** without marks, blemishes, etc. **3** easy to hear or understand **4** certain: *a clear case of murder* **5** open; empty: *The road's clear of snow.* **6** free; no longer touching: *We're clear of danger now.* **7** free of guilt or blame **8** (of wages or profit) remaining after all taxes, etc. have been paid ♦ *n* **in the clear** free from guilt, debt, etc. ♦ *adv* **1** in a clear way **2** completely: *The prisoner got clear away.* **3** out of the way: *jump clear of the train* ♦ *v* **1** *vi/t* become clear; remove something unwanted **2** *vt* get past without touching: *clear a fence* **3** *vt* give official approval to **4** *vt* free from blame **5** *vt* earn as clear profit or wages: *She clears £10,000 a year.* **clear away** *phr vt* make an area tidy by removing **clear off** *phr vi* go away **clear out** *phr v* **1** *vi* go away **2** *vt* empty **clear up** *phr v* **1** *vt* explain: *clear up the mystery* **2** *vi/t* tidy **~ly** *adv* **1** in a clear way: *speak clearly* **2** undoubtedly: *clearly wrong*

clearance *n* **1** official approval **2** distance between objects **3** also **security clearance** official acceptance that one is in no way an enemy of one's country **4** also **clearance sale** time when a shop sells goods cheaply so as to get rid of as many as possible

clear-cut *adj* clear in meaning

clear-headed *adj* **1** not confused; sensible **2** having no illusions

clearing *n* area cleared of trees

clearing house *n* **1** central agency for the collection and distribution of material **2** establishment run by banks for settling their accounts with one another

clear-sighted *adj* perceptive

clearway *n BrE* road on which vehicles may stop only in an emergency

cleat *n* **1** piece of rubber, iron, etc. fastened to the sole of a shoe to prevent slipping **2** two-pronged metal fixture to which a rope can be tied **3** wedge-shaped block

cleavage *n* **1** division caused by splitting **2** space between a woman's breasts as seen when she is wearing a dress

cleave *vt* **cleaved** *or* **cleft** *or* **clove, cleaved** *or* **cleft** *or* **cloven** divide or make by a cutting blow **cleave to** *phr vt lit* remain loyal to **~r** *n* butcher's heavy-bladed implement for jointing carcasses

clef *n* sign at the beginning of a line of written music to show the pitch (of) notes

cleft *past t of* cleave

cleft palate *n* congenital gap in the roof of the mouth

cleft stick *n* **(caught) in a cleft stick** (caught) in a very awkward position

clematis *n* climbing perennial with large flowers

clemency *n fml* mercy **–ent** *adj* (of weather) not severe
clench *vt* close tightly
clerestory *n* part of a wall above an adjoining roof
clergy *pl n* priests
clergyman *n* **-men** Christian priest
cleric *n* clergyman **~al** *adj* **1** of priests **2** of clerks
clerk *n* **1** office worker **2** official in charge of court records, etc.
clever *adj* **1** quick at learning **2** showing skill; ingenious **~ly** *adv* **~ness** *n*
cliché *n* expression or idea used so often it has lost much of its force
click *n* slight short sound, as of a camera ♦ *v* **1** *vi/t* make a click **2** *vi* fall into place; understand **3** *vi* be a success
client *n* **1** person who pays for advice from a professional person **2** customer
clientele /ˌklee·onˈtel/ *n* clients; customers
cliff *n* steep rock face, esp. on a coast
cliffhanger *n* **1** competition, game, etc., whose result is in doubt until the very end **2** story told in parts, each of which ends at a moment of exciting uncertainty
climactic *adj* forming a climax
climate *n* **1** average weather conditions **2** condition of opinions: *political climate* **–matic** *adj*
climax *n* **1** most powerful part of a story, usu. near the end **2** orgasm ♦ *vi/t* bring or come to a climax
climb *v* **1** *vi/t* move over a vertical or inclined surface esp. using hands and feet **2** *vi* rise **3** *vi* (of a plant) grow upwards **climb down** *phr vi infml* admit that one has been wrong ♦ *n* **1** journey by climbing **2** place to climb **~er** *n* person or thing that climbs
clime *n* also **climes** *pl* climate; region
clinch¹ *vt* settle (an agreement) firmly
clinch² *n* embrace
cling *vi* **clung** hold tightly **~ing** *adj* **1** (of clothes) tight-fitting **2** (of a person) too dependent
clingfilm *n* plastic film for wrapping foodstuffs
clinic *n* place for specialized medical treatment **~al** *adj* **1** of clinics or hospitals **2** coldly scientific
clink *vi/t* (cause to) make a sound like pieces of glass knocking together **clink** *n*
clinker *n* fused coal residues
clinker-built *adj* (of a boat) having a hull made of overlapping planks
clip¹ *n* small esp. metal object for holding things together **clip** *vt* **-pp-**
clip² *vt* **-pp- 1** cut with scissors, etc. **2** *sl* hit ♦ *n* **1** cutting **2** *sl* quick blow: *a clip round the ear* **~pers** *pl n* scissor-like tool **~ping** *n* **1** piece cut off **2** cutting (2)
clipboard *n* board with a clip at one end for holding papers
clip joint *n sl* place, e.g. a nightclub, that overcharges
clipper *n* fast commercial sailing ship
clique /kleek/ *n derog* closely united group of people
clitoris *n* small front part of the female sex organ
Cllr *BrE abbrev. for:* councillor
cloak *n* loose outer garment without sleeves ♦ *vt* keep secret
cloak-and-dagger *adj* (of stories, etc.) dealing with adventure and mystery
cloakroom *n* room where coats, etc., may be left
clobber¹ *vt sl* **1** attack severely **2** defeat completely
clobber² *n BrE sl* one's belongings
cloche *n* **1** usu. glass cover to protect young plants **2** woman's close-fitting, round-domed hat
clock *n* **1** instrument for measuring time **2 around/round the clock** all day and all night **3 put the clock back** return to old-fashioned ideas **4 watch the clock** think continually of how soon work will end **5 work against the clock** work very quickly in order to finish a job before a certain time ♦ *vt* record (time, speed, distance, etc.) **clock in/out** *phr vi* record the time of arriving at/leaving work **clock up** *phr vt infml* **1** record (a distance travelled,

a speed reached, etc.) **2** succeed in getting
clockwise *adv* in the direction of the movement of a clock
clockwork *n* **1** machinery wound up with a key **2 like clockwork** without trouble
clod *n* lump or mass of clay or earth
clog[1] *n* wooden shoe
clog[2] *vi/t* **-gg-** (cause to) become blocked or filled
cloisonné *adj, n* (having) enamel decoration in cells formed by a network of metal wires
cloister *n* covered passage usu. forming part of a college, monastery, etc. **~ed** *adj* sheltered from the world
clone *n* non-sexually produced descendant of a single plant or animal **clone** *vt*
close[1] *v* **1** *vi/t* shut **2** *vt* bring to an end: *close a bank account* **3 close a deal (with)** settle a business agreement **close down** *phr vi/t* (of a factory, etc.) stop operating **close in** *phr vi* surround gradually ♦ *n* end of a period of time
close[2] *adj* **1** near **2** thorough **3** without fresh air; too warm **4** decided by a small difference: *a close finish to the race* ♦ *adv* **1** near: *close behind/together* **2 close on** almost **3 close to home** near the (usu. unpleasant) truth **4 (sail) close to the wind** (be) near to dishonesty or improper behaviour ♦ *n* **1** courtyard **2** blind alley **~ly** *adv* **~ness** *n*
close call *n* narrow escape
close-cropped *adj* with hair cut short
closed circuit *n* a television installation where the signal is transmitted by wire to a limited number of receivers **closed-circuit** *adj*
closed shop *n* place of work where one must belong to a particular trade union
close-fisted *adj* tight-fisted
close-hauled *adj* with sails set for sailing into the wind
close-knit also **closely-knit** *adj* tightly bound together by social, political, etc., beliefs and activities
close season *n* period when it is illegal to kill certain kinds of game and fish
close-set *adj* set close together: *close-set eyes*
close shave *n infml* situation in which something dangerous or very unpleasant is only just avoided
closet *n esp. AmE* built-in cupboard ♦ *adj* not publicly admitted; secret ♦ *vt* enclose (esp. oneself) in a private room
close-up *n* photograph taken from very near
closure *n* closing
clot *n* **1** lump formed from liquid **2** *sl esp. BrE* fool ♦ *vi/t* **-tt-** form into clots
cloth *n* (piece of) material made by weaving
clothe *vt* provide clothes for
clothes *pl n* things to cover the body; garments
clotheshorse *n* **1** *BrE* framework on which clothes are hung to dry, usu. indoors **2** *infml esp. AmE* person who is very interested in clothes and fashion
clothing *n* clothes
cloud *n* **1** white or grey mass floating in the sky which is formed from very small drops of water **2** similar floating mass: *clouds of smoke/mosquitoes* **3** something threatening: *the clouds of war* **4 under a cloud** out of favour ♦ *v* **1** *vi/t* cover with clouds **2** *vt* confuse: *cloud the issue* **~y** *adj* **1** full of clouds **2** not clear
cloudburst *n* heavy fall of rain
clout *n* **1** blow with the hand **2** influence, esp. political ♦ *vt* strike, esp. with the hand
clove[1] *past t. of* cleave
clove[2] *n* dried flower of a tropical tree used in cooking
clove[3] *n* any of the smallest pieces into which the root of the garlic plant can be divided
clove hitch *n* knot for attaching a rope to a branch or spar
cloven *past p. of* cleave
cloven hoof *n* animal's foot or hoof divided into two parts at the end

farthest from the body

clover *n* **1** three-leafed plant often grown as food for cattle **2 in clover** living in comfort

cloverleaf *n* **-leafs** *or* **-leaves** major road intersection whose lay-out resembles a four-leaved clover

clown *n* **1** comic circus performer **2** person acting like this ♦ *vi* behave foolishly

cloy *vi/t* (of food) become unpleasant because too sweet

club *n* **1** society of people who meet for amusement; building where they meet **2** heavy stick used as a weapon **3** stick for striking the ball in golf **4** playing card with one or more black three-leafed figures on it ♦ *vt* **-bb-** hit with a heavy stick **club together** *phr vi* share the cost of something with others

club foot *n* foot misshapen from birth

cluck *vi* make the noise a hen makes **cluck** *n*

clue *n* **1** something that helps to find the answer to a problem **2 not have a clue** know nothing; be unable to understand **~less** *adj* stupid

clued up *adj infml* very well-informed

clump[1] *n* group of trees, etc.

clump[2] *vi* walk heavily

clumsy *adj* **1** awkward in movement **2** tactless **–sily** *adv* **–siness** *n*

clung *past t. and p. of* cling

cluster *n* group of things close together ♦ *vi* form a close group

clutch[1] *v* **1** *vt* hold tightly **2** *vi* try to seize: *He clutched at a branch.* ♦ *n* **1** act of clutching **2** apparatus connecting and disconnecting the working parts of a car engine **clutches** *pl n* control: *in the clutches of the enemy*

clutch[2] *n* **1** (chickens born from) a number of eggs laid by one bird **2** group

clutter *vt* make untidy ♦ *n* scattered disorderly things

cm *abbrev. for:* centimetre(s)

CND *n* Campaign for Nuclear Disarmament

co- *prefix* **1** with; together: *co-exist* **2** associate; fellow: *co-author/co-founder*

Co. *abbrev. for:* company (1)

C.O. *n* Commanding Officer; person in the armed forces in charge of others

c/o *abbrev. for:* **1** care of **2** carried over

coach *n* **1** *BrE* long-distance bus **2** railway carriage **3** large horse-drawn carriage **4** person who trains people for sports, or gives private lessons ♦ *vt* train; teach

coachman *n* driver of a horse-drawn carriage

coachwork *n* outside body of a car

coagulate /koh'agyoolayt/ *vi/t* change from a liquid to a solid **–lant** *n* substance which causes coagulation **–lation** *n*

coal *n* (piece of) black mineral that can be burnt

coalesce /ˌkoh·ə'les/ *vi fml* grow together; unite

coalface *n* surface where coal is cut in a mine

coalfield *n* area where there is coal under the ground

coalition *n* union of political parties for a special purpose

coarse *adj* **1** not fine; lumpy **2** rough in manner; insensitive **~ly** *adv* **~ness** *n* **coarsen** *vi/t*

coarse fish *n esp. BrE* freshwater fish other than salmon and trout **~ing** *n*

coast *n* **1** seashore **2 the coast is clear** all danger has gone ♦ *vi* go downhill on a bicycle, etc., without effort or power **~al** *adj*

coaster *n* **1** ship which sails in coastal waters **2** small round mat placed under a glass or bottle

coastguard *n* **1** police organization responsible for the coast and nearby sea **2** member of the coastguard

coastline *n* shape of a coast

coat *n* **1** outer garment with sleeves, fastened at the front **2** animal's fur **3** covering on a surface ♦ *vt* cover (a surface) **~ing** *n* thin covering

coat hanger *n* hanger

coat of arms *n* **coats of arms** patterns or pictures, usu. on a shield, used by a family, town, etc., as their special sign

coax *vt* **1** persuade gently **2** obtain (something) by gently persuading

coaxial cable *n* cable containing two conductors, the one surrounded by, but insulated from, the other

cob *n* **1** long hard central part of an ear of corn **2** strong short-legged horse **3** male swan **4** round loaf

cobalt *n* **1** silver-white metallic element **2** blue colour obtained from cobalt

cobber *n AustrE infml* male friend

cobble[1] also **cobblestone** *n* rounded stone used for road surfaces **–bled** *adj* covered with cobbles

cobble[2] *vt* put together quickly and roughly

cobbler *n* shoe repairer

cobblers *n BrE sl* nonsense

COBOL *n* high-level computer language for commercial use

cobra *n* kind of poisonous snake

cobweb *n* a spider's net of spun threads

cocaine *n* addictive drug formerly used as an anaesthetic, now mainly as a pleasurable stimulant

coccyx /ˈkoksiks/ *n* **coccyges** *or* **coccyxes** end of the spinal column

cochineal *n* scarlet dye made from the dried body of a Mexican insect

cochlea *n* **-leas** *or* **-leae** spiral tube in inner ear

cock *n* **1** fully-grown male bird, esp. a chicken **2** hammer of a gun **3** tap for controlling the flow of liquid in a pipe **4** *sl* penis ♦ **1** *vi/t* raise up: *The horse cocked its ears.* **2** *vt* set (the hammer of a gun) in the correct position for firing **3 cock a snook (at)** *BrE infml* show open disrespect (for) **cock up** *phr vt sl* make a mess of

cockade *n* badge worn on a hat

cock-a-hoop *adj infml* triumphant

cock-and-bull story *n* improbable story

cockatoo *n* **-toos** Australian bird with a large crest on its head

cockchafer *n* large European beetle

cockerel *n* young cock

cockeyed *adj* **1** stupid **2** crooked

cockle *n* small shellfish used for food

Cockney *n* **1** person from the industrial parts of London **2** the way Cockneys talk

cockpit *n* part of a plane where the pilot sits

cockroach *n* large black insect which lives esp. in dirty or old houses

cocksure *adj* too self-confident

cocktail *n* **1** mixed alcoholic drink **2** mixture of fruit or seafood

cock-up *n BrE sl* **1** blunder **2** fiasco

cocky *adj sl* too sure of oneself **.cockily** *adv*

cocoa *n* **1** brown powder tasting of chocolate **2** hot drink made from this

coconut *n* (flesh of) a very large tropical nut

coconut shy *n* fairground stall where balls are thrown to dislodge coconuts

cocoon *n* silky covering that protects some insects in their inactive stage ♦ *vt* protect from hardship

cod *n* **cod** *or* **cods** large sea fish

COD *abbrev for:* cash on delivery

coddle *vt* treat (someone) too tenderly

code *n* **1** system of signs, or of secret writing: *computer code* **2** collection of laws or social customs ♦ *vt* translate into a code

codeine *n* painkiller derived from morphine

codex *n* manuscript of an ancient text

codger *n infml* (old) man

codicil *n* addition to a will

codify *vt* arrange (laws) in a system

codpiece *n* prominent bag covering the front opening in men's breeches

codswallop *n sl* nonsense

coed *n AmE* female student in a college open to both sexes ♦ *adj* coeducational

coeducation *n* education of boys and girls together **~al** *adj*

coefficient *n* **1** number by which a variable is multiplied **2** number that serves as measure of a characteristic of e.g. a process: *the coefficient of expansion of a metal*

coerce *vt* force to do something **–ercive** *adj* **–ercion** *n*

coexist *vi* exist at the same time **~ence**

n (esp. of countries) existing together peacefully

C of E *n* **1** Church of England **2** Council of Europe

coffee *n* (drink made by pouring boiling water onto) the (crushed) berries of a tropical tree

coffee table *n* low table

coffer *n* large chest for money, etc.

cofferdam *n* watertight enclosure which is pumped out to allow construction work e.g. on a river bed

coffin *n* box in which a dead person is buried

cog *n* **1** tooth on the edge of a wheel that moves another wheel **2 cog in the machine** unimportant person in a very large organization

cogent *adj fml* forceful; convincing **~ly** *adv* **cogency** *n*

cogitate *vi fml* think carefully **–tation** *n*

cognac *n* kind of French brandy

cognate *adj fml* related: *cognate languages*

cognition *n fml* act or experience of knowing **–nitive** *adj*

cognizance /ˈkɒgnɪz(ə)ns/ *n fml* **take cognizance of** take notice of; take into consideration

cognoscenti *pl n* (art) experts and connoisseurs

cohabit *vi fml* live together as though married **~ation** *n* **~ant** *n* cohabiting person

coherent /kohˈhɪərənt/ *adj* (of speech, ideas, etc.) reasonably connected; clear **-ence** *n* **~ly** *adv*

cohesive *adj* sticking together **–sion** *n*

cohort *n* **1** group (esp. of Roman soldiers) **2** *esp. AmE* crony; accomplice

COHSE *n* Confederation of Health Service Employees

coif *n* close-fitting cap worn by medieval women

coiffure *n* hairstyle

coil *vi/t* twist into a circle ♦ *n* **1** connected set of twists: *coil of rope* **2** twisted wire that carries an electric current **3** coil of metal or plastic which is fitted inside the uterus as a contraceptive

coin *n* piece of metal money ♦ *vt* **1** make (coins) **2** invent (new words) **3 coin (the) money (in)** also **coin it (in)** make or earn a lot of money very quickly

coincide *vi* **1** happen at the same time **2** (of opinions, etc.) agree

coincidence *n* accidental and surprising combination of events **–dental** *adj* **–dentally** *adv*

coition *also* **coitus** *n fml* sexual intercourse

coke *n* **1** substance left after gas has been removed from coal **2** *sl* cocaine

col *n* high mountain pass

colander *n* bowl with holes, for separating liquid from food

cold *adj* **1** low in temperature **2** unfriendly **3** (of cooked food) allowed to get cool **4** unconscious **5 get/have cold feet** lose courage **6 give/get the cold shoulder** treat/be treated unsympathetically ♦ *n* **1** low temperature **2** illness of the nose and throat **3 (out) in the cold** not noticed; unwanted **~ly** *adv* **~ness** *n*

cold-blooded *adj* **1** (of reptiles, etc.) having a body temperature that varies with the surroundings **2** cruel; without feeling

cold comfort *n* no consolation

cold cream *n* (scented) skin-cleansing cream

cold-hearted *adj* unkind **~ly** *adv*

cold storage *n* **1** preservation of perishable goods at very low temperatures **2** state of being set aside temporarily

cold turkey *n sl* (the unpleasant sick feeling caused by) the sudden stopping of the use of a drug by an addict

cold war *n* severe political struggle without actual fighting

coleslaw *n* salad of raw chopped cabbage

coley *n* **-ley** or **-leys** N Atlantic fish used as food

colic *n* severe pain in the stomach and bowels **~ky** *adj*

collaborate *vi* **1** work together **2** help the enemy **–rator** *n* **–ration** *n*

collage *n* picture made by gluing various materials or objects onto a surface
collapse *v* **1** *vi* fall down suddenly **2** *vi* fall helpless **3** *vi/t* fold flat ♦ *n* collapsing: *the collapse of the peace talks* **-lapsible** *adj* that can be folded for packing, etc.
collar *n* **1** part of a garment that fits round the neck **2** band put round an animal's neck ♦ *vt* seize and hold
collarbone *n* bone joining the ribs to the shoulders
collate *vt fml* **1** compare (copies of books, etc.) to find the differences **2** arrange (the sheets) of (esp. a book) in the proper order
collateral *n* property promised as security for a debt
collation *n fml* light meal
colleague *n* fellow worker
collect[1] *v* **1** *vi/t* gather together **2** *vt* save (stamps, coins, etc.) as a hobby **3** *vt* fetch: *collect one's skirt from the cleaners* **4** *vt* regain control of (oneself, one's thoughts, etc.) **~ed** *adj* controlled; calm **~ive** *adj* shared by many people: *collective ownership* **~ive** *n* business owned and controlled by the people who work in it **~ively** *adv* jointly; as a group **~or** *n* person who collects something **~ion** *n* **1** collecting **2** set of things, sum of money, etc., collected
collect[2] *adj, adv AmE* to be paid for by the receiver: *Call me collect.*
collect[3] *n* short prayer
collective bargaining *n* talks between unions and employers about working conditions, etc.
colleen *n IrE* girl
college *n* **1** school for higher education; part of a university **2** group of people with a common profession or purpose: *the Royal College of Nursing*
collide *vi* **1** crash violently **2** come into conflict
collie *n* breed of sheepdog
collier *n* **1** coal miner **2** ship for carrying coal
colliery *n* coal mine
collision *n* colliding
collocate *vi* (of words) go naturally together **-cation** *n*
colloquial *adj* (of words, style, etc.) suitable for informal conversation **~ly** *adv* **~ism** *n* colloquial expression
colloquy /ˈkoləkwi/ *n* formal conversation
collude *vi fml* act in collusion
collusion *n fml* secret agreement to deceive
collywobbles *pl n infml* **1** stomach ache **2** feeling of nervous apprehension
cologne *n* eau de cologne
colon[1] *n* lower part of the bowels
colon[2] *n* the mark (:)
colonel /ˈkuhnl/ *n* army or (US) airforce officer of middle rank
Colonel Blimp *n* pompous, reactionary man
colonial *adj* of or about colonies ♦ *n* person living or having lived in a colony **~ism** *n* principle of having colonies
colonize, **-ise** *vt* make into a colony; settle (6) **-nist** *n* person living in a new colony **-nization** *n*
colonnade /ˌkoləˈnayd/ *n* row of pillars
colony *n* **1** place lived in and controlled by people from a distant country **2** group of people of the same kind, living together
color *n AmE* colour
colossal *adj* extremely large
colossus *n* **-suses** *or* **-si** very large person or thing
colostrum *n* milky secretion from a mother's breast in the first few days after giving birth
colour, *AmE* **color** *n* **1** red, blue, green, etc. **2** paint or dye **3** appearance of the skin **4** interesting details of a place, thing, or person ♦ *v* **1** *vt* give colour to **2** *vi* blush **3** *vt* change; influence **~ed** *adj* **1** having colours; not just white, or black and white **2** (of people) black or brown **3** (*often cap.*) *S AfrE* of mixed race **~ful** *adj* **1** brightly coloured **2** exciting **~ing** *n* **1** substance giving

colour **2** skin colour, showing health **~less** *adj* **1** without colour **2** dull **colours** *pl n* **1** official flag **2** something worn as the sign of a club, team, etc. **3 show one's true colours** show one's real nature or character

colour bar *n* customs or laws that prevent people of different colours from mixing

colour-blind *adj* unable to see the difference between colours

colourfast *adj* having colour that will not fade or run

colour scheme *n* choice and arrangement of colours esp. in a room

colour supplement *n* magazine printed in colour and given free with a newspaper, esp. a Sunday one

colt *n* young male horse **~ish** *adj* frisky; playful

columbine *n* flower of the buttercup family

column *n* **1** pillar **2** vertical arrangement esp. of figures **3** a division of a page **4** newspaper article **5** long narrow formation: *a column of troops* **~ist** *n* writer of a newspaper column

coma *n* unnatural deep sleep

comatose *adj* **1** in a coma **2** inactive and sleepy

comb *n* **1** toothed implement for tidying the hair or worn in the hair as an ornament **2** act of combing **3** honeycomb ♦ *vt* **1** tidy (hair) with a comb **2** search (a place) thoroughly

combat *n* struggle; fight **combat** *vt/i* **-tt-** (*AmE* **-t-** *or* **-tt-**) **~ant** *n* person who fights **~ive** *adj* fond of fighting

combination *n* **1** combining: *We worked well in combination.* **2** people or things combined **3** numbers needed to open a special lock **combinations** *pl n* one-piece woollen undergarment covering the whole body

combine *vi/t* join together; unite ♦ *n* **1** group of people, businesses, etc., acting together **2** also **combine harvester** machine that cuts and threshes grain

combo *n* small jazz band

combustible *adj* burning easily

combustion *n* process of burning

come *vi* **came, come 1** move towards the speaker; arrive **2** reach a particular point **3** have a particular position **4** happen **5** begin **6** become **7** be offered, produced, etc. **8** *sl* have an orgasm **9 come and go** pass or disappear quickly **10 how come?** how did it happen (that)? **11 to come** in the future **come about** *phr vi* happen **come across** *phr vi* be effective and well received **come across/upon** *phr vt* find by chance **come along** *phr vi* **1** improve; advance **2** arrive by chance **3 Come along!** Hurry up! **come apart** *phr vi* break into pieces without the need of force **come at** *phr vt* advance towards in a threatening manner **come away** *phr vi* become disconnected without being forced **come between** *phr vt* cause trouble between **come by** *phr vt* obtain; receive **come down** *phr vi* **1** fall **2 come down in the world** fall to a lower standard of living **3 come down in favour of/on the side of** decide to support **come down on** *phr vt* punish **come down to** *phr vt* be no more than: *It all comes down to a question of money.* **come down with** *phr vt* catch (an infectious illness) **come forward** *phr vi* offer oneself to fill a position, give help to police, etc. **come in** *phr vi* **1** become fashionable **2 come in handy/useful** be useful **come in for** *phr vt* receive (esp. blame) **come in on** *phr vt* take part in **come into** *phr vt* **1** inherit **2** begin to be in (a state or activity) **come of** *phr vt* result from **come off** *phr v* **1** *vi* happen as planned **2** *vt* **come off it!** stop lying or pretending **come on** *phr vi* **1** improve; advance **2** (of weather, illness, etc.) begin **3 Come on!** Hurry up! **come out** *phr vi* **1** appear **2** become known **3** (of colour, etc.) be removed **4** strike **5** (of a photograph) be successful **6** declare oneself to be homosexual **7** make one's first appearance in society **come out against** *phr vt* declare one's opposition to **come out in** *phr vt* be partly covered by (marks caused by an illness) **come**

out with *phr vt* say, esp. suddenly **come over** *phr v* **1** *vt* (of feelings, etc.) influence suddenly: *What's come over you?* **2** *vi* make a short informal visit **3** *vi BrE infml* become: *I came over dizzy.* **come round** *phr vi* **1** also **come to** regain consciousness **2** change one's opinions **3** happen as usual **come through** *phr v* **1** *vi* (of news, etc.) become known **2** *vi/t* survive **come to** *phr vt* **1** occur to **2** concern: *He's ignorant when it comes to politics.* **3** come round **come under** *phr vt* **1** be in (a particular class): *Rabbits come under the heading of pets.* **2** be governed or controlled by **come up** *phr vi* **1** happen **2** come near **come up against** *phr vt* meet (difficulties) **come up with** *phr vt* think of (a plan, reply, etc.); produce

comer *n* **1** *esp. AmE* person who appears likely to be successful in their job **2 all comers** everyone who comes and tries **coming** *n* arrival ♦ *adj* future; next in sequence

comeback *n* **1** return to strength or fame **2** retort **3** subsequent criticism or complaint **4** means of redress

Comecon *n* Council for Mutual Economic Assistance; an association of Communist countries

comedian *n* **1** actor who makes people laugh **2** amusing person

comedienne *n* female comedian

comedown *n* fall in importance

comedy *n* **1** (type of) funny play, film, etc. **2** amusing quality of something

come-hither *adj* sexually inviting

comely /ˈkʌmli/ *adj lit* good-looking

comestibles *pl n lit* food

comet *n* bright heavenly body with a tail

come-uppance *n* well-deserved punishment or misfortune

comfit *n arch.* sugar-covered sweet with fruit or a nut at the centre

comfort *n* **1** lack of pain or anxiety; physical satisfaction **2** something that satisfies physical needs **3** (person or thing that brings) help for an unhappy person ♦ *vt* make less unhappy **~er 1** person who comforts **2** dummy (2) **3** *BrE* woollen scarf

comfortable *adj* **1** giving comfort **2** feeling comfort; not suffering or anxious **-bly** *adv*

comfortably off *adj* fairly rich

comfort station *n AmE euph* public toilet

comfy *adj infml* comfortable

comic *adj* **1** funny **2** of comedy ♦ *n* **1** magazine consisting mainly of stories in the form of comic strips **2** comedian **~al** *adj* funny **comics** *pl n AmE* part of a newspaper with cartoons

comic strip *n* set of drawings telling a usu. short funny story

comma *n* the sign (,)

command *v* **1** *vi/t* order; direct **2** *vt* deserve and get: *command respect* **3** *vt* control (a place) from above ♦ *n* **1** order, instruction **2** control: *take command of the army* **3** division of an army, air force, etc. **4** ability to use something: *a good command of spoken English* **~er** *n* **1** naval officer of middle rank **2** any officer in command **3 commander in chief** person in overall command of a country's armed forces

commandant *n* officer in charge of a military organization

commandeer /ˌkɒmənˈdɪə/ *vt* seize (private property) for public use

commandment *n* law given by God

command module *n* part of a space vehicle from which operations are controlled

commando *n* **-dos** *or* **-does** (member of) a fighting force trained to make quick raids

command performance *n* special performance given at the request of the head of state

comme il faut *adj* correct; in accordance with the dictates of etiquette or propriety

commemorate *vt* honour the memory of **-rative** *adj* issued, held, erected, etc. in honour of **-ration** *n*

commence *vi/t fml* begin; start **~ment** *n*

commend *vt fml* **1** praise **2** put into someone's care **~able** *adj* worthy of praise **~ation** *n* **1** praise **2** official prize

commensurate *adj fml* equal; suitable: *a job commensurate with his abilities*

comment *n* written or spoken opinion ♦ *vi/t* make a comment

commentary *n* **1** collection of opinions on a book, etc. **2** description broadcast during an event

commentate *vi* broadcast a description **-tator** *n*

commerce *n* buying and selling; trade

commercial *adj* **1** of or used in commerce **2** producing profit **3** (of television or radio) paid for by charges made for advertisements ♦ *n* television or radio advertisement **~ly** *adv* **~ize, -ise** *vt* make into a matter of profit rather than religion, art, etc.

commercial traveller *n* person who travels from place to place trying to get orders for a firm's goods

commie *n, adj infml usu. derog* communist

commiserate with *phr vt* express sympathy for **-ration** *n*

commissar *n* official responsible for political education in Communist countries

commissariat /ˌkomiˈseəri·ət/ *n* army department that organizes food supplies

commission *n* **1** payment for selling goods, made to the salesman **2** job or duty given to someone **3** group officially appointed to find out and report on facts **4** paper appointing an officer in the armed forces **5 out of commission 1** (of a ship) not ready for active service **2** out of order ♦ *vt* **1** give a job to **2** place an order for: *commission a portrait* **3** appoint as an officer in the armed forces **~er** *n* **1** member of a commission **2** government representative in certain countries

commissionaire *n esp. BrE* uniformed attendant at the entrance to a cinema, hotel, etc.

commit *vt* **-tt- 1** do (something wrong) **2** send (someone) to prison or a mental hospital **3** consign **4 commit oneself: a** make a firm decision, promise, agreement, etc. **b** give a firm opinion **~ted** *adj* **1** loyal; dedicated **2** bound by an undertaking **~ment** *n* **1** dedication **2** obligation; duty **~tal** *n* committing someone to prison, etc.

committee *n* group chosen to do special business

committee stage *n* stage between the second and third readings of a parliamentary bill when it is examined in detail by a committee

commode *n* **1** chest of drawers **2** seat built over a compartment holding a chamber pot

commodious *adj lit* comfortable; spacious

commodity *n* article of trade; product

commodore *n* **1** high-ranking naval officer **2** president of a sailing club

common *adj* **1** ordinary; usual **2** shared in a group **3** rough in manner; vulgar ♦ *n* **1** area of grassland with no fences which all people are free to use **2 in common** in shared possession **~ly** *adv*

common denominator *n* quality or belief shared by all the members of a group

commoner *n* person who is not a member of a noble family

common law *n* unwritten law based on custom and court decisions rather than on laws made by Parliament **common-law** *adj*

Common Market *n* the EEC

common-or-garden *adj BrE infml* ordinary

commonplace *adj* ordinary; dull

common room *n* room in a school or college for recreational use by staff or students

commons *pl n* **1** the ordinary people as opposed to the rulers **2 on short commons** not being given enough to eat

Commons *n* the House of Commons

common sense *n* practical good sense gained from experience

Commonwealth *n* **1** association of independent states that used to be parts of the British Empire **2** official title of certain countries, such as Australia

commotion *n* noisy confusion

communal *adj* shared by a group **~ly** *adv*

commune¹ *n* **1** group who live and work together and share their possessions **2** local government division in France

commune² *vi* exchange thoughts, ideas or feelings: *commune with nature*

communicable *adj* (esp. of ideas, thoughts, illnesses, etc.) that can be (easily) passed from one person to another

communicant *n* person who takes Communion

communicate *v* **1** *vi/t* make (opinions, etc.) known **2** *vt* pass on (a disease) **3** *vi* (of rooms) be connected **–cator** *n* person who communicates **–cation** *n* **1** communicating **2** *fml* message, letter, etc. **–cations** *pl n* ways of travelling or sending messages

communication cord *n BrE* emergency alarm in a railway carriage

communicative *adj* willing to give information

communion *n* **1** *fml* sharing of beliefs, feelings, etc. **2** (*cap.*) Christian ceremony of sharing bread and wine

communiqué /kəˈmyoohniˌkay/ *n* official report

communism *n* **1** social and political system by which the state owns the means of production **2** (*cap.*) one-party system of government on this principle **–nist** *n, adj*

community *n* **1** group of people with shared interests **2** people in general; the public **3** shared possession

community centre *n* building for educational and recreational use by the community

commutation ticket *n AmE* reduced-price ticket for a fixed number of trips on public transport

commute *v* **1** *vi* travel regularly between home and work **2** *vt* make (a punishment) less severe **–muter** *n* person who commutes to work

compact¹ *adj* neatly packed into a small space ♦ *n* **1** container for face powder **2** *AmE* small car

compact² *n fml* agreement between two or more parties, countries, etc.

compact disc *n* small circular piece of plastic on which sound, information, etc., can be stored

companion *n* **1** person who spends time with another **2** handbook **~able** *adj* friendly **~ship** *n* friendly company

companionway *n* staircase between decks on a ship

company *n* **1** business firm; people working together **2** group of about 120 soldiers **3 a** presence of companions: *I was grateful for her company.* **b** companions, esp. guests **4 be good/bad company** be a good/bad person to be with

company secretary *n* high-ranking member of a business firm who deals with accounts, legal matters, etc.

comparable *adj* similar **–bly** *adv*

comparative *adj* **1** expressing an increase in quality or quantity: *'Worse' is the comparative form of 'bad'.* **2** measured or judged by a comparison that is not stated: *She's a comparative newcomer to television* **3** making a comparison: *a comparative study of European languages* ♦ *n* comparative form of an adjective or adverb **~ly** *adv*

compare *v* **1** *vt* judge (one thing) against another thing, to show likeness or difference **2** *vt* show the likeness between (two things) **3** *vi* be worthy of comparison

comparison *n* **1** (statement of) comparing **2** likeness

compartment *n* separate division of a space; small room in a railway carriage, etc.

compartmentalize, -ise *vt* separate into different compartments or categories

compass *n* **1** instrument for showing direction, with a needle that points to the north **2** *fml* range; limit **compasses** *pl n* instrument for drawing circles

compassion *n* sympathy; pity **~ate** *adj* **~ately** *adv*
compassionate leave *n* special leave from work or military service for personal reasons, e.g. the death of a relative
compatible *adj* able to exist or work together **–bly** *adv* **–bility** *n*
compatriot *n* person of the same nationality as another
compeer *n lit* equal
compel *vt* **-ll-** force to do something **~ling** *adj* important; urgent
compendious *adj* brief, but including a great deal (of information) **–dium** *n* **1** summary **2** collection of indoor games and puzzles
compensate *vi/t* pay, or give something, to balance a loss **–sation** *n* something given to compensate **–satory** *adj*
compere *n BrE* person who introduces a stage, radio or television show **compere** *vi/t*
compete *vi* try to win in a competition
competence *n* **1** ability to do what is needed **2** legal powers or scope **3** *arch* income sufficient to live on **–tent** *adj* **–tently** *adv*
competition *n* **1** test of strength, skill, etc. **2** rivalry **3** person or people against whom one competes
competitive *adj* **1** decided by competition **2** liking to compete **~ly** *adv*
competitor *n* person, firm, etc., that competes
compile *vt* make (e.g. a book) from collected facts **–piler** *n* **–pilation** *n* **1** act of compiling **2** something compiled
complacency *n* unwarranted feeling of satisfaction **–cent** *adj* **–cently** *adv*
complain *vi/t* say that one is unhappy: *to complain that the room is too hot* **~ant** *n* plaintiff
complaint *n* **1** (statement of) complaining **2** illness
complaisant /kəmˈplays(ə)nt/ *adj* willing to please; ready to agree **~ly** *adv* **–sance** *n*
complement *n* **1** something that completes **2** full number needed **3** noun or adjective after a verb such as 'be' or 'become' ♦ *vt* make complete or perfect **~ary** *adj* supplying what is needed
complete *adj* **1** having all necessary parts; whole **2** finished; ended **3** total; thorough ♦ *vt* **1** make whole **2** finish **~ly** *adv* in every way **–pletion** *n*
complex *adj* **1** difficult to understand **2** made of many connected parts ♦ *n* **1** system of many connected parts: *new sports complex* **2** group of unconscious fears or feelings **~ity** *n*
complexion *n* **1** natural appearance of the skin **2** general character of a situation
compliance *n* complying **–ant** *adj*
complicate *vt* make difficult to deal with **–cated** *adj* complex **–cation** *n* added difficulty
complicity *n fml* taking part with someone else in a crime
compliment *n* expression of praise ♦ *vt* express admiration of **compliments** *pl n* good wishes **~ary** *adj* **1** expressing admiration **2** given free
compline *n* last service of the day in the Roman Catholic church
comply *vi* agree to do something; obey
component *n* any part of a whole machine or system
comport *vt fml* behave (oneself) **~ment** *n*
compose *v* **1** *vi/t* write (music, poetry, etc.) **2** *vt* get (oneself) under control **3** **be composed of** consist of **–posed** *adj* calm **–poser** *n* writer of music
composite / ˈkompəzit, -ziet/ *n, adj* (something) made up of different parts
composition *n* **1** act of writing music, poetry, etc. **2** something written **3** mixture or arrangement of parts
compositor *n* person who arranges material for printing
compos mentis *adj* of sound mind
compost *n* decayed plant matter, used to improve the soil
composure *n* calmness
compote *n* fruit stewed in syrup and eaten cold
compound[1] *n, adj* (thing, esp. a chemi-

cal substance) made up of two or more parts ♦ *vt* **1** make by combining parts **2** make worse: *compound an error*
compound² *n* enclosed area containing buildings
compound eye *n* eye made up of many small visual units
compound fracture *n* fracture in which the broken bone makes an open wound in the flesh
compound interest *n* interest calculated on the original sum plus accumulated interest
comprehend *vt* **1** understand **2** *fml* include
comprehension *n* **1** power of understanding **2** exercise to test student's understanding of a passage **–sible** *adj* understandable **–sibly** *adv*
comprehensive *adj* **1** thorough; including a lot **2** *BrE* teaching pupils of all abilities together ♦ *n* a comprehensive school **~ly** *adv*
compress *vt* **1** force into less space **2** put (ideas, etc.) into fewer words **~ion** *n* **~or** *n* machine for compressing gases
comprise *v* consist of; have as parts
compromise *n* agreement reached by each side agreeing to some of the other side's demands ♦ *v* **1** *vi* make a compromise **2** *vt* put into a dishonourable position
comptroller *n* (in titles) controller
compulsion *n* **1** force that makes a person do something **2** strong desire **–sive** *adj* caused by a compulsion **–sively** *adv*
compulsory *adj* that must be done by law, etc. **–rily** *adv*
compunction *n* feeling of guilt
compute *vt* calculate
computer *n* electronic machine that stores, recalls, and processes information **~ate** *infml* able to use a computer **~ize, -ise** *vt* use or begin to use a computer to control (an operation) **~ization** *n*
comrade *n* **1** close companion **2** fellow member of a union or political party **~ship** *n*
con *vt* **-nn-** trick (a trusting person) ♦ *n infml* confidence trick
Con *abbrev. for:* Conservative Party
concatenation *n fml* a linked series e.g. of events
concave *adj* curved inwards
conceal *vt* hide **~ment** *n*
concede *vt* **1** admit as true **2** give as a right **3** end a game or match by admitting defeat
conceit /kən'seet/ *n* too high an opinion of oneself **~ed** *adj*
conceive *v* **1** *vt* think of; imagine **2** *vi/t* become pregnant **–ceivable** *adj* imaginable; possible **–ceivably** *adv*
concentrate *v* **1** *vi* direct all one's attention **2** *vi/t* bring or come together in one place **3** *vt* make (a liquid) stronger ♦ *n* concentrated liquid
concentration *n* **1** close attention **2** close gathering
concentration camp *n* large prison for political prisoners
concentric *adj* (of circles) having the same centre
concept *n* general idea; notion **~ual** *adj* of or based on (the formation of) concepts **~ualize, -ualise** *vi/t* form a concept (of)
conception *n* **1** understanding **2** forming of an idea **3** starting of a new life by the union of a male and female sex cell
concern *vt* **1** be about (a subject) **2** be of importance to **3** worry ♦ *n* **1** something that matters to someone **2** worry **3** business; firm **~ing** *prep* about
concert *n* **1** musical performance **2 in concert: a** working together **b** playing at a concert
concerted *adj* done together by agreement
concert grand *n* grand piano used for concerts
concertina *n* small accordion ♦ *vi* (esp. of a vehicle) become pressed together as the result of a crash
concertmaster *n AmE* leader of an orchestra
concerto *n* **-tos** piece of music for one

instrument supported by an orchestra
concert pitch *n* **1** standard pitch to which orchestral instruments are tuned **2** state of complete readiness or fitness
concession *n* **1** something conceded after a disagreement **2** official permission to do something: *oil concessions in the North Sea* **~ary** *adj* given as a concession **~aire** *n* holder of an official permit
conch *n* (large spiral shell of) a marine mollusc
conchie *n sl* conscientious objector
concierge *n* caretaker and porter of a building esp. in France
conciliate *vt* remove the anger of **-ation** *n* **-atory** *adj* trying to conciliate
concise *adj* expressing a lot in a few words **~ly** *adv* **~ness** *n*
conclave *n* **1** private meeting **2** assembly of cardinals to elect a new Pope
conclude *v fml* **1** *vi/t* bring or come to an end **2** *vt* come to believe **3** *vt* settle: *conclude an agreement*
conclusion *n* **1** decision; settlement **2** end **-sive** *adj* ending all doubt
concoct *vt* **1** make by mixing parts **2** invent (something false) **~ion** *n* mixture
concomitant /kon'komit(ə)nt/ *adj* existing or happening together **~ly** *adv* **-tance** *n*
concord *n* **1** friendly agreement; harmony **2** grammatical agreement esp. between verb and subject **~ance** *n* index of instances of the use of a particular word in e.g. the Bible **~ant** *adj* consonant; harmonious **~at** *n* treaty
concourse *n* place where crowds can gather
concrete *adj* **1** real or solid; not abstract **2** clear; particular: *concrete proposals* ♦ *n* building material made of sand, cement, etc. ♦ *vt* cover (a path, wall, etc.) with concrete
concrete jungle *n* unlovely modern urban environment
concubine *n* mistress; secondary wife, or mistress, of an Eastern ruler **-inage** *n*
concupiscence /kəng'kyoohpis(ə)ns/ *n fml* lust **-scent** *adj*
concur *vi* **-rr-** *fml* **1** agree **2** happen at the same time **~rence** *n* **~rent** *adj* **~rently** *adv*
concuss *vt* damage (the brain) by a heavy blow **~ion** *n*
condemn *vt* **1** express disapproval of **2** state the punishment for: *condemn him to death* **3** doom; force to: *She was condemned to life in a wheelchair.* **4** declare (a building, etc.) unfit for use **~ation** *n*
condemned cell *n* cell in which a prisoner awaiting execution is held
condense *vi/t* **1** make (a gas) liquid **2** make (a liquid) thicker **3** put into fewer words **-denser** *n* **-densation** *n* **1** act of condensing **2** drops of water formed when steam condenses
condescend *vi* **1** do something unsuited to one's social or professional position **2** *derog* behave as though one is grander than others **-scension** *n*
condign /kən'dien/ *adj fml* deserved; appropriate
condiment *n* something used for giving taste to food
condition *n* **1** state; way of being: *a car in poor condition* **2** something necessary for something else: *I'll come on condition that John comes too.* **3** illness **4 in/out of condition** thoroughly fit/not fit **5 on no condition** never ♦ *vt* **1** control; determine **2** train to behave in a certain way **conditions** *pl n* surrounding circumstances: *better working conditions* **-tional** *adj* depending on conditions **-tionally** *adv* **~ing** *n* (result of) being trained to act in a certain way
conditioned reflex *n* an involuntary response to a stimulus, which is the result of earlier conditioning
condolence *n* expression of sympathy
condom *n* sheath worn over the penis during sexual intercourse, as a contraceptive and as a protection against disease
condominium also *infml* **condo** *n AmE*

block of flats which are each owned by the people living in them
condone *vt* forgive (wrong behaviour)
condor *n* very large S American vulture
conducive /kən'dyoohsiv/ *adj fml* likely to produce: *conducive to health*
conduct *v* **1** *vt* direct; lead **2** *vi/t* direct the playing of (musicians) **3** *vt* be the path for (electricity, etc.) **4 conduct oneself** behave ♦ *n* **1** behaviour **2** management of something **~ive** *adj* able to conduct electricity, etc. **~ion** *n* passage of electricity, etc.
conductor *n* **1** person who conducts musicians **2** person who collects payments on a bus **3** *AmE* guard on a train **4** substance that conducts electricity
conductress *n* woman bus conductor
conduit /'kondit, 'kondwit/ *n* pipe for water, gas, etc.
cone *n* **1** hollow or solid object with a round base and pointed top **2** fruit of a pine or fir tree
confab *also* **confabulation** *n* a private conversation
confection *n fml* sweet-tasting food **~ery** *n* sweets, cakes, etc. **~er** *n* person who sells these
confederacy *n* **1** union of people, parties, or states **2** (*usu. cap.*) the southern states in the American Civil War
confederate *n* **1** accomplice **2 a** member of a confederacy **b** (*usu. cap.*) supporter of the Confederacy **confederate** *adj* **-ration** *n* confederacy (1)
confer *v* **-rr-** *fml* **1** *vi* talk together **2** *vt* give (a title, etc.) to
conference *n* meeting for the exchange of ideas
confess *vi/t* admit (one's faults) **~or** *n* priest who hears one's confession **~ion** *n* telling of one's faults **~ional** *n* place where one makes one's confession to a priest
confetti *n* bits of coloured paper thrown at weddings
confidant *n* person to whom one tells secrets
confidante *n* female confidant
confide *vt* tell (a secret) trustingly **confide in** *phr vt* talk freely to
confidence *n* **1** faith; trust **2** belief in one's own ability **3** something told secretly **4 in confidence** secretly **-dent** *adj* **1** sure **2** self-confident
confidence trick *n* trick played in order to cheat a trusting person of money
confidential *adj* **1** told in secret **2** ted with secrets **~ly** *adv* **~ity** *n*
configuration *n* shape; arrangement
confine *vt* **1** keep shut in **2** keep within the limits **~ment** *n* **1** being shut up **2** giving birth to a child **3** limits
confirm *vt* **1** support; give proof of: *confirm a telephone message in writing* **2** admit (a person) to membership of the Christian church **~ed** *adj* firmly settled; unlikely to change **~ation** *n* **1** proof **2** religious service in which someone is confirmed
confiscate *vt* seize (private property) officially, without payment **-cation** *n* **-catory** *adj*
conflagration *n* large destructive fire
conflate *vi/t* combine **-flation** *n*
conflict *n* **1** disagreement; argument **2** war ♦ *vi* be in opposition
confluence *n* place where two or more rivers flow together
conform *vi* obey established rules or customs **~able** similar (to) **~ist** *n* person who conforms **~ity** *n*
confound *vt* confuse and surprise **~ed** *adj* damned
confraternity *n* association of men with common aims; lay religious brotherhood
confront *vt* face (up to); meet **~ation** *n* angry opposition **~ational** *adj* aggressive
Confucian *n, adj* (follower) of Confucius **~ism** *n* ethical system of the Chinese philosopher Confucius
confuse *vt* **1** cause to be mixed up in the mind **2** be unable to tell the difference between **3** make less clear: *confusing the issue* **-fused** *adj* muddled; mixed-up **-fusion** *n*
confute *vt* prove to be wrong **-futation** *n*

conga *n* **1** Latin American line dance **2** tall bass drum played with the hands

congeal *vi/t* (of a liquid, esp. blood) become solid

congenial *adj* pleasant; in agreement with one's tastes **~ly** *adv*

congenital *adj* (of diseases) existing from one's birth

conger *n* large sea eel

congeries /ˈkonjəreez/ *fml* (disordered) collection

congested *adj* too full; blocked **–tion** *n*

conglomerate *n* large business firm producing many kinds of goods **–ration** *n* mixed coherent mass

congratulate *vt* express pleasure at (someone's) success or good luck **–lations** *interj, also infml* **congrats** I congratulate you **–lations** *pl n* expressions of praise and pleasure **–latory** *adj*

congregate *vi* gather together **–gation** *n* group of people gathered together in church

Congregational *adj* of a Protestant denomination in which each church or congregation is self-governing **~ism** *n*

congress *n* **1** formal meeting to exchange information **2** (*cap.*) highest lawmaking body of the US, consisting of the Senate and the House of Representatives **~ional** *adj*

congressman *n* **-men** member of Congress

congresswoman *n* **-women** female member of Congress

congruent *adj* **1** having the same size and shape as (each other): *congruent triangles* **2** congruous **–ence** *n*

congruous *adj fml* suitable; proper **–gruity** *n*

conical *adj* cone-shaped

conifer *n* tree that bears cones

conjecture *vi/t, n fml* guess **–tural** *adj*

conjoin *vi/t fml* unite for a common purpose **~t** *adj fml* united; joint

conjugal *adj fml* of marriage

conjugate *vt* give the forms of (a verb) **–gation** *n* class of verbs conjugated in the same way

conjunction *n* **1** word such as 'but' or 'while' **2 in conjunction with** in combination with

conjunctivitis *n* painful eye disease

conjure *v* **1** *vi* do clever tricks that seem magical **2** *vt* cause to appear (as if by magic): *conjure up memories of the past* **–jurer, -juror** *n* person who does conjuring tricks

conk *n sl* nose

conker *n* fruit of horse chestnut tree

conkers *pl n* child's game played with a conker attached to a string

conk out *phr vi infml* break down (2)

conman *n infml* confidence trickster; swindler

connect *v* **1** *vi/t* join together **2** *vt* think of as related

connection also *BrE* **connexion** *n* **1** being connected; relationship **2** plane, train, etc. planned to take passengers arriving by another one **3** person connected to others by family or business **4 in connection with** with regard to

conning tower *n* **1** raised observation tower on a submarine **2** control position on a warship

connive at *phr vt* make no attempt to stop (something wrong); secretly sympathize with **–nivance** *n*

connoisseur /ˌkonəˈsuh/ *n* person with special knowledge of art, wine, etc.

connote *vt fml* (of a word) suggest something more than its ordinary meaning **–notation** *n* implied meaning: *'Skinny' has bad connotations.*

connubial *adj fml* of marriage

conquer *vt* **1** defeat; overcome **2** take (a place) by force **~or** *n*

conquest *n* **1** conquering **2** something conquered, esp. land gained in war

conquistador *n* **-dors** *or* **-dores** member of the Spanish forces which conquered Latin America

consanguineous /ˌkonsangˈgwini·əs/ *adj fml* related by birth **–guinity** *n*

conscience *n* **1** knowledge of right and wrong, esp. as regards one's own actions, thoughts, etc. **2 on one's conscience** causing one to feel guilty

conscience clause *n* clause exempting objectors on moral or religious grounds
conscience money *n* payment made to ease a feeling of guilt
conscientious *adj* careful and honest **~ly** *adv* **~ness** *n*
conscientious objector *n* person who refuses to serve in the armed forces because of moral or religious beliefs
conscious *adj* **1** awake and able to think **2** knowing; aware **3** intentional: *conscious effort* **~ly** *adv* **~ness** *n*
consciousness raising *n* increasing people's awareness (esp. of social ethical and political issues) **consciousness-raising** *adj*
conscript *vt* make someone serve in the armed forces ♦ *n* conscripted person **~ion** *n* practice of conscripting people
consecrate *vt* **1** declare as holy **2** set apart solemnly for a particular purpose: *consecrate one's life to helping the poor* **-cration** *n*
consecutive *adj* following in unbroken order **~ly** *adv*
consensus *n* general agreement
consent *vi* give permission ♦ *n* permission
consequence *n* **1** result **2** importance: *It's of no consequence to me.*
consequent *adj* following as a result **~ly** *adv*
consequential *adj* **1** consequent **2** important
conservancy *n* **1** conservation **2** court or commission with jurisdiction over a river, port, area of countryside, etc.
conservation *n* **1** protection of animals, plants, ancient buildings, etc. **2** careful use of a limited supply, to prevent waste **~ist** *n* **~ism** *n*
conservative *adj* **1** not liking change **2** kept rather low: *a conservative estimate* **3** (*cap.*) of a British political party opposed to sudden change ♦ *n* **1** person who dislikes change **2** (*cap.*) member of the Conservative Party **~ly** *adv* **-tism** *n*
Conservative Party *n* British political party which tends to be opposed to sudden change
conservatoire *n* conservatory (2)
conservatory *n* **1** greenhouse; glass-walled extension to a house **2** school of music or acting
conserve *vt* use carefully; preserve ♦ *n* fruit preserved by cooking in sugar; jam
consider *v* **1** *vi/t* think about **2** *vt* take into account; remember **3** *vt* believe to be **~ed** reached after careful thought **~ing** *prep* if one takes into account: *She did well, considering her age.*
considerable *adj* fairly large **-bly** *adv* much
considerate *adj* kind and thoughtful **~ly** *adv*
consideration *n* **1** thoughtful attention **2** fact to be remembered when deciding something **3** payment; reward **4 take something into consideration** remember when making a judgment
consign *vt* **1** send (goods) for sale **2** give into someone's care **~ment** *n* **1** goods consigned **2** act of consigning **~ee** *n* person to whom something is consigned **~or** *n* person who consigns
consistency *n* **1** state of always behaving in the same way **2** degree of thickness of a liquid **-tent** *adj* **1** not changing **2** in agreement **-tently** *adv*
consist in *phr vt fml* have as a base; depend on
consist of *phr vt* be made up of
consistory *n* church court or council, esp. one made up of the Pope and cardinals
consol *n* interest-bearing British government bond redeemable on demand
consolation prize *n* prize given to a loser or a runner-up
console[1] *vt* make less unhappy **-solation** *n* (person or thing giving) comfort
console[2] *n* **1** control panel **2** keyboard(s), stops, etc. of an organ **3** ornamental wall bracket
consolidate *vi/t* **1** (cause to) become stronger **2** combine into one **-dation** *n*

consommé *n* clear soup
consonant¹ *n* (letter representing) a speech sound such as b, m, s, made by stopping the breath
consonant² *adj* in agreement **-nance** *n*
consort *n* wife or husband of a ruler
consort with *phr vi* spend time in company
consortium *n* **-tiums** *or* **-tia** combination of a number of companies, banks, etc.
conspectus *n* **-tuses** *fml* survey; summary
conspicuous *adj* easily seen; noticeable **~ly** *adv*
conspiracy *n* (plan made by) conspiring
conspiracy of silence *n* agreement to keep silent to protect one's own interests
conspirator *n* person who conspires **~ial** *adj* like a conspirator; furtive **~ially** *adv*
conspire *vi* **1** plan something bad together secretly **2** (of events) combine in a bad way
constable *n* British policeman or police officer
constabulary *n* police force of an area
constant *adj* **1** happening all the time **2** unchanging **3** continuous **4** loyal ♦ *n* something that never varies **~ly** *adv* **-stancy** *n* **1** freedom from change **2** loyalty
constellation *n* named group of stars
consternation *n* great shock and fear
constipation *n* being unable to empty the bowels properly **-ted** *adj*
constituency *n* (voters in) an area that elects a representative to Parliament
constituent *n* **1** voter **2** necessary part ♦ *adj* helping to make a whole
constituent assembly *n* body of representatives elected to draw up or change a constitution
constitute *vt* **1** form when added together **2** establish
constitution *n* **1** laws and principles by which a country is governed **2** person's physical condition **3** structure of something **~al** *adj* **1** by or of a political constitution **2** of a person's constitution **~ally** *adv*
constrain *vt fml* force (someone) to do something
constraint *n* **1** compulsion (1) **2** restriction
constrict *vt* make narrower or tighter **~ion** *n* **~or** *n* **1** muscle that constricts **2** large snake that squeezes its prey to death
construct *vt* make out of parts; build **~ion** *n* **1** building; the building industry **2** something built **3** meaning given to something: *put the wrong construction on his behaviour* **-ive** *adj* helpful: *constructive suggestions* **~or** *n*
construe *vt* place a certain meaning on
consubstantiation *n* the doctrine of the presence of the body and blood of Christ in Communion bread and wine
consul *n* **1** representative of a government in a foreign city **2** chief magistrate in ancient Rome **~ar** *adj* **~ate** *n* consul's office
consult *vt* go to (a person, book, etc.) for advice **~ation** *n*
consultant *n* **1** person who gives professional advice **2** *BrE* high ranking hospital doctor who gives specialist advice **-tancy** *n* **-tative** *adj* giving advice
consume *vt fml* **1** eat or drink **2** use up; destroy **-suming** *adj* passionate; engrossing **-sumer** *n* person who buys goods
consumer durable *n* large article that is bought only infrequently, e.g. a car
consumer goods *pl n* goods made for sale to the public rather than to industry
consummate *adj* perfect; complete ♦ *vt* **1** complete (a marriage) by having sex **2** make perfect **-mation** *n*
consumption *n* **1** consuming; amount consumed **2** tuberculosis **-tive** *adj* suffering from tuberculosis
cont *abbrev. for:* continued
contact *n* **1** meeting; relationship: *Have you been in contact with the disease?* **2** person one knows who can help one **3** electrical part that touches another to

carry electric current ♦ *vt* reach (someone) by telephone, letter, etc.
contact lens *n* plastic lens shaped to fit over the eye to improve eyesight
contagion /kən'tayj(ə)n/ *n* **1** spreading of a disease by touch **2** harmful influence **–gious** *adj*
contain *vt* **1** have within itself **2** keep under control: *I can't contain myself.* **3** keep from spreading or gaining ground **~ment** *n* keeping within bounds
container *n* **1** box, bottle, etc., used to contain something **2** large metal box in which goods are packed to be carried on ships, etc. **~ize, –ise** *vt* **1** to transport in containers **2** to convert to the use of containers **~ization, –isation** *n*
contaminate *vt* make impure or dirty: *contaminated water* **–nation** *n*
contemplate *vt* **1** think about; consider as possible **2** look solemnly at **–plation** *n* deep thought **–plative** *adj*
contemplative order *n* religious group devoted entirely to prayer, as opposed to practical work
contemporaneous *adj* contemporary (2)
contemporary *adj* **1** modern; of the present **2** happening, existing, etc., at the same time ♦ *n* person of the same age, or living at the same time
contempt *n* complete lack of respect **~ible** *adj* deserving contempt **~uous** *adj* showing contempt
contempt of court *n* offence of disobeying a judge in court
contend *v* **1** *vi* compete; struggle **2** *vt* claim; declare **~er** *n* competitor
content[1] *adj* satisfied; happy ♦ *vt* make happy **~ed** *adj* quietly happy **~edly** *adv* **~ment** *n* quiet happiness
content[2] *n* **1** subject matter of a book **2** amount contained in something: *a high fat content* **contents** *pl n* **1** what something contains **2** index of a book
contention *n* **1** claim; point of view **2** struggle **–tious** *adj* **1** causing argument **2** quarrelsome
contest *n* struggle; competition ♦ *vt* **1** compete for **2** argue about the rightness of **~ant** *n* competitor
context *n* **1** words that surround a word or phrase **2** surrounding conditions
contiguous /kən'tigyoo·əs/ *adj* **1** touching **2** neighbouring **~ly** *adv*
continent[1] *adj* **1** able to control the bowels and bladder **2** exercising self-restraint, esp. in sexual matters **–nence** *n*
continent[2] *n* **1** large land mass; Europe, Asia, etc. **2** (*cap.*) Europe without Britain **~al** *adj*
continental breakfast *n* light breakfast usu. of bread, butter, jam and coffee
continental drift *n* theory that earth's continents have split off from a single land mass
continental quilt *n BrE* duvet
continental shelf *n* shallow sea bed surrounding the edge of a continent
contingency *n* possible event that might cause problems
contingent *adj* **1** dependent on something uncertain **2** happening by chance ♦ *n* **1** part of a larger force of soldiers, ships, etc. **2** part of a larger gathering of people
continual *adj* regular; frequent **~ly** *adv*
continue *vi/t* **1** go on doing something **2** start again after stopping **–uation** *n* **1** act of continuing **2** something which continues from something else
continuity *n* uninterrupted connection
continuo *n* **–nuos** bass instrumental accompaniment to baroque music
continuous *adj* continuing unbroken: *The brain needs a continuous supply of blood.* **~ly** *adv*
continuous assessment *n* judging the quality of a student's work throughout his/her course
continuum *n* **-uums** *or* **-ua** **1** something which is without parts and the same from beginning to end **2** something that changes gradually without sudden breaks
contort *vt* twist out of shape **~ion** *n*
contortionist *n* **1** acrobat who twists into unnatural positions **2** person who twists words and meanings, esp. in

order to get out of a difficult situation

contour *n* **1** shape of the edges of something, such as a coast **2** line on a map linking points of equal height

contra- *prefix* **1** against; contrasting: *contraflow* **2** pitched lower than normal: *contrabass*

contraband *n* goods that it is not legal to bring into a country

contrabass *n* double bass

contraception *n* (methods for) preventing pregnancy **–tive** *n, adj* (drug, etc.) used for contraception

contract *n* formal agreement to do something ♦ *v* **1** *vi/t* arrange by formal agreement **2** *vi/t* (cause to) become smaller **3** *vt* get (a disease) **–contract in/out** *phr vi* promise, esp. officially to/not to take part **~ion** *n* **1** process of getting smaller **2** shortened form of a word **3** strong tightening of a muscle **~ual** *adj* by or relating to a formal agreement

contract bridge *n* form of the game, bridge, in which only the points made on tricks bid by the declarer count towards game

contractor *n* firm that provides supplies and/or workers, esp. for building work

contradict *v* **1** *vi/t* say the opposite of; declare to be wrong **2** *vt* (of a statement, fact, etc.) be opposite to (another) **~ory** *adj* **~ion** *n*

contradistinction *n fml* **in contradistinction to** as opposed to; in contrast to

contraflow *n* arrangement by which traffic in both directions on a road can use only one side

contrail *n* vapour trail left by aircraft

contraindicated *adj* (of a drug or treatment) unsuitable, given the patient's condition **–ation** *n* symptom or condition which makes a certain treatment inadvisable

contralto *n* **-tos** female alto

contraption *n* strange-looking apparatus.

contrapuntal *adj* of or in counterpoint

contrariwise *adv* **1** conversely **2** in the opposite way or direction

contrary *n* **1** opposite **2 on the contrary** no, not at all **3 to the contrary** to the opposite effect ♦ *adj* **1** completely different; opposed **2** (of a person) unreasonable **–riety** *n* opposition; disagreement **–rily** *adv* **–riness** *n* **–riwise** *adv* **1** conversely **2** vice versa

contrast *v* **1** *vt* compare so that differences are made clear **2** *vi* show a difference: *sharply contrasting attitudes* ♦ *n* noticeable difference

contravene *vt* break (a law) **–vention** *n*

contretemps /ˈkon(h)trəˌtonh/ *n* **-temps** **1** unlucky and unexpected event **2** disagreement; quarrel

contribute *v* **1** *vi/t* join with others in giving something **2** *vi* help in causing: *contribute to good health* **3** *vt* write (an article) for a magazine **–utor** *n* person who contributes **–utory** *adj* **–ution** *n*

contrite *adj fml* sorry for having done wrong **~ly** *adv* **–trition** *n*

contrive *vt* **1** succeed in doing something **2** invent; create **–trivance** *n* clever plan or invention **–trived** *adj* unnatural and forced

control *vt* **-ll-** **1** direct; have power over **2** hold back; restrain ♦ *n* power to control **2** means of controlling **3** instruments by which something is controlled: *controls of a plane* **4** standard against which the results of a study are measured **5 out of control** in(to) a state of not being controlled **6 under control** working properly **~ler** *n* person who directs something

controversy /ˈkontrəˌvuhsi, kənˈtrovəsi/ *n* fierce argument **–sial** *adj* causing controversy **–sially** *adv*

contumacy /ˈkontyoomәsi/ *fml n* stubborn disobedience **–acious** *adj*

contumely *n fml* abusive and contemptuous language or treatment **–elious** *adj*

contusion *n fml* bruise

conundrum *n* **1** riddle **2** difficult problem

conurbation *n* number of towns joined into one large city or network

convalesce *vi* spend time getting well

after an illness **–lescence** *n* time spent getting well **–lescent** *n, adj* (person) spending time getting well

convection *n* (heat transfer by) the circulation of currents in a gas or liquid **–or** *n* a heater which uses convection

convene *v* **1** *vi* meet together **2** *vt* call (a group) to meet **–vener**, **-venor** *n* person who convenes meetings

convenience *n* **1** fitness; suitableness **2** useful tool or apparatus **3** toilet **4** personal comfort **–ent** *adj* **1** suited to one's needs **2** near **–ently** *adv*

convenience food *n* food that can be stored for use at any time and needs little or no preparation

convent *n* **1** place where nuns live **2** school run by nuns

convention *n* **1** accepted social custom **2** meeting of a group with a shared purpose **3** formal political agreement **~al** *adj* following accepted customs **~ally** *adv*

converge *vi* come together and meet **–vergence** *n*

conversant *adj* having knowledge or experience

conversation *n* informal talk **~al** *adj* (of language) used in conversation

conversation piece *n* **1** object that provokes conversation **2** group portrait

converse[1] *vi fml* talk informally

converse[2] *adj, n fml* opposite **~ly** *adv*

conversion *n* act of converting

convert *vi/t* **1** change into another form: *convert dollars into pounds* **2** change to a particular religious, political, etc. belief ♦ *n* person who has accepted a particular belief **~er** *n* apparatus that converts something, esp. information to be put into a computer **~ible** *adj* (esp. of money) able to be converted **~ible** *n* car with a roof that can be folded back

convex *adj* curved outwards **~ity** *n*

convey *vt* **1** take; carry **2** make (feelings, etc.) known **~er, –or** *n*

conveyance *n* **1** *fml* vehicle **2** legal paper giving the right to property **–ancing** *n* branch of law concerned with legal conveyances **–ancer** *n*

conveyer belt, conveyor belt *n* endless moving belt carrying objects from one place to another

convict *vt* prove (someone) to be guilty of a crime ♦ *n* convicted person who is sent to prison

conviction *n* **1** being convicted of a crime **2** firm belief

convince *vt* cause to feel sure of something **–vincing** *adj* **–vincingly** *adv*

convivial *adj* merry and friendly **~ity** *n*

convoke *vt* call together (for a formal meeting) **convocation** *n*

convoluted *adj* **1** twisted **2** difficult to understand **–lution** *n* twist

convolvulus *n* genus of plants with twining stems

convoy *n* **1** group of ships or vehicles travelling together, esp. for safety **2** protecting force of warships, etc. ♦ *vt* go with and protect

convulse *vt* shake violently **–vulsive** *adj* **–vulsion** *n*

cony *n* rabbit (fur)

coo *vi* **1** make the soft cry of a dove **2** speak lovingly

cook *v* **1** *vi/t* prepare (food) by using heat **2** *vi* (of food) be cooked **3** *vt* change (accounts, etc.) dishonestly **4 cook somebody's goose: a** spoil someone's chances **b** bring about someone's downfall **cook up** *phr vt* concoct; improvise ♦ *n* person who cooks food **~er** *n* stove for cooking on

cookery *n* art of cooking

cookie *n esp. AmE* **1** biscuit **2** person: *a smart/tough cookie*

cool *adj* **1** pleasantly cold **2** calm; unexcited **3** not very friendly **4** (used to add force to an expression): *a cool £1,000 a month* ♦ *n* **1** cool temperature: *the cool of the evening* **2** calmness: *lose one's cool* ♦ *vi/t* make or become cool **cool down/off** *phr vi/t* (cause to) become calmer ♦ *adv* **play it cool** act calmly **~ness** *n* **~ly** *adv*

coolant *n* fluid used to cool an engine or machine

cooler *n* **1** container that keeps things cool **2** *sl* prison
coolie *n* unskilled labourer or porter in oriental countries
coon *n* **1** *taboo* coloured person **2** *AmE infml* raccoon
coop *n* cage for small creatures **coop up** *phr vt* shut into a small space
cooperate *vi* work together for a shared purpose **–rative** *adj* helpful **–rative** *n* firm, farm, etc., owned by its workers **–ration** *n*
co-opt *vt* (of an elected group) choose as a fellow member **~ion** *n*
coordinate *vt* cause to work together effectively: *coordinate our efforts* **–nation** *n*
coordinates *pl n* separate garments in matching colours that can be worn together
cop *n sl* **1** policeman **2** arrest ♦ *vt* **-pp- 1** get; catch **2 cop it** *sl esp. BrE* be in serious trouble **cop out** *phr vi sl* avoid responsibility
cope *vi* deal with something successfully
copier *n* machine for making paper copies
coping *n* top course of brick, stone, etc. on a wall
copious /ˈkohpi·əs/ *adj* plentiful **~ly** *adv*
cop-out *n* evasion of responsibility
copper¹ *n* **1 a** soft reddish-brown metal **b** its colour **2** copper coin
copper² *n sl* policeman
copra *n* dried flesh of the coconut
copse also **coppice** *n* small group of trees
copula *n* verb (e.g. *be* or *seem*) which links a noun and its complement
copulate *vi fml* have sex **–lation** *n*
copy *n* **1** thing made to be like another **2** single example of a book, newspaper, etc. **3 good copy** interesting news ♦ *v* **1** *vt* make a copy of **2** *vt* do the same as **3** *vi/t* cheat in an examination, etc., by copying
copy-book *adj BrE* entirely suitable or correct
copycat *n derog infml* person who copies other people's behaviour, dress, work, etc.
copyright *n* legal right to be the only seller of a book, etc.
copywriter *n* person who writes the text of advertisements or publicity material
coquette *n* flirtatious woman **–ttish** *adj* **coquetry** *n*
coracle *n* small round boat made of wicker covered with skins
coral *n* white, pink, or red substance formed by small sea creatures
cor anglais *n* woodwind instrument like a large oboe
corbel *n* stone wall-bracket
cord *n* **1** thick string or thin rope **2** electric wire **~less** *adj* battery-operated
cordial¹ *adj* warm and friendly **~ly** *adv* **1** in a cordial manner **2 dislike/hate each other cordially** dislike/hate each other very strongly
cordial² *n* nonalcoholic fruit drink
cordite *n* explosive used as propellant for bullets and shells
cordon *n* ring of police, etc., surrounding an area **cordon off** *phr vt* protect with a cordon
cordon bleu *adj, n* (of) high-class (French) cuisine
cords *pl n infml* trousers made from corduroy
corduroy /ˈkawd(ə)roy/ *n* strong cotton cloth with raised lines on it
core *n* **1** central part **2 to the core** thoroughly ♦ *vt* remove the core of (a fruit)
co-respondent *n* person alleged to have committed adultery with the respondent in a divorce case
corgi *n* short-legged Welsh dog with a foxy face
coriander *n* **1** plant of the carrot family **2** its leaves or seeds used as flavouring
cork *n* **1** bark of a tree (the **cork oak**) **2** piece of this used for closing a bottle ♦ *vt* close with a cork
corm *n* plant stem base from which e.g. crocuses and anemones are grown

cormorant *n* large fish-eating seabird, famed for its voracity

corn[1] *n* **1** *BrE* (seed of) various grain plants, esp. wheat **2** *AmE* (seed of) a tall plant with long bunches of yellow seeds

corn[2] *n* painful lump of hard skin on the foot

cornea *n* protective covering on the front surface of the eye

corned beef *n* kind of pressed cooked beef in tins

cornelian *n* reddish stone used in jewellery

corner *n* **1 a** point where two lines, edges, or roads meet **b** angular space enclosed by two meeting lines, walls, etc. **2** remote, secluded or humble place **3** also **corner kick** (in football) kick taken from the corner of the field **4 around/round the corner** near ♦ *v* **1** *vt* force into a difficult position **2** *vt* gain control of (by buying, selling, or production of goods) **3** *vi* (of a vehicle) turn a corner

cornerstone *n* **1** stone set at one bottom corner of a building **2** something of great importance, on which everything else is based

cornet *n* **1** musical instrument like a trumpet **2** *BrE* cone-shaped eatable container for ice-cream

cornflakes *pl n* breakfast cereal of crushed corn

cornflour *n* finely ground maize flour used for thickening

cornice *n* decorative border at the top edge of the front of a building, a column, or the walls of a room

Cornish pasty *n* folded pastry case baked with chopped meat and vegetables inside

corn pone *n* maize bread originally made by American Indians

cornucopia *n* **1** abundance **2** horn-shaped container

corny *adj sl* too common; old-fashioned

corollary /kəˈrɒləri/ *n* something that naturally follows from something else

corona *n* **1** halo of light esp. around the moon **2** long straight-sided cigar

coronary thrombosis also **coronary** *n* stopping of the blood supply to the heart; kind of heart attack

coronation *n* ceremony of crowning a king or queen

coroner *n* official who enquires into the cause of a person's death if it is not clearly known

coronet *n* small crown worn by nobles, etc.

corporal[1] *adj fml* of the human body: *corporal punishment*

corporal[2] *n* noncommissioned officer in an army or air force

corporate *adj* **1** shared by a whole group **2** of a corporation

corporation *n* **1** large business organization **2** town council **3** *infml* pot-belly

corporeal *adj* physical; tangible

corps /kaw/ *n* **1 a** trained army group **b** branch of the army equal to two divisions **2** group with the same activity: *the press corps*

corps de ballet *n* ballet dancers who perform as a group

corpse *n* dead body

corpulent *adj* very fat **–lence** *n*

corpus *n* **-pora 1** collection of writings or works **2** main part

corpuscle *n* any of the red and white cells in the blood

corral *n* enclosed area (esp. in Western America) for cattle and horses ♦ *vt* **-ll-** put in a corral

correct *adj* **1** without mistakes; true **2** proper **~ly** *adv* **~ness** *n* ♦ *vt* make right; show the mistakes in **~ive** *adj, n* **~ion** *n* **1** correcting **2** change that improves something **3** punishment

correlate *vi/t* (show to) have a close connection **–ation** *n* close connection

correspond *vi* **1** be equal; match **2** exchange letters **~ing** *adj* matching; equal

correspondence *n* **1** letter-writing; letters **2** equality between things; likeness **–dent** *n* **1** person with whom one exchanges letters **2** someone employed by a newspaper, television or radio station, etc., to report news from a distant area

corridor *n* passage between rows of rooms

corrigenda /ˌkoriˈjendə/ *pl n* (list of) printing errors shown side by side with correct forms

corroborate *vt* support (an opinion, etc.) by proof **–ration** *n*

corroboree *n AustrE* **1** Aborigine festival **2** noisy festivity

corrode *vi/t* destroy slowly, esp. by chemical action

corrosion *n* **1** corroding **2** rust, etc., produced by corroding **–sive** *adj*

corrugated *adj* having wavelike folds **–gation** *n*

corrupt *adj* **1** morally bad, esp. dishonest **2** containing mistakes ♦ *vi/t* make or become corrupt **~ly** *adv* **~ion** *n*

corsage *n* flowers worn on a woman's bodice

corsair *n* pirate

corselet *n* **1** also **corselette** combined corset and bra **2** also **corslet** piece of armour enclosing the body above the waist

corset also **corsets** *pl n* tight-fitting undergarment worn esp. by women

cortege *n* funeral procession

cortex *n* **-tices** *or* **-texes 1** outer layer, esp. of the brain **2** plant bark

cortisone *n* (synthetically produced) steroid hormone used esp. in treating rheumatic diseases

corundum *n* hard mineral used in powder form for polishing and sharpening

coruscate *vi* sparkle; flash

corvette *n* small escort warship

cosh *vt, n BrE* (hit with) a short heavy pipe or filled rubber tube

cosine *n* ratio of the length of the side adjacent to an angle in a right-angled triangle to the length of the hypotenuse

cos lettuce *n* long-leaved lettuce

cosmetic *n* cream, powder, etc., for the skin or hair ♦ *adj* **1** of, related to, or causing increased beauty **2** dealing only with the outside appearance rather than the central part of something

cosmic *adj* of the whole universe

cosmic rays *pl n* electromagnetic rays from space

cosmology *n* study of the origin and nature of the universe

cosmonaut *n* a Soviet astronaut

cosmopolitan *adj* **1** consisting of people from many parts of the world **2** not narrow-minded ♦ *n* cosmopolitan person

cosmos *n* the whole universe

Cossack *n* member of a tribe from south-east Russia which served as cavalry under the Tsars

cosset *vt* **-tt-** treat too kindly

cost *n* **1** price of something **2** what is needed to gain something **3 at all costs** whatever it may cost **4 at cost** at cost price **5 to one's cost** from one's own unpleasant experience ♦ *vt* **1** (*past t. and p.* **cost**) have as a price **2** cause to lose, suffer: *The mistake cost him his job.* **3** (*past t. and p.* **costed**) calculate the price to be charged for (a job) **~ly** *adj* expensive **costs** *pl n* cost of taking a matter to a court of law

co-star *n* famous actor or actress who appears with another famous actor or actress in a film, etc. **co-star** *vi*

cost-effective *adj* bringing the best possible profits or advantages for the lowest possible cost **~ly** *adv* **~ness** *n*

costive *adj* constipated

cost price *n* price paid for an article by the retailer

costume *n* clothes, esp. as worn in plays

costume drama *n* play(s) set in a historical period and requiring costume

costume jewellery *n* precious-looking jewellery made from cheap materials

cosy also *AmE* **cozy** *adj* warm and comfortable ♦ *n* covering for a teapot, eggcup, etc. to keep the contents warm **–sily** *adv* **–siness** *n*

cot *n* **1** *BrE* bed for a small child **2** *AmE* light narrow bed which folds flat

cot death *n* unexplained death of a healthy baby

cote *n* small shelter for animals or birds

coterie *n* clique; in-group
coterminous *adj fml* **1** having a common boundary **2** the same in scope or duration
cotoneaster *n* garden shrub with red or orange berries
cottage *n* small house, esp. in the country
cottage cheese *n* soft white cheese made from skimmed milk
cottage industry *n* industry in which workers produce goods at home on their own equipment
cottage pie *n* shepherd's pie
cotton *n* **1** soft white hair of a tropical plant **2** thread or cloth made from this **3** *AmE* cotton wool **cotton on** *phr vi infml* understand
cotton wool *n BrE* soft mass of cotton for cleaning wounds, etc.
cotyledon *n* first leaf developed by the embryo of a seed plant
couch *n* long seat like a bed ♦ *vt* express: *His refusal was couched in unfriendly terms.*
couchette /kooh'shet/ *n* folding bed on a train
cougar *n* large American wild cat
cough *v* **1** *vi* push air out noisily from the lungs **2** *vt* produce by doing this: *cough up blood* ♦ *n* **1** act of coughing **2** illness that makes a person cough **cough up** *phr vt infml* produce (money or information) unwillingly
could *v aux* **1** *past t. of* can: *He could read when he was four.* **2** (used in indirect speech): *She asked if she could smoke.* **3** (used to show what is possible): *I think the accident could have been prevented.* **4** (used to make a request): *Could you help me?*
couldn't *short for:* could not
coulomb *n* unit of electrical charge
council *n* group of people appointed or elected to manage something ♦ *adj* owned by British local government **~lor** *n* member of a council
councilman *n* **-men** *AmE* councillor
councilwoman *n* **-women** *AmE* female councillor
counsel *n* **counsel 1** *law* barrister acting for someone **2** advice ♦ *v* **-ll-** (*AmE* **-l-**) advise **~lor,** *AmE* **~or 1** adviser **2** *AmE* lawyer
count[1] *v* **1** *vi/t* name (numbers) in order: *count (to) 20* **2** *vt* find the total of **3** *vt* include: *six people, counting me* **4** *vt* consider to be: *count yourself lucky* **5** *vi* have value: *Every moment counts* **count down** *phr vt* count backwards to zero, esp. before sending a spacecraft into space **count in** *phr vt* include **count on/upon** *phr vt* depend on; expect **count out** *phr vt* **1** put down in turn while counting **2** not include **3** declare (a boxer who fails to get up after 10 seconds) to be a loser of a fight ♦ *n* **1** act of counting; total **2** item in an indictment: *guilty on all counts* **3 be out for the count** (in boxing) be counted out; be unconscious **4 keep/lose count** know/no longer know the exact number **~able** *adj* that can be counted: *Egg is a countable noun.* **~less** *adj* very many
count[2] *n* European nobleman
countdown *n* counting towards zero of time before an event
countenance *n fml* **1** face **2** support; approval ♦ *vt fml* give approval to
counter[1] *n* **1** table where people in a shop, etc., are served **2** object used in some games instead of money **3** machine that counts **4 over the counter** (when buying drugs) without a prescription **5 under the counter** secretly and often unlawfully
counter[2] *vi/t* **1** take defensive or retaliatory measures against an attack **2** oppose ♦ *adv, adj* opposed; opposite: *act counter to all advice*
counter- *prefix* **1** opposite: *counterproductive* **2** retaliatory: *counterattack* **3** corresponding: *counterpart* **4** duplicate: *counterfoil*
counteract *vt* reduce the effect of: *counteract a poison*
counterattack *vi/t, n* (make) an attack to oppose another
counterattraction *n* rival show, display, meeting, etc.

counterbalance *vt, n* (act as) a force that balances another
counterblast *n* strongly-worded reaction or refutation
counterclockwise *adj, adv AmE* anticlockwise
counterespionage *n* secret police work aimed at foiling enemy espionage
counterfeit /ˈkowntəfit, -feet/ *n, adj* (thing) made as a copy of something else, to deceive ♦ *vt* make a counterfeit of
counterfoil *n* part of a cheque, ticket, etc., kept as a record
counterinsurgency *n* military action to put down a rebellion
countermand *vt* declare (a command already given) ineffective
counterpane *n* bedspread
counterpart *n* person or thing that matches another, but in a different system
counterpoint *n* (art of) combining two or more melodies in a single texture
counterpoise *vt, n* counterbalance
counterproductive *adj* having an opposite effect from the one intended
Counter-Reformation *n* reform movement in the Roman Catholic church intended to counteract the effects of the Reformation
countersign *vt* add another signature to (a paper already signed)
countersink *vt* enlarge (a hole) to take the head of a screw
countertenor *n* male alto
countervailing *adj* acting with equal force but opposite effect
countess *n* **a** woman who holds the rank of count or earl for herself **b** wife of a count or earl
country *n* **1** nation, with its land and population **2** also **countryside** land outside towns **3 go to the country** *esp. BrE* (of a government) call a general election ♦ *adj* of, in, or from the country
country and western also **country music** *n* popular music in the style of the southern and western US
country cousin *n* person unused to city life
country dance *n* traditional dance for groups of couples
countryman *n* **-men 1** compatriot **2** man who lives in, or comes from, the country
country seat *n* family mansion or estate in the country
countrywoman *n* **-women 1** compatriot **2** woman who lives in, or comes from, the country
county *n* subdivision of a country for purposes of local government
coup *n* **1** clever effective action **2** also **coup d'état** sudden and violent seizure of state power by a small group
coup de grace *n* finishing blow
coupé *n* closed car with two doors and a sloping back
couple *n* **1** two things of the same kind **2** two people, esp. a husband and wife **3** a few ♦ *v* **1** *vt* join (two things) together **2** *vi* (of animals) mate **–plet** *n* two successive lines of poetry **–pling** *n* something that joins two things, esp. two railway carriages
coupon *n* ticket showing the right of the holder to receive something
courage *n* ability to control fear; bravery **–ageous** *adj* brave **–ageously** *adv*
courgette *n BrE* small green marrow
courier *n* **1** person who looks after travellers on a tour **2** official messenger **3** person who transports drugs or contraband **4** employee of a private postal company
course *n* **1** path along which something moves **2** area for races or certain sports **3** plan of action **4 a** set of lessons, treatments, etc. **b** university studies: *a four year course* **5** any of several parts of a meal **6 in the course of** during **7 of course** certainly **8 run/take its/their course** (of an illness, etc.) continue to its natural end ♦ *vi* (of liquid) flow quickly
court *n* **1 a** room (**courtroom**) or building where law cases are judged **b** people gathered together there **2** area for certain ball games such as tennis **3** king or

queen with the royal family, officials, etc. **4 a** short street surrounded by buildings on three sides **b** block of flats **c** courtyard ♦ *vt* **1** try to win the favour of **2** visit and pay attention to (a woman a man hopes to marry) **3** risk foolishly: *to court disaster*

court card *n* king, queen or jack

courteous /ˈkuhtyəs/ *adj fml* polite and kind **~ly** *adv*

courtesan *n* high-class prostitute

courtesy /ˈkuhtəsi/ *n* **1** polite behaviour **2 by courtesy of** with the permission of

courtier *n* person in attendance at a royal court

court-martial *n* (trial before) a court for offences against military law ♦ *vt* **-ll-** (*AmE* **-l-**) try (someone) in a court-martial

Court of Session *n* highest civil court in Scotland

courtship *n* (period of) trying to attract someone to oneself, esp. with the aim of marriage

courtyard *n* open space surrounded by buildings

couscous *n* crushed wheat which is cooked by steaming

cousin *n* **1** child of one's uncle or aunt **2** related person or thing

cove *n* small bay

coven *n* band of witches

covenant *n* **1** formal agreement **2** written promise to pay a fixed regular sum of money to a church, charity, etc. ♦ *vt* agree (to pay)

Coventry *n* **send someone to Coventry** refuse to speak to someone as a punishment

cover 1 *vt* spread something over; hide in this way **2** *vt* lie on the surface of; spread over (something): *The town covers five square miles.* **3** *vt* travel (a distance) **4** *vt* include: *a talk covering the whole history of medicine* **5** *vt* report (an event) for a newspaper **6** *vt* be enough money for **7** *vt* protect from loss; insure **8** *vt* keep a gun aimed at **9** *vi/t* act in place of (someone who is absent) **cover up** *phr vt* prevent (something) from being noticed **cover up for** *phr vt* hide something wrong or shameful in order to save (someone else) from punishment, blame, etc. ♦ *n* **1** anything that protects or hides by covering **2** outside of a book or magazine **3** shelter; protection **4** insurance against loss, etc. **5 under plain/separate cover** in a plain/separate envelope **~age** *n* time and space given to reporting an event **~ing** *n* something that covers or hides

coveralls *pl n AmE* overalls

cover charge *n* charge made by a restaurant in addition to the cost of the food and drinks or of the service

covered wagon *n* horse-drawn wagon with a rounded cloth roof, used by 19th-century American settlers

covering letter *n* letter or note containing an explanation or additional information, sent with a parcel or another letter

cover note *n* provisional insurance document

covert *adj* hidden; secret **~ly** *adv*

cover-up *n* attempt to conceal e.g. an error or a crime

covet /ˈkovit, ˈku-/ *vt* desire (esp. someone else's possessions) eagerly **~ous** *adj* **~ousness** *n*

covey *n* small group (of birds)

cow[1] *n* female of cattle and some other large animals

cow[2] *vt* frighten into obedience

coward *n* person afraid of pain or danger **~ly** *adj*

cowardice *n* lack of courage

cowboy *n* **1** man who looks after cattle on horseback in N America **2** *BrE sl* someone who is careless and dishonest in business

cowcatcher *n* metal frame attached to the front of a locomotive to push obstacles off the track

cower *vi* bend low from fear or shame

cowl *n* monk's hood

cowlick *n* tuft of hair that sticks up

cowling *n* cover for an aircraft engine

cowpat *n* lump of cow dung

cowrie, -ry *n* (mollusc with) a brightly marked shell formerly used as money in parts of Africa and Asia
cowslip *n* wild flower of the primrose family
cox *n* person who guides and controls a rowing boat, esp. in races ♦ *vi/t* act as cox
coxcomb *n* conceited foolish person; fop
coy *adj* pretending not to be self-confident **~ly** *adv*
coyote /ˈkoyoht, -ˈohti/ *n* small wolf
cozen *vt arch.* cheat
cozy *adj, n AmE* cosy
cp *abbrev. for:* **1** candlepower **2** compare
CP *abbrev. for:* **1** Cape Province **2** Communist Party
CPU *abbrev. for:* central processing unit
crab *n* 10-legged edible shellfish
crab apple *n* (tree which bears) a small sour-tasting wild apple
crabby *adj* bad-tempered
crack *v* **1** *vi/t* break without dividing into pieces **2** *vi/t* make a sudden explosive sound: *crack a whip* **3** *vi/t* cause to break open: *crack a safe* **4** *vi* (of a voice) change suddenly in level **5** *vi/t* hit suddenly **6** *vi* lose strength or control: *crack (up) under the strain* **7** make (a joke) **8** discover the secret of (a code) **9** (cause to) strike with a sudden blow **10 cracked up to be** believed to be **11 get cracking** be or become busy doing something in a hurried way **crack down** *phr vi* take strong action against something ♦ *n* **1** thin line caused by breaking **2** explosive sound **3** sudden sharp blow **4** sudden change in the level of the voice **5** quick joke; clever remark **6** *sl* extremely pure form of cocaine **7 at the crack of dawn** very early in the morning ♦ *adj* very skilful: *crack troops*
crack-brained *adj* crackpot
crackdown *n* severe or repressive disciplinary action
cracked *adj infml* slightly mad
cracker *n* **1** unsweetened biscuit **2** paper tube that makes a noise when pulled apart
crackers *adj BrE infml* mad
crackle *vi* make small sharp sounds: *The fire crackled.* **crackle** *n*
crackling *n* crisp skin of roast pork
crackpot *adj* strange; mad ♦ *n* crackpot person
crackup *n* nervous breakdown
cradle *n* **1** small bed for a baby **2** origin of something: *the cradle of Western civilization* **3** frame to support something ♦ *vt* hold gently
craft *n* **1** (trade needing) skill, esp. with one's hands **2** craftiness **3 craft** boat, aircraft, or spacecraft
craftsman *n* **-men** skilled worker **~ship** *n*
craftswoman *n* **-women** skilled female worker
crafty *adj* cleverly deceitful **-ily** *adv* **-iness** *n*
crag *n* high steep rock **~gy** *adj* **1** steep and rough **2** (esp. of a man's face) rough in appearance
cram *v* **-mm- 1** *vt* force into a small space; fill too full **2** *vi* study hard for a short time
cramp *n* **1** sudden painful tightening of a muscle **2** clamp to hold timbers or masonry together ♦ *vt* **1** cause to have a cramp **2** prevent natural growth or development **3 cramp someone's style** prevent someone from showing their abilities to the full **~ed** *adj* limited in space
crampon *n* set of spikes fixed to a boot for climbing ice slopes
cranberry *n* (shrub with) an edible sour red berry
crane *n* **1** machine with a movable arm for lifting heavy objects **2** tall water-bird with long legs ♦ *vi/t* stretch out one's neck to see better
cranium *n* **-niums** *or* **-nia** bony part of the head, covering the brain **-al** *adj*
crank *n* **1** L-shaped handle for turning **2** person with strange ideas ♦ *vt* **1** move by turning a crank **2** use a crank to start a car **~y** *adj* **1** (of people or ideas) peculiar **2** *AmE* bad-tempered

crankshaft *n* shaft driving or driven by a crank
cranny *n* small narrow opening in a wall, etc.
crap *n taboo sl* **1** (act of passing) solid waste from the bowel **2** nonsense ♦ *vi* **-pp-** *taboo sl* defecate **~py** *adj* bad; inferior
craps *pl n* gambling game played with dice **crap** *adj*
crapulent, **crapulous** *adj* drunken; hard-drinking
crash *v* **1** *vi/t* fall or hit violently **2** *vi* make a sudden loud noise **3** *vi* move violently and noisily **4** *vi* fail suddenly in business ♦ *n* **1** violent vehicle accident **2** sudden loud noise **3** sudden business failure ♦ *adj* intended to get quick results: *a crash diet/course* ♦ *adv* with a crash **~ing** *adj* utter; absolute
crash barrier *n* safety barrier along the centre of a motorway, around a racetrack, etc.
crash-dive *vi* (of plane or submarine) dive at great speed
crash helmet *n* protective helmet worn by motorcyclists, etc.
crash-land *vi/t* (cause a plane) to crash in a controlled way **crash landing** *n*
crass *adj* showing great stupidity and a complete lack of feeling or respect for others
crate *n* large wooden or plastic box for bottles, etc.
crater *n* **1** mouth of a volcano **2** hole made by an explosion **3** flat-bottomed round hole on the moon's surface
cravat *n* wide piece of cloth worn like a tie
crave *vi/t* have a very strong desire for (something) **craving** *n*
craven *adj* cowardly
crawl *vi* **1** move slowly, esp. with the body close to the ground **2** be (as if) covered by, or swarming with, crawling insects **3** have an unpleasant sensation, as of insects, etc., moving slowly over one's skin: *The idea makes my flesh crawl.* **4** *infml* try to win the favour of someone by being too nice to them ♦ *n* **1** very slow movement **2** rapid way of swimming **~er** *n* **1** something, esp. a vehicle, that goes slowly **2** servile person
crayfish *n* freshwater crustacean resembling a lobster
crayon *n* pencil of coloured chalk or wax **crayon** *vi/t*
craze *n* popular fashion that lasts a short time ♦ *vt* make excited or mad
crazy *adj* **1** mad; foolish **2** wildly excited **-zily** *adv* **-ziness** *n*
crazy paving *n BrE* surface made up of irregularly shaped paving stones
creak *vi, n* (make) the sound of a badly-oiled door **~y** *adj*
cream *n* **1** thick liquid that rises to the top of milk **2** soft mixture like this: *face cream* **3** best part: *the cream of the students* ♦ *adj* yellowish-white ♦ *vt* **1** make into a soft mixture: *creamed potatoes* **2** take cream from the surface of (milk) **cream off** *phr vt* take the best part **~er** *n* cream jug **~y** *adj* **1** containing cream **2** like cream
cream cheese *n* soft white cheese made from full milk
creamery *n* dairy
cream of tartar *n* white powder used in baking powders or laxatives
crease *n* **1** line made by folding **2** line marked on the ground for certain games ♦ *vi/t* press into creases
create *vt* **1** cause (something new) to exist; make **2** appoint to a rank **-ator** *n* **1** person who creates something **2** (*cap.*) God **-ation** *n* **1** act of creating **2** something created **3** the whole universe
creative *adj* able to make new things; inventive **~ly** *adv* **-tivity** *n*
creature *n* person, animal, or being
creature comforts *pl n* material or bodily comforts
crèche /kresh/ *n BrE* public nursery for babies
credence *n* acceptance as true; belief
credentials *pl n* written proof of a person's ability and trustworthiness
credibility gap *n* difference between

what someone, esp. a politician, says and what they really mean or do
credible *adj* that can be believed **-bly** *adv* **-bility** *n*
credit *n* **1** system of buying things and paying later **2** quality of being likely to repay debts **3** amount of money in someone's bank account **4** belief; trust **5** (cause of) public honour: *get credit for an invention|He's a credit to his team.* **6** unit of a student's work **7 to someone's credit: a** in someone's favour **b** to/in someone's name ♦ *vt* **1** believe **2** add to an account **~able** *adj* deserving approval **~ably** *adv* **credits** *n* names of actors, etc., which appear at the beginning or end of a film or television show
credit card *n* plastic card allowing one to buy goods without paying cash
creditor *n* person to whom money is owed
credo *n* **-dos** creed
credulous *adj* too willing to believe **~ly** *adv* **-lity** *n*
creed *n* system of (esp. religious) beliefs
creek *n* **1** *BrE* narrow piece of water reaching in from the sea **2** *AmE* small stream
creel *n* wicker basket for fish
creep *vi* **crept 1** move slowly and quietly; crawl **2** (of a plant) grow along the ground or a surface **3** crawl (3) ♦ *n* *infml* unpleasant servile person **~er** *n* creeping plant **~y** *adj* strange and frightening **creeps** *pl n* feeling of fear and strangeness
creepy-crawly *n infml esp. BrE* a creeping insect
cremate *vt* burn (a dead person) **-mation** *n*
crematorium *n* place where bodies are cremated
crème de la crème *n* the very best
crème de menthe *n* sweet green mint-flavoured liqueur
crenellated, *AmE* **crenelated** *adj* having battlements
Creole *n* **1** (in West Indies and Latin America) a person of European, or mixed European and Negro, descent **2** hybrid language ♦ **Creole** *adj*
creosote *n* brown oily liquid used for preserving wood **creosote** *vt*
crepe *n* **1** cloth, paper or rubber with a lined and folded surface **2** very thin pancake
crept *past t. and p. of* creep
crepuscular *adj* of or resembling the twilight
crescendo /krəˈshendoh/ *n* **-dos** gradual increase of force or loudness, esp. in music
crescent *n* **1** curved shape of the new moon **2** something shaped like this, such as a curved street
cress *n* small green salad plant
crest *n* **1** growth of feathers on a bird's head **2** decoration like this on a soldier's helmet **3** top of a hill, wave, etc. **4** picture used as a personal mark on letters, etc.
crestfallen *adj* disappointed
cretin *n* **1** *sl* very stupid person **2** *med* kind of idiot
cretonne *n* heavy printed cotton cloth
crevasse *n* deep crack in ice
crevice *n* narrow crack in rock, wall, etc.
crew *n* **1 a** all the people working on a ship or plane **b** all of these except the officers **2** group working together: *a camera crew* ♦ *vi* act as ship's crew
crew cut *n* all-over short bristly haircut
crew neck *n* plain round neck esp. on a jumper
crib *n* **1** *AmE* cot **2** book supplying a translation ♦ *vt* **-bb-** copy (someone's work) dishonestly
cribbage *n* card game in which scores are kept by small sticks inserted in a board
crick *n* painful stiffening of the muscles, esp. in the back or the neck **crick** *vt*
cricket[1] *n* **1** outdoor ball game played by two teams of 11 players each **2 not cricket** *BrE* unfair **~er** *n* cricket player
cricket[2] *n* jumping insect that makes a loud noise

cried *past t. and p. of* cry
cries *pres. t. of* cry ♦ *n pl of* cry
crikey *interj BrE* (mild, rather old-fashioned expression of surprise)
crime *n* **1** offence that is punishable by law **2** a shame
criminal *adj* of crime ♦ *n* person who is guilty of crime **~ly** *adv*
crimp *vt* **1** to make wavy or curly **2** to seal by pressing together
Crimplene *tdmk* crease-resistant synthetic material
crimson *n, adj* deep red
cringe *vi* **1** bend low from fear; cower **2** be servile towards; fawn on
crinkle *n* fold made by crushing ♦ *vi/t* make or get crinkles
crinoline *n* (stiff petticoat or hooped framework used to support) a very full skirt
cripple *n* person who cannot use the limbs, esp. the legs, properly ♦ *vt* **1** make into a cripple **2** damage seriously: *crippling debts*
crisis *n* **-ses** moment of great danger or difficulty
crisp *adj* **1** hard, dry, and easily broken **2** (of weather) cold and dry **3** (of style, manners, etc.) quick and clear ♦ *n BrE* thin piece of dry cooked potato ♦ *vi/t* cook until crisp **~ly** *adv* **~ness** *n* **~y** *adj*
crisscross *vi/t, n* (make) a network of crossed lines
criterion /krie'tiəri·ən/ *n* **-ria** *or* **-rions** standard on which a judgment is based
critic *n* **1** person who gives judgments about art, music, etc. **2** person who expresses disapproval **~al** *adj* **1** finding fault **2** of a critic's work **3** of or at a crisis: *critical decisions* **~ism** *n* **1** work of a critic **2** disapproval **~ize, -ise** *vi/t* **1** make judgments **2** find fault
critique *n* book or article criticizing the work of esp. a writer
croak *vi/t, n* **1** (make) the deep low noise a frog makes **2** speak with a rough voice as if one has a sore throat
crochet *n* type of knitting done with a single, hooked needle ♦ *vi/t* do (in) crochet
crock¹ *n* pot; jar
crock² *n infml* old broken-down vehicle or person
crockery *n* cups, plates, pots, etc.
crocodile *n* **1** large tropical river reptile **2** its skin, used as leather **3** line of people, esp. children, walking in pairs
crocodile tears *pl n* insincere sorrow
crocus *n* small spring plant with purple, yellow, or white flowers
croft **1** small farm, esp. in Scotland **2** small field **~er** *n* farmer working a croft
croissant *n* crescent-shaped flaky roll
cromlech *n* dolmen
crone *n derog* wizened, witchlike old woman
crony *n infml, derog* friend or companion
crook¹ *n* **1** *infml* thief **2** bend or curve: *the crook of her arm* ♦ *vi/t* bend **~ed** *adj* **1** not straight **2** dishonest
crook² *adj AustrE infml* **1** unpleasant **2** not in working order **3** ill
croon *vi/t* sing gently in a low soft voice
crop *n* **1** plant grown by a farmer **2** amount gathered in a season ♦ *vt* **-pp- 1** (of animals) bite off the tops of (grass etc.) **2** cut (hair, etc.) short **crop up** *phr vi* happen unexpectedly
cropper *n infml* **come a cropper** fall heavily; fail
croquet /'krohkay/ *n* garden game in which players knock wooden balls through hoops
croquette *n* small ball of minced meat, mashed potato, etc., coated in breadcrumbs
crosier *n* bishop's staff
cross *n* **1** the mark X or + **2 a** upright post with a bar across it, esp. that on which Christ died **b** this shape as a sign of the Christian faith **3** sorrow; pain **4** mixture of two things ♦ *v* **1** *vi/t* go or put across **2** *vt* oppose (someone's wishes, etc.) **3** *vi* (of letters) pass in opposite directions **4** *vt* mix different breeds of (animals or plants) **5** *vt* draw two lines across (a cheque) to show that

it must be paid into a bank account **6** **cross oneself** make the sign of the cross with the hand **7** **cross one's mind** come into one's thoughts **cross off/out** *phr vt* draw a line through (writing) ♦ *adj* angry **~ly** *adv* **~ness** *n* **~ing** *n* **1** journey across the sea **2** place where a road, etc., may be crossed **~wise** *adv* across

cross- *prefix* going between the things specified

crossbar *n* horizontal bar esp. one forming the top of a goal

crossbenches *pl n* seats in Parliament on which members sit who do not belong to the official government or opposition parties

crossbow *n* weapon, consisting of a small bow fixed crosswise on a stock, fired by a trigger from the shoulder

crossbreed *n* animal or plant of mixed breed **-bred** *adj*

crosscheck *vt* test (a calculation, etc.) by using a different method

cross-country *adj, adv* across the fields or open country ♦ *n* cross-country race or racing

crosscut saw *n* saw for cutting across the grain

cross-dressing *n* transvestism

cross-examine *vt* question (esp. a witness in court) closely, to test answers given before

cross-eyed *adj* with the eyes looking in towards the nose

cross-fertilization *n* **1** fertilization of a plant by pollen from another **2** productive interaction

crossfire *n* gunfire across one's direction of movement

cross-grained *adj* **1** (of a piece of wood) with the grain running across rather than along **2** argumentative

cross-legged *adj* having the knees wide apart and ankles crossed

crosspatch *n infml* bad-tempered person

crosspiece *n* horizontal beam, bar, etc. forming part of a structure

crossply *n, adj* (vehicle tyre) with the cords arranged crosswise

cross-purposes *n* **be at cross-purposes** misunderstand one another

cross-question *vt* cross-examine

cross-reference *n* note directing the reader to another place in the book

crossroads *n* **-roads** **1** place where roads cross **2** point where a decision must be taken

cross-section *n* **1** (drawing of) a surface made by cutting across **2** typical example of a whole

cross-stitch *n* (needlework using) an X-shaped stitch

cross-talk *n* **1** *BrE* repartee esp. between two comedians **2** interference by voices from another line or channel during a radio programme or telephone conversation

crossword *n* printed game in which words are fitted into numbered squares

crotch *n* place between the tops of a person's legs

crotchet *n* a musical note

crotchety *adj infml* bad-tempered

crouch *vi* lower the body by bending the knees

croup[1] *n* rump (of a horse)

croup[2] *n* serious throat condition in infants

croupier *n* person who collects and pays out money at a casino

crouton *n* small cube of fried or toasted bread

crow[1] *n* **1** large shiny black bird **2** **as the crow flies** in a straight line

crow[2] *vi* **1** make the loud cry of a cock **2** speak proudly

crowbar *n* iron bar for raising heavy objects

crowd *n* **1** large number of people together **2** particular social group ♦ *v* **1** *vi* come together in a crowd **2** *vt* (esp. of people) fill: *a crowded bus*

crown *n* **1** ring-shaped head decoration, esp. for a king or queen **2** royal power **3** top of a head, hat, hill, etc. **4** old British coin worth 25p ♦ *vt* **1** place a crown on the head of **2** cover the top of: *mountains crowned with snow* **3** com-

plete worthily **4 to crown it all** to complete good or bad luck **~ing** *adj* above all things
Crown Court *n* local criminal court in England and Wales
crown prince *n* heir to the throne
crow's feet *pl n* line at the outer corner of a person's eye; wrinkle
crow's nest *n* small shelter near top of a ship's mast for a look-out
crozier *n* crosier
crucial *adj* of the greatest importance **~ly** *adv*
crucible *n* pot for melting metals in
crucifix *n* cross with a figure of Christ on it
crucifixion *n* death by nailing to a cross
cruciform *adj* cross-shaped
crucify *vt* **1** kill by crucifixion **2** be very cruel to, esp. publicly
crud *n infml* encrusted dirt, muck, or residue **~dy** *adj*
crude *adj* **1** in a natural state; untreated **2** without sensitive feeling; coarse **3** badly made ♦ *n* crude oil **~ly** *adv* **crudity** *n*
cruel *adj* **-ll- 1** liking to cause suffering **2** causing suffering: *cruel disappointment* **~ly** *adv* **~ty** *n*
cruet *n* set of containers for pepper, salt, etc., at meals
cruise *v* **1** *vi* sail slowly for pleasure **2** *vi* (of a car, etc.) move at a steady speed **3** *vi/t* look (in public places) for a sexual partner, esp. a homosexual ♦ *n* sea voyage for pleasure **cruiser** *n* **1** fast heavily-armed warship **2** motorboat with a cabin
cruise missile *n* low-flying subsonic guided missile
crumb *n* **1** small piece of dry food, esp. bread **2** small amount (of information, comfort, etc.)
crumble *v* **1** *vi/t* break into small pieces **2** *vi* come to ruin **-bly** *adj* easily crumbled
crummy *adj sl* of poor quality
crumpet *n* **1** small round bun with a perforated surface and breadlike texture **2** *sl* women collectively viewed as sex objects
crumple 1 *vi/t* crush into irregular folds **2** *vi* lose strength
crunch *v* **1** *vt* crush (food) noisily with the teeth **2** *vi* make a crushing noise ♦ *n* **1** crunching sound **2** crisis; decisive moment
crupper *n* loop from the back of a saddle passing under a horse's tail
crusade *n* **1** Christian war against the Muslims in the Middle Ages **2** any united struggle ♦ *vi* take part in a crusade **-sader** *n*
crush *v* **1** *vi/t* break or spoil by pressure **2** *vi* press; push **3** *vt* destroy or humiliate completely ♦ *n* **1** crowd of people pressed together **2** strong foolish and short-lived love for someone
crush barrier *n* barrier used to divide up or control a large crowd
crust *n* hard outer surface of something, esp. bread **~y** *adj* **1** with a hard crust **2** bad-tempered
crustacean /kru'staysh(ə)n/ *n* shellfish
crutch *n* **1** stick to help someone to walk **2** something that gives moral support: *He uses religion as a crutch.* **3** crotch
crux *n* central part of a problem
cry *v* **1** *vi* produce tears from the eyes **2** *vi/t* call out loudly **3** *vi* (of a bird or animal) make its natural sound **4 cry one's eyes out** cry very bitterly **5 for crying out loud** *sl* (used to give strength to a demand, etc.): *Oh, for crying out loud, shut that door!* **cry off** *phr vi* refuse to fulfil a promise **cry out for** *phr vt* need very badly ♦ *n* **1** shout expressing something **2** period of crying **3** bird's or animal's natural sound **4 a far cry from** a great deal different from (something)
crybaby *n* person who cries too readily with little cause
cryogenics *n* branch of physics dealing with (phenomena occurring at) very low temperatures
crypt *n* room under a church
cryptic *adj* **1** with a hidden meaning **2** obscure; mysterious

crypto- *prefix* secret; hidden
cryptogam *n* plant that does not produce seed, e.g. fungus or fern **~ous** *adj*
cryptogram *n* coded message **–graphy** *n* the science of analysing codes
crystal *n* **1** (piece of) transparent ice-like mineral **2** expensive colourless glass **3** regular shape formed naturally by some substances such as sugar **4** *AmE* transparent cover of a clock or watch face **~lize**, **–lise** *v* **1** *vi/t* form into crystals **2** *vi/t* make (ideas, etc.) fixed in form **3** *vt* preserve (fruit) with sugar **~line** *adj* comprised of crystal or crystals
crystal ball *n* ball used by fortune-tellers to look into the future
crystal clear *adj* completely clear
crystal gazing *n* attempting to foretell the future
CSE *abbrev. for:* Certificate of Secondary Education
CS gas *n* gas causing weeping and choking, used in riot control
cub *n* **1** young lion, bear, etc. **2** also **cub scout** junior member of the Scout movement
cubbyhole *n* small room or cupboard
cube *n* **1** solid object with six equal square sides **2** result of multiplying a number by itself twice ♦ *vt* multiply a number by itself twice: *3 cubed is 27.*
cubic *adj* multiplying length by width and height
cubicle *n* small division of a large room
cubism *n* early 20th century school of art which combines different views of the same object in a single picture and makes great use of geometric forms
cubit *n* ancient measure of length based on the distance from the elbow to the tip of the middle finger
cuckold *n* man whose wife is unfaithful to him ♦ *vt* make a cuckold
cuckoo *n* bird that lays its eggs in other birds' nests and makes a noise like its name
cucumber *n* long green vegetable eaten raw
cud *n* food swallowed and brought up again by cows, etc., for further eating
cuddle *vi/t* hold lovingly in one's arms
cuddle up *phr vi* lie close and comfortably ♦ *n* cuddling; hug **–dly** *adj* suitable for cuddling
cudgel *n* club (2)
cue[1] *n* **1** signal for the next actor to speak in a play **2** example of how to behave
cue[2] *n* stick for pushing the ball in billiards
cuff[1] *n* **1** end of a sleeve **2 off the cuff** (of an answer, remark etc.) without preparation
cuff[2] *vt* hit lightly; smack **cuff** *n*
cuff link *n* button-like object used for fastening cuffs
cuirass *n* piece of armour covering the chest and back
cuisine *n* style of cooking
cul-de-sac *n* street closed at one end
culinary *adj* of or related to the kitchen or cooking
cull 1 *vt* gather (information, etc.) **2** *vi/t* take from a group and kill (a weak or unproductive animal) ♦ *n* **1** act of culling **2** animals killed this way
cullender *n* colander
culminate in *phr vt* reach the last and highest point **–nation** *n*
culottes *pl n* woman's knee-length wide trousers
culpable *adj fml* deserving blame **–bly** *adv* **–bility** *n*
culprit *n* guilty person
cult *n* **1** system of worship **2** popular fashion: *cult films*
cultivate *vt* **1 a** prepare (land) for crops **b** grow (crops) **2** improve or develop by careful attention, study, etc. **3** pay friendly attention to (people) **–vated** *adj* educated and well-mannered **–vation** *n*
culture *n* **1** art, thought, and customs of a society **2** high development in art and thought **3** raising animals and growing plants **–tural** *adj* **–tured** *adj* **1** cultivated **2** produced by humans: *cultured pearls*

culvert *n* drainage tunnel under a road, railway, etc.
cum *prep* (used to indicate the dual nature or purpose of something): *a garage-cum-workshop*
cumbersome *adj* heavy and awkward to carry
cumin *n* plant whose seeds are used as a spice
cummerbund *n* sash worn around the waist with men's formal evening wear
cumulative /ˈkyoohmyooləliv/ *adj* increasing by one addition after another **~ly** *adv*
cumulus *n* **-li** massive fleecy cloud with a flat base
cuneiform /ˈkyoohni,fawm/ *adj* **1** wedge-shaped **2** written in ancient wedge-shaped characters ◆ *n* cuneiform writing
cunnilingus *n* stimulation of the female sex organ with the lips and tongue
cunning *adj* clever in deceiving ◆ *n* quality of being cunning **~ly** *adv*
cunt *n taboo* **1** vagina **2** foolish or nasty person
cup *n* **1** container, usu. with a handle, to drink from **2** cup-shaped thing: *bra cups* **3** gold or silver container given as a prize in competitions **4** *AmE* hole in golf ◆ *vt* **-pp-** form (one's hands) into a cup shape
cupboard *n* piece of furniture with doors
cupboard love *n BrE* show of love for what can be got out of it
cup cake *n* small cake baked in a cup-shaped case
cup final *n BrE* (esp. in football) last match to decide the winning team in a competition
Cupid *n* Roman god of love represented as a winged boy (sometimes blind) with a bow and arrow
cupidity *n lit* greed
cupola *n* dome on top of a roof
cur *n* **1** mongrel **2** despicable person
curable *adj* that can be cured
curaçao *n* orange-flavoured liqueur
curate *n* clergyman who assists a parish priest
curative *n, adj* (substance) that cures (a disease)
curator *n* person in charge of a museum
curb *n* **1** controlling influence; check **2** *AmE* kerb ◆ *vt* hold back; control
curd *n* thick soft substance that separates from milk when it becomes sour
curdle *vi/t* (cause to) form into curds; (cause to) thicken
cure *vt* **1 a** bring back to health **b** make (a disease, problem, etc.) go away **2** preserve (food, skin, tobacco) by drying, etc. ◆ *n* **1** something that cures a person or disease **2** a return to health after illness
curette *n* surgical scoop **-ttage** *n* scraping or cleaning with a curette
curfew *n* time or signal for people to stay indoors
curia *n* papal court and government
curie *n* unit for measuring radioactivity
curio *n* **-os** rare or beautiful small object
curiosity *n* **1** desire to know **2** interesting rare object
curious *adj* **1** eager to learn **2** peculiar **~ly** *adv*
curl *n* **1** hanging twist of hair **2** thing this shape ◆ *vi/t* twist; wind **curl up** *phr vi/t* (cause to) lie comfortably with the limbs drawn close to the body **~y** *adj* having curls
curlew *n* large wading bird with a long curved beak
curling *n* sport in which heavy stones are slid along on ice
curmudgeon *n* mean and bad-tempered person **~ly** *adj*
currant *n* **1** dried grape **2** kind of black, red, or white berry
currency *n* **1** money in use in a country **2** state of being generally believed
current *adj* **1** of the present time **2** commonly accepted **3** (of money) used as currency ◆ *n* **1** flow of liquid, gas, or electricity **2** general tendency or course of events
current account *n BrE* bank account from which money can be taken out at

any time

curriculum *n* **-la** *or* **-lums** course of study in a school, etc.

curriculum vitae /kəˈrikyooləm veetie/ *n* a CV

curry¹ *n* hot-tasting Indian dish of meat, vegetables, etc. flavoured with **curry powder** ♦ *vt* make into curry

curry² *vt* **1** groom (a horse) with a special comb (**currycomb**) **2 curry favour** try to win approval dishonestly

curse *n* **1** words calling for evil to come to someone **2** cause of misfortune: *Foxes are a curse to farmers.* **3** word or words used in swearing ♦ *vi/t* **1** call down evil upon **2** use violent language (against) **3 be cursed with** suffer from **cursed** *adj* hateful; annoying

cursive *adj* (of handwriting) joined-up

cursor *n* mark which can move around a computer screen to point to a particular position

cursory *adj* (of work, reading, etc.) not thorough **-rily** *adv*

curt *adj* (of speech) impolitely short **~ly** *adv* **~ness** *n*

curtail *vt* shorten; reduce **~ment** *n*

curtain *n* **1** cloth hung over a window, or in front of a theatre stage **2** something that acts as a barrier or screen **curtains** *pl n sl* the end, esp. of a person's life

curtain call *n* appearance by an actor or actors to acknowledge applause at the end of a play

curtain raiser *n* **1** short play preceding the main one **2** preliminary

curtsy *vi, n* (make) a woman's act of bending the knees and lowering the head to show respect

curvaceous /kuhˈvayshəs/ *adj infml* (of a woman's figure) shapely; attractive

curvature *n* state of being curved

curve *n* line that is not straight and has no angles ♦ *vi/t* move in, or have the shape of, a curve

cushion *n* **1** bag filled with something soft, for lying or sitting on **2** anything that resembles a cushion or has a cushioning effect ♦ *vt* **1** lessen the force of **2** protect from hardship

cushy *adj* (of a job, style of life, etc.) easy

cusp *n* **1** pointed end esp. of the crescent moon or a tooth **2** period of transition from one sign of the zodiac to the next

cuspidor *n AmE* spittoon

cuss *n infml* **1** curse **2** person ♦ *vi* curse

custard *n* sweet yellow mixture of eggs and milk

custard pie *n* pie, usu. filled with an artificial creamy substance, thrown at people as a joke, esp. on stage

custodian /kuˈstohdi·ən/ *n* person in charge of a public building

custody *n* **1** right to look after someone **2** being guarded or imprisoned **–dial** *adj* (of a sentence) involving detention

custom *n* **1** established social behaviour **2** something someone does regularly **3** regular support given to a shop by its customers **customs** *pl n* **1** taxes on goods entering or leaving a country **2** place where these taxes are collected

customary *adj* established by custom; usual

custom-built *adj* made especially for one person or group of people

customer *n* person who buys things from a shop

customize *vt* make or alter to suit an individual's requirements

cut¹ *v* **cut, -tt- 1** *vt/i* use something sharp to divide, remove, shorten, make a hole, etc. **2** *vi* **a** be able to be cut **b** (of a knife, etc.) be sharp **3** *vt* make shorter or smaller: *cut a long speech* **4** *vt* make (esp. a public service) less in size, amount, etc.: *They're cutting postal deliveries* **5** *vt* stay away on purpose **6** *vt* put (a film) into final form **7** *vt* refuse to acknowledge or speak to **8** *vt* (of a line, path, etc.) cross **9** *vi* stop filming a scene **10 cut both ways** have both advantages and disadvantages **11 cut corners** do something quickly and cheaply but not perfectly **12 cut it fine** leave oneself too little time or money **13 cut no/not much ice** have no/little influence or effect **14 cut one's losses** stop doing something before one loses any more money **cut across** *phr vt* **1** go across instead of round **2** disregard (established groupings, procedures, etc.): *cut across party lines* **cut back** *phr v* **1** *vt* prune (a plant) **2** *vi/t* reduce **cut down** *phr v* **1** *vt* bring down by cutting **2** *vi/t* reduce: *cut down (on) smoking* **3** knock down or kill (someone) **4 cut down to size** reduce from too great importance to true or suitable importance **cut in** *phr vi* **1** interrupt **2** drive between moving vehicles –**cut off** *phr vt* **1** separate by cutting **2** disconnect (telephone, gas, electricity, etc.) **3** separate from others: *cut off by floods* **4** *lit* kill: *cut off in his prime* **5** disinherit **cut out** *phr v* **1** *vt* remove by cutting **2** *vt* make by cutting: *cut out a dress* **3** *vt/i* stop: *cut out smoking|engine keeps cutting out* **4 not cut out for** not suitable for ♦ *n* **1** opening made by cutting **2** piece e.g. of meat, cut off **3** reduction **4** way in which clothes, hair, etc., are shaped **5** *infml* someone's share of a profit **6 a** act of removing a part, to improve or shorten **b** part removed **7 a cut above** better than

cut-and-dried *adj* unlikely to change; fixed

cut and thrust *n* the strong methods of arguing or behaving typical of a very competitive activity

cutaway *n* **1** tailcoat **2** drawing or model of an object with part of the casing missing to show the internal structure or works

cutback *n* planned reduction

cute *adj* **1** delightfully pretty **2** (too) clever **~ly** *adv* **~ness** *n*

cut glass *n* glass with a decorative pattern of grooves cut into it

cuticle *n* skin at the base of one's nails

cutlass *n* short sword with a curved blade

cutler *n* person who makes or sells cutlery

cutlery *n* knives, forks, spoons, etc.

cutlet *n* small piece of meat

cutoff *n* **1** fixed limit; stopping point **2** device that cuts off the flow or supply of something

cut-price *adj* (of goods) cheap

cutter *n* **1** person or tool that cuts **2** small fast boat

cutthroat *adj* fierce; unprincipled: *cutthroat competition*

cutting *n* **1** piece cut from a plant to form a new one **2** *BrE* piece cut from a newspaper **3** unroofed passage cut through a hill esp. for a railway ♦ *adj* **1** sharp; piercing **2** hurtful

cutting edge *n* **1** trenchant quality in speech or writing **2** area where the most significant advances in e.g. technology are taking place

cuttlefish *n* sea creature with ten tentacles resembling a squid

cut up *adj* upset; distressed

CV, cv *n* short written account of a person's education and past employment

cwt *abbrev for:* hundredweight

-cy *suffix* (makes nouns from words usu. ending in *-t* or *-te*) **1** action or state of: *piracy/bankruptcy* **2** rank or class of: *magistracy*

cyanide /ˈsie·ənied/ *n* strong poison

cybernetics *n* science of how information is dealt with by machines and the brain

cyclamate *n* artificial sweetener

cyclamen *n* (pot) plant with showy turned-back petals

cycle¹ *n* (time needed for) a set of events in regularly repeated order **cyclical** *adj* happening in cycles

cycle² *v, n* bicycle **cyclist** *n*

cyclone *n* very violent wind moving rapidly in a circle

cyclostyle *vt, n* (reproduce with) a duplicating machine that uses a special stencil

cyclotron *n* apparatus which separates subatomic particles out from nuclei by whirling them around in a strong magnetic field

cygnet *n* young swan

cylinder *n* **1** object or container with a circular base and straight sides **2** tube

for a piston in an engine
cymbal *n* one of a pair of metal plates struck together to make a noise in music
cynic *n* person who sees little good in anything and shows it by making unkind remarks **~al** *adj* **~ally** *adv* **~ism** *n*
cynosure *n lit* centre of attraction
cypress *n* evergreen tree with dark green leaves and hard wood
Cyrillic alphabet *n* alphabet used for Russian, Bulgarian and other Slavonic languages
cyst *n* hollow growth in the body, containing liquid
cystitis *n* disease of the bladder
cytology *n* the biology of cells
czar *n* tsar
Czech *n, adj* (inhabitant) of Czechoslovakia

D

D, d the 4th letter of the English alphabet
D *abbrev. for:* **1** died **2** diameter **3** penny (2)
-d *suffix* -ed
DA *n* district attorney
dab¹ *vi/t* **-bb-** touch or cover lightly ♦ *n* small quantity of paint, etc.
dab² *n* small flatfish
dabble *v* **1** *vi* work at something not professionally: *dabble in politics* **2** *vt* move (one's feet, etc.) playfully about in water
dab hand *n BrE infml* person who is clever or good at something
dachshund /ˈdaksənd/ *n* small dog with short legs and a long body
dad *n infml* father
daddy *n infml* (child's word for) father
daddy longlegs *n* insect with very long thin legs
dado /ˈdaydoh/ *n* lower part of a wall, if separately lined or painted
daemon *n* **1** demigod in Greek mythology **2** guardian spirit
daffodil *n* bell-shaped yellow spring flower
daft *adj BrE* silly **~ly** *adv* **~ness** *n*
dagga *n SAfrE* hemp smoked as a drug
dagger *n* **1** short knife used as a weapon **2 look daggers at** look angrily at
dago *n* **-gos** *or* **-goes** *derog* Spanish or Portuguese person
daguerrotype *n* early type of photograph
dahlia *n* big bright garden flower
Dáil *n* lower house of the Irish parliament
daily *adj, adv* every day ♦ *n* **1** newspaper sold every day but Sunday **2** also **daily help** *infml esp. BrE* someone, esp. a woman, who comes to clean a house daily
dainty *adj* small, pretty, and delicate **-tily** *adv* **-tiness** *n*
daiquiri *n* cocktail made of rum, lime juice and sugar
dairy *n* place where milk, butter, cheese, etc., are produced or sold
dairy cattle *pl n* cows kept for milk, not meat
dais *n* raised floor at one end of a hall
daisy *n* common small white flower that grows in grass
Dalai Lama *n* spiritual head of Tibetan Buddhism
dale *n* valley
dalliance *n lit* flirtation
dally *vi* waste time **dally with** *phr vt* play with (an idea)
dalmatian *n* medium-sized dog which is white with black or brown spots
dam¹ *n* wall built to keep back water ♦ *vt* **-mm-** make a dam across **dam up** *phr vt* control (a feeling, esp. of anger) in an unhealthy way
dam² *n* (used esp. in relation to domestic animals) mother
damage *n* harm; loss ♦ *vt* cause damage to **damages** *pl n* money paid for

damage done

damask *n* lustrous fabric

dame *n* **1** *AmE sl* woman **2** (*cap.*) British rank of honour for a woman

damn *vt* **1** (of God) punish **2** declare to be bad **3** ruin: *damning evidence* **4 Well, I'll be damned!** *infml* I'm very surprised ♦ *n* even the smallest bit: *don't care a damn* ♦ *interj* (used in curses) **damn**, also **~ ed** *adj, adv* (used for giving force to an expression): *run damned fast|He's a damn fool.* **~able** *adj* very bad **~ation** *n* **1** act of damning **2 in damnation** (used for giving force to an expression of anger): *What in damnation do you mean?* **~edest** *n* **do one's damnedest** do everything possible **~ing** *adj* leading to condemnation or ruin

damp *adj* rather wet ♦ *n* slight wetness ♦ also **dampen** *vt* **1** wet slightly **2** reduce (eagerness, enthusiasm, etc.) **damp down** *phr vt* make (a fire) burn more slowly **~ness** *n*

damp course *n* material built into a wall to stop wetness from coming up

damper *n* **1** metal plate controlling the flow of air to a fire **2** influence reducing eagerness

damp-proof *vt* treat (a wall) to prevent damp **~ing** *n*

damp squib *n* something which is intended to be exciting, effective, etc., but which fails and disappoints

damsel *n lit* young unmarried woman of noble birth; young girl

damson *n* kind of small plum

dance *n* **1** (music for) a set of movements performed to music **2** party with dances **3** art of dancing ♦ *vi/t* do a dance **dancer** *n*

D and C *n* dilatation and curettage; scraping clean of the womb

dandelion *n* common bright yellow flower

dander *n* **get one's/someone's dander up** become or make angry

dandle *vt* move (a small child) up and down on one's knee or in one's arms

dandruff *n* bits of dead skin in the hair

dandy *n* man who is almost too well dressed **-dify** *vt*

Dane *n* native or citizen of Denmark

danger *n* **1** possibility of harm **2** cause of danger **~ous** *adj* not safe **~ously** *adv*

danger money *n* additional pay for dangerous work

dangle *vi/t* **1** hang loosely **2 keep someone dangling** keep someone waiting and not knowing what the result will be

Danish *adj* of Denmark or the Danes ♦ *n* also **Danish pastry** puff pastry case with a sweet filling

dank *adj* unpleasantly wet and cold

dapper *adj* neatly dressed

dappled *adj* having cloudy spots of colour or shadow

dare *v* **1** *vi* be brave enough (to) **2** *vt* challenge to do something ♦ *n* challenge: *She jumped for a dare.*

daredevil *n* foolishly adventurous person

daren't *short for*: dare not

daresay *v* **I daresay** *esp. BrE* I suppose (that); perhaps

daring *n* adventurous bravery ♦ *adj* **1** brave **2** shocking **~ly** *adv*

dark *adj* **1** without (much) light **2** tending towards black: *dark green* **3** secret; hidden: *keep it dark* **4** evil; sad ♦ *n* **1** absence of light **2 after/before dark** after/before night **3 in the dark** not knowing something **~en** *vi/t* make or become darker **~ly** *adv* **~ness** *n*

Dark Ages *pl n* period in Europe between about AD 476 to AD 1000

dark horse *n* unknown competitor who may win

dark lantern *n* lantern with sliding panel to hide or dim its light

darkroom *n* room where photographs are processed

darky *n taboo* black person

darling *adj, n* dearly loved (person)

darn[1] *vi/t* mend (holes in cloth) ♦ *n* darned hole

darn[2] *n, adj, adv, interj* damn

dart *n* **1** pointed object like a small arrow **2** quick movement ♦ *vi/t* move

or send suddenly
dartboard *n* circular board divided into different scoring areas at which darts are thrown
darts *pl n* game in which darts are thrown at a dartboard
Darwinian *adj* relating to (the theory of evolution of) Charles Darwin
dash *v* **1** *vi* run quickly **2** *vi/t* strike violently: *The waves dashed the boat against the rocks.* **3** *vt* destroy (hopes, etc.) ♦ *n* **1** sudden quick run or short race **2** small amount added: *a dash of pepper* **3** the mark (-) **4** combination of bravery and style **~ing** *adj* spirited and stylish
dashboard *n* instrument board in a car
dastard *n* coward and bully **~ly** *adj*
data *n* facts; information, esp. as stored in a computer's **data bank** for **data processing**
database *n* computer's collection of data
date¹ *n* **1** day, month, or year of an event **2** arrangement to meet **3** person of the opposite sex whom one arranges to meet socially **4 out of date: a** old-fashioned **b** no longer valid **5 to date** up till now **6 up to date** modern ♦ *v* **1** *vt* guess the date of **2** *vt* write the date on **3** *vi* become old-fashioned **4** *vi/t* make a social date with **date from** also **date back to** *phr vt* have lasted since **~d** *adj* old-fashioned
date² *n* small tropical fruit with a long stone
dative *n* grammatical case principally indicating that a word is the indirect object of a verb
daub *v* **1** *vi/t* pain crudely **2** *vt* cover with something sticky ♦ *n* crude painting
daughter *n* someone's female child
daughter-in-law *n* **daughters-in-law** son's wife
daunt *vt* discourage **~less** *adj* not discouraged
dauphin /ˈdohfanh/ *n* eldest son of a king of France
davit *n* one of a pair of curved poles with tackle used for raising and lowering esp. boats over a ship's side
Davy Jones's locker *n infml* the bottom of the sea, considered as the grave of drowned seamen
Davy lamp *n* early miner's safety lamp
dawdle *vi* waste time; be slow
dawn *n* **1** first light of morning **2** first appearance: *the dawn of civilization* ♦ *vi* begin to grow light **dawn on** *phr vt* become known to
day *n* **1** period of 24 hours **2** time between sunrise and sunset **3** hours that one works **4** period; time: *the present day* **5** period of success **6 call it a day** finish (working for the day) **7 day after day** also **day in, day out** continuously **8 make someone's day** make someone very happy **9 one's days** one's life
dayboy *n* boy who attends a boarding school but lives at home
daybreak *n* dawn
daycare *n BrE* daytime supervision and care for e.g. children or old people
daydream *vi, n* (have) pleasant dream-like thoughts
daygirl *n* girl who attends a boarding school but lives at home
daylight *n* **1** light **2** dawn **3 beat/knock/scare the (living) daylights out of** hit/frighten (someone) very severely
daylight saving *n* setting clocks one hour ahead of standard time
day release course *n BrE* educational course attended by workers during the usual working day
day return *n BrE* bus or train ticket that one can use to go and come back on the same day
day-to-day *adj* **1** happening each day **2** planning for one day at a time
daze *vt* make unable to think clearly ♦ *n* dazed condition
dazzle *vt* **1** make unable to see because of too strong light **2** cause wonder to: *dazzled by success*
dB *abbrev. for:* decibel
DBE *abbrev. for:* Dame Commander of the (Order of the) British Empire
DC *abbrev. for:* **1** Detective Constable **2**

direct current **3** District of Columbia **4** District Council

D day *n* day for launching an operation, esp. the Allied invasion of Europe in 1944

DDT *n* insecticide

de- *prefix* **1** do the opposite of: *decentralize* **2** remove (from): *dethrone; debug* **3** reduce: *devalue*

deacon *n* Christian church officer below a priest

deaconess *n* female deacon

dead *adj* **1** no longer alive **2** no longer used or usable **3** complete: *dead silence* **4** without activity **5** numb **6** (of sound or colour) dull ♦ *adv* **1** completely: *stop dead* **2** directly: *dead ahead* ♦ *n* the least active period of **~en** *vt* cause to lose (strength, feeling, brightness)

dead-and-alive *adj infml* dull and lifeless

deadbeat *n* lazy aimless person

dead centre *n* exact centre

dead end *n* end (of a street) with no way out: *We've reached a dead end in our talks.*

dead heat *n* race in which two or more competitors finish together

deadline *n* fixed date for finishing something

deadlock *n* disagreement that cannot be settled

deadly *adj* **1** likely to cause death **2** total: *deadly enemies* **3** *infml* very dull ♦ *adv* **1** like death: *deadly pale* **2** very: *deadly dull*

deadly nightshade *n* bush with poisonous black berries

dead man's handle *n* device which automatically brings a train to a halt if the pressure on it is released

deadpan *adj, adv* with no show of feeling, esp. when telling jokes

dead reckoning *n* calculation of a ship's or aircraft's position from its known movements without the use of navigational aids

dead ringer *n* someone who looks exactly like someone else

dead set *adj* absolutely determined ♦ *n* determined effort (to get something)

deadweight *n* whole weight of something that does not move

dead wood *n* useless people or things

deaf *adj* **1** unable to hear **2 deaf to** unwilling to listen to **~en** *vt* (of loud noises) make unable to hear: *The noise was deafening.* **~ness** *n*

deaf-aid *n BrE* hearing aid

deaf-mute *n, adj* (person) who is deaf and cannot speak

deal[1] *vi/t* **dealt** /delt/ **1** give out (esp. playing cards) as a share **2** strike: *deal someone a blow* **deal in** *phr vt* trade in; sell **deal with** *phr vt* **1** trade with **2** take action about **3** be about ♦ *n* **1** business arrangement **2** one's turn to deal cards **3 a good/great deal** a fairly/very large amount **~er** *n* **1** person who deals cards **2** trader **~ing** *n* methods of business or personal relations **~ings** *pl n* personal or business relations

deal[2] *n* pine timber

dean *n* **1** Christian priest in charge of a cathedral **2** important university official **~ery** *n* office or residence of a dean

dear *adj* **1** loved; precious **2** (at the beginning of letters): *Dear Sir* **3** expensive ♦ **1** *n* loved person **2 a** (used when speaking to someone you love) **b** (used informally as a friendly form of address, esp. by or to a woman) **3** lovable, helpful, etc. person ♦ *interj* (expressing surprise, sorrow, etc.): *Oh dear!* **~ly** *adv* **1** with much feeling **2** at terrible cost

dearth *n fml* lack

death *n* **1 a** end of life **b** extinction; disappearance **2** state of being dead **3** cause of death: *Drinking will be the death of him.* **4 at death's door** in danger of dying; about to die **5 like death warmed up** *infml* very ill or tired **6 put to death** kill, esp. officially **7 to death** beyond proper limits: *sick/bored/worried to death* **~less** *adj* unforgettable **~ly** *adj, adv* like death

death duty *n BrE* tax paid on property after death

death mask *n* cast taken from a dead person's face
death row *n esp. AmE* part of prison reserved for prisoners awaiting execution
death's head *n* human skull as a symbol of death
death trap *n* very dangerous thing or place
deathwatch beetle *n* beetle that bores into wood
débâcle /diˈbahkəl/ *n* sudden complete failure
debar from *phr vt* **-rr-** officially prevent from
debase *vt* make lower in value **~ment** *n*
debate *n* (process of) discussion ♦ *vi/t* **1** hold a debate about **2** think about; wonder **debatable** *adj* doubtful; questionable
debauch *vt* lead away from moral conduct, esp. in relation to sex and alcohol ♦ *n* orgy **~ed** *adj* **~ee** *n* debauched person **~ery** *n*
debenture *n BrE* loan secured on the assets of a company
debilitate *vt* make weak **–ity** *n fml* weakness
debit *n* record of money owed ♦ *vt* charge against an account
debonair *adj* cheerful and fashionably dressed
debouch /diˈbowch/ *vi* issue out of (a narrow into a broader place)
debrief *vt* find out information from (someone on one's own side) by thorough questioning after an action
debris /ˈdebri/ *n* broken remains; ruins
debt *n* something owed; state of owing **~or** *n* person who owes money
debug *vt infml* **1** remove the surveillance bugs from a room or building **2** search for and remove the bugs in (a computer program)
debunk *vt* point out the truth about a wrong idea
debut *n* first public appearance **~ante** *n* young woman making her first formal entrance to society
deca-, **dec-** *prefix* ten
decade *n* period of 10 years
decadent *adj* falling to a lower level of morals **–dence** *n*
decaffeinate *vt* remove the caffeine from (e.g. coffee)
decal *n* transfer (3)
Decalogue *n* the Ten Commandments
decamp *vi* go away quickly and esp. secretly
decanal *adj* of a dean
decant *vt* pour (liquid) into another container **~er** *n* glass container for liquid, esp. wine
decapitate *vt* behead
decathlon *n* athletic contest in which each competitor competes in 10 separate events
decay *vi* **1** go bad: *decayed teeth* **2** lose health, power, etc. ♦ *n* process of decaying
deceased *adj fml* dead ♦ *n fml* the dead person
deceit *n* dishonesty **~ful** *adj* dishonest **~fully** *adv*
deceive *vt* cause to believe something false **deceiver** *n*
decelerate *vi/t* (cause to) go slower **–ration** *n*
December *n* the 12th and last month of the year
decennial *adj* **1** lasting 10 years **2** occurring every 10 years ♦ *n* 10th anniversary
decent *adj* **1** socially acceptable; proper **2** good enough: *a decent meal* **3** kind **decency** *n* **1** propriety **2** kindness **~ly** *adv*
decentralize, **-ise** *vi/t* move (a business, etc.) from a central office or place to several smaller ones **–ization**, **–isation** *n*
deception *n* **1** deceiving **2** trick **–tive** *adj* misleading **–tively** *adv*
deci- *prefix* one tenth
decibel *n* unit of loudness
decide *v* **1** *vi/t* make a choice or judgment: *She decided to go.* **2** *vt* make (someone) decide **3** *vi/t* end uncertainty **decide on** *phr vt* decide in

favour of **decided** *adj* **1** easily seen: *decided improvement* **2** sure of oneself **decidedly** *adv* certainly

deciduous *adj* (of trees) losing their leaves in autumn

decimal *adj* based on the number 10 ♦ *n* fraction such as .5 or .6 **~ize**, **-ise** *vi/t* change to a decimal system of money, etc.

decimate *vt* destroy a large part of

decipher *vt* read (something difficult, esp. a code)

decision *n* **1** deciding; choice: *reach a decision* **2** firmness of judgment

decisive *adj* **1** firm in judgment **2** leading to a clear result **~ly** *adv* **~ness** *n*

deck *n* **1** floor of a ship or bus **2** *AmE* pack of playing cards **3** upper surface, including playing mechanism, of a gramophone or tape recorder **4** *infml* the ground ♦ *vt* decorate

deckchair *n* folding chair with a cloth seat

declaim *vt* say loudly, like an actor **declamation** *n* **declamatory** *adj*

declaration *n* **1** declaring **2** official statement

declare *vt* **1** make known officially: *declare war* **2** state clearly **3** tell customs officials about (taxable goods) **4** announce (e.g. a trump suit) in a card game **~r** *n*

declassify *vt* declare (esp. political and military information) no longer secret

declination *n* angle between the direction in which a compass needle points and true north

decline *v* **1** *vi* become worse or less **2** *vi/t* refuse (an invitation, etc.) politely ♦ *n* process or period of decrease or deterioration: *Interest in the arts is on the decline.*

declivity *n fml* downward slope

declutch *vi* step on the clutch of a car before changing gear

decoct *vt* extract the essence of by boiling **~ion** *n*

decode *vt* read (something written in code)

decoke *vt* remove sooty waste from (an internal-combustion engine)

décolleté *adj* (wearing a dress which is) low-cut

decolonize, **-ise** *vt* give political independence to **-nization** *n*

decommission *vt* **1** dismantle and make safe (e.g. a nuclear power station) at the end of its useful life **2** take (a warship) out of active service

decompose *vi* go bad; decay **-position** *n*

decompress *vt* reduce air pressure on **~ion** *n*

decongestant *n, adj* (something e.g. a drug) that relieves congestion

decontaminate *vt* remove dangerous substances from **-nation** *n*

décor *n* decoration and furnishings of a place

decorate *v* **1** *vt* add something beautiful to **2** *vi/t* paint, put paper, etc., on rooms **3** *vt* give a mark of honour, e.g. a medal, to **-rator** *n* person who paints houses **-rative** *adj* beautiful; attractive **-ratively** *adv* **-ration** *n* **1** decorating **2** something that decorates **3** mark of honour; medal

decorous *adj* (of appearance or behaviour) correct **~ly** *adv*

decorum *n* correct behaviour

decoy *n, vt* (something used) to lure a person or bird into a trap

decrease *vi/t* (cause to) become less ♦ *n* **1** process of decreasing **2** amount by which something decreases

decree *n* official command or decision ♦ *vt* order officially

decree absolute *n* final decree of divorce

decree nisi /di,kree 'neezi, 'niesie/ *n* provisional decree of divorce

decrement *n fml* diminution

decrepit *adj* weak from old age

decriminalize, **-ise** *vt* make no longer a crime

decry *vt fml* speak disapprovingly of

dedicate *vt* **1** give to a serious purpose: *dedicate her life to medical research* **2** declare (a book, etc.) to be in honour of someone, by printing their name at the front **–cation** *n* **1** act of dedicating **2** words used in dedicating a book **–cated** *adj* **1** devoted to a cause, ideal or purpose **2** (of computers) given over to a specific purpose

deduce *vt* reach (a piece of knowledge) by reasoning

deduct *vt* take away (part) from a total **~ible** *adj*

deduction *n* **1** example of deducing; knowledge deduced **2** process of deducting; something deducted

deed *n* **1** *lit* something done; action **2** *law* signed agreement

deed poll *n* deed signed when changing one's name

deem *vt* consider; judge

deep *adj* **1** going far down from the top, or in from the outside **2** (of colour) dark **3** (of sound) low **4** strong; extreme: *deep sleep|deep distrust* **5** difficult to understand **6 a** wise **b** mysterious **7 go off the deep end** *sl* lose one's temper **8 in/into deep water** *infml* in/into serious trouble **9 (thrown) in at the deep end** (of a beginner) being expected to tackle difficult tasks from the outset ♦ *adv* far down; far in **~en** *vi/t* make or become deeper **~ly** *adv* **~ness** *n*

deep freeze *vt* freeze food quickly in order to preserve it ♦ *n* freezer

deep fry *vt* fry completely under the surface of oil or fat

deep-rooted *adj* firmly established

deep-seated *adj* **1** existing below the surface **2** deep-rooted

deer *n* **deer** large fast animal of which the males have antlers

deerstalker *n* cap with peaks at the front and rear and earflaps which can be folded down

deface *vt* spoil the surface of **~ment** *n*

de facto /di 'faktoh, day/ *adj, adv fml* in actual fact, though not by law

defame *vt fml* attack the good reputation of **defamation** *n* **defamatory** *adj*

default *n* **1** failure to fulfil a contract, pay a debt, etc. **2 by default** through the absence of some other person **default** *vi* **~er** *n*

defeat *vt* **1** win a victory over **2** cause to fail ♦ *n* (example or act of) defeating or being defeated **~ism** *n* practice of thinking or behaving in expectation of defeat **~ist** *n*

defecate *vi fml* pass waste matter from the bowels

defect[1] *n* imperfection; fault **~ive** *adj*

defect[2] *vi* desert one's political party, country, etc. **~or** *n* **~ion** *n*

defence, *AmE* **defense** *n* **1** act or process of defending **2** something used in defending **3** *law* **a** arguments used in defending someone in court **b** lawyers who defend someone **~less** *adj* unable to defend oneself

defend *vt* **1** keep safe; protect **2** act as a lawyer for (someone charged with a crime) **3** argue in favour of

defendant *n* person against whom a legal charge or claim is brought

defensible *adj* that can be defended

defensive *adj* **1** used in defence **2** (of someone) who always seems to be expecting attack ♦ *n* **on the defensive** prepared for attack **~ly** *adv* **~ness** *n*

defer *vt* **-rr-** postpone **defer to** *phr vt* accept the decision of **~ment** *n*

deference *n* respect for another's wishes **–ential** *adj* showing deference **–entially** *adv*

defiance *n* open disobedience; resistance **–ant** *adj* **–antly** *adv*

deficiency *n* lack **–cient** *adj*

deficit *n* amount by which something, esp. money, is too little

defile[1] *vt* make dirty

defile[2] *n* narrow pass; gorge

define *vt* **1** give the meaning of; explain exactly **2** set, mark or show the limits of: *a clearly-defined shape*

definite *adj* clear; without uncertainty **~ly** *adv* **1** in a clear way **2** certainly

definite article *n* (in English) the word 'the'

definition *n* **1** (statement) defining something **2** clearness of shape: *The photograph lacks definition.*

definitive *adj* that cannot be questioned;

not needing change

deflate *v* **1** *vt* let air or gas out of (a tyre, etc.) **2** *vt* undermine a person's self-confidence or self-importance **3** *vi/t* reduce the supply of money in a country **deflation** *n* **deflationary** *adj*

deflect *vi/t* turn aside from a straight course: *to deflect someone from their purpose* **~ion** *n*

deflower *vt lit* deprive (a woman) of virginity

defoliant *n* chemical which strips the leaves from plants **–iate** *vt*

deforest *vt* clear of trees

deform *vt* spoil the shape of **~ity** *n* imperfection of the body

defraud *vt* deceive so as to get something: *They defrauded him of £50.*

defray *vt fml* pay for

defrock *vt* unfrock

defrost *vt* remove ice from; unfreeze

deft *adj* effortlessly skilful **~ly** *adv*

defunct *adj* dead

defuse *vt* **1** remove the fuse from (a bomb, etc.) **2** reduce the potential for harm or violence in

defy *vt* **1** refuse to obey **2** challenge to do something impossible **3** remain unreachable by all efforts at or from: *It defies description.*

degenerate *adj* having become worse than before; corrupt ♦ *n* degenerate person ♦ *vi* become worse **–rative** *adj* **–ration** *n*

degrade *v* **1** *vt* bring shame to **2** *vi/t* change to a simpler chemical form **degradation** *n*

degree *n* **1** unit of measurement of angles, or of temperature **2** stage; level: *getting better by degrees* **3** title given to a university student

dehisce *vi* burst open releasing seeds **~nt** *adj*

dehumanize, **-ise** *vt* **1** deprive of human qualities; brutalize **2** make artificial or mechanical

dehydrate **1** *vt* remove water from **2** *vi* lose fluid from (the body) **–ation** *n*

de-ice *vt* remove ice from or prevent ice forming on (e.g. aircraft wings) **~r** *n*

deify /ˈdee·ifie, ˈday-/ *vt* make a god of

deign *vt derog* condescend

deism *n* belief in a God whose existence is deducible by reason rather than revealed by scripture and who does not intervene in the workings of the universe **deist** *n* **deistic** *adj*

deity /ˈdee·əti, ˈday-/ *n* god or goddess

déjà vu *n* sense that one is remembering something though experiencing it for the first time

dejected *adj* low in spirits; sad **~ly** *adv* **–tion** *n*

de jure /ˌdi ˈjooəri/ *adj, adv* by legal right

dekko *n BrE infml* **have/take a dekko** have/take a look

delay *v* **1** *vt* make later **2** *vi* act slowly ♦ *n* **1** delaying **2** example or time of being delayed

delectable *adj* delightful; delicious **–tation** *n lit* enjoyment

delegate *n* person chosen to act for others ♦ *v* **1** *vi/t* give (power, etc.) to someone else **2** *vt* appoint (someone) as a delegate **–gation** *n* **1** act of delegating **2** group of delegates

delete *vt* take out (written words) **deletion** *n*

deleterious /ˌdeliˈtiəri·əs/ *adj fml* harmful

deli *n infml* delicatessen

deliberate *adj* **1** done on purpose **2** (of speech, movement, etc.) slow; unhurried ♦ *vi/t* consider carefully **~ly** *adv* **–ration** *n fml* **1** (process of) deliberating **2** being slow and unhurried

delicacy *n* **1** being delicate **2** something good to eat

delicate *adj* **1** easily damaged, hurt, or made ill **2** soft and fine **3** needing careful treatment: *a delicate situation* **4** pleasing but not easy to recognize: *a delicate flavour* **5** sensitive: *delicate instruments* **~ly** *adv*

delicatessen *n* shop that sells foreign foods ready cooked

delicious *adj* (esp. of taste or smell) delightful **~ly** *adv*

delight *n* **1** great pleasure; joy **2** cause

of great pleasure ♦ *v* **1** *vt* give delight to **2** *vi* find delight: *He delights in scandal.* **~ful** *adj* very pleasing **~fully** *adv*

delimit *vt* mark or prescribe the boundaries of

delineate *vt* show by drawing

delinquent *n, adj* (person) who breaks a law **–quency** *n*

deliquesce /ˌdeliˈkwes/ *vi* melt away **–quescence** *n* **–quescent** *adj*

delirious *adj* excited and dreamy, esp. because of illness **~ly** *adv* **–ium** *n* excited dreamy state

delirum tremens *n* violent delirum with tremors induced by chronic alcoholism

deliver *vt* **1** take (goods, letters, etc.) to people's houses **2** help in the birth of **3** give (a blow, kick, etc.) **4** say (a speech, etc.) **5** *fml* rescue **~er** *n fml* rescuer **~ance** *n fml* saving; rescue **~y** *n* **1** delivering things; things delivered **2** birth of a child **3** style of public speaking

dell *n* small hollow or valley

delouse *vt* remove lice from (people, clothing, etc.)

delphinium *n* garden plant with tall spikes of usu. blue flowers

delta *n* land in the shape of a triangle at the mouth of a river

delude *vt* mislead; deceive

deluge *n* heavy rain; flood **deluge** *vt*

delusion *n* **1** deluding **2** false belief

de luxe *adj* of very high quality

delve *vi* **1** search deeply **2** dig (around)

Dem *abbrev. for:* Democrat

demagnetize, **-ise** *vt* deprive of magnetic properties

demagogue *n* leader who gains power by exciting the crowds **–goguery**, **–gogy** *n* **–gic**, **–gical** *adj*

demand *n* **1** demanding; claim **2** desire for things that people can pay for: *a great demand for teachers* ♦ *vt* **1** ask for firmly; claim **2** need: *problems demanding your attention* **~ing** *adj* needing a lot of attention or effort

demarcation *n* limits; separation

demarcation dispute *n* disagreement between trade unions about who is to do a job

démarche *n* (esp. diplomatic) move or manoeuvre

demean *vt fml* bring shame to; degrade

demeanour, *AmE* **-nor** *n fml* behaviour; outward manner

demented *adj* mad **~ly** *adv*

demerara sugar *n* unrefined brown sugar

demerit *n fml* fault

demesne *n* **1** lands attached to a manor house **2** (law) legal possession of land

demi- *prefix* half

demigod *n* lesser god; being half divine, half mortal

demijohn *n* large narrow-necked bottle

demilitarize, **–ise** *vt* remove armed forces from (an area) **–rization** *n*

demimonde *n* (mistresses and courtesans on) the shadier fringes of esp. 19th century society

demise *n* death

demist *vt* remove steam from (car windows) **~er** *n*

demo *n infml* **demos** demonstration (2)

demob *vt BrE infml* demobilze ♦ *n* demobilization

demobilize, **–ise** *vi/t* send home the members of (an armed force), usu. at the end of a war **–ization** *n*

democracy *n* **1** government by elected representatives of the people **2** country governed in this way **3** social equality

democrat *n* **1** person who believes in democracy **2** (*cap.*) member of the Democratic Party in the US, or the Social and Liberal Democratic Party in the UK **~ic** *adj* **1** of or favouring democracy **2** (*cap.*) of a US political party (the **Democratic Party**) **~ically** *adv*

démodé *adj* out-of-date

demography *n* study of the numbers and movement of human population **–phic** *adj* **–pher** *n* person who studies demography

demolish *vt* **1** pull down (buildings, etc.); destroy **2** *infml* eat up hungrily **–molition** *n*

demon *n* **1** evil spirit **2** very active

skilful person **~ic** *adj* of, by or like a demon **~ically** *adv*
demoniac, -acal *adj* **1** (as if) possessed by a devil; frantic, frenzied **2** devilish **~ally** *adv*
demonstrable *adj* easily proved **-bly** *adv*
demonstrate *v* **1** *vt* show clearly **2** *vi* take part in a public demonstration **-strator** *n* **-stration** *n* **1** showing something **2** public show of opinion, by marching, etc.
demonstrative *adj* showing feelings openly **~ly** *adv*
demoralize, -ise *vt* destroy the courage and confidence of **-ization** *n*
demote *vt* reduce in rank **demotion** *n*
demotic *adj* of the common people
demur *vi* **-rr-** *fml* show opposition to a plan ♦ *n* **1** hesitation **2** objection
demure *adj* quiet and modest **~ly** *adv*
den *n* **1** home of a wild animal **2** secret or private place **3** small, quiet room in a house
denationalize, -ise *vt* remove from state ownership **-ization** *n*
denature *vt* **1** change the nature of **2** make (alcohol) unfit for human consumption **3** make (nuclear material) unusable in nuclear weapons
denial *n* **1** denying **2** statement that something is false
denier *n* unit of the fineness of nylon, rayon or silk
denigrate *vt* declare to be worthless **-ation** *n*
denim *n* strong cotton cloth **denims** *pl n* jeans
denizen *n lit* inhabitant
denominate *vt lit* designate
denomination *n* **1** religious group **2** unit of value
denominator *n* figure below the line in a fraction
denote *vt* be the name or sign of; mean
denouement /day'noohmonh/ *n* end of a story, when everything is explained
denounce *vt* speak or write publicly against **~ment** *n*
dense *adj* **1** closely packed **2** hard to see through **3** stupid **~ly** *adv* **density** *n*
dent *n* small hollow in a surface, made by a blow ♦ *vt* make a dent
dental *adj* of the teeth
dental floss *n* waxed thread for cleaning between teeth
dentifrice *n* substance for cleaning the teeth
dentine *n* hard bonelike substance of which teeth are mainly formed
dentist *n* person trained to treat the teeth **~ry** *n*
dentures *pl n* false teeth
denude *vt fml* remove the covering from: *a hill denuded of trees*
denunciation *n* act or example of denouncing
deny *vt* **1** declare untrue **2** refuse to allow
deodorant *n* chemical that hides bad smells **-rize, -rise** *vt*
deontology *n* science of ethics **-logical** *adj* **-logist** *n*
Deo volente *interj* God willing
depart *vi fml* **1** leave; go away **2 depart this life** *lit* to die **depart from** *phr vt* turn or move away from **~ed** *adj* **1** bygone **2** dead
department *n* **1** division of a government, business, college, etc. **2** *infml* activity or subject for which a person is responsible **~al** *adj*
department store *n* large shop divided into departments
departure *n* **1** going away **2** change from a usual course of action
depend *v* vary according to; be decided by **depend on/upon** *phr vt* **1** trust **2** be supported by **3** vary according to
dependable *adj* that can be trusted **-bly** *adv*
dependant, -dent *n* person supported by another
dependence *n* **1** being dependent **2** trust **3** need to have certain drugs regularly
dependent *adj* that depends on
depict *vt* show in a picture, or in words **~ion** *n*

depilatory /diˈpilət(ə)ri/ *n, adj* (substance) that gets rid of unwanted hair
deplete *vt* lessen (supplies, stocks, etc.) greatly **depletion** *n*
deplore *vt* be very sorry about (and consider wrong) **-rable** *adj* very bad **-rably** *adv*
deploy *vt* arrange for effective action **~ment** *n*
depopulate *vt* greatly reduce the population of **-lation** *n*
deport *vt* send (an unwanted foreigner) out of the country **~ation** *n*
deportment *n* way a person stands and walks
depose *vt* remove (a ruler) from power
deposit *vt* **1** put down **2** (of a river, etc.) leave (soil, etc.) lying **3** put in e.g. a bank, for safety ♦ *n* **1** material deposited by a natural process **2** first part of a payment for something, to show that an agreement will be kept **~or** *n* person who deposits money
deposit account *n BrE* bank account which earns interest but from which money cannot be taken out at once
depot *n* **1** storehouse for goods **2** bus garage **3** *AmE* railway station
depraved *adj* wicked **depravity** *n*
deprecate /ˈdeprikayt/ *vt* express (mild) disapproval of **-catory** *adj* **1** apologetic **2** disapproving
depreciate *vi* (esp. of money) fall in value **-ation** *n*
depredations *pl n fml* acts of destruction
depress *vt* **1** sadden **2** make less active **3** press down **~ed** *adj* **1** sad **2** suffering from low levels of business activity **~ing** *adj*
depression *n* **1** sad feeling **2** period of reduced business activity **3** hollow in a surface **4** area of low air pressure
deprive *vt* prevent from having something **~d** *adj* without food, money or decent living conditions **deprivation** *n*
depth *n* **1** (degree of) being deep **2 in depth** done thoroughly **3 out of one's depth: a** in water deeper than one's height **b** beyond one's understanding
depths *pl n* deepest or most central part of: *the depths of winter/despair*
depth charge *n* underwater explosive device used against submarines
deputation *n* group sent to act on behalf of others
deputy *n* person given power to act for another **-tize, -tise** *v* **1** *vi* act as a deputy **2** *vt AmE* appoint as a (sheriff's) deputy
derail *vt* cause (a train) to run off the line **~ment** *n*
deranged *adj* unbalanced in the mind **-ment** *n*
derby *n* **1** (*usu. cap.*) premier English flat race held annually at Epsom **2** *BrE* contest between local rivals **3** *AmE* race open to anyone **4** *AmE* bowler hat
deregulate *vt* remove from control by law **-lation** *n*
derelict *adj* fallen into ruin ♦ *n* person, esp. an alcoholic, who has no home and no legal means of support **~ion** *n* **1** state of being derelict **2** failure to do one's duty
deride *vt* laugh unkindly at
de rigueur *adj* required by custom, fashion or etiquette
derision *n* unkind laughter **-sive** *adj* mocking **-sively** *adv* **-sory** *adj* deserving derision; ridiculously small
derivative *adj derog* not original or new
derive *v* **1** *vt* obtain from somewhere: *derive pleasure from one's work* **2** *vi* have something as an origin: *words that derive from Latin* **derivation** *n*
dermatitis *n* skin disease with redness and swelling
dermatology *n* study of (diseases of) the skin **-logist** *n* doctor who specializes in treating skin complaints **-logical** *adj*
dermis *n* (sensitive inner layer of) the skin
derogatory *adj fml* (of words) showing disapproval
derrick *n* **1** large mechanical crane **2** tower over an oil well
derring-do *n* daring and heroism
derringer *n* small pistol

derv *n* diesel fuel
dervish *n* member of ascetic Muslim sect, noted for frenzied, whirling dancing
DES *abbrev. for:* Department of Education and Science
desalinate *vt* remove the salt from (sea water) **~ation** *n*
descant *n* vocal line sung above the melody ♦ *vi* talk or write at length (on)
descend *vi/t* **1** go down **2 be descended from** have as an ancestor **descend on/upon** *phr vt* **1** arrive suddenly **2** attack suddenly **~ant** *n* person descended from another
descent *n* **1** going down **2** downward slope **3** family origins
describe *vt* **1** say what something is like **2** *fml* draw or move in the shape of: *describe a circle*
description *n* **1** statement that describes **2** sort: *birds of every description* **–tive** *adj* **1** that describes **2** saying how a language is used **–tively** *adv*
descry *vt lit* catch sight of esp. at a distance
desecrate *vt* spoil (a holy thing or place) **–cration** *n*
desegregate *vt* end racial segregation in **–ation** *n*
deselect *vt BrE* refuse to nominate (a sitting MP) for re-election
desensitize *vt* make less sensitive
desert[1] *n* large area of dry sandy land
desert[2] *v* **1** *vt* leave (a place) empty **2** *vt* leave (people) cruelly **3** *vi* leave military service without permission **~er** *n* person who deserts from the armed forces **~ion** *n*
deserts *pl n* what someone deserves
deserve *vt* be worthy of **deservedly** *adj* rightly **deserving** *adj*
deshabille /ˌdayzəˈbeel/ *n* partial undress
desiccate *vi/t* dry up
desideratum *n* **-rata** desirable or necessary thing
design *vt* **1** draw a plan for (something to be made) **2** plan (something) for a purpose: *books designed for use in colleges* ♦ *n* **1** plan drawn for making something **2** art of designing things **3** decorative pattern **4** plan in the mind **designs** *pl n* evil plans: *designs on your life*
designate *vt* choose for a particular job or purpose ♦ *adj* chosen for an office but not yet officially placed in it
designer *n* person who makes plans or designs ♦ *adj* **1** made by a designer: *designer jeans* **2** *humor* or *derog* intended to make the user appear extremely fashionable: *designer stubble/socialism*
desirable *adj* worth having; attractive **–bly** *adv* **–bility** *n*
desire *vt* wish for; want very much ♦ *n* **1** strong wish **2** strong wish for sexual relations with **3** something desired **desirous** *adj* feeling or having a desire
desist *vi* cease doing
desk *n* table at which one writes or does business
desktop *adj* being or using a small computer: *desktop publishing*
desolate *adj* sad and lonely **~ly** *adv* **–lation** *n*
despair *vi* lose all hope ♦ *n* loss of hope **~ingly** *adv*
despatch *n, vt* dispatch
desperado *n* **-oes** *or* **-os** reckless criminal
desperate *adj* **1** ready for any wild act because of despair **2** very dangerous and without much hope of success **~ly** *adv* **-ation** *n*
despicable *adj* deserving to be despised **–bly** *adv*
despise *vt* regard as worthless
despite *prep* in spite of
despoil *vt* ravage; plunder
despondent *adj* without hope; discouraged **~ly** *adv* **–dency** *n*
despot /ˈdespot/ *n* ruler with total power who governs cruelly **~ic** *adj* **~ism** *n*
dessert *n* sweet food served at the end of a meal
dessertspoon *n* middle-sized spoon
destabilize, **–ise** *vt* make (a government, country, etc.) unstable

destination *n* place to which someone or something is going
destined *adj* intended, esp. by fate: *He was destined to become famous.*
destiny *n* fate; what must happen
destitute *adj* **1** without food, clothes, shelter, etc. **2** lacking in: *destitute of feeling* **–tution** *n*
destroy *vt* **1** make useless; ruin **2** kill (esp. an animal) **~er** *n* **1** someone who destroys **2** small fast warship
destruction *n* destroying; ruin **–tive** *adj* **1** causing destruction **2** not helpful: *destructive criticism*
desuetude /ˈdeswityoohd/ *n lit* disuse
desultory /ˈdesəlt(ə)ri/ *adj* passing from one thing to another without plan or purpose **–torily** *adv*
detach *vt* separate from something larger **~ed** *adj* **1** (of a house) not joined to others **2** not influenced by personal feelings **~ment** *n* **1** being emotionally detached **2** group of soldiers, etc.
detail *n* **1** small fact about something **2** small working party of e.g. soldiers ♦ *vt* **1** describe fully: *a detailed account* **2** appoint (soldiers, etc.) for special work
detain *vt* **1** prevent (someone) from leaving **2** keep in custody
detainee *n* person detained officially in a camp or prison
detect *vt* notice; discover **~able** *adj* **~ive** *n* person who hunts criminals **~or** *n* instrument for finding something **~ion** *n*
détente *n* calmer political relations between unfriendly countries
detention *n* act of preventing a person from leaving
deter *vt* **-rr-** discourage from doing something
detergent *n* (esp. soapless) product for washing things
deteriorate *vi* become worse **–ration** *n*
determinant *n* something that decides, fixes, or limits
determinate *adj fml* **1** limited **2** conclusively settled or fixed
determination *n* **1** strong will to succeed **2** firm intention **3** finding out
determine *vt* **1** form a firm intention **2** limit; fix **3** find out; calculate
determiner *n* word that describes a noun and comes before any adjectives that describe the same noun (such as ‘his’ in ‘his new car’)
determinism *n* belief that everything is preordained and unalterable **–ist** *n* **–istic** *adj*
deterrent *n, adj* (something) that deters
detest *vt* hate very much **~able** *adj* **~ation** *n*
dethrone *vt* remove (a king or queen) from power
detonate *vi/t* explode **–nator** *n* piece of equipment used for detonating **–nation** *n*
detour *n* way round something
detract from *phr vt* lessen the value or beauty of
detractor *n* person who says bad things about another
detrain *vi/t* (cause to) leave a train
detriment *n fml* harm; damage **~al** *adj* **~ally** *adv*
detritus /diˈtrietəs/ *n* debris; loose residues
de trop *adj* unwanted; superfluous
deuce *n* (in tennis) 40 points to each player **2** the 2 in a suit of cards **3** *euph* the devil **~d** *adj, adv euph* damned
deus ex machina *n lit* person or thing that appears unexpectedly and resolves a crisis
Deutschmark also **Deutsche Mark** *n* standard currency unit of West Germany
devalue *vi/t* **1** reduce the exchange value of (money) **2** make (a person or action) seem less valuable or important **–uation** *n*
devastate *vt* **1** destroy completely **2** shatter (2) **–station** *n*
develop *v* **1** *vi/t* (cause to) grow or become more advanced **2** *vt* use (land) for building on **3** *vt* begin to have: *develop measles* **4** *vt* cause (a photograph) to appear on paper **~er** *n* **1** person who develops land **2** chemical used to develop photographs **~ment** *n*

1 developing **2** new event **3** developed piece of land
developing country *n* poor country that is trying to improve its industry and living conditions
development area *n BrE* area of high unemployment given government assistance to establish new industries
deviant *adj* different from an accepted standard **-ance** *n*
deviate *vi* turn away from what is usual **-ation** *n* noticeable difference
device *n* **1** instrument or tool **2** plan; trick **3 leave someone to their own devices** leave (someone) alone, without help
devil *n* **1** evil spirit **2** *sl* person: *You lucky devil!* **~ish** *adj* evil; like the devil **~ishly** *adv* very: *devilishly hard work* **~ment** *n* mischief
devil-may-care *adj* reckless; happy-go-lucky
devil's advocate *n* person who opposes an idea or plan to test how good it is
devious *adj* not direct; not very honest **~ly** *adv* **~ness** *n*
devise *vt* plan; invent
devoid *adj* **devoid of** empty of: *devoid of human feeling*
devolution *n* giving of power to someone else
devolve on/upon *phr vt* (of power or work) be passed to
devote *vt* give completely to something **devoted** *adj* loyal; loving **devotion** *n* **1** great love **2** devoutness **devotions** *pl n* prayers
devotee *n* person who admires someone or something
devour *vt* **1** eat up hungrily **2** read, look at, etc. eagerly **3** completely take up the attention of: *devoured by hate*
devout *adj* **1** seriously religious **2** deeply felt: *a devout hope* **~ly** *adv*
dew *n* drops of water that form on cold surfaces in the night **~y** *adj* wet (as if) with dew: *a dewy-eyed look*
dewlap *n* hanging fold of skin under an animal's neck
dexterity *n* quick cleverness, esp. with one's hands **-terous, -trous** *adj*
dextrose *n* form of sugar found in some fruits
DF *abbrev. for:* Defender of the Faith
DFC *abbrev. for:* Distinguished Flying Cross
DFM *abbrev. for:* Distinguished Flying Medal
dhoti *n* loincloth worn by Hindu men
dhow *n* Arab boat with lateen rig
DHSS *abbrev. for:* Department of Health and Social Security
DI *abbrev for:* Detective Inspector
di- *prefix* **1** twice; double **2** containing two atoms
diabetes *n* disease in which there is too much sugar in the blood **-tic** *n, adj* (person) suffering from this
diabolical *adj* **1** very cruel or bad **2** very unpleasant and annoying: *The train service was diabolical.* **~ly** *adv*
diaconal *adj* of a deacon or deaconess
diacritic *n* accent (2)
diadem *n lit* crown
diaeresis /dieˈerisis/ *AmE* **dieresis** *n* **-ses** mark (¨) placed over the second of two adjacent vowels to indicate that it should be pronounced separately
diagnose *vt* discover the nature of (a disease)
diagnosis *n* **-ses** (judgment made by) diagnosing **-nostic** *adj*
diagonal *adj* (of a straight line) joining opposite corners of a square, oblong, etc. **~ly** *adv*
diagram *n* plan drawn to explain a machine, idea, etc. **~matic** *adj*
dial *n* **1** marked face of a clock, etc. **2** wheel with holes on a telephone ♦ *vi/t* **-ll-** (*AmE* **-l-**) operate a telephone dial (to call a particular number)
dialect *n* variety of a language, spoken in one part of a country
dialectic *n* method of arguing by moving from one idea to its antithesis and then seeking to resolve the two **-ical** *adj*
dialogue *AmE* **-log** *n* **1** conversation in a book or play **2** exchange of opinion
dialysis *n* process by which solid sub-

stances are removed from a liquid, used esp. for purifying the blood of people with kidney disorders
diamanté *n, adj* (fabric) encrusted with tiny glittering stones
diameter *n* distance across a circle, measured through the centre
diametrically *adv* completely: *diametrically opposed/opposite*
diamond *n* **1** hard valuable precious stone **2** figure with four equal sides, standing on one of its points **3** red diamond-shaped figure on a playing card
diamond jubilee *n* 60th anniversary of some important event
diamond wedding *n* 60th wedding anniversary
diaper *n AmE* nappy
diaphanous *adj* almost transparent
diaphragm *n* **1** muscle separating the lungs from the stomach **2** thin plate in a telephone, camera, etc **3** Dutch cap
diarrhoea, -rhea *n* illness in which the bowels are emptied too often and the faeces are abnormally fluid
diary *n* (book for) a daily record of events in one's life **-rist** *n* writer of a diary
Diaspora *n* the dispersion of the Jews in countries other than their homeland
diastole *n* dilation of the chambers of the heart
diatonic *adj* being, or composed in, the regular major or minor scale
diatribe *n* violent attack in words
dibber, dibble *n* pointed garden tool for making holes in the ground
dice *n* **dice** small six-sided block with spots on it, used in games ♦ *vt* **1** cut (food) into small squares **2 dice with death** take a great risk **dicey** *adj* risky and uncertain
dichotomy /die'kotəmi/ *n fml* division into two opposite parts or groups
dick *n taboo sl* **1** penis **2** *sl* detective
dickens *n BrE infml* (used to give force to an expression): *What the dickens is that?*
dicky *adj infml BrE* weak
dickybird *n* **1** (used to children) little bird **2 not a dickybird** *infml* not a word; nothing
Dictaphone *n tdmk for* office recording machine used esp. for giving dictation
dictate *vi/t* **1** say (words) for someone else to write down **2** give (orders) ♦ *n* order (esp. from within ourselves): *the dictates of your own conscience* **-tion** *n* **1** dictating **2** piece of writing dictated
dictator *n* ruler with complete power **~ship** *n* (country with) government by a dictator **~ial** *adj*
diction *n* way in which someone pronounces words
dictionary *n* book giving a list of words in alphabetical order, with their meanings
dictum *n* **-ta** *or* **-tums** formal statement of opinion
did *past t. of* do
didactic *adj fml* intending to teach
diddle *vt infml* cheat
didgeridoo *n* long wooden Australian wind instrument
didn't *short for:* did not
die[1] *vi* **died,** *pres p.* **dying 1** stop living; become dead: *My love will never die.* **2 be dying for/to** want very badly **3 die hard** (of beliefs, customs, etc.) take a long time to disappear **die away** *phr vi* fade and then cease **die down** *phr vi* become less: *The excitement soon died down.* **die off** *phr vi* die one by one **die out** *phr vi* become extinct
die[2] *n* metal block for shaping or stamping e.g. coins **2** *esp. AmE* dice (*sing.*) **3 the die is cast** an irrevocable decision or step has been taken
diehard *n* person who strongly opposes change
dieresis *n AmE* diaeresis
diesel *n* heavy oil used instead of petrol, esp. in buses and trains
diet *n* **1** food and drink usually taken **2** limited list of food and drink that someone is allowed for medical reasons **3 (be/go) on a diet** (be/start) living on a limited list of food usu. in order to lose weight ♦ *vi* eat according to a diet

~ary *adj*
differ *vi* **1** be different **2** disagree
difference *n* **1** way or fact of being different **2** slight disagreement
different *adj* **1** unlike **2** separate: *They go to different schools.* **3** various: *It comes in different colours.* **4** unusual **~ly** *adv*
differential *n* **1** amount of difference between things: *pay differentials* **2** also **differential gear** device that allows the rear wheels of a vehicle to turn at different speeds while turning corners
differential calculus *n* branch of mathematics dealing with the rate of change of functions with respect to their variables
differentiate *vi/t* **1** see a difference between **2** make different
difficult *adj* **1** hard to do, understand, etc. **2** (of people) not easily pleased
difficulty *n* **1** being difficult; trouble **2** something difficult; problem
diffident *adj* lacking confidence in oneself **~ly** *adv* **–dence** *n*
diffract *vt* break up (a beam of light) into the spectrum **~ion** *n*
diffuse *vi/t fml* spread freely in all directions ♦ *adj* **1** diffused **2** using too many words **–fusion** *n*
dig *vi/t* **dug**, *pres p.* **digging 1** break up and move (earth) **2** make (a hole) in this way **3** *sl* like or understand **4 dig someone in the ribs** touch someone with one's elbow, as to share a joke **dig at** *phr vt* speak to (someone) in an unpleasant way: *Stop digging at me!* **dig in** *phr v* **1** *vi/t* dig a protective place for oneself; get firmly settled **2** *vi* start eating **dig up** *phr vt* find (something hidden or buried) by careful searching; bring to light: *dig up an old scandal* ♦ *n* **1** quick push **2** place being uncovered by archaelogists **3** unpleasant remark **digs** *pl n BrE* lodgings
digest *vt* **1** change (food) so that the body can use it **2** arrange (facts) in one's mind ♦ *n* short summary **~ible** *adj* **~ive** *adj* of or helping in digesting food **~ion** *n* ability to digest food
digit *n* **1** any number from 0 to 9 **2** *fml* finger or toe **~al** *adj* using digits: *digital watch* **~ize, -ise** *vt* use digits to express information
digitalis *n* (drug prepared from the dried leaves of) the foxglove
digital recording *n* (record made by) a sound recording process which converts audio signals into electrical pulses corresponding to varying voltage levels
dignified *adj* having dignity **–ify** *vt* make dignified
dignitary *n* person of high rank
dignity *n* **1** nobleness of character **2** formal grand behaviour **3 beneath one's dignity** below one's standard of moral or social behaviour
digress *vi* (of a writer or speaker) move away from the subject **~ion** *n*
dike, dyke *n* **1** bank to hold back water **2** ditch **3** *sl. derog* lesbian
diktat *n* arbitrary decree
dilapidated *adj* falling to pieces
dilate *vi/t* (cause to) become wider by stretching: *eyes dilated with terror* **dilation** *n*
dilatory /ˈdilət(ə)ri/ *adj* too slow in action
dildo *n* **-os** artificial penis
dilemma *n* difficult choice between two things
dilettante /ˌdiliˈtanti/ *n, adj* (person) who enjoys art or a branch of study but does not take it seriously
diligence *n* steady effort **–gent** *adj* **–gently** *adv*
dill *n* herb with aromatic foliage and seeds
dillydally *vi infml* dawdle
dilute *vt* make (liquid) weaker and thinner **dilution** *n*
dim *adj* **-mm- 1** (of light) not bright **2** not easy to see **3** *sl* stupid **4 take a dim view of** think badly of ♦ *vi/t* **-mm-** make or become dim **~ly** *adv* **~mer** *n* device for dimming electric lights **~ness** *n*
dime *n* coin of US and Canada worth 10 cents
dimension *n* **1** measurement of

breadth, length, or height **2** particular site or part of a problem, subject, etc. **–dimensional** *adj* having (so many) dimensions: *two-dimensional* **dimensions** *pl n* size
diminish *vi/t* make or become smaller
diminished responsibility *n* state of not being fully responsible for one's (criminal) actions because of a mental disorder
diminishing returns *pl n* smaller increases in output or profit despite constant increases in effort or production
diminuendo *n* gradual decrease in force or volume esp. in music
diminution *n* diminishing
diminutive *adj* very small
dimity *n* corded cotton fabric
dimple *n* small hollow in the cheek, etc.
dim sum *n* Chinese food consisting of steamed parcels of pastry containing small pieces of meat or vegetables
dimwit *n* stupid person **~ted** *adj*
din *n* loud unpleasant noise **din into** *phr vt* repeat (something) forcefully over and over again to (someone)
dine *vi* eat dinner **dine out on** *phr vt* gain social success with (news or a story)
diner *n* **1** person dining **2** dining car **3** *AmE* small roadside restaurant
dingdong *n* **1** ringing noise **2** *infml* noisy fight ♦ *adj* hard-fought
dinghy *n* small open boat
dingle *n* small wooded valley
dingo *n* **-gos** wild dog of Australia
dingy *adj* dirty and faded
dining car *n* railway carriage where meals are served
dining table *n* table for having meals on
dinkum *adj AustrE infml* real; genuine
dinky *adj* **1** *esp. BrE* dainty **2** *esp. AmE* small and insignificant
dinner *n* main meal of the day, eaten either at midday or in the evening
dinner jacket *n* man's black (or white) coat for formal evening occasions
dinosaur *n* **1** large extinct reptile **2** something very large and old-fashioned that no longer works well
dint *n* **by dint of** by means of
diocese *n* area controlled by a bishop **–cesan** *adj*
diode *n* semiconductor which converts alternating to direct current
dioxide *n* compound containing two oxygen atoms
dioxin *n* toxic byproduct of weedkiller production
dip *v* **-pp- 1** *vt* put into a liquid for a moment **2** *vt* lower slightly: *dip your headlights* **3** *vi* go down; slope downward **dip into** *phr vt* **1** read (a book) for a short time **2** make inroads into (money) ♦ *n* **1** quick bathe **2** downward slope **3** sauce into which food is dipped at parties **4** (liquid for) dipping animals: *sheep dip*
diphtheria /dif'thiəri·ə, dip-/ *n* serious infectious disease of the throat
diphthong /'difthong, dip-/ *n* compound vowel sound
diploma *n* official paper showing success in studying something
diplomacy *n* **1** management of relations between countries **2** skill at dealing with people
diplomat *n* person (e.g. an ambassador) whose profession is diplomacy **~ic** *adj* of or having diplomacy **~ically** *adv*
diplomatic relations *pl n* connection between two countries that each keep an embassy in the other country
dipsomania *n* uncontrollable craving for alcohol **–maniac** *n*
dipstick *n* graduated rod for showing the depth of liquid in a container
dire *adj* terrible
direct *vt* **1** tell (someone) the way to a place **2** control; manage **3** command; order **4** aim **5** *vi/t* act as the director of (a play, film, etc.) ♦ *adj* **1** going straight **2** with nothing coming between: *direct result* **3** honest; clearly expressed **4** exact: *direct opposite* ♦ *adv* without turning aside **~ly** *adv* **1** in a direct way **2** at once **~ness** *n*
direction *n* **1** point towards which a person or thing moves or faces **2** control; management **directions** *pl n*

instructions
direction finder *n* aerial used to determine the direction of incoming radio waves
directive *n* official order
direct object *n* the noun, noun phrase, or pronoun that is needed to complete the meaning of a transitive verb: *In 'I saw Mary', 'Mary' is the direct object.*
director *n* **1** senior manager of a firm **2** person who directs a play or film **~ship** *n* company director's position
Director of Public Prosecutions *n* British government lawyer who in doubtful cases decides whether people should stand trial
directory *n* book or list of names, facts, etc.
direct speech *n* actual words of a speaker
dirge *n* slow sad song
dirigible *n* airship
dirk *n* Highlander's dagger
dirndl *n* full skirt with a tight waistband
dirt *n* **1** unclean matter **2** soil **3** obscenity **4** *infml* scandal **~y** *adj* **1** not clean **2** sordid; base **3** unfair **4** obscene; indecent **5** unpleasant ♦ *vt* make dirty **~ily** *adv*
dirt cheap *adj* extremely cheap
dirt road *n* road made of compacted earth
dirt track *n* loose surface, esp. for motorcycle racing
dirty old man *n* older man with an unhealthy interest in sex
dirty trick *n* instance of mean, spiteful or treacherous treatment **dirty tricks** *pl n* dubious undercover operations intended esp. to discredit an opponent
dirty work *n* **1** unpleasant tasks **2** *infml* dishonest or illicit activity
dis- *prefix* **1** de- (1), (2) **2** opposite or absence of: *disbelief* **3** not: *disagreeable*
disability *n* **1** being disabled **2** handicap (1)
disable *vt* make unable to use one's body properly **-abled** *adj* **~ment** *n*
disabuse *vt* free (someone) from a wrong idea
disadvantage *n* unfavourable condition **~ous** *adj* **disadvantaged** *adj* suffering from a disadvantage with regard to one's social position, family background, etc.
disaffected *adj* lacking (esp. political) loyalty **-fection** *n*
disaffiliate *vi/t* sever one's connection with
disagree *vi* **1** have different opinions **2** be different **disagree with** *phr vt* (of food, etc.) make ill **~able** *adj* unpleasant **~ably** *adv* **~ment** *n* difference of opinion
disallow *vt* **1** prohibit **2** refuse to recognize as valid: *the referee disallowed the goal*
disappear *vi* **1** go out of sight **2** cease to exist **~ance** *n*
disappoint *vt* fail to fulfil hopes **~ed** *adj* sad at not seeing hopes fulfilled **~ing** *adj* **~ingly** *adv* **~ment** *n* **1** being disappointed **2** something disappointing
disapprove *vi* have an unfavourable opinion **-proval** *n*
disarm *v* **1** *vt* take away weapons from **2** *vi* reduce a nation's military strength **3** *vt* drive away the anger of: *a disarming smile* **~ingly** *adv*
disarmament *n* act or principle of reducing armaments
disarrange *vt* disorder
disarray *n fml* disorder
disassociate *vt* dissociate
disaster *n* **1** sudden serious misfortune **2** fiasco; failure **-trous** *adj* **-trously** *adv*
disavow *vt fml* refuse to admit (knowledge, responsibility, etc.)
disband *vi/t* break up (a group)
disbar *vt* expel from the legal profession
disbelief *n* lack of belief
disbelieve *vi/t* refuse to believe
disburse *vt fml* make a payment for
disc, *AmE* **disk** *n* **1** anything round and flat, such as a plate or record **2** flat piece of cartilage in one's back **3** disk (2)
discard *v* **1** *vt* get rid of; throw away **2** *vi/t* lay down (a card) ♦ *n* something

discarded, esp. a card
disc brakes *pl n* brakes which function by the pressure of two pads against a disc which revolves with the wheel
discern *vt* see or understand esp. with difficulty **~ible** *adj* **~ing** *adj* able to decide and judge; having good taste **~ment** *n*
discharge *v* **1** *vt* send (a person) away **2** *vi/t* let out (gas, liquid, etc.) **3** *vt* perform (a duty or promise) **4** *vt* pay (a debt) **5** *vt* fire (a gun, etc.) ♦ *n* **1** discharging **2** something discharged **3** release or dismissal (e.g. after military service)
disciple *n* follower of a (religious) leader
disciplinarian *n* person who can make others obey and believes in firm discipline
disciplinary *adj* connected with punishment: *take disciplinary action*
discipline *n* **1** training to produce obedience and self-control **2** control gained by this training **3** punishment **4** branch of learning ♦ *vt* **1** train to be obedient **2** punish
disc jockey *n* broadcaster who introduces records of popular music
disclaim *vt* deny: *disclaim responsibility* **~er** *n* written statement which disclaims
disclose *vt* make (a secret) known
disclosure *n* **1** act of disclosing **2** disclosed secret
disco *n* **-cos 1** club where people dance to recorded music **2** music of the kind played at discos **3** mobile equipment for playing music at a disco
discography *n* list of gramophone recordings
discolour *AmE* **-or** *vi/t* change colour for the worse **-oration** *n*
discombobulate *vt esp. AmE infml* throw into confusion
discomfit *vt lit* **1** thwart; foil **2** disconcert
discomfort *n* (cause of) being uncomfortable
discommode *vt lit* inconvenience
discompose *vt* unsettle, disconcert
disconcert *vt* worry; upset **~ing** *adj* **~ingly** *adv*
disconnect *vt* undo the connection of **~ed** *adj* (of thoughts and ideas) badly arranged
disconsolate *adj* hopelessly sad **~ly** *adv*
discontent *n* restless unhappiness **~ed** *adj* **~edly** *adv*
discontinue *vi/t* stop; end
discord *n* **1** *fml* disagreement between people **2** lack of musical harmony **~ant** *adj*
discotheque *n fml* disco
discount *n* reduction in cost ♦ *vt* **1** regard (information) as unimportant or untrue **2** deduct from the usual price
discountenance *vt fml* **1** embarrass **2** discourage
discourage *vt* **1** take away hope from **2** persuade not to do something **~ment** *n*
discourse *n* serious conversation or speech
discourteous /disˈkuhtyəs/ *adj* not polite **~ly** *adv* **-tesy** *n*
discover *vt* find; find out **~er** *n* **~y** *n* **1** discovering **2** something found
discredit *vt* **1** stop people from believing in **2** damage the reputation of ♦ *n* (source of) shame or disgrace **~able** *adj* bringing shame
discreet *adj* not saying too much; showing good sense and judgment **~ly** *adv*
discrepancy *n* difference between amounts, facts, etc.
discrete *adj fml* separate; not continuous
discretion *n* **1** being discreet **2** ability to decide what to do: *use your own discretion* **~ary** *adj* left to someone's decision
discriminate *vi/t* recognize a difference
discriminate against/in favour of *phr vt* treat worse/better than others **-nating** *adj* (of a person) able to choose the best by seeing small differences **-natory** *adj* **-nation** *n*
discursive *adj* (of a piece of writing) casually passing from one topic to the

next; rambling

discus *n* heavy plate to be thrown as a sport

discuss *vt* talk about **~ion** *n*

disdain *n* contempt ♦ *vt* regard with disdain; be too proud for **~ful** *adj* **~fully** *adv*

disease *n* illness **-eased** *adj* ill

disembark *vi/t* (cause to) leave a ship **~ation** *n*

disembodied *adj* existing with no body: *a disembodied voice*

disembowel *vt* remove the entrails of

disembroil *vt* release from a tangle

disenchanted *adj* having lost belief in the value of something **-chantment** *n*

disenfranchise *vt* disfranchise **~ment** *n*

disengage *vi/t* **1** come loose and separate **2** stop fighting

disentangle *vt* **1** make free from knots **2** extricate; separate out

disestablish *vt* deprive (a church) of its established status **~ment** *n*

disfavour *n* dislike; disapproval

disfigure *vt* spoil the beauty of **~ment** *n*

disfranchise *vt* take away the right to vote from **~ment** *n*

disgorge *vi/t* (cause to) flow out

disgrace *n* (cause of) shame or loss of respect ♦ *vt* bring disgrace to **~ful** *adj* **~fully** *adv*

disgruntled*adj* annoyed and disappointed

disguise *vt* change the appearance of, to hide or deceive ♦ *n* **1** something worn to disguise someone **2** being disguised

disgust *n* dislike caused esp. by a bad smell or taste or bad behaviour ♦ *vt* cause disgust in **~ingly** *adv*

dish *n* **1** large plate **2** cooked food of one kind **3** *infml, esp. BrE* good-looking person ♦ *vt BrE infml* ruin; spoil **dish out** *phr vt* **1** serve out to several people **2 dish it out** punish or express disapproval of someone else, esp. thoughtlessly or unjustly **dish up** *phr vi/t* put (a meal) into dishes **~y** *adj BrE infml* attractive

dishabille *n* deshabille

dishcloth *n* cloth for washing or drying dishes

dishearten *vt* discourage

dishevelled *adj* (esp. of someone's hair) untidy

dishonest *adj* not honest **~ly** *adv* **~y** *n*

dishonour *AmE* **-or** *n fml* (person or thing bringing) loss of honour ♦ *vt*

dishwater *n* water (that has been) used for washing dishes

disillusion *vt* tell the unpleasant truth to **~ed** *adj* **~ment** *n*

disincentive *n* something that discourages effort

disinclined *adj* unwilling

disinfect *vt* make (things and places) free from infection **~ant** *n* chemical that disinfects

disinfest *vt* rid of vermin

disingenuous /ˌdisinˈjenyoo·əs/ *adj* not sincere; slightly dishonest **~ly** *adv*

disinherit *vt* take away the right to inherit from

disintegrate *vi/t* break up into small pieces **-gration** *n*

disinter *vt* **1** exhume **2** unearth

disinterested *adj* not influenced by personal advantage **~ly** *adv*

disinvestment *n* reduction of investment by selling things, etc.

disjointed *adj* (of words, ideas, etc.) not well connected **~ly** *adv*

disk *n* **1** *AmE* disc **2** flat circular piece of plastic used for storing computer information

disk drive *n* piece of electrical equipment used for passing information to and from a disk

diskette *n* small floppy disk

dislike *vt* not like **dislike** *n*

dislocate *vt* **1** put (a bone) out of place **2** put (traffic, plans, etc.) into disorder **-cation** *n*

dislodge *vt* force out of a position

disloyal *adj* not loyal **~ly** *adv* **~ty** *n*

dismal *adj* sad; hopeless **~ly** *adv*

dismantle *vt* take to pieces

dismast *vt* break or knock down the masts of (a ship)

dismay *vt, n* (fill with) great fear and

hopelessness
dismember *vt* cut or tear (a body) apart
dismiss *vt* **1** *fml* remove from a job **2** send away **3** refuse to think seriously about **3** (of a judge) stop (a court case) **~al** *n* **~ive** *adj* contemptuous **~ively** *adv*
disobedient *adj* refusing to obey **~ly** *adv* **–ence** *n*
disobey *vi/t* not obey
disoblige *vt* go against the wishes of
disorder *n* **1** confusion **2** public violence **3** illness of the body or mind ♦ *vt* put into disorder **~ly** *adj*
disorderly house *n* brothel
disorganize, –ise *vt* throw into confusion **–ization** *n*
disorientate also **disorient** *vt* cause (someone) to lose sense of time, direction, etc.; confuse
disown *vt* say that one has no connection with
disparage *vt* speak without respect of **–agingly** *adv*
disparate /ˈdispərət/ *adj fml* that cannot be compared; quite different **–rity** *n* **1** inequality **2** difference
dispassionate *adj* calm and fair; not taking sides **~ly** *adv*
dispatch *vt* **1** send **2** finish (work, etc.) quickly **3** kill ♦ *n* **1** message sent **2** sending **3** speed and effectiveness
dispatch box *n* box for official papers, esp. the one on the central table in the House of Commons beside which leading Members of Parliament stand to make their speeches
dispel *vt* **-ll-** drive away; scatter
dispensation *n* **1** permission to disobey a rule **2** *fml* dispensing
dispensation *n* **1** way in which things are ordered by God or nature **2** religious or political system **3** exemption
dispense *vt* **1** give out to people **2** prepare (medicines) **dispense with** *phr vt* do without **dispensary** *n* place where medicines are dispensed **~r** *n* **1** machine that dispenses things **2** person who prepares medicines
disperse *vi/t* scatter in different directions **dispersal, dispersion** *n*
dispirited *adj lit* discouraged **~ly** *adv*
displace *vt* **1** force out of the proper place **2** take the place of **~ment** *n*
displaced person *n* refugee
display *vt* show; arrange for viewing ♦ *n* **1** presentation; show **2** ostentation **3** eye-catching arrangement **4** information shown on e.g. a VDU screen
displease *vt fml* annoy **–pleasure** *n* annoyance
disport *vt* **disport oneself** *lit* frolic
disposable *adj* **1** to be used once and then thrown away **2** able to be used: *disposable income* ♦ *n* disposable article
disposal *n* **1** removal **2 at one's disposal** for one to use
dispose *v* **1** *vt* put in order **2** *vi lit* decide on a matter **dispose of** *phr vt* **1** get rid of **2** deal with conclusively
disposed *adj* **1** willing: *I don't feel disposed to help.* **2** having a tendency
disposition *n* **1** person's natural character **2** arrangement; ordering
dispossess *vt* take property away from
disproportionate *adj* too much or too little **~ly** *adv*
disprove *vt* prove to be false
dispute *v* **1** *vi/t* argue (about) **2** *vt* question the truth of **3** *vt* struggle over or about (esp. in defence): *disputed territory* ♦ *n* argument; quarrel **–tant** *n* person engaged in a dispute **-tation** *n* (formal) argument **–tatious** *adj* argumentative
disqualify *vt* **1** make unfit to do something **2** declare ineligible **–fication** *n*
disquiet *vt fml* make anxious ♦ *n* also **disquietude** anxiety
disquisition *n* (over-)lengthy speech or report
disregard *vt* pay no attention to ♦ *n* lack of proper attention
disrepair *n* need for repair
disreputable /disˈrepyootəbl/ *adj* having a bad reputation
disrepute *n* loss of people's good opinion

disrespect *n* rudeness **~ful** *adj*
disrobe *vi* take off (ceremonial) clothing
disrupt *vt* throw into disorder **~ive** *adj* **~ively** *adv* **~ion** *n*
dissatisfy *vt* fail to satisfy; displease **-faction** *n*
dissect *vt* cut up (a body) so as to study it **~ion** *n*
dissemble *v lit* **1** *vi/t* conceal by pretence **2** *vt* simulate
disseminate *vt fml* spread (ideas, etc.) widely **-nation** *n*
dissension *n* disagreement; argument
dissent *vi* disagree with an opinion ♦ *n* refusal to agree **~er** *n*
dissertation *n* long (written) account of a subject
disservice *n* harm or harmful action
dissident *n, adj* (person) who disagrees: *political dissidents*
dissimilar *adj* not similar
dissipate *v* **1** *vi/t* disperse; scatter **2** *vt* squander **~d** *adj* dissolute; debauched **-pation** *n*
dissociate *n* separate in one's mind **-ation** *n*
dissoluble *adj* that can be broken up
dissolute *n, adj* (person) who leads a bad or immoral life **~ly** *adv* **~ness** *n*
dissolution *n* dispersal or breaking up, esp. of a group or assembly
dissolve *vi/t* **1** make (a solid) become liquid **2** cause (a group) to break up: *dissolve Parliament* **3** fade out or away gradually: *his strength/the clouds dissolved* **4** lose one's self-control under the influence of strong feeling: *dissolve into tears/laughter*
dissonance *n* **1** combination of musical notes which do not sound pleasant together **2** lack of agreement between beliefs and actions **-nant** *adj* **-nantly** *adv*
dissuade *vt* persuade not to **-suasion** *n*
distaff *n* **1** stick for holding the thread in spinning **2 the distaff side** female line or side of a family
distance *n* **1** separation in space between places **2** distant place: *watch from a distance* **3 go the distance** (in sports) keep playing, etc. till the end of the match **4 keep one's distance** stay far enough away **5 keep someone at a distance** treat someone without much friendliness ♦ *vt* separate (esp. oneself) esp. in the mind or feelings
distant *adj* **1** far off **2** not close: *distant relations* **3** unfriendly **~ly** *adv*
distaste *n* dislike **~ful** *adj* unpleasant
distemper *n* **1** water-based paint for walls **2** infectious disease of animals
distend *vi/t* swell
distil also *AmE* **-till** *vt* **-ll- 1** make (a liquid) into gas and then make the gas into liquid, as when making alcoholic drinks **2** extract the most important part(s) of (a book, an idea, etc.) **~lery** *n* place where e.g. whisky is distilled **~lation** *n*
distinct *adj* **1** different; separate **2** clearly noticed **~ly** *adv*
distinction *n* **1** difference **2** unusual excellence **3** mark of honour **-tive** *adj* showing a difference **-tively** *adv*
distinguish *v* **1** *vi/t* recognize a difference **2** *vi/t* see clearly **3** *vt* make different **4 distinguish oneself** perform noticeably well **~able** *adj* **~ed** *adj* excellent; famous
distort *vt* **1** twist out of the natural shape **2** give a false account of **~ion** *n*
distract *vt* take (someone's attention) away **~ed** *adj* anxious and confused **~ion** *n* **1** something that distracts one's attention **2** amusement **3** madness
distrain *vt* seize (goods or property) for payment of a debt **~t** *n*
distrait /di'stray/ *adj* absent-minded
distraught /di'strawt/ *adj* very anxious and troubled
distress *n* **1** great suffering or sorrow **2** serious danger ♦ *vt* cause suffering to **~ed** *adj* **1** suffering pain or sorrow **2** suffering hardship **3** (of materials) made to look old and worn
distribute *vt* **1** give out **2** scatter **-utor** *n* **1** person who distributes goods **2**

instrument that distributes electric current in an engine **–ution** *n*
district *n* area of a country or city
distrust *vt* have no trust in ♦ *n* lack of trust **~ful** *adj* **~fully** *adv*
disturb *vt* **1** interrupt **2** worry **3** alter the position or arrangement of **~ance** *n* **1** act of disturbing **2** noisy disorder **~ed** *adj* having or showing signs of mental illness
disunity *n* disagreement; quarrelling
disuse *n* state of no longer being used **–used** *adj*
ditch *n* passage cut for water to flow through ♦ *vt sl* get rid of
dither *vi* be unable to decide **dither** *n*
ditto *n* **-tos** the same
ditty *n* short simple song
diuretic *n, adj* (substance) which increases the flow of urine
diurnal *adj* **1** *fml* daily; taking a day **2** active during the day
divan *n* bed with no back
dive *vi* **dived,** *AmE also* **dove, dived 1** jump head first into water **2** go under water **3** (of a plane or bird) go down steeply and swiftly **4** go down quickly: *dive under the table* **5** enter quickly into some matter or activity ♦ *n* **1** act of diving **2** not very respectable club, etc. **3 take a dive** *sl* agree to lose a match dishonestly **diver** *n* **1** person who dives, or works on the sea bottom **2** large fish eating diving bird
dive-bomb *vt* bomb from an aircraft diving steeply towards its target **~er** *n*
diverge *vi* separate; get further apart **divergence** *n* **divergent** *adj*
divers *adj arch.* various
diverse *adj* of different kinds **diversity** *n* variety
diversify *vi/t* make diverse: *diversify our range of products* **–fication** *n*
diversion *n* **1** diverting **2** something that amuses people **3** detour **~ary** *adj* intended to divert attention: *diversionary tactics*
divert *vt* turn to another direction: *divert a river*
divertimento *n* **-ti** *or* **-tos** piece of light chamber music in several movements
divest *vt* take away from someone
divide *vi/t* **1** separate into parts **2** find out how many times one number is contained in another **3** be an important cause of disagreement between ♦ *n* something that divides **dividers** *pl n* instrument for measuring lines, angles, etc.
dividend *n* **1** part of profit that is divided among shareholders **2 pay dividends** produce an advantage
divine *adj* **1** of God or a god **2** excellent ♦ *vi/t* **1** *fml* find out; guess **2** find (water or minerals) underground using a Y-shaped stick **(divining rod)** ♦ *n* clergyman **diviner** *n* dowser **divinity** *n* **1** quality or state of being divine **2** god or goddess **3** theology
Divine Office *n* prescribed form of the prayers said daily by Roman Catholic priests
divine right *n* **1** theory that a king is answerable to, and derives his right to rule from, God alone **2** unquestionable right
divingboard *n* high board off which people dive into the water
divisible *adj* that can be divided
division *n* **1** separation or sharing **2** one of the parts into which a whole is divided: *the firm's export division* **3** something that separates **4** disagreement **5** process of dividing numbers **6** vote in Parliament **~al** *adj*
divisive *adj* causing disunity
divisor *n* demoninator
divorce *n* **1** legal ending of a marriage **2** separation ♦ *v* **1** *vi/t* end a marriage by law **2** *vt* separate completely **divorcée** *n* divorced woman
divot *n* piece of turf
divulge *vt* tell (a secret)
divvy *n BrE infml* dividend
dixie *n BrE* (soldier's) cooking pot
Dixie *n* the southern states of the USA
Dixieland *n* **1** Dixie **2** traditional jazz
DIY *abbrev. for:* do-it-yourself
dizzy *adj* **1** feeling as if things are going round and round **2** causing this feeling:

dizzy heights **3** silly **–zily** *adv* **–ziness** *n*
DJ *n* **1** disc jockey **2** dinner jacket
djinn *n* genie
DM *abbrev. for:* Deutschmark
DNA *n* acid which carries genetic information in a cell
D notice *n* (in UK) official request that information should not be made public
do *v aux* **did, done 1** (used with another verb): *Do you like it?|He doesn't know.|Do be careful!* **2** (used instead of another verb): *He walks faster than I do.|She likes it, and so do I.|She sings, doesn't she?* ♦ *v* **1** *vt* perform (an action); work at or produce **2** *vi* **a** advance: *do well/badly* **b** behave: *Do as you're told!* **3** *vi/t* be enough or suitable (for): *Will £5 do (you)?|That will do!* **4** *vt sl* cheat: *We've been done!* **5 do well by** treat well **6 How do you do?** (used when one is introduced to someone) **7 That does it!** (expression showing that enough, or too much has been done) **8 What do you do (for a living)?** What is your work? **do away with** *phr vt* **1** abolish **2** kill or murder (someone or oneself) **do down** *phr vt* **1** cause to feel ashamed or less proud of oneself **2** say bad things about (someone not present) **3** cheat **do for** *phr vt* **1** kill or ruin **2** *BrE infml* keep house or do cleaning for (someone) **do in** *phr vt* **1** kill **2** tire completely **3** injure; wreck **do out of** *phr vt* cause to lose, by cheating **do over** *phr vt sl* attack and wound **do up** *phr vt* **1** fasten or wrap **2** repair; improve **do with** *phr vt* **1** need; want **2** cause (oneself) to spend time doing: *I don't know what to do with myself since you've gone.* **3 have/be to do with** be connected with **do without** *phr vi/t* manage without ♦ *n infml* **1** *esp. BrE* a big party **2 dos and don'ts** rules of behaviour
dob in *phr vt AustrE sl* inform against
doc *n infml* doctor
docile *adj* quiet and easily taught **~ly** *adv* **–ility** *n*
dock¹ *n* **1** place where ships are loaded and unloaded, or repaired **2** place in a court of law where a prisoner stands ♦ *vi/t* **1** (cause to) sail into, or remain at, a dock **2** (cause spacecraft) to join in space **~er** *n* person who works at a dock, loading and unloading ships
dock² *vt* **1** cut off the end of **2** make a deduction from: *dock someone's wages*
dock³ *n* broad-leaved weed
docket *n* paper sent with e.g. a package giving details of contents, delivery instructions, etc. ♦ *vt* fix a docket to
dockland *n* also **docklands** *pl* area around the docks
dockyard *n* shipyard
Doc Martens *n tdmk for* over-ankle lace- up boots with thick soles
doctor *n* **1** person trained in medicine **2** person holding one of the highest university degrees ♦ *vt* **1** change dishonestly: *doctor the accounts* **2** neuter
doctorate *n* academic degree of a doctor
doctrinaire *adj* (obstinately) concerned with implementing a doctrine or principle; not practical: *doctrinaire socialism*
doctrine *n* belief; set of teachings **–trinal** *adj*
docudrama *n* film or TV dramatization of real events
document *n* paper giving information, proof, etc. ♦ *vt* prove or support with documents **~ation** *n* documents used as proof
documentary *adj* **1** of documents **2** based on factual material ♦ *n* documentary film, broadcast, etc.
doddering **doddery** *adj* weak, shaky and slow esp. because of age
doddle *n infml BrE* something that is very easy to do
dodge *v* **1** *vi/t* avoid (something) by suddenly moving aside **2** *vt* avoid dishonestly ♦ *n* **1** evasive movement **2** clever trick **dodger** *n* **dodgy** *adj* risky
dodgem *n* small electric car driven around a rink at a fairground, bumping other cars
dodo *n* extinct flightless bird

doe *n* female of esp. the deer, rat, and rabbit
DOE *abbrev. for:* Department of the Environment
does *3rd pers. sing. pres. of* do
doesn't *short for:* does not
doff *vt* take off (hat, cap, etc.) as a mark of respect
dog *n* **1** common four-legged animal, useful to humans **2** male of this and similar animals **3** person, esp. a contemptible person **4** *AmE* something inferior **5** *sl* unattractive woman **6 a dog's dinner** *or* **breakfast** mess **7 a dog's life** a very unhappy life **8 like a dog's dinner** very smartly (dressed) **9 dog in the manger** someone who does not want others to use something even though they themselves do not need it ♦ *vt* **-gg-** follow closely; pursue: *dogged by bad luck* **dogs** *pl n* **1** dog races **2 go to the dogs** be ruined
dog collar *n* **1** neckband for a dog **2** *infml* priest's stiff collar
dog days *pl n* hottest days of the year
doge *n* chief magistrate of former Venetian republic
dogeared *adj* (of pages) bent down with use
dog-eat-dog *adj* having, showing or marked by cruel self-interest
dogend *n* cigarette butt
dogfight *n* close-quarters combat between fighter aircraft
dogfish *n* smallish fish of the shark family
dogged *adj* refusing to give up; determined **~ly** *adv*
doggerel *n* loosely styled esp. comic poetry
doggo *adv* **lie doggo** remain quietly in hiding
doggone, -goned *adj AmE euph.* damned ♦ *interj* (used to express surprise or annoyance)
doggy bag *n* bag in which left-over food can be taken home from a restaurant
doghouse *n* **1** *AmE* kennel **2 in the doghouse** in a state of disfavour or shame
dogleg *n* sharp bend
dogma *n* (religious) belief to be accepted without reasoning **~tic** *adj* trying to force one's beliefs on other people **~tically** *adv* **~tism** *n*
do-gooder *n derog* person who tries to do good things for others
dog paddle also **doggy paddle** *n* simple swimming stroke
dog rose *n* wild European rose
dogsbody *n BrE* person in a low position who does the dull work
dog-tired *adj* very tired
doily, doiley *n* decorative mat placed under food, esp. cakes
do-it-yourself *n* doing repairs, painting the house, etc., oneself, rather than paying workmen
Dolby *n tdmk* system for reducing unwanted noise on sound recordings
doldrums *pl n* **in the doldrums** sad and dull
dole *n* unemployment benefit **dole out** *phr vt* give in small shares
doleful *adj* unhappy; mournful **~ly** *adv*
doll *n* **1** small toy figure of a person **2** *AmE sl* person that one likes **doll up** *phr vt* dress prettily
dollar *n* **1** unit of money, as used in the US, Canada, and other countries **2** piece of paper, coin, etc., of this value
dollop *n* shapeless mass, esp. of food
dolmen *n* prehistoric stone monument shaped like a table
dolour, *AmE* **dolor** *n* mental anguish **~ous** *adj*
dolphin *n* marine mammal of the whale family, two to three metres long, which swims in groups
dolt *n* stupid person
-dom *suffix* **1** condition of being: *freedom* **2** rank or domain: *dukedom* **3** class of people: *officialdom*
domain *n* **1** area of interest or knowledge **2** land controlled by one ruler
dome *n* rounded roof **domed** *adj* like or covered with a dome
domestic *adj* **1** of the house, home, or family **2** not foreign: *domestic policies* **3** (of animals) not wild ♦ *n* house servant

~ally *adv*
domicile /ˈdomisiəl/ *n fml* place where one lives **domicile** *vt*
dominant *adj* most noticeable or important; dominating **–nance** *n* controlling influence; importance
dominate *vi/t* **1** have power (over); control **2** have the most important place (in) **3** rise or be higher than: *The castle dominated the whole town.* **–nation** *n*
domineer *vi* try to control others unpleasantly
Dominican *n, adj* (member) of an order of friars founded by St. Dominic
dominion *n* **1** *lit* power to rule **2** land under one government **2** *(usu. cap.)* self-governing Commonwealth country
domino *n* **-noes** small flat piece of wood with spots on it, used with others in a game (**dominoes**)
domino effect *n* situation in which one event causes similar ones to happen one after another
don[1] *n BrE* university teacher
don[2] *vt* **-nn-** put on (e.g. clothes)
donate *vt* give (money, etc.), esp. for a good purpose **donation** *n*
done *past p. of* do **1** finished **2** *esp. BrE* socially acceptable
donga *n SAfrE* steep-sided gully
Don Juan *n* accomplished and inveterate seducer of women
donkey *n* **1** animal like a small horse, with long ears **2** fool **3 donkey's years** a very long time
donor *n* person who gives or donates: *blood donor*
don't *short for:* do not
doodle *vi/t* draw lines, figures, etc., aimlessly while thinking of something else **doodle** *n*
doodlebug *n infml* flying bomb
doom *n* **1** unavoidable destruction **2 doom and gloom** hopelessness **~ed** *adj* destined to something bad
Doomsday *n* **1** end of the world **2 till Doomsday** forever
door *n* **1** thing that closes an entrance **2** doorway **3** (in some fixed phrases) house or building: *live next door/two doors away* **4 be on the door** have some duty at the door, such as collecting tickets **5 by the back door** secretly or by a trick **6 shut/close the door to/on** make impossible **7 out of doors** outdoors
do-or-die *adj* determined and reckless or desperate (attempt, effort)
doorkeeper *n* person who guards the main door to a building
doormat *n* **1** mat placed behind a door for people to wipe their shoes on **2** *infml* person who passively allows him- or herself to be bullied or exploited
doorstep *n* step in front of a door
doorstepping *n, adj* (practice of) causing people inconvenience in their homes, etc., in order to find stories for newspapers
door to door *adv* **1** calling at every house in turn **2 a** collecting from and delivering to addresses specified e.g. by a client **b** from the precise point of departure to the precise destination **door-to-door** *adj*
doorway *n* opening for a door
dope *n* **1** harmful drug **2** fool ♦ *vt* give dope to **~y** *adj* **1** sleepy and unable to think clearly, (as if) because of drugs **2** stupid
doppelgänger *n* ghostly double of a living person
dormant *adj* inactive
dormer *also* **dormer window** *n* gabled structure with a vertical window projecting from a sloping roof
dormitory *n* bedroom for several people
dormouse *n* **-mice** small mouse
dorp *n SAfrE* small town
dorsal *adj* of or on the back or top surface of
dosage *n fml* amount of a dose
dose *n* measured amount of medicine to be taken at a time ♦ *vt* give medicine to
doss *vi BrE sl* be lazy **doss down** *phr vi sl, esp. BrE* sleep, esp. not in a proper bed **~er** *n* **1** person who sleeps in doss-houses **2** *infml* lazy person

dosshouse *n* **-houses** *esp. BrE* very cheap lodging-house
dossier *n* set of papers containing facts about a person or subject
dot *n* **1** small spot **2 on the dot** at the exact moment ♦ *vt* **-tt- 1** mark with a dot **2** cover with dots **3 dotted about** scattered **4 sign on the dotted line** agree to something quickly and unconditionally **~ty** *adj* slightly mad
dotage /ˈdohtij/ *n* weakness of the mind caused by old age
dote on *phr vt* be too fond of
double *adj* **1** with two parts or uses **2** for two people **3** twice as much or many ♦ *adv, predeterminer* twice: *buy double the amount* ♦ *n* **1** something that is twice the size, quantity, value, etc. of something else **2** person who looks just like another **3** stand-in **4** bet on two races **5** success in two games, competitions, etc. **6 at the double** quickly ♦ *v* **1** *vi/t* make or become twice as much **2** *vt* fold in half **double as** *phr vt* have as a second use or job **double back** *phr vi* return along the same path **double up** *phr v* **1** *vi/t* bend (the body) at the waist: *doubled up with pain* **2** *vi infml* share accommodation **doubly** *adv* twice as **doubles** *pl n* two pairs of players
double agent *n* spy who, while pretending to work for one country, is actually working for another
double-barrelled *adj* **1** (of a gun) having two barrels **2** (of a name) having two parts
double bass *n* largest stringed musical instrument of the violin family, with a very deep sound
double-breasted *adj* (of a coat) crossing over in front, with two rows of buttons
double-check *vi/t* examine (something) twice for exactness or quality
double chin *n* fold of loose skin between the face and neck
double cream *n* thick cream suitable for whipping
double-cross *vt* cheat; betray **~er** *n*
double-dealer *n* dishonest person **–ing** *adj, n*
double-decker *n* **1** bus with two levels **2** sandwich with two fillings between three slices of bread
double-dutch *n* speech or writing that one cannot understand
double entendre *n* phrase which can be understood two ways, one of which is usu. sexual
double-glazing *n* two thicknesses of glass in a window **–glaze** *vt*
double-jointed *adj* having joints that move backwards as well as forwards
double park *vi/t* park beside an already parked vehicle on a public road
double-quick *adj, adv* very quick(ly)
double stopping *n* playing on two strings (of e.g. a violin) simultaneously
doublet *n* man's close-fitting tunic of the 15th-17th centuries
double take *n* delayed movement of surprise, usu. for comic effect
double-talk *n* **1** use of elaborate language to mislead someone **2** gibberish
doublethink *n* holding or expressing two contradictory ideas at the same time
doubloon *n* old Spanish coin
doubt *vt* **1** feel uncertain about **2** consider unlikely ♦ *n* **1** (feeling of) uncertainty **2 no doubt** probably **~ful** *adj* **1** uncertain **2** not likely **~less** *adv* **1** without doubt **2** probably
douche /doohsh/ *n* (instrument for injecting) a jet or spray of water to cleanse part of the body
dough *n* **1** mixture for making bread **2** *sl* money
doughnut *n* ring-shaped cake cooked in fat
doughty *adj* stalwart
dour *adj* hard and cold in one's nature; unfriendly **~ly** *adv*
douse *vt* **1** throw water over **2** put out (a light)
dove[1] *n* **1** kind of pigeon **2** person in favour of peace
dove[2] *past t. (esp. AmE) of* dive
dovecote *n* building or loft for housing pigeons

dovetail *n* close-fitting joint for two pieces esp. of wood ♦ *v* **1** *vt* join two pieces of wood with a dovetail **2** *vi* fit skilfully or perfectly together

dowager /ˈdowəjə/ *n* grand old lady, esp. a nobleman's widow

dowdy *adj* **1** dully dressed **2** (of clothes) dull **–dily** *adv*

dowel *n* wooden or metal peg which joins two parts of a structure internally

down[1] *adv* **1** to or at a lower level **2** to the south: *come down from Scotland* **3** on paper: *write it down* **4** from the past: *jewels handed down in the family* **5** (shows reduction): *Profits are down.*| *Turn the radio down.* **6 Down with** ... Let's get rid of... ♦ *prep* **1** to or at a lower level on **2** along **3** to: *I'm just going down to the shops.* ♦ *adj* **1** at a lower level, esp. lying on the ground **2** directed down: *the down escalator* **3** finished: *8 down and 2 to go* **4** sad **5** not working: *The computer/phone is down.* **6 down on** having a low opinion or dislike for ♦ *vt* **1** knock down; defeat **2** drink quickly **~er** *n sl* **1** drug that reduces activity **2** experience or state of affairs which is saddening

down[2] *n* soft feathers or hair **~y** *adj*

down-and-out *adj, n* (person who is) suffering from misfortune, lack of money, etc.

downbeat *adj* **1** relaxed; informal **2** pessimistic

downcast *adj* **1** downhearted **2** (of eyes) looking down

downdraught *n* downward current of air

downfall *n* sudden ruin

downgrade *vt* reduce to a lower position

downhearted *adj* low in spirits; sad

downhill *adj, adv* **1** down a slope **2 go downhill** become worse

Downing Street *n* the government of Great Britain

download *vt* transfer (data) from one computer to another

down-market *adj* produced for the lower social groups; usu. low in price, quality, tastefulness and prestige

down payment *n* part of the full price paid at the time of buying, with the rest to be paid later

downpour *n* heavy fall of rain

downright *adj* **1** plain; honest **2** (of something bad) complete ♦ *adv* thoroughly: *downright rude*

downs *pl n* low grassy hills

Down's syndrome *n* congenital mental deficiency; mongolism

downstage *adv, adj* at or towards the front of the stage

downstairs *adv, adj* on or to a lower floor

downstream *adv, adj* **1** moving with the current of a river **2** further down a river

downtime *n* time during which a computer is not operating

down-to-earth *adj* practical; sensible

downtown *adv, adj* to or in the town centre

downtrodden *adj* treated badly by those in power

downturn *n* downward trend in e.g. economic activity

downward *adj* going down **–wards** *adv*

downwind *adv, adj* **1** in the direction that the wind is blowing **2** on the leeward side

dowry /ˈdowri/ *n* property that a woman's father gives to her husband when she marries

dowse *vi* search for water or minerals with a divining rod **~r** *n*

doyen *n* senior, or most experienced, member, exponent, etc.

doyenne *n* senior, or most experienced, woman member, exponent, etc.

doze *vi* sleep lightly **doze** *n*

dozen *determiner, n* **dozen** *or* **dozens 1** twelve **2 talk, speak, etc., nineteen/twenty/forty to the dozen** talk quickly and continuously

DP *abbrev. for:* **1** data processing **2** displaced person

DPP *abbrev. for:* Director of Public Prosecutions

Dr *abbrev. for:* Doctor

drab *adj* dull **~ness** *n*

drachm *n* unit of weight equal to 1/16 oz

drachma /ˈdrakmə/ *n* monetary unit of Greece

draconian *adj (often cap.)* (of a law or punishment) unusually or excessively severe

draft *n* **1** first rough plan of something **2** written order for money from a bank **3** *AmE* draught **4** *AmE* conscription ♦ *vt* **1** make a first plan of **2** *AmE* conscript[1]

draftsman *n* **-men 1** person who drafts new laws **2** *AmE* draughtsman

draftswoman *n* **-women 1** drafter of new laws **2** *AmE* draughtswoman

drag *v* **1** *vt* pull (something heavy) along **2** *vi* move too slowly: *The meeting dragged on for hours.* **3** *vt* cause to come or go unwillingly: *They dragged me to a party.* **4** *vi* move along while touching the ground: *Her long dress dragged in the dust.* **5** *vt* search the bottom of (water) with a net **6 drag one's feet/heels** act intentionally in a slow or ineffective way **drag in** *phr vt* introduce (unconnected subject) **drag on** *phr vi* last an unnecessarily long time **drag out** *phr v* **1** *vi/t* (cause to) last an unnecessarily long time **2** *vt* force (something) to be told **drag up** *phr vt* raise (a subject) unnecessarily ♦ *n* **1** someone or something that makes progress hard **2** *sl* dull event or person **3** *sl* the clothing of one sex worn by the other **4** *sl* act of breathing in cigarette smoke

dragée *n* sugar coated sweet

dragon *n* **1** mythical fire-breathing animal **2** fierce old woman

dragonfly *n* brightly-coloured, slender-bodied winged insect which lives near water

dragoon *n* mounted infantryman ♦ *vt* coerce; pressgang

drain *vi/t* **1** (cause to) flow away **2** make or become dry by removing liquid: *drain a field* **3** empty by drinking the contents of **4** make weak and tired ♦ *n* **1** ditch or pipe to carry water away **2** something that uses up money, etc. **3 down the drain** used wastefully or brought to nothing **~age** *n* system for draining

draining board *n* sloping board on which dishes are placed to dry

drake *n* male duck

Dralon *n* acrylic upholstery fabric

dram *n* **1** tot of whisky **2** drachm

drama *n* **1** theatrical play **2** plays as a group **3** exciting situation **~tic** *adj* **1** of the theatre **2** exciting **~tically** *adv* **~tist** *n* writer of plays **~tize, -tise** *vt* **1** turn (a story, etc.) into a play **2** present (facts) in an exciting way

dramatic irony *n* situation in a play where the audience know that the characters hold mistaken ideas or expectations

dramatis personae *n* (list of) characters in a play

drank *v past t. of* drink

drape *vt* **1** hang (cloth) in folds **2** cause to hang or stretch out loosely or carelessly **~r** *n BrE* dealer in cloth, sewing materials, etc. **~ry** also **drapes** *AmE n* cloth, curtains, etc.

drastic *adj* sudden and violent **~ally** *adv*

draught *n* **1** current of air **2** amount of liquid swallowed **3** depth of water a ship needs **4** *BrE* round object used in playing a board game (**draughts**) ♦ *adj* **1** (of beer, etc.) drawn from a barrel **2** (of animals) used for pulling loads **~y** *adj* with cold draughts

draughtsman *n* **-men 1** person who draws parts of a new machine or building **2** person who draws well

draughtswoman *n* female draughtsman

draw *v* **drew, drawn 1** *vi/t* make (pictures) with a pen or pencil **2** *vt* cause to come, go, or move by pulling **3** *vt* take or pull out: *draw his sword|draw £100 from the bank|draw blood* **4** *vt* attract: *The play drew big crowds.* **5** *vi* move steadily: *The car drew ahead.* **6** *vt* make or get by reasoning: *draw a comparison/lesson* **7** *vi* end a game without either side winning **8** *vi/t* take (breath) in **9 draw a blank** be unsuccessful **10 draw the line (at)** refuse to do or accept **draw away** *phr v* **1** *vi/t* move (something) away **2** *vi* get further and further ahead **draw back** *phr vi* be unwilling to fulfil something **draw in** *phr vi* **1** (of days) become shorter **2** arrive **draw into** *phr vt* encourage, persuade, or force to join in **draw on** *phr vt* **1** make use of **2** approach in time **draw out** *phr v* **1** *vi* (of days) become longer **2** *vt* persuade to talk **draw up** *phr v* **1** *vt* draft (a plan, document, etc.) **2** *vi* (of a vehicle) arrive and stop **3 draw oneself up** stand up straight ♦ *n* **1** result with neither side winning **2** lottery **3** person or thing that attracts the public **drawn** *adj* stretched out of shape: *face drawn with sorrow* **~ing** *n* **1** art of drawing pictures **2** picture

drawback *n* disadvantage

drawbridge *n* bridge that can be raised esp. to defend the entrance to a castle

drawer *n* sliding container in a piece of furniture

drawing pin *n BrE* short pin with a broad flat head used esp. for pinning up notices

drawing room *n* living room

drawl *vi/t* speak or say slowly and with lengthened vowels **drawl** *n*

drawn *past p. of* draw

dray *n* low cart without sides used esp. by brewers

dread *vt* fear greatly ♦ *n* great fear **~ful** *adj* terrible **~fully** *adv*

dreadlocks *pl n* long matted locks of hair worn by Rastafarians

dream *n* **1** image experienced during sleep **2** something hopefully desired **3** something very beautiful ♦ *vi/t* **dreamed** *or* **dreamt 1** have a dream **2** imagine (something) **3 not dream of** refuse to consider **dream up** *phr vt* invent (esp. something silly) **~er** *n* **1** person who dreams **2** impractical person **~less** *adj* (of sleep) peaceful **~y** *adj* **1** seeming half asleep **2** peaceful and beautiful

dreamboat *n sl* very attactive person

dreary *adj* sad and dull **-ily** *adv* **-iness** *n*

dredge[1] *vi/t* bring up mud, etc. from the bottom of water **dredge up** *phr vt* **1** bring to the surface of water **2** produce or bring up (usu. something unpleasant): *dredge up the past*

dredge[2] *vt* sprinkle with flour, sugar, etc.

dregs *pl n* **1** bits of matter that sink to the bottom of liquid **2** worthless part: *the dregs of society*

drench *vt* make thoroughly wet

dress *v* **1** *vi/t* put clothes on **2** *vi* put on formal evening clothes **3** *vt* clean and cover (a wound) **4** *vt* arrange; prepare: *dress a salad/a shop window* **5 dressed to kill** dressed in one's best clothes **dress up** *phr v* **1** *vi/t* put special clothes on **2** *vt* make (something or someone) seem different or more attractive ♦ *n* **1** woman's one-piece outer garment **2** clothing **~ing** *n* **1** covering for a wound **2** sauce, stuffing, etc. **~y** *adj* showy or too ornamental

dressage /ˈdresahzh/ *n* execution of precise movements by a trained horse

dresser[1] *n* person who helps an actor to dress

dresser[2] *n* sideboard with shelves above it

dressing-down *n* strong reprimand

dressing gown *n* loose coat for wearing indoors

dressing room *n* room where people, esp. actors, dress

dressing table *n* table with a mirror, in a bedroom

dressmaker *n* person who makes clothes

dress rehearsal *n* final rehearsal before public performance

drew *past t. of* draw

drey *n* squirrel's nest

dribble *v* **1** *vi* let saliva flow out slowly from the mouth **2** *vi/t* let (liquid) flow slowly **3** *vi/t* move (a ball) by many short kicks or strokes **dribble** *n*

dribs *pl n* **dribs and drabs** *infml* small amounts
dried *past t. and p. of* dry
drift *n* **1** mass of something blown together **2** aimless movement **3** general meaning: *the drift of his argument* ♦ *vi* **1** be driven by wind or water **2** move or live aimlessly *n* **~er** person who lives aimlessly
driftwood *n* wood floating or washed up on shore
drill[1] *n* tool for making holes ♦ *vi/t* use a drill (on)
drill[2] *n* training by repeating and following orders: *army drill* ♦ *vi/t* do or give drill
drill[3] *n* **1** (seed sown in) a shallow furrow **2** planting machine
drily *adv* tersely; ironically
drink *v* **drank, drunk 1** *vi/t* swallow (liquid) **2** *vi* take in (too much) alcohol **drink to** *phr vt* wish (someone or something) good health or success ♦ *n* **1** liquid to drink **2** alcohol to drink **~able** *adj* **~er** *n* person who drinks too much alcohol
drip *vi/t* **1** fall or let fall in drops **2** overflow with or as if with liquid: *She was dripping with diamonds.* ♦ *n* **1** (sound of) liquid falling in drops **2** dull person **~ping** *adj* very wet
drip-dry *adj* (of clothes) that will dry smooth if hung while wet
dripping *n* fat from roasted meat
drive *v* **drove, driven 1** *vi/t* guide (a wheeled vehicle) **2** *vt* take (someone) in a vehicle **3** *vt* force (animals, etc.) to go **4** *vt* be the power for **5** *vt* send by hitting **6** *vt* force (someone) into a bad state: *The pain's driving me mad.* **7** *vi* (esp. of rain) move violently **8 be driving at** mean; hint ♦ *n* **1** journey in a vehicle **2** road through a park or garden **3** stroke in a ball game **4** campaign **5** force of mind: *He lacks drive.* **6** important natural need which must be fulfilled **driver** *n* **1** person who drives vehicles or animals **2** golf club for hitting long shots
drive-in *n, adj* (place) that people can use while remaining in their cars
drivel *n* nonsense ♦ *vi* **-ll-** (*AmE also* **-l-**) talk nonsense
driveway *n* drive (2)
drizzle *n* fine misty rain **drizzle** *vi*
drogue *n* **1** small parachute used to assist aircraft or spacecraft on landing **2** cone-shaped device on the end of the fuel line from a tanker aircraft **3** target towed behind an aircraft **4** sea anchor
droll /drohl/ *adj* odd and amusing **~y** *adv*
dromedary *n* camel with one hump
drone *vi, n* (make) a continuous low dull sound **drone on** *phr vi* speak for a long time in an uninteresting manner
drongo *n* **1** tropical bird with black plumage **2** *AustrE* fool
drool *vi* **1** let liquid flow from the mouth **2** show pleasure in a foolish way
droop *vi* hang downwards **droop** *n*
drop *n* **1** small round mass of liquid **2** small round sweet **3 a** distance or fall straight down **b** fall in quantity: *a drop in sales* **4 at the drop of a hat** suddenly ♦ *v* **-pp- 1** *vi/t* fall or let fall **2** *vi/t* (cause to) become less **3** *vt* let (someone) get out of a vehicle **4** *vt* stop; give up: *drop a subject* **5** *vt* say or write informally: *drop a hint/a note* **6** *vt* leave out (from a team) **drop back/behind** *phr vi* get further away by moving more slowly **drop in/by/round** *phr vi* make an unexpected visit **drop off** *phr vi* **1** get less **2** fall asleep **drop out** *phr vi* **1** stop taking part **2** become a dropout **drops** *n* liquid medicine taken drop by drop
dropout *n* **1** person who leaves a college, school, etc., without finishing the course **2** person who opts out of conventional society
droppings *pl n* waste matter from the bowels of animals or birds
dropsy *n* illness in which tissues are swelled by excess liquid
dross *n* waste or impure matter
drought /drowt/ *n* long period of dry weather when there is not enough water
drove[1] *past t. of* drive

drove[2] *n* group; crowd: *droves of tourists* **~r** *n* person who drives sheep or cattle esp. to or from market

drown *v* **1** *vi/t* die or kill by being under water **2** *vt* cover completely with water **3** *vt* cover up (a sound) with a louder one **4 drown one's sorrows** drink alcohol in an attempt to forget one's troubles

drowse *vi* fall into a light sleep **drowsy** *adj* sleepy **-sily** *adv* **-siness** *n*

drub *vt* beat decisively

drudge *vi* do hard dull work ♦ *n* person who drudges **~ry** *n* hard uninteresting work

drug *n* **1** medicine **2** substance which induces a sense of well-being or hallucinations and is often addictive ♦ *vt* **-gg- 1** add harmful drugs to **2** give drugs to **~gist** *AmE* pharmacist

drugget *n* coarse fabric used esp. as a floor covering

drugstore *n AmE* pharmacy that also sells simple meals

druid *n* priest of the ancient Celtic pre-Christian religion

drum *n* **1** musical instrument made of a skin stretched over a circular frame **2** container, etc., shaped like this ♦ *vi* **-mm- 1** beat a drum **2** make drumlike noises **3 drum something into someone** make someone remember something by saying it often **drum out** *phr vt* send away formally and disapprovingly **drum up** *phr vt* obtain by continuous effort and esp. by advertising **~mer** *n* person who plays a drum

drum major *n* leader of a marching band

drum majorette *n* **1** female leader of a marching band **2** majorette

drumstick *n* **1** stick for beating a drum **2** *infml* lower part of the leg of cooked chicken, turkey, etc.

drunk *past p. of* drink ♦ *adj* under the influence of alcohol ♦ *n* also **drunkard** person who is (habitually) drunk

drunken *adj* **1** drunk **2** resulting from or connected with too much drinking: *a drunken sleep* **~ly** *adv* **~ness** *n*

dry *adj* **1** not wet **2** (of wine) not sweet **3** not allowing the sale of alcohol **4** amusing without appearing to be so; quietly ironic: *dry wit* **5** uninteresting ♦ *v* **1** *vi/t* make or become dry **2** *vt* preserve (food) by removing liquid **3** *vi sl* forget one's lines **dry out** *phr vi/t* **1** (cause to) give up dependence on alcohol **2** (cause to) become completely dry **dry up** *phr vi* **1** (of a supply) stop coming **2** *sl* shut up; stop talking **~er, drier** *n* machine that dries **~ly, drily** *adv* **~ness** *n*

dry-clean *vt* clean (clothes) with chemicals instead of water **~er's** *n* cleaner's **~ing** *n* **1** action or industry of dry-cleaning clothes **2** clothes that need to be or have just been dry-cleaned

dry dock *n* place where a ship is held while water is pumped out

dry goods *pl n AmE* drapery esp. as opposed to hardware or groceries

dry ice *n* solid carbon dioxide

dry rot *n* disease that turns wood into powder

dry run *n* dummy run

dry-shod *adj, adv* keeping one's shoes or feet dry

DSC *abbrev. for:* Distinguished Service Cross

DSc *abbrev. for:* Doctor of Science

DSO *abbrev. for:* Distinguished Service Order

DTI *abbrev. for:* Department of Trade and Industry

DTs *pl n infml* delirium tremens

dual *adj* having two parts; double **~ity** *n*

dual carriageway *n BrE* road with a separate carriageway for each direction of traffic

dub *vt* **-bb- 1** give (a name) to **2** change the spoken language of (a film)

dubbin *n* grease for softening and waterproofing leather

dubious *adj* feeling or causing doubt **~ly** *adv*

ducal *adj* of a duke

ducat *n* old European gold coin

duchess *n* **a** wife of a duke **b** woman

who holds the rank of duke in her own right

duchy *n* lands of a duke or duchess

duck *n* **1** common swimming bird **2** its meat **3** *infml, esp. BrE* (used for addressing) a person one likes **4** (in cricket) failure to make any runs at all ♦ *v* **1** *vi/t* lower (one's head) quickly **2** *vt* push (someone) under water **3** *vt* try to avoid responsibility

duckling *n* young duck

duct *n* tube that carries liquids, air, etc.

ductile *adj* easily shaped; malleable

dud *adj, n sl* useless (thing or person): *a dud cheque*

dude *n sl* **1** *AmE* city-dweller **2** (smart) guy

dudgeon *n lit* **in high dudgeon** very angry or indignant

due *adj* **1** owed **2** suitable; proper **3** expected: *The train is due any minute.* **4** **due to** caused by ♦ *adv* (before **north, south, east, west**) exactly ♦ *n* something that rightfully belongs to one: *give him his due* **dues** *pl n* official payments

duel *n* fight arranged between two people **duel** *vi* **-ll-** (*AmE* **-l-**)

duenna *n* older woman employed as a governess and chaperone esp. formerly in Spain and Portugal

duet *n* piece of music for two performers

duff *adj BrE infml* dud

duffel coat *n* loose heavy coat, often with a hood

duffer *n infml* incompetent person

dug[1] *past t. and p. of* dig

dug[2] *n* nipple, udder or breast

dugong *n* whalelike mammal found in shallow tropical waters

dugout *n* **1** boat made of a hollow log **2** shelter dug in the ground

duke *n* British nobleman of the highest rank **~dom** *n* rank or lands of a duke

dulcet /ˈdulsit/ *adj* sweetly soothing

dull *adj* **1** not bright or shining **2** slow in thinking **3** not sharp: *a dull pain* **4** uninteresting ♦ *vt* make dull **~ness** *n*

dullard *n* stupid or obtuse person

duly *adv* properly; as expected

dumb *adj* **1** unable to speak **2** unwilling to speak; silent **3** *sl* stupid **~ly** *adv* **~ness** *n*

dumbbell *n* **1** weight for exercising consisting of two metal balls connected by a short bar **2** *AmE* stupid person

dumbfound *vt* make dumb from surprise

dumdum *n* soft-nosed bullet that expands on impact

dummy *n* **1** object made to look like a real thing or person **2** *BrE* baby's rubber teat for sucking **3** *sl* stupid person

dummy run *n* practice attempt made before the real thing

dump *vt* **1** drop carelessly **2** sell (goods) abroad more cheaply than at home ♦ *n* place for dumping waste **2** stored supply **3** *sl* dirty untidy place **4** **in the dumps** sad **~er** *n* large vehicle for carrying earth and stones **~y** *adj* short and fat

dumpling *n* ball of boiled dough

dun[1] *n* brownish grey colour

dun[2] *n* debt-collector ♦ *vt* make persistent demands for payment

dunce *n* slow learner

dunderhead *n* blockhead

dune *n* long low sandhill piled up by the wind

dung *n* animal manure

dungarees *pl n* **1** *BrE* trousers with a bib, usu. made of heavy cotton **2** *AmE* jeans for working in

dungeon *n* underground prison

dunk *vt* dip (esp. food) into liquid while eating

duo *n* a pair, esp. of musicians

duodenum *n* first part of the small intestine

duologue *n* (theatrical) dialogue between two people

dupe *vt* trick; deceive ♦ *n* person who is duped

duplex *adj* double, twofold ♦ *n AmE* **1** flat on two floors **2** semi-detached house

duplicate *n, adj* (something that is)

exactly like another ♦ *vt* copy exactly **–cator** *n* machine that copies **–cation** *n*
duplicity *n* dishonesty
durable *adj* long-lasting **durables** *pl n* goods expected to last for years
durance *n lit* captivity
duration *n fml* **1** time during which something lasts **2 for the duration** as long as something lasts
duress *n* threats: *promise under duress*
Durex *n tdmk* condom
during *prep* **1** all through (a length of time) **2** at some moment in: *die during the night*
dusk *n* time when daylight fades
dusky *adj* rather dark in colour
dust *n* powder made of earth or other matter ♦ *vt* **1** clean the dust from **2** cover with powder **dust off** *phr vt* begin to use or practise again, after a period of not doing so **~er** *n* cloth for removing dust **~y** *adj* covered with dust
dustbin *n BrE* container for waste materials
dustbowl *n* area that suffers from drought and dust storms
dustcart *n BrE* vehicle that collects the contents of dustbins
dust jacket *n* loose paper cover on a hardback book
dustman *n* **-men** *BrE* person employed to empty dustbins
dustpan *n* flat container into which house dust is swept
dustsheet *n* large sheet used to cover furniture, etc., to keep off dust
dust-up *n infml* quarrel
Dutch *adj* **1** of the Netherlands (Holland) **2 go Dutch (with someone)** share expenses
Dutch cap *n* female contraceptive that fits over the neck of the womb
Dutch courage *n infml* bravery due to drinking
Dutch oven *n* large stewing pan
Dutch treat *n* outing on which everybody shares expenses
Dutch uncle *n* **talk (to someone) like a Dutch uncle** criticize or admonish (someone) sternly
duty *n* **1** something one must do **2** tax **3 on/off duty** required/not required to work **dutiable** *adj* on which duty has to be paid **dutiful** *adj* showing respect and obedience **dutifully** *adv*
duty-free *adj, adv* (of goods) allowed to enter a country without tax
duvet /ˈdoovay/ *n* large bag of feathers used as a bed covering
DV *abbrev. for:* Deo volente
dwarf *n* **dwarfs** *or* **dwarves** very small person, animal, or plant ♦ *vt* cause to look small
dwell *vi* **dwelled** *or* **dwelt** *lit* live (in a place) **dwell on** *phr vt* think or speak a lot about **~er** *n* person or animal that lives somewhere: *city-dwellers* **~ing** *n fml* home
dwindle *vi* become gradually fewer or smaller
dye *n* substance used to colour cloth, etc. ♦ *vi/t* **dyes, dyed, dyeing** colour with dye
dyed-in-the-wool *adj* impossible to change (as to the stated or known quality): *a dyed-in-the-wool Republican*
dying *present p. of* die
dyke *n* dike
dynamic *adj* **1** powerful and active **2** of force that causes movement **~ally** *adv*
dynamics *n* science that deals with matter in movement **–ism** *n* being dynamic
dynamite *n* **1** powerful explosive **2** something or someone that will cause great shock, admiration, etc. ♦ *vt* blow up with dynamite
dynamo *n* **-mos** machine that turns movement into electricity
dynasty *n* line of rulers of the same family **–stic** *adj*
dys- *prefix* **1** abnormal **2** painful
dysentery /ˈdis(ə)ntri/ *n* painful bowel disease
dyslexia *n* inability to read, from difficulty in recognizing letter shapes **–ic** *adj*
dyspepsia *n* indigestion **–peptic** *adj*

E

E, e the 5th letter of the English alphabet
E *abbrev. for:* east(ern)
each *determiner, pron* every one separately ♦ *adv* for or to each: *They cost fifty cents each.*
each other *pron* with each doing something to the other
each way *adj, adv* (of a bet) for a win or a place
eager *adj* keen; wanting very much **~ly** *adv* **~ness** *n*
eager beaver *n* someone who is very, or excessively, enthusiastic and industrious
eagle *n* large meat-eating bird with a hooked beak **~-eyed** *adj* having very good eyesight
eaglet *n* young eagle
-ean *suffix* **-ian**
ear[1] *n* **1** either of the two parts of the head with which we hear **2** good recognition of sounds: *an ear for music* **3 all ears** listening eagerly **4 play by ear** play music without written notes **5 up to one's ears in** deep in; very busy with
ear[2] *n* head of a grain-producing plant
earache *n* pain inside the ear
eardrum *n* tight skin inside the ear which allows one to hear sound
earful *n infml* **1** sharp scolding **2** outpouring of news or gossip
earl *n* British nobleman of high rank **~dom** *n* rank or lands of an earl
earlobe *n* lobe (1)
early *adv, adj* **1** sooner than usual or expected **2** near the beginning **3 at the earliest** and not sooner
early bird *n* person who gets up or arrives early
early warning system *n* radar network that gives advance information of enemy air attack
earmark *vt* set aside (money, etc.) for a particular purpose
earn *v* **1** *vi/t* get (money) by working **2** *vt* deserve (what one has worked for) **~er** *n* **~ings** *pl n* money earned
earnest *adj* determined and serious ♦ *n* **in earnest: a** in a determined way **b** not joking **~ly** *adv* **~ness** *n*
earphones *pl n* headphones
earpiece *n* **1** flap on a cap or hat, which covers the ear **2** piece of a spectacle frame which hooks over the ear
earplug *n* soft thing put into the ear to keep out noise, etc.
earring *n* decoration for the ear
earshot *n* **within/out of earshot** within/beyond the distance at which a sound can be heard
earth *n* **1** (*often cap.*) the world we live on **2** its surface, as opposed to the sky **3** soil **4** wild animal's hole **5** *BrE* safety wire carrying electricity to the ground ♦ *vt BrE* connect (electrical apparatus) to the ground **~ly** *adj* **1** of this world, not heaven **2** possible: *no earthly reason* **~y** *adj* **1** like soil **2** crude; coarse
earthbound *adj* **1** unable to leave the surface of the Earth **2** unimaginative
earthenware *n* (pots, etc., made of) baked clay
earthling *n* (in science fiction) inhabitant of the Earth
earthquake *n* sudden violent shaking of the earth's surface
earth-shaking *adj* of tremendous importance
earthwork *n* large structure of earth used as a protection against enemies
earthworm *n* common type of worm that burrows in soil
ear trumpet *n* primitive trumpet-shaped hearing aid
earwig *n* insect with two curved parts on its tail
ease *n* **1** ability to do something easily **2** state of being comfortable **3 ill at ease**

uncomfortable ♦ *v* **1** *vi/t* make or become less painful or difficult **2** *vt* make less anxious **3** *vt* move slowly and carefully into a different position **ease off/up** *phr vi* become less active or severe
easel *n* wooden frame to support a picture or blackboard
east *n* (*often cap.*) direction from which the sun rises ♦ *adj* **1** in the east **2** (of wind) from the east ♦ *adv* to the east **~ward** *adj, adv*
Easter *n* holy day in memory of Christ's death
Easter egg *n* chocolate, or painted hard-boiled egg given as a present at Easter
easterly *adj* east
eastern *adj* of the east part of the world or of a country
easy *adj* **1** not difficult **2** comfortable; without worry ♦ *adv* **go easy on: a** be less severe with **b** not use too much of **–sily** *adv* **1** without difficulty **2** without doubt: *easily the best*
easy chair *n* an armchair
easygoing *adj* pleasantly calm and unhurried
easy street *n infml* **on easy street** in comfortable (financial) circumstances
easy virtue *n* **a woman of easy virtue** *lit* promiscuous woman
eat *v* **ate, eaten 1** *vi/t* take in (food) through the mouth **2** *vt* destroy by chemical action **3 be eaten up with** be full of (violent feeling) **4 eat one's words** admit that one was wrong **5 eat out of someone's hand** be very willing to agree with or obey somebody **6 eat your heart out** *infml* be very jealous **~able** *adj* **~er** *n*
eats *n infml* food
eau de cologne *n* toilet water
eaves *pl n* edges of a roof, beyond the walls
eavesdrop *vi* **-pp-** listen secretly to conversation **~per** *n*
ebb *vi* grow less or lower: *His courage ebbed away.* ♦ *n* **1** the going out of the tide **2 at a low ebb** in a bad state
ebb tide *n* outward flow of the sea
ebony *adj, n* (of the colour of) hard black wood
ebullient /iˈbulli·ənt/ *adj* full of happy excitement **–ence** *n*
eccentric /ikˈsentrik/ *adj* **1** (of people) unusual; peculiar **2** (of circles) not having the same centre ♦ *n* eccentric person **~ity** *n.*
ecclesiastical *adj* of the Christian church
ECG *abbrev. for:* **1** electrocardiogram **2** electrocardiograph
echelon /ˈeshəlon/ *n* level within an organization
echo *n* **-oes** sound sent back from a surface ♦ *v* **1** *vi* come back as an echo **2** *vt* copy or repeat (words, ideas, etc.)
echo sounder *n* sonar
éclair *n* finger-shaped cake with cream inside
éclat /ayˈklah/ *n* **1** brilliant success **2** ostentation
eclectic *adj fml* using ideas from many different systems **~ism** *n*
eclipse *n* disappearance of the sun's light (cut off by the moon) or of the moon's light (cut off by the Earth) ♦ *vt* **1** cause an eclipse of **2** make (something) less important by comparison
ecliptic *n* the sun's apparent path around the Earth
eclogue *n* pastoral poem usu. in the form of a conversation
ecology *n* relations of living things to their surroundings **–gist** *n* **–gical** *adj*
economic *adj* **1** connected with trade, industry, and wealth **2** profitable **~al** *adj* not wasteful **~ally** *adv*
economics *n* study of the way in which wealth is produced and used **-nomist** *n*
economize, –mise *vi* avoid waste
economy *n* **1** economic system of a country **2** avoidance of waste ♦ *adj* cheap: *an economy class air ticket*
ecosystem *n* all the living things in an area and the relationship between them
ecstasy *n* great joy **ecstatic** *adj* **ecstatically** *adv*
ECT *abbrev. for:* electro-convulsive

therapy

ectoplasm *n* substance supposedly emitted by a spiritualistic medium in a trance

ecumenical /ˌekyooˈmenikl, eek-/ *adj* favouring Christian unity

eczema /ˈeks(i)mə/ *n* red swollen condition of the skin

-ed *suffix* **1** (makes regular past tense and participle of verbs) **2** having or wearing the stated thing: *bowler-hatted*

Edam *n* mild yellow Dutch cheese made in balls with a red wax rind

eddy *n* circular movement of water, smoke, etc. ♦ *vi* move in eddies

edelweiss *n* alpine plant with woolly white leaves and yellowish flowers

Eden *n* (garden where Adam and Eve lived in) a state of perfect happiness

edge *n* **1** cutting part of a knife, etc. **2** narrowest part along the outside of an object: *the edge of a coin* **3** place where something begins or ends: *the water's edge* **4 have the edge on** be better than **5 on edge** nervous **6 take the edge off** *infml* make less severe ♦ *v* **1** *vt* put a border on **2** *vi/t* move gradually, esp. sideways **~ways** *adj, adv* sideways **edging** *n* border **edgy** *adj* nervous **edgily** *adv*

edible *adj* that can be eaten

edict *n* official public command

edification *n* improvement of character or mind **edify** *vt*

edifice *n fml* large fine building

edit *vt* prepare (a newspaper, film, etc.) for printing or showing **~or** *n* person who edits

edition *n* **1** one printing, esp. of a book **2** form in which a book is printed: *a paperback edition*

editorial *adj* of an editor ♦ *n* newspaper article giving the paper's opinion

EDP *abbrev. for:* electronic data processing

educate *vt* teach; train

educated guess *n* guess based on information and experience

education *n* (knowledge resulting from) teaching or training **~al** *adj*

Edwardian *adj* of, or dating from, the reign of Edward VII

-ee *suffix* **1** person to whom the stated thing is done: *trainee* **2** person who is or does the stated thing: *absentee*

EEC *n* European Economic Community; West European organization to encourage trade and friendly relations

EEG *abbrev. for:* **1** electroencephalogram **2** electroencephalograph

eel *n* long snake-like fish with a smooth slimy skin

-eer *suffix* person who does the stated thing: *auctioneer*

eerie *adj* frightening because of being strange: *an eerie silence* **eerily** *adv*

efface *vt fml* rub out

effect *n* **1** result; what happens because of a cause **2 in effect: a** in operation **b** in fact **3 take effect** come into operation ♦ *vt* produce; cause **effects** *pl n* **1** sounds, etc., produced in a film or play **2** personal belongings

effective *adj* **1** producing the desired result: *very effective new laws* **2** actual: *the effective strength of our army* **~ly** *adv* **~ness** *n*

effeminate *adj* (of a man) too like a woman **~nacy** *n*

effervesce *vi* form bubbles of gas **–vescence** *n* **–vescent** *adj*

effete *adj* weak; effeminate

efficacy *n* effectiveness **–cacious** *adj*

efficient *adj* working well: *an efficient secretary/machine* **~ly** *adv* **-ciency** *n*

effigy *n* wooden, stone, etc., likeness of someone

effing and blinding *n* using obscene language

efflorescence *n lit* flowering; blossoming

effluent *n* liquid chemical or human waste

effluvium *n* **-via** bad smell given off by something

effort *n* **1** use of strength **2** attempt **~less** *adj* successful without effort **~lessly** *adv*

effrontery *n* rudeness without any feeling of shame

effulgent *adj lit* radiant; brilliant **–ence** *n*
effusive *adj* showing too much feeling **~ly** *adv*
EFL *abbrev. for:* English as a foreign language
EFTA *abbrev. for:* European Free Trade Association
e.g. *abbrev. for:* for example
egalitarian *adj* believing in social equality **~ism** *n*
egg *n* **1** round object with a shell, containing a baby bird, snake, etc. **2** (the contents of) an egg when used as food: *a boiled egg* **3** female cell producing young **4 have egg on one's face** seem foolish **egg on** *phr vt* encourage someone, esp. to do wrong
eggcup *n* container for a boiled egg
egghead *n derog* a highbrow
eggplant *n* large purple vegetable; aubergine
egg timer *n* device, usu. a miniature hourglass, for timing the boiling of an egg
ego *n* **egos 1** one's opinion of oneself **2** *tech* one's conscious self
egocentric *adj* thinking only about oneself; selfish
egoism *n* selfishness **-ist** *n*
egotism *n* believing that one is more important than other people **-tist** *n* **–tistic, -tistical** *adj*
ego trip *n* act or set of acts done mainly because it makes one feel proud of oneself
egregious /iˈgreej(y)əs/ *adj fml* noticeably bad
egress *n* way out
egret *n* wading bird similar to a heron
Egyptian *n, adj* (inhabitant) of Egypt
eiderdown *n* bed covering filled with feathers esp. from an **eider duck**
eight *determiner, n, pron* 8 **eighth** *determiner, adv, n, pron* 8th
eighteen *determiner, n, pron* 18 **~th** *determiner, adv, n, pron* 18th
eighty *determiner, n, pron* 80 **-tieth** *determiner, adv, n, pron* 80th
eisteddfod *n* Welsh-language competitive festival of music and poetry
either *determiner, pron, conj* **1** one or the other **2** each of two: *houses on either side of the road* ♦ *adv* (used with negative expressions) also: *I haven't been to France, or Germany either.*
ejaculate *vi/t* **1** throw out (sperm) suddenly from the body **2** cry out suddenly **-lation** *n*
eject *vt* throw out **~ion** *n*
ejector seat, *AmE* **ejection seat** *n* seat that throws one out of a crashing plane
eke out *phr vt* **1** make (supplies) last as long as possible **2** supplement **3** earn (a living) with difficulty
elaborate *adj* full of detail ♦ *vi* add more detail **-ration** *n* **~ly** *adv*
élan /ayˈlon, -ˈlan/ *n* liveliness; vigour
eland *n* large African antelope
elapse *vi* (of time) pass
elastic *adj* able to spring back into shape after stretching or bending ♦ *n* elastic material **~ity** *n*
elastic band *n BrE* rubber band
Elastoplast *tdmk* (strip of) elastic adhesive plaster
elate *vt* cause to become elated
elated *adj* proud and happy **-ion** *n*
elbow *n* joint where the arm bends ♦ *vt* push with the elbows
elbow grease *n* hard work with the hands
elbow room *n* space to move freely
elder¹ *adj* (of a family member) older ♦ *n* **1** older of two people **2** person in a respected official position **~ly** *adj* rather old
elder² small tree with black berries **(elderberries)** and white flowers **(elderflowers)**
elder statesman *n* old and respected person who is asked for advice because of his or her experience
eldest *n, adj* (person who is) the oldest of three or more
El Dorado *n* mythical place of fabulous wealth
elect *vt* **1** choose by voting **2** *fml* decide: *She elected to go.* ♦ *adj* chosen, but not yet at work; *president elect* **–ive** *adj* **1**

chosen by election **2** optional **~or** *n* person with the right to vote **~oral** *adj* **~orally** *adv*

election *n* (occasion of) choosing representatives by voting

electioneering *n* activity of persuading people to vote for a political party

electoral college *n* body of electors, esp. those chosen by each state to elect the president of the USA

electorate *n* all the electors

Electra complex *n* (in Freudian psychology) a girl's unconscious sexual desire for her father and hatred of her mother

electric *adj* **1** worked by or producing electricity **2** *infml* very exciting **~al** *adj* concerned with or using electricity: *an electrical fault* **~ally** *adv*

electric blanket *n* blanket containing a heating element

electric chair *n* (device for) executing a criminal by electrocution

electrician *n* person who fits and repairs electrical apparatus

electricity *n* **1** power from moving electrons **2** electric power supply

electric shock therapy *or* **treatment** *n* electroconvulsive therapy

electrify *vt* **1** use electric power for **2** excite greatly **-fication** *n*

electro- *prefix* electric or electrically

electrocardiogram *n* tracing made by an **electrocardiograph**, an instrument that records the electrical activity of the heart

electroconvulsive therapy *n* treatment of mental illness by passing a small electric current through the brain

electrocute *vt* kill by passing electric current through the body **-cution** *n*

electrode *n* point at which current enters or leaves a battery

electroencephalogram *n* tracing made by an **electroencephalograph**, an instrument that records brain waves

electrolysis /ˌelekˈtroləsis/ *n* the use of electricity **a** for separation of a liquid into its chemical parts or **b** for destruction of hair roots **-lytic** *adj*

electromagnet *n* iron or steel core magnetized by a current passed through a coil of wire wound round it **~ic** *adj*

electron *n* small particle of matter that moves round the nucleus of an atom

electronic *adj* of, using, or produced by equipment that works by means of an electric current passing through chips transistors, etc. (for example, televisions, computers, etc.) **~ally** *adv* **electronics** *n* study or making of such equipment

electron microscope *n* microscope which uses a beam of electrons

eleemosynary *adj lit* supported by, or giving, charity

elegant *adj* graceful; stylish **~ly** *adv* **-gance** *n*

elegy *n* sad or reflective poem, esp. one expressing sorrow for a dead person **elegaic** *adj*

element *n* **1** simple substance consisting of only one kind of atom **2** small amount: *an element of truth in what you say* **3** part of a whole: *Honesty is an important element in his character.* **4** heating part of a piece of electric apparatus **5 in/out of one's element** doing/not doing what one is best at **elements** *pl n* **1** (bad) weather **2** first things to study in a subject **elemental** *adj* of the forces of nature

elementary *adj* **1** easy **2** concerned with the beginning of something

elementary school *n AmE* school for the first six to eight years of a child's education

elephant *n* very large animal with tusks and a long trunk **~ine** *adj* heavy and awkward

elephantiasis *n* **-ses** tropical disease causing enormous swellings

elevate *vt fml* **1** raise **2** improve (the mind)

elevation *n* **1** *fml* act of elevating **2** height above sea-level **3** drawing of one side of a building **4** angle made with the horizon, e.g. by a gun

elevator *n* **1** *AmE* lift (2) **2** machine for raising grain, liquids, etc.

eleven *determiner, n, pron* 11 **~th** *determiner, adv, n, pron* 11th

eleven-plus *n* (former) British examination to determine whether a pupil should attend a grammar school or secondary modern school

elevenses *n BrE infml* coffee, tea, or a light meal at about 11 o'clock in the morning

eleventh hour *n* the very last moment

elf *n* **elves** small usu. male fairy **~in** *adj* like an elf

elicit *vt* get (information, response, etc.) from someone

elide /iˈlied/ *vt* leave out (a sound) in pronunciation

eligible *adj* fulfilling the conditions; suitable **-bility** *n*

eliminate *vt* remove; get rid of **-nation** *n*

elite /iˈleet/ *n* favoured powerful group in society **elitism** *n* (*usu. derog.*) belief in the virtue of having elites and in their entitlement to special treatment **elitist** *n, adj*

elixir /iˈliksə/ *n* something with magical curative powers

Elizabethan *adj* of the reign of Elizabeth I

elk *n* very large deer

ellipse *n* oval shape

ellipsis *n* (mark indicating) the omission of letters or words

elliptical *adj* **1** oval **2** concise (to the point of obscurity)

elm *n* large broad-leaved tree

elocution *n* (the art of) good clear speaking

elongate *vt* make longer

elope *vi* run away to get married **~ment** *n*

eloquent *adj* **1** able to influence people by using language well **2** showing something very strongly: *an eloquent reminder of the horrors of wars* **-quence** *n*

else *adv* **1** more; as well **2** apart from (what is mentioned) **3** otherwise: *pay or else go to prison*

elsewhere *adv* at, in, from, or to another place

ELT *n* English language teaching

elucidate *vt fml* explain **-dation** *n*

elude *vt* escape from

elusive *adj* hard to find or remember

elver *n* young eel

elves *pl. of* elf

Elysium *n* paradise

em- *prefix* en-

emaciated *adj* extremely thin **-ation** *n*

emanate from *phr vi fml* come out (from somewhere) **-nation** *n*

emancipate *vt* free from slavery, restraint, etc. **-pation** *n*

emasculate *vt* **1** weaken **2** castrate **-lation** *n*

embalm *vt* preserve (a dead body) with chemicals, etc. **~er** *n*

embankment *n* wall that holds back water or carries a road or railway

embargo *n* **-goes** official order forbidding trade ♦ *vt* put an embargo on

embark *vi/t* go or put onto a ship **embark on/upon** *phr vt* start (something new) **~ation** *n*

embarrass *vt* make ashamed or socially uncomfortable: *an embarrassing question/silence* **~ingly** *adv* **~ment** *n*

embassy *n* **1** offices or residence of an ambassador **2** official mission to a foreign country

embattled *adj* surrounded by enemies or difficulties

embed *vt* **-dd-** fix firmly in surrounding material

embellish *vt* **1** decorate **2** add (esp. untrue) details to **~ment** *n*

ember *n* piece of red-hot coal, etc., in a dying fire

Ember days *pl n* days set aside by the church for prayer and fasting

embezzle *vi/t* steal (money placed in one's care) **~ment** *n* **-zler** *n*

embitter *vt* make sad and angry

emblazon *vt* **1** display conspicuously **2** adorn, esp. with coats of arms

emblem *n* sign representing something: *The emblem of England is a rose.* **~atic** *adj*

embody *vt* give physical expression to

-iment *n* something in physical form: *She's the embodiment of evil.*
embolism *n* (obstruction of a blood vessel by) a blood clot
emboss *vt* decorate with a raised pattern
embrace *v* **1** *vi/t* take (someone) lovingly in one's arms **2** *vt* include **3** *vt* become a believer in: *embrace the Muslim faith* ♦ *n* act of embracing: *a warm embrace*
embrasure *n* splayed door or window aperture
embroider *vi/t* **1** decorate (cloth) with needlework **2** embellish **~y** *n*
embroiled *adj* mixed up in something troublesome: *to get embroiled in an argument*
embryo *n* **-os 1** creature in its first state before birth **2 in embryo** still incomplete **~nic** *adj* **~logy** *n* study of embryos
emcee *n AmE* compere
emend *vt* take mistakes out of (something written) **~ation** *n*
emerald *n* (colour of) a bright green precious stone
emerge *vi* **1** come out **2** (of facts) become known **emergence** *n* **emergent** *adj* beginning to develop: *emergent nations*
emergency *n* dangerous happening which must be dealt with at once
emeritus *adj* retired but retaining one's title: *emeritus professor*
emery *n* hard powder used for polishing
emetic *n, adj* (substance) which induces vomiting
emigrant *n* person who emigrates
emigrate *vi* leave one's own country to live in another **-gration** *n*
émigré *n* refugee
eminence *n* great importance
éminence grise *n* someone who secretly has great influence, but does not have an official position of power
eminent *adj* (of a person) famous and admired **~ly** *adv fml* extremely
emir *n* Muslim ruler **~ate** *n* lands, etc., of an emir
emissary *n fml* person sent with a message or to do special work
emission *n fml* **1** act of emitting **2** something emitted
emit *vt* **-tt-** send out: *to emit smoke*
Emmenthaler, -taler *n* mild hard Swiss cheese with holes in it
Emmy *n* **-mys** *or* **-mies** US award for outstanding TV performances or productions
emollient *n, adj* (substance) which softens or gives relief
emoluments *pl n fml* pay; wages
emote *vi* express emotion (theatrically)
emotion *n* **1** strong feeling, such as love, sorrow, etc. **2** strength of feeling: *a voice shaking with emotion* **~al** *adj* **1** concerning the emotions **2** having feelings that are (too) strong **~ally** *adv*
emotive *adj* causing strong feeling
empanel *vt* **-ll-** (*AmE* **-l-**) **1** enroll on a panel **2** select as a member of a jury
empathy *n* ability to imagine oneself in the position of another person **-thize, -thise** *vi*
emperor *n* ruler of an empire
emphasis *n* **-ses** special force or attention given to something important
emphasize, -sise *vt* place emphasis on
emphatic *adj* strongly emphasized **~ally** *adv*
emphysema /ˌemfiˈseemə/ *n* lung disease causing breathlessness and wheezing
empire *n* group of countries under one government
empiricism /emˈpirisiz(ə)m/ *n* **1** belief that all knowledge must be derived from observation and experience **2** use of empirical methods **-cal** *adj* based on observation and experience **-cally** *adv*
emplacement *n* gun platform
employ *vt* **1** give paid work to **2** *fml* use **~able** *adj* suitable as a worker **~ee** *n* employed person **~er** *n* person who employs others **~ment** *n* **1** paid work **2** *fml* useful activity
emporium *n* **-riums** *or* **-ria** large shop
empower *vt* give a legal power to
empress *n* female ruler of an empire

empty *adj* **1** containing nothing **2** insincere: *empty promises* ♦ *n* empty container ♦ *vi/t* make or become empty **-tiness** *n*
empty-handed *adj* having gained nothing
empty-headed *adj* silly
EMS *abbrev. for:* European Monetary System
emu *n* large Australian flightless bird
emulate *vt* try to do as well as or better than **-lation** *n*
emulsion *n* creamy liquid mixture, esp. paint
en- *prefix* cause to be (more): *enlarge*
-en *suffix* **1** (in adjectives) made of: *wooden* **2** (in verbs) make or become (more): *sweeten*
enable *vt* make able
enact *vt* make (a law)
enamel *n* **1** glassy covering on metal, etc. **2** hard surface of the teeth ♦ *vt* **-ll-** (*AmE* **-l-**) cover with enamel
enamoured, *AmE* **-ored** *adj* very fond (of an idea, person, etc.)
en bloc *adv* all together as a single unit
encampment *n* military camp
encapsulate *vt* express in a short form
encase *vt* cover completely
-ence *prefix* -ance
encephalitis /inˌsefəˈlietəs/ *n* inflammation of the brain
enchant *vt* **1** delight **2** use magic on **~ing** *adj* delightful **~ingly** *adv* **~ment** *n*
enchilada *n* Mexican dish consisting of a tortilla rolled around a filling and covered with chilli sauce
encircle *vt* surround
enclave *n* part of a country surrounded by another
enclose *vt* **1** surround with a fence, etc. **2** put (something else) into an envelope
enclosure *n* **1** enclosed place **2** something put in with a letter **3** act of enclosing
encomium *n* **-miums** *or* **-mia** *fml* expression or speech of praise
encompass *vt* include; be concerned with
encore *interj, n* (word calling for) a repeated performance
encounter *vt* meet (something dangerous or unexpected) ♦ *n* sudden (esp. unpleasant) meeting
encounter group *n* group who develop self-awareness and sensitivity by frank interaction guided by a leader or therapist
encourage *vt* **1** inspire with courage, confidence, or hope **2** foster; promote **3** urge; spur on **-ging** *adj* causing feelings of hope and confidence **-gingly** *adv* **~ment** *n*
encroach *vi* go beyond limits; intrude on: *encroach on their territory* **~ment** *n*
encrusted *adj* thickly covered: *encrusted with jewels/mud*
encumber *vt* load; burden **-brance** *n*
-ency *suffix* quality or state of: *dependency*
encyclical /enˈsiklikl/ *n* papal letter to all bishops
encyclopedia, -paedia *n* book of many facts in alphabetical order **-dic** *adj* wide and full
end *n* **1** point where something stops or finishes **2** little piece remaining: *cigarette ends* **3** aim; purpose **4 in the end** at last **5 make ends meet** get just enough money **6 no end of** an endless amount of **7 on end: a** continuously: *for hours on end* **b** upright **9 put an end to** stop ♦ *vi/t* finish **end up** *phr vi* finish one's journey **~ing** *n* end (of a story, etc.) **~less** *adj* never finishing **~lessly** *adv*
endanger *vt* cause danger to
endear make (someone or oneself) loved by **~ment** *n* expression of love
endeavour, *AmE* **-or** *vi* try ♦ *n* effort
endemic *adj* (esp. of something bad) often happening in a place
endgame *n* final stages of a chess game
endive *n* salad plant with curly, bitter leaves
endocrine gland *n* gland that secretes hormones directly into the bloodstream

endogenous *adj* developing or originating within an organism
endorse *vt* **1** express approval of (opinions, etc.) **2** write one's name on (a cheque) **3** record a driving offence on (a driver's licence) **~ment** *n*
endow *vt* give a continuing income to (a school, etc.) **endow with** *phr vt* provide with (an ability or attribute) **~ment** *n*
endowment mortgage *n* mortgage in which the principal is repaid by an endowment policy
endowment policy *n* insurance policy under which an agreed amount is paid out to the holder after a specified period, or to a beneficiary in the event of his or her death
endue with *phr vt fml* endow with; imbue with
endurance *n* power of enduring
endure *v* **1** *vt* suffer (pain, etc.) patiently **2** *vi* continue to exist
endways, endwise *adv* **1** with the end forward; lengthways **2** end to end
enema *n* putting of a liquid, esp. a medicine, into the bowels through the rectum
enemy *n* **1** person who hates or opposes another person **2** country with which one is at war
energetic *adj* very active **~ally** *adv*
energy *n* **1** ability to be active and work hard **2** power that drives machines, provides heat, etc. **-gize, -gise** *vt* give energy to
enervate *vt fml* debilitate
en famille /on faˈmeeː/ *adv* together as a family
enfant terrible /ˌonfonh teˈreeblə/ *n* shocking but also often interesting and amusing person
enfeebled *adj* made weak
enfilade *vt, n* (attack with) gunfire directed along a line or position from the flank
enfold *vt* **1** envelop **2** take into one's arms
enforce *vt* cause (a law etc.) to be obeyed **~able** *adj* **~ment** *n*
enfranchise *vt* give the right to vote to **~ment** *n*
engage *v* **1** *vt* arrange to employ **2** *vi/t* lock (machine parts) together **engage in** *phr vt* (cause to) take part in
engaged *adj* **1** having agreed to marry **2** busy or in use **~ment** *n* **1** agreement to marry **2** arrangement to meet someone **3** *fml* battle
engagé *adj* (politically) active and committed
engaging *adj* charming **~ly** *adv*
engender *vt* cause; produce
engine *n* **1** machine that turns power into movement **2** machine that pulls a train
engineer *n* **1** person who plans machines, roads, bridges, etc. **2** person who controls engines ♦ *vt* cause by secret planning **~ing** *n* profession of an engineer
English *adj* of England
English breakfast *n* a breakfast of esp. bacon and eggs, toast and marmalade
engrave *vt* cut (words, etc.) on a hard surface **-ver** *n* **-ving** *n* **1** picture printed from an engraved piece of metal **2** work of an engraver
engross *vt* completely fill the attention of
engulf *vt* swallow up
enhance *vt* increase (something good) **~ment** *n*
enigma *n* mystery; riddle **~tic** *adj* **~tically** *adv*
enjoin *vt* **1** command **2** prohibit
enjoy *vt* **1** get pleasure from **2** possess (something good) **3 enjoy oneself** be happy **~able** *adj* pleasant **~ably** *adv* **~ment** *n*
enlarge *vi/t* (cause to) become larger **enlarge on/upon** *phr vt* say more about **~ment** *n*
enlighten *vt* make free from false beliefs **~ment** *n*
enlist *v* **1** *vi/t* (cause to) join the armed forces **2** *vt* obtain (help, sympathy, etc.) **~ment** *n*
enlisted man *n AmE* private
enliven *vt* make more active or cheerful
en masse *adv* all together; in a body

enmesh *vt* catch as if in a net
enmity *n* hatred; hostility
ennoble *vt* **1** make finer; elevate (2) **2** raise to the nobility
ennui *n* boredom; dissatisfaction
enormity *n* **1** enormous size **2** great wickedness
enormous *adj* very large **~ly** *adv* extremely
enough *determiner, pron, adv* **1** as much or as many as is needed **2 oddly/strangely enough . . .** and this is strange, but . . .
en passant /ˌon pa'sonh/ *adv* in passing; by the way
enquire *vi/t* inquire **enquiry** *n*
enrage *vt* make very angry
enrapture *vt* make very happy
enrich *vt* **1** make rich **2** improve by adding something **~ment** *n*
enrol, enroll *vi/t* **-ll-** (cause to) jon a group officially **~ment** *n*
en route *adv* on the way; travelling
ensconced *adj* comfortably seated or settled
ensemble *n* **1** small group of musicians **2** *fml* set of things
enshrine *vt fml* preserve as if holy
enshroud *vt* shroud
ensign *n* **1** ship's flag **2** US naval officer
enslave *vt* make into a slave **~ment** *n*
ensnare *vt* catch (as if) in a snare
ensue *vi* happen afterwards or as a result
en suite *adv* (of rooms) forming a set, esp. by opening directly off a main room
ensure *vt* make (something) certain to happen
-ent *suffix* -ant
entablature *n* upper section of a wall in a classical building usu. supported on columns
entail *vt* **1** necessitate; involve **2** restrict (the inheritance of property) to designated heirs
entangle *vt* cause to become twisted with something else **~ment** *n*
entente /on'tont/ *n* friendly relationship between countries
enter *v* **1** *vi/t* come or go in or into **2** *vt* become a member of **3** *vt* put into a book, list, etc. **enter into** *phr vt* take part in **enter on/upon** *phr vt fml* begin
enteritis *n* inflammation of the intestine usu. causing diarrhoea
enterprise *n* **1** project, esp. one that needs courage **2** willingness to take risks **3** business organization **-prising** *adj* having initiative
entertain *v* **1** *vi/t* amuse and interest **2** *vi/t* provide food and drink for (guests) **3** *vt* (be willing to) consider (ideas) **~er** *n* person who amuses people professionally **~ment** *n* **1** act of entertaining **2** public amusement
enthral, enthrall *vt* **-ll-** hold the complete attention of
enthrone *vt* put (a ruler) on a throne
enthuse *vi* speak with enthusiasm
enthusiasm *n* great interest and admiration **-ast** *n* person who is keen on something **-astic** *adj* full of enthusiasm **-astically** *adv*
entice *vt* persuade, esp. to do wrong **~ment** *n*
entire *adj* complete **~ly** *adv* **~ty** *n*
entitle *vt* **1** give a right (to) **2** give a title to (a book, etc.) **~ment** *n*
entity *n* thing with separate existence
entomb *vt lit* put (as if) in a tomb
entomology *n* study of insects **–gist** *n*
entourage /'ontooˌrahzh/ *n* people who surround someone important
entr'acte *n* (entertainment given during) the interval between two acts of a play
entrails *n* bowels
entrain *vi/t* (cause to) board a train
entrance¹ *n* **1** door, gate, etc., by which one enters **2** act of entering, esp. onto the stage **3** right to enter
entrance² *vt* fill with delight
entrant *n* person who enters a race, profession, etc.
entrap *vt* **1** catch (as if) in a trap **2** lure into an incriminating act or statement
entreat *vt fml* beg; implore **~y** *n* act of entreating
entrecote *n* beefsteak cut from between

the ribs
entree *n* **1** freedom to enter **2 a** *esp. BrE* small meat dish eaten before the main dish of a meal **b** *esp. AmE* main dish of a meal
entrenched *adj* (of beliefs, etc.) firmly established
entre nous /ˌontrə ˈnooh/ *adv* between ourselves
entrepreneur /ˌontrəprəˈnuh/ *n* person who starts a firm, etc., and takes business risks **~ial** *adj*
entresol *n* mezzanine
entropy *n* the tendency of all energy in the universe to spread out evenly and become inert
entrust *vt* give to someone to take care of
entry *n* **1** act of coming or going in **2** something written in a list
entwine *vt* twist together or round
E number *n* number with the letter E in front of it, used to show the additives contained in food
enumerate *vt* name one by one **-ration** *n*
enunciate *vt/i* pronounce (words) clearly **-ation** *n*
envelop *vt* cover completely **~ment** *n*
envelope *n* paper container for a letter
envenom *vt* **1** put poison into or onto **2** embitter
enviable *adj* very desirable **-bly** *adv*
envious *adj* feeling envy **~ly** *adv*
environment *n* conditions in which people, animals, etc., live **~al** *adj* **~ally** *adv* **~alist** *n* person who tries to keep our natural surroundings from being spoilt
environs *pl n* surrounding neighbourhood
envisage, also *AmE* **envision** *vt* see in the mind; expect
envoy *n* messenger; representative
envy *n* **1** bad feeling one has towards someone who has better luck than oneself **2 the envy of (someone)** something which other people want to have or to be ♦ *vt* feel envy towards or because of
enzyme *n* substance produced by living cells that causes chemical change
eon *n* aeon
epaulet, **-lette** *n* shoulder decoration on a uniform
épée *n* (fencing with) a sharp-pointed, thin-bladed sword with a bowl-shaped guard
ephemeral /iˈfem(ə)rəl/ *adj* lasting only a short time
epi- *prefix* **1** outer: *epidermis* **2** above: *epigraph* **3** in addition: *epilogue*
epic *n* **1** long poem, film, etc., about the deeds of gods or great men **2** *derog* event needing a lot of time and energy ♦ *adj* (of stories) full of bravery and excitement
epicentre, *AmE* **-center** *n* point on the earth's surface above the place of origin of an earthquake
epicure *n lit* gourmet
epicurean *n* person who believes pleasure to be the greatest good in life
epidemic *n* many cases of an infectious disease at the same time
epidermis *n* outer layer of the skin
epidural *n* spinal anaesthetic given esp. during labour
epiglottis *n* flap of cartilage which covers the entrance to the windpipe when food is being swallowed
epigram *n* short amusing poem or saying
epigraph *n* **1** inscription **2** quotation introducing a book, poem, or chapter
epilepsy *n* disease of the brain causing sudden unconsciousness **-leptic** *adj, n*
epilogue *n* concluding part of a play or book
Epiphany *n* church festival commemorating the coming of the magi
episcopal /iˈpiskəpl/ *adj* of or governed by bishops
episode *n* one separate event or period of time **-sodic** *adj* **1** made up of episodes **2** occasional; sporadic
epistle *n fml* letter (1)
epistolary *adj lit* relating to or consisting of letters

epitaph *n* words written above a grave
epithet *adj* descriptive and usu. abusive word or phrase
epitome /iˈpitəmi/ *n* something that perfectly shows a particular quality: *My son is the epitome of laziness.* **-mize, -mise,** *vt* be typical of
epoch /ˈeepok/ *n* period of historical time, esp. one in which some remarkable event happened **~-making** *adj* extremely important
Epsom salts *pl n* white powder used as a purgative
equable *adj* even and regular **-bly** *adv*
equal *adj* **1** the same in size, value, etc. **2 equal to** having enough ability, etc., for ♦ *n* person equal to another ♦ *vt* **-ll-** (*AmE* **-l-**) be the same as **~ize, -ise** *vt* make equal **~ly** *adv* **~ity** *n*
equanimity *n fml* calmness of mind
equate *vt* consider as equal
equation *n* statement that two quantities are equal: $2x + 1 = 7$ *is an equation.*
equator *n* imaginary line round the world, halfway between the North and South Poles **~ial** *adj*
equerry *n* officer in personal attendance on a member of the royal family
equestrian *adj* of horse-riding
equi- *prefix* equally
equidistant *adj* equally distant from two or more places
equilateral *adj* having all sides equal
equilibrium *n* balance (1)
equine *adj* of or resembling the horse
equinox *n* time of year when day and night are of equal length
equip *vt* **-pp-** provide with what is necessary **~ment** *n* things needed for an activity
equipoise *n* **1** even balance **2** counterbalance
equitable *adj* fair and just: *an equitable division of the money* **-bly** *adv*
equitation *n fml* horse-riding
equity *n* **1** *fml* fairness **2** legal system which is based on natural justice and supplements the common law **3** ordinary shareholders' interest in a company **equities** *pl n tech* firm's ordinary shares, on which no fixed amount of interest is paid
equivalent *n, adj* (something) the same in value
equivocal *adj* doubtful in meaning; questionable **-cate** *vi fml* speak in an equivocal way on purpose
ER *abbrev. for:* Elizabeth Regina (Queen Elizabeth)
-er[1] *suffix* (forming comparative of adjectives and adverbs) more
-er[2] *suffix* **1** person or thing that does the stated thing: *driver; mincer* **2** native or resident of: *Londoner* **3** something that has the thing stated: *three-wheeler*
era *n* period of historical time, marked esp. by particular developments
eradicate *vt* root out; eliminate **-cation** *n*
erase *vt* rub out **eraser** *n* rubber (2)
ere *prep, conj* before
erect *adj* upright ♦ *vt* **1** put upright: *erect a tent* **2** build: *erect a monument* **~ion** *n* **1** the act of erecting something **2** a building **3** (an example of) the state of the penis when upright **~ly** *adv* **~ness** *n*
erg *n* unit of work or energy
ergo *adv* therefore
ergonomics *n* study of how people work best with machines **-ic** *adj* **-ically** *adv*
ergot *n* **1** (disease of grain caused by) a type of fungus **2** drug made from this fungus used e.g. to treat migraine
ermine *n* (white fur of) the stoat
Ernie *n* Electronic Random Number Indicator Equipment; a computer that randomly selects winning Premium Bond numbers
erode *vt* (of acids, water, etc.) wear away; reduce **erosion** *n*
erogenous *adj* sexually sensitive
erotic *adj* of sexual love **~ism** *n* **~a** *pl n* literature or art on erotic themes
err *vi* make a mistake
errand *n* short journey to do or esp. buy something
errant *adj fml* wandering away and misbehaving

erratic *adj* changeable; not regular **~ally** *adv*
erratum *n* **-ta** printing error to be corrected
erroneous *adj* (of a belief) incorrect **~ly** *adv*
error *n* **1** mistake **2** state of being mistaken
ersatz *adj derog* used instead of something else; artificial
erstwhile *adj lit* former
erudite *adj fml* full of learning
erupt *vi* (of a volcano) explode suddenly **~ion** *n*
-ery *suffix* **1** -ness **2** art or practice: *cookery* **3** place where something is done: *brewery*
erysipelas *n* infectious disease causing red sore patches on the skin
-es *suffix* (forming plural or 3rd person sing. of verbs) -s
escalate *vi/t* (cause to) grow greater or more serious **-lation** *n*
escalator *n* set of moving stairs
escalope *n* thin slice of meat
escapade *n* wild dangerous act
escape *v* **1** *vi/t* get out; get free (from) **2** *vt* avoid (something dangerous): *to escape death* **3** *vt* be forgotten by: *His name escapes me.* ♦ *n* (act of) getting free
escapement *n* device which regulates the movement of the mechanism of a wind-up clock or watch
escape velocity *n* speed a body must attain to escape from the gravitational pull of e.g. a planet
escapism *n* activity providing escape from dull reality **-ist** *adj, n*
escapology *n* art of escaping from bags, chains etc. as a theatrical performance **–logist** *n*
escarpment *n* long cliff
eschatology *n* theological study of, or beliefs concerning, the end of the world **–logical** *adj*
eschew *vt fml* avoid
escort *n* **1** person or people who go with another as a protection or honour **2** social companion, esp. a man ♦ *vt* go with as an escort
escritoire *n* writing desk
escutcheon *n* shield with a coat of arms on it
-ese *suffix* **1** inhabitant or language of: *Chinese* **2** (*usu. derog.*) style or diction of a particular group: *journalese*; *officialese*
Eskimo *n* Inuit
ESL *abbrev. for:* English as a second language
esoteric /ˌeesəˈterik/ *adj* having deep and secret meanings understood only by a few people **~ally** *adv*
ESP *n* extrasensory perception; knowledge obtained without using one's ordinary five senses
espalier *n* (tree or shrub trained to grow flat against) a railing, trellis, etc. **espalier** *vt*
especially *adv* **1** to a particularly great degree: *not especially hot* **2** in particular: *I like fruit, especially apples.*
Esperanto *n* artificial international language
espionage *n* spying
esplanade *n* promenade (1)
espouse *vt* **1** *fml* support (an aim, etc.) **2** *arch* marry **espousal** *n*
espresso *n* **-sos** (cup of) coffee made by forcing steam through ground coffee beans
esprit de corps *n* loyalty to a group
espy *vt* catch sight of
Esq. *abbrev for:* esquire (used as courtesy title for a man replacing Mr): *Simon Phipps Esq.*
-esque *suffix* in the manner or style of: *Kafkaesque*; *picturesque*
-ess *suffix* female: *actress*; *lioness*
essay *n* short piece of writing on a subject **~ist** *n* writer of essays
essence *n* **1** most important quality of something **2** liquid, etc., with some particular strong taste or smell: *coffee essence* **3 of the essence** extremely important
essential *adj* **1** necessary **2** fundamental ♦ *n* something necessary **~ly** *adv* basically

-est *suffix* (forming superlative of adjectives and adverbs) most
establish *vt* **1** begin; create (an organization, set of rules, etc.) **2** settle (esp. oneself) firmly in a particular state or position: *the film which established her reputation as a director* **3** make certain of (a fact, etc.) **~ment** *n* **1** act of establishing **2** *fml* place run as a business **3** (*cap.*) *often derog* the powerful people who control public life
established church *n* church recognized as a national institution
estate *n* **1** piece of land in the country, with one owner **2** *BrE* piece of land built on in a planned way: *a housing estate* **3** *law* whole of a person's property, esp. as left after death
estate agent *n BrE* person who buys and sells houses and land for people
estate car *n BrE* car with a door at the back and folding back seats
esteem *n fml* respect: *I hold him in high esteem.* ♦ *vt* **1** respect greatly **2** *fml* consider to be **estimable** *adj* worthy of respect
ester *n* compound formed by the reaction between an acid and an alcohol
estimate *vt/i* calculate; form an opinion about (cost, etc.) ♦ *n* calculation of cost, number, etc. **-mation** *n* judgment; opinion
estrange *vt* make unfriendly **~ment** *n*
estuary *n* mouth of a river, into which the sea flows
ETA *abbrev. for:* estimated time of arrival
et al *adv* and others
etc., also **etcetera** *adv* and the rest; and other things
etch *vi/t* draw with a needle and acid on metal **~ing** *n*
eternal *adj* lasting for ever **~ly** *adv*
eternal triangle *n* difficult situation resulting from the love of two people, usu. of the same sex, for another person, usu. of the other sex
eternity *n* **1** endless time after death **2** an extremely long time
-eth *suffix* -th
ether *n* **1** liquid that easily changes to a gas **2** upper levels of the air
ethereal /iˈthiəri·əl/ *adj* extremely light and delicate
ethic *n* system of moral behaviour **~al** *adj* **1** of morals **2** morally good **~ally** *adv* **ethics** *n* **1** science of morals **2** moral rules
Ethiopian *n, adj* (inhabitant) of Ethiopia
ethnic *adj* of or related to a racial, national, or tribal group **~ally** *adv*
ethnocentric *adj* based on a belief in the superiority of one's own race, nation or culture **–trism** *n*
ethnology *n* study of different races **–gical** *adj* **-gically** *adv* **–gist** *n*
ethos *n* characteristic moral beliefs of a person or group
ethyl alcohol *n* ordinary alcohol which can be drunk
etiolated *adj* **1** (of a plant) white and spindly through lack of sunlight **2** sickly; feeble
etiquette *n* formal rules of conduct
-ette *suffix* **1** small: *kitchenette* **2** female: *usherette*
etymology *n* study of the origins of words
eucalyptus *n* tree whose oil is used as medicine for colds
Eucharist *n* (bread and wine consecrated at) Holy Communion
eugenics *n* science of selective breeding to improve a race or stock **eugenic** *adj*
eulogy *n* **1** *fml* speech in praise of someone **2** *AmE* formal speech given at a person's funeral **-gize** ,**-gise** *vt* praise highly **-gistic** *adj* full of praise
eunuch *n* man who has been castrated
euphemism *n* (use of) a pleasanter, less direct word for something unpleasant **-mistic** *adj* **–mistically** *adv*
euphonious /yoohˈfohnyəs/ *adj fml* pleasant-sounding **–phony** *n*
euphonium *n* brass instrument like a small tuba
euphoria *n* state of happiness and cheerful excitement **-ric** *adj*
euphuism *n* very ornate and high-flown style of writing

Eurasian *n, adj* (person) of mixed European and Asian origin
eureka *interj* (humorously) triumphant cry of discovery
Euro- *prefix* of Europe, esp. of the EEC
Eurocrat *n infml often derog* EEC official
Eurodollar *n* US dollar held by a European bank
European *adj* of or from Europe ♦ **1** inhabitant of Europe **2** person of European (racial) origin
eustachian tube *n* tube connecting the middle ear to the throat
euthanasia *n* painless killing of very ill or very old people
evacuate *vt* take all the people away from (a dangerous place) **–ation** *n* **–uee** *n* person who has been evacuated
evade *vt* avoid; escape from
evaluate *vt* calculate the value of **–ation** *n*
evanescent /ˌevəˈnes(ə)nt/ *adj* fleeting; vanishing like vapour **evanesce** *vi* **–scence** *n*
Evangelical *n, adj* **1** (member) of those Christian churches that believe in studying the Bible rather than in ceremonies **2** (person) showing very great eagerness in spreading certain beliefs
evangelist *n* travelling Christian religious teacher **-lism** *n* **~ic** *adj*
evaporate *vi/t* change into steam and disappear **-ration** *n*
evasion *n* the act of evading: *tax evasion* **-sive** *adj* **–sively** *adv*
eve *n* **1** (*usu. cap.*) day before a (religious) holiday **2** time just before any event: *on the eve of the election*
even *adv* **1** (shows that something is unexpected and surprising): *John's a very good swimmer, but even he doesn't swim in the river* **2** (makes comparisons stronger): *It's even colder than yesterday.* **3 even if** it does not matter if **4 even now/so/then** in spite of that: *I explained, but even then he didn't understand.* **5 even though** though ♦ *adj* **1** smooth and regular: *an even surface/temperature* **2** (of things that can be compared) equal: *an even chance* **3** (of numbers) that can be divided by two **even out** *phr vi/t* (cause to) become level or equal **~ly** *adv* **~ness** *n*
even-handed *adj* giving fair and equal treatment to all sides
evening *n* time between afternoon and bedtime
evening dress *n* **1** formal clothes for the evening **2** woman's formal long dress
evensong *n* evening service in the Anglican church
event *n* **1** (important) happening **2** one race, etc., in a day's sports **3 at all events** in spite of everything **4 in the event** when it actually happened **5 in the event of . . .** if (something) happens **~ful** *adj* full of important events
eventual *adj* happening at last **~ly** *adv* in the end **~ity** *n fml* possible event
eventuate *vi fml* result
ever *adv* **1** at any time **2** always: *the ever-increasing population* **3** (gives force to a question): *What ever is that?* **4 ever so/such** *infml* very
evergreen *n, adj* (tree) that does not lose its leaves in winter
everlasting *adj* lasting for ever
every *determiner* **1** each **2** (of things that can be counted) once in each: *I go every three days.* **3** as much as is possible: *I have every reason to trust him.* **4 every other** the 1st, 3rd, 5th, etc., or the 2nd, 4th, 6th, etc.: *Take the pills every other day* **5 every now and then** also **every so often** sometimes, but not often
everybody *pron* everyone
everyday *adj* ordinary; common
everyone *pron* **1** every person **2** all the people usually here: *Where is everyone?*
everything *pron* **1** each thing **2** all that matters: *Money isn't everything.*
everywhere, also *AmE* **everyplace** *adv* at or to every place
every which way *adv AmE* in every direction
evict *vt* force to leave a place by law **~ion** *n*
evidence *n* **1** proof **2** answers given in a court of law **3 in evidence** present

and easily seen
evident *adj* plain and clear **~ly** *adv*
evil *adj* harmful; wicked ♦ *n* wickedness or misfortune **~ly** *adv*
evil eye *n* supposed power to put a spell on people by looking at them
evince *vt fml* show clearly; reveal
eviscerate /iˈvisərayt/ *vt fml* disembowel
evocative *adj* conjuring up memories, feelings, etc.
evoke *vt* produce (a memory, feeling, etc.)
evolution *n* gradual development, esp. of living things from earlier and simpler forms **~ary** *adj*
evolve *vi/t* develop gradually
ewe *n* female sheep
ewer *n* water jug esp. for holding water for washing or shaving
ex *n infml* former wife, husband, girlfriend or boyfriend
ex- *prefix* **1** former: *ex-wife* **2** out of; outside
exacerbate /ekˈsasəbayt/ *vt* make (something bad) worse **-ation** *n*
exact *adj* correctly measured; precise: *the exact time* ♦ *vt* demand and obtain by force **~ing** *adj* demanding great effort **~ly** *adv* **1** correctly **2** (as a reply) I agree! **3 not exactly** not really **~ness, ~itude** *n* **~ion** *n* **1** harsh demand esp. for money **2** something exacted
exaggerate *vi/t* make (something) seem larger, more important, etc., than it is **-ration** *n*
exalt *vt fml* **1** praise highly **2** raise in rank **~ation** *n* great joy because of success **~ed** *adj* of high rank
exam *n* test of knowledge
examination *n* **1** exam **2** act of examining
examine *vt* **1** look carefully at **2** ask questions, to find out something or to test knowledge **-iner** *n*
example *n* **1** something that shows a general rule: *a typical example* **2** something to be copied: *Her courage is an example to us all.* **3 for example** here is one of the things just spoken of **4 make an example of someone** punish someone to frighten others
exasperate *vt* annoy very much **-ratedly** *adv* **-ratingly** *adv* **-ration** *n*
ex cathedra *adj, adv* **1** (made) with authority **2** (of papal pronouncements) to be accepted by Catholics as infallibly true
excavate *vt* **1** dig (a hole) **2** uncover by digging **-vator** *n* person or machine that excavates **-vation** *n*
exceed *vt* **1** be greater than **2** do more than: *to exceed the speed limit* **~ingly** *adv* extremely
excel *v* **-ll- 1** *vi* be extremely good (at something) **2** *vt* surpass
Excellency *n* (title of some people of high rank in the state or church)
excellent *adj* very good **-lence** *n* **~ly** *adv*
except *prep* not including; but not ♦ *vt* leave out; not include
exception *n* **1** (a case of) leaving out or being left out: *Everyone, without exception, must attend.* **2 take exception to** be made angry by **~al** *adj* unusual, esp. because very good **~ally** *adv*
exceptionable *adj* likely to cause offence
excerpt *n* piece taken from a book, etc.
excess *n, adj* (an amount that is) greater than is usual or allowed: *an excess of violence in the film* **~ive** *adj* too much **~ively** *adv* **excesses** *pl n* extremely bad, cruel, etc., behaviour
exchange *vt* give and receive in return: *I exchanged my dollars for pounds.* ♦ *n* **1** act of exchanging **2** changing of money: *the rate of exchange* **3** place where **a** telephone wires meet **b** business people meet: *the Stock Exchange* **4** short period of fighting or talking
Exchequer *n* government department responsible for taxation and revenue
excise¹ *n* tax on goods produced inside a country
excise² *vt fml* remove by cutting
excite *vt* **1** cause to have strong (pleasant) feelings **2** cause (feelings): *to*

excite interest **~ment** *n* **excitable** *adj* easily excited **excited** *adj* pleasantly aroused or expectant **exciting** *adj*
exclaim *vi/t* speak or say suddenly
exclamation *n* word(s) exclaimed
exclamation mark, *AmE* **exclamation point** *n* punctuation mark (!) written after an exclamation
exclude *vt* **1** keep out or leave out **2** shut out from the mind: *Don't exclude that possibility.* **–uding** *prep* not including **–usion** *n*
exclusive *adj* **1** keeping out unsuitable people **2** not shared ♦ *n* story appearing in only one newspaper **~ly** *adv* only: *exclusively for women*
excogitate *vt fml* think out; devise
excommunicate *vt* exclude from the Christian Church **-cation** *n*
excoriate *vt fml* criticise scathingly
excrement *n* solid waste from the bowels
excrescence *n* unnatural outgrowth
excreta *pl n fml* excrement and/or urine
excrete *vt* pass out (waste matter)
excruciating *adj* (of pain) very bad **~ly** *adv*
exculpate *vt fml* free from blame
excursion *n* **1** short journey for pleasure **2** digression
excuse *vt* **1** forgive: *Please excuse my bad handwriting.* **2** make (bad behaviour) seem less bad **3** free from a duty **4 Excuse me** (said when starting to speak to a stranger, or when one wants to get past a person, or to apologize for something) **5 excuse oneself** ask permission to be absent ♦ *n* **1** reason given when asking to be excused **2** justification **3** *infml* inferior version of something **excusable** *adj* that can be forgiven
ex-directory *adj* (of a telephone number) omitted from the directory at the subscriber's request
execrable *adj fml* very bad **–bly** *adv*
execrate *vt lit* **1** detest **2** curse; damn **–ation** *n*
execute *vt* **1** kill as a legal punishment **2** carry out; perform: *execute a plan* **–cutant** *n* performer **-cution** *n* **1** legal killing **2** carrying out; performance **-cutioner** *n* official who executes criminals
executive *adj* concerned with managing, or carrying out decisions ♦ *n* **1** person in an executive position in business **2** branch of government that carries out the law
executor *n* person who carries out the orders in a will
executrix *n* woman executor
exegesis *n* explanation of the meaning of esp. biblical texts
exemplary *adj* **1** suitable to be copied; model **2** intended as a warning **exemplar** *n* something that serves as a model or example
exemplify *vt* be or give an example of **-fication** *n*
exempt *adj* freed from a duty, etc. ♦ *vt* make exempt **~ion** *n*
exequies *pl n lit* funeral rites
exercise *n* **1** use of the powers of the body to improve it: *go swimming for exercise* **2** something done for training; *naval exercises* **3** use (of a power or right) ♦ **1** *vi/t* take or give physical exercise **2** *vt* use (a power or right)
exercise bike or **cycle** *n* stationary machine like a bicycle which one pedals as a way of keeping fit
exert *vt* **1** use (strength, etc.) **2 exert oneself** make an effort **~ion** *n*
exeunt *v* (used in stage directions) they go out
ex gratia /eks ˈgraysh(i)ə/ *adj* (of a payment) made as a favour, and not because one has a legal duty to make it
exhale *vi/t* breathe out **–lation** *n*
exhaust *vt* **1** tire out **2** use up completely ♦ *n* pipe by which gases escape from an engine **~ive** *adj* thorough **~ively** *adv* **~ion** *n*
exhibit *vt* **1** show publicly for sale, etc. **2** *fml* show that one has (a quality) ♦ *n* something shown in e.g. a museum **~or** *n* person showing exhibits
exhibition *n* **1** public show of objects **2** act of exhibiting **~ism** *n* **1** behaviour

of someone who wants to be looked at **2** indecent exposure **~ist** *n*
exhilarate *vt* make cheerful and excited **-ration** *n*
exhort *vt fml* urge strongly **~ation** *n*
exhume *vt* dig up (a dead body) **exhumation** *n*
exigency /ˈeksij(ə)nsi, igˈzij(ə)nsi/ *n fml* urgent need
exiguous *adj fml* scanty; meagre
exile *n* **1** unwanted absence from one's country **2** someone forced into this ♦ *vt* send into exile
exist *vi* have life; be real **~ence** *n* **1** state of being real **2** way of living: *lead a miserable existence* **~ent** *adj* existing; present
existential *adj* **1** related to existence **2** existentialist
existentialism *n* philosophy which deals with human experience in relation to the world, esp. questions of freedom and responsibility **–ist** *n, adj*
exit *n* **1** way out of a building **2** act of leaving ♦ *vi* (used as a stage direction) he/she/it goes out
exodus *n* going away of many people
ex officio *adv, adj* by virtue of an office held
exogamy *n* marriage with someone from outside one's own tribe or group
exonerate *vt* free (someone) from blame **-ration** *n*
exorbitant *adj* (of cost) too much **~ly** *adv*
exorcize, –cise *vt* drive out (an evil spirit, etc.) by prayers **-cism** *n* act or art of exorcizing **-cist** *n*
exotic *adj* excitingly strange or unusual ♦ *n* exotic person or thing **~ally** *adv*
expand *vi/t* (cause to) grow larger or more detailed **expand on/upon** *phr vt* make more detailed
expanse *n* wide open space
expansion *n* act of expanding **~ism** *n* policy of expanding one's territory, influence, etc. **~ist** *n, adj*
expansive *adj* friendly and willing to talk **~ly** *adv*
expatiate on/upon /ikˈspayshiˌayt/ *phr vt* speak a lot about
expatriate *n, adj* (person) living abroad
expect *vt* think or believe that something will happen **~ing** *adj infml* pregnant **~ation** *n* **1** state of expecting **2** something expected
expectant *adj* **1** waiting hopefully **2** pregnant **~ly** *adv* **-tancy** *n* hope
expectorate *vi fml* spit **–rant** *n* cough medicine that gets rid of phlegm
expedient *adj* (of an action) useful, esp. for one's own purposes ♦ *n* useful plan, esp. one thought of in a hurry because of urgent need **~ly** *adv* **-ency** *n*
expedite /ˈekspiˌdiet/ *vt fml* make (a plan) go faster
expedition *n* (people making) a journey for a purpose: *an expedition to the North Pole* **~ary** *adj* (of an army) sent abroad to fight
expeditious *adj fml* speedy **~ly** *adv*
expel *vt* **-ll- 1** dismiss officially from a school, etc. **2** force out from a container
expend *vt* spend; use up **~able** *adj* that can be used up without worrying
expenditure *n* spending
expense *n* **1** cost **2 at someone's expense: a** with someone paying **b** (of a joke) against someone **expenses** *pl n* money for a purpose: *We'll pay his travelling expenses.*
expense account *n* (record of) expenses which will be paid by one's employer
expensive *adj* costing a lot **~ly** *adv*
experience *n* **1** knowledge gained by practice **2** something that happens to a person ♦ *vt* suffer or learn by experience **–enced** *adj* having experience
experiment *n* test carried out to learn something ♦ *vi* perform experiments **~al** *adj* used for or based on experiments **~ation** *n*
expert *n, adj* (person) with special skill or training **~ly** *adv*
expertise *n* skill in a particular field
expert system *n* computer system which contains information on a particular subject, used to solve problems

expiate *vt fml* pay for (a crime) by accepting punishment **-ation** *n*
expire *vi* **1** (of something that lasts for a time) come to an end **2** *lit* die **expiry** also **expiration** *n*
explain *v* **1** *vi/t* make (a meaning) clear **2** *vt* be the reason for **explain away** *phr vt* give an excuse for (something) in order to avoid blame **explanation** *n* **1** act of explaining **2** something that explains **explanatory** *adj* (of a statement) explaining
expletive *n* swearword
explicable *adj fml* (of behaviour, etc.) understandable
explicate *vt fml* explain
explicit *adj* (of a statement, etc.) clearly and fully expressed **~ly** *adv* **~ness** *n*
explode *v* **1** *vi/t* blow up; burst **2** *vi* show violent feeling **~d** *adj* **1** (of a drawing, diagram, etc.) showing the parts of e.g. a machine separately, but in correct relationship to each other **2** (of a theory) discredited
exploit *n* brave successful act ♦ *vt* **1** use (people) unfairly for profit **2** use (things) fully for profit **~er** *n* **~ation** *n* **~ative** *adj* tending to exploit
explore *vt* **1** travel through (a place) for discovery **2** examine (a subject) carefully **explorer** *n* **exploration** *n* **exploratory** *adj*
explosion *n* **1** (noise of) exploding **2** sudden increase: *the population explosion*
explosive *n, adj* (substance) that explodes **~ly** *adv*
exponent *n* someone who expresses or supports a belief
exponential *adj* produced by multiplying a set of quantities by themselves
export *vi/t* send (goods) abroad for sale ♦ *n* **1** (business of) exporting **2** something exported **~er** *n*
expose *vt* **1** uncover; leave without protection **2** make known (a secret crime, etc.) **3** uncover (photographic film) to the light **4 expose oneself** show one's sexual parts on purpose, in the hope of shocking people **exposure** *n*
exposé *n* public statement of something shameful
exposition *n* explaining; explanation
ex post facto *adj, adv* **1** after the event **2** having retrospective effect
expostulate *vi fml* complain loudly and firmly
expound *vt* describe (a belief, etc.) in detail
express *vt* **1** make known by words or looks: *She expressed surprise at his decision.* **2 express oneself** speak or write one's thoughts or feelings ♦ *adj* **1** going quickly **2** clearly stated: *her express wish* ♦ *n* express train ♦ *adv* by express post **~ly** *adv* **1** clearly **2** on purpose
expression *n* **1** act of expressing **2** word or phrase **3** look on someone's face **4** quality of showing feeling: *singing without much expression* **~less** *adj* without expression
expressionism *n* style of art which attempts to depict the artist's subjective emotions rather than external reality **-ist** *n, adj*
expressive *adj* showing feelings **~ly** *adv*
expressway *n AmE* motorway
expropriate *vt fml* take away for public use **-ation** *n*
expulsion *n* act of expelling
expunge *vt* remove completely from a list, etc.
expurgate /ˈekspuhˌgayt/ *vt* remove improper words, etc., from
exquisite *adj* beautifully made or done **~ly** *adv*
extant *adj* still existing
extempore /ikˈstempəri/ *adj, adv* off the cuff; impromptu **-poraneous** *adj* extempore **-porize, -ise** *vi/t* improvise on the spur of the moment
extend *v* **1** *vt* make longer or larger **2** *vt* stretch out (part of one's body) to the limit **3** *vt* offer, give: *extend a welcome* **4** *vi* (of land) reach **~able, -ible** *adj*
extended family *n* the nuclear family plus other close relations, e.g. grand-

parents and cousins, thought of as a group

extension *n* **1** act of extending **2** part added **3** telephone line inside a set of offices

extensive *adj* large in amount or area **~ly** *adv*

extent *n* **1** amount or length **2** degree: *to a large extent*

extenuating *adj* giving good reasons (for bad behaviour): *extenuating circumstances*

exterior *adj, n* outside (of something)

exterminate *vt* kill all of **-nation** *n*

external *adj* outside **~ize, -ise** *vt* give outward expression to **~ly** *adv*

externals *pl n* outward forms and appearances

extinct *adj* **1** (of a kind of animal) no longer existing **2** (of a volcano) no longer active **~ion** *n* state of being or becoming extinct

extinguish *vt fml* **1** put out (a fire, etc.) **2** destroy (hope, etc.) **~er** *n* apparatus for putting out fires

extirpate /ˈekstuh,payt/ *vt fml* destroy completely

extol *vt* **-ll-** praise highly

extort *vt* obtain by force or threats **~ion** *n* **~ionist** *n*

extortionate *adj* exorbitant

extra *adj, adv* beyond what is usual or necessary ♦ *n* **1** extra thing **2** film actor in a crowd scene **3** special edition of a newspaper

extra- *prefix* not included in; beyond; outside

extract *vt* **1** pull out, esp. with difficulty **2** get (a substance) from another substance ♦ *n* **1** piece of writing taken from a book, etc. **2** product obtained by extracting: *beef extract* **~ion** *n* **1** act or example of extracting **2** family origin: *of Russian extraction* **~or** *n* apparatus for removing stale air, fumes, etc. from e.g. a building

extracurricular *adj* outside the ordinary course of work in a school or college

extradite *vt* send (a foreign criminal) home for trial **-ditable** *adj* **-dition** *n*

extramarital *adj* (of sexual relationships) outside marriage

extramural *adj* connected with but outside an organization

extraneous *adj* not directly connected

extraordinary *adj* **1** very strange **2** beyond what is ordinary: *a man of extraordinary ability* **-narily** *adv*

extrapolate *vi/t* guess from facts already known

extrasensory perception *n* ESP

extraterrestrial *adj* (from) outside the Earth

extravagant *adj* **1** wasteful of money, etc. **2** (of ideas, behaviour, etc.) beyond what is reasonable **~ly** *adv* **-gance** *n*

extravaganza *n* very grand and expensive piece of entertainment

extreme *adj* **1** furthest or greatest possible: *extreme cold* **2** *often derog* beyond the usual limits: *extreme opinions* ♦ *n* furthest possible degree: *He's gone from one extreme to the other.* **~ly** *adv* very

extreme unction *n* sacrament of anointing and praying over a dying person

extremism *n derog* holding of (politically) extreme opinions **-ist** *n, adj*

extremity *n* **1** highest degree **2** desperate situation **extremities** *pl n* human hands and feet

extricate *vt* set free from something that is hard to escape from

extrinsic *adj* not forming part of **~ally** *adv*

extrovert, extravert *n, adj* (person who is) confident, cheerful, and sociable

extrude *vt* **1** force out **2** shape by forcing through a die

exuberant *adj* overflowing with life and excitement **~ly** *adv* **-rance** *n*

exude *vi/t* (cause to) flow out slowly in all directions

exult *vi* show great delight **~ant** *adj* **~antly** *adv* **~ation** *n*

-ey *suffix* (esp. after 'y') -y

eye *n* **1** either of the two parts of the head with which we see **2** power or way of seeing: *an experienced eye* **3** hole in a needle **4** ring into which a hook fits **5**

calm area in the centre of a storm **6 an eye for an eye** punishment equivalent to the crime **7 have an eye for** be able to judge **8 in the eyes of** in the opinion of **9 keep an eye on** watch carefully **10 one in the eye for** *infml* a defeat for **11 see eye to eye** agree completely **12 up to one's eyes in** *infml* very busy with **13 with an eye to a** intending to **b** bearing in mind; with reference to ♦ *vt* look at closely

eyeball *n* the whole of the eye, including the part inside the head ♦ *vt esp. AmE* look directly at

eyebrow *n* line of hairs above each eye

eyebrow pencil *n* coloured cosmetic pencil for shading and shaping the eyebrows

eye-catching *adj* unusual and attractive to look at

eye contact *n* looking into someone's eyes and having the look returned

eyeful *n infml* **1** look (1): *get an eyeful of that* **2** attractive sight, esp. a good-looking person

eyeglass *n* monocle

eyelash *n* hair on the edge of the eyelid

eyelet *n* hole in fabric or leather with a ring around it, through which a lace or cord can be passed

eyelid *n* piece of skin that moves to close the eye

eye-opener *n* something surprising that changes one's ideas about something

eyepiece *n* lens nearest the eye of someone looking through e.g. a microscope

eye shadow *n* coloured make-up used on the eyelids

eyesight *n* power of seeing

eyesore *n* something ugly to look at

eyewash *n sl* nonsense

eyewitness *n* person who was present at an event and can describe what happened

eyot *n BrE* small island in a river

eyrie, eyry *n* high nest of an eagle

F

F, f the 6th letter of the English alphabet

F *abbrev. for:* **1** fahrenheit **2** farad **3** fluorine

f *abbrev. for:* **1** fathom **2** female

FA *abbrev. for:* **1** Football Association **2** *BrE* (*euph*) fuck-all

Fabian *n, adj* (member) of a British socialist society

fable *n* **1** short story that teaches a lesson **2** legend **3** lie **fabled** *adj* legendary

fabric *n* **1** woven cloth **2** structure of a building

fabricate *vt* **1** construct; manufacture **2** invent (esp. something false) **-cation** *n*

fabulous *adj* **1** existing in fables **2** extraordinary **3** *infml* very good, fine, or enjoyable **~ly** *adv* extremely

facade *n* **1** front of a building **2** false appearance

face¹ *n* **1** front part of the head **2** expression on the face **3** *infml* make-up **4** front; surface: *miners at the coal face* **5** dignity; personal prestige: *afraid of losing face* **6** effrontery **7 face to face** in someone's direct presence **8 in the face of** in opposition to; despite **9 on the face of it** apparently **10 to someone's face** openly in their presence ♦ *v* **1** *vi/t* turn the face towards **2** *vt* meet and oppose: *face danger* **3** *vt* cover the front of: *a building faced with stone* **face up to** *phr vt* be brave enough to deal with **~less** *adj* with no clear character

face card *n AmE* court card

facecloth *n* small cloth for washing the face

face-lift *n* **1** plastic surgery to make the face look younger **2** renovations; refurbishment

face-pack *n* mixture applied to the face to improve the complexion
face-saving *adj* allowing self-respect to be kept
facet *n* aspect of a subject
facetious /fəˈseeshəs/ *adj* (meant to be) funny; flippant **~ly** *adv*
face value *n* **1** value shown on the face of e.g. a postage stamp **2** value of something as it first appears
facial *adj* of the face ♦ *n* facial beauty treatment
facile *adj* (of words) superficial; glib
facilitate *vt* make easy
facility *n* **1** ability to do things easily **2** something provided for use: *shopping/sporting facilities*
facing *n* **1** outer covering of a wall **2** material sewn in to stiffen a garment **~s** *pl n* collar, cuffs, etc. of a uniform
facsimile /fakˈsiməli/ *n* exact copy
fact *n* **1** something known to be true **2** truth **3 in fact** really
faction[1] *n* **1** group within a larger (esp. political) one **2** dissention within a group **factious** *adj* **1** caused by faction **2** apt to split up into factions (and quarrel)
faction[2] *n* drama which is a blend of fact and fiction
factitious /fakˈtishəs/ *adj* artificial; sham
factor *n* **1** influence that helps to produce a result **2** (*maths*) one of the numbers multiplied to form a product
factory *n* place where goods are made by machinery
factory farm *n often derog.* farm where eggs, meat, or milk are produced intensively
factotum *n* general servant
facts of life *pl n* **1** the details of sex and birth **2** the realities of a situation
factual *adj* based on fact **~ly** *adv*
faculty *n* **1** natural power of the mind or body **2 a** university department **b** teachers in such a department
fad *n* **1** short-lived interest in something **2** usu. quirky individual taste **~dish** *adj* **~dy** *adj*
fade *v* **1** *vi/t* (cause to) lose colour or freshness **2** *vi* disappear gradually **fade in/out** *phr vi/t* (in film making and broadcasting) (cause to) appear/disappear slowly
faeces /feeseez/ *pl n* solid waste from the bowels
fag *n BrE* **1** *infml* tiring job **2** *sl* cigarette **3** *AmE derog sl* homosexual **4** public-schoolboy acting as servant to a senior boy **fagged (out)** *adj BrE sl* very tired
fag end *n infml* **1** *BrE* cigarette butt **2** last (and least lively, interesting, etc.) part of something
faggot, *AmE* **fagot** *n* **1** ball of minced meat **2** bunch of sticks for burning **3** *AmE* fag (3)
Fahrenheit *n* scale of temperature in which water freezes at 32° and boils at 212°
faience /fieˈahns/ *n* earthenware with a tin glaze
fail *v* **1** *vi/t* be unsuccessful or unable **2** *vi* not do what is wanted: *The crops/business failed.* **3** *vt* judge to be unsuccessful in a test **4** *vt* disappoint or leave (someone) at a bad time: *My courage failed me.* **5** *vi* lose strength: *His health is failing.* ♦ *n* **without fail** certainly
failing *n* fault; weakness ♦ *prep* in the absence of
fail-safe *adj* made so that any failure will stop the machine
failure *n* **1** lack of success **2** person or thing that fails **3** non-performance; inability
fain *adv* **would fain** *arch.* would like to
faint *adj* **1** likely to lose consciousness **2** lacking strength or courage **3** not clear or bright **4** slight ♦ *vi* lose consciousness ♦ *n* act of fainting **~ly** *adv* **~ness** *n*
faint-hearted *adj* cowardly
fair[1] *adj* **1** just and honest: *fair play* **2** quite good: *a fair knowledge of French* **3** having a good, clean appearance: *a fair copy of the report* **4** (of skin or hair) not dark **5** (of weather) not stormy ♦ *adv* **1** honestly **2 fair and square: a** honestly

b directly **3 fair enough** *infml* all right **~ly** *adv* **1** honestly **2** rather
fair[2] *n* **1** *BrE* funfair **2** market for farm produce **3** large show of goods: *book fair*
fair copy *n* clean perfect copy
fair dinkum *adj, adv AustrE* honest(ly); real(ly)
fair game *n* **a** something that it is reasonable to attack **b** person, idea, etc., which can easily be laughed at and criticized
fairground *n* open space for a funfair
fairing *n* streamlined cover
fairway *n* part of a golf course along which one hits the ball
fair-weather friend *n* friend who deserts one in times of trouble
fairy *n* **1** small imaginary person with magical powers **2** *derog* homosexual man
fairy godmother *n* person who helps, and esp. saves, someone who is in trouble
fairyland *n* **1** land where fairies live **2** place of magical beauty
fairy light *n* small coloured light for decorating a Christmas tree, etc.
fairy tale *n* **1** story about magic **2** untrue story **fairy-tale** *adj* magically wonderful
fait accompli *n* **faits accomplis** something that has happened and cannot now be changed
faith *n* **1** confident trust **2** religious belief **3** loyalty to a promise **~ful** *adj* **1** loyal **2** true to the facts: *faithful copy* **~ful** *pl n* religious people **~fully** *adv* **Yours faithfully** (used for ending letters to strangers) **~less** *adj fml* disloyal
faith healing *n* method of treating diseases by prayer
fake *n* person or thing that is not what he/she/it looks like or pretends to be ♦ *vi/t* **1** make or copy (e.g. a work of art) to deceive **2** pretend ♦ *adj* counterfeit; phoney
fakir *n* Hindu or Muslim holy man
falchion *n arch.* sword
falcon *n* bird that can be trained to hunt **~er** *n* person who trains falcons **~ry** *n* hunting with falcons
fall *vi* **fell, fallen 1** come or go down freely: *She fell into the lake.* **2** hang loosely: *Her hair falls over her shoulders.* **3** become lower: *The temperature fell.* **4** (of land) slope down **5** happen: *Christmas falls on a Friday.* **6** become: *fall asleep/in love* **7** be wounded or killed in battle **8** be defeated **9** (of the face) take on a look of sadness, etc. **10 fall flat** produce no result **11 fall foul of** get into trouble with **12 fall short** fail to reach a standard **fall about** *phr vi* lose control of oneself (with laughter) **fall back** *phr vi* retreat **fall back on** *phr vt* use when there is failure or lack of other means **fall behind** *phr vi/t* not keep up (with) **fall for** *phr vt* **1** be attracted by **2** accept and be cheated by **fall off** *phr vi* become less **fall on** *phr vt* attack eagerly **fall out** *phr vi* quarrel **fall through** *phr vi* (of a plan) fail ♦ *n* **1** act of falling **2** something that has fallen: *a heavy fall of snow* **3** *AmE* autumn **falls** *pl n* waterfall
fallacy *n* false belief or reasoning **-lacious** *adj fml* based on fallacy
fall guy *n* **1** dupe **2** scapegoat
fallible *adj* able to make mistakes **-bility** *n*
falling star *n* shooting star
fallopian tube *n* tube through which eggs pass to the womb
fallout *n* **1** dangerous dust left in the air after a nuclear explosion **2** concomitant effects
fallow *adj* **1** (of land) dug but left unplanted **2** dormant; unproductive
fallow deer *n* small European deer with spotted coat
false *adj* **1** not true or correct **2** disloyal **3** not real **4** careless; unwise: *One false move and I'll shoot* **~ly** *adv* **~ness** *n* **~hood** *n* lying; lie
false alarm *n* warning of something bad that does not happen
false pretences *pl n* behaviour intended to deceive
false start *n* unsuccessful beginning

that means one must start again
falsetto *n* **-tos** (man with an) unnaturally high voice
falsies *pl n* pads worn to make the breasts look larger
falsify *vt* make false **–fication** *n*
falsity *n fml* falseness
falter *vi* **1** move or behave uncertainly **2** speak unsteadily **~ingly** *adv*
fame *n* condition of being well known
famed *adj* famous
familial *adj* of a family
familiar *adj* **1** often seen; common **2** too friendly **3** closely acquainted **~ly** *adv* **~ity** *n* **~ize**, **–ise** *vt* make well informed
family *n* **1** one's parents, children, aunts, etc. **2** one's children **3** people descended from the same ancestor **4** division of living creatures or languages ♦ *adj* suitable for children: *a family film*
family credit *n* welfare payments to poor families in the UK
family man *n* **1** man with a wife and children **2** man who is fond of home life
family planning *n* controlling of the number of children in a family by contraception
family tree *n* drawing showing the relationship of family members
famine *n* serious lack of food
famished *adj* very hungry
famous *adj* very well known **~ly** *adv* very well
fan[1] *n* instrument for making a flow of air ♦ *vt* **-nn- 1** send cool air onto **2** spread in a half circle
fan[2] *n* keen supporter
fanatic *n* person who is too keen on something: *religious fanatics* **~al** *adj* **~ally** *adv* **~ism** *n*
fan belt *n* belt driving a fan to cool an engine
fancier *n* person with a particular interest, esp. in breeding a particular type of animal or growing a particular type of plant: *a pigeon fancier*
fanciful *adj* **1** showing imagination rather than reason **2** imaginary **~ly** *adv*
fancy *n* **1** imagination **2** opinion not based on fact **3 take a fancy to** become fond of ♦ *vt* **1** wish for; like **2** imagine: *Fancy that!* **3** believe: *I fancy he's Dutch.* **4** *infml* be attracted to **5 fancy oneself** have a very high opinion of oneself ♦ *adj* **1** decorative and unusual **2** extravagant; exorbitant
fancy dress *n* amusing clothes worn for a party, etc.
fancy-free *adj* not involved in a binding relationship
fancy man *n infml derog.* woman's lover
fancy woman *n infml derog.* mistress (2)
fandango *n* **-gos** (music for) a lively Spanish dance
fanfare *n* short loud piece of trumpet music to introduce a person or event
fang *n* long sharp tooth
fanlight *n* small window over a door
fan mail *n* letters to a famous person from fans
fanny *n sl* **1** *AmE* bottom (2) **2** *BrE taboo* female genitals
fantasia *n* musical or literary composition in a free style
fantasize, -ise *vi/t* have fantasies (about)
fantastic *adj* **1** *sl* wonderful **2** (of ideas) not practical **3** wild and strange **~ally** *adv*
fantasy *n* (a product of the) imagination
fanzine *n* a magazine for fans
far *adv, adj* **farther** *or* **further, farthest** *or* **furthest 1** a long way (away) **2** very much **3** (of a political position) extreme **4 as/so far as** to the degree that: *So far as I know, he's coming.* **5 far and away** by a great deal or amount: *She's far and away the best actress.* **6 far be it from me to** I certainly would not want to **7 so far** until now
faraway *adj* **1** distant **2** (of a look in someone's eyes) dreamy
farce *n* **1** light, boisterous comedy **2** absurd situation **farcical** *adj*
fare *n* **1** money charged for a journey **2** *fml* food ♦ *vi* get on; succeed: *fare badly*
Far East *n* countries east of India

farewell *interj, n* goodbye
farfetched *adj* hard to believe
far-flung *adj* spread over a great distance
far-gone *adj* in an advanced state, esp. of something bad
farina *n* starchy flour or meal **farinaceous** *adj*
farm *n* area of land and buildings where crops are grown and animals raised ♦ *vi/t* use (land) as a farm **farm out** *phr vt* send (work) for other people to do
farmer *n* person who owns or manages a farm
farmhand *n* worker on a farm
farmhouse *n* main house on a farm
farmyard *n* yard surrounded by farm buildings
far-off *adj* distant
far-out *adj infml* **1** very unconventional **2** extremely good
farrago /fəˈrahgoh/ *n* **-oes** hotchpotch
far-reaching *adj* having a wide influence
farrier *n* blacksmith
farrow *n* litter of pigs ♦ *vi/t* give birth to pigs
farsighted *adj* able to judge future effects
fart *vi taboo* send out air from the bowels ♦ *n taboo* **1** escape of air from the bowels **2** *sl* extremely unpleasant person
farther *adv, adj* further
farthest *adv, adj* furthest
farthing *n* British coin worth 1/4 of an old penny
farthingale *n* hoop worn under skirts
fasces *pl n* bundle of rods around an axe, used as a symbol of authority in ancient Rome and as the emblem of the Fascist party
fascia /ˈfayshə/ *n* **1** nameboard of shop **2** *BrE* dashboard
fascinate *vt* attract and interest strongly **–nating** *adj* **–nation** *n*
fascism /ˈfashiz(ə)m/ *n* political system marked by total state control under a single leader, and support of one's own nation and race **fascist** *n, adj*
fashion *n* **1** way of dressing or behaving that is popular at a certain time **2** *fml* manner of doing something: *in an orderly fashion* **3 after a fashion** not very well ♦ *vt* make; shape **~able** *adj* in the latest fashion **~ably** *adv*
-fashion *suffix* in the way of: *Indian-fashion*
fast¹ *adj* **1** quick **2** firmly fixed: *fast colours* **3** (of a clock) showing time later than the right time **4 a** dissipated **b** forward; promiscuous ♦ *adv* **1** quickly **2** firmly **3 fast asleep** sleeping deeply
fast² *vi* eat no food, esp. for religious reasons ♦ *n* period of fasting
fasten *vi/t* make or become firmly fixed **fasten on** *phr vt* take eagerly and use **~er** *n* thing that fastens things together **~ing** *n* something that holds things shut
fast food *n* restaurant food (e.g. fried chicken) that is easily prepared
fast forward *n* device that enables one to move rapidly to a later point in a cassette tape
fastidious *adj* difficult to please; disliking anything dirty or nasty **~ly** *adv* **~ness** *n*
fastness *n* **1** being fixed or colourfast **2** fortified or remote and inaccessible place
fat *n* **1** material under the skins of animals and human beings which helps keep them warm **2** this substance used in cooking **3 the fat of the land** the best and richest things to eat and drink ♦ *adj* **-tt- 1** having a lot of fat on the body **2** thick and well-filled: *fat book* ♦ *vt* **-tt-** feed up for slaughter **~ness** *n*
fatal *adj* causing death or ruin **~ly** *adv*
fatalism *n* belief that events are controlled by fate **–ist** *n* **–istic** *adj*
fatality *n* **1** violent death **2** being fatal
fat cat *n esp. AmE* rich powerful person
fate *n* **1** power beyond human control that decides events **2** end, esp. death **3** the future **~ful** *adj* important (esp. in a bad way) for the future: *fateful decision* **~fully** *adv* **fated** *adj* **1** caused by fate

2 *infml* very unlucky
fathead *n BrE* fool
father *n* **1** male parent **2** (*usu. cap.*) priest ♦ *vt* become the father of **~hood** *n* **~less** *adj* **~ly** *adj* like a good father
fathers *pl n* forefathers
Father Christmas *n esp. BrE* Santa Claus
father figure *n* older man on whom one depends for advice
father-in-law *n* **fathers-in-law** father of one's wife or husband
fatherland *n* one's native land
fathom *n* unit of measurement (6 feet) for the depth of water ♦ *vt* understand fully
fatigue *n* **1** tiredness **2** weakness in metals caused by repeated bending **3** (in the army) a job of cleaning or cooking **~s** *pl n* clothes worn while doing army fatigue ♦ *vt* make tired
fatten *vt* make fatter
fatty *adj* containing fat ♦ *n sl* fat person
fatuous *adj* silly: *fatuous remarks* **~ly** *adv*
faucet *n AmE* tap[1]
fault *n* **1** mistake or imperfection **2** crack in the Earth's surface **3 at fault** in the wrong **4 find fault with** complain about **5 one's fault** something one can be blamed for **6 to a fault** (of good qualities) too; too much ♦ *vt* find mistakes in **~less** *adj* perfect **~y** *adj*
fauna *n* animals of a particular area or period
faux pas /ˌfoh ˈpah/ *n* **faux pas** social mistake
favour *n* **1** approval; goodwill **2** kind act: *do me a favour* **3** partiality **4** *arch.* token of love or allegiance **5 in favour of a** in support of **b** (of a cheque) payable to **6 in one's favour** to one's advantage ♦ *vt* **1** approve of **2** be unfairly fond of; treat with favour **~able** *adj* **1** showing or winning approval **2** advantageous **~ably** *adv*
favourite, *AmE* **-vorite** *n* **1** person or thing loved above all others **2** horse expected to win a race ♦ *adj* most loved **-ritism** *n* unfairly generous treatment of one person
fawn *n* **1** young deer **2** light yellowish-brown colour
fawn on *phr vt* try to gain the favour of, by being too attentive
fax *vt* send (copies of printed material) in electronic form along a telephone line ♦ *n* **1** machine which faxes **2** faxed document
fay *n lit* fairy
faze *vt esp. AmE* shock into silence
FBI *n* Federal Bureau of Investigation; US police department under central control
FC *abbrev. for:* Football Club
fealty /ˈfee·əlti/ *n* **1** loyalty to a feudal lord **2** allegiance
fear *n* **1** anxiety; dread **2 No fear!** Certainly not! ♦ *vi/t fml* be afraid (of) **~ful** *adj* **1** terrible; shocking **2** *fml* afraid **~less** *adj* not afraid **~lessly** *adv* **~some** *adj lit* frightening
feasible *adj* able to be done; possible **-bility** *n*
feast *n* **1** splendid meal **2** religious festival ♦ *vi* **1** eat and drink very well **2 feast one's eyes on** look at with delight
feat *n* difficult action successfully done
feather *n* **1** one of a bird's many light skin coverings **2 a feather in one's cap** honour to be proud of ♦ *vt* **1** put feathers on or in **2 feather one's nest** make oneself dishonestly rich while in a trusted position **~y** *adj* soft and light
featherbed *vt* overprotect; pamper
featherbrained *adj* silly and thoughtless
featherweight *n* lightweight boxer ♦ *adj* unimportant
feature *n* **1** noticeable quality **2** part of the face **3** long newspaper article **4** full-length film ♦ *v* **1** *vt* include as a performer **2** *vi* play an important part **~less** *adj* uninteresting
feature-length *adj* being of the normal length for a feature film
febrile *adj* feverish
February *n* the second month of the year
feces *n AmE* faeces

feckless *adj* worthless and irresponsible
fecund *adj fml* fertile
fed[1] *past t. and p. of* feed
fed[2] *n AmE infml* federal officer
federal *adj* **1** of or being a federation **2** of the central US government as opposed to the States **~ism** *n* **~ist** *n*
Federal Bureau of Investigation *n* FBI
federation *n* **1** united group of states, organizations, etc. **2** action or result of uniting in this way
fedora *n* man's hat, similar to a trilby, formerly very popular in the USA
fed up *adj sl* tired and discontented
fee *n* money paid for professional services, to join a club, etc.
feeble *adj* weak **feebly** *adv*
feebleminded *adj* with low intelligence
feed *v* **fed 1** *vt* give food to **2** *vi* (esp. of animals) eat **3** *vt* supply; provide: *feed information into a computer* ♦ *n* **1** animal's or baby's meal **2** food for animals **3** pipe, etc., through which a machine is fed
feedback *n* **1** information about the results of an action, passed back to the person in charge **2** return to the input of part of the output of a machine, e.g. an amplifier
feeding bottle *n* baby's bottle with a rubber teat
feel *v* **felt 1** *vt* learn about with the fingers **2** *vt* experience (the touch of something) **3** *vi* search with the fingers **4** *vi* be consciously: *feel hungry/happy* **5** *vt* suffer because of: *feel the cold* **6** *vi* give a sensation: *This sheet feels wet.* **7** *vt* believe without reasoning: *I feel they won't come.* **8 feel like** wish for; want **feel for** *phr vt* be sorry for ♦ *n* **1** sensation caused by touching **2** act of feeling **3 get the feel of** become used to and skilled at
feeler *n* **1** thread-like part of an insect's head, with which it touches things **2** suggestion made to test opinion
feeling *n* **1** consciousness of something felt **2 a** belief not based on reason **b** opinion **3** power to feel **4** emotion **5** sympathy
feet *pl of* foot
feign *vt fml* pretend to have or be
feint[1] /faynt/ *n* false attack or blow ♦ *vi* make a feint
feint[2] *adj* (of rulings on paper) faint
feisty /ˈfiesty/ *adj AmE* excited and quarrelsome
feldspar *n* white or pink mineral
felicitate *vt* congratulate **-tation** *n*
felicitous *adj* apt; well-chosen
felicity *n fml* happiness
feline *adj* of or like a cat
fell[1] *past t. of* fall
fell[2] *vt* cut or knock down: *fell a tree*
fell[3] *n* high rocky country in the north of England
fell[4] *adj lit* **1** fierce; destructive **2 at one fell swoop** all at once
fellah *n* **-ahin** *or* **-aheen** Arab peasant
fellatio /fəˈlayshioh/ *n* oral stimulation of the penis
feller *n sl* fellow; man
fellow *n* **1** man **2** member of a learned society or college **3** companion: *schoolfellows* ♦ *adj* another of the same group: *fellow prisoners* **~ship** *n* **1** group or society **2** companionship **3** position of a college fellow
fellow feeling *n* sympathy for someone like oneself
fellow traveller *n* someone who is sympathetic to Communism without actually joining the party
felony *n* serious crime (e.g. murder) **felon** *n* person guilty of a felony
felspar *n* feldspar
felt[1] *past t. and p. of* feel
felt[2] *n* thick cloth made of pressed wool
felt-tip pen *n* pen with felt nib
female *adj* **1** of the sex that produces young **2** (of plants) producing fruits **3** having a hole into which something fits: *female plug* ♦ *n* woman or female animal
feminine *adj* **1** suitable for a woman **2** of the word class including most words for females **-ninity** *n* being feminine
feminism *n* principle that women should have the same rights as men

–**nist** *n, adj*
femme fatale *n* seductive woman, esp. one who lures men into dangerous situations
femur *n* thigh bone –**oral** *adj* of the thigh
fen *n* area of low wet land
fence *n* **1** wall made of wood or wire **2** someone who buys and sells stolen goods **3 sit on the fence** avoid taking sides in an argument ♦ *v* **1** *vt* surround or separate with a fence **2** *vi* **a** fight with a long thin sword as a sport **b** avoid giving an honest answer **fencer** *n*
fencing *n* **1** sword-fighting as a sport **2** material for making fences
fender *n* **1** low metal surround for a fireplace **2** *AmE* wing (4)
fend for *phr vt* look after: *fend for oneself*
fend off *phr vt* push away
fenestration *n* arrangement of windows in a building
fennel *n* yellow-flowered herb with edible root
fenugreek *n* (aromatic seeds of) an Asiatic plant
feral *adj* not domesticated: *feral cat*
ferment *vi/t* **1** change chemically so that sugar becomes alcohol **2** make or become excited ♦ *n* trouble and excitement ~**ation** *n*
fern *n* plant with feathery green leaves
ferocious *adj* fierce; violent ~**ly** *adv*
ferocity *n* ferociousness
ferret *n* small fierce animal that hunts rats and rabbits ♦ *vi/t* search; find by searching
ferris wheel *n* big wheel at fairgrounds
ferro- *prefix* containing iron: *ferroconcrete*
ferrous *adj* of or containing iron
ferrule *n* metal ring or cap used to strengthen e.g. the end of a stick
ferry also **ferryboat** *n* boat that carries people and things across a narrow piece of water ♦ *vt* carry (as if) on a ferry
fertile *adj* **1** producing young, crops, etc. **2** (of a person's mind) inventive –**tility** *n*
fertilize, -ise *vt* make fertile –**lizer** *n* plant food –**lization** *n*
fervent *adj* showing strong feeling ~**ly** *adv*
fervid *adj* impassioned; ardent
fervour, *AmE* **-vor** *n* zeal
festal *adj lit* festive
fester *vi* (of a wound) become infected
festival *n* **1** time for public celebration: *Christmas is a festival of the church.* **2** group of musical, theatrical, etc., performances held regularly
festive *adj* joyful
festivity *n* festive activity
festoon *vt* decorate with chains of flowers, ribbons, etc.
fetch *vt* **1** go and get and bring back **2** be sold for **3 fetch and carry** do the small duties of a servant **fetch up** *phr vi infml* end up ~**ing** *adj* pretty; attractive
fete *n* day of public amusement held esp. to collect money ♦ *vt* honour publicly
fetid *adj* foul-smelling
fetish *n* **1** object of obsessive concern **2** object used to obtain sexual gratification ~**ism** *n* ~**ist** *n*
fetlock *n* (tuft of hair on) a projection behind and just above a horse's hoof
fetter *n* chain for a prisoner's foot ♦ *vt* tie; prevent from moving ~**s** *pl n* bonds; restrictions
fettle *n* condition: *He's in fine fettle.*
fetus *n* foetus
feud *n* violent continuing quarrel ♦ *vi* have a feud
feudal *adj* of the system of holding land in return for work, as practised in Europe from the 9th to the 15th century ~**ism** *n*
fever *n* **1** (disease causing) high body temperature **2** excited state ~**ish** *adj* **1** of or having fever **2** unnaturally fast ~**ishly** *adv*
few *determiner, pron, n* **1** some: *Let's invite a few friends.* **2** not many: *She has few friends.*
fey *adj* **1** otherworldly; scatty **2** clair-

voyant **3** *esp. Scots* doomed
fez *n* flowerpot-shaped hat
ff *abbrev. for:* **1** and following (pages) **2** fortissimo
fiancé (*masc.*), **fiancée** (*fem.*) *n* person one is engaged to
fiasco *n* **-cos** complete failure
fiat *n* command; decree
fib *vi, n* **-bb-** (tell) a small lie **~ber** *n*
fibre, *AmE* **fiber** *n* **1** thin thread-like plant or animal growth **2** mass of threads **3** person's inner character **fibrous** *adj*
fibreboard, *AmE* **fiberboard** *n* board made of compressed e.g. wood fibres
fibreglass, *AmE* **fiberglass** *n* material of glass fibres used for making boats, etc.
fibre optics *n* a technology using glass or plastic fibres to transmit light signals
fibrositis *n* rheumatic disorder of the muscles
fibula *n* **-lae** *or* **-las** outer bone of the lower leg
fickle *adj* not loyal; often changing
fiction *n* **1** stories **2** untrue story **~al** *adj* **~alize,~ alise** *vt*
fictitious *adj* untrue: invented
fiddle *n* **1** dishonest practice **2** violin **3** **(as) fit as a fiddle** perfectly healthy ♦ *v* **1** *vi* move things aimlessly **2** *vi* play the violin **3** *vt sl* falsify; lie about **4** *vt sl* obtain by deception **-dler** *n*
fiddling *adj* small and silly
fiddly *adj* needing delicate use of the fingers
fidelity *n* **1** faithfulness **2** closeness to an original
fidget *vi* move one's body around restlessly ♦ *n* someone who fidgets
fiduciary *adj* relating to a trust or trustee
fie *interj arch.* (exclamation indicating severe disapproval or distaste)
fief *n* **1** feudal estate **2** something entirely under somebody's control
field *n* **1** piece of farming land **2** open area **3** branch of knowledge **4** place where practical operations actually happen: *study tribal languages in the field* **5** area where a force is felt: *gravitational field* ♦ *v* **1** *vi/t* (in cricket, etc.) catch or stop (the ball) **2** *vt* deal with by giving an answer off the cuff **3** *vt* produce (a team or army) **~er** *n*
field day *n* **1** a day for military manoeuvres or outdoor activities **2** **have a field day** enjoy oneself very much
field event *n* competitive sports event, such as weight-throwing or jumping
field glasses *pl n* binoculars
field hockey *n AmE* hockey played on grass
field marshal *n* British army officer of highest rank
field of vision *n* whole space within seeing distance
field-test *vt* try (something) out under actual operating conditions
field trip *n* excursion or visit made for study purposes
fieldwork *n* study done in the field
fiend *n* **1** devil **2** *infml* someone very keen on something **~ish** *adj* **~ishly** *adv*
fierce *adj* **1** angry, violent, and cruel **2** severe **~ly** *adv* **~ness** *n*
fiery /ˈfie·əri/ *adj* **1** like fire **2** violent
fiesta *n* religious holiday with public dancing, etc.
fife *n* small flute
fifteen *determiner, n, pron* 15 **~th** *determiner, adv, n, pron* 15th
fifth *determiner, n, pron, adv* 5th
fifth column *n* group of people who secretly help the enemies of their country in war
fifty *determiner, n, pron* 50 **~tieth** *determiner, adv, n, pron* 50th
fifty-fifty *adj, adv* (of shares or chances) equal(ly)
fig *n* (tree that bears) a soft sweet fruit with small seeds
fig. *abbrev. for:* **1** figurative **2** figure[1] (5)
fight *vi/t* **fought 1** use violence (against); struggle **2** argue **fight back** *phr vi* **1** recover from a bad or losing position **2** defend oneself by fighting **fight off** *phr*

vt keep away with an effort **fight out** *phr vt* settle (a quarrel) by fighting ♦ *n* **1** battle **2** power or wish to fight **3** boxing match **~er** *n* **1** person who fights professionally **2** courageous and determined person **3** small military aircraft

fighting chance *n* small but real chance if great effort is made

fig leaf *n* something that hides something else, esp. dishonestly

figment *n* something not real

figurative *adj* (of words, phrases, etc.) metaphorical **~ly** *adv*

figure *n* **1** (shape of) a human body **2** person **3** (sign for) a number **4** price **5** diagram ♦ *v* **1** *vi* take a part **2** *vt esp. AmE* believe **3 That figures** *infml* That seems reasonable **figure on** *phr vt esp. AmE* plan on; include in one's plans **figure out** *phr vt* discover by thinking

figured bass *n* bass line of music with figures above each note to indicate what chord should be played

figurehead *n* **1** carved figure on the prow of a sailing ship **2** someone who is the chief in name only

figure of eight also *esp. AmE* **figure eight** *n* something, e.g. the pattern made by a moving figure, shaped like an 8

figure of speech *n* figurative expression

figurine *n* statuette

filament *n* thin thread, esp. in an electric light bulb

filbert *n* a hazel nut

filch *vt* steal (something of small value)

file[1] *n* steel tool for rubbing or cutting hard surfaces ♦ *vt* rub or cut with a file: *file one's nails*

file[2] *n* **1** arrangement for storing papers **2** store of papers on one subject ♦ *vt* put in a file **file for** *phr vt law* request officially

file[3] *n* line of people or things one behind the other ♦ *vi* move in a file

filet mignon *n* small tender boneless cut of beef

filial *adj* suitable to a son or daughter

filibeg *n* kilt

filibuster *vi* delay parliamentary action by making long speeches **filibuster** *n*

filigree *n* decorative wire work

filing cabinet *n* piece of office furniture for storing papers in

filings *pl n* very small sharp bits that have been rubbed off a metal surface with a file

Filipino *n, adj* (inhabitant) of the Philippines

fill *v* **1** *vi/t* make or become full **2** *vt* go or be put into: *fill a vacancy* **3** *vt* fulfil **fill in** *phr vt* **1** put in (what is necessary): *fill in a form* **2** supply the most recent information **3** take someone's place **fill out** *phr v* **1** *vi* get fatter **2** *vt* fill in (1) **fill up** *phr vi/t* make or become full ♦ *n* full supply **~er** *n* **1** thing added to increase size **2** substance used to fill holes in walls, wood, etc. **~ing** *n* **1** material to fill a hole, esp. in a tooth **2** food mixture folded inside pastry, sandwiches, etc.

fillet *n* piece of meat or fish without bones ♦ *vt* remove bones from

filling station *n* place that sells petrol and oil and may also do repairs

fillip *n* stimulus; lift[2] (4)

filly *n* young female horse

film *n* **1** (roll of) thin material used in photography **2** *esp. BrE* cinema picture **3** thin covering: *film of oil* ♦ *vi/t* make a film (of) **~y** *adj* very thin

film star *n* famous cinema actor or actress

filmstrip *n* length of photographic film that shows drawings, etc., separately as still pictures

filter *n* **1** apparatus through which liquids are passed to clean them **2** glass that changes the colour or amount of light ♦ *vi/t* go or send (as if) through a filter

filter tip *n* (cigarette with) an end that filters smoke

filth *n* **1** very nasty dirt **2** something obscene or vile **3** *sl* the police **~y** *adj*

filtration *n* process of filtering: *filtration plant*

fin *n* **1** winglike part of a fish **2** thing shaped like this on an aircraft, car, etc.

final *adj* **1** last **2** (of a decision, etc.) that cannot be changed ♦ *n also* **finals** *pl.* *n* **1** last of a set of matches **2** last and most important examinations in a college course **~ist** *n* player in a final match **~ize, -ise** *vt* give final form to **~ly** *adv* **1** at last **2** allowing no further change

finale /fiˈnahli/ *n* last division of a piece of music; last number, act, etc. in a show

finance *n* **1** management of (public) money **2** money, esp. provided by a bank, to help run an organization or buy something ♦ *vt* provide money for **~s** *pl n* money at one's disposal **-cial** *adj* **-cially** *adv*

financial year *n* yearly period over which accounts are calculated

financier *n* someone who controls large sums of money

finch *n* small songbird

find *vt* **found 1** get (something lost or not known) by searching **2** learn by chance or effort **3** obtain by effort: *find time to study* **4** (of a thing) arrive at: *Water finds its own level.* **5** know to exist: *Elephants are found in Africa.* **6** *law* decide to be: *find someone guilty* **find against** *phr vt* give judgement against **find for** *phr vt* give judgement in favour of **find out** *phr vt* discover ♦ *n* something good or valuable that is found **~er** *n* **~ing** *n* **1** what is learnt by enquiry **2** *law* decision made in court **3** something learnt as the result of an official enquiry

fin de siècle *adj* characteristic of the end of the 19th century

fine[1] *adj* **1** good; beautiful **2** very thin or small **3** subtle **4** (of weather) bright; not wet **5** healthy ♦ *adv* **1** very well **2** very thin **~ly** *adv* **1** into small bits **2** delicately: *finely tuned*

fine[2] *n* money paid as a punishment ♦ *vt* take a fine from

fine arts *pl n* painting, music, etc.

finery *n* beautiful clothes

fines herbes *pl n* mixture of finely chopped green herbs

finesse *n* delicate skill

fine-tune *vt* make delicate adjustments to in order to achieve optimum performance

finger *n* **1** any of the five end parts of the hand **2** part of a glove made to fit one of these parts **3 be/feel all fingers and thumbs** be/feel unable to control one's hands **4 (have) a finger in every pie** (have) a part in everything that is going on **5 keep one's fingers crossed** hope for the best **6 put one's finger on** define exactly ♦ *vt* feel with one's fingers **~ing** *n* (marks to show) use of the fingers when playing music

fingerboard *n* part of a stringed instrument on which the fingers press the strings to vary their pitch

finger bowl *n* water bowl for rinsing the fingers in at table

fingerpost *n* signpost

fingerprint *n* mark made by a finger pressed onto a surface ♦ *vt* take (someone's) fingerprints

fingerstall *n* protective cover for an injured finger

fingertip *n* end of a finger

finial /ˈfieni·əl/ *n* architectural ornament in the form of a small pointed turret or pinnacle

finicky *adj* hard to please; choosy

finis *n* the end

finish *v* **1** *vi/t* come or bring to an end **2** *vt* eat or drink the rest of **3** *vt* complete; give a proper finish to **4** kill; defeat **finish off** *phr vt* kill **finish with** *phr vt* have no more use for ♦ *n* **1** last part **2** appearance or condition of having been properly polished, painted, etc.

finishing school *n* private school where rich young girls learn how to behave in social life

finite /ˈfieniet/ *adj* **1** limited **2** (of a verb) changing according to tense and subject **~ly** *adv*

Finn *n* inhabitant of Finland

finnan haddie or **haddock** *n* haddock split and smoked

Finnish *n* of Finland

fiord *n* fjord

fir *n* evergreen tree of the pine family
fire *n* **1** condition of burning **2** something burning, on purpose or by accident **3** gas or electrical heater **4** destruction by fire **5** gunfire **6 catch fire** start to burn **7 on fire** burning **8 open/cease fire** start/stop shooting **9 set fire to** cause to burn **10 under fire** being shot at ♦ *v* **1** *vi/t* shoot off (bullets or arrows) **2** *vt* dismiss from a job **3** *vt* excite: *fire one's imagination* **4** *vt* bake (clay things) in a kiln
fire alarm *n* signal that warns people of fire
firearm *n* gun
fireball *n* **1** centre of a nuclear explosion **2** lightning in the shape of a ball **3** large meteor
firebomb *n* incendiary bomb ♦ *vt* attack with an incendiary device
firebrand *n* trouble-maker; agitator
firebreak *n* strip of cleared land to stop a fire from spreading
firebug *n* arsonist
firedamp *n* (explosive mixture of air and) gas which forms in mines
firedog *n* andiron
fire drill *n* practice in leaving a burning building safely
fire engine *n* vehicle that carries a fire brigade and their equipment
fire escape *n* outside stairs for leaving a burning building
fire fighting *n* **1** action to put out large fires **2** actions taken to discover and remove causes of sudden trouble in organizations, etc.
firefly *n* flying insect which glows in the dark
fireguard *n* protective framework round a fireplace
fire irons *pl n* household tongs, poker, shovel, etc.
fireman *n* **-men 1** person who puts out fires **2** stoker
fireplace *n* opening for a fire in a room
firepower *n* ability to deliver gunfire
fireproof *adj* unable to be damaged by fire **fireproof** *vt*
fire-raising *n* crime of starting fires on purpose
fire ship *n* burning vessel sent in amongst an enemy fleet
fireside *n* area around the fireplace
fire station *n* building for a fire brigade
fire storm *n* huge uncontrollable fire started usu. by bombs and kept burning by inrushing winds
firetrap *n* building which is dangerous either because it could easily catch fire or because it would be difficult to escape from if it caught fire
firewood *n* wood cut to be used on fires
firework *n* container of explosive powder, burnt to make coloured lights **~s** *pl n* **1** show of fireworks **2** show of anger **3** show of virtuosity
firing line *n* position of maximum exposure during an attack
firing squad *n* group of soldiers ordered to shoot an offender
firkin *n* wooden cask usu. of nine gallon capacity
firm[1] *adj, adv* **1** solidly fixed **2** not likely to change **3** determined; resolute **~ly** *adv* **~ness** *n*
firm[2] *n* business company
firmament *n lit* the sky
firmware *n* computer program stored on a chip inside the computer
first *determiner, adv* **1** before the others **2** for the first time **3** rather than do something else **4 first thing** at the earliest time in the morning **5 the first** the slightest: *They haven't the first idea what it means.* ♦ *n, pron* **1** person or thing before others **2** *BrE* university examination result of highest quality **3 at first** at the beginning **~ly** *adv* before anything else
first aid *n* treatment given by an ordinary person to someone hurt in an accident, etc.
firstborn *adj, n* eldest (child)
first class *n* best travelling conditions on a train, etc. **first-class** *adj* of the best quality
first cousin *n* child of one's aunt or uncle
first floor *n* **1** *BrE* floor above the

ground floor **2** *AmE* ground floor
firsthand *adj, adv* (of information) directly from its origin
first lady *n* **1** (in the US) wife of the President **2** woman preeminent in any field
first name *n* name that stands before one's family name
first night *n* premiere of play, opera, etc.
first-past-the-post *adj* (of an electoral system) in which the person who polls most votes in a constituency is its sole representative in parliament
first person *n* form of verb, pronoun, etc. used by a speaker to refer to him-/herself
first-rate *adj* of the best quality
first strike *n* attack made on your enemy before they (can) attack you
first-string *adj* being a regular member of a team, not a reserve
firth *n* Scottish river estuary
fiscal *adj fml* of public money, taxes, etc.
fish *n* **fish** *or* **fishes 1** cold-blooded creature that lives in water **2** its flesh as food ♦ *v* **1** *vi* try to catch fish **2** *vi* search indirectly: *fish for compliments* **3** *vt* bring out or up: *He fished a key from his pocket.* **~y** *adj* **1** like fish **2** dubious; arousing suspicion
fisherman *n* **-men** man who catches fish, esp. as a job
fishery also **-ries** *pl* part of the sea where fishing is practised
fish-eye lens *n* convex lens which covers a very wide angle of view
fish farm *n* place where fish are bred in tanks or pools
fish finger *n* small oblong of fish coated with breadcrumbs
fishing *n* sport or job of catching fish
fishmonger *n BrE* someone who sells fish in a shop
fishnet *n* netlike fabric: *fishnet stockings*
fishplate *n* metal plate connecting e.g. two rails
fish slice *n* spatula with usu. perforated blade, used for turning food during cooking
fishwife *n* vulgarly abusive or scolding woman
fission *n* splitting of a cell or atom **-sile** *adj* capable of being split or undergoing nuclear fission
fissure *n* deep crack esp. in rock
fist *n* hand when closed tightly
fisticuffs *pl n humorous* fighting with the fists
fistula *n* long narrow pipe-like ulcer
fit[1] *v* **-tt- 1** *vi/t* be the right size and shape (for) **2** *vt* put in place **3** *vt* make suitable for **fit in** *phr v* **1** *vi* match; harmonize **2** *vt* make room or time for **fit out** *phr vt* equip; furnish ♦ *n* **1** quality of fitting well **2** way that something fits **~ted** *adj* fixed in place **~ter** *n* **1** person who fits machine parts **2** person who cuts out and fits clothes
fit[2] *adj* **1** suitable, right: *fit to eat|Do as you think fit.* **2** physically healthy **3** ready to: *laugh fit to burst* **~ness** *n*
fit[3] *n* **1** short attack of illness; passing mood, emotion, etc. **2** sudden loss of consciousness **3 by fits and starts** not regularly **4 have a fit** *infml* be very angry **~ful** *adj* restlessly irregular **~fully** *adv*
fitment *n* piece of fitted furniture
fitting *adj fml* suitable ♦ *n* **1** something fixed into a building **2** occasion of trying whether clothes fit
five *determiner, n, pron* 5 **fiver** *n* £5 note
five o'clock shadow *n infml* dark regrowth of stubble visible on the face of a man who has not shaved since morning
fix *vt* **1** fasten firmly **2** arrange; decide on **3** repair **4** tidy **5** *esp. AmE* prepare (food or drink) **6** arrange the result of (something) dishonestly **fix on** *phr vt* choose **fix up** *phr vt* **1** provide **2** repair, change or improve ♦ *n* **1** awkward situation **2** *sl* injection of a drug **3** (determination of) navigational position **~ative** *n* chemical for sticking things in position **~ation** *n* obsession **~er** *n* person who is good at arranging that something happens, esp. by using influence or dishonesty

fixture *n* **1** something fixed into a building **2** sports event on an agreed date
fizz *vi, n* (make) a sound of bubbles in a liquid **~y** *adj*
fizzle out *phr vi* end disappointingly
fjord /fyawd/ *n* narrow arm of the sea between steep cliffs, esp. in Norway
flab *n infml* soft loose flesh
flabbergasted *adj* surprised and shocked
flabby *adj* **1** (of muscles) too soft **2** lacking force or effectiveness **–biness** *n*
flaccid /ˈflaksid/ *adj* not firm enough
flag[1] *n* **1** piece of coloured cloth used as the symbol e.g. of a country or to make signals **2** flagstone ♦ *vt* -**gg**- put a flag on **flag down** *phr vt* signal (a vehicle) to stop
flag[2] *vi* -**gg**- become weak
flag day *n BrE* day on which small flags or stickers are sold for charity
flagellate *vt* whip esp. as religious punishment or for sexual gratification **–lant** *n* person who whips him-/herself **–lation** *n*
flageolet *n* musical instrument similar to a recorder
flag of convenience *n* flag of a country in which a ship is registered to avoid the taxes and regulations of the shipowner's home country
flagon *n* large container for liquids
flagpole *n* long pole to raise a flag on
flagrant *adj* openly bad **~ly** *adv*
flagship *n* chief naval ship in a group
flagstaff *n* flagpole
flagstone *n* flat stone for a floor or path
flag-waving *n* noisy expression of national feeling
flail *n* wooden implement used for threshing corn by hand ♦ *vi* wave violently but aimlessly about
flair *n* natural ability to do something
flak *n* **1** antiaircraft fire **2** severe opposition
flake *n* **1** small leaf-like bit **2** *AmE* a person who is not with it; an eccentric or crazy person ♦ *v* **1** *vi* fall off in flakes **2** *vt* form into flakes; chip **flake out** *phr vi* fall asleep or faint because of great tiredness **flaky** *adj* **1** made up of flakes or tending to flake **2** *AmE infml* eccentric **flakiness** *n*
flamboyant *adj* **1** brightly coloured **2** (of a person) showy and bold **–ance** *n* **~ly** *adv*
flame *n* **1** (tongue of) burning gas **2 in flames** burning ♦ *vi* **1** burn brightly **2** break out with sudden violence
flamenco *n* -**cos** (music for) a vigorous Spanish dance
flame-thrower *n* weapon that shoots out a stream of burning liquid
flaming *adj* **1** in flames **2** very bright **3** *sl* (used for giving force to a remark): *flaming cheek!*
flamingo *n* -**gos** *or* -**goes** long-legged tropical water bird with pink plumage
flammable *adj* inflammable (1)
flan *n* open pastry case filled with fruit, etc.
flange *n* projecting edge of a wheel
flank *n* side of an animal, person, or moving army ♦ *vt* be placed beside
flannel *n* **1** loosely woven woollen cloth **2** facecloth **3** *infml, esp. BrE* meaningless words used to avoid giving a direct answer ♦ *vi/t* speak evasively (in order to deceive somebody) **~s** *pl n* flannel trousers **~ette** *n* thick soft cotton flannel
flap *n* **1** flat part of anything that covers an opening **2** movable part of the wing of an aircraft **3** sound of flapping **4 in a flap** excited and anxious ♦ *v* **1** *vi/t* wave slowly up and down **2** *vi* get excited and anxious
flapjack *n* **1** *BrE* biscuit made with oats and syrup **2** *esp. AmE* pancake
flapper *n* emancipated, pleasure-loving young woman of the 1920s
flare[1] *vi* burn brightly but unsteadily **flare up** *phr vi* become suddenly hotter, more violent, etc. ♦ *n* **1** flaring light **2** bright light used as a signal
flare[2] *vi/t* widen towards the bottom **flare** *n* a flared shape **~s** *pl n* flared trousers
flarepath *n* illuminated landing strip for

aircraft
flare-up *n* outbreak of violence
flash *v* **1** *vi/t* shine for a moment **2** *vi* move very fast **3** *vt* send by radio, telegraph, etc. **4** *vi* expose oneself (to) ♦ *n* **1** sudden bright light **2** sudden burst of e.g. inspiration **3** short news report **4** flashlight (1) **5 in a flash** at once ♦ *adj* **1** sudden: *flash flood* **2** modern and expensive-looking **~er** *n* **1** flashing light **2** *sl* man who exposes himself **~y** *adj* unpleasantly big, bright, etc.
flashback *n* scene in a film, etc., that goes back in time
flashbulb *n* bright electric lamp for photography
flashcube *n* cube holding four flash bulbs
flashgun *n* device holding a photographic flashlight
flashlight *n* **1** apparatus for taking photographs in the dark **2** *esp. AmE* torch (1)
flash point *n* point or place at which violence may be expected
flask *n* **1** narrow-necked bottle **2** flat bottle for carrying drinks in one's pocket **3** bottle with a vacuum between its two walls, for keeping liquids hot or cold
flat *n* **1** low level plain **2** flat part or side (of) **3** (in music) flat note **4** flat piece of stage scenery **5** *BrE* set of rooms on one floor of a building **6** a flat tyre ♦ *adj* **-tt-** **1** smooth and level **2** spread out fully **3** not very thick **4** (of a tyre) without enough air in it **5** (of a battery) having lost electrical power **6** (of beer, etc.) having lost its gas **7** dull and lifeless **8** (in music) below the right note **9** firm; with no more argument: *a flat refusal* ♦ *adv* **1** into a flat or level position **2** below the right note **3** and no more: *three minutes flat* **4 flat broke** with no money at all **5 flat out** at full speed
flat-chested *adj* having small breasts
flat feet *n* feet that rest too flat on the ground **flat-footed** *adj*
flatfish *n* a seafish, e.g. sole or plaice, with a flat body
flatmate *n BrE* person who shares a flat with another
flat race *n* horse race with no jumps
flat rate *n* one charge including everything
flatten *vi/t* make or become flat
flatter *vt/i* **1** praise too much or insincerely **2** give pleasure to **3** make (a person) seem more beautiful **~er** *n* **~y** *n* flattering remarks
flatulence *n fml* wind[1] (3) **–lent** *adj*
flaunt *vt derog* show for admiration: *flaunt her wealth*
flautist *n BrE* flute-player
flavour, *AmE* **flavor** *n* **1** taste **2** particular characteristic **3 flavour of the month** *infml* person or thing currently popular ♦ *vt* give taste to **~ing** *n* something added to improve the taste **~less** *adj*
flaw *n* fault or weakness ♦ *vt* make a flaw in **~less** *adj* **~lessly** *adv*
flax *n* (thread made from the stem of) a plant with blue flowers used for making linen
flaxen *adj lit* (of hair) pale yellow
flay *vt* **1** remove the skin from **2** attack fiercely in words
flea *n* wingless jumping insect that feeds on blood
fleabag *n* **1** scruffy and decrepit-looking person or animal **2** *AmE* cheap dirty hotel
fleabite *n* insignificant injury, loss, etc. **–bitten** *adj* scruffy; shabby
flea market *n* street market where used goods are sold
fleapit *n BrE* cheap dirty cinema or theatre
fleck *n* small spot or grain ♦ *vt* mark with flecks
fledgling *n* **1** young bird learning to fly **2** inexperienced person
flee *vi/t* **fled** hurry away (from); escape
fleece *n* sheep's woolly coat ♦ *vt* rob by a trick; charge too much **fleecy** *adj* woolly
fleet[1] *n* **1** number of ships under one command **2** group of buses, etc. under one control

fleet² *adj lit* swift **~ing** *adj* not lasting long **~ingly** *adv*

flesh *n* **1** soft part of a person or animal that covers the bones **2** soft part of a fruit **3** the body as opposed to the soul **4 flesh and blood a** human beings **b** one's relatives **5 in the flesh** in real life; actually present **~y** *adj* fat

fleshings *pl n* ballet dancers' flesh-coloured tights

fleshpots *pl n* (places providing) physical pleasures

fleur-de-lis /ˌfluh dəˈlee/ *n* **fleurs-de-lis** heraldic three-petalled lily

flew *past t. of* fly

flex¹ *n BrE* electric wire in a protective covering

flex² *vt* bend or stretch (one's muscles)

flexible *adj* **1** easily bent **2** easily changed **–bility** *n*

flexitime *n* British system by which people can choose their hours of work

flibbertigibbet *n* flighty, gossiping person, usu. a woman

flick *n* light sudden blow or movement ♦ *vt* touch or strike lightly

flicker *vi* **1** burn unsteadily **2** move backwards and forwards ♦ *n* **1** flickering **2** short-lived feeling

flickknife *n BrE* pocket knife with a blade that flicks out when a button is pressed

flier *n* person (esp. a pilot) or thing that flies

flies *pl n* covered front opening on trousers

flight¹ *n* **1** flying: *birds in flight / flights of fancy.* **2** journey by air **3** aircraft making a journey **4** group of birds or aircraft **5** set of stairs **~less** *adj* unable to fly

flight² *n* (an example of) the act of running away; escape

flight deck *n* **1** deck of an aircraft carrier **2** cockpit (1)

flight path *n* course through the air of an aircraft, etc.

flight recorder *n* black box

flighty *adj* (of a person) too influenced by sudden desires or ideas

flimsy *adj* light and thin; easily destroyed **–sily** *adv*

flinch *vi* move back in pain or fear

fling *vt* **flung** throw violently ♦ *n* short time of enjoyment, often with no sense of responsibility

flint *n* **1** hard stone that makes sparks **2** bit of metal in a cigarette lighter that lights the gas or petrol **~y** *adj* **1** like flint **2** hard; cruel

flintlock *n* gun in which the charge is lit by sparks from a flint

flip 1 *vt* send spinning into the air **2** *vi* become mad or very angry ♦ *n* **1** quick light blow **2** drink containing beaten egg ♦ *adj* flippant

flip-flop *n* **1** *BrE* a rubber sandal held on by a strap between the toes **2** an electronic circuit capable of assuring either of two stable states **3** *esp. AmE* complete change of policy; U-turn

flippant *adj* disrespectful about serious subjects **~ly** *adv* **–pancy** *n*

flipper *n* **1** flat limb of a seal, etc. **2** rubber shoe shaped like this, for swimming

flip side *n* less interesting side of a record

flirt *vi* behave as if sexually attracted **flirt with** *phr vt* **1** consider, but not seriously **2** risk, esp. needlessly or lightly ♦ *n* person who flirts **~ation** *n* **~atious** *adj* liking to flirt

flit *vi* **-tt-** fly or move quickly and lightly

flitch *n* a side of bacon

float *v* **1** *vi/t* (cause to) stay on the surface of liquid or be held up in air **2** *vt* establish (a business) by selling shares **3** *vi/t* (allow to) vary in exchange value **4** suggest ♦ *n* **1** light object that floats **2** flat vehicle drawn in a procession **3** money kept for use if an unexpected need arises **~ing** *adj* not fixed

floating voter *n* person who does not always vote for the same political party

flocculent *adj* woolly (1); flaky (1)

flock¹ *n* **1** group of sheep, goats, or birds **2** crowd **3** priest's congregation ♦ *vi* move in large numbers

flock² *n* **1** small pieces of wool, cotton,

etc. used for stuffing mattresses **2** short fibres used for making a raised pattern on e.g. wallpaper
floe *n* floating ice
flog *vt* **-gg-** **1** beat severely **2** *sl* sell **3 flog to death** *infml* spoil (a story, idea, etc.) by repeating too often
flood also **floods** *pl n* **1** water covering a place that is usu. dry **2** large quantity: *floods of tears* ♦ *vi/t* **1** fill or cover with water **2** overflow **3** arrive in large numbers
floodgate *n* gate for controlling water
floodlight *n* powerful light thrown on the outside of buildings, etc. ♦ *vt* **-lit** light with floodlights
flood tide *n* flow of the tide inwards
floor *n* **1** surface one stands on indoors: *dance floor* **2** level of a building **3** part of a parliament, etc. where members sit and speak **4 go through the floor** *infml* (of a price) sink to a very low level **5 take the floor: a** speak in a debate **b** start dancing ♦ *vt* **1** provide with a floor **2** knock down; defeat **3** confuse **~ing** *n* material for floors
floorboard *n* board in a wooden floor
floor show *n* cabaret
floozy, floozie *n derog* disreputable woman; prostitute
flop *vi* **-pp-** **1** fall awkwardly **2** fail ♦ *n* **1** awkward fall **2** failure **~py** *adj* soft and loose: *floppy hat* **~ piness** *n*
flophouse *n AmE* cheap hotel
floppy disk *n* plastic circle on which computer information is stored
flora *n* plants of a particular area or period
floral *adj* of flowers
floret *n* small flower forming part of a composite head of e.g. cauliflower
floribunda *n* variety of rose whose flowers grow in large sprays
florid *adj* **1** over-decorated **2** having a red face
florin *n* two-shilling piece in pre-decimal British coinage
florist *n* person who sells flowers
floss *n* **1** short silky fibres **2** dental floss **~y** *adj*
flotation *n* act of floating a business
flotilla *n* group of small ships
flotsam *n* floating wreckage
flotsam and jetsam *n* **1** miscellaneous and usu. useless odds and ends **2** vagrants
flounce[1] *vi* move violently to express anger or attract attention ♦ *n* flouncing movement
flounce[2] *n* gathered strip of fabric attached to the hem of a skirt or dress
flounder[1] *vi* **1** make wild movements, esp. in water **2** lose control when speaking, etc.
flounder[2] *n* a flatfish
flour *n* powder of crushed grain, used for making bread, etc.
flourish *v* **1** *vi* grow healthily **2** *vt* brandish ♦ *n* noticeable fancy movement
flout *vt* treat (rules, etc.) without respect
flow *vi* move or proceed smoothly ♦ *n* steady stream or supply **~ing** *adj* curving or hanging gracefully
flowchart *n* drawing showing how the parts of a process are connected
flower *n* **1** part of a plant that produces seeds **2** plant grown for its coloured petals or flowers **3** *lit* best part: *the flower of the nation's youth* **~less** *adj* **~y** *adj* **1** decorated with flowers **2** (of language) florid ♦ *vi* produce flowers
flowerbed *n* small piece of ground where flowers are grown
flowerpot *n* pot in which a plant is grown
flown *past p.* of fly
fl oz *abbrev. for:* fluid ounce
flu *n* infectious disease like a bad cold but more serious
fluctuate *vi fml* (of levels, etc.) change continually **-ation** *n*
flue *n* pipe through which smoke or heat passes
fluent *adj* **1** able to speak easily **2** (of speech) coming easily **~ly** *adv* **-ency** *n*
fluff *n* **1** soft light pieces from woolly material **2** soft fur or hair on a young animal or bird **3** *infml* slip of the tongue ♦ *vt* **1** shake or brush **2** do

(something) badly or unsuccessfully **~y** *adv* covered with fluff

fluid *adj* **1** able to flow **2** smooth and graceful **3** liable to change ♦ *n* liquid

fluke[1] *n* piece of accidental good luck

fluke[2] *n* **1** part of an anchor which sticks into the sea bed **2** flat wing-like part of a whale's tail

flume *n* a sloping channel for water

flummery *n* **1** pudding containing cream and whisky **2** meaningless flattery; humbug (1)

flummox *vt* confuse completely

flung *past t. and p. of* fling

flunk *v esp. AmE* **1** *vi/t* fail (an examination, etc.) **2** *vt* mark as unsatisfactory

flunkey, flunky *n* **1** liveried servant **2** yes-man

fluorescent /flooəˈres(ə)nt, flaw-/ *adj* giving out electromagnetic radiation in the form of bright light **–cence** *n*

fluoride *n* chemical compound said to protect teeth against decay **–ridate** *vt* add fluoride to **–ridation** *n*

flurry *n* **1** sudden rush of rain, snow, etc. **2** nervous excitement ♦ *vt* make nervous

flush *n* **1** (cleaning with) a rush of water **2** redness of the face **3** feeling of eager excitement **4** hand of cards all of the same suit ♦ *v* **1** *vt* clean with a rush of water **2** *vi* blush **3** *vt* make (someone) leave a hiding place ♦ *adj* **1** level **2** *sl* having plenty of money **~ed** *adj* proud and excited

fluster *vt* make nervous ♦ *n* nervous state

flute *n* woodwind instrument played by blowing sideways across it

flutist *n AmE* flautist

flutter *vi/t* **1 a** move (wings) quickly and lightly **b** fly by doing this **2** move in a quick irregular way ♦ *n* **1** fluttering or shaking movement **2** state of excitement

fluvial *adj* of rivers

flux *n* **1** *fml* continual change **2** substance used to promote fusion of metals e.g. when soldering

fly[1] *v* **flew, flown 1** *vi* move through the air as a bird or aircraft does **2** *vt* control (an aircraft) **3** *vt* raise (a flag) **4** *vi* flee **5** *vi* go fast **6 fly in the face of** defy **7 fly into a rage/temper** become suddenly angry **8 fly off the handle** *infml* become suddenly and unexpectedly angry **9 let fly** attack with words, bullets or blows

fly[2] *n* **1** winged insect **2** hook that is made to look like a fly, used in fishing **3 fly in the ointment** *infml* something that spoils the perfection of something **4 there are no flies on someone** *BrE infml* someone is not a fool and cannot be tricked

fly[3] *n* flies

fly[4] *adj infml* sharp; hard to fool

flyaway *adj* (of hair) light, loose and difficult to keep in place

flyblown *adj* **1** covered with flies' eggs **2** old and worthless

flyby *n* **1** *AmE* flypast **2** close-range observation of e.g. a planet by a spacecraft

fly-by-night *adj infml* unreliable; transitory

flyer *n* flier

fly-fishing *n* fishing using an artificial fly as bait

fly half *n* (in rugby) pivotal player who initiates movements by the threequarters

flying boat *n* large aircraft that takes off from and lands on water

flying buttress *n* arched buttress

flying colours *pl n* **with flying colours** very successfully; splendidly

flying doctor *n* doctor who visits patients in remote areas by aeroplane

flying fish *n* tropical fish with long fins enabling it to glide short distances above the water

flying fox *n* fruit bat

flying picket *n* someone who travels to picket a place of work other than their own

flying saucer *n* disc-shaped UFO

flying squad *n* special police kept ready for quick action

flying start *n* very good beginning

flying visit *n* very short visit

flyleaf *n* **-leaves** empty page at the beginning or end of a book
flyover *n BrE* place where two roads cross at different levels
flypaper *n* paper coated with a sticky substance to trap flies
flypast *n BrE* ceremonial low flight by aircraft over a public gathering
flysheet *n* **1** circular **2** outer sheet covering a tent
flyweight *n* boxer of the lightest class
flywheel *n* heavy wheel which keeps a machine working at a constant speed
FM *n, adj* frequency modulation
foal *n* young horse ♦ *vi* give birth to a foal
foam *n* **1** mass of bubbles **2** foam rubber ♦ *vi* produce foam **~y** *adj*
foam rubber *n* soft rubber full of bubbles
fob *n* **1** pocket at the waistband of trousers **2** watch chain or strap
fob off *phr vt* **-bb-** deceive (someone) into accepting (something)
fo'c'sle /ˈfohks(ə)l/ *n* forecastle
focus *n* **-cuses** *or* **-ci 1** point at which beams of light, etc., meet **2** centre of attention **3 in/out of focus** giving a clear/unclear picture ♦ *vi/t* **-s-** *or* **-ss- 1** come or bring to a focus **2** direct (attention) **focal** *adj*
fodder *n* **1** food for farm animals **2** anything that supplies a continuous demand
foe *n lit* enemy
foetus /ˈfeetəs/ *n* creature before birth, at a later stage than an embryo
fog *n* (period of) thick mist ♦ *vi/t* **-gg-** (cause to) become covered with fog **foggy** *adj* **1** misty **2** not clear: *I haven't the foggiest idea.*
fogbound *adj* prevented by fog from travelling
foghorn *n* horn used for warning ships in fog
fog lamp *n* bright lamp on a vehicle, for driving through fog
fogy *n derog* slow uninteresting old person
foible *n* foolish little personal habit
foil[1] *vt* prevent (someone) from succeeding in a plan
foil[2] *n* **1** thin sheet metal **2** person or thing that provides a contrast to another
foil[3] *n* thin sword for fencing
foist *vt* force someone to accept
-fold *suffix* multiplied by the stated number: *fourfold*
fold[1] *v* **1** *vt* bend back on itself **2** *vi* be able to be folded **3** *vt* cross (one's arms) **4** *vi* (of a business) fail ♦ *n* line made by folding **~er** *n* cardboard holder for papers
fold[2] *n* enclosure for sheep
foliage *n* leaves
folio *n* **-lios 1** page size produced by folding a large sheet of paper once **2** a book with pages this size
folk *n* **1** people **2** folk music ♦ *adj* of music, art, etc. that has grown up among ordinary people **~s** *pl n* one's relatives
folklore *n* beliefs long preserved among a tribe or nation
follicle *n* tiny skin cavity from which a hair grows
follow *v* **1** *vi/t* come or go after **2** *vt* go along: *follow the river* **3** *vt* attend or listen to carefully **4** *vi/t* understand **5** *vt* act according to **6** *vi* be a necessary result **7 as follows** as now to be told **8 follow suit** do what someone else has done **follow through** *phr vt* carry out to the end **follow up** *phr vt* take action to continue or add to the effect of something done before **~er** *n* someone who follows or supports **~ing** *adj* **1** next **2** to be mentioned now **~ing** *n* group of supporters
follow-through *n* continuation of a movement esp. in sport beyond the point at which contact is made with the ball or the ball is released from the hand
follow-up *n* action, consultation, investigation, etc. supplementary to an initial undertaking
folly *n fml* foolishness
foment *vt fml* help (something bad) to

develop

fond *adj* **1** loving **2** foolishly hopeful: *fond belief* **3** having a great liking or love (for) **~ly** *adv* **~ness** *n*

fondant *n* (sweet made from) creamy mixture of flavoured sugar and water

fondle *vt* touch lovingly

font[1] *n* container for water for baptism

font[2] *n AmE* fount[2]

food *n* **1** something, esp. solid, that creatures eat **2 food for thought** something to think about carefully

foodstuff *n* substance used as food

fool *n* **1** silly person **2 make a fool of oneself** behave in a silly way ♦ *v* **1** *vt* deceive **2** *vi* behave in a silly way **3** *vi* joke **~ish** *adj* silly **~ishly** *adv* **~ishness** *n*

foolhardy *adj* taking unwise risks

foolproof *adj* that cannot fail

foolscap *n* a size of paper, usu, 17 × $13\frac{1}{2}$ in

fool's errand *n* wild-goose chase

fool's gold *n* iron pyrites

fool's paradise *n* carelessly happy state in spite of a threat of change

foot *n* **feet 1** end part of the leg **2** bottom: *foot of the stairs* **3** (measure of length equal to) 12 inches **4** a unit of verse consisting of a combination of stressed and unstressed syllables **5 a foot in the door** favourable position from which to advance, gain influence, etc. **6 on foot** walking **7 put one's foot down** speak firmly **8 put one's foot in it** , *esp. AmE* **put one's foot in one's mouth** *infml* say the wrong thing ♦ *vt* **1 foot it a** walk **b** dance **2 foot the bill** *infml* pay the bill **~ing** *n* **1** firm placing of the feet **2** position in relation to others

footage *n* (length in feet of) cinema film used to record a scene, event etc.

foot-and-mouth disease *n* very contagious and often fatal disease of cattle, sheep and goats

football *n* **1** *BrE* field game for two teams of 11 players using a round ball that is kicked **2** ball used in this game **3** *AmE* American football

football pools *pl n* pools

footbridge *n* narrow bridge for pedestrians only

footfall *n* sound of a footstep

footfault *vi, n* overstep(ping) the baseline while serving at tennis

foothill *n* low hill at the foot of a mountain

foothold *n* **1** place where a foot can stand **2** position from which to advance

footle *vi* waste time in ineffectual activity **-ling** *adj* **1** bungling **2** fiddling

footlights *pl n* lights along the front of a stage floor

footloose *adj* free to go wherever one wants and do what one likes

footman *n* **-men** uniformed servant who opens doors, etc.

footnote *n* note at the bottom of a page

footpath n narrow path for walking on

footplate *n* place where the driver of a railway engine stands

footprint *n* mark made by a foot

footsie *n infml* **1** sexy touching with the feet **2** *AmE* clandestine dealings

footslog *vi* **-gg-** march or walk long distances

footsore *adj* having sore feet from too much walking

footstep *n* **1** sound of a person's step **2 follow in someone's footsteps** follow an example set by someone else in the past

footstool *n* low structure for resting the feet on

footwear *n* shoes, etc.

footwork *n* use of the feet in sports, etc.

fop *n* dandy **~pish** *adj*

for *prep* **1** intended to be given to, used by, or used in: *a present for you|cake for tea* **2** in order to help: *lift it for you* **3** (shows purpose): *What's this knife for?* **4** in support of; representing **5** towards: *set off for school* **6** so as to get: *wait for the bus* **7** (shows price or amount): *buy it for £1* **8** (shows meaning): *Red is for danger.* **9** (shows distance or time): *stay for a week* **10** because of **11** in regard to: *good for his health* **12** considering: *tall for his age* **13 for it** blamed or punished ♦ *conj fml* because

forage *n* food for horses and cattle ♦ *vi* search about

foray *n* **1** sudden rush into enemy country **2** attempt to enter a sphere of activity

forbear[1] *vi* **-bore**, **-borne** *fml* hold oneself back from doing something **~ance** *n* patient forgiveness

forbear[2] *n* forebear

forbid *vt* **-bade** *or* **-bad, -bidden** refuse to allow **~ding** *adj* looking dangerous

force *n* **1** strength; violence **2** influence **3** power that produces change **4** group of soldiers, police, etc. **5 in force** in large numbers **6 in(to) force** in/into operation **7 join forces (with)** unite (with) for a purpose ♦ *vt* **1** use (physical) force on **2** produce with effort: *forced laughter* **3** hasten growth of (plants) **4 force someone's hand** make someone act as one wishes or before they are ready **~s** *pl n* a country's army, navy, and airforce **~ful** *adj* (of people, words, etc.) powerful **~fully** *adv* **forcible** *adj* done by physical force **forcibly** *adv*

force-feed *vt* force food or liquid down a person's or animal's throat

force majeure *n* disruptive event which cannot reasonably be anticipated

forcemeat *n* type of stuffing consisting esp. of breadcrumbs and meat

forceps *pl n* medical instrument for holding objects

ford *n* place where one can cross a river without a bridge ♦ *vt* cross at a ford

fore *adj* front ♦ *n* **1** front **2 come to the fore** become well-known or noticeable

fore- *prefix* **1** (occurring) earlier or beforehand: *forewarn* **2 a** situated at the front: *foreground* **b** front part of: *forearm*

fore-and-aft *adj* aligned lengthwise along a ship

forearm *n* arm between the hand and elbow

forebear *n* ancestor

foreboding *n* feeling of coming evil

forecast *vt* **-cast** *or* **-casted** say in advance (what will happen in future) ♦ *n* prediction

forecastle /ˈfohks(ə)l/ *n* raised deck at ship's bow; sailors' quarters

foreclose *vi/t* take back property because a mortgage has not been repaid

forecourt *n* courtyard in front of a building

forefathers *pl n* ancestors

forefinger *n* finger next to the thumb

forefront *n* leading position

forego *vt* forgo

foregoing *n, adj* (statement, paragraph, etc.) immediately preceding

foregone conclusion *n* result that is certain from the start

foreground *n* nearest part of a view

forehand *n, adj* (tennis stroke) with the inner part of hand and arm turned forward

forehead *n* face above the eyes

foreign *adj* **1** of a country that is not one's own **2** coming or brought in from outside **3 foreign to** not natural in **~er** *n* foreign person

foreign affairs *pl n* matters concerning international relations and the interests of one's own country in foreign countries

foreign exchange *n* (practice of buying and selling) foreign money

foreknowledge *n* knowledge of an event before it occurs

foreland *n* headland

forelock *n* lock of hair above the forehead

foreman *n* **-men 1** worker in charge of others **2** leader of a jury

foremost *adj* most important

forename *n* first name

forenoon *n fml* morning

forensic *adj* used in the law and the tracking of criminals

foreplay *n* erotic stimulation before intercourse

forerunner *n* person or thing that prepares the way for another

foresee *vt* **-saw**, **-seen** see in advance **~able** *adj* that can be foreseen

foreshadow *vt* be a sign of (what will happen)
foreshore *n* shore between the sea and ordinary land
foreshorten *vt* **1** shorten (object depicted) to create the illusion of depth **2** make more compact
foresight *n* ability to imagine the future; wise planning
foreskin *n* fold of skin covering the tip of the penis
forest *n* area covered with trees **~er** *n* person who works in a forest **~ry** *n* work of planting and caring for trees
forestall *vt* prevent (a person or plan) by acting first
foretaste *n* first experience of something that will come later
foretell *vt* **-told** prophesy
forethought *n* wise planning for the future
forever *adv* **1** for all future time **2** continually **3 take forever** take an extremely long time
forewarn *vt* warn of coming danger
forewent *past t. of* forego
forewoman *n* **-men** female foreman
foreword *n* short introduction to a book
forfeit *vt* lose as a punishment ♦ *n* something forfeited **~ure** *n* forfeiting
forgather *vi* come together, assemble
forgave *past t. of* forgive
forge *vt* **1** copy in order to deceive **2** form (metal) by heating and hammering **3** create **forge ahead** *phr vi* move with a sudden increase of speed and power ♦ *n* place where metal is forged
forger *n* person who forges papers, etc. **~ry** *n* **1** forging of papers, etc. **2** forged paper, etc.
forget *vi/t* **-got, -gotten 1** fail to remember **2** stop thinking about **~ful** *adj* in the habit of forgetting
forget-me-not *n* plant with light blue flowers
forgive *vi/t* **-gave, -given** stop blaming (someone for something) **–givable** *adj* **–giving** *adj* willing to forgive **~ness** *n* act of forgiving
forgo, fore- *vt* **–went, –gone** *fml* give up; dispense with
fork *n* **1** instrument with prongs, for lifting food to the mouth **2** farm or gardening tool with prongs **3** place where a road, etc., divides; one of the divisions ♦ *v* **1** *vt* lift, etc., with a fork **2** *vi* divide into branches **3** *vi* (of a person) turn (left or right) **~ed** *adj* that divides into two or more points at the end **fork out** *phr vi/t* pay (money) unwillingly
forklift truck *n* small vehicle with movable prongs for lifting goods
forlorn *adj lit* **1** alone and unhappy **2 forlorn hope** undertaking which has very little chance of success **~ly** *adv*
form *n* **1** shape **2** plan; kind **3** way in which a work of art is put together **4** official paper with spaces for answering questions **5** class in a British school **6** long seat with no back **7** degree of skill, fitness, etc. **8** correct practice ♦ *v* **1** *vi* begin to exist **2** *vt* make from parts; shape **3** *vt* have the shape or substance of **~less** *adj* shapeless
formal *adj* **1** suitable for official occasions **2** regular in shape **3** stiff in manner and behaviour **4** official; following established procedure **~ly** *adv* **~ize, -ise** *vt* make formal **~ity** *n* **1** compliance with rules **2** observance required by custom or established procedure **3** ceremoniousness, stiffness
formaldehyde *n* gas used chiefly as a disinfectant and preservative
formalin *n* solution of formaldehyde in water
format *n* size, shape, or arrangement of something ♦ *vt* **-tt-** arrange (a book, computer information, etc.) in a particular format
formation *n* **1** shaping of something **2** arrangement; structure
formative *adj* giving shape: *a child's formative years*
forme *n* block of type assembled ready for printing
former *adj* of an earlier period ♦ *n* first of two things mentioned **~ly** *adv* in earlier time

Formica *adj, n tdmk* (made of) laminated plastic sheet used for heat-resistant surfaces
formic acid *n* acid obtained from ants
formidable *adj* **1** large and frightening **2** hard to defeat **–bly** *adv*
formula *n* **-las** *or* **-lae 1** rule expressed in a short form by letters, numbers, etc. **2** list of substances used in making something; recipe **3** combination of suggestions, plans, etc. **4** set form or method **5** classification for racing cars **~ic** *adj*
formulate *vt* **1** express exactly **2** invent (a plan) **–lation** *n*
fornicate *vi* have sex outside marriage **–cation** *n*
forsake *vt* **-sook, -saken** *lit* desert[2] (2)
forswear *vt* **1** renounce **2** perjure (oneself)
forsythia *n* yellow-flowered shrub
fort *n* **1** building for military defence **2 hold the fort** look after everything while someone is away
forte[1] /ˈfawti, -tay/ *n* something someone does particularly well
forte[2] *adj, adv* (of music) loud(ly)
forth *adv lit* **1** forward **2 and (so on and) so forth** etc.
forthcoming *adj* **1** happening soon **2** supplied when needed: *No answer was forthcoming.* **3** ready to be helpful
forthright *adj* speaking plainly; direct
forthwith *adv fml* at once
fortieth *determiner, n, pron, adv* 40th
fortify *vt* **1** strengthen against attack **2** make stronger **–fication** *n* **1** towers, etc., for defence **2** act of fortifying
fortitude *n* uncomplaining courage
fortnight *n BrE* two weeks **~ly** *adj, adv* happening once a fortnight
FORTRAN *n* computer programming language used esp. for mathematical and scientific purposes
fortress *n* large fort
fortuitous /fawˈtyooh·itəs/ *adj fml* **1** accidental **2** lucky
fortunate *adj* lucky **~ly** *adv*
fortune *n* **1** good or bad luck **2** that which will happen to a person in the future **3** great sum of money
fortune-teller *n* person who claims to be able to tell people their future
forty *determiner, n, pron* 40
forty-five *n* **1** .45 calibre pistol **2** record that revolves at 45 rpm
forty winks *pl n* short sleep in the daytime
forum *n* place for public argument
forward *adj* **1** towards the front or future **2** advanced in development **3** too bold, often in sexual matters ♦ *vt* **1** send (e.g. letters) to a new address **2** send (goods) ♦ *n* attacking player in football, rugby, etc. ♦ *adv* also **forwards** towards the front or future **~ness** *n*
forwent *past t. of* forgo
fosse *n* moat; ditch
fossick *vi AustrE* **1** rummage around **2** search for gold by picking over old workings **~er** *n*
fossil *n* **1** part or print of an ancient animal or plant, preserved in rock, ice, etc. **2** old person with unchanging ideas **~ize, -ise** *vi/t* **1** change into a fossil **2** (cause to) become very fixed (in ideas, etc.)
foster *vt* **1** *fml* encourage to develop **2** take (a child) into one's home for a while
foster- *prefix* giving or receiving parental care though not of the same family: *foster-mother*
fought *past t. and p. of* fight
foul *adj* **1** very unpleasant **2** against the rules ♦ *n* act that is against the rules ♦ *vi/t* **1** make dirty **2** be guilty of a foul
foul up *phr vt infml* spoil (an occasion, etc.)
foul-mouthed *adj* habitually using obscene or abusive language
foul play *n* **1** (in sports) unfair play **2** criminal violence, esp. murder
foul-up *n* mistake; blunder
found[1] *past t. and p. of* find
found[2] *vt* **1** establish; build **2** base **~er** *n* person who establishes something
foundation *n* **1** founding of an organization **2** basis **3** organization that gives out money **4** cream, lotion, etc., applied

as a base for other make-up **~s** *pl n* base that supports a building
foundation garment *n* girdle, corset, etc.
foundation stone *n* first stone of a new building, often laid with public ceremony
founder *vi* (of a ship) fill with water and sink
foundling *n* abandoned infant
foundry *n* place where metal is melted and poured into shapes
fount[1] *n lit* source
fount[2] *n* set of type of one particular variety and size
fountain *n* **1** decorative structure from which water springs up **2** flow of liquid
fountain pen *n* pen with ink reservoir inside
four *determiner, n, pron* 4
four-letter word *n* obscene word, esp. one consisting of four letters
four-poster *n* bed with four tall posts usu. supporting a canopy
foursome *n* group of four people, esp. playing a game together
foursquare *adj* **1** solid and steadfast **2** forthright
four-stroke *adj* (of an internal-combustion engine) making four piston strokes at every explosion in a cylinder
fourteen *determiner, n, pron* 14 **~th** *determiner, adv, n, pron* 14th
fourth *determiner, adv, n, pron* 4th
fourth dimension *n* time (1)
fourth estate *n* the press
fowl *n* **fowls** *or* **fowl** **1** farmyard bird, esp. a hen **2** any bird
fox *n* wild animal of the dog family ♦ *vt* confuse; deceive **~y** *adj* **1** crafty; cunning **2** *AmE* sexually attractive
foxglove *n* tall plant with white or purple flowers
foxhole *n* hole where soldiers shelter from enemy fire
foxhunting *n* hunting of foxes by special dogs (**foxhounds**) and people on horses **-ter** *n*
foyer *n* entrance hall of a theatre, etc.
Fr *abbrev. for:* **1** Father **2** French **3** Friar
fracas /ˈfrakah/ *n* noisy quarrel
fraction *n* **1** division of a whole number (e.g. $\frac{1}{3}$) **2** small part **~al** *adj* so small as to be unimportant
fractious *adj* restless and complaining
fracture *n* break esp. in a bone or pipe ♦ *vi/t* break
fragile *adj* **1** easily broken **2** having a small thin body or weak in health **-gility** *n*
fragment *n* piece broken off ♦ *vi/t* break into pieces **~ation** *n* **~ary** *adj* incomplete
fragrant *adj* sweet-smelling **~ly** *adv* **-grance** *n*
frail *adj* weak, esp. in body **~ty** *n* **1** quality of being frail **2** fault of character
frame *n* **1** border into which something fits **2** structure on which something is built **3** human or animal body **4** single photograph in a cinema film **5 frame of mind** state of mind at a particular time ♦ *vt* **1** put in a frame **2** give shape to; express: *frame a question* **3** *infml* make (a guiltless person) seem guilty of a crime
frame-up *n infml* carefully prepared plan to incriminate an innocent person
framework *n* supporting structure
franc *n* the basic money unit of France, Belgium, Switzerland, etc.
franchise *n* **1** the right to vote **2** the right to sell a product
Franciscan *n* member of religious order founded by St. Francis of Assissi
Franco- *prefix* **1** of France or the French: *Francophile, Francophone* **2** French and: *Franco-German*
frangipani *n* tropical American shrub with waxy flowers and a very strong scent
Franglais *n* French with a lot of English words mixed up in it
frank[1] *adj* open and honest **~ly** *adv* **~ness** *n*
frank[2] *vt* stamp (a letter) by machine
frankfurter *n* red smoked sausage
frankincense *n* fragrant gum resin burnt as incense

frantic *adj* wildly anxious, afraid, happy, etc. **~ally** *adv*

frappé *n* **1** partly frozen drink **2** liqueur served over crushed ice **3** *AmE* thick milk shake

fraternal *adj* brotherly

fraternity *n* **1** people joined by common interests **2** *AmE* college society **3** *fml* brotherly feeling

fraternize, -ise *vi* meet and be friendly (with someone) **–nization** *n*

fratricide *n* murder of one's brother or sister

fraud *n* **1** criminal deceit to make money **2** person who falsely claims to be something

fraudulent *adj* deceitful; got or done by fraud **~ly** *adv*

fraught *adj* **1** full of: *fraught with danger* **2** *infml* **a** (of a person) worried **b** (of conditions) difficult

fray[1] *vi/t* **1** develop loose threads by rubbing **2** strain; irritate

fray[2] *n lit* battle

frazzle *vt infml* make exhausted and irritable ♦ *n* exhausted and irritable condition

freak *n* **1** strange unnatural creature or event **2** person who takes a special interest in the stated thing: *a film freak* **~ish** *adj* unreasonable; unusual

freckle *n* small brown spot on the skin **freckled** *adj*

free *adj* **1** able to act as one wants; not in prison or controlled by rules **2** not busy or being used **3** without payment **4** (of a way or passage) not blocked **5** not fixed; loose **6 free and easy** unworried **7 free from/of** untroubled by; without **8 free with** ready to give **9 make free with** use (something) without respect or as if it is one's own ♦ *adv* **1** without payment **2** without control **3** in a loose position ♦ *vt* **freed** set free **~ly** *adv* **1** readily; openly **2** in great amounts

-free *suffix* without: *fatfree; troublefree*

free-base *vi sl* smoke a specially prepared mixture of cocaine

freebie, -bee *n infml* something that is given or received without payment

freeboard *n* distance between the waterline and the top of the side of a ship

freebooter *n* pirate

Free Church *adj, n* Nonconformist (church)

free collective bargaining *n* negotiation between unions and employers subject to no government controls

freedom *n* **1** state of being free **2** certain rights, often given as an honour: *the freedom of the city*

free enterprise *n* social system in which private trade, business, etc., is carried on without much government control

free-fall *n* **1** being subject solely to the force of gravity **2** part of a parachute jump before the parachute opens

freefone *n BrE* arrangement whereby all calls to a certain number are paid for by the subscriber holding that number

free-for-all *n* quarrel, etc., in which many people join

freehand *adj, adv* drawn without instruments

free hand *n* unlimited freedom of action

freehold *adj, adv, n* (with) unconditional ownership of land or buildings

free house *n BrE* public house that can sell products of more than one brewery

free kick *n* (in football) unopposed kick awarded because of an infringement by the other team

freelance, freelancer *n* self-employed person who works for many employers

freelance *adj, adv* working as or done by a freelance ♦ *vi* work as a freelance

freeload *vi* selfishly exploit other people's generosity **~er** *n*

Freemason *n* man belonging to an ancient society whose members help each other **~ry** *n*

free port *n* port into which goods from all countries are admitted without paying taxes

free-range *adj* being or produced by hens kept under natural conditions

free rein *n* complete freedom of action

free speech *n* right to express one's ideas in public
freestanding *adj* standing unsupported; not integrated with other units
freethinker *n* sceptic rationalist esp. in religious matters
free trade *n* system of allowing foreign goods freely into a country
free verse *n* poetry without rhyme or conventional metre
freeway *n AmE* motorway
freewheel *vi* travel downhill without using power **~ing** *adj infml* not greatly worrying about rules, responsibilities, etc.
free will *n* **1** ability to decide freely what to do **2** belief that human effort can influence events, and they are not fixed in advance by God
free world *n* all the non-communist countries
freeze *v* **froze, frozen 1** *vi/t* harden into ice **2** *vi* (of weather) be at the temperature at which ice forms **3** *vi/t* stop working properly because of cold **4** *vi* feel very cold **5** *vt* preserve (food) at low temperatures **6** *vi/t* stop moving **7** *vt* fix (prices, wages, etc.) **freeze out** *phr vt infml* prevent from being included **freeze over** *phr vi/t* (cause to) turn to ice on the surface ♦ *n* **1** period of freezing weather **2** fixing of prices or wages **~er** *n* machine that freezes food
freight /frayt/ *n* goods carried by ship, plane, etc. **~er** *n* ship or plane that carries goods
French *adj* of France ♦ *n* **1** the language of France **2** *pl* the people of France **~man** *n* **~woman** *n*
French dressing *n* salad dressing of oil and vinegar with seasonings
French fries *pl n esp. AmE* chips (3)
French horn *n* circular valved brass instrument
French kiss *n* open-mouthed kiss usu. with tongue contact
French leave *n infml* unauthorized absence from duty
French letter *n BrE infml* condom
French polish *n* solution of shellac used as wood polish
French toast *n esp. AmE* bread dipped in beaten egg and fried
French windows *pl n* glass doors
frenetic *adj* overexcited; feverish
frenzy *n* violent excitement
frequency *n* **1** frequent occurrence **2** rate at which something happens or is repeated **3** particular number of radio waves per second
frequency modulation *n* modulation of the frequency of a radio wave by the characteristics of the signal carried
frequent *adj* happening often ♦ *vt* go to (a place) often **~ly** *adv*
fresco *n* **-coes** *or* **-cos** picture painted on wet plaster
fresh *adj* **1** recently made, found, etc.; not stale **2** (of food) not frozen or tinned **3** (of water) not salt **4** new and different **5 a** (of wind) rather strong **b** (of weather) cool and windy **6** not tired **7** too bold with someone of the opposite sex ♦ *adv* **1** just; newly **2 fresh out of** *infml, esp. AmE* having just used up one's supplies of **~ly** *adv* **~ness** *n*
freshen *vi/t* **1** make or become fresh **2** (of wind) become stronger **freshen up** *phr vi/t* **1** (cause to) feel less tired, look more attractive, etc. **2** (of a drink) add more liquid, esp. alcohol, to it
freshman also **fresher** *n* **-men** student in the first year at college or university
freshwater *adj* of a river or lake, not the sea
fret *vi/t* **-tt-** worry about small things **~ful** *adj* anxious and complaining **~fully** *adv*
fretsaw *n* tool for cutting patterns in wood
fretwork *n* patterns cut with a fretsaw
Freudian *adj* **1** (of the psychoanalytic theory and practice) of Sigmund Freud **2 Freudian slip** a slip of the tongue that reveals one's unconscious thought
friable *adj* easily crumbled
friar *n* member of a Christian religious order combining monastic life with outside religious activity
fricassee *n* stewed meat served in a

white sauce

fricative *n, adj* (consonant sound) made by forcing air out through a narrow opening e.g. between the lips

friction *n* **1** rubbing of one surface against another **2** disagreement within a group

Friday *n* the 5th day of the week

fridge *n* refrigerator

friend *n* **1** person whom one likes but who is not related **2** helper; supporter **3** **make friends** form a friendship **~less** *adj* without friends **~ly** *adj* **1** acting as a friend **2** not causing unpleasant feelings in competitions, etc. **~liness** *n* **~ship** *n* friendly relationship

-friendly *suffix* adapted to the needs of: *user-friendly*

friendly society *n BrE* association to which members pay regular sums in return for old-age pensions, sickness benefits, etc.

fries *n* French fries

Friesian /ˈfreezh(ə)n/ *n* any of a breed of large black-and-white dairy cattle

frieze *n* decorative border along the top of a wall

frig *vi taboo* **1** masturbate **2** have sexual intercourse **~ging** *adj* (used to express annoyance with something)

frigate *n* small fast warship

fright *n* feeling of fear

frighten *vt* fill with fear **~ed** *adj* **~ingly** *adv*

frightful *adj* terrible; very bad **~ly** *adv*

frigid *adj* **1** (of a woman) disliking sex **2** very cold **~ly** *adv* **-gidity** *n*

frill *n* **1** decorative wavy edge on cloth **2** unnecessary decoration **~y** *adj*

fringe *n* **1** decorative edge of hanging threads on a curtain, etc. **2** hair hanging over the forehead **3** edge **4** not official; not conventional: *fringe theatre* ♦ *vt* be the border of

fringe benefit *n* something given with a job, besides wages

frippery *n* tawdry finery

Frisbee *tdmk* plastic disc which players throw to one another

frisk *v* **1** *vi* jump about playfully **2** *vt* search (someone) for hidden weapons **~y** *adj* joyfully playful

frisson /ˈfreesonh/ *n* feeling of excitement caused by fear

fritter *n* piece of cooked batter with fruit, meat, etc., inside

fritter away *phr vt* waste

frivolity *n* **1** quality of being frivolous **2** frivolous act or remark

frivolous *adj* not serious enough; silly **~ly** *adv*

frizzy *adj* (of hair) very curly

frock *n* woman's dress

frock coat *n* knee-length coat worn by men in the 19th century

frog *n* **1** small jumping creature that lives on land and in water **2** **a frog in the/one's throat** difficulty in speaking because of roughness in the throat

frogman *n* **-men** skilled underwater swimmer who uses breathing apparatus

frogmarch *vt* force (a person) to move forward with the arms held together firmly from behind

frog spawn *n* mass of frog's eggs

frolic *vi* **-ck-** jump about happily ♦ *n* lighthearted entertainment or game **~some** *adj* playful

from *prep* **1** starting at (a place or time) **2** given or sent by **3** away: *subtract 10 from 15* **4** using **5** because of: *suffer from heart disease* **6** out of **7** (indicating release, protection, prevention, etc.): *She saved the child from drowning.* **8** judging by: *From what John tells me, they're very rich.*

frond *n* leaf of a fern or palm

front *n* **1** part in the direction that something moves or faces **2** line where fighting takes place in war **3** road beside the sea in a holiday town **4** line dividing cold from warmer air **5** (often false) outward appearance **6** combined effort or movement against opposing forces **7** particular area of activity: *They have made little progress on the employment front.* **8** *infml* person, group or thing used for hiding the real nature of a secret or unlawful activity **9** **in front** : **a**

ahead **b** in the most forward position **10 in front of** : **a** ahead of **b** in the presence of **11 up front** *infml* as payment in advance ♦ *vi/t* face (towards): *The hotel fronts onto the lake.* **~al** *adj* at, of, or from the front

frontage *n* front width of a building or piece of land

frontbench *n* either of the two rows of seats in the British parliament on which the most important politicians of the two major parties sit **~er** *n*

frontier *n* **1** edge of a country **2** also **frontiers** *pl* furthest limit: *the frontiers of knowledge*

frontiersman *n* **-men** pioneer living on the edge of settled territory, esp. in the early American West

frontispiece *n* illustration usu. facing the title page of a book

front line *n* **1** military front **2** most advanced position **front-line** *adj*

front man *n* someone who explains the views or future plans of esp. a large company to the public

front-page *adj* very interesting; worthy of being on the front page of a newspaper

front-runner *n* person who has the best chance of success in competing for something

frost *n* **1** white powder that forms on things below freezing point **2** (period of) freezing weather ♦ *v* **1** *vi/t* (cause to) become covered with frost **2** *vt* roughen the surface of (glass) **~y** *adj* **1** very cold **2** unfriendly

frostbite *n* harmful swelling etc., of the limbs, caused by cold **-bitten** *adj*

froth *n* **1** mass of small bubbles **2** *derog* light empty show of talk or ideas ♦ *vi* produce froth **~y** *adj* covered with froth

frown *vi* draw the eyebrows together in anger or effort **frown** *n*

frowsty *adj esp. BrE* stuffy (1)

frowzy, frowsy *adj* slovenly; unkempt

froze *past t. of* freeze

frozen *past p. of* freeze

FRS *abbrev. for:* Fellow of the Royal Society

fructify *v fml* **1** *vi* bear fruit **2** *vt* make fruitful or productive

frugal *adj* **1** not wasteful **2** small and cheap **~ly** *adv* **~ity** *n*

fruit *n* **1** seed-containing part of a plant, often edible **2** also **fruits** *pl* result or reward ♦ *vi* bear fruit **~ful** *adj* useful; successful **~fully** *adv* **~less** *adj* unsuccessful **~lessly** *adv* **~y** *adj* **1** like fruit **2** (of a voice) rich and deep

fruit bat *n* tropical, fruit-eating bat

fruitcake *n* **1** cake containing small dried fruits, nuts, etc. **2** *infml* a mad, silly person

fruiterer *n* someone who sells fruit in a shop

fruition /ˈfroohˈish(ə)n/ *n fml* fulfilment of plans, etc.

fruit machine *n BrE* one-armed bandit

frump *n* dowdy woman **~ish, ~y** *adj*

frustrate *vt* **1** disappoint and annoy **2** prevent the fulfilment of (plans) **-tration** *n*

fry[1] *vi/t* cook in hot fat or oil

fry[2] *n* very small fish

frying pan *n* **1** flat pan for frying **2 out of the frying pan into the fire** out of a bad position into an even worse one

fry-up *n BrE infml* simple esp. impromptu meal of fried food

ft *written abbrev. for:* foot[1] (3)

fuchsia /ˈfyoohshə/ *n* garden shrub with bell-shaped pink, red, or purple flowers

fuck *vi/t taboo* have sex (with) ♦ *n taboo sl* **1** act of having sex **2 not care/give a fuck** not care at all **fuck off** *phr vi taboo sl* go away **fuck up** *phr vt taboo sl* spoil; ruin

fuck-all *n taboo sl* nothing

fuck-up *n taboo sl* mess; fiasco

fuddled *adj* **1** confused **2** unable to think clearly (esp. because of drinking)

fuddy-duddy *adj, n infml* old-fashioned, conservative, fussy (person)

fudge[1] *n* creamy brown sweet made of sugar, milk, butter, etc.

fudge[2] *v* **1** *vt* put together roughly or dishonestly **2** *vi/t* avoid taking firm

action (on)
fuel *n* material (e.g. coal) that produces heat or power ♦ *v* **-ll-** (*AmE* **-l-**) **1** *vt* provide with fuel **2** *vi* take in fuel
fug *n* stuffy atmosphere **~gy** *adj*
fugitive *n* person escaping from something
fugue *n* piece of music in which different parts enter in succession with the same tune
-ful *suffix* **1** having or giving: *sinful; restful* **2** amount contained by: *handful; spoonful*
fulcrum *n* **-crums** *or* **-cra** point on which a lever turns
fulfil, *AmE* **fulfill** *vt* **-ll- 1** perform (a promise, duty, etc.) **2** develop fully the character and abilities of (oneself) **~ment** *n*
full *adj* **1** holding as much or as many as possible **2** well fed **3** complete **4** highest possible **5** (of a garment) loose **6** rounded; plump **7 full of** thinking only of ♦ *n* **1 in full** completely **2 to the full** thoroughly ♦ *adv* **1** straight; directly **2** very **~ly** *adv* **1** at least: *It's fully an hour since he left.* **2** completely **~ness, fulness** *n*
fullback *n* defensive player usu. rearmost (apart from the goalkeeper) in any on-field formation
full-blooded *adj* **1** of unmixed ancestry **2** thoroughgoing; whole-hearted **3** vigorous
full-blown *adj* **1** (of a flower) completely open **2** fully developed
full-grown *adj* completely developed
full house *n* **1** crowd or audience that fills a venue to capacity **2** poker hand consisting of three cards of one value and a pair of another value
full-length *adj* **1** (of a painting, etc.) showing someone from head to foot **2** not shorter than usual
full moon *n* the moon when seen as a circle
full-scale *adj* **1** (of a model, etc.) as big as the object represented **2** (of an activity) not lessened: *full-scale war*
full stop *n* **1** a mark (.) showing esp. the end of a sentence **2 come to a full stop** stop completely
full-time *adj* working or studying all the usual hours
fully-fashioned *adj* tailored to the shape of the body
fully-fledged *adj* **1** (of a bird) having grown all its feathers **2** completely trained
fulmar *n* large arctic seabird
fulminate *vi* denounce or criticize vehemently
fulsome *adj* praising too much
fumble *vi* use the hands awkwardly
fume *vi* show great anger
fumes *pl n* strong-smelling gas or smoke
fumigate *vt* disinfect by means of smoke or gas
fun *n* **1** playfulness **2** (cause of) amusement; enjoyment **3 for fun** also **for the fun of it** for pleasure **4 in fun** not seriously **5 make fun of** laugh unkindly at
function *n* **1** natural purpose of something or someone **2** important social gathering **3** (*maths*) quantity whose value depends on that of another variable ♦ *vi* be in action; work **~al** *adj* **1** made for use, not decoration **2** functioning **~ality** *n*
fund *n* also **funds** *pl n* supply of money for a purpose ♦ *vt* provide money for
fundamental *adj* central; very important ♦ *n* basic rule **~ly** *adv* **~ism** *n* **1** belief in the literal truth of the Bible **2** precise observance of the tenets of a religion **~ist** *n, adj*
funeral *n* ceremony of burying or cremating a dead person **-real** *adj* gloomy; solemn
funeral director *n* undertaker
funeral parlour also *AmE* **funeral home** *n* undertaker's place of business
funfair *n esp. BrE* travelling show, with amusements and rides
fungicide *n* chemical for destroying fungus
fungus *n* **-gi** *or* **-guses** leafless plant e.g. mould, mushroom, toadstool

funicular /fyooh'nikyoolə/ *n* mountain railway worked by a cable
funk *n* fear; panic ♦ *vt* not do (something) out of fear
funky *adj infml, esp. AmE* **1** (of jazz or similar music) having a simple direct style and feeling **2** attractive and fashionable
funnel *n* **1** wide-mouthed tube for pouring liquids through **2** chimney on a steam engine or steamship ♦ *vi/t* **-ll-** (*AmE* **-l-**) pass (as if) through a funnel
funny *adj* **1** amusing **2** strange **–nily** *adv*
funny bone *n* tender part of the elbow
funny business *n infml* trickery; underhand behaviour
funny farm *n AmE infml* mental hospital
fur *n* **1** soft thick hair of a cat, rabbit, etc. **2** (garment made of) the fur-covered skin of an animal **3** hard covering on the inside of pots, hot-water pipes, etc. **~ry** *adj*
furious *adj* **1** very angry **2** wild; uncontrolled **~ly** *adv*
furl *vt* roll or fold up (a sail, flag, etc.)
furlong *n* a measure of length equal to 220 yards (201 metres)
furlough *n* leave² (1)
furnace *n* **1** enclosed space where metals, etc., are heated **2** enclosed fire to make hot water
furnish *vt* **1** put furniture in **2** supply **~ings** *pl n* furniture, etc., for a room
furniture *n* beds, chairs, etc.
furore /fyoo'rawri/ *n* sudden burst of public interest
furphy /'fuhfi/ *n esp. AustrE infml* absurd rumour
furrier *n* person who makes or sells fur garments
furrow *n* **1** track cut by a plough **2** wrinkle ♦ *vt* make furrows in
further *adv, adj* **1** (*comparative of* far) at or to a greater distance or more distant point **2** more **3 further to** continuing the subject of **4 go further** give, do, or say more ♦ *vt* help to advance **~ance** *n fml* advancement **~most** *adj* farthest
further education *n BrE* post-secondary school education other than at a university, polytechnic, etc.
furthermore *adv* also
furthest *adv, adj* (*superlative of* far) at or to the greatest distance or degree
furtive *adj* trying to escape notice **~ly** *adv* **~ness** *n*
fury *n* **1** great anger **2** wild force
furze *n* gorse
fuse¹ *n* wire that melts to break an electric connection ♦ *vi/t* **1** stop working because a fuse has melted **2** join by melting
fuse² *n* **1** pipe, cord, etc., that carries fire to an explosive article **2** part of a bomb that makes it explode
fuselage /'fyoohzi,lahzh/ *n* body of an aircraft
fusilier *n* British infantryman formerly armed with a light musket
fusillade *n* rapid continuous firing of shots
fusion *n* **1** joining together by melting **2** blend
fuss *n* **1** unnecessary show of excitement or annoyance **2 make a fuss of** pay loving attention to ♦ *vi* show unnecessary anxiety **~y** *adj* too concerned about details **2** (of dress, etc.) overdecorated
fusspot *adj infml* fussy person
fustian *n* **1** rough heavy cotton material **2** *lit* bombastic speech or writing
fusty *adj* **1** old and smelling bad **2** old-fashioned
futile *adj* unsuccessful; useless **futility** *n*
futon /'foohton/ *n* Japanese-style fold-away mattress
future *n* **1** time after the present **2** that which will happen to someone or something **3** likelihood of success **4** future tense **5 in future** from now on ♦ *adj* **1** that will be, occur etc. in the future **2** (of verbs) expressing what will happen in the future **~s** *pl n* (contracts for) commodities bought at the current price but to be delivered at a later date
futuristic *adj* of strange modern design
fuzz *n* fluff **~y** *adj* **1** (of hair) standing

up in a light short mass **2** not clear in shape **3** (of cloth, etc.) having a raised soft hairy surface **-ily** *adv* **-iness** *n*

FYI *abbrev. for:* (*AmE*) for your information

G

G, g the 7th letter of the English alphabet

g *abbrev. for:* gram(s)

G *abbrev. for* **1** gravity; unit of gravitational force exerted on a body **2** *AmE sl* one thousand dollars

gab *vi, n* chatter

gabardine, -erdine *n* (raincoat made from) strong cloth

gabble *vi/t* speak or say too quickly to be heard **gabble** *n*

gable *n* three-cornered top of a wall between sloping roofs

gad about *phr vi* travel for enjoyment

gadfly *n* **1** fly which pesters livestock **2** lightweight but annoying critic

gadget *n* small useful machine or tool **~ry** *n* gadgets

gadzooks *interj arch.* (expressing surprise or other strong feeling)

Gaelic *adj, n* (of or being) any of the Celtic languages, esp. those of Scotland, Ireland, or the Isle of Man

gaff *n* pole with a hook attached for landing large fish

gaffe *n* social mistake

gaffer *n* man in charge, esp. of lighting for a film

gag *n* **1** something put over someone's mouth to stop them from talking **2** joke ♦ *vt* **-gg-** put a gag on

gaga *adj* senile

gage[1] *n, v AmE* gauge

gage[2] *n* **1** *arch.* glove or other token thrown down as a challenge to combat **2** *lit* pledge

gaggle *n* **1** group of geese **2** group of noisy people

gaiety *n* cheerfulness

gaily *adv* cheerfully

gain *v* **1** *vi/t* obtain (something useful) **2** *vi* (of a clock) go too fast **3** *vt* succeed in reaching **gain on** *phr vt* get close to (someone ahead in a race) ♦ *n* increase in wealth or amount; profit **~ful** *adj* profitable **~fully** *adv* **~er** *n*

gainsay *vt* **-said** *fml* deny

gait *n* way of walking

gaiter *n* covering for the lower leg

gal *n* girl

gala *n* festive event

galah *n* **1** type of cockatoo **2** *AustrE sl* fool

galaxy *n* large group of stars **-actic** *adj*

gale *n* **1** strong wind **2** noisy outburst

gall[1] *n* daring rudeness; audacity ♦ *vt* cause to feel annoyed disappointment or anger

gall[2] *n* diseased growth on a plant

gallant *adj* **1** brave **2** (of a man) polite to women **~ly** *adv* **~ry** *n*

gall bladder *n* hollow organ in which bile is stored

galleon *n* sailing ship, esp. Spanish, of the 15th to 18th centuries

gallery *n* **1** place where works of art are shown **2** upper floor of a hall or church **3** passage in a mine **4** top floor in a theatre

galley *n* **1** ancient ship rowed by slaves **2** ship's kitchen

Gallic *adj* typical of France

gallivant *vi* gad about

gallon *n* (a measure for liquids equal to) **a** (in Britain) 4 quarts **b** (in America) 231 cubic inches

gallop *vi* (of a horse) move at its fastest speed ♦ *n* galloping

gallows *n* **gallows** wooden frame on which criminals are hanged

gallows humour *n* jokes about the unpleasant side of life

gallstone *n* hard stone that forms in the gall bladder

Gallup poll *n* survey of public opinion

galore *adj* in plenty: *bargains galore*
galoshes *pl n* rubber overshoes
galumph *vi esp. humorous* walk heavily and clumsily
galvanize, -ise *vt* **1** cover (another metal) with zinc **2** shock into action
gambit *n* action done to produce a future advantage, esp. an opening move in a game, conversation, etc.
gamble *v* **1** *vi/t* bet **2** *vi* take a risk ♦ *n* risky matter **–bler** *n*
gambol *vi* **-ll-** (*AmE* **-l-**) jump about playfully
game *n* **1** form of play or sport **2** single part of a match (e.g. in tennis) **3** wild animals and birds hunted for food and sport **4** *infml* profession or activity: *the advertising game* ♦ *adj* brave and willing **~ly** *adv* **games** *pl n* sports competitions
gamekeeper *n* man who looks after game birds
gamelan *n* Javanese percussion orchestra
gamesmanship *n* art of winning by using rules to one's own advantage but without cheating
gamete *n* reproductive cell, esp. an egg or sperm
game theory *n* theoretical analysis of conflict and its resolution
gamin, gamine *adj* (of a woman or her looks) impish, tomboyish
gaming *n* gambling
gamma ray *n* electromagnetic ray of shorter wavelength than X-rays
gammon *n* smoked or salted ham
gammy *adj infml* (esp. of a leg) lame
gamut *n* range
gamy *adj* high smelling or tasting, like game that has been hung for several days
-gamy *suffix* marriage: *polygamy*
gander *n* male goose
gang *n* **1** group of people working together, esp. criminals **2** group of friends **gang up** *phr vi* work together (against someone); conspire
gang-bang *n sl* occasion when several men have sex with the same woman; multiple rape
gangland *n* world of professional, esp. violent crime
gangling *adj* tall, thin, and awkward
ganglion *n* **1** small harmless tumour **2** dense mass of nerve cells
gangplank *n* movable bridge for getting into or out of a ship
gangrene *n* decay of a body part because blood has stopped flowing there **–grenous** *adj*
gangster *n* member of a criminal gang
gangway *n* **1** large gangplank **2** *BrE* passage between rows of seats
ganja *n* cannabis
gannet *n* large black and white seabird
gantry *n* frame supporting movable heavy machinery
gaol *n, v BrE* jail **~er** *n*
gaolbird *n BrE* jailbird
gap *n* **1** empty space between two things **2** break in continuity
gape *vi* **1** look hard in surprise **2** be or become very wide: *gaping hole*
garage *n* **1** building in which motor vehicles are kept **2** place that repairs them, and sells petrol and oil ♦ *vt* put in a garage
garb *n fml* clothes
garbage *n esp. AmE* rubbish
garbage can *n AmE* dustbin
garble *vt* give a confused account of
garden *n* **1** piece of land for growing flowers and vegetables **2** also **gardens** *pl* public park ♦ *vi* work in a garden **~er** *n*
garden centre *n* place where plants and gardening equipment are sold
garden city *n* planned town with grass and open spaces
gardenia *n* (white or yellow flower from) a tropical bush
garden party *n* formal party held in a garden
gargantuan /gahˈgantyoo·ən/ *adj* extremely large
gargle *vi* wash the throat by blowing through liquid ♦ *n* (liquid for) gargling
gargoyle *n* figure of an ugly creature on a church roof, esp. used as a rain water

spout

garish *adj* unpleasantly bright **~ly** *adv*

garland *n* circle of flowers for decoration ♦ *vt* put garlands on

garlic *n* plant like an onion, used in cooking

garment *n fml* article of clothing

garner *vt lit* collect

garnet *n* red jewel

garnish *vt* decorate (food) ♦ *n* something used to garnish

garret *n lit* small usu. unpleasant room at the top of a house

garrison *n* **1** soldiers living in a town or fort **2** fort or camp where such soldiers live ♦ *vt* send (a group of soldiers) to guard (a place)

garrotte *vt* strangle, esp. with a metal collar or wire

garrulous /ˈgar(y)ooləs/ *adj fml* talking too much **~ly** *adv* **–rulity** *n*

garter *n* elastic band to keep a stocking up

gas *n* **-s-** *or* **-ss-** **1** substance like air **2** gas used for heating, cooking, poisoning, anaesthetizing, etc. **3** *AmE* petrol ♦ *v* **1** *vt* kill with gas **2** *vi infml* talk a long time **~eous** *adj* of or like gas

gasbag *n infml* person who talks too much

gas fitter *n* workman who instals gas pipes, repairs cookers, etc.

gash *vt, n* (wound with) a long deep cut

gasholder *n* large container from which gas is piped to buildings

gasket *n* flat piece of material placed between surfaces to prevent liquid or gas from escaping

gaslight *n* light from burning gas

gasman *n* **-men** official who visits houses to see how much gas has been used

gas mask *n* breathing apparatus that protects the wearer against poisonous gas

gasoline, -lene *n AmE* petrol

gasp *v* **1** *vi* breathe quickly and with effort **2** *vt* say while gasping **gasp** *n*

gas pedal *n AmE* accelerator

gas station *n AmE* filling station

gassy *adj* full of gas **-siness** *n*

gastric *adj* of the stomach: *gastric juices*

gastritis /gaˈstrietəs/ *n* inflammation of the lining of the stomach

gastroenteritis /ˌgastrohˌentəˈrietəs/ *n* inflammation of the stomach lining and bowels

gastronomy *n* art of good eating **–nome** *n* person who enjoys eating well

gastropod *n* snail, slug, or related animal

gasworks *n* **gasworks** place where gas is made from coal

gate *n* **1** frame closing an opening in a wall, fence, etc. **2** way in or out at an airport **3** (money paid by) the number of people attending a match

gâteau *n* **-teaux** large rich cake

gatecrash *vi/t* go to (a party) uninvited **~er** *n*

gateleg table *n* table with drop sides and supports which swing out underneath to hold them up

gatepost *n* post from which a gate is hung

gateway *n* **1** opening for a gate **2** way of finding: *the gateway to success*

gather *v* **1** *vi/t* come or bring together **2** *vt* increase gradually: *gather speed* **3** *vt* collect (flowers, crops, etc.) **4** *vt* have been informed **5** *vt* draw (cloth) into small folds **~ing** *n* meeting

gauche /gohsh/ *adj* socially awkward **~ly** *adv* **~ness** *n*

gaucho *n* **-os** S American cowboy

gaudy *adj* too bright; overdecorated **–dily** *adv*

gauge, also *AmE* **gage** *n* **1** instrument for measuring **2** (measure of) thickness or width **3** distance between the rails of a railway ♦ *vt* **1** measure **2** make a judgment about

gaunt *adj* **1** thin, as if ill or hungry **2** (of a place) bare and unattractive **~ness** *n*

gauntlet *n* long glove protecting the wrist

gauss *n* unit of density of a magnetic field

gauze *n* thin net-like cloth

gave *past t. of* give

gavel *n* small hammer used by a chairman, auctioneer, etc., to get attention
gavotte *n* fast French dance or its music
gawky *adj* awkward in movement **–kiness** *n*
gawp *vi* look at something in a foolish way
gay *adj* **1** homosexual **2** bright: *gay colours* **3** cheerful ♦ *n* homosexual
gaze *vi* look steadily ♦ *n* steady fixed look
gazebo /gə'zeeboh/ *n* **-os** shelter or hut placed to command a view
gazelle *n* small African or Asian antelope
gazette *n* official government newspaper giving important notices
gazetteer *n* geographical list of names
gazump *vt BrE* cheat (someone who has agreed to buy a house) by selling it to someone else who offers more money
GB *abbrev. for:* Great Britain
GBH *abbrev. for:* grievous bodily harm
GCHQ *abbrev. for:* Government Communications Headquarters
GCSE *n* General Certificate of Secondary Education; British exam for children of 16 or over
GDP *n* Gross Domestic Product; the total value of everything produced in a country, usu. in a single year
GDR *abbrev. for:* German Democratic Republic
gear *n* **1 a** set of toothed wheels in a machine **b** particular adjustment of engine speed to vehicle speed: *in fourth gear* **2** equipment: *football gear* **3** apparatus or mechanism: *the landing gear of an aircraft* **gear to** *phr vt* make appropriate to: *education geared to the needs of industry* **gear up** *phr vt infml* put into a state of readiness
gearbox *n* case containing the gears of a vehicle
gear lever *n* rod that controls the gears of a vehicle
gecko *n* **-os** *or* **-oes** small tropical lizard
geese *pl of* goose
gee up *phr v* **1** *vi* (tells a horse to move ahead) **2** *vt infml* instil greater vigour into
geezer *n infml* man, fellow
Geiger counter *n* instrument that measures radioactivity
geisha /'gayshə/ *n* (in Japan) girl trained to provide company and entertainment for men
gel *n* semi-solid jelly-like substance ♦ *vi* **-ll-** become more definite
gelatine also *AmE* **-tin** *n* gluey material used in making jelly **–nous** *adj* thick and sticky
geld *vt* remove the sexual organs of (a male animal) **~ing** *n* gelded animal, esp. a horse
gelignite *n* powerful explosive
gem *n* **1** jewel **2** very valuable thing or person
gendarme *n* French policeman
gender *n* **1** (in grammar) (division into) masculine, feminine, or neuter **2** division into male and female; sex
gender-bender *n* person who dresses, behaves, etc., like the opposite sex
gene *n* material in a cell controlling heredity
genealogy /ˌjeeni'aləji/ *n* (study of) the history of a family, often shown in a tree diagram **–gical** *adj*
genera *pl of* genus
general *adj* **1** concerning all: *the general feeling* **2** not detailed: *a general idea* **3** (in titles) chief: *Postmaster-General* ♦ *n* **1** army officer of very high rank **2 in general** usually **~ly** *adv* **1** usually **2** by most people **3** without considering details **–rality** *n* **1** general statement **2** being general
general election *n* election in which the whole country takes part
generalissimo *n* **-mos** supreme commander
generalize, -ise *vi* make a general statement **-ization** *n* (statement formed by) generalizing
general practitioner *n* community doctor who treats all diseases
general staff *n* officers who assist an army commander
general strike *n* nationwide stopping of

work
generate *vt* produce: *generate heat* **-rator** *n* machine that generates esp. electricity **-rative** *adj* able to produce
generation *n* **1** length of time in which a child grows up and has children **2** people of about the same age **3** act of generating
generation gap *n* difference in attitudes between older and younger people and the resultant lack of understanding between them
generic *adj* shared by a whole class **~ally** *adv*
generosity *n* **1** quality of being generous **2** generous act
generous *adj* **1** giving freely **2** more than enough **~ly** *adv*
genesis *n* origin
genetic engineering *n* artificial alteration of the genetic make-up of an organism (e.g. to produce disease-free plants)
genetics *n* study of heredity **genetic** *adj* **-ically** *adv*
genial *adj* cheerful and kind **~ly** *adv*
genie *n* (in Arab folklore) spirit serving whoever calls it
genitalia *pl n* genitals
genitals *pl n* outer sex organs **genital** *adj*
genitive *adj, n* (of or in a) grammatical case expressing possession
genius *n* **1** exceptional powers of thought, skill, or imagination **2** person with this ability
genocide *n* killing of a whole race of people
genre /ˈzhonh·rə/ *n* class; kind
gent *n infml* gentleman **gents** *n BrE* men's public toilet
genteel *adj* affectedly polite
gentian *n* plant with deep blue flowers
gentile *n, adj* (person who is) not Jewish
gentility *n* being genteel
gentle *adj* not rough or violent **~ness** *n* **-tly** *adv*
gentleman *n* **-men 1** man who behaves well and can be trusted **2** any man **~ly** *adj* like a gentleman
gentleman's agreement *n* unwritten agreement made between people who trust each other
gentlewoman *n* **-women** lady
gentrify *vt* make more suitable to middle-class tastes
gentry *pl n* people of high social class
genuflect *vi fml* bend one's knee in worship **~ion** *n*
genuine *adj* not false or falsified; real **~ly** *adv* **~ness** *n*
genus /ˈjeenəs/ *n* **genera** division of plants or animals
geo- *prefix* connected with the study of the Earth and its surface
geocentric *adj* having or regarding the earth as the centre
geodesic dome *n* light hemispherical structure made out of struts forming polygonal patterns
geography *n* study of the countries of the world and of seas, towns, etc. **-pher** *n* **-phical** *adj* **-phically** *adv*
geology *n* study of the Earth's history as recorded in rocks **-gist** *n* **-gical** *adj* **-gically** *adv*
geometry *n* mathematical study of lines, angles, and surfaces and their relationships **geometric** *adj* **geometrically** *adv*
geopolitical *adj* **1** concerning the effects of geographical and demographic factors on politics **2** relating to global politics **-tics** *n*
Geordie *n* person from northeast England
georgette *n* thin strong crepe fabric
Georgian *adj* **1** of Georgia in the USSR **2** (in the style) of the reigns of Kings George I, II and III **3** (of poetry) in the late romantic style of the early 20th century
geostationary *adj* always staying in the same place above the Earth
geranium *n* plant with pink or blue flowers and round leaves
gerbil *n* mouselike desert rodent
geriatrics *n* medical care of old people **geriatric** *adj*
germ *n* **1** bacterium carrying disease **2**

beginning of something (e.g. an idea)
German *n, adj* (inhabitant) of Germany
germane *adj fml* relevant
German measles *n* infectious disease with high temperature and a rash
German shepherd *n esp. AmE* Alsatian
germicide *n* chemical for killing germs
germinate *vi/t* start or cause (a seed) to start growing **–nation** *n*
gerontology *n* scientific study of (the effects of) old age
gerrymandering *n* electoral malpractice, esp. in the dividing up of voting areas
gerund *n* verbal noun
Gestapo *n* sadistic secret police force esp. in Nazi Germany
gestation *n* period between conception and birth
gesticulate *vi* wave the hands and arms about to express something **–lation** *n*
gesture *n* **1** movement of the body to express something **2** action done to show one's feelings
get *v* **got**, *esp. BrE* **got**, *AmE* **gotten**, *pres. p.* **getting** **1** *vt* receive; obtain **2** *vt* collect; bring **3** *vt* catch (an illness) **4** *vi* arrive: *get home* **5** become: *get married* **6** *vt* hear or understand: *I don't get you.* **7** *vt* confuse; puzzle: *That's got you!* **8** *vt* annoy **9 get something done** cause something to be done: *get one's shoes mended* **10 have got** have: *He's got red hair* **get around/round to** *phr vt* find time for; do at last **get at** *phr vt* **1** mean; imply **2** say unkind things about **get away with** *phr vt* escape punishment for **get by** *phr vi* **1** continue to live; survive **2** be adequate **get down** *phr vt* depress **get down to** *phr vt* begin to work at **get off** *phr vi/t* (cause to) escape punishment **get on** *phr vi* **1** progress **2** be friendly: *They don't get on together* **get round** *phr vt* **1** avoid; circumvent **2** persuade to do something **get up** *phr vt* **1** organize **2** decorate or change the appearance of in the stated way **get up to** *phr vt* do (something bad)
getaway *n* escape
get-together *n* friendly informal meeting
getup *n infml* set of clothes
get-up-and-go *n infml* enthusiastic energy
gewgaw *n* bauble; trinket
geyser /ˈgeezə/ *n* **1** natural spring of hot water **2** *BrE* water-heating tank
ghastly *adj* **1** very bad; terrible **2** pale and ill-looking
ghat *n* (in India and Pakistan) **1** pass[2] (4) **2** mountain **3** steps leading down to a river or lake **4** place where dead bodies are ceremonially burnt
ghee *n* melted (and resolidified) butter used in Indian cooking
gherkin *n* small green cucumber
ghetto *n* **-os** *or* **-oes** part of city where poor people or foreigners live
ghetto-blaster *n* large tape recorder that can be carried around
ghost *n* **1** (spirit of) a dead person who appears again **2** also **ghost writer** person who writes material for another person whose name appears as author **3 the ghost of a** the slightest **~ly** *adj* like a ghost ♦ *vt* write (something) as a ghost
ghost town *n* empty town that was once busy
ghoul *n* person with morbid interests **~ish** *adj*
GHQ *abbrev. for:* General Headquarters
GI *n* US soldier
giant *n* big strong person or creature ♦ *adj* very large
giantess *n* female giant
giant killer *n* weak or inferior opponent that defeats a more powerful one
gibber *vi* talk very fast and meaninglessly
gibberish *n* meaningless talk
gibbet *n* gallows
gibbon *n* animal like a monkey with no tail and long arms
gibbous *adj* (of the moon) showing more than half but less than the whole disc
gibe *n* remark that makes someone look foolish **gibe at** *phr vt* make gibes

about
giblets *pl n* bird's heart, liver, etc., taken out before cooking
giddy *adj* **1** causing or having a feeling of unsteady movement **2** (of a person) not serious **-diness** *n*
gift *n* **1** something given freely; present **2** talent **3 the gift of the gab** *infml* ability to speak well continuously, and esp. to persuade people **~ed** *adj* talented
gift-wrap *vt* **-pp-** wrap up in decorative paper
gig[1] *n* musician's performance
gig[2] *n* **1** long light ship's boat **2** light two-wheeled carriage
gigantic *adj* very large
giggle *vi* laugh in a silly way **giggle** *n* **1** act of giggling **2** *infml, esp. BrE* something that amuses
gigolo *n* **-os** woman's paid lover and companion
gild *vt* **1** cover with gold or gold paint **2 gild the lily** try to improve something that is already good enough, so spoiling the effect
gill[1] *n* organ through which a fish breathes
gill[2] *n* measure of liquid
gilt *n* material with which things are gilded
gilt-edged *adj* (of government shares) having a fixed interest rate and therefore safe
gimbals *pl n* device that enables an object, e.g. a ship's compass, to remain level even when its support is tilted
gimcrack /ˈjimˌkrak/ *adj* showy and insubstantial
gimlet *n* tool for making holes for screws
gimmick *n* trick, phrase, etc., used to draw attention **-y** *adv*
gin *n* colourless alcoholic drink
ginger *n* **1** plant whose hot-tasting root is used in cooking **2** orange-brown colour: *ginger hair* **ginger up** *phr vt* make more exciting
ginger ale *n* non-alcoholic drink with a mild ginger flavour
ginger beer *n* ginger-flavoured non-alcoholic drink
gingerbread *n* cake with ginger in it
ginger group *n* group that agitates for stronger action
gingerly *adv* carefully ♦ *adj* careful
ginger nut also *esp. AmE* **ginger snap** *n* hard ginger-flavoured biscuit
gingham /ˈging·əm/ *n* cotton cloth with a pattern of squares
gingivitis /ˌjinjiˈvietəs/ *n* inflammation of the gums
ginseng *n* plant with a root used as a tonic
gipsy, gypsy *n* member of a dark-haired people who often travel about in caravans
giraffe *n* long-necked African animal
gird *vt* **girded** *or* **girt** *fml* fasten with a belt
girder *n* metal beam supporting a roof, bridge, etc.
girdle *n* **1** woman's light corset **2** *lit* something that surrounds ♦ *vt lit* go all round
girl *n* young female person **~hood** *n* time of being a girl **~ish** *adj* like a girl
girl Friday *n* female secretary or general assistant
girlfriend *n* **1** man's female companion **2** woman's female friend
giro *n* **-os 1** banking system handled by one central computer **2** *BrE* social security payment (by cheque)
girt *past t. and p. of* gird
girth *n* **1** band round a horse's middle to hold the saddle firm **2** thickness measured round something
gist *n* main points of something
git *n BrE sl* unpleasant person
give *v* **gave, given 1** *vt* cause or allow someone to have **2** *vt* pay **3** *vi* supply money: *give to charity* **4** *vt* provide: *Cows give milk* **5** *vt* perform (an action): *give an order/a sign* **6** *vt* offer (an amusement, etc.): *give a party* **7** *vi* bend or stretch under pressure **8 give or take** more or less (a certain amount) **9 give way (to): a** admit defeat in an argument or fight **b** break **c** be superseded by **d** allow oneself to show (a feel-

ing) **give away** *phr vt* **1** give freely **2** show the truth about **give in** *phr vi* surrender **give off** *phr vt* emit (esp. a smell) **give out** *phr v* **1** *vt* distribute **2** *vi* come to an end; fail **give up** *phr v* **1** *vi/t* stop: *give up smoking* **2** *vi* surrender **3** *vi* stop trying to guess **4** *vt* regard as lost or hopeless ♦ *n* quality of bending or stretching under pressure **giver** *n*

give-and-take *n* willingness to compromise

giveaway *n* something unintentional that reveals a secret ♦ *adj* (of a price) very low

given *adj* **1** fixed and stated: *a given time* **2 be given to** have a tendency to ♦ *prep* if one takes into account

given name *n AmE* first name

gizzard *n* part of a bird's digestive tract, used for grinding food

glabrous *adj lit* smooth and hairless

glacé *adj* (of fruit) sugar-coated

glacial *adj* of ice or an ice age

glaciation *n* formation of glaciers or ice sheets

glacier *n* mass of ice that flows slowly down a valley

glad *adj* **-dd- 1** pleased **2** *lit* causing happiness **~ly** *adv* willingly **~ness** *n*

gladden *vt* make glad

glade *n* open space in a forest

glad eye *n infml* sexually inviting look

glad hand *vt, n* (give someone) a warm welcome from ulterior motives

gladiator *n* (in ancient Rome) man who fought in public as an entertainment

gladiolus *n* **-li** iris-like garden plant with colourful flowers and long thin leaves

glad rags *pl n infml* smart clothes

Gladstone bag *n* old-fashioned usu. leather travelling bag

glamorize, -ise *vt* make (something) appear more attractive than it really is

glamour, *AmE* **-or** *n* **1** sexual attraction **2** exciting but illusory attractiveness **~ous** *adj*

glance *vi* give a rapid look **glance off** *phr vi/t* (esp. of a blow) hit and move off at an angle ♦ *n* **1** rapid look **2 at a glance** at once **-cing** *adj* striking at an angle

gland *n* body organ that secretes substances into the bloodstream **~ular** *adj* of the glands

glandular fever *n* infectious disease causing long-lasting tiredness

glare *vi* **1** look fiercely **2** shine too strongly **glare** *n* **glaring** *adj* **1** too bright **2** noticeably bad: *glaring injustice*

glasnost *n* Soviet policy of greater openness

glass *n* **1** hard transparent material used in windows, etc. **2** glass container for drinking from **~y** *adj*

glassblower *n* person who shapes hot glass by blowing through a tube

glasses *pl n* two glass lenses in a frame, worn to improve a person's sight

glass fibre *n* fibreglass

glasshouse *n BrE* greenhouse

glassware *n* glass objects generally

glassworks *n* **glassworks** factory where glass is made

glaucoma /glawˈkohmə/ *n* eye disease leading gradually to blindness

glaucous *adj* **1** *lit* bluish-green **2** (of a leaf, fruit, etc.) having a waxy or powdery coating

glaze *v* **1** *vt* put a shiny surface on (pottery) **2** *vt* fit (a window) with glass **3** *vi* (of the eyes) become dull ♦ *n* shiny surface

glazier *n* workman who fits glass into windows

gleam *n* **1** gentle light **2** sudden sign of something: *a gleam of interest* ♦ *vi* send out a gleam

glean *vt* gather (information) in small amounts

glebe *n* **1** *lit* earth, soil **2** land belonging to a parish church

glee *n* joyful satisfaction **~ful** *adj* **~fully** *adv*

glen *n* narrow valley, esp. in Scotland

glib *adj* **-bb-** speaking or spoken too easily; superficial: *glib excuses* **~ly** *adv* **~ness** *n*

glide *vi* move smoothly and noiselessly ♦ *n* gliding movement **glider** *n* plane with no engine
glimmer *vi* shine faintly ♦ *n* **1** faint light **2** small uncertain sign: *a glimmer of hope*
glimpse *n* quick incomplete view of something ♦ *vt* see for a moment
glint *vi, n* (give out) a small flash of light
glissando *n* **-di** *or* **-dos** rapid sliding movement up or down a musical scale
glisten *vi* shine as if wet
glister *vi lit* glitter
glitch *n* small fault in the operation of something
glitter *vi* flash brightly: *glittering diamonds* ♦ *n* brightness
glitterati *pl n* fashionable people whose social activities are widely reported
glitz *n infml* ostentatious glamour **~y** *adj*
gloaming *n lit* twilight
gloat *vi* regard something with unpleasant satisfaction **~ingly** *adv*
global *adj* **1** of the whole world **2** taking account of all considerations **~ly** *adv*
globe *n* **1** object in the shape of a ball, esp. one with a map of the Earth painted on it **2** the Earth
globetrotter *n* person who travels widely **-ting** *adj, n*
globular *adj* shaped like a ball
globule *n* drop of liquid
glockenspiel *n* percussion instrument played with sticks
gloom *n* **1** darkness **2** sadness; hopelessness **~y** *adj* **~ily** *adv*
glorify *vt* **1** praise; worship **2** cause to seem more important: *Her cottage is just a glorified hut.* **-fication** *n*
glorious *adj* **1** having great honour: *glorious victory* **2** splendid **~ly** *adv*
glory *n* **1** great honour **2** splendid beauty **glory in** *phr vt* enjoy, often selfishly
glory hole *n BrE infml* place, e.g. a cupboard or drawer, where little-used or unwanted articles are dumped
gloss *n* **1** shiny brightness **2** explanation of a piece of writing ♦ *vt* write an explanation of **gloss over** *phr vt* hide (faults) **~y** *adj* shiny
glossary *n* list of explanations of words
glossy magazine *n* magazine printed on shiny paper with lots of pictures, esp. of clothes
glottal stop *n* indeterminate speech sound made by opening and closing the glottis (as when one pronounces 'glottis' as 'glo'is')
glottis *n* (structures surrounding) the space between the vocal chords
glove *n* covering for the hand
glove compartment *n* small storage compartment in the dashboard of a car
glow *vi* give out heat or light without flames ♦ *n* glowing light **~ing** *adj* strongly favourable: *a glowing account*
glower *vi* look angrily
glow-worm *n* insect that gives out a greenish light
glucose *n* sugar found in fruit
glue *n* sticky substance for joining things ♦ *vt pres. p.* **gluing** *or* **glueing** **1** join with glue **2** **glued to** watching or doing with deep concentration **~y** *adj*
glue-sniffing *n* harmful breathing in of glue fumes for their intoxicating effect
glum *adj* **-mm-** sad; gloomy **~ly** *adv*
glut *vt* **-tt-** supply with too much ♦ *n* too large a supply
gluten *n* sticky protein found in wheat flour
glutinous /ˈgloohtinəs/ *adj fml* sticky
glutton *n* **1** person who eats too much **2** person with a great capacity for something: *a glutton for punishment* **~ous** *adj* greedy **~y** *n* habit of eating too much
glycerine, glycerin *n* colourless liquid used in making soap, medicines, and explosives
gm *abbrev. for:* gram
GM *abbrev. for:* George Medal
GMT *abbrev. for:* Greenwich Mean Time
gnarled *adj* rough and twisted
gnash *n* strike or grind (one's teeth) together
gnat *n* small flying insect that stings

gnaw *vi/t* bite or chew steadily (at)
gneiss /nies/ *n* coarse-grained banded rock
gnome *n* **1** (in stories) little (old) man who lives under the ground **2** (stone or plastic) figure representing this **3 gnomes of Zurich** certain powerful bankers, esp. Swiss ones
gnomic *adj fml* characterized by pithy sayings **~ally** *adv*
gnomon *n* arm that projects a shadow on a sundial
gnostic *adj fml* relating to, or possessing, (spiritual) knowledge
GNP *n* Gross National Product; total value of everything produced in a country, usu. in a single year
gnu /noo/ *n* large ox-like African antelope
go *v* **went, gone 1** *vi* leave a place **2** *vi* move; travel: *go by bus|go shopping* **3** *vi* lead; reach: *This road goes to London.* **4** *vi* start an action **5** *vi* become: *go mad* **6** *vi* match; fit: *4 into 3 won't go.|Your dress goes with your eyes.* **7** *vi* (of machines) work **8** *vt* make (a particular noise): *Ducks go 'quack'.* **9** *vi* happen or develop in the stated way: *The party went well.* **10 be going to** (shows the future): *Is it going to rain?* **11 to go** left; remaining: *only three more days to go* **go ahead** *phr vi* **1** begin **2** continue **go along with** *phr vt* agree with **go around** *phr vi* be enough for everyone **go back on** *phr vt* break (a promise) **go down** *phr vi* **1** be accepted: *His speech went down well.* **2** be recorded: *This day will go down in history.* **go for** *phr vt* **1** attack **2** like or be attracted by **go in for** *phr vt* **1** enter (a competition) **2** have a habit of **go into** *phr vt* **1** enter (a profession) **2** explain or examine thoroughly **go off** *phr vi* **1 a** explode **b** ring or sound loudly **2** have the stated success **go on** *phr vi* **1** happen **2** continue: *Go on with your work* **go out** *phr vi* spend time with someone of the opposite sex **go over** *phr vt* **1** examine **2** repeat **go round** *phr vi* go around **go through** *phr v* **1** *vi* be approved officially **2** *vt* suffer or experience **3** *vt* search **go through with** *phr vt* continue to a finish **go to** *phr vt* make oneself have: *go to a lot of trouble* **go with** *phr vt* **1** match **2** be often found with **go without** *phr vi/t* do without ♦ *n* **1** quality of being very active **2** attempt **3** turn, esp. in a game **4 make a go of** *infml* make a success of **5 on the go** very busy
goad *vt* urge by continuous annoyance ♦ *n* stick for driving cattle
go-ahead *n* permission to take action ♦ *adj* active in using new methods
goal *n* **1** one's aim or purpose **2 a** place where the ball must go to score in football, hockey, etc. **b** score made by sending the ball there
goalkeeper *n* player responsible for keeping the ball out of a team's goal
goalpost *n* one of the two posts between which the ball must go to score a goal
goat *n* horned animal like a sheep
goatee *n* small pointed beard
gob *n BrE sl* mouth
gobbet *n* lump or piece of something, esp. food
gobble *vi/t* eat quickly and often noisily
gobbledygook *n* meaningless official language
go-between *n* person who takes messages from one person or side to another
goblet *n* glass or metal drinking cup with a stem and no handle
goblin *n* unkind fairy that plays tricks on people
god *n* **1** being who is worshipped **2** (*cap.*) (in the Christian, Jewish, and Muslim religions) the maker and ruler of the world **~less** *adj* not showing respect for or belief in God **~like** *adj* like a god **~ly** *adj* religious; leading a good life
godchild *n* boy (**godson**) or girl (**goddaughter**) for whom someone makes promises at baptism
goddess *n* female god
godfather *n* male godparent
god-fearing *adj fml* good and well-

behaved

godforsaken *adj* (of places) sad and empty

godmother *n* female godparent

godown *n IndE* warehouse

godparent *n* person who takes responsibility for a new Christian at baptism

gods *pl n* seats high up at the back of a theatre

godsend *n* unexpected lucky chance or thing

gofer *n* person whose job is to fetch or take things for other people

go-getter *n* enterprising person

goggle *vi* stare with the eyes wide open

goggles *pl n* glasses to protect the eyes

goggle box *n BrE infml* television set

go-go *adj* **1** of or being a form of fast dancing with sexy movements **2** energetic and enterprising

going *n* speed or condition of travel ♦ *adj* operating at present

going-over *n* **goings-over** *infml* **1** examination and/or treatment or repair **2** severe beating

goings-on *pl n* undesirable activities

goitre, *AmE* **-ter** /ˈgoytə/ *n* abnormal swelling in the neck caused by lack of certain chemicals

go-kart *n* small low racing car

gold *n* **1** valuable yellow metal **2** gold coins **3** the colour of gold

golden *adj* **1** of or like gold **2** very favourable: *a golden opportunity*

golden age *n* (mythical) period of great happiness, prosperity or creativity

golden eagle *n* eagle with golden-brown plumage, native to the British isles

golden handshake *n* large amount of money given to someone leaving a firm

golden jubilee *n* 50th anniversary of an important event

golden rule *n* very important rule of behaviour

golden syrup *n esp. BrE* sweet thick liquid made from sugar

golden wedding *n* 50th wedding anniversary

goldfield *n* area where gold can be found

goldfish *n* **goldfish** small orange fish kept as a pet

gold leaf *n* thin sheets of gold

goldmine *n* **1** mine where gold is found **2** profitable business

gold rush *n* rush to newly discovered goldmines

goldsmith *n* person who makes things out of gold

golf *n* game in which people hit a ball into holes with golf clubs **~er** *n*

golf ball *n* **1** small hard ball used in golf **2** metal sphere on which letters are carried in an electric typewriter

golf club *n* **1** long-handled stick for hitting the ball in golf **2** club for golfers with buildings and land

golliwog *n* doll made of fabric with black face and hair

golly *interj infml* (expresses surprise)

gonad *n med* sex gland (e.g. an ovum or testicle)

gondola *n* long narrow Venetian boat rowed with one oar **-lier** *n* person who rows a gondola

gone *past p. of* go

goner *n infml* person or thing sure to die, fail, etc.

gong *n* **1** metal disc that makes a ringing sound when struck **2** *BrE sl* medal

gonorrhea, -rhoea /ˌgonəˈriə/ *n* disease passed on during sexual activity

goo *n* **1** sticky material **2** sentimentalism

good *adj* **better, best 1** satisfactory; pleasant **2** beneficial: *Milk is good for you.* **3** clever: *good at maths* **4** well-behaved **5** morally right: *good deeds* **6 a good** at least: *a good three hours* **7 a good deal** quite a lot **8 as good as** almost the same as **9 in good time** early **10 make good** be successful ♦ *n* **1** something good or beneficial **2 for good** forever **~ness** *n* **1** quality of being good **2** (used in expressions of surprise and annoyance): *Goodness me!*

good afternoon *interj* (used when meeting someone in the afternoon)

Good Book *n* the Bible

goodbye *interj* (used when leaving someone)
good day *interj* (used when meeting someone in the morning or afternoon)
good evening *interj* (used when meeting someone in the evening)
good-for-nothing *adj, n* useless (person)
Good Friday *n* Friday before Easter
good-humoured *adj* cheerful and friendly
good-looking *adj* attractive; beautiful
goodly *adj* **1** large **2** satisfying
good morning *interj* (used when meeting someone in the morning)
good-natured *adj* cheerful and cooperative
goodnight *interj* (used when leaving someone at night, or going to sleep)
good offices *pl n* intervention or mediation to help someone out of a difficulty
goods *pl n* **1** things for sale **2** things carried by train, lorry, etc.
good Samaritan *n* person who helps people in trouble
goodwill *n* **1** kind feelings **2** popularity of a business, as part of its value
goody *n* something very pleasant, esp. to eat
goody-goody *adj, n derog* insufferably virtuous
gooey *adj* **1** sticky and sweet **2** sentimental
goof *n infml* **1** foolish person **2** silly mistake ♦ *vi infml, esp. AmE* make a silly mistake **goof off** *phr vi AmE infml* waste time or avoid work **~y** *adj* stupid-looking
googly *n* (in cricket) a ball bowled to look as if it will go in one direction after it bounces but actually going in the other direction
goon *n* **1** silly person **2** *esp. AmE* hired thug
goosander *n* type of duck
goose *n* **geese 1** bird like a large duck **2** silly person
gooseberry *n* **1** garden bush with prickly green berries **2** unwanted companion of two lovers
gooseflesh *n* condition in which the skin rises up in small bumps
goosestep *n* way of marching with stiff straight legs
GOP *n* Grand Old Party; the Republican Party in US politics
gopher *n* ratlike burrowing American rodent
gore[1] *vt* wound with horns or tusks
gore[2] *n lit* blood **gory** *adj*
gorge *n* **1** steep narrow valley **2 make someone's gorge rise** make someone feel sickened ♦ *vi/t* eat or feed eagerly
gorgeous *adj* wonderful; beautiful **~ly** *adv*
gorgon *n* fearsome woman
Gorgonzola *n* pungent Italian blue cheese
gorilla *n* largest of the apes
gormless *adj BrE infml* foolish
gorse *n* spiny yellow-flowered shrub
gosh *interj* (expressing surprise)
gosling *n* young goose
go-slow *n BrE* industrial action involving working slowly
gospel *n* **1** *(cap.)* any of four accounts of Christ's life in the Bible **2** something completely true
gossamer *n* thin silky thread
gossip *n* **1** talk about other people's private lives **2** person who likes this kind of talk ♦ *vi* spend time in gossip
got *past t. and p. of* get
Gothic *adj* **1** of a style of building common from the 12th to 16th centuries, with pointed arches and tall pillars **2** of a style of writing in the 18th century which produced novels set in lonely frightening places
gotten *AmE past p. of* get
gouache /gooˈahsh/ *n* (picture painted by) a method using colours mixed with water and a sort of glue
Gouda *n* mild-flavoured yellow Dutch cheese
gouge out *phr vt* push or dig out violently
goulash *n* meat stew seasoned with paprika
gourd *n* hard outer shell of a fruit, esp. as used for carrying water

gourmand *n* person who is extremely fond of food and drink
gourmet /ˈgawmay/ *n* person who knows a lot about food and drink
gout *n* disease that makes the toes and fingers swell painfully
govern *v* **1** *vi/t* exercise political authority (over) **2** *vt* control **~ance** *n fml* governing
governess *n* woman who teaches children in their home
government *n* **1** group of people who govern: *the Swiss government* **2** act or process of governing **3** form or method of governing **~al** *adj*
governor *n* person who controls a place or organization: *the governor of the prison* **~ship** *n*
governor-general *n* **governors-general** *or* **governor-generals** representative of the British monarch in Commonwealth countries which are not republics
gown *n* **1** woman's long dress **2** loose outer garment worn by judges, teachers, surgeons, etc.
GP *abbrev. for:* general practitioner
grab *vt/i* **-bb-** seize suddenly and roughly ♦ *n* **1** sudden attempt to seize something **2 up for grabs** *infml* ready for anyone to take or win
grab bag *n AmE* lucky dip
grace *n* **1** beauty of movement or shape **2** delay allowed as a favour: *give them a week's grace* **3** prayer of thanks for meals **4 with (a) good/bad grace** willingly/unwillingly ♦ *vt* give honour or beauty to **~ful** *adj* **1** having grace **2** suitably expressed **~fully** *adv* **~less** *adj* awkward
gracious *adj* **1** polite and pleasant **2** having those qualities made possible by wealth: *gracious living* **~ly** *adv* **~ness** *n*
gradation *n* successive stage or degree
grade *n* **1** level of quality **2** *AmE* **a** form[1] (5) **b** mark given for schoolwork **c** gradient **3 make the grade** succeed; reach the necessary standard ♦ *vt* separate into levels of quality
grade crossing *n AmE* level crossing
grade school *n AmE* elementary school
gradient *n* degree of slope, as on a road
gradual *adj* happening slowly; not sudden **~ly** *adv* **~ness** *n*
graduate *n* **1** person with a university degree **2** *AmE* person who has completed any school or college course ♦ *v* **1** *vi* become a graduate **2** mark with degrees for measurement **-ation** *n* **1** (ceremony of) becoming a graduate **2** mark of measurement
graffiti *pl n* drawings or writings on a wall
graft *n* **1** piece from one plant fixed inside another to grow there **2** piece of skin or bone similarly fixed into the body **3** *esp. AmE* corrupt obtaining of money or advantage **4** *BrE infml* work ♦ *vt* put onto as a graft
grail *n* cup used by Christ and sought by knights in medieval legend
grain *n* **1** single seed of rice, wheat, etc. **2** crops from food plants like these **3** small hard piece **4** natural arrangement of threads or fibres in wood, cloth, etc. **5 be/go against the grain** be counter to one's inclinations
gram, gramme *n* (measure of weight equal to) 1/1000 of a kilogram
grammar *n* rules describing the way language works
grammarian *n* person who studies and knows about grammar
grammar school *n* British secondary school providing academic education
grammatical *adj* **1** of grammar **2** correct according to the rules of grammar
gramophone *n BrE* record player
gran *n BrE infml* grandmother
granary *n* storehouse for grain
grand *adj* **1** splendid; impressive **2** (of people) important **3** pleasant; delightful ♦ *n* **1** grand piano **2** (*pl* **grand**) *sl* 1,000 pounds or dollars
grandad *n infml* grandfather
grandchild *n* **grandchildren** boy (**grandson**) or girl (**granddaughter**) who is the child of the stated person's son or daughter

grandee *n* Spanish or Portuguese nobleman

grandeur /ˈgranjə, -dyə/ *n* quality of being grand; magnificence

grandfather *n* male grandparent

grandfather clock *n* tall clock that stands on the floor

grandiloquent /granˈdiləkwənt/ *adj* using (too many) long words **-ence** *n*

grandiose *adj* intended to seem splendid and important

grand jury *n* (in the US) jury which decides whether a suspect should be tried

grandma *n infml* grandmother

grandmother *n* female grandparent

grand opera *n* opera(s) on serious dramatic themes with no spoken dialogue

grandparent *n* parent of someone's father or mother

grand piano *n* large piano with strings set parallel to the ground

grand prix *n* **grand prix** one of a series of racing car races

grand slam *n* the winning of all of a set of important sports competitions

grandstand *n* seats arranged in rising rows, for people watching sport, races, etc.

grand total *n* complete amount

grand tour *n* extended tour of Europe, formerly undertaken as part of the education of a young English nobleman

grange *n* large farmhouse

granite *n* hard usu. grey rock

granny, -nie *n infml* grandmother ♦ *adj* for old people: *a granny flat*

granny knot *n* botched attempt at a reef knot

grant *vt* **1** *fml* give: *grant permission* **2** admit the truth of **3 take something for granted** accept it without question ♦ *n* money granted esp. officially

granulated *adj* (of sugar) in the form of not very fine powder

granule *n* small grain **~lar** *adj* made of granules

grape *n* green or purple fruit from which wine is made

grapefruit *n* large yellow fruit like a sour orange

grapeshot *n* cannon charge of small iron balls

grapevine *n* unofficial way of spreading news

graph *n* diagram showing the relationship between two changing values

graphic *adj* **1** clear and detailed **2** of drawing, printing, etc. **~ally** *adv* **1** clearly **2** using graphs **graphics** *pl n* visual representations

graphite *n* black substance used in pencils

graphology *n* study of handwriting as an indicator of a person's character

grapnel *n* grappling iron

grapple with *phr vt* **1** seize and struggle with **2** try to deal with (something difficult)

grappling iron *n* iron shaft with several hooks radiating from one end, attached to a rope

grasp *vt* **1** take firm hold of **2** succeed in understanding ♦ *n* **1** firm hold **2** understanding **~ing** *adj* too eager for money

grass *n* **1** common green plant grown in lawns and eaten by animals **2** *sl* someone who grasses **3 out to grass: a** feeding on this plant **b** no longer working **~y** *adj* ♦ *vi BrE sl* (esp. of a criminal) inform the police about the activities of (other) criminals

grasshopper *n* insect which can jump high and makes a sharp noise by rubbing its legs against its body

grass roots *pl n* ordinary people, not those with political power

grass widow *n* woman whose husband is away for a period of time

grate[1] *n* metal frame in a fireplace

grate[2] *v* **1** *vt* rub into pieces on a rough surface **2** *vi* make a sharp unpleasant sound **grater** *n* tool for grating food

grateful *adj* feeling or showing thanks **~ly** *adv* **~ness** *n*

gratify *vt* please; satisfy **~ing** *adj* pleasing **-fication** *n*

grating *n* network of bars to protect an opening
gratis *adv, adj fml* without payment; free
gratitude *n* gratefulness
gratuitous *adj fml* not deserved or necessary: *gratuitous insults* **~ly** *adv*
gratuity /grəˈtyooh·əti/ *n fml* tip for a service done
grave¹ *n* hole where a dead person is buried
grave² *adj* serious; solemn **~ly** *adv*
gravel *n* small stones, as used for making paths **~ly** *adj* **1** covered with gravel **2** having a low rough hard sound
gravestone *n* stone over a grave
graveyard *n* cemetery
gravitate *vi* be attracted (as if) by gravity **-tation** *n*
gravity *n* **1** force by which objects are drawn towards each other **2** seriousness: *the gravity of his illness*
gravy *n* juice that comes out of meat in cooking
gravy train *n* something from which many people can profit without much effort
gray *adj, n, v AmE* grey
graze¹ *vi* (of animals) eat growing grass
graze² *vt* **1** rub the skin from **2** rub lightly while passing ♦ *n* surface wound
grease *n* soft fat or oil ♦ *vt* **1** put grease on **2 grease someone's palm** bribe someone **3 like greased lightning** *infml* extremely fast **greasy** *adj*
greasepaint *n* theatrical make-up
greaseproof *adj BrE* (of paper) not letting grease pass through it
great *adj* **1** excellent and important; outstanding **2** large **3** keen; active: *a great filmgoer* **4** *infml* splendid: *a great idea* **5 great-: a** parent of someone's grandparent: *his great-grandfather* **b** child of someone's grandchild: *his great-granddaughter* **~ly** *adv* very much **~ness** *n*
Great Bear *n* large constellation which includes the Plough
greatcoat *n* heavy overcoat
Great Dane *n* very tall, powerful, smooth-haired dog
grebe *n* ducklike water bird
Grecian *adj* of ancient Greece
greed *n* desire for too much food, money, etc. **~y** *adj* **~ily** *adv*
Greek *n, adj* (inhabitant) of Greece
green *adj* **1** of a colour between yellow and blue; of the colour of leaves and grass **2** (of fruit, plants, etc.) young or unripe **3** inexperienced and easily deceived **4** very jealous ♦ *n* **1** green colour **2** smooth area of grass **~ness** *n* **greens** *pl n* green vegetables
greenback *n AmE infml* bank note
green belt *n* stretch of countryside round a town where building is not allowed
greenery *n* green leaves and plants
green-eyed monster *n* jealousy
green fingers *pl n esp. BrE* natural skill in making plants grow
greenfly *n* **-fly** *or* **-flies** small green insect harmful to plants
greengage *n* kind of green plum
greengrocer *n esp. BrE* person who sells fruit and vegetables
greenhorn *n* inexperienced and/or gullible person
greenhouse *n* glass building for growing plants in
greenhouse effect *n* heating of the atmosphere due to atmospheric pollution
green light *n* (official) permission to begin
green thumb *n AmE* green fingers
Greenwich Mean Time *n* time at 0° longitude, used as a standard of measurement
greet *vt* **1** welcome **2** react to; receive **3** be suddenly seen or heard by **~ing** *n* **1** words used on meeting or writing to someone **2** a good wish: *Christmas greetings*
gregarious /griˈgeəri·əs/ *adj* fond of companionship
Gregorian calendar *n* system of dividing up and numbering years

introduced by Pope Gregory in 1582 and still in general use

Gregorian chant *n* rhythmically free unison chanting developed by the medieval church

gremlin *n* cause of unexplained malfunction

grenade *n* small bomb thrown by hand **–dier** *n* soldier in a regiment formerly armed with grenades

grew *past t. of* grow

grey *adj* **1** of the colour of black mixed with white **2** having grey hair ♦ *n* grey colour ♦ *vi* become grey

grey area *n* part of a subject or situation which remains undefined or unsettled

greyhound *n* thin dog with long legs, which can run quickly

grey matter *n* **1** the brain **2** *infml* power of thought

grid *n* **1** grating **2** *BrE* network of electricity supply wires **3** system of numbered squares on a map

griddle *n* flat metal plate for cooking over a fire

gridiron *n* **1** frame for cooking meat over a fire **2** field marked for American football

grief *n* **1** (cause of) great sorrow **2 come to grief** suffer harm; fail

grievance *n* cause for complaint

grieve *v* **1** *vi* suffer grief **2** *vt* make unhappy

grievous *adj fml* (of something bad) very great; severe **~ly** *adv*

grievous bodily harm *n* (criminal offence of causing) serious injury to another person

griffin, griffon *n* mythical animal, part lion, part eagle

grill *v* **1** *vi/t* cook under or over direct heat **2** *vt* question severely ♦ *n BrE* **1** shelf under direct heat, for grilling food **2** meat cooked this way: *a mixed grill*

grille *n* framework of bars forming a screen, esp. in a bank or post office

grim *adj* **-mm- 1** serious; terrible: *grim news* **2** showing determination: *grim smile* **~ly** *adv* **~ness** *n*

grimace *vi* twist the face to express pain, etc. **grimace** *n*

grime *n* black dirt on a surface **grimy** *adj*

grim reaper *n* (name for death, considered as a person)

grin *vi* **-nn- 1** smile widely **2 grin and bear it** suffer without complaint **grin** *n*

grind *vt* **ground 1** crush into powder **2** rub (the teeth) together **3** make smooth or sharp by rubbing **4 grind to a halt** stop noisily **grind down** *phr vt* keep in a state of suffering and hopelessness **grind out** *phr vt derog* produce (esp. writing or music) continually but unimaginatively ♦ *n infml* **1** hard dull work **2** *AmE* swot **~er** *n* person or machine that grinds

grindstone *n* round stone that is turned to sharpen tools

gringo *n* **-os** foreigner in Latin America

grip *vi/t* **-pp- 1** seize tightly **2** hold someone's attention: *a gripping story* ♦ *n* **1** tight hold **2** thing that grips: *hairgrip* **3** *AmE* traveller's small bag **4 come/get to grips with** deal seriously with

gripe *vi sl* complain continuously ♦ **gripe** *n*

grisly *adj* shocking and sickening; horrifying

grist *n* **1** grain for grinding **2 (all) grist to one's mill** something that can be turned to one's own advantage

gristle *n* cartilage in cooked meat

grit *n* **1** small stones and sand **2** unyielding courage; determination ♦ *vt* **-tt- 1** put grit on (esp. a road) **2 grit one's teeth** show determination **~ty** *adj*

grizzle *vi BrE infml* **1** whimper **2** complain self-pityingly

grizzled *adj* grey-haired

grizzly bear *n* large N American bear

groan *vi, n* (make) a loud deep sound of suffering

grocer *n* shopkeeper who sells dry foods and other things for the home

groceries *pl n* goods sold by a grocer

grog *n* rum or other spirits

groggy *adj* weak and unsteady from illness or tiredness **-giness** *n*

groin *n* **1** place where the legs meet the front of the body **2** *AmE* groyne

groom *n* **1** person who looks after horses **2** bridegroom ♦ *vt* **1** brush and clean (horses) **2** make (oneself) neat and tidy **3** prepare (someone) for a future role

groove *n* long hollow mark in a surface
groovy *adj sl* (fashionably) wonderful

grope *v* **1** *vi* search about with the hands as in the dark **2** *vt sl* (try to) feel the body of (a person) to get sexual pleasure **grope** *n*

gross¹ *adj* **1** unpleasantly fat **2** rough; rude **3** (of something bad) obviously great; severe **4** total ♦ *vt* gain as total profit **~ly** *adv* **~ness** *n*

gross² *determiner, n* **gross** *or* **grosses** 144

grotesque /groh'tesk/ *adj* strange and ugly **~ly** *adv*

grotto *n* **-oes** *or* **-os** cave

grotty *adj sl* nasty and in bad condition

grouch *n* **1** complaint **2** person who is always complaining **~y** *adj*

ground¹ *past t. and p. of* grind

ground² *n* **1** surface of the Earth **2** soil **3** piece of land used for a particular purpose: *a playground* **4** basis for argument **5** area of knowledge **6 get off the ground** make a successful start **7 to ground** into hiding to escape ♦ *v* **1** *vi* (of a boat) strike against the bottom of the sea, a river, etc. **2** *vt* cause (a plane or pilot) to stay on the ground **3** *vt* base: *arguments grounded on experience* **~ing** *n* first necessary training in something **~less** *adj* without reason: *groundless fears* **~lessly** *adv*

ground crew *n* people who maintain and service aircraft

ground floor *n* **1** *BrE* part of a building at ground level **2** first stage of an activity

groundnut *n* peanut (plant)

ground plan *n* **1** plan of the ground floor of a building **2** general basic plan

ground rule *n* basic principle or rule of procedure

grounds *pl n* **1** solid bits at the bottom of a liquid **2** area round a building **3** reason: *grounds for divorce*

groundsel *n* weed with small yellow flowers

groundsheet *n* waterproof sheet to spread on the ground

groundsman *n* **–men** *esp. BrE* man employed to look after a sports ground

ground staff *n BrE* **1** workers employed to look after a sports ground **2** ground crew

ground stroke *n* (in tennis) stroke played to a ball after it has bounced

groundswell *n* **1** movement of the sea to its depths caused by e.g. a distant gale or earthquake **2** rapidly-developing undercurrent of feeling or opinion

groundwork *n* work on which further study is based

group *n* connected set of people or things ♦ *vi/t* form into groups

groupie *n* pop fan who follows performers around

group practice *n* working partnership of several doctors

grouse¹ *vi, n* grumble

grouse² *n* **grouse** smallish fat bird which is shot for food and sport

grout *vt, n* (fill with) thin mortar

grove *n* small group of trees

grovel *vi* **-ll-** (*AmE* **-l-**) **1** lie flat in fear or obedience **2** be shamefully humble and obsequious **~ler** *n*

grow *v* **grew, grown 1** *vi* get bigger **2** *vi* (of plants) live and develop **3** *vt* cause (plants) to grow **4** become: *grow old*
grow on *phr vt* become more pleasing to **grow out of** *phr vt* get too big or old for **grow up** *phr vi* **1** develop from child to adult **2** arise and develop
grown *adj* adult: *grown men*

growing pains *n* **1** aches and pains in the limbs of growing children **2** problems associated with development

growl *vi, n* (make) the threatening noise of an angry dog

grown-up *adj, n* adult

growth *n* **1** process of growing; increase

2 something that has grown, esp. an abnormal lump in the body
groyne, *AmE* **groin** *n* wall-like structure built out into the sea
grub[1] *n* **1** insect larva **2** *sl* food
grub[2] *vi/t* **-bb-** dig with the hands or paws
grubby *adj* rather dirty **-biness** *n*
grubstake *n* money provided to develop a new business
grudge *vt* be unwilling to give ♦ *n* continuing feeling of resentment **grudgingly** *adv*
gruel *n* thin porridge
gruelling , *AmE* **grueling** *adj* very tiring
gruesome *adj* very shocking and sickening; horrifying **~ly** *adv*
gruff *adj* (of the voice) deep and rough **~ly** *adv* **~ness** *n*
grumble *vi* complain ♦ *n* complaint
grumpy *adj* bad-tempered **–ily** *adv* **–iness** *n*
grunt *vi, n* (make) the short deep sound that pigs make
Gruyère *n* hard Swiss cheese with holes in it
G string *n* minimal covering for the genitals consisting of a small piece of material and a thong
guano *n* fertilizer made from bird droppings
guarantee *n* **1** written promise to replace or repair an article if it is imperfect **2** agreement to be responsible for a debt **3** assurance that something is or will be as it should be ♦ *vt* **1** give a guarantee about **2** promise
guarantor *n law* person who agrees to be responsible for a debt
guard *n* **1** state of watching against attack: *soldiers on guard* **2** person or people keeping guard **3** protective apparatus: *a fireguard* **4** *BrE* railway official on a train ♦ *vt* **1** defend **2** watch (prisoners) to prevent escape **guard against** *phr vt* take preventive action against legally **~ed** *adj* cautious in speech
guardhouse *n* building used by soldiers on guard duty or for imprisoning soldiers
guardian *n* person responsible for a child **~ship** *n*
guardroom *n* (room in a) guardhouse
guava *n* pink-fleshed tropical fruit
gubernatorial /ˌgyoohbənəˈtawri·əl/ *adj* of a governor
Guernsey *n* **1** (one of) a breed of dairy cattle **2** close-fitting woollen sweater
guerrilla *n* member of an unofficial army which attacks in small groups
guess *v* **1** *vi/t* form an opinion (on) without knowing all the facts **2** *vt infml, esp. AmE* suppose; consider likely ♦ *n* **1** opinion formed by guessing **2** attempt to guess
guesstimate *n* rough estimate made by guesswork
guesswork *n* guessing
guest *n* **1** person invited to someone's home, or staying in a hotel **2** person invited to take part in a television show, film, etc. ♦ *vi esp. AmE* take part as a guest performer
guesthouse *n* small private hotel
guff *n infml* nonsense
guffaw *vi* laugh loudly and esp. rudely **guffaw** *n*
guidance *n* help; advice
guide *n* **1** person who shows the way **2** something that is indicative of what is happening, what should be done, etc. **3** also **guide book** book of information for travellers **4** instruction book **5** member of an association (the **Guides**) for training girls in character and self-help ♦ *vt* act as a guide to
guided missile *n* missile whose flight is controlled electronically
guidelines *pl n* main points on how to deal with something
guild *n* association of people in the same business or with the same interests
guilder *n* unit of money in the Netherlands
guile *n* deceit **~ful** *adj* **~less** *adj*
guillemot *n* black and white seabird with a long narrow bill
guillotine /ˈgilәteen/ *n* **1** machine for cutting off the heads of criminals **2**

machine for cutting paper **3** time limit fixed for discussion in Parliament ♦ *vt* use a guillotine on

guilt *n* **1** fact of having done wrong **2** feeling of being to blame **~y** *adj* having done wrong

guinea *n* (formerly) £1.05 in British money

guinea fowl *n* plump grey African bird

guinea pig *n* **1** small tailless furry animal sometimes used in scientific tests **2** person on whom something is tested

guise *n fml* outer appearance

guitar *n* stringed musical instrument played with the fingers

gulag *n* labour or prison camp in the USSR

gulch *n AmE* ravine

gulf *n* **1** piece of sea partly surrounded by land **2** division, esp. between opinions

gull *n* any of several kinds of large seabird

gullet *n* food-carrying passage in the throat

gullible *adj* easily tricked **~ bility** *n*

gully *n* channel cut by running water

gulp *vi/t* swallow hastily **gulp** *n*

gum¹ *n* flesh in which the teeth are fixed

gum² *n* **1** sticky plant substance **2** hard jelly-like sweet **3** chewing gum ♦ *vt* **-mm-** stick with gum **~my** *adj* sticky

gumboil *n infml* abscess on the gum

gumboot *n esp. BrE* wellington

gumdrop *n* hard jelly-like sweet

gumption *n* **1** practical good sense **2** courage

gumshoe *n AmE sl* detective

gumtree *n* **1** *esp. AustrE* eucalyptus **2** **up a gumtree** *BrE infml* in a very awkward situation

gun *n* weapon that fires bullets or shells through a tube-shaped barrel **gun down** *phr vt* kill or wound by shooting **gun for** *phr vt* pursue with determination

gunboat *n* small heavily armed warship

gunboat diplomacy *n* using (the threat of) military intervention to support a claim or complaint against another country

gunfire *n* (sound of) shooting

gunge *n BrE infml* unpleasantly messy material **–gy** *adj*

gung-ho *adj* showing extreme or excessive enthusiasm esp. to attack an enemy

gunman *n* **-men** armed criminal

gunner *n* soldier in the artillery

gunpoint *n* **at gunpoint** under a threat of death by shooting

gunpowder *n* explosive powder

gunrunner *n* person who illegally and secretly brings guns into a country **–ning** *n*

gunwale, gunnel *n* upper edge of the side of a boat

gurgle *vi, n* (make) the sound of water flowing unevenly

Gurkha *n* Nepalese soldier in the Indian or British army

guru *n* **1** Indian religious teacher **2** greatly respected person whose ideas are followed

gush *v* **1** *vi/t* flow out or send (liquid) out in large quantities **2** *vi* express admiration too effusively ♦ *n* sudden flow

gusset *n* piece of material sewn into a garment to strengthen or widen it

gust *n* sudden rush of wind **~y** *adj*

gustatory *adj fml* of the sense of taste

gusto *n* eager and vigorous enjoyment

guts *pl n* **1** bowels **2** bravery and determination **gut** *vt* **-tt-** **1** take out the internal organs of **2** destroy the inside of (a building) **gut** *adj* coming from feelings rather than thought: *gut reactions* **gutsy** *n* brave **~less** *adj* cowardly

gutter *n* **1** ditch or pipe that carries away rainwater **2** the poorest level of society

gutter press *n* newspapers which tend to be full of shocking stories

guttersnipe *n derog* **1** ragged urban child **2** unprincipled person

guttural *adj* (of speech) coming from deep in the throat

guy *n* **1** *sl* **a** man **b** *esp. AmE* person, male or female: *Come on, you guys!* **2** figure of a man burnt in Britain on

November 5th
guzzle *vi/t* eat or drink eagerly
gybe *vi, n* (do a) sailing manoeuvre to change direction by swinging the sail to the other side of the boat
gym *n* **1** gymnasium **2** gymnastics
gymkhana *n esp. BrE* local sports meeting, esp. for horse riding by children
gymnasium *n* hall with apparatus for indoor exercise
gymnast *n* person trained in gymnastics
gymnastics *n* training of the body by physical exercises **–tic** *adj*
gymslip *n* plain sleeveless dress formerly worn as part of school uniform
gynaecology, *AmE* **gynecology** /ˌgienəˈkoləji/ *n* medical study and treatment of the female sex organs **–gist** *n* **–gical** *adj* **–gically** *adv*
gyp[1] *n BrE infml* severe pain
gyp[2] *vt* **-pp-** cheat, swindle
gypsum *n* chalklike mineral used in plaster
gypsy *n* gipsy
gyrate *vi fml* swing round and round **gyration** *n*
gyroscope *n* wheel that spins inside a frame, used for keeping ships, aircraft, etc., steady

H

H, h the 8th letter of the English alphabet
habeas corpus /ˌhaybi·əs ˈkawpəs/ *n* written order that a person in prison must be brought before a court
haberdasher *n* **1** *BrE* shopkeeper who sells articles used in sewing **2** *AmE* shopkeeper who sells men's hats, gloves, etc. **~y** *n* haberdasher's goods
habiliments *pl n lit* clothing
habit *n* **1** person's usual behaviour **2** clothes worn by a monk or nun
habitable *adj* fit to be lived in
habitat *n* natural home of an animal or plant
habitation *n fml* living in: *houses fit for habitation*
habitual *adj* **1** usual **2** (done) by habit **~ly** *adv*
habitué *n* regular attender
hacienda *n* (main house of a) ranch in a Spanish-speaking country
hack[1] *vi/t* cut roughly
hack[2] *n* **1** writer who does a lot of poor quality work **2** horse for riding **3** tired old horse
hacker *n* someone who uses or changes information in a computer system without permission
hacking cough *n* cough with a rough, unpleasant sound
hackles *n* **make someone's hackles rise** make someone very angry
hackneyed *adj* (of a saying) meaningless because used too often
hacksaw *n* tool with a fine-toothed blade used esp. for cutting metal
hackwork *n* (poor-quality) writing done solely to earn money
had *past t. and p. of* have
haddock *n* **haddock** common fish, used as food
hadn't *short for:* had not
haem-, haema-, haemo- *prefix* hem-
haft *n* handle of a weapon or tool
hag *n derog* ugly old woman
haggard *adj* (of the face) lined and hollow from tiredness
haggis *n* Scottish dish of sheep's offal cooked inside its stomach
haggle *vi* argue over a price
hagiography *n* **1** biography of saints **2** biography full of uncritical praise
ha-ha *n* wall or fence built in a ditch so as not to interrupt a view
haiku /ˈhieˌkooh/ *n* 3-line Japanese poem
hail[1] *n* **1** frozen rain drops **2** sudden massed discharge ♦ *vi* (of hail) fall
hail[2] *vi* **1** call out to: *hail a taxi* **2**

acclaim **hail as** *phr vt* recognize as (something good) **hail from** *phr vt* originate

hail-fellow-well-met *adj* very hearty and informal from the first moment of greeting

hailstone *n* single piece of hail

hair *n* **1** threadlike growth from the skin **2** mass of these growths **3 let one's hair down** behave unrestrainedly **~y** *adj* **1** covered with hair **2** *infml* exciting in a way that causes fear; dangerous **~iness** *n*

hairdo *n* **-dos** style a person's hair is shaped into

hairdresser *n* person who cuts and shapes hair

hairgrip *n BrE* flat pin with the ends pressed together, for the hair

hairline *n* **1** line around the head where the hair starts growing **2** very fine line

hairpiece *n* small wig for a bald patch

hairpin bend *n* U-shaped curve on a road

hair-raising *adj* very frightening

hair restorer *n* substance supposed to make the hair grow again

hair's breadth *n* very short distance

hair shirt *n* shirt of rough cloth worn next to the skin as a penance, esp. by monks

hairsplitting *n derog* act or habit of paying too much attention to unimportant differences and details

hair trigger *n* trigger that needs to be pressed only very lightly

hake *n* **hake** sea fish used for food

halal *n* meat from animals slaughtered according to Muslim law

halberd *n* spear with an axelike head

halcyon /ˈhalsi·ən/ *adj lit* peaceful and happy: *halcyon days*

hale *adj* **hale and hearty** very healthy

half *n* **halves 1** either of 2 equal parts; 1/2 **2** either of 2 parts into which something is divided: *He's in the bottom half of the class.* **3** coin, ticket, drink, etc., of 1/2 the value or amount **4 by halves** incompletely; half-heartedly **5 go halves** share something equally ♦ *predeterminer, adj* 1/2 in amount: *half a kilo of rice.* ♦ *adv* **1** partly **2 half and half** 1/2 one and 1/2 the other **3 not half** *BrE infml* **a** very **b** not at all

half back *n* player in football, hockey, etc. positioned directly behind the forwards

half-baked *adj* (esp. of ideas) not sensible

half-brother *n* brother related through only one parent

half-caste also **half-breed** *n, adj* (person) with parents of different races

half cock *n* **go off at half cock** fail or only partially succeed esp. because of inadequate preparation

half-hearted *adj* showing not much interest

half-life *n* time it takes for half the atoms in a radioactive substance to decay

halflight *n* dim light, esp. at dawn or dusk

half-mast *n* point near the middle of a flag-pole where the flag flies as a sign of mourning

half measures *pl n derog* insufficient or half-hearted action

half nelson *n* wrestling hold in which an opponent's arm is pinned behind his back

halfpenny *n* (in Britain before 1985) small bronze coin, two of which made a penny

half-sister *n* sister related through only one parent

half-timbered *adj* having a visible timber framework filled in with plaster

half time *n* rest period in the middle of e.g. a football match

half volley *n* ball hit, kicked, etc. just after it bounces

halfway *adj, adv* at the midpoint between two things

halfway house *n* **1** position or thing midway between two points **2** rehabilitation centre for e.g. discharged prisoners or mental patients

half-wit *n* weak-minded, stupid person **~ted** *adj*

halibut *n* **halibut** large flatfish used for food
halitosis *n* bad breath
hall *n* **1** passage inside the entrance of a house **2** large room for meetings, entertainments, etc.
halleluja *interj* (expression of praise to God)
hallmark *n* **1** mark proving that something is really silver or gold **2** distinguishing characteristic
hallo *interj, n* **-os** *BrE* hello
hall of residence *n* university or college building providing living accommodation for students
hallowed *adj fml* holy
Hallowe'en *n* October 31st, when children play tricks and dress in strange clothes
hallucinate *vi* see things that are not there **–natory** *adj* **–nation** *n* (experience of seeing) something which is not really there, seen because of illness or drugs
hallucinogen *n* a drug that produces hallucinations **~ic** *adj*
halo *n* **-oes** *or* **-os** **1** circle of light represented round the heads of saints **2** circle of light round the sun or moon
halogen *n* any of five related elements including chlorine and iodine
halt[1] *vi/t, n* stop
halt[2] *adj arch.* lame
halter *n* rope for leading a horse
halterneck *n* (garment with) strings that are tied behind the wearer's neck leaving the back and arms bare
halting *adj* stopping and starting uncertainly
halve *vt* **1** reduce by half **2** divide into halves
halves *pl of* half
halyard *n* rope for raising a sail, flag, etc.
ham *n* **1** preserved meat from a pig's thigh **2** actor whose performance is unnatural **3** non-professional radio operator ♦ *vi/t* perform like an actor
hamburger *n* flat round cake of small bits of meat, eaten in a bread roll
ham-fisted *adj* awkward in using the hands
hamlet *n* small village
hammer *n* **1** tool with a metal head for driving nails into wood **2** part of a piano that hits the strings **3 be/go at it hammer and tongs** fight or argue violently ♦ *v* **1** *vi/t* hit with a hammer **2** *vt* defeat thoroughly **3** *vi* make repeated or persistent efforts **hammer out** *phr vt* talk about in detail and come to a decision about
hammer and sickle *n* symbol of Communism
hammerhead shark *n* shark with a broad flattened snout
hammock *n* cloth or net hung up to sleep in
hamper[1] *vt* cause difficulty in movement
hamper[2] *n* large basket with a lid
hamster *n* small mouselike animal often kept as a pet
hamstring *n* cordlike tendon at the back of the leg ♦ *vt* **-strung** make powerless
hand *n* **1** movable part at the end of the arm **2** pointer on a clock, dial, etc. **3** set of playing cards held by one player **4** handwriting **5** worker: *factory hands* **6** help: *give/lend a hand* **7** control: *get out of hand* **8** applause **9 at hand** near in time or place **10 by hand: a** not typed or printed **b** delivered directly, not by post **11 hand in hand: a** holding each other's hands **b** in close connection **12 have a hand in** be partly responsible for **13 have one's hands full** be very busy **14 in hand** being dealt with **15 on hand** ready for use or to take part **16 on the one/other hand** (used for comparing two things) **17 (out of/off) one's hands** (no longer) one's responsibility **18 to hand** within reach ♦ *vt* **1** give with one's hand(s) **2 (have to) hand it to someone** (have to) admit the high quality or success of someone **hand down** *phr vt* give to those who come later **hand in** *phr vt* deliver **hand on** *phr vt* give to someone else **hand out** *phr vt* **1** give out to several people **2**

give freely **hand over** *phr vt* give control of

handbag *n* woman's small bag for money and personal things

handball *n* (ball used in) a game in which players hit a ball against a wall with their hands

handbill *n* small printed notice or advertisement distributed by hand

handbook *n* book of instructions

handbrake *n* brake worked by the driver's hand, not by the foot

handcart *n* simple cart that can be pushed or pulled by hand

handcuffs *pl n* pair of metal rings for fastening a criminal's wrists **handcuff** *vt* put handcuffs on

handful *n* **1** as much as can be held in one hand **2** small number (of people) **3** *infml* person or animal that is hard to control

hand grenade *n* grenade

handgun *n* pistol

handhold *n* something to hold onto for support

handicap *n* **1** disability of the body or mind **2** disadvantage, esp. one given to the stronger competitors in a sport ♦ *vt* **-pp-** **1** give a disadvantage to **2** (of a disability of body or mind) prevent (someone) from acting or living as most people do

handicraft *n* skill, such as weaving, which uses the hands

handiwork *n* **1** work demanding the skilful use of the hands **2** result of someone's action

handkerchief *n* cloth or paper for blowing the nose

handle *n* part of a door, cup, etc., that one holds ♦ *v* **1** *vt* touch or move with the hands **2** *vt* control; deal with: *handle the accounts* **3** *vi* (of a car, boat, etc.) respond to controlling movements in the stated way **-dler** *n* person who controls an animal

handlebars *pl n* curved bar above front wheel of a bicycle which controls its direction

handmaiden *n* personal female servant

hand-me-down *n BrE infml* article of clothing handed down from one person to another

handout *n* **1** something given free **2** printed sheet of information given out

handpicked *adj* carefully chosen

handset *n* part of a telephone held in the hand

handshake *n* act of grasping each other's hand as a greeting

handsome *adj* **1** good-looking **2** plentiful; *a handsome reward* **~ly** *adv*

hands-on *adj* involving much personal involvement and intervention

handstand *n* position in which the body is supported upside down on the hands

hand-to-hand *adj* (of fighting) involving physical contact **hand to hand** *adv*

hand-to-mouth *adj* (of a way of life) with just enough food, money, etc., to live

handwriting *n* (style of) writing done by hand **-written** *adj* written by hand

handy *adj* **1** useful **2** clever with one's hands **3** easily reached **-ily** *adv*

handyman *n* **-men** person who does small repairs

hang *v* **hung** **1** *vi/t* fix or be fixed from above so that the lower part is free **2** *vt* stick (wallpaper) on a wall **3** *vt* (*past t. and p.* **hanged**) kill by dropping with a rope round the neck **4** **hang one's head** appear ashamed **hang about/around** *phr vi* wait without purpose **hang back** *phr vi* be unwilling to move **hang on** *phr v* **1** *vi* keep hold of something **2** *vi* wait **3** *vt* depend on **hang onto** *phr vt* try to keep **hang out** *phr vi infml* live or spend a lot of time **hang up** *phr v* **1** *vi* finish a telephone conversation **2** *vt* put on a hook **3** **be hung up on/about** *sl* be anxious or have a fixed idea about ♦ *n* **get/have the hang of something** understand how something works

hangar *n* building where aircraft are kept

hang-dog *adj* **1** dejected **2** shamefaced

hanger *n* hook and crosspiece to hang a garment from

hanger-on *n* **hangers-on** person who tries to be friendly in the hope of

advantage
hang gliding *n* sport of gliding using a large kite instead of a plane
hangings *pl n* curtains or wall-coverings that hang
hangman *n* **-men** man whose work is hanging criminals
hangover *n* **1** feeling of sickness, headache, etc., the day after drinking too much alcohol **2** condition or effect resulting from an earlier event or state
hangup *n sl* something about which a person gets unusually worried
hank *n* looped bundle of hair, rope, etc.
hanker after also **hanker for** *phr vt* desire strongly **hankering** *n*
hankie, -ky *n* handkerchief
hanky-panky *n* improper behaviour, esp. deceit, of a not very serious kind
Hansard *n* official record of debates in the British parliament
hansom cab *n* 19th-century horse-drawn cab
haphazard *adj* unplanned; disorderly **~ly** *adv*
hapless *adj lit* unlucky
happen *vi* **1** (of an event) take place **2** be or do by chance: *We happened to meet.* **3** be true (as if) by chance: *As it happens, we do know each other.* **happen on** *phr vt* find by chance **~ing** *n* event
happy *adj* **1** pleased; contented **2** causing pleasure: *a happy occasion* **3** (of thoughts, remarks, etc.) suitable **–pily** *adv* **–piness** *n*
happy-go-lucky *adj* unworried; carefree
happy hour *n* limited period when alcoholic drinks are sold at lower than usual prices
hara-kiri *n* Japanese ritual suicide
harangue *vt, n* (attack or try to persuade with a) long angry speech
harass *vt* worry repeatedly **~ment** *n*
harbinger /ˈhahbinjə/ *n* person or thing foreshadowing what is to come
harbour, *AmE* **-bor** *n* sheltered area where ships are safe ♦ *vt* **1** give protection to **2** keep (thoughts or feelings) secretly in the mind
hard *adj* **1** firm and stiff **2** difficult **3** needing or using effort: *hard work/worker* **4** unpleasant; severe: *hard winter* **5** containing minerals that stop soap lathering easily **6** (of drugs) dangerous and addictive ♦ *adv* **1** with great effort **2** heavily: *raining hard* **3** **hard at it** working hard **4 hard done by** unfairly treated **5 hard put (to it)** having great difficulty **6 hard up** *infml* not having enough (esp. money) **~ness** *n*
hard-and-fast *adj* (of rules) fixed
hardback *n,adj* (book) with a stiff cover
hardball *n AmE* **1** baseball **2 play hardball** be uncompromising or ruthless in pursuit of one's own ends
hard-bitten *adj* (of a person) toughened by hard experience
hardboard *n* stiff cardboard, used like wood
hard-boiled *adj* **1** (of eggs) boiled till the yolk is hard **2** (of people) not showing feeling
hard copy *n* readable information from a computer, esp. printed on paper
hardcore *n* small unchanging group within an organization **hard-core** *adj* **1** very strongly following a particular belief or activity **2** showing or describing sexual activity very explicitly
hard currency *n* money that can be freely exchanged
hard disk *n* inflexible data-storage disk for a computer
harden *vi/t* make or become hard or firm **harden to** *phr vt* make (someone) less sensitive to
hardheaded *adj* tough and practical
hard-hearted *adj* not kind or gentle
hard-hitting *adj* forceful and effective
hardihood *n lit* boldness
hard labour *n* (punishment which consists of) hard physical work such as digging
hard landing *n* landing which destroys the spacecraft involved
hard line *n* firm unchanging opinion or policy **hard-liner** *n*
hard luck *n* bad luck

hardly *adv* **1** almost not: *I can hardly wait.* **2** not at all: *You can hardly blame me.*
hard-nosed *adj* ruthlessly practical
hard of hearing *adj* rather deaf
hard-on *n esp. AmE taboo* erection (3)
hard-pressed *adj* experiencing severe or continual difficulties
hard sell *n* method of selling by putting pressure on buyers
hardship *n* difficult conditions of life, such as lack of money, food, etc.
hard shoulder *n esp. BrE* hard surface beside a motorway where cars may stop if in difficulty
hardtop *n* car with a fixed metal roof
hardware *n* **1** pans, tools, etc., for the home **2** machinery which makes up a computer **3** military weapons
hardwearing *adj* (esp. of clothes) lasting a long time
hardwood *n* strong wood from trees such as the oak
hardy *adj* able to bear cold, hard work, etc. **-diness** *n*
hare *n* fast-running animal like a large rabbit ♦ *vi* run fast
harebrained *adj* impractical; foolish
harelip *n* top lip divided into two parts
harem *n* (women living in) the women's part of a Muslim house
haricot *n* bean with edible seeds and pods
hark *vi lit* listen **hark back** *phr vi* talk about the past
harlot *n arch.* prostitute
harm *n* **1** damage; injury **2 out of harm's way** safe ♦ *vt* cause harm to **~ful** *adj* **~less** *adj* not dangerous
harmonica *n* mouthorgan
harmonium *n* musical instrument like a small organ
harmonize, -ise *vi/t* (cause to) be in agreement, esp. in style, colour, etc.
harmony *n* **1** musical notes pleasantly combined **2** peaceful agreement **3** pleasant combination of colours, styles, etc. **-nious** *adj* **-niously** *adv*
harness *n* **1** leather bands and chains that fasten a horse to a cart **2** similar arrangement for tying someone to something: *safety harness* ♦ *vt* **1** fasten with a harness **2** use (wind, water, etc.) to produce esp. electrical power
harp *n* large stringed musical instrument played with the fingers **harp on** *phr vt* keep returning to (a subject) tediously **~ist** *n*
harpoon *vt, n* (strike with) a spear on a rope, for hunting whales, seals, etc.
harpsichord /ˈhahpsiˌkawd/ *n* kind of early keyboard instrument
harpy *n* rapacious woman
harridan *n* ill-tempered woman
harrier *n* **1** kind of hawk **2** hound used in hunting hares
harrow *vt, n* (break up the soil with) a farm machine set with sharp teeth or discs
harrowing *adj* causing painful feelings
harry *vt* trouble continually
harsh *adj* **1** painful to the senses **2** cruel **~ly** *adv* **~ness** *n*
hart *n* stag
harum-scarum /ˌheərəm ˈskeərəm/ *adj infml* scatty; irresponsible
harvest *n* **1** (time of) gathering crops **2** amount of crops gathered ♦ *vt* gather (crops)
harvest festival *n* church service of thanksgiving for the harvest
harvest home *n* ceremonial meal formerly provided for farm workers after the harvest
has *3rd person sing. pres. t. of* have
has-been *n infml* outdated person or thing
hash *n* **1** meal of (re-cooked) cut up meat **2 make a hash of** do badly
hashish *n* strongest form of the drug cannabis
hasn't *short for:* has not
hasp *n* hinged metal fastening strap
hassle *n infml* a lot of trouble ♦ *vt* cause trouble or difficulties for
hassock *n* cushion for kneeling on to pray
haste *n* quick movement or action
hasten **1** *vi/t fml* hurry **2** *vi* be quick (to say): *I hasten to add that no one was*

hurt.

hasty *adj* **1** done (too) quickly **2** (of people) too quick in acting or deciding **-ily** *adv*

hat *n* **1** covering for the head **2 keep under one's hat** keep secret **3 take one's hat off to** show admiration for **~ter** *n* maker of hats

hatch[1] *v* **1** *vi/t* (cause to) be born from an egg **2** *vt* form (a plan)

hatch[2] *n* (cover over) a hole in a wall or floor

hatchback *n* car with a door at the back that opens upwards

hatchet *n* small axe

hatchet-faced *adj* having a gaunt severe face

hatchet job *n* vicious attack in speech or writing

hatchet man *n* **1** person who does unpleasant jobs for e.g. an employer **2** severe critic

hate *vt* **1** dislike very much **2** be sorry: *I hate to tell you.* ♦ *n* strong dislike **~ful** *adj* very unpleasant **~fully** *adv*

hatred *n* hate

hat trick *n* (in sport) three successes of the same kind one after the other

haughty /ˈhawti/ *adj* too proud; arrogant **-tily** *adv* **-tiness** *n*

haul *vi/t* pull with effort ♦ *n* **1** amount of something gained **2** distance that something travels or is carried

haulage *n* **1** carrying of goods by road **2** charge for this

haulier *n* transporter of goods by lorry

haunch *n* fleshy part of the body between the waist and knee

haunt *vt* **1** (of a ghost) appear in **2** visit regularly **3** remain in the thoughts of: *haunting tune* ♦ *n* place often visited

haute couture /ˌoht koohˈtyooə/ *n* business of making high-fashion clothes for women

hauteur *n* haughtiness

Havana *n* quality cigar from Cuba

have *v aux, pres. t. I/you/we/they* **have,** *he/she/it* **has** *past t.* **had 1** (forms perfect tenses) **2 had better (do/not do)** ought (not) to **3 have (got) to** be forced to; must **4 have had it** *infml* have done all one can ♦ *vt* **1** also **have got** possess **2** experience or enjoy: *have a party/a holiday* **3** receive: *I had some good news today.* **4** eat, drink, or smoke **5** allow: *I won't have all this noise.* **6** cause to be done: *have one's hair cut* **7** give birth to **8 have done with** finish **9 have to do with** have a connection with **have on** *phr vt* deceive playfully **have out** *phr vt* settle by argument **have up** *phr vt BrE* prosecute

haven *n* calm safe place

have-nots *pl n* poor people

haven't *short for:* have not

haver *vi esp. BrE* be indecisive

haversack *n* rucksack

havoc *n* widespread damage

haw *n* (berry of the) hawthorn

hawk[1] *n* **1** medium-sized bird of prey **2** person who believes in use of force, esp. military **~ish** *adj* favouring aggressive policies

hawk[2] *vt* sell (goods) in the street or from door to door **~er** *n*

hawk-eyed *adj* **1** having good eyesight **2** very watchful or observant

hawser *n* large rope or cable on a ship

hawthorn *n* thorny flowering tree or shrub

hay *n* dried grass for animal food

hay fever *n* illness like a bad cold, caused by breathing in pollen

haystack *n* large pile of stored hay

haywire *adj* **go haywire** (esp. of plans) become badly disordered

hazard *n* danger; risk ♦ *vt* **1** offer (a guess or suggestion) **2** put in danger **~ous** *adj* dangerous

haze *n* light mist **hazy** *adj* **1** misty **2** uncertain; vague

hazel *n* (small round nut of a) tree of the birch family ♦ *adj* greenish brown

H-bomb *n* hydrogen bomb

he *pron* (used for the male subject of a sentence)

head *n* **1** part of the body containing the eyes, mouth, and brain **2** top or front end **3** mind: *Don't put ideas into his head.* **4** power to be in control of oneself: *keep/lose one's head* **5** ruler; chief **6 a/per head** for each person **7 above/over one's head** too hard to understand **8 bring/come to a head** reach a critical point **9 go to someone's head** make someone drunk or too excited or proud **10 head and shoulders above** very much better than **11 head over heels: a** turning over headfirst **b** completely: *head over heels in love* **12 make head or tail of** manage to understand **13 off one's head** *infml* mad ♦ *v* **1** *vt* be at the top or front of: *head a procession* **2** *vt* strike (a ball) with the head **3** *vi* go in a particular direction **head off** *phr vt* **1** cause to change direction **2** prevent **heads** *n* front of a coin

headache *n* **1** pain in the head **2** problem

headband *n* fabric band worn round the head

headbanger *n infml* randomly violent person

headboard *n* board at the head of a bed

headdress *n* decorative head covering

header *n* act of propelling a ball with the head

headfirst *adj, adv* with the rest of the body following the head

headgear *n* covering for the head

headhunter *n* person who tries to find suitable people for important jobs

heading *n* words written as a title at the top of a page

headland *n* piece of land sticking out into the sea

headlight also **headlamp** *n* strong light on the front of a vehicle

headline *n* **1** heading above a newspaper story **2** main point of the news on radio

headlong *adj, adv* **1** headfirst **2** in foolish haste

headmaster *n* head teacher in a school

headmistress *n* female head teacher

head-on *adv, adj* with the front parts meeting, usu. violently

headphones *pl n* listening apparatus that fits over the ears

headquarters *n* **-ters** central office of an organization

headrest *n* support for the head

headroom *n* space to stand or move under something

headset *n* headphones esp. with a small microphone attached

headship *n* post of headmaster or headmistress

head start *n* advantage in a race or competition

headstone *n* stone marking the top end of a grave

headstrong *adj* impetuous and stubborn; wilful

headway *n* **make headway** advance; make progress

headwind *n* wind blowing directly against one

heady *adj* **1** making one drunk **2** exciting

heal *vi/t* make or become healthy again **~er** *n*

health *n* **1** state of being well, without disease **2** condition of body or mind: *in poor health* **~y** *adj* enjoying or producing good health

health centre *n* building where several doctors hold surgeries

health food *n* naturally-grown additive-free food

health visitor *n* trained person who gives health care in people's homes

heap *n* untidy pile ♦ *vt* pile up **heaps** *pl n infml* lots

hear *v* **heard 1** *vi/t* perceive (sounds) with the ears **2** *vt* be told or informed: *I hear they're married.* **3 won't/wouldn't hear of** refuse(s) to allow **hear from** *phr vt* receive news from, esp. by letter **hear of** *phr vt* know about: *I've never heard of him.* **hear out** *phr vt* listen to, till the end

hearing *n* **1** ability to hear sound **2** chance to explain **3** *law* trial of a case

hearing aid *n* small electric device to improve hearing

hearken *vi lit* listen

hearsay *n* things heard but unproved

hearse *n* car for carrying a body to a funeral

heart *n* **1** organ that pumps blood round the body **2** centre of a person's feelings: *a kind heart* **3** centre: *heart of a lettuce/of the city/of the matter* **4** red heart-shaped figure on a playing card **5** courage *lose heart* **6 by heart** from memory **7 set one's heart on** want very much **8 take something to heart** feel something deeply
heartache *n* deep sorrow
heart attack *n* dangerous malfunction of the heart
heartbeat *n* pumping movement of the heart
heartbreak *n* terrible sorrow **~ing** *adj* causing heartbreak
heartbroken *adj* broken-hearted
heartburn *n* unpleasant feeling of burning in the chest, caused by indigestion
hearten *vt* encourage
heart failure *n* stopping of the heart's functions, esp. when leading to death
heartfelt *adj* sincere
hearth *n* area round the fire in a home
heartland *n* central and most important area
heartless *adj* cruel **~ly** *adv* **~ness** *n*
heartrending *adj* causing great pity **~ly** *adv*
heart-searching *n* examining one's feelings or conscience
heartstrings *pl n* deepest feelings of love and pity
heartthrob *n infml* man who is very attractive and with whom girls fall in love
heart-to-heart *n* open talk about personal details **heart-to-heart** *adj*
heartwarming *adj* causing pleasant feelings
hearty *adj* **1** friendly and cheerful **2** healthy **3** (of meals) large **4** *BrE* (too) cheerful in a loud way **–ily** *adv* **1** in a hearty way **2** very
heat *n* **1** (degree of) hotness **2** part of a race, whose winners will then race against others **3 on heat** (of female animals) ready for sexual intercourse ♦ *vi/t* make or become hot **~ed** *adj* excited and angry **~er** *n* machine for heating air or water **~ing** *n* system for keeping rooms warm
heath *n* piece of open wild land
heathen *n, adj* (person) not belonging to one of the large established religions
heather *n* plant which grows on moors and has small pink or purple flowers
Heath Robinson *adj* (of a machine or contraption) elaborate, ramshackle-looking, ingenious and impractical
heat shield *n* covering that protects a spacecraft on its re-entry into the Earth's atmosphere
heatstroke *n* sunstroke
heat wave *n* period of unusually hot weather
heave[1] *v* **1** *vi/t* pull or lift with effort **2** *vt* throw (something heavy) **3** *vi* rise and fall regularly **4 heave a sigh** sigh
heave[2] *vi* **hove 1** (esp. of a ship) move; come **2 heave into sight/view** come into one's view **heave to** *phr vi* (of a ship) stop moving
heaven *n* **1** home of God or the gods **2** wonderful place or state **3** *pl lit* sky **~ly** *adj* **1** of heaven **2** wonderful
heavensent *adj* occurring opportunely
heavy *adj* **1** of great weight **2** unusually large in amount: *heavy rain* **3** needing effort: *heavy work* **4** serious and dull **5** (of food) too solid **6** (of the sea) with big waves ♦ *adv* in a troublesome, dull way ♦ *n* serious usu. male part in a play, film, etc., esp. a bad character **–ily** *adv* **–iness** *n*
heavy-duty *adj* (of clothes, machines, etc.) strong enough for rough treatment
heavy-handed *adj* awkward; not careful
heavyhearted *adj* sad
heavy industry *n* industry that produces large goods, or materials such as coal, steel, etc., that are used in the production of other goods
heavy metal *n* loud style of rock music with a heavy beat
heavy petting *n* kissing, caressing, etc. stopping just short of sexual intercourse

heavy-set *adj* thickset (and inclining to fat)
heavyweight *n, adj* **1** (fighter) of the heaviest category in boxing **2** (a person or thing) **a** of more than average weight **b** having great importance or influence
hebdomadal *adj fml* weekly
Hebrew *n* language used by the Jews
heckle *vi/t* interrupt (a speaker) disapprovingly at a meeting **–ler** *n*
hectare *n* (measure of area of land equal to) 10,000 square metres
hectic *adj* full of hurry and excitement
hecto- *prefix* hundred: *hectolitre*
hector *vi/t* bully
he'd *short for:* **1** he would **2** he had
hedge *n* **1** row of bushes dividing gardens or fields **2** protection: *a hedge against inflation* ♦ *v* **1** *vt* make a hedge round **2** *vi* refuse to answer directly **3 hedge one's bets** protect oneself against loss by favouring or supporting more than one side
hedgehog *n* small prickly animal
hedgerow *n* row of bushes, esp. along roads, separating fields
hedonism *n* idea that pleasure is the only important thing in life **–ist** *n* **–istic** *adj*
heebie-jeebies *pl n infml* nervous anxiety
heed *vt fml* give attention to ♦ *n fml* attention **~less** *adj*
heel *n* **1** back of the foot **2** raised part of a shoe under the foot **3** unpleasant person, who treats others badly **4 down at heel** untidy and poor-looking **5 to heel** under control ♦ *vt* put a heel on (a shoe)
hefty *adj* big and powerful
hegemony /hiˈgeməni/ *n fml* power of one state over others
Hegira *n* Mohammed's escape from Mecca, the date of which marks the beginning of the Islamic **Hegira calendar**
heifer /ˈhefə/ *n* young cow
height *n* **1** (degree of) being high **2** measurement from top to bottom **3 a** highest degree: *the height of fashion* **b** main or most active point: *the height of the storm.*
heighten *vi/t* make or become greater in degree
heinous /ˈhaynəs, ˈheenəs/ *adj fml* (of wickedness) extreme
heir *n* person inheriting property
heir apparent *n* **heirs apparent** person certain to succeed to a title or property if they outlive the present holder or owner
heiress *n* female heir
heirloom /ˈeəloohm/ *n* valuable object bequeathed to succeeding generations
heir presumptive *n* **heirs presumptive** person who will succeed to a title or property if no child with a superior claim is born
heist /hiest/ *n AmE sl* armed robbery
held *past t. and p. of* hold
helicopter *n* aircraft that flies by means of fast-turning blades on top
heliotrope *n* plant with purplish flowers which turn towards the sun
heliport *n* place for helicopters to land
helium *n* very light gas used in airships, balloons, etc.
helix *n* spiral
hell *n* **1** place where the wicked are said to be punished after death **2** terrible place **3** *sl* (used in anger or to give force): *What the hell's that?* **4 like hell** *sl* **a** very much **b** not at all ♦ *interj* (an expression of anger or disappointment) **~ish** *adj* terrible **~ishly** *adv*
he'll *short for:* he will
hell-bent *adj* stubbornly or recklessly determined
Hellenic *adj* of (ancient) Greece
hello *interj, n* **-os 1** (used in greeting) **2** *esp. BrE* (an expression of surprise)
hell's angel *n* member of a motorcycle gang, usu. with leather clothes
helm *n* **1** wheel or tiller that guides a ship **2 at the helm** in control
helmet *n* protective head covering
help *v* **1** *vi/t* make it possible for (someone) to do something; be useful (to) **2** *vt* avoid; prevent: *I couldn't help laughing.* **3** *vt* serve (oneself) with some-

thing; take **help out** *phr vi/t* give help to (someone) at a time of need ♦ *n* **1** act of helping; aid **2** someone or something that helps **~ful** *adj* useful **~fully** *adv* **~less** *adj* unable to look after oneself **~lessly** *adv* **~er** *n* person who helps **~ing** *n* serving of food

helpmate, -meet *n* helpful companion; spouse

helter-skelter *adv, adj* in confused haste ♦ *n* spiral slide at a fairground

hem *n* bottom edge of a garment turned under and sewn ♦ *vt* **-mm-** put a hem on **hem in** *phr vt* surround closely

hem-, hema-, hemo- *prefix* of the blood

he-man *n* strong virile man

hemisphere *n* **1** half a sphere **2** half of the Earth **–ric, –rical** *adj*

hemistich *n* half of a line of verse

hemline *n* length of a skirt or dress

hemlock *n* poisonous plant

hemoglobin *n* protein that transports oxygen in the blood

hemophilia *n* disease that makes the sufferer bleed badly after only a small cut **–iac** *n* person suffering from hemophilia

hemorrhage *n* instance of severe bleeding ♦ *vi* bleed heavily

hemorrhoid *n* swollen blood vessel at the lower end of the bowel

hemp *n* plant used for making rope, rough cloth, and cannabis

hemstitch *n* decorative edging stitch usu. for hems

hen *n* female bird, esp. a chicken kept for its eggs on farms

hence *adv fml* **1** for this reason **2** from here or now

henceforth, -forward *adv fml* from now on

henchman *n* **-men** faithful supporter who may use violent methods

henna *n* reddish-brown dye

henpecked *adj* (of a man) persistently nagged by his wife

hepatic *adj med* of the liver

hepatitis *n* serious disease of the liver

heptagon *n* flat figure with seven sides and seven angles **~al** *adj*

her *pron* (used for the female object of a sentence) ♦ *determiner* of her **hers** *pron* of her; her one(s)

herald *n* (in former times) person who brought important news ♦ *vt* be a sign of (something coming) **~ic** *adj* of a herald or heraldry

heraldry *n* study of coats of arms

herb *n* any plant used in medicine or to improve the taste of food **~al** *adj* of herbs **~alist** *n* person who uses herbs, esp. to treat disease

herbaceous *adj* (of a plant) soft-stemmed

herbivorous *adj* (of an animal) eating grass or other plants

Herculean *adj* needing great strength or determination

herd *n* **1** group of animals together **2** people generally, thought of as acting all alike ♦ *vt* drive (as if) in a herd

herdsman *n* person who looks after livestock

here *adv* **1** at, in, or to this place **2 here and there** scattered about **3 Here's to** (said when drinking a toast)

hereabouts *adv* somewhere near here

hereafter *adv fml* in the future ♦ *n* life after death

hereby *adv fml* by this means

hereditament /ˌheriˈditəmənt/ *n law* property that can be inherited

hereditary *adj* that can be inherited

heredity *n* transmission of characteristics from parent to child

herein *adv fml* in this

hereinafter *adv* subsequently in this document

heresy *n* (religious) belief that goes against what is officially accepted

heretic *n* person guilty of heresy **~al** *adj*

herewith *adv fml* with this

heritage *n* something passed down within a family or nation

hermaphrodite /huhˈmafrədiet/ *n* animal or plant that is both male and female **~tic** *adj*

hermetic *adj* airtight **~ally** *adv*

hermit *n* person who lives alone, esp. for

religious reasons
hermitage *n* hermit's home
hernia *n* condition in which an organ, esp. the bowel, pushes through its covering wall
hero *n* **-roes 1** someone admired for bravery **2** most important character in a story **~ic** *adj* very brave **~ically** *adv* **~ics** *pl n* grand speech or actions that mean nothing **~ism** *n* courage
heroic couplet *n* two rhyming lines of iambic pentameter
heroin *n* drug made from morphine
heroine *n* female hero
heron *n* large long-legged bird of rivers and lakes
herpes *n* very infectious skin disease
herring *n* sea fish used for food
herringbone *n* repeated V-shaped pattern
herself *pron* (*reflexive or strong form of* she): *She hurt herself.*
hertz *n* **hertz** unit of radio frequency
he's *short for:* **1** he is **2** he has
hesitant *adj* tending to hesitate **-tancy** *n* **~ly** *adv*
hesitate *vi* **1** pause because one is uncertain **2** be unwilling **-ation** *n*
hessian *n* coarse fabric, as used for sacks
heterodox *adj fml* (of beliefs) against accepted opinion **~y** *n*
heterogeneous /ˌhetərəˈjeeniəs/ *adj* of many different kinds
heterosexual *adj, n* (person) attracted to people of the other sex **~ity** *n*
het up *adj infml* nervous and excited
heuristic /ˌhyooəˈristik/ *adj* solving problems by trial and error **~ally** *adv*
hew *vi/t* **hewed, hewed** *or* **hewn** *lit* cut with a heavy tool
hex *n AmE* evil spell; jinx ♦ *vt* put a hex on
hex-, hexa- *prefix* six
hexagon *n* figure with six sides **~al** *adj*
hexameter *n* a line of verse with six feet
hey *interj* (attracts attention, or for exclaiming)
heyday *n* time of greatest success
hey presto *interj* (way of announcing that one has accomplished something very deftly and quickly, used esp. by conjurers)
HGV *abbrev. for:* heavy goods vehicle
hiatus /hieˈaytəs/ *n fml* space where something is missing
hibernate *vi* (of some animals) sleep during the winter **-nation** *n*
hibiscus *n* tropical plant with large colourful flowers
hiccup, hiccough *n* sudden stopping of the breath with a sharp sound **hiccup** *vi*
hickory *n* American tree with edible nuts
hide[1] *v* **hid, hidden 1** *vt* put out of sight **2** *vi* keep oneself from being seen ♦ *n* place where one may watch animals, birds, etc., without being seen by them
hide[2] *n* animal's skin
hide-and-seek *n* game in which one player has to find others who have hidden
hidebound *adj* not willing to consider new ideas
hideous *adj* very ugly; horrible **~ly** *adv*
hideout also **hideaway** *n* place where one can go to avoid people
hiding[1] *n* beating
hiding[2] *n* state of being hidden
hie *vi arch.* hurry
hierarchy *n* organization with higher and lower ranks **-chical** *adj*
hieroglyphics *pl n* writing that uses pictures, as in ancient Egypt
hi-fi *n* high-quality equipment for reproducing recorded sound
higgledy-piggledy *adj, adv* in confusion; disordered
high *adj* **1** far above the ground **2** great: *high cost* **3** good: *high standards* **4** (of a musical note) not deep **5** (of food) not fresh **6** *infml* drunk or drugged ♦ *adv* **1** to or at a high level **2 high and dry** deserted **3 high and low** everywhere ♦ *n* **1** high point or level **2** state of great excitement **~ly** *adv* **1** very **2** very well: *highly paid*
high-and-mighty *adj infml* arrogant
highball *n esp. AmE* whisky or brandy

served with water or a mixer and ice usu. in a tall glass
highbrow *n, adj* (person) knowing a lot about art, books, etc.
high chair *n* chair with long legs that brings a baby up to the level of a table
High Church *adj* of the part of the Church of England which is closest to the Roman Catholic Church in its beliefs and forms of worship
high-class *adj* **1** of good quality **2** of high social position
high commissioner *n* person representing one Commonwealth country in another
high court *n* superior court of justice
higher education *n* education at a university or college
higher-up *n infml* more important official person
high explosive *n* very powerful explosive (e.g. TNT)
highfalutin *adj* pretentious; pompous
high fidelity *adj* able to reproduce sound almost perfectly
high-flier, -flyer *n* clever and ambitious person
high-flown *adj usu. derog.* extravagant; pretentious
high-grade *adj* of high quality
high-handed *adj* using power too forcefully **~ly** *adv* **~ness** *n*
high horse *n* **on one's high horse** *infml derog* behaving as if one knows best, or more than others
high jinks *pl n infml* high-spirited fun and games
high jump *n* **1** sport of jumping over a bar **2 be for the high jump** *BrE* be punished or severely rebuked
highlands *pl n* mountainous area
high-level *adj* in or at a position of high importance
high-life *n* enjoyable life of the rich and fashionable
highlight *n* **1** most important detail **2** lightest area on a picture, or in the hair ♦ *vt* throw attention onto
highly-strung *adj* nervous; excitable
high-minded *adj* having high principles
Highness *n* (title of some royal persons)
high point *n* high spot
high-powered *adj* having great force or ability; dynamic
high-rise *adj* (of buildings) with many floors
high road *n* **1** *BrE* main road or high street **2** most direct way
high school *n esp. AmE* school for children over 14
high seas *pl n* oceans that do not belong to any particular country
high-season *n* time of year when business is greatest and prices are highest
high-spirited *adj* lively and adventurous
high spot *n* most remembered part of an activity, esp. because pleasurable
high street *n BrE* main street of a town
high table *n* (raised) dining table where college teaching staff sit
hightail *v* **hightail it** *esp. AmE* leave quickly
high tea *n BrE* early-evening meal
high tech, hi-tech *adj* of or using high technology
high technology *n* use of the most modern machines, processes, etc., in business or industry
high-water mark *n* **1** mark showing the highest level reached by the tide **2** highest point or stage
highway *n* broad main road
Highway Code *n* official rules for road users in Britain
highwayman *n* **-men** (in former times) man who used to stop people on the roads and rob them
hijack *vt* **1** take control of (esp. an aircraft) by force **2** stop and rob (a train, coach, etc.) **~er** *n*
hike *vi, n* (go for) a long country walk **hiker** *n*
hilarious *adj* full of or causing laughter **~ly** *adv*
hilarity *n* cheerful laughter
hill *n* **1** raised piece of land, not as high as a mountain **2** slope on a road **~y** *adj*
hillbilly *n AmE* unsophisticated country person

hillock *n* small hill
hilt *n* **1** handle of a sword **2 (up) to the hilt** completely
him *pron* (used for the male object of a sentence)
himself *pron* **1** (*reflexive or strong form of* he): *He shot himself.*
hind[1] *adj* (of animals' legs) back
hind[2] *n* **hinds** *or* **hind** female deer
hinder *vt* delay the progress of **–drance** *n*
hindmost *adj* furthest behind
hindquarters *pl n* animal's back legs
hindsight *n* ability to understand the past, and esp. what went wrong
Hindu *n* **-dus** person whose religion is Hinduism **Hindu** *adj*
Hinduism *n* chief religion of India, notable for its caste system and belief in reincarnation
hinge *n* metal joint on which a door, gate, etc., swings ♦ *vt* fix on hinges **hinge on/upon** *phr vt* depend on
hint *n* **1** small or indirect suggestion **2** useful advice **3** slight trace *vi/t* suggest indirectly
hinterland *n* inner part of a country
hip[1] *n* fleshy part where the legs join the body
hip[2] *n* berry-like fruit of a rose
hip bath *n* portable bath one can sit but not lie in
hippie, -py *n* (young) person who is against the standards of ordinary society
Hippocratic oath *n* oath taken by doctors
hippodrome *n* **1** arena for equestrian performances **2** theatre
hippopotamus also **hippo** *n* **-muses** *or* **-mi** large African river animal
hire *vt* get the use or services of (something or someone) for a limited time, for payment: *hire a car* ♦ *n* (money for) being hired
hireling *n derog* person who works only for financial gain
hire purchase *n BrE* system of paying small sums regularly for goods already received
hirsute /huh'syooht/ *adj fml* hairy
his *determiner* of him ♦ *pron* of him; his one(s)
Hispanic *adj* of Spain, Portugal or Latin America
hiss *vi/t* make a sound like 's', esp. to show disapproval **hiss** *n*
histamine *n* chemical (e.g. in pollen or insect stings) which causes an allergic reaction
histology *n* study of the microscopic structure of animal and plant tissue **–logical** *adj*
historian *n* person who studies history
historic *adj* important in history
historical *adj* about history **~ly** *adv*
historiography *n* study of the writing of history **–pher** *n*
history *n* **1** study of past events **2** account of past events **3** record of someone's past: *her medical history* **4 make history** do something important which will be remembered
histrionics *pl n* insincere behaviour, like a theatrical performance **histrionic** *adj*
hit *vt* **hit,** *pres. p.* **hitting 1** come; strike or bring hard against **2** *infml* reach: *hit the main road* **3** have a bad effect on **4 hit it off** have a good relationship **5 hit the nail on the head** say or do the right thing **6 hit the roof** be intensely angry **hit back** *phr vi* reply forcefully to an attack on oneself **hit on** *phr vt* find by chance **hit out at/against** *phr vt* attack in words ♦ *n* **1** blow **2** successful performance
hit-and-miss *adj* depending on chance
hitch *v* **1** *vt* fasten by hooking a rope or metal part on something **2** *vi* hitchhike **3 get hitched** *infml* get married ♦ *n* **1** difficulty or delay **2** kind of knot **hitch up** *phr vt* pull up into place
hitchhike *vi* travel by getting rides in other people's cars **~r** *n*
hi-tech *adj* of or using high technology
hither *adv fml* to this place
hitherto *adv fml* until now
hit list *n infml* list of people or organizations against whom some (bad) action

is planned
hit man *n infml, esp. AmE* criminal who is employed to kill someone
hit-or-miss *adj* hit-and-miss
hit parade *n* list of top-selling pop records
HIV *n* virus carried in the blood that usually develops into the disease AIDS
hive *n* **1** container in which bees are kept **2** crowded busy place **hive off** *phr vt* separate from a larger organization
hives *pl n* itchy red patches on the skin
HM *abbrev. for* His or Her Majesty('s)
HMS *abbrev. for:* His/Her Majesty's Ship; title for a ship in the British Navy
hoard *n* (secret) store of something valuable ♦ *vt* save; store, esp. secretly
hoarding *n BrE* high board fence, esp. for sticking advertisements on
hoarfrost *n* white surface frost
hoarse *adj* (of a voice) sounding rough **~ly** *adv* **~ness** *n*
hoary *adj* **1** (of hair) white with age **2** hackneyed
hoax *n* trick to deceive someone **hoax** *vt*
hob *n* flat top of a modern cooker
hobble *n* **1** *vi* walk with difficulty **2** *vt* tie two legs of (a horse)
hobbledehoy *n* awkward youth
hobby[1] *n* pleasant activity for one's free time
hobby[2] *n* small falcon
hobbyhorse *n* **1** children's toy like a horse's head on a stick **2** fixed idea to which a person keeps returning in conversation
hobgoblin *n* goblin
hobnail *n* heavy nail in the sole of a boot or shoe
hobnob *vi* **-bb-** have a social relationship (with)
hobo *n* **-oes** *AmE* tramp
Hobson's choice *n* apparent choice that offers no real alternative
hock[1] *n esp. BrE* German white wine
hock[2] *vt sl for* pawn[2]
hock[3] *n* middle joint of an animal's back leg
hockey *n* **1** field team game played with sticks and a ball **2** *esp. AmE* ice hockey
hocus-pocus *n* trickery; mystifying jargon
hod *n* box on a stick, for carrying bricks
hoe *n* garden tool for breaking up the soil **hoe** *vi/t*
hog *n* **1** pig **2** person who eats too much ♦ *vt derog* take and keep all (of something) for oneself
Hogmanay *n* New Year's Eve in Scotland
hogshead *n* large barrel for beer, wine, etc.
hogwash *n infml* nonsense
hoick *vt infml* lift or pull abruptly
hoi polloi *pl n* the common people
hoist *vt* pull up on a rope ♦ *n* **1** upward push **2** apparatus for lifting heavy goods
hoity-toity *adj* haughty
hold[1] *v* **held 1** *vt* keep in the hands **2** *vt* keep in a particular position: *hold one's head up* **3** *vt* not allow to leave **4** *vt* not use: *hold one's breath* **5** *vt* defend against attack **6** *vi* remain unchanged: *What I said still holds.* **7** *vt* have room for **8** *vt* possess: *hold the office of chairman* **9** *vt* believe **10** *vt* cause to happen: *hold an election* **11 Hold it!** *infml* Don't move. **12 hold one's own** keep one's (strong) position **13 hold one's tongue** not talk **14 hold water** seem to be true **hold against** *phr vt* allow (something bad) to influence one's feelings about (someone) **hold back** *phr v* **1** *vt* control **2** *vt* keep secret **3** *vi* be unwilling to act **hold down** *phr vt* **1** keep (a job) **hold forth** *phr vi* talk at length **hold off** *phr vi/t* delay **hold on** *phr vi* **1** wait (esp. on the telephone) **2** continue in spite of difficulties **hold out** *phr vi* continue to exist; last **hold out for** *phr vt* demand firmly and wait in order to get **hold over** *phr vt* postpone **hold up** *phr vt* **1** delay **2** rob by force **hold with** *phr vt* approve of ♦ *n* **1** holding **2** something to hold, esp. in climbing **3** influence
hold[2] *n* compartment below decks where a ship's cargo is stored

holdall *n* bag for travelling
holder *n* **1** person who possesses something **2** container
holding *n* land, shares, etc., that one possesses
holdup *n* **1** delay, as in traffic **2** attempt at armed robbery
hole *n* **1** empty space in something solid **2** home of a small animal **3** *infml* difficult position **4** (in golf) hollow place in the ground into which the ball must be hit ♦ *v* **1** *vt* make a hole in **2** *vi/t* hit (the ball) into a hole in golf **hole up** *phr vi infml* hide as a means of escape
holiday *n* time of rest from work ♦ *vi* have a period of holiday **~maker** *n* person on holiday
holier-than-thou *adj derog* thinking oneself to be morally superior to other people
holiness *n* **1** being holy **2** (*cap.*) (title of the Pope)
holistic *adj* concerning the whole of something or someone, not just its parts: *holistic medicine*
holler *vi esp. AmE* shout
hollow *adj* **1** having an empty space inside **2** lacking flesh: *hollow cheeks* **3** (of sounds) as if made by striking an empty container **4** insincere ♦ *n* wide hole ♦ *vt* make hollow
holly *n* tree whose red berries are used for Christmas decoration
hollyhock *n* tall garden plant with colourful flowers
holocaust *n* great destruction and the loss of many lives, esp. by burning
hologram *n* picture made with laser light so that it appears to be solid rather than flat
holography /hoˈlɒgrəfi/ *n* science of producing holograms
holster *n* leather holder for a pistol
holy *adj* **1** connected with, or serving, religion **2** leading a pure and blameless life
Holy Ghost also **Holy Spirit** *n* God in the form of a spirit; the third person of the Trinity
holy of holies *n* sanctum
Holy Week *n* week before Easter day
Holy Writ *n* **1** the Bible **2** any piece of writing (humorously) regarded as being authoritative
homage *n* signs of great respect
homburg *n* man's soft hat
home *n* **1** place where one lives **2** one's house and family **3 a** place where a plant or animal is found **b** place where something was originally discovered, made, or developed **4** place for the care of people or animals **5 at home** comfortable and at ease ♦ *adv* **1** to or at one's home **2 bring/come home to one** make/become clearly understood **3 home and dry** *infml, esp. BrE* having safely or successfully completed something ♦ *adj* **1** of or related to one's home or origin **2** not foreign **3** (of a sports match) played on one's own, not an opponent's, pitch **home in on** *phr vt* aim exactly towards **~less** *adj*
homebody *n infml* person who enjoys being at home
homebrew *n* homemade beer
homecoming *n* arrival home, esp. after a long absence
Home Counties *pl n* the counties surrounding London
home from home *AmE* **home away from home** *n* place which is as comfortable, welcoming, etc. as one's own home
home front *n* (activities of) civilians in their own country during a war
home help *n* someone sent in by the British Social Services to help with domestic work
homeland *n* **1** country where one was born **2** area set aside for the South African black population
homely *adj* **1** simple and plain **2** *AmE* not good-looking
homemade *adj* made at home or by one's own efforts
homeopathy, homoeo- *n* system of treating disease with small amounts of substances that in larger amounts would produce a similar illness **–thic** *adj*
home rule *n* self-government

home run *n* baseball hit that enables the batter to run around all four bases
homesick *adj* unhappy because away from home **~ness** *n*
homespun *adj* unsophisticated
homestead *n* house with surrounding land used as a simple farm
home truth *n* unpleasant fact about someone
homeward *adj* going towards home **homewards** also *AmE* **homeward** *adv*
homework *n* **1** schoolwork done outside the classroom **2** preparations done before taking part in an important activity
homey, homy *adj AmE infml* pleasant, like home
homicide *n fml* murder **-cidal** *adj*
homily *n* long speech on moral behaviour
homing *adj* of or having the ability to **a** guide oneself home **b** (of machines) guide themselves towards the place they are aimed at
hominid *n* human being or extinct related species
homogeneous *adj fml* formed of parts of the same kind
homogenize, -ise *vt* make (the parts of a whole, esp. a mixture) become evenly spread
homograph *n* word with the same spelling as another
homonym *n* word pronounced the same but with different meaning
Homo sapiens *n* the human race
homosexual *n, adj* (person) sexually attracted to people of the same sex **~ity** *n*
hone *vt* sharpen
honest *adj* not likely to lie or cheat **~ly** *adv* **1** in an honest way **2** really
honesty *n* quality of being honest
honey *n* **1** sweet substance that bees make **2** *esp. AmE* darling
honeycomb *n* wax structure that bees make to store honey
honeymoon *n* **1** holiday taken by two people who have just got married **2** short period of good relations at the beginning of something ♦ *vi* spend one's honeymoon **~er** *n*
honeysuckle *n* climbing plant with sweet-smelling flowers
honk *vi, n* (make) the sound of a car horn
honky-tonk *adj, n* (of or being a) form of ragtime piano playing
honorarium /ˌɒnəˈreəri·əm/ *n* **~s** *or* **-ia** voluntary fee for professional services
honorary *adj* **1** (of a rank, title, etc.) given as an honour **2** unpaid: *honorary chairman*
honorific /ˌɒnəˈrifik/ *adj* (of a title) showing respect or honour
honour, *AmE* **honor** *n* **1** great public respect **2** high standards of behaviour: *men of honour* **3** person or thing that brings pride ♦ *vt* **1** bring honour to **2** keep (an agreement) **honours** *pl n* **1** marks of respect **2** specialized university degree
honourable, *AmE* **honorable** *adj* **1** bringing or showing honour **2** (*cap.*) (title for certain high officials, children of noblemen, etc.) **-bly** *adv*
hooch *n AmE sl* strong alcoholic drink
hood *n* **1** covering for the head and neck **2** folding cover over a car **3** *AmE* bonnet (2)
-hood *suffix* condition or period: *childhood*
hoodoo *n* **-oos** bringer of bad luck; jinx
hoodwink *vt infml* deceive
hoof *n* **hoofs** *or* **hooves** horny foot of a horse, cow, etc.
hoo-ha *n infml* fuss (1)
hook *n* **1** curved piece of metal or plastic for catching, hanging, or fastening things **2** (in boxing) punch with the elbow bent **3 off the hook** no longer in a difficult situation ♦ *vt* catch, hang, or fasten with a hook **~ed** *adj* **1** hook-shaped **2** dependent (e.g. on drugs)
hookah *n* smoking pipe drawing the smoke through water
hooker *n esp. AmE sl* prostitute
hookup *n* (temporary) linking of e.g. electronic circuits
hooky *n* **play hooky** *esp. AmE infml* play

truant
hooligan *n* noisy violent destructive person **~ism** *n*
hoop *n* circular band of wood or metal
hooray *interj, n* hurray
Hooray Henry *n sl* young upper-class man with a hearty manner
hoot *n* **1** sound made by an owl or a car's horn **2** shout of dislike ♦ *vi/t* (cause to) make a hoot **~er** *n* horn, whistle, etc.
Hoover *n tdmk BrE* (type of) vacuum cleaner ♦ *vi/t* clean with a vacuum cleaner
hooves *pl of* hoof
hop[1] *vi* **-pp- 1** (of people) jump on one leg **2** (of small creatures) jump **3** get into or onto a vehicle **4 Hop it!** Go away! ♦ *n* **1** jump **2 on the hop** unprepared
hop[2] *n* climbing plant used for giving taste to beer
hope *n* **1** expectation that something good will happen **2** person or thing that may bring success ♦ *vi/t* wish and expect **~ful** *adj* feeling or giving hope **~fully** *adv* **1** in a hopeful way **2** if our hopes succeed **~less** *adj* **1** feeling or giving no hope **2** not skilled **~lessly** *adv*
hopper *n* large funnel for grain or coal
hopscotch *n* children's game involving jumping between squares
horde *n* large moving crowd
horizon *n* **1** line where the sky seems to meet the earth or sea **2** also **horizons** *pl* range of one's experience
horizontal *adj* flat; level ♦ *n* horizontal line, surface, or position **~ly** *adv*
hormone *n* substance produced in the body that influences growth and other functions **–nal** *adj*
horn *n* **1** pointed growth on an animal's head **2** material that this is made of **3** apparatus, e.g. in a car, that makes a warning sound **4** musical instrument played by blowing **~y** *adj* **1** hard and rough **2** *taboo sl* sexually excited
hornbill *n* tropical bird with a very large curved beak
hornet *n* large stinging insect
hornet's nest *n* **stir up a hornet's nest** provoke an angry and hostile reaction
hornpipe *n* dance performed esp. by sailors
horoscope *n* set of ideas about someone's character, life, and future gained by knowing the position of the stars or planets at time of their birth
horrendous *adj* really terrible **~ly** *adv*
horrible *adj* **1** causing horror **2** very unpleasant **–bly** *adv*
horrid *adj* nasty
horrific *adj* horrifying **~ally** *adv*
horrify *vt* fill with horror
horror *n* **1** (something causing) great shock and fear **2** unpleasant person, usu. a child **3 have a horror of** hate ♦ *adj* frightening: *horror films*
horror-stricken also **horror-struck** *adj* deeply shocked
hors de combat *adj* injured and unable to fight
hors d'oeuvre /ˌaw ˈduhv/ *n* **hors d'oeuvres** small dish served at the beginning of a meal
horse *n* **1** large 4-legged animal that people ride on **2** apparatus for jumping over **3 from the horse's mouth** (of information) directly from the person concerned **horse around/about** *phr vi infml* play roughly or waste time in rough play
horseback *n* **on horseback** riding a horse ♦ *adj, adv esp. AmE* on the back of a horse
horsebox *n* vehicle in which a horse can travel
horselaugh *n* loud rude laugh
horseman *n* **-men** person riding a horse
horseplay *n* rough noisy behaviour
horsepower *n* **horsepower** unit measuring the power of an engine
horseradish *n* plant with a very pungent root, used as a condiment
horse sense *n* common sense
horseshit *n AmE taboo* bullshit
horseshoe *n* U-shaped shoe for a horse, believed to bring good luck
horse-trading *n infml* mutual concessions in bargaining
horsewoman *n* **–men** female

horseman

horsy *adj* **1** interested in horses **2** looking like a horse

horticulture *n* science of growing fruit, flowers, and vegetables **–tural** *adj*

hosanna *n* (in hymns, the Bible, etc.) cry of adoration

hose[1] also **hosepipe** *n* tube used for watering gardens ♦ *vt* use a hose on

hose[2] *n* socks and stockings

hosiery *n* socks, stockings, etc.

hospice *n* hospital for people with incurable illnesses

hospitable *adj* offering a friendly welcome to guests **–bly** *adv*

hospital *n* place where people who are ill or injured are treated **~ize, –ise** *vt* put into hospital

hospitality *n* being hospitable

host[1] *n* **1** man who receives guests **2** person who introduces performers, e.g. on a TV show ♦ *vt* act as a host of or at

host[2] *n* large number: *a host of difficulties*

hostage *n* prisoner kept by an enemy so that the other side will obey demands or pay ransom

hostel *n* building where students or travellers can live and eat

hostelry *n* pub

hostess *n* **1** female host **2** airhostess **3** young woman who acts as companion, dancing partner, etc., in a nightclub

hostile *adj* **1** unfriendly **2** belonging to an enemy

hostility *n* unfriendliness **–ties** *pl n* war

hot *adj* **-tt- 1** having a high temperature **2** having a burning taste: *hot pepper* **3** fierce; excitable: *hot temper* **4** well-informed about and interested in **6 hot and bothered** worried by a feeling that things are going wrong **6 hot on someone's trail** following someone closely **7 not so hot** *infml* not very good **hot up** *phr vi* **-tt-** become more exciting or dangerous **~ly** *adv* **1** angrily **2** eagerly: *hotly pursued*

hot air *n* meaningless talk

hotbed *n* place where something bad can develop

hot-blooded *adj* passionate

hotchpotch *n* confused mixture

hot-cross bun *n* spicy bun marked with a cross usu. eaten on Good Friday

hot dog *n* frankfurter in a long bread roll

hotel *n* building where people can stay in return for payment

hotelier *n* hotel manager

hot flush *n* flushing and feeling of heat usu. associated with the menopause

hotfoot *adv* fast and eagerly

hot-gospeller *n infml* preacher who aims to rouse his audience to a high state of excitement

hothead *n* person who acts in haste, without thinking **~ed** *adj*

hothouse *n* heated greenhouse

hot line *n* direct telephone line between heads of government

hotplate *n* metal surface on which food is cooked

hot rod *n* car rebuilt for high performance

hot seat *n infml* position of difficulty from which one must make important decisions

hot spot place where there is likely to be unrest and perhaps war

hot stuff *n infml* **1** something or someone (sexually) exciting **2** something or someone of outstanding ability

hot-tempered *adj* easily angered

hot water *n* trouble: *get into hot water*

hot-water bottle *n* rubber container for hot water, to warm a bed

hound *n* hunting dog ♦ *vt* chase and worry

hour *n* **1** period of 60 minutes **2** period: *my lunch hour* **3 after hours** later than the usual times of work **~ly** *adj, adv* once every hour

hourglass *n* 8-shaped container through which sand falls to measure time

houri *n* desirable young woman in the Muslim heaven

house *n* **1** building for people to live in, esp. on more than one level **2** building for a stated purpose: *a hen house* **3** (*of-*

ten cap.) noble or royal family **4** division of a school **5 bring the house down** cause loud admiration **6 get on like a house on fire** be very friendly **7 keep house** do or control the cleaning, cooking, etc. **8 on the house** (of drinks) paid for by the management ♦ *vt* provide a home, or space, for

house arrest *n* confinement to one's own home as a form of punishment usu. for political offences

houseboat *n* boat for living in

housebound *adj* unable to leave one's home

housebreaker *n* thief who enters a house by force

housebroken *adj AmE* house-trained

housecoat *n* garment worn by women at home

household *n* all the people living in a house ♦ *adj* concerned with the management of a house **~er** *n* person who owns or is in charge of a house

household name also **household word** *n* person or thing that is very well known or talked about by almost everyone

housekeeper *n* person paid to run a house

housekeeping *n* **1** work of running a house **2** money set aside for food and other household necessities

house lights *pl n* auditorium lights in a theatre

housemaid *n* female servant who does housework

houseman *n* **-men** *BrE* low-ranking doctor completing hospital training

housemaster *n* teacher in charge of a school house

House of Commons *n* the lower but more powerful of the two parts of the British or Canadian parliament

House of Lords *n* the upper but less powerful of the two parts of the British parliament, consisting of non-elected peers

House of Representatives *n* the larger and lower of the two parts of the national legislature in such countries as New Zealand, Australia, and the US

house-proud *adj* keeping one's home very clean and tidy

house-to-house *adj* door-to-door

house-trained *adj BrE* (of pets) trained to urinate and defecate outdoors

housewarming *n* party given for friends when one has moved into a new house

housewife *n* **-wives** woman who works at home for her family, cleaning, cooking, etc.

housework *n* cleaning, etc., in a house

housey-housey *n* bingo

housing *n* **1** places to live **2** protective cover for a machine

hove *past t. and p. of* heave[2]

hovel *n* dirty little house or hut

hover *vi* **1** (of birds, helicopters, etc.) stay in the air in one place **2** (of people) wait around

hovercraft *n* **-craft** *or* **-crafts** boat that moves over land or water supported on a cushion of air

how *adv* **1** (used in questions) **a** in what way **b** in what state of health: *How are you?* **c** (in questions about number, size, etc.): *How big is it?* **2** (showing surprise): *How kind of you!* **3 How do you do?** (formal greeting)

howdah *n* (roofed) seat for a rider on an elephant

however *adv* **1** in whatever degree or way **2** in spite of this **3** in what way (showing surprise): *However did you get here?*

howitzer *n* gun firing shells at a high trajectory

howl *vi/t, n* (make) a long loud cry **~er** *n infml* silly laughable mistake

hoyden *n* boisterous girl **~ish** *adj*

HP *abbrev. for:* **1** horsepower **2** hire purchase

HQ *n* headquarters

hr, hrs *abbrev. for:* hour(s)

HRH *abbrev. for:* His/Her Royal Highness; title for certain members of the British royal family

hub *n* **1** centre of a wheel **2** centre of activity

hubbub *n* mixture of loud noises

hubby *n infml* husband

hubcap *n* metal covering for the centre of a wheel on a car
hubris /ˈhyoohbris/ *n* overconfidence (preceding a fall)
huckster *n derog* **1** pedlar **2** high-pressure salesman
huddle *vi/t* crowd together ♦ *n* crowded group
hue *n fml* colour
hue and cry *n* public outcry
huff *n* fit of resentment **~y** *adj*
hug *vt* **-gg-** **1** hold tightly in one's arms **2** travel along beside: *The boat hugged the coast.* **hug** *n*
huge *adj* very big **~ly** *adv* very much
hugger-mugger *n lit* **1** secrecy **2** disorder **hugger-mugger** *adj, adv*
huh *interj* (used for asking a question or for expressing surprise or disapproval)
hula *n* Hawaiian dance
Hula Hoop *n tdmk for* plastic hoop swung around on the hips as a form of exercise
hulk *n* **1** old dilapidated ship **2** heavy, awkward person or creature
hulking *adj* big and awkward
hull *n* body of a ship or aircraft
hullabaloo *n infml* uproar
hullo *interj, n* **-os** *BrE* hello
hum *v* **-mm-** **1** *vi* buzz (1) **2** *vi/t* sing with closed lips **3** *vi* be full of activity **hum** *n*
human *adj* **1** of or being people **2** kind, compassionate, etc., as people should be ♦ *n* person **~ism** *n* system of belief based on people's needs, and not on religion **~ize, -ise** *vt* make human or humane **~ly** *adv* according to human powers: *not humanly possible*
humane *adj* **1** showing human kindness and the qualities of a civilized person **2** trying not to cause pain: *humane killing* **~ly** *adv*
humanitarian *n, adj* (person) trying to improve conditions of life for people **~ism** *n*
humanity *n* **1** being human or humane **2** people in general **humanities** *pl n* cultural subjects of study, e.g. literature and history
humanoid *adj* having human form or characteristics
humble *adj* **1** low in rank; unimportant **2** having a low opinion of oneself; not proud ♦ *vt* make humble **-bly** *adv*
humbug *n* **1** insincere nonsense **2** impostor; hypocrite **3** *BrE* hard boiled sweet
humdinger *n infml* something excellent or remarkable
humdrum *adj* dull and ordinary
humerus *n med* bone of the upper arm
humid *adj* (of air) damp and warm **~ify** *vt* make humid **~ity** *n*
humiliate *vt* cause to feel ashamed **-ation** *n*
humility *n* quality of being humble (2)
humming bird *n* tiny long-beaked tropical American bird
hummock *n* hillock
humorist *n* person who makes jokes or writes humorously
humorous *adj* funny **~ly** *adv*
humour, *AmE* **humor** *n* ability to cause amusement or be amused ♦ *vt* keep (someone) happy by acceptance of their foolish wishes, behaviour, etc.; indulge
hump *n* **1** round lump, esp. on a camel's back **2** *BrE infml* feeling of bad temper ♦ *v* **1** *vt infml* carry (something heavy), esp. with difficulty **2** *vi/t taboo sl* have sex (with)
humus /ˈhyoohməs/ *n* decomposed soil-forming material
hunch[1] *n* idea based on feeling rather than reason
hunch[2] *vt* pull (esp. the shoulders) into a rounded shape
hunchback *n* (person with) a back misshaped by a round lump **~ed** *adj*
hundred *determiner, n, pron* **-dred** *or* **-dreds** 100 **~th** *determiner, adv, n, pron* 100th
hundredweight *n* **-weight** (measure of weight equal to) **a** 45.36 kilograms or **b** 50.8 kilograms
hung *past t. and p. of* hang
Hungarian *n, adj* (inhabitant) of Hungary

hunger *n* **1** need for food **2** strong wish **–gry** *adj* feeling hunger **–grily** *adv*
hunger strike *n* refusal to eat as a protest
hunk *n* **1** thick piece, esp. food **2** *infml* good-looking man
hunt *vi/t* **1** chase (animals) for food or sport **2** search (for) ♦ *n* **1** chasing or searching **2** people hunting foxes **hunt down/out/up** *phr vt* find by searching **~er** *n*
huntsman *n* **–men** hunter, esp. hunting foxes
hurdle *n* **1** frame to jump over in a race **2** difficulty to be dealt with
hurdy-gurdy *n* small barrel organ
hurl *vt* throw violently
hurling *n* Irish game similar to hockey
hurly-burly *n* noisy activity
hurray *interj*, *n* (shout of joy or approval)
hurricane *n* violent storm with a strong fast circular wind
hurricane lamp *n* lamp with a glass over its flame
hurry *vi/t* (cause to) go or do something (too) quickly ♦ *n* **1** quick activity **2** need to hurry **–ried** *adj* done (too) quickly **–riedly** *adv*
hurt *v* **hurt 1** *vt* cause pain or damage to **2** *vt* cause pain to (the feelings) of (a person) **3** *vi* feel pain **4** *vi/t* matter (to): *It won't hurt (you) to wait.* ♦ *n* harm; damage **~ful** *adj* **~fully** *adv*
hurtle *vi* move or rush with great force
husband *n* man to whom a woman is married
hush *vi/t* (cause to) be silent **hush up** *phr vt* keep secret ♦ *n* silence
husk *n* dry outer covering of some fruits and seeds
husky[1] *adj* **1** (of a voice) hoarse **2** (of a person) big and strong **–kily** *adv*
husky[2] *n* hardy working dog used by polar explorers
hussar *n* member of various cavalry regiments
hussy *n* impertinent or promiscuous young woman
hustings *pl n* proceedings, (e.g. speeches) before an election
hustle *vt* **1** push or drive hurriedly **2** persuade forcefully, esp. to buy something ♦ *n* hurried activity **hustler** *n* **1** *infml* busy active person, esp. one who tries to persuade people to buy things **2** *sl, esp. AmE* prostitute
hut *n* small simple building
hutch *n* cage for small animals (e.g. rabbits)
hyacinth *n* garden plant with fragrant flowers that grows from a bulb
hybrid *n* animal or plant of mixed breed
hydra *n* **1** mythical many-headed serpent **2** evil thing difficult to destroy **3** small freshwater polyp
hydrangea *n* garden shrub with clusters of usu. pink flowers
hydrant *n* water pipe in the street
hydraulic /hieˈdrolik/ *adj* using water pressure
hydro- *prefix* of or using water
hydrocarbon *n* organic compound of hydrogen and carbon
hydrochloric acid *n* a strong corrosive acid
hydroelectric *adj* producing electricity by water power
hydrofoil *n* large motor boat which raises itself out of the water on floats as it moves
hydrogen *n* light gas that burns easily
hydrogen bomb *n* bomb made using hydrogen which explodes when the nuclei of the atoms join together
hydrometer *n* instrument for measuring the relative density of liquids
hydrophobia *n* (abnormal fear of water, esp. as a symptom of) rabies
hydrotherapy *n* use of water in the treatment of disease
hyena *n* doglike carrion-eating African animal
hygiene /ˈhieˌjeen/ *n* cleanness, to prevent the spreading of disease **–nic** *adj*
hygrometer *n* instrument for measuring the humidity of the air
hymen *n* membrane partly enclosing the vagina of a virgin

hymn *n* song of praise to God
hype *vt infml* publicize extravagantly **hype** *n* extravagant publicity
hyped up *adj infml* very excited and anxious
hyper- *prefix* very or too much
hyperactive *adj* unable to rest or be quiet
hyperbole /hieˈpuhbəli/ *n fml* exaggeration
hypermarket *n BrE* very large supermarket
hypertension *n med* high blood pressure
hyphen *n* mark (-) joining words or word parts **~ate** *vt* join with a hyphen
hypnosis *n* sleep-like state in which a person can be influenced by the person who produced the state **–otic** *adj* **–otism** *n* production of hypnosis **–otist** *n* **~otize, –otise** *vt* produce hypnosis in
hypocaust *n* ancient Roman underfloor heating
hypochondriac /ˌhiepəˈkondriak/ *n* someone who worries unnecessarily about their health
hypocrisy *n* pretence of moral superiorty
hypocrite *n* person who practises hypocrisy **–critical** *adj*
hypodermic *adj*, *n* (of) a needle for injecting drugs
hypotenuse *n* longest side of a right-angled triangle which is opposite the right angle
hypothermia *n* abnormally low body temperature
hypothesis *n* idea put forward to explain facts **–etical** *adj* not yet proved
hysterectomy *n* surgical removal of the womb
hysteria *pl n* uncontrolled nervous excitement **–rical** *adj* **–rics** *n* attack(s) of hysteria
Hz *abbrev. for:* hertz

I

I[1] **, I** the 9th letter of the English alphabet
I[2] *pron* (used for the person speaking, as the subject of a sentence)
iamb *n* unit of verse consisting of one short or unstressed syllable followed by one long or stressed one
IBA *abbrev. for:* Independent Broadcasting Authority
Iberian *adj* of Spain and Portugal
ibex *n* wild mountain goat
ibis *n* wading bird with long curved beak
ICBM *n* intercontinental ballistic missile
ice *n* **1** frozen water **2** frozen sweet food **3 skating on thin ice** taking risks **4 keep something on ice** take no immediate action about something ♦ *vt* **1** make cold with ice **2** cover with icing **ice over/up** *phr vi* become covered with ice
ice age *n* period when ice covered many northern countries
ice axe *n* tool like a small pickaxe used by mountaineers
iceberg *n* mass of floating ice in the sea
icebox *n* **1** box where food is kept cool with ice **2** *AmE* fridge
icebreaker *n* **1** ship that cuts through floating ice **2** action which makes people who have just met more relaxed
ice cap *n* lasting covering of ice, e.g. at the Poles
ice cream *n* frozen creamy food mixture
ice floe *n* large area of floating ice
ice hockey *n* game like hockey played on ice
ice lolly *n BrE* piece of flavoured ice on a stick

ice pack *n* bag of ice to put on the body
ice pick *n* tool for breaking ice
ice-skate *n* skate (1) **ice-skate** *vi*
ice water *n* ice-cold water for drinking
icicle *n* tapering mass of ice, formed when water freezes as it runs down
icing *n* mixture of powdered sugar with liquid, used to decorate cakes
icon *n* **1** devotional picture of a saint, Christ, etc. **2** symbol used on computer screens
iconoclast *n* person who attacks established beliefs **~ic** *adj*
icy *adj* **1** very cold **2** covered with ice **icily** *adv*
id *n* instinctual, unconscious part of the mind
I'd *short for:* **1** I would **2** I had
ID *n infml* means of identification: *ID card*
idea *n* **1** plan, thought, or sugestion for a possible course of action **2** picture in the mind; conception **3** opinion or belief
ideal *adj* **1** perfect; as one would wish **2** too good to exist ♦ *n* **1** (belief in) high principles or perfect standards **2** perfect example **~ist** *n* **~ize, -ise** *vt* imagine as perfect **~ly** *adv* **1** in an ideal way: *ideally suited* **2** if things were perfect
idealism *n* quality or habit of living according to one's ideals, or the belief that such a way of life is possible **-ist** *n* **-istic** *adj* **-istically** *adv*
idée fixe *n* obsessive idea
identical *adj* **1** exactly alike **2** the same **~ly** *adv*
identify *vt* show the identity of **-fication** *n* **1** identifying **2** document, card, etc. that proves who one is **dentify with** *phr vt* **1** consider (someone) to be connected with **2** feel sympathy for
identikit *n* set of pictures of facial features for making a composite portrait
identity *n* **1** who or what a person or thing is **2** sameness
ideogram *n* symbol representing a thing or idea (e.g. a Chinese character)
ideologue *n* advocate of an ideology
ideology *n* set of (political or social) ideas **-ogical** *adj*
idiocy *n* **1** stupidity **2** stupid act
idiom *n* **1** particular use or variety of language **2** phrase with a metaphorical meaning
idiomatic *adj* typical of natural speech **~ally** *adv*
idiosyncrasy *n* personal peculiarity **-atic** *adj* **-atically** *adv*
idiot *n* fool **~ic** *adj*
idle *adj* **1** not working **2** lazy **3** useless: *idle threats* ♦ *vi* **1** waste time **2** (of an engine) run slowly because it is disconnected **idle away** *phr vt* waste (time) **~ness** *n* **idly** *adv* **idler** *n*
idol *n* **1** image worshipped as a god **2** someone greatly admired **~ize, -ise** *vt* worship as an idol
idolatry /ie'dolətri/ *n* worship of idols **-trous** *adj* **-ater** *n*
idyll *n* poem or prose work evoking (rural) contentment **~ic** *adj* simple and happy
i.e. that is; by which is meant
if *conj* **1** on condition that **2** even though **3** whether **4** that: *I'm sorry if she's annoyed.*
iffy *adj infml* uncertain; dubious
-ify *suffix* (*in verbs*) make or become: *simplify*
igloo *n* **-oos** dome-shaped Inuit house made of ice
igneous *adj* (of rock) formed from molten material
ignis fatuus *n* **ignes fatui** moving light seen over marshy ground
ignite *vi/t fml* start to burn
ignition *n* **1** electrical apparatus that starts an engine **2** *fml* action of igniting
ignoble /ig'nohbl/ *adj fml* not honourable **-bly** *adv*
ignominy /'ignəmini/ *n* disgrace **-nious** *adj*
ignoramus /ˌignə'rayməs/ *n* ignorant person
ignorant *adj* **1** without knowledge **2** rude, esp. because of lack of social training **-rance** *n*

ignore *vt* refuse to notice
iguana *n* large tropical American lizard
il- *prefix* (before *l*) not
ileum *n* lower part of the small intestine
ilk *n* sort; type: *books of that ilk*
ill *adj* **worse, worst 1** sick **2** bad: *ill luck* ♦ *adv* **1** badly: *ill-treated* **2** not enough: *ill fed* ♦ *n* evil circumstance; trouble
I'll *short for:* I will or I shall
ill-advised *adj* unwise
ill-assorted *adj* not well matched, going badly together
ill-bred *adj* impolite
illegal *adj* against the law **~ly** *adv* **~ity** *n*
illegible *adj* impossible to read **-bility** *n*
illegitimate *adj* **1** born to unmarried parents **2** against the rules **~ly** *adv*
ill-fated *adj* destined to fail
ill feeling *n* animosity
ill-gotten *adj* dishonestly obtained
illiberal *adj fml* **1** bigoted **2** mean
illicit *adj* against the law or the rules **~ly** *adv*
illiterate *adj* unable to read or write **-racy** *n*
ill-mannered *adj* rude
ill-natured *adj* bad-tempered
illness *n* disease
illogical *adj* against logic; not sensible **~ly** *adv* **-lity** *n*
ill-omened *adj* seemingly fated to turn out badly
ill-timed *adj* inopportune
ill-treat *vt* be cruel to
illuminate *vt* **1** give light to **2** decorate with lights **3** (esp. in former times) decorate with gold and bright colours **-ating** *adj* helping to explain **-ation** *n* **-ations** *pl n* coloured lights to decorate a town
illumine *vt lit* illuminate (1)
illusion *n* something perceived wrongly; false sight or idea **-sory** *adj* unreal
illustrate *vt* **1** add pictures to **2** explain by giving examples **-ator** *n* person who draws pictures for books **-ation** *n* **1** picture **2** example **3** illustrating **-trative** *adj* used as an example
illustrious *adj* famous
ill will *n* animosity
I'm *short for:* I am
im- *prefix* (before *b, m, p*) not
image *n* **1** picture in the mind, or seen in a mirror **2** general opinion about a person, company etc., that has been formed or intentionally created in people's minds **3** exact likeness **4** idol (1) **~ry** *n* metaphors in literature
imaginary *adj* unreal
imagine *vt* **1** form (an idea) in the mind **2** believe; suppose **-nable** *adj* **-native** *adj* good at imagining **-nation** *n* **1** ability to imagine **2** something only imagined
imago *n* final perfected form of an insect
imam *n* **1** prayer leader in a mosque **2** (*cap.*) Shiite Muslim leader
imbalance *n* lack of balance or equality
imbecile *n* idiot **-cility** *n* **1** being an imbecile **2** foolish act
imbibe *vi/t fml* drink or take in
imbroglio /im'brohlioh/ *n* **-os** confused situation
imbue with *phr vt* fill with (a feeling)
IMF *abbrev. for:* International Monetary Fund
imitate *vt* **1** copy **2** take as an example **-tor** *n* **-tive** *adj* following an example; not inventive **-tion** *n* **1** (act of) imitating **2** copy of the real thing
immaculate *adj* **1** clean; pure **2** perfect **~ly** *adv*
Immaculate Conception *n* Roman Catholic belief that the Virgin Mary was conceived without original sin
immanent *adj fml* present in or throughout something
immaterial *adj* **1** unimportant **2** without physical substance
immature *adj* not fully formed or developed **-rity** *n*
immeasurable *adj* too big to be measured **-ly** *adv*
immediate *adj* **1** done or needed at once **2** nearest **~ly** *adv* **1** at once **2** with nothing between **~ly** *conj* as soon as **-acy** *n* nearness or urgent presence of

something
immense *adj* very large **~ly** *adv* very much **-sity** *n*
immerse *vt* **1** put deep into liquid **2** engross; absorb **-sion** *n*
immersion heater *n* electric water heater in a tank
immigrate *vi* come to live in a country **-ant** *n* person who does this **-ation** *n*
imminent *adj* going to happen soon **~ly** *adv*
immobile *adj* unmoving; unable to move **-ility** *n* **-ilize, -ilise** *vt* make immobile
immolate *vt* kill, esp. sacrificially **~ation** *n*
immoral *adj* **1** not good or right **2** sexually improper **~ity** *n*
immortal *adj* living or remembered for ever ♦ *n* immortal being **~ity** *n* endless life **~ize,~ise** *vt* give endless life or fame to
immune *adj* unable to be harmed; protected **-nity** *n* **-nize, -ise** *vt* protect from disease
immune system *n* bodily system that fights substances that cause disease
immunology *n* study of biological immunity **-gical** *adj* **-gist** *n*
immunosuppressive *adj* that suppresses the immune system **-sant** *adj, n*
immure *vt fml* enclose within walls, esp. in prison
immutable *adj fml* unchangeable
imp *n* **1** little devil **2** troublesome child **~ish** *adj*
impact *n* **1** force of one object hitting another **2** influence; effect
impair *vt* spoil; weaken
impala *n* large African antelope
impale *vt* push something sharp through
impalpable *adj fml* not easily felt or understood
impart *vt fml* **1** convey; transmit **2** make known
impartial *adj* fair; just **~ly** *adv* **~ity** *n*
impassable *adj* (of roads, routes, etc.) impossible to travel over
impasse /'ampas, impəs/ *n* point where further movement is blocked
impassioned *adj* full of deep feelings
impassive *adj* showing no feelings; calm **~ly** *adv*
impatient *adj* **1** not patient **2** eager **~ly** *adv* **-ence** *n*
impeach *vt* charge with a crime against the state **~ment** *n*
impeccable *adj* faultless **-bly** *adv*
impecunious *adj fml* without money; poor
impede *vt* get in the way of
impediment *n* something that makes action difficult or impossible
impedimenta *pl n* **1** equipment **2** encumbrances
impel *vt* **-ll-** (of an idea, feeling, circumstance, etc.) cause (someone) to act
impending *adj* (esp. of something bad) about to happen
impenetrable *adj* **1** that cannot be gone through **2** impossible to understand
impenitent *adj* feeling no remorse **~ly** *adv*
imperative *adj* urgent; that must be done ♦ *n* verb form expressing a command (e.g. *Come!*) **~ly** *adv*
imperceptible *adj* (so slight or gradual as to be) undetectable by the senses **-tibly** *adv*
imperfect *adj* not perfect ♦ *n* verb form showing incomplete action in the past (e.g. *was walking*) **~ly** *adv* **~ion** *n* **1** imperfect state **2** fault
imperial *adj* of an empire or its ruler **~ly** *adv* **~ism** *n* (belief in) the making of an empire **~ist** *n, adj*
imperil *vt* **-ll-** (*AmE* **-l-**) put in danger
imperious *adj fml* (too) commanding; expecting obedience from others **~ly** *adv*
imperishable *adj* **1** incapable of wearing out **2** immortal
impersonal *adj* without personal feelings **~ly** *adv*
impersonate *vt* pretend to be (another person) **-ation** *n*
impertinent *adj* not properly respectful **~ly** *adv* **-ence** *n*

imperturbable *adj* unworried; calm **–ly** *adv*
impervious *adj* **1** not letting esp. water through **2** not easily influenced: *impervious to criticism*
impetigo /ˈimpəˈtiegoh/ *n* skin disease producing pustules
impetuous *adj* acting quickly but without thought **~ly** *adv* **–osity** *n*
impetus *n* **1** force of something moving **2** stimulus
impinge on *phr vt* have an effect on
impious /ˈimpi·əs/ *adj* without respect for religion **~ly** *adv* **–iety** *n*
implacable *adj* impossible to satisfy or placate
implant *vt* fix deeply into
implausible *adj* seeming to be untrue or unlikely
implement *n* tool or instrument ♦ *vt* carry out (e.g. a plan)
implicate *vt* show (someone or something) to be involved, esp. in something bad
implication *n* **1** (example of) implying **2** possible later effect of something **3** act of implicating
implicit *adj* **1** meant though not expressed **2** unquestioning: *implicit trust* **~ly** *adv*
implode *vi* explode inwards
implore *vt* beg; request strongly
imply *vt* **1** express indirectly **2** make necessary
impolitic *adj* unwise, injudicious
imponderable *n, adj* (thing) whose effects cannot be measured exactly
import *vt* bring in (goods) from abroad ♦ *n* **1** something imported **2** *fml* importance; significance **~er** *n* **~ation** *n*
important *adj* mattering very much **~ly** *adv* **–ance** *n*
importune *vt fml* bother with repeated requests **–nate** *adj* persistently demanding
impose *v* **1** *vt* establish (a tax) **2** *vt* force the acceptance of **3** *vi* take unfair advantage **-sing** *adj* large and impressive **-sition** *n* act of imposing
impossible *adj* **1** not possible **2** hard to bear **–bly** *adv* **–bility** *n*
impost *n fml* tax
impostor *n* someone who deceives by pretending to be someone else
impotent *adj* **1** powerless **2** (of a man) unable to perform the sex act **~ly** *adv* **–ence** *n*
impound *vt* take away officially
impoverish *vt* make poor
impracticable *adj* that cannot be used in practice
impractical *adj* not practical; not sensible or reasonable
imprecation *n fml* curse
impregnable *adj* impossible to enter by attack
impregnate *vt* **1** make wet; saturate **2** *fml* make pregnant
impresario *n* **-os** person who arranges theatre or concert performances
impress *vt* **1** fill with admiration **2** tell someone forcefully **~ive** *adj* causing admiration **~ively** *adv* **~ion** *n* **1** effect produced on the mind **2** mark left by pressing **3** (theatrical) imitation of a person's appearance or behaviour **~ionable** *adj* easily influenced
impressionism *n* 19th-century (French) art movement stressing the effect of light on things seen **–ist** *adj, n*
imprimatur /ˌimpriˈmahtə, -maytə/ *n* formal approval
imprint *vt* press (a mark) on ♦ *n* **1** mark left on or in something **2** name of the publisher as it appears on a book
imprison *vt* put in prison **~ment** *n*
improbable *adj* unlikely **–bly** *adv* **–bility** *n*
impromptu *adj, adv* without preparation
improper *adj* **1** not suitable or correct **2** socially unacceptable; rude **~ly** *adv*
impropriety *n* being improper
improve *vi/t* make or become better **~ment** *n* (sign of) improving
improvident *adj* wasteful; thriftless
improvise *vi/t* **1** do (something one has not prepared for) **2** invent (music) while one plays **–sation** *n*
impudent *adj* shamelessly disrespectful

~ly *adv* **-ence** *n*
impugn /im'pyoohn/ *vt fml* cast doubt on, esp. unfairly
impulse *n* **1** sudden urge **2** wave of energy: *nerve impulses* **-sive** *adj* acting on impulse
impunity *n* **with impunity** without being punished
impure *adj* **1** mixed with something else **2** morally bad **-rity** *n*
impute *vt fml* ascribe, esp. unjustly
in *prep* **1** contained or surrounded by **2** (of time) **a** during **b** at the end of **3** included as part of **4** wearing **5** using **6** (shows the way something is done or happens): *in public|in a hurry* **7** **in all** as the total ♦ *adv* **1** (in order to be) contained or surrounded; away from the outside **2** towards or at home or the usual place **3** into a surface **4** fashionable **5** in power **6** **be in for** be about to have (esp. something bad) **7** **be in on** take part in **8** **be in with** *infml* be friendly with ♦ *adj* **1** *infml* fashionable **2** shared by only a few favoured people: *an in joke* ♦ *n* **ins and outs** *infml* details (of a complex or difficult situation)
in- *prefix* not: *inedible*
inability *n* lack of power or skill
inaccessible *adj* impossible to reach
inaccurate *adj* not correct **~ly** *adv* **-acy** *n*
inaction *n* state of doing nothing
inactive *adj* not active **~ly** *adv* **-vity** *n*
inadequate *adj* not good enough **~ly** *adv*
inadmissible *adj* not able to be accepted or considered, esp. in a court of law
inadvertent *adj* done by accident **~ly** *adv* **-tency** *n*
inalienable *adj fml* (of rights) that cannot be taken away
inamorata *n* woman one loves
inane *adj* stupid **~ly** *adv* **-nity** *n*
inanimate *adj* not living
inappropriate *adj* not suitable **~ly** *adv* **~ness** *n*
inapt *adj* not suitable
inarticulate *adj* **1** (of speech) not clear **2** (of people) not speaking clearly **~ly** *adv*
inasmuch as *conj fml* to the degree that; because
inaugurate *vt* **1** start or introduce with a special ceremony **2** be the beginning of (a period of time) **-ral** *adj* **-ration** *n*
inauspicious *adj* suggesting an unfavourable outcome
inboard *adj* inside a boat
inborn *adj* present from one's birth
inbred *adj* **1** inborn **2** produced by inbreeding
inbreeding *n* breeding between closely related family members
inbuilt *adj* inherent
inc *adj* incorporated; (of a US firm) formed into a legal corporation
incalculable *adj* too great to be counted **-bly** *adv*
in camera *adv* (of a court case) held in private
incandescent *adj* shining brightly when heated **-ence** *n*
incantation *n* words used in magic
incapacitate *vt* make unable to do something **-city** *n* lack of ability
incarcerate *vt fml* imprison **-ation** *n*
incarnate *adj* in human form **-nation** *n* **1** being incarnate **2** any of a person's many lives **3** (*cap.*) (in Christianity) the coming of God to Earth in the body of Jesus Christ
incendiary *adj* **1** causing fires **2** causing violence; inflammatory ♦ *n* **1** bomb which sets fire to buildings **2** arsonist
incense *n* substance burnt to make a sweet smell
incensed *adj* extremely angry
incentive *n* encouragement to get things done
inception *n* beginning
incessant *adj* (of something bad) never stopping **~ly** *adv*
incest *n* sexual relationship between close relatives **~uous** *adj*
inch *n* **1** a measure of length equal to 2.54 centimetres **2** small amount **3** **every inch** completely ♦ *vi/t* move slowly
inchoate /'inkoh·ayt/ *adj fml* imperfect-

ly formed; incomplete
incidence *n* rate of happening: *a high incidence of disease*
incident *n* **1** (unusual) event **2** event that includes or leads to violence, danger, or serious disagreement
incidental *adj* happening in connection with something else ♦ *n* something (esp. a fact or detail) that is unimportant **~ally** *adv* (used to introduce a new subject in talking)
incidental music *n* music played between the scenes of a play or to accompany the action on stage
incinerate *vt* burn (unwanted things) **–rator** *n* container for burning things in
incipient *adj fml* at an early stage
incise *vt* cut into **–sor** *n* front cutting tooth **–sive** *adj* going directly to the point **–sion** *n* (act of making) a cut, esp. in a surgical operation
incite *vt* encourage (violence, or people to be violent) **~ment** *n*
inclement *adj* (of weather) bad
incline *v* **1** *vt* encourage to feel or think **2** *vi* tend: *I incline to take the opposite view.* **3** *vi/t* slope **4** *vt* move or bend downward ♦ *n* slope **~ed** *adj* **1** disposed **2** tending **–nation** *n* **1** liking **2** tendency **3** act of inclining
include *vt* **1** have as a part **2** put in with something else **–usion** *n* **–usive** *adj* including everything
incognito /ˌinkogˈneetoh/ *adj, adv* taking another name as a disguise
incoherent *adj* not clearly expressed **~ly** *adv* **–ence** *n*
income *n* money received regularly
income tax *n* tax on one's income
incoming *adj* coming in, starting a period in office
incommunicado *adv* (of people) prevented from giving or receiving messages
incomparable *adj* unequalled; very great **–ly** *adv*
incompatible *adj* not suitable to be together **–bility** *n*
incompetent *adj* not skilful **–ence** *n* **~ly** *adv*
incomprehensible *adj* impossible to understand **–bility** *n* **–sion** *n* failure to understand
inconceivable *adj* impossible to imagine **–bly** *adv*
inconclusive *adj* leading to no conclusion or definite result
incongruous *adj* out of place **–uity** *n*
inconsequential *adj* **1** unimportant **2** not relevant **~ly** *adv*
inconsiderate *adj* not thinking of other people **~ly** *adv*
inconsistent *adj* lacking consistency **~ly** *adv*
inconsolable *adj* too sad to be comforted **-bly** *adv*
inconspicuous *adj* not readily noticeable **~ly** *adv*
inconstant *adj* **1** liable to change **2** *lit* unfaithful
incontestable *adj* indisputable
incontinent *adj* unable to control one's bowels and bladder **–ence** *n*
incontrovertible *adj fml* which cannot be disproved **–bly** *adv*
inconvenient *adj* causing difficulty or annoyance because unsuitable or at the wrong time **~ly** *adv* **–ence** *n* (cause of the) state of being inconvenient **–ence** *vt* cause inconvenience to
incorporate *vt* include in something larger **–ation** *n*
incorrect *adj* wrong **~ly** *adv*
incorrigible *adj* bad, and impossible to improve **–bly** *adv*
incorruptible *adj* **1** not subject to decay **2** too honest to be bribed or influenced by personal motives
increase *vi/t* (cause to) become larger ♦ *n* rise in amount, numbers, or degree **–singly** *adv* more and more
incredible *adj* **1** unbelievable **2** *infml* wonderful **–bly** *adv*
incredulous *adj* not believing **~ly** *adv* **–lity** *n* disbelief
increment *n* increase in money or value
incriminate *vt* cause (someone) to seem guilty of a crime or fault **–atory** *adj* **–ation** *n*
incubate *vt* keep (eggs) warm until they

hatch **–tor** *n* apparatus for keeping eggs warm, or for keeping premature babies alive **–tion** *n* **1** act of incubating **2** period between infection and the appearance of a disease

incubus *n* **-es** *or* **-i** **1** male spirit that has sex with a sleeper **2** oppressive influence

inculcate *vt* fix (ideas) in someone's mind

incumbent *adj* being a moral duty of ♦ *n* person holding a (political) office

incunabulum /ˌinkyooˈnabyooləm/ *n* **-a** early printed book

incur *vt* **-rr-** bring (esp. something bad) on oneself

incurable *adj* that cannot be cured **–bly** *adv*

incurious *adj fml* lacking curiosity; uninterested

incursion *n* sudden brief invasion

indaba *n SAfrE* gathering

indebted *adj* grateful **~ness** *n*

indecent *adj* **1** sexually offensive **2** unsuitable **~ly** *adv* **–ency** *n*

indecent assault *n* sexual attack which does not include rape

indecent exposure *n* deliberate exposure of usu. the genitals in public

indecipherable *adj* unable to be read or understood

indecision *n* inability to decide

indecorous /inˈdek(ə)rəs/ *adj fml* in bad taste **–orum** *n*

indeed *adv* **1** certainly; really **2** (used with **very** to make the meaning stronger): *It's very cold indeed.* **3** (showing surprise)

indefatigable *adj* tireless **–bly** *adv*

indefensible *adj* that cannot be defended

indefinable *adj* impossible to describe **–bly** *adv*

indefinite *adj* not clear or fixed **~ly** *adv* for an unlimited period

indefinite article *n* (in English) 'a' or 'an'

indelible *adj* that cannot be rubbed out **-bly** *adv*

indelicate *adj* not polite or modest **~ly** *adv* **–acy** *n*

indemnify *vt* pay (someone) in case of loss **–nity** *n* protection against loss; payment for loss

indent *vi/t* start (a line of writing) further into the page than the others **~ation** *n* **1** (act of making) a space at the beginning of a line of writing **2 a** dent or notch **b** recessed space

indentures *pl n* contract of employment or esp. apprenticeship **–ed** *adj*

independent *adj* **1** self-governing **2** not depending on advice, money, etc., from others ♦ *n* (*often cap.*) person who does not always favour the same political party **~ly** *adv* **–ence** *n*

in-depth *adj* very thorough

indescribable *adj* that cannot be described **–bly** *adv*

indestructible *adj* too strong to be destroyed

indeterminate *adj* not fixed as one thing or another

index *n* **-dexes** *or* **-dices** **1 a** alphabetical list of subjects mentioned in a book **b** also **card index** similar alphabetical list, e.g. of books and writers that can be found in a library, written on separate cards **2 a** sign by which something can be measured **b** ratio used for comparisons ♦ *vt* make, include in, or provide with an index

index finger *n* forefinger

index-linked *adj* rising and falling with the cost-of-living index

Indian *n, adj* **1** (inhabitant) of India **2** (member) of the original peoples of North, South, or Central America, except the Inuit

Indian club *n* bottle-shaped club used esp. in gymnastic exercises

Indian corn *n* maize

Indian summer *n* warm period in late autumn

India rubber *n* rubber[1]

indicate *v* **1** *vt* point at; show **2** *vt* be a sign of **3** *vi* show the direction in which one is turning in a vehicle by hand signals, lights, etc. **–ator** *n* **1** flashing light on a car that shows which way it will turn **2** needle or pointer showing

measurement **-ation** *n* sign or suggestion indicating something **-ative** *adj* showing
indices /ˈindiseez/ *pl of* index
indict *vt* charge officially with a crime **~able** *adj* for which one can be indicted **~ment** *n*
indifferent *adj* **1** not interested **2** not very good **~ly** *adv* **-ence** *n*
indigenous /inˈdij(ə)nəs/ *adj* native to a place: *indigenous plants*
indigent *adj lit* poor
indigestion *n* discomfort from not being able to digest food
indignant *adj* angry, esp. at something unjust **~ly** *adv* **-ation** *n* indignant feeling
indignity *n* humiliating treatment
indigo *n* dark blue (dye)
indirect *adj* **1** not straight; not directly connected **2** (of taxes) paid by increasing the cost of goods or services **3** allusive **~ly** *adv*
indirect object *n* person or thing that the direct object of a verb is given to, made for, done to, etc.
indirect speech *n* speech reported without repeating all the actual words
indiscreet *adj* not acting carefully or politely **~ly** *adv* **-cretion** *n* **1** being indiscreet **2** indiscreet act
indiscriminate *adj* not choosing or chosen carefully **~ly** *adv*
indispensable *adj* necessary
indisposed *adj fml* **1** not very well **2** unwilling **-sition** *n*
indisputable *adj* beyond doubt **-bly** *adv*
indistinguishable *adj* impossible to tell apart
indium *n* silvery metallic element
individual *adj* **1** single; separate **2** (of a way of doing things) particular to a person, thing, etc. ♦ *n* single person (in a group) **~ly** *adv* separately **~ism** *n* belief in the rights of each person in society **~ist** *n, adj* (person) independent and unlike other people **~istic** *adj* **~ity** *n* qualities that make a person different from others
indivisible *adj* not dividable
indoctrinate *vt* train to accept ideas without question **-ation** *n*
Indo-European *adj* of the language family including English, French, Russian, Hindi, etc.
indolent *adj fml* lazy **-ence** *n* **~ly** *adv*
indomitable *adj* too strong to be discouraged **-ly** *adv*
Indonesian *n, adj* (inhabitant or language) of Indonesia
indoor *adj* inside a building **indoors** *adv*
indubitable *adj fml* unquestionable **-bly** *adv*
induce *vt* **1** persuade **2** cause; produce **~ment** *n* (something, esp. money, which provides) encouragement to do something
induction *n* **1** act or ceremony of introducing a person to a new job, organization, etc. **2** (action of causing) birth of a child which has been hastened by the use of drugs **3** way of reasoning using known facts to produce general laws
indulge *v* **1** *vt* allow to do or have something nice **2** *vi* allow oneself pleasure: *indulge in a cigar* **-gence** *n* **1** habit or activity of indulging **2** something in which one indulges **-gent** *adj* (too) kind
industrial *adj* of or having industry **~ly** *adv* **~ism** *n* system in which industries are important **~ist** *n* owner or manager of an industry **~ize, ~ise** *vi/t* (cause to) become industrially developed
industrial action *n esp. BrE* action by workers to try to make their employers agree to their demands (e.g. a strike)
industrial estate *n BrE* area where factories are built
industrial relations *pl n* dealings between management and unions
industrial revolution *n* period of change from an economy based on agriculture to one based on manufacturing industry
industrious *adj* hard-working **~ly** *adv*

industry *n* **1** (branch of) the production of goods for sale **2** continual hard work
-ine *suffix* **1** of or concerning: *equine* **2** made of; like: *crystalline*
inebriated *adj fml* drunk
inedible *adj* unsuitable for eating
ineffable *adj fml* too great to be described **–bly** *adv*
ineffective *adj* unable to produce the right results **~ly** *adv* **~ness** *n*
ineffectual *adj* which does not give a good enough effect, or who is not able to get things done **~ly** *adv*
inefficient *adj* not working well **~ly** *adv* **–ency** *n*
inelegant *adj* not graceful or refined
ineligible *adj* not fulfilling the conditions **–bility** *n*
ineluctable *adj fml* inevitable
inept *adj* **1** foolishly unsuitable **2** totally unable to do things **~ly** *adv* **~itude** *n*
inequality *n* lack of fairness or equality
ineradicable *adj fml* not removable
inert *adj* **1** unable to move **2** not acting chemically: *inert gases*
inertia /iˈnuhshə/ *n* **1** force that keeps a thing in the same state until pushed **2** laziness
inertia reel *n* wound-up length esp. of seat belt in a car that unwinds freely except when jerked suddenly forward
inertia selling *n esp. BrE* sending of unrequested goods and then demanding payment
inescapable *adj* unavoidable
inessential *n, adj* (something) of little importance
inestimable *adj fml* too good to be measured **–bly** *adv*
inevitable *adj* **1** unavoidable **2** *infml* expected and familiar **–bly** *adv* **–bility** *n*
inexcusable *adj* unforgivable **–bly** *adv*
inexhaustible *adj* that cannot be used up
inexorable *adj fml* impossible to change or prevent **–bly** *adv*
inexperience *n* lack of experience **~d** *adj*
inexpert *adj* not skilful; clumsy
inexplicable *adj* too strange to be explained **–bly** *adv*
inexpressible *adj* too great to be expressed **–bly** *adv*
inextricable *adj fml* impossible to escape from, or to untie **–bly** *adv*
infallible *adj* **1** never making mistakes **2** always effective **–bility** *n*
infamous /ˈinfəməs/ *adj* wicked **–my** *n* wickedness
infancy *n* early childhood
infant *n* very young child
infanticide *n* (person who commits) the crime of killing a child
infantile *adj* childish
infantry *n* foot soldiers
infantryman *n* **-men** soldier in the infantry
infarction *n* death of an area of tissue (e.g. in the heart)
infatuated *adj* foolishly loving **–ation** *n*
infect *vt* **1** give disease to **2** cause something to spread rapidly to (others) **~ion** *n* (disease spread by) infecting **~ious** *adj* able to infect: *infectious laughter*
infer *vt* **-rr-** draw (meaning) from facts **~ence** *n*
inferior *adj* less good; low(er) in rank ♦ *n* inferior person **~ity** *n*
infernal *adj* terrible; like hell
inferno *n* **-os** place of very great heat and large uncontrollable flames
infertile *adj* not fertile **–ility** *n*
infest *vt* (of something bad) be present in large numbers in
infidel *n* person of another (esp. non-Muslim) religion
infidelity *n* **1** (act of) disloyalty **2** (act of) sex with someone other than one's marriage partner
infield *n* (fielders in) the area close to the wicket (in cricket) or enclosed by the bases (in baseball) **~er** *n*
infighting *n* disagreement between members of a group
infiltrate *vt* enter secretly, with an unfriendly purpose **–tion** *n*
infinite *adj* without limits; endless **~ly**

adv
infinitesimal *adj* minute
infinitive *n* verb form that can follow other verbs and be preceded by **to**
infinity *n* endless space or quantity
infirm *adj fml* weak in body or mind **~ity** *n*
infirmary *n* **1** hospital **2** room where sick people are given treatment
in flagrante delicto *adv* red-handed
inflame *vt* make violent **inflamed** *adj* red and swollen
inflammable *adj* **1** which can easily be set on fire and which burns quickly **2** easily excited or made angry
inflammation *n* inflamed condition
inflammatory *adj* likely to inflame: *inflammatory speeches*
inflatable *adj* able to be inflated ♦ *n* large inflatable object esp. for children to play on
inflate *v* **1** *vt* blow up (e.g. a tyre) **2** *vi/t* increase the supply of money in (a country's economy) **-d** *adj* too big
inflation *n* **1** inflating or being inflated **2** rise in prices caused by increased production costs or an increase in money supply **~ary** *adj* likely to cause price increases
inflection *n* **1** change in the form of a word to show difference in its use **2** movement up or down of the voice
inflexible *adj* impossible to bend or change **–bly** *adv* **–bility** *n*
inflict *vt* force (something unpleasant, e.g. punishment) on **~ion** *n*
in-flight *adj* done or provided while in flight
inflorescence *n* cluster of flowers
inflow *n* flowing in
influence *n* **1** (power to have) an effect **2** someone with this power: *She's a bad influence on you.* **3 under the influence** drunk ♦ *vt* have an influence on
influential *adj* having great influence
influenza *n fml* flu
influx *n* arrival in large numbers or quantities
info *n infml* information
inform *vt* give information to **inform against/on** *phr vt* tell the police that (someone) is guilty **~ant** *n* person who gives information **~ed** *adj* **1** knowing things **2** using suitable knowledge: *an informed guess* **~er** *n* person who tells the police about someone
informal *adj* not formal; without ceremony **~ly** *adv* **~ity** *n*
information *n* knowledge given; facts
information technology *n* science of collecting and using information by means of computer systems
informative *adj* telling one useful things
infraction *n fml* infringement
infrared *adj* of or being the heat-giving light rays of longer wave-length than the visible spectrum
infrastructure *n* underlying systems (e.g. of power, roads, laws, banks) needed to keep a country going
infrequent *adj* rare **~ly** *adv* **–nce** *n*
infringe *vt/i fml* go against (a law, or someone's rights) **~ment** *n*
infuriate *vt* make very angry
infuse *vt* **1** fill (someone) with a quality **2** put (e.g. tea) into hot water to make a drink **infusion** *n* (liquid made by) infusing
-ing *suffix* (makes present participles and verbal nouns): *sleeping*
ingenious *adj* clever at making or inventing **~ly** *adv* **–nuity** *n*
ingenue /ˌanzhayˈnooh/ *n* (role of a) naive young woman
ingenuous /inˈjenyoo·əs/ *adj* simple and inexperienced **~ly** *adv*
ingest *vt* take in (as if) as food
inglenook *n* fireside corner (seat)
inglorious *adj lit* shameful **~ly** *adv*
ingot *n* (brick-shaped) lump of metal
ingrained *adj* deeply fixed: *ingrained dirt/habits*
ingrate *n lit* ungrateful person
ingratiate *vt* make (oneself) pleasant, so as to gain favour **–ating** *adj* **–atingly** *adv*
ingratitude *n* ungratefulness
ingredient *n* one of a mixture of things, esp. in baking
ingress *n* act of entering; right of entry

in-group *n* group that treats members better than non-members

inhabit *vt* live in (a place) **~ant** *n* person living in a place

inhale *vi/t* breathe in **~r** *n* apparatus for inhaling medicine to make breathing easier **–lation** *n*

inherent *adj* necessarily present: *problems inherent in the system* **~ly** *adv*

inherit *vi/t* receive (property) from someone who has died **~ance** *n* **1** something inherited **2** inheriting **~or** *n*

inhibit *vt* prevent; hinder **~ion** *n* feeling of being unable to do what one really wants to

inhospitable *adj* **1** not welcoming **2** harsh and barren

in-house *adj* within a group or organization

inhuman *adj* cruel **~ity** *n*

inhumane *adj* unkind; not humane **~ly** *adv*

inimical *adj* hostile; harmful

inimitable *adj* too good to be copied **–bly** *adv*

iniquitous *adj* very unjust or wicked **~ly** *adv* **–ty** *n*

initial *adj* at the beginning ♦ *n* first letter of someone's name ♦ *vt* **-ll-** (*AmE* **-l-**) write one's initials on **~ly** *adv* at first

initiate *vt* **1** start (something) working **2** introduce (someone) into a group ♦ *n* person instructed or skilled in some special field **–ation** *n*

initiative *n* **1** ability to act without help or advice **2** first step: *take the initiative*

inject *vt* **1** put (esp. a drug) into someone with a needle **2** introduce; instil **~ion** *n*

injudicious *adj* indiscreet, unwise

injunction *n* official order

injure *vt* hurt; damage **~d** *adj*, *n* hurt (people) **injury** *n* **1** harm; damage **2** wound

injustice *n* (act of) unfairness

ink *n* coloured liquid for writing, printing, etc. **~y** *adj* black

inkling *n* slight idea

inkwell *n* container for ink

inlaid *adj* set ornamentally into another substance

inland *adj*, *adv* inside a country

Inland Revenue *n* (in Britain) office that collects taxes

in-laws *pl n* relatives by marriage

inlay *n* inlaid material

inlet *n* narrow piece of water reaching into the land

in loco parentis *adv* having the responsibilities of a parent

inmate *n* person living in a prison, hospital, etc.

in memoriam *prep* in memory of

inmost also **innermost** *adj* furthest inside; most well-hidden

inn *n* small pub or hotel, esp. one built many centuries ago

innards *pl n* inside parts, esp. of the stomach

innate *adj* (of a quality) present from birth **~ly** *adv*

inner *adj* **1** on the inside; close to the middle **2** secret, esp. if of the spirit: *inner meaning/life*

inner city *n* central (run-down) area of a city

inner tube *n* inflatable tube inside a tyre

inning *n* period of play in baseball

innings *n* **1** period when a cricket team or player bats **2** *BrE infml* time when one is active

innkeeper *n* manager of an inn

innocent *adj* **1** not guilty **2** harmless **3** unable to recognize evil; simple **~ly** *adv* **–ence** *n*

innocuous *adj* harmless **~ly** *adv*

innovation *n* **1** new idea **2** introducing new things **–vate** *vi* make changes **–vator** *n* **–vative, -vatory** *adj*

Inns of Court *pl n* London law societies to one of which an English barrister must belong

innuendo *n* **-oes** *or* **-os** unpleasant indirect remark(s)

innumerable *adj* too many to count

innumerate *adj BrE* unable to calculate with numbers **–acy** *n*

inoculate *vt* introduce a weak form of a disease into (someone) as a protection **–lation** *n*
inoffensive *adj* not causing dislike; not rude **~ly** *adv*
inoperable *adj* not curable by an operation
inoperative *adj* **1** (of a machine) not working **2** (of a law, rule, etc.) not taking effect
inopportune *adj fml* at the wrong time **~ly** *adv*
inordinate *adj fml* beyond reasonable limits **~ly** *adv*
inorganic *adj* **1** not composed of or concerned with living substances **2** not showing natural growth
in-patient *n* patient being treated inside a hospital
input *n* something put in for use, esp. information into a computer ♦ *vt* **-tt-**; *past t. and p.* **inputted** *or* **input** put (information) into a computer
inquest *n* official inquiry, esp. when someone dies unexpectedly
inquire *vi/t* ask for information (about) **inquire into** *phr vt* look for information about **–ring** *adj* that shows an interest in knowing **–ry** *n* **1** (act of) inquiring **2** investigation to find out why something happened
inquisition *n* thorough and esp. cruel inquiry **–sitor** *n* person who conducts an inquisition **–sitorial** *adj*
inquisitive *adj* asking too many questions **~ly** *adv*
inquorate *adj* not having a quorum present
inroads *pl n* **1** attack on or advance into a new area **2** effort or activity that lessens the quantity or difficulty of what remains afterwards
ins and outs *pl n* details (of a situation, problem, etc.)
insane *adj* mad **~ly** *adv* **–nity** *n*
insanitary *adj* dirty enough to cause disease
insatiable *adj* impossible to satisfy **–bly** *adv*
inscribe *vt fml* write (words) on **inscription** *n* piece of writing inscribed, esp. on stone
inscrutable *adj* mysterious **–bly** *adv*
insect *n* small creature with six legs
insecticide *n* substance used to kill insects
insectivore *n* insect-eating animal **–orous** *adj*
insecure *adj* **1** not safe **2** not sure of oneself **~ly** *adv* **–rity** *n*
insemination *n* putting of male sperm into a female
insensible *adj* **1** unconscious **2** lacking knowledge: *insensible of the danger* **–bility** *n*
insensitive *adj* not sensitive **~ly** *adv* **–vity** *n*
inseparable *adj* impossible to separate
insert *vt* put into something ♦ *n* written or printed material put in between pages of a book **~ion** *n*
in-service *adj* (taking place) during one's work
inset *n* picture, map, etc., in the corner of a larger one
inshore *adj, adv* at sea but near the shore
inside *n* **1** part nearest to the middle, or that faces away from the open air **2** also **insides** *pl. infml* one's stomach **3** **inside out: a** with the inside parts on the outside **b** thoroughly ♦ *adj* **1** facing or at the inside **2** from or involving someone closely concerned: *inside information* ♦ *adv* to or in the inside, esp. indoors ♦ *prep* **1** to or on the inside of **2** in less time than
insider *n* person accepted in a social group, esp. someone with special information or influence
insider dealing also **insider trading** *n* illegal share-dealing by people who use their knowledge of the business affairs of the companies they work for
inside track *n AmE* advantageous position in a competition
insidious *adj* gradually and secretly causing harm **~ly** *adv*
insight *n* (penetrative) understanding
insignia *pl n* objects worn as signs of

rank

insignificant *adj* not important **~ly** *adv* **–ance** *n*

insinuate *vt* **1** suggest (something unpleasant) indirectly **2** gain acceptance for (esp. oneself) stealthily or subtly **–tion** *n*

insipid *adj derog* lacking a strong character, taste, or effect

insist *vi/t* **1** order **2** declare firmly **~ent** *adj* repeatedly insisting **~ence** *n*

in situ *adv* in its original place

in so far as *conj* to the degree that

insolent *adj* disrespectful; rude **–ence** *n* **~ly** *adv*

insoluble *adj* **1** impossible to answer **2** impossible to dissolve

insolvent *n, adj* (someone) unable to pay their debts **–ency** *n*

insomnia *n* inability to sleep **~c** *n* someone who habitually cannot sleep

insouciance /inˈsoohsyəns/ *n* light-hearted unconcern **–ant** *adj*

inspect *vt* examine closely **~or** *n* **1** official who inspects something **2** police officer of middle rank **~ion** *n*

inspire *vt* **1** encourage to act **2** fill with a particular feeling **–ration** *n* **1** inspiring or being inspired **2** something that inspires **3** sudden good idea **~d** *adj* very clever

inst *BrE fml* of the current month: *your letter of the 12th inst*

instability *n* **1** unsteadiness **2** (of people) tendency to act unpredictably

install *vt* **1** put (esp. a machine) in place **2** settle (someone) in a position **~ation** *n* **1** installing **2** apparatus installed

instalment *n* **1** single part of a story that appears in regular parts **2** single regular payment

instance *n* **1** example (1) **2 for instance** for example ♦ *vt* give as an example

instant *n* moment of time ♦ *adj* happening or produced at once **~ly** *adv* at once

instantaneous *adj* happening at once **~ly** *adv*

instead *adv* **1** in place of that **2 instead of** in place of

instep *n* upper surface of the foot

instigate *vt fml* cause to happen or be done; initiate **–ator** *n* **–ation** *n*

instil *vt* **-ll-** put (ideas) into someone's mind

instinct *n* natural tendency to act in a certain way **~ive** *adj* **~ively** *adv*

institute *n* society formed for a special purpose ♦ *vt fml* start; establish

institution *n* **1** (building for) a hospital, school, etc., where people are looked after **2** established custom **3** act of instituting **~al** *adj* **~alize, ~alise** *vt* **1** make into an established custom **2** cause to become unable to live or work anywhere except in an institution

instruct *vt* **1** give orders to **2** teach **3** *law* inform officially **~ive** *adj* teaching something useful **~or** *n* teacher

instruction *n* **1** order **2** act of instructing; teaching **instructions** *pl n* advice on how to do something

instrument *n* **1** thing that helps in work **2** device for playing music **~al** *adj* **1** for musical instruments **2** helpful; causing: *information instrumental in catching the thief* **~alist** *n* player of a musical instrument **~ation** *n* **1** set of instruments e.g. for controlling a vehicle or machine **2** arrangement of a piece of music for different instruments

insubordinate *adj* disobedient **–ation** *n*

insubstantial *adj* not firm or solid

insufferable *adj* unbearable **–bly** *adv*

insufficient *adj* not enough **~ly** *adv* **–ency** *n*

insular *adj* **1** narrow-minded **2** of an island **~ity** *n*

insulate *vt* **1** cover, to prevent the escape of heat, electricity, etc. **2** protect from experiences **–ator** *n* **–ation** *n* (material for) insulating

insulin *n* hormone controlling blood-sugar levels

insult *vt* be rude to ♦ *n* rude remark or action

insuperable /inˈs(y)oohprəbl/ *adj* impossible to deal with

insupportable *adj* unbearable

insurance *n* **1** agreement to pay money in case of loss, damage, etc. **2** protection against something
insure *vt* protect by insurance
insurgent *n, adj* rebel **–ency** *n*
insurmountable *adj* too large, difficult, etc., to deal with
insurrection *n* rebellion
intact *adj* undamaged
intaglio /inˈtahlioh/ *n* **-os** design cut into a hard surface
intake *n* **1** amount or number taken in **2** pipe to let in gas, water, etc.
intangible *adj* **1** which cannot be perceived by the senses or described **2** which is hidden or not material, but known to be real: *intangible assets* **–bly** *adv* **–bility** *n*
integer *n* whole number
integral *adj* necessary to complete something; essential
integrate *vi/t* (cause to) mix with other people or ethnic groups **–ation** *n* **–ationist** *n* believer in integration
integrated circuit *n* set of electrical connections printed esp. on a computer chip
integrity *n* **1** honesty; trustworthiness **2** wholeness
integument *n* enclosing layer of skin, membrane, etc
intellect *n* ability to think **~ual** *adj* **1** of the intellect **2** clever and well-educated **~ual** *n* intellectual person **~ually** *adv*
intelligence *n* **1** ability to learn and understand **2** (people who gather) information about enemies **–ent** *adj* clever **–ently** *adv*
intelligentsia *pl n* intellectuals as a social group
intelligible *adj* understandable **–bly** *adv* **–bility** *n*
intemperate *adj* rash; unbridled
intend *vt* have as one's purpose; mean
intense *adj* strong (in quality or feeling) **~ly** *adv* **–sity** *n* quality or appearance of being intense
intensify *vi/t* make or become more intense **–fication** *n*
intensive *adj* giving a lot of attention **~ly** *adv*
intensive care *n* continuous hospital treatment for a seriously ill patient
intent *n* **1** purpose **2 to all intents and purposes** in almost every way ♦ *adj* **1** with fixed attention **2** determined
intention *n* plan; purpose **~al** *adj* done on purpose **~ally** *adv*
inter *vt* **-rr-** *fml* bury
inter- *prefix* between: *international*
interact *vi* have an effect on each other **~ion** *n*
interactive *adj* **1** that interacts **2** allowing the exchange of information between a computer and a user while a program is in operation
inter alia *adv fml* among other things
interbreed *vi/t* breed between closely related species or individuals
intercede *vi* speak in favour of someone
intercept *vt* stop (someone or something moving between two places) **~ion** *n*
intercession *n* **1** interceding **2** prayer which asks for other people to be helped
interchange *vi/t* exchange **~able** *adj* ♦ *n* **1** (act of) interchanging **2** system of smaller roads connecting main roads
intercity *adj* travelling fast between cities
intercom *n* indoor communication system with microphones and loudspeakers
interconnect *vi/t* connect with each other
intercontinental *adj* between continents
intercontinental ballistic missile *n* long-range ballistic missile with a nuclear warhead
intercourse *n* **1** sexual intercourse **2** *fml* conversation, meetings, etc., between people
interdependent *adj* depending on each other **~ly** *adv*
interdict *n* official order forbidding something ♦ *vt* prohibit officially
interest *n* **1** willingness to give attention **2** quality that makes people give attention **3** activity or subject that one likes to give time to **4** also **interests** *pl*

advantage: *in one's interests* **5** money paid for the use of money **6** share in a business ♦ *vt* cause to feel interest **~ed** *adj* **1** feeling interest **2** personally concerned or connected **~ing** *adj* having interest

interface *n* point where two systems meet and act on each other ♦ *vi/t* connect or be connected by means of an interface

interfere *vi* **1** enter into a matter that does not concern one and in which one is not wanted **2** prevent something from working properly **interfere with** *phr vt* **1** get in the way of **2** touch or move (something) in a way that is not allowed **3** annoy or touch sexually **-ference** *n* **1** interfering **2** noises, visual patterns, etc., that stop radio or television from working properly

interferon *n* protein which inhibits the action of a virus

intergalactic *adj* between the galaxies

interim *adj* done as part of something to follow later; provisional

interior *n* inside of something **interior** *adj*

interject *vi/t fml* make (a sudden remark) between others **~ion** *n* **1** word or phrase interjected, such as *'Good heavens!'* **2** interjecting

interlace *vi/t* join by twisting under and over each other

interlard *vt* intersperse, esp. with something irrelevant

interleave *vt* insert between pages or layers

interlock *vi/t* fasten or be fastened together

interlocutor /ˌintəˈlokyootə/ *n fml* person one is talking with

interloper *n* person found in a place, esp. among others, with no right to be there

interlude *n* period of time between two parts or activities

intermarry *vi* (of groups of people) become connected by marriage **-riage** *n*

intermediary *n* person who persuades opposing sides to agree

intermediate *adj* between two others; halfway

interment *n fml* burial

intermezzo /ˌintəˈmetsoh/ *n* **-zzi** *or* **-zzos** short piece of music coming between sections of an opera

interminable *adj* long and dull; (seeming) endless **-bly** *adv*

intermingle *vi/t* mix together with something else

intermission *n esp. AmE* interval (2)

intermittent *adj* not continuous **~ly** *adv*

intern[1] *vt* put in prison, esp. in wartime **~ment** *n*

intern[2] *n esp. AmE* person who has recently completed professional training, esp. in medicine, and is gaining practical experience, esp. in a hospital

internal *adj* **1** inside **2** not foreign; domestic **~ly** *adv* **~ize** *vt* make (values or attitudes) one's own as a result of learning or experience

internal-combustion engine *n* engine which produces its own heat to turn into energy

Internal Revenue *n* (in the US) government department that collects taxes

international *adj* between nations ♦ *n* **1** international sports match **2** person who plays for his or her country's team **~ly** *adv* **~ism** *n* principle that nations should work together

international date line *n* north-south line running through the Pacific to the west of which the date is one day earlier than it is to the east of it

internecine /ˌintəˈneesien/ *adj fml* (of fighting, disagreement, etc.) inside a group

interplay *n* interaction

Interpol *n* international police organization which assists national police forces

interpolate *vt fml* put in (words); interrupt **-ation** *n*

interpose *vt fml* put or say between things

interpret *v* **1** *vt* understand or explain the meaning of **2** *vi/t* turn (spoken

words) into another language **~er** *n* person who interprets between languages **~ation** *n* **1** explanation **2** performance of music, drama, etc., by someone giving their own idea of the composer's, writer's, etc., intentions
interracial *adj* between different races
interregnum *n* interval without government
interrelate *vi/t* (cause to) be mutually related **-ationship** *n*
interrogate *vt* **1** question formally, esp. for a long time and often with the use of threats or violence **2** (try to) get direct information from: *interrogate a computer* **-gation** *n* **-gative** *adj* asking a question
interrupt *vi/t* break the flow of (speech, thoughts, action, etc.) **~ion** *n*
intersect *vi/t* cut across: *intersecting paths* **~ion** *n* **1** intersecting **2** crossroads
intersperse *vt* put here and there among other things
interstate *adj* connecting, or happening between, different states, esp. in the US
interstice /in'tuhstis/ *n* small space or crack between things placed close together
intertwine *vi/t* twist together
interval *n* **1** time between events **2** *BrE* time between the parts of a play, concert, etc. **3** distance between things
intervene *vi* **1** interrupt so as to stop something **2** (of time) happen between events **-vention** *n*
interview *n* meeting at which someone is asked questions ♦ *vt* ask (someone) questions in an interview **~ee** *n* person who is (to be) interviewed, esp. for a job **~er** *n* person who interviews
intestate *adj law* not having made a will
intestine also **-ines** *pl n* bowels **-inal** *adj*
intimacy *n* **1** state of being intimate **2** remark or action of a kind that happens only between people who know each other very well **3** the act of sex
intimate[1] *adj* **1** having a close relationship: *intimate friends* **2** private: *her intimate thoughts* **3** resulting from close study: *intimate knowledge* **~ly** *adv*
intimate[2] *vt fml* make known, esp. indirectly; suggest **-ation** *n*
intimidate *vt* frighten by threats **-ation** *n* **-atory** *adj*
into *prep* **1** so as to be in **2** against: *bump into a tree* **4** (used when dividing): *7 into 11 won't go.*
intolerable *adj* unbearable **-bly** *adv*
intolerant *adj* not tolerant **-ance** *n*
intonation *n* rise and fall of the voice in speech
intone *vi/t* say (e.g. a prayer) in a level voice
in toto *adv* as a whole; entirely
intoxicate *vt* **1** make drunk **2** overwhelm with excitement; elate **-ation** *n*
intra- *prefix* **1** within: *intrauterine* **2** into: *intravenous*
intractable *adj* difficult to control or deal with **-bly** *adv*
intransigent *adj* refusing to change; stubborn **-gence** *n*
intransitive *adj* (of a verb) having a subject but no object
intrauterine device *n* IUD
intravenous *adj* into a vein **~ly** *adv*
intrepid *adj* fearless **~ly** *adv*
intricacy *n* **1** being intricate **2** something intricate
intricate *adj* having many details; complicated **~ly** *adv*
intrigue *v* **1** *vt* interest greatly **2** *vi* make plots ♦ *n* **1** act or practice of secret planning **2** plot **-guing** *adj* very interesting, esp. because of some strange quality; fascinating
intrinsic *adj* belonging to the essential nature of something; inherent **~ally** *adv*
intro *n* **intros** *infml* **1** introduction to a person **2** introductory speech **3** introductory section of a piece of music
intro- *prefix* into; inwards: *introvert*
introduce *vt* **1** make (people) known to each other **2** bring or put in **-duction** *n* **1** act of introducing **2** occasion of telling people each other's names **3** ex-

planation at the beginning of a book, lecture, etc. **4** simple book about a subject **–ductory** *adj* happening or said at the beginning, explaining what is to come

introit *n* hymn or anthem, sung at the beginning of a church service

introspection *n* thinking about one's own thoughts and feelings **–ive** *adj*

introvert *n* quiet introspective person **~ed** *adj*

intrude *vi* come in when not wanted **~r** *n* person who intrudes, esp. intending to steal **–usive** *adj* intruding **–usion** *n*

intuit *vt* apprehend by intuition

intuition *n* **1** power of knowing something without reasoning or learned skill **2** something known in this way **–tive** *adj* **–tively** *adv*

Inuit *n* member of a people living in the icy far north of N America; Eskimo

inundate *vt* **1** flood **2** overwhelm **–ation** *n*

inured *adj* accustomed (by long experience)

invade *vt* **1** attack and take control of (a country) **2** crowd into **~r** *n* **–asion** *n*

invalid *adj* not valid ♦ *n* person weakened by illness **invalid out** *phr vt* allow to leave the armed forces because of ill-health **~ate** *vt* make invalid **~ation** *n*

invaluable *adj* too valuable for the worth to be measured

invariable *adj* unchanging **–bly** *adv* always

invective *n fml* angry abusive language

inveigh against /in'vay/ *phr vt fml* attack bitterly in words

inveigle into /in'vaygl/ *phr vt* trick (someone) into (doing something)

invent *vt* **1** produce for the first time **2** think up (something untrue, e.g. an excuse) **~ive** *adj* clever at inventing **~or** *n* **~ion** *n* **1** inventing **2** something invented

inventory *n* list, esp. one of all the goods in a place

inverse *n, adj* opposite

invert *vt* turn upside down **–ersion** *n*

invertebrate *n* animal without a backbone

inverted comma *n BrE* quotation mark

inverted snob *n* person who asserts the social superiority of the lower classes

invest *vt* **1** use (money) to make more money **2** *lit* surround; besiege **invest in** *phr vt* buy **invest with** *phr vt fml* give officially to; confer on **~ment** *n* **1** investing **2** (something bought with) money invested **~or** *n*

investigate *vi/t* inquire carefully (about) **–ator** *n* **–ative** *adj* **–ation** *n*

investiture *n* ceremony of investing someone with rank

inveterate *adj* fixed in a bad habit

invidious *adj* tending to cause ill-will or make people unnecessarily offended or jealous

invigilate *vi/t BrE* watch over (students in an examination) **–ator** *n*

invigorate *vt* give a feeling of energy and liveliness to

invincible *adj* too strong to be defeated **–bly** *adv*

inviolable *adj* impossible to violate

inviolate *adj fml* not violated

invisible *adj* that cannot be seen **–bly** *adv* **–bility** *n*

invite *vt* **1** ask to come **2** ask politely for: *invite questions* **–iting** *adj* attractive **–itingly** *adv* **–itation** *n* **1** request to come **2** act of inviting **3** encouragement to an action

in vitro *adj* (done) outside a living body, in a piece of scientific equipment

invocation *n fml* **1** invoking **2** prayer for help

invoice *vt, n* (send) a bill for goods received

invoke *vt fml* **1** call to (God, the law) for help **2** beg for **3** cause to appear by magic

involuntary *adj* done without intention **–rily** *adv*

involuted *adj* **1** coiled in upon itself **2** very complex and intricate

involve *vt* **1** have as a necessary result

2 cause to become connected or associated **–d** *adj* **1** complicated **2** (of a person) having a (sexual) relationship (with) **~ment** *n*

invulnerable *adj* that cannot be harmed

inward *adj, adv* **1** on or towards the inside **2** of the mind or spirit **~ly** *adv* **~s** *adv*

iodine *n* chemical used to prevent infection in wounds

ion *n* atom with an electrical charge **~izer, ~iser** *n* machine that produces negative ions, believed to make the air more healthy

ionosphere *n* part of the atmosphere which is used in helping to send radio waves around the Earth

iota *n* very small amount

IOU *n* 'I owe you'; signed piece of paper saying one owes money

IPA *abbrev. for:* International Phonetic Alphabet; a system of signs representing the sounds made in speech

ipso facto *adv fml* (proved) by the fact itself

IQ *n* intelligence quotient; measure of intelligence

ir- *prefix* (before *r*) not: *irregular*

IRA *n* Irish Republican Army; illegal organization whose aim is to unite Northern Ireland and the Republic of Ireland

Iranian *n, adj* (inhabitant) of Iran

Iraqi *n, adj* (inhabitant) of Iraq

irascible /iˈrasibl/ *adj fml* easily angered; quick-tempered

irate *adj* angry **~ly** *adv*

ire *n lit* anger

iridescent /iriˈdes(ə)nt/ *adj* changing colour as light falls on it **–ence** *n*

iris *n* **1** tall yellow or purple flower **2** coloured part of the eye

Irish *adj* of Ireland

Irish coffee *n* coffee with whiskey and cream

Irish stew *n* stew of meat, potatoes, and onions

irk *vt* annoy **~some** *adj* annoying

iron *n* **1** common hard metal used in making steel **2** heavy heated metal implement for making cloth smooth **3 have several irons in the fire** have various different interests, activities, or plans at the same time ♦ *adj* very firm: *iron will* ♦ *vt* make smooth with an iron **iron out** *phr vt* remove (difficulties, misunderstandings, etc.) **irons** *pl n* chains for a prisoner

Iron Age *n* time in the history of mankind when iron was used for tools

Iron Curtain *n* border between western Europe and the Communist countries

iron-grey *adj* dark grey

ironic, ironical *adj* expressing irony **~ally** *adv*

ironing board *n* narrow table for ironing clothes on

iron lung *n* machine fitted over the body which helps one breathe in and out

ironmonger *n BrE* person who sells hardware

iron pyrites *n* pale yellow mineral

iron rations *pl n* emergency food rations

irony *n* **1** intentional use of words which are opposite to one's real meaning, in order to be amusing or show annoyance **2** event or situation which is the opposite of what one expected

irradiate *vt* **1** treat with X-rays or similar radiation **2** treat (food) with X-rays to kill bacteria and make it last longer **–ation** *n*

irrational *adj* not reasonable **~ly** *adv*

irreconcilable *adj* impossible to bring into agreement **–bly** *adv*

irrecoverable *adj* that cannot be recovered or retrieved **–bly** *adv*

irredeemable *adj* **1** irrecoverable **2** hopeless

irrefutable /ˌiriˈfyoohtəbl/ *adj fml* too strong to be disproved

irregular *adj* **1** uneven **2** *fml* against the usual rules **3** not following the usual pattern **~ly** *adv* **~ity** *n*

irrelevant *adj* not relevant **–ance** *n*

irreligious *adj* hostile or indifferent to religion

irreparable *adj* too bad to be put right **–bly** *adv*

irreplaceable *adj* too special for any-

thing else to replace it
irrepressible *adj* impossible to repress –**ibility** *n* –**bly** *adv*
irreproachable *adj* faultless –**bly** *adv*
irresistible *adj* so attractive, powerful, etc., that one cannot resist it –**bly** *adv*
irresolute *adj* unable to make decisions ~**ly** *adv*
irrespective *adv* **irrespective of** without regard to
irresponsible *adj* not trustworthy; careless –**bly** *adv* –**bility** *n*
irretrievable *adj* impossible to get back or put right –**bly** *adv*
irreverent *adj* not respectful, esp. of holy things ~**ly** *adv* –**ence** *n*
irreversible *adj* impossible to reverse –**ibly** *adv*
irrevocable /iˈrevəkəbl/ *adj* unchangeable once made or started –**bly** *adv*
irrigate *vt* supply water to (land) –**ation** *n*
irritable *adj* easily annoyed –**bly** *adv* –**bility** *n*
irritate *vt* **1** annoy **2** make sore –**ation** *n* –**tant** *n* something that irritates
irruption *n fml* violent rush or bursting into something
is *3rd person sing. present tense of* be
ISBN *abbrev. for:* International Standard Book Number
-ise *suffix* -ize
-ish *suffix* **1** of a particular country: *Swedish* **2** typical of: *girlish* **3** rather: *reddish*
isinglass *n* gelatin made from the air bladders of fish, esp. sturgeons
Islam *n* (people and countries that practise) the Muslim religion ~ **ic** *adj*
island *n* **1** piece of land surrounded by water **2** raised place where people can wait in the middle of a road for traffic to pass ~**er** *n* person living on an island
isle *n lit* island
-ism *suffix* **1** set of beliefs **2** quality: *heroism*
isn't *short for:* is not
isobar *n* line joining points of equal atmospheric pressure
isolate *vt* keep separate from others ~**d** *adj* single, without others: *an isolated case* –**ation** *n*
isomer *n* chemical compound, group, etc. with the same number of atoms but in a different arrangement
isosceles triangle *n* triangle with two equal sides
isotherm *n* line joining points of equal temperature
isotope *n* atom of an element with the same number of protons in its nuclei but a different number of neutrons
Israeli *n, adj* (inhabitant) of Israel
Israelite *n, adj* (member) of the ancient tribes or kingdom of Israel
issue *n* **1** subject to be talked or argued about **2** particular number of a magazine **3** *law* children ♦ *vt* produce or provide officially
-ist *suffix* **1** player, operator, etc.: *pianist* **2** (follower) of a set of beliefs 3 discriminating: *ageist*
isthmus *n* narrow piece of land joining two larger pieces
it *pron* **1** that thing already mentioned **2** (used in statements about weather, time, or distance): *It's raining.* ♦ *n infml* a very important person: *He thinks he's it.*
IT *n* information technology
Italian *n, adj* (inhabitant) of Italy
italics *pl n* sloping printed letters –**cize, -cise** *vt* print in italics
itch *vi* **1** have the feeling of wanting to scratch the skin **2 be itching to/for** want very much ♦ *n* **1** itching feeling **2** strong desire ~**y** *adj*
itchy feet *pl n infml* desire to travel
itchy palm *n infml* great desire for money, esp. as payment for unfair favours
it'd *short for:* **1** it would **2** it had
-ite *suffix* -ist (2)
item *n* **1** single thing on a list, agenda, etc. **2** piece of news ~**ize,** ~**ise** *vt* make a detailed list of
iterate *vt fml* say or do again –**ation** *n*
itinerant *adj* travelling from place to place
itinerary *n* plan for a journey
-itis *suffix med* disease or inflammation

of: *bronchitis*
it'll *short for:* it will
its *determiner* of it
it's *short for:* **1** it is **2** it has
itself *pron* (*reflexive or strong form of* it)
itsy-bitsy *adj infml* tiny
-itude *suffix* (in nouns) the state or degree of being: *exactitude*
-ity *suffix* -ness: *stupidity*
IUD *n* plastic or metal object fitted inside a woman's womb as a form of contraception
-ive *suffix* tending to: *supportive*
I've *short for:* I have
ivory *n* **1** hard white substance of which elephants' tusks are made **2** creamy white colour of this
ivory tower *n* place where people avoid the difficult realities of ordinary life
ivy *n* climbing plant with shiny leaves
Ivy League *adj AmE* belonging to or typical of a group of old and respected universities of the eastern US
-ize *suffix* make or become: *modernize*

J

J, j the 10th letter of the English alphabet
jab *vi/t* **-bb-** push forcefully, esp. with something pointed ♦ *n* **1** sharp forceful push **2** *infml, esp. BrE* injection
jabber *vi/t* talk or say quickly and often unintelligibly **jabber** *n*
jack *n* **1** apparatus for lifting a car **2** playing card between the 10 and the queen **jack in** *phr vt BrE sl* stop; be unwilling to continue **jack up** *phr vt* lift with a jack
jackal *n* kind of wild dog
jackass *n* **1** *infml* stupid person **2** male ass
jackboot *n* **1** high military boot **2** cruel military rule
jackdaw *n* bird of the crow family
jacket *n* **1** short coat with sleeves **2** potato skin **3** cover for a machine, pipe, etc. **4** loose paper cover for a book
jackhammer *n AmE* pneumatic drill
jack-in-the-box *n* box from which a toy figure springs out
jack knife *n* large pocket knife, the blade of which folds into the handle
jack-knife *vi* (of an articulated vehicle) bend suddenly in the middle
jack-of-all-trades *n* versatile person
jackpot *n* biggest money prize to be won in a game
Jacobean *adj* of the time when James I was king of England (1603-25)
Jacobite *adj, n* (of or being) a supporter of James II and his descendants in their claim to the English throne
Jacuzzi /jəˈkoohzi/ *n tdmk* bath fitted with a system of hot water currents
jade[1] *n* (colour of) a green precious stone
jade[2] *n arch.* **1** worn-out old horse **2** disreputable woman
jaded *adj* tired because of having had too much of something, esp. experience
jagged *adj* with a rough uneven edge
jaguar *n* large spotted wild cat of S America
jail *n* prison ♦ *vt* put in jail **~er** *n* person in charge of prisoners
jailbird *n* person who is, or has been, in prison
jalopy *n infml* dilapidated old car
jam[1] *n* fruit boiled in sugar, for spreading on bread
jam[2] *v* **-mm-** **1** *vt* crush or press tightly **2** *vi* get stuck: *The door jammed.* **3** *vt* block (radio messages) ♦ *n* **1** closely jammed mass **2** difficult situation
jamb *n* door- or window-post
jamboree *n* large party or gathering
jammy *adj BrE infml* **1** (undeservedly) lucky **2** easy
jam-packed *adj* with many people or things very close together
jam session *n* impromptu jazz session
jangle *vi/t* (cause to) make the noise of

metal striking metal
janitor *n* caretaker
January *n* the 1st month of the year
Japanese *adj* of Japan
jape *n* prank
japonica *n* bush with red or white flowers
jar[1] *n* short wide pot or bottle
jar[2] *vi/t* **-rr-** **1** *vi* make an unpleasant sound **2** *vt* give an unpleasant shock to **3** *vi* go badly together: *jarring colours*
jardinière *n* ornamental pot or trough for plants
jargon *n* language used by a particular group
jasmine *n* climbing shrub with fragrant flowers
jasper *n* red, yellow, brown or green semi-precious stone
jaundice *n* disease that makes the skin yellow **~d** *adj* mistrustful and cynical
jaunt *n* short pleasure trip **~y** *adj* cheerful and confident
javelin *n* light spear for throwing
jaw *n* one of the two bony structures where the teeth are fixed ♦ *vi infml* talk for a long time **jaws** *pl n* **1** animal's mouth **2** two parts of a tool that hold things tightly
jawbreaker *n infml* word that is hard to pronounce
jay *n* fawn bird of the crow family
jaywalk *vi* cross streets carelessly
jazz *n* music with a strong beat, originated by black Americans **jazz up** *phr vt* make brighter or more interesting **~y** *adj* brightly coloured
JCB *tdmk for* earth-moving and excavating machine
jealous *adj* **1** unhappy at not being liked as much as someone else: *jealous husband* **2** very envious **3** wanting to keep what one has **~ly** *adv*
jealousy *n* jealous feeling
jeans *pl n* strong cotton trousers
jeep *n* (military) car for travelling on rough ground
jeer *vi/t* laugh rudely (at) **jeer** *n* **~ingly** *adv*
Jehovah *n* God (in the Old Testament)
Jehovah's Witness *n* member of a fundamentalist Christian sect that believes the end of the world is coming soon
jejune /ji'joohn/ *adj* dull; unsatisfying
jejunum *n* middle section of the small intestine
jell *vi AmE* gel
jello *n AmE* jelly (1)
jelly *n* **1** soft semisolid food made with gelatine, or from fruit juice boiled with sugar **2** any material between a liquid and a solid state
jellyfish *n* sea animal with a soft saucer-shaped body
jemmy *n* short crowbar used by burglars
jeopardize, -ise /'jepədiez/ *vt* put in danger
jeopardy *n* danger
jerboa *n* jumping rodent with long hind legs
jeremiad *n lit* long dismal complaint
jerk[1] *n* sudden quick pull or movement ♦ *vi/t* pull or move with a jerk **~y** *adj* not smooth in movement
jerk[2] *n sl* foolish and ungraceful person
jerkin *n* short sleeveless coat
jeroboam *n* very large wine bottle
jerry-built *adj* built cheaply and badly
jersey *n* sweater
jest *vi, n fml* joke **~er** *n* man kept formerly to amuse a ruler
Jesuit *n* member of a Roman Catholic missionary and teaching order (the **Society of Jesus**) **jesuitical** *adj* clever, esp. in intrigue or persuasion
jet[1] *n* **1** narrow stream of gas or liquid forced out of a hole **2** aircraft whose engine (**jet engine**) works on this principle ♦ *vi* **-tt-** **1** come in a jet of gas or liquid **2** travel by jet plane
jet[2] *n* hard shiny black mineral
jetfoil *n* hydrofoil
jet lag *n* tiredness after flying to a place where the time is different
jet set *n* international social group of rich fashionable people
jet stream *n* current of strong winds high in the atmosphere

jettison *vt* throw away or out
jetty *n* small pier
Jew *n* member of a people who lived in Israel in ancient times, and have established the modern state of Israel
jewel *n* **1** precious stone **2** very valuable person or thing **~ler,** *AmE* **~er** *n* person who sells jewellery **~lery,** *AmE* **~ry** *n* jewels worn as decoration
Jew's harp *n* musical instrument held between the teeth and struck with one finger
jib *n* long arm of a crane from which the hook hangs down **jib at** *phr vt* be unwilling to do; balk at
jibe *n, v* gibe
jiffy *n infml* moment
Jiffy bag *tdmk for* padded envelope
jig *n* (music for) a quick merry dance ♦ *vi* jump up and down
jiggery-pokery *n BrE infml* underhand dealings
jiggle *vi/t* shake from side to side
jigsaw also **jigsaw puzzle** *n* picture cut into pieces to be fitted together for fun
jihad *n* Islamic holy war
jilt *vt* unexpectedly refuse (an accepted lover)
jingle *n* **1** sound as of small bells ringing **2** simple poem used esp. for advertisement ♦ *vi/t* (cause to) sound with a jingle
jingoism *n derog* extreme warlike nationalism
jink *n* move with elusive twists and turns
jinx *vi* something that brings bad luck
jitterbug *vi, n* (do) a fast active dance of the 1940s
jitters *pl n* anxiety before an event **-ery** *adj*
jive *n* (dance performed to) a kind of popular music with a strong beat ♦ *vi* dance to jive music
Jnr *abbrev. for:* Junior
job *n* **1** regular paid employment **2** piece of work **3** *sl* crime, esp. a robbery **4** something hard to do: *You'll have a job to open it.* **5 just the job** exactly the thing wanted or needed **~ber** *n* member of the Stock Exchange who does not deal directly with the public **~bing** *adj* paid by the job **~less** *adj* unemployed
job centre *n* office where people can find work
job lot *n* group of things of different kinds bought or sold together
Job's comforter *n* person whose attempts to cheer someone up have the opposite effect
jobsharing *n* dividing a full-time job between two people
jock *n AmE infml* athlete
jockey *n* professional rider in horse races ♦ *vi/t* try by all possible means to get into a good position
jockstrap *n* support for the genitals worn by sportsmen
jocose *adj fml* humorous
jocular *adj* joking; not serious **~ly** *adv* **~ity** *n*
jocund *adj lit* merry
jodhpurs *pl n* trousers for horse riding
joey *n AustrE* young kangaroo
jog *v* **-gg- 1** *vt* knock slightly **2** *vi* run slowly for exercise **3 jog someone's memory** make someone remember **jog along** *phr vi* move slowly and uneventfully **jog** *n* **~ger** *n* someone who jogs
john *n AmE infml* lavatory
John Bull *n lit* England; the English
John Doe *n AmE* unidentified person or corpse
johnny *n BrE* **1** *infml* man **2** *sl* condom
join *v* **1** *vt* fasten; connect **2** *vi/t* come together (with); meet: *join me for a drink* **3** *vt* become a member of **join in** *phr vi* take part in an activity **join up** *phr vi* offer oneself for military service ♦ *n* place where two things are joined
joiner *n* maker of doors, window frames, and other wooden fittings for buildings **~y** *n* trade of a joiner
joint *n* **1** place where things (esp. bones) join **2** *BrE* large piece of meat **3** *sl* bar, nightclub, etc. **4** *sl* cigarette containing cannabis ♦ *adj* shared **~ly** *adv*
joist *n* beam supporting a floor
jojoba /hə'hohbə/ *n* American shrub

with seeds that give a liquid wax

joke *n* something said or done to amuse people ♦ *vi* tell jokes **~r** *n* **1** person who makes jokes **2** additional playing card with no fixed value

jolly *adj* happy; pleasant ♦ *adv infml* very: *jolly difficult* **jolly along** *phr vt* encourage in a joking or friendly way

Jolly Roger *n* pirate flag with a skull and crossed bones on it

jolt *vi/t* shake or shock **jolt** *n*

Jonah *n* person who seems to bring bad luck

Joneses *n* **keep up with the Joneses** *derog* compete with one's neighbours socially, esp. by buying the same expensive new things that they buy

josh *vt esp. AmE infml*, tease; make gentle fun of

joss stick *n* stick of incense

jostle *vi/t* knock or push (against)

jot *n* slightest amount ♦ *vt* **-tt-** write quickly **~ter** *n* notebook **~ting** *n* rough note

joule *n* unit of energy or work

journal *n* **1** magazine **2** diary **~ism** *n* profession of writing for newspapers **~ist** *n* person whose profession is journalism

journalese *n derog* language of newspapers

journey *n* long trip, esp. by land ♦ *vi lit* travel

journeyman *n* **-men 1** trained workman esp. one paid by the day **2** competent but not outstanding practitioner

joust *vi* fight in a tournament

jovial *adj* friendly and cheerful **~ly** *adv* **~ity** *n*

jowl *n* lower part of the face

joy *n* **1** great happiness **2** something that causes joy **3** *BrE infml* success **~ful** *adj* full of or causing joy **~fully** *adv* **~ous** *adj lit* joyful

joyride *n* ride for pleasure in a (stolen) car

joystick *n* upright lever used to control an aircraft in flight or when playing computer games

JP *n* Justice of the Peace; magistrate

Jr *abbrev. for:* Junior

jubilant *adj* delighted, esp. because of success; exultant **-ation** *n* rejoicing **~ly** *adv*

jubilee *n* time of rejoicing at an anniversary

Judaism *n* religion of the Jews

Judas *n* traitor

judder *vi BrE* (of a vehicle) shake violently

judge *n* **1** public official who decides legal cases **2** person who decides in a competition **3** person who can give a valuable opinion: *I'm no judge of music.* ♦ *vi/t* act as a judge (in); form an opinion (about)

judgment, judgement *n* **1** ability to decide correctly **2** opinion **3** decision of a judge or court of law

judgment day *n* day when God will judge everyone

judicature *n* administration of justice

judicial *adj* of law courts and judges **~ly** *adv*

judiciary /jooh'dishəri/ *n* all the judges, as a group

judicious /jooh'dishəs/ *adj* sensible; discerning **~ly** *adv*

judo *n* type of self-defence, from Asia

jug *n esp. BrE* pot for liquids, with a handle and a lip for pouring

juggernaut *n BrE* very large lorry

juggle *vi/t* **1** keep (objects) in the air by throwing and catching them **2** play tricks (with), esp. to deceive: *juggling the figures* **~r** *n*

jugular vein *n* vein at the side of the neck

juice *n* liquid from fruit, vegetables, or meat **juicy** *adj* **1** having a lot of juice **2** *infml* interesting esp. because providing details about scandal

jujitsu *n* Japanese art of wrestling and self-defence

juju *n* (power associated with) a W African idol

jujube *n* small jelly-like sweet or throat lozenge

jukebox *n* coin-operated music machine

julep *n* sweetened alcoholic American

drink usu. flavoured with mint

July *n* the 7th month of the year

jumble *vi/t* mix in disorder ♦ *n* **1** disorderly mixture **2** *BrE* things for a jumble sale

jumble sale *n BrE* sale of used articles, esp. to get money for charity

jumbo *adj* very large

jumbuck *n AustrE* sheep

jump *v* **1** *vi* push oneself off the ground with one's leg muscles **2** *vt* cross in this way: *jump a stream* **3** *vi* move suddenly: *The noise made me jump.* **4** *vi* rise sharply: *Oil prices have jumped.* **5** *vt* attack suddenly **6** *vt* leave, pass or escape from (something) illegally **7 jump the gun** start something too soon **8 jump the queue** get something before those who have waited longer **jump at** *phr vt* accept eagerly ♦ *n* **1** act of jumping **2** thing to jump over **3 one jump ahead** in a position of advantage through anticipating one's competitors **~y** *adj* nervously excited

jumped-up *adj* having too great an idea of one's own importance

jumper *n* **1** *BrE* sweater **2** horse or person that jumps

jumping-off point *n* starting point

jumpsuit *n* a one-piece garment combining top and trousers

junction *n* place of joining

juncture *n fml* point in time

June *n* the 6th month of the year

jungle *n* thick tropical forest

junior *n, adj* **1** (someone) younger **2** (someone) of low or lower rank

Junior *adj esp. AmE* the younger (of two men in the same family with the same name)

junior school *n BrE* school for children between 7 and 11 years old

juniper *n* evergreen shrub of the cypress family

junk[1] *n* **1** old useless things **2** *sl* dangerous drug, esp. heroin ♦ *vt infml* get rid of as worthless

junk[2] *n* flat-bottomed Oriental boat with squarish sails

junket *n* **1** *infml, often derog* trip, esp. one made by a government official and paid for with government money **2** kind of thick sweet milk

junk food *n infml* unhealthy food

junkie, -y *n sl* person who takes heroin

junk mail *n* mail, usu. for advertising, sent to people although they have not asked for it

junta /ˈjuntə, ˈhoontə/ *n* (military) government that has seized power by armed force

Jupiter *n* the largest planet, 5th in order from the sun

jurisdiction *n* legal power

jurisprudence *n* science or philosophy of law

jurist *n* legal expert

juror *n* member of a jury

jury *n* **1** group of people chosen to decide questions of fact in a court of law **2** group of people chosen to judge a competition of any kind

just *adv* **1** exactly: *sitting just here* **2** completely: *It's just perfect!* **3** at this moment: *I'm just coming.* **4** only a short time (ago): *just after breakfast* **5** almost not *just in time* **6** only **7 just now: a** at this moment **b** a moment ago ♦ *adj* fair; according to what is deserved **~ly** *adv*

justice *n* **1** quality of being just; fairness **2** the law: *court of justice* **3** judge (1)

Justice of the Peace *n* magistrate

justify *vt* give or be a good reason for **–iable** *adj* **–iably** *adv* **–ication** *n* good reason

jut *vi* **-tt-** stick out or up further than the things around it

jute *n* plant fibre used for sacking or twine

juvenile *n* **1** young person **2** actor or actress who plays such a person ♦ *adj* **1** of or for juveniles **2** childish or foolish

juvenile delinquency *n* crimes by juveniles **–nt** *n*

juxtapose *vt* put side by side **–osition** *n*

K

K, k the 11th letter of the English alphabet

K *abbrev. for:* **1** 1024 bytes of computer data **2** *infml* one thousand

kaffir *n SAfrE offensive* black African

kaftan *n* caftan

Kalashnikov *n* Soviet automatic rifle

kale, kail *n* type of cabbage with curly leaves

kaleidoscope *n* tube containing mirrors, and often bits of coloured glass, turned to produce changing patterns **-opic** *adj* changing quickly and often

kamikaze *n* Japanese suicide pilot in World War 2

kangaroo *n* Australian animal that jumps along on its large back legs, and carries its young in a pocket

kangaroo court *n* unofficial court at which someone is given an unfair 'trial'

kaolin *n* fine white clay used in medicine

kapok *n* cotton-like material used to fill sleeping bags, mattresses, etc.

kaput *adj infml* completely destroyed or broken

karat *n* carat

karate *n* Asian style of fighting using the hands and feet

karma *n* force generated by a person's actions, which in Hindu and Buddhist belief affects their next reincarnation

kaross *n SAfrE* blanket made of animal skins

kayak *n* light covered canoe

K.C. *n* (title, while a king is ruling, for) a British lawyer of high rank

kebab *n* small pieces of meat cooked on a stick

kedge *n* small anchor

kedgeree *n* dish of rice, fish, and eggs

keel *n* beam along the bottom of a boat **keel over** *phr vi* fall over sideways

keelhaul *vt* drag under a ship's keel as a punishment

keen *adj* **1** having a strong interest: *keen on football* **2** (of the five senses) good, strong, quick, etc.: *keen eyesight* **3** (of edges) sharp; cutting **~ly** *adv* **~ness** *n*

keep *v* **kept 1** *vt* continue to have; not lose or give back **2** *vi/t* (cause to) continue being: *keep them warm|Keep off the grass!* **3** *vi* continually do something: *He keeps complaining.* **4** *vt* fulfil (a promise) **5** *vt* prevent **6** *vt* not tell (a secret) **7** *vt* make records of or in: *keep a diary* **8** *vt* own or manage: *keep chickens/a shop* **9** *vi* remain fresh **10 keep (oneself) to oneself** not mix with or talk to other people very much **11 keep one's head** remain calm **12 keep someone company** remain with someone **keep at** *phr vt* continue working at (something) **keep back** *phr vt* not tell or give; withhold **keep down** *phr vt* **1** prevent from increasing **2** oppress **keep from** *phr vt* **1** not tell (someone) about (something) **2** prevent oneself from (doing something) **keep in with** *phr vt* remain friendly with **keep on** *phr v* **1** *vi* continue **2** *vi* continue talking **3** *vt* continue to employ (someone) **keep on at** *phr vt* ask repeatedly **keep to** *phr vt* **1** limit oneself to **2** keep (something) private to (oneself) **keep up** *phr v* **1** *vi* stay level **2** *vt* continue doing ♦ *n* **1** (cost of) what is necessary for daily living, esp. food **2** central tower of a castle **3 for keeps** *infml* for ever

keeper *n* person who guards or looks after

keeping *n* **1** care; charge: *left in my keeping* **2 in/out of keeping with** suitable/not suitable for

keepsake *n* thing kept to remind one of the giver

keg *n* small barrel

kelp *n* large brown seaweed
kelvin *n* unit of temperature defined by the **Kelvin scale**
ken *n* **beyond one's ken** outside one's knowledge
kennel *n* house for a dog **kennels** *n* place where dogs are bred or looked after
kept *past t. and p. of* keep
keratin *n* protein forming nails, claws, hoofs, etc.
kerb *n BrE* stone edge of a pavement
kerb crawler *n* man who drives slowly looking for a prostitute
kerchief *n* piece of cloth worn as a head covering or scarf
kerfuffle *n BrE infml* fuss
kernel *n* **1** centre of a nut, seed, etc. **2** important part of a subject
kerosene *n AmE* paraffin
kestrel *n* red-brown European bird of prey
ketch *n* two-masted sailing vessel
ketchup *n* thick liquid made from tomato juice
kettle *n* pot with a spout, for boiling water
kettledrum *n* large metal drum
key *n* **1** shaped piece of metal for locking things **2** something that explains or helps one to understand **3** any of the parts of a piano, typewriter, etc., to be pressed to produce the desired sound or effect **4** musical notes starting at a particular base note: *the key of C* ♦ *adj* very important; necessary: *key industries* ♦ *vt* **1** make suitable: *factories keyed to military needs* **2** keyboard **3 keyed up** excited and nervous
keyboard *n* **1** row of keys on a typewriter, piano, etc. **2** electronic musical instrument with a keyboard which produces a wide variety of sounds ♦ *vt* put (information) into a machine by working a keyboard
keyhole *n* hole for a key
keynote *n* central idea (e.g. of a speech)
key signature *n* sharps and flats which indicate which key a piece is played in
keystone *n* **1** stone at the top of an arch **2** something on which others depend
kg *abbrev. for:* kilogram(s)
khaki /ˈkahki/ *n* **1** yellowish-brown colour **2** cloth of this colour, esp. as worn by soldiers
khan *n* medieval Asiatic ruler
khedive /kiˈdeev/ *n* ruler of Egypt 1867-1914
kibbutz *n* **-zim** *or* **-zes** farm or settlement in Israel where many families live and work together
kibosh *n* **put the kibosh on** prevent; put an end to
kick *v* **1** *vt* hit with the foot **2** *vi* move the feet as if to kick **3** *vi* (of a gun) move violently when fired **4** *vt sl* stop or give up (a harmful activity) **5 kick the bucket** *sl* die **kick off** *phr vi* begin **kick out** *phr vt* remove or dismiss (someone), esp. violently **kick up** *phr vt* make (trouble) ♦ *n* **1** act of kicking **2** *sl* excitement: *drive fast for kicks* **3** *infml* strength
kickback *n infml* money received in return for favours
kickoff *n* first kick in football
kick-start *vt* start (a motorcycle) by pressing down on a pedal
kid¹ *n* **1** child or young person **2** (leather from) a young goat
kid² *vi/t* **-dd-** *sl* pretend; deceive
kid gloves *pl n* gentle methods of dealing with people
kidnap *vt* **-pp-** take (someone) away by force, so as to demand money **~per** *n*
kidney *n* organ that separates waste liquid from the blood
kidney machine *n* hospital machine that can do the work of human kidneys
kill *vt* **1** cause to die **2 kill time** make time pass quickly **3 kill two birds with one stone** get two good results from one action ♦ *n* **1** bird or animal killed **2** act or moment of killing **~er** *n* **~ing** *n* **1** murder **2 make a killing** make a lot of money suddenly
killer whale *n* small black and white carnivorous whale
killjoy *n* person who spoils other people's pleasure
kiln *n* apparatus for baking pots, bricks,

etc., or for drying
kilo *n* **-os** kilogram
kilo- *prefix* thousand
kilobyte *n* 1000 or 1024 bytes of computer information
kilogram, -gramme *n* (measure of weight equal to) 2.2 pounds
kilometre, *AmE* **-ter** *n* (measure of length equal to) 0.62 of a mile
kilowatt *n* 1000 watts
kilt *n* short skirt worn esp. by Scotsmen
kilter *n* **out of kilter** not in working order
kimono *n* **-os 1** long loose Japanese garment **2** loose dressing gown
kin *pl n* closest relative(s)
kind[1] *n* **1** type; sort **2 a kind of** an unclear or unusual sort of: *a kind of feeling* **3 in kind** (of payment) in goods, not money **4 kind of** *infml* in a certain way; rather
kind[2] *adj* helpful and friendly **~ness** *n* **1** quality of being kind **2** kind act
kindergarten *n* school for young children, usu. between the ages of four and six
kind-hearted *adj* having a kind nature **~ly** *adv* **~ness** *n*
kindle *vt/i* (cause to) start burning **-ling** *n* materials for starting a fire
kindly *adv* **1** in a kind way **2** (showing annoyance) please **3 take kindly to** accept willingly ◆ *adj* kind
kindred *adj* **1** related **2 kindred spirit** person with almost the same habits, interests, etc.
kine *pl n arch.* cattle
kinetic *adj fml* of or about movement
king *n* **1** (title of) the male ruler of a country **2** most important man or animal **3** playing card with a picture of a king
kingdom *n* **1** country governed by a king or queen **2** any of the three divisions of natural objects: *the animal kingdom*
kingfisher *n* fish-eating river bird
kingmaker *n* person with great influence on the appointment of people to high office
kingpin *n* most important person in a group
kingpost *n* main upright beam supporting the ridge of a roof
king-size *adj* above the standard size
kink *n* **1** twist in hair, a pipe, etc. **2** strangeness of character **~y** *adj* sexually unnatural
kinsman *n* **-men** relative
kinswoman *n* **-men** female relative
kiosk *n* **1** small open hut for selling newspapers, cigarettes, etc. **2** *BrE* public telephone box
kip *n, vi* **-pp-** *BrE sl* sleep
kipper *n* smoked salted herring
kirk *n* **1** Scottish church **2** (*usu. cap.*) the Church of Scotland
kirsch *n* cherry-flavoured liqueur
kismet *n* fate
kiss *vi/t* touch with the lips as a sign of love or a greeting **kiss** *n* act of kissing
kiss of death *n infml* something that makes failure certain
kiss of life *n esp. BrE* method of preventing death of a person by breathing into his/her mouth
kit *n* **1** necessary clothes, tools, etc.: *a sailor's/carpenter's kit* **2** set of pieces to be put together: *model aircraft kit* **kit out/up** *phr vt* **-tt-** supply with necessary clothes and equipment
kit bag *n* bag for carrying a soldier's or sailor's kit
kitchen *n* room for cooking in
kitchenette *n* very small kitchen
kitchen garden *n* vegetable garden
kitchen-sink drama *n* serious drama depicting working-class domestic life realistically
kite *n* **1** frame covered with paper or cloth, for flying in the air **2** kind of hawk
Kite mark *n* mark of approval of the British Standards Institution
kith and kin *pl n* one's friends and relatives
kitsch *n* objects, works of literature, etc. which pretend to be art but are considered silly, funny, or worthless
kitten *n* young cat
kitty *n* money collected by several

people for an agreed purpose
kiwi *n* **1** flightless New Zealand bird **2** *infml* New Zealander
kiwi fruit *n* oval green-fleshed fruit
klaxon *n* powerful electric horn
Kleenex *n tdmk* paper handkerchief
kleptomania *n* compulsive desire to steal **–ac** *n* person with kleptomania
klutz *n AmE sl* idiot
km *abbrev. for:* kilometre(s)
knack *n infml* special skill
knacker *n* person who slaughters old horses
knackered *adj BrE sl* very tired
knackers *pl n BrE sl* testicles
knapsack *n* bag carried on the back
knave *n* **1** jack (2) **2** *arch.* dishonest man
knead *vt* mix (dough) by pressing with the hands **2** press and rub (muscles) to cure pain, stiffness, etc.
knee *n* **1** middle joint of the leg **2** part of a pair of trousers that covers the knee **3 bring someone to his knees** defeat someone completely ♦ *vt* hit with the knee
kneecap *n* bone at the front of the knee ♦ *vt* **-pp-** shoot the kneecaps of (someone), usu. as an unofficial punishment
knee-deep *adj* **1** deep enough to reach the knees **2** deeply occupied or troubled
knee-high *adj* reaching up to one's knees
knee-jerk *adj derog* (of opinion) held without thought
kneel *vi* **knelt** *or* (*esp. AmE*) **kneeled** go down on one's knees
knees-up *n BrE infml* boisterous party with dancing
knell *n* sound of a bell rung slowly for a death
knew *past t. of* know
knickerbockers *pl n* short trousers fitting tightly below the knees
knickers *pl n BrE* women's underpants
knick-knack *n* small decorative object
knife *n* **knives** blade with a handle, for cutting ♦ *vt* wound with a knife
knife-edge *n* **1** something sharp and narrow **2 on a knife-edge** in an extremely uncertain position
knight *n* **1** (in former times) noble soldier **2** man who has been given the British title 'Sir' **3** piece in chess **~hood** *n* rank of a knight ♦ *vt* make (someone) a knight
knit *vi/t* **knitted** *or* **knit 1** make (esp. clothes) by forming a network of threads with long needles **(knitting needles) 2** join closely; grow together **~ting** *n* something being knitted
knitwear *n* knitted clothing
knives *pl of* knife
knob *n* **1** round handle or control button **2** round lump
knobbly, *AmE* **knobby** *adj* protruding and lumpy
knobkerrie *n* native African club
knock *v* **1** *vi/t* hit **2** *vt infml* criticize **3** *vi* (of a car engine) make a noise like hitting **knock about/around** *phr v* **1** *vi/t* be present or active (in) **2** *vt* treat roughly **knock back** *phr vt* drink quickly **knock down** *phr vt* reduce (a price) **knock off** *phr v* **1** *vi/t* stop (work) **2** *vt* take from a total payment **3** *vt sl* steal **4** *vt* finish quickly **5** *vt sl* murder **knock out** *phr vt* **1** make unconscious by hitting **2** (of a drug) make (someone) go to sleep **3** eliminate from a competition **4** *sl* fill with great admiration **knock up** *phr v* **1** *vt BrE* make quickly **2** *vt BrE* awaken by knocking **3** *vt AmE sl* make pregnant **4** *vi BrE* practise before beginning a real game ♦ *n* **1** blow **2** sound of knocking **3** *infml* piece of bad luck
knockdown *adj* (of a price) the lowest possible
knocker *n* **1** instrument fixed to a door, for knocking **2** *derog* person who criticizes
knock-kneed *adj* with knees that touch when walking
knock-on *adj* marked by a set of events, actions, etc., each of which is caused by the one before
knockout *n* **1** act of knocking a boxer unconscious **2** competition from which

losers are eliminated **3** *infml* person or thing causing admiration ♦ *adj infml* wonderful

knoll *n* small round hill

knot *n* **1** fastening made by tying rope, string, etc. **2** hard lump in wood **3** small group of people **4** a measure of the speed of a ship, about 1853 metres per hour ♦ *vt* **-tt- 1** make a knot in; join with a knot **2 Get knotted!** *BrE sl* (expresses great annoyance at a person) **~ty** *adj* **1** (of wood) with knots **2** difficult: *knotty problem*

know *v* **knew, known 1** *vi/t* have (information) in the mind **2** *vt* have learnt **3** *vt* be familiar with: *Do you know Paris well?* **4** *vt* be able to recognize: *You'll know him by his red hair.* **know apart** *phr vt* be able to tell the difference between **know backwards** *phr vt* know or understand perfectly **know of** *phr vt* have heard of or about ♦ *n* **in the know** well-informed

know-all *n* person who behaves as if he/she knows everything

know-how *n* practical ability

knowing *adj* having secret understanding **~ly** *adv* **1** in a knowing way **2** intentionally

knowledge *n* **1** understanding **2** learning **3** information about something **4 to the best of one's knowledge** so far as one knows

knowledgeable *adj* well-informed

known *past p. of* know ♦ *adj* **1** publicly recognized: *known criminals* **2 known as: a** generally recognized as **b** also publicly called

knuckle *n* finger joint **knuckle down** *phr vi* start working hard **knuckle under** *phr vi* be forced to submit

knuckle-duster *n* piece of metal fitting round the fist, used as a weapon

knurled *adj* ridged to give a better grip

KO *n* **KOs** *infml* knockout (1)

koala *n* small Australian animal like a bear

kohl *n* black cosmetic powder used esp. by Asian women to darken the eyelids

kohlrabi *n* cabbage with an enlarged edible stem

kookaburra *n* large Australian kingfisher

kooky *adj AmE infml* eccentric

kopeck *n* money unit of the USSR

kopje, kopple *n SAfrE* small hill

Koran *n* the holy book of the Muslims

Korean *n, adj* (inhabitant) of Korea

kosher *adj* **1** (of food) prepared according to Jewish law **2** *infml* honest and trustworthy

kowtow /ˈkowˌtow/ *vi* obey without question

kraal *n SAfrE* **1** African village with a fence **2** fenced cattle pen

kraut *n sl offensive* German

Kremlin *n* (buildings containing) the government of the Soviet Union

krill *n* minute shrimplike animals, eaten by whales

Krugerrand *n* S African gold coin

krypton *n* colourless gas used in fluorescent lighting

Kt *abbrev. for:* knight

kudos /ˈk(y)oohdos/ *n* prestige

kulak *n* rich peasant in Russia

kumquat *n* small orange

kung fu *n* Chinese style of fighting, like karate

kw *abbrev. for:* kilowatt(s)

kwashiorkor *n* tropical disease of children resulting from protein deficiency

kyrie *n* (musical setting of) a short prayer beginning 'Lord have mercy'

L

L, l the 12th letter of the English alphabet

l *abbrev. for:* **1** litre(s) **2** line **3** (*often cap.*) lake

laager *n* fortified encampment in Africa

lab *n* laboratory
Lab *abbrev. for:* Labour Party
label *n* piece of paper, card, etc.,fixed to something to say what it is, who owns it, etc. ♦ *vt* **-ll-** (*AmE* **-l-**) **1** fix a label on **2** describe as, esp. unjustly
labial *adj* of the lips
laboratory *n* building or room where a scientist works
laborious *adj* needing great effort **~ly** *adv*
labour, *AmE* **labor** *n* **1** hard work **2** workers as a group **3** act of giving birth ♦ *adj* (*cap.*) of the Labour Party ♦ *v* **1** *vi* work hard **2** *vt* treat in too great detail: *labour the point* **labour under** *phr vt* suffer from: *labour under a delusion* **~er** *n* man who does heavy unskilled work **~ed** *adj* needing or showing much effort
labour-intensive *adj* needing a lot of workers
Labour Party *n* political party in favour of social improvement for esp. workers and less wealthy people
laboursaving *adj* reducing the amount of (manual) work required
labrador *n* large dog for retrieving shot game
laburnum *n* tree with bright yellow flowers
labyrinth /ˈlabərinth/ *n* maze
lace *n* **1** netlike decorative cloth **2** cord for fastening shoes, clothes, etc. ♦ *vt* **1** fasten with a lace **2** make (a drink) stronger by adding alcohol **lacy** *adj* like lace
lacerate *vt fml* cut; wound **–ation** *n*
lachrymal /ˈlakriməl/ *adj* of tears
lachrymose /ˈlakrimohs/ *adj fml* **1** in the habit of weeping **2** tending to cause weeping
lack *vt* be without (enough of) ♦ *n* absence; need **~ing** *adj* **1** missing **2 be lacking in** without the usual or needed amount of
lackadaisical *adj* without enough effort; careless
lackey *n derog* person who obeys without question
lacklustre, *AmE* **-ter** *adj* lifeless; dull
laconic *adj fml* using few words **~ally** *adv*
lacquer *n* transparent substance that makes a hard shiny surface, or keeps hair in place ♦ *vt* cover with lacquer
lacrosse *n* field game for two teams, using sticks with nets at the end
lactation *n* secretion of milk
lactic *adj* of or obtained from milk
lactose *n* sugary substance present in milk
lacuna *n* **-nae** *or* **-nas** *fml* gap, esp. in written matter or knowledge
lad *n* **1** boy; youth **2** *infml* playfully rude man **lads** *pl n BrE infml* group of men one knows and likes
ladder *n* **1** bars joined to each other by steps, for climbing **2** *BrE* ladder-shaped fault in a stocking, tights, etc. ♦ *vi/t* (of tights, etc.) develop a ladder (in)
laden *adj* heavily loaded
la-di-da, lah-di-dah *adj BrE infml* affectedly refined
ladies *n* women's lavatory
ladle *n* large spoon for serving liquids ♦ *vt* serve with a ladle **ladle out** *phr vt* give out freely
lady *n* **1** woman **2** woman of good manners or high social rank **3** (*cap.*) (title for) a woman of noble rank **~like** *adj* (of a woman) behaving like a lady with good manners or high social rank **~ship** *n* (title for) a woman called 'Lady'
ladybird *n* small beetle with red and black wing cases
lady-in-waiting *n* **ladies-in-waiting** lady attendant to a queen or princess
lady-killer *n infml* man who (thinks he) is irresistibly attractive to women
lag[1] *vi* **-gg-** move too slowly: *lag behind the others*
lag[2] *vt* **-gg-** cover (water pipes, tanks, etc.) to prevent loss of heat
lager *n* light kind of beer
lager lout *n* beer-swilling hooligan
laggard *n* one who lags behind
lagoon *n* lake of sea water, (partly) separated from the sea

laid *past t. and p. of* lay[2]
laid-back *adj infml* cheerfully informal and unworried
lain *past p. of* lie[2]
lair *n* home of a wild animal
laird *n* Scottish landowner
laissez-faire *n* non-interference
laity /ˈlayəti/ *pl n* people who are not priests
lake *n* large mass of water surrounded by land
lama *n* Tibetan Buddhist monk
lamb *n* **1** young sheep **2** its meat **3** harmless gentle person ♦ *vi* give birth to lambs
lambaste, lambast *vt infml* beat or attack fiercely
lambent *adj lit* softly flickering
lame *adj* **1** unable to walk properly **2** (of an excuse) weak; unconvincing ♦ *vt* make lame **~ly** *adv* **~ness** *n*
lamé *n* fabric with shiny metallic threads
lame duck *n* **1** weak and ineffective person or business **2** *esp. AmE* political official whose period in office will soon end
lament *vi/t* express grief or sorrow (for) ♦ *n* song, poem, etc., expressing sorrow **~able** *adj* **1** unsatisfactory **2** worthy of blame **~ation** *n fml*
laminated *adj* made by joining thin sheets of a material
lamp *n* **1** apparatus for giving light **2** apparatus for producing health-giving sorts of heat
lampoon *n* written attack that makes someone look foolish **lampoon** *vt*
lamppost *n* post supporting a street lamp
lampshade *n* cover for a lamp
lance *n* long spearlike weapon ♦ *vt* cut open with a lancet
lance corporal *n* soldier just above a private in rank
lancet *n* doctor's knife for cutting flesh
land *n* **1** solid dry part of the Earth's surface **2** country; nation ♦ *v* **1** *vi/t* come or bring to land **2** *vi* succeed in getting: *land the top job* **land in** *phr vt* bring (someone) into (an undesirable state or position) **land up** *phr vi* reach the stated (often undesirable) state or position; end up **land with** *phr vt* give (someone) (something unwanted) **~ed** *adj* owning a lot of land
landau *n* four-wheeled horsedrawn carriage
landfall *n* first sight of, or arrival on, land during a sea voyage
landing *n* **1** level space at the top of a set of stairs **2** arrival on land from air or sea
landing craft *n* flat boat for landing soldiers and their vehicles on shore
landing gear *n* wheels and undercarriage of an aircraft
landing stage *n* platform for landing passengers or cargo
landlady *n* **1** woman **a** who runs a small hotel **b** from whom one rents a room **2** female landlord
landlocked *adj* surrounded by dry land
landlord *n* **1** person from whom one rents land or buildings **2** man who owns or runs a pub
landlubber *n infml* person unused to the sea
landmark *n* **1** recognizable object from which one can tell one's position **2** important event, discovery, etc.
landmine *n* bomb hidden usu. just below the ground
landscape *n* (picture of) country scenery ♦ *vt* make (land) into a garden
landscape gardening *n* art of arranging the layout of a garden or grounds for picturesque effect
landslide *n* **1** sudden fall of earth and rocks **2** great success in an election
lane *n* **1** narrow road **2** division of a wide road, to keep fast and slow vehicles apart **3** path used regularly by ships or aircraft **4** path marked for each competitor in a race
language *n* **1** system of human expression by means of words **2** particular system as used by a people or nation: *the English language*
language laboratory *n* room where

foreign languages are taught using audiovisual aids, e.g. tape recorders
languid *adj* lacking energy; listless **~ly** *adv*
languish *vi fml* **1** experience long suffering **2** become weak
languor /ˈlaŋ·gə/ *n* **1** tiredness of mind or body **2** pleasant or heavy stillness
lank *adj* (of hair) straight and limp
lanky *adj* ungracefully tall and thin
lanolin *n* fatty wax that coats wool
lantern *n* container round the flame of a candle or other light
lantern-jawed *adj* having a long, hollow-looking face
lanyard *n* **1** rope fastening on board ship **2** cord attached to a whistle, knife, etc.
lap[1] *n* front of a seated person between the waist and the knees
lap[2] *v* **-pp- 1** *vt* drink as a cat does **2** *vi* (of water) move with soft sounds **lap** *n*
lap[3] *n* single journey round a race track ♦ *v* **-pp- 1** *vt* pass (another racer) so as to be one lap ahead **2** *vi* race completely round the track
laparoscopy *n* medical examination inside the abdomen through a thin tube
lap dog *n* **1** small docile dog **2** *derog* subservient person
lapel *n* part of the front of a coat that is joined to the collar and folded back
lapidary *adj fml* elegantly precise
lapis lazuli *n* blue semiprecious stones
Lapp *n* member of a nomadic N Scandinavian people
lapse *n* **1** small fault or mistake **2** failure in correct behaviour, belief, etc. **3** passing away of time ♦ *vi* **1** sink gradually; subside: *lapse into silence* **2** (of time) pass **3** (of business agreements, treaties, etc.) come to an end **~d** *adj* **1** no longer practising, esp. one's religion **2** *law* no longer in use
laptop *n* small portable personal computer
lapwing *n* small bird with a raised crest
larceny *n law* (an act of) stealing
lard *n* pig's fat used in cooking ♦ *vt* embellish (one's speech or writing) with striking phrases
larder *n* storeroom or cupboard for food
large *adj* **1** big **2 at large: a** free **b** as a whole: *the country at large* **~ly** *adv* mostly
largesse *n* money given generously
largo *n, adj, adv* (piece of music) played at a very slow broad tempo
lariat *n esp. AmE* lasso
lark[1] *n* small bird that sings in flight
lark[2] *n* bit of fun; joke **lark about/around** *phr vi* play rather boisterously
larrikin *n AustrE* hooligan
larva *n* **-vae** wormlike young of an insect
laryngitis /ˌlarin·jietəs/ *n* painful swelling of the larynx
larynx *n* part of the windpipe in the throat, where voice is produced by the vocal cords
lasagna, -gne *n* pasta in broad flat ribbons
lascar *n* East Indian sailor
lascivious /ləˈsi·vi·əs/ *adj* causing, showing or feeling uncontrolled sexual desire **~ly** *adv*
laser *n* apparatus producing a strong narrow beam of light
lash *v* **1** *vi/t* whip **2** *vi/t* move about violently **3** *vt* tie firmly **lash out** *phr vi* **1** attack violently **2** spend money extravagantly ♦ *n* **1** (a hit with) the thin striking part of a whip **2** eyelash
lashings *pl n esp. BrE* plenty; lots
lass *n* girl
lassitude *n fml* tiredness
lasso *n* **-s** looped rope for catching horses and cattle ♦ *vt* catch with a lasso
last[1] *determiner, adv* **1** after the others **2** only remaining: *my last £5* **3** most recent(ly): *When did we last meet?* **4** least suitable or likely **5 have the last laugh** be proved right after being ridiculed **6 on one's/its last legs: a** very tired **b** nearly worn out or dead ♦ *n, pron* **1** person or thing after all others **2** the one or ones before the present one **3 at (long) last** in the end **~ly** *adv* in the end
last[2] *v* **1** *vi* continue **2** *vi/t* be enough

(for) **~ing** *adj* continuing for a long time
last³ *n* block shaped like a human foot used in making and repairing shoes
last-ditch *adj* done as one last effort before accepting defeat
last post *n BrE* bugle call played esp. at military funerals
last rites *pl n* (esp. in the Roman Catholic church) ceremonies and prayers for those near death
last straw *n* problem or circumstance that makes the total unbearable when it is added to one's previous difficulties
Last Supper *n* meal shared by Jesus and his disciples on the evening before his crucifixion
last word *n* **1** remark that ends an argument **2** most modern example of something
latch *n* **1** small bar for fastening a door, gate, window, etc. **2** spring lock for a house door which can be opened from outside with a key **latch on** *phr vi* understand **latch onto** *phr vt* **1** understand **2** refuse to leave (someone)
latchkey *n* key to an outside (esp. front) door
latchkey child *n* **-children** child whose parents are usu. out (working) when he/she returns from school
late *adj, adv* **1** after the usual time **2** near the end: *in late September* **3** recently dead **4** recent: *the latest fashions* **5 of late** lately **~ly** *adv* not long ago
lateen *adj* (of rigging) having a triangular sail hung on a short mast and long spar
latent *adj* existing but not yet noticeable or developed **–ency** *n*
lateral *adj* of, from, or to the side **~ly** *adv*
lateral thinking *n* making of unusual connections in the mind to find a new and clever answer to a problem
latex *n* liquid from which natural rubber is made
lath *n* strip of wood to which tiles or plaster are fixed
lathe *n* machine that turns a piece of wood or metal to be shaped
lather *n* **1** froth made with soap and water **2 in a lather** *infml* worried ♦ *v* **1** *vi* make a lather **2** *vt* cover with lather
Latin *adj, n* (of) the language of the ancient Romans
Latin American *adj* of the Spanish- or Portuguese-speaking countries of Central and S America
latitude *n* **1** distance north or south of the equator, measured in degrees **2** freedom of choice **latitudes** *pl n* area at a particular latitude
latitudinarian *adj* marked by a liberal and tolerant attitude esp. in religious matters
latrine *n* outdoor toilet in a camp, barracks, etc.
latter *adj* of a later period ♦ *n fml* second of two things mentioned **~ly** *adv* recently
latter-day *adj* modern
lattice *n* wooden or metal frame used as a fence, screen, etc.
laud *vt lit* praise **~able** *adj* deserving praise **~ably** *adv* **~atory** *adj* praising
laudanum *n* solution of opium in alcohol
laugh *vi* **1** express amusement, happiness, etc., by breathing out forcefully so that one makes sounds with the voice, usu. while smiling **2 no laughing matter** serious ♦ *n* **1** act or sound of laughing **2** something done for a joke **~able** *adj* foolish **~ably** *adv*
laughing-stock *n* someone or something regarded as foolish
laughter *n* laughing
launch *vt* **1** send (a newly-built boat) into the water **2** send (a rocket, missile, etc.) into the sky **3** begin (an activity): *launch an attack/a company* **launch into** *phr vt* begin with vigour, enthusiasm, etc. **launch out** *phr vi* begin something new ♦ *n* **1** act of launching **2** large motorboat **~er** *n*
launching pad *n* base from which spacecraft, missiles, etc., are launched
launder *vt* **1** wash and iron (clothes) **2**

give (money obtained illegally) the appearance of being legal
launderette *n* place where members of the public pay to wash their clothes in machines
laundry *n* **1** place where clothes are laundered **2** clothes (needing to be) laundered
laureate *n* **1** poet laureate **2** winner of a very high award
laurel *n* evergreen bush with shiny leaves **laurels** *n* honour gained for something done
lava *n* molten rock that flows from a volcano
lavatory *n* toilet
lave *vt lit* wash; flow around
lavender *n* (pale purple colour of) a plant with strong-smelling flowers
lavish *adj* **1** generous **2** given or produced in (too) great quantity ♦ *vt* give freely or extravagantly **~ly** *adv*
law *n* **1** rule(s) made by a government **2** statement of what always happens in certain conditions: *the laws of physics* **3 be a law unto oneself** do exactly what one wishes **~ful** *adj* allowed or recognized by law **~fully** *adv* **~less** *adj* not governed by laws **~lessness** *n*
law-abiding *adj* obeying the law
lawman *n* **-men** *AmE* law-enforcing official
lawn *n* area of closely cut grass
lawnmower *n* machine for mowing a lawn
lawn tennis *n* tennis played on a grass court
lawsuit *n* non-criminal case in a law court
lawyer *n* person whose profession is the law
lax *adj* careless and uncontrolled **~ity** *n*
laxative *n, adj* (medicine) helping the bowels to empty
lay[1] *past t. of* lie[2]
lay[2] *v* **laid 1** *vt* **a** put, esp. carefully, in a flat position: *lay one's coat on the bed* **b** set in proper order or position: *lay bricks* **2** *vt* arrange for use: *lay the table for dinner* **3** *vt* cause to settle or disappear: *lay his fears to rest* **4** *vi/t* (of a bird, insect, etc.) produce (eggs) **5** *vt* make (a statement, claim, charge, etc.) formally or officially **6 lay hold of** catch and hold firmly **7 lay waste** destroy completely **lay down** *phr vt* **1** state firmly: *lay down the law* **2** give up (one's life) **lay in** *phr vt* get and store a supply of **lay into** *phr vt* attack physically or verbally **lay low** *phr vt* **1** knock down **2** make ill **lay off** *phr vt* **1** stop employing **2** give up **lay on** *phr vt* **1** provide: *lay on lunch* **2 lay it on** exaggerate **lay out** *phr vt* **1** arrange or plan **2** knock (someone) down **3** spend (money) **lay up** *phr vt* **1** keep in bed with an illness **2** collect and store for future use
lay[3] *adj* **1** of or by people who are not priests **2** not professional
lay[4] *n* ballad
layabout *n* lazy person
lay-by *n* **-bys** *BrE* space next to a road where vehicles may park
layer *n* **1** thickness of some substance laid over a surface **2** bird that lays eggs
layette *n* clothing and equipment for a baby
lay figure *n* jointed model of the human body used by artists
layman *n* **-men 1** person who is not a priest **2** person who is not a professional
lay-off *n* stopping of a worker's employment
layout *n* (planned) arrangement
lay reader *n* lay person empowered to conduct certain (parts of) religious services
lazar *n lit* leper
laze *vi* rest lazily
lazy *adj* **1** avoiding work **2** spent in inactivity **–zily** *adv* **–ziness** *n*
lazybones *n* lazy person
lb *abbrev. for:* pound[1] (1)
lbw *abbrev. for:* leg before wicket
LCD *n* liquid crystal display: device on which figures are shown by passing an electric current through a special liquid

LCM *abbrev. for:* lowest common multiple

L-driver *n BrE* person learning to drive

lea *n lit* meadow

leach *vi* pass out or through by percolation

lead[1] *v* **led 1** *vi/t* guide, esp. by going first **2** *vi* (of a road, path, etc.) go in the stated direction **3** *vt* influence: *What led you to do it?* **4** *vt* control or govern **5** *vi/t* be ahead (of) in sports **6** *vt* experience (a kind of life) **lead on** *phr vt* influence (someone) to do something wrong or believe something untrue **lead up to** *phr vt* be a preparation for ♦ *n* **1** guiding suggestion **2 a** chief or front position **b** distance by which one competitor is ahead **3** (person playing) the main acting part in a play or film **4** strap, chain, etc., for leading a dog **6** wire carrying electrical power **~ing** *adj* most important: chief

lead[2] *n* **1** heavy greyish metal used e.g. for water pipes **2** graphite used in pencils **3** weight on the end of a sounding line **~s** *pl n* sheets of lead used for covering a roof

leaden *adj* **1** dull grey **2** heavy and sad

leader *n* **1** person who leads **2** *BrE* editorial **~ship** *n* position or qualities of a leader

lead-in *n* introductory remarks

leading article *n BrE* editorial

leading light *n* person of importance

leading question *n* question formed so as to suggest the answer

lead time *n* period between starting and completion

leaf *n* **leaves 1** flat green part of a plant, joined to its stem **2** sheet of paper or metal **3** part of a tabletop that can be slid or folded out **4 take a leaf out of someone's book** follow someone's example **leaf through** *phr vt* turn the pages (of a book, magazine, etc.) quickly without reading much **~y** *adj*

leaflet *n* small sheet of printed matter ♦ *vi/t* give out (political) leaflets (to)

leaf mould *n* decaying leaves forming a rich top layer to the soil

league[1] *n* **1** group of people, countries, etc., joined together for a shared aim **2** group of sports clubs that play against each other **3** level of quality **4 in league (with)** working together secretly

league[2] *n arch.* distance of about three miles

leak *n* **1** accidental hole through which something flows **2** disclosure of secrets ♦ *v* **1** *vi/t* (allow to) pass through a leak **2** *vt* make (secrets) publicly known **~y** *adj*

leakage *n* process or amount of leaking

lean[1] *v* **leant** *or* **leaned 1** *vi* bend from an upright position **2** *vi/t* support or rest in a sloping position: *lean a ladder against a tree* **3 lean over backwards** make every possible effort (to) **lean on** *phr vt* **1** depend on **2** *infml* influence (someone) by threats **lean towards** *phr vt* favour (a plan or opinion) **~ing** *n* tendency

lean[2] *adj* **1** not fat **2** producing little profit: *a lean year for business*

lean-burn *adj* (of an engine) burning lower-than-average amounts of fuel

lean-to *n* **-os** small building constructed against a wall

leap *n* **1** jump **2** sudden increase in number, quantity, etc. **3 by leaps and bounds** very quickly **4 a leap in the dark** action or risk taken without knowing what will happen ♦ *vi/t* **leapt** *or* **leaped** jump

leapfrog *n* game in which players jump over each other ♦ *vi/t* **-gg-** go ahead of (each other) in turn

leap year *n* a year, every 4th year, in which February has 29 days

learn *vi/t* **learned** *or* **learnt 1** gain (knowledge or skill): *learn to swim* **2** fix in the memory: *learn a poem* **3** become informed (of): *learn of his success* **~ed** *adj* having great knowledge **~er** *n* **~ing** *n* knowledge gained by study

lease *n* contract for the use of a place in return for rent ♦ *vt* give or take (a place) on a lease

lease-back *n* arrangement by which the giver or seller of a piece of property

subsequently rents it back from the new owner
leasehold *adj, adv* (of a place) held on a lease **~er** *n* person who has a place on a lease
leash *n* lead (4)
least *determiner, pron* **1** smallest number, amount, etc. **2 at least: a** not less than **b** if nothing else: *At least it's legal.* **3 in the least** at all ♦ *adv* (*superlative of* little) **1** less than anything else or than any others **2 not least** partly, and quite importantly
leather *n* preserved animal skin used for making shoes, bags, etc. **~y** *adj* stiff like leather
leave *v* **left 1** *vi/t* go away (from) **2** *vt* allow to remain: *Is there any coffee left?* **3** *vt* fail to take or bring **4** *vt* give by a will **5** *vt* have remaining after subtraction **leave off** *phr vi/t* stop (doing something) **leave out** *phr vt* **1** not include **2 Leave it out!** *BrE sl* Stop lying, pretending, etc. ♦ *n* **1** time spent away from work **2** *fml* permission **3 take leave of** say goodbye to **~r** *n*
leaven /ˈlev(ə)n/ *vt* **1** make (dough) rise by adding yeast or a similar substance **2** make less dull
leaves *pl of* leaf
leave-taking *n* act of saying goodbye
leavings *pl n* residue; leftovers
lecher *n derog* lecherous man
lecherous *adj derog* sexually insatiable **~ly** *adv*
lechery *n derog* being lecherous
lectern *n* sloping table to hold a book
lecture *n* **1** speech given as a method of teaching **2** long solemn scolding or warning ♦ *vi/t* give a lecture (to) **~r** *n* person who gives (university) lectures **~ship** *n* post as a lecturer
led *past t. and p. of* lead[1]
LED *n* light emitting diode; semiconductor which becomes luminous when an electric current is passed through it
ledge *n* shelf sticking out from a wall, rock, etc.
ledger *n* account book of a business
ledger line *n* short line added above or below the musical stave
lee *n* shelter from the wind ♦ *adj* on the side away from the wind
leech *n* **1** wormlike creature that sucks blood **2** person who makes profit from others **3** *arch.* doctor
leek *n* vegetable with a long fleshy stem and broad leaves that tastes slightly of onions
leer *vi, n* (look with) an unpleasant smile
leery *adj infml* wary
lees *pl n* dregs in a wine barrel
leeward *adj* **1** with or in the direction of the wind **2** away from the wind
leeway *n* **1** amount of time, distance, etc. by which one thing lags behind another **2** amount of freedom to act
left[1] *past t. and p. of* leave
left[2] *adj* **1** on the side of the body that contains the heart **2** in the direction of one's left side **3** belonging to or favouring the left in politics ♦ *n* **1** left side or direction **2** political parties that favour more change and more state control ♦ *adv* towards the left **~ist** *n, adj* (a supporter) of the political left
left-hand *adj* on the left side **~ed** *adj* using the left hand for most actions **~er** *n* left-handed person
left luggage office *n BrE* place in a station where one can leave one's bags
leftovers *pl n* food remaining uneaten after a meal
left wing *n* the political left
leg *n* **1** limb that includes the foot, used for walking **2** part of a garment that covers this **3** support of a table, chair, etc. **4** single stage of a journey **5 not have a leg to stand on** have no good reason or excuse
legacy *n* **1** money or other property left in someone's will **2** aftereffect
legal *adj* of, allowed by, or demanded by the law **~ly** *adv* **~ize** *vt* make legal **~ity** *n*
legal aid *n* payment to help those who cannot afford legal representation
legalistic *adj derog* placing too great an importance on keeping exactly to what

the law says

legal tender *n tech* money that must by law be accepted in payment

legate *n* emissary usu. from the Pope

legation *n* offices of a minister below the rank of ambassador, representing one country in another country

legato *n, adv, adj* (piece of music) played with smoothly connected notes

legend *n* **1** story from the past which may not be true **2** such stories collectively **3** famous person or act **4** caption **~ary** *adj* famous in legends

legerdemain *n* sleight of hand

leggings *pl n* outer coverings to protect the legs

legible *adj* that can be read easily **-bly** *adv* **-bility** *n*

legion *n* **1** division of an army, esp. in ancient Rome **2** large group of people ♦ *adj fml* very many **~ary** *n* member of a legion in an army

legionnaire's disease *n* serious infectious disease of the lungs

legislate *vi* make laws **-ator** *n* **-ation** *n* **1** law or set of laws **2** act of making laws

legislative *adj* having the power and duty to make laws: *a legislative assembly*

legislature *n* body of people who make the laws

legit *adj infml* legitimate (1), (3)

legitimate *adj* **1** legally correct **2** born of parents married to each other **3** reasonable: *a legitimate conclusion* **~ly** *adv* **-acy** *n*

legitimize, -ise also **legitimatize, -ise** *BrE vt* **1** make legal or acceptable **2** make (a child) legitimate

legless *adj infml, esp. BrE* very drunk

Lego *n tdmk* construction toy consisting of pieces of plastic with studs on them which fit into other pieces

legroom *n* space for one's legs while sitting

leg side *n* (in cricket) the part of the field behind a batsman as he faces the bowler

leguminous /li'gyoohminəs/ *adj* of the pea and bean family

leg-warmer *n* woollen covering for the lower part of the leg

legwork *n infml* (work that involves) walking about

leisure *n* **1** free time **2 at one's leisure** at a convenient time **~d** *adj* **1** having leisure **2** leisurely

leisurely *adj* unhurried

leitmotiv /'lietmoh,teef/ *n* recurring symbolic theme, esp. in music

lekker *adj S Afr infml* pleasant; nice

lemming *n* small northern mammal which takes part in mass migrations

lemon *n* **1** sour fruit with a hard yellow skin **2** light bright yellow **3** *sl* something unsatisfactory or worthless

lemonade *n* **1** drink made of lemons, sugar, and water **2** *BrE* fizzy drink tasting of lemons

lemur *n* tree-dwelling mammal esp. from Madagascar

lend *v* **lent** /lent/ **1** *vi/t* give something for a limited time **2** *vt* give; add: *The flags lent colour to the streets.* **3 lend a hand** give help **4 lend itself to** be suitable for **~er** *n*

length *n* **1** measurement of something from one end to the other or of its longest side **2** quality or condition of being long **3** distance from front to back of a horse or boat in a race: *win by 3 lengths* **4** amount of time from beginning to end **5** piece of something: *a length of string* **6 at length: a** in many words **b** *fml* finally **7 go to any/great lengths** be prepared to do anything **~y** *adj* (too) long

lengthen *vi/t* make or become longer

lengthways, lengthwise *adv* in the direction of the longest side

lenient *adj* not severe in judgment, punishment, etc. **~ly** *adv* **-ence, -ency** *n*

lenitive *n, adj* (drug which is) soothing or mildly laxative

lenity *n lit* mildness; clemency

lens *n* **1** curved piece of glass in a camera, microscope, etc. **2** part of the eye that can focus light **3** contact lens

lent *past t. and p. of* lend
Lent *n* the 40 days before Easter
lentil *n* small beanlike seed used for food
lento *adv, adj* played in slow tempo
leonine *adj* like a lion
leopard *n* large spotted catlike animal
leopardess *n* female leopard
leotard *n* close fitting one-piece garment worn e.g. by dancers
leper *n* **1** person with leprosy **2** person avoided by other people for social or moral reasons
lepidoptera *pl n* order of insects including butterflies and moths
leprechaun /ˈleprik(h)awn/ *n* mischievous Irish elf
leprosy *n* disease in which the skin becomes rough, flesh and nerves are destroyed and fingers, toes, etc., drop off **–rous** *adj*
lesbian *adj, n* (of or being) a woman homosexual **~ism** *n*
lese majesty *n* violation of (royal) power or dignity
lesion /ˈleezh(ə)n/ *n med* wound
less *determiner, pron* (*comparative of* little) *n* **1** smaller amount **2 less and less** (an amount) that continues to become smaller ♦ *adv* **1** not so; to a smaller degree (than) **2** not so much: *work less* **3 less and less** increasingly rarely **4 much/still less** and certainly not ♦ *prep* minus
-less *suffix* without: *windless*
lessee *n* person who leases a property
lessen *vi/t* make or become less
lesser *adj, adv* not so great or severe
lesson *n* **1** (period of) teaching something, e.g. in school **2** experience from which to learn: *teach someone a lesson* **3** short passage read from the Bible
lest *conj fml* for fear that
-let *suffix* small: *a flatlet*
let[1] *vt* **let**; *pres. p.* **letting 1** allow (to do or happen) **2** give the use of (a place) for rent **3 let alone** and certainly not **4 let/leave go** stop holding **5 let oneself go: a** behave unrestrainedly **b** stop taking care of one's appearance **6 let's, let us** (used when making suggestions) **7 let someone go: a** set someone free **b** dismiss someone from a job **8 let someone know** tell someone, esp. later **let down** *phr vt* disappoint **let in for** *phr vt* cause (esp. oneself) to have (something unwanted) **let into/in on** *phr vt* allow to share (a secret) **let off** *phr vt* **1** excuse from punishment **2** explode **let on** *phr vi* tell a secret **let up** *phr vi* lessen or stop
let[2] **1** point that must be replayed in tennis **2** *fml* obstruction: *without let or hindrance*
letdown *n* disappointment
lethal *adj* causing death **~ly** *adv*
lethargy *n* tiredness and laziness **–gic** *adj* **–gically** *adv*
let-off *n infml* escape from punishment or misfortune
letter *n* **1** written message sent to someone **2** sign representing a sound **3** actual words of something: *the letter of the law* **~ing** *n* style and size of written letters **letters** *pl n fml* literature
letter bomb *n* small bomb posted in an envelope
letterbox *n esp. BrE* **1** hole in a door for letters **2** box in a post office or street, in which to post letters
letterhead *n* name and address printed at the top of the owner's writing paper
letting *n esp. BrE* house or flat to be rented
lettuce *n* green leafy vegetable, eaten raw
letup *n* lessening of activity
leucocyte *n* white blood cell
leucotomy *n* lobotomy
leukemia, -kae- *n* type of cancer in which the blood has too many white cells
levee[1] *n* formal reception of visitors
levee[2] *n AmE* river embankment
level *adj* **1** flat; horizontal **2** equal e.g. in score **3 (at) level pegging** *infml* having the same score **4 one's level best** all that one can do ♦ *n* **1** line or surface parallel with the ground; position of height in relation to a flat

surface **2** standard of quality or quantity: *increase production levels* **3 on the level** honest(ly) ♦ *vi/t* **-ll-** (*AmE* **-l-**) make or become level **level at/against** *phr vt* **1** aim (a weapon) at **2** bring (a charge) against (someone) **level off/out** *phr vi* stop rising or falling **level with** *phr vt infml* speak truthfully to

level crossing *n BrE* place where a road and a railway cross, usu. protected by gates

level-headed *adj* calm and sensible

leveller *n* person who seeks political, social, etc. equality

lever *n* **1** bar that turns on its middle point, to lift things **2** rod that works a machine **3** something used for influencing ♦ *vt* move with a lever

leverage *n* **1** power of a lever **2** influence

leveret *n* young hare

leviathan *adj, n* (of) a large or formidable thing

levitate *vi* rise into the air as if by magic **-ation** *n*

levity *n fml* lack of proper seriousness

levy *vt* demand and collect (esp. taxes) officially

lewd *adj* sexually improper; obscene **~ly** *adv* **~ness** *n*

lexical *adj* of words **~ly** *adv*

lexicography *n* writing of dictionaries **-pher** *n*

lexicon *n* dictionary or wordlist

liability *n* **1** condition of being liable **2** debt that must be paid **3** someone or something that limits one's activities or freedom

liable *adj* **1** responsible in law **2 liable to** having a tendency to

liaise /lee'ayz/ *vi* form a liaison for the purpose of communication

liaison *n* **1** working association between groups **2** sexual relationship between an unmarried couple

liana *n* climbing jungle plant

liar *n* person who tells lies

lib *n* liberation

Lib *written abbrev. for:* Liberal Party

libation *n* drink poured on the ground as an offering to the gods

libel *n* damaging written statement about someone ♦ *vt* **-ll-** (*AmE* **-l-**) publish a libel against **~lous** (*AmE* **~ous**) *adj*: *a libellous remark*

liberal *adj* **1** willing to respect the opinions of others **2** given freely or generously: *liberal supplies* **4** (*cap.*) of the Liberal Party ♦ *n* (*cap.*) member of the Liberal Party **~ism** *n* liberal opinions **~ize, ~ise** *vt* make less restrictive **~ization** *n*

liberality *n fml* **1** generosity **2** broadness of mind

Liberal Party *n* former British political party, now part of the Social and Liberal Democrats

liberate *vt fml* set free **-d** *adj* socially and sexually free **-ator** *n* **-ation** *n*

liberation theology *n* Roman Catholic movement advocating greater political freedom

libertarian *n* believer in freedom of thought **~ism** *n*

libertine *n* man who leads a (sexually) immoral life

liberty *n* **1** personal or political freedom **2** chance or permission to do or use something **3 at liberty** free **4 take liberties** behave too freely

libidinous /li'bidinəs/ *adj fml* lascivious **~ly** *adv*

libido /li'beedoh/ *n* **-dos** *tech* the sexual urge

librarian *n* person in charge of a library **~ship** *n*

library *n* (room or building with) a collection of books, records, etc.

libretto *n* **-os** *or* **-tti** text of an opera **-tist** *n* writer of a libretto

lice *pl of* louse

licence *AmE* **license** *n* **1** (document showing) official permission to do something **2** *fml* uncontrolled freedom

license also *AmE* **licence** *vt* give a licence to **licensee** *n* person with a licence, esp. to sell alcohol

licentious *adj* sexually uncontrolled **~ly** *adv* **~ness** *n*

lichen *n* primitive plant which grows in flat patches on walls and trees

licit *adj* legal; permissible **~ly** *adv*

lick *vt* **1** move the tongue across **2** (of flames or waves) pass lightly over **3** *infml* defeat ◆ *n* **1** act of licking **2** small amount, e.g. of paint **3** *BrE infml* speed

licorice *n* liquorice

lid *n* **1** movable cover of a container **2** eyelid

lido *n* **-os** place for swimming and lying in the sun

lie[1] *vi, n* **lied**, *pres. p.* **lying** (make) a false statement

lie[2] *vi* **lay, lain**, *pres. p.* **lying 1** be or remain in a flat position on a surface **2** be or remain in a particular position or state: *The town lies two miles to the east.* **3** be the responsibility of someone: *The decision lies with you.* **4 lie low** be in hiding or avoid being noticed **5 take something lying down** suffer something bad without complaining or trying to stop it ◆ *n* **1** way something lies **2 lie of the land** *BrE* **a** appearance, slope, etc., of a piece of land **b** state of affairs at a particular time **lie about** *phr vi* be lazy; do nothing **lie behind** *phr vt* be the reason for

lie detector *n* instrument that is said to show when someone is telling lies

lie-down *n BrE infml* a short rest

lief *adv arch.* gladly

liege also **liege lord** *n* person owed service under the feudal system

lie-in *n infml, esp. BrE* a stay in bed later than usual in the morning

lieu *n* **in lieu (of)** instead (of)

lieutenant /lef'tenənt/ *n* officer of low rank in the armed forces

life *n* **lives 1** active force that makes animals and plants different from stones or machines **2** living things: *There is no life on the moon.* **3** human existence: *Life is full of surprises.* **4** period or way of being alive **5** activity; movement; liveliness: *full of life* **6** also **life imprisonment** punishment of being put in prison for a long time **7** biography **8** person or thing that is the cause of enjoyment in a group: *the life and soul of the party* **9 come to life: a** regain one's senses after fainting **b** show or develop interest, excitement, etc. **10 take one's life** kill oneself **11 take one's life in one's hands** be in continual danger **12 take someone's life** kill someone **~less** *adj* **1** dead **2** not active; dull **~lessly** *adv* **~like** *adj* like a real person **~r** *n infml* prisoner serving a life sentence

life belt *n* belt worn to keep a person from sinking in water

lifeblood *n* something that gives continuing strength

lifeboat *n* boat for saving people in danger at sea

life buoy *n* floating ring to hold onto in the water

life cycle *n* all the stages of development through which a creature passes during its life

life expectancy *n* number of years a person can expect to live, based on statistics

lifeguard *n* swimmer employed to help other swimmers in danger

life insurance also *BrE* **life assurance** *n* form of insurance in which money is paid to a beneficiary on the death of the policyholder

life jacket *n* garment worn to support a person in water

lifeline *n* **1** rope for saving life **2** something on which one's life depends

lifelong *adj* lasting all one's life

life peer *n* British peer whose title is not hereditary

life preserver *n AmE* life belt, life jacket or similar device for saving life

life science *n* biology, medicine, etc.

life-size, life-sized *adj* (of a work of art) as big as what it represents

lifespan *n* length of a creature's life

lifestyle *n* way of living

life-support system *n* equipment needed to keep e.g. a person who is very ill or a space traveller alive

lifetime *n* time during which someone is alive

lift *v* **1** *vt* raise to a higher level **2** *vt* improve: *lift my spirits* **3** *vi* (esp. of clouds) disappear **4** *vt* bring to an end: *lift a ban* **5** *vt* steal **lift off** *phr vi* (of an aircraft or spacecraft) leave the ground ♦ *n* **1** act of lifting **2** *BrE* apparatus in a building for taking people and goods from one floor to another **3** free ride in a vehicle **4** feeling of increased strength, higher spirits, etc.

lift-off *n* vertical takeoff by an aircraft or missile

ligament *n* band of tissue that joins bones together

ligature *n* thread used for tying, esp. in medicine

light[1] *n* **1** force by which we see things: *sunlight* **2** something (e.g. a lamp) that gives light **3** (something that will make) a flame **4** way in which something is regarded: *see it in a different light* **5 bring/come to light** make or become known **6 in the light of** taking into account ♦ *v* **lit** *or* **lighted 1** *vi/t* (cause to) start burning **2** *vt* give light to: *lighted streets* **light up** *phr v* **1** *vi/t* make or become bright **2** *vi* start smoking ♦ *adj* **1** not dark: *a light room* **2** pale: *light green* **~ing** *n* system or quality of lights in a place

light[2] *adj* **1** not heavy **2** small in amount: *light meals/traffic* **3** easy to bear or do: *light duties* **4** gentle: *light touch* **5** quick and graceful **6** not serious: *light reading* **7 make light of** treat as of little importance ♦ *adv* with few travelling cases or possessions: *travel light* **~ly** *adv* **1** gently **2** slightly **3** not seriously **~ness** *n*

light[3] *vt* **lit** *or* **lighted** come down from flight and settle **light on** *phr vt* find by chance

light bulb *n* bulb (2)

lighten *vi/t* make or become **a** brighter **b** less heavy, or **c** more cheerful

lighter *n* instrument for lighting esp. cigarettes

light-fingered *adj infml* having the habit of stealing small things

light-headed *adj* **1** unable to think clearly **2** not sensible

light-hearted *adj* cheerful **~ly** *adv*

lighthouse *n* tower with a powerful light to guide ships

lightning *n* electric flash of light in the sky ♦ *adj* very quick, short, or sudden

lightning conductor *n BrE* wire leading from the top of a building to the ground, as a protection against lightning

lights *pl n* lungs esp. of slaughtered animals

lightship *n* ship with a powerful light moored near e.g. rocks or sandbanks to warn other ships

lightweight *n* **1** person or thing of less than average weight **2** someone who does not think deeply or seriously **lightweight** *adj*

light year *n* **1** distance that light travels in a year **2** *infml* a very long time

ligneous *adj fml* like wood

lignite *n* brown woody coal

likable, likeable *adj* (esp. of people) pleasant; attractive

-like *suffix* typical of: *childlike*

like[1] *vt* **1** regard with pleasure or fondness **2** be willing (to): *I don't like to ask.* **3** wish or choose (to have): *I'd like a boiled egg.* **liking** *n* **1** fondness **2 to one's liking** which suits one's ideas or expectations **likes** *pl n* things that one likes; preferences

like[2] *prep* **1** in the same way as; similar to **2** typical of: *It's not like her to be late.* **3** such as: *Houses like that are expensive.* **4 something like** about ♦ *n* **1** something of the same kind **2 the likes of** people or things of the stated type ♦ *adj fml* similar ♦ *conj infml* as

likelihood *n* probability

likely *adj* probable ♦ *adv* **1 most/very likely** probably **2 Not likely!** *infml* Certainly not!

like-minded *adj* having the same ideas, interests, etc.

liken *vt* point out similarities; compare

likeness *n* similarity in appearance

likewise *adv* similarly; also

lilac *n* **1** bush with pinkish-purple or white flowers **2** pinkish-purple

lilliputian /ˌliliˈpyoohsh(ə)n/ *adj* tiny
Lilo *n tdmk BrE* inflatable mattress
lilt *n* pleasant pattern of rising and falling sound **~ing** *adj*
lily *n* plant with large esp. white flowers
lily-livered *adj lit* cowardly
lily-white *adj* **1** pure white **2** pure and blameless
limb *n* **1** leg, arm, or wing **2** branch of a tree **3 out on a limb** alone without support
limber up *phr vi* exercise the muscles before exertion
limbo[1] *n* state of uncertainty
limbo[2] *n* **-os** dance involving passing under a low bar
lime[1] *n* white substance used in making cement
lime[2] *n* tree with sweet-smelling yellow flowers
lime[3] *n* sour fruit like a lemon
limelight *n* the centre of public attention
limerick *n* funny poem with five lines
limey *n AmE sl* British person
limit *n* **1** farthest point or edge **2** *infml* someone or something too bad to bear **3 off limits** where one is not allowed to go **4 within limits** up to a reasonable point ♦ *vt* keep below a limit **~ed** *adj* **1** small; having limits **2** (*abbrev.* **Ltd**) (of a British firm) having a reduced liability to pay back debts **~less** *adj* endless
limitation *n* **1** limiting **2** condition that limits
limn *vt lit* draw; paint
limousine /ˌliməˈzeen/ *n* expensive car with the driver's seat separated from the back
limp[1] *vi, n* (walk with) an uneven step
limp[2] *adj* lacking firmness; not stiff **~ly** *adv*
limpet *n* kind of shellfish that holds tightly to rocks
limpid *adj lit* clear and transparent
linchpin *n* person or thing that keeps something together
linctus *n BrE* liquid cough medicine
linden *n* lime tree
line[1] *n* **1** long narrow mark on a surface **2** limit; border: *the finishing line in a race* **3 a** row: *standing in (a) line* **b** row of words on a printed page: *The actor forgot his lines.* **4** direction followed: *the line of fire* **5** piece of string, wire, etc.: *fishing line* **6** telephone connection: *Hold the line, please.* **7** railway **8** method of action: *on the right lines* **9** type of goods: *a new line in hats* **10 in line for** being considered for **11 in line with** in accordance with **12 out of line** beyond what is allowed or usual ♦ *vt* **1** mark with lines or wrinkles: *lined paper* **2** form rows along: *crowds lining the streets* **line up** *phr v* **1** *vi/t* form into a row **2** *vt* arrange
line[2] *vt* **1** cover the inside of (something) with material **2 line one's pocket(s)/purse** make money for oneself **lining** *n*
lineage *n fml* line of descent from one person to another in a family
lineal *adj* in a direct line of descent
lineament *n* contour, outline
linear *adj* **1** in lines **2** of length: *linear measurements*
line judge *n* person who indicates whether a ball falls inside or outside the court in tennis
lineman *n* **-men** person who repairs telephone wires or railway tracks
linen *n* **1** cloth made from flax **2** sheets, tablecloths, etc.
line printer *n* machine that prints computer information
liner *n* **1** large passenger ship **2** something used to line something
linesman *n* **-men** (in sport) official who says whether a ball has gone outside the limits
lineup *n* **1** set of people, esp. side by side in a line looking forward **2** competitors in a race or game **3** set of events
ling[1] *n* fish with a long body
ling[2] *n* heather
linger *vi* be slow to disappear; delay going
lingerie /ˈlonh·zhəri/ *n fml* women's underclothes
lingo *n* **-oes** *sl* language

lingua franca *n* language used for communication between people speaking different native languages
linguist *n* **1** person who studies and is good at foreign languages **2** person who studies language in general **~ic** *adj* of language **~ics** *n* study of language
liniment *n* liquid for rubbing on stiff muscles
link *n* **1** connection **2** one ring of a chain ♦ *vi/t* join; connect
linkage *n* system or way of connection
linkman *n* **-men** broadcaster who introduces and links separate items esp. in news programmes
links *n* **links** golf course
linkwoman *n* **-women** female linkman
linnet *n* small singing finch
linocut *n* (print made from) a design cut into a piece of linoleum
linoleum also **lino** *n* smooth hard floor-covering
linseed oil *n* oil from the seeds of flax
lint *n* soft material for protecting wounds
lintel *n* beam above a door or window
lion *n* **1** large yellow catlike animal **2** famous and important person: *a literary lion* **3 the lion's share** the biggest part **~ize, ~ise** *vt* treat (someone) as important
lioness *n* female lion
lip *n* **1** edge of the mouth **2** edge of a cup, glass, etc.
lipid *n* fatty, waxy substance in living cells
lip-read *vi/t* understand speech by watching lip movements
lip service *n* **pay lip service to** support in words, but not in fact
lipstick *n* (stick of) coloured cosmetic put on the lips
liquefy *vi/t* make or become liquid **-faction** *n*
liqueur *n* strong sweet alcoholic drink
liquid *n* substance which is not a solid or a gas, which flows freely and is wet ♦ *adj* **1** in the form of a liquid **2** clear and wet-looking **3** (of sounds) pure and flowing **4** easily exchanged for money: *liquid assets* **~ize, ~ise** *vt* crush into juice **~izer** *n BrE* blender
liquidate *v* **1** *vt* kill **2** *vi/t* arrange the end of (an unsuccessful company) **-ation** *n*
liquidity *n* **1** state of being liquid **2** state of having liquid assets
liquor *n* alcoholic drink
liquorice *n* black substance used in medicine and sweets
lira *n* **-re, -ras** money unit of Italy
lisp *vi* pronounce 's' to sound like 'th' **lisp** *n*
lissom, lissome *adj* supple, lithe
list[1] *n* set of things written in order: *shopping list* ♦ *vt* put into a list
list[2] *vi* (of a ship) lean or slope to one side **list** *n*
listen *vi* give attention in hearing **listen in** *phr vi* **1** listen to the radio **2** eavesdrop **~er** *n*
listless *adj* tired and not interested **~ly** *adv* **~ness** *n*
list price *n* price suggested for an article by the makers
lit *past t. and p. of* light[1] or light[3]
litany *n* long series of prayers included in a church service
litchi *n* lychee
liter *n AmE* litre
literacy *n* being literate
literal *adj* **1** reproduced word for word; verbatim **2** following the usual meaning of words **~ly** *adv* **1** really **2** word by word
literary *adj* of literature or writers
literate *adj* **1** able to read and write **2** well-educated
literati *pl n fml* people with an expert knowledge of literature
literature *n* **1** written works of artistic value **2** printed material giving information: *sales literature*
lithe *adj* (of people or animals) gracefully supple
lithium *n* very light metal
lithograph *n* picture printed from stone or metal **~y** *n*
litigation *n* process of taking legal

action, in non-criminal matters **–gant** *n* person involved in litigation **–gate** *vi*

litigious /li'tijəs/ *adj fml, often derog* fond of litigation

litmus *n* substance that turns red in acid and blue in alkali

litre, *AmE* **-ter** *n* (a measure of liquid equal to) 1.76 pints

litter *n* **1** paper, bottles, tins, etc., scattered untidily **2** family of young animals ♦ *vt* scatter litter on

little *adj* **1** small **2** short: *a little while* **3** young **4** unimportant ♦ *adv* **1** not much: *little-known facts* **2** *fml* not at all: *I little realized* ♦ *determiner, pron, n* **less, least 1** some but not much: *a little milk* **2 little by little** gradually

little finger *n* smallest finger on the hand

littoral *adj, n* (of the) sea shore

liturgy *n* form of Christian worship **–gical** *adj*

live *v* **1** *vi* be alive **2** *vi* remain alive: *The doctor says he'll live.* **3** *vi* have one's home: *live in Paris* **4** *vt* lead (a kind of life) **5 live and let live** be tolerant **6 live it up** *infml* have a good time **live down** *phr vt* cause (a bad action) to be forgotten, by later good behaviour **live together** *phr vi* live as if married **live up to** *phr vt* keep to the high standards of **live with** *phr vt* **1** live as if married with **2** accept (an unpleasant thing) ♦ *adj* **1** alive **2** able to explode or shock: *live bomb/wire* **3** (of broadcasting) seen or heard as it happens

livelihood *n* way one earns one's money

livelong /ˈliv,long/ *adj lit* whole, entire

lively *adj* **1** full of quick movement and thought **2** bright; vivid **–liness** *n*

liven up *phr vi/t* make or become lively

liver *n* **1** organ in the body that cleans the blood **2** animal's liver as food **~ish** *adj* feeling unwell, esp. after eating or drinking too much

livery *n* uniform worn by servants

livery stable *n* stable where horses are kept for hire

lives *pl of* life

livestock *pl n* farm animals

live wire *n* very lively person

livid *adj* **1** bluish-grey **2** very angry

living *adj* **1** alive **2** still in use: *living language* ♦ *n* **1** livelihood **2** manner of life

living memory *n* as long as anyone now living can remember

living room *n* main room for general use in a house

lizard *n* four-legged reptile with a long tail

ll *abbrev. for:* lines

llama *n* S American animal related to the camel

lo *interj arch.* (attracts attention)

load *n* **1** something being carried **2 a** amount vehicle can carry **b** weight borne by the frame of a building **3** amount of work to be done **4 a load off someone's mind** the removing of a great worry **5 loads of** *infml* a lot of ♦ *vi/t* **1** put a load on or in **2** put a bullet, shell, etc., into (a gun) or film into (a camera) **~ed** *adj* **1** containing a hidden trap: *a loaded question* **2** *sl* very rich **3** *sl* drunk

loaf[1] *n* **loaves 1** single mass of baked bread **2** minced food prepared in a solid piece: *meat loaf* **3** *sl* brains; common sense

loaf[2] *vi* waste time **~er** *n*

loam *n* crumbly fertile soil

loan *n* **1** something lent **2** amount of money lent **3 on loan** being borrowed ♦ *vt* lend

loath, loth *adj* unwilling

loathe *vt* hate very much

loathsome *adj* disgusting

loaves *pl of* loaf

lob *vt* **-bb-** send (a ball) in a high curve ♦ *n* lobbed ball

lobby *n* **1** hall or passage in a public building **2** group of people who try to influence those in power ♦ *vt* **1** meet (a member of Parliament) in order to persuade him/her to do something **2** *vi* be publicly active in trying to bring about change **~ist** *n*

lobe *n* **1** lower fleshy part of the ear **2** division of the brain or lungs

lobelia *n* small garden plant with blue flowers

lobotomy *n* operation to cut some of the main nerves in the brain

lobster *n* eight-legged sea animal with claws

lobster pot *n* cage for trapping lobsters

local *adj* **1** of a certain place: *our local doctor* **2** limited to one part: *local anaesthetic* ♦ *n* **1** person living in a place **2** *BrE* local pub **~ly** *adv*

local authority *n BrE* government of a particular town, county, etc.

local colour *n* details that give realism to the description of a place

locale *n* particular place, esp. where something is set

locality *n* place; area

localize, -ise *vt* keep inside a small area

locate *vt* **1** find out the position of **2** fix in a particular place: *offices located in the town centre* **location** *n* **1** position **2** act of locating **3 on location** in a town, country, etc., to make a film

loch *n ScotE* lake

loci *pl of* locus

lock¹ *n* **1** apparatus for fastening a door, window, etc. **2** piece of water closed off by gates, so that the level can be raised or lowered **3** *BrE* amount that a steering wheel can be turned **4 lock, stock, and barrel** completely ♦ *v* **1** *vi/t* fasten with a lock **2** *vi* become immovable **lock onto** *phr vt* (esp. of a missile) find and follow (its target) closely **lock up** *phr v* **1** *vi/t* make (a building) safe by locking the doors **2** *vt* put in a safe place (e.g. prison) and lock the door

lock² *n* small piece of hair

locker *n* small cupboard for clothes and other belongings esp. at school, in a sports building, etc.

locker room *n esp. AmE* room for changing clothes

locket *n* case for a small picture worn on a chain round the neck

lockjaw *n* tetanus

locknut *n* nut screwed on top of another to prevent it moving

lockout *n* act of preventing workers from going to work in order to make them agree to the employer's terms

lockup *n* **1** *BrE* place, e.g. shop or garage, that can be locked up **2** (small) jail **lock-up** *adj*

loco¹ *n* **-os** *infml* locomotive

loco² *adj AmE sl* crazy

locomotion *n fml* movement from place to place

locomotive *adj tech* of movement ♦ *n* railway engine

locum *n esp. BrE* doctor or priest doing the work of another who is away

locus *n* **loci** set of mathematical points or lines whose position is determined by stated conditions

locus classicus *n* **loci classici** *fml* best-known passage dealing with a particular topic

locust *n* large flying insect that destroys crops

locution *n fml* phrase, expression

lode *n* seam of metal ore

lodestar *n lit* guiding star

lodestone *n* piece of magnetic stone

lodge *v* **1** *vi* stay somewhere and pay rent **2** *vi/t* (cause to) become fixed **3** *vt* make (a report, complaint, etc.) officially **4** *vt* put in a safe place: *lodged with the bank* ♦ *n* **1** small house in the grounds of a larger one **2** house in wild country for hunters, skiers, etc. **lodger** *n* person who pays to live in someone's house

lodging *n* place to stay **lodgings** *pl n* rented furnished rooms

loft *n* attic

lofty *adj* **1** (of ideas, ambitions, etc.) noble **2** proud **3** *lit* high **–ily** *adv*

log *n* **1** thick piece of wood from a tree **2** official record of a journey **3 like a log** (of sleeping) deeply without moving ♦ *vt* **-gg-** record in a log **log in/on** *phr vi* begin a period of using a computer system by performing a fixed set of operations **log off/out** *phr vi* finish a period of using a computer system by performing a fixed set of operations

loganberry *n* fruit like a large raspberry

logarithm *n* number of times a number must be multiplied by itself to produce a particular number
logbook *n* **1** log (2) **2** *BrE* registration document
loggerheads *n* **at loggerheads** always disagreeing
loggia *n* roofed gallery with open arches along its side(s)
logic *n* **1** science of formal reasoning **2** good sense **~al** *adj* **~ally** *adv*
logistics *pl n* detailed planning of an operation
logjam *n* **1** mass of tightly-packed floating logs **2** impasse
logo *n* **-os** design, pattern, etc., representing a business firm
-logy *suffix* 1 science or study of: *sociology* **2** body of writing on a certain subject: *trilogy*
loin *n* (piece of) meat from the lower part of an animal **loins** *pl n* human body between the waist and legs
loincloth *n* cloth worn round the loins
loiter *vi* stand somewhere for no clear reason **~er** *n*
loll *vi* **1** lie lazily **2** hang down loosely
lollipop *n* hard sweet made of boiled sugar or frozen fruit juice on a stick
lollipop lady, lollipop man *n BrE* person who controls the traffic where children cross busy roads
lollop *vi* walk or run awkwardly
lolly *n BrE* **1** ice lolly **2** *infml* money
lone *adj* alone; single
lonely *adj* **1** alone and unhappy **2** (of places) without people **-liness** *n*
lonely hearts *adj* for people looking for a boyfriend or girlfriend
loner *n* person who prefers to be alone
lonesome *adj* lonely
long[1] *adj* **1** large when measured from beginning to end **2** (of a drink) cool, containing little or no alcohol, and served in a tall glass ◆ *adv* **1** (for) a long time: *long ago* **2 as/so long as** on condition that **3 no longer/(not) any longer** (not) any more **4 so long** goodbye for now ◆ *n* **1** a long time: *It won't take long.* **2 before long** soon **3 the long and (the) short of it** *infml* the general result, expressed in a few words
long[2] *vi* wish very much **long for** *phr vt* want very much **~ing** *adj, n* (showing) a strong wish **~ingly** *adv*
long-drawn-out *adj* lasting too long
longevity /lɒnˈjevəti/ *n fml* long life
longhand *n* ordinary writing by hand
longitude *n* distance east or west of Greenwich, measured in degrees **-tudinal** *adj* going along, not across
long johns *pl n infml* long-legged men's underpants
long jump *n* sport of jumping as far as possible across the ground
long-range *adj* covering a long distance or time
longship *n* Viking warship driven by oars and a sail
longshoreman *n* **-men** *AmE* docker
long shot *n* something unlikely to be successful
longsighted *adj* able to see things only when they are far away
long-standing *adj* having existed for a long time
longsuffering *adj* patient under continued difficulties
long-term *adj* for or in the distant future
longueur *n lit* boring part or period
long wave *n* radio broadcasting on waves of more than 1000 metres
longwinded *adj* saying too much; dull
loo *n* **loos** *BrE infml* toilet
loofah *n* long thin bath sponge
look[1] *v* **1** *vi* use the eyes to see something **2** *vi* seem; appear: *You look tired.* **3** *vi* face: *The window looks east.* **4 look as if/like** seem probable **look after** *phr vt* take care of **look ahead** *phr vi* plan for the future **look at** *phr vt* **1** watch **2** consider; examine **look back** *phr vi* recall the past **look down on** *phr vt* despise **look for** *phr vt* try to find **look forward to** *phr vt* expect to enjoy **look in** *phr vi infml* make a short visit **look into** *phr vt* examine; investigate **look on** *phr v* **1** *vi* watch **2** *vt* regard as **look out** *phr vi* take care; keep watching

look over *phr vt* examine quickly **look round** *phr vi/t* examine (a place) **look through** *phr vt* examine for points to be noted **look to** *phr vt* **1** depend on: *I look to you for support.* **2** pay attention to **look up** *phr v* **1** *vi* improve **2** *vt* find (information) in a book **3** *vt* find and visit **look up to** *phr vt* respect ♦ *n* **1** act of looking **2** appearance **looks** *pl n* person's (attractive) appearance

look-alike *n* person or thing that closely resembles another

looker *n infml* good-looking woman

look-in *n* chance to take part or succeed

looking glass *n* mirror

lookout *n* **1** state of watching **2** person who keeps watch **3** one's own problem or responsibility

loom[1] *n* machine for weaving cloth

loom[2] *vi* appear in a threatening way

loony *n, adj sl* lunatic

loony bin *n sl* mental hospital

loop *n* (shape of) a piece of string, cotton, etc., curved back on itself ♦ *vi/t* make (into) a loop

loophole *n* way of escape: *loopholes in the tax laws*

loose *adj* **1** not firmly fixed **2** free from control: *loose cattle* **3** not packed together: *loose biscuits* **4** (of clothes) too wide **5** not exact: *a loose translation* **6** without sexual morals **7 at a loose end** having nothing to do **~ly** *adv*

loose-leaf *adj* (having pages) which can be put in and taken out

loosen *vi/t* make or become looser

loot *n* goods taken illegally by soldiers, rioters, etc. ♦ *vi/t* take loot (from) **~er** *n*

lop *vt* **-pp-** cut (branches) from a tree

lop-sided *adj* with one side lower than the other

loquacious /lə'kwayshəs/ *adj fml* talking a great deal **~ly** *adv* **–city** *n*

loquat *n* (yellow plumlike fruit of) an evergreen tree growing mainly in China and Japan

lord *n* **1** ruler; master **2** nobleman **3** (*cap.*) God **4** (*cap.*) (title for certain official people): *Lord Mayor* **~ship** *n* (title for) a Lord

lordly *adj* proud; grand

lore *n* accumulated traditional knowledge or information

lorgnette /law'nyet/ *n* pair of glasses with a handle

lorry *n BrE* large motor vehicle for carrying loads

lose *v* **lost 1** *vt* be unable to find **2** *vt* have taken away: *lose one's job* **3** *vi/t* be defeated (in): *lose a battle* **4** *vt* have less of: *lose weight/money* **5** *vi* (of a clock) go too slowly **6** *vt* (cause to) fail to hear, see, or understand **lose out** *phr vi* **1** make a loss **2** be defeated **loser** *n* person who loses

loss *n* **1** act of losing; failure to keep **2** person, thing, or amount lost **3** failure to make a profit **4 at a loss** uncertain what to do or say

loss adjuster *n* employee of an insurance company who decides the extent of a loss and the amount of compensation payable

loss leader *n* something sold cheaply to encourage further sales

lost *past t. and p. of* lose

lost cause *n* something which has no chance of success

lot[1] *n* **1** a great number or amount **2** group or amount: *a new lot of students* **3 a lot** much **4 lots** much: *lots better* **5 the lot** the whole; all

lot[2] *n* **1** article sold at an auction **2** *esp. AmE* piece of land **3** (use of) different objects picked at random to make a decision **4** *fml* one's fate

loth *adj* loath

lothario *n* **-os** *infml* frequent seducer of women

lotion *n* liquid mixture for the skin or hair to make it clean and healthy

lottery *n* system of giving prizes to people who bought numbered tickets, chosen by chance

lotus *n* large tropical water lily

louche /loohsh/ *adj* disreputable

loud *adj* **1** producing a lot of sound **2** unpleasantly colourful ♦ *adv* in a loud way **~ly** *adv* **~ness** *n*

loudhailer *n BrE* megaphone
loudmouth *n infml* person who talks too much or reveals secrets
loudspeaker *n* part of a radio or record player from which the sound comes out
lough *n* Irish lake or inlet
lounge *vi* stand or sit lazily ♦ *n* comfortable room to sit in
lounge bar *n BrE* saloon bar
lounge suit *n* man's daytime suit
lour *vi* lower[2]
louse *n* **lice 1** insect that lives on people's and animals' bodies **2** worthless person
lousy *adj* **1** very bad **2** covered with lice
lout *n* rough awkward man or boy **~ish** *adj*
louvre, *AmE* **louver** *n* (slat which is or can be set at an angle and forms part of) an arrangement for doors or windows which keeps out wind and rain but allows some light and air in
lovable *adj* deserving, causing, or worthy of love
love *n* **1** great fondness for someone **2** warm interest: *a love of music* **3** loved person or thing **4** (in tennis) nil **5 make love (to)** have sex (with) ♦ *v* **1** *vi/t* feel love (for) **2** *vt* like very much: *I'd love a drink.* **loving** *adj* fond
love affair *n* sexual relationship
love child *n euph* illegitimate child
lovely *adj* **1** beautiful **2** very pleasant: *lovely dinner* **–liness** *n*
lovemaking *n* sexual intercourse
lover *n* **1** person (usu. a man) who has a sexual relationship with another person outside marriage **2** person who is fond of the stated thing: *art lovers*
lovesick *adj* sad because of unreturned love
low *adj* **1** not high **2** (of a supply) nearly finished **3** (of sounds) **a** deep **b** not loud **4** unhappy **5** not fair or honest: *a low trick* **6** for a slow speed: *a low gear* ♦ *adv* to or at a low level: *bend low* ♦ *n* low point or level
lowbrow *n, adj* (person) not interested in art, books, etc.
Low Church *adj* of the evangelical wing of the Anglican church
lowdown *n sl* the plain facts
low-down *adj* worthless; dishonourable
lower[1] *adj* at or nearer the bottom ♦ *vt* **1** make less high **2 lower oneself** bring oneself down in people's opinion
lower[2] *vi* **1** be dark and threatening **2** frown severely
lower-case *adj* (of letters) which are not capitals
lower class *n* social class of lowest rank **lower-class** *adj*
low-key *adj* quiet and controlled
lowlands *pl n* land lower than its surroundings
lowly *adj* low in rank; humble **–liness** *n*
low-rise *adj* (of a building) having only two or three stories
low season *n* time of year when business is least and prices are lowest
low-spirited *adj* unhappy
loyal *adj* faithful to one's friends, country, etc. **~ist** *n* person who remains loyal to a ruler **~ly** *adv*
loyalty *n* **1** being loyal **2** connection that binds one to a person or thing to which one is loyal
lozenge *n* medical sweet
LP *n* record that plays for about 20 minutes each side
L-plate *n* letter L, fixed to a British vehicle to show that the driver is a learner
LSD *n* illegal drug that causes hallucinations
Lt *abbrev. for:* lieutenant
Ltd *abbrev. for:* limited (2)
lubricant *n* substance (e.g. oil) that lubricates
lubricate *vt* make (machine parts) work without rubbing
lubricious *adj fml* lecherous
lucerne *n* leguminous plant grown esp. as fodder
lucid *adj* **1** easy to understand **2** able to think clearly **~ly** *adv* **~ity** *n*
Lucifer *n* Satan
luck *n* **1** what happens to someone by chance **2** success: *wish them luck* **3 be in/out of luck** have/not have good for-

tune **~y** *adj* having or bringing good luck **~ily** *adv*

lucky dip *n BrE* box or tub containing gifts for people to pick at random

lucrative *adj* profitable

lucre *n derog.* money

luddite *n derog* someone who is opposed to change, esp. the introduction of new work methods and machinery

ludicrous *adj* causing laughter; foolish **~ly** *adv*

ludo *n* board game played with counters and a dice

lug *vt* **-gg-** pull or carry with difficulty

luggage *n* bags, cases, etc., of a traveller

lughole *n BrE sl* ear

lugubrious *adj fml* sorrowful **~ly** *adv*

lukewarm *adj* **1** (of liquid) neither warm nor cold **2** not eager

lull *vt* cause to rest ♦ *n* calm period

lullaby *n* song to make a child go to sleep

lumbago *n* pain in the lower back

lumbar *adj med* of the lower part of the back

lumber *v* **1** *vi* move heavily and awkwardly **2** *vt* give (someone) an unwanted object or job ♦ *n* **1** useless articles stored away **2** *AmE* timber

lumberjack *n* person who cuts down trees

luminary *n fml* famous respected person

luminescence *n* (emission of) light produced at low temperatures

luminous *adj* shining in the dark **–nosity** *n*

lummox *n infml* clumsy person

lump *n* **1** solid mass **2** hard swelling **3** **lump in the throat** tight sensation in the throat caused by unexpressed pity, sorrow, etc. ♦ *v* **lump it** accept bad conditions without complaint **lump together** *phr vt* consider (two or more things) as a single unit **~y** *adj*

lump sum *n* money given as a single payment rather than in parts

lunacy *n* madness

lunar *adj* of the moon

lunatic *adj, n* mad or foolish (person)

lunatic fringe *n* section of an esp. political group holding the most extreme or unreasonable opinions

lunch also *fml* **luncheon** *n* meal eaten at about midday **lunch** *vi*

luncheon meat *n* compressed mixture of meat and cereal, usu. tinned

lung *n* either of the two breathing organs in the chest

lunge *vi, n* (make) a sudden forward movement

lupin *n* plant with long spikes of flowers also used as cattle food

lurch *vi* move irregularly ♦ *n* **1** lurching movement **2 in the lurch** alone and in difficulty

lure *n* something that attracts ♦ *vt* attract into trouble

lurid *adj* **1** unnaturally bright **2** shocking; unpleasant **~ly** *adv*

lurk *vi* wait in hiding, esp. for a bad purpose

luscious /ˈlushəs/ *adj* **1** having a ripe sweet taste **2** sexually attractive

lush¹ *adj* (of plants) growing thickly

lush² *n sl, esp. AmE* alcoholic

lust *n* strong (sexual) desire **lust** *vi* **~ful** *adj*

lustre, *AmE* **-ter** *n* **1** brightness of a polished surface **2** glory **–rous** *adj*

lusty *adj* strong and healthy **–tily** *adv*

lute *n* ancient stringed musical instrument played by plucking

luxuriant *adj* growing well and thickly **~ly** *adv* **–ance** *n*

luxuriate *vi* enjoy oneself lazily

luxurious *adj* comfortable and esp. expensive **~ly** *adv* **~ness** *n*

luxury *n* **1** great comfort, as provided by wealth **2** something pleasant, but not necessary and not often had or done

-ly *suffix* in the stated way: *sadly*

lychee *n* Asian fruit with white juicy flesh

lychgate *n* roofed gateway to a churchyard

lying *v pres. p. of* lie¹ and lie²

lying-in *n* confinement (2)

lymph *n* clear body fluid which carries substances (e.g. proteins) to the blood

lynch *vt* (esp. of a crowd) kill without a

legal trial
lynx *n* **lynx** *or* **lynxes** wild cat with mottled coat and tufted ears
lyre *n* ancient Greek harp
lyric *n, adj* (short poem) expressing strong feelings in songlike form **~al** *adj* full of joyful feeling **lyrics** *pl n* words of a popular song **~ism** *n* lyrical quality

M

M,m the 13th letter of the English alphabet
m *abbrev. for:* **1** metre(s) **2** mile(s) **3** million **4** married **5** male
ma *n infml* mother
ma'am *n* (polite way of addressing a woman)
mac *n BrE* coat that keeps out the rain
macabre *adj* causing fear, esp. because connected with death
macadam *n* road surface of small bits of stone pressed hard together **~ize, ~ise** *vt*
macaroni *n* pasta in the shape of hollow tubes
macaroon *n* small cake made of ground almonds
macaw *n* large S American parrot
mace[1] *n* ceremonial rod carried by an official
mace[2] *n* spice made of dried nutmeg shell
macerate *vt* make soft by soaking **-ation** *n*
Mach /mak/ also **Mach number** *n* number giving the ratio of the speed of an aircraft to the speed of sound
machete /mə'sheti/ *n* large heavy knife
Machiavellian /ˌmaki·ə'veli·ən/ *adj* skilful in using indirect means to get what one wants
machinations /ˌmaki'naysh(ə)nz/ *pl n* secret efforts or plans to do harm **-ate** *vi*
machine *n* **1** instrument or apparatus that uses power to work **2** group that controls and plans activities of a political party ♦ *vt* make or produce by machine **-nist** *n*
machine code *n* system of coding information in a form understood by a computer
machinegun *n* gun that fires continuously
machine-readable *adj* in a form that can be understood and used by a computer
machinery *n* **1** machines **2** working parts of a machine or engine **3** operation of a system or organization
machine tool *n* power-driven tool for cutting or shaping metal, wood, etc.
machismo /mə'kizmoh, -'chiz-/ *n usu. derog* quality of being macho
macho /'machoh, -koh/ *adj* (trying to seem) strong, brave and masculine
mackerel *n* **-el** *or* **-els** sea fish, often eaten
mackintosh *n* mac
macramé *n* (art of making) decorative work of knotted string
macro- *prefix* **1** long: *macrodiagonal* **2** large: *macrospore*
macrobiotic *adj* of a type of food (esp. vegetable products grown without chemicals) thought to produce good health
mad *adj* **-dd- 1** ill in the mind **2** very foolish **3** angry **4** filled with strong interest: *She's mad about politics.* **5 like mad** very hard, fast, loud, etc. **~ly** *adv* **~ness** *n* **~den** *vt* annoy extremely
Madam *n* (polite way of addressing a woman)
Madame *n* **Mesdames** (title of a married French-speaking woman)
madder *n* (plant which yields) a red dye
made *v past t. and p. of* make
Madeira *n* strong sweet wine
Mademoiselle *n* **Mesdemoiselles** (title of an unmarried French-speaking

woman)
madonna *n* (picture or figure of) Mary, the mother of Christ
madras *n* fine cotton cloth, usu. brightly checked
madrigal *n* song for several singers without instruments
maelstrom /ˈmaylstrohm/ *n* **1** violent whirlpool **2** destructive force of events
maestro /ˈmiestroh/ *n* **-tros** great or famous musician
mafia *n* **1** (*usu. cap.*) organization of criminals, esp. in the US **2** influential group who support each other: *the medical mafia*
magazine *n* **1** sort of book with a paper cover, containing writing, photographs, and advertisements, that is printed every week or month **2** part of a gun in which bullets are stored
magenta /məˈjentə/ *adj* dark purplish red
maggot *n* larva of flies and other insects
magic *n* **1** use of strange unseen forces, or of tricks, to produce effects **2** special wonderful quality: *the magic of the theatre* ♦ *adj* caused by or used in magic **~al** *adj* strange and wonderful **~ly** *adv*
magic eye *n* photoelectric cell
magician *n* person who practises magic
magisterial *adj* showing complete and undoubted control
magistrate *n* official who judges cases in the lowest law courts
maglev *n* railway system in which a train is held above the track by powerful magnets
magma *n* molten rock from beneath the earth's crust
magnanimous *adj* very generous **~ly** *adv* **–mity** *n*
magnate *n* wealthy and powerful person
magnesia *n* white oxide of magnesium used as a mild laxative
magnesium *n* silver-white metal
magnet *n* **1** piece of iron or steel that draws other metal objects towards it **2** person or thing that attracts or interests people greatly **~ism** *n* magnetic force **~ize, –ise** *vt* **~ic** *adj* **~ically** *adv*
magnetic pole *n* point near the North Pole or South Pole towards which a compass needle points
magnetic tape *n* tape on which sound or other information can be recorded
magneto *n* apparatus, containing magnets, and used to produce electricity
magnificent *adj* extremely fine or good **–cence** *n* **~ly** *adv*
magnify *vt* cause to look or seem larger **–fication** *n*
magnifying glass *n* curved lens for magnifying things
magniloquent /magˈniləkwənt/ *adj* grandiloquent
magnitude *n* degree of size or importance
magnolia *n* tree with large sweet-smelling flowers
magnum *n* (large wine bottle containing) a measure of about 1.5 litres
magpie *n* black and white bird of the crow family
magus *n* **magi 1** priest of ancient Persia **2** one of the three wise men of the Nativity story **3** magician
maharajah *n* (title of) an Indian prince
maharani *n* (title of) the wife of a maharaja
mahatma *n* wise and holy man in India
mahogany *n* dark reddish wood used for furniture
mahout *n* person who trains and rides elephants
maid *n* **1** female servant **2** maiden
maiden *n lit* young unmarried woman ♦ *adj* **1** first: *the ship's maiden voyage* **2** unmarried: *my maiden aunts*
maidenhair *n* small, delicate fern
maidenhead *n lit* virginity
maiden name *n* family name a woman has or had before marriage
maid of honour *n* **1** chief bridesmaid **2** small almond-flavoured tart
mail[1] *n* **1** the postal system **2** letters, etc., that one posts or receives ♦ *vt esp. AmE* post[2]

mail² *n* soldiers' protective clothing in former times, made of small metal rings
mail order *n* sale of goods by mail
mailshot *n* sending of advertisements, etc., to large numbers of people by post
maim *vt* wound very seriously and usu. lastingly
main¹ *adj* chief; most important **~ly** *adv*
main² *n* **1** large pipe or wire supplying water, gas, or electricity **2 in the main** mainly; mostly
main chance *n* possibility of making money or other personal gain
mainframe *n* the largest and most powerful kind of computer
mainland *n* a land mass, considered without its islands **mainland** *adj*
mainline *vi/t* inject an illegal drug into a vein
mainspring *n* **1** chief spring in a watch **2** chief force or reason that makes something happen
mainstay *n* someone or something which provides the chief means of support
mainstream *n* main or usual way of thinking or acting
maintain *vt* **1** keep in good condition **2** support with money **3** continue to have or do **4** continue to say, believe, or argue
maintenance *n* **1** keeping in good condition **2** money given to wives and/or children by a husband/father who does not live with them
maisonette *n* flat that is part of a larger house
maize *n esp. BrE* corn (2)
majesty *n* **1** (*cap.*) (used as a title for kings and queens) **2** *fml* grandness **-tic** *adj* **-tically** *adv*
major *adj* of great importance or seriousness: *a major problem|major surgery* ♦ *n* army officer, above captain **major in** *phr vt esp.AmE* study as the chief subject(s) for a university degree
majordomo *n* **-mos** man in charge of a large household staff
majorette *n* girl or woman with a baton who marches with a band or dances to band music
major general *n* officer of high rank in the army or US air force
majority *n* **1** most **2** difference in number between a large and small group: *win by a majority of 300 votes*
make *vt* **made 1** produce: *make a cake* **2** cause to be: *It made me happy.* **3** force; cause: *I can't make him understand.* **4** earn (money) **5** calculate or be counted as: *What time do you make it?* **6** add up to: *2 and 2 make 4* **7** tidy (a bed that has been slept in) **8** have the qualities of: *That story makes good reading.* **9** reach: *We made harbour by night fall.* **10** complete: *That picture really makes the room.* **11 make believe** pretend **12 make do** use something for lack of anything better: *We had to make do with water.* **13 make it: a** arrive in time **b** succeed **make for** *phr vt* **1** move in the direction of: *I made for the exit.* **2** result in: *Large print makes for easy reading.* **make off** *phr vi* leave in a hurry **make out** *phr v* **1** *vt* write in complete form **2** *vt* see, hear, or understand properly **3** *vt* claim; pretend **4** *vi* succeed **5** *vt* argue: *make out a case* **make over** *phr vt* **1** pass over to someone else, esp. legally **2** *esp. AmE* remake **make up** *phr v* **1** *vt* invent (a story, etc.), esp. to deceive **2** *vi/t* use special paint and powder on the face to look beautiful or change the appearance **3** *vt* prepare for use: *A pharmacist made up the doctor's prescriptions.* **4** *vt* form as a whole: *Oil makes up half of our exports.* **5** *vi* become friends again after a quarrel **6** *vi* compensate ♦ *n* **1** type of product **2 on the make** searching for personal gain **maker** *n* **1** person who makes something: *a watchmaker* **2** (*usu. cap.*) God **making** *n* **1 be the making of** cause to improve greatly **2 have the makings of** have the possibility of developing into
make-believe *n* pretending

makeshift *adj* used because there is nothing better
make-up *n* **1** paint, powder, etc., worn on the face **2** combination of members or qualities
mal- *prefix* bad or badly; wrong or wrongly: *malnourished / malodorous*
maladjusted *adj* not fitting in well with other people or with life generally
maladroit *n* clumsy
malady *n lit* illness
malaise *n* **1** failure to be active and successful **2** feeling of not being well
malapropism *n* amusing misuse of a word, esp. one like the intended word but meaning something completely different
malaria *n* tropical disease passed on by mosquitoes
Malay *n* (the language of) an inhabitant of the Malay peninsula **Malay** *adj*
Malaysian *n, adj* (inhabitant) of Malaysia
malcontent *n fml* dissatisfied person who is likely to make trouble
male *n, adj* (person or animal) of the sex that does not give birth
male chauvinist *n derog* man who assumes that women are inferior to men
malediction *n fml* curse
malefactor /ˈmælɪˌfæktə/ *n fml or lit* person who does evil
malefic /məˈlefɪk/ *adj fml* malign **~ent** *adj* **~ence** *n*
malevolent *adj lit* wishing to do evil to others **~ly** *adv* **–lence** *n*
malfeasance *n* wrongdoing, esp. by a government official
malformed *adj* made or shaped badly: *a malformed limb* **–formation** *n*
malfunction *n* fault in operation, fail to operate properly **malfunction** *vi*
malice *n* desire to hurt or harm **–icious** *adj* **–iciously** *adv*
malign *adj* bad; causing harm ♦ *vt* say bad things about
malignant *adj* **1** (of disease) likely to kill **2** malign **~ly** *adv* **–ncy** *n*
malinger *vi* avoid work by pretending to be ill **~er** *n*
mall *n AmE* area of streets with no cars, where one can shop
mallard *n* wild duck
malleable *adj* easy to shape; soft **~ness** *n* **–bility** *n*
mallet *n* wooden hammer
mallow *n* plant with pink or purple flowers
malnourished *adj* suffering from malnutrition
malnutrition *n* lack of (proper) food
malodorous *adj fml* smelling bad
malpractice *n* failure to do one's professional duty properly or honestly
malt *n* partly grown grain used esp. for making beer and whisky
Maltese *n* (the language of) an inhabitant of Malta **Maltese** *adj*
maltreat *vt* treat roughly or cruelly **~ment** *n*
mama *n AmE infml or BrE lit* mother
mamba *n* very poisonous African tree snake
mammal *n* animal of the sort fed on the mother's milk when young
mammary *adj* of the breasts
mammary gland *n* large milk-producing gland in a female mammal
mammoth *n* extinct hairy elephant ♦ *adj* extremely large
man *n* **men 1** adult male person **2** the human race: *Man must change in a changing world.* **3** person: *All men must die.* **4** male of low rank: *officers and men* **5** object used in board games: *chess men* ♦ *vt* **-nn-** provide with people for operation **~hood** *n* quality or time of being a (brave) man
man-about-town *n* (rich) man who attends many fashionable social events
manacle *n* metal ring for fastening a prisoner's hands or feet
manage *v* **1** *vt* be in charge of; run **2** *vi/t* succeed in doing: *I only just managed to get out of the way.* **3** *vi* succeed in living, esp. on a small amount of money: *We don't earn much, but we manage.* **~able** *adj* easy or possible to deal with **~ment** *n* **1** managing **2** the people in charge **manager** *n* person who runs

an organization, e.g. a business, hotel, or sports team **–agerial** *adj*

Mancunian *n, adj* (inhabitant) of Manchester

mandarin *n* **1** high-ranking government official in the former Chinese empire **2** *often derog* high-ranking official **3** small orange

mandate *n* government's right or duty to act according to the wishes of the electors

mandatory *adj fml* which must be done

mandible *n med* jaw **–bular** *adj*

mandolin *n* 8-stringed musical instrument

mandrake *n* plant with a forked root formerly used in medicine

mandrill *n* large baboon with a brightly-coloured face

mane *n* long hair on a horse's or lion's neck

maneuver *n, v AmE* manoeuvre

man Friday *n* male assistant

manfully *adv* bravely and determinedly

manganese *n* greyish white metallic element

mange /manj, maynj/ *n* skin disease of animals which causes loss of fur

mangel-wurzel, mangel *n* large orange root vegetable grown as cattle feed

manger *n* long open container for animals' food

mangetout /ˈmonzhtooh/ *n* pea with edible pods

mangle[1] *vt* crush and tear so as to ruin

mangle[2] *vt, n* (put through) machine with rollers for squeezing water from laundry

mango *n* **-goes** *or* **-gos** tropical fruit with sweet yellow flesh

mangrove *n* tropical tree that grows in or near water and puts down new roots from its branches

mangy /ˈmanji, ˈmaynji/ *adj* **1** suffering from mange **2** scruffy

manhandle *vt* hold or move forcefully or roughly

manhole *n* opening in the road leading to underground pipes, wires, etc.

manhour *n* the amount of work done by one person in one hour

mania *n* **1** madness **2** extreme interest or desire: *soccer mania* **maniac** *n* **~cal** *adj*

manic *adj* **1** *tech* of or suffering from mania **2** wildly excited

manic-depressive *n, adj* (a person) suffering from extreme changes of mood, between cheerful excitement and depression

manicure *vt, n* (give) treatment for the hands, esp. the fingernails, including cleaning and cutting **–curist** *n*

manifest *adj* plain to see or understand ♦ *vt* show plainly **~ation** *n* **~ly** *adv*

manifesto *n* **-tos** *or* **-toes** statement of intentions or opinions, esp. as made by a political party before an election

manifold *adj* many in number or kind ♦ *n tech* pipe with holes, to allow gases to enter or escape from an engine, such as in a car

manikin, manni- *n* **1** little man **2** mannequin (1)

manilla, manila *n* strong brown paper

manipulate *vt* **1** handle skilfully **2** control and influence for one's own purposes **–lative** *adj* **–lation** *n*

mankind *n* human beings

manly *adj* having qualities suitable to a man **–liness** *n*

man-made *adj* **1** produced by people **2** (of materials) not made from natural substances

manna *n* **1** (in the Bible) food miraculously given to the Israelites **2** something good that comes unexpectedly

mannequin *n* **1** dummy used by artists or in making or displaying clothese **2** woman who models clothes

manner *n* **1** way: *a meal prepared in the Japanese manner* **2** way of behaving towards people: *a rude manner* **3 all manner of** *fml* every sort of **manners** *pl n* (polite) social practices **~ly** *adj*

mannerism *n* way of behaving that has become a habit

manoeuvre, *AmE* **maneuver** *n* **1** skilful movement **2** secret trick to gain a purpose **3 on manoeuvres** doing battle training ♦ *vt* move or turn, esp. skilfully or deceivingly: *The car manoeuvres well in wet weather.* **–vrable**, *AmE* **–verable** *adj*

man of straw *n* **1** *esp. BrE* person of weak character **2** *esp. AmE* imaginary opponent whose arguments can easily be defeated

man-of-war, man-o'-war *n arch.* warship

manometer *n* instrument for measuring the pressure of gases **–tric** *adj* **–trically** *adv*

manor *n* area of land owned by the local lord in former times

manpower *n* number of workers needed

manqué /ˈmongˌkay/ *adj fml* that failed to become the stated thing

mansard, mansard roof *n* roof sloping gently at the top and then more steeply

manse *n* house of a Presbyterian or Baptist clergyman

mansion *n* large grand house

man-sized *adj* large

manslaughter *n* crime of killing someone unintentionally

mantelpiece *n* shelf above a fireplace

mantilla *n* light scarf worn over the head esp. by Spanish women

mantle *n* **1** covering: *a mantle of snow* **2** (sign of) general or official recognition: *the mantle of world heavyweight champion* **3** sheath of incandescent fabric in a gas lamp **4** the part of the earth between the crust and the core ♦ *vt* cover as with a mantle

man-to-man *adj, adv* open(ly) and honest(ly)

mantra *n* word or phrase repeated in religious chanting or in meditation (e.g. in Hinduism or Buddhism)

manual *adj* of or using the hands ♦ *n* book giving information or instructions **~ly** *adv*

manufacture *vt* make in large quantities using machinery ♦ *n* manufacturing: *goods of foreign manufacture* **~turer** *n*

manure *n* animal waste matter put on land to make crops grow ♦ *vt* put manure on

manuscript *n* **1** first copy of a book, etc., handwritten or typed **2** old book written by hand

Manx *n, adj* (the language or people) of the Isle of Man

Manx cat *n* type of cat with no tail

many *determiner, pron* a large number (of): *I haven't got as many as you.|many people* ♦ *adv* to a great extent: *many more*

Maoism *n* theories of Mao Tse Tung, the first Communist leader of China **–ist** *adj, n*

Maori *n* (the language of) an indigenous inhabitant of New Zealand **Maori** *adj*

map *n* representation of (part of) the Earth's surface as if seen from above: *a map of France* ♦ *vt* **-pp-** make a map of

maple *n* tree with many-pointed leaves

mar *vt* spoil

marabou, -bout *n* large African stork

maracas *pl n* pair of rattles used in Latin American music

maraschino *n* **-nos** (cherry preserved in) a wild cherry liqueur

marathon *n* **1** running race of about 26 miles (42 kilometres) **2** (hard) activity that lasts a long time: *a marathon speech*

maraud *vi/t* (roam in search of places to) attack and plunder **–er** *n*

marble *n* **1** hard smooth usu. white stone used for statues or buildings **2** small glass ball rolled against others in a game (**marbles**) ♦ *vt* decorate with a streaky pattern

march *v* **1** *vi* walk with regular forceful steps like a soldier **2** *vt* force to go: *They marched him off to prison.* ♦ *n* **1** act of marching **2** tune to accompany marching

March *n* the 3rd month of the year

marching orders *pl n* being told officially that one must leave

marchioness *n* **1** wife of a marquess **2** woman with the rank of a marquess

Mardi Gras *n* (carnival finishing on) Shrove Tuesday

mare *n* female horse

margarine *n* butter-like food substance

margin *n* **1** space down the edge of a page, with no writing or printing in it **2** amount by which one thing is greater than another: *We won by a decisive margin.* **3** area on the outside edge of a larger area: *the margin of the stream*

marginal *adj* **1** small in importance or amount: *a marginal difference* **2** (of a seat in parliament) in danger of being lost to another party in an election **~ly** *adv* **~ize** *vt* push out to the edge of (a group)

marguerite *n* large white daisy

marigold *n* plant with golden-yellow flowers

marijuana /ˌmarəˈwahnə/ *n* form of the drug cannabis

marina *n* small harbour for pleasure boats

marinade *n* mixture of oil, wine, herbs and spices in which food is soaked before being cooked **–nate** *vt* soak in a marinade

marine *adj* **1** of the sea **2** of ships and sailing ♦ *n* soldier who serves on a naval ship

mariner *n* sailor

marionette *n* puppet with strings

marital *adj* of marriage

maritime *adj* **1** marine **2**. near the sea

marjoram *n* herb of the mint family

mark[1] *n* **1** something on or put onto a surface: *dirty marks on the wall|tyre marks in the snow* **2** a number that represents a judgment of quality: *The top mark in the test was 8 out of 10.* **3** something that shows a quality: *They all stood as a mark of respect.* **4** printed or written sign: *punctuation mark* **5** particular type of machine: *the new Mark 4 gun* **6 make one's mark (on)** gain success, fame, etc., (in) **7 quick/slow off the mark** *infml* quick/slow in understanding or acting **8 up to the mark: a** of an acceptable standard **b** in good health **9 wide of the mark** not correct or close to the subject♦ *v* **1** *vi/t* spoil with marks: *Hot cups have marked the table.|The table marks easily.* **2** *vt* give marks to **3** *vt* stay close to (an opposing player) to spoil their play **4** *vt* be a sign of: *A cross marks his grave.* **5 mark time** spend time on work, etc., without making any advance **mark down/up** *phr vt* lower/raise the price of **mark out** *phr vt* **1** also **mark off** draw lines round (an area) **2** show or choose as likely to become (successful) or gain (success) **~ed** *adj* **1** having marks **2** definite: *a marked American accent* **3** under attack or suspicion: *a marked man* **~edly** *adv*

mark[2] *n* German unit of money

marker *n* **1** tool for making marks **2** object for marking a place

market *n* **1** (place for) a gathering of people to buy and sell goods **2** desire to buy; demand: *There's no market for coats at this time of year.* **3** area where goods are sold: *the foreign/domestic market* **4** trade: *the tea market* **5 play the market** buy and sell business shares to try to make a profit ♦ *vt* present and offer for sale **~ing** *n* **1** skills of advertising, supplying, and selling goods **2** *AmE* shopping **~able** *adj* **~ability** *n*

market forces *pl n* operation of business and trade without government controls

market garden *n BrE* area for growing vegetables and fruit for sale

marketplace *n* **1** place where a market is held **2** activities of buying and selling

market research *n* study of what people buy and why

marking *n* natural marks on an animal's fur or feathers

marksman *n* person who can shoot well **~ship** *n*

markup *n* price increase by a seller

marl *n* soil formed of clay and lime

marlin *n* large sea fish

marline *n* thin rope used on board ship

marmalade *n* jam made from oranges

marmoreal *adj* of or like marble

marmot *n* European burrowing rodent

maroon[1] *vt* abandon in a lonely or dangerous place, without help

maroon[2] *adj* dark red
marquee *n* very large tent
marquess, marquis *n* nobleman ranking below a duke
marquetry *n* (art of making) decorative patterns of inlaid wood
marram grass *n* coarse grass that grows by the sea
marriage *n* **1** ceremony to marry people **2** state of being husband and wife **~able** *adj* suitable for marriage
marrow *n* **1** large long vegetable of the cucumber family **2** soft tissue inside bones
marrowfat *n* large pea
marry *v* **1** *vi/t* take (as) a husband or wife: *He never married.|She married a soldier.* **2** *vt* join in marriage: *The priest married them.* **3** *vt* cause to get married: *They married their daughter (off) to a young diplomat.* **married** *adj*
Mars *n* the planet 4th in order from the sun
Marsala *n* sweet strong wine from Sicily
Marseillaise *n* national anthem of France
marsh *n* (area of) soft wet land **~y** *adj*
marshal *n* **1** US law official, like a sheriff **2** military officer of very high rank **3** organizer of an event, such as a ceremony or race ♦ *vt* **-ll-** (*AmE* **-l-**) **1** arrange (esp. facts) in good order **2** lead (people) carefully
marshalling yard *n* place where railway coaches and engines are assembled into trains
marshmallow *n* type of soft round sweet
marsupial *n* animal that carries its young in a pouch of skin and does not develop a placenta
marsupium *n* pouch of a marsupial
mart *n* market
marten *n* carnivorous tree-dwelling animal like a large weasel
martial *adj fml* of war, soldiers, etc.
martial art *n* Eastern fighting sport: *Judo is a martial art.*
martial law *n* government by the army under special laws
Martian *n, adj* (creature) from Mars
martinet *n* very strict person
martini *n* cocktail of gin and vermouth
martyr *n* **1** someone who dies or suffers for their (religious) beliefs **2 make a martyr of oneself** give up one's own wishes to help others, or in the hope of being praised ♦ *vt* kill as a martyr
marvel *n* wonderful thing or example: *the marvels of modern science* ♦ *vi* **-ll-** (*AmE* **-l-**) be filled with surprise and admiration **~lous,** *AmE* **~ous** *adj* very pleasing or good **~lously** *adv*
Marxism *n* teaching of Karl Marx on which Communism is based **–ist** *n, adj*
marzipan *n* sweet paste made from almond
masc. *abbrev. for:* masculine
mascara *n* dark substance for colouring the eyelashes
mascot *n* object, animal, or person thought to bring good luck
masculine *adj* **1** (in grammar) referring to males **2** of or like a man **–linity** *n*
maser *n* device that produces a powerful beam of microwaves
mash *vt* crush into a soft substance ♦ *n* **1** mashed potatoes **2** crushed malt mixed with hot water to ferment **3** bran mixed with hot water as food for livestock
mask *n* covering for the face, to hide or protect it ♦ *vt* hide **~ed** *adj* wearing a mask
masking tape *n* sticky tape used when painting to protect unpainted areas
masochism *n* **1** gaining pleasure from being hurt **2** wish to be hurt so as to gain sexual pleasure **–chist** *n* **–chistic** *adj*
mason *n* **1** stonemason **2** (*usu. cap.*) Freemason **~ic** *adj*
masonry *n* stone building blocks
masque *n* **1** masquerade (2) **2** play performed by masked actors
masquerade /ˌmaskə·rayd/ *vi* pretend: *thieves masquerading as bank employees* ♦ *n* **1** hiding of the truth **2** dance where people wear masks
mass *n* **1** large lump, heap, or quantity:

a mass of clouds **2** also **masses** *pl infml* lots: *masses of work to do* **3** (in science) amount of matter in a body ♦ *vi/t* gather in large numbers or quantity **masses** *pl n* ordinary people in society
Mass *n* (in the Catholic and Orthodox churches) important religious ceremony
massacre *n* killing of large numbers of people **massacre** *vt*
massage *n* (act of) pressing and rubbing someone's body, esp. to cure pain or stiffness ♦ *vt* **1** give a massage to **2** change (facts, figures, etc.) usu. in a dishonest way
masseur *n* person who gives massages
masseuse *n* female masseur
massif *n tech* group of mountains forming one mass
massive *adj* extremely big **~ly** *adv* **~ness** *n*
mass media *n* the media
mass-produce *vt* produce (goods) in large numbers to the same pattern **mass production** *n*
mast *n* **1** long upright pole for carrying sails **2** tall framework for aerials
mastectomy *n* operation for the removal of a breast
master *n* **1** person in control of people, animals, or things **2** teacher **3** great artist, writer, or musician **4** captain of a ship **5** something from which copies are made: *a master tape* ♦ *vt* **1** learn or gain as a skill: *master the art of public speaking* **2** control and defeat: *He mastered his fear of heights.* **~ful** *adj* able or eager to control others **~fully** *adv* **~ly** *adj* showing great skill. **~y** *n* **1** power to control **2** great skill or knowledge
master key *n* key that will open several different locks
mastermind *vt* plan cleverly: *mastermind a crime* ♦ *n* very clever person
master of ceremonies *n* person who introduces speakers or performers at a public event
masterpiece *n* piece of work, esp. of art, done with extreme skill
masthead *n* **1** top of a mast **2** name of a newspaper shown at the top of its first page
masticate *vi/t* chew **-ation** *n*
mastiff *n* large powerful dog
mastitis /ma'stietəs/ *n* inflammation of the breast or udder
mastodon *n* extinct animal like an elephant
mastoid *adj, n* (of or near) a small bone behind the ear
masturbate *vi/t* excite the sex organs (of) by handling, rubbing, etc. **–bation** *n*
mat *n* **1** piece of strong material for covering part of a floor **2** small piece of material for putting under objects on a table
matador *n* person who kills the bull in a bullfight
match¹ *n* **1** sports or other competition between two people or sides; game: *a football match* **2** one who is equal to or better than another: *I'm no match for her at maths.* **3** good combination: *The hat and shoes are a perfect match.* **4** marriage: *Both her daughters made good matches.* ♦ *v* **1** *vi/t* be similar (to) or combine well (with): *The curtains and carpets don't match.* **2** *vt* be equal to or find an equal for: *a restaurant that can't be matched for service* **~maker** *n* person who tries to arrange others' love affairs
match² *n* short thin stick that burns when its end is rubbed against a rough surface **~box** *n* box for holding matches **~wood** *n* wood broken into small pieces
matchless *adj* without equal
matchlock *n* musket ignited by a match
match point *n* situation in a game, esp. tennis, in which the player who wins the next point will win the match
mate¹ *n* **1** friend, or person one works or lives with: *We're mates/schoolmates/flatmates.* **2** either of a male-female pair **3** officer on a non-navy ship **4** *BrE sl* (used for addressing a man) ♦ *vi* (esp. of animals) join sexually to produce

young **~y** *adj* friendly
mate² *n, v* checkmate
maté *n* tea made from the leaves and shoots of a South American holly plant
matelot *n* sailor
material *n* **1** substance of which things are or can be made **2** cloth **3** knowledge of facts from which a (written) work may be produced: *She's collecting material for a book.* ♦ *adj* **1** of matter or substance, not spirit **2** *fml* important or necessary **~ly** *adv*
materialism *n* (too) great interest in the pleasures of the world, money, etc. **–ist** *n* **–istic** *adj*
materialize, -ise *vi* **1** become able to be seen **2** become real or actual: *Her hopes never materialized.* **3** come; arrive **–ization** *n*
maternal *adj* **1** of or like a mother **2** related through the mother's part of the family: *my maternal grandmother*
maternity *n* motherhood ♦ *adj* for women who are going to give birth: *a maternity hospital*
matey *adj infml* friendly
mathematics also *BrE* **maths**, *AmE* **math** *n* science of numbers **–ical** *adj* **–ically** *adv* **–ician** *n*
matinée *n* afternoon performance of a play or film
matins *n* morning service in the Anglican church
matri- *prefix* mother: *matriarch*
matriarch *n* woman who controls a (family) group **~al** *adj* ruled by women **~y** *n*
matricide *n* murder of one's mother
matriculate *vi* become a member of a university **–lation** *n*
matrimony *n* being married **–nial** *adj*
matrix *n* **1** (in mathematics) an arrangement of numbers in a square **2** mould[1] **3** substance in which something takes shape
matron *n* **1** chief nurse **2** woman in charge of living arrangements in a school **3** *lit* older married woman, esp. of quiet behaviour **~ly** *adj* **1** (of a woman) rather fat **2** with the dignity of an older woman
matt *adj* not shiny
matted *adj* twisted in a thick mass
matter *n* **1** subject; affair: *several important matters to discuss* **2** trouble; cause of pain: *Is anything the matter?* **3** substance of which things are made: *all the matter in the universe* **4** things of a particular kind or for a particular purpose: *reading matter* **5 a matter of: a** a little more or less than: *It's only a matter of hours before the doctor arrives.* **b** needing as a part: *Learning is a matter of concentration.* **6 a matter of course** a usual event **7 as a matter of fact** in fact; really **8 for that matter** (used when mentioning another possibility) **9 no matter** ... it makes no difference: *No matter how hard I tried, I couldn't move it.* ♦ *vi* be important
matter-of-fact *adj* without feelings or imagination
matting *n* rough woven material, esp. for the floor
mattins *n* matins
mattock *n* digging tool with a point and a blade
mattress *n* large filled cloth case for sleeping on
mature *adj* **1** fully developed **2** sensible, like a mature person **3** carefully thought about ♦ *vi/t* become or make mature **–turation** *n* **–turity** *n*
maudlin *adj* stupidly sad, esp. when drunk
maul *vt* hurt by handling roughly: *mauled by a lion*
maunder *vi* speak in a disordered or unclear way
Maundy Thursday *n* the Thursday before Easter
mausoleum *n* grand building containing a grave
mauve *adj* pale purple
maverick *n* person who acts differently from the rest of a group
maw *n* **1** an animal's throat or stomach **2** something that seems to swallow things up
mawkish *adj* expressing love and ad-

miration in a silly way
maxi- *prefix* unusually large or long
maxim *n* rule for sensible behaviour
maximize, -ise *vt* make as big as possible
maximum *n, adj* **-ma** *or* **-mums** largest (amount, number, etc.): *our maximum offer* **–mal** *adj* **–mize** *vt*
may *v aux* **1** (shows a possibility): *He may come and he may not.* **2** have permission to; be allowed to: *You may come in now.|May we go home, please?* **3** (used when expressing a wish): *May you live happily ever after!* **4 may as well** have no strong reason not to: *It's late, so I may as well go to bed.*
May *n* the 5th month of the year
maybe *adv* perhaps
mayday *n* (radio signal used as) a call for help
May Day *n* the first day of May, celebrated as a spring festival or a workers' festival
mayfly *n* water insect with a very short life in its winged, adult form
mayhem *n* violent disorder and confusion
mayonnaise *n* salad dressing made from eggs and oil
mayor *n* person elected each year by a town council to be head of that city or town **~alty** *n* (term of) office of a mayor
mayoress *n* **1** woman who is a mayor **2** wife of a mayor
maypole *n* tall pole with ribbons, round which people dance on May Day
maze *n* arrangement of twisting paths in which one becomes lost
mazurka, mazourka *n* (music for) a Polish folk dance
MC *n* **1** master of ceremonies **2** Member of Congress
MCP *abbrev. for:* male chauvinist pig
MD *abbrev. for:* **1** Doctor of Medicine **2** Managing Director
me *pron* (object form of **I**)
mead *n* alcoholic drink made from honey
meadow *n* field of grass
meadowsweet *n* tall plant with fragrant, cream-coloured flowers
meagre, *AmE* **-ger** *adj* not big enough **~ly** *adv* **~ness** *n*
meal[1] *n* (food eaten at) an occasion for eating
meal[2] *n* crushed grain **~y** *adj*
mealie *n SAfr* (an ear of) maize
mealy-mouthed *adj* expressing (unpleasant) things too indirectly
mean[1] *vt* **meant** **1** (of words, signs, etc.) represent an idea: *'Melancholy' means 'sad'.|The red light means 'stop'.* **2** intend: *He said Tuesday, but meant Thursday.|I said I'd help and I meant it.* **3** be a sign of: *This could mean war.* **4** be of importance to the stated degree: *Her work means everything to her.* **5 be meant to** *esp. BrE* ought to; be supposed to **6 mean business** act with serious intentions **7 mean well** act with good intentions **~ing** *n* **1** idea intended to be understood, esp. from words: *'Measure' has several meanings.* **2** importance or value: *His life lost its meaning when his wife died.* **~ing** *adj* suggesting a hidden thought: *a meaning look* **~ingful** *adj* **~ingless** *adj*
mean[2] *adj* **1** ungenerous **2** unkind; nasty **3** *esp. AmE* bad-tempered **4 no mean** very good: *He's no mean cook.* **~ly** *adv* **~ness** *n*
mean[3] *n, adj* average
meander *vi* **1** wander **2** (of a stream) flow slowly and twistingly ♦ *n* winding of a stream
means *n* **means** **1** method; way **2** money, esp. enough to live on **3 by all means** (a polite way of giving permission) **4 by means of** using; with **5 by no means** not at all **6 live beyond/within one's means** spend more than/not more than one can afford
means test *n* inquiry into the amount of money someone has, esp. to find out if they need money from the state
meant *v past t. and p. of* mean[1]
meantime *n* **in the meantime** meanwhile (1)
meanwhile *adv* **1** in the time between

two events **2** during the same period of time

measles *n* infectious disease in which the sufferer has small red spots on the skin

measly *adj sl* too small

measure *vt* **1** find or show the size, amount, degree, etc., of:*Measure the (height of the) cupboard first.*|*A clock measures time.* **2** be of the stated size: *The river measured 200 metres from side to side.* **measure off/out** *phr vt* take from a longer length or larger quantity **measure up** *phr vi* show good enough qualities (for) ♦ *n* **1** measuring system **2** unit in such a system **3** amount: *She's had a certain measure of success.* **4** act to bring about an effect: *The government was forced to take strong measures.* **5** rhythm in poetry or music **6 for good measure** in addition **7 take someone's measure/get the measure of someone** judge what someone is like **-sured** *adj* careful and steady **~ment** *n* **1** act of measuring **2** length, height, etc., measured **-surable** *adj* **-surably** *adv*

meat *n* **1** flesh of animals (not fish) for eating **2** valuable matter, ideas, etc.: *It was a clever speech, but there was no real meat in it.* **~y** *adj*

meatball *n* ball of minced meat

mecca *n* place that many people wish to reach

mechanic *n* person skilled in using or repairing machinery

mechanical *adj* **1** of or worked or produced by machinery **2** without new thought or strong feeling **~ly** *adv*

mechanics *n* **1** science of the action of forces on objects **2** science of machinery **3** way in which something works

mechanism *n* machine or the way it works

mechanistic *adj* regarding all actions of living things as governed by scientific laws

mechanize, -ise *vt* (start to) use machines for or in **-ization** *n*

med. *abbrev. for:* **1** medicine; medical **2** medieval **3** medium

medal *n* usu. coinlike object given as a mark of honour, esp. for bravery **~list,** *AmE* **~ist** *n* person who has won a medal, esp. in sport

medallion *n* large medal, or piece of jewellery like a medal

meddle *vi* take action in a matter which does not concern one **~dler** *n*

meddlesome *adj* inclined to meddle

media *pl n* television, radio, newspapers, etc.

mediaeval *adj* medieval

medial *tech* in the middle position

median *n* **1** number or amount at the mid-point of a series **2** line from a point of a triangle to the centre of the opposite side ♦ *adj tech* in or passing through the middle

mediate *vi* act so as to bring agreement after a quarrel **-ator** *n* **-ation** *n*

medic *n infml* doctor or medical student

Medicaid *n* (in the US) system by which the government helps to pay the medical costs of people on low incomes

medical *adj* of or for the treatment of illness♦ *n* medical examination of the body **~ly** *adv*

medicament *n* medicine

Medicare *n* (in the US) system of medical care provided by the government, esp. for old people

medication *n* medicine, esp. a drug **-ive** *adj*

medicinal *adj* as medicine; curing **~ly** *adv*

medicine *n* **1** substance for treating illness **2** science of treating illness

medicine man *n* (in certain tribes) man with magical powers, esp. for curing people

medico *n* **-os** *infml* medic

medieval *adj* of the Middle Ages

mediocre /ˌmeediˈohkə/ *adj* rather bad **-crity** *n*

meditate *v* **1** *vi* think deeply, esp. before making a decision **2** *vi* empty the mind of thought, esp. as a religious practice **3** *vt* plan or consider carefully **-tation** *n* **-tative** *adj* thoughtful

Mediterranean *adj* of or characteristic of the Mediterranean sea or the countries round it
medium[1] *adj* of middle size, amount, quality, etc.
medium[2] *n* **-dia** *or* **-diums 1** method of artistic expression or of giving information **2** condition or surroundings in which things exist **3** middle position or state
medium[3] *n* **-diums** person who claims to receive messages from the spirits of the dead
medlar *n* (small tree that bears) a fruit like a wild apple
medley *n* mass of different types mixed together
meek *adj* gentle and uncomplaining **~ly** *adv* **~ness** *n*
meerkat *n* South African mongoose that lives in groups
meerschaum *n* (tobacco pipe made of) a white clayey mineral
meet *v* **met** /met/ **1** *vi/t* come together (with) **2** *vi/t* be introduced (to) **3** *vt* find or experience: *She met her death in a plane crash.* **4** *vt* follow (as if) in answer: *His speech was met with boos.* **5** *vt* satisfy: *Their offer meets all our needs.* **6** *vt* pay: *Have you enough money to meet your debts?* **7 meet someone halfway** make an agreement which partly satisfies both sides **meet up** *phr vi infml* meet, esp. by informal arrangements **meet with** *phr vt* **1** experience: *I met with an accident.* **2** esp. *AmE* have a meeting with ♦ *n* gathering of people for **a** *BrE* foxhunting **b** *AmE* sports events **~ing** *n* occasion of coming together, esp. to talk
mega- *prefix* **1** million: *megawatt* **2** very great: *megastar*
megadeath *n* one million deaths (used in calculations about nuclear warfare)
megalith *n* huge block of stone used in prehistoric monuments **~ic** *adj*
megalomania *n* delusions of personal power and importance **-niac** *n*
megaphone *n* horn-shaped device to amplify the voice
megaton *n* an explosive force equal to that of one million tons of TNT
megrim *n* migraine
melancholia /ˌmelənˈkohli·ə/ *n* mental disorder with strong feelings of depression and worthlessness
melancholy *adj*, *n* sad(ness) **–ic** *adj*
mélange *n* mixture
meld *vi/t AmE* merge
melee *n* riotous or disorderly crowd
meliorate *vt* improve **–ative** *adj* **–ation** *n*
mellifluous *adj* sounding smooth and sweet
mellow *adj* **1** suggesting gentle ripeness **2** (of colour) soft and warm ♦ *vi/t* become or make mellow **~ness** *n*
melodrama *n* **1** play or film full of action and passion **2** episode of sensational events or emotional overreaction **~tic** *adj* **~tically** *adv*
melody *n* **1** tune **2** song **–dic** *adj* of or having melody **–dious** *adj* tuneful
melon *n* large round juicy fruit
melt *v* **1** *vi/t* become or make liquid: *The sun melted the ice.* **2** *vi* go away: disappear **3** *vi* become more sympathetic **melt down** *phr vt* make (a metal object) liquid by heating
meltdown *n* dangerous situation in which material burns through the bottom of an atomic reactor
melting point *n* temperature at which a solid melts
melting pot *n* **1** place where many different things are mixed together **2 in the melting pot** not fixed or decided
member *n* **1** someone who belongs to a group, esp. an organized group **2** part of the body, such as an organ or limb **~ship** *n* **1** state of being a member of an organization **2** all the members of an organization
membrane *n* soft thin skin
memento *n* **-tos** object that brings back pleasant memories
memo *n* **-os** note from one person or office to another within an organization
memoirs *pl n* autobiography

memorabilia *pl n* interesting things connected with a famous person or event
memorable *adj* worth remembering, esp. because good **–bly** *adv*
memorandum *n fml* memo
memorial *n* something, esp. a stone monument, in memory of a person or event
memorize, -ise *vt* learn and remember on purpose
memory *n* **1** ability to remember: *She's got a good memory.* **2** example of remembering: *one of my earliest memories* **3** time during which things happened which can be remembered: *within living memory* **4** opinion held of someone after their death: *to praise his memory* **5** part of a computer in which information is stored
memsahib *n* European woman living in India
men *n pl. of* man
menace *n* **1** threat; danger **2** troublesome person or thing ♦ *vt* threaten
ménage à trois /meˌnahzh ah ˈtrwah/ *n* relationship in which two people and the lover of one of them live together
menagerie *n* collection of wild animals kept privately or for the public to see
mend *v* **1** *vt* repair **2** *vi* regain one's health **3 mend one's ways** improve one's behaviour ♦ *n* **1** repaired place **2 on the mend** regaining one's health **~er** *n*
mendacity *n fml* untruthfulness **–cious** *adj*
mendicant *n* beggar **–cancy** *n*
menial *adj* (of a job) humble and not interesting or important ♦ *n* someone who does menial work
meningitis *n* serious brain illness
meniscus *n* **-ci** *or* **-cuses** curved surface of a body of liquid
menopause *n* time of life when a woman stops menstruating
menses *pl n* the flow of blood in menstruation
menstruation *n* monthly discharge of blood from the womb of a woman of childbearing age **–ate** *vi* **–al** *adj*
mensuration *n fml* measurement, esp. of area and volume
-ment *suffix* act or result of doing the stated thing: *enjoyment*
mental *adj* **1** of or in the mind: *a mental picture* **2** of or for illness of the mind: *a mental hospital* **3** *infml* mad **~ly** *adv*
mental age *n* measure of someone's mental ability, according to the age at which an average child would display similar ability
mentality *n* **1** abilities and powers of the mind **2** person's character and way of thought
menthol *n* substance which smells and tastes of mint **~ated** *adj*
mention *vt* tell of or about, esp. in a few words ♦ *n* **1** short remark about **2** naming of someone, esp. to honour them **~able** *adj*
mentor *n* person who habitually advises another
menu *n* list of food one can order in a restaurant
MEP *abbrev. for:* Member of the European Parliament
mercantile *adj* of trade and business **–tilism** *n*
Mercator's projection *n* way of representing the map of the world as a rectangle evenly marked out by the lines of latitude and longitude
mercenary *adj* influenced by the wish for money ♦ *n* soldier who fights for whoever will pay him
mercer *n BrE* dealer in (esp. fine quality) textile fabrics
mercerize, ise *vt* improve (cotton yarn) by treatment with an alkali
merchandise *n* things for sale
merchant *n* person who buys and sells goods in large amounts ♦ *adj* used in trade, not war: *the merchant navy*
merchant bank *n* bank that provides banking services for businesses rather than for ordinary people
merchantman *n* ship carrying goods for trade

merchant navy *n BrE* (the personnel of) commercial ships
mercury *n* **1** silvery liquid metal **2** (*cap.*) the planet nearest the sun **-rial** *adj* quick, active, and often changing
mercy *n* **1** willingness to forgive, not to punish; kindness and pity **2** fortunate event **3 at the mercy of** defenceless against **merciful** *adj* **merciless** *adj*
mere *adj* only; nothing more than: *a mere child* **~ly** *adv* only
meretricious /ˌmerəˈtrishəs/ *adj fml* (seeming) attractive but of no real value **~ly** *adv* **~ness** *n*
merge *v* **1** *vi* combine, esp. gradually, so as to become a single thing **2** *vi/t* join together: *The two companies merged.* **merger** *n* joining together of two or more companies
meridian *n* **1** imaginary line over the Earth's surface from pole to pole, used on maps **2** highest point, esp. of a star
meringue *n* (light cake made from) a mixture of sugar and egg whites
merino *n* **1** (one of) a breed of sheep with fine wool **2** soft wool or wool and cotton fabric or yarn
merit *n* good quality ♦ *vt* deserve **~orious** *adj* deserving praise
meritocracy *n* social system which gives the highest positions to those with the most ability
merlin *n* small falcon
mermaid *n* (in stories) woman with a fish's tail
merry *adj* **1** full of or causing laughter and fun **2** *BrE infml* rather drunk **-rily** *adv* **-riment** *n*
merry-go-round *n* machine with large model animals on which children ride round and round
mesa *n* level-topped hill, esp. in US
mescalin, -ine *n* drug obtained from a cactus **(mescal)**, which causes hallucinations
mesh *n* **1** net, esp. with small holes **2** threads in such a net ♦ *vi* (of the teeth of gears) to connect
mesmerism *n* hypnotism **-ist** *n*
mesmerize, -ise *vt* hold the complete attention of, as if by a strong force **-ric** *adj*
Mesozoic *adj, n* (of) an era of geological history between about 230 million and 65 million years ago
mess *n* **1** (state of) untidiness or dirt **2** bad situation; trouble **3** room where a group of people, esp. soldiers eat ♦ *vi* **1** take meals in a mess **2** make a mess **3** interfere: *Don't mess with my things!* **mess about/around** *phr v* **1** *vi* act or speak stupidly **2** *vi* spend time with no particular plan or purpose **3** *vt* treat badly **mess up** *phr vt* ruin; spoil **~y** *adj*
message *n* **1** piece of information passed from one person to another **2** main moral idea of a story, picture, etc. **3 get the message** understand what is meant
messenger *n* person who brings a message
messiah *n* **1** new leader in a religion **2** (*cap.*) Jesus Christ
mestizo *n* **-os** person with one Spanish and one American Indian parent
met *v past t. and p. of* meet
meta- *prefix* **1** situated beyond: *metacarpus* **2** change: *metamorphosis* **3** transcending: *metaphysics*
metabolism *n* process by which a body lives, esp. by changing food into energy **-lic** *adj* **-ize, -ise** *vi/t*
metal *n* usu. solid shiny material, such as iron, copper, or silver **~lic** *adj*
metalloid *n* element having some of the properties of a metal ♦ *adj* **1** resembling a metal **2** of a metalloid
metallurgy *n* scientific study of metals **-gist** *n* **-gical** *adj*
metalwork *n* making of metal objects
metamorphosis *n* **-ses** complete change from one form to another **-phic** *adj* **-phose** *vi/t*
metaphor *n* (use of) a phrase which describes one thing by stating another thing with which it can be compared (as in *the roses in her cheeks*) **~ical** *adj* **~ically** *adv*
metaphysics *n* philosophy of being and knowing **-ical** *adj* concerned with

metaphysics **2** (of ideas) at a high level and difficult to understand

meteor *n* small piece of matter that flies through space and can be seen burning if it comes near the Earth **~ic** *adj* very fast: *a meteoric rise to fame* **~ically** *adv*

meteorite *n* meteor that lands on the Earth

meteorology *n* scientific study of weather **-gist** *n* **-gical** *adj*

mete out *phr vt lit* give (esp. punishment)

meter *n* **1** machine that measures something: *a gas meter* **2** *AmE* metre

methane *n* gas that burns easily

methanol *n* poisonous liquid alcohol

methinks *v* **-thought** *arch* I think

method *n* **1** way of doing something **2** proper planning and arrangement **~ical** *adj* careful; using an ordered system **~ically** *adv*

Methodism *n* form of Protestantism influenced by John Wesley **-ist** *n, adj*

methodology *n* set of methods

methyl alcohol also **wood alcohol** *n* poisonous alcohol found in some natural substances

methylated spirits also *BrE* **meths** *n* alcohol for burning in lamps and heaters

meticulous *adj* very careful, with great attention to detail **~ly** *adv*

métier *n fml* one's type of work

metre, *AmE* **meter** *n* **1** a measure of length equal to 39.37 inches **2** arrangement of beats in poetry **~ic, ~ical** *adj*

metric *adj* using a measured system (**metric system**) based on the metre and kilogram **~ation** *n* changing to a metric system

metro *n* **-ros** underground railway in France and certain other countries

metronome *n* instrument that marks exact time for music

metropolis *n* main or capital city **-litan** *adj*

mettle *n* **1** *fml* will to continue bravely in spite of difficulties **2 on one's mettle** ready to make the best possible effort **~some** *adj* spirited

mew *vi, n* (make) the crying sound a cat makes

mews *n* **mews** small city street with houses and flats, at the back of larger houses

Mexican *n* (inhabitant) of Mexico

mezzanine /ˈmezəneen/ *n* low-ceilinged storey between two main storeys of a building

mezzo[1] *adv* (in music) quite; not very

mezzo[2] also **mezzo-soprano** *n* **mezzos, mezzo-sopranos** (person with) a singing voice lower than soprano but higher than alto

mezzotint *n* (print produced by) an engraving method which involves burnishing parts of a metal plate and leaving others rough

mg *abbrev. for:* milligram(s)

MHR *abbrev. for:* Member of the House of Representatives

MHZ *abbrev. for:* megahertz

MI5 *n* branch of British military intelligence that combats espionage

MI6 *n* branch of British military intelligence that organizes espionage

miaow *vi, n* (make) the crying sound a cat makes

miasma /miˈazmə/ *n* **1** heavy mist **2** strong harmful influence

mica *n* glasslike substance used in making electrical instruments

mice *pl of* mouse

Michaelmas *n* the feast of St Michael on 29th September

Michaelmas daisy *n* tall garden plant with white, blue, or purple daisy-shaped flowers

mick *n derog* Irishman

mickey *n* **take the mickey (out of)** *sl* tease

Mickey Finn *n* alcoholic drink to which a drug has been added to make the drinker unconscious

Mickey Mouse *adj infml* small and unimportant, not to be taken seriously

micro- *prefix* **1** extremely small: *microcomputer* **2** using a microscope: *microsurgery* **3** millionth part: *microsecond*

microbe *n* bacterium
microbiology *n* scientific study of very small living creatures **-gist** *n*
microchip *n* chip (4)
microcomputer also **micro** *infml n* the smallest type of computer, used esp. in the home, in schools, or by small businesses
microcosm *n* something small that represents all the qualities of something larger
microfiche *n* microfilm holding very small photographs of printed pages
microfilm *n* film for photographing something in a very small size ♦ *vt* photograph on microfilm
microlight n aeroplane weighing not more than 150 kg
micrometer *n* instrument for measuring very small distances
microorganism *n* bacterium
microphone *n* electrical instrument for collecting sound, so as to amplify or broadcast it
microprocessor *n* central controlling chip in a small computer
microscope *n* scientific instrument that magnifies extremely small things **-scopic** *adj* **1** very small **2** using a microscope **-scopically** *adv*
microwave *n* band of very short electric waves
microwave oven also **microwave** *n* oven that cooks food using microwaves
mid- *prefix* middle; in the middle of: *midsummer*
midair *n* point up in the sky
midday *n* 12 o'clock in the morning
midden *n* heap of farmyard manure or household rubbish
middle *adj*, *n* (in or at) the centre or a point halfway between two ends
middle age *n* period between youth and old age **middle-aged** *adj*
middle aged spread *n* increase of flesh round the waist which tends to happen as people grow older
Middle Ages *pl n* period between about AD 1100 and 1500 in Europe
middlebrow *n* person who likes books and works of art that are of average quality but not too difficult **middlebrow** *adj*
middle class *n* social class between the upper and lower classes, including business and professional people, office workers, etc. **middle-class** *adj*
middle distance *n* part of a view between what is close and what is far away
Middle East *n* countries in Asia west of India **~ern** *adj*
middleman *n* **-men** someone who buys from a producer and sells to a customer
middle name *n* **1** name coming between the first name and the surname **2** *infml* something for which a person is well known: *'Generosity's my middle name'*.
middle-of-the-road *adj* favouring a course of action that most people would agree with
middleweight *n* boxer heavier than a welterweight and lighter than a heavyweight
middling *adj* average
midge *n* small winged insect that bites
midget *adj*, *n* very small (person)
Midlands *pl n* central parts of England, between the North and the South
mid-life crisis *n* depression and uncertainty suffered by someone in middle age
midnight *n* 12 o'clock at night
midriff *n* front of the body below the chest
midshipman *n* (rank of) a young person training to become a naval officer
midst *n* **in the midst of** in the middle of; among
midsummer *n* (time around) the summer solstice on 22nd June
Midsummer Day *n* 24th June
midway *adj*, *adv* halfway
midwife *n* **-wives** nurse who helps women giving birth **-wifery** *n*
mien /meen/ *n* look or manner (of a person)
miffed *adj infml* slightly angry
might[1] *v aux* **1** (used for expressing slight possibility): *He might come, but it's unlikely.* **2** *past t. of* may: *I thought*

it might rain. **3** ought; should: *You might have offered to help!*

might² *n* power; strength **~y** *adj* very great **~ily** *adv*

migraine *n* very severe headache

migrant *n* migrating person or bird: *migrant workers*

migrate *vi* **1** (of birds or fish) travel regularly from one part of the world to another, according to the season **2** move from one place to another, esp. for a limited period **–gration** *n* **–gratory** *adj*

mike *n sl* microphone

milch *adj* giving milk

mild *adj* not strong, forceful, or severe; gentle **~ly** *adv* **~ness** *n*

mildew *n* whitish growth on plants and on things stored in damp conditions **~ed** *adj*

mile *n* a measure of length equal to 1.609 kilometres

mileage *n* **1** distance travelled, measured in miles **2** fixed amount of money paid for each mile travelled **3** amount of use: *The newspapers are getting a lot of mileage out of the royal wedding.*

mileometer *n BrE* instrument that tells how far a vehicle has travelled

milestone *n* **1** stone beside the road, saying how far to the next town **2** important event

milieu /ˈmeelyuh/ *n* **-s** *or* **-x** person's social surroundings

militant *n, adj* (person) taking a strong active part in a struggle **~ly** *adv* **–tancy** *n*

militarism *n derog* belief in the use of armed force **–rist** *n* **–ristic** *adj*

military *adj* of, for, or by soldiers, armies, or war ♦ *n* the army

militate against *phr vt* act, serve, or have importance as a reason against

militia *n* force trained to be soldiers in time of special need

milk *n* **1** white liquid produced by human or animal females to feed their young **2** white liquid produced by certain plants: *coconut milk* ♦ *v* **1** *vt* take milk from (e.g. cow) **2** *vi* (e.g. of a cow) give milk **3** *vt* get money or knowledge from (someone or something) by clever or dishonest means **4** *vt* get poison from (a snake) **~y** *adj*

milk float *n* light vehicle carrying milk for domestic delivery

milkmaid *n* (esp. in former times) woman who milks cows

milkman *n* **-men** person who delivers milk to houses

milk run *n infml* familiar and frequently travelled journey

milk shake *n* milk drink flavoured with fruit, chocolate, etc.

milksop *n* weak cowardly man

milk tooth *n* tooth of a child or small mammal that is replaced later

Milky Way *n* broad faint band of light seen in the sky at night

mill *n* **1** (building containing) a machine for crushing grain to flour **2** factory: *a cotton mill* **3** small machine for crushing: *a coffee mill* **4 through the mill** through (a time of) hard training or experience ♦ *vt* **1** crush or produce in a mill **2** mark (metal) with grooves

mill about/around *phr vi* move purposelessly in large numbers **~er** *n* person who owns or works a flourmill

millennium *n* **-nnia** **1** 1,000 years **2 the millennium** future age in which everyone will be happy

millet *n* small seeds of a grasslike plant, used as food

milli- *prefix* thousandth part: *millilitre*

millibar *n* unit of atmospheric pressure

milligram, –gramme *n* a measure of weight equal to 0.001 grams

millimetre, *AmE* **-ter** *n* a measure of length equal to 0.001 metres

milliner *n* maker of women's hats **~y** *n* articles made and sold by a milliner

million *determiner, n, pron* **million** *or* **millions 1** 1,000,000 **2** also **millions of** very large number **~th** *determiner, n, pron, adv*

millionaire *n* person who has a million or more pounds or dollars; very wealthy person

millionairess *n* female millionaire
millipede *n* small wormlike creature with many legs
millrace *n* (channel for) the current of water that turns a mill wheel
millstone *n* **1** circular crushing stone in a flourmill **2** crushing burden
millwheel *n* large waterwheel that drives a mill
milometer *n* mileometer
milt *n* sperm of fish
mime *n* use of actions without language to show meaning, esp. as a performance ♦ *n* actor who does this ♦ *vi/t* act in mime
mimeograph *vt, n AmE* (copy using) a duplicator
mimetic *adj* mimicking
mimic *vt* **-ck- 1** copy (someone or something) amusingly **2** appear very like (something else) ♦ *n* person who mimics others ♦ *adj* not real **~ry** *n*
mimosa *n* shrub with small round esp. yellow flowers
minaret *n* tall thin tower in a mosque
minatory /ˈminət(ə)ri/ *adj fml* threatening
mince *v* **1** *vt* cut (esp. meat) into very small pieces **2** *vi* walk in an affected way **3 mince one's words** avoid using plain direct language ♦ *n* **1** *BrE* meat that has been cut into very small pieces **2** *AmE* mincemeat
mincemeat *n* mixture of dried fruit used as a filling for pastry
mince pie *n* small pastry case filled with mincemeat
mind[1] *n* **1** person's (way of) thinking or feeling; thoughts: *She has a very quick mind.* **2** memory: *I'll keep it in mind.* **3** attention: *Keep your mind on your work.* **4** intention: *Nothing was further from my mind.* **5** opinion: *We are of one mind on this matter.* **6** person considered for his/her ability to think well: *She's one of the finest minds in the country.* **7 on one's mind** causing anxiety **8 out of one's mind** mad **9 speak one's mind** express plainly one's thoughts and opinions ♦ *v* **1** *vi/t* be opposed to (a particular thing): *'Coffee or tea?' 'I don't mind.'* **2** *vi/t* be careful (of): *Mind the step!* **3** *vt* take care of; look after **4 mind you** also **mind** take this into account also **~er** *n* person who looks after: *a childminder* **~ful** *adj* giving attention **~less** *adj* not needing or using thought; stupid **~lessly** *adv* **~lessness** *n*
mind-bending *adj* hard to believe or understand
mind-blowing *adj* **1** (causing sensations) like the effect of psychedelic drugs **2** strange and exhilarating
mind-boggling *adj sl* very surprising
mind reader *n* someone who is good at knowing what another person is thinking without being told **mind reading** *n*
mind's eye *n* imagination; memory
mine[1] *pron* belonging to me; my one(s): *This pen's mine, not yours.*
mine[2] *n* **1** place where coal or metal is dug from the ground: *a goldmine* **2** sort of bomb placed just under the ground or in the sea ♦ *v* **1** *vi/t* dig or get from a mine **2** *vt* put military mines in or under **3** *vt* destroy by military mines
miner *n* worker in a mine
minefield *n* **1** place where military mines have been put **2** something full of hidden dangers
minelayer *n* ship or aircraft for laying mines
mineral *n* substance formed naturally in the earth, such as stone, metal, coal, salt, or oil
mineralogy *n* scientific study of minerals **-gist** *n*
mineral oil *n* oil obtained from minerals
mineral water *n* **1** water from a spring, containing minerals **2** *BrE* fizzy bottled drink
minestrone *n* vegetable soup containing pasta
minesweeper *n* ship for finding and destroying mines
mingle *v* **1** *vi/t* mix so as to form an undivided whole **2** *vi infml* talk to different people at a party
mingy *adj* stingy

mini *n* anything that is smaller than other things of the same kind: *a mini (skirt)*
mini- *prefix* unusually small or short: *miniskirt*
miniature *adj, n* very small (thing, esp. a copy of a bigger one, or picture) **–turize, –ise** *vt* **–turist** *n* artist who paints small pictures
minibus *n* small bus for between 6 and 12 people
minicab *n* taxi which can be hired by telephone
minicomputer *n* computer smaller than a mainframe, used e.g. by business organizations
minim *n* musical note half as long as a semibreve
minimal *adj* as little as possible **~ly** *adv*
minimize, -ise *vt* **1** reduce as much as possible **2** treat as if not serious
minimum *n, adj or* **-mums** smallest (amount or number)
minimum wage *n* lowest wage permitted by law or by agreement
mining *n* digging minerals out of the earth
minion *n* slavelike helper
miniscule *adj* extremely small
minister *n* **1** politician in charge of a government department **2** Christian priest ♦ *v* **minister to** *phr vt* help: *ministering to the sick* **~ial** *adj*
ministrant *n* person giving help
ministration *n* giving of help and service
ministry *n* **1** government department **2** job of being a priest
mink *n* **mink** (valuable brown fur of) a small fierce animal
minnow *n* small freshwater fish
minor *adj* **1** of small importance or seriousness **2** being or based on a musical scale with a semitone between the second and third notes ♦ *n law* person too young to be held responsible
minority *n* **1** less than half **2** small part of a population different from the rest **3** *law* state or time of being a minor
Minotaur *n* (in Greek mythology) a flesh-eating monster half man and half bull
minster *n* great or important church: *York Minster*
minstrel *n* travelling singer in former times
mint[1] *n* **1** peppermint **2** herb with fresh-smelling leaves used in food **~y** *adj*
mint[2] *n* **1** place where coins are made **2** **make a mint** earn a lot of money ♦ *vt* make (a coin) ♦ *adj* unused and in perfect condition
minuet *n* (music for) a slow graceful dance
minus *prep* **1** made less by: *10 minus 4 is 6.* **2** below freezing point: *It was minus 10 today.* **3** *infml* without ♦ *n* also **minus sign** sign (-) showing a number less than zero, or that one number is to be taken away from another ♦ *adj* less than zero
minuscule *adj* extremely small
minute[1] *n* **1** 60th part of an hour **2** short time: *Wait a minute!* **3** 60th part of a degree of angle **4** short note of an official nature, such as on a report **5 the minute (that)** as soon as ♦ *vt* record in the minutes
minute[2] *adj* very small **~ness** *n* **~ly** *adv* with great attention to detail
minutes *pl n* written record of a meeting
minute steak *n* thin piece of steak that can be cooked very quickly
minutiae /miˈnyoohshiˌee/ *pl n* small exact details
minx *n* flirtatious girl
miracle *n* **1** unexplainable but wonderful act or event, esp. as done by a holy person **2** wonderful example (of a quality, ability, etc.): *a miracle of modern science* **–culous** *adj* **–culously** *adv*
miracle play *n* mystery play
mirage *n* optical illusion, esp. as caused by the hot desert air
mire *n esp. lit* deep mud
mirror *n* piece of glass in which one can see oneself ♦ *vt* reflect truly (as if) in a mirror
mirror image *n* image in which the right side appears on the left, and the left side on the right

mirth *n* laughter **~ful** *adj* **~less** *adj*
mis- *suffix* **1** bad or badly; wrong or wrongly: *mistreat / misconduct* **2** lack of; opposite of: *mistrust*
misadventure *n* accident or piece of bad luck
misalliance *n* unsuitable alliance between people, esp. an unsuitable marriage
misandry *n* hatred of men
misanthropic *adj* disliking everyone **~ally** *adv* **–ope**, **–opist** *n*
misapply *vt* use wrongly or for a wrong purpose **–lication** *n*
misapprehension *n* mistaken belief; misunderstanding **misapprehend** *vt*
misappropriate *vt* take dishonestly (and use) **–ation** *n*
misbegotten *adj* **1** badly planned **2** (of a person) worthless
misbehave *vi/t* behave (oneself) badly **–haviour** *n*
misc. *abbrev. for:* miscellaneous
miscalculate *vi* calculate wrongly; form a wrong judgment of something **–lation** *n*
miscarriage *n* giving birth to a child too early for it to live
miscarriage of justice *n* unjust legal decision
miscarry *vi* **1** have a miscarriage **2** *fml* (of a plan) go wrong
miscast *vt* **1** give an unsuitable part to (an actor) **2** cast actors badly in (a play or film)
miscegenation /ˌmisˌejiˈnaysh(ə)n/ *n derog* interbreeding of races
miscellaneous *adj* of many different kinds
miscellany *n* mixture of various kinds
mischance *n fml* (piece of) bad luck
mischief *n* **1** slightly bad behaviour, esp. by children **2** damage; harm
mischievous *adj* **1** playfully troublesome **2** causing harm, esp. intentionally **~ly** *adv*
miscible *adj* (of a liquid) capable of being mixed
misconceive *vt* **1** make (a plan) badly **2** misunderstand
misconception *n* case of wrong understanding
misconduct *n fml* bad behaviour, esp. sexual
misconstruction *n* wrong understanding **misconstrue** *vt*
miscreant *adj, n lit* (of a) person of bad character
misdeed *n fml* wrong act
misdemeanour, *AmE* **-nor** *n* crime or wrong act which is not very serious
misdirect *vt* **1** send to the wrong place: *a misdirected letter* **2** use (e.g. one's abilities) wrongly **3** (of a judge) advise a jury wrongly
mise-en-scène *n* **mise-en-scènes 1** arrangement of scenery on a stage **2** circumstances in which something happens
miser *n* person who loves money and hates spending it **~liness** *n* **~ly** *adj*
miserable *adj* **1** very unhappy **2** causing lack of cheerfulness: *miserable weather* **3** very low in quality or very small in amount: *a few miserable pounds* **–bly** *adv*
misery *n* **1** great unhappiness or suffering **2** *esp. BrE* complaining person
misfire *vi* **1** (of a gun) not fire properly **2** (of a plan or joke) not have the intended effect
misfit *n* someone who cannot live or work happily in their surroundings
misfortune *n* **1** bad luck, esp. of a serious nature **2** very unfortunate event or condition
misgiving *n* apprehension about a future event
misguided *adj* showing bad judgment; foolish **~ly** *adv*
mishap *n* slight unfortunate happening
mishit *vt* **-hit, -tt-** hit (a ball or stroke) badly **mishit** *n*
mishmash *n* jumble
misinform *vt* give wrong information to **–mation** *n*
misinterpret *vt* understand or explain incorrectly
misjudge *vt* judge wrongly, esp. form a wrong or unfairly bad opinion

-**judgement** *n*

mislay *vt* -**laid** lose for a short time

mislead *vt* -**led** cause to think or act mistakenly

mismanage *vt* control or deal with (private, public or business affairs) badly ~**ment** *n*

mismatch *vt* combine wrongly or unsuitably, esp. in marriage **mismatch** *n*

misnomer *n* unsuitable name

misogynist *n* woman-hater

misogyny *n* hatred of women

misplace *vt* **1** put in the wrong place **2** mislay

misprint *n* mistake in printing

misquote *vt* make a mistake in reporting (a person, or a person's words)

misread *vt* **1** make a mistake in reading **2** judge wrongly: *He misread the situation.*

misreport *vt* give an incorrect account of

misrepresent *vt* give an intentionally untrue account or explanation of ~**ation** *n*

misrule *n* **1** bad government **2** disorder; anarchy

miss[1] *v* **1** *vi/t* fail to hit, catch, meet, see, hear, etc. **2** *vt* feel unhappy at the absence or loss of **miss out** *phr v* **1** *vt* fail to include **2** *vi* lose a chance to gain advantage or enjoyment ♦ *n* **1** failure to hit, etc. **2 give something a miss** *esp. BrE* not do, take, etc., something ~**ing** *adj* not in the proper place; lost

Miss[2] *n* (title of a girl or unmarried woman): *Miss Browne*

missal *n* book containing the forms of service of the mass

misshapen *adj* not of the usual or ordinary shape

missile *n* **1** explosive flying weapon **2** object or weapon thrown: *They threw bottles and other missiles at the police.*

missing link *n* **1** fact needed to complete a chain of reasoning **2** creature that some people think once existed, at a stage of development between early man and the anthropoid apes

mission *n* **1** special job, duty, or purpose: *They were sent on a secret mission.* **2** group of people sent abroad: *a trade mission* **3** place where missionaries work

missionary *n* person sent abroad to teach and spread religion

missis *n* missus

missive *n lit* letter

misspent *adj* wasted

misstate *vt* state wrongly or falsely ~**ment** *n*

missus *n infml* **1** wife **2** (used to address a married or older woman)

mist *n* thin fog ♦ *vi/t* cover (as if) with mist: *The windscreen had misted up.* ~**y** *adj*

mistake *vt* -**took**, -**taken 1** have a wrong idea about: *He mistook my meaning.* **2** fail to recognize **mistake for** *phr vt* think wrongly that (a person or thing) is (someone or something else): *I mistook him for his brother.* ♦ *n* something done through carelessness or lack of knowledge

mistaken *adj* wrong; incorrect ~**ly** *adv*

mister *n* **1** (sometimes written instead of *Mr*) **2** (informal way of addressing an unknown man) **3** ordinary man without social or occupational title

mistime *vt* do or say at an inappropriate time

mistle thrush *n* large thrush with large dark spots on its breast

mistletoe *n* plant with white berries, used for Christmas decorations

mistral *n* cold northerly wind of southern France

mistress *n* **1** woman in control **2** man's unmarried female sexual partner **3** *esp. BrE* female teacher

mistrial *n* trial that is declared to be legally void, because it was not properly carried out

mistrust *vt* not trust ♦ *n* lack of trust ~**ful** *adj*

misunderstand *vi/t* -**stood** understand wrongly ~**ing** *n* **1** lack of correct understanding **2** slight disagreement

misuse *vt* **1** put to wrong use **2** maltreat **misuse** *n*

mite *n* **1** very small arachnid **2** small coin or sum of money **3** small thing, esp. a child
mitigate *vt* lessen the severity of –**gation** *n*
mitre, *AmE* **miter** *n* **1** bishop's tall pointed hat **2** also **mitre joint** joint between two pieces of wood each of which is cut at an angle ♦ *vt* fit together in a mitre joint
mitt *n* type of protective mitten
mitten *n* glove without separate finger parts
mix *v* **1** *vi/t* combine so that the parts no longer have a separate shape, appearance, etc.: *Oil and water don't mix.* **2** *vi* be or enjoy being in the company of others **~ed** *adj* **1** of different kinds **2** for both sexes **~er** *n* ♦ *n* mixture (1): *cake mix*
mixed bag *n* collection of things of many different kinds (and qualities)
mixed blessing *n* something that is bad as well as good
mixed economy *n* operation of a country's money supply, industry, and trade by a mixture of capitalist and socialist principles
mixed metaphor *n* use of two metaphors together with a foolish or funny effect
mixture *n* **1** set of substances (to be) mixed together **2** combination: *a mixture of amusement and disbelief* **3** act of mixing
mix-up *n* state of disorder and confusion
ml *abbrev. for:* **1** mile **2** millilitre
Mlle *abbrev. for:* Mademoiselle
mm *abbrev. for:* millimetres
Mme *abbrev. for:* Madame
mnemonic /niˈmonik/ *n, adj* (something) used for helping one to remember
MO *abbrev. for:* **1** medical officer **2** modus operandi
moa *n* very large extinct flightless bird of New Zealand
moan *vi, n* (make a) **a** low sound of pain **b** discontented complaint
moat *n* usu. water-filled trench round esp. a castle
mob *n* **1** noisy (violent) crowd **2** group of criminals ♦ *vt* **-bb-** gather round **a** to attack **b** because of interest or admiration
mobile *adj* (easily) movable; not fixed –**bility** *n*
mobilize, -ise *vt* bring into action, esp. ready for war –**ization** *n*
moccasin *n* simple soft leather shoe
mocha *n* **1** fine coffee **2** coffee and chocolate flavour
mock *vt* laugh at unkindly or unfairly ♦ *adj* not real; pretended: *a mock battle*
mockery *n* **1** mocking **2** something unworthy of respect **3 make a mockery of** show to be foolish or untrue
mockingbird *n* American bird that mimics the songs of other birds
mock-up *n* full-size model of something to be built
MoD *abbrev. for:* Ministry of Defence
modal auxiliary *n* verb that goes in front of another, such as *can, may,* or *would*
mod con *n* **all mod cons** (esp. in newspaper advertisements for houses) with all modern conveniences (such as central heating)
mode *n* way of doing something
model *n* **1** small copy: *a model aeroplane* **2** person who models clothes **3** person to be painted or photographed **4** person or thing of the highest quality: *a model student* **5** type of vehicle, machine, weapon, etc.: *His car is the latest model.* ♦ *v* **-ll-** (*AmE* **-l-**) **1** *vt* make a small copy **2** *vi/t* wear (clothes) to show them to possible buyers **model on** *phr vt* form as a copy of: *She modelled herself on her mother.*
modem *n* electronic apparatus for changing information from a form which a computer understands into a form which can be sent e.g. along a telephone line to another computer
moderate *adj* **1** neither too much nor too little; middle **2** not politically extreme ♦ *vi/t* lessen in force, degree, etc. ♦ *n* person whose opinions are moderate **~ly** *adv* not very –**ration** *n*

1 self-control **2** reduction in force or degree **3 in moderation** within sensible limits

moderato *n, adj* **-os** (music) played at an average even speed **moderato** *adv*

moderator *n* **1** someone who arbitrates **2** someone who presides over an assembly

modern *adj* **1** of the present time **2** new and different from the past **~ize, -ise** *v* **1** *vt* make suitable for modern use **2** *vi* start using more modern methods **~ization** *n* **~ism** *n* way of thought characteristic of modern times, esp. in art or theology

modest *adj* **1** not too proud **2** not large **3** not sexually improper **~ly** *adv* **~y** *n*

modicum *n* small amount

modify *vt* **1** change, esp. slightly **2** make (a claim, condition, etc.) less hard to accept or bear **3** (esp. of an adjective or adverb) go with and describe (another word) **-fication** *n*

modish *adj* fashionable **~ly** *adv*

modulate *vt* vary the strength, nature, etc., of (a sound) **-lation** *n*

module *n* **1** standard part used in building, making furniture, etc. **2** part of a spacecraft for independent use **-ular** *adj*

modus operandi *n* method of doing something

modus vivendi *n* way of living (together)

mogul *n* person of very great power and wealth

MOH *abbrev. for:* Medical Officer of Health

mohair *n* (cloth from) the long silky wool of a sort of goat

Mohammedan *n, adj* Muslim

moiety /ˈmoyəti/ *n* a half share

moist *adj* slightly wet **~en** *vi/t* make or become moist **~ure** *n* liquid in or on something **~urize, -ise** *vt* remove the dryness from

moke *n BrE infml* donkey

molar *adj, n* (of a) large back tooth

molasses *n* sweet dark liquid produced in sugar refining

mold *n, v AmE* mould

molder *v AmE* moulder

mole[1] *n* **1** small furry animal that lives underground **2** *BrE* spy who works inside an organization

mole[2] *n* small, dark brown mark on the skin

mole[3] *n* (harbour formed by) a very large man-made breakwater

molecule *n* smallest natural unit of matter, made of 2 or more atoms **-cular** *adj*

molehill *n* small pile of earth thrown up by a mole

molest *vt* **1** attack; harm **2** attack (esp. a woman or child) sexually **~ation** *n*

moll *n infml* **1** prostitute **2** criminal's girlfriend

mollify *vt* make less angry

mollusc, *AmE* **mollusk** *n* any of a class of soft-bodied invertebrate animals, usu. with a shell

mollycoddle *vt* take too much care of (a person or animal)

Molotov cocktail *n* petrol-filled bottle used as a bomb

molt *vi AmE* moult

molten *adj* (of metal or rock) melted

molto *adv* (in music) very

molybdenum *n* metallic element used in hardening steel

moment *n* **1** very short period of time **2** particular point in time **3** importance: *a matter of great moment* **~ary** *adj* lasting a moment **~arily** *adv* **1** for just a very short time **2** *esp. AmE* very soon; in a moment

moment of truth *n* moment when something important will happen

momentous *adj* extremely important **~ness** *n*

momentum *n* measurable quantity of movement in a body

mommy *n AmE* mummy [1]

monarch *n* (non-elected, royal) ruler **~y** *n* **1** rule by a monarch **2** country ruled by a monarch **~ist** *n* supporter of monarchy

monastery *n* building in which monks live

monastic *adj* of monks or monasteries
Monday *n* the 1st day of the week, between Sunday and Tuesday
monetarism *n* (in economics) belief that the best way of controlling the economy of a country is to control its money supply **-rist** *n, adj*
monetary *adj* of or about money
money *n* **1** something used for paying, esp. coins or paper notes **2** wealth **-eyed, -ied** *adj* rich
moneybags *n* rich person
moneybox *n* container for saving small amounts of money
moneychanger *n* person whose business is exchanging different kinds of currency
money-grubber *n* person unpleasantly determined to gain money
moneylender *n* person whose business is lending money and charging interest on it
money-spinner *n* something that brings in a lot of money
money supply *n* all the money that exists and is being paid and spent in a country in the form of coins, notes, and credit
Mongol *n* **1** inhabitant of Mongolia or the Mongolian People's Republic **2** (*not cap.*) person with Down's syndrome **~ian** *n* (language of) an inhabitant of Mongolia **~ian** *adj* **~ism** (*not cap.*) Down's syndrome
mongoose *n* **-gooses** *or* **-geese** ferret-sized African or Asian mammal that hunts snakes and rodents
mongrel *n* **1** dog of mixed breed **2** person or thing of mixed race or origin
monitor *vt* watch or listen to carefully for a special purpose ♦ *n* **1** television used to show the view seen by a television camera **2** instrument for monitoring a bodily condition: *a heart monitor* **3 a** screen for use with a computer **b** parts of a computer operation that make sure that the computer system is working properly **4** person who listens to foreign radio news, etc., and reports on its content **5** pupil chosen to help the teacher: *dinner money monitor*
monk *n* member of an all-male religious group that lives together
monkey *n* **1** small tree-climbing long-tailed animal **2** *infml* child full of playful tricks **monkey about/around** *phr vi* play foolishly
monkey business *n infml* deviousness which causes trouble
monkeynut *n* peanut
monkey-puzzle *n* evergreen tree with stiff sharp leaves covering the branches
monkey wrench *n* adjustable spanner
mono *adj* (of sound) coming from only one place: *a mono record*
mono- *prefix* one; single: *monosyllable*
monochrome *adj* **1** in only one colour **2** in black and white only
monocle *n* lens for one eye only, to help the sight
monogamy *n* having only one husband or wife at a time **-mous** *adj*
monoglot *adj* monolingual
monogram *n* combined letters, esp. someone's initials **~med** *adj*
monolingual *adj* knowing or using only one language
monolith *n* large stone pillar **~ic** *adj* **1** like a monolith **2** *often derog* forming a large unchangeable whole
monologue *n* long speech by one person
mononucleosis *n* glandular fever
monopoly *n* unshared control or right to do or produce something **-lize, -ise** *vt* keep unshared control of **-list** *n*
monorail *n* railway with one rail
monosodium glutamate *n* chemical compound added to certain foods, to make their taste stronger
monosyllable *n* word of one syllable **-bic** *adj*
monotheism *n* belief that there is only one God **-ist** *n* **-istic** *adj*
monotone *n* way of speaking or singing in which the voice continues on the same note
monotony *n* dull sameness **-onous** *adj* dull; boring **-onously** *adv*
Monsieur *n* **Messieurs** (used as a title

for a French-speaking man)
Monsignor *n* (used as a title for a Roman Catholic priest of high rank)
monsoon *n* (time of) very heavy rains in and near India
monster *n* **1** strange usu. large and frightening creature **2** very evil person ♦ *adj* unusually large: *a monster potato*
monstrance *n* ceremonial dish holding holy bread in the Mass
monstrosity *n* something very ugly and usu. large
monstrous *adj* **1** extremely bad; shocking **2** unnaturally large, strange, etc. **~ly** *adv*
mons veneris *n* rounded mass of flesh just above and in front of a woman's vulva
montage *n* picture made from separate parts combined
month *n* 12th part of a year; four weeks **~ly** *adj*
monument *n* **1** something built in honour of a person or event **2** historical old building or place **3** work, esp. a book, worthy of lasting fame **~al** *adj* **1** intended as a monument **2** very large **3** (esp. of something bad) very great in degree **~ally** *adv* extremely
moo *vi,n* (make) the sound of a cow
mooch *vt AmE sl* get by asking for it **mooch about/around** *phr vi* wander about rather unhappily with no purpose
mood[1] *n* **1** state of feeling: *in a cheerful mood* **2** state of feeling in which one is bad-tempered or angry **~y** *adj* often having bad moods **~ily** *adv*
mood[2] *n* any of the three sets of verb forms that express **a** a fact or action (indicative), **b** a command (imperative), or **c** a doubt, wish, etc. (subjunctive)
moon *n* **1** large body that moves round the Earth and shines at night **2** body that moves round a planet other than the Earth **3** *infml* **over the moon** very happy ♦ *v* **moon about/around** *phr vi* wander about in an aimless unhappy way
moonbeam *n* beam of light from the moon
moonlight light of the moon ♦ *vi* have a second job in addition to a regular one, esp. without the knowledge of the tax office
moonscape *n* desolate landscape like the surface of the moon
moonshine *n* **1** moonlight **2** nonsense **3** illegally distilled spirits, esp. whisky
moon shot *n* launching of a spacecraft towards the moon
moonstone *n* milky-white gem
moonstruck *adj* slightly crazy
moor[1] also **moors** *pl*, **moorland** *n esp. BrE* (area of) high hilly usu. treeless land
moor[2] *vi/t* fasten (a boat) to land, etc., by means of ropes, etc. **~ings** *pl n* **1** ropes, anchors, etc., for mooring **2** also **mooring** place where a boat is moored
Moor *n* member of the mixed Arab and Berber people who conquered Spain in the 8th century AD **~ish** *adj*
moorhen *n* blackish bird that nests near water
moose *n* **moose** large North American deer
moot *vt* state (a question, matter, etc.) for consideration
moot point *n* undecided matter, on which people have different opinions
mop *n* **1** long stick with thick string or a sponge at one end, for washing floors **2** thick untidy mass of hair ♦ *vt* **-pp-** wash or dry (as if) with a mop **mop up** *phr vt* **1** remove liquid, dirt, etc., with a mop **2** finish dealing with: *mop up small enemy groups*
mope *vi* be continuously sad
moped *n* small motorcycle
moppet *n infml* small girl
moquette *n* upholstery fabric with a velvety pile
moraine *n* earth and stones deposited by a glacier
moral *adj* **1** of or based on the difference between good and evil or right and wrong **2** pure and honest in character and behaviour ♦ *n* lesson

that can be learnt from a story or event **~ize, -ise** *vi* give one's opinions on right and wrong, esp. when unwelcome **morals** *pl n* standards of (sexual) behaviour **~ity** *n* rightness or pureness of behaviour or of an action **~ist** *n*

morale *n* pride and confidence, esp. in relation to a job to be done

moral majority *n* a movement, esp. in the US, that favours very severe Christian religious principles and is against political change

moral support *n* encouragement

morass *n* **1** muddle **2** marsh

moratorium *n* **-ria** official period of delay

morbid *adj* unhealthily interested in death **~ly** *adv* **~ity** *n*

mordant *n* **1** chemical that fixes a dye **2** corrosive substance used in etching ♦ *adj* **1** cruel and cutting in speech **2** acting as a mordant **–ncy** *n*

more *adv* **1** (forms comparatives): *more difficult* **2** to a greater degree: *He likes this one more than that one.* **3** again: *Do it just once more.* ♦ *determiner, pron* (*comparative of* **many, much**) **1** a greater or additional number or quantity (of): *He wants more food.* **2** **more or less: a** nearly **b** about

morello *n* **-os** large sour cherry

moreover *adv* in addition; besides

mores *pl n* fixed moral customs in a social group

morganatic *adj tech* (of a marriage) between a person of high and one of lower rank, and not conferring any rights or titles on the person of lower rank or the children **~ally** *adv*

morgue *n* mortuary

moribund *adj* completely inactive and near to the end of existence

Mormon *n* member of the Church of Jesus Christ of the Latter Day Saints, founded in the US in 1830

morn *n lit* morning

morning *n* **1** time between sunrise and midday **2** **in the morning** tomorrow morning

morning-after pill *n* contraceptive pill taken by a woman within 72 hours of having sex

morning dress *n* formal dress worn by a man at official or social ceremonies in the morning or afternoon

morning glory *n* climbing plant with blue, trumpet-shaped flowers

Morning Prayer *n* matins

morning sickness *n* nausea felt esp. in the morning during early pregnancy

morning star *n* bright planet, esp. Venus, seen in the eastern sky at sunrise

Moroccan *n, adj* (inhabitant) of Morocco

morocco *n* fine soft leather

moron *n* very stupid person **~ic** *adj*

morose *adj* angry and silent **~ly** *adv*

morphine, morphia *n* powerful drug for stopping pain

morphology *n* **1** (biology of) the form and structure of animals and plants **2** (study of) the system of word formation in a language **3** (study of) the structure and form of something **–logist** *n* **–logical** *adj*

morris dance *n* traditional English dance performed by a group of men

Morse code *n* system of sending messages with letters represented by combinations of long and short signals

morsel *n* small piece, esp. of food

mortal *adj* **1** that will die **2** of human beings **3** causing death: *a mortal wound* ♦ *n* human being **~ly** *adv* **1** so as to cause death **2** very much: *mortally offended* **~ity** *n* **1** rate or number of deaths **2** state of being mortal

mortal sin *n* sin so great that it cuts the doer off from God's mercy

mortar[1] *n* mixture of lime, sand, and water, used in building

mortar[2] *n* **1** apparatus for firing small bombs **2** thick bowl in which things are crushed

mortarboard *n* **1** board for holding mortar **2** academic cap with a flat square top

mortgage *n* **1** agreement to borrow money to buy esp. a house, which belongs to the lender until the money is repaid **2** the amount borrowed ♦ *vt* give up the ownership of (a house, etc.) for a time in return for money lent **–gee** *n* **–gor** *n*

mortician *AmE* undertaker

mortify *vt* make ashamed **–fication** *n*

mortise, -ice *vt, n* (join by) a cavity cut in a piece of material (e.g. wood) to take a matching part sticking out from another piece

mortise lock *n* lock that fits into a cavity cut in the side of a door

mortuary *n* place where dead bodies are kept until a funeral

mosaic *n* pattern or picture formed by small pieces of coloured stone or glass

Mosaic *adj* of Moses

moselle *n* white German wine

mosey *vi AmE infml* saunter

Moslem *n, adj* Muslim

mosque *n* building in which Muslims worship

mosquito *n* **-tos** *or* **-toes** small blood-sucking flying insect

moss *n* (thick flat mass of) a small usu. green plant of wet places

most *adv* **1** (forms superlatives): *the most difficult question* **2** more than anything else: *He likes bananas most of all.* **3** *fml* very: *I was most upset.* ♦ *determiner, pron* (*superlative of* **many, much**) **1** nearly all: *Most people dislike him.* **2 at (the) most** not more than **3 for the most part** mainly **4 make the most of** get the best advantage from **~ly** *adv* mainly

-most *suffix* –est: *topmost*

MOT *n* (in Britain) regular official examination of cars to make sure they are in good enough condition to be driven

mote *n* small particle, esp. of dust floating in air

motel *n* hotel specially built for motorists

moth *n* large-winged insect that flies mainly at night

mothball *n* **1** ball of strong-smelling chemical for keeping moths away from clothes **2 in mothballs** stored and not used

moth-eaten *adj* **1** (of clothes) eaten by the young of moths **2** very worn out

mother *n* **1** female parent **2** (*usu. cap.*) female head of a convent ♦ *vt* care for or protect (too) lovingly **~hood** *n* **~ly** *adj* like a good mother

motherboard *n* device enabling a computer to operate peripherals

mother country *n* country one was born in or came from originally

mother-in-law *n* **mothers-in-law** *or* **mother-in-laws** wife's or husband's mother

mother-of-pearl *n* shiny substance from inside certain shells, used decoratively

mother superior *n* head of a convent

mother tongue *n* first language one spoke

motif *n* (repeated) artistic or musical pattern

motion *n* **1** act, way, or process of moving **2** single movement **3** suggestion formally made at a meeting **4 go through the motions** do something without care or interest ♦ *vi/t* signal or direct by a movement of esp. the hand **~less** *adj* unmoving

motion picture *n AmE* film (2)

motivate *vt* **1** give (someone) a (strong) reason for doing something; encourage **2** be the reason why (something) was done **–vation** *n*

motive *n* reason for action

mot juste /ˌmoh ˈzhoohst/ *n* **mots justes** the exactly right word or phrase

motley *adj usu. derog* of many different kinds and qualities ♦ *n* bright clothes worn by a jester

motocross *n* motorcycle racing across rough country

motor *n* **1** machine that changes power into movement: *an electric motor* **2** *BrE infml* a car ♦ *adj* **1** driven by an engine: *a motor mower* **2** of cars, etc.: *the motor trade* ♦ *vi* go by car **~ist** *n* car driver **~ize, –ise** *vt* equip with a motor or with motor-driven transport

motorcade *n* procession of cars

motorcar *n BrE* car
motorcycle *n* also *BrE infml* **motorbike** large heavy bicycle driven by an engine
motor scooter *n* scooter (2)
motorway *n BrE* wide road for fast long-distance travel
mottled *adj* irregularly marked with colours and/or shapes
motto *n* **-toes** *or* **-tos** phrase or short sentence used as a guiding principle
mould[1], *AmE* **mold** *n* shaping container into which a soft substance is poured to set ♦ *vt* shape or form (esp. something solid): *moulded her character* **~ing** *n* decorative stone, plastic, or wood band(s)
mould[2], *AmE* **mold** *n* soft often greenish growth on damp or decaying matter **~y** *adj*
mould[3] *n* **1** crumbling soil good for plants **2** *lit* earth
moulder, *AmE* **molder** *vi* decay gradually
moult, *AmE* **molt** *vi* (of a bird or animal) lose most of its feathers or fur
mound *n* **1** pile **2** small hill
mount *v* **1** *vi* rise: *Costs mounted.* **2** *vt* get on (a horse, bicycle, etc.) **3** *vt* provide with a horse: *the mounted police* **4** *vt* prepare and produce: *mount an exhibition* **5** *vt* fix on a support or in a frame **6** *vt* go up; climb ♦ *n* **1** animal for riding **2** frame or backing to which something is fixed
Mount *n* (used before names of mountains): *Mount Everest*
mountain *n* **1** very high rocky hill **2** very large amount **3 make a mountain out of a molehill** make a problem seem more difficult than it is **~ous** *adj* **1** full of mountains **2** extremely large
mountain ash *n* rowan
mountaineer *n* mountain climber **~ing** *n*
mountain lion *n* puma
mountebank /ˈmowntiˌbangk/ *n* charlatan
Mountie *n* member of the Royal Canadian Mounted Police
mourn *vi/t* feel or express grief (for), esp. when someone dies **~er** *n* **~ful** *adj* (too) sad **~ing** *n* **1** grief **2** funeral clothes, usu. black
mouse *n* **mice 1** long-tailed furry animal, like a rat but smaller **2** quiet nervous person **3** small box connected to a computer by a wire which, when moved by hand, causes a cursor to move around on a VDU ♦ *vi* hunt for mice **mousy** *adj* **1** (of hair) dull pale brown **2** (of a person) unattractively plain and quiet
moussaka *n* Greek dish of minced meat and eggplant
mousse *n* dish made from flavoured cream and eggs
moustache *n* hair on the upper lip
mouth *n* **mouths 1** opening in the face for eating and speaking **2** opening; entrance: *the mouth of the cave* **3 down in the mouth** not cheerful ♦ *vt* **1** say by moving the lips soundlessly **2** repeat without understanding or sincerity
mouthful *n* **1** amount put into the mouth **2** long word or phrase, difficult to say
mouthorgan *n* small rectangular musical instrument played by breathing in and out
mouthpiece *n* **1** part of e.g. a musical instrument or telephone held in or near the mouth **2** person or thing (e.g. newspaper) that expresses the opinions of another
mouth-watering *adj* (of food) very attractive
movable, -eable *n, adj* (property) that can be moved
movable feast *n* annual church festival not celebrated on the same date each year, e.g. Easter
move *v* **1** *vi/t* (cause to) change place or position **2** *vi* act: *I had to move fast to clinch the deal.* **3** *vi* also **move house** change one's home **4** *vt* cause to have strong feelings, esp. of pity: *a very moving story* **5** *vi/t* make (a formal suggestion) at a meeting **move on** *phr v* **1** *vi* change (to something new) **2** *vi/t* go away to another place or position **move**

out *phr vi* leave one's former home **move over** *phr vi* change position in order to make room for someone or something else ♦ *n* **1** change of position or place, esp. in games like chess **2** set of actions to bring about a result: *new moves to settle the dispute* **3 on the move a** travelling about **b** having started to move or happen **~ment** *n* **1** (act of) moving **2** group of people in a united effort: *the trade-union movement* **3** separate part of a large piece of music

movie *n esp. AmE* film (2) **movies** *pl n esp. AmE for* cinema

mow *vt* **mowed, mowed** *or* **mown** cut (grass, corn, etc.) **mow down** *phr vt* knock down or kill, esp. in large numbers **~er** *n*

MP *n* **1** Member of Parliament **2** (member of) the military police

mpg *abbrev. for:* miles per gallon

mph *abbrev. for:* miles per hour

Mr *n* (ordinary man's title): *Mr Smith*

Mrs *n* (married woman's title)

Ms *n* (unmarried or married woman's title)

MS *abbrev. for:* **1** left hand (used in music) **2** manuscript **3** multiple sclerosis

MSc *abbrev. for:* Master of Science

MSS *abbrev. for:* manuscripts

Mt *abbrev. for:* Mount

much *adv* **1** a lot: *much better* **2** to the stated degree: *I liked it very much.* **3** in most ways: *much the same as usual* **4 much as** although **5 much less** and certainly not ♦ *determiner, pron* **more, most 1** large amount or part (of): *He gave me too much cake.* **2 I thought as much** I had expected that the stated usu. bad thing would happen **3 make much of: a** treat as important **b** understand: *I couldn't make much of his explanation* **4 too much for** too difficult for

mucilage *n* gummy liquid obtained from plants **–ginous** *adj*

muck *n* **1** dirt **2** worthless or improper material **3** manure ♦ *v* **muck about/around** *phr vi esp. BrE* **1** behave in a silly way **2** treat without consideration **muck in** *phr vi* join in work or activity (with others) **muck up** *phr vt* **1** spoil or do wrong **2** make dirty **~y** *adj*

muckraking *n derog* finding and telling unpleasant stories about well-known people **muckraking** *adj* **–er** *n*

mucous membrane *n* smooth wet skin, as inside the mouth

mucus *n* slippery body liquid, as produced in the nose

mud *n* very wet earth **~dy** *adj* **1** covered in mud **2** dull-looking **3** confused **muddy** *vt* make cloudy, dull, or confused

muddle *n* state of confusion and disorder ♦ *vt* **1** put into disorder **2** confuse the mind of **muddle along** *phr vi* continue confusedly, with no plan **muddle through** *phr vi* succeed in spite of having no plan or good method

mudflat *n* muddy area of ground covered at high tide

mudguard *n* protective cover over a cycle wheel

mudpack *n* health treatment in which mud is put on the face

muesli *n* breakfast dish of grain, nuts, and fruit, usu. eaten with milk

muezzin /mooh'ezin/ *n* mosque official who calls the faithful to prayer

muff *n* fur or cloth cover to keep the hands or ears warm ♦ *vt* spoil a chance to do (something) well

muffin *n* light round bun

muffle *vt* make (sound) less easily heard

muffler *n* **1** scarf worn to keep one's neck warm **2** *AmE* silencer

mufti *n* **1** Muslim lawyer **2** civilian clothes worn by people usually in uniform

mug[1] *n* **1 a** large straight-sided drinking cup with a handle **b** the contents of this: *a mug of tea* **2** *BrE sl* foolish person **3** *sl* face

mug[2] *vt* **-gg-** rob violently **~ger** *n*

muggy *adj* (of weather) unpleasantly warm with heavy damp air

mugshot *n sl* photograph, esp. one of a criminal that is part of police records

mug up *vi/t infml* study hard
mugwump *n AmE derog* person who tries to be independent of the leaders in politics
Muhammadan *adj, n* Muslim
mulatto /myooh'latoh/ *n* **-tos** *or* **-toes** *lit* person with one black parent and one white one
mulberry *n* (tree bearing) small dark purple fruit
mulch *vt, n* (cover with) a layer, e.g. of compost, that protects earth against drought and weeds
mulct *vt, n* (punish by) a fine
mule[1] *n* animal that is the young of a donkey and a horse **muleteer** *n* driver of mules **mulish** *adj* stubborn
mule[2] *n* backless slipper
mull[1] *vt* heat (wine) with sugar and spices
mull[2] *n ScotE* peninsula
mullah *n* Muslim religious teacher
mullet *n* **mullet** *or* **mullets** edible sea fish
mulligatawny *n* rich spicy soup
mullion *n* vertical bar between two panes of a window
mullock *n AustrE* rubbish; refuse
mull over *phr vt* consider carefully
multi- *prefix* many: *multipurpose*
multifarious /,multi'feəri·əs/ *adj fml* of many different types
multilateral *adj* including more than 2 groups or countries **~ly** *adv*
multinational *n, adj* (a company) having factories, offices, etc., in many different countries
multiple *adj* of many different types or parts ♦ *n* number which can be divided exactly by a smaller number
multiple sclerosis *n* serious nerve disease in which one can no longer control one's bodily movements and actions
multiplicity *n* large number or great variety
multiply *v* **1** *vt* add (a number) to itself the stated number of times: *2 multiplied by 3 is 6.* **2** *vi/t* increase in number or amount **3** *vi* breed **-plication** *n*
multitude *n* **1** large number **2** large crowd
multitudinous *adj* very many
mum[1] *n* mother
mum[2] *adj infml* not saying or telling anything
mumble *vi/t* speak or say unclearly
mumbo jumbo *n derog* meaningless talk or actions, esp. in religion
mummify *vi/t* (cause to) be dried and preserved as or like a mummy
mumming *n* performance in a traditional comic play **-er** *n*
mummy[1] *n BrE* (child's word for) mother
mummy[2] *n* dead body preserved from decay, esp. in ancient Egypt
mumps *n* infectious illness with swelling in the throat
munch *vi/t* eat (something hard) with a strong jaw movement
mundane *adj* **1** familiar and dull; ordinary **2** worldly
municipal *adj* of a town or its local government
municipality *n* town, city, etc., with its own local government
munificent /myooh'nifis(ə)nt/ *adj fml* very generous **-cence** *n*
munitions *pl n* bombs, guns, etc.; war supplies
mural *n* painting done directly on a wall
murder *n* **1** crime of killing someone intentionally **2** very difficult or tiring experience ♦ *vt* kill illegally and intentionally **~er** *n* **~ous** *adj* **1** intending or likely to cause murder **2** violent (in appearance)
murk *n* darkness
murky *adj* unpleasantly dark
murmur *n* **1** soft low continuous sound **2** complaint ♦ *vi/t* make or express in a murmur
Murphy's Law *n* Sod's Law
muscat *n* sweet grape **~el** *n* **1** sweet wine from muscat grapes **2** raisin from muscat grapes
muscle *n* **1** (one of) the pieces of elastic material in the body which can tighten to produce movement **2** strength ♦ *v*
muscle in *phr vi* force one's way into

(esp.) a group activity
muscle-bound *adj* having large stiff muscles
Muscovite *n* person from Moscow
muscular *adj* **1** of muscles **2** with large muscles; strong
muscular dystrophy *n* disease that causes progressive wasting of the muscles
muse[1] *vi* think deeply
muse[2] *n* **1** (*often cap.*) any of nine ancient Greek goddesses each representing an art or science **2** force or person that seems to help a creative artist
museum *n* building where objects of historic, scientific, or artistic interest are kept and shown
mush *n* soft mass of semi-liquid material **~y** *adj*
mushroom *n* type of fungus that is often eaten ♦ *vi* grow and develop fast
music *n* **1** sounds arranged in patterns, usu. with tunes **2** art of making music **3** printed representation of music **~ian** *n*
musical *adj* **1** of music **2** skilled at music ♦ *n* play or film with songs and usu. dances **~ly** *adv*
musical box *n* box containing a clockwork mechanism that plays a tune
musical chairs *n* party game in which people have to find seats when the music stops
music hall *n* (in Britain in former times) (theatre for) performances of songs, jokes, acts of skill, etc.
musk *n* strong-smelling substance used in perfumes **~y** *adj*
musket *n* early type of long-barrelled gun
muskrat *n* large N American water rat
Muslim *n, adj* (follower) of the religion started by Mohammed
muslin *n* very fine thin cotton
musquash *n* (fur of) the muskrat
muss *vt infml* make untidy
mussel *n* sea mollusc with a long, dark shell
must *v aux* **1** (shows what is necessary): *It's an order; you must obey.* **2** (shows what is likely): *You must be cold.* ♦ *n* something that should be done or seen
mustache *n AmE* moustache
mustachio *n* **-os** large curly moustache **~ed** *adj*
mustang *n* wild horse
mustard *n* hot-tasting yellow substance made from the seeds of a plant with yellow flowers
mustard gas *n* poisonous gas used in the First World War
muster *vt* gather; collect ♦ *n* assembly
mustn't *short for:* must not
musty *adj* with an unpleasant smell as if old **-iness** *n*
mutable *adj* changeable
mutant *n* new type of creature resulting from mutation
mutation *n* (example or result of) a process of change in living cells, causing a new part or type **-tate** *vi*
mutatis mutandis *adv* after making the necessary changes; after taking obvious differences into account
mute *adj* not speaking or spoken; silent ♦ *n* **1** person who cannot speak **2** object put on or in a musical instrument to make it sound softer **~ly** *adv* **muted** *adj* (of sound or colour) softer than usual
mutilate *vt* wound and make ugly or useless **-lation** *n*
mutineer *n* person who mutinies
mutiny *n* (an example of) revolt esp. by sailors or soldiers against officers **-nous** *adj* **1** taking part in a mutiny **2** angrily disobedient **-nously** *adv* ♦ *vi* take part in a mutiny
mutt *n* dog of no particular breed
mutter *vi/t* speak or say quietly and unclearly
mutton *n* meat from a sheep
muttonchops also **muttonchop whiskers** *n* whiskers shaved to form a widening band on each side, running from the ear to the corner of the mouth
mutual *adj* **1** equal for both sides: *their mutual dislike* **2** shared by both: *mutual interests* **~ly** *adv*
mutual fund *n AmE* unit trust

Muzak *n tdmk* recorded background music played in public places
muzzle *n* **1** animal's nose and mouth **2** covering for an animal's muzzle, to stop it biting **3** front end of a gun barrel ♦ *vt* **1** put a muzzle on (an animal) **2** force to keep silent
muzzy *adj* confused
MW *abbrev. for:* **1** medium wave **2** megawatt
mW *abbrev. for:* milliwatt
my *determiner* of me: *my parents* ♦ *interj* (expresses surprise)
mycology *n* biology of fungi **–gist** *n* **–gical** *adj*
mynah, myna *n* Asian starling sometimes kept as a talking bird
myopia *n* shortsightedness **–pic** *adj*
myriad *n, adj* large and varied number (of)
myrrh *n* bitter aromatic gum resin
myself *pron* **1** (*reflexive form of* I): *I hurt myself.* **2** (*strong form of* I): *I'll do it myself.* **3** (in) my usual state of mind or body: *I'm not myself today.*
mystery *n* **1** something which cannot be explained or understood **2** strange secret quality **–rious** *adj* **1** unexplainable: *his mysterious disappearance* **2** hiding one's intentions **–riously** *adv* **-riousness** *n*
mystery play *n* medieval play based on part of the Bible
mystic *n* person who practises mysticism
mysticism *n* gaining of direct personal religious knowledge **mystical, mystic** *adj* **mystically** *adv*
mystify *vt* cause (someone) to be puzzled: *her mystifying disappearance*
mystique *n* special quality that makes a person or thing seem mysterious and different, esp. causing admiration
myth **1** story from ancient times, dealing with the beginning of the world and society **2** widely believed false story or idea **~ical** *adj* **1** of myths **2** not real
mythology *n* body of myths, esp. those of a particular people **–gical** *adj*
myxomatosis *n* fatal disease of rabbits

N

N, n the 14th letter of the English alphabet
N *abbrev. for:* north(ern)
nab *vt* **-bb-** *sl* **1** arrest **2** get; take
nabob *n* **1** local governor in 17th-18th century India **2** very rich man, esp. an Englishman who made money in India in the 18th or 19th century
nacelle *n* casing for an aircraft engine
nacre *n* mother-of-pearl **~ous** *adj*
nadir *n* lowest point of misfortune, failure, etc.
naevus *n* birthmark
naff *adj BrE sl* (of things, ideas, behaviour, etc.) of poor quality and esp. in bad taste
nag[1] *vi/t* **-gg-** continuously complain (at) **~ging** *adj* continuously hurting or worrying
nag[2] *n* old horse
naiad *n* (in Greek and Roman myths) water nymph
nail *n* **1** thin pointed piece of metal for hammering into wood **2** hard flat piece at the end of each finger and toe ♦ *vt* **1** fasten with a nail **2** *sl* catch; trap **nail down** *phr vt* force to be definite
nail-biting *adj* causing excitement and anxiety
nail varnish *n* liquid for giving a hard shiny surface on finger and toenails
naive *adj* **1** without experience of life **2** too willing to believe without proof **~ly** *adv* **~ty** *n* naive quality
naked *adj* **1** with no clothes on **2** uncovered: *a naked light* **3 with the naked eye** without a microscope, telescope, etc. **~ness** *n*
namby-pamby *adj* too weak, childish,

or easily frightened
name *n* **1** what someone (or something) is called **2** usu. offensive term for someone: *call someone names* **3** opinion others have of one; reputation **4 name of the game** quality or object which is most necessary or important ♦ *vt* **1** give a name to **2** identify by name **3** appoint; choose **~less** *adj* **1** whose name is not known or told **2** too terrible to mention **~ly** *adv* and that is/they are: *There are two factors, namely cost and availability*
name day *n* feast day of the saint after whom a person is named
namedrop *vi* **-pp-** *derog* mention famous people as if one knew them well **~per** *n*
namesake *n* person with the same name
nanny *n* woman employed to take care of children
nanny goat *n* female goat
nano- *prefix* thousand millionth part of: *nanosecond*
nap¹ *n* short sleep ♦ *vi* have a nap **~ping** *adj* unprepared
nap² *n* soft furry surface of cloth
napalm /ˈnay,pahm/ *n* fiercely burning petrol jelly, used in bombs
nape *n* back (of the neck)
naphtha /ˈnafthə/ *n* inflammable liquid made from petroleum
napkin *n* piece of cloth or paper used at meals for protecting clothes and cleaning the lips and fingers
nappy *n BrE* cloth worn by a baby to absorb urine and faeces
narcissism *n* too great love for one's own appearance or abilities **-sist** *n* **-sistic** *adj*
narcissus *n* **-ses** *or* **-si** daffodil or related plant
narcotic *n* sleep-producing drug, harmful in large amounts
nark *n sl* **1** *BrE* police informer **2** *AustrE* annoying person or thing ♦ *v* **1** *vi* act as an informer **2** *vt* annoy
narky *adj BrE sl* bad-tempered
narrate *vt* tell (a story) or describe (events) **-rator** *n* **-ration** *n*
narrative *n* **1** *fml* story **2** art of narrating
narrow *adj* **1** small from one side to the other **2** limited **3** only just successful: *a narrow escape* **4** not open to new ideas: *a narrow mind* ♦ *vi/t* become or make narrower **narrow down** *phr vt* reduce, limit **~ly** *adv* only just **~ness** *n*
narrow-minded *adj* unwilling to respect the opinions of others when different from one's own **~ness** *n*
narrow squeak *n infml* close shave
NASA *n* National Aeronautics and Space Administration: US space agency
nasal *adj* of the nose **~ly** *adv*
nascent *adj fml* starting to develop
nasturtium *n* trailing garden plant with reddish flowers
nasty *adj* **1** not nice; unpleasant **2** dangerous or painful: *a nasty cut* **-tily** *adv* **-tiness** *n*
natal *adj fml* of birth
nation *n* (all the people belonging to) a country
national *adj* **1** of or being a nation, esp. as opposed to any of its individual parts or to other nations **2** owned or controlled by the central government of a country ♦ *n* person from a particular country **~ly** *adv* **~ism** *n* **1** love of and pride in one's country **2** desire to become a separate independent country **~ist** *adj, n* **~istic** *adj* showing too great nationalism **~ity** *n* fact of being a citizen of a particular country
national debt *n* amount of money owed by the government of a country
National Front *n* extreme right-wing British political party
National Guard *n* state militia of the US
National Health Service *n* NHS
National Insurance *n* British system of social security, in which workers and employers pay contributions to insure individuals against sickness and unemployment and to provide pensions
nationalize, -ise *vt* take (a business or

industry) into government control **–ization** *n*

national park *n* area of land conserved by the state

national service *n* compulsory military service

nationwide *adj, adv* happening over the whole country

native *adj* **1** of or being one's place of birth **2** found naturally in a place: *native species* **3** not learned: *native ability* ♦ *n* **1** person born in a place **2** local person, esp. non-European

Nativity *n* the birth of Christ

NATO *n* North Atlantic Treaty Organization; a group of western countries which give military help to each other

natter *vi, n BrE* (have) a long unimportant talk

natty *adj infml* neat in appearance or esp. dress **–tily** *adv*

natural *adj* **1** existing or happening ordinarily in the world, esp. not made by people: *death from natural causes* **2** usual; to be expected **3** existing from birth; not learned: *a natural talent* **4** having natural skill ♦ *n* person with natural skill **~ly** *adv* **1** as a natural skill **2** in an ordinary way **3** of course **~ist** *n* person who studies animals and plants **~istic** *adj* representing things exactly as they are **~istically** *adv*

natural gas *n* gas obtained from the Earth's crust, esp. that used as fuel

natural history *n* study of animals and plants

naturalize, -ise *vt* make (someone born elsewhere) a citizen of a country **–ization** *n*

natural selection *n* process by which creatures well suited to their conditions continue to exist and those less well suited die out

nature *n* **1** everything that exists in the world independently of people, such as animals and plants, the land, and the weather **2** character: *a kind nature* **3** *fml* kind; sort

naturism *n* nudism

naturopathy *n* treatment of disease e.g. with herbal medicine to stimulate natural healing processes **–thic** *adj*

naught *n arch.* nothing

naughty *adj* **1** (esp. of a child) behaving badly **2** sexually improper **–tily** *adv* **–tiness** *n*

nausea *n* feeling of sickness and desire to vomit **–eous** *adj* **–ate** *vt* **1** cause to feel nausea **2** sicken; disgust

nautical *adj* of ships or sailing

nautical mile *n* unit of distance used for sea and air navigation, 1853 metres

nautilus *n* **-ses** *or* **-li** ocean mollusc with a spiral shell

naval *adj* of a navy or warships

nave *n* long central part of a church

navel *n* small sunken place in the middle of the stomach

navigable *adj* (of a river, channel, etc.) deep and wide enough to let ships pass

navigate *vi/t* direct the course of (a ship, aircraft, etc., or a car) **–gator** *n* **–gation** *n*

navvy *n BrE* unskilled labourer

navy *n* ships and sailors for fighting

navy blue *n* dark blue

nay *adv esp. arch.* no

Nazi *n* member of the German fascist party 1933-45 **–ism** *n*

NB (used in writing) take notice (of this)

NCO abbrev. for: noncommissioned officer

Neanderthal man *n* type of prehistoric human being

Neapolitan *n, adj* (inhabitant) of Naples

neapolitan *adj* (of ice cream) made in layers of different colours and flavours

neap tide *n* low tide twice a month

near *adj* **1** at a short distance; close **2** **nearest and dearest** one's family ♦ *adv, prep* not far (from) ♦ *vi/t* come closer (to) **~ly** *adv* **1** almost **2 not nearly** not at all **~ness** *n*

nearby *adj, adv* near

Near East *n* countries round the Eastern Mediterranean Sea, including Turkey and North Africa

near miss *n* something that comes close to succeeding or (of a bomb) hitting

nearside *adj, n* (on) the left-hand side, esp. of a vehicle
nearsighted *adj esp. AmE* shortsighted
near thing *n* something bad that nearly happened but didn't
neat *adj* **1** tidy **2** simple and effective: *a neat trick* **3** (of an alcoholic drink) not diluted **~ly** *adv* **~ness** *n*
neath *prep lit* beneath
nebula *n* **-as** *or* **-ae** galaxy (as seen from Earth)
nebulous *adj* not clear, esp. in meaning or expression **~ly** *adv*
necessary *adj* that is needed or must be done **-rily** *adv* in a way that must be so; inevitably
necessitate *vt fml* make necessary
necessitous *adj fml* needy
necessity *n* **1** condition of being necessary; need **2** something necessary, esp. for life
neck *n* **1** part of the body joining the head to the shoulders **2** part of a garment that goes round this **3** narrow part sticking out from a broader part: *the neck of a bottle* **4 neck and neck** doing equally well in a competition **5 neck of the woods** *infml* area or part of the country **6 up to one's neck** deeply involved or implicated ♦ *vi infml* kiss and cuddle
necklace *n* decorative chain or string of jewels, worn round the neck
necktie *n esp. AmE* tie
necromancy *n* evil magic; sorcery **-cer** *n*
necrophilia *n* sexual interest in corpses **-iac** *adj, n*
nectar *n* **1** sweet liquid collected by bees from flowers **2** sweet and delicious drink
nectarine *n* peach-like fruit
née *adj* (used to show a woman's name before she married): *Sheila Smith, née Brown*
need *n* **1** condition in which something necessary or desirable is missing **2** necessary duty: *There's no need for you to come.* **3** something one must have **4** state of lacking food, money, etc.: *children in need* **5 if need be** if necessary ♦ *v* **1** *vt* have a need for; require **2** *vi* have to; must: *You needn't come* **~less** *adj* unnecessary **~lessly** *adv* **~y** *adj* poor
needle *n* **1** thin pointed pin or rod used in sewing or knitting **2** something long, thin, and sharp, such as a leaf, a pointer on a compass, or the part of a hypodermic which is pushed into someone's skin **3** stylus ♦ *vt* annoy
needlework *n* sewing
ne'er-do-well *n lit* useless lazy person
nefarious /niˈfeəri·əs/ *adj fml* wicked **~ly** *adv*
negate *vt* cause to have no effect **-ation** *n*
negative *adj* **1** saying or meaning 'no' **2** not useful or encouraging **3** less than zero **4** (of electricity) of the type carried by electrons ♦ *n* **1** word, expression, or statement saying or meaning 'no' **2** film showing dark areas as light and light as dark
neglect *vt* **1** give too little attention or care to **2** fail (to do something), esp. because of carelessness ♦ *n* neglecting or being neglected **~ful** *adj* tending to neglect things **~fully** *adv* **~fulness** *n*
negligee /ˈneglizhay/ *n* light thin nightdress
negligent *adj* not taking enough care **~ly** *adv* **-ence** *n*
negligible *adj* too slight or unimportant to worry about
negotiable *adj* **1** that can be settled or changed by being negotiated **2** that can be travelled through, along, etc.
negotiate *v* **1** *vi/t* talk to someone in order to try to get (an agreement) **2** *vt* travel safely along or through **-ator** *n* **-ation** *n*
Negress *n* female Negro
Negro *n* **-oes** black person
negroid *adj* like a Negro in appearance
neigh *vi, n* (make) the sound of a horse
neighbour, *AmE* **-bor** *n* someone who lives near another **~hood** *n* **1** area in a town **2 in the neighbourhood of** about; roughly **~ing** *adj* (of a place) near **~ly** *adj* friendly

neither *determiner, pron, conj* not one and not the other ♦ *adv* also not
nematode *n* type of (parasitic) worm
nem con *adv* (used of a proposal that is voted on) without any opposition: *The motion is carried nem con.*
nemesis *n lit* (force bringing) just and unavoidable punishment
neo- *prefix* new; recent
neoclassical *adj* done recently, but in the style of ancient Greece and Rome
neocolonialism *n derog* indirect control of smaller countries by more powerful ones
Neolithic *adj* of a period about 10,000 years ago
neologism *n* new word or expression
neon *n* gas used in making bright electric lights
neophyte *n fml* beginner
neoplasm *n* tumour **-stic** *adj*
nephew *n* son of one's brother or sister
nephritis *n* inflammation of the kidneys
nepotism *n* giving unfair favour and advantages to one's relatives
Neptune *n* planet 8th in order from the sun
nerd *n sl* fool
nerve *n* **1** threadlike part in the body that carries feelings and messages to and from the brain **2** courage **3** disrespectful rudeness; cheek ♦ *vt* give courage to (someone, esp. oneself) **nerves** *pl n* **1** great nervousness **2 get on someone's nerves** make someone annoyed or bad-tempered **nervous** *adj* **1 a** rather frightened **b** easily excited and worried **2** of the nerves: *the nervous system* **-ously** *adv* **-ousness** *n*
nerve centre *n* place from which a system, organization, etc., is controlled
nerve-racking *adj* that causes great worry or fear
nervous breakdown *n* serious medical condition of deep worrying, anxiety, and tiredness which stops one working
nervy *adj infml* **1** nervous **2** bold
ness *n* headland
-ness *suffix* quality or state: *tiredness*
nest *n* **1** hollow place built or used by a bird as a home and a place to keep its eggs **2** group of similar objects which fit closely into or inside one another: *a nest of tables* ♦ *vi* build or use a nest
nest egg *n* amount of money saved for special future use
nestle *vi/t* settle, lie, or put in a close comfortable position
nestling *n* very young bird
net[1] *n* (piece of) material made of strings, wires, etc., tied together with regular spaces between them ♦ *vt* **-tt-** catch in a net **~ting** *n* string, wire, etc., made into a net
net[2], nett *adj* left after nothing further is to be taken away: *a net profit* ♦ *vt* **-tt-** gain as a profit
netball *n* women's team game in which points are scored by throwing a ball into a net
nether *adj lit* lower; under
nethermost *adj* lowest
nettle *n* wild plant with stinging leaves ♦ *vi* irritate
network *n* **1** large system of lines, wires, etc., that cross or meet each other **2** group of radio or television stations ♦ *vi/t* connect (computers) to form a network to share information
neural *adj* of the nerves
neuralgia *n med* sharp pain along the length of a nerve **-gic** *adj*
neurology *n* scientific study of nerves and their diseases **-gist** *n*
neurosis /nyoo(ə)ˈrohsis/ *n* **-ses** mental disorder in which one suffers from strong unreasonable fears and emotional instability **-rotic** *adj* of or suffering from a neurosis
neuter *adj* (in grammar) belonging to the class of words that mainly includes things rather than males or females ♦ *vt* remove part of the sex organs of (an animal)
neutral *adj* **1** not supporting either side in a war, argument, etc. **2** having no strong or noticeable qualities: *a neutral colour* ♦ *n* **1** position of a car's gears in which the engine is not connected with the wheels **2** a neutral person or

country **~ize, -ise** *vt* cause to have no effect **~ity** *n*
neutrino *n* **-os** very small particle of matter with no mass or electrical charge
neutron *n* very small particle of matter that is part of an atom and carries no electricity
neutron bomb *n* nuclear bomb producing much radiation
never *adv* not ever
nevermore *adv lit* never again
never-never *n BrE sl* hire purchase
nevertheless *adv* in spite of that; yet
new *adj* **1** only recently made or begun **2** different from the one before **3 new to** just beginning to know about or do; unfamiliar with ♦ *adv* recently: *new-laid eggs* **~ly** *adv* that has just happened or been done; recently **~ness** *n*
new blood *n* new members of a group, bringing new ideas, energy, etc.
newborn *adj* recently born
new broom *n esp. BrE* newly appointed person who is eager to make changes
newcomer *n* someone who has just arrived
newfangled *adj* new but neither necessary nor better
newlywed *n* recently married person
new moon *n* **1** time when the dark side of the moon faces the earth **2** thin crescent moon seen for a few days after this
New Right *n* movement against the welfare state by some Conservatives in the 1980s
news *n* **1** facts that are reported about a recent event **2** regular report of recent events on radio or television
newsagent, *AmE* **news dealer** *n* someone who sells newspapers in a shop
newscaster also **newsreader** *n* person who reads the news on television
newshound *n* very eager newspaper reporter
newsletter *n* printed sheet of news about an organization sent regularly to its members
newspaper *n* paper printed with news, notices, advertisements, etc., that comes out every day or every week
newspeak *n* language whose meanings are slightly changed to make people believe things that are not quite true
newsprint *n* paper on which newspapers are printed
newsworthy *adj* important or interesting enough to be reported as news
newt *n* four-legged animal living both on land and water
New Testament *n* second part of the Christian Bible, containing the earliest Christian writings
New World *n* western hemisphere
New Year *n* year which has just begun or will soon begin
next *adj* **1** with nothing before or between; nearest **2** the one following or after: *next week* ♦ *adv* **1** just afterwards **2** the next time: *when next we meet* **3 next to** almost
next door *adv* **1** in the next building **2 next door to** *infml* almost the same as
nexus *n* connection or link
NHS *n* National Health Service; the British system of medical treatment for everyone, paid for by taxes
nib *n* pointed piece on the end of a pen, out of which ink flows
nibble *vi/t* eat with small bites ♦ *n* small bite
nice *adj* **1** good; pleasant **2** showing or needing careful understanding; subtle **3** *infml* bad: *a nice mess* **~ly** *adv* **~ness** *n*
nicety *n* fine or delicate point; detail
niche /neesh, nich/ *n* **1** hollow place in a wall, where something is put **2** suitable place, job, etc.
nick¹ *n* **1** small cut **2** *BrE infml* prison **3 in the nick of time** only just in time; almost too late ♦ *vt* **1** make a small cut in **2** *BrE sl* arrest **3** *BrE infml* steal
nick² *n BrE sl* stated condition: *in good nick*
nickel *n* **1** hard silver-white metal **2** US 5-cent coin
nicker *n* **nicker** *BrE sl* pound (in money)
nicknack *n* knick-knack
nickname *n* informal name used in-

stead of someone's real name ♦ *vt* give (someone) a nickname

nicotine *n* poisonous chemical found in tobacco

niece *n* daughter of one's brother or sister

niff *n BrE infml* bad smell **~y** *adj*

nifty *adj infml* very good, attractive, or effective

Nigerian *n, adj* (inhabitant) of Nigeria

niggardly *adj* very mean; stingy **niggard** *n* mean person

nigger *n taboo* black person

niggle *vi* be continually annoying or troubling

nigh *adj, adv lit* near

night *n* dark part of the day, between sunrise and sunset

night blindness *n* inability to see in a poor light

nightcap *n* drink before going to bed

nightclub *n* restaurant open late at night where people may drink, dance, and see a show

nightdress also **nightie** *n* woman's garment worn in bed

nightfall *n* beginning of night

nightingale *n* bird with a beautiful song

nightlife *n* evening entertainment or social activity

nightly *adj, adv* (happening, done, etc.) every night

nightmare *n* **1** frightening dream **2** terrible experience or event

nightshade *n* types of plant with bell-shaped flowers, often poisonous

nightshirt *n* man's long loose shirt worn in bed

night soil *n* human excrement collected for fertilizing the soil

nightstick *n AmE* truncheon

night watchman *n* man who guards a building at night

nihilism /ˈnie·əˌliz(ə)m/ *n* belief that nothing has meaning or value **-ist** *n*

nil *n* nothing; zero

nimble *adj* quick, light, and neat in movement **-bly** *adv* **~ness** *n*

nimbus *n* **-bi** *or* **~es** large rain cloud

nincompoop *n infml* fool

nine *determiner, n, pron* 9 **ninth** *determiner, adv, n, pron* 9th

nine days' wonder *n* thing or event that causes excitement for a short time and is then forgotten

ninepins *n* **like ninepins** (falling or being destroyed) quickly and in large numbers

nineteen *determiner, n, pron* 19 **~th** *determiner, adv, n, pron* 19th

ninety *determiner, n, pron* 90 **-tieth** *determiner, adv, n, pron* 90th

ninny *n* fool

nip[1] *v* **-pp- 1** *vt* catch in a sharp tight usu. painful hold **2** *vi BrE* go quickly; hurry **3 nip something in the bud** stop something before it has properly started ♦ *n* **1** sharp tight hold or bite **2** coldness: *a nip in the air*

nip[2] *n* small drink of spirits

nipper *n infml* child

nipple *n* round pointed dark-skinned area on a breast, through which milk is secreted

nippy *adj infml* **1** cold **2** quick in movement

Nirvana *n* (in Buddhism and Hinduism) calm state of union with the spirit of the universe

nit[1] *n BrE* silly person

nit[2] *n* egg of a louse found in someone's hair

nitpicking *n, adj* (habit of) paying too much attention to small unimportant details

nitrate *n* chemical used esp. to fertilize the soil

nitric acid *n* powerful acid which destroys other materials

nitrogen *n* gas that forms most of the Earth's air

nitroglycerine *n* powerful liquid explosive

nitty-gritty *n infml* difficult, practical, and important part of a matter

nitwit *n* silly person

nix *n infml* nothing ♦ *adv AmE* no ♦ *vt AmE* forbid

no *adv* **1** (used for refusing or disagreeing) **2** not any: *no better* ♦

determiner **1** not a; not any **2** (shows what is not allowed): *No smoking* ♦ *n* **noes, nos** answer or decision of no

no. *abbrev. for:* number

No 10 Number Ten

nob *n BrE infml* upper-class person

nobble *vt BrE sl* **1** prevent (a racehorse) from winning by using drugs **2** get or persuade dishonestly

Nobel prize *n* annual international prize for oustanding achievement

nobility *n* **1** people of high social rank with titles **2** state of being noble

noble *adj* **1** of high moral quality; fine and unselfish **2** grand **3** of high social rank ♦ *n* lord in former times **-bly** *adv*

nobleman *n* **-men** member of the nobility

noblewoman *n* **-men** female member of the nobility

nobody *pron* no one ♦ *n* unimportant person

no-claim bonus *n* reduction in insurance premiums given to someone who has not made any claims within a particular period

nocturnal *adj* happening or active at night **~ly** *adv*

nocturne *n* piece of dreamy piano music

nod *vi/t* **-dd-** bend (one's head) forward and down, esp. to show agreement or give a sign **nod off** *phr vi* fall asleep unintentionally ♦ *n* act of nodding

nodding acquaintance *n* slight familiarity

node *n* point from which lines branch

nodule *n* small round lump or swelling

Noel *n* Christmas

noggin *n* **1** small amount of a strong alcoholic drink **2** *infml* head

nohow *adv infml* in no way

noise *n* sound, esp. loud and unpleasant

noisy *adj* making a lot of noise **-ily** *adv* **-iness** *n*

noisome *adj fml* repellent

nomad *n* member of a tribe that does not settle long in one place **~ic** *adj*

no-man's-land *n* land no one owns or controls, esp. between two armies or borders

nom de plume *n* **noms de plume** pen name

nomenclature /noˈmenklәchә/ *n* system of naming things

nominal *adj* **1** not really what the name suggests **2** (of an amount of money) very small **3** of or being a noun **~ly** *adv*

nominate *vt* to suggest officially that (someone) should be chosen or elected **-ation** *n*

nominative *adj* being the grammatical case of the subject of a sentence

nominee *n* person who has been nominated

non- *prefix* not

nonagenarian *n* person between 90 and 99 years old

nonaligned *adj* (of a country) not supporting any particular powerful nation

nonce *n* **for the nonce** for now

nonchalant /ˈnonshәlәnt/ *adj* calm and usu. uninterested **~ly** *adv* **-ance** *n*

noncombatant *n* person attached to an army who does not fight

noncommissioned officer *n* person in the army, navy, etc., below the rank of officer but with some power to command others

noncommittal *adj* not showing what you really think or intend **~ly** *adv*

nonconformist *n, adj* **1** (person) not following customary ways of living, thinking, etc. **2** (*cap.*) (member) of a Christian group separated from the Church of England

nondescript *adj* very ordinary-looking and dull

none *pron* not any ♦ *adv* **1 none the** not at all: *none the worse* **2 none too** not very

nonentity *n* person without much ability, character, or importance

nonetheless *adv* in spite of that; nevertheless

non-event *n* something much less important, interesting, etc., than expected

nonfiction *n* writing about facts, not stories

no-nonsense *adj* practical and direct

nonpareil *n lit* person or thing without

an equal
nonplus *vt* **-ss-** surprise (someone) so much that they do not know what to think or do
nonsense *n* **1** meaningless words **2** foolish words, ideas, or actions **-sensical** *adj* foolish
non sequitur *n* statement that does not follow logically from what has been said before
non-specific urethritis *n* NSU
nonstarter *n BrE* person or idea with no chance of success
nonstick *adj* with a special surface that food will not stick to when cooked
nonstop *adj, adv* without a pause or interruption
non-U *adj* not typical of the upper classes
nonviolence *n* peaceful means to gain political or social ends
noodle *n* long thin piece of pasta, cooked in soup or boiling water
nook *n* **1** sheltered private place **2 nooks and crannies** hidden or little-known places
noon *n* midday
no one *pron* not anyone; no person
noose *n* ring formed by the end of a rope, which closes tighter as it is pulled
nope *adv infml* no
nor *conj* and also not
Nordic *adj* Scandinavian
norm *n* usual or average way of happening or behaving
normal *adj* according to what is usual, expected, or average **~ly** *adv* **~ity** also *AmE* **~cy** *n*
normalize, -ise *vi/t* (cause to) become normal, esp. to bring or come back to a good or friendly state **-ization** *n*
Norman *n, adj* (person) of Normandy
normative *adj fml* being or prescribing a norm
Norse *adj* Scandinavian, esp. in medieval times
north *n* (*often cap.*) direction which is on the left of a person facing the rising sun ♦ *adj* **1** in the north **2** (of wind) from the north ♦ *adv* towards the north **~ward** *adj, adv*
northeast *n, adj, adv* (direction) halfway between north and east **~ern** *adj*
northerly *adj* towards or in the north
northern *adj* of the north part of the world or of a country **~er** *n* person who lives in or comes from the northern part of a country
northwest *n, adj, adv* (direction) halfway between north and west **~ern** *adj*
Norwegian *n, adj* (inhabitant) of Norway
nos. *abbrev. for:* numbers
nose *n* **1** the part of the face above the mouth that is used for breathing and smelling **2** (pointed) front end: *the nose of the rocket* **3** ability to find out: *a nose for trouble* **4 under someone's (very) nose** quite openly in front of someone ♦ *vi* **1** move ahead slowly and carefully **2** try to find out about things that do not concern you
nosebag *n* bag hung around a horse's head to hold its food
nosebleed *n* case of bleeding from the nose
nosecone *n* pointed front part of a spacecraft or missile
nosedive *vi* **1** (of a plane) drop suddenly, front end first **2** fall suddenly and greatly: *Prices nosedived.* **nosedive** *n*
nosegay *n lit* small bunch of flowers
nosh *n BrE sl* meal, food
no-show *n* person who makes a booking but does not attend
nostalgia *n* fondness for past things **-gic** *adj*
nostril *n* either of the two openings in the nose
nostrum *n* facile or questionable remedy
nosy, nosey *adj* interested in things that do not concern one
nosy parker *n BrE infml* nosy person
not *adv* **1** (used for showing the opposite meaning) **2 not at all** (a polite answer to thanks)
notable *adj* unusual or good enough to be especially noticed **-bly** *adv* particularly

notary *n* public official who witnesses the signing of documents and makes them official
notation *n* system of signs for writing something down
notch *n* V-shaped cut ♦ *vt* **1** make a notch in **2** gain (a victory)
note *n* **1** short written record to remind one of something **2** short piece of additional information in a book **3** short informal letter **4** piece of paper money **5** (sign representing) a musical sound **6** stated quality or feeling: *a note of anger in his voice* **7** *fml* fame; importance **8 take note of** pay attention to ♦ *vt* **1** record in writing **2** notice and remember **~d** *adj* famous
notebook *n* book of plain paper in which one writes notes
notepaper *n* paper for writing letters on
noteworthy *adj* notable
nothing *pron* **1** not any thing: *There's nothing in this box — it's empty.* **2** something of no importance **3 for nothing** : **a** free **b** with no good result **4 nothing like** not nearly **~ness** *n*
notice *n* **1** written or printed sign giving information **2** information that something is going to happen; warning: *changed without notice* **3** attention; regard: *Don't take any notice of him.* ♦ *vi/t* see, hear, etc., so as to be conscious of and remember **~able** *adj* big enough to be noticed **~ably** *adv*
notify *vt* tell (someone), esp. formally **-fication** *n*
notion *n* idea; opinion
notional *adj* **1** theoretical **2** imaginary **~ly** *adv*
notoriety *n* state of being notorious
notorious *adj* famous for something bad **~ly** *adv*
notwithstanding *adv fml* in spite of that
nougat *n* sweet made of sugar, nuts, fruit, etc.
nought *n BrE* zero
noughts and crosses *n BrE* game in which two players write O or X in a pattern of squares and try to make a row of three Os or Xs
noun *n* word that is the name of a thing, quality, action, etc., and can be used as the subject or object of a verb
nourish *vt* **1** keep alive and healthy by giving food **2** keep (a feeling, plan, etc.) alive **~ment** *n* food
nous /nows/ *n BrE* good practical judgment
nouveau riche *n, adj* **nouveaux riches** (person who is) wealthy but obviously not accustomed to being so
nouvelle cuisine *n* style of cooking emphasizing natural ingredients and attractive presentation
nova *n* **-ae** *or* **-as** sudden explosion of a star
novel[1] *n* long written story **~ist** *n* novel writer
novel[2] *adj* new and rather clever
novelette *n derog* short bad romantic novel
novella *n* **-las** *or* **-le** story shorter than a novel and longer than a short story
novelty *n* **1** interesting newness **2** something new and unusual **3** small cheap object, usu. not very useful
November *n* the 11th month of the year
novice *n* person who has just begun and has no experience
novitiate *n* (period of) being a novice
now *adv* **1** at this present time **2** (used for attracting attention or giving a warning) **3 (every) now and again/then** at times; sometimes ♦ *conj* in view of the fact that
nowadays *adv* in these modern times
no way *adv, interj sl* no; certainly not
nowhere *adv* **1** not anywhere **2 nowhere near** not at all near or nearly
nowise *adv arch.* not at all
noxious *adj* harmful; poisonous
nozzle *n* short tube at the end of a pipe for controlling the flow of a liquid
NSU *n* non-specific urethritis; type of venereal disease
nth *adj* **to the nth degree** to the highest, greatest, furthest, etc., degree or form
nuance /ˈnyooh,ons/ *n* slight delicate difference in meaning, colour, etc.
nub *n* most important point

nubile *adj* (of a young woman) sexually attractive

nuclear *adj* **1** being, using, or producing the great power you get by splitting atoms **2** using nuclear weapons: *a nuclear war*

nuclear family *n* family unit that consists only of husband, wife, and children, without grandmothers, uncles, etc.

nuclear winter *n* period of extreme cold and darkness following a nuclear war

nucleic acid *n* complex acid (e.g. DNA or RNA) found in the cells of all living things

nucleus *n* **-clei 1** central part of **a** an atom **b** a cell (2) **2** original part round which the rest is built

nude *adj* with no clothes on ♦ *n* **1** (piece of art showing a) naked person **2 in the nude** with no clothes on

nudge *vt* push gently, esp. with the elbow **nudge** *n*

nudism *n* practice of going around with no clothes on, usu. in a special place (**nudist camp**) **nudist** *n*

nudity *n* state of being nude

nugatory /ˈnyoohgət(ə)ri/ *adj fml* worthless, trifling

nugget *n* **1** small rough lump **2** small item, esp. of information

nuisance *n* annoying person, animal, thing, or situation

nuke *vt infml* attack with nuclear weapons

null *adj tech* of, being, or concerning zero

null and void *adj* having no legal effect

nullify *vt* cause to have no effect

nullity *n* **1** state of being null and void in law **2** lack of meaning or significance

numb *adj* unable to feel **numb** *vt* **~ness** *n*

number *n* **1** (written sign for) a member of the system used in counting and measuring **2** quantity; amount: *a large number of people* **3** (copy of) a magazine printed at a particular time **4** piece of music **5 have someone's number** have knowledge useful in annoying or defeating someone ♦ *vt* **1** give a number to **2** reach as a total: *The audience numbered over 5000.* **3** *fml* include: *I number him among my friends.* **~less** *adj* too many to count

number one *n* **1** chief person or thing **2** oneself and no one else

numberplate *n* sign on a vehicle showing its registration number

Number Ten *n* home of the British prime minister, in London

numeral *n* sign that represents a number

numerate *adj* able to calculate with numbers **–acy** *n*

numeration *n* system of counting

numerator *n tech* number above the line in a fraction

numerical *adj* of or using numbers **~ly** *adv*

numerous *adj* many

numinous *adj* giving a sense of holiness and mystery

numismatics *n* coin collecting **–tist** *n*

numskull, numbskull *n* foolish person

nun *n* member of an all-female religious group that lives together **~nery** *n* building where they live

nuncio *n* **-cios** papal ambassador

nuptial /ˈnupsh(ə)l/ *adj fml* of marriage **nuptials** *pl n fml* wedding

nurse *n* person who takes care of sick, hurt, or old people, esp. in hospital ♦ *vt* **1** take care of as or like a nurse **2** hold in the mind: *nurse a grudge* **3** handle carefully or lovingly **4** feed (a baby) with breast milk **nursing** *n* job of being a nurse

nursemaid *n* woman employed to take care of a young child

nursery *n* **1** place where young children are taken care of **2** area where garden plants are grown to be sold

nursery rhyme *n* song or poem for young children

nursery school *n* school for young children of two to five years of age

nursing home *n* place where old or sick people can live and be looked after

nurture *vt lit* give care and food to, so as

to help development

nut *n* **1** fruit with a hard shell and a softer dry seed inside which is eaten **2** small piece of metal with a hole through it for screwing onto a bolt **3** *sl* mad person **4 do one's nut** *infml* be very worried and/or angry **5 off one's nut** *sl* mad **nuts** *adj sl* mad **~ty** *adj* **1** like or full of nuts **2** *sl* mad

nutcase *n sl* mad person

nutcracker *n* tool for cracking the shell of a nut

nutmeg *n* large hard fragrant seed used as a spice

nutrient *n, adj* (a chemical or food) providing for life or growth

nutrition *n* process of giving or getting food **–tious** *adj* valuable to the body as food

nutritive *adj tech* of nutrition

nuts and bolts *pl n* the simple facts or skills of a subject or job

nutshell *n* **in a nutshell** described in as few words as possible

nuzzle *vi/t* press closely, esp. with the nose

nylon *n* strong synthetic material made into cloth, plastic, etc.

nymph *n* (in Greek and Roman myths) goddess of nature living in trees, streams, mountains, etc.

nymphet *n* girl in early adolescence who is sexually attractive

nymphomania *n* (excessively) strong sexual desire in a woman **–niac** *n* woman with nymphomania

O

O, o **1** the 15th letter of the English alphabet **2** (in speech) zero

oaf *n* rough stupid awkward person **~ish** *adj*

oak *n* large broad tree with hard wood and curly leaves

oak apple *n* round swelling on oak twigs, caused by an insect

oaken *adj lit* made of oak

oakum *n* tarry fibre used for filling gaps, esp. on wooden ships

OAP *n BrE* old age pensioner

oar *n* **1** long pole with a flat blade, used for rowing a boat **2 put/shove/stick one's oar in** *infml* interfere

oarsman *n* **-men** rower

oarswoman *n* **-men** female rower

oasis *n* **-ses** place with water and trees in a desert

oasthouse *n* building for drying hops

oath *n* **oaths 1** solemn promise **2** use of bad angry words; curse **3 be on/under oath** have promised to tell the truth

oatmeal *n* crushed oats

oats *pl n* sort of grain used as food

obbligato *n* **-os** *or* **-ti** musical accompaniment

obdurate *adj fml* unwilling to think or act differently; stubborn **~ly** *adv* **–acy** *n*

OBE *abbrev. for:* Order of the British Empire

obeah *n* magical practices of the West Indies

obedient *adj* doing what one is told to do **~ly** *adv* **–ence** *n*

obeisance /oʊˈbay(i)səns/ *n fml* show of respect and obedience, esp. by bowing

obelisk *n* tall pointed stone pillar

obese *adj fml* unhealthily fat **–ity** *n*

obey *vi/t* do what one is told to do (by someone in a position of power)

obfuscate *vt fml* make unclear; obscure **–ation** *n*

obiter dictum *n* **obiter dicta** incidental remark

obituary *n* report e.g. in a newspaper of someone's death

object[1] *n* **1** thing that can be seen or felt **2** purpose **3** word or words that represent the person or thing affected by the action of a verb **4** person or thing that produces the stated feeling: *an object of pity* **5 be no object** not be a

difficulty
object[2] *vi* be opposed to something or someone
objection *n* **1** statement or feeling of dislike or opposition **2** reason or argument against
objectionable *adj* unpleasant **–bly** *adv*
objective *adj* **1** not influenced by personal feelings; fair **2** existing outside the mind; real ♦ *n* purpose of a plan **–tivity** *n*
object lesson *n* event or story from which one can learn how or how not to behave
objet d'art *n* **objets d'art** small object of some value as art
oblate *adj* (of a sphere) flattened at each end
oblation *n* religious offering (e.g. worship)
obligate *vt* make obliged
obligation *n* what one has to do; duty **–tory** *adj*
oblige *vt fml* **1** make it necessary for (someone) to do something **2** do a favour for **3 much obliged** (used for thanking someone politely)
obliging *adj* kind and eager to help **~ly** *adv*
oblique *adj* **1** indirect: *an oblique hint* **2** sloping
obliterate *vt* remove all signs of; destroy **–ation** *n*
oblivion *n* **1** state of being completely forgotten **2** state of being unconscious or not noticing one's surroundings
oblivious *adj* not noticing
oblong *n* right-angled figure with four sides, two long and two shorter ones **oblong** *adj*
obloquy /ˈobləkwi/ *n fml* **1** (abusive) condemnation **2** discredit
obnoxious *adj* extremely unpleasant **~ly** *adv*
oboe *n* woodwind instrument with a plaintive tone **oboist** *n* player of an oboe
obscene *adj* very offensive or shocking, esp. sexually **obscenity** *n* obscene word or behaviour
obscurantist *n, adj derog* (person) deliberately making things obscure
obscure *adj* **1** hard to understand; not clear **2** not well known ♦ *vt* hide **obscurity** *n* state of being obscure
obsequies *pl n* funeral rites
obsequious /əbˈseekwi·əs/ *adj fml* too eager to obey or serve **~ly** *adv* **~ness** *n*
observance *n fml* **1** doing something in accordance with a law, custom, etc. **2** part of a religious ceremony
observant *adj* quick at noticing things **~ly** *adv*
observation *n* **1** action of noticing **2** ability to notice things **3** *fml* remark, esp. about something noticed **4 under observation** being carefully watched during a period of time
observatory *n* place where scientists look at and study the stars, moon, etc.
observe *vt* **1** watch carefully **2** *fml* act in accordance with (a law, custom, etc.) **3** *fml* say **observer** *n* **1** someone who observes **2** someone who attends meetings, conferences, etc., only to listen, not take part
obsess *vt* completely fill (someone's) mind, so they cannot think about anything else **~ive** *adj* that is an obsession **~ion** *n* fixed and often unreasonable idea or pattern of behaviour
obsidian *n* shiny black volcanic glass
obsolescent *adj* becoming obsolete **–ence** *n*
obsolete *adj* no longer used; out of date
obstacle *n* something that prevents action, movement, or success
obstetrician *n* doctor concerned with obstetrics
obstetrics *n* branch of medicine concerned with the birth of children
obstinate *adj* **1** not willing to obey or change one's opinion; stubborn **2** difficult to control or defeat: *obstinate resistance* **~ly** *adv* **–acy** *n*
obstreperous *adj* noisy and uncontrollable **~ly** *adv* **~ness** *n*
obstruct *vt* **1** block **2** put difficulties in the way of **~ive** *adj* intentionally ob-

structing **~ion** *n* **1** obstructing **2** something that obstructs
obtain *vt fml* get; acquire **~able** *adj*
obtrude *vt* **1** stick out **2** assert (oneself) aggressively
obtrusive *adj fml* unpleasantly noticeable **~ly** *adv*
obtuse *adj* **1** *fml* annoyingly slow to understand **2** (of an angle) more than 90° **~ly** *adv* **~ness** *n*
obverse *n* **1** front side of a coin, medal, etc. **2** opposite
obviate *vt fml* make unnecessary
obvious *adj* easy to see and understand; clear **~ly** *adv*
ocarina *n* simple oval wind instrument
occasion *n* **1** time when something happens **2** *fml* reason: *He had no occasion to be so rude.* **3** special event or ceremony **4 on occasion** occasionally ♦ *vt fml* cause
occasional *adj* happening sometimes; not regular **~ly** *adv*
occidental *n, adj* (person) of the western part of the world
occipital /ok'sipitl/ *n adj med* of the back of the skull
occlude *vt* **1** *fml* block; hinder **2** *tech* form into an occlusion
occlusion *n* boundary formed by a cold air mass overtaking and lifting a warm one
occult *n, adj* (world of the) supernatural
occupant *n* person who is living in a house, room, etc. **-ancy** *n* (period of) being an occupant
occupation *n* **1** job **2** something done to pass time **3** taking possession of a country, city, etc. **~al** *adj* of one's job
occupational therapy *n* activities to help patients recover
occupy *vt* **1** be in (a position, seat, etc.) **2** fill (space or time) **3** take possession of (a country, city, etc.) militarily **4** keep busy **-pier** *n*
occur *vi* **-rr- 1** happen **2** be found; exist
occur to *phr vt* (of an idea) come to (someone's) mind **~rence** *n* **1** event **2** process of occurring
ocean *n* (any of the) great seas which cover most of the Earth **~ic** *adj*
~ography *n* study of oceans
ocelot /'osə,lot/ *n* medium-sized American wild cat
oche *n* line behind which a darts player must stand
ochre, *AmE* **-er** *n* dark yellow colour
ocker *n AustrE infml* (vulgarly aggressive) Australian
o'clock *adv* (used in telling the time when it is exactly a numbered hour)
octagon *n* flat figure with eight sides and eight angles **~al** *adj*
octane *n* number showing the power and quality of petrol: *high-octane fuel*
octave *n* space of eight degrees between musical notes
octavo *n* **-os** book format of paper sheets folded into eight pages
octet *n* (music for) eight musicians
October *n* the 10th month of the year
octogenarian *n* a person who is between 80 and 90 years old
octopus *n* deep-sea creature with eight limbs
ocular *adj* of or seen with the eyes
oculist *n* optician
O.D. *abbrev. for:* overdose
odalisque *n* female slave in a harem
odd *adj* **1** strange; unusual **2** (of a number) that cannot be exactly divided by two **3** separated from its pair or set: *an odd shoe* **4** not regular: *doing odd jobs* **5** rather more than the stated number: *20-odd years ago* **~ly** *adv* strangely **~ity** *n* **1** strange thing, person, etc. **2** strangeness
oddball *n, adj* (someone or something) eccentric or peculiar
odd man out *n* person or thing different from or left out of a group
oddment *n* something left over
odds *pl n* **1** probability of something happening, esp. as calculated for gambling **2 at odds** in disagreement
odds and ends *pl n* small articles of various kinds
odds-on *adj* with a good chance of success
ode *n* long poem

odious *adj fml* very unpleasant
odium *n fml* widespread hatred
odometer *n* mileometer
odoriferous *adj* having a smell
odorous *adj* having a smell
odour, -or *n fml* smell
odyssey *n* long adventurous journey
oedema /iˈdeemə/ *n* swelling of tissue due to fluid
Oedipus complex *n* (in Freudian psychology) a child's sexual desire for one parent and jealousy of the other parent
oesophagus /eeˈsofəgəs/ *n med* muscular tube from the mouth to the stomach
oestrogen /ˈeestrəj(ə)n/ *n* substance in females that changes the body ready for reproduction
oestrus /ˈeestrus/ *n* cycle of bodily changes in preparation for reproduction
of *prep* **1** belonging to **2** made from **3** containing: *a bag of potatoes* **4** (shows a part or amount): *two pounds of sugar* **5** in relation to; in connection with: *fond of swimming* **6 a** done by: *the plays of Shakespeare* **b** done about: *a picture of Shakespeare*
off *adv, adj* **1** disconnected; removed **2** (esp. of electrical apparatus) not lit or working **3** away **4** away or free from work **5** so as to be finished or destroyed: *They were all killed off.* **6** not going to happen after all: *The party's off!* **7** no longer good to eat or drink **8** provided with what you need: *They're not well off.* **9** not busy: *the off season* **10** **off and on** sometimes **11 on the off ch[illegible]ce** just in case ♦ *prep* **1** away from **2** [illegible]road) turning away from (a lar[illegible] [illegible] not wanting: *She's off her* [illegible]

[illegible] organs of an animal

[illegible]tional
[illegible]ll **2** sexually
[illegible]ng up a
[illegible]

esp. a crime **2** cause for hurt feelings: *take offence*
offend *v* **1** *vt* hurt the feelings of; upset **2** *vt* displease greatly **3** *vi* do wrong **~er** *n* person who offends, esp. a criminal **~ing** *adj* causing displeasure, discomfort, or inconvenience
offensive *adj* **1** extremely unpleasant **2** for attacking ♦ *n* **1** continued military attack **2 on the offensive** attacking **~ly** *adv* **~ness** *n*
offer *v* **1** *vi/t* say one will give or do **2** *vt* provide; give: *The situation doesn't offer much hope.* ♦ *n* **1** statement offering something **2** what is offered **~ing** *n* something offered
offertory *n* offering of something to God during a church service
offhand *adv, adj* **1** careless; disrespectful **2** without time to think or prepare
office *n* **1** room or building where written work is done **2** place where a particular service is provided: *a ticket office* **3** government department: *the Foreign Office* **4** important job or position of power
officer *n* **1** person in command in the army, navy, etc. **2** person in a government job: *a local government officer* **3** policeman
official *adj* of, from, or decided by someone in a position of power and responsibility ♦ *n* person who holds an important job **~ly** *adv* **1** formally by an official **2** as stated publicly (but perhaps not really) **~dom** *n* officials as a group **~ese** *n infml* language of government officials, considered unnecessarily obscure
officiate *vi* perform official duties
officious /əˈfishəs/ *adj* too eager to give orders **~ly** *adv* **~ness** *n*
offing *n* **in the offing** coming soon
off-licence *n BrE* shop where alcoholic drink is sold to be taken away
off-line *adj* not directly controlled by a computer
off-load *vt BrE* get rid of (something unwanted)
off-peak *adj* **1** less busy **2** existing

during less busy periods
offprint *n* separate printing of one part, e.g. one article from a magazine **offprint** *vt*
off-putting *adj esp. BrE* unpleasant and making one not want to continue
offset *vt* **-set**, *present p.* **-setting** make up for; balance
offshoot *n* subsidiary or additional branch
offshore *adv, adj* **1** in the sea near the coast: *offshore islands* **2** away from the coast: *offshore winds*
offside *adj, adv* **1** (in certain sports) ahead of the ball, which is against the rules **2** on the right-hand side, esp. of a vehicle
offspring *n* **offspring** *fml* someone's child
offstage *adj, adv* out of sight of the audience
off-the-record *adj, adv* unofficial and not to be formally recorded
off-the-wall *adj esp. AmE* amusingly foolish
off-white *adj* greyish or yellowish white
oft *adv lit* often
often *adv* **1** many times **2** in many cases **3 as often as not** at least 50% of the time **4 every so often** sometimes
ogle *vi/t* look (at) with great sexual interest
ogre *n* **1** fierce giant in fairy stories **2** frightening person
ogress *n* female ogre
oh *interj* (expresses surprise, fear, etc.)
ohm *n* measure of electrical resistance
-oid *suffix* (something) resembling: *humanoid*
oil *n* thick fatty inflammable liquid esp. petroleum ♦ *vt* put oil on or into **~y** *adj* **1** like or covered with oil **2** too polite
oils *pl n* paints containing oil
oil cake *n* block of seeds from which oil has been pressed
oilfield *n* area with oil underneath it
oil painting *n* painting done using paint made with oil
oilrig *n* large apparatus for getting oil up from under the sea
oilskin *n* (garment made of) cloth treated with oil so as to be waterproof
oil slick *n* film of oil on water
oil well *n* hole made in the ground to get oil
oink *vi, n* (make) the noise that a pig makes
ointment *n* oily usu. medicinal substance rubbed on the skin
okapi *n* African mammal related to the giraffe but with a shorter neck and black and cream rings on the legs
okay, OK *adj, adv* **1** all right; satisfactory **2** (expresses agreement or permission) ♦ *n* approval; permission ♦ *vt* give permission for
okra *n* vegetable consisting of sticky green pods
old *adj* **1** having lived or existed a long time **2** of a particular age: *2 years old* **3** having been so a long time: *an old friend* **4** former: *his old job* **5 of old: a** in the past **b** for a long time ♦ *pl n* old people
old age *n* part of one's life when one is old
old age pension *n* money paid regularly by the state to old people **~er** *n*
old-boy network *n BrE* tendency of former pupils of the same (public) school to favour each other, esp. in gaining jobs
olden *adj lit* past; long ago
olde worlde *adj BrE* of a (too) consciously old-fashioned style
old-fashioned *adj* once usual or fashionable but now less common
old flame *n* someone with whom one used to be in love
old guard *n* group of people with old-fashioned ideas who are against change
old hand *n* very experienced person
old hat *adj* old-fashioned
old maid *n* old unmarried woman
old master *n* (picture by) an important painter of esp. the 15th to 18th centuries
Old Nick *n* the devil
old school *n* traditional (but superseded) way of doing things

Old Testament *n* the part of the Christian Bible that is also the Jewish scriptures

old timer *n* **1** person who has been somewhere or done something for a long time **2** *AmE* old man

old wives' tale *n* ancient and not necessarily true belief

Old World *n* eastern hemisphere

oleaginous /ˌohliˈajinəs/ *adj fml* oily

oleander *n* evergreen shrub with white or pink flowers

O level *abbrev for:* Ordinary Level

olfactory *adj med* of the sense of smell

oligarchy /ˈoligahki/ *n* **1** government by a small usu. unrepresentative group **2** state governed in this way

olive *n* **1** small fruit of Mediterranean tree, eaten raw or made into oil for cooking **2** dull pale green

olive branch *n* sign of a wish for peace

-ology *suffix* science or study of

Olympic Games *pl n* international sports competition held every four years

O & M *abbrev. for:* organization and method

ombudsman *n* **-men** person who deals with complaints about an organization

Omega *n* final letter of the Greek alphabet

omelette *n* flat round mass of eggs beaten together and cooked

omen *n* sign of something that will happen

ominous *adj* seeming to show that something bad will happen **~ly** *adv*

omission *n* **1** omitting **2** something left out

omit *vt* **1** not include; leave out **2** *fml* not do; fail: *They omitted to tell me.*

omnibus *n* **1** book containing several works, esp. by one writer **2** *fml* bus

omnipotent /omˈnipət(ə)nt/ *adj fml* having unlimited power **–ence** *n*

omnipresent *adj* present everywhere **–nce** *n*

omniscient /omˈnisi·ənt/ *adj* knowing everything **–ence** *n*

omnivorous *adj* (esp. of an animal) eating anything

on *prep* **1** touching, supported by, hanging from, or connected with **2** directed towards: *a tax on beer* **3** in (a large vehicle): *on a train* **4** (shows when something happens): *on Tuesday.* **5** about: *a book on golf* **6** by means of: *A car runs on petrol.* **7** in a state of: *on fire|on holiday* **8** paid for by: *The drinks are on me!* ◆ *adv, adj* **1** continuously, instead of stopping: *keep on* **2** further; forward **3** (so as to be) wearing **4** with the stated part in front: *head on* **5** in(to) a vehicle **6** (esp. of electrical apparatus) lit or working **7** (of something arranged) happening or going to happen: *What's on at the cinema?* **8** with the stated part forward: *sideways on* **9 be on about/at** talk persistently and annoyingly about/to **10 not on** impossible; not acceptable **11 on and off** from time to time **12 on and on** without stopping

once *adv* **1** one time **2** formerly **3 at once: a** now; without delay **b** together **4 once and for all** now, so as to be settled, with no further change **5 once in a while** sometimes, but not often **6 once more** again ◆ *conj* from the moment that

onceover *n infml* a quick look or examination

oncoming *adj* coming towards you

one *determiner, n* **1** (the number) 1 **2** a certain: *They'll come back one day.* **3** the same: *They all ran in one direction.* **4 at one** *fml* in agreement **5 be one up (on)** have the advantage (over) **6 for one** as one out of several **7 in one** combined **8 one and all** every one **9 one and the same** exactly the same ◆*pron* **1** single thing or person of the sort mentioned **2** *fml* any person; you: *One should do one's duty.*

one another *pron* each other

one-armed bandit *n* machine with a long handle, into which people put money to try to win more money

one-liner *n* brief witty remark or joke

one-man band *n* **1** street musician who plays different instruments simul-

taneously **2** activity which someone does all on their own
one-night stand *n* **1** performance of music or a play given only once in each of a number of places **2** sexual relationship which lasts only one night
one-off *adj esp. BrE* **1** happening or done only once **2** made as a single example **one-off** *n*
one-piece *adj* made in one piece only
onerous /ˈohnərəs, ˈon-/ *adj fml* difficult; hard to bear
oneself *pron* **1** (*reflexive or strong form of* one (2)) **2 (all) by oneself: a** alone **b** without help **3 to oneself** not shared
one-sided *adj* with one side stronger or more favoured than the other
onetime *adj* former
one-to-one *adj, adv* **1** matching one another exactly **2** between only two people
one-upmanship *n* art of getting an advantage without actually cheating
one-way *adj* moving or allowing movement in one direction only
ongoing *adj* continuing
onion *n* strong-smelling round white vegetable
online *adj* directly connected to and/or controlled by a computer **online** *adv*
onlooker *n* person watching something happen
only *adj* **1** with no others in the same group **2** best: *She's the only person for this job.* ♦ *adv* **1** and no one or nothing else **2 if only** (expresses a strong wish) **3 only just: a** a moment before **b** almost not **4 only too** very; completely ♦ *conj* except that; but: *She wants to go, only she hasn't got enough money.*
o.n.o. *abbrev. for:* or nearest offer
onomatopoeia /ˌonəˌmatəˈpee·ə/ *n* formation of words which sound like their meaning (e.g. *buzz*) **–ic** *adj*
onrush *n* strong movement forward
onset *n* start, esp. of something bad
onshore *adv, adj* towards the coast
onside *adj, adv* not offside
onslaught *n* fierce attack
onstream *adv, adj* (esp. of an oil well) in(to) production
onto *prep* **1** to a position or point on **2 be onto** have found out about (someone or something wrong or illegal)
ontology *n* philosophical study of the nature of existence **–gical** *adj*
onus *n* duty; responsibility
onward *adj, adv* forward in space or time
onyx *n* translucent quartz with bands of colour
oodles *pl n infml* lots
oomph *n infml* energy
ooze *v* **1** *vi* (of thick liquid) pass or flow slowly **2** *vt* have (liquid) oozing out **3** *vt* exude: *ooze charm* ♦ *n* mud or thick liquid
op *n infml* operation (3, 4)
op. *abbrev. for:* opus
opacity /ohˈpasəti/ *n* opaqueness
opal *n* white precious stone with iridescent colours in it
opalescent *adj* like an opal
opaque *adj* which you cannot see through **~ness** *n*
op art *n* art using geometric shapes to create optical illusions
OPEC *n* Organization of Petroleum Exporting Countries
open *adj* **1** not shut **2** not surrounded by anything: *open country* **3** without a roof **4** not completely decided or answered: *an open question* **5** not hiding or hidden; honest **6** that anyone can enter: *an open competition* **7 open to: a** not safe from: *open to criticism* **b** willing to receive: *open to suggestions* ♦ *n* **1** the outdoors **2 in(to) the open** (of opinions, secrets, etc.) so as to be generally known ♦ *vi/t* **1** make or become open **2** start: *The story opens in a country village.* **3** (cause to) begin business **4 open fire** start shooting **5 open someone's eyes** make someone realize something **open into/onto** *phr vt* provide a means of entering or reaching **open out** *phr vi* speak more freely **open up** *phr v* **1** *vt* make possible the development of **2** *vi* open the door **3** *vi* speak more freely **~ly** *adv* not secretly

~**ness** *n* ~**er** *n*

open-air *adj* of or in the outdoors

open-and-shut *adj* easy to prove

open-cast *adj* where coal is dug from an open hole in the ground and not mined underground

open-door policy *n* idea of allowing traders from all countries to trade freely in a certain country

open-ended *adj* with no limit set in advance

open-handed *adj* generous

open-heart *adj* (of surgery) performed while the heart is cut open, and its functions are carried out by a machine

openhearted *adj* generous

opening *n* **1** hole or clear space **2** favourable set of conditions **3** unfilled job ♦ *adj* first; beginning

open letter *n* letter addressed to one person, but published or circulated for many to see

open-minded *adj* ready to consider new ideas

open-plan *adj* (of a large room) not divided into a lot of little rooms

open prison *n* prison without high walls and other strict security measures

open sandwich *n* sandwich without a top slice of bread

open season *n* time when it is legal to kill fish or game

open secret *n* fact tacitly known by many people

open sesame *n* key

open shop n establishment whose workers need not belong to a union

open verdict *n* (in a coroner's court) verdict leaving the cause of death undecided

opera *n* musical play in which (most of) the words are sung ~**tic** *adj*

operable *adj* (of a disease or condition) that can be cured by an operation

opera glasses *pl n* small binoculars for use at a theatre

operate *v* **1** *vi/t* (cause to) work: *operate the controls* **2** *vi* carry on trade or business **3** *vi* cut the body to cure or remove diseased parts, usu. in a special room (**operating theatre**) **4** *vi* produce effects: *The new law operates in our favour.*

operating system *n* set of programs inside a computer that controls the way it works and helps it to handle other programs

operation *n* **1** condition or process of working **2** thing (to be) done; activity **3** cutting of the body to cure or remove a diseased part **4** planned military movement ~**al** *adj* **1** of operations: *operational costs* **2** ready for use

operative *adj* **1** (of a plan, law, etc.) working; producing effects **2** most significant or crucial ♦ *n* worker

operator *n* person who works a machine, apparatus, or esp. telephone switchboard

operetta *n* light opera

ophthalmic /ofˈthalmik/ *adj med* of or near the eye

ophthalmology *n* branch of medicine dealing with the eye **–gist** *n*

opiate *n* **1** drug derived from opium **2** something that makes one calm

opine *vt* state as an opinion

opinion *n* **1** what someone thinks about something, based on personal judgment rather than facts **2** what people in general think about something **3** professional judgment or advice ~**ated** *adj* too sure that what one thinks is right

opium *n* sleep-producing drug

opossum *n* small marsupial of America and Australia

opponent *n* **1** person who takes the opposite side in a competition or fight **2** person who opposes someone or something

opportune *adj fml* **1** (of time) right for a purpose **2** coming at the right time ~**ly** *adv*

opportunism *n* taking advantage of every chance for success, sometimes to other people's disadvantage **–ist** *n*

opportunity *n* favourable moment; chance

oppose *vt* be or act against

opposed *adj* **1 opposed to:** against **2 as opposed to** and not
opposite *adj* **1** as different as possible from **2** facing: *the houses opposite* ♦ *n* opposite thing or person ♦ *prep* facing
opposite number *n* one that is equivalent or does the same things, but in a different group
opposition *n* **1** act or state of opposing **2** people who are against one **3** (*often cap.*) political parties opposed to the government
oppress *vt* **1** rule in a hard cruel way **2** cause to feel ill or sad **~ive** *adj* **1** cruel; unjust **2** causing feelings of illness and depression **~or** *n* **~ion** *n*
opprobrium *n fml* strong public disapproval or contempt **-rious** *adj* showing opprobrium
opt for *phr vt* choose
optic *adj* of the eyes
optical *adj* of the sense of sight
optical character reader *n* electronic device that can 'read' by recognizing patterns of light
optical fibre *n* very thin glass fibre that transmits light
optical illusion *n* something that deceives the sense of sight
optician *n* person who makes and sells glasses, contact lenses, etc.
optics *n* scientific study of light
optimist *n* person who expects good things to happen **-mism** *n* **~ic** *adj*
optimize, -ise *vt* make as perfect or effective as possible
optimum also **optimal** *adj* most favourable
option *n* **1** freedom to choose **2** possible course of action that can be chosen **3** right to buy or sell something at a stated time in the future **~al** *adj* which you can choose to have or not to have
opt out *phr vi* decide not to take part
opulent *adj* **1** showing great wealth **2** in good supply **-ence** *n*
opus *n* piece of work done, esp. a piece of music written
or *conj* **1** (shows different possibilities) **2** if not: *Wear your coat or you'll be cold.*
-or *suffix* -er: *actor*
oracle *n* (in ancient Greece) person through whom a god answered human questions
oracular *adj* (like the sayings) of an oracle
oral *adj* **1** spoken, not written: *an oral exam* **2** *med* of the mouth **~ly** *adv*
orange *n* common round reddish-yellow fruit ♦ *adj* of the colour of an orange
orangeade *n* orange-flavoured drink
orangutang *n* large ape with reddish hair and no tail
oration *n* solemn formal public speech
orator *n* public speaker
oratorio *n* **-os** piece of music for singers and orchestra, telling a (religious) story
oratory[1] *n* eloquent public speaking
oratory[2] *n* (Roman Catholic) chapel
orb *n* **1** *lit* sphere **2** jewelled ball carried in coronations
orbit *n* **1** path of something going round something else, esp. in space **2** area of power or influence ♦ *vi/t* go round in an orbit **~al** *adj*
orchard *n* place where fruit trees are grown
orchestra *n* large group of musicians playing different instruments **~l** *adj*
orchestrate *vt* **1** arrange (music) to be played by an orchestra **2** plan (something with many parts) for best effect **-ation** *n*
orchid *n* plant with bright strange-shaped flowers
ordain *vt* **1** make (someone) a priest **2** *fml* (of God, the law, etc.) order
ordeal *n* difficult or painful experience
order *n* **1** way in which things are arranged: *alphabetical order* **2** fitness for use: *out of order.* **3** condition in which laws and rules are obeyed: *keep order* **4** command **5** request to supply goods **6** decoration given to someone in) a group of specially honoured people: *the Order of Merit* **7** *fml* kind; sort: *courage of the highest order* **8 in order that** *fml* so that **9 in order to** with the purpose of

♦ *v* **1** *vt* command **2** *vi/t* ask for (something) to be supplied **3** *vt* arrange **order about** *phr vt* give many commands to, unpleasantly

orderly *adj* **1** well-arranged **2** liking tidy arrangement **3** peaceful and well-behaved ♦ *n* helper in a hospital **-liness** *n*

order paper *n* programme of the day's business in a parliament

ordinal number *n* one of the numbers (1st, 2nd, 3rd, etc.) that show order rather than quantity

ordinance *n* formal decree or order

ordinary *adj* not unusual; common **-narily** *adv* usually

Ordinary level *n* former examination for secondary school pupils usu. taken at 16

ordination *n* act of ordaining a priest

ordnance *n* heavy guns; artillery

ordure *n* excrement

ore *n* rock from which metal is obtained

oregano *n* plant of the mint family used as a herb

organ *n* **1** part of an animal or plant that has a special purpose, such as the heart **2** large musical instrument played by blowing air through pipes **~ist** *n* organ player

organdie, organdy *n* stiff fine transparent muslin

organ grinder *n* street musician who plays a barrel organ

organic *adj* **1** of living things or bodily organs **2** made of parts with related purposes **3** (of food) grown without chemicals **~ally** *adv*

organism *n* **1** living creature **2** whole made of related parts

organization, -isation *n* **1** group of people with a special purpose, such as a business or club **2** organizing; arrangement

organize, -ise *vt* **1** arrange into a good system **2** make necessary arrangements for: *to organize a party* **-izer** *n*

orgasm *n* highest point of sexual pleasure

orgiastic *adj* of or like an orgy

orgy *n* **1** wild party where people get drunk and have sex **2** *infml* unrestrained bout

oriel window *n* projecting window in an upper storey

Orient *n esp. lit* the eastern part of the world; Asia

orient *vt esp. AmE* orientate

oriental *n, adj* (person) of or from the Orient

orientate *vt* **1** arrange or direct with a particular purpose: *an export-orientated company* **2** find out where you are **-ation** *n*

orienteering *n* sport which involves finding one's way across country

orifice *n tech* opening, esp. in the body

origami *n* Japanese art of paper folding

origin *n* **1** starting point **2** also **origins** *pl* parents and conditions of early life: *humble origins*

original *adj* **1** first; earliest **2** new and different **3** not copied ♦ *n* the one from which copies have been made **~ly** *adv* **1** in the beginning, before changing **2** in a new and different way **~ity** *n* quality of being new and different

original sin *n* (Christian doctrine of) man's natural wickedness

originate *vi/t* (cause to) begin **-nator** *n*

orison *n arch.* prayer

ormolu *n* gilded metal used in furniture

ornament *n* decorative object(s) ♦ *vt* decorate **~al** *adj* **~ation** *n*

ornate *adj* having (too) much ornament

ornery *adj esp. AmE* bad-tempered

ornithology *n* scientific study of birds **-gist** *n*

orotund *adj* **1** full-sounding **2** pompous

orphan *n* child with no parents ♦ *vt* cause to be an orphan **~age** *n* place where orphans live

orthodontics *n* skill or process of correcting the growth of children's teeth **orthodontic** *adj*

orthodox *adj* **1** generally or officially accepted or used; conventional **2** holding orthodox opinions **~y** *n*

Orthodox *adj* **1** belonging to a group of Eastern Christian churches **2** belong-

ing to a strictly orthodox branch of Judaism
orthography *n* (system of) spelling **–phic** *adj*
orthopaedic, -pedic *adj* of the branch of medicine (**orthopaedics**) concerned with putting right disorders of the body's bone and muscle structure
-ory *suffix* involving or constituting: *congratulatory*
oryx *n* African antelope with long straight horns
Oscar *n* gold statuette awarded for excellence in films
oscillate /ˈosiˌlayt/ *vi* **1** move regularly from side to side **2** vary between opposing choices **–ation** *n*
osculate *vt fml* kiss **–ation** *n*
osier *n* (twig from a) willow tree
-osis *suffix* (diseased) condition: *thrombosis*
osmosis *n* gradual passing of liquid through a membrane **–otic** *adj*
osprey *n* fish-eating eagle
osseous *adj* bony
ossify *vi/t* **1** turn to bone **2** make or become rigidly conventional
ostensible *adj* (of a reason) seeming or pretended, but perhaps not really true **–bly** *adv*
ostentation *n* unnecessary show of wealth, knowledge, etc. **–ious** *adj*
osteo- *prefix* bone
osteopath *n* person who treats diseases by manipulating bones and muscles **~y** *n* treatment of disease by this method
ostler *n* (in former times) man who took care of guests' horses at an inn
ostracize, -cise *vt* exclude from social acceptance or from one's group **–cism** *n*
ostrich *n* extremely large long-legged flightless African bird
other *determiner, pron* **1** the remaining one of a set; what is left as well as that mentioned **2** additional **3** not this, not oneself, not one's own, etc.: *He likes spending other people's money.* **4 other than: a** except **b** anything but: *I can't be other than grateful.*
otherwise *adv* **1** differently **2** apart from that **3** if not: *Go faster, otherwise we'll be late.*
otherworldly *adj* more concerned with spiritual than practical things
otic *adj* of or near the ear
otiose *adj fml* having no purpose
otter *n* small fish-eating swimming mammal
ottoman *n* upholstered seat without back or arms
Ottoman *adj* Turkish
ouch *interj* (expresses sudden pain)
ought *v aux* **1** have a (moral) duty (to do something) **2** (shows what is right or sensible): *You ought to see a doctor.* **3** will probably
ouija board *n* board marked with the alphabet, used in séances
ounce *n* measure of weight equal to 28.35 grams
our *determiner* of us
ours *pron* of us; our one(s)
ourselves *pron* (*reflexive or strong form of* we)
-ous *suffix* having; full of: *dangerous*
oust *vt* force (someone) out
out *adv* **1** away from the inside **2** away from home or the usual place **3** away from a surface **4** to lots of people or places: *Hand out the drinks.* **5** (of a fire or light) no longer burning **6** completely: *tired out* **7** aloud: *Call the names out.* **8** so as to be clearly seen, understood, etc. **9** wrong in calculating or guessing **10** no longer fashionable **11 out of: a** from inside; away from **b** from among: *4 out of 5 people preferred it.* **c** not having; without: *out of petrol* **d** because of: *I came out of interest.* **e** (shows what something is made from) **12 out of it** (sad because) excluded **13 out to** trying to ♦ *adj* **1** directed outward **2 out-and-out** complete; total
out- *prefix* better or more than others
outback *n* remote bush country (of Australia)
outboard motor *n* motor fixed to the stern of a small boat

outbreak *n* sudden appearance or start of something bad
outburst *n* sudden powerful expression of feeling
outcast *n* someone forced from their home or friendless
outcaste *n, adj* (person) belonging to no caste
outclass *vt* be very much better than
outcome *n* effect; result
outcrop *n* rock or rocks on the surface of the ground
outcry *n* public show of anger
outdated *adj* no longer in general use
outdo *vt* **-did**, **-done**, *3rd person sing. pres. t.* **-does** do or be better than
outdoor *adj* existing, happening, or used outside **~s** *adv*
outer *adj* on the outside; furthest from the middle
outermost *adj* furthest from the centre
outer space *n* area where the stars are
outface *vt* **1** deal with bravely **2** outstare
outfield *n* (players in) the part of a cricket or baseball field furthest from the batter
outfit *n* **1** set of things, esp. clothes, for a particular purpose **2** group of people working together ♦ *vt* **-tt-** provide with a set of esp. clothes **~ter** *n*
outflank *vt* go round the side of (an enemy) to attack
outfox *vt* outwit
outgoing *adj* **1** finishing a period in office **2** friendly; extrovert **outgoings** *pl n* money spent
outgrow *vt* **-grew**, **-grown** grow too big, too old, or too fat for **-growth** *n* process or product of growing out
outhouse *n* small building near a larger main building
outing *n* short journey for pleasure, esp. by a group
outlandish *adj* noticeably unusual; bizarre **~ly** *adv* **~ness** *n*
outlast *vt* last longer than
outlaw *n* (in former times) criminal being hunted ♦ *vt* declare (something) illegal
outlay *n* money spent on something
outlet *n* **1** way out for liquid or gas **2** way of relieving or satisfying something
outline *n* **1** line showing the shape of something **2** main ideas or facts, without details ♦ *vt* draw or describe in outline
outlive *vt* live longer than
outlook *n* **1** view from a place **2** future probabilities **3** one's general point of view
outlying *adj* distant; far from a main centre
outmanoeuvre *vt* defeat by more subtle or devious skill
outmoded *adj* no longer in fashion or use
outmost *adj* outermost
outnumber *vt* be more in numbers than
out-of-date *adj* no longer in use or in fashion
out-of-the-way *adj* **1** distant **2** unusual
outpatient *n* person treated at a hospital but not staying there
outplay *vt* defeat in a game
outpost *n* group of people or settlement far from the main group or settlement
output *n* (industrial) production
outrage *n* **1** very wrong or cruel act **2** anger caused by such an act ♦ *vt* offend greatly **~ous** *adj* **1** very offensive **2** wildly unexpected and unusual **~ously** *adv*
outrank *vt* have a higher rank than
outré /ˈoohtray/ *adj* bizarre
outride *vt* ride faster or further than
outrider *n* guard or attendant riding beside or ahead of a vehicle
outrigger *n* canoe-shaped support to stop a boat capsizing
outright *adv* **1** without qualification; completely: *outright win* **2** without delay: *killed outright* **3** openly; frankly ♦ *adj* complete and clear: *an outright lie*
outset *n* beginning
outshine *vt* **-shone 1** shine more brightly than **2** be much better than
outside *n* **1** part furthest from the middle, or that faces away from one or

towards the open air **2 at the outside** at the most ♦ *adj* **1** facing or at the outside **2** from elsewhere: *an outside broadcast* **3** (of a chance or possibility) slight ♦ *adv* to or on the outside, esp. in the open air: *go outside* ♦ *prep* **1** to or on the outside of **2** beyond the limits of

outsider *n* **1** person not accepted in a social group **2** participant not expected to win

outsize *adj* larger than the standard sizes

outskirts *pl n* outer areas or limits of a town

outsmart *vt* defeat by being cleverer

outspoken *adj* expressing thoughts or feelings openly and frankly **~ly** *adv* **~ness** *n*

outstanding *adj* **1** much better than others **2** not yet done or paid **~ly** *adv*

outstare *vt* stare at (somebody) until they look away

outstay *vt* stay longer than

outstrip *vt* **-pp-** do better than

out-take *n* piece of film that is cut out during editing

outward *adj, adv* **1** away: *the outward journey* **2** on the outside but perhaps not really **~ly** *adv* **~s** *adv*

outweigh *vt* be more important than

outwit *vt* **-tt-** defeat by being cleverer

outwork *n* **1** military fortification at some distance from a main one **2** work for a business that is done by people in their homes **~er** *n*

outworn *adj* (of an idea, custom, etc.) no longer used or useful

ouzo *n* Greek spirit flavoured with aniseed

ova *pl of* ovum

oval *n, adj* (something) egg-shaped

ovary *n* part of a female that produces eggs **–rian** *adj*

ovation *n* joyful expression of public approval

oven *n* closed box for cooking, baking clay, etc.

ovenware *n* dishes in which food can be cooked in an oven

over *prep* **1** higher than but not touching **2** so as to cover **3** from side to side of, esp. by going up and down: *climb over a wall* **4** down across the edge of: *fell over the cliff* **5** in; throughout **6** in control of **7** more than: *over 10 years ago* **8** while doing, eating, etc.: *a meeting over lunch* **9** by means of: *I heard it over the radio.* **10** about: *an argument over money* **11 over and above** as well as ♦ *adv* **1** downwards from an upright position: *fall over* **2** across an edge or distance: *boil over* **3** so that another side is seen: *Turn the page over.* **4** beyond a particular quantity **5** so as to be covered **6** remaining: *left over* **7** (shows something is repeated) **8** in all details: *Think it over* ♦ *adj* ended

over- *prefix* too much

overall *adj, adv* including everything; total ♦ *n* **1** *BrE* loose coat worn to protect clothes **2** *AmE* overalls (1)

overalls *pl n* **1** *BrE* garment for the whole body, to protect one's clothes **2** *AmE* dungarees

overarm *adj, adv* with the arm moving above the shoulder

overawe *vt* make quiet because of respect and fear

overbalance *vi* become unbalanced and fall over

overbearing *adj* forcefully trying to tell others what to do

overblown *adj derog* inflated; pretentious

overboard *adv* **1** over the side of a boat into the water **2 go overboard** become very or too keen

overcast *adj* dark with clouds

overcharge *vt* **1** charge too much **2** overload

overcoat *n* long warm coat

overcome *vt* **-came, -come 1** defeat **2** make helpless

overcrop *vt* spoil (farmland) by growing too many crops

overcrowd *vt* put or allow too many people or things in (one place)

overdo *vt* **-did, -done,** *3rd person sing. pres. t.* **-does** do, decorate, perform, etc., too much

overdose *n* too much of a drug ♦ *vi* take an overdose
overdraft *n* money lent by a bank to an overdrawn person
overdrawn *adj* having withdrawn more money from one's bank account than it contains
overdrive *n* gear that allows a car to go fast on less than full power
overdue *adj* late
overestimate *vi/t* make too high an estimate (of) **overestimate** *n*
overflow *vi/t* **1** flow over the edge (of) **2** go beyond the limits (of): *The crowd overflowed into the street.* ♦ *n* (pipe for carrying away) something that overflows
overfly *vt* fly over
overgrown *adj* **1** covered with plants growing uncontrolled **2** grown too large
overhand *adj, adv* overarm
overhang *vi/t* **-hung** hang or stick out over (something) ♦ *n* overhanging rock, roof, etc.
overhaul *vt* **1** examine thoroughly (and repair) **2** overtake ♦ *n* thorough examination
overhead *adj, adv* above one's head
overheads *pl n* money spent regularly to keep a business running
overhear *vi/t* **-heard** hear (what others are saying) without them knowing
overjoyed *adj* extremely pleased
overkill *n* something that goes beyond the desirable or safe limits
overladen *past p. of* overload
overland *adj, adv* across land and not by sea or air
overlap *vi/t* **-pp- 1** cover (something) partly and go beyond it **2** be partly the same (as) ♦ *n* part that overlaps
overlay *n* something (e.g. a design) laid over something else
overleaf *adv* on the other side of the page
overload *vt* **-loaded** *or* **-laden 1** load too heavily **2** put too much electricity through **overload** *n*
overlook *vt* **1** give a view of from above **2** not notice; miss **3** forgive
overlord *n* supreme ruler
overly *adv esp. AmE* too
overmanned *adj* having more workers than are needed for a job **-ning** *n*
overmuch *adv, determiner, pron* **1** too much **2** very much: *I don't like him overmuch.*
overnight *adj, adv* **1** for or during the night **2** instant(ly)
overpass *AmE for* flyover
overplay *vt* make (something) appear more important than it really is
overpower *vt* defeat by greater power **~ing** *adj* very strong
overran *past t. of* overrun
overrate *vt* give too high an opinion of
overreach *v* **1** *vt* defeat (oneself) by trying to do too much **2** *vi* reach too far
overreact *vi* react too strongly to something
override *vt* **-rode**, **-ridden** declare invalid; set aside **–riding** *adj* taking precedence over all others
overrule *vt* officially reverse (something already decided)
overrun *v* **-ran**, **-run 1** *vt* spread over and cause harm **2** *vi/t* continue beyond (a time limit)
overseas *adv, adj* in, to, or from a foreign country across the sea
oversee *vt* **-saw**, **-seen** watch to see that work is properly done **-seer** *n*
oversell *vt* praise too highly
oversexed *adj* with unusually strong sexual impulses
overshadow *vt* **1** make worried and sadder **2** make appear less important
overshoes *pl n* galoshes
overshoot *vi/t* **-shot** go too far or beyond, and miss
oversight *n* unintended failure to notice or do something
oversimplify *vt* represent too simply **–fication** *n*
oversleep *vi* **-slept** wake up too late
overspill *n esp. BrE* people who leave a crowded city and settle elsewhere
overstate *vt* express too strongly
overstep *vt* **-pp-** go beyond (the limits of

what is proper or allowed)
overt *adj* not hidden; open **~ly** *adv*
overtake *v* **-took, -taken 1** *vi/t* pass (a vehicle in front) **2** *vt* (of something unpleasant) affect suddenly and unexpectedly
overthrow *vt* **-threw, -thrown** remove from power by force **overthrow** *n*
overtime *n, adv* (money paid for or time spent working) beyond the usual working time
overtone *n* **1** higher musical note sounding together with a basic note **2** suggestion of another colour present in a basic colour
overtones *pl n* things suggested but not stated clearly
overtook *past t. of* overtake
overture *n* musical introduction, esp. to an opera **overtures** *pl n* offer to begin talks
overturn *v* **1** *vi/t* turn over **2** *vt* bring (esp. a government) to an end suddenly
overview *n* usu. short account (of something) which gives a general picture but no details
overweening *adj fml* over-confident **~ly** *adv*
overweight *adj* weighing too much
overwhelm *vt* **1** defeat or make powerless by much greater numbers **2** (of feelings) make completely helpless
overwrought /ohvəˈrawt/ *adj* too nervous and excited
oviparous /ohˈviparəs/ *adj* producing eggs that hatch outside the mother's body
ovoid *adj* shaped like an egg
ovulate *vi* produce eggs from the ovary **–ation** *n*
ovum *n* **ova** egg (3)
ow *interj* (expresses sudden slight pain)
owe *vt* **1** have to pay **2** feel grateful for: *We owe a lot to our parents.*
owing *adj* **1** still to be paid **2 owing to** because of
owl *n* night bird with large eyes
own *determiner, pron* **1** belonging to the stated person and no one else: *room of my own.* **2 come into one's own** begin to be properly respected for one's qualities **3 have/get one's own back (on someone)** succeed in doing harm (to someone) in return for harm done to oneself **4 on one's own** : **a** alone **b** without help ♦ *vt* possess, esp. by legal right **own to** *phr vt* admit **own up** *phr vi* admit a fault or crime **~er** *n* **~ership** *n*
own goal *n esp. BrE* **1** (in football) goal scored by a player against his own team **2** *infml* mistake that harms oneself and makes one look foolish
ox *n* **oxen** large animal of the cattle type, esp. a castrated male
oxide *n* chemical compound containing oxygen
oxidize, ise *vi/t* chemically affect or be affected by oxygen
oxyacetylene *adj* using a mixture of gases to produce a very hot flame
oxygen *n* gas present in the air, necessary for life
oxygenate *vt* add oxygen to
oxymoron *n* combination of contradictory words, e.g. *deafening silence*
oyster *n* flat shellfish, often eaten
oystercatcher *n* black and white wading bird
oz *abbrev. for:* ounce(s)
ozone *n* **1** sea air that is pleasant to breathe **2** type of oxygen

P

P, p the 16th letter of the English alphabet
p *abbrev. for:* **1** page **2** *BrE* penny/pence
PA *abbrev. for:* **1** personal assistant **2** public address (system)
pace *n* **1** speed, esp. of walking or running **2** (distance moved in) a single step **3 keep pace with** go as fast as **4 put**

someone through his/her paces make someone do something in order to show his/her abilities, qualities, etc. **5 set the pace** fix the speed for others to copy ♦ *v* **1** *vi/t* walk (across) with slow regular steps **2** *vt* control (oneself) so as not to do too much too quickly **pace out/off** *phr vt* measure by taking steps

pacemaker *n* **1** person who sets a speed or example for others to follow **2** machine used to make weak or irregular heartbeats regular

pachyderm /ˈpakiduhm/ *n tech* large thick-skinned mammal (e.g. an elephant)

pacific *adj fml* **1** peace-loving **2** soothing

pacifier *n* **1** person who pacifies **2** *AmE for* dummy (2)

pacifist *n* person who believes war is wrong and refuses to fight **–fism** *n*

pacify *vt* make calm and quiet, esp. less angry **–fication** *n*

pack *n* **1** number of things wrapped or tied together or put in a case **2** *esp. AmE* packet **3** group of hunting animals **4** collection, group: *a pack of lies/thieves* **5** complete set of playing cards ♦ *v* **1** *vi/t* put (things) into cases, boxes, etc., for taking somewhere or storing **2** *vi/t* fit or push tightly into a space **3** *vt* cover, fill, or surround closely with protective material **4 pack a punch** *infml* be very forceful or vigorous **pack in** *phr vt infml* **1** stop doing **2** attract in large numbers **pack off** *phr vt infml* bundle off **pack up** *phr v infml* **1** *vi* finish work **2** *vi esp. BrE* (of a machine) stop working **3** *vt* stop **~ed** *adj* full of people

package *n* **1** number of things packed together; parcel **2** set of related things offered as a unit ♦ *vt* **1** make into a package **2** put in a special container for selling

package deal *n* offer or agreement where a number of things must all be accepted together

package tour *n* holiday where all travel, hotels, food, etc., are paid for together

packaging *n* **1** packing **2** presentation

pack animal *n* animal, such as a **packhorse**, used for carrying loads

packet *n* **1** small container or parcel: **2** *sl* large amount of money

pack ice *n* area of ice on the sea

packing *n* **1** putting things in cases or boxes **2** protective material for packing things

packing case *n* strong wooden box

pact *n* solemn agreement

pad[1] *n* **1** something made or filled with soft material, for protection or to give shape **2** many sheets of paper fastened together **3** launching pad **4** *sl* one's home **5** thick-skinned underpart of the foot of some animals ♦ *vt* **-dd-** **1** protect, shape, or make more comfortable with a pad **2** make longer by adding unnecessary words **~ding** *n* **1** material used to pad something **2** unnecessary words or sentences

pad[2] *vi* **-dd-** walk steadily and usu. softly

paddle[1] *n* short pole with a wide blade at the end(s), for rowing a small boat ♦ *vi/t* **1** row with a paddle **2 paddle one's own canoe** *infml* depend on oneself and no one else

paddle[2] *vi* walk about in water a few inches deep ♦ *n* act of paddling

paddle steamer *n* steamship propelled by two large **paddle wheels** at the sides

paddock *n* small field where horses are kept

paddy[1] *n* field where rice is grown in water

paddy[2] *n infml* fit of temper or anxiety

padlock *n* removable lock fastened with a U-shaped bar, for locking gates, bicycles, etc. ♦ *vt* fasten or lock with a padlock

padre *n* clergyman

paean /ˈpee·ən/ *n* joyful song (of praise)

paederast *n* pederast

paediatrics /ˌpeediˈatriks/ *n* pediatrics

paedophilia *n* sexual desire for children **–phile** *n*

paella *n* Spanish dish of rice, seafood, meat, etc.

pagan *n, adj* (person) not believing in

(a) religion **~ism** *n*
page[1] *n* one or both sides of a sheet of paper in a book, newspaper, etc.
page[2] *n* **1** boy servant at a hotel, club, etc. **2** boy attendant at a wedding ♦ *vt* summon **a** by repeated calling, esp. over a public-address system **b** by a signal emitted esp. by a radio transmitter
pageant *n* splendid public show or ceremony **~ry** *n* splendid show of ceremonial grandness
pager *n* radio apparatus for paging people by coded signals
pagination *n* numbering of pages
pagoda *n* tall towerlike Buddhist or Hindu temple
paid *past t. and p. of* pay
paid-up *adj* having paid in full (esp. so as to continue being a member)
pail *n* bucket
pailiasse *n* palliasse
pain *n* **1** (particular instance of) bodily suffering or discomfort **2** also **pain in the neck** *infml* person, thing, or happening that makes one angry or tired **3** **on/under pain of** *fml* at the risk of suffering (a punishment) if something is not done ♦ *vt fml* cause pain to **~ed** *adj* displeased or hurt in one's feelings **~ful** *adj* **~less** *adj* **pains** *pl n* effort; trouble: *take pains* **painstaking** *adj* very careful and thorough
painkiller *n* medicine for providing relief from pain
paint *n* liquid colouring matter for decorating surfaces or making pictures ♦ *vi/t* **1** put paint on (a surface) **2** make a picture (of) with paint **3 paint the town red** go out and have a good time **~ing** *n* **1** act or art of painting **2** painted picture **paints** *pl n* set of small containers of different-coloured paint, for painting pictures
painter[1] *n* person who paints pictures, or houses, rooms, etc.
painter[2] *n* rope for tying up a small boat
paintwork *n* painted surface
pair *n* **1** two of the same kind **2** something made of two similar parts: *a pair of scissors* **3** two people closely connected ♦ *vi/t* form into one or more pairs
pair up *phr vi/t* (cause to) join in pairs, esp. for work or sport
paisley *n, adj* (soft fabric) with curved tear-shaped patterns
pajamas *n esp. AmE* pyjamas
Pakistani *n, adj* (inhabitant) of Pakistan
pal *n infml* friend
PAL *n* system of colour television transmission
palace *n* large grand house, esp. where a king or president lives
palace revolution *n* removal of a president, king, etc., from power by people who worked closely with him/her
paladin *n* champion
Palaeolithic *adj* of the earliest period of the Stone Age
palanquin *n* enclosed chair or bed carried on poles
palatable *adj fml* **1** good to taste **2** acceptable; pleasant
palate *n* **1** the top inside part of the mouth **2** ability to judge good food or wine
palatial /pəˈlaysh(ə)l/ *adj* (of a building) large and splendid **~ly** *adv*
palaver *n* trouble over unimportant matters; fuss
pale[1] *adj* **1** not bright or dark **2** (of a face) rather white ♦ *vi* **1** become pale **2** seem less important, clever, etc., when compared with others
pale[2] *n* limit of proper behaviour: *beyond the pale*
paleface *n* white person
Paleolithic *adj* Palaeolithic
paleontology *n* study of fossils **-gist** *n*
palette *n* board on which a painter mixes colours
palfrey *n arch.* quiet horse for riding
palimony *n* money paid by court order to support a former lover
palindrome *n* word or phrase spelled the same backwards and forwards
palings *pl n* (fence made of) pointed pieces of wood
palisade *n* defensive fence
pall[1] *vi* become uninteresting or dull

pall² *n* **1** heavy or dark covering: *a pall of smoke* **2** cloth spread over a coffin
Palladian *adj* of a 16th-century Italian or 18th-century English style of architecture
pallbearer *n* person who walks beside or helps carry a coffin
pallet *n* large flat frame used with a forklift for lifting heavy goods
palliasse *n* thin straw mattress
palliate *vt fml* cause to be or seem less unpleasant or wrong **-ative** *n, adj*
pallid *adj* (of skin) unhealthily pale **~ness** *n*
pallor *n* pallidness
pally *adj* friendly
palm¹ *n* tall tropical tree with no branches and a mass of large leaves at the top
palm² *n* lower surface of the hand **palm off** *phr vt* **1** get rid of by deception **2** deceive into accepting
palmetto *n* **-tos** *or* **-toes** small palm tree
palmist *n* person who tells someone's future by looking at the palm of their hand **~ry** *n* palmist's art
palmy *adj* (of past periods) most pleasant and successful
palomino *n* **-os** light tan or cream horse
palpable *adj fml* easily and clearly known; obvious **-bly** *adv*
palpate *vt med* examine by touching
palpitate *vi* (of the heart) beat fast and irregularly **-tations** *pl n*
palsy /ˈpawlzi/ *n* paralysis
paltry *adj* worthlessly small or unimportant
pampas *n* wide treeless plains in South America
pampas grass *n* tall grass with large silky flower heads
pamper *vt* treat too kindly
pamphlet *n* small book with paper covers
pan *n* **1** round metal container for cooking, usu. with a long handle **2** *esp. BrE* bowl of a lavatory ♦ *v* **-nn- 1** *vt infml* criticize very severely **2** *vi/t* move (a camera) to follow the action being recorded on film or television **pan out** *phr vi* happen in a particular way
pan- *prefix* all; whole
panacea *n* something that will put right all troubles
panache *n* flamboyant splendid way of doing things
panatela *n* long thin cigar
pancake *n* thin flat batter cake cooked in a pan
pancreas *n* bodily organ that helps in changing food chemically for use by the body
panda *n* black-and-white bearlike animal from China
Panda car *n BrE* police car
pandemic *n* disease affecting many people over a wide area
pandemonium *n* wild and noisy disorder
pander to *phr vt* satisfy unworthily
Pandora's box *n* source of a large number of problems accidentally let loose
p and p *abbrev for:* postage and packing
pane *n* sheet of glass in a window
panegyric /ˌpaniˈjirik/ *n fml* speech or writing full of great praise
panel *n* **1** flat piece of wood in a door or on a wall **2** board with instruments fixed in it: *an aircraft's control panel* **3** small group of people who answer questions on esp. a radio or television show **4** group of experts or advisers ♦ *vt* **-ll-** (*AmE* **-l-**) decorate with panels: **~ling**, *AmE* **~ing** *n* panels (1)
pang *n* sudden sharp feeling of pain or conscience
panhandle *vi* beg **~r** *n*
panic *n* sudden uncontrollable quickly-spreading fear or terror ♦ *vi/t* **-ck-** (cause to) feel panic **~ky** *adj* suddenly afraid
panic stations *n* state of confused anxiety because something needs to be done in a hurry
panic-stricken *adj* filled with panic
panjandrum *n humorous* grand personage or self-important official
pannier *n* **1** basket, esp. either of a pair on a bicycle **2** petticoat or draped material giving extra width to a skirt at

the sides
panoply *n* splendid ceremonial show or dress
panorama *n* **1** complete view of a wide stretch of land **2** general representation in words or pictures **–ramic** *adj*
pan-pipes *pl n* musical instrument made of short pipes joined together
pansy 1 small flowering garden plant **2** *infml derog* **a** effeminate young man **b** male homosexual
pant *vi* breathe quickly, with short breaths ♦ *n* quick short breath
pantaloons *pl n* (baggy) trousers
pantechnicon *n BrE* large van esp. for transporting furniture
pantheism *n* religious idea that God and the universe are the same thing **–ist** *n*
pantheon *n* gods of a particular religion
panther *n* leopard, esp. a black one
panties *pl n* women's or children's short undergarment worn below the waist
pantograph *n* instrument for scaling drawings up or down
pantomime also *infml* **panto** *n* play for children based on a fairy story, produced at Christmas
pantry *n* small room with shelves where food is kept
pants *pl n* **1** *BrE* panties or underpants **2** *esp. AmE* trousers **3 with one's pants down** *sl* awkwardly unprepared
pantyhose *pl n esp. AmE* tights
panzer *n* German tank
pap *n* **1** soft liquid food for babies or sick people **2** *esp. AmE* low-grade reading matter or entertainment intended only for amusement
papa *n BrE lit or AmE* father
papacy *n* power and office of the pope
papadum *n* popadum
papal *adj* of the pope
paparazzo /ˌpapəˈratsoh/ *n* **-zi** newspaper writer or photographer who follows famous people about hoping to find out interesting or shocking stories about them
papaya *n* pawpaw
paper *n* **1** material in thin sheets for writing or printing on, wrapping things in, etc. **2** newspaper **3** set of questions to be answered in an examination **4** piece of writing for specialists, often read aloud **5 on paper** as written down, but not yet tried out in reality ♦ *vt* cover with wallpaper
papers *pl n* official documents
paperback *n* book with a thin cardboard cover
paperboy *n* boy who delivers newspapers
paper chase *n* game in which players follow a trail of scattered paper
paper clip *n* piece of curved wire for holding papers together
paper tiger *n* enemy that seems or wishes to seem powerful or threatening but is really not so
paperweight *n* heavy object put on papers to stop them being scattered
paperwork *n* writing reports and letters, keeping records, etc.
papier-mâché *n* light modelling material made from pulped wastepaper
papist *n derog* Roman Catholic
papoose *n* **1** North American Indian baby **2** device for carrying a baby on one's back
paprika *n* hot-tasting red powder from a plant, used in cooking
papyrus /pəˈpie·ərəs/ *n* (manuscript on a piece of) paperlike material made from reeds
par *n* **1** (nearly) equal level **2** average number of hits in golf **3 under par** *infml* not in the usual or average condition of health
parable *n* short simple story which teaches a moral lesson
parabola /pəˈrabələ/ *n* curved line, like a thrown ball rising and falling **–olic** *adj*
paracetamol *n* painkilling drug
parachute *n* piece of cloth on long ropes, fastened to someone to allow them to fall slowly and safely from an aircraft ♦ *vi/t* drop by means of a parachute **–tist** *n*

parade *n* **1** informal procession **2** ceremonial gathering of soldiers to be officially inspected ♦ *v* **1** *vi* walk or gather in a parade **2** *vi* walk ostentatiously **3** *vt* show in order to be admired: *parading her knowledge*

paradigm /ˈparədiem/ *n* set of all a word's inflections **–matic** *adj*

paradise *n* **1** (*usu. cap.*) Heaven **2** place or state of perfect happiness

paradox *n* **1** statement that says two opposite things but has some truth in it **2** strange combination of opposing qualities, ideas, etc. **~ical** *adj* **~ically** *adv*

paraffin *n BrE* sort of oil burned for heating and lighting

paragon *n* person who is or seems to be a perfect model to copy

paragraph *n* division of a piece of writing that begins a new line

parakeet *n* small parrot

parallel *adj* **1** (of lines) always the same distance apart **2** comparable ♦ *n* **1** comparable person or thing **2** (point of) similarity **3** line of latitude ♦ *vt* **-ll-** (*AmE* **-l-**) be similar to

parallelogram *n* four-sided figure with opposite sides equal and parallel

paralyse, *AmE* **-yze** *vt* **1** cause paralysis in **2** stop all work or functioning in

paralysis *n* loss of movement in (some of) the body muscles **paralytic** *adj* **1** suffering from paralysis **2** *infml, esp. BrE* very drunk

paramedic *n esp. AmE* someone, such as an ambulance driver, who helps in the care of sick people but is not a doctor or nurse

parameter *n* any of the established limits within which something must operate

paramilitary *adj* acting like an army, esp. illegally

paramount *adj* greater than all others in importance

paramour *n arch.* lover

paranoia *n* disease of the mind in which you think esp. that other people are trying to harm you **–noid** *adj* (as if) suffering from paranoia

paranormal *adj* not explainable by science

parapet *n* low protective wall at the edge of a roof, bridge, etc.

paraphernalia *n* small articles of various kinds

paraphrase *vt, n* (make) a re-expression of (something written or said) in different words

paraplegia *n* paralysis of both legs **–gic** *adj, n*

parapsychology *n* scientific study of psychic abilities

paraquat *n* poisonous weedkiller

paras *pl n infml* paratroops

parasite *n* **1** animal or plant that lives and feeds on another **2** useless person supported by others' efforts **–sitic** *adj*

parasol *n* sunshade

paratroops *pl n* soldiers who drop from aircraft using parachutes

paratyphoid *n* disease like typhoid but less dangerous

parboil *vt* boil briefly

parcel *n* something wrapped up in paper and fastened ♦ *v* **-ll-** (*AmE* **-l-**) **parcel out** *phr vt* divide into parts or shares **parcel up** *phr vt* wrap and tie

parch *vt* make hot and dry

parchment *n* treated animal skin, used formerly for writing on

pardon *n* (act of) forgiving, esp. of a guilty person, so they will no longer be punished ♦ *vt* give pardon to ♦ *interj* (used to ask for something not fully heard to be repeated) **~able** *adj* that can be forgiven

pare *vt* **1** cut off the edge or thin covering of **2** reduce

parent *n* father or mother **~tal** *adj*

parentage *n* having certain parents

parenthesis *n* **-ses 1** bracket (2) **2** words introduced as an added explanation or thought

parenthetic *adj* introduced as an explanation **~ally** *adv*

par excellence *adj* without equal

pariah /pəˈrie·ə/ *n fml* person not

accepted by society
parish *n* area for which a priest has responsibility
parishioner *n* person who lives in a parish
parity *n fml* being equal
park *n* large usu. grassy enclosed piece of land in a town, used by the public for pleasure and rest ♦ *vi/t* put (a vehicle) for a time
parka *n* (hooded) warm waterproof coat
parking meter *n* apparatus into which one puts money, allowing one to park near it for a time
Parkinson's disease *n* nervous disease in which one becomes weak and shakes
parkland *n* large grassy area surrounding a large country house
parky *adj BrE infml* chilly
parlance *n fml* particular way of speaking or use of words
parley *vi, n* (hold) a talk, esp. with an enemy to make peace
parliament *n* body of people elected or appointed to make laws **~ary** *adj*
parliamentarian *n* **1** experienced member of a parliament **2** *cap.* Roundhead
parlour, *AmE* **-lor** *n* **1** shop: *an ice-cream parlour* **2** living room
parlour game *n* game played sitting down indoors
parlous *adj fml* in danger of failing
Parmesan *n* hard strong Italian cheese
parochial /pəˈrohki·əl/ *adj* **1** only interested in one's own affairs **2** of a parish
parody *n* copy of a writer's or musician's style, made to amuse ♦ *vt* make a parody of
parole *n* letting someone out of prison before their sentence has ended ♦ *vt* let out of prison on parole
paroxysm *n* sudden sharp expression of feeling or attack of pain **~al** *adj*
parquet /ˈpahkay/ *n* small wooden blocks making a floor
parricide *n* (the act of) someone who murders a parent or close relative
parrot *n* tropical bird with a curved beak and usu. brightly coloured feathers ♦ *vt* repeat (someone else's words or actions) without thought or understanding
parry *vt* turn aside (a blow or weapon)
parse *vt* describe or analyse grammatically
parsec *n* unit of distance in space, about $3\frac{1}{4}$ light years
Parsi, Parsee *n, adj* (member) of the Zoroastrian community in India
parsimonious *adj* unwilling to spend money; stingy **~ly** *adv* **~ness** *n*
parsimony *n fml* ungenerousness
parsley *n* small plant used in cooking
parsnip *n* plant with a long white root used as a vegetable
parson *n* priest in charge of a parish
parsonage *n* parson's house
parson's nose *n* fleshy piece at the tail end of a cooked chicken
part[1] *n* **1** any of the pieces into which something is divided **2** share in an activity: *take part in something* **3** (words of) a character acted in a play or film **4 for the most part: a** mostly **b** in most cases **5 in part** partly **6 on the part of** of or by (someone) **7 part and parcel of** inseparable and essential part of ♦ *adv* partly **~ly** *adv* **1** not completely **2** in some degree **parts** *pl n* area of a country
part[2] *v* **1** *vi/t* separate **2** *vt* separate (hair on the head) along a line **3 part company (with): a** end a relationship (with) **b** no longer be together (with) **c** disagree (with) **part with** *phr vt* give away; stop having **~ing** *n* **1** leaving **2** line on the head where the hair is parted
partake *vi* **-took, -taken** *fml* eat or drink something offered
parthenogenesis *n tech* reproduction without fertilization
partial *adj* **1** not complete **2** (unfairly) favouring one more than another **3 partial to** very fond of **~ly** *adv* **~ity** *n* **1** unfair favouring of one more than another **2** fondness
participant *n* person who participates
participate *vi* take part or have a share

in an activity **–pation** *n* **–patory** *adj*

participle *n* past or present participle

particle *n* very small piece

parti-coloured *adj* showing different colours or tints

particular *adj* **1** special; unusual **2** single and different from others: *this particular case* **3** showing (too) much care over small matters **4 in particular** especially ♦ *n* small single part of a whole; detail **~ly** *adv* especially

parting shot *n* remark or action made when leaving

partisan *n, adj* **1** (person) giving strong unreasoning support to one side **2** member of an armed group that fights in secret against an occupying enemy

partition *n* **1** thin wall indoors **2** division, esp. of a country ♦ *vt* divide up **partition off** *phr vt* separate with a partition

partner *n* person you are with, doing something together ♦ *vt* act as a partner to **~ship** *n* **1** being a partner **2** business owned by two or more partners

part of speech *n* class of word, such as 'noun' or 'verb'

partook *past t. of* partake

partridge *n* small plump game bird

part-song *n* song in which three or more musical lines are sung together

part-time *adj, adv* (working) during only part of the regular working time

parturition *n fml* giving birth

party *n* **1** gathering of people for food and amusement **2** association of people with the same political aims **3** group of people doing something together: *a search party* **4** *esp. law* person or group concerned in a matter **5 be (a) party to** take part in or know about (some action or activity) ♦ *vi infml, esp. AmE* enjoy oneself, esp. at a party or parties

party line *n* **1** telephone line shared by two or more households **2** policy of a political party

party piece *n* song, poem, etc., that is someone's usual choice when asked to give a performance, e.g. at a party

party wall *n* wall shared by two buildings

parvenu *n derog* person newly powerful or wealthy; upstart

PASCAL *n* computer programming language

Paschal *adj* **1** of the Passover **2** of Easter

pas de deux *n* (in ballet) dance for two performers

pass *v* **1** *vi/t* reach and move beyond **2** *vi/t* (cause to) go: *I passed a rope around the tree.* **3** *vi* come to an end **4** *vt* give: *Please pass me the salt.* **5** *vt* (in sport) kick, throw, etc. (esp. a ball) to a member of one's own side **6 a** *vi* (of time) go by **b** *vt* spend (time) **7** *vt* accept officially: *Parliament passed a new law.* **8** *vi/t* succeed in (an examination) **9** *vt* give (a judgment, opinion, etc.) **10 let something pass** leave (a wrong statement, mistake, etc.) without putting it right **11 pass the time of day (with)** greet and talk (to) **pass away** *phr vi* die **pass by** *phr vt* disregard **pass for** *phr vt* be (mistakenly) accepted or considered as **pass off** *phr v* **1** *vt* present falsely **2** *vi* take place and be completed **pass on** *phr vi* **1** pass away **2** move on **pass out** *phr vi* faint **pass over** *phr vt* fail to choose **pass up** *phr vt* fail to take advantage of; miss ♦ *n* **1** successful result in an examination **2** official document showing that one is allowed to do something **3** act of giving the ball to someone else in sport **4** way by which one can travel through or over a place, esp. a range of mountains **5** act of trying to interest someone sexually: *He made a pass at me.*

passable *adj* **1** (just) good enough **2 a** (of a road) fit to be used **b** (of a river) fit to be crossed **–bly** *adv*

passage *n* **1** long narrow connecting way, esp. a corridor **2** way through **3** *fml* going across, through, etc.: *the bill's passage through Parliament* **4** onward flow (of time) **5** (cost of) a journey by sea or air **6** short part of a speech, piece of music, etc.

passbook *n* **1** record of a building society account **2** identity document for non-white S Africans
passé *adj* old-fashioned
passenger *n* person being taken in a vehicle
passerby *n* **passersby** person who is going past a place
passim *adv tech* throughout a book, text, etc.
passing *n* **1** going by **2** ending; disappearance **3** death **4 in passing** while talking about something else ♦ *adj* **1** moving or going by **2** brief
passion *n* **1** strong deep feeling, esp. of love or anger **2** a strong liking: *a passion for tennis* **3** (*cap.*) the suffering and death of Christ
passionate *adj* filled with passion **~ly** *adv*
passionflower *n* genus of climbing plants, some of which bear egg-shaped, strong-tasting **passionfruit**
passive *adj* **1** suffering something bad without (enough) opposition **2** (of verbs or sentences) expressing an action which is done to the subject of a sentence ♦ *n* passive form of a verb **~ly** *adv* **~ness**, **-sivity** *n*
passive smoking *n* inhaling of smoke from others' cigarettes, etc.
passkey *n* **1** key given to only a few people **2** key that will open many different locks
Passover *n* Jewish festival commemorating how Moses led the Jews from Egypt
passport *n* **1** small official book allowing you to enter foreign countries **2** something that lets you get something else easily
password *n* secret word which you have to know to be allowed into a building, camp, etc.
past *adj* **1** (of time) earlier than the present: *the past few days* **2** ended: *Winter is past.* **3** expressing past time: *the past tense* **4** former: *a past president of our club* ♦ *n* **1** (what happened in) the time before the present **2** secret former life containing wrong-doing of some kind ♦ *prep* **1** up to and beyond: *They rushed past us.* **2** beyond in time or age: *It's 10 minutes past four.* **3** beyond the possibility of: *I'm past caring.* **4 past it** *infml* no longer able to do the things one could formerly do ♦ *adv* by: *run past*
pasta *n* food made in different shapes from flour paste
paste *n* **1** soft mixture of powder and liquid **2** liquid mixture, usu. with flour, for sticking paper together ♦ *vt* fasten with paste
pasteboard *n* board made by pasting sheets of paper together
pastel *adj* soft and light in colour
pasteurize, **-ise** *vt* heat (a liquid) to destroy bacteria **-ization** *n*
pastiche *n* work of art made of, or in the style of, other works of art
pastille *n* small hard sweet, esp. containing throat medicine
pastime *n* something done to pass one's time pleasantly
pasting *n* severe beating or defeat
past master *n* very skilled person
pastor *n* Christian priest in charge of a church
pastoral *adj* **1** of a priest's duties amongst his religious group **2** of simple country life
past participle *n* form of a verb used in compounds to show the passive or the perfect tenses
pastrami *n* highly seasoned smoked beef
pastry *n* **1** a mixture of flour, fat, and liquid, eaten when baked **2** article of food made from this
pasture *n* (piece of) grassy land where farm animals feed ♦ *vt* put in a pasture to feed
pasty[1] *n* small pastry case filled usu. with meat
pasty[2] *adj* (of the face) unhealthily white
pat[1] *vt* **-tt-** strike gently and repeatedly with a flat hand ♦ *n* **1** light friendly stroke with the hand **2** small shaped

mass of butter **3 pat on the back** expression of praise or satisfaction for something done

pat² *adj, adv* (too) easily or quickly answered or known

patch *n* **1** irregularly shaped part of a surface different from the rest **2** small piece of material to cover a hole **3** small piece of ground: *a cabbage patch* **4** piece of material worn to protect a damaged eye **5** period: *going through a bad patch* **6 not a patch on** *BrE infml* not nearly as good as ♦ *vt* put a patch of material on **patch up** *phr vt* **1** repair **2** become friends again after (a quarrel)

patchwork *n* (piece of) sewn work made by joining small bits of different materials

patchy *adj* **1** in or having patches: *patchy fog* **2** incomplete or only good in parts **–ily** *adv* **–iness** *n*

pâté *n* food made by mincing or pureeing meat, esp. liver

patella *n* **–llae** *or* **–llas** kneecap

patent *n* (official document giving someone) the exclusive right to make or sell a new invention ♦ *adj* **1** protected by a patent **2** *fml* obvious ♦ *vt* obtain a patent for **~ly** *adv fml* clearly

patent leather *n* very shiny leather, usu. black

paternal *adj* **1** of or like a father **2** protecting people like a father but allowing them no freedom **3** related to a person through the father's side of the family **~ly** *adv*

paternalism *n* dominatingly protective way of controlling people **–istic** *adj* **–istically** *adv*

paternity *n esp. law* origin from the male parent

path *n* **1** track or way where you can walk **2** line along which something moves: *the path of an arrow*

Pathan *n, adj* (member) of the chief ethnic group of Afghanistan

pathetic *adj* **1** causing pity or sorrow **2** *derog* hopelessly unsuccessful **~ally** *adv*

pathogen *n* disease-causing agent e.g. a bacterium or virus

pathology *n* study of disease **–gist** *n* specialist in pathology, esp. one who examines a dead body to find the cause of death **-gical** *adj* **1** of pathology **2** caused by disease, esp. of the mind **3** great and unreasonable: *pathological jealousy* **–gically** *adv*

pathos *n* quality that causes pity and sorrow

pathway *n* path (1)

patience *n* **1** ability to wait calmly, to control oneself when angered, or to accept unpleasant things without complaining **2** card game for one player

patient *adj* showing patience ♦ *n* person being treated medically **~ly** *adv*

patina *n* pleasingly smooth shiny surface

patio *n* **-os** stone-floored space next to a house, for sitting out on in fine weather

patisserie *n* (shop selling) cakes and sweet foods made from pastry

patois /ˈpatwah/ *n* **-tois** local form of speech

patrial *n* person with a legal right to live in Britain

patriarch *n* **1** old and much-respected man **2** chief bishop of the Eastern Churches **~al** *adj* **1** ruled only by men **2** of a patriarch

patrician *n, adj* (person) of high social rank

patricide *n* **1** murder of one's father **2** person guilty of this

patrimony *n* property one gets from one's dead father, grandfather, etc.

patriot *n* someone who loves their country **~ism** *n* **~ic** *adj* **~ically** *adv*

patrol *n* **1** (period of) patrolling: *on patrol* **2** small group on patrol ♦ *vi/t* **-ll-** go round (an area, building, etc.) repeatedly to see that there is no trouble

patron *n* **1** person who gives money for support **2** *fml* customer in a shop, pub, etc., esp. regularly **~age** *n* **1** support given by a patron **2** right to appoint people to important positions

patronize, -ise *vt* **1** behave condescendingly towards **2** *fml* be a customer of

patron saint *n* saint giving special protection to a particular place, activity, etc.

patronymic *n* name derived from that of a father

patsy *n infml esp. AmE* dupe, sucker

patter[1] *vi, n* (run with or make) the sound of something striking lightly, quickly, and repeatedly

patter[2] *n* fast continuous amusing talk

pattern *n* **1** regularly repeated arrangement, esp. with a decorative effect **2** way in which something develops: *the usual pattern of the illness* **3** shape used as a guide for making something (e.g. a dress) ♦ *vt* make a decorative pattern on

patty *n* small pie

paucity /ˈpawsəti/ *n fml* less than is needed; lack

paunch *n* fat stomach **~y** *adj*

pauper *n* very poor person

pause *n* short but noticeable break in activity, speech, etc. ♦ *vi* make a pause

pavane *n* slow 16th-century dance

pave *vt* **1** cover with a hard level surface, esp. of paving stones **2 pave the way (for/to)** prepare for or make possible

pavement *n BrE* paved path at the side of a road

pavilion *n* **1** *esp. BrE* building beside a sports field, for the players and watchers **2** large public building usu. put up for only a short time, used e.g. for exhibitions

paving *n* **1** (material for making) a paved surface **2** paving stone

paving stone *n* flat stone for making pavements or other paved areas

paw *n* **1** animal's foot with claws **2** *infml* human hand ♦ *vi/t* **1** (of an animal) touch or strike with the foot **2** handle rudely or roughly

pawky *adj esp. BrE* dryly humorous

pawn[1] *n* **1** least valuable piece in chess **2** unimportant person used for someone else's advantage

pawn[2] *vt* leave with a pawnbroker in return for money lent ♦ *n* state of being pawned

pawnbroker *n* person who lends money in return for things one brings, which he keeps if one does not repay the money

pawpaw *n* yellow edible tropical fruit

pay *v* **paid 1** *vi/t* give (money) to (someone) in return for goods bought, work done, etc. **2** *vt* settle (a bill, debt, etc.) **3** *vi/t* be profitable (to); be worth the trouble (to) **4** *vt* give, offer, or make: *pay attention* | *pay a visit* **5 pay one's way** pay money for things as one buys them so as not to get into debt ♦ *n* **1** money received for work **2 in the pay of** employed by **pay back** *phr vt* **1** return (what is owing) to (someone) **2** return bad treatment, rudeness, etc., to **pay for** *phr vt* suffer or be punished for **pay off** *phr v* **1** *vt* pay all of (a debt) **2** *vt* pay and dismiss **3** *vt* pay (someone) to keep silent about a wrong act **4** *vi* be successful **pay out** *phr v* **1** *vi/t* make (a large payment) **2** *vt* allow (a rope) to be pulled out gradually **pay up** *phr vi* pay a debt in full, esp. unwillingly or late **~er** *n*

payable *adj* that must or can be paid

paybed *n* hospital bed paid for by the occupant

pay dirt *n AmE* valuable discovery

PAYE *n* pay as you earn; income-tax payment by deduction from salary

payee *n tech* person to whom money is or should be paid

payload *n* amount carried in a vehicle, esp. a spacecraft

paymaster *n* person who pays someone, and can therefore control their actions

payment *n* **1** act of paying **2** amount of money (to be) paid

payoff *n* **1** payment made to settle matters **2** ending to something, when everything is explained

pay packet *n* (envelope containing) wages

payphone *n* coin-operated telephone

payroll *n* **1** list of workers employed **2** total amount of wages paid in a

particular company
pc *abbrev. for:* **1** per cent **2** personal computer
PC *abbrev. for:* **1** police constable **2** privy councillor
PE *n* physical education; development of the body by games, exercises, etc.
pea *n* large round green seed used as food
peace *n* **1** period free of war **2** calmness; quietness **3** good order in a country **4** lack of anxiety: *peace of mind* **5 make one's peace with** settle a quarrel with **~ful** *adj* **1** quiet; untroubled **2** without war **~fully** *adv* **~fulness** *n*
peacetime *n* time when a nation is not at war
peach *n* round soft juicy yellowish-red fruit
peacock *n* large bird with long beautifully coloured tail feathers
peahen *n* the dark-coloured female of the peacock
peak *n* **1** highest point, level, etc. **2** sharply pointed mountain top **3** part of a cap which sticks out in front ♦ *adj* highest; greatest ♦ *vi* reach the highest point, level, etc.
peaky *adj* pale and ill-looking
peal *n* **1** loud long sound: *peals of laughter* **2** sound of bells ringing ♦ *vi* (of a bell) ring loudly
peanut *n* nut that grows in a shell underground **peanuts** *pl n sl* very little money
pear *n* sweet, juicy fruit, narrow at the stem end and wide at the other
pearl *n* round silvery-white jewel formed in the shell of oysters
pearly gates *pl n* gates of Heaven
peasant *n* **1** person who works on the land in a poor country or in former times **2** *infml derog* uneducated or bad-mannered person
peasantry *n* all the peasants in a place
pease pudding *n* dish of dried peas, boiled and mashed
peashooter *n* small tube for blowing peas from
peat *n* partly decayed plant material in the earth, used for growing things or burning **~y** *adj*
pebble *n* small stone **–bly** *adj*
pebbledash *n* wall covering of small stones in plaster
pecan *n* edible nut like a long walnut
peccadillo *n* **-oes** *or* **-os** unimportant wrongdoing
peccary *n* American wild pig
peck *v* **1** *vi/t* (of a bird) strike with the beak **2** *vt* kiss hurriedly ♦ *n* **1** stroke or mark made by pecking **2** hurried kiss
pecking order *n* social order, showing who is more and less important
peckish *adj* slightly hungry
pectin *n* substance found in fruit which helps jam to set
pectoral *adj* of or on the chest
peculate *vt fml* embezzle **–ation** *n*
peculiar *adj* **1** strange, esp. in a displeasing way **2** belonging only to a particular place, time, etc.: *a plant peculiar to these islands* **3** rather mad **4** rather ill **~ly** *adv* **1** especially **2** strangely **~ity** *n* **1** being peculiar **2** something belonging to a particular time, place, etc. **3** strange or unusual habit, custom, etc.
pecuniary *adj fml* financial; monetary
pedagogical /ˌpedəˈgojik(ə)l/ *adj* of teaching or the study of teaching methods **~ly** *adv*
pedagogue /ˈpedəgog/ *n* teacher who is too much concerned with rules
pedal *n* part pushed with the foot to drive or control a machine ♦ *v* **-ll-** (*AmE* **-l-**) **1** *vi* work pedals **2** *vi/t* ride (a bicycle)
pedant *n* person who overvalues small details and formal rules **~ic** *adj* **~ically** *adv*
pedantry *n* fussy concern with rules and details
peddle *vt* try to sell by going from place to place
peddler *n* **1** person who peddles illegal drugs **2** *AmE* pedlar
pederast *n* person who has anal intercourse with a boy
pedestal *n* **1** base on which a pillar or

statue stands **2 put someone on a pedestal** treat someone as better or nobler than anyone else
pedestrian *n* walker ♦ *adj* **1** dull and ordinary **2** for pedestrians
pediatrics *n* branch of medicine concerned with children **-rician** *n* children's doctor
pedicure *n* foot-care treatment
pedigree *n* (an official description of) the set of people or animals from whom a person or animal is descended ♦ *adj* (of an animal) specially bred from a high-quality family of animals
pediment *n* triangular piece of wall above a doorway
pedlar *n* person who peddles small articles
pee *vi infml* urinate ♦ *n infml* **1** act of peeing **2** urine
peek *vi, n* (take) a quick look
peel *v* **1** *vt* remove (the outer covering) from (esp. a fruit or vegetable) **2** *vi* come off in small pieces: *My skin is peeling.* **3 keep one's eyes peeled** keep careful watch ♦ *n* outer covering of fruits and vegetables
peep[1] *vi, n* (take) a quick often secret look
peep[2] *n* **1** short weak high sound **2** sound, esp. something spoken
peephole *n* small hole to look through
peeping Tom *n* man who looks at people who think they are unobserved (e.g. women undressing); voyeur
peepshow *n* exotic entertainment (viewed through a small hole)
peer[1] *n* **1** lord or lady **2** *fml* one's equal in rank, quality, etc.
peer[2] *vi* look very carefully or hard
peerage *n* **1** rank of a peer **2** all the peers
peeress *n* **1** female peer **2** wife of a peer
peerless *adj* better than any other
peeve *vt* annoy
peevish *adj* bad-tempered **~ly** *adv* **~ness** *n*
peewit *n* lapwing
peg *n* short piece of wood, metal, etc., for fastening things, hanging things on, etc. ♦ *vt* **-gg-** fasten as if with a peg **peg out** *phr vi infml, esp. BrE* die
peg leg *n infml* artificial leg
pejorative *adj* (of a word or expression) saying that something is bad or worthless **~ly** *adv*
pekingese, pekinese *n* small dog with long silky hair
pelican *n* **-cans** *or* **-can** large water bird with a large beak in which it stores fish to eat
pelican crossing *n* (in Britain) place where pedestrians wishing to cross the road can stop the traffic by working special traffic lights
pellagra *n* deficiency disease characterized by dermatitis and nervous symptoms
pellet *n* **1** small ball of soft material **2** small bullet
pell-mell *adv* in confused haste
pellucid *adj* very clear
pelmet *n esp. BrE* strip above a window to hide curtain tops
pelota *n* Spanish ball game played by throwing and catching with a basket
pelt[1] *v* **1** *vt* attack by throwing things **2** *vi* (of rain) fall very heavily **3** *vi* run very fast ♦ *n* **(at) full pelt** very fast
pelt[2] *n* animal's skin with its fur
pelvis *n* bowl-shaped frame of bones at the base of the spine **-vic** *adj*
pemmican *n* dried, pressed meat
pen[1] *n* instrument for writing with ink
pen[2] *n* enclosed piece of land for keeping animals in ♦ *vt* **-nn-** shut in a pen or small space
penal *adj* of or being legal punishment, esp. in prison
penalize, -ise *vt* **1** put in an unfavourable or unfair situation **2** punish with a penalty
penalty *n* **1** punishment or disadvantage suffered, esp. for doing wrong **2** (in sports) disadvantage suffered by a player or team for breaking a rule
penance *n* willing self-punishment, to show one is sorry for doing wrong
pence *pl of* penny
penchant /ˈpenchənt, ˈpon(h)shonh/ *n*

liking for something

pencil *n* narrow pointed writing instrument containing a thin stick of black material ♦ *v* **-ll-** (*AmE* **-l-**) **pencil in** *phr vi* include for now, with the possibility of being changed later

pendant *n* hanging piece of jewellery, esp. round the neck

pendent *adj* hanging

pending *adj* waiting to be decided ♦ *prep* until

pendulous *adj fml* hanging down loosely **~ly** *adv*

pendulum *n* weight hanging so as to swing freely, esp. as used to control a clock

penetrate *v* **1** *vi/t* go (into or through) **2** *vt* see into or through **-trating** *adj* **1** (of sight, a question, etc.) sharp and searching **2** able to understand clearly and deeply **-tration** *n* **1** penetrating **2** ability to understand clearly and deeply

pen friend *n* usu. foreign friend that you write to but have usu. never met

penguin *n* black-and-white flightless seabird of the Antarctic

penicillin *n* drug that kills bacteria

peninsula *n* piece of land almost surrounded by water

penis *n* male sex organ

penitent *adj* feeling sorry and intending not to do wrong again **-ence** *n* **~ly** *adv*

penitential *adj* of penance or penitence

penitentiary *n* prison, esp. in the US

penknife *n* **-knives** small knife with a folding blade

pen name *n* false name used by a writer instead of his/her real name

pennant *n* long narrow pointed flag

penniless *adj* having no money

pennon *n* pennant

penny *n* **pennies** *or* **pence 1** (in Briain since 1971) unit of money equal to 1/100th of a pound **2** (in Britain before 1971) unit of money equal to one twelfth of a shilling **3 the penny (has) dropped** *BrE infml* the meaning (of something said) has at last been understood

penny dreadful *n* cheap, sensational novel

penny-farthing *n* bicycle with a very large front wheel and very small back wheel

penny-pinching *n, adj* (quality of being) unwilling to spend money

penology *n* science of how to run prisons and treat offenders

pension¹ *n* money paid regularly to someone who can no longer earn (enough) money by working, esp. because of old age or illness **pension off** *phr vt* dismiss from work and pay a pension to **~er** *n* person receiving a pension

pension² *n* house in a non-English speaking country where one can get a room and meals

pensive *adj* deeply or sadly thoughtful **~ly** *adv* **~ness** *n*

pentagon *n* five-sided figure

pentameter *n* line of verse with five beats

pentathlon *n* sports event in which the competitors take part in five different sports

Pentecost *n* **1** Jewish festival 50 days after Passover **2** Christian festival celebrating the coming of the Holy Spirit

penthouse *n* set of rooms built on top of a tall building

pent up *adj* not allowed to be free or freely expressed

penultimate *adj* next to the last

penumbra *n fml* slightly dark area between full darkness and full light

penury /ˈpenyoori/ *n fml* being very poor **-rious** *adj*

peony *n* garden plant with large usu. red flowers

people *n* **1** *pl* persons other than oneself; persons in general **2** *pl* all the ordinary members of a nation **3** race; nation: *the peoples of Africa* ♦ *vt* **1** live in (a place) **2** fill with people

pep *n infml* keen activity and forcefulness ♦ *v* **-pp- pep up** *phr vt infml* make more active or interesting

pepper *n* **1** hot-tasting powder made

from the fruit of a tropical plant **2** hollow slightly hot-tasting vegetable ♦ *vt* hit repeatedly with shots
pepper-and-salt *adj* speckled black and white
peppercorn rent *n BrE* very small amount of money paid as rent
peppermint *n* **1** plant with a special strong taste **2** sweet with this taste
pep pill *n* pill taken to make one livelier or happier for a short time
pepsin *n* enzyme in the stomach that breaks down proteins
pep talk *n* talk intended to make people work harder, more quickly, etc.
peptic *adj* of or caused by the digestive juices
per *prep* for each: *two per year*
peradventure *adv arch.* **1** perhaps **2** by chance
perambulator *n fml* pram
per annum *adv* each year
per capita *adj, adv* for or by each person
perceive *vt* (come to) have knowledge of, esp. by seeing or understanding
per cent *n, adv, adj* (one part) in or for each 100
percentage *n* **1** number stated as if it is part of a whole which is 100 **2** *infml* advantage; profit
perceptible *adj* noticeable **–bly** *adv*
perception *n* **1** perceiving **2** keen natural understanding
perceptive *adj* having or showing natural understanding **~ly** *adv*
perch¹ *n* **1** branch, rod, etc., where a bird sits **2** high position or place ♦ *v* **1** *vi* (of a bird) sit **2** *vi/t* put or be in a high or unsafe place
perch² *n* European freshwater fish
perchance *adv lit* possibly
percipient /pəˈsipiˌənt/ *adj fml* perceptive **–ence** *n*
percolate *vi* pass slowly (as if) through a material with small holes **–lator** *n* pot in which coffee is made by hot water percolating through the crushed beans **–ation** *n*
percussion *n* musical instruments played by being struck
perdition *n fml* everlasting punishment after death
peregrinations *pl n lit* long journey (abroad)
peregrine falcon *n* medium-sized fast bird of prey
peremptory *adj fml* **1** impolitely quick and unfriendly **2** (of a command) that must be obeyed **–rily** *adv*
perennial *adj* **1** lasting forever or for a long time **2** (of a plant) living for more than two years ♦ *n* perennial plant **~ly** *adv*
perfect *adj* **1** of the very best possible kind, standard, etc. **2** with nothing missing; full: *a perfect set of teeth* **3** complete : *a perfect fool* **4** (of a verb tense) expressing an action that has happened and finished ♦ *vt* make perfect **~ly** *adv* **~ible** *adj*
perfection *n* **1** being perfect **2** making perfect **3** perfect example
perfectionist *n* someone not satisfied with anything not perfect
perfidious /ˌpuhˈfidi·əs/ *adj fml* disloyal **~ly** *adv* **–fidy** *n* treachery
perforate *vt* **1** make a hole through **2** make a line of holes in (paper) to make it easier to tear **–ration** *n*
perforce *adv fml* necessarily, unavoidably
perform *v* **1** *vt* do (a piece of work, ceremony, etc.): *perform an operation* **2** *vi/t* act or show (a play, piece of music, etc.), esp. in public **3** *vi* work or carry out an activity (in the stated way): *a car that performs well on hills* **~ance** *n* **1** action or manner of performing **2** (public) show of music, a play, etc. **~er** *n* actor, musician, etc.
perfume *n* (liquid having) a sweet smell ♦ *vt* cause to smell sweet **~ry** *n* place where perfume is made or sold
perfunctory *adj* done hastily and without interest or care **–rily** *adv* **–riness** *n*
pergola *n* framework for overhanging plants
perhaps *adv* it may be; possibly
perigee /ˈperiˌjee/ *n* point where an

orbit is closest to the Earth
peril *n* (something that causes) great danger **~ous** *adj* **~ously** *adv*
perimeter *n* (length of) the border round an enclosed area, esp. a camp or airfield
period *n* **1** stretch of time **2** division of a school day **3** monthly flow of blood from a woman's womb ♦ *adv infml* (used at end of a sentence) and that is all I'm going to say on the matter **~ic** *adj* repeated and regular **~ical** *n* magazine that comes out regularly **~ically** *adv*
periodic table *n* list of chemical elements in order of atomic weight
peripatetic *adj fml* travelling about, esp. to work
periphery /pəˈrif(ə)ri/ *n* outside edge **-ral** *adj* **1** on the periphery **2** marginal; slight **-ral** *n* piece of equipment, e.g. a VDU or printer, attached to a computer
periphrasis /pəˈrifrəsis/ *n* **-ses** *fml* (use of) indirect phrasing **-astic** *adj*
periscope *n* long tube with mirrors so that people lower down can see what is above them, esp. in submarines
perish *v* **1** *vi fml* die **2** *vi/t* (cause to) decay or lose natural qualities **~able** *adj* (of food) that will decay quickly **~ing, ~ ed** *adj* very cold
peristalsis *n* muscle movements that force food through the intestine **-altic** *adj*
peritoneum *n* membrane covering organs in the abdomen
peritonitis *n* inflammation of the peritoneum
periwinkle *n* small evergreen plant with blue flowers
perjure *vt* **perjure oneself** tell lies in a court of law **-ury** *n* lying in court
perk *n* money, goods, etc., that one gets from an employer in addition to one's pay
perk up *phr vi/t infml* make or become more cheerful
perky *adj* confidently cheerful **-kily** *adv* **-kiness** *n*
perm[1] *n BrE* act of putting artificial curls into hair ♦ *vt* give a perm to
perm[2] *vt infml* permute
permafrost *n* layer of permanently frozen ground
permanent *adj* lasting a long time or for ever **~ly** *adv* **-ence** *n*
permanganate *n* chemical salt containing manganese, esp. **potassium permanganate,** used as a disinfectant
permeable *adj* that can be permeated
permeate *vt* spread or pass through or into every part of
permissible *adj* allowed **-bly** *adv*
permission *n* act of allowing
permissive *adj* allowing (too) much freedom, esp. in sexual matters **~ly** *adv* **~ness** *n*
permit[1] *vi/t* **-tt-** allow ♦ *n* official document allowing something
permute *vt* rearrange in a different order **-utation** *n*
pernicious *adj fml* very harmful **~ly** *adv* **~ness** *n*
pernickety *adj* worrying too much about small things
peroration *n fml* **1** last part of a speech **2** grand, long, but meaningless speech
peroxide *n* oxide with a high proportion of oxygen, esp. **hydrogen peroxide,** used as a bleach and disinfectant
peroxide blonde *n* woman with bleached hair
perpendicular *adj* **1** exactly upright **2** at an angle of 90° to another line or surface ♦ *n* perpendicular line or position
perpetrate *vt fml* be guilty of **-rator** *n*
perpetual *adj* lasting (as if) for ever **~ly** *adv*
perpetuate *vt* make (something) continue to exist for a long time **-ation** *n*
perpetuity /ˌpuhpiˈtyooh·əti/ *n* **in perpetuity** *fml* for ever
perplex *vt* make (someone) feel confused by being difficult to understand; puzzle **~ity** *n*
perquisite /ˈpuhkwizit/ *n fml* perk
perry *n* alcoholic drink made from pears
per se *adv* considered alone and not in connection with other things

persecute *vt* **1** cause to suffer, esp. for religious beliefs **2** trouble or harm continually **-utor** *n* **-ution** *n*
persevere *vi* continue firmly in spite of difficulties **-erance** *n*
Persian *adj* of Persia or Iran ♦ *n* **1** Persian person **2** Persian language
Persian cat *n* cat with long silky hair
persiflage /ˈpuhsiˌflahzh/ *n fml* light-hearted talk
persimmon *n* globular orange fruit with several seeds
persist *vi* **1** continue firmly in spite of opposition or warning **2** continue to exist **~ent** *adj* persisting **~ently** *adv* **~ence** *n*
person *n* **1** single human being **2** form of a verb or pronoun, showing the speaker (**first person**), the one spoken to (**second person**), or the one spoken about (**third person**) **3 in person** personally; oneself **4 on/about one's person** carried around with one
persona *n* outward character a person takes on
personable *adj fml* attractive
personage *n* character in a play or book, or in history
personal *adj* **1** of, for, or by a particular person **2** private **3** rude **4** *fml* of the body: *personal cleanliness* **~ly** *adv* **1** directly and not through a representative **2** privately
personal column *n* part of a newspaper that gives or asks for messages, news, etc., about particular people
personality *n* **1** whole nature or character of a person **2** (person with) forceful, lively, and usu. attractive qualities of character **3** well-known person
personality cult *n* practice of giving too great admiration to a particular person, esp. a political leader
personal pronoun *n* pronoun showing the grammatical person, such as *I* or *you*
personal stereo *n* small machine for playing cassettes, which has earphones and is carried around with the user
personify *vt* **1** be a good example of (a quality) **2** represent as being human **-fication** *n*
personnel *n* **1** *pl* all employed people in a company, army, etc. **2** department that deals with these people and their problems
perspective *n* **1** effect of depth, distance, and solidity in drawing and painting **2** proper relationship of each part of a matter
perspex *n* strong glasslike plastic
perspicacious *adj fml* showing good judgment and understanding **~ly** *adv* **~ness, -acity** *n*
perspicuous *adj fml* clearly and accurately expressed
perspire *vi* sweat **-spiration** *n* **1** sweat **2** act of sweating
persuade *vt* make (someone) do something by reasoning, arguing, begging, etc.
persuasion *n* **1** (skill in) persuading **2** particular belief: *her political persuasions*
persuasive *adj* able to persuade others **~ly** *adv* **~ness** *n*
pert *adj* amusingly disrespectful **~ly** *adv* **~ness** *n*
pertain to *phr vt fml* be about or connected with
pertinacious *adj fml* holding firmly to an opinion or action **~ly** *adv* **~ness, ~acity** *n*
pertinent *adj fml* directly connected; relevant **~ly** *adv* **-ence** *n*
perturb *vt* worry **~ation** *n*
peruse *vt fml* read carefully **perusal** *n*
Peruvian *n, adj* (person) of Peru
pervade *vt fml* spread all through
pervasive *adj* pervading; widespread **~ly** *adv* **~ness** *n*
perverse *adj* **1** purposely doing wrong or unreasonable things **2** awkward and annoying **~ly** *adv*
perversion *n* **1** perverted form of what is true, reasonable, etc. **2** unnatural sexual act **3** perverting
perversity *n* **1** being perverse **2** perverse act

pervert *vt* **1** lead into wrong or unnatural (sexual) behaviour **2** use for a bad purpose ♦ *n* person who commits unnatural sexual acts
peseta *n* money unit of Spain
peso *n* **-os** money unit of several S American countries
pessary *n* **1** vaginal suppository **2** device worn in the vagina to support the womb or as a contraceptive
pessimist *n* person who expects bad things to happen **–ism** *n* **-istic** *adj*
pest *n* **1** animal or insect that harms food products **2** annoying person
pester *vt* annoy continually, esp. with demands
pesticide *n* chemical to kill harmful insects or animals
pestilence *n fml* terrible disease killing many people
pestilent, pestilential *adj* **1** *fml* causing a pestilence **2** unpleasantly annoying
pestle *n* implement for crushing things in a thick bowl
pet *n* **1** animal kept as a companion **2** person specially favoured ♦ *v* **-tt- 1** *vi* kiss and touch sexually **2** *vt* touch lovingly
petal *n* coloured leaflike part of a flower
peter out *phr vi* gradually end
petit bourgeois *adj* lower middle class
petite *adj* (esp. of a woman) having a small and neat figure
petit four *n* small fancy cake or biscuit
petition *n* request or demand to a government, ruler, etc., signed by many people ♦ *vi/t* make or send a petition **~er** *n*
petit mal *n* mild form of epilepsy
pet name *n* name for someone you like, instead of their real name
petrel *n* gull-like seabird
petrify *vt* **1** frighten extremely **2** turn into stone
petrochemical *n* chemical obtained from petroleum
petrodollar *n* US dollar earned by the sale of oil, esp. by oil-producing countries in the Middle East
petrol *n BrE* liquid obtained from petroleum and used for producing power in engines
petroleum *n* mineral oil obtained from below the ground
petrology *n* scientific study of rocks **–gist** *n*
petrol station *n BrE* filling station
petticoat *n* skirtlike undergarment
pettifogging *n, adj* quibbling over small details
pettish *adj* petulant
petty *adj* **1** unimportant (by comparison) **2** showing a narrow and ungenerous mind **–tiness** *n*
petty bourgeois *adj* petit bourgeois
petty cash *n* money kept for small payments
petty officer *n* person of middle rank in the navy
petulant *adj* showing childish bad temper **~ly** *adv* **–ance** *n*
petunia *n* small garden plant with funnel-shaped flowers
pew *n* seat in a church
pewit *n* lapwing
pewter *n* greyish metal made from lead and tin
pfennig *n* money unit of Germany
PG *abbrev. for:* parental guidance; (of a film) which may in parts be unsuitable for children under 15
pH *n* number representing the degree of acidity or alkalinity
phagocyte *n* cell that destroys harmful material in the body
phalanx *n* group packed closely together, esp. for attack or defence
phallus *n* image of the male sex organ **–lic** *adj*
phantasm *n lit* something unreal or illusory
phantasmagoria *n* confusing succession of scenes
phantom *n* **1** ghost **2** something that is not really there
phantom pregnancy *n* symptoms of pregnancy when not actually pregnant
pharaoh /ˈfeərəʊ/ *n* ruler of ancient Egypt
pharisee *n* hypocrite **–saic, -saical** *adj*

Pharisee *n* member of a strict Jewish sect in the time of Christ
pharmaceutical *adj* of (the making of) medicine
pharmacist *n* **1** person who makes medicines **2** *BrE* chemist (2)
pharmacology *n* study of medicine and drugs **–gist** *n*
pharmacopoeia /ˌfahməkəˈpee·ə/ *n* official list of drugs
pharmacy *n* **1** shop where medicines are sold **2** making or giving out of medicines
pharyngitis *n med* sore throat
pharynx *n med* throat
phase *n* **1** stage of development **2** way the moon looks at a particular time ♦ *vt* arrange in separate phases **phase in/out** *phr vt* introduce/withdraw gradually
phatic *adj tech* communicating a general atmosphere rather than specific ideas
PhD *abbrev. for:* doctor of philosophy; (someone with) a degree for advanced postgraduate work
pheasant *n* large bird often shot for food
phenol *n* poisonous chemical used as a disinfectant
phenomenal *adj* very unusual **~ly** *adv*
phenomenon *n* **-na 1** fact or event in the world as it appears or is experienced by the senses, esp. an unusual one **2** very unusual person, thing, etc.
pheromone *n* chemical given off by animals to attract others
phew *interj* (expresses relief, surprise, or exhaustion)
phial *n* small thin bottle
philanderer *n arch.* man who has many casual love affairs **–ing** *n*
philanthropist *n* kind person who gives money to those who are poor or in trouble **–py** *n* **–pic** *adj*
philately /fiˈlatəli/ *n* stamp collecting **–list** *n*
-phile *suffix* (person) with a liking for: *Francophile*
philistine *n* person who does not understand and actively dislikes art, music, beautiful things, etc.
philology *n* study of the history of languages
philosopher *n* **1** person who studies philosophy **2** philosophical person
philosopher's stone *n* imaginary substance thought in former times to change any metal into gold
philosophize, -ise *vi* talk or write like a philosopher
philosophy *n* **1** study of the nature and meaning of existence, reality, morals, etc. **2** system of thought **–phical** *adj* **1** of philosophy **2** accepting things with calm courage **–phically** *adv*
philtre, *AmE* **-ter** *n* love potion
phlebitis *n* inflammation of a vein
phlegm /flem/ *n* **1** thick liquid produced in the nose and throat **2** *fml* calmness
phlegmatic /flegˈmatik/ *adj* calm and unexcitable **~ally** *adv*
-phobe *suffix* person afraid of
phobia *n* strong (unreasonable) fear and dislike
-phobia *suffix* fear of: *Francophobia*
phoenix *n* mythical bird that burnt itself up and was born again from its ashes
phon- *prefix* sound; speech
phone *n, vi/t* telephone
phone book *n* book with a list of all telephone numbers in an area
phone box *n* hut containing a public telephone
phone-in *n* show in which telephoned questions or comments from the public are broadcast
phoneme *n* unit of speech sound
phone-tapping *n* listening secretly to other people's telephone conversations by means of electronic equipment
phonetic *adj* of the sounds of human speech **~ally** *adv*
phonetics *n* study and science of speech sounds **–ician** *n*
phoney *n, adj* (someone or something) pretended or false
phoney war *n* period during which a state of war officially exists but there is

no actual fighting
phonograph *n AmE* record player
phonology *n* study of the system of speech sounds in a language **–gical** *adj*
phosphate *n* chemical made from phosphoric acid, esp. as used for making plants grow better
phosphorescent *adj* shining faintly in the dark by a natural process **–ence** *n*
phosphorus *n* yellowish waxlike chemical that burns when brought into the air **–ric** *adj*
phot- *prefix* light
photo *n* **-os** photograph
photocall *n* session for taking (publicity) photographs
photocopy *vi/t, n* (make) a photographic copy
photoelectric *adj* using light to trigger an electrical effect
photoelectric cell *n* (apparatus worked by) a device that uses light to start or control an electric current
photo finish *n* very close finish to a race, where a photograph is needed to show the winner
Photofit *n tdmk* system of making a composite photograph of someone's face from individual features
photogenic *adj* that looks good when photographed
photograph *n* picture taken with a camera and film ♦ *vt* take a photograph of **~er** *n* **~y** *n* art or business of producing photographs or films **~ic** *adj*
photon *n* minute particle of light
photosensitive *adj* changing under the action of light
Photostat *n tdmk* machine for making photographic copies
photosynthesis *n* process by which plants make food using sunlight
phrasal *adj* of or being a phrase
phrasal verb *n* group of words that acts like a verb and consists usu. of a verb with an adverb and/or a preposition
phrase *n* **1** group of words without a finite verb **2** short (suitable) expression ♦ *vt* express in the stated way
phrasebook *n* book explaining foreign phrases, for use abroad
phraseology *n* choice and use of words
phylactery *n* small box containing scriptures, worn by Jews
phylum *n* **-la** category of plants or animals
physic *n arch.* medicine
physical *adj* **1** of or being matter or material things (not the mind or spirit) **2** of the body **~ly** *adv* **1** with regard to the body **2** according to the laws of nature: *physically impossible*
physician *n fml* doctor
physicist *n* person who studies or works in physics
physics *n* science dealing with matter and natural forces
physio *n infml* physiotherapist
physiognomy *n fml* facial features
physiology *n* science of how living bodies work **–gist** *n* **–gical** *adj*
physiotherapy *n* exercises, massage, etc., to treat sick people **–pist** *n*
physique *n* shape and quality of a person's body
pianissimo *adj, adv* played very quietly
piano *n* **-os** large musical instrument with wire strings, played by pressing black and white keys
pianoforte *n fml* piano
piazza /piˈatsə/ *n* public square, esp. in Italy
picador *n* man on horseback who helps the matador in a bullfight
picaninny *n taboo* black child
picaresque *adj* (of a story) dealing with a character of whom one disapproves but who is not usu. wicked
piccalilli *n* pickled vegetables in a mustard sauce
piccolo *n* **-os** small flute
pick[1] *vt* **1** choose **2** pull off from a plant: *picking fruit* **3** take up with the fingers, a beak, or a pointed instrument **4** remove unwanted pieces from: *picking her teeth* **5** steal from **6** open (a lock) without a key **7** cause (a fight, quarrel etc.) intentionally **8 pick and choose** choose very carefully **9 pick holes in**

find the weak points in **10 pick one's way** walk carefully **11 pick someone's brains** make use of someone's knowledge **pick at** *phr vt* eat (a meal) with little interest **pick off** *phr vt* shoot one by one **pick on** *phr vt* choose unfairly for punishment or blame **pick out** *phr vt* **1** choose specially **2** see among others, esp. with difficulty **pick up** *phr v* **1** *vt* take hold of and lift up **2** *vt* gather together: *Pick up your toys.* **3** *vi/t* (cause to) start again **4** *vt* acquire **5** *vt* go and meet or collect **6** *vi* improve, esp. in health **7** *vt* become friendly with for sexual purposes **8** *vt* be able to hear or receive (on a radio) ♦ *n* **1** choice: *Take your pick!* **2** best **~er** *n* **~ings** *n* additional money or profits

pick² *n* **1** pickaxe **2** sharp, pointed, usu. small instrument

pickaxe also *AmE* **-ax** *n* large tool with two sharp points, for digging up roads

picket *n* **1** person or group outside a place of work trying to persuade others not to work there during a strike **2** soldier guarding a camp **3** strong pointed stick fixed in the ground ♦ *vt* surround with or as pickets during industrial action

pickle *n* **1** vinegar or salt water for preserving foods **2** vegetable preserved in this **3** dirty, difficult, or confused condition ♦ *vt* preserve in pickle **~d** *adj infml* drunk

pick-me-up *n infml* something, esp. a drink or medicine, that makes one feel stronger, happier, etc.

pickpocket *n* person who steals from people's pockets

pick-up *n* **1** needle and arm of a record player **2** light van having an open body with low sides

picky *adj* difficult to please; fussy

picnic *n* informal outdoor meal ♦ *vi* **-ck-** have a picnic

pictorial *adj* having or expressed in pictures **~ly** *adv*

picture *n* **1** representation made by painting, drawing, or photography **2** what is seen on the television screen **3** cinema film **4** image in the mind **5** person or thing that is beautiful **6** perfect example: *He's the picture of health.* **7 in the picture: a** knowing all the facts **b** receiving much attention ♦ *vt* **1** imagine. **2** paint or draw **pictures** *pl n* **1** the cinema **2** the film industry

picturesque *adj* **1** charming to look at **2** (of language) unusually forceful and descriptive

piddling *adj infml* small and unimportant

pidgin *n* language which is a mixture of other languages

pie *n* baked dish of pastry filled with meat or fruit

piebald *n, adj* (horse) coloured black and white

piece *n* **1** separate part or bit **2** single object that is an example of its kind or class: *a piece of paper/music/advice* **3** small object used in board games **4** *BrE* coin **5 give someone a piece of one's mind** *infml* tell someone angrily what you think of them **6 go to pieces** *infml* lose the ability to think or act clearly **7 in one piece** unharmed **8 of a piece** similar; in agreement **piece together** *phr vt* complete by finding all the bits and putting them together

pièce de résistance *n* **pièces de résistance** the best or most important thing or event, coming at the end

piecemeal *adj, adv* (done) only one part at a time

piece of cake *n infml* something very easy to do

piecework *n* work paid for by the amount done rather than by the hours worked

pie chart *n* circle divided into several parts showing the way in which something, e.g. money or population, is divided up

piecrust *n* pastry of a pie

pied *adj* marked with different colours

pied-à-terre *n* **pieds-à-terre** small additional home

pie-eyed *adj infml* drunk

pier *n* **1** long structure built out into the

sea, esp. with entertainments on it **2** supporting pillar

pierce *vt* make a hole in or through with a point **piercing** *adj* **1** (of wind) very strong and cold **2** (of sound) unpleasantly sharp and clear **3** searching: *a piercing look*

pietà *n* statue or picture of Mary holding the dead Christ

piety /ˈpie·əti/ *n* deep respect for God and religion

piezoelectric *adj* producing electricity by pressure on a crystal

piffle *n infml* nonsense

piffling *adj infml* useless; worthless

pig *n* **1** fat short-legged animal with no fur, kept on farms for food **2** *infml* person who is dirty or rude or eats too much

pigeon *n* **1** quite large light-grey bird **2** responsibility: *It's not my pigeon.*

pigeon-chested *adj* having a chest that sticks out in the middle

pigeonhole *n* **1** boxlike division for putting papers in **2** neat division which separates things too simply ♦ *vt* **1** put aside and do nothing about **2** assign to a category

pigeon-toed *adj* having feet that point inwards

piggery *n* **1** place where pigs are kept **2** disgusting behaviour

piggish *also* **piggy** *adj* like a pig, esp. greedy

piggyback *n* ride on someone's back **piggyback** *adv*

piggybank *n* small usu. pig-shaped container used by children for saving coins

pigheaded *adj* very stubborn

pig iron *n* impure form of iron

piglet *n* young pig

pigment *n* **1** dry coloured powder for making paint **2** natural colouring matter in plants and animals **~ation** *n*

pigmy *n* pygmy

pigsty *n* **1** small building for pigs **2** very dirty room or house

pigswill *n* waste food given to pigs

pigtail *n* length of twisted hair hanging down the back

pike[1] *n* **pikes** *or* **pike** large fish-eating river fish

pike[2] *n* long-handled spear

pilaf *n* dish of rice

pilchard *n* small sea fish, often eaten

pile[1] *n* **1** tidy heap **2** also **piles** *pl. infml* lots **3** *infml* very large amount of money ♦ *v* **1** *vt* make a pile of **2** *vi* come or go in a (disorderly) crowd **pile up** *phr vi* form into a mass or large quantity

pile[2] *n* soft surface of short threads on carpets or cloth

pile[3] *n* heavy supporting post hammered into the ground

piles *pl n* hemorrhoids

pileup *n* traffic accident with many vehicles

pilfer *vi/t* steal (small things)

pilgrim *n* person on a journey to a holy place **~age** *n* pilgrim's journey

pill *n* **1** small ball of medicine **2** (*often cap.*) pill taken as birth control

pillage *vi/t* steal things violently from (a place taken in war)

pillar *n* **1** tall upright round post, usu. of stone, used esp. as a support for a roof **2** important member and active supporter

pillar-box *n BrE* large round box in the street for posting letters

pillbox *n* **1** small round box for pills **2** concrete shelter with a gun inside it

pillion *n* passenger seat on a motorcycle

pillock *n BrE sl* fool

pillory *n* wooden frame in which wrongdoers were locked up in public ♦ *vt* **1** put in a pillory **2** attack with words, esp. in public

pillow *n* filled cloth bag for supporting the head in bed ♦ *vt* rest (esp. one's head) on something

pillowcase *n* cloth cover for a pillow

pilot *n* **1** person who flies a plane **2** person who guides ships into a harbour ♦ *adj* intended to try something out: *a pilot survey* ♦ *vt* act as the pilot of

pilot light *n* **1** small gas flame to light a main flame **2** small electric light to show an apparatus is turned on

pimento *n* **-os** red pepper, esp. as used

for stuffing olives
pimp *n* man who controls and gets money from prostitutes
pimpernel *n* small wild plant with esp. red flowers
pimple *n* small raised diseased spot on the skin
pin *n* **1** short thin pointed piece of metal for fastening things **2** *AmE* brooch **3** *infml* leg ♦ *vt* **-nn- 1** fasten with a pin **2** keep in one position, esp. by weight from above **3. pin one's hopes on** depend on **pin down** *phr vt* **1** force to give clear details, make a firm decision, etc. **2** prevent from moving
piña colada *n* drink made from pineapple juice and rum
pinafore *n* loose garment worn over (the front of) a dress to keep it clean
pinball *n* game in which small balls are rolled into holes to score points
pince-nez *n* **pince-nez** glasses held to the nose with a spring
pincer *n* footlike part of a crab, lobster, etc., for seizing things **pincers** *pl n* tool for holding things tightly
pincer movement *n* simultaneous attack from opposite directions
pinch *v* **1** *vt* press tightly between two surfaces or between finger and thumb **2** *vi* hurt by being too tight **3** *vt infml* steal **4** *vt infml* arrest ♦ *n* **1** act of pinching **2** amount picked up with finger and thumb: *a pinch of salt* **3** suffering through not having enough, esp. of money: *feel the pinch* **4 at a pinch** if necessary
pinchbeck *adj, n* (of) an alloy of copper and zinc used to imitate gold
pincushion *n* small filled bag for sticking pins into until needed
pine[1] *n* tall tree with thin sharp evergreen leaves
pine[2] *vi* **1** lose strength and health through grief **2** have a strong desire, esp. that is impossible to fulfil
pineal gland *n* small gland in the brain
pineapple *n* large tropical fruit with sweet juicy yellow flesh
ping *vi, n* (make) a short sharp ringing sound
ping-pong *n* table tennis
pinion[1] *vt* prevent from moving by tying or holding the limbs
pinion[2] *n* small wheel fitting against a larger one for turning
pinion[3] *n* (outer joint of) a bird's wing
pink[1] *adj* pale red ♦ *n* **in the pink** in perfect health
pink[2] *vi* (of an engine) make sharp sounds when not working properly
pink gin *n* gin flavoured with bitters
pinkie, -y *n ScotE or AmE* little finger
pinko *n* **-os** *or* **-oes** *derog* left-wing person
pin money *n* money earned by doing small jobs
pinnace *n* small sailing boat
pinnacle *n* highest point or degree
pinny *n infml* pinafore
pinochle /ˈpeeˌnukl/ *n* US card game
pinpoint *vt* find or describe exactly
pins and needles *pl n* slight pricking sensation in a limb
pinstripe *n* **1** any of a pattern of parallel pale lines on dark cloth **2 pinstripes** *pl,* also **pinstripe suit** suit made of pinstripe cloth
pint *n* **1** a measure of liquids equal to 20 fluid ounces **2** pint of beer
pintable *n* pinball machine
pint-size *adj derog* small
pinup *n* picture of an attractive or admired person such as a popular singer, esp. as stuck up on a wall
pinyin *n* system for writing Chinese with Western letters
pioneer *n* person who does something first, preparing the way for others ♦ *vt* act as a pioneer in
pious *adj* **1** having deep respect for God and religion **2** unlikely to be fulfilled: *a pious hope* **~ly** *adv*
pip[1] *n* small seed of an apple, orange, etc.
pip[2] *n* short high-sounding note, esp. as given on the radio to show the exact time
pip[3] *vt BrE* **pip at the post** just beat at the end of some struggle

pipe *n* **1** tube carrying liquid or gas **2** small tube with a bowl-like container, for smoking tobacco **3** simple tubelike musical instrument ♦ *vt* **1** carry in pipes **2** play music on a pipe or pipes **pipe down** *phr vi infml* stop talking or being noisy **pipe up** *phr vi* suddenly start to speak **pipes** *pl n* bagpipes
piper *n* player of bagpipes
piped music *n* quiet recorded music played continuously in public places
pipe dream *n* impossible hope, plan, or idea
pipeline *n* **1** line of joined pipes, esp. for carrying oil or gas **2 in the pipeline** about to arrive or appear; being prepared
pipette, *AmE* **pipet** *n* small glass tube for sucking up and measuring liquids
piping¹ *n* pipes carrying liquid or gas
piping² *adv* **piping hot** very hot
pipit *n* small songbird
pippin *n* type of apple
pipsqueak *n infml* small or insignificant person
piquant /ˈpeekənt/ *adj* **1** having a pleasant sharp taste **2** interesting and exciting to the mind **–ancy** *n*
pique *n* annoyance and displeasure because of hurt pride ♦ *vt* offend
piracy *n* robbery by pirates
piranha *n* fierce S. American flesh-eating river fish
pirate *n* **1** person who sails around robbing ships **2** person who pirates things ♦ *vt* make and sell (a book, record, etc., by someone else) without permission or payment
pirouette *n* very fast turn on one foot by a dancer **pirouette** *vi*
piss *vi taboo sl* urinate **piss about/around** *phr vi taboo sl* waste time; act in a foolish way **piss off** *phr v taboo sl* **1** *vi* go away **2** *vt* **a** annoy **b** cause to lose interest ♦ *n taboo sl* **1** urine **2 take the piss out of** make fun of **~ed** *adj taboo sl* drunk
piss artist *n BrE derog sl* person who does not do things seriously
pistachio /piˈstahshi·oh/ *n* **-os** green-fleshed nut
piste *n* skiing track
pistil *n* female reproductive organ of a flowering plant
pistol *n* small gun held in one hand
piston *n* short cylindrical part of an engine that goes up and down inside a tube and sends power to the engine
pit *n* **1** hole in the ground **2** coal mine **3** small dent on a surface **4** space in front of a stage where musicians sit **5** *esp. AmE* stone of certain fruit **6 pit of the stomach** place where fear is thought to be felt **pits** *pl n* **1** place beside the track where cars are repaired during a race **2** *infml* the worst possible example of something ♦ *vt* **-tt-** mark with small dents **pit against** *phr vt* set against in competition or fight
pit-a-pat *n, adv* pitter-patter
pitch¹ *v* **1** *vt* set up (a camp or tent) **2** *vi* (of a ship or aircraft) move along with the front and back going up and down **3** *vt* set the pitch of (a sound, music, etc.) **4** *vt* throw **5** *vi/t* (cause to) fall suddenly forwards **pitch in** *phr vi* **1** start eagerly **2** add one's help or support ♦ *n* **1** *BrE* marked-out area for playing sport **2** degree of highness and lowness of a (musical) sound **3** level; degree: *a high pitch of excitement* **4** place (e.g. in a market) where somebody regularly performs, sells, etc. **5** *infml* salesman's special way of talking about goods he/she is trying to sell
pitch² *n* black substance used for keeping out water
pitch-black *adj* very dark
pitchblende *n* mineral which is the chief ore of uranium
pitched battle *n infml* fierce and long quarrel or argument
pitcher¹ *n* **1** *BrE* large old-fashioned container for holding and pouring liquids **2** *AmE* jug
pitcher² *n* (in baseball) player who throws the ball towards the batter
pitchfork *n* long-handled fork for lifting hay on a farm ♦ *vt* put without warning

or against someone's will
piteous *adj fml* causing pity **~ly** *adv*
pitfall *n* unexpected difficulty or danger
pith *n* soft white substance in the stems of some plants and under the skin of oranges, grapefruit, etc. **~y** *adj* **1** full of pith **2** strongly and cleverly stated in few words; succinct
pithead *n* entrance to a coal mine
pitiable *adj* **1** deserving pity **2** pitiful **-bly** *adv*
pitiful *adj* **1** causing or deserving pity **2** worthless; weak **~ly** *adv*
pitiless *adj* merciless; cruel **~ly** *adv*
piton /piˈton(h)/ *n* spike used by mountaineers for gaining a hold
pit prop *n* support for the roof of a mine
pitta *n* flat oval bread
pittance *n* very small amount of pay or money
pitter-patter *adv, n* (with) a quick succession of light sounds
pituitary *n* small organ near the brain which helps to control growth
pity *n* **1** sympathy and sorrow for others' suffering or unhappiness **2** unfortunate state of affairs **3 for pity's sake** (used to add force to a request) please **4 more's the pity** unfortunately ♦ *vt* feel pity for
pivot *n* central point on which something turns ♦ *vi/t* turn on or provide with a pivot **~al** *adj*
pixel *n* tiny individual element of the image on a television screen
pixie, pixy *n* small fairy that plays tricks
pizza *n* flat round dough baked with cheese, tomatoes, etc., on top
pizzazz *n infml* exciting, forceful quality
pizzicato *n, adv* **-ti** (music) played by plucking strings
pl *abbrev. for:* plural
placard *n* board put up or carried around publicly, with information on it
placate *vt* cause to stop feeling angry
place *n* **1** particular position in space **2** particular town, building, etc. **3** usual or proper position: *Put it back in its place.* **4** position in the result of a competition, race, etc. **5** a leading place, usu. second or third, in a race **6** position of employment, in a team, etc. **7** numbered point in an argument, discussion, etc.: *In the first place, I can't afford it.* **8** duty: *It's not my place to tell them what to do.* **9 go places** *infml* be increasingly successful **10 in/out of place: a** in/not in the usual or proper position **b** suitable/unsuitable **11 in place of** instead of **12 put someone in his/her place** show someone that he/she is not as important as he/she would like to be **13 take place** happen **14 take the place of** replace ♦ *vt* **1** put in the stated place **2** make (an order for goods one wants to buy) **3** remember fully who (someone) is **~ment** *n*
placebo /pləˈseeboh/ *n* **-os** *or* **-oes** substance given instead of real medicine, without the person who takes it knowing that it is not real
place mat *n* mat for a plate
placenta *n* **-as** *or* **-ae** thick mass inside the womb joining the unborn child to its mother
placid *adj* not easily angered or excited **~ly** *adv* **~ness, -dity** *n*
plagiarize, -rise *vt* take (words, ideas, etc.) from (someone else's work) and use them in one's own writings without admitting that one has done so **-ism** *n*
plague *n* **1** quickly spreading disease that kills many people **2** widespread uncontrollable mass or number: *a plague of locusts* ♦ *vt* trouble or annoy continually
plaice *n* **plaice** flat fish, often eaten
plaid /plad/ *n* (piece of) thick cloth with a pattern of coloured squares
plain *adj* **1** without decoration or pattern; simple **2** easy to see, hear, or understand **3** expressing thoughts clearly, honestly, and exactly **4** rather ugly ♦ *adv* completely **~ly** *adv* **~ness** *n* ♦ *n* large stretch of flat land
plain clothes *pl n* ordinary clothes, not uniform
plain sailing *n* something easy to do

plainsong *n* chanting church music
plainspoken *adj* (too) frank
plaint *n lit* expression of sorrow
plaintiff *n* person who brings a legal charge or claim
plaintive *adj* sad-sounding **~ly** *adv*
plait *vt esp. BrE* twist together into a ropelike length ♦ *n esp. BrE* plaited length of esp. hair
plan *n* **1** arrangement for carrying out a (future) activity **2** (maplike drawing showing) an arrangement of parts in a system ♦ *vi/t* **-nn-** make a plan (for) **~ner** *n*
plane¹ *n* **1** aircraft **2** level; standard: *on a friendly plane* **3** *maths* flat surface ♦ *adj maths* completely flat
plane² *n* tool with a sharp blade for making wood smooth ♦ *vt* use a plane on
plane³ *n* broad-leaved tree common in towns
planet *n* large body in space that moves round a star, esp. the sun **~ary** *adj*
planetarium *n* building with stars, planets, etc. displayed on the ceiling
plangent *adj fml* (of a sound) expressing sorrow **~ly** *adv* **-ency** *n*
plank *n* **1** long narrow wooden board **2** main principle of a political party's policy **~ing** *n* (floor) planks
plankton *n* extremely small sea animals and plants
plant *n* **1** living thing with leaves and roots **2** factory or other industrial building **3** industrial machinery **4** *infml* **a** person placed secretly in a group in order to discover facts about them **b** thing hidden on someone to make them seem guilty ♦ *vt* **1** put (plants or seeds) in the ground **2** *infml* hide (illegal goods) on someone to make them seem guilty **3** *infml* put (a person) secretly in a group **4** place firmly or forcefully **~er** *n*
plantain¹ *n* weed with small green flowers
plantain² *n* banana-like vegetable
plantation *n* area where large plants are grown as a business
plaque *n* **1** flat metal or stone plate with writing on it, usu. fixed to a wall **2** film of mucus and bacteria on a tooth
plasma *n* liquid part of blood, containing the cells
plaster *n* **1** mixture of lime, water, sand, etc., which hardens when dry **2** (a thin band of) material that can be stuck to the skin to protect small wounds **3 in plaster** in a plaster cast ♦ *vt* **1** put plaster on (e.g. a wall) **2** cover too thickly **~ed** *adj infml* drunk **~er** *n*
plasterboard *n* board of light material bonded to plaster
plaster cast *n* **1** copy of a statue in plaster of paris **2** case of plaster of paris supporting a broken bone
plaster of paris *n* white powder mixed with water to form a hard substance
plastic *n* light artificial material used for making various things ♦ *adj fml* **1** easily formed into various shapes **2** connected with the art of making models, statues, etc. **~ity** *n*
plastic bullet *n* piece of plastic fired from a gun to disperse crowds
plastic explosive *n* soft mouldable explosive
Plasticine *n tdmk for* coloured claylike substance played with by children
plastic surgery *n* repair of body parts with pieces of skin or bone taken from other parts
plate *n* **1** flat dish from which food is eaten or served **2** flat, thin, usu. large piece of something hard **3** metal covered with gold or silver **4** picture in a book, usu. coloured **5 on a plate** with too little effort **6 on one's plate** to deal with ♦ *vt* cover (a metal article) thinly with gold, silver, or tin
plateau *n* **-eaus** *or* **-eaux 1** large area of level high land **2** steady unchanging level, period, or condition
plate glass *n* clear glass in large thick sheets
platelayer *n* workman who builds or repairs railway tracks
platelet *n* small particle in blood that thickens it to stop bleeding

platform *n* **1** raised area beside the track at a railway station **2** raised floor for speakers or performers **3** policy of a political party, esp. as stated before an election

platinum *n* very valuable greyish-white metal

platinum blonde *n* woman with silvery-blond hair

platitude *n* statement that is true but not new or interesting

platonic *adj* (of friendship, esp. between a man and woman) not sexual

platoon *n* small group of soldiers

platter *n* **1** *AmE* dish **2** large flat esp. wooden dish

platypus *n* small Australian animal that has a beak and lays eggs

plaudits *pl n* show of pleased approval

plausible *adj* seeming true; believable **–bly** *adv*

play *n* **1** activity for fun, esp. by children **2** story written to be acted **3** action in a sport **4** action; effect: *bring all one's experience into play* ♦ *v* **1** *vi* amuse oneself with a game, toys, etc. **2** *vi/t* produce sounds or music (from) **3** *vi/t* take part in (a sport or game) **4** *vi/t* perform (in) **5** *vt* plan and carry out: *play a trick* **6** pretend to be: *playing the fool* **7** *vt* strike and send (a ball) **8** *vt* place (a playing card) face upwards on the table **9** *vt* aim; direct: *They played their hoses on the blaze.* **10** *vi* move lightly and irregularly **11 play a part in** have an influence on **12 play ball** *infml* cooperate **13 play for time** delay in order to gain time **14 play into someone's hands** behave in a way that gives someone an advantage **15 play it by ear** act according to changing conditions, rather than making fixed plans in advance **16 play (it) safe** act so as to avoid trouble **play along** *phr vi* pretend to agree, esp. to avoid trouble **play at** *phr vt* do in a way that is not serious **play back** *phr vt* listen to or look at (something just recorded) **play down** *phr vt* cause to seem less important **play off** *phr v* **1** *vt* set (people or things) in opposition, esp. for one's own advantage **2** *vi* play another match in order to decide who wins **play on** *phr vt* try to use or encourage (others' feelings) for one's own advantage **play up** *phr v* **1** *vi/t* cause trouble or suffering (to) **2** *vt* give special importance to **play up to** *phr vt* act so as to win the favour of **play with** *phr vt* **1** consider (an idea) not very seriously **2 to play with** that one can use; available **~er** *n* person playing a sport or a musical instrument

play-act *vi* behave with an unreal show of feeling

playback *n* playing of something just recorded, esp. on television

playboy *n* wealthy (young) man who lives for pleasure

play dough *n* small children's modelling material

playful *adj* **1** full of fun **2** not intended seriously **~ly** *adv* **~ness** *n*

playground *n* piece of ground for children to play on

playgroup *n* informal school for very young children

playhouse *n* **1** theatre **2** small house for children to play in

playing card *n fml* card (1a)

playing field *n* ground marked out for a team game

playmate *n* child's friend who shares in games

play-off *n* second match played to decide who wins

playpen *n* enclosed frame for a baby to play in

plaything *n* **1** toy **2** person treated without consideration

playwright *n* writer of plays

plaza *n* public square or marketplace

plc *abbrev. for:* public limited company

plea *n* **1** urgent or serious request **2** *law* statement by someone in a court saying whether they are guilty or not

plea bargaining *n* practice of agreeing to say in a court of law that one is guilty of a small crime in exchange for not being charged with a greater one

plead *v* **1** *vi* make continual and deeply felt requests **2** *vi/t law* say officially in court that one is (guilty or not guilty) **3** *vt* offer as an excuse

pleasant *adj* pleasing; nice **~ly** *adv*

pleasantry *n fml* politely amusing remark

please *v* **1** *vi/t* make (someone) happy or satisfied **2** *vi* want; like: *Do as you please.* ♦ *interj* (used when asking politely for something) **~d** *adj* happy; satisfied

pleasurable *adj fml* enjoyable **–bly** *adv*

pleasure *n* **1** happy feeling; enjoyment **2** something that gives one pleasure **3** something that is not inconvenient and that one is pleased to do: *'Thank you.' 'My pleasure.'*

pleat *n* flattened narrow fold in cloth ♦ *vt* make pleats in

pleb *n derog* plebeian

plebeian /plɪˈbeeən/ *n, adj* (member) of the lower social classes

plebiscite /ˈplebɪˌsiet/ *n* vote by the people of a country to decide a matter

plectrum *n* small piece of plastic, metal, etc., for plucking the strings of a guitar

pledge *n* **1** solemn promise **2** something valuable left with someone as a sign that one will fulfil an agreement **3** something given as a sign of love ♦ *vt* make a solemn promise of

plenary *adj fml* (of powers or rights) full; limitless

plenipotentiary *n fml* official or representative with full powers

plenitude *n fml* **1** completeness **2** abundance

plenteous *adj lit* plentiful **~ness** *n*

plentiful *adj* in large enough quantities **~ly** *adv*

plenty *pron* as much as or more than is needed

pleonasm *n* (phrase) using more words than are needed **–stic** *adj*

plesiosaur *n* large marine dinosaur

plethora /ˈplethərə/ *n fml* too much

pleurisy *n* inflammation of the inside of the chest

pliable *adj* **1** easily bent **2** able and willing to change; adaptable **3** pliant (1) **–bility** *n*

pliant *adj* **1** (too) easily influenced **2** pliable (1) **–ancy** *n*

pliers *pl n* small tool for holding small things or cutting wire

plight[1] *n* bad or serious condition or situation

plight[2] *v* **plight one's troth** *arch.* make a promise of marriage

plimsoll *n BrE* light shoe with a cloth top

Plimsoll line *n* line on a ship showing the depth to which it can go down in the water when loaded

plinth *n* square block which a statue stands on

plod *vi* **-dd- 1** walk slowly and with effort **2** work steadily, esp. at something dull **~der** *n* slow, steady, not very clever worker

plonk[1] *vt infml* put, esp. heavily or with force

plonk[2] *n infml BrE* cheap wine

plonker *n BrE sl* fool

plop *vi, n* **-pp-** (make or fall with) a sound like something falling smoothly into liquid

plot *n* **1** set of connected events on which a story is based **2** secret plan to do something bad **3** small piece of ground for building or growing things ♦ *v* **-tt- 1** *vi/t* plan together secretly (something bad) **2** *vt* mark (the course of a ship or aircraft) on a map **3** *vt* mark (a line showing facts) on a graph **~ter** *n*

plough, *AmE* **plow** *n* farming tool for breaking up earth and turning it over ♦ *v* **1** *vi/t* break up and turn over (earth) with a plough **2** *vi* go forcefully or roughly **plough back** *phr vt* put (money earned) back into a business

Plough *n* constellation of seven bright stars, seen from the northern hemisphere

ploughman's lunch *n* bread and cheese

ploughshare *n* blade of a plough

plover *n* wading bird with a short beak and compact build

ploy *n* something done to gain an advantage, sometimes deceivingly

pluck *vt* **1** pull the feathers off (a bird to be cooked) **2** pull out or pick up sharply **3** play an instrument by pulling (its strings) **4** *lit* pick (a flower) **pluck up** *phr vt* show (courage) in spite of fear ♦ *n* courage **~y** *adj* brave

plug *n* **1** small usu. round thing for blocking a hole, esp. in a bath, sink, etc. **2** small object for connecting an apparatus with a supply of electricity **3** favourable comment on a product on radio, television, etc., intended to make people want to buy it ♦ *vt* **-gg- 1** block or fill with a plug **2** give a recommendation **plug in** *phr vt* connect to a supply of electricity

plughole *n BrE* hole in a bath, sink, etc., where a plug fits

plum *n* roundish usu. dark red fruit with a hard seed in the middle ♦ *adj* very desirable: *a plum job*

plumage *n* feathers on a bird

plumb *vt* **1** (try to) find the meaning of **2 plumb the depths** reach the lowest point ♦ *adv* exactly

plumber *n* person who fits and repairs water pipes

plumbing *n* **1** all the water pipes and containers in a building **2** work of a plumber

plumb line *n* string with a weight on it, for finding the depth of water or whether something is upright

plume *n* **1** (large or showy) feather **2** rising feathery shape: *a plume of smoke* **~d** *adj*

plummet *vi* fall steeply or suddenly

plummy *adj* **1** full of plums **2** (of a voice) affectedly full and rich **3** plum

plump *adj* pleasantly fat **plump up** *phr vt* make rounded and soft by shaking **~ness** *n*

plump for *phr vt BrE infml* choose

plunder *vi/t* steal or rob in time of war ♦ *n* (goods seized by) plundering **~er** *n*

plunge *vi/t* move suddenly forwards and/or downwards **-ging** *adj* (of the neck of a woman's garment) having a low front or v-neck showing quite a large area of chest ♦ *n* **1** act of plunging **2 take the plunge** at last do something one had delayed **~r** *n* part of a machine that moves up and down

plunk *vi/t infml* play in a twanging or jangling way

pluperfect *n* verb tense that expresses action completed before a particular time, formed in English with *had*

plural *n, adj* (word or form) that expresses more than one

pluralism *n* condition or policy of having several rather than exclusively one **-ist** *adj, n*

plurality *n* **1** being plural **2** pluralism

plus *prep* with the addition of: *3 plus 2 is 5.* ♦ *adj* **1** greater than zero **2** additional and desirable ♦ *n* **1** sign (+) for adding **2** *infml* welcome or favourable addition

plus fours *pl n* trousers gathered at the knee

plush[1] *adj* looking very splendid and expensive

plush[2] *n* cloth with a deep pile

Pluto *n* the planet ninth in order from the sun

plutocrat *n* powerful wealthy person **~ic** *adj*

plutonium *n* substance used in producing atomic power

ply[1] *n* measure of the number of threads in wool, rope, etc., or the number of sheets in plywood

ply[2] *v* **1** *vi* travel regularly for hire or other business **2** *vt* work at (a trade) **ply with** *phr vt* keep giving (esp. food) to

plywood *n* material made of thin sheets of wood stuck together

pm, PM *abbrev. for:* post meridiem; after midday (used after numbers expressing time)

P M *n infml* prime minister

PMT *abbrev. for:* premenstrual tension; irritability, headaches, etc. just before menstruation

pneumatic *adj* **1** worked by air pressure **2** filled with air: *a pneumatic tyre*

pneumatic drill *n* tool driven by compressed air that hammers rapidly and noisily to break e.g. a road surface
pneumoconiosis *n* serious lung disease caused by breathing dust
pneumonia *n* inflammation of the lungs
P.O. *abbrev. for:* **1** post office **2** postal order
poach[1] *vi/t* **1** catch or kill (animals) illegally on someone else's land **2** take (something) unfairly or by deception **~er** *n*
poach[2] *vt* cook in gently boiling water
pocked *adj* pockmarked
pocket *n* **1** small baglike part in or on a garment **2** container for thin things in a case, inside a car door, etc. **3** small separate area or group **4** (supply of) money: *beyond my pocket* **5 in each other's pockets** *infml* (of two people) always together **6 out of pocket** *BrE* having spent money without any good result ♦ *adj* small enough to put into one's pocket ♦ *vt* **1** put into one's pocket **2** take (money) dishonestly
pocketbook *n* small notebook
pocket money *n* money given regularly to a child by its parents
pockmark *n* hollow mark on the skin where a diseased spot has been **~ed** *adj*
pod *n* long narrow seed container of peas and beans
podgy *adj* short and fat
podiatry /poˈdie·ətri/ *n AmE* chiropody **–trist** *n*
podium *n* **-ums** *or* **-dia** raised part for a speaker or performer to stand on
poem *n* piece of writing in patterns of lines and sounds
poesy *n lit* poetry (1, 2)
poet *n* writer of poetry **~ic** *adj* **1** of poetry **2** graceful **~ical** *adj* **1** written as poetry **2** poetic **~ically** *adv*
poetaster *n* inferior poet
poetic justice *n* something suitably bad happening to a wrong-doer
poetic licence *n* poet's freedom to change facts, not to obey the usual rules of grammar, etc.
poet laureate *n* poet appointed to the British royal court, who writes poems on important occasions
poetry *n* **1** art of a poet **2** poems **3** graceful quality
po-faced *adj BrE infml* absurdly solemn, esp. in showing disapproval
pogey *n Can E infml* dole
pogrom *n* planned killing of large numbers of people
poignant /ˈpoynyənt/ *adj* sharply sad **~ly** *adv* **~ancy** *n*
poinsettia *n* plant with red flowerlike leaves
point *n* **1** sharp end **2** particular place or moment: *a weak point in the plan|At that point I left.* **3** unit for recording the score in a game **4** single particular idea or part of an argument or statement **5** main idea, which gives meaning to the whole: *beside the point* **6** purpose; advantage **7** particular quality or ability: *Spelling isn't her strong point.* **8** sign (.) to the left of decimals **9** socket **10 in point of fact** actually **11 make a point of** take particular care to **12 on the point of** just about to **13 to the point of** so as to be almost ♦ *v* **1** *vi* show or draw attention to something by holding out a finger, stick, etc., in its direction **2** *vi/t* aim or be aimed **3** *vt* fill in and make smooth the spaces between (bricks of a wall) with cement **point out** *phr vt* draw attention to **~ed** *adj* **1** having a sharp end **2** directed against a particular person: *a pointed remark* **~edly** *adv* **points** *pl n BrE* short rails for moving a train from one track to another
point-blank *adj, adv* **1** fired from a very close position **2** forceful and direct
pointer *n* **1** stick for pointing at things **2** thin piece that points to numbers on a measuring apparatus **3** piece of helpful advice **4** type of hunting dog
pointillism /ˈpwantiˌliz(ə)m/ *n* painting technique using tiny dots of colour **–ist** *adj, n*
pointless *adj* meaningless; useless **~ly** *adv* **~ness** *n*

point of view *n* particular way of considering something
point-to-point *n* cross-country horse race
poise *n* **1** quiet confidence and self-control **2** well-balanced way of moving ♦ *vt* put lightly in a place where it is hard to be steady **~d** *adj* **1** ready: *poised to attack* **2** showing poise
poison *n* substance that can kill or cause illness ♦ *vt* **1** give poison to or put poison in **2** have a damaging or evil effect on **~ous** *adj*
poison ivy *n* US wild climbing plant that causes a painful rash when touched
poison-pen letter *n* malicious or abusive (anonymous) letter
poison pill *n* tactic to deter a company from taking over another
poke *vi/t* **1** push out sharply **2** push a pointed thing (into) **3 poke fun at** cause (unkind) laughter at **4 poke one's nose into something** enquire into something which does not concern one ♦ *n* act of poking
poker[1] *n* thin metal rod for poking a fire to make it burn better
poker[2] *n* card game
poker face *n* expression that hides someone's thoughts or feelings
pokerwork *n* (art of making) pictures burnt into wood or leather with a hot tool
poky *adj* uncomfortably small and unattractive
polar *adj* of or near the North or South Pole
polar bear *n* large white bear that lives near the North Pole
polarity *n fml* having or developing two opposite qualities
polarize, -ise *vi/t* form into groups based on two directly opposite principles **–ization** *n*
Polaroid *n tdmk* **1** substance that makes sunshine less bright, used in sunglasses **2** camera that produces finished photographs in seconds
Pole *n* Polish person
pole[1] *n* long straight thin stick or post
pole[2] *n* **1** (*often cap.*) point furthest north and south on the Earth **2** either end of a magnet **3** either of the points on a battery where wires are fixed **4** either of two positions that are as far apart as they can be **5 poles apart** widely separated in character, opinion, etc.
poleaxe *vt* cause to fall (as if) by a heavy blow
polecat *n* small fierce animal with an unpleasant smell
polemic /pəˈlemɪk/ *n fml* fierce argument defending or attacking ideas or opinions **~al** *adj*
pole vault *n* jump over a high bar using a long pole
police *pl n* official body for making people obey the law, catching criminals, etc. ♦ *vt* control or keep a watch on (as if) with policemen
policeman *n* **-men** male police officer
police officer *n* member of the police
police state *n* country where people are controlled by (secret) political police
police station *n* local police office
policewoman *n* **–men** female police officer
policy *n* **1** what a government, company, political party, etc., intends to do about a particular matter **2** insurance contract
polio *n* serious infectious nerve disease, esp. of the spine, which often prevents movement
polish *vt* **1** make smooth and shiny by rubbing **2** make as perfect as possible ♦ *n* **1** liquid, paste, etc., for polishing **2** act of polishing **3** fine quality **~ed** *adj* **1** (of a piece of artistic work, a performance, etc.) done with great skill and control **2** polite and graceful **polish off** *phr vt* finish (food, work, etc.) quickly or easily **polish up** *phr vt* improve by practising **~er** *n*
Polish *n, adj* (language) of Poland
politburo *n* **-os** chief Communist decision-making committee
polite *adj* having good manners **~ly** *adv* **~ness** *n*
politic *adj fml* sensible; advantageous

political *adj* **1** of or concerning government and public affairs **2** of (party) politics **3** very interested or active in politics **~ly** *adv*
political asylum *n* official protection given to someone who has left their country because they oppose its government
politician *n* person whose business is politics
politicize, -ise *vt* make political
politicking *n derog* taking part in political activity
politico *n* **-os** or **-oes** *derog* politically influential person
politics *n* **1** the activity of winning and using government power, in competition with other parties **2** art and science of government **3** *pl* political opinions **4** activity within a group by which some members try to gain an advantage: *office politics*
polity *n tech* form of government
polka *n* quick simple dance for people dancing in pairs
polka dot *n* circular spot forming a pattern on fabric
poll *n* **1** attempt to find out the general opinion about something by questioning a number of people chosen randomly **2** election **3** number of votes given ♦ *vt* **1** receive (a stated number of votes) **2** question in a poll
pollard *vt* cut the branches from (a tree)
pollen *n* yellow dust that makes plants produce seeds
pollinate *vt* bring pollen to (a flower) **-ation** *n*
polling station *n* place where votes are cast in an election
pollster *n* person who carries out polls
poll tax *n* tax of a fixed amount per person
pollutant *n* polluting substance, esp. one produced by human activity
pollute *vt* make dangerously impure or unfit for use **-ution** *n* **1** polluting **2** polluting substance
polo *n* game played on horses by hitting a ball with a long-handled mallet
polonaise *n* (music for) a stately dance
polo neck *n* round rolled collar
poltergeist *n* spirit that makes noises and throws things around
poly *n* **polys** *BrE infml* polytechnic
poly- *prefix* many: *polygon*
polyandry *n* having two or more husbands at one time **-drous** *adj*
polyanthus *n* garden primrose with several brightly-coloured flowers on each stem
polyester *n* artificial material used for cloth
polyethylene *n* polythene
polygamy /pəˈlɪgəmi/ *n* having two or more wives at one time **-mist** *n* **-mous** *adj*
polyglot *adj fml* speaking or including many languages
polygon *n* figure with five or more straight sides
polygraph *n* lie detector
polymath *n fml* person who knows a lot about many subjects
polymer *n* simple chemical compound with large molecules
polymorphous *also* **polymorphic** *adj fml or tech* existing in various different forms
polyp *n* **1** very simple small water animal **2** small diseased bodily growth
polyphony *n* music with two or more simultaneous related melodic lines **-nic** *adj*
polystyrene *n* light plastic that keeps heat in
polysyllabic *adj* with many syllables
polytechnic *n* place of higher education giving training in science, industry, etc.
polytheism *n* belief in many gods
polythene *n* strong plastic used for making many common articles
polyunsaturated *adj* (of fat or oil) having chemicals combined in a way that is thought to be good for the health when eaten
polyurethane *n* polymer used to make foams, paints, and varnish
pomade *n* perfumed ointment for the

hair or scalp
pomegranate *n* fruit with small red seeds inside
pommel *n* rounded part at the front of a saddle
pommy *n AustrE sl* English person
pomp *n* grand solemn ceremonial show
pompom *n* small decorative woollen ball
pompous *adj* foolishly solemn and thinking oneself important **~ly** *adv* **~ness**, **-posity** *n*
ponce *n BrE* **1** pimp **2** *derog* man who behaves foolishly, showily, or womanishly **ponce about/around** *phr vi BrE derog* behave foolishly, showily, or womanishly
poncho *n* **-os** cloth worn over the shoulders, with a hole for the head
pond *n* small area of still water
ponder *vi/t* spend time considering
ponderous *adj* **1** heavy, slow, and awkward **2** dull and solemn **~ly** *adv*
pong *vi, n BrE infml* (make) a bad smell **~y** *adj*
pontiff *n* pope
pontificate *vi* give one's opinion as if it were the only right one
pontoon[1] *n* floating hollow container connected with others to support a floating bridge
pontoon[2] *n BrE* card game
pony *n* small horse
ponytail *n* hair tied in a bunch at the back of the head
pooch *n infml* dog
poodle *n* dog with curling hair, often cut in shapes
poof *n BrE derog sl* male homosexual
poofter *n BrE derog sl* poof
pooh *interj* (used when something smells bad)
pooh-pooh *vt* treat as not worth considering
pool[1] *n* **1** small area of water in a hollow place **2** small amount of liquid on a surface **3** swimming pool
pool[2] *n* **1** shared supply of money, goods, workers, etc. **2** American game like snooker ♦ *vt* combine; share
pools *pl n* arrangement (esp. in Britain) for gambling on the results of football matches
poop *n* raised structure above the stern of a ship
poor *adj* **1** having very little money **2** less or worse than usual or than expected: *poor health* **3** unlucky; deserving pity: *poor chap* **~ness** *n* low quality
poorly *adv* not well; badly ♦ *adj infml* ill
poor relation *n* one regarded as the least important among a group of similar ones
pop[1] *vi/t* **-pp-** **1** (cause to) make a small explosive sound **2** come, go, or put quickly **3** **pop the question** *infml* make an offer of marriage **pop up** *phr vi* happen or appear suddenly ♦ *n* **1** small explosive sound **2** sweet fizzy drink
pop[2] *n* modern popular music with a strong beat
pop[3] *n esp. AmE* **1** father **2** (used as a form of address to an old man)
pop[4] *abbrev. for:* population
popadum *n* very thin crisp Indian bread
pop art *n* modern art showing objects from everyday life
popcorn *n* maize seeds heated so that they swell
pope *n* the head of the Roman Catholic Church
pop-eyed *adj* with wide-open eyes
popgun *n* toy gun that shoots e.g. corks
popish *adj derog* Roman Catholic
poplar *n* tall straight thin tree
poplin *n* strong cotton cloth
popper *n* press-stud
poppet *n infml* lovable person or animal
poppy *n* plant with bright flowers, usu. red
poppycock *n* nonsense
Popsicle *n AmE tdmk for* ice lolly
populace *n* all the (ordinary) people of a country
popular *adj* **1** liked by many people **2** common; widespread **3** of the general public: *popular opinion* **~ly** *adv* by most people **~ize**, **~ise** *vt* **~ity** *n*
populate *vt* live in as a population
population *n* (number of) people (or

animals) living in a particular area or country
populist *n* person who claims to support the aims of ordinary people in politics
populous *adj fml* having a large population
porcelain *n* (cups, plates, etc., made from) fine hard thin claylike substance
porch *n* roofed entrance built out from a house or church
porcine /ˈpɔːsaɪn/ **1** of or like pigs **2** obese
porcupine *n* animal with long needle-like hairs on its back
pore *n* small hole in the skin, through which sweat passes
pore over *phr vt* read with close attention
pork *n* meat from pigs
porn *n infml, esp. BrE* pornography
pornography *n derog* books, films, etc. showing or describing sexually exciting scenes **-phic** *adj*
porous *adj* allowing liquid to pass slowly through
porpoise *n* large fishlike sea animal
porridge *n* soft breakfast food of oatmeal
port[1] *n* harbour
port[2] *n* left side of a ship or aircraft
port[3] *n* strong sweet red wine from Portugal
port[4] *n* point for connecting other pieces of equipment to a computer
portable *adj* that can be carried
portals *pl n* grand entrance to a building
portcullis *n* castle gate that can be raised and lowered
portend *vt fml* be a sign of (a future undesirable event)
portent *n fml* sign of a future strange or undesirable event
portentous *adj fml* **1** threatening **2** solemnly self-important
porter *n esp. BrE* **1** person who carries loads, esp. travellers' bags, or goods in a market **2** person in charge of the entrance to a hotel, hospital, etc.
portfolio *n* **1 a** flat case for carrying drawings **b** drawings carried in this **2** collection of business shares owned **3** office and duties of a government minister
porthole *n* window in a ship or aircraft
portico *n* **-oes** *or* **-os** grand pillared entrance to a building
portion *n* **1** part **2** share **3** quantity of food for one person **portion out** *phr vt* share
portly *adj* (of a person) fat
portmanteau *n* **-eaus** *or* **-eaux** large case for carrying clothes
port of call *n* **1** port where a ship stops **2** place one visits
portrait *n* **1** picture of a person **2** lifelike description in words
portray *vt* **1** represent, describe **2** act the part of **~al** *n*
Portuguese *adj* of Portugal ♦ *n* **1** *pl* Portuguese people **2** Portuguese language
Portuguese man-of-war *n* jellyfish with long stinging tentacles
pose *v* **1** *vi* stand or sit in a particular position to be drawn, photographed, etc. **2** *vt* cause (a problem) **3** *vt* ask (a question) ♦ *n* **1** position when posing **2** pretended way of behaving **pose as** *phr vt* pretend to be
poser *n* **1** hard question **2** poseur
poseur *n* person who behaves unnaturally to produce an effect
posh *adj* **1** fashionable and splendid **2** of the upper social classes
posit *vt fml* suggest as being possible
position *n* **1** place where something is or should be **2** way in which something is placed or stands, sits, etc. **3** situation; state: *the company's current financial position* **4** place in a rank or group **5** *fml* job **6** *fml* opinion ♦ *vt* place
positive *adj* **1** leaving no possibility of doubt **2** having no doubt; sure **3** effective; actually helpful **4** more than zero **5** (of electricity) of the type carried by protons **6** complete; real: *a positive delight* **~ly** *adv* **1** in a positive way **2** really; indeed
positive discrimination *n* practice or principle of favouring people who are

often treated unfairly, esp. because of their sex or race

positron *n* particle of matter like an electron but carrying a positive electrical charge

posse /ˈposi/ *n* **1** group of people gathered together to help find a criminal **2** gang

possess *vt* **1** *fml* have; own **2** (of a feeling or idea) seem to control all (someone's) actions **~ed** *adj* wildly mad **~or** *n*

possession *n* **1** state of possessing; ownership **2** something one owns **3** control by an evil spirit

possessive *adj* **1** unwilling to share one's own things **2** (of a word) showing ownership **~ly** *adv* **~ness** *n*

possibility *n* **1** (degree of) likelihood **2** fact of being possible **3** something possible

possible *adj* **1** that can exist, happen, or be done **2** acceptable; suitable ♦ *n* **1** that which can exist, happen, or be done **2** person or thing that might be suitable **-bly** *adv* **1** in accordance with what is possible **2** perhaps

possum *n* small tree-climbing animal from America and Australia

post- *prefix* after: *postwar*

post¹ *n* **1** strong thick upright pole fixed in position **2** finishing place in a race ♦ *vt* **1** put up a notice about **2** report as being: *The ship was posted missing.*

post² *n esp. BrE* **1** official system for carrying letters, parcels, etc. **2** (a single official collection or delivery of) letters, parcels, etc., sent by this means ♦ *vt* **1** send by post **2 keep someone posted** continue to give someone all the latest news about something **~al** *adj* **1** of the post **2** sent by post

post³ *n* **1** job **2** special place of duty, esp. of a soldier **3** military base ♦ *vt* **1** place (soldiers, policemen, etc.) on duty **2** send to a job, esp. abroad

postage *n* charge for carrying a letter, parcel, etc., by post

postage stamp *n fml* stamp

postal order *n* official paper sent by post, to be exchanged for money by the receiver

postbag *n* **1** postman's bag **2** number of letters received

postbox *n* box into which people put letters for posting

postcard *n* card for sending messages by post without an envelope

postcode *n BrE* letters and numbers added to an address to make it more exact for delivering letters

postdate *vt* write a date later than the actual date of writing on (esp. a cheque)

poster *n* large printed notice or picture

poste restante *n BrE* system for collecting letters from a post office, rather than having them delivered

posterior *adj fml* nearer the back ♦ *n* bottom (2)

posterity *n* people or times after one's death

poster paint *n* bright-coloured artist's paint

postgraduate *n, adj* (person doing university studies) after getting a first degree

posthaste *adv fml* very quickly

posthumous /ˈpostyoomәs/ *adj* after death **~ly** *adv*

postilion, postillion *n* person who rides on the near horse of one of the pairs attached to a carriage to guide the horses

postman *n* **-men** person who delivers letters, parcels etc.

postmark *n* official mark on a letter, parcel etc., showing where and when it was posted **postmark** *vt*

postmodern *adj* rejecting modernism (e.g. in architecture) and returning to traditional approaches

postmortem *n* **1** tests to find out why someone died **2** finding out why something failed

postnatal *adj* of or for the time just after a birth

post office *n* place where stamps are sold, letters can be posted, and various sorts of government business are done

postpone *vt* move to a later time **~ment** *n*

postprandial *adj fml* after a meal
postscript *n* remark(s) added at the end of a letter
postulant *n* person preparing to become a monk or nun
postulate *vt fml* accept as true, as a basis for reasoning
posture *n* **1** bodily position **2** manner of behaving or thinking on some occasion ♦ *vi* **1** place oneself in fixed bodily positions, esp. in order to make other people admire one **2** pretend to be something one is not
posy *n* small bunch of flowers
pot *n* **1** round container **2** *sl* marijuana **3 go to pot** *infml* become ruined or worthless ♦ *v* **-tt- 1** *vi/t* shoot, esp. for food or sport **2** *vt* plant in a pot **~ted** *adj* **1** (of meat, fish, etc.) made into a paste **2** (of a book) in a short simple form **pots** *n infml* large amount (of money)
potable *adj* drinkable
potash *n* sort of potassium used in farming and industry
potassium *n* soft silver-white metal common in nature and necessary for life
potato *n* **-oes** common roundish brown or yellowish vegetable that grows underground
potbelly *n infml* fat stomach
potboiler *n* book, picture etc., produced quickly just to earn money
poteen *n* illegally distilled whiskey
potent *adj* powerful **~ly** *adv* **-ency** *n*
potentate *n* powerful ruler
potential *adj* that may become so; not (yet) actual ♦ *n* possibility for developing **~ly** *adv* **~ity** *n*
pothole *n* **1** deep hole going far underground **2** unwanted hole in the road **-holing** *n* sport of climbing down underground potholes
potion *n* liquid mixture intended as a medicine, poison, or magic charm
potluck *n* **take potluck** choose without enough information; take a chance
pot plant *n* plant grown (indoors) in a pot
potpourri /ˌpohpəˈree/ *n* **1** miscellaneous collection **2** mixture of dried flowers and herbs which give off a pleasant frangrance
potshot *n* carelessly aimed shot
potter[1] *n* person who makes pottery
potter[2] *vi* move or act slowly or purposelessly **potter about/around** *phr vi* spend time in activities that demand little effort
potter's wheel *n* revolving disc on which clay is shaped into pots
pottery *n* (pots, dishes, etc., made of) baked clay
potting shed *n* small shed where a gardener works and stores things
potty[1] *adj BrE infml* **1** slightly mad **2** having a strong uncontrolled interest or admiration
potty[2] *n* pot for children to urinate into
pouch *n* **1** small leather bag **2** baglike part of an animal
pouffe *n* large cushion used as a seat
poultice *n* soft wet heated mass placed on the skin to lessen pain
poultry *n* (meat from) farmyard birds such as hens, ducks, etc.
pounce *vi* fly down or jump suddenly to seize **pounce on** *phr vt* seize or accept eagerly
pound[1] *n* **1** standard unit of money, in Britain containing 100 pence **2** measure of weight equal to 0.4536 kilograms
pound[2] *v* **1** *vt* crush **2** *vi/t* strike repeatedly and heavily **3** *vi* move with quick heavy steps
pound[3] *n* place where lost animals are kept until their owners take them back
pour *v* **1** *vi/t* (cause to) flow fast and steadily **2** *vi* rush together in large numbers **3** *vi* (of rain) fall hard **pour out** *phr vt* tell freely and with feeling
pout *vi* push the lips forwards, esp. to show displeasure **pout** *n*
poverty *n* **1** being poor **2** *fml* lack
poverty-stricken *adj* extremely poor
poverty trap *n* earning slightly too much to be able to receive welfare pay-

ments but not enough to live comfortably on
POW *abbrev. for:* prisoner of war
powder *n* **1** very fine dry grains **2** pleasant-smelling substance like this, used on the skin **3** gunpowder ♦ *vt* put powder on **~ed** *adj* produced in the form of powder **~y** *adj*
powder puff *n* soft ball for putting on powder
powder room *n* women's public toilet
power *n* **1** strength **2** force used for driving machines, producing electricity, etc.: *nuclear power* **3** control over others; influence **4** what one can do; (natural) ability: *the power of speech* **5** (legal) right to act **6** person, nation, etc., that has influence or control **7** a large amount (of good) **8 the powers that be** *infml* the unknown people in important positions who make decisions that have an effect on one's life ♦ *vt* supply power to (a machine) ♦ *adj* done to impress people with one's influence or status: *power dressing*
powerboat *n* fast boat for racing
powerful *adj* **1** full of force **2** great in degree: *a powerful smell* **3** having much control or influence **4** having a strong effect: *powerful drugs* **~ly** *adv*
powerless *adj* lacking strength or ability
power of attorney *n* right to act for someone else in business or law
power plant *n* engine supplying power to a factory, aircraft, etc.
power point *n* electrical socket
power-sharing *n* giving of some (government) power to minority groups
power station *n* building where electricity is made
powwow *n* meeting or council of North American Indians
pox *n infml* syphilis
pp *abbrev. for:* pages
PR *n* **1** public relations **2** proportional representation
practicable *adj* that can be done **–bility** *n*
practical *adj* **1** concerned with action or actual conditions, rather than ideas **2** effective or convenient in actual use **3** clever at doing things and dealing with difficulties; sensible **~ly** *adv* **1** usefully; suitably **2** almost **~ity** *n*
practical joke *n* trick played on someone to amuse others
practice, also *AmE* **-ise** *n* **1** regular or repeated doing of something, to gain skill **2** experience gained by this **3** actual doing of something: *put a plan into practice* **4** business of a doctor or lawyer **5** something regularly done **6 in/out of practice** having/not having practised enough
practise, also *AmE* **-ice** *v* **1** *vi/t* do (an action) or perform on (esp. a musical instrument) repeatedly to gain skill **2** *vi/t* do (the work of a doctor, lawyer, etc.) **3** *vt* act in accordance with (a religion) **4** *vt fml* do (habitually) **–tised** *adj* skilled through practice
practitioner *n* person who works in a profession, esp. a doctor
praesidium /priˈsidi·əm/ *n* **-iums** *or* **-ia** presidium
pragmatic *adj* concerned with actual effects rather than general principles **~ally** *adv* **–ism** *n*
prairie *n* wide grassy plain, esp. in North America
praise *vt* **1** speak of with admiration **2** worship ♦ *n* expression of admiration
praiseworthy *adj* deserving praise
praline *n* crisp confection of sugar and nuts
pram *n* small four-wheeled hand-pushed carriage for a baby
prance *vi* **1** (of an animal) jump on the back legs **2** move happily or flamboyantly
prank *n* playful but foolish trick
prat *n BrE sl* fool
prate *vi fml* talk excessively and tiresomely
prattle *vi* talk continually about unimportant things ♦ *n* foolish or unimportant talk
prawn *n* small 10-legged sea creature,

often eaten

pray *vi* **1** speak to God or a god, often silently, often asking for something **2** wish or hope strongly

prayer *n* **1** (form of words used in) a solemn request to God or a god **2** praying

prayer wheel *n* revolving cylinder containing written prayers, used by esp. Tibetan Buddhists

praying mantis *n* large carnivorous insect

pre- *prefix* before: *prewar*

preach *v* **1** *vi/t* make (a religious speech) in public **2** *vt* urge others to accept: *preaching revolution* **3** *vi* offer unwanted moral advice **~er** *n*

preamble *n* something said or written before getting to the main part

prebendary *n* priest who works at a cathedral

precarious *adj* not firm or steady; full of danger **~ly** *adv*

precaution *n* action done to avoid possible trouble **~ary** *adj*

precede *vt* come (just) before **–ceding** *adj* previous

precedence *n* (right to) a particular place before others, esp. because of importance

precedent *n* **1** what has usu. been done before **2** earlier act which shows what may be done now

precept *n fml* guiding rule of behaviour

precinct *n* **1** part of a town limited to the stated use: *a shopping precinct* **2** *AmE* division of a town for election or police purposes **precincts** *pl n* space around a large (old) building, usu. inside walls

preciosity /ˌpres(h)iˈosəti/ *n fml* quality of being unnaturally fine or perfect

precious *adj* **1** of great value **2** *fml* (of words, manners, etc.) unnaturally fine or perfect ♦ *adv* very: *precious few* **~ness** *n*

precipice *n* very steep side of a mountain or cliff

precipitate *vt* **1** *fml* make (an unwanted event) happen sooner **2** *fml* throw down suddenly **3** separate (solid matter) from liquid chemically ♦ *n* precipitated matter ♦ *adj fml* too hasty **~ly** *adv* **–ation** *n fml* **1** precipitating **2** rain, snow, etc. **3** unwise speed

precipitous /priˈsipitəs/ *adj fml* **1** dangerously steep **2** precipitate **~ly** *adv* **~ness** *n*

précis *n* **précis** shortened form of something written or said

precise *adj* **1** exact **2** (too) careful and correct about small details **~ly** *adv* **1** exactly **2** yes, that is correct

precision *n* exactness ♦ *adj* **1** done with exactness **2** giving exact results

preclude *vt fml* prevent

precocious *adj* developing unusually early **~ly** *adv* **~ness**, **-cocity** *n*

precognition *n fml* knowing about things before they happen

preconception *n* opinion formed in advance without (enough) knowledge **–ceived** *adj*

precondition *n* thing that must be agreed to if something is to be done

precursor *n* one that came before and led to a later thing

predate *vt* be earlier in history than

predatory *adj* **1** killing and eating other animals **2** living by attacking and robbing **-ator** *n* predatory animal

predecease *vt law* die before

predecessor *n* one that came before

predestination *n* belief that everything in the world has been decided by God, and that no human effort can change it

predestine *vt* settle in advance, esp. as if by fate or the will of God

predetermine *vt* **1** fix unchangeably from the beginning **2** arrange in advance

predeterminer *n* word (e.g. *all*) that can be used before a determiner

predicament *n* difficult situation

predicate *n* part of a sentence which makes a statement about the subject

predicative *adj* coming after a verb

predict *vt* say in advance (what will happen) **~able** *adj* **1** that can be predicted **2** not doing anything unexpected **~ably** *adv* **~ion** *n* predicting or

something predicted
predilection /preedi'leksh(ə)n/ *n* special liking for something
predispose *vt fml* make (someone) likely to do or have **-position** *n*
predominant *adj* most powerful, noticeable, important, etc. **~ly** *adv* **-ance** *n*
predominate *vi* **1** have the main power or influence **2** be greatest in numbers
preeminent *adj* better than any others **~ly** *adv* **-ence** *n*
preempt *vt* prevent by taking action in advance **~ive** *adj*
preen *vi/t* (of a bird) clean (itself or its feathers) with its beak
prefab *n* prefabricated building
prefabricate *vt* make (the parts of a building, ship, etc.) in advance in a factory and put them together later
preface *n* introduction to a book ♦ *vt* introduce (speech or writing) in the stated way
prefatory /'prefət(ə)ri/ *adj fml* acting as a preface
prefect *n* **1** older pupil who keeps order among younger ones **2** (esp. in France) public official with government or police duties
prefecture *n* governmental area or headquarters of a prefect
prefer *vt* **-rr- 1** like better; choose rather **2** *law* make (a charge) officially **~able** *adj* better, esp. because more suitable **~ably** *adv*
preference *n* **1** liking for one thing rather than another **2** special favour shown to one person, group, etc.
preferential *adj* giving or showing special favour **~ly** *adv*
preferment *n fml* appointment or promotion to a particular job
prefigure *vt* be a sign of (something about to happen)
prefix *n* wordlike part added at the beginning of a word to change its meaning (as in *un*tie) ♦ *vt* **1** add a prefix to **2** add (something) to the beginning (of)
pregnant *adj* **1** having an unborn child or young in the body **2** full of hidden meaning **-ancy** *n*
prehensile *adj* able to hold things
prehistoric *adj* of times before recorded history **~ally** *adv*
prehistory *n* prehistoric times
prejudge *vt* form an opinion about before knowing all the facts
prejudice *n* **1** unfair feeling against something **2** *fml* damage; harm ♦ *vt* **1** cause to have a prejudice **2** weaken; harm
prejudicial *adj fml* harmful
prelate *n* priest of high rank
preliminary *adj* coming before (and preparing for) esp. the main one ♦ *n* preliminary act or arrangement
prelude *n* **1** something that is followed by something larger or more important **2** short piece of music introducing a large musical work
premarital *adj* happening before marriage
premature *adj* happening before the proper time **~ly** *adv*
premeditated *adj* planned in advance **-ation** *n*
premenstrual *adj* happening just before menstruation
premier *n* prime minister ♦ *adj fml* first in importance
premiere, -ère *n* first public performance of a film or play ♦ *vt* give a premiere of (a play or film)
premise *n fml* statement or idea on which reasoning is based
premises *pl n* building and its land, considered as a piece of property
premium *n* **1** money paid for insurance **2** additional charge **3 at a premium** rare or difficult to obtain **4 put a premium on** cause to be an advantage
premium bond *n* British government bond that earns no interest but is entered in a recurring lottery
premonition *n* feeling that something is going to happen
prenatal *adj* antenatal
preoccupation *n* **1** being preoccupied **2** something that takes up all one's attention
preoccupy *vt* fill (someone's) thoughts,

taking attention away from other things
preordain *vt* predestine
prep *n BrE* homework
preparation *n* **1** preparing **2** arrangement for a future event **3** *fml* (chemical) mixture for a certain purpose
preparatory *adj* done to get ready
preparatory school *n* **1** (esp. in Britain) private school for pupils up to the age of 13 **2** (in the US) private school that makes pupils ready for college
prepare *vi/t* **1** get or make ready **2** put (oneself) into a suitable state of mind **~d** *adj* willing: *not prepared to help*
preponderance *n fml* larger number; state of being more
preposition *n* word (e.g. *in* or *by*) used with a noun or pronoun to show its connection with another word **~al** *adj*
prepossessing *adj fml* very pleasing; charming
preposterous *adj* foolishly unreasonable or improbable **~ly** *adv*
preppy *adj AmE infml* typical of (former) students of expensive private schools in the US, esp. in being neat and well-dressed
prequel *n* book, film, etc. describing events previous to those in another
prerequisite *n fml* something needed before something else can happen
prerogative *n* special right belonging to someone
presage /ˈpresij, priˈsayj/ *vt fml* be a warning or sign of (a future event)
Presbyterian *n, adj* (member) of a Protestant church governed by a body of equal-ranking officials
prescient /ˈpresi·ənt/ *adj fml* seeming to know in advance **-ence** *n*
prescribe *vt* **1** order as a medicine or treatment **2** *fml* state (what must be done)
prescription *n* **1** (doctor's written order for) a particular medicine or treatment **2** prescribing
prescriptive *adj* saying how a language ought to be used
presence *n* **1** fact of being present **2** *fml* personal appearance and manner, as having a strong effect on others
presence of mind *n* ability to act quickly, calmly, and wisely when necessary
present[1] *vt* **1** give, esp. ceremonially **2** be the cause of: *That presents no difficulties.* **3** offer for consideration: *to present a report* **4** provide for the public to see in a theatre, cinema, etc. **5** introduce and take part in (a radio or television show) **6** introduce (someone) esp. to someone of higher rank **7 present itself** (of something possible) happen ♦ *n* gift **~er** *n*
present[2] *adj* **1** here/there: *I was not present at the meeting.* **2** existing or being considered now: *my present address* **3** (of a word, tense, etc.) expressing an existing state or action ♦ *n* **1** the present time **2 at present** at this time **3 for the present** now, but not necessarily in the future
presentable *adj* fit to be seen publicly **-bly** *adv*
presentation *n* **1** presenting **2** way something is shown, explained, etc., to others
present-day *adj* existing now; modern
presentiment *n* strange feeling that something (bad) is going to happen
presently *adv* **1** soon **2** *esp. AmE* now
present participle *n* participle that is formed in English by adding *-ing* to the verb
preservation *n* **1** preserving **2** condition after a long time
preservative *n, adj* (substance) used to preserve food
preserve *vt* **1** keep from decaying or being destroyed or lost **2** treat (food) so it can be kept a long time ♦ *n* **1** jam **2** something limited to one person or group
preside *vi* be in charge, esp. at a meeting
presidency *n* office of president
president *n* **1** head of state (and government) in countries that do not have a king or queen **2** head of a business firm, government department, club,

etc. **~ial** *adj*
presidium *n* **-iums** *or* **-ia** ruling political committee, esp. in Communist countries
press *v* **1** *vt* push firmly and steadily **2** *vt* direct weight onto to flatten, shape, get liquid out, etc. **3** *vi* move strongly, esp. in a mass **4** *vt* urge strongly **press for** *phr vt* demand urgently **press on** *phr vi* continue with determination ♦ *n* **1** (writers for) the newspapers **2** treatment given in the newspapers: *The play got a good press.* **3** act of pushing steadily **4** printing machine **5** apparatus for pressing something **6 go to press** (esp. of a newspaper) start being printed **~ed** *adj* not having enough: *pressed for time* **~ing** *adj* urgent
press box *n* place where newspaper reporters sit at sports events
press conference *n* meeting where someone answers reporters' questions
pressgang *vt* force to do something unwillingly
press release *n* prepared statement given out to news services and newspapers
press-stud *n* fastener for clothes, with a knob on one piece fitting a socket on the other
press-up *n* form of exercise where one lies face down and pushes with one's arms
pressure *n* **1** (force produced by) pressing **2** forcible influence; strong persuasion **3** conditions of anxiety in life or work ♦ *vt* pressurize (1)
pressure cooker *n* closed metal pot in which food is cooked quickly in hot steam
pressure group *n* group who work to convince the public and the government of the importance of their concerns
pressurize, -ise *vt* **1** (try to) make (someone) do something by forceful demands **2** control the air pressure inside
prestidigitation *n* conjuring **–ator** *n*
prestige *n* quality of being widely admired, esp. because of being the best or connected with high rank **–tigious** *adj* having or bringing prestige
prestressed *adj* (of concrete) strengthened by incorporating steel cables under tension
presumably *adv* it may reasonably be supposed that
presume *v* **1** *vt* take as true without proof **2** *vi fml* be disrespectful enough; dare
presumption *n* **1** act of supposing **2** *fml* disrespectful behaviour
presumptive *adj law* probable
presumptuous *adj* disrespectful and with too high an opinion of oneself **~ly** *adv*
presuppose *vt* **1** accept as true in advance without proof **2** need according to reason: *A child presupposes a mother.* **–position** *n*
pretence, also *AmE* **-tense** *n* **1** false appearance or reason **2** claim to possess: *little pretence to fairness*
pretend *v* **1** *vi/t* give an appearance of (something untrue), to deceive or as a game **2** *vi* attempt; dare
pretender *n* person who makes a (doubtful or unproved) claim to some high position
pretension *n fml* claim to possess a skill, quality, etc.
pretentious *adj* claiming importance, rank, or artistic value one does not have **~ly** *adv* **~ness** *n*
preterite /ˈpretərit/ *adj* (of a verb tense) expressing the past
preternatural /ˌpreetəˈnachərəl/ *adj fml* beyond what is usual or natural **~ly** *adv*
pretext *n* false reason
pretty *adj* pleasing to look at ♦ *adv* **1** rather; quite **2 pretty penny** rather large amount of money **3 pretty well** almost **–tily** *adv*
pretzel *n* crisp salted biscuit
prevail *vi fml* **1** win **2** exist; be widespread **~ing** *adj* **1** (of wind) that usu. blows **2** common or general (in some place or time) **prevail upon** *phr*

vt fml persuade
prevalent *adj fml* common in a place or at a time **~ly** *adv* **–ence** *n*
prevaricate *vi fml* try to hide the truth **–ation** *n*
prevent *vt* stop (something) happening or (someone) doing something **~ion** *n*
preventive also **preventative** *adj* that prevents esp. illness
preview *n* private showing or short description of film, show, etc., before it is publicly seen ♦ *vt* give a preview of
previous *adj* before this one **~ly** *adv*
prewar *adj* of the period before a war
prey *n* **1** animal hunted and eaten by another **2** such hunting and eating: *birds of prey* **prey on** *phr vt* **1** hunt and eat as prey **2** trouble greatly
price *n* **1** money (to be) paid for something **2 at a price** at a high price **3 not at any price** not at all ♦ *vt* fix the price of
priceless *adj* **1** extremely valuable **2** *infml* very funny
price tag *n* **1** small ticket showing the price of an article **2** a (fixed or stated) price
pricey *adj infml, esp. BrE* expensive
prick *v* **1** *vt* make a small hole in with something sharp-pointed **2** *vi/t* (cause to) feel a light sharp pain on the skin **3 prick up one's ears** start to listen carefully ♦ *n* **1** small sharp pain **2** mark made by pricking **3** *taboo* penis **4** *taboo sl* foolish worthless man
prickle *n* **1** small sharp point on an animal or plant **2** pricking sensation on the skin ♦ *vi/t* prick (2) **–ly** *adj* **1** covered with prickles **2** that gives one a prickling sensation **3** difficult to deal with
prickly heat *n* irritating skin rash caused by tropical conditions
prickly pear *n* (fruit of) a cactus
pride *n* **1** pleasure in what you (or someone connected with you) can do or have done well **2** reasonable self-respect **3** too high an opinion of yourself **4** most valuable one : *the pride of my collection* **5 pride of place** *esp. BrE* highest or best position **pride oneself on** *phr vt* be proud of oneself because of
priest *n* **1** (in the Christian Church, esp. in the Roman Catholic Church) specially trained person who performs religious ceremonies and other religious duties **2** specially trained person in certain non-Christian religions **~hood** *n* **1** position of being a priest **2** all the priests
priestess *n* female non-Christian priest
prig *n* unpleasantly moral person **~gish** *adj*
prim *adj* **-mm-** easily shocked by rude things **~ly** *adv*
primacy *n fml* being first in importance, rank, etc.
prima donna *n* **1** main female opera singer **2** someone who thinks they are very important and often gets excited and angry
primaeval *adj* primeval
prima facie /ˌpriemə ˈfayshi/ *adj, adv law* based on what seems true
primal *adj* belonging to the earliest times
primarily *adv* mainly
primary *adj* **1** chief; main **2** earliest in time or order of development ♦ *n* (esp. in the US) election in which candidates for a political office are chosen
primary colour *n* red, yellow, or blue
primary school *n* **1** *BrE* school for children between five and 11 years old **2** *AmE* elementary school
primate *n* **1** member of the most highly developed group of mammals which includes human beings, monkeys, and related animals **2** archbishop in the Church of England
prime¹ *n* time when someone is at their best ♦ *adj* **1** main **2** best
prime² *vt* **1** put primer on **2** instruct in advance **3** put explosive powder into (a gun)
prime minister *n* chief minister and government leader
prime number *n* number that can only be divided by itself and 1
primer¹ *n* **1** paint put on before the main painting **2** tube containing explosive,

esp. to set off a bomb
primer² *n* simple book for beginners
prime time *n* time when most people are thought to watch television
primeval *adj* very ancient
primitive *adj* **1** of the earliest stage of development **2** roughly made or done **3** old-fashioned and inconvenient **~ly** *adv*
primogeniture /ˌpriemohˈjenichə/ *n* system by which a dead man's property goes to his eldest son
primordial *adj* existing from or at the beginning of time
primrose *n* pale yellow spring flower
primula *n* garden variety of primrose
Primus stove *n tdmk for* small metal cooking apparatus
prince *n* **1** king's son **2** royal ruler of a small country **~ly** *adj* **1** of a prince **2** splendid; generous
Prince Charming *n* ideal suitor
prince consort *n* **princes consort** husband of a queen reigning in her own right
princely *adj* magnificent; lavish
princess *n* **1** king's daughter **2** prince's wife
principal *adj* main ♦ *n* **1** head of a college, school, etc. **2** money lent, on which interest is paid **~ly** *adv*
principal boy *n* chief male character in a pantomime, played by a woman
principality *n* country ruled by a prince
principal parts *pl n* main forms of a verb (e.g. infinitive, past tense, and past participle)
principle *n* **1** general truth or belief: *the principle of free speech* **2** moral rule which guides behaviour **3** high personal standard of right and wrong **4** general rule which governs the way something works or is done **5 in principle** as an idea, if not in fact **6 on principle** for a moral reason
print *n* **1** printed letters, words, etc. **2** mark made on a surface: *a thumbprint* **3** photograph printed on paper **4** picture printed from a metal sheet **5 in/out of print** (of a book) that can still/no longer be obtained ♦ *v* **1** *vi/t* press (letters or pictures) on (esp. paper) with ink- or paint-covered shapes **2** *vt* make (a book, magazine, etc.) by doing this **3** *vt* cause to be included in or produced as a newspaper, magazine etc. **4** *vt* copy (a photograph) from film onto paper **5** *vi/t* write without joining the letters **~able** *adj* suitable for reading by anyone **~er** *n* **1** person who prints books, newspapers, etc. **2** printing machine
printout *n* printed record produced by a computer
prior¹ *adj* **1** earlier **2** more important **3 prior to** before
prior² *n* head of a priory
prioritize, -ise *vt* give (something) priority
priority *n* **1** (right of) being first in position or earlier in time **2** something that needs attention before others
priory *n* (building for) a religious group
prise *vt esp. BrE* prize²
prism *n* transparent three-sided block that breaks up light into different colours
prismatic *adj* **1** of or being a prism **2** brilliantly coloured
prison *n* large building where criminals are kept for punishment
prison camp *n* guarded camp for prisoners of war
prisoner *n* person kept in prison
prisoner of war *n* soldier caught by the enemy in war
prissy *adj infml* annoyingly exact or proper **-ssily** *adv*
pristine *adj fml* fresh and clean
prithee *interj arch.* please
privacy *n* **1** (desirable) state of being away from other people **2** secrecy
private *adj* **1** not (to be) shared with others; secret **2** just for one person or a small group, not everyone **3** not connected with or paid for by government **4** not connected with one's work or rank; unofficial **5** quiet; without lots of people ♦ *n* soldier of the lowest rank **~ly** *adv*
private detective *n* person, not a

policeman, hired to follow people, report on their actions, etc.
private enterprise *n* capitalism
privateer *n* (in former times) (sailor on a) private warship
private eye *n infml* private detective
private parts *pl n* outer sexual organs
private sector *n* those industries and services that are owned and run by private companies, not by the state
privation *n fml* lack of things necessary for life
privatize, -ise *vt* sell (a government-owned industry or organization) into private ownership **-ization** *n*
privet *n* bush often used for hedges
privilege *n* **1** special advantage limited to a particular person or group **2** unfair possession of such advantages because of wealth, social rank, etc. **~d** *adj* having (a) privilege
privy *adj fml* sharing secret knowledge (of) ♦ *arch.* toilet
Privy Council *n* body of important people who advise the British king or queen
prize¹ *n* something awarded for winning, doing well, etc. ♦ *vt* value highly ♦ *adj* **1** that has gained or is worthy of a prize **2** given as a prize
prize² *vt* lift or force with a tool or metal bar
prizefight *n* public boxing match in former times **~er** *n*
pro *n* **pros** *infml* professional
pro- *prefix* in favour of; supporting: *pro-American*
pro-am *n, adj* (competition) including both professionals and amateurs
probability *n* **1** likelihood **2** probable event or result
probable *adj* that has a good chance of happening or being true; likely **-bly** *adv*
probate *n* legal process of declaring someone's will properly made
probation *n* **1** (period of) testing someone's suitability **2** system of not sending law-breakers to prison if they behave well for a time
probation officer *n* person who watches and advises law-breakers on probation
probe *vi/t* search or examine carefully (as if) with a long thin instrument ♦ *n* **1** metal tool for probing **2** spacecraft for searching through space **3** thorough inquiry
probity *n fml* perfect honesty
problem *n* difficulty that needs attention and thought
problematic *adj* full of or causing problems
proboscis /prəˈbosis/ *n* long movable nose of certain animals
procedure *n* **1** set of actions for doing something **2** way a meeting, trial, etc., is (to be) run **-ural** *adj*
proceed *vi fml* **1** begin or continue in a course of action **2** walk or travel in a particular direction
proceedings *pl n* legal action taken against someone
proceeds *pl n* money gained from the sale of something
process *n* **1** set of actions that produce continuation, change, or something new **2** method, esp. for producing goods **3 in the process of** actually doing (the stated thing) at the time ♦ *v* **1** *vt* treat and preserve (food): *processed cheese* **2** *vt* print a photograph from (film) **3** *vt* deal with; examine **4** *vi* walk in a procession
procession *n* line of people or vehicles moving along, esp. ceremonially
processor *n* microprocessor
proclaim *vt* declare publicly and officially
proclamation *n* **1** official public statement **2** proclaiming
proclivity *n fml* strong natural liking or tendency
proconsul *n* governor of a dependent territory, esp. in the ancient Roman empire **~ar** *adj* **~ate, ~ship** *n*
procrastinate *vi fml* delay (annoyingly) **-ation** *n*
procreate *vi fml* produce young **-ation** *n*
procurator-fiscal *n* (in Scotland) local

public prosecutor

procure *v* **1** *vt fml* obtain **2** *vi/t* provide (a woman) for sexual pleasure **~r** *n*

prod *v* **-dd- 1** *vi/t* push with a pointed object **2** *vt* urge sharply **prod** *n*

prodigal *adj fml* **1** carelessly wasteful, esp. of money **2** giving or producing (something) freely and in large amounts **~ity** *n*

prodigious /prəˈdijəs/ *adj* wonderfully large, powerful, etc. **~ly** *adv*

prodigy *n* **1** person with wonderful abilities **2** a wonder in nature

produce *vt* **1** bring into existence; give **2** make (goods for sale) **3** give birth to **4** bring out and show **5** prepare and bring before the public ♦ *n* something produced, esp. on a farm

producer *n* **1** person, company, etc., that produces goods **2** person in charge of the business of putting on a play, film, etc.

product *n* **1** something made or produced **2** result

production *n* **1** producing **2** process of making products **3** amount produced **4** play, film, or broadcast that is produced

production line *n* arrangement of factory workers and machines for producing goods

productive *adj* **1** that produces a lot **2** causing or producing (a result) **~ly** *adv*

productivity *n* rate of producing goods, crops, etc.

prof *n infml* professor

profane *adj* **1** showing disrespect, esp. for holy things **2** (esp. of language) socially shocking **3** *fml* concerned with human life in this world; secular ♦ *vt* treat disrespectfully **~ly** *adv*

profanity *n* profane behaviour or speech

profess *vt fml* **1** declare openly **2** claim, usu. falsely **3** have as one's religion **~ed** *adj* **1** self-declared **2** pretended

profession *n* **1** form of employment, esp. a socially respected one like law or medicine **2** people in a particular profession **3** *fml* open declaration

professional *adj* **1** working in a profession **2** doing for payment what others do for fun **3** showing high standards of work ♦ *n* professional person **~ism** *n* skill or quality of professionals

professor *n* university teacher of highest rank **~ial** *adj*

proffer *vt fml* offer

proficient *adj* very good at doing something **~ly** *adv* **-iency** *n*

profile *n* **1** side view, esp. of someone's head **2** state of being noticed by other people around one: *keep a low profile* **3** short description ♦ *vt* draw or write a profile of

profit *n* **1** money gained **2** advantage gained from some action **profit by/from** *phr vt* gain advantage or learn from

profitability *n* state of being profitable or the degree to which a business is profitable

profitable *adj* producing profit **-bly** *adv*

profiteer *n* person who makes unfairly large profits **profiteer** *vi*

profiterole *n* small usu. cream-filled bun

profit margin *n* difference between production cost and selling price

profit sharing *n* workers sharing the profits of a business

profligate *adj fml* **1** foolishly wasteful **2** shamelessly immoral **-acy** *n*

profound *adj* **1** very strongly felt; deep **2** having thorough knowledge and understanding **~ly** *adv* **-fundity** *n*

profuse *adj* produced in great quantity **~ly** *adv* **-fusion** *n* (too) great amount

progenitor *n* one in the past from which someone or something is descended

progeny *n fml* **1** descendants **2** children

progesterone *n* bodily substance that prepares the uterus for its work

prognathous /progˈnaythəs/ *adj tech* having jaws that stick out

prognosis *n* **-ses 1** doctor's opinion of how an illness will develop **2** description of the future

prognosticate *vt fml* say (what is going

to happen) **–ation** *n*
program *n* **1** set of instructions for making a computer do something **2** *AmE* programme ♦ *vt* **-mm-** or **-m-** **1** supply (a computer) with a program **2** *AmE* programme **~mable** *adj* controllable by means of a computer program **~mer** *n*
programme, *AmE* **-gram** *n* **1** list of performers or things to be performed **2** television or radio show **3** plan for future action ♦ *vt* plan or arrange
progress *n* **1** continual improvement or development **2** forward movement in space **3 in progress** happening or being done ♦ *vi* make progress
progression *n* **1** progressing **2** set of numbers that vary in a particular way
progressive *adj* **1** developing continuously or by stages **2** favouring change or new ideas **3** (of a verb form) showing action that is continuing ♦ *n* person with progressive ideas, esp. about social change **~ly** *adv*
prohibit *vt fml* **1** forbid by law or rule **2** prevent **~ory** *adj* prohibitive
prohibition *n* **1** prohibiting something, esp. the sale of alcohol **2** *fml* order forbidding something
prohibitive *adj* **1** preventing **2** (of prices, expense, etc.) too high **~ly** *adv*
project[1] *n* long piece of planned work
project[2] *v* **1** *vi/t* stick out beyond a surface **2** *vt fml* aim and throw through the air **3** *vt* direct (sound or light) into space or onto a screen **4** *vt* make plans for **5** *vt* judge or calculate using the information one has: *projected sales figures* **6** *vi/t* express (oneself or one's beliefs, ideas, etc.) outwardly, esp. to have a favourable effect on others
projectile *n* object or weapon thrown or fired
projection *n* **1** projecting **2** something that sticks out **3** guess of future possibilities based on known facts
projectionist *n* person who works a projector, esp. in a cinema
projector *n* apparatus for projecting films, slides, etc.
prolapse *vi fml* (of an internal body organ) slip out of its right place
prole *n infml derog* proletarian
proletarian *n, adj* (member) of the proletariat
proletariat *n* class of unskilled wage-earning workers
proliferate *vi* increase rapidly in numbers **–ation** *n*
prolific *adj* producing a lot **~ally** *adv*
prolix *adj fml* using too many words
prologue, *AmE* **-log** *n* **1** introduction to a play, long poem, etc. **2** event that leads up to another, bigger one
prolong *vt* lengthen **~ed** *adj* long
prom *n BrE* **1** promenade (1) **2** promenade concert
promenade *n* **1** wide path along the coast in a holiday town **2** *fml* unhurried walk ♦ *vi* walk slowly up and down
promenade concert *n* (esp. in Britain) concert where some listeners stand
prominent *adj* **1** sticking out **2** noticeable **3** famous **~ly** *adv* **-ence** *n*
promiscuous *adj* **1** not limited to one sexual partner **2** *fml* being of many sorts mixed together **–uity** *n*
promise *n* **1** statement, which one wishes to be believed, of what one will do **2** signs of future success, good results, etc. ♦ *v* **1** *vi/t* make a promise **2** *vt* cause one to expect or hope for **–ising** *adj* showing good potential
Promised Land *n* hoped-for condition which will bring happiness
promissory note *n* written promise to pay a sum of money
promontory /ˈpromənt(ə)ri/ *n* point of land stretching out into the sea
promote *vt* **1** raise to a higher position or rank **2** help to arrange (a business, concert, etc.) **3** advertise **4** *fml* help to bring about **~r** *n* person whose job is to promote events, activities, etc.
promotion *n* **1** raising of rank or position **2** act of furthering the growth or development of something **3** advertising activity
prompt *vt* **1** cause; urge **2** remind (an actor) of forgotten words **prompt, ~er**

n person who prompts actors ♦ *adj* acting or done quickly or at the right time **~ly** *adv* **~ness** *n*

promulgate *vt fml* **1** bring (e.g. a law) into effect by official public declaration **2** spread (e.g. a belief) widely **-ation** *n* **-tor** *n*

prone *adj* **1** likely to suffer the stated undesirable thing **2** lying face downwards

prong *n* **1** pointed part of a fork **2** subdivision **~ed** *adj*

pronominal *adj* of a pronoun

pronoun *n* word used instead of a noun, such as *he* or *it*

pronounce *vt* **1** make the sound of (a letter, word, etc.) **2** *fml* declare officially **~ment** *n* solemn declaration **~d** *adj* very strong or noticeable

pronto *adv infml* without delay

pronunciation *n* way in which a language or word is pronounced

proof *n* **1** way of showing that something is true **2** test or trial **3** test copy of something to be printed **4** standard of strength for certain alcoholic drinks ♦ *adj* having or giving protection

-proof *suffix* **1** *(in adjectives)* treated or made so as not to be harmed by the stated thing: *bulletproof* **2** *(in verbs)* to treat or make in this way

proofread *vi/t* read and put right mistakes in printers' proofs **~er** *n*

prop¹ *n* support for something heavy ♦ *vt* **-pp-** support or keep in a leaning position

prop² *n* small article used on stage

propaganda *n* information spread to influence public opinion **-dize, -dise** *vi/t* distribute propaganda (to) **-dist** *n, adj*

propagate *v* **1** *vi/t* (cause to) increase in number by producing young **2** *vt fml* spread (e.g. ideas) **-ation** *n*

propane *n* inflammable gas used as a fuel

propel *vt* **-ll-** move or push forward

propellant *n* explosive for firing a shell or rocket

propeller *n* two or more blades on a central bar that turns to drive an aircraft or ship

propensity *n fml* natural tendency

proper *adj* **1** right; suitable; correct **2** socially acceptable **3** complete: *a proper fool* **~ly** *adv*

proper noun *n* name of a particular thing or person, spelt with a capital letter

property *n* **1** something owned; possession(s) **2** (area of) land and/or building(s) **3** natural quality or power

prophecy *n* (statement) telling what will happen in the future

prophesy *vi/t* say (what will happen in the future)

prophet *n* **1** person who makes known and explains God's will **2** person who tells about the future **~ic** *adj* **~ically** *adv*

prophylactic /ˌprofiˈlaktik/ *adj fml* for preventing disease ♦ *n* something prophylactic, esp. a condom

propinquity /prəˈpingkwəti/ *n fml* nearness

propitiate /prəˈpishiˌayt/ *vt fml* make (an angry or unfriendly person) more friendly **-ation** *n*

propitious *adj fml* favourable; advantageous **~ly** *adv*

proponent *n fml* person who advises the use of something

proportion *n* **1** relationship between one thing or part and another in size, importance, etc. **2** part of a whole **3** **in/out of proportion** according/not according to real importance ♦ *vt fml* make in or put into suitable proportion **~al** *adj* in correct proportion **proportions** *pl n* size and shape

proportional representation *n* system of voting in elections by which parties are represented in parliament according to the proportion of votes they receive

proposal *n* **1** plan; suggestion **2** offer of marriage

propose *v* **1** *vt* suggest **2** *vt* intend **3** *vi/t* make an offer of (marriage)

proposition *n* **1** statement giving an unproved judgment **2** suggested offer

or arrangement **3** person or situation to be dealt with **4** suggested offer to have sex with someone ♦ *vt infml* make a (esp. sexual) proposition to (someone)
propound *vt fml* put forward (an idea)
proprietary *adj* **1** privately owned **2** of or like an owner
proprietor *n* owner of a business
propriety *n fml* **1** social or moral correctness **2** rightness or reasonableness
propulsion *n* force that propels **–sive** *adj*
pro rata *adv, adj* according to a fair share for each
prorogue /prəˈrohg, ˌproh-/ *vt* end the meetings of (a parliament) for a time **–gation** *n*
prosaic *adj* dull **~ally** *adv*
pros and cons *pl n* reasons for and against
proscenium *n* front arch of a theatre stage
proscribe *vt fml* forbid, esp. by law
proscription *n fml* proscribing
prose *n* ordinary written language (not poetry)
prosecute *vi/t* bring a criminal charge (against) in court **–utor** *n* **–ution** *n* **1** prosecuting **2** group of people prosecuting someone in court **3** *fml* the carrying out of something that needs to be done
proselyte /ˈprosiliet/ *n fml* new member of a religion
proselytize, -ise /ˈprosiliˌtiez/ *vi fml* try to persuade people to become proselytes
prosody *n* arrangement of sounds and rhythms in poetry
prospect *n* **1** reasonable hope of something happening **2** something which is likely soon **3** wide or distant view ♦ *vi* try to find gold, oil, etc. **~or** *n*
prospective *adj* likely to become
prospectus *n* small book advertising a product, college, new business, etc.
prosper *vi* **1** become successful and esp. rich **2** grow well **~ous** *adj* successful and rich **~ity** *n* success and wealth
prostate *n* male bodily organ producing a sperm-carrying liquid
prosthesis *n* artificial body part
prostitute *n* someone who has sex with people for money ♦ *vt fml* use dishonourably for money **–ution** *n*
prostrate *adj* **1** lying face downwards, esp. in worship **2** without any strength or courage ♦ *vt* make prostrate
protagonist *n* **1** main supporter of a new idea **2** someone taking part
protean *adj fml* continually changing
protect *vt* keep safe **~or** *n* **~ion** *n* **1** protecting or being protected **2** something that protects
protectionism *n* helping one's own country's trade by taxing foreign goods
protection racket *n* getting money from shop owners by threatening to damage their property
protective *adj* **1** that protects **2** wishing to protect **~ly** *adv*
protectorate *n* country controlled and protected by another country
protégé *n* person guided and helped by another
protein *n* food substance that builds up the body and keeps it healthy
pro tem *adv* for the present time only
protest *n* **1** strong expression of disapproval, opposition, etc. **2 under protest** unwillingly ♦ *v* **1** *vi* make a protest **2** *vt* declare strongly against opposition **~er** *n*
Protestant *n, adj* (member) of a branch of the Christian church that separated from the Roman Catholic Church in the 16th century
protestation *n fml* **1** solemn declaration **2** protesting
proto- *prefix* first; original: *prototype*
protocol *n* fixed rules of behaviour
proton *n* very small piece of matter that is part of an atom and carries positive electricity
protoplasm *n* substance from which all plants and creatures are formed
prototype *n* first form of a machine, afterwards developed
protozoan *n* minute single-celled animal

protract *vt* cause to last an (unnecessarily) long time **~ion** *n*
protractor *n* instrument for measuring and drawing angles
protrude *vi fml* stick out **-trusion** *n*
protuberance *n fml* swelling; bulge **-ant** *adj*
proud *adj* **1** showing proper and reasonable self-respect **2** having too high an opinion of oneself **3** having or expressing personal pleasure in something connected with oneself: *proud of her new car* **4** splendid; glorious ♦ *adv* **do someone proud** treat someone, esp. a guest, splendidly **~ly** *adv*
prove *v* **1** *vt* show to be true **2** be (later) found to be; turn out to be
proven *adj* tested and shown to be true
provenance *n fml* (place of) origin
provender *n* food for horses or cattle
proverb *n* short well-known wise saying **~ial** *adj* **1** widely known and spoken of **2** of, concerning, or like a proverb
provide *vt* arrange for someone to get; supply **provide for** *phr vt* **1** supply with necessary things **2** (of the law) make possible **~d** *conj* on condition that **-viding** *conj* provided
providence *n* the kindness of fate
provident *adj fml* careful to save for future needs **~ly** *adv*
providential *adj fml* lucky **~ly** *adv*
province *n* **1** main division of a country **2** area of knowledge, activity, etc. **-incial** *adj* **1** of a province **2** narrow or old-fashioned in interest, customs, etc. **provinces** *pl n* parts of a country far from the main city
proving ground *n* **1** place for scientific testing **2** situation where something new is tried out
provision *n* **1** providing **2** preparation against future risks or for future needs **3** condition in an agreement or law **provisions** *pl n* food supplies
provisional *adj* for use now, but likely to be changed **~ly** *adv*
proviso /prəˈviezoh/ *n* **-os** condition made in advance
provocation *n* **1** provoking **2** something annoying
provocative *adj* likely to cause **a** anger **b** sexual interest **~ly** *adv*
provoke *vt* **1** make angry **2** cause (a feeling or action)
provost *n* **1** chief canon in a cathedral **2** chief magistrate in a Scottish town **3** head of a college
provost marshal *n* military police commander
prow *n* front part of a ship
prowess *n fml* great ability or courage
prowl *vi/t* move about quietly and threateningly **prowl** *n*
proximity *n fml* nearness
proxy *n* **1** right to act for another person, esp. as a voter **2** person given this right
prude *n* person easily offended by rude things, esp. connected with sex **prudish** *adj* **-dery** *n*
prudent *adj* sensible and careful **~ly** *adv* **-ence** *n*
prudential *adj* showing or resulting from prudence, esp. in business **~ly** *adv*
prune¹ *n* dried plum
prune² *vt* **1** cut off parts of (a tree or bush) to improve shape and growth **2** remove unwanted parts of
prurient *adj fml* unhealthily interested in sex **-ence** *n*
pruritis *n med* severe itching
prussic acid *n* highly poisonous acid
pry¹ *vi* try to find out about someone's private affairs
pry² *vt esp. AmE* prize²
P.S. *n* note added at the end of a letter
psalm *n* religious song or poem, esp. as in the Bible
psaltery *n* ancient stringed instrument
psephology /seˈfoləji/ *n* study of the way people vote in elections **-gist** *n*
pseud *n BrE infml* person who falsely claims knowledge, social position, etc.
pseudo- *prefix* only pretending to be; false: *pseudo-intellectuals*
pseudonym *n* invented name, esp. of a writer **~ous** *adj*

psittacosis *n* serious bird disease catchable by people
psoriasis *n* skin disease producing scales
psst *interj* (used for quietly gaining someone's attention)
psyche /ˈsieki/ *n fml* human mind or spirit
psychedelic *adj* **1** (of a drug) causing strange and powerful feelings **2** having strong patterns of colour, lines, moving lights, noise, etc.
psychiatry *n* study and treatment of diseases of the mind **–trist** *n* **–tric** *adj*
psychic *adj* **1** having strange powers, such as the ability to see into the future **2** of the mind **3** connected with the spirits of the dead **~ally** *adv*
psycho- *prefix* connected with (illness of) the mind: *psychotherapy*
psychoanalysis *n* way of treating disorders of the mind by finding their causes in the patient's past life **–lyse** also *AmE* **-lyze** *vt* **–analyst** *n*
psychokinesis *n* power to move objects without touching them **–etic** *adj*
psychological *adj* **1** of or connected with the way the mind works **2** *infml* not real; imagined
psychological warfare *n* spreading fear, different political beliefs, etc., among the enemy
psychology *n* study of how the mind works **–gist** *n*
psychopath *n* mad person who may be violent **~ic** *adj*
psychosis *n* **-ses** serious disorder of the mind **–chotic** *n, adj*
psychosomatic *adj* (of an illness) caused by anxiety, not a real disorder of the body
psychotherapy *n* treatment of mind disorders by psychological methods (not drugs, etc.) **–pist** *n*
psych out *phr vt sl, esp. AmE* **1** understand by intuition **2** frighten **psych up** *phr vt sl, esp. AmE* make (esp. oneself) keen and ready
pt *abbrev. for:* **1** part **2** pint(s) **3** point **4** port
PTA *abbrev. for:* parent-teacher association
ptarmigan /ˈtahmigən/ *n* northern game bird that turns white in winter
Pte *abbrev. for:* private (in the army)
pterodactyl *n* extinct flying reptile
PTO *abbrev. for:* please turn over; look at the next page
ptomaine *n* substance formed by bacteria, that causes food poisoning
Pty *AustrE, NZE, & SAfrE abbrev. for:* Proprietary; Ltd
pub *n* building where alcohol may be bought and drunk
pub-crawl *n infml esp. BrE* visit to several pubs
puberty *n* period of change from childhood to the adult state in which one can produce children
pubic *adj* of or near the sexual organs
public *adj* **1** of or for people in general or everyone; not private **2** of the government **3** not secret **4 in the public eye** often seen in public or on television, or mentioned in newspapers ♦ *n* **1** people in general **2 in public** openly **~ly** *adv*
public-address system *n* microphones and loudspeakers for making announcements
publican *n* **1** person who runs a pub **2** tax collector in the ancient Roman empire
publication *n* **1** act of publishing **2** book, magazine, etc.
public bar *n BrE* plainly furnished room in a pub, hotel, etc., where drinks are cheaper than in the saloon bar
public company *n* business company that offers shares in itself for sale on the stock exchange
public convenience *n BrE* public toilet
public house *n fml* pub
publicist *n* person who publicizes something, esp. products
publicity *n* **1** public notice or attention **2** business of publicizing things; advertising
publicize, -ise *vt* bring to public notice
public opinion *n* what most people think

about something
public prosecutor *n* lawyer who prosecutes on behalf of the state
public relations *n* **1** forming of a favourable public opinion of an organization **2** *pl* good relations between an organization and the public
public school *n* British school for older children, not run by the state
public sector *n* those industries and services that are owned and run by the state
public spirit *n* willingness to do what is helpful for everyone **~ed** *adj*
public works *pl n* buildings, roads, etc. constructed by the government for public use
publish *vt* **1** bring out (a book, newspaper, etc.) **2** make known generally **~er** *n*
puce *adj* dark brownish purple
puck *n* hard flat piece of rubber used instead of a ball in ice hockey
pucker *vi/t* tighten into folds
puckish *adj* harmlessly playful
pudding *n* **1** *BrE* sweet dish served at the end of a meal **2** boiled dish with a covering made from flour, fat, etc.
puddle *n* small amount of water, esp. rain, lying in a hollow place in the ground
pudendum *n* **-da** *med* outer sexual organs
pudgy *adj* podgy
pueblo *n* mud or stone house made by N American Indians
puerile *adj fml* childish; silly
puerperal *adj med* of, after, or caused by giving birth
puff[1] *v* **1** *vi* breathe rapidly and with effort **2** *vi/t* send out or come out as little clouds of smoke or steam **puff out/up** *phr vi/t* swell ♦ *n* **1** sudden light rush of air, smoke, etc. **2** hollow piece of light pastry filled with a soft, sweet mixture **3** *infml* piece of writing praising a person or entertainment **~y** *adj* rather swollen **~ed** *adj infml* out of breath
puffball *n* ball-like fungus
puffin *n* seabird with a large brightly coloured beak
puff pastry *n* light air-filled pastry
pug *n* small dog with a broad wrinkled face
pugilist *n fml* boxer **-ism** *n*
pugnacious *adj fml* fond of quarrelling and fighting
puke *vi infml* vomit
pukka *adj* real; genuine
pulchritude /ˈpulkriˌtyoohd/ *n fml* beauty **-dinous** *adj*
pull *v* **1** *vi/t* bring (something) along behind one **2** *vi/t* move (someone or something) towards oneself **3** *vt* take with force: *He had a tooth pulled (out).* **4** *vt* stretch and damage: *pull a muscle* **5** *vi* move in or as a vehicle: *The train pulled out.* **6** *vt* attract **7 pull a face** make an expression with the face to show rude amusement, disagreement, etc. **8 pull a fast one (on)** get the advantage (over) by a trick **9 pull one's punches** not criticize as severely as one might **10 pull someone's leg** make fun of someone playfully **11 pull the wool over someone's eyes** trick someone by hiding the facts **pull off** *phr vt* succeed in doing (something difficult) **pull out** *phr vi/t* (cause to) stop taking part **pull through** *phr vi/t* **1** (cause to) live in spite of illness or wounds **2** (help to) succeed in spite of difficulties **pull together** *phr v* **1** *vi* work together to help a shared effort **2** *vt* control the feelings of (oneself) **pull up** *phr vi* (of a vehicle) stop *n* **1** (act of) pulling **2** rope, handle, etc., for pulling something: *a bellpull* **3** difficult steep climb **4** special (unfair) influence
pullet *n* young hen
pulley *n* apparatus for lifting things with a rope
Pullman *tdmk for* very comfortable railway carriage
pullover *n* sweater pulled on over the head
pullulate /ˈpulyooˌlayt/ *vi fml* swarm with small crawling or writhing things
pulmonary *adj* of the lungs

pulp *n* **1** soft almost liquid mass, esp. of plant material **2** book, magazine, etc., cheaply produced and containing matter of bad quality ♦ *vt* make into pulp

pulpit *n* raised enclosure from which a priest speaks in church

pulsar *n* starlike object that sends out regular radio signals

pulsate *vi* **1** shake very rapidly and regularly **2** pulse **–ation** *n*

pulse¹ *n* **1** regular beating of blood in the body's blood vessels **2** strong regular beat **3** short sound or electrical charge ♦ *vi* move or flow with a strong beat

pulse² *n* (seeds of) beans, peas, etc., used as food

pulverize, -ise *vt* **1** crush to a powder **2** defeat thoroughly

puma *n* **-mas** or **-ma** large fierce American wild cat

pumice *n* very light rough rock

pummel *vt* **-ll-** (*AmE* **-l-**) hit repeatedly

pump¹ *n* machine for forcing liquid or gas into or out of something ♦ **1** *vt* empty or fill with a pump **2** *vt* put in or remove with a pump **3** *vi* **a** work a pump **b** work like a pump: *My heart was pumping fast.* **4** *vt* try to get information from with questions

pump² *n* light shoe for dancing

pumpernickel *n* coarse dark rye bread

pumpkin *n* extremely large round dark yellow vegetable

pun *n* amusing use of a word or phrase with two meanings

punch¹ *vt* **1** hit hard with the fist **2** cut a hole in with a special tool ♦ *n* **1** hard blow with the fist **2** forcefulness **3** tool for cutting holes, or for driving in nails **~y** *adj infml* **1** forceful **2** punch-drunk

punch² *n* mixed sweet fruit drink usu. made with alcohol

punch-drunk *adj* suffering brain damage from blows in boxing

punch line *n* funny part at the end of a joke

punch-up *n BrE infml* fight

punctilio *n* **-os** *fml* small detail of correct behaviour

punctilious *adj fml* very exact about details, esp. of behaviour **~ly** *adv*

punctual *adj* coming, happening, etc., at exactly the right time **~ly** *adv* **~ity** *n*

punctuate *vt* **1** divide into sentences, phrases, etc., with punctuation marks **2** repeatedly break the flow of **–ation** *n* **1** act or system of punctuating **2** punctuation marks

punctuation mark *n* sign used in punctuating, e.g. a full stop or a comma

puncture *n* small hole, esp. in a tyre ♦ *vi/t* (cause to) get a puncture

pundit *n* expert who is often asked to give an opinion

pungent *adj* (of a taste or smell) strong and sharp

punish *vt* **1** cause (someone) to suffer for (a crime or fault) **2** deal roughly with **~ment** *n* **1** punishing **2** way in which someone is punished

punishing *adj* that makes one thoroughly tired and weak

punitive /ˈpyoohnətiv/ *adj* **1** intended as punishment **2** very severe

punk *n* (since the 1970's) young person with strange clothes and often coloured hair who likes loud violent music

punnet *n esp. BrE* small square basket in which fruit is sold

punt¹ *n* long narrow flat-bottomed river boat moved along with a pole

punt² *n* long kick in football **punt** *vt*

punt³ *n* unit of money in Ireland

punter *n esp. BrE* **1** person who bets on horse races **2** *infml* customer

puny *adj* small and weak

pup *n* puppy

pupa *n* **-pas** or **-pae** form of an insect in a covering preparing to become an adult **~l** *adj*

pupate *vi* become a pupa

pupil¹ *n* person being taught

pupil² *n* small round black opening in the middle of the eye

puppet *n* **1** toylike figure of a person or animal that is made to move as if it were alive **2** person or group that is

controlled by someone else: *a puppet government*
puppy *n* young dog
puppy fat *n* temporary fatness in children
puppy love *n* young boy's or girl's short-lived romantic affection
purblind *adj* **1** partly blind **2** lacking insight; obtuse
purchase *vt fml* buy ♦ *n fml* **1** buying **2** something bought **3** firm hold on a surface
purdah *n* system of keeping women out of public view, esp. among Muslims
pure *adj* **1** not mixed with anything else **2** clean **3** free from evil **4** complete; thorough: *by pure chance* **~ly** *adv* wholly; only
puree *n* soft half-liquid mass of food ♦ *vt* make (fruit or vegetables) into a puree
purgative *n* medicine that empties the bowels
purgatory /ˈpuhgət(ə)ri/ *n* **1** (in the Roman Catholic Church) place where the soul of a dead person is made pure and fit to enter heaven **2** situation of great suffering
purge *vt* **1** get rid of (an unwanted person) from (a state, group, etc.) by driving out, killing, etc. **2** make clean and free from (something evil) **3** empty (the bowels) with medicine ♦ *n* act of purging
purify *vt* make pure **–fication** *n*
purist *n* someone who tries to make sure things are always done correctly and not changed, esp. in matters of grammar
puritan *n* **1** person with hard fixed standards of behaviour who thinks pleasure is wrong **2** (*cap.*) member of a former Christian group which wanted to make religion simpler and less ceremonial **~ical** *adj*
purity *n* being pure
purl *n* knitting stitch done backwards ♦ *vi/t* use a purl stitch (on)
purler *n BrE infml* heavy fall
purlieus /ˈpuhlyoohz/ *pl n fml* neighbourhood, vicinity
purloin *vt fml* steal
purple *adj* of a colour that is a mixture of red and blue
purple heart *n infml* amphetamine pill
Purple Heart *n* medal given to US soldiers wounded in battle
purple passage *n* (too) splendid part in the middle of a dull piece of writing
purport *n fml* meaning ♦ *vt* have an intended appearance of being
purpose *n* **1** reason for doing something **2** use; effect; result **3** determined quality; willpower **4 on purpose** intentionally **~ful** *adj* determined **~fully** *adv* intentionally
purpose-built *adj esp. BrE* originally made to be the stated thing
purr *vi* make the low continuous sound of a pleased cat
purse *n* **1** small flat bag for carrying coins **2** amount of money offered, esp. as a prize **3** *AmE* handbag ♦ *vt* draw (esp. the lips) together in little folds
purser *n* ship's officer responsible for money and travellers' arrangements
purse strings *pl n* control of the spending of money
pursuance *n* **in the pursuance of** *fml* doing
pursuant *adj* **pursuant to** *fml* in accordance with
pursue *vt* **1** follow in order to catch **2** *fml* continue steadily with **~r** *n*
pursuit *n* **1** pursuing **2** *fml* activity, esp. for pleasure
purulent /ˈpyooərələnt/ *adj fml* containing pus
purvey *vt fml* supply (food or other goods) **~or** *n*
purview *n fml* limit of one's concern, activity, or knowledge
pus *n* thick yellowish liquid produced in an infected part of the body
push *v* **1** *vi/t* use sudden or steady pressure to move (someone or something) forward, away from oneself, or to a different position **2** *vt* try to force (someone) by continual urging **3** *vt* sell (illegal drugs) **4 be pushing** *infml* be nearly (a stated age) **5 push one's luck**

take a risk **push around** *phr vt* treat roughly and unfairly **push for** *phr vt* demand urgently and forcefully **push off** *phr vi infml* go away ♦ *n* **1** act of pushing **2** large planned attack and advance **3 give/get the push** *infml* dismiss/be dismissed from a job **~ed** *adj* not having enough: *pushed for time* **~er** *n* seller of illegal drugs

push-bike *n BrE infml* bicycle

push-button *n* small button pressed to operate something

pushchair *n BrE* small chair on wheels for a child

pushover *n infml* **1** something very easy to do or win **2** someone easily influenced or deceived

push-start *vt* start (a motor vehicle) by pushing it

pushy *adj* too forceful in getting things done, esp. for one's own advantage **-shily** *adv*

pusillanimous /ˌpyoohsiˈlaniməs/ *adj fml* cowardly **-mity** *n*

pussy[1] also **puss, pussycat** *n* (child's name for) a cat

pussy[2] *n taboo sl* the female sex organ

pussyfoot *vi* act too carefully

pussy willow *n* (tree with) small grey furry flowers

pustule *n med* small raised diseased spot on the skin

put *vt* **put**, *pres. p.* **-tt- 1** move, place, or fix to, on, or in the stated place **2** cause to be: *put something right* **3** express in words **4** submit officially for judgment **5** write down **6 put paid to** *BrE* ruin **put across** *phr vt* cause to be understood **put aside** *phr vt* save (money) **put away** *phr vt* **1** *infml* eat (usu. large quantities of food) **2** place (someone) in prison or a mental hospital **put back** *phr vt* delay **put by** *phr vt* put aside **put down** *phr vt* **1** control; defeat: *put down a rebellion* **2** record in writing **3** kill (an old or sick animal) **4** cause to feel unimportant; humiliate **put down to** *phr vt* state that (something) is caused by **put forward** *phr vt* suggest **put in for** *phr vt* make a formal request for **put off** *phr vt* **1** delay; postpone **2** discourage **3** cause to dislike **put on** *phr vt* **1** increase: *She's put on weight.* **2** provide: *They're putting on another train.* **3** pretend to have (a feeling, quality, etc.) **4** deceive playfully **put onto** *phr vt* give information about **put out** *phr vt* **1** trouble or annoy **2** broadcast or print **3 put oneself out** take trouble **put over** *phr vt* put across **put over on** *phr vt* **put one over on** deceive **put to** *phr vt* **1** ask (a question) of or make (an offer) to **2** suggest to (someone) that **3 be hard put to it to** find it difficult to **put up** *phr vt* **1** put in a public place: *put up a notice* **2** provide food and lodging for **3** make; offer: *He didn't put up much of a fight.* **4** offer for sale **5** supply (money needed) **put up to** *phr vt* give the idea of doing (esp. something bad) **put up with** *phr vt* suffer without complaining

putative *adj fml* generally supposed to be or to become

put-down *n infml* words that make someone feel unimportant or hurt

put-on *n AmE infml* something not intended seriously or sincerely

putrefy *vi fml* decay **-faction** *n*

putrescent *adj fml* decaying

putrid *adj* **1** very decayed and bad-smelling **2** worthless; greatly disliked

putsch *n* sudden attempt to remove a government by force

putt *vi/t* (in golf) hit (the ball) along the ground towards or into the hole **~er** *n* **1** golf club for putting **2** person who putts

putty *n* soft oily paste, esp. for fixing glass to window frames

put-up job *n infml* something dishonestly arranged in advance

put-upon *adj* (of a person) used for someone else's advantage

puzzle *v* **1** *vt* cause (someone) difficulty in the effort to understand **2** *vi* try hard to find the answer ♦ *n* **1** game or toy to exercise the mind **2** something that puzzles one **puzzle out** *phr vt* find the answer to by thinking hard

PVC *n* type of plastic

pygmy *n* **1** (*usu. cap.*) member of an African race of very small people **2** very small person
pyjamas, *esp. AmE* **pajamas** *pl n* soft loose-fitting trousers and short coat worn in bed
pylon *n* tall structure supporting electricity-carrying wires
pyorrhoea *n* inflammation of the gums
pyramid *n* **1** solid figure with three-angled sides that slope up to meet at a point **2** large stone building in this shape, used as the burial place of kings in ancient Egypt
pyramid selling *n* method of selling involving a succession of agents, with the one who actually makes the sale getting the least commission
pyre *n* high mass of wood for burning a dead body
Pyrex *n tdmk for* strong glass used in making cooking containers
pyrography *n* pokerwork
pyromaniac *n* person with an urge to start fires
pyrotechnic *adj* of fireworks **~s** *pl n* a (too) splendid show of skill in words, music, etc.
Pyrrhic victory *n* costly victory
python *n* large tropical snake that crushes the animals it eats

Q

Q, q the 17th letter of the English alphabet
Q.C. *n* (title, while a queen is ruling, for) a senior British barrister
QED there is the proof of my argument
qua *prep fml* thought of only as
quack[1] *vi, n* (make) the sound ducks make
quack[2] *n* **1** person dishonestly claiming to be a doctor **2** *BrE infml* doctor
quad[1] *n BrE* square open space with buildings round it
quad[2] *n* quadruplet
quadrangle *n* **1** quadrilateral **2** *fml* quad [1] **–angular** *adj*
quadrant *n* **1** quarter of a circle **2** instrument for measuring angles
quadraphonic *adj* giving sound from four different places
quadrilateral *n, adj* (flat figure) with four straight sides
quadrille *n* old dance for four couples
quadruped *n* four-legged creature
quadruple *vi/t* multiply by four ♦ *adj, adv* four times as big
quadruplet *n* any of four children born at the same time
quaff *vt fml* drink deeply
quagmire /ˈkwagˌmie·ə, ˈkwog/ *n* soft wet ground
quail[1] *n* **quail** *or* **quails** (meat of) a type of small bird
quail[2] *vi fml* be afraid; tremble
quaint *adj* charmingly old-fashioned **~ly** *adv* **~ness** *n*
quake *vi* shake; tremble
Quaker *n* member of a Christian religious group that opposes violence
qualification *n* **1** something that limits the force of a statement **2** act of qualifying **3** proof that one has passed an examination **qualifications** *pl n* (proof of having) the necessary ability, experience, or knowledge
qualify *v* **1** *vi/t* (cause to) reach a necessary standard **2** *vt* limit the force or meaning of (a statement) **–fied** *adj* **1** having suitable qualifications **2** limited: *qualified approval*
qualitative *adj* of or about quality **~ly** *adv*
quality *n* **1** (high) degree of goodness **2** something typical of a person or thing
qualm *n* uncomfortable feeling of uncertainty
quandary *n* feeling of not knowing what to do
quango *n* **-os** (in Britain) independent body with legal powers, set up by the

government
quantifier *n* (in grammar) word or phrase used with a noun to show quantity, such as *much, few*, and *a lot of*
quantify *vt fml* measure **–fiable** *adj*
quantitative *adj* of or about quantity **~ly** *adv*
quantity *n* **1** the fact of being measurable **2** amount; number
quantum *n* **-ta** (in physics) fixed amount
quantum leap *n* very large and important advance or improvement
quantum theory *n* idea that energy travels in quanta
quarantine *n* period when a sick person or animal is kept away from others so the disease cannot spread ♦ *vt* put in quarantine
quark *n* smallest possible piece of material forming the substances of which atoms are made
quarrel *n* **1** angry argument **2** cause for or point of disagreement ♦ *vi* **-ll-** (*AmE* **-l-**) have an argument **quarrel with** *phr vt* disagree with **~some** *adj* likely to argue
quarry[1] *n* place where stone, sand, etc., are dug out ♦ *vt* dig from a quarry
quarry[2] *n* person or animal being hunted
quart *n* a measure of amount equal to two pints
quarter *n* **1** a 4th part of a whole **2** 15 minutes: *a quarter to ten* **3** three months of the year **4** part of a town **5** person or place from which something comes **6** *fml* giving of life to a defeated enemy ♦ *vt* **1** divide into four parts **2** provide lodgings for **quarters** *pl n* lodgings
quarter day *n* day on which a quarter of the year officially begins
quarterdeck *n* top part of a ship, used only by officers
quarterfinal *n* any of four matches whose winners play in semifinals
quartering *n* division, section, or emblem in a section of a heraldic shield
quarterly *adj, adv* (happening) four times a year ♦ *n* quarterly magazine
quartermaster *n* military officer in charge of supplies
quarterstaff *n* **–staffs** *or* **–staves** long stout pole used as a weapon
quartet *n* (music for) four musicians
quarto *n* large size of paper for books
quartz *n* hard mineral used in making very exact clocks
quasar *n* very bright very distant star-like object
quash *vt* **1** officially refuse to accept **2** put an end to: *quash a rebellion*
quasi- *prefix* seeming to be; almost like
quatercentenary *n* 400 years after a particular event
quatrain *n* four lines of poetry
quaver *vi* (of a voice or music) shake ♦ *n* **1** a shaking in the voice **2** musical note equal in duration to 1/8 semibreve **~y** *adj*
quay *n* place in a harbour where ships tie up and unload
queasy *adj* **1** feeling one is going to be sick **2** uncertain about the rightness of doing something **–sily** *adv* **–siness** *n*
queen *n* **1 a** female ruler **b** king's wife **2** leading female: *a beauty queen* **3** leading female insect in a group **4** *sl* male homosexual **~ly** *adj* like, or suitable for, a queen
queen mother *n* mother of a ruler
Queensberry rules *n* basic rules of boxing
Queen's Counsel *n* Q.C.
queer *adj* **1** strange **2** *infml* slightly ill **3** *infml derog* homosexual ♦ *n infml derog* male homosexual
quell *vt* defeat; crush
quench *vt* **1** satisfy (thirst) by drinking **2** put out (flames)
quern *n* primitive stone corn grinder
querulous /ˈkwer(y)ooləs/ *adj* complaining **~ly** *adv* **~ness** *n*
query *n* question or doubt ♦ *vt* express doubt or uncertainty about
quest *n fml* long search
question *n* **1** sentence or phrase asking for information **2** matter to be settled; problem **3** doubt: *beyond question* **4 in question** being talked about **5 out of the**

question impossible **6 there's no question of** there's no possibility of ♦ *vt* **1** ask (someone) questions **2** have doubts about **~able** *adj* **1** uncertain **2** perhaps not true or honest **~ably** *adv* **~er** *n*

question mark *n* mark (?) written at the end of a question

question master *n* person who asks questions in a quiz game

questionnaire *n* set of questions asked to obtain information

queue *n BrE* line of people, vehicles, etc., waiting to do something in turn ♦ *vi* wait in a queue

queue-jump *vi* join a queue in front of others who were there before you

quibble *vi* argue about small unimportant points **quibble** *n*

quiche *n* flat pastry case filled with eggs, cheese, vegetables, etc.

quick[1] *adj* **1** fast **2** easily showing anger: *a quick temper* ♦ *adv* fast **~ly** *adv* **~en** *vi/t* make or become quicker **~ness** *n*

quick[2] *n* flesh to which fingernails and toenails are joined

quickfire *adj* coming in rapid succession

quickie *n* something made or done in a hurry

quicklime *n* lime[1]

quicksand *n* wet sand which sucks things down

quicksilver *n arch.* mercury ♦ *adj lit* fast (and ever-changing)

quickstep *n* dance with fast steps

quick-witted *adj* swift to understand and act **~ly** *adv* **~ness** *n*

quid *n* **quid** *BrE infml* pound in money

quid pro quo *n* something given in fair exchange

quiescent /kwi'es(ə)nt/ *adj fml* inactive (for the present) **~ly** *adv* **-ence** *n*

quiet *adj* **1** with little noise **2** calm; untroubled: *a quiet life* ♦ *n* **1** quietness **2 on the quiet** secretly **~en** *vi/t* make or become quiet **~ly** *adv* **~ness** *n*

quietism *n* religious mysticism involving peaceful contemplation **-tist** *n*

quietude *n fml* calmness; stillness

quietus *n fml* **1** death **2** removal from activity

quiff *n* hair standing up over the forehead

quill *n* **1** long feather **2** pen made from this **3** sharp prickle on some animals, esp. the porcupine

quilt *n* cloth covering for a bed, filled with feathers, cotton wool, etc. **~ed** *adj* made with cloth containing soft material with stitching across it

quin *n* quintuplet

quince *n* hard apple-like fruit

quinine *n* drug used for treating malaria

quinsy /'kwinzi/ *n* throat infection

quintal *n* a measure of weight equal to 100 kilograms

quintessence *n fml* perfect type or example **-ential** *adj* **-entially** *adv*

quintet *n* (music for) five musicians

quintuplet *n* any of five children born at the same time

quip *n* clever amusing remark ♦ *vi* **-pp-** make a quip

quire *n* 24 sheets of paper

quirk *n* **1** strange happening or accident **2** strange habit or way of behaving **~y** *adj*

quisling *n* traitor

quit *vi/t* **quitted** *or* **quit**, *pres. p.* **-tt-** stop (doing something) and leave **~ter** *n* person who lacks the courage to finish things when he/she meets difficulties

quite *predeterminer, adv* **1** completely; perfectly **2** to some degree; rather **3** *esp. BrE* (used for showing agreement) **4 quite a/an** an unusual: *quite a party*

quits *adj* back on an equal level with someone after an argument, repaying money, etc.

quittance *n* (document proving) release from a debt or obligation

quiver[1] *vi* tremble a little **quiver** *n*

quiver[2] *n* container for arrows

qui vive *n* **on the qui vive** careful to notice; watchful

quixotic /kwik'sotik/ *adj* doing foolishly brave things in order to be helpful

~ally *adv*
quiz *n* **-zz-** game where questions are put ♦ *vt* **-zz-** ask questions of (someone), esp. repeatedly
quizmaster *n esp. AmE* question master
quizzical *adj* (of a smile or look) suggesting a question or secret knowledge **~ly** *adv* **~ity** *n*
quod *n sl* prison
quoit *n* ring to be thrown over a small post in a game
quondam *adj fml* former
quorate *adj* (of a meeting) having a quorum present
quorum *n* number of people who must be present for a meeting to be held
quota *n* amount officially to be produced, received, etc., as one's share
quotation *n* **1** words quoted **2** act of quoting **3** price quoted
quotation mark *n* mark (' or ') showing the start or end of a quotation
quote *v* **1** *vi/t* repeat the words of (a person, book, etc.) in speech or writing **2** *vt* offer as a price for work to be done ♦ *n* **1** *infml* quotation (1, 3) **2 in quotes** in quotation marks
quoth *v past arch.* said
quotidian /kwoˈtidi·ən/ *adj fml* daily, humdrum
quotient /ˈkwohsh(ə)nt/ *n* number got by dividing
Qur'an *n* the Koran
q.v. (used for telling readers to look in another place in the same book to find something out)
qwerty *adj* (of a keyboard with letters) having the standard arrangement of letters

R

R, r the 18th letter of the English alphabet
R *written abbrev. for:* river
rabbet /ˈrabit/ *vt, n* (fix with) a groove cut in a piece of wood
rabbi *n* Jewish priest
rabbinic, rabbinical *adj* of rabbis
rabbit[1] *n* common small long-eared animal, often kept as a pet
rabbit[2] *vi BrE infml* talk continuously and annoyingly
rabbit punch *n* punch to the back of the neck
rabble *n* disordered noisy crowd
rabble-rousing *adj* causing hatred and violence among a crowd of listeners
Rabelaisian *adj* full of jokes about sex and the body that are shocking but harmless
rabid *adj* **1** suffering from rabies **2** (of feelings or opinions) unreasoningly violent **~ly** *adv* **~ness, ~ity** *n*
rabies *n* disease passed on by the bite of an infected animal and causing madness and death
raccoon *n* small North American animal with a black-ringed tail
race[1] *n* competition in speed ♦ *vi/t* **1** compete in a race (against) **2** (cause to) go very fast
race[2] *n* **1** (any of) the main divisions of human beings, each of a different physical type **2** group of people with the same history, language, etc.: *the German race* **3** breed or type of animal or plant
racecourse *n* track round which horses race
racehorse *n* horse bred and trained for racing
raceme *n* stalk with flowers growing up it
race meeting *n* occasion when horse races are held
racetrack *n* track round which horses, runners, cars, etc. race
racial *adj* **1** of a race of people **2** between races of people: *racial tension* **~ly** *adv*
racism *n* **1** belief that one's own race is best **2** dislike or unfair treatment of

other races **racist** *adj, n*

rack[1] *n* **1** frame or shelf with bars, hooks, etc., for holding things **2** instrument of torture for stretching people's bodies **3** bar with teeth, moved along by a wheel with similar teeth ♦ *vt* **1** cause great pain or anxiety to **2 rack one's brains** think very hard

rack[2] *n* **rack and ruin** ruined condition, esp. of a building

rack[3] *n* front ribs of lamb, usu. roasted

racket[1], **racquet** *n* implement with a netlike part for hitting the ball in games like tennis

racket[2] *n* **1** loud noise **2** dishonest business

racketeer *n* someone involved in dishonest business **racketeer** *vi*

rackets *pl n* game played with a ball and rackets on a four-walled court

rack rent *vt, n* (charge) a very high rent

raconteur *n* someone good at telling stories

racoon *n* raccoon

racy *adj* (e.g. of a story) amusing, lively and perhaps dealing with sex **racily** *adv* **raciness** *n*

radar *n* apparatus or method of finding solid objects by receiving and measuring the speed of radio waves seen on a screen

raddled *adj* showing the effects of a life of debauchery

radial *adj* like a wheel ♦ also **radial tyre** *n* car tyre with cords inside the rubber that go across the edge of the wheel rather than along it, so as to give better control

radian *n* angle formed by two lines drawn from the edge of a circle, one radius-length apart, to the centre

radiant *adj* **1** sending out light or heat in all directions **2** (of a person) showing love and happiness **~ly** *adv* **–ance** *n*

radiate *vt* send out (light, heat, etc.)

radiation *n* **1** (act of) radiating something **2** radioactivity

radiator *n* **1** apparatus, esp. of hot-water pipes, for heating a building **2** apparatus that keeps a car's engine cool

radical *adj* **1** (of a change) thorough and complete **2** in favour of complete political change ♦ *n* politically radical person **~ly** *adv*

radii *pl. of* radius

radio *n* **1** sending or receiving sounds through the air by electrical waves **2** apparatus to receive such sounds **3** radio broadcasting industry

radioactivity *n* **1** quality, harmful in large amounts to living things, that some elements have of giving out energy by the breaking up of atoms **2** the energy given out in this way **–tive** *adj*

radio astronomy *n* astronomy using radio telescopes

radiogram *n* **1** picture made by radiography **2** combined radio receiver and record player

radiography *n* taking of photographs made with X-rays, usu. for medical reasons **–pher** *n* person who practises radiography

radiology *n* study and medical use of radioactivity **–gist** *n*

radiotelephone *n* telephone using radio waves rather than wires

radio telescope *n* radio receiver for following the movements of stars and other objects in space

radiotherapy *n* treatment of disease by X-rays **-pist** *n*

radish *n* small plant with a round red root, eaten raw

radium *n* radioactive metal used in the treatment of certain diseases

radius *n* **-dii 1** (length of) a straight line from the centre of a circle to its side **2** stated circular area measured from its centre point: *within a ten-mile radius*

raffia *n* soft string-like substance from leaves of a palm tree, used e.g. to make baskets

raffish *adj* (of a person) happy, wild, and not very respectable **~ly** *adv* **~ness** *n*

raffle *n* way of getting money by selling chances to win prizes ♦ *vt* offer as a raffle prize

raft[1] *n* flat, usu. wooden, floating structure, used esp. as a boat
raft[2] *n esp. AmE* large number or amount
rafter *n* large sloping beam that holds up a roof
rag[1] *n* **1** small piece of old cloth **2** old worn-out garment **3** *infml derog* newspaper
rag[2] *n esp. BrE* amusing public event held by college students to collect money for charity
rag[3] *vt esp. BrE* make fun of
rag[4] *n* (piece of music in) ragtime
raga /ˈrahgə/ *n* (piece of music based on) a traditional Indian melodic pattern
ragamuffin *n* scruffy child
ragbag *n* confused mixture
rage *n* **1** (sudden feeling of) extreme anger **2 all the rage** very fashionable ♦ *vi* **1** be in a rage **2** (of bad weather, pain, etc.) be very violent
ragged *adj* **1** old and torn **2** dressed in old torn clothes **3** rough; uneven **~ly** *adv* **~ness** *n*
raglan *adj* (of an arm of a garment) joined at the neck rather than at the shoulder
ragout /ˈragooh/ *n* thick meat stew
rag-rolling *n* mottled painting of walls using a rag
ragtime *n* popular music of the 1920s, in which the strong notes of the tune come just before the main beats
rag trade *n infml* garment industry
raid *n* **1** quick attack on an enemy position **2** unexpected visit by the police in search of crime ♦ *vi/t* make a raid (on) **~er** *n*
rail[1] *n* **1** fixed bar, esp. to hang things on or for protection **2** line of metal bars which a train runs on **3** railway ♦ *vt* enclose or separate with rails **~ing** *n* rail in a fence
rail[2] *vi fml* curse or complain angrily
rail[3] *n* small wading bird
railhead *n* **1** end of a railway line **2** place where (military) supplies are unloaded from trains
raillery /ˈrayl(ə)ri/ *n* good-humoured teasing
railroad *vt* **1** hurry (someone) unfairly **2** pass (a law) or carry out (a plan) quickly in spite of opposition ♦ *n AmE* railway
railway *n BrE* **1** track for trains **2** system of such tracks
raiment *n arch.* clothing
rain *n* water falling from the clouds ♦ *v* **1** *vi* (of rain) fall **2** *vi/t* (cause to) fall thickly, like rain **~y** *adj* **1** with lots of rain **2 for a rainy day** for a time when money may be needed
rainbow *n* arch of different colours that appears in the sky after rain
rainbow trout *n* large European and North American trout
rain check *n AmE* request to claim later something offered now
raincoat *n* waterproof overcoat
rainfall *n* amount of rain that falls in a certain time
rain forest *n* wet tropical forest
rain gauge *n* instrument for measuring rainfall
raise *vt* **1** lift **2** make higher in amount, size, etc. **3** collect together: *raise an army* **4** produce and look after (children, animals, or crops) **5** mention or introduce (a subject) for consideration **6** bring into being: *raise doubts* **7** bring to an end (something that controls or forbids): *raise a siege* **8 raise Cain/hell/the roof** *infml* become very angry ♦ *n AmE* wage increase
raisin *n* dried grape
raison d'etre *n* reason for existing
raj *n* British rule in India
rajah, raja *n* (title of) Indian ruler
rake[1] *n* gardening tool with a row of points at the end of a long handle ♦ *vt* **1** gather, loosen, or level with a rake **2** examine or shoot in a continuous sweeping movement **rake in** *phr vt infml* earn or gain a lot of (money) **rake up** *phr vt* **1** produce with difficulty by searching **2** remember and talk about (something that should be forgotten)

rake[2] *n* inclination from the vertical or horizontal **~d** *adj* (steeply) sloping

rake[3] *n* man who leads a wild life with regard to drink and women

rake-off *n infml* usu. dishonest share of profits

rakish *adj* wild and informal **~ly** *adv* **~ness** *n*

rallentando *n* **-os** gradual decrease in musical speed

rally *n* **1** large esp. political public meeting **2** motor race over public roads **3** long exchange of hits in tennis ♦ *v* **1** *vi/t* come or bring together (again) for a shared purpose **2** *vi* recover **rally round** *phr vi* help in time of trouble

ram *n* **1** adult male sheep that can be the father of young **2** any machine that repeatedly drops or pushes a weight onto or into something ♦ *vt* **-mm- 1** run into (something) very hard **2** force into place with heavy pressure

RAM *n* Random-Access Memory; computer memory holding information that is needed by the computer for a limited period, and can be searched in any order one likes

Ramadan *n* month of Muslim fasting

ramble *n* (long) country walk for pleasure ♦ *vi* **1** go on a ramble **2** talk or write in a disordered wandering way **-bler** *n* **-bling** *adj* **1** (of speech or writing) disordered and wandering **2** (of a street, house, etc.) of irregular shape; winding **3** (of a plant) growing loosely in all directions

rambunctious *adj AmE* boisterous **~ly** *adv* **~ness** *n*

rambutan /ram'boohtn/ *n* spiny red tropical fruit

ramekin /'ram(i)kin/ *n* small dish for baking in

ramification *n* **1** branch of a system with many parts **2** any of the results that may follow from an action or decision

ramify *vi/t* (cause to) separate into branches or parts

ramp *n* artificial slope connecting two levels

rampage *vi* rush about wildly or angrily ♦ *n* **on the rampage** rampaging

rampant *adj* (of crime, disease, etc.) widespread and uncontrollable **~ly** *adv* **-ancy** *n*

rampart *n* wide bank or wall protecting a fort or city

ramrod *n* stick for pushing ammunition into or cleaning a gun

ramshackle *adj* (of a building or vehicle) falling to pieces

ran *past t. of* run

ranch *n* large American farm where animals are raised

rancid *adj* (of butter, cream, etc.) unpleasant because not fresh **~ness, ~ity** *n*

rancour, *AmE* **-cor** *n fml* bitter unforgiving hatred **-orous** *adj*

rand *n* **rand** money unit of S Africa

R and B *n* rhythm and blues; mixture of blues and more lively black American music

R and D *n* research and development; part of a business concerned with studying new ideas, planning new products, etc.

random *adj* without any fixed plan ♦ *n* **at random** in a random way **~ly** *adv* **~ness** *n*

randy *adj infml, esp. BrE* full of sexual desire **-iness** *n*

ranee, rani *n* (title of) **a** a female Indian ruler **b** the wife of a rajah

rang *past t. of* ring

range *n* **1** distance over which something has an effect or limits between which it varies **2** area where shooting is practised or missiles are tested **3** connected line of mountains or hills **4** (in N America) stretch of grassy land where cattle feed **5** set of different objects of the same kind, esp. for sale **6** (formerly) iron fireplace and stove set into a chimney in a kitchen ♦ *v* **1** *vi* vary between limits **2** *vi* wander freely **3** *vt* put in position

range finder *n* instrument for indicating or finding the distance between a gun or camera and the thing it is aimed at

ranger *n* forest or park guard

rangy *adj* tall and thin

rani *n* ranee

rank[1] *n* **1** position in the army, navy, etc. **2** (high) social position **3** line of people or things **4 keep/break rank(s)** (of soldiers) stay in line/fail to stay in line ♦ *v* **1** *vi/t* be or put in a certain class **2** *vt* arrange in regular order **ranks** *pl n* ordinary soldiers below the rank of sergeant

rank[2] *adj* **1** (of a plant) too thick and widespread **2** (of smell or taste) very strong and unpleasant **3** (of something bad) complete

rank and file *n* ordinary people in an organization, not the leaders

rankle *vi* continue to be remembered with bitterness and anger

ransack *vt* **1** search thoroughly and roughly **2** search and rob

ransom *n* money paid to free a prisoner ♦ *vt* free by paying a ransom

rant *vi* talk wildly and loudly

rap[1] *n* **1** quick light blow **2 take the rap (for)** *infml* receive the punishment (for someone else's crime) ♦ *v* **-pp- 1** *vi/t* strike quickly and lightly **2** *vt* say sharply and suddenly

rap[2] *vi* **-pp-** *sl, esp. AmE* **1** talk **2** speak the words of a song to a musical accompaniment with a steady beat

rapacious /rəˈpayshəs/ *adj fml* taking all one can, esp. by force **~ly** *adv* **~ness, -city** *n*

rape[1] *vt* have sex with (someone) against their will ♦ *n* **1** act of raping **2** spoiling **rapist** *n*

rape[2] *n* plant grown for the oil produced from its seeds

rapid *adj* fast **~ly** *adv* **~ity** *n*

rapid-fire *adj* (of questions, comments, etc.) coming quickly one after the other

rapids *pl n* fast-flowing rocky part of a river

rapier *n* long thin sharp sword

rapine *n lit* pillaging

rapport /raˈpaw/ *n* close agreement and understanding

rapporteur *n* person who prepares and presents reports

rapprochement /raˈproshmonh/ *n* reestablishment of good relations

rapscallion *n* rascal

rapt *adj* giving one's whole mind; deeply concentrated **~ly** *adv* **~ness** *n*

rapture *n fml* great joy and delight **–turous** *adj* **–turously** *adv*

rare[1] *adj* uncommon **~ly** *adv* not often **~ness** *n*

rare[2] *adj* (of meat) lightly cooked

rare earth *n* any of a group of rare metallic elements

rarefied /ˈreərified/ *adj* **1** (of air in high places) with less oxygen than usual **2** very high or grand

raring *adj* very eager

rarity *n* **1** quality of being uncommon **2** something uncommon

rascal *n* **1** misbehaving child **2** dishonest person

rash[1] *adj* without thinking enough of the (possibly bad) results **~ly** *adv* **~ness** *n*

rash[2] *n* **1** red spots on the skin, caused by illness **2** sudden large number

rasher *n* thin piece of bacon

rasp *vt* **1** rub with something rough **2** say in a rough voice ♦ *n* **1** tool for smoothing metal, wood, etc. **2** rasping sound **~ing** *adj* (of a sound) unpleasantly rough

raspberry *n* **1** red berry, often eaten **2** rude sound made by putting one's tongue out and blowing

Rastafarian also **Rasta** *n* follower of a religion from Jamaica **~ism** *n*

raster *n* pattern of lines from which a television picture is formed

rat *n* **1** animal like a large mouse **2** worthless disloyal person ♦ *vi* **-tt-** act disloyally **~ty** *adj BrE sl* bad-tempered

ratbag *n BrE and AustrE sl* nasty or worthless person

ratchet *n* toothed wheel or bar that allows a part of a machine to move past it in one direction only

rate *n* **1** amount measured in relation to another **2** payment fixed according to a

standard scale **3** of the (numbered) quality: *a first-rate performer* **4 at any rate** in any case **rates** *pl n* local tax paid in Britain by owners of buildings ♦ *vt* **1** have the stated opinion about **2** deserve **3** *infml* have a good opinion of
rateable value *n* amount used for calculating the rates to be charged on a building
rate-cap *vt* **-pp-** *BrE* (of a central government) limit the amount of rates to be charged by (a local council)
rather *predeterminer, adv* **1** to some degree **2** more willingly: *I'd rather have tea.* **3** more exactly
ratify *vt* approve (a formal agreement) and make it official **–fication** *n*
rating *n* British sailor who is not an officer **ratings** *pl n* list of the positions of popularity given to television shows
ratio *n* **-os** way one amount relates to another
ratiocination *n fml* exact and careful reasoning
ration *n* amount of something allowed to one person for a period ♦ *vt* **1** limit (someone) to a fixed ration **2** limit and control (supplies) **rations** *pl n* supplies of food
rational *adj* **1** (of ideas and behaviour) sensible **2** (of a person) able to reason **~ly** *adv* **~ ity** *n*
rationale *n* reasons and principles on which a practice is based
rationalist *adj, n* (typical of) someone who relies on reason rather than religious faith, feelings, or immediate impressions **~ic** *adj* **~ism** *n*
rationalize, -ise *vi/t* **1** give or claim a rational explanation for (esp. strange behaviour) **2** *esp. BrE* make (a system) more modern and sensible **–ization** *n*
rat race *n* endless competition for success in business
rattan *n* stem of a palm tree, used for canes and wickerwork
rattle *v* **1** *vi/t* (cause to) make continuous quick hard noises **2** *vt* make anxious or afraid **rattle off** *phr vt* repeat quickly and easily from memory **rattle on/away** *phr vi* talk quickly and continuously **rattle through** *phr vt* perform quickly ♦ *n* **1** toy or other instrument that rattles **2** rattling noise
rattlesnake *n* poisonous American snake that rattles its tail
rattletrap *n* noisy old car
rat trap *n AmE* dirty old building that is in very bad condition
raucous *adj* unpleasantly loud and rough **~ly** *adv* **~ness** *n*
raunchy *adj infml* sexy **–ily** *adv* **–iness** *n*
ravage *vt* **1** ruin and destroy **2** rob (an area) violently **ravages** *pl n* destroying effects
rave *vi* **1** talk wildly as if mad **2** talk with extreme admiration ♦ *adj* full of enthusiastic praise **raving** *adj, adv* wildly (mad)
ravel *vt* **-ll-** (*AmE* **-l-**) unravel, disentangle
raven *n* large black bird of the crow family
ravening *adj* predatory
ravenous *adj* very hungry **~ly** *adv*
raver *n infml* modern person who leads an exciting life with sexual and social freedom
rave-up *n infml, esp. BrE* wild party
ravine *n* deep narrow steep-sided valley
ravioli *n* small filled pasta cases
ravish *vt fml* **1** *lit* rape[1] **2** fill with delight **~ing** *adj* very beautiful
raw *adj* **1** not cooked **2** not yet treated for use **3** not yet trained or experienced **4** (of skin) painful; sore **5** (of weather) cold and wet **~ness** *n*
raw-boned *adj* large but without much flesh or muscle
raw deal *n* unfair treatment
rawhide *n* untanned leather
Rawlplug *n tdmk for* small piece of hollow plastic or wood put into a hole to make a tight fit for a screw
ray¹ *n* narrow beam of light or other force
ray² *n* flat-bodied sea fish
rayon *n* silklike material made from plant substances

raze *vt fml* flatten (buildings, cities, etc.)

razor *n* sharp instrument for removing hair, esp. from a man's face

razzle *n* **on the razzle** *infml* having noisy fun

razzmatazz *n infml* noisy showy activity

RC *abbrev. for:* Roman Catholic

Rd *written abbrev. for:* Road

re *prep fml* on the subject of; with regard to

re- *prefix* again

-'re *short for:* are: *We're ready.*

reach *v* **1** *vt* arrive at **2** *vi* stretch out an arm or hand for some purpose esp. in order to touch or get (something) **3** *vi/t* stretch (as far as): *The garden reaches down to the lake.* **4** *vt* get a message to ♦ *n* **1** distance one can reach **2** part of a river

react *vi* **1** act or behave as a result **2** change when mixed with another substance

reaction *n* **1** (way of) reacting **2** change back to former condition **3** quality of being reactionary

reactionary *n, adj* (person) strongly opposed to change

reactive *adj* **1** liable to react chemically **2** happening as a reaction

reactor *n* large machine that produces energy from atoms

read *v* **read 1** *vi/t* look at and understand (something printed or written) **2** *vi/t* say (written words) to others **3** *vt* (of a measuring instrument) show **4** *vt* study at university **5 read between the lines** find hidden meanings **6 read the riot act** warn (esp. a child) to behave well **7 take something as read** accept something as true without any need to consider it further **~able** *adj* interesting or easy to read

reader *n* **1** someone who reads **2** British university teacher of high rank **3** schoolbook for beginners **~ship** *n* number or type of readers

reading *n* **1** act or practice of reading **2** opinion about the meaning of something **3** figure shown by a measuring instrument **4** (in Parliament) one of the three official occasions on which a proposed new law is read and considered

readout *n* information produced from a computer in readable form

ready *adj* **1** prepared and fit for use **2** willing **3** (of thoughts or their expressions) quick: *a ready wit* ♦ *adv* in advance ♦ *n* **at the ready** ready (1) **–ily** *adv* **1** willingly **2** easily **–iness** *n*

ready-made *adj* prepared in advance

ready money *n* coins and notes that can be paid at once

ready-reckoner *n BrE* arithmetical table to help in calculating

reafforest *vt* plant again with trees **~ation** *n*

reagent /ri'ayj(ə)nt/ *n* chemical that shows the presence of a particular substance

real *adj* **1** actually existing **2** complete: *a real idiot* ♦ *adv AmE* very **~ly** *adv* **1** in fact; truly **2** very **3** (shows interest, doubt, or displeasure)

real estate *n esp. AmE* houses to be bought

realign *vt* reorganize, esp. in a new grouping **~ment** *n*

realism *n* **1** accepting the way things really are in life **2** (in art and literature) showing things as they really are **–list** *n* **–listic** *adj* **–listically** *adv*

reality *n* **1** real existence **2** something or everything real **3 in reality** in actual fact

realize, -ise *v* **1** *vi/t* (come to) have full knowledge and understanding (of) **2** *vt* make (a purpose, fear, etc.) real **3** *vt* be sold for **–lization** *n*

realm *n* **1** *fml* kingdom **2** area of activity; world

realpolitik /ray'ahlpoliteek/ *n* realistic policy for advancing a country's own interests

real tennis *n* original form of tennis

real-time *adj* of or being very quick information handling by a computer

realtor *n AmE* estate agent
ream[1] *n* 480 sheets of paper **reams** *pl n* a lot of writing
ream[2] *vt* enlarge (a hole) with a cutting tool **~er** *n*
reap **1** *vi/t* cut and gather (a crop of grain) **2** *vt* gain (a resulting reward) **~er** *n*
rear[1] *n, adj* **1** back (part) **2 bring up the rear** be last
rear[2] *v* **1** *vt* care for until fully grown **2** *vi* rise upright on the back legs **3** *vt* raise (the head)
rear admiral *n* officer below an admiral in rank
rearguard *n* soldiers protecting the rear of an army
rearguard action *n* fight by the rearguard of an army being driven back by a victorious enemy
rearm *vi/t* arm (oneself or others) again, esp. with better weapons
rearmament *n* providing a nation with weapons again, or with new weapons
rearward *adj, n* (in or towards) the rear **rearwards**, **–ward** *adv*
reason *n* **1** why something is or was done; cause **2** power to think, understand, and form opinions **3** sanity **4** good sense **5 within reason** not beyond sensible limits ♦ *v* **1** *vi* use one's powers of reason **2** *vt* give as an opinion based on thought and understanding **reason with** *phr vt* try to persuade by fair argument **~ing** *n* steps in thinking about or understanding something
reasonable *adj* **1** showing fairness or good sense **2** quite cheap **–bly** *adv* **1** sensibly **2** quite
reassure *vt* comfort and make free from worry **–surance** *n*
rebarbative *adj fml* unattractive
rebate *n* official return of part of a payment
rebel *n* person who rebels ♦ *vi* **-ll-** oppose or fight against those in control
rebellion *n* (act of) rebelling **–ious** *adj* **–iously** *adv* **–iousness** *n*
rebirth *n fml* renewal of life; change of spirit
reborn *adj fml* as if born again
rebound *vi* bounce back after hitting something **rebound on** *phr vt* (of a bad action) harm (the doer) ♦ *n* **on the rebound: a** while rebounding **b** while in an unsettled state of mind as a result of failure in a relationship
rebuff *n* rough or cruel answer or refusal **rebuff** *vt*
rebuke *vt fml* speak to angrily and blamingly **rebuke** *n*
rebus *n* puzzle in which pictures or symbols suggest the sounds of a word or words
rebut *vt fml* prove the falseness of **~tal** *n*
recalcitrant *adj fml* refusing to obey **–ance** *n*
recall *vt* **1** remember **2** send for or take back ♦ *n* **1** ability to remember **2** call to return
recant *vi/t fml* say publicly that one no longer holds (a religious or political opinion) **~ation** *n*
recap *vi/t* **-pp-** repeat (the chief points of something said) **recap** *n*
recapitulate *vi/t fml* recap **–ation** *n*
recapture *vt* **1** capture (an escapee) **2** experience again
recast *vt* do again in a different form
recce /ˈreki/ *n infml* reconnaissance
recede *vi* move back or away
receipt *n* **1** written statement that one has received money **2** *fml* receiving **receipts** *pl n* money received from a business
receive *vt* **1** get; be given **2** accept as a visitor or member **3** turn (radio waves) into sound or pictures **~d** *adj* generally accepted **~r** *n* **1** part of a telephone that is held to the ear **2** radio or television set **3** official who looks after the affairs of a bankrupt **4** person who buys and sells stolen property
receiving end *n* position of being a victim
recension *n* revision or version of a text
recent *adj* that happened or started only a short time ago **~ly** *adv* not long ago

receptacle *n fml* container
reception *n* **1** welcome **2** large formal party **3** place where visitors to a hotel or other large building are welcomed **4** quality of radio or television signals received **~ist** *n* person who welcomes and deals with visitors to a hotel, shop, etc.
reception room *n* **1** waiting room for a doctor's or dentist's patients **2** room in a private house for general use
receptive *adj* willing to consider new ideas **~ness, -ivity** *n*
receptor *n* something that receives a signal, stimulus, etc.
recess *n* **1** pause for rest during a working period **2** space in an inside wall for shelves, cupboards, etc. **3** secret inner place ♦ *vt* make or put into a recess in a wall
recession *n* **1** period of reduced business activity **2** act of receding
recessive *adj* (of a gene) suppressed if the dominant gene produces a different effect
recharge *vt* put a new charge of electricity into (a battery) **recharge** *n* **~r** *n* **~able** *adj*
recherché /rəˈsheəshay/ *adj* rare and strange
recidivist *n fml* person who returns to criminal habits **recidivist, -istic** *adj* **-ism** *n*
recipe *n* set of cooking instructions
recipient *n fml* person who receives something
reciprocal *adj fml* given and received in return; mutual **~ly** *adv*
reciprocate *vi/t fml* give or do (something) in return **-ation** *n*
reciprocity /ˌresiˈprosəti/ *n* reciprocal relationship
recital *n* performance of music or poetry by one person or a small group
recitative /ˌresitəˈteev/ *n* passage (e.g. in opera) sung in natural speech rhythm
recite *v* **1** *vi/t* say (something learned) aloud in public **2** *vt fml* give a detailed account or list of **recitation** *n*
reck *vt arch.* worry about; care
reckless *adj* not caring about danger **~ly** *adv* **~ness** *n*
reckon *vt* **1** consider; regard **2** guess; suppose **3** calculate; add up **reckon on** *phr vt* make plans in expectation of **reckon with** *phr vt* **1** have to deal with **2** take account of in one's plans **3 to be reckoned with** to be taken seriously as a possible opponent, competitor, etc. **~ing** *n* **1** calculation **2** punishment: *a day of reckoning*
reclaim *vt* **1** ask for the return of **2** make (land) fit for use **reclamation** *n*
réclame /ˌrayˈklahm/ *n* fashionable fame
recline *vi fml* lie back or down; rest
recluse *n* someone who lives alone on purpose **-sive** *adj* **-sion** *n*
recognizance *n* (money given as security for) a bond entered into before a court
recognize, -ise *vt* **1** know again (as someone or something one has met before) **2** accept as being legal or real **3** be prepared to admit **4** show official gratefulness for **-izable** *adj* **-ition** *n*
recoil *vi* **1** move back suddenly in fear or dislike **2** (of a gun) spring back when fired **recoil** *n*
recollect *vi/t* remember **~ion** *n* memory
recommend *vt* **1** praise as being good for a purpose **2** advise **3** (of a quality) to make (someone or something) attractive **~ation** *n*
recompense *n fml* reward or payment for trouble or suffering ♦ *vt fml* give recompense to
reconcile *vt* **1** make friendly again **2** find agreement between (two opposing things) **reconcile to** *phr vt* cause (someone) to accept (something unpleasant) **-ciliation** *n*
recondite *adj* (of something) little known or obscure **~ly** *adv* **~ness** *n*
recondition *vt* repair and bring back into working order
reconnaissance /riˈkonəs(ə)ns/ *n* (act of) reconnoitring
reconnoitre, *AmE* **-ter** /ˌrekəˈnoytə/ *vi/t*

go near (the place where an enemy is) to find out information
reconsider *vi/t* think again and change one's mind (about) **~ation** *n*
reconstitute *vt* bring back to a former condition, esp. by adding water **–ution** *n*
reconstruct *vt* **1** build up again **2** form an idea of (something unknown) from available evidence **~ion** *n*
record *v* **1** *vt* write down so that it will be known **2** *vi/t* preserve (sound or a television show) so that it can be heard or seen again **3** *vt* (of an instrument) show by measuring ♦ *n* **1** written statement of facts, events, etc. **2** known facts about past behaviour **3** best yet done **4** circular piece of plastic on which sound is stored for playing back **5 for the record** to be reported as official **6 off the record** unofficial(ly) **7 on the record: a** (of facts or events) (ever) recorded **b** (of a person) having publicly said, as if for written records ♦ *adj* better, faster, etc., than ever before
recorded delivery *n* postal service in which the delivery of an item is recorded
recorder *n* **1** simple musical instrument played by blowing **2** tape recorder
recording *n* recorded performance, speech, or piece of music
record player *n* machine for producing sounds from records
recount[1] *vt* count (esp. votes) again **recount** *n*
recount[2] *vt fml* tell
recoup *vt* get back (something lost, esp. money)
recourse *n* **have recourse to** *fml* make use of
recover *v* **1** *vt* get back (something lost or taken away) **2** *vi* return to the proper state of health, strength, ability, etc. **~able** *adj* **~y** *n*
recreant *n, adj arch.* (person who is) cowardly and disloyal
recreate *vt* create again, esp. **a** make a copy of **b** remember vividly
recreation *n* (form of) amusement; way of spending free time **~al** *adj*
recrimination *n* (act of) quarrelling and blaming one another
recrudescence /ˌreekroohˈdes(ə)ns/ *n fml* new occurrence **recrudesce** *vi* **–escent** *adj*
recruit *n* new member of an organization, esp. the army, navy, etc. ♦ *vi/t* get recruits or as a recruit **~ment** *n*
rectal *adj* of the rectum
rectangle *n* flat shape with four straight sides forming four 90° angles **–gular** *adj*
rectify *vt fml* put right
rectilinear *adj* in a straight line
rectitude *n fml* moral pureness
recto *n* **-os** right-hand page
rector *n* priest in charge of a parish **~y** *n* rector's home
rectum *n med* lowest end of the bowel, where food waste passes out
recumbent *adj fml* lying down on the back or side **~ly** *adv* **–ency** *n*
recuperate *vi* get well again after illness **–ative** *adj* helping one to recuperate **-ation** *n*
recur *vi* **-rr-** happen again **–currence** *n* **–current** *adj*
recusant /ˈrekyooz(ə)nt/ *n, adj* (person) refusing to obey (religious) authority **–ancy** *n*
recycle *vt* treat (a used substance) so that it is fit to use again
red *adj* **-dd- 1** of the colour of blood **2** (of hair) brownish orange **3** (*cap.*) *infml* Communist ♦ *n* **1** red colour **2** (*cap.*) *infml* Communist **3 in the red** in debt **~den** *vi/t* make or become red
red admiral *n* black and red butterfly
red-blooded *adj* forceful and vigorous
redbrick *adj* (of an English University) founded between 1800 and 1939
red carpet *n* special ceremonial welcome to a guest
redcoat *n* British soldier of around 1750-1850
Red Cross *n* international organization that looks after the sick and wounded
red deer *n* large European and

Asian deer

redeem *vt* **1** buy back (something given for money lent) **2** *fml* make (something bad) slightly less bad **3** *fml* fulfil (e.g. a promise) **Redeemer** *n* Christ

redemption *n* redeeming

redeploy *vt* rearrange (soldiers, workers in industry, etc.) in a more effective way **~ment** *n*

red giant *n* very large cool star

red-handed *adj* in the act of doing wrong

redhead *n* person with red hair

red herring *n* something introduced to draw people's attention away from the main point

red-hot *adj* so hot that it shines red

Red Indian *n* American Indian

red lead *n* red oxide of lead

red-letter day *n* specially good day

red light *n* signal indicating that vehicles should stop

red-light district *n* area where prostitutes work

red meat *n* dark-coloured meat, e.g. beef or lamb

redneck *n infml, esp. AmE* person who lives in the country, esp. one who is uneducated and has strong unreasonable opinions

redolent *adj fml* making one think (of); suggesting **-ence** *n*

redouble *vi/t* increase greatly

redoubt *n fml* small fort

redoubtable *adj* greatly respected and feared **-bly** *adv*

redound to *phr vt fml* increase (fame, honour, etc.)

redress *vt fml* **1** put right (a wrong, injustice, etc.) **2 redress the balance** make things equal again ♦ *n* something, such as money, that puts right a wrong

red shift *n* increase in the wavelength of radiation produced by a body moving away in space

redskin *n derog* Red Indian

red tape *n* silly detailed unnecessary rules

reduce 1 *vt* make less **2** *vi* (of a person) lose weight on purpose **reduce to** *phr vt* bring to (a less favourable state): *The child was reduced to tears.* **-duction** *n*

reductio ad absurdum *n* logical but absurd consequence

redundant *adj* **1** *esp. BrE* no longer employed because there is not enough work **2** *fml* not needed **-ancy** *n*

reduplicate *vt* copy, repeat

redwing *n* European thrush

redwood *n* extremely tall American coniferous tree

reecho *vi* produce or come back as repeated echoes

reed *n* **1** grasslike plant growing in wet places **2** thin piece of wood or metal in certain musical instruments, blown across to produce sound **~y** *adj* **1** full of reeds **2** (of a sound) thin and high

reef[1] *n* line of sharp rocks at or near the surface of the sea

reef[2] *vt* reduce the area of (a sail)

reefer *n infml* cigarette containing marijuana

reefer jacket *n* short close-fitting jacket of thick cloth

reef knot *n* double knot that will not undo easily

reek *vi, n* (have) a strong unpleasant smell

reel[1] *n* **1** round object on which cotton, cinema film, etc., can be wound **2** length of time it takes to show this amount of film ♦ *vt* bring, take, etc., by winding **reel off** *phr vt* say quickly and easily from memory

reel[2] *vi* **1** walk unsteadily as if drunk **2** be shocked or confused **3** seem to go round and round

reel[3] *n* lively Scottish dance

reentry *n* entering again, esp. into the Earth's atmosphere

reeve *n* medieval English manor officer

ref *n infml* referee (1)

refectory *n* eating room in a school, college, etc.

referee *n* **1** person in charge of a game **2** person who gives a job reference

reference *n* **1** (act of) mentioning **2** (act of) looking at something for informa-

tion **3** information about someone's character and ability, esp. when they are looking for a job **4 in/with reference to** *fml* about
reference book *n* book for finding information
referendum *n* **-da** *or* **-dums** direct vote by all the people to decide something
referent *n* thing that a symbol stands for
refer to *phr vt* **-rr- 1** mention; speak about **2** be about or directed towards **3** look at for information **4** send to (a person or place) for information, a decision, etc. **~ral** *n*
refill *vt* fill again ♦ *n* (container holding) a fresh supply to refill something **~able** *adj*
refine *vt* make pure **~d** *adj* **1** made pure **2** showing education, delicacy of feeling, and good manners **~ment** *n* **1** clever addition or improvement **2** refining **3** quality of being refined
refinery *n* place where oil, sugar, etc., is refined
refit *vt* **-tt-** repair and put new machinery into (a ship) **refit** *n*
reflate *vi/t* increase the supply of money in (a money system) **-flation** *n*
reflect *v* **1** *vt* throw back (heat, sound, or an image) **2** *vt* give an idea of; express **3** *vi* think carefully **reflect on** *phr vt* cause to be considered in a particular way **~ive** *adj* thoughtful **~ively** *adv* **~or** *n*
reflection *n* **1** reflected image **2** reflecting of heat, sound, etc. **3** deep and careful thought
reflex *n* unintentional movement made in response to a stimulus
reflexive *n, adj* (word, such as *myself*) showing effect on oneself
reflexology *n* foot massage to cure illness in other body parts **-gist** *n*
reforest *vt* reafforest
reform *vi/t* make or become (morally) right; improve ♦ *n* action to improve conditions, remove unfairness, etc. **~er** *n*
re-form *vi/t* (cause to) form again, esp. into ranks
reformation *n* **1** (moral) improvement **2** (*cap.*) 16th-century religious movement leading to the establishment of Protestant churches
reformatory *n* place where young criminals are sent for discipline and training
refract *vt* bend (light passing through) **~ion** *n*
refractory *adj fml* disobedient and troublesome
refrain¹ *vi fml* not do something
refrain² *n* part of a song that is repeated
refresh *vt* **1** cause to feel fresh or active again **2 refresh one's memory** help oneself to remember again **~ing** *adj* **1** producing comfort and new strength **2** pleasingly new and interesting **~ingly** *adv* **~ment** *n* **~ments** *pl n* food and drink
refresher course *n* course to instruct people about new developments in their field of work
refrigerant *n* substance used to refrigerate
refrigerate *vt* make (food, drink, etc.) cold to preserve it **-ation** *n*
refrigerator *n fml* fridge
refuel *vi/t* fill up again with fuel
refuge *n* (place providing) protection or shelter
refugee *n* person forced to leave their country because of (political) danger
refulgent *adj fml* brightly shining **-ence** *n*
refund *n* repayment ♦ *vt* pay (money) back
refurbish *vt* make fit for use again **~ment** *n*
refusal *n* (case of) refusing
refuse¹ *vi/t* not accept, do, or give
refuse² *n* waste material; rubbish
refusenik *n* Soviet Jew not allowed to emigrate
refute *vt fml* prove that (someone or something) is mistaken **-utation** *n*
regain *vt* get or win back
regal *adj fml* like a king or queen; very splendid **~ly** *adv*
regale with *phr vt* entertain with

regalia /rɪˈgaylyə/ *n* ceremonial clothes and decorations

regard *vt* **1** look at or consider in the stated way **2** *fml* pay respectful attention to ♦ *n* **1** respect **2** respectful attention; concern **3 in/with regard to** in connection with **~less** *adv* **1** whatever may happen **2 regardless of** without worrying about **regards** *pl n* good wishes **~ing** *prep* in connection with

regatta *n* meeting for boat races

regency *n* rule by a regent, esp. (*cap.*) from 1811 to 1820 in Britain

regenerate *vi/t* grow again **–ation** *n*

regent *n* person who governs in place of a king or queen who is ill, still a child, etc.

reggae *n* West Indian popular dance and music

regicide *n* **1** killing a king or queen **2** person who does this

regime *n* **1** (system of) government **2** regimen

regimen *n fml* fixed plan of food, exercise, etc., to improve health

regiment *n* large military group ♦ *vt* control too firmly **~al** *adj* **~ally** *adv*

Regina *n BrE law* (used when a queen is reigning) the state as prosecutor in a criminal trial

region *n* **1** quite large area or part **2 in the region of** about **~al** *adj* **regions** *pl n* parts of the country away from the capital

register *n* **1** (book containing) a record or list **2** range of the voice or of a musical instrument ♦ *v* **1** *vt* record or list **2** *vi* put one's name on a list, esp. of those who will take part **3** *vt* (of a measuring instrument) show **4** *vt* (of a person or face) express **5** *vt* send by registered post **6** *vi* be noticed; have an effect

registered post *n* system for posting valuable things, which protects the sender against loss

registrar *n* keeper of official records

registration *n* registering to take part in something

registration number *n BrE* official number shown on a vehicle

registry office also **register office** *n* (esp. in Britain) office where marriages can legally take place and where births, marriages, and deaths are officially recorded

regnant *adj tech* reigning

regress *vi fml* go back to a former and usu. worse condition, way of behaving, etc. **~ion** *n* **~ive** *adj* **~ively** *adv*

regret *vt* **-tt-** be sorry about and wish one had (not) done ♦ *n* unhappiness at the loss of something, because of something one has done or not done, etc. **~ful** *adj* **~fully** *adv* **~table** *adj* that one should regret **~tably** *adv*

regroup *vi/t* form into new groups

regular *adj* **1** not varying **2** happening (almost) every time **3** correct or usual **4** evenly shaped **5** employed continuously: *a regular soldier* **6** following a standard grammatical pattern **7** *infml* complete; thorough **8** *esp. AmE* pleasant and honest: *a regular guy* ♦ *n* regular visitor, customer, etc. **~ly** *adv* at regular times **~ize, ~ise** *vt* make lawful **–larity** *n*

regulate *vt* **1** control, esp. by rules **2** make (a machine) work in a certain way **–atory** *adj fml* having the purpose of regulating **–ator** *n*

regulation *n* **1** (official) rule **2** control

regulo *n BrE* temperature in a gas oven, expressed as a number from 1/4 to 9

regurgitate *vt fml* **1** bring back (swallowed food) through the mouth **2** repeat (something heard or read) in one's own work, without thought or change **–ation** *n*

rehabilitate *vt* **1** make able to live an ordinary life again **2** put back into good condition **3** put back to a former high rank, position, etc. **–ation** *n*

rehash *vt* use (old ideas) again **rehash** *n*

rehear *vt* hear (a trial or lawsuit) over again **~ing** *n*

rehearse *vi/t* practise for later performance **rehearsal** *n*

rehouse *vt* put into new or better housing

Reich *n* German empire
reify *vt* **1** regard (something abstract) as a material thing **2** regard or treat (a person) as a thing
reign *n* period of reigning ♦ *vi* **1** be the king or queen **2** exist (noticeably): *Silence reigned.*
reign of terror *n* period of widespread official killing
reimburse *vt* pay (money) back to **~ment** *n*
rein *n* also **reins** *pl* **1** long narrow (leather) band for controlling a horse **2** means of (control)
reincarnate *vt* cause to return to life in a new form after death **-ation** *n*
reindeer *n* **reindeer** large deer from northern parts of the world
reinforce *vt* strengthen with additions **~ment** *n* **~ments** *pl n* more soldiers sent to reinforce an army
reinforced concrete *n* concrete strengthened by metal bars
reinstate *vt* put back into a position formerly held **~ment** *n*
reissue *vt* issue again, esp. print again after a time
reiterate *vt fml* repeat several times **-ation** *n*
reject *vt* refuse to accept ♦ *n* something thrown away as useless or imperfect **~ion** *n*
rejig *vt* **-gg-** rearrange, esp. so as to perform different work or to work more effectively
rejoice *vi* **1** feel or show great joy **2** **rejoice in the name of** be called (used when the name sounds foolish) **rejoicing** *n* (public) show of joy
rejoin[1] *vi/t* join again
rejoin[2] *vt* answer, esp. angrily
rejoinder *n* (rude) answer
rejuvenate *vt* make young again **-ation** *n*
relapse *vi* return to a bad state of health or way of life **relapse** *n*
relate *vt* **1** see or show a connection between **2** *fml* tell (a story) **relate to** *phr vt* **1** connect (one thing) with (another) **2** *infml* understand and accept **~d** *adj* of the same family or kind; connected
relation *n* **1** member of one's family **2** connection **3** **in/with relation to** *fml* with regard to **~ship** *n* **1** friendship or connection between people **2** connection **relations** *pl n* dealings between (and feelings towards) each other
relative *n* relation (1) ♦ *adj* compared to each other or something else **~ly** *adv* quite
relative clause *n* clause joined on by a relative pronoun
relative pronoun *n* pronoun which joins a clause to the rest of a sentence, such as *who*, *which*, or *that*
relativism *n* theory that knowledge and moral principles have no objective standard **~ist** *n*
relativity *n* relationship between time, size, and mass, said to change with increased speed
relax *vi/t* make or become **a** less active and worried **b** less stiff, tight, or severe **~ation** *n* **1** (something done for) rest and amusement **2** act of making or becoming less severe
relay *n* **1** group that takes the place of another to keep work going continuously **2** race between teams of runners who each run part of the distance **3** (broadcast sent out by) an electrical connection for receiving and passing on signals ♦ *vt* pass by means of a relay
release *vt* **1** set free **2** allow to be seen or read publicly **3** press (a handle) so as to let something go ♦ *n* **1** setting free **2** new film, record, or piece of information that has been released
relegate *vt* put into a lower or worse place **-ation** *n*
relent *vi* become less cruel or severe **~less** *adj* continuously cruel or severe
relevant *adj* directly connected with the subject **~ly** *adv* **-ance** *n*
reliable *adj* that may be trusted **-ably** *adv* **-ability** *n*
reliant *adj* dependent (on) **-ance** *n* **1** dependence **2** trust

relic *n* **1** something old that reminds us of the past **2** part of or something that belonged to a dead saint

relict *n* **1** *tech* plant or animal that remains when others like it are extinct **2** *arch.* widow

relief *n* **1** comfort at the ending of anxiety, pain, or dullness **2** help for people in trouble **3** person who takes over another's duty **4** decoration that stands out above the rest of the surface it is on **5** *BrE* permission not to pay tax on a part of one's income

relief map *n* map showing the height of land

relieve *vt* **1** lessen (pain or trouble) **2** take over duties from **3** give variety or interest to **4 relieve oneself** urinate or defecate **relieve of** *phr vt* free from **~d** *adj* no longer worried

religion *n* (system of) belief in and worship of one or more gods

religiose *adj* affectedly religious **-osity** *n*

religious *adj* **1** of religion **2** obeying the rules of a religion **3** performing the stated duties very carefully **~ly** *adv* regularly

relinquish *vt* give up (something to someone)

reliquary /ˈrelikwəri/ *n* something in which relics of saints are kept

relish *n* **1** great enjoyment **2** substance eaten with a meal, to add taste and interest ♦ *vt* enjoy

relive *vt* experience again in the imagination

relocate *vi/t* move to or establish in a new place

reluctant *adj* unwilling **~ly** *adv* **-ance** *n*

rely on *phr vt* **1** trust **2** depend on

REM *n* rapid eye movement, occurring when a sleeper dreams

remain *v* **1** *vi* stay or be left behind after others have gone **2** continue to be **remains** *pl n* **1** parts of something which are left **2** *fml* dead body

remainder *n* what is left over ♦ *vt* sell (esp. books) cheap so as to get rid of them quickly

remake *vt* make (esp. a film) again **remake** *n*

remand *vt* send back to prison from a court of law, to be tried later ♦ *n* being remanded

remark *n* spoken or written opinion ♦ *vt* say **remark on** *phr vt fml* mention

remarkable *adj* unusual or noticeable **-bly** *adv*

rematch *n* second match between the same opponents

remediable *adj* that can be put right or cured

remedial *adj* providing a remedy

remedy *n* way of curing something ♦ *vt* put (something bad) right

remember *v* **1** *vt* call back into the mind **2** *vi/t* take care not to forget **3** *vt* give money or a present to **remember to** *phr vt* send greetings from (someone) to

remembrance *n* **1** act of remembering **2** something given or kept to remind one

Remembrance Day also **Remembrance Sunday** *n* Sunday nearest to November 11th, when people in Britain remember those who died in the two world wars

remind *vt* cause to remember **remind of** *phr vt* cause to remember by seeming the same **~er** *n* something to make one remember

reminisce /ˌremiˈnis/ *vi* talk pleasantly about the past **-iscence** *n* **-iscences** *pl n* written or spoken account of one's past life **-iscent** *adj* that reminds one (of); like

remiss *adj fml* careless about a duty

remission *n* **1** lessening of the time someone has to stay in prison **2** *fml* period when an illness is less severe

remit *vt* -**tt**- *fml* **1** send (money) by post **2** free someone from (a debt or punishment) **~tance** *n* **1** money remitted **2** *fml* act of remitting money

remnant *n* part that remains

remodel *vt* change the shape of

remonstrate *vi fml* express disapproval **-ation, ~ance** *n* **-ative** *adj* **-atively** *adv*

remorse *n* sorrow for having done wrong **~ful** *adj* **~fully** *adv* **~less** *adj* **1** showing no remorse **2** threateningly unstoppable **~lessly** *adv*

remote *adj* **1** far distant in space or time **2** quiet and lonely **3** widely separated; not close: *a remote connection* **4** slight: *a remote chance of success* **5** not showing interest in others **~ly** *adv* at all: *not remotely interested* **~ness** *n*

remote control *n* controlling machinery by radio signals

remount *v* **1** *vi/t* mount again **2** *vt* provide with fresh horses ♦ *n* a fresh horse

remove *vt* **1** take away; get rid of **2** *fml* dismiss **3 removed from** distant or different from ♦ *n* degree of separation or difference **removal** *n* **~r** *n*

remunerate *vt fml* pay **–ative** *adj* well-paid **–ation** *n*

renaissance *n* renewal of interest in art, literature, etc., esp. (*cap.*) in Europe between the 14th and 17th centuries

renal *adj med* of the kidneys

renascent *adj fml* returning or becoming stronger again

rend *vt* **rent** *lit* **1** split **2** pull violently

render *vt fml* **1** cause to be **2** give **3** perform **~ing** also **rendition** *n* performance

rendering *n* covering, usu. of cement, sand, and lime, applied to exterior walls **render** *vt*

rendezvous /ˈrendiˌvooh/ *n* **–vous 1** (arrangement for) a meeting **2** meeting place ♦ *vi* meet by arrangement

renegade *n* person who disloyally leaves one country or belief to join another

renege, renegue /riˈneeg, riˈnayg/ *vi fml* break a promise

renew *vt* **1** do again; repeat **2** give new life and freshness to **3** get something new of the same kind to take the place of **~al** *n*

rennet *n* substance for thickening milk to make cheese

renounce *vt* say formally that one does not own or has no more connection with

renovate *vt* put back into good condition **–ation** *n*

renown *n* fame **~ed** *adj* famous

rent[1] *n* money paid regularly for the use of a house, television etc. ♦ *vt* **1** pay rent for the use of **2** allow to be used in return for rent **~al** *n* sum of money fixed to be paid as rent

rent[2] *n* large tear

rent[3] *past t. and p. of* rend

rent boy *n BrE infml* young male prostitute

rentier *n* person living on investment income

renunciation *n* (act of) renouncing something

reorganize, -ise *vi/t* organize in a new and better way **–ization** *n*

Rep *abbrev. for:* Republican

rep[1] *n infml* sales representative

rep[2] *n* repertory (company)

rep[3] *n* cloth with ridges running across it

repair[1] *vt* mend ♦ *n* **1** (act or result of) mending **2** condition: *in good repair*

repair[2] *vi fml* go

reparable *adj* capable of being repaired

reparation *n fml* repayment for loss or damage

repartee *n* quick amusing talk

repast *n fml* meal

repatriate *vt* send (someone) back to their own country **–ation** *n*

repay *vt* **repaid 1** pay (money) back to (someone) **2** reward **~ment** *n*

repeal *vt* end (a law) **repeal** *n*

repeat *vt* **1** say or do again **2 repeat oneself** keep saying the same thing ♦ *n* performance broadcast a second time **~ed** *adj* done again and again **~edly** *adv*

repel *vt* **-ll- 1** drive away (as if) by force **2** cause feelings of extreme dislike in **~lent** *adj* extremely nasty **~lent** *n* substance that repels esp. insects

repent *vi/t fml* be sorry for (wrongdoing) **~ant** *adj* **~antly** *adv* **~ance** *n*

repercussion *n* far-reaching effect

repertoire *n* set of things one can perform
repertory *n* performing several plays one after the other on different days with the same actors
répétiteur *n* person who coaches opera singers
repetition *n* repeating **-tious, -tive** *adj* containing parts that are repeated too much
rephrase *vt* put into different (clearer) words
repine *vi fml* feel miserable or regretful
replace *vt* **1** put back in the right place **2** take the place of **3** get another (better) one instead of **~ment** *n* **1** replacing **2** one that replaces someone or something
replay *vt* play again ♦ *n* something played again (e.g. on a video recording)
replenish *vt* fill up again **~ment** *n*
replete *adj fml* very full, esp. of food **-pletion** *n*
replica *n* close copy
replicate *vt fml* copy exactly
reply *vi, n* answer
report *n* **1** account of events, business affairs, etc. **2** what is said generally but unofficially **3** noise of an explosion ♦ *v* **1** *vi/t* provide information (about); give an account of, esp. for a newspaper or radio or television **2** *vi* go somewhere and say that one is there (and ready for work) **3** *vt* make an official complaint about **~er** *n* person who reports news
reportage *n* (writing, film, etc., in) the style of reporters
reportedly *adv* according to what is said
reported speech *n* indirect speech
repose *n fml* rest ♦ *vi/t fml* rest; lie; lay **repose in** *phr vt fml* place (trust, hope, etc.) in
repository *n* place where things are stored
repossess *vt* take back, esp. when rent has not been paid **~ion** *n*
reprehensible *adj fml* deserving blame; bad **-bly** *adv*
represent *v* **1** *vt* act or speak officially for (someone else) **2** *vt* be a picture or statue of; show **3** *vt* be a sign of; stand for **4** be: *This represents a considerable improvement.* **~ation** *n* **1** representing or being represented **2** a picture, statue, etc. that represents something else
representational *adj* (of painting or sculpture) realistic
representative *adj* **1** typical **2** (of government) in which the people and their opinions are represented ♦ *n* person who officially represents others
repress *vt* control; hold back **~ive** *adj* hard and cruel **~ively** *adv* **~ion** *n* pushing unwelcome feelings into one's unconscious mind, with odd effects on behaviour
reprieve *vt* give a reprieve to ♦ *n* official order not to carry out the punishment of death (yet)
reprimand *vt* express severe official disapproval of **reprimand** *n*
reprint *vi/t* print or be printed again **reprint** *n*
reprisal *n* (act of) punishing others for harm done to oneself
reprise *n* repeating of a piece of music
reproach *n* **1** (word of) blame **2 above/beyond reproach** perfect ♦ *vt* blame, not angrily but sadly **~ful** *adj* **~fully** *adv*
reprobate *n fml* person of bad character
reprocess *vt* process again (to make suitable for reuse)
reproduce *vi/t* **1** produce the young of (oneself or one's kind) **2** produce a copy (of) **-duction** *n* **-ductive** *adj* concerned with producing young
reprography /ri'prɒgrəfi/ *n* copying of graphic material (e.g. by photocopying)
reproof *n fml* (expression of) blame or disapproval
reprove *vt fml* speak blamingly or disapprovingly to
reptile *n* animal, such as a snake, with blood that changes temperature **-tilian** *adj*
republic *n* state ruled by a president and usu. an elected parliament, not by a king

republican *adj* belonging to or supporting a republic ♦ *n* person who favours republics **~ism** *n* beliefs or practices of republicans
Republican *n* member or supporter of the **Republican Party**, one of the two largest political parties of the US
repudiate *vt fml* **1** state that (something) is untrue **2** refuse to accept **–ation** *n*
repugnant *adj fml* causing extreme dislike; nasty **–ance** *n*
repulse *vt* **1** refuse coldly **2** drive back (an attack) **–pulsive** *adj* extremely unpleasant **–pulsion** *n* **1** extreme dislike **2** natural force by which one body drives another away from it
reputable *adj* having a good reputation **–bly** *adv*
reputation *n* opinion which people in general have about someone or something
repute *n fml* **1** reputation **2** good reputation **~d** *adj* generally supposed, but with some doubt **~dly** *adv*
request *n* **1** polite demand **2** something asked for ♦ *vt* demand politely
request stop *n* place where you can get a bus to stop by signalling
requiem *n* (music for) a Christian ceremony for a dead person
require *vt* **1** need **2** *fml* order, expecting obedience **~ment** *n* something needed or demanded
requisite /ˈrekwizit/ *adj* needed for a purpose
requisition *n* formal demand, esp. by the army ♦ *vt* demand or take officially, esp. for the army
requite *vt fml* **1** return (feelings, esp. love); share **2** avenge
reredos /ˈriəˌdos/ *n* ornamental screen behind an altar
rerun *vt* show (a film or television programme) again **rerun** *n*
reschedule *vt tech* arrange for postponed repayment of (a loan or debt)
rescind /riˈsind/ *vt* end (a law) or take back (a decision, order, etc.) **~ment** *n*
rescript *n* official order or announcement
rescue *vt* save or set free from harm or danger **rescue** *n* **~r** *n*
research *n* advanced and detailed study, to find out (new) facts ♦ *vi/t* do research (on or for) **~er** *n*
resection *n* surgical removal of a body part
resemble *vt* look or be like **–blance** *n* likeness
resent *vt* feel hurt and angry because of **~ful** *adj* **~fully** *adv* **~ment** *n*
reservation *n* **1** limiting condition(s) **2** private doubt in one's mind **3** arrangement to have or use something **4** area set apart for particular people to live in
reserve *vt* **1** keep apart for a special purpose **2** arrange to have or use: *reserve hotel rooms* ♦ *n* **1** quantity kept for future use **2** piece of land kept for the stated purpose **3** player who will play if another cannot **4** being reserved **5** also **reserves** *pl* military forces kept for use if needed **6 without reserve** *fml* completely **~d** *adj* not liking to show one's feelings or talk about oneself **~dly** *adv* **~dness** *n*
reservist *n* soldier in a military reserve
reservoir *n* **1** artificial lake for storing water **2** large supply (still unused)
reset *vt* **1** set (esp. a broken bone or a piece of printing) again **2** change (e.g. a clock) to show a different reading
resettle *vi/t* (help to) go to live in a new country or area **~ment** *n*
reshuffle *vt* change around the positions of people working in **reshuffle** *n*
reside *vi fml* have one's home
residence *n fml* **1** (large grand) house **2** residing
residency *n* official residence
resident *n, adj* (person) who lives in a place **~ial** *adj* **1** consisting of private houses **2** for which one must live in a place: *a residential course*
residual *adj* left over; remaining
residual current device *n* device which shuts off electrical current when a wire is cut

residuary *adj* **1** residual **2** receiving what is left over
residue *n* what is left over
resign *vi/t* leave (one's job or position) **resign to** *phr vt* cause (oneself) to accept calmly (something which cannot be avoided) **~ed** *adj* calmly suffering without complaint **~edly** *adv*
resignation *n* **1** (act or written statement of) resigning **2** being resigned
resilient *adj* **1** able to spring back to its former shape **2** able to recover quickly from misfortune **~ly** *adv* **–ence** *n*
resin *n* **1** thick sticky liquid from trees **2** man-made plastic substance
resist *vt* **1** oppose; fight against **2** remain unharmed by **3** force oneself not to accept
resistance *n* **1** resisting or ability to resist **2** force opposed to movement: *wind resistance* **3** secret army fighting against an enemy in control of its country **–ant** *adj* showing resistance
resistor *n* piece of wire for reducing the power of an electrical current
resit *vt* take (an examination) again **resit** *n*
resolute *adj* firm; determined in purpose **~ly** *adv*
resolution *n* **1** formal decision at a meeting **2** firm decision **3** quality of being resolute **4** resolving (a problem)
resolve *vt* **1** find a way of dealing with (a problem); settle **2** decide firmly **3** make a formal or firm decision ♦ *n fml* resolution (2, 3)
resonant *adj* **1** (of a sound) full, clear, and continuing **2** producing resonance in another body **–ance** *n* **1** quality of being full, clear and continuing **2** sound produced in a body by sound waves from another
resonate *vi* **1** produce resonance in something **2** (of a sound) be resonant
resonator *n* something that resonates, esp. a device for increasing the resonance of a musical instrument
resort[1] *n* **1** holiday place **2** something made use of: *a last resort when all else fails* **resort to** *phr vt* make use of, esp. when there is nothing else
resound *vi* **1** be loud and clearly heard **2** be filled (with sound) **~ing** *adj* very great and complete
resource *n* **1** something useful that one possesses **2** resourcefulness **~ful** *adj* able to find a way round difficulties **~fully** *adv*
respect *n* **1** great admiration and honour **2** attention; care; consideration **3** detail; aspect **4 with respect to** with regard to; about ♦ *vt* feel or show respect for **~ing** *prep* in connection with **respects** *pl n* polite formal greetings
respectable *adj* **1** socially acceptable **2** adequate **–bly** *adv* **–bility** *n*
respectful *adj* feeling or showing admiration and honour **~ly** *adv*
respective *adj* particular and separate **~ly** *adv* each separately in the order mentioned
respiration *n fml* breathing **–atory** *adj*
respirator *n* apparatus to help people breathe
respire *vi tech* breathe
respite *n* **1** short rest from effort, pain, etc. **2** delay before something unwelcome happens
resplendent *adj* gloriously bright and shining **~ly** *adv* **–ence** *n*
respond *vi* **1** answer **2** act in answer **respond to** *phr vt* (esp. of a disease) get better as a result of
respondent *n* one who responds, esp. a defendant ♦ *adj* responding
response *n* **1** answer **2** action done in answer
responsibility *n* **1** condition or quality of being responsible **2** something for which one is responsible **3** trustworthiness
responsible *adj* **1** having done or caused something (bad); guilty **2** having a duty to do or look after something **3** trustworthy **4** (of a job) needing a trustworthy person to do it **–bly** *adv*
responsive *adj* answering readily with words or feelings **~ly** *adv* **~ness** *n*
rest[1] *n* **1** (period of) freedom from

action or from something tiring **2** not moving: *come to rest* **3** support, esp. for the stated thing: *a headrest* **4 set/put at rest** free from anxiety ♦ *v* **1** *vi/t* (allow to) take a rest **2** *vt* lean; support **3** *vi* lie buried **4 rest assured** be certain **rest on** *phr vt* **1** (of a proof, argument, etc.) depend on **2** (of eyes) be directed towards **rest with** *phr vt* be the responsibility of **~ful** *adj* peaceful; quiet **~fully** *adv*

rest[2] *n* ones that still remain; what is left

restate *vt* state again, esp. in a different way **~ment** *n*

restaurant *n* place where meals are sold and eaten

restaurateur /ˌrest(ə)rəˈtuh/ *n* restaurant owner

restitution *n fml* giving something back to its owner, or paying for damage

restive *adj* unwilling to keep still or be controlled **~ly** *adv* **~ness** *n*

restless *adj* **1** giving no rest or sleep **2** unable to stay still, esp. from anxiety or lack of interest **~ ly** *adv* **~ness** *n*

restoration *n* **1** restoring **2** (*cap.*) period after 1660 in Britain

restorative *n, adj* (food, medicine, etc.) that brings back health and strength

restore *vt* **1** give back **2** bring back into existence **3** bring back to a proper state, esp. of health **4** put back into a former position **5** repair (an old painting, building, etc.) **~r** *n*

restrain *vt* prevent from doing something; control **~ed** *adj* calm and controlled **~edly** *adv* **restraint** *n* **1** quality of being restrained or act of restraining oneself **2** something that restrains

restrict *vt* keep within a certain limit **~ive** *adj* that restricts one **~ively** *adv* **~ion** *n*

restrictive practice *n BrE* **1** working method which harms efficiency **2** trading agreement against the public interest

rest room *n AmE* public toilet

restructure *vt* arrange (a system or organization) in a new way

result *n* **1** what happens because of an action or event **2** (a) noticeable good effect **3** situation of defeat or victory at the end of a game **4** answer to a sum ♦ *vi* happen as an effect or result **result in** *phr vt* cause **~ant** *adj* resulting

resume *v* **1** *vi/t* begin again after a pause

résumé *n* **1** summary of a speech, book, etc. **2** *esp. AmE* curriculum vitae

resumption *n* resuming

resurface *v* **1** *vt* put a new surface on **2** *vi* come to the surface again

resurgence *n* becoming active again

resurrect *vt* bring back into use or fashion **~ion** *n* **1** renewal **2** return of dead people to life at the end of the world **3** (*cap.*) (in the Christian religion) return of Christ to life after his death

resuscitate *vt* bring back to life **-ation** *n*

retail *n* sale of goods in shops to customers, not for reselling to anyone else ♦ *adv* from or by a retailer ♦ *vi/t* **1** sell by retail **2** *fml* tell; recount **~er** *n*

retain *vt* **1** keep; avoid losing **2** hold in place **3** employ (esp. a lawyer)

retainer *n* **1** servant **2** money paid for advice and help

retake *vt* **1** recapture **2** record or film again ♦ *n* act of filming or recording again

retaliate *vi* pay back evil with evil **-atory** *adj* **-ation** *n*

retard *vt* make slow or late **~ed** *adj* slow in development of the mind

retch *vi* try unsuccessfully to be sick

retd *abbrev. for:* retired

retention *n* retaining

retentive *adj* able to remember things well **~ness** *n*

rethink *vt* **rethought** think again and perhaps change one's mind about **rethink** *n*

reticent *adj* unwilling to say much **~ly** *adv* **-ence** *n*

reticulated *adj* forming or marked with a network **-tion** *n* network

reticule *n* small decorative handbag

retina *n* area at the back of the eye which receives light

retinue *n* group travelling with and helping an important person

retire *vi* **1** leave one's job, usu. because of age **2** leave a place of action **3** *fml* go away, esp. to a quiet place **4** *fml* go to bed **~ment** *n* **~d** *adj* having stopped working **retiring** *adj* liking to avoid company

retort[1] *n* quick or angry reply ♦ *vt* make a retort

retort[2] *n* long-necked bottle for heating chemicals

retouch *vt* improve (a picture) with small additions

retrace *vt* go back over

retract *vi/t* **1** draw back or in **2** take back (a statement or offer one has made) **~able** *adj* **~ion** *n*

retractile *adj tech* retractable

retread *n* tyre with a new covering of rubber **retread** *vt*

retreat *vi* **1** move backwards, esp. when forced **2** escape (from something unpleasant) ♦ *n* **1** (act of) retreating **2** place one goes to for peace and safety

retrench *vi fml* arrange to lessen one's spending **~ment** *n*

retrial *n* new trial of a law case

retribution *n fml* deserved punishment **-tive** *adj*

retrieve *vt* **1** find and bring back **2** *fml* put right **retrieval** *n* retrieving **~r** *n* dog that retrieves shot birds

retro *adj infml* nostalgically recreating fashions of the (recent) past

retro- *prefix* **1** backwards **2** behind

retroactive *adj* having an effect on the past

retroflex *adj* **1** bent backwards **2** pronounced with the tip of the tongue curled back

retrograde *adj* moving back to an earlier and worse state

retrogression *n fml* going back to an earlier and worse state **-sive** *adj* **-sively** *adv*

retro-rocket *n* rocket on a spacecraft fired to slow it down or change its direction

retrospect *n* **in retrospect** looking back to the past **~ive** *adj* **1** thinking about the past **2** (of a law) having an effect on the past **3** showing the work of a painter, sculptor, etc., from his or her earliest years up to the present time **~ively** *adv*

retroussé *adj* (of a nose) turned up at the end

retsina *n* Greek wine flavoured with resin

return *v* **1** *vi* come or go back **2** *vt* give or send back **3** *vt* elect to parliament **4** *vt* give (a verdict) ♦ *n* **1** (act of) coming or giving back **2** profit **3** official statement or set of figures: *a tax return* **4 by return of post** by the next post **5 in return for** in exchange (for) ♦ *adj BrE* (of a ticket) for a journey to a place and back again

returning officer *n* official who arranges an area's parliamentary election and gives out the result

return match *n* second game between the same sides

reunion *n* **1** meeting of former fellow-workers or friends after a separation **2** state of being brought together again

reuse *vt* use again, esp. after reclaiming or reprocessing **-sable** *adj*

rev *vt* **-vv-** increase the speed of (an engine) ♦ *n* revolution (3)

Rev *abbrev. for:* Reverend

revalue *vt* give a new (higher) value to

revamp *vt* give a new and improved form to

reveal *vt* allow to be seen or known

reveille /rɪˈvæli/ *n* signal to waken soldiers in the morning

revel *v* **-ll-** (*AmE*) *lit* pass the time in dancing, feasting, etc. **revel in** *phr vt* enjoy greatly **~ler**, *AmE* **~er** *n* person taking part in revelry **~ry** *n* wild noisy dancing and feasting

revelation *n* **1** making known of something secret **2** (surprising) fact made known

revenge *n* punishment given in return

for harm done to oneself ♦ *vt* do something in revenge for
revenue *n* income, esp. received by the government
reverberate *vi* (of sound) be continuously repeated in waves **-ation** *n*
revere *vt fml* respect and admire greatly
reverence *n fml* great respect and admiration
Reverend *n* (title of respect for) a Christian priest
Reverend Mother *n* (title of respect for) the nun in charge of a convent
reverent *adj* showing (religious) reverence **~ly** *adv*
reverential *adj* showing reverence **~ly** *adv*
reverie *n* pleasant dreamlike state while awake
revers /rɪˈvɪə/ *n* **revers** lapel, esp. on a woman's coat
reversal *n* **1** (case of) being reversed **2** defeat or piece of bad luck
reverse *adj* opposite in position ♦ *n* **1** opposite **2** position of a vehicle's controls that causes backward movement **3** reversal (2) **4** rear side of a coin, medal, etc. ♦ **1** *vi/t* go or cause (a vehicle) to go backwards **2** *vt* change round or over to the opposite **3 reverse the charges** make a telephone call to be paid for by the receiver
reversion *n* return to a former condition or habit
revert to *phr vt* go back to (a former condition, habit, or owner)
review *vt* **1** consider and judge (an event or situation) **2** hold a review of armed forces **3** give a review of (a book, play, etc.) ♦ *n* **1** (act of) considering and judging **2** grand show of armed forces, in the presence of a king, queen, general, etc. **3 a** (written) expression of judgment on a new book, play, etc. **b** magazine containing such judgments **~er** *n*
revile *vt fml* say bad things about **~ment** *n*
revise *v* **1** *vt* improve and make corrections to (written material) **2** *vt* change (an opinion, intention, etc.) **3** *vi/t esp. BrE* restudy (something already learned), esp. before an examination
revision *n* **1** (act of) revising **2** revised piece of writing
revisionism *n* questioning of the main beliefs of a (Marxist) political system **-ist** *n*
revitalize, -ise *vt* put new strength or power into
revive *v* **1** *vi/t* become or make conscious or healthy again **2** *vi/t* come or bring back into use or existence **3** *vt* perform (an old play) again after many years **revival** *n* **1** renewal **2** new performance of an old play
revivify *vt fml* revive
revocation *n* revoking
revoke *vt* put an end to (a law, decision, permission, etc.)
revolt *v* **1** *vi* (try to) take power violently from those in power **2** *vt* cause to feel sick and shocked ♦ *n* (instance of) revolting **~ing** *adj* extremely nasty **~ingly** *adv*
revolution *n* **1** (time of) great social change, esp. of a political system by force **2** complete change in ways of thinking or acting **3** one complete circular movement **~ary** *adj* **1** of a political revolution **2** completely new and different ♦ *n* person who favours or joins in a revolution **~ize, ~ise** *vt* cause a complete change in
revolve *vi* spin round on a central point
revolve around *phr vt* have as a centre or main subject
revolver *n* small gun with a revolving bullet-container
revue *n* theatrical show with short acts, songs, jokes, etc.
revulsion *n* feeling of being revolted
reward *n* **1** (something gained in) return for work or service **2** money given for helping the police ♦ *vt* give a reward to or for **~ing** *adj* giving personal satisfaction
rewind *vt* wind back onto a spool
rewire *vt* provide (e.g. a house) with

new electric wiring
reword *vt* express again in different words
rework *vt* put (music, writing, etc.) into a new or different form (in order to use again)
rewrite *vt* revise (written material)
Rex *n BrE law* (used when a king is reigning) the state as prosecutor in a criminal trial
rhapsodize, -ise *vi* express eager and excited approval
rhapsody *n* **1** expression of too great praise and excitement **2** piece of music of irregular form **-dic** *adj*
rhea /ˈrɪə/ *n* large flightless S American bird
rheostat *n* adjustable resistor
rhesus factor *n* substance in most people's blood, harmful to those who do not have it
rhetoric /ˈretərik/ *n* **1** art of speaking persuadingly **2** fine-sounding but insincere or meaningless words **~al** *adj* **1** asked or asking only for effect, and not expecting an answer: *a rhetorical question* **2** of or showing rhetoric **~ally** *adv*
rheumatic fever *n* severe disease, esp. of children, which can damage the heart
rheumatism *n* disease causing joint or muscle pain **-matic** *adj* of, suffering from, or being rheumatism
rheumatoid arthritis *n* long-lasting disease causing pain and stiffness in the joints
Rh factor *n* rhesus factor
rhinestone *n* diamond-like jewel made from glass or a transparent rock
rhino *n* **-os** rhinoceros
rhinoceros *n* large thick-skinned African or Asian animal with either one or two horns on its nose
rhizome *n* thick rootlike stem of certain plants
rhododendron *n* large bush with large bright flowers
rhomboid *n* parallelogram **rhomboid, ~al** *adj* in the shape of a rhombus
rhombus *n* figure with four equal straight sides
rhubarb *n* large-leaved plant whose thick red stems are eaten
rhyme *v* **1** *vi* (of words or lines in poetry) end with the same sound **2** *vt* put together (words) ending with the same sound ♦ *n* **1** (use of) rhyming words at line-ends in poetry **2** word that rhymes with another **3** short simple rhyming poem **4 rhyme or reason** (any) sense or meaning
rhyming slang *n* use of a rhyming phrase to stand for another word (e.g. *trouble and strife* for *wife*)
rhythm *n* regular repeated pattern of sounds or movements **~ic, ~ical** *adj* **~ically** *adv*
rhythm and blues *n* R and B
rhythm method *n* method of contraception which depends on having sex only at a time when the woman is not likely to conceive
rial *n* riyal
rib *n* **1** any of the curved bones enclosing the chest **2** curved rod for strengthening a frame **3** thin raised line in a pattern ♦ *vt* **-bb-** make fun of (someone) **~bed** *adj* having a pattern of thin raised lines
ribald /ˈrib(ə)ld, ˈrie-/ *adj fml* (of jokes or laughter) rude and disrespectful **~ry** *n*
ribbon *n* long narrow band of cloth
ribbon development *n* (building) houses along main roads leading out of a city
rib cage *n* all one's ribs
riboflavin *n* vitamin of the B complex, occurring esp. in milk and liver
rice *n* (plant with) a seed that is widely eaten
rice paper *n* sort of edible paper
rich *adj* **1** having a lot of money or property **2** having a lot: *a city rich in ancient buildings* **3** expensive, valuable, and beautiful **4** (of food) containing a lot of cream, eggs, sugar, etc. **5** (of a sound or colour) deep, strong, and beautiful **6** *infml* amusing but often rather annoying ♦ *pl n* rich people **~ly** *adv* **1** splendidly **2** fully **~ness** *n*

riches *n esp. lit* wealth
Richter scale *n* scale of severity of earthquakes
rick[1] *vt* twist (part of the body) slightly
rick[2] *n* large pile of straw or hay
rickets *n* children's disease in which bones become soft and bent
rickety *adj* weak and likely to break
rickshaw *n* small East Asian carriage pulled by a man
ricochet /ˈrikəshay/ *n* sudden change of direction by a bullet, stone, etc., when it hits a hard surface ♦ *vi* **-t-** *or* **-tt-** change direction in a ricochet
ricotta *n* Italian sheep's-milk cottage cheese
rictus *n* unnatural gaping grin
riddance *n* **good riddance** (said when one is glad that someone or something has gone)
-ridden *suffix* **1** suffering from the effects of: *guilt-ridden* **2** too full of: *mosquito-ridden*
riddle[1] *n* **1** difficult and amusing question **2** mystery
riddle[2] *n* coarse seive **riddle with** *phr vt* make full of holes
ride *v* **rode, ridden 1** *vi/t* travel along on (a horse, donkey, etc., a bicycle, or a motorcycle) **2** *vi* travel on a bus **3** *vt* remain safe (and floating) through: *a ship riding a storm* **4 let something ride** let something continue, taking no action **5 ride high** have great success **6 ride roughshod over** act in a hurtful way towards **ride out** *phr vt* come safely through (bad weather, trouble) **ride up** *phr vi* (of clothing) move upwards or out of place ♦ *n* **1** journey on an animal, in a vehicle, etc. **2 take someone for a ride** deceive someone **~r** *n* **1** person riding esp. a horse **2** statement added to esp. an official declaration or judgment
ridge *n* long narrow raised part, where two slopes meet
ridicule *n* unkind laughter ♦ *vt* laugh unkindly at
ridiculous *adj* silly **~ly** *adv*
riding *n* **1** former administrative district of Yorkshire **2** electoral district of a commonwealth country e.g. Canada
rid of *phr vt* **rid** *or* **ridded**, *pres. p.* **-dd- 1** make free of **2 get rid of** : **a** free oneself from **b** drive or throw away or destroy
Riesling *n* medium-dry white wine
rife *adj* (of a bad thing) widespread; common
riff *n* repeated jazz phrase
riffle through *phr vt* turn over (esp. papers) quickly, searching
riffraff *n derog* worthless badly-behaved people
rifle[1] *n* gun with a long barrel, fired from the shoulder
rifle[2] *vt* search through and steal from
rift *n* **1** crack **2** break in friendship
rift valley *n* long valley formed by subsidence
rig[1] *vt* **-gg-** fit (a ship) with sails, ropes, etc. **rig out** *phr vt* dress in special or funny clothes **rig up** *phr vt* make quickly and roughly ♦ *n* **1** way a ship's sails and masts are arranged **2** apparatus: *a drilling rig* **~ging** *n* all the ropes, chains, etc., holding up a ship's sails
rig[2] *vt* **-gg-** arrange dishonestly for one's own advantage
right *adj* **1 a** on the side of the body away from the heart **b** in the direction of one's right side: *the right bank of the river* **2** just; proper; morally good **3** correct **4** in a proper or healthy state ♦ *n* **1** right side or direction **2** what is just and proper **3** morally just or legal claim **4** political parties that favour less change and less state control **5 in one's own right** because of a personal claim that does not depend on anyone else ♦ *adv* **1** towards the right side **2** correctly **3** exactly **4** completely **5** yes; I will **6** *BrE sl or arch.* very **7 right away** at once ♦ *vt* put back to a correct position or condition **~ness** *n*
right angle *n* angle of 90 degrees
righteous *adj* **1** morally good **2** having just cause **~ly** *adv* **~ness** *n*
rightful *adj* according to a just or legal

claim **~ly** *adv* **~ness** *n*
right-hand *adj* on the right side **~ed** *adj* using the right hand for most actions **~er** *n* right-handed person
right-hand man *n* most useful and valuable helper
rightist *n, adj* (supporter) of the right in politics
rightly *adv* **1** correctly **2** justly
right-minded *adj* having the right opinions, principles, etc.
righto *interj esp. BrE* right (5)
right of way *n* **rights of way 1** right of a vehicle to go first **2** (right to follow) a path across private land
rights *pl n* **1** political, social, etc., advantages to which someone has a just claim, morally or in law **2 by rights** in justice; if things were done properly **3 set/put to rights** make just, healthy, etc. **4 the rights and wrongs of** the true facts of **5 within one's rights** not going beyond one's just claims
right-wing *adj* favouring the right in politics
rigid *adj* **1** stiff **2** not easy to change **~ly** *adv* **~ity** *n*
rigmarole *n* long confused story or set of actions
rigor mortis *n* stiffening of the muscles after death
rigorous *adj* **1** careful and exact **2** severe **~ly** *adv*
rigour, *AmE* **-or** *n* **1** severity **2** *fml* exactness and and clarity of thought
rig-out *n infml* set of clothes
rile *vt infml* annoy
rill *n lit* small stream
rim *n* edge, esp. of a round object ♦ *vt* **-mm-** be round the edge of
rime *n lit* white frost
rind *n* thick outer covering of certain fruits, or of cheese or bacon
ring[1] *n* **1** (metal) circle worn on the finger **2** circular band, mark, or arrangement **3** enclosed space where things are shown, performances take place, or people box or wrestle **4** group of people who work together, esp. dishonestly **5 make/run rings round** do things much better and faster than ♦ *vt* form or put a ring round
ring[2] *v* **rang, rung 1** *vi/t* cause (a bell) to sound **2** *vi* (of a bell, telephone, etc.) sound **3** *vi/t esp. BrE* telephone **4** *vi* be filled with sound **5 ring a bell** remind one of something **6 ring the changes** introduce variety **7 ring true/false** sound true/untrue **ring off** *phr vi BrE* end a telephone conversation **ring out** *phr vi* (of a voice, bell, etc.) sound loudly and clearly **ring up** *phr vt* **1** record (money paid) on a cash register **2** telephone ♦ *n* **1** bell-like sound **2** certain quality: *a ring of truth* **3** *esp. BrE* telephone call **~er** *n*
ring binder *n* binder for loose sheets of paper, with metal rings to hold them in place
ringleader *n* person who leads others to do wrong
ringlet *n* long hanging curl of hair
ringmaster *n* person who directs circus performances
ring-pull *n* ring-shaped handle for pulling open a sealed tin
ring road *n BrE* road that goes round a town
ringside *adj, adv, n* (at) the edge of a ring, e.g. a boxing ring, where performances are held
ringworm *n* disease causing red rings on the skin
rink *n* specially prepared surface for skating
rinse *vt* wash in clean water, so as to get rid of soap, dirt, etc. ♦ *n* **1** act of rinsing **2** liquid hair colouring
riot *n* **1** noisy violent crowd behaviour **2** plentiful show: *a riot of colour* **3** *infml* very funny and successful occasion or person **4 run riot**: **a** become violent and uncontrollable **b** (of a plant) grow too thick and tall ♦ *vi* take part in a riot **~er** *n* **~ous** *adj* wild and disorderly **~ously** *adv*
rip *vi/t* **-pp- 1** tear quickly and violently **2 let something rip** *infml* remove control and let things develop in their own way **rip off** *phr vt infml* **1** charge

too much **2** *esp. AmE* steal ♦ *n* long tear

RIP *abbrev. for:* rest in peace; words written on a gravestone

ripcord *n* cord pulled to open a parachute

ripe *adj* **1** (fully grown and) ready to be eaten **2** ready; suitable: *land ripe for industrial development* **~ness** *n*

ripen *vi/t* make or become ripe

rip-off *n infml* **1** act of charging too much **2** act of stealing

riposte *vi, n* (make) a quick clever (unfriendly) reply

ripple *vi* **1** move in small waves **2** make a sound like gently running water ♦ *n* **1** very small wave or gentle waving movement **2** sound of or like gently running water

rip-roaring *adj* noisy and exciting

ripsnorter *n infml* something unusually exciting or powerful

rise *vi* **rose, risen 1** go up; get higher **2** (of the sun) come above the horizon **3** (of land) slope upward **4** stand up **5** *fml* get out of bed **6** (of wind) get stronger **7** rebel **8** come back to life after being dead **9** (esp. of a river) begin **10 rise to the occasion** show that one can deal with a difficult matter ♦ *n* **1** increase **2** act of growing greater or more powerful **3** *BrE* wage increase **4** upward slope **5 give rise to** cause **rising** *n* uprising **rising** *prep* nearly (the stated age)

risible *adj fml* deserving to be laughed at **–bility** *n*

rising damp *n* water that comes up into the walls of a building

risk *n* **1** chance that something bad may happen **2** (in insurance) (a person or thing that is) a danger **3 at risk** in danger **4 at one's own risk** agreeing to bear any loss or danger ♦ *vt* **1** place in danger **2** take the chance of **~y** *adj* dangerous

risotto *n* rice dish with meat, vegetables, etc.

risqué *adj* (of a joke) slightly rude

rissole *n* small round flat mass of cut-up meat

rite *n* ceremonial (religious) act with a fixed pattern

rite of passage *n* ritual connected with an important change in someone's life (e.g. puberty)

ritornello *n* **-li** *or* **-os** musical passage played by accompanying instruments

ritual *n* (ceremonial) act or acts always repeated in the same form ♦ *adj* done as a rite

ritzy *adj infml* glamorous; chic

rival *n* person with whom one competes ♦ *adj* competing ♦ *vt* **-ll-** (*AmE* **-l-**) be as good as **~ry** *n* competition

riven *adj fml* split violently apart

river *n* wide natural stream of water

rivet *n* metal pin used for fastening heavy metal plates together ♦ *vt* **1** fasten with rivets **2** attract and hold (someone's attention) strongly **~ing** *adj* very interesting

riviera *n* stretch of coast where people take holidays

rivulet *n lit* very small stream

riyal *n* unit of money in Saudi Arabia

RN *abbrev. for:* Royal Navy

RNA *n* acid which carries genetic information in a cell

roach[1] *n* European freshwater fish

roach[2] *n AmE* **1** cockroach **2** *sl* butt of a marijuana cigarette

road *n* smooth prepared track for wheeled vehicles

roadblock *n* something placed across a road to stop traffic

road hog *n* fast selfish careless driver

roadhouse *n* inn beside a main road

roadie *n* organizer of a rock group's tour

roadstead *n* sheltered stretch of water near the shore

roadster *n* open sports car

road tax *n* tax vehicle owners must pay

roadway *n* middle part of a road, where vehicles drive

road works *pl n* road repairing

roadworthy *adj* (of a vehicle) in safe condition to drive **–thiness** *n*

roam *vi/t* wander around with no clear purpose

roan *n, adj* (horse) of mixed colour
roar *n* deep loud continuing sound ♦ *v* **1** *vi* give a roar **2** *vt* say forcefully **3** *vi* laugh loudly **~ing** *adj, adv* **1** very great: *a roaring trade* **2** very: *roaring drunk*
roast *vt* cook (esp. meat) in an oven or over a fire ♦ *adj* roasted ♦ *n* large piece of roasted meat
rob *vt* **-bb-** steal something from **~ber** *n* **~bery** *n* (example of) the crime of robbing
robe *n* long flowing garment
robin *n* small brown bird with a red front
robot *n* machine that can do some of the work of a human being **~ics** *n* study of the making and use of robots
robust *adj* strong (and healthy) **~ly** *adv* **~ness** *n*
roc *n* huge legendary bird
rock[1] *n* **1** stone forming part of the Earth's surface **2** large piece of stone **3** *AmE* a stone **4** (in Britain) hard sticky kind of sweet made in long round bars **5** *sl, esp. AmE* a diamond **6** rock 'n' roll **7 on the rocks** : **a** (of a marriage) likely to fail soon **b** (of a drink) with ice but no water
rock[2] *v* **1** *vi/t* move regularly backwards and forwards or from side to side **2** *vt* shock greatly **3 rock the boat** spoil the existing good situation
rock and roll *n* rock 'n' roll
rock bottom *n* the lowest point
rockbound *adj* bordered with rocks
rock cake *n* small hard cake
rocker *n* **1** curved piece of wood on which something rocks **2** *esp. AmE* rocking chair **3 off one's rocker** *infml* mad
rockery *n* (part of) a garden laid out with rocks and small plants
rocket *n* **1** tube-shaped object driven through the air by burning gases, used for travelling into space, or as a missile or firework **2** *BrE infml* severe scolding ♦ *vi* rise quickly and suddenly
rocking chair *n* chair with rockers
rocking horse *n* wooden horse with rockers, for a child to ride on
rock 'n' roll *n* popular modern music with a strong loud beat
rock salmon *n BrE* (name used by shopkeepers for) any of various types of food fish
rock salt *n* common salt mined from the earth
rocky *adj* **1** full of rocks **2** *infml* unsteady; not firm
rococo *adj* with much curling decoration
rod *n* long thin stiff pole or bar
rode *past t. of* ride
rodent *n* small plant-eating animal with long front teeth, such as a mouse, rat, or rabbit
rodeo *n* **-os** (in America) public entertainment with horse riding, cattle catching, etc.
rodomontade /ˌrodəmonˈtayd, -ˈtahd/ *n fml* boastful speech
roe *n* mass of fish eggs, often eaten
roebuck *n* male roe deer
roe deer *n* small European and Asian deer
roentgen ray /ˈrontgən, ˈrentgen/ *n* X-ray
roger *interj* (used in radio and signalling to say one has understood)
rogue *n* dishonest person ♦ *adj* **1** (of a wild animal) bad-tempered and dangerous **2** not following the usual or accepted standards **roguish** *adj* playful and fond of playing tricks
rogues' gallery *n* collection of (pictures of) criminal or unpleasant people
roister *vi arch.* engage in noisy merrymaking **~er** *n*
role *n* **1** character played by an actor **2** part someone takes in an activity
role-playing *n* adoption of a particular type of behaviour, esp. to help with psychological problems
roll *v* **1** *vi/t* turn over and over or from side to side **2** *vt* form into esp. a tube by curling round and round **3** *vi* move steadily and smoothly (as if) on wheels **4** *vi* swing from side to side on the sea **5** *vt* flatten with a roller or rolling pin **6**

vi make a long deep sound **7** *vt* cause (esp. film cameras) to begin working **8** *vt* cause (the eyes) to move round and round **roll in** *phr vi* arrive in large quantities **roll on** *phr vi* come soon; hurry up **roll out** *phr vt* unroll **roll up** *phr vi* **1** arrive **2** (used esp. asking people to see a show at a circus, fair, etc.) come in ♦ *n* **1** act of rolling **2** rolled tube **3** small loaf for one person **4** long deep sound (as if) of a lot of quick strokes **5** official list of names **~ing** *adj* **1** (of land) with long gentle slopes **2 rolling in it** *infml* extremely rich

roll call *n* calling a list of names to see who is there

roller *n* **1** tube-shaped part for pressing, smoothing, shaping, etc., **2** long heavy wave on the coast

roller coaster *n* small railway with sharp slopes and curves, found in amusement parks

roller skate *n* arrangement of four small wheels on a shoe, for moving along on **roller-skate** *vi*

roller towel *n* continuous towel hung from a roller

rollicking *adj* noisy and merry ♦ *n BrE infml* severe scolding

rolling mill *n* factory or machine in which metal is rolled into plates and bars

rolling pin *n* tube-shaped implement for flattening pastry

rolling stock *n* carriages, engines, etc., of a railway

rolling stone *n* person with no fixed home or responsibilities

rollmop *n* pickled herring

roll-on roll-off *adj* (of a ferry) that large vehicles can drive on to and off

roly-poly *adj infml* (of a person) fat and round

ROM *n* read-only memory; computer memory holding information that is continuously needed by the computer

Roman *n, adj* (citizen) of Rome, esp. ancient Rome

Roman candle *n* firework that shoots out coloured stars

Roman Catholic *n, adj* (member) of the branch of the Christian religion led by the pope **~ism** *n*

romance *n* **1** love affair **2** romantic quality **3** story of love, adventure, etc.

Romance *adj* (of language) developed from Latin

Romanesque *adj* of a style of European architecture of around 1000 AD, characterized by round arches

Roman nose *n* prominently curved nose

Roman numeral *n* any of the signs (such as I, II, V, X, L) used for numbers in ancient Rome and sometimes now

Romansh, Romansch *n* language spoken in E Switzerland

romantic *adj* **1** showing warm feelings of love **2** of or suggesting love, adventure, strange happenings, etc. **3** highly imaginative; not practical **4** showing romanticism ♦ *n* romantic person **~ally** *adv* **~ism** *n* admiration of feeling rather than thought in art and literature **~ize, ~ise** *vt* make (something) seem more interesting or romantic than it really is

Romany *n* **1** gipsy **2** gipsies' language

Romeo *n* **-os** romantic male lover

romp *vi* play noisily and roughly **romp through** *phr vt* succeed in, quickly and easily ♦ *n* **1** occasion of romping **2** *infml* piece of amusing entertainment with plenty of action

rompers *pl n* one-piece garment for babies

rondeau /ˈrondoh/ *n* **-deaux** 15-line 3-stanza poem with recurring lines and rhymes

rondo *n* **-os** piece of music with a recurring refrain

roo *n* **roos** *AustrE infml* kangaroo

rood *n arch.* crucifix

roof *n* **1** top covering of a building, vehicle, etc. **2** upper part of the inside (of the mouth) ♦ *vt* put or be a roof on **~ing** *n* roof material

roof rack *n* metal frame on top of a car, for carrying things

rooftop *vt* **1** roof **2 from the rooftops**

loudly, so that everyone can hear

rook[1] *n* large black bird, like a crow

rook[2] *n* castle (2)

rook[3] *vt sl* cheat

rookery *n* group of rooks' nests

rookie *n esp. AmE* new soldier or policeman

room *n* **1** division of a building, with its own floor, walls, and ceiling **2** (enough) space **3** need or possibility for something to happen; scope: *room for improvement* ♦ *vi AmE* have lodgings; have a room or rooms **~y** *adj* with plenty of space inside

room service *n* hotel service providing food, drink, etc., in people's rooms

roost *n* place where a bird sleeps ♦ *vi* **1** (of a bird) sit and sleep **2 come home to roost** (of a bad action) have a bad effect on the doer, esp. after a period of time

rooster *n esp. AmE* cock (1)

root *n* **1** part of a plant that goes down into the soil for food **2** part of a tooth, hair, etc., that holds it to the body **3** cause; beginning; origin **4** (in grammar) base part of a word to which other parts can be added **5** number that when multiplied by itself a stated number of times gives another stated number **6 root and branch** (of something bad to be got rid of) thoroughly ♦ *v* **1** *vi/t* (cause to) form roots **2** *vi* search by turning things over **root for** *phr vt* support strongly **root out** *phr vt* get rid of completely **~less** *adj* without a home **roots** *pl n* (one's connection with) one's place of origin

root beer *n AmE* sweet fizzy drink flavoured with roots and herbs

rope *n* **1** (piece of) strong thick cord **2** fat twisted string of jewels **3** hanging as a punishment **4 give someone (plenty of) rope** allow someone (plenty of) freedom to act ♦ *vt* tie with a rope **rope in** *phr vt infml* persuade or force to join an activity **rope off** *phr vt* separate or enclose with ropes **ropes** *pl n* rules, customs, and ways of operating

rope ladder *n* ladder made (partly) from rope

ropy, ropey *adj BrE infml* of bad quality or condition

Roquefort /ˈrok(ə)ˌfaw/ *n* strong French sheep's-milk cheese

Rorschach test *n* psychological test in which someone interprets random shapes

rosary *n* string of beads used by Roman Catholics for counting prayers

rose[1] *past t. of* rise

rose[2] *n* **1** (brightly coloured sweet-smelling flower of) a prickly-stemmed bush **2** pale to dark pink colour **3 be not all roses** *infml* (of a job, situation, etc.) include some unpleasant things

rosé *n* light pink wine

roseate *adj lit* pink

rose-coloured also **rose-tinted** *adj* providing or being a falsely optimistic impression

rose hip *n* berry of a rose

rosemary *n* shrubby plant used as a herb

rosette *n* flat flower-like arrangement of cloth, worn as a sign of something

rose window *n* circular decorative church window

rosewood *n* dark tropical wood used for furniture

rosin *n* substance rubbed on the bows of stringed musical instruments

roster *n* list of people's names and duties

rostrum *n* **-trums** *or* **-tra** raised place for a public performer

rosy *adj* **1** (esp. of skin) pink **2** (esp. of the future) giving hope **rosily** *adv* **rosiness** *n*

rot *vi/t* **-tt-** decay ♦ *n* **1** decay **2** process of getting worse or going wrong **3** *infml* foolish nonsense

rota *n* list of things to be done by different people taking turns

rotary *adj* rotating

rotate *vi/t* **1** turn round a fixed point **2** (cause to) take turns or come round regularly **-ation** *n* **1** rotating **2** one complete turn **3 in rotation** taking regular turns

Rotavator *n tdmk for* machine for

breaking up the soil for planting
rote *n fml* repeated study using memory rather than understanding
rotgut *n infml* strong low-quality alcoholic drink
rotisserie *n* rotating spit for roasting
rotor *n* **1** rotating part of a machine **2** set of helicopter blades
rotten *adj* **1** decayed; gone bad **2** *infml* nasty or unpleasant
rotter *n infml, esp. BrE* despicable person
rottweiler *n* German dog with short black hair, used for guarding
rotund *adj fml* (of a person) fat and round **~ness, ~ity** *n*
rotunda *n* round building
rouble *n* unit of money in the USSR
roué *n* debauched (old) man
rouge *n* red substance for colouring the cheeks
rough *adj* **1** having an uneven surface **2** stormy and violent **3** lacking gentleness, good manners, or consideration **4** (of food and living conditions) not delicate; simple **5** not detailed or exact **6** unfortunate and/or unfair **7** *infml* unwell **8 rough and ready** simple and without comfort ♦ *adv* in uncomfortable conditions: *sleeping rough* ♦ *n* **1** areas of long grass on a golf course **2 take the rough with the smooth** accept bad things as well as good things uncomplainingly ♦ *v* **rough it** *infml* live simply and rather uncomfortably **rough up** *phr vt infml* attack roughly, usu. as a threat **~ly** *adv* **1** in a rough manner **2** about; not exactly **~en** *vi/t* make or become rough **~ness** *n*
roughage *n* coarse matter in food, which helps the bowels to work
rough-and-tumble *n* noisy fighting
roughcast *n* surface of little stones on the outside of a building
rough diamond *n* very kind person with rough manners
rough-hewn *adj* (of wood or stone) roughly cut
roughhouse *n infml* brawl
roughneck *n* person who handles drilling-rig equipment
rough paper *n* paper for making informal notes or drawings
rough stuff *n BrE* violent behaviour
rough trade *n sl* coarse or uncouth men sought by homosexuals
roulette *n* game of chance played with a small ball and a spinning wheel
round *adj* **1** circular **2** ball-shaped **3** (of parts of the body) fat and curved **4** (of a number) expressed to the nearest 10, 100, 1000, etc. ♦ *adv* **1** with a circular movement **2** surrounding a central point: *Gather round.* **3** to various places: *travelling round* **4** so as to face the other way **5** everywhere or to everyone **6** to a particular place: *invite someone round* **7 round about** a little more or less than ♦ *prep.* **1** with a circular movement about **2** surrounding **3** into all parts of **4** not going straight but changing direction **5** near (a place or amount): *Do you live round here?* ♦ *n* **1** number or set (of events): *a continual round of parties* **2** regular delivery journey **3** number of esp. alcoholic drinks bought for everyone present **4 a** (in golf) complete game **b** (in boxing) period of fighting in a match **c** (in tennis, football, etc.) stage in a competition **d** one single shot from a gun **5** long burst: *a round of applause* **6** type of song for three or four voices, in which each sings the same tune, one starting a line after another has just finished it **7** *esp. BrE* sandwich made with two whole pieces of bread ♦ *vt* **1** go round **2** make round **round down** *phr vt* reduce to a whole number **round off** *phr vt* end suitably and satisfactorily **round on** *phr vt* turn and attack **round up** *phr vt* **1** gather together (scattered things) **2** increase (an exact figure) to the next highest whole number **~ness** *n*
roundabout *n BrE* **1** area of circular traffic flow where several roads meet **2** merry-go-round ♦ *adj* indirect
roundarm *adj, adv* done with a horizontal swing of the arm
roundel *n* circular figure or object

roundelay *n* simple song with a refrain
rounders *n* children's game where a player hits the ball and then runs round a square area
Roundhead *n* (in England) supporter of Parliament against Charles I
roundly *adv fml* **1** completely **2** forcefully
round robin *n* letter signed by many people
roundsman *n* tradesman who makes rounds
round-table *adj* at which everyone can meet and talk equally
round-the-clock *adj* happening both day and night
round trip *n* journey to a place and back again
roundup *n* gathering together of scattered things, animals, or people
rouse *vt* **1** *fml* waken **2** make more active, interested, or excited **rousing** *adj* that makes people excited
roustabout *n AmE* man who does heavy unskilled work
rout *n* complete defeat ♦ *vt* defeat completely
route *n* way from one place to another ♦ *vt* send by a particular route
route march *n* soldiers' long training march
routine *n* **1** regular fixed way of doing things **2** set of dance steps, songs, etc. ♦ *adj* **1** regular; not special **2** dull **~ly** *adv*
roux /rooh/ *n* **roux** mixture of flour and fat for thickening sauces
rove *vi esp. lit* wander
roving commission *n* job that takes one to many places
roving eye *n* sexual interests that pass quickly from one person to another
row[1] *n* **1** neat line of people or things **2 in a row** one after the other without a break
row[2] *vi/t* move (a boat) through the water with oars **~er** *n*
row[3] *n* **1** noisy quarrel **2** noise ♦ *vi* quarrel (noisily)
rowan *n* tree with small red berries
rowdy *adj* noisy and rough **-dily** *adv* **-diness** *n* **~ism** *n* rowdy behaviour
rowel *n* revolving disc at the end of a spur
row house *n AmE* terraced house
rowlock /ˈrolək *or* (*not tech*) ˈroh-ˌlok/ *n* fastener for an oar on the side of a boat
royal *adj* of a king or queen ♦ *n* member of the royal family **~ly** *adv* splendidly
royal assent *n* (in Britain) formal acceptance of a new law by the sovereign
royal blue *adj* of a purplish-blue colour
royalist *n* supporter of rule by kings and queens
royal jelly *n* nutritious secretion of the honey-bee
royalty *n* **1** people of the royal family **2** payment made to the writer of a book, piece of music, etc., out of the money from its sales
rozzer *n BrE sl* policeman
rpm *abbrev. for:* revolutions per minute
RSJ *n* rolled-steel joist; metal beam used in building
RSVP please reply (written on invitations)
rub *vi/t* **-bb- 1** press against (something or each other) with a repeated up-and-down or round-and-round movement **2 rub it in** *infml* keep talking about something that another person wants to forget **3 rub salt in the wound** make someone's suffering even worse **4 rub shoulders with** *infml* meet socially and treat as equals **5 rub up the wrong way** *infml* annoy **rub down** *phr vt* **1** dry by rubbing **2** make smooth by rubbing **rub in** *phr vt* make (liquid) go into a surface by rubbing **rub off** *phr vi* **1** come off a surface (onto another) by rubbing **2** be influential through contact or example **rub out** *phr vt BrE* erase with a rubber ♦ *n* **1** act of rubbing **2** cause of difficulty: *There's the rub.* **~bing** *n* copy made by rubbing paper laid over the top
rubato *adj* (of music) played with expressive changes of speed
rubber[1] *n* **1** elastic substance used for keeping out water, making tyres, etc. **2**

BrE piece of this for removing pencil marks **~y** *adj*
rubber² *n* competition, esp. in cards, which usu. consists of an odd number of games
rubber band *n* thin circle of rubber for fastening things together
rubber bullet *n* bullet made of rubber, for riot control
rubber cheque *n humorous* cheque which a bank will not cash because there is not enough money in the account
rubberneck *n AmE infml* **1** nosy person **2** sightseer
rubber plant *n* decorative large-leaved house plant
rubber-stamp *n* piece of rubber with raised letters or figures, for printing ♦ *vt* approve or support (a decision) officially, without really thinking about it
rubbish *n BrE* **1** waste material to be thrown away **2** nonsense
rubble *n* broken stone and bricks, esp. from a destroyed building
rubdown *n* act of rubbing something down
rubella *n* German measles
rubicund /ˈroohbikənd/ *adj fml* fat, red, and healthy-looking **~ity** *n*
ruble *n* rouble
rubric *n* set of printed instructions
ruby *n* deep red precious stone
ruche *n* pleated strip of fabric
ruck *n* **1** ordinary level of life **2** (in rugby) a loose group of players trying to get the ball
rucksack *n* large bag carried on the back, esp. by walkers, climbers, etc.
ruck up *phr vi* crease
ruckus *n AmE* rumpus
ructions *pl n infml* noisy complaints and anger
rudder *n* blade at the back of a boat or aircraft to control its direction
ruddy *adj* **1** (of the face) pink and healthy **2** *lit* red **3** *BrE infml* (used for adding force to an expression) **-diness** *n*
rude *adj* **1** not polite; bad-mannered **2** concerned with sex **3** sudden and violent: *a rude shock* **4** *old use* roughly made **~ly** *adv* **~ness** *n*
rudimentary *adj* **1** (of facts, knowledge, etc.) at the simplest level **2** small and not fully usable
rudiments *pl n* simplest parts of a subject, learnt first
rue *vt* be very sorry about **~ful** *adj* feeling or showing that one is sorry about something **~fully** *adv*
ruff *n* stiff wheel-shaped white collar
ruffian *n* unpleasant violent man
ruffle *vt* **1** make uneven **2** trouble; upset
rug *n* **1** thick floor mat **2** warm woollen covering to wrap round oneself
rugby *n* type of football played with an egg-shaped ball which can be handled
rugged *adj* large, rough, and strong-looking **~ly** *adv* **~ness** *n*
rugger *n infml* rugby
ruin *n* **1** destruction **2** also **ruins** *pl* remains of a building that has fallen down or been (partly) destroyed ♦ *vt* **1** spoil **2** cause total loss of money to **~ed** *adj* (of a building) partly or wholly destroyed **~ous** *adj* causing destruction or total loss of money
ruination *n* (cause of) being ruined
rule *n* **1** something that tells you what you must do **2** period or way of ruling **3** ruler (2) **4 as a rule** usually ♦ *v* **1** *vi/t* be in charge of (a country, people, etc.) **2** *vi* give an official decision **3** *vt* draw (a line) with a ruler **4 rule the roost** be in charge **rule out** *phr vt* **1** remove from consideration **2** make impossible **ruling** *n* official decision
rule of thumb *n* quick inexact way of calculating or judging
ruler *n* **1** person who rules **2** narrow flat rod for measuring or drawing straight lines
rum¹ *n* strong alcoholic drink made from sugar
rum² *adj* **-mm-** *infml* strange
rumba *n* lively Latin American dance
rumble¹ *vi, n* (make) a deep continuous rolling sound
rumble² *vt BrE infml* not be deceived by

rumbustious *adj* noisy, cheerful, and lively **~ness** *n*
ruminant *n, adj* (animal) that ruminates
ruminate *vi* **1** think deeply **2** (of an animal) bring food back from the stomach and chew it again **-ative** *adj* seeming thoughtful
rummage *vi* turn things over untidily in searching
rummy *n* simple card game
rumour, *AmE* **-or** *n* (piece of) information, perhaps untrue, spread from person to person **~ed** *adj* reported unofficially
rump *n* part of an animal above the back legs
rumple *vt* make untidy; disarrange
rumpus *n* noisy angry argument or disagreement
run *v* **ran, run,** *pres. p.* **-nn- 1** *vi* (of people and animals) move faster than a walk **2** *vt* take part in (a race) by running **3** *vi/t* (cause to) move quickly: *The car ran into a tree.* **4** *vi/t* (cause to) work **5** *vt* control (an organization or system) **6** *vi* go; pass: *The road runs south.* **7** *vi* continue in operation, performance, etc. **8** *vi* (cause liquid) to flow: *run a bath* **9** *vi* pour out liquid **10** *vi* (melt and) spread by the action of heat or water **11** become: *Supplies are running low.* **12** *vi esp. AmE* try to get elected **13** *vt* bring into a country illegally and secretly **14** *vi esp. AmE* ladder **15** *vt* take somewhere in a vehicle **run across** *phr vt* meet or find by chance **run after** *phr vt* **1** chase **2** try to gain the attention and company of **run along** *phr vi* go away **run away** *phr vi* go away (as if) to escape **run away/off with** *phr vt* **1** (of feelings) gain control of **2** go away with (a lover) **3** steal **run down** *phr v* **1** *vt* knock down and hurt with a vehicle **2** *vt* chase and catch **3** *vi* (esp. of a clock or battery) lose power and stop working **4** *vt* say unfair things about **run into** *phr vt* meet by chance **run off** *phr vt* print (copies) **run out** *phr vi* **1** come to an end, so there is none left **2** have none left **run over** *phr v* **1** *vt* knock down and drive over **2** *vi* overflow **run through** *phr vt* **1** repeat for practice **2** read or examine quickly **3** push one's sword right through **run to** *phr vt* be or have enough to pay for **run up** *phr vt* **1** raise (a flag) **2** make quickly, esp. by sewing **3** cause oneself to have (bills or debts) **run up against** *phr vt* be faced with (a difficulty) ♦ *n* **1** act of running **2** continuous set of similar events, performances, etc. **3** eager demand to buy or sell **4** freedom to use something **5** animal enclosure: *a chicken run* **6** scoring unit in cricket **7** sloping course: *a ski run* **8** *AmE* ladder (2) **9 run for one's money: a** plenty of opposition in a competition **b** good results for money spent or effort made **10 on the run** trying to escape
run-about *n infml* small light car
run-around *n sl* delaying or deceiving treatment
runaway *adj* **1** out of control **2** having escaped by running
rundown *n infml* detailed report
run-down *adj* **1** tired, weak, and ill **2** in bad condition
rune *n* letter in an alphabet formerly used in Northern Europe **runic** *adj*
rung[1] *past p. of* ring[2]
rung[2] *n* cross-bar in a ladder or on a chair
run-in *n infml* quarrel or disagreement, esp. with the police
runnel *n esp. lit* small stream
runner *n* **1** person or animal that runs **2** smuggler: *a gunrunner* **3** thin blade on which something slides on ice or snow **4** stem with which a plant spreads itself along the ground
runner bean *n* bean with long edible seed pod
runner-up *n* **runners-up** one that comes second in a race or competition
running *n* **1** act or sport of running **2 in/out of the running** with some/no hope of winning **3 make the running** set the speed at which something develops ♦ *adj* **1** (of water) flowing **2** continuous: *a running commentary* **3** (of

money) spent or needed to keep something working **4 in running order** (of a machine) working properly ♦ *adv* in a row
running-mate *n* (in US politics) person with whom one is trying to get elected for a pair of political positions of greater and lesser importance
runny *adj* **1** in a more liquid form than usual **2** (of the nose or eyes) producing liquid
run-of-the-mill *adj* ordinary; dull
runt *n* **1** small badly-developed animal **2** *derog* small unpleasant person
run-through *n* act of repeating something for practice
run-up *n* period leading up to an event
runway *n* surface on which aircraft land and take off
rupee *n* unit of money in India, Pakistan, etc.
rupture *n* **1** *fml* sudden breaking **2** hernia ♦ *v* **1** *vi/t fml* break suddenly **2** *vt* give (oneself) a hernia
rural *adj* of the country (not the town)
Ruritanian *adj* characterized by the dated finery or intrigue of central European minor royalty
ruse *n* deceiving trick
rush[1] *v* **1** *vi/t* go or take suddenly and very quickly **2** *vi* hurry **3** *vt* deal with (too) hastily **4** *vt* force (someone) to do something hastily **5** *vt* attack suddenly and all together ♦ *n* **1** sudden rapid movement **2** (need for) (too much) hurrying **3** sudden demand **4** period of great and hurried activity
rush[2] *n* grasslike water plant
rushes *pl n* (in film making) the first print of a film
rush hour *n* busy period when most people are travelling to or from work
rusk *n* hard biscuit for babies
russet *adj esp. lit* brownish red
Russian *adj* of Russia or the USSR ♦ *n* **1** Russian person **2** language of Russia
Russian roulette *n* dangerous game in which one fires a gun at one's head without knowing whether it is loaded
Russo- *prefix* **1** of Russia: *Russophile* **2** Russian and: *Russo-Japanese*
rust *n* **1** reddish brown surface formed on iron, steel, etc., that has been wet **2** the colour of this ♦ *vi/t* (cause to) become covered with rust **~y** *adj* **1** covered with rust **2** *infml* lacking recent practice
rustic *adj* typical of the country, esp. in being simple ♦ *n usu. derog* person from the country
rusticate *vt* suspend (a student) from university
rustle *v* **1** *vi/t* (cause to) make slight sounds like dry leaves moving **2** *vt esp. AmE* steal (cattle or horses) **~r** *n*
rustle up *phr vt* provide quickly
rut[1] *n* **1** deep narrow track left by a wheel **2** dull fixed way of life **~ted** *adj* having ruts
rut[2] *n* (season of) sexual excitement in deer ♦ *vi* **-tt-** (of an animal) be in a rut
rutabaga *n AmE* swede
ruthless *adj* doing cruel things without pity **~ly** *adv* **~ness** *n*
-ry *suffix* -ery: *wizardy*
rye *n* grass plant with grain used esp. for flour

S

S, s the 19th letter of the English alphabet
S *abbrev. for:* south(ern)
-s *suffix* makes **a** the pl of nouns **b** the 3rd person pres. sing. of verbs
-'s *suffix* makes the possessive case of nouns
-s' *suffix* makes the possessive case of pl nouns
Sabbath *n* religious day of rest, esp. Saturday (for Jews) or (for Christians) Sunday
sabbatical *n, adj* (period) with pay

when one is free to leave one's ordinary job to travel and study
sable *n* (dark fur from) a small animal related to the weasel ♦ *adj lit* black
sabot *n* wooden shoe
sabotage *n* intentional damage carried out secretly ♦ *vt* perform sabotage against
saboteur *n* person who practises sabotage
sabra *n* native-born Israeli
sabre, *AmE* **saber** *n* heavy military sword, usu. curved
sabre-rattling *n* talking about (military) power in a threatening way
sabre-toothed tiger *n* extinct tiger with long fangs
sac *n* pouchlike part in an animal or plant
saccharin /ˈsak(ə)rin/ *n* very sweet-tasting chemical used instead of sugar ♦ *adj derog* sentimentally sweet
sacerdotal /ˌsasəˈdohtl/ *adj* of a priest
sachet *n* small plastic bag holding an amount of liquid, etc.
sack[1] *n* **1** large simple bag of strong material **2** *BrE* dismissal from a job **3** *infml esp. AmE* bed ♦ *vt BrE* dismiss from a job **~ing** *n* sackcloth (1)
sack[2] *vt* destroy and rob (a defeated city) **sack** *n*
sack[3] *n* dry white Spanish wine of Shakespeare's time
sackbut *n* trombone of Renaissance times
sackcloth *n* **1** rough cloth for making sacks **2 sackcloth and ashes** *lit* sign of sorrow for what one has done
sacrament *n* important Christian ceremony, such as baptism or marriage **~al** *adj*
Sacrament *n* bread (and wine) received at Communion
sacred *adj* **1** connected with religion **2** holy because connected with God or gods **3** that is solemn and must be respected **~ness** *n*
sacred cow *n derog* thing so much accepted that not even honest doubts about it are allowed
sacrifice *n* **1** offering to gods, esp. of an animal killed ceremonially **2** loss or giving up of something of value ♦ *v* **1** *vi/t* offer (as) a sacrifice to gods **2** *vt* give up or lose, esp. for some good purpose **–ficial** *adj*
sacrilege *n* treating a holy place or thing without respect **–legious** *adj*
sacristan *n* person in charge of a sacristy
sacristy *n* room where a church's ceremonial equipment is kept
sacroiliac /ˌsaykrohˈiliak/ *adj, n* (of) the place where the spine joins the pelvis
sacrosanct *adj* too holy or important to be treated disrespectfully or harmed
sacrum /ˈsaykrəm/ *n* **-ra** bottom of the spine
sad *adj* **-dd- 1** unhappy **2** unsatisfactory **~ly** *adv* **~den** *vt* make or become sad **~ness** *n*
saddle *n* **1** rider's seat on a horse, bicycle, etc. **2** piece of meat from the back of a sheep or deer **3 in the saddle** in control (of a job) ♦ *vt* put a saddle on (a horse) **saddle with** *phr vt* give (someone) (an unpleasant or difficult duty, responsibility, etc.)
saddlesore *adj* sore from riding
sadhu *n* Hindu holy man
sadism *n* unnatural fondness for cruelty to others, sometimes to gain sexual pleasure **–ist** *n* **–istic** *adj*
sadomasochism *n* the gaining of (sexual) pleasure from hurting oneself (or other people)
s.a.e. *abbrev. for:* stamped addressed envelope
safari *n* journey to hunt or photograph animals, esp. in Africa
safari park *n* park where wild animals are kept and can be looked at
safari suit *n* suit made of a light material, esp. strong cotton, including a **safari jacket** with belt and breast pockets
safe *adj* **1** out of danger **2** not likely to cause danger or harm **3** (of a seat in Parliament) certain to be won in an election by a particular party **4 on the**

safe side being more careful than may be necessary ♦ *n* thick metal box with a lock, for keeping valuable things in **~ly** *adv* **~ness** *n*

safe-conduct *n* official protection given to someone passing through an area

safe-deposit box *n* small box for storing valuable objects, esp. in a bank

safeguard *n* means of protection against something unwanted ♦ *vt* protect

safekeeping *n* protection from harm or loss

safety *n* condition of being safe

safety catch *n* lock on a gun to prevent it from being fired accidentally

safety lamp *n* miner's lamp made so that the flame cannot ignite inflammable gas

safety match *n* match which will only ignite on a specially prepared surface

safety net *n* **1** net to catch tightrope walkers, acrobats, etc. who fall **2** safeguard

safety pin *n* bent pin with a cover at one end, used for fastening things

safety valve *n* **1** means of getting rid of possibly dangerous forces (in a machine) **2** something that allows strong feelings to be expressed in a non-violent way

saffron *n* **1** deep orange substance got from a flower, used for giving colour and taste to food **2** orange-yellow colour

sag *vi* **-gg- 1** sink or bend downwards out of the usual position **2** become less active, happy, etc. **sag** *n*

saga *n* **1** old story, esp. about the Vikings **2** long story

sagacious /sə'gayshəs/ *adj fml* wise **~ly** *adv* **-city** *n*

sage[1] *adj lit* wise, esp. from long experience ♦ *n* wise person, esp. an old man

sage[2] *n* herb with grey-green leaves

sagebrush *n* bushy plant covering large areas of the plains of the western US

sago *n* white plant substance used for making sweet dishes

sahib *n* (used formerly in India as a title of respect for a European man)

said *past t. and p. of* say ♦ *adj law* just mentioned

sail *n* **1** piece of strong cloth that allows the wind to move a ship through the water **2** trip in a boat **3** wind-catching blade of a windmill **4 set sail** begin a sea journey ♦ *v* **1** *vi/t* travel (across) by boat **2** *vt* direct or command (a boat) on water **3** *vi* begin a voyage **4** *vi* move smoothly or easily **~ing** *n* sport of riding in or directing a small boat with sails

sailboard *n* floating board with a sail, ridden in windsurfing

sailcloth *n* **1** heavy canvas used in sails and tents **2** lightweight canvas used for clothing

sailor *n* person who works on a ship

sailplane *n* glider which rises on upward air currents

saint *n* **1** person officially recognised after death as especially holy by the Christian church **2** *infml* very good and completely unselfish person **~ly** *adj* very holy

Saint Bernard *n* large Swiss dog used for helping lost travellers

saith *v arch.* says

sake[1] *n* **1 for the sake of** : **a** in order to help, improve, or bring advantage to **b** for the purpose of **2 for Christ's/God's/goodness/pity('s) sake** *infml* (used to give force to urgent request or sometimes an expression of annoyance)

sake[2] /'sahki/ *n* Japanese alcoholic drink made from rice

salaam *vi, n* (in Eastern countries) (perform) a low bow, touching the forehead with the hand

salacious /sə'layshəs/ *adj fml* showing a strong (improper) interest in sex **~ly** *adv* **~ness** *n*

salad *n* mixture of usu. raw vegetables served cold, sometimes with other food added

salad days *pl n* one's time of youth and inexperience

salamander *n* small animal like a lizard
salami *n* large salty sausage with a strong taste of garlic
salary *n* fixed regular pay each month for a job, esp. for workers of higher rank **–ried** *adj* receiving a salary (as opposed to wages)
salchow /ˈsalkow/ *n* jump in skating, turning round in the air
sale *n* **1** (act of) selling **2** special offering of goods at low prices **salable** *adj* that can be sold
sales *adj* of or for selling: *a sales forecast*
salesclerk *n AmE* shop assistant
salesman *n* **-men** male salesperson
salesmanship *n* skill in selling
salesperson *n* **-people 1** sales representative **2** shop assistant, esp. a skilled one
sales representative *n* person who goes from place to place, usu. within a particular area, selling and taking orders for their firm's goods
sales resistance *n* unwillingness to buy
sales talk *n* talking intended to persuade people to buy
saleswoman *n* **–women** female salesperson
Salic law *n* rule excluding females from succeeding to the throne
salient[1] *adj fml* most noticeable or important
salient[2] *n* outwardly projecting part of a fortification or line of defence
saline *adj* containing salt
saliva *n* natural liquid produced in the mouth **~ry** *adj*
sallow[1] *adj* (of the skin) yellow and unhealthy-looking **~ness** *n*
sallow[2] *n* type of willow tree
sally *n* **1** quick short attack **2** sharp, clever remark ♦ **sally forth** *phr vi often humorous* go out, esp. to meet a difficulty
salmon *n* **salmon** *or* **salmons** large pink-fleshed fish highly valued as food
salmonella /ˌsalməˈnelə/ *n* bacteria that causes food poisoning
salmon trout *n* large trout with pink flesh
salon *n* stylish or fashionable small shop
saloon *n* **1** large grandly furnished room for use of ship's passengers **2** *BrE* large car with a fixed roof **3** *AmE* public drinking place
saloon bar *n BrE* comfortably furnished room in a pub, with more expensive drinks than in the public bar
salsa *n* Latin American blend of jazz and rock music
salsify *n* vegetable with a long edible root
salt *n* **1** common white substance used for preserving food and improving its taste **2** chemical compound of an acid and a metal **3** *infml* old, experienced sailor **4 the salt of the earth** person or people regarded as admirable and dependable ♦ *vt* put salt on **salt away** *phr vt* save (money), esp. for the future
saltcellar *n* small pot with a hole for shaking salt on to food
saltlick *n* **1** large salty block for cattle to lick **2** place where animals get salt from the ground
saltpan *n* hollow or vessel in which salt is left when salty water evaporates
saltpetre, *AmE* **–ter** *n* chemical used in making gunpowder and matches
saltwater *adj* of or living in salty water or the sea
salty *adj* containing or tasting of salt
salubrious *adj* **1** socially desirable or respectable **2** *fml* health-giving
saluki *n* tall slender N African hunting dog
salutary /ˈsalyoot(ə)ri/ *adj* causing an improvement in character, future behaviour, health, etc.
salutation *n* **1** *fml* expression of greeting by words or actions **2** word or phrase such as 'Ladies and Gentlemen', 'Dear Sir', 'Dear Miss Jones', at the beginning of a speech or letter
salute *n* **1** military sign of recognition, esp. raising the hand to the forehead **2** ceremonial firing of guns to honour someone ♦ *v* **1** *vi/t* make a military

salute (to) **2** *vt fml* honour and praise **3** *vt fml* greet

salvage *vt* save (goods or property) from wreck or destruction ♦ *n* salvaging

salvation *n* **1** (esp. in the Christian religion) saving or state of being saved from sin **2** something or someone that saves one from loss or failure

Salvation Army *n* Christian organization with military uniforms and ranks, that helps poor people

salve *n* medicinal paste for putting on a wound, sore place, etc. ♦ *vt fml* make (esp. feelings) less painful

salver *n* fine metal plate for serving food, drink, etc., formally

salvia *n* garden plant of the mint family

salvo *n* **-os** *or* **-oes** firing of several guns together

sal volatile *n* type of smelling salts

SAM *n* missile fired from the ground against aircraft

Samaritan *n* member of an organization (**the Samaritans**) that helps people in despair with no one to talk to

samba *n* quick dance of Brazilian origin

same *adj* **1** not changed or different; not another or other **2** alike in (almost) every way **3 in the same boat** in the same unpleasant situation **4 just/all the same** in spite of this ♦ *pron* the same thing, person, condition, etc. ♦ *adv* **the same (as)** in the same way (as) **~ness** *n* **1** very close likeness **2** lack of variety

samey *adj infml* lacking variety; monotonous

samite *n* rich medieval fabric

samizdat *n* system of distributing banned literature in the USSR

samosa *n* (in Indian cookery) small triangular filled pastry case

samovar *n* Russian water boiler for making tea

sampan *n* small flat-bottomed oriental boat

samphire *n* edible fleshy plant that grows near the sea

sample *n* small part representing the whole ♦ *vt* take and examine a sample of

sampler *n* piece of cloth with pictures, letters, etc., stitched on it with thread, done to show one's skill at sewing

samurai /ˈsam(y)ooˌrie/ *n* **samurai** member of the medieval military aristocracy of Japan

sanatorium *n* **-ums** *or* **-a** sort of hospital for sick people who are getting better but still need treatment, rest, etc.

sanctify *vt* make holy

sanctimonious *adj fml* disapproving of others because one thinks one is good, right, etc., and they are not **~ly** *adv* **~ness** *n*

sanction *n* **1** *fml* formal or official permission, approval, or acceptance **2** action taken against a person or country that has broken a law or rule **3** something that forces people to keep a rule ♦ *vt fml* **1** accept, approve, or permit, esp. officially **2** make acceptable

sanctity *n* holiness

sanctuary *n* **1** part of a (Christian) church considered most holy **2** (place of) protection for someone being hunted by officers of the law **3** area where animals are protected

sanctum *n* **1** holy place inside a temple **2** *infml* private place or room where one can be quiet and alone

sand *n* loose material of very small grains, found on seacoasts and in deserts ♦ *vt* **1** make smooth by rubbing with esp. sandpaper **2** put sand on, esp. to stop slipping **sands** *pl n* **1** area of sand **2** moments in time (as if measured by sand in an hourglass) **~y** *adj* **1** consisting of sand or having sand on the surface **2** (of hair) yellowish brown

sandal *n* light shoe with a flat bottom and bands to hold it to the foot

sandalwood *n* fragrant wood of an E Asian tree

sandbag[1] *n* sand-filled bag, esp. for forming a protective wall

sandbag[2] *vt* **1** protect or block with sandbags **2** hit with a sandbag

sandbank *n* ridge of sand deposited by

the sea or a river
sandblast *vt, n* (cut or clean with) a jet of sand propelled by air or steam **~er** *n*
sandcastle *n* small model, esp. of a castle, built of sand
sander also **sanding machine** *n* machine with a rough rotating disc, for smoothing surfaces
sand fly *n* small biting fly
sandpaper *n* paper covered with fine grainy material, for rubbing surfaces to make them smoother ♦ *vt* rub with sandpaper
sandpiper *n* small wading bird with a long bill
sandshoe *n* light canvas shoe
sandstone *n* soft rock formed from sand
sandstorm *n* desert windstorm in which sand is blown about
sandwich *n* two pieces of bread with other food between them ♦ *vt* fit (with difficulty) between two other things
sandwich board *n* advertising signs hung at the front and back of someone who walks about in public
sandwich course *n BrE* course of study including a period of work in business or industry
sane *adj* **1** healthy in mind; not mad **2** sensible **~ly** *adv* **~ness** *n*
sang *past t. of* sing
sangfroid /ˌsongˈfrwah/ *n* composure under stress
sangria *n* Spanish drink of red wine with fruit juice
sanguine *adj fml* quietly hopeful
sanitary *adj* **1** concerned with preserving health, esp. by removing dirt **2** not dangerous to health; clean
sanitary towel *n* small mass of soft paper worn to take up menstrual blood
sanitation *n* methods of protecting public health, esp. by removing and treating waste
sanitize, -ise *vt derog* make less unpleasant, dangerous, strongly expressed, etc., in order not to offend people
sanity *n* quality of being sane
sank *past t. of* sink
sansculotte /ˌsanzkyooˈlot/ *n* extreme political radical
Sanskrit *n* ancient language of India
Santa Claus *n* imaginary old man believed by children to bring presents at Christmas
sap[1] *n* watery food-carrying liquid in plants
sap[2] *vt* **-pp-** weaken or destroy, esp. over a long time
sapient *adj fml* wise **~ly** *adv* **-ence** *n*
sapling *n* young tree
sapper *n* soldier who digs trenches, lays mines, etc.
sapphire *n* bright blue precious stone
saraband *n* (music for) a slow 17th-18th-century court dance
Saracen *n* Muslim at the time of the Crusade
sarcasm *n* saying the clear opposite of what is meant, in order to be (amusingly) offensive **-astic** *adj* **-astically** *adv*
sarcophagus *n* **-gi** *or* **-guses** stone box for a dead body
sardine *n* **1** small young fish often preserved in oil for eating **2 like sardines** packed very tightly together
sardonic *adj* seeming to regard oneself as too important to consider a matter, person, etc., seriously **~ally** *adv*
sarge *n infml for* sergeant
sari *n* dress consisting of a length of cloth, worn by Hindu women
sarky *adj BrE infml* sarcastic
sarnie *n BrE infml* sandwich
sarong *n* Malayan skirt consisting of a length of cloth
sarsaparilla /ˌsahs(ə)pəˈrilə/ *n* fizzy drink made from plant extracts
sarsen *n* large mass of eroded sandstone
sartorial *adj fml* of (the making of) men's clothes
SAS *n* Special Air Service: British force of commandos
sash[1] *n* length of cloth worn round the waist or over one shoulder
sash[2] *n* window frame, esp. in a sort of window with two frames that slide up and down

sashay *vi AmE infml* **1** saunter **2** strut
sassafras *n* tall N American tree with aromatic bark
sassy *adj esp. AmE infml* saucy
sat *past t. and p. of* sit
Satan *n* the Devil
satanic *adj* **1** very evil or cruel **2** of satanism **~ally** *adv*
satanism *n* worship of the devil **-ist** *n*
satchel *n* small bag carried over the shoulders
sate *vt fml* satisfy with more than enough of something
sateen *n* shiny cotton cloth
satellite *n* **1** heavenly body that moves round a larger one **2** man-made object moving round the Earth, moon, etc. **3** country or person that depends on another
satiate *vt fml* satisfy (too) fully **–ation** *n* **–able** *adj*
satiety *n fml* state of being satiated
satin *n* smooth shiny cloth made mainly from silk
satinwood *n* (hard smooth wood of) an East Indian tree
satire *n* (piece of writing, picture, etc. aimed at) showing the foolishness or evil of something in an amusing way **–irical** *adj* **–irize, –irise** *vt*
satisfaction *n* **1** (something that gives) a feeling of pleasure **2** *fml* fulfilment of a need, desire, etc. **3** *fml* certainty: *proved to my satisfaction* **4** *fml* chance to defend one's honour
satisfactory *adj* **1** pleasing **2** good enough **–rily** *adv*
satisfy *vt* **1** please **2** fulfil (a need, desire, etc.) **3** *fml* fit (a condition, rule, standard, etc.) **4** persuade fully
satrap /ˈsatrəp/ *n* (despotic) subordinate ruler
satsuma *n* type of mandarin orange
saturate *vt* **1** make completely wet **2** fill completely **~d** *adj* (of fat or oil) having chemicals unhealthily combined **–ation** *n*
Saturday *n* the 6th day of the week, between Friday and Sunday
Saturn *n* the planet 6th in order from the sun, with large rings round it
saturnalia *n* **-lias** *or* **-lia** orgy
saturnine /ˈsatəˌnien/ *adj fml* sad and solemn, often in a threatening way
satyr *n* **1** manlike Greek woodland god with goat's legs and horns **2** lecher
sauce *n* **1** quite thick liquid put on food **2** rude disrespectful talk **saucy** *adj* **1** amusingly disrespectful or rude **2** producing sexual interest in an amusing way
sauceboat *n* container for pouring sauce at table
saucepan *n* metal cooking pot with a handle
saucer *n* small plate for putting a cup on
sauerkraut *n* brine-pickled cabbage
sauna *n* (room or building for) a Finnish type of bath in steam
saunter *vi* walk unhurriedly
saurian *adj, n* (like) a lizard
sausage *n* minced meat in a tube of thin skin
sausage roll *n* small piece of sausage in a pastry covering
sauté *vt* **-téed** *or* **-téd** fry in a little fat
Sauternes *n* sweet white wine
savage *adj* **1** forcefully cruel or violent **2** uncivilized ♦ *n* member of an uncivilized tribe ♦ *vt* attack and bite fiercely **~ly** *adv*
savagery *n* (act of) savage behaviour
savanna *n* flat grassy land in a warm part of the world
savant *n* learned person
save¹ *v* **1** *vt* make safe from danger or destruction **2** *vi/t* keep and add to an amount of (money) for later use **3** *vt* avoid the waste of (money, time, etc.) **4** *vt* keep for future use or enjoyment later **5** *vt* make unnecessary **6** *vt* (of a goalkeeper) stop (a shot) from going in the net **7 save one's skin/neck/bacon** *infml* escape from a serious danger ♦ *n* act of saving a goal **saver** *n* **savings** *pl n* money saved, esp. in a bank
save² *prep fml* except
saveloy *n* dry precooked sausage
saving grace *n* the one good thing that makes something acceptable

savings and loan association *n AmE* building society
saviour, *AmE* **-vior** *n* **1** one who saves from danger or loss **2** (*usu. cap.*) Jesus Christ
savoir-faire *n* ability to do or say the proper thing on every social occasion
savory *n* herb used in cooking
savour, *AmE* **-vor** *n* **1** taste or smell **2** (power to excite) interest ♦ *vt* enjoy slowly and purposefully
savoury, *AmE* **-vory** *adj* **1** not sweet; tasting of meat, cheese, etc. **2** *fml* morally good ♦ *n* a small salty dish
savoy *n* curly-leaved cabbage
savvy *vi sl* know; understand ♦ *n* common sense ♦ *adj* astute
saw[1] *past t. of* see
saw[2] *n* thin-bladed tool with teeth for cutting hard materials ♦ *vi/t* **sawed, sawed** *or* **sawn** cut (as if) with a saw
saw[3] *n* short well-known saying
sawbones *n infml* doctor
sawdust *n* wood dust made by a saw in cutting
sawhorse *n* frame to hold wood for sawing
sawmill *n* factory or machine that cuts wood
saxifrage /ˈsaksifrij, -frayj/ *n* plant grown in rockeries
Saxon *n* member of a Germanic people who invaded England in the 5th century AD
saxophone also *infml* **sax** *n* metal musical instrument of the woodwind family, used esp. in jazz
say *v* **said 1** *vt* pronounce (a sound, word, etc.) **2** *vi/t* express (a thought, opinion, etc.) in words **3** *vt* give as a general opinion; claim **4** *vt* suppose; suggest **5 go without saying** be clear; not need stating **6 say to oneself** think **7 that is to say** expressed another (more exact) way **8 to say nothing of** including ♦ *n* **1** power or right of (sharing in) acting or deciding **2 have one's say** (have the chance to) express one's opinion
saying *n* well-known wise statement
say-so *n* **1** personal statement without proof **2** permission
scab *n* **1** hard mass of dried blood formed over a wound **2** *derog* one who works while others are on strike
scabbard *n* tube for holding a sword, knife, etc.
scabies *n* skin disease
scabious *n* plant with dense blue flower heads
scabrous *adj fml* improper; salacious
scads *pl n AmE infml* large number or quantity
scaffold *n* raised platform for the execution of criminals **~ing** *n* structure of poles and boards round a building for workmen to stand on
scald *vt* burn with hot liquid **scald** *n*
scale[1] *n* **1** set of marks on an instrument, used for measuring **2** set of figures for measuring or comparing: *a temperature scale* **3** relationship between a map or model and the thing it represents **4** size or level in relation to other or usual things: *a large-scale business operation* **5** set of musical notes at fixed separations ♦ *vt* **1** climb up **2** increase/reduce, esp. by a fixed rate
scale[2] *n* also **scales** *pl n* weighing apparatus
scale[3] *n* **1** any of the small flat stiff pieces covering fish, snakes, etc. **2** greyish material formed inside hot water pipes, pots in which water is boiled, etc. ♦ *vt* remove the scales from
scalene *adj* (of a triangle) having three sides of different lengths
scallion *n* spring onion
scallop *n* edible shellfish with a round flat shell
scalloped *adj* (of an edging) shaped in a row of small outward curves
scallywag *n* trouble-making child
scalp *n* **1** skin on top of the head **2** (symbol of) defeat ♦ *vt* cut off the scalp of
scalpel *n* small sharp knife used in surgical operations
scam *n sl* clever and dishonest plan or

course of action
scamp *n* playfully trouble-making child
scamper *vi* run quickly and usu. playfully
scampi *n BrE* (dish of) large prawns
scan *v* **-nn- 1** *vt* examine closely, esp. making a search **2** *vt* look at quickly without careful reading **3** *vi* (of poetry) have a regular pattern of repeated beats ♦ *n* act of scanning **~ner** *n* instrument for scanning
scandal *n* **1** (something causing) a public shock **2** talk which brings harm or disrespect to someone **~ize, -ise** *vt* offend (someone's) feelings of what is right or proper **~ous** *adj* morally shocking **~ously** *adv*
scandalmonger *n* someone who spreads scandal
Scandinavian *adj* of Denmark, Norway, Sweden, Finland, and/or Iceland
scansion *n* way a line of a poem scans
scant *adj* hardly enough
scanty *adj* hardly (big) enough **–ily** *adv*
scapegoat *n* one who takes the blame for others' faults
scapula *n* **-lae** *or* **-las** *med* shoulder blade
scar *n* mark left when a wound heals ♦ *vt* **-rr-** mark with a scar
scarab *n* large black beetle
scarce *adj* **1** less than is wanted; hard to find **2 make oneself scarce** *infml* go away or keep away, esp. in order to avoid trouble **~ly** *adv* **1** hardly; almost not **2** (almost) certainly not **scarcity** *n* being scarce; lack
scare *vt* frighten ♦ *n* **1** sudden fear **2** (mistaken or unreasonable) public fear
scary *adj* frightening
scarecrow *n* figure dressed in old clothes set up in a field to scare birds away from crops
scaremonger *n* person who spreads reports causing public anxiety
scarf[1] *n* **scarves** *or* **scarfs** piece of cloth worn round the neck or head
scarf[2] *n* piece of wood cut at an angle to fit against another
scarify *vt* make small cuts or scratches on the surface of **–fication** *n*
scarlet *adj* bright red
scarlet fever *n* serious disease marked by a painful throat and red spots on the skin
scarlet pimpernel *n* small red wild flower
scarlet woman *n* prostitute
scarp *n* line of inland cliffs
scarper *vi BrE sl* run away
scat[1] *vi* **-tt-** *infml* go away fast
scat[2] *n* improvised jazz singing
scathing *adj* bitterly cruel in judgment **~ly** *adv*
scatology *n* (writing with) obscene interest in excrement **–ogical** *adj*
scatter *v* **1** *vi/t* separate widely **2** *vt* spread widely (as if) by throwing **~ed** *adj* far apart; irregularly separated
scatterbrain *n* careless or forgetful person **~ed** *adj*
scatty *adj BrE* slightly mad or scatterbrained
scavenge *vi/t* **1** (of an animal) feed on (waste or decaying flesh) **2** search for or find (usable objects) among unwanted things **~r** *n*
scenario *n* **-os 1** written description of the action in a film or play **2** description of a possible course of events
scene *n* **1** (in a play) division (within an act) **2** single piece of action in one place in a play or film **3** stage background for the action of a play **4** place where something happens: *the scene of the crime* **5** event regarded as like something in a play or film: *scenes of merrymaking* **6** show of angry feelings, esp. between two people in public **7** an area of activity: *the political scene* **8 behind the scenes** secretly **9 on the scene** present **10 set the scene** prepare
scenery *n* **1** natural surroundings, esp. in the country **2** painted background and other articles used on stage
scenic *adj* showing attractive natural scenery
scent *n* **1** pleasant smell **2** smell followed by hunting animals **3** *esp. BrE* perfume ♦ *vt* **1** tell the presence of by

smelling **2** get a feeling of the presence of **3** fill with pleasant smells
sceptic /ˈskeptik/ *n* sceptical person **~al** *adj* unwilling to believe **~ally** *adv* **~ism** *n* doubt
sceptre, *AmE* **-ter** /ˈseptə/ *n* ceremonial rod carried by a ruler
schedule *n* **1** planned list or order of things to be done **2** planned or expected time **3** *esp. AmE* timetable of trains, buses, etc. ♦ *vt* plan for a certain future time **~d** *adj* being a regular service
schema *n* **-ata** diagram
schematic *adj* showing the main parts but leaving out details **~ally** *adv*
schematize *vt* **-ise 1** organize systematically **2** represent (too) simply
scheme *n* **1** plan in simple form; system **2** *BrE* official or business plan **3** clever dishonest plan ♦ *vi* make clever dishonest plans
scherzo /ˈskeətsoh/ *n* **-zos** quick piece of music
schilling *n* money unit of Austria
schism *n* separation between parts originally together, esp. in the church **~atic** *adj*
schist /shist/ *n* rock that splits into layers
schizoid /ˈskitsoyd/ *adj* of schizophrenia
schizophrenia *n* disorder in which the mind becomes separated from the feelings **-phrenic** *adj*, *n* (of) someone with schizophrenia
schlep *v* **-pp-** *AmE infml* **1** *vt* carry or drag (something heavy) **2** *vi* spend a lot of time and effort in getting from one place to another
schmaltz, schmalz *n infml* oversentimental art or esp. music **~y** *adj*
schmuck *n AmE infml* fool
schnapps *n* strong alcoholic spirit
schnitzel *n* thin cutlet
schnozzle *n infml* nose
scholar *n* **1** person with great knowledge of a (non-science) subject **2** holder of a scholarship **~ly** *adj* **1** concerned with serious detailed study **2** of or like a scholar
scholarship *n* **1** payment so that someone can attend a college **2** exact and serious study
scholastic *adj* of schools and teaching **~ism** *n*
school[1] *n* **1** (attendance or work at) a place of education for children **2** teaching establishment: *a driving school* **3** university department concerned with a particular subject **4** *AmE* university **5** group of people with the same methods, style, etc. ♦ *vt fml* teach, train, or bring under control
school[2] *n* large group of fish swimming together
schoolmarm *n* old-fashioned, bossy, and easily shocked woman
schoolmaster *n* teacher at a school
schoolmate *n* a child at the same school
schoolmistress *n* female teacher at a school
school of thought *n* group with the same way of thinking, opinion, etc.
schooner *n* **1** large fast sailing ship **2** tall drinking glass esp. for sherry or beer
schwa *n* vowel sound as in the second syllable of *gala* shown in this dictionary as /ə/
sciatica *n* pain in the lower back
science *n* **1** (study of) knowledge which depends on testing facts and stating general natural laws **2 a** branch of such knowledge, such as physics, chemistry, or biology **b** anything which may be studied exactly
science fiction *n* stories about imaginary future (scientific) developments
science park *n* area where there are a lot of companies concerned esp. with new technology and scientific study
scientific *adj* **1** of science **2** needing or showing exact knowledge or use of a system **~ally** *adv*
scientist *n* person who works in a science
scientology *n* religious movement founded by L. Ron Hubbard, stressing cleansing of the mind through recollection

scimitar /ˈsimitə/ *n* curved sword
scintilla *n* minute amount; jot
scintillate *vi* **1** (esp. of conversation) be quick, witty, and interesting **2** throw out quick flashes of light
scion /ˈsie·ən/ *n fml* descendant, offspring
scissors *pl n* cutting tool with two joined blades
sclerosis *n med* hardening of some usu. soft bodily organ
scoff[1] *vi* speak laughingly and disrespectfully
scoff[2] *vt infml* eat eagerly and fast
scold *vt* speak angrily and complainingly to (a wrong-doer)
sconce *n* bracket candlestick
scone *n* small round breadlike cake
scoop *n* **1** sort of deep spoon for lifting and moving liquids or loose material **2** news report printed, broadcast, etc., before one's competitors can do so ♦ *vt* **1** take up or out (as if) with a scoop **2** make a news report before (another newspaper)
scoot *vi* go quickly and suddenly
scooter *n* **1** child's two-wheeled vehicle pushed along by one foot **2** low vehicle with two small wheels, an enclosed engine, and usu. a wide curved part at the front to protect the legs
scope *n* **1** area within the limits of a question, subject, etc. **2** space or chance for action or thought
-scope *suffix* observing instrument
scorch *v* **1** *vt* burn the surface of (something) without destroying completely **2** *vi infml* travel very fast ♦ *n* scorched place **~er** *n infml* **1** very hot day **2** something very exciting, angry, fast, etc.
scorched earth policy *n* destruction by an army of all useful things, esp. crops, in an area before leaving it to an advancing army
score[1] *n* **1** number of points won in a game, examination, etc. **2 a** written copy of a piece of music **b** music for a film or play **3** reason: *Don't worry on that score.* **4** old disagreement or hurt kept in the mind ♦ *v* **1** *vi/t* make (a point) in a game **2** *vi* record the points made in a game **3** *vt* gain (a success, victory, etc.) **4** *vi/t* make (a clever point) esp. in an argument **5** *vt* arrange (music) for a particular combination of instruments **6** *vt* cut one or more lines on **7** *vi sl* (usu. of a man) have sex with someone **8** *vi sl* obtain and use unlawful drugs **~r** *n* person who makes or records points in a game
score[2] *determiner, n* **score** *or* **scores** *esp. lit* 20 **scores** *pl n* a lot
scoreboard *n* board on which a game's score is recorded
scorn *n* strong (angry) disrespect ♦ *vt* refuse to accept or consider because of scorn or pride **~ful** *adj* **~fully** *adv*
scorpion *n* small animal with a long poisonous stinging tail
Scot *n* Scottish person
scotch *vt fml* put an end to
Scotch *adj* Scottish ♦ *n* whisky made in Scotland
Scotch egg *n* cooked egg covered in sausage meat
Scotch mist *n* very fine light drizzle
scot-free *adj* without harm or esp. punishment
Scotland Yard *n* (head office of) the criminal investigation department of the London police force
Scots *adj* Scottish
Scottish *adj* of Scotland
scoundrel *n* wicked, selfish, or dishonest man **~ly** *adj*
scour[1] *vt* search (an area) thoroughly
scour[2] *vt* clean by hard rubbing with a rough material **~er** *n* pad of rough nylon for cleaning pots and pans
scourge *n* cause of great harm or suffering ♦ *vt* cause great harm or suffering to
Scouse *adj BrE infml* of Liverpool
scout *n* **1** member of an association (**the scouts**) for training boys in character and self-help **2** soldier sent ahead of an army to find out about the enemy **3** person who seeks out good young sportspeople, actors, etc., for new

teams, shows, etc. ♦ *vi* go looking for something
scout car *n* small armoured vehicle
scouting *n* activities of the scouts
scoutmaster *n* adult leader in the scouts
scow *n* barge for transporting material in bulk
scowl *n* angry frown ♦ *vi* make a scowl
scrabble *vi* scramble (1, 2)
scrag *vt* **-gg-** *BrE infml* seize and hit
scrag end *n* bony part of a sheep's neck
scraggy *adj* thin and bony
scram *vi* **-mm-** *infml* get away fast
scramble *v* **1** *vi* move or climb quickly and untidily **2** *vi* struggle or compete eagerly or against difficulty **3** *vt* cook (an egg) while mixing the white and yolk together **4** *vt* mix up (a radio or telephone message) so that it cannot be understood ♦ *n* **1** act of climbing quickly **2** motorcycle race over rough ground
scrap[1] *n* **1** small piece **2** unwanted material (to be) thrown away ♦ *vt* **-pp-** get rid of **~py** *adj* not well arranged or planned
scrap[2] *n* sudden short fight or quarrel ♦ *vi* **-pp-** fight or quarrel
scrapbook *n* book of empty pages on which esp. cut-out pictures are stuck
scrape *v* **1** *vi/t* (cause to) rub roughly against a surface **2** *vt* remove or clean by pulling or pushing an edge repeatedly across a surface **3** *vi* live, keep a business, etc., with no more than the necessary money **4** *vi* succeed by doing work of the lowest acceptable quality **scrape up/together** *phr vt* gather (enough money) with difficulty ♦ *n* **1** act or sound of scraping **2** mark or wound made by scraping **3** difficult situation
scrap heap *n* **1** pile of waste material, esp. metal **2** imaginary place where unwanted things, people, or ideas go
scrap paper, also *AmE* **scratch paper** *n* used paper for making notes, shopping lists, etc.
scratch *vi/t* **1** rub and tear or mark with something pointed or rough **2** rub (a part of the body) lightly and repeatedly **3** remove (oneself, a horse, etc.) from a race or competition **4 scratch the surface** deal with only the beginning of a matter or only a few of many cases ♦ *n* **1** mark or sound made by scratching **2** act of scratching part of the body **3 from scratch** (starting) from the beginning **4 up to scratch** at/to an acceptable standard **~y** *adj* **1** (e.g. of a record) spoiled by scratches **2** (of clothes) hot, rough, and uncomfortable
scrawl *vt* write carelessly or awkwardly ♦ *n* (piece of) careless or irregular writing
scrawny *adj* unpleasantly thin
scream *v* **1** *vi/t* cry out in a loud high voice **2** *vi* make a shrill sound ♦ **1** sudden loud cry **2** *infml* very funny person, thing, joke, etc.
scree *n* small loose stones on a mountainside
screech *vi* make an unpleasant high sharp sound (as if) in terror or pain ♦ *n* very high unpleasant noise
screech owl *n* owl with a harsh, shrill cry
screed *n* long (dull) piece of writing
screen *n* **1** something, esp. a movable upright frame, that protects, shelters, or hides **2** surface on which a cinema film is shown **3** the cinema industry **4** front glass surface of an electrical instrument, esp. a television, on which pictures or information appear ♦ *vt* **1** shelter, protect, or hide (as if) with a screen **2** test so as to remove those that do not reach the proper standard **3** show or broadcast (a film or television show) **~ing** *n* **1** (a) showing of a film **2** process of quality testing
screenplay *n* story written for a film
screen test *n* test of someone's suitability for a film role
screw *n* **1** metal pin having a head with a cut across it, a point at the other end, and a raised edge winding round it so that when twisted into e.g. wood it holds firmly **2** act of turning one of these **3** propeller, esp. on a ship **4** *taboo*

sl **a** act of having sex **b** someone considered as a person to have sex with **5 have a screw loose** *humorous* be slightly mad **6 put the screws on someone** *infml* force someone to do as one wishes, esp. by threatening ♦ *v* **1** *vt* fasten with one or more screws **2** *vi/t* tighten or fasten by turning **3** *vi/t taboo sl* have sex (with) **4** *vt sl* cheat **screw up** *phr v* **1** *vt* twist (a part of the face) to express disapproval or uncertainty **2** *vt* carelessly twist (e.g. paper) into a ball **3** *vt sl* ruin **4** *vi/t* deal with badly **5 screw up one's courage** stop oneself from being afraid **6 screwed up** *infml* very worried and confused

screwball *n AmE* screwy person

screwdriver *n* tool with a blade that fits into the top of a screw, for turning it

screwy *adj infml* strange or slightly mad

scribble *v* **1** *vi* write meaningless marks **2** *vt* write carelessly or hastily ♦ *n* meaningless or careless writing

scribe *n* person employed to copy things in writing

scrimmage *n* confused fight

scrimp *vi* **scrimp and save** save money slowly and with great difficulty

scrimshank *vi BrE sl* avoid one's work

scrip *n* share certificate(s)

script *n* **1** written form of a play, film, or broadcast **2** particular alphabet: *Arabic script* **3** *fml* handwriting **~ed** *adj* having a script

scripture also **scriptures** *pl* **1** the Bible **2** holy book(s) of a particular religion **-tural** *adj*

scrofula *n* tuberculosis of glands in the neck

scroll *n* **1** rolled-up piece of paper, esp. as used for an official document **2** decoration or shape like this in stone or wood

scrooge *n* extremely ungenerous person

scrotum *n* **-ta** *or* **-tums** bag of flesh holding the testicles

scrounge *vi/t* get (something) without work or payment or by persuading others **~r** *n*

scrub[1] *v* **-bb- 1** *vi/t* clean or remove by hard rubbing **2** *vt* no longer do or have; cancel ♦ *n* act of scrubbing

scrub[2] *n* low-growing plants covering the ground thickly

scrubber *n* **1** apparatus for removing impurities from gases **2** *sl* promiscuous woman

scrubby *adj* **1** covered in scrub **2** small or unimportant

scruff[1] *n* flesh at the back (of the neck)

scruff[2] *n BrE infml* dirty and untidy person

scruffy *adj* dirty and untidy

scrum *n* **1** group of players trying to get the ball in rugby **2** disorderly struggling crowd

scrummage *vi, n* (take part in) a scrum

scrumptious *adj infml* (of food) extremely good

scrumpy *n BrE* dry strong cider

scrunch *vt* crush, crumple

scruple *n* **1** moral principle which keeps one from doing something **2** conscience

scrupulous *adj* **1** *fml* very exact **2** exactly honest **~ly** *adv*

scrutineer *n* person who scrutinizes

scrutiny *n* careful and thorough examination **-ize** *vt* examine closely

scuba *n* aqualung

scud *vi* **-dd-** (esp. of clouds and ships) move along quickly

scuff *vt* make rough marks on the smooth surface of (shoes, a floor, etc.) ♦ *n* mark made by scuffing

scuffle *n* disorderly fight among a few people **scuffle** *vi*

scull *vi/t* row (a small light boat) **~er** *n*

scullery *n* room next to a kitchen, where pots and dishes are washed

scullion *n arch.* kitchen servant

sculpt *vt* make by shaping

sculptor *n* artist who makes sculptures

sculpture *n* **1** art of shaping solid representations **2** (piece of) work produced by this ♦ *vt* sculpt

scum *n* **1** (unpleasant) material formed on the surface of liquid **2** *pl often taboo*

worthless immoral people
scupper *vt BrE* **1** sink (one's own ship) intentionally **2** wreck or ruin (a plan)
scuppers *pl n* openings in a ship's side for draining water from the deck
scurf *n* small bits of dead skin, esp. in the hair
scurrilous *adj fml* containing very rude, improper, and usu. untrue statements **~ly** *adv* **~ness** *n*
scurry *vi* hurry, esp. with short quick steps ♦ *n* movement or sound of scurrying
scurvy *n* disease caused by lack of vitamin C
scuttle[1] *n* sort of bucket for holding and carrying coal
scuttle[2] *vi* rush with short quick steps
scuttle[3] *vt* sink (a ship) by making holes in the bottom
scythe *n* grass-cutting tool with a long curving blade fixed to a handle ♦ *vt* cut (as if) with a scythe
SDI *n* Strategic Defence Initiative; a US government plan for the use of special weapons to destroy enemy missiles in space
SDP *abbrev. for:* Social Democratic Party
sea *n* **1** great body of salty water that covers much of the Earth's surface **2** particular (named) part of this **3** broad plain on the Moon **4** large quantity spread out in front of one: *a sea of faces* **5 at sea** *infml* not understanding
sea anchor *n* device, usu. a canvas cylinder, towed by a ship to slow down its drifting
sea anemone *n* simple flower-like sea animal
seaboard *n* the part of a country along a seacoast
sea change *n lit* a complete but usu. gradual change
sea dog *n lit* experienced sailor
seafaring *adj* connected with the sea and sailing
seafood *n* fish and fishlike animals from the sea which can be eaten, esp. shellfish
seafront *n* part of a coastal (holiday) town on the edge of the sea, often with a broad path along it
seagull *n* gull
seahorse *n* small fish with a head and neck like those of a horse
seal[1] *n* **1** official mark put on an official document, often by pressing a pattern into red wax **2** something fastened across an opening to protect it **3** tight connection to keep gas or liquid in or out **4 set the seal on** bring to an end in a suitable way ♦ *vt* **1** fix a seal onto **2** fasten or close (as if) with a seal **3** make (more) certain, formal, or solemn **4 seal someone's doom/fate** *fml* make someone's death or punishment certain **seal off** *phr vt* close tightly so as not to allow entrance or escape
seal[2] *n* large smooth-bodied sea animal with broad flat limbs for swimming
sea legs *pl n* ability to walk comfortably on a moving ship
sea level *n* average height of the sea, used as a standard for measuring heights on land
sealing wax *n* hard easily-melted substance used for seals
sea lion *n* large seal of the Pacific Ocean
Sealyham *n* short-legged Welsh terrier
seam *n* **1** line of stitches joining two pieces of cloth **2** narrow band of coal between other rocks
seaman *n* **-men 1** sailor, esp. of low rank **2** man skilled in handling ships at sea **~ship** *n* skill in handling a ship and directing its course
sea mile *n* nautical mile
seamstress *n* woman who sews
seamy *adj* rough and immoral **–iness** *n*
séance /ˈsay·on(h)s/ *n* meeting where people try to talk to the spirits of the dead
seaplane *n* aircraft which can land on the sea
sear *vt* burn with sudden powerful heat **~ing** *adj* **1** burning **2** causing or describing very strong feelings esp. of a sexual kind

search *vi/t* **1** look through or examine (a place or person) carefully and thoroughly to try to find something **2 search me** ! *infml* I don't know! ♦ *n* (act of) searching **~ing** *adj* sharp and thorough: *a searching look* **~er** *n*

searchlight *n* large powerful light that can be turned in any direction

search party *n* group of searchers, esp. for a lost person

search warrant *n* official written order allowing the police to search a place

seascape *n* picture of the sea

seashore *n* land along the edge of the sea

seasick *adj* sick because of a ship's movement **~ness** *n*

seaside *n esp. BrE* coast, esp. as a holiday place

season *n* **1** spring, summer, autumn, or winter **2** period of the year marked by a particular thing: *the cricket season* **3 in/out of season** (of food) at/not at the best time of year for eating ♦ *vt* **1** give a special taste to (a food) by adding salt, pepper, a spice, etc. **2** dry (wood) gradually for use **~able** *adj fml* suitable or useful for the time of year **~al** *adj* happening or active only at a particular season **~ally** *adv* **~ed** *adj* having much experience **~ing** *n* something that seasons food

season ticket *n* ticket usable for a number of journeys, performances, etc., during a fixed period of time

seat *n* **1** place for sitting **2** the part on which one sits **3** place as a member of an official body (e.g. a parliament) **4** place where a particular activity happens ♦ *vt* **1** cause or help to sit **2** have room for seats for **~ing** *n* seats

seat belt *n* protective belt round a seated person in a car, plane, etc.

sea urchin *n* small ball-shaped sea animal with a prickly shell

seaweed *n* plant that grows in the sea

seaworthy *adj* (of a ship) fit for a sea voyage **-thiness** *n*

sebaceous *adj* of or producing **sebum**, an oily substance secreted by glands in the skin

sec[1] *n BrE infml* second[2] (2)

sec[2] *adj* (of wine) dry

secant /ˈseekənt/ *n* straight line cutting a curve at two or more points

secateurs *pl n BrE* strong garden scissors

secede /siˈseed/ *vi* formally leave an official group or organization **secession** *n*

seclude *vt fml* keep (esp. oneself) away from other people **~d** *adj* very quiet and private **seclusion** *n*

second[1] *determiner, adv, pron* 2nd ♦ *n* **1** helper of a boxer or duellist **2** imperfect article sold cheaper **3** British university examination result of middle to good quality **4 second to none** *infml* the best **seconds** *pl n infml* 2nd servings of food at a meal

second[2] *n* **1** length of time equal to $^1/_{60}$ of a minute **2** *infml* moment

second[3] *vt* support formally (a formal suggestion at a meeting) **~er** *n*

second[4] *vt BrE fml* move from usual duties to a special duty **~ment** *n*

secondary *adj* **1** (of education or a school) for children over 11 **2** not main **3** developing from something earlier: *a secondary infection* **-rily** *adv*

secondary modern *n* (esp. formerly) a British secondary school for academically less able children

secondary picket *n* picket not directly involved in the industrial dispute in question

second best *adj* not as good as the best

second childhood *n* dotage

second class *n* travelling conditions cheaper than first class on a train, aircraft, etc. **second-class** *adj* below the highest quality

Second Coming *n* the return of Christ to judge the world

second cousin *n* child of one's parent's cousin

second-guess *vt AmE infml* **1** make a judgment about (someone or something) only after an event has taken place **2** try to say in advance what (someone) will do, how (something) will happen, etc.

second-hand *adj, adv* **1** owned or used by someone else before; not new **2** (of information) not directly from its origin

second nature *n* very firmly fixed habit

second-rate *adj* of low quality

second sight *n* supposed ability to know about future or distant things

second-string *adj* being a substitute or reserve rather than a regular

second thought *n* thought that a past decision or opinion may not be right

second wind *n* return of one's strength during hard physical activity, when it seemed one had become too tired to continue

secrecy *n* **1** keeping secrets **2** being secret

secret *adj* **1** that no one else knows or must know about **2** undeclared ♦ *n* **1** matter kept hidden or known only to a few **2** special way of doing something well: *the secret of baking perfect bread* **3** mystery **4 in secret** in a private way or place **~ly** *adv*

secret agent *n* person gathering information secretly, esp. for a foreign government

secretariat *n* official office or department concerned with the running of a large organization

secretary *n* **1** person who prepares letters, keeps records, arranges meetings, etc., for another **2** government minister or high non-elected official **3** officer of an organization who keeps records, writes official letters, etc. **-rial** *adj*

secrete[1] *vt* (esp. of an animal or plant organ) produce (a usu. liquid substance) **secretion** *n* (production of) a usu. liquid substance

secrete[2] *vt fml* hide **secretion** *n*

secretive *adj* hiding one's thoughts or plans **~ly** *adv* **~ness** *n*

secret service *n* government department dealing with special police work, esp. (in the US) protecting high government officers

sect *n* small group within or separated from a larger (esp. religious) group

sectarian *adj* of or between sects, esp. as shown in great strength and narrowness of beliefs **~ism** *n*

section *n* **1** separate part of a larger object, place, group, etc. **2** representation of something cut through from top to bottom **~al** *adj* **1** in sections (to be) put together **2** limited to one particular group or area

sector *n* **1** part of a field of activity, esp. in business or trade **2** area of military control

secular *adj* not connected with or controlled by a church **~ism** *n*

secure *adj* **1** protected against danger or risk **2** fastened firmly **3** having no anxiety ♦ *vt* **1** close tightly **2** make safe **3** *fml* get **~ly** *adv*

security *n* **1** state of being secure **2** (department concerned with) protection, esp. against lawbreaking, violence, enemy acts, escape from prison, etc. **3** property of value promised to a lender in case repayment is not made **4** share, bond, or similar form of investment

sedan *n AmE* saloon (1)

sedan chair *n* seat carried through the streets on poles in former times

sedate *adj* calm or quiet ♦ *vt* make sleepy or calm, esp. with a drug **-ation** *n*

sedative *n* drug that makes one calm, esp. by causing sleep

sedentary /ˈsed(ə)ntri/ *adj fml* used to or needing long periods of sitting and only slight activity

sedge *n* grasslike marsh plant

sediment *n* solid material that settles to the bottom of a liquid **~ary** *adj*

sedimentation *n* forming or depositing of sediment

sedition *n* speaking, actions, etc., encouraging people to disobey the government **-ious** *adj*

seduce *vt* **1** persuade to have sex with one **2** persuade to do esp. something bad by making it seem attractive **~r** *n* **seduction** *n* **seductive** *adj* very desirable or attractive **seductively** *adv*

sedulous *adj fml* showing steady attention, care, and determination **~ly** *adv*

see[1] *v* **saw, seen 1** *vi* have or use the power of sight **2** *vt* notice, recognize, or examine by looking **3** *vi/t* come to know or understand: *I can't see why you don't like it.* **4** *vt* envisage **5** *vt* visit, meet, or receive as a visitor **6** *vi/t* (try to) find out: *I'll see if he's there.* **7** *vt* make sure; take care **8** *vt* go with: *I'll see you home.* **9** *vt* be the occasion of (an event or course in history) **10** *vt* have experience of: *That sofa has seen better days.* **11 let me see** (used for expressing a pause for thought) **12 see fit** decide to **13 see red** become very angry **14 see the light: a** understand or accept an idea **b** have a religious experience which changes one's belief **c** come into existence **15 see things** think one sees something that is not there **see about** *phr vt* **1** deal with **2** consider further **see in** *phr vt* find attractive in **see off** *phr vt* **1** go to the airport, station, etc., with (someone who is starting a trip) **2** chase away **3** remain firm until (something dangerous) stops **see out** *phr vt* **1** last until the end of **2** go to the door with (someone who is leaving) **see through** *phr vt* **1** not be deceived by **2** provide for, support, or help until the end of (esp. a difficult time) **see to** *phr vt* attend to; take care of

see[2] *n* area governed by a bishop

seed *n* **1** usu. small hard plant part that can grow into a new plant **2** something from which growth begins: *seeds of future trouble* **3** seeded player **4 go/run to seed: a** (of a plant) produce seed after flowers have been produced **b** (of a person) lose one's freshness, esp. by becoming lazy, careless, old, etc. ♦ *vt* **1** plant seeds in (a piece of ground) **2** place (esp. tennis players at the start of a competition) in order of likelihood to win **~less** *adj*

seedbed *n* **1** ground specially prepared for seeds **2** place where something develops

seedcorn *n* **1** grain kept for planting **2** something useful for future development

seedling *n* young plant grown from a seed

seedsman *n* person who grows and sells seeds

seedy *adj* **1** looking poor, dirty, and uncared for **2** *infml* slightly unwell and/or in low spirits **-iness** *n*

seeing also **seeing that** *conj* as it is true that; since

seek *v* **sought** *fml or lit* **1** *vi/t* search (for) **2** *vt* ask for **3** *vt* try

seem *v* give the idea or effect of being; appear **~ing** *adj* that seems to be, but perhaps is not real **~ingly** *adv* according to what seems to be so (but perhaps is not)

seemly *adj fml* (socially) suitable **-liness** *n*

seen *past p. of* see

seep *vi* (of liquid) flow slowly through small openings in a material **~age** *n* slow seeping flow

seer *n lit* someone who knows about the future

seersucker *n* light fabric used for clothing

seesaw *n* **1** board balanced in the middle for people to sit on at opposite ends so that when one end goes up the other goes down **2** up and down movement ♦ *vi* move up and down esp. between opponents or opposite sides

seethe *vi* **1** be in a state of anger or unrest **2** (of a liquid) move about as if boiling

see-through *adj* (esp. of a garment) that can be (partly) seen through

segment *n* any of the parts into which something may be cut up or divided ♦ *vt* divide into segments **~ation** *n*

segregate *vt* separate or set apart, esp. from a different social or racial group **-ation** *n*

seigneur /say'nyuh/ *n* feudal lord

seine *n* fishing net which hangs vertic-

ally in the water
seismic /ˈsiezmik/ *adj* of or caused by earthquakes
seismograph *n* instrument for measuring the force of earthquakes **~er** *n* **~y** *n* **~ic** *adj*
seize *vt* **1** take possession of by force or official order **2** take hold of eagerly, quickly, or forcefully **seize up** *phr vt BrE* (of part of a machine) become stuck and stop working **seizure** *n* **1** act of seizing **2** sudden attack of illness
seldom *adv* not often; rarely
select *vt* choose as best, most suitable, etc., from a group ♦ *adj* **1** limiting to members of the best quality or class **2** of high quality **~or** *n* **~ion** *n* **1** selecting or being selected **2** something or someone selected **3** collection of things to choose from
selective *adj* **1** careful in choosing **2** having an effect only on certain things **~ly** *adv* **-tivity, ~ness** *n*
selenium *n* chemical similar to sulphur
self *n* **selves** whole being of a person, including their nature, character, abilities, etc.
self- *prefix* of or by oneself or itself
self-abnegation *n* self-denial
self-absorbed *adj* paying all one's attention to oneself and one's own affairs
self-addressed *adj* addressed for return to the sender
self-appointed *adj* chosen by oneself to do something, unasked and usu. unwanted
self-assertive *adj* forceful in making others take notice of one or in claiming things for oneself **-tion** *n*
self-assured *adj* confident **-surance** *n*
self-centred *adj* interested only in oneself **~ness** *n*
self-confessed *adj* openly acknowledged by oneself; admitted
self-confident *adj* sure of one's own power to succeed **~ly** *adv* **-ence** *n*
self-conscious *adj* nervous and uncomfortable about oneself as seen by others **~ly** *adv* **~ness** *adj*
self-contained *adj* **1** complete in itself; independent **2** not showing feelings or depending on others' friendship
self-control *n* control over one's feelings **-trolled** *adj*
self-defence *n* act or skill of defending oneself
self-denial *n* limited the enjoyable things one allows oneself to do
self-determination *n* country's right to govern itself
self-effacing *adj* not drawing attention to oneself; humble
self-employed *adj* earning money from one's own business, rather than being paid by an employer
self-esteem *n* one's good opinion of one's own worth
self-evident *adj* plainly true without need of proof **~ly** *adv*
self-explanatory *adj* easily understood
self-fulfilling prophecy *n* statement about what may happen in the future which comes true because it has been made
self-important *adj* having too high an opinion of one's own importance **-ance** *n* **~ly** *adv*
self-indulgent *adj* too easily allowing oneself pleasure or comfort **-ence** *n* **~ly** *adv*
self-interest *n* concern for what is best for oneself **~ed** *adj*
selfish *adj* concerned with one's own advantage without care for others **~ly** *adv* **~ness** *n*
selfless *adj* concerned with others' advantage without care for oneself **~ly** *adv* **~ness** *n*
self-made *adj* having gained success and wealth by one's own efforts alone
self-possessed *adj* calm and confident **-session** *n*
self-raising flour *n* flour containing a chemical to make it puff up in cooking
self-reliant *adj* not depending on others' help **-ance** *n*
self-respect *n* proper pride in oneself **~ing** *adj*
self-righteous *adj* (too) proudly sure of one's own rightness or goodness **~ly**

adv **~ness** *n*

self-sacrifice *n* the giving up of things that one cares deeply about, esp. in order to help others

selfsame *adj* exactly the same

self-satisfied *adj* too pleased with oneself

self-seeking *n, adj* (practice of) working only for one's own advantage

self-service *adj, n* (working by) the system in which buyers collect what they want and pay at a special desk

self-starter *n* **1** usu. electrical apparatus for starting a car engine **2** person able to work alone on their own ideas

self-styled *adj* given the stated title by oneself, usu. without any right to it

self-sufficient *adj* able to provide everything one needs without outside help **–ency** *n*

self-will *n* strong unreasonable determination to follow one's own wishes **~ed** *adj*

sell *v* **sold 1** *vi/t* give (property or goods) to someone in exchange for money **2** *vi* be bought **3** *vt* make acceptable or desirable by persuading **4 sell one's soul** act dishonourably in exchange for money, power, etc. **5 sell someone down the river** put someone in great trouble by being disloyal to them **6 sell something/someone short** value something or someone too low **sell off** *phr vt* get rid of by selling, usu. cheaply **sell out** *phr v* **1** *vi/t* sell all of (what was for sale) **2** *vi* be disloyal or unfaithful, esp. for payment **sell up** *phr vi* sell something (esp. a business) completely ♦ *n infml* deception **~er** *n*

Sellotape *n BrE tdmk for* band of thin clear sticky material ♦ *vt* put together or mend with Sellotape

sell-out *n* **1** performance, match, etc., for which all tickets have been sold **2** act of disloyalty or unfaithfulness

seltzer *n* fizzy mineral water

selvage *n* strengthened edge of fabric

selves *pl. of* self

semantic *adj* of meaning in language **~ally** *adv* **–ics** *n* study of meaning

semaphore *n* system of sending messages with flags

semblance *n* appearance; outward form or seeming likeness

semen *n* sperm-carrying liquid, passed into the female during the sexual act

semester *n* either of the two teaching periods in the year at US colleges

semi *n BrE infml* semidetached

semi- *prefix* **1** half **2** partly; incomplete(ly)

semibreve *n* long musical note equal to four crotchets

semicircle *n* half a circle

semicolon *n* mark (;) used to separate independent parts of a sentence

semiconductor *n* substance which allows the passing of an electric current more easily at high temperatures

semidetached *adj, n* (being) one of a pair of joined houses

semifinal *n* either of two matches whose winners play in a final

seminal *adj* **1** *fml* influencing future development in a new way **2** containing or producing semen

seminar *n* small study group

seminary *n* college for training esp. Roman Catholic priests

semiology /ˌsemiˈɒlədʒi, see-/ *n* study of signs and symbols **–gical** *adj* **–gist** *n*

semiotics *n* semiology **–tic** *adj*

semiprecious *adj* (of a jewel) not of the kinds which have the highest commercial value

semiquaver *n* short musical note

Semitic *adj* of a race of people including Jews and Arabs

semitone *n* interval between two musical notes corresponding to two notes next to each other on the piano

semolina *n* ground wheat used esp. for pasta and cooked milky dishes

Senate *n* **1** higher of the two parts of the law-making body in the US, France, etc. **2** highest council of state in ancient Rome **3** governing council in some universities **–ator** *n* member of a senate **–atorial** *adj*

send *v* **sent 1** *vt* cause to go or be taken, without going oneself **2** *vt* cause to become: *It sent him mad* **send down** *phr vt BrE* dismiss (a student) from a university for bad behaviour **2** *infml* send to prison **send for** *phr vt* ask or order to come **send off** *phr vt* **1** post (a letter, parcel, etc.) **2** *BrE* (in sport) order (a player) to leave the field because of a serious breaking of the rules **send up** *phr vt* **1** *BrE* make fun of by copying **2** *AmE infml* send down (2) **~er** *n*

send-off *n* show of good wishes at the start of a journey, new business, etc.

send-up *n BrE* something which makes fun of someone or something

senescent /si'nes(ə)nt/ *adj fml* growing old **–ence** *n*

seneschal /'senish(ə)l/ *n* agent in charge of a lord's estate in medieval times

senile *adj* of or showing old age, esp. in weakness of mind **senility** *n*

senior *n, adj* **1** (someone) older **2** (someone) of high or higher rank **~ity** *n* **1** being senior **2** official advantage gained by length of service in an organization

Senior *adj esp. AmE* the older, esp. of two men in the same family who have the same name

senior citizen *n* person beyond retirement age

senna *n* dried pods of a plant of the pea family, used as a laxative

señor *n* **-es** (title of) a Spanish man

señora *n* (title of) a married Spanish woman

señorita *n* (title of) an unmarried Spanish woman or girl

sensation *n* **1** feeling, such as of heat or pain, coming from the senses **2** general feeling in the mind or body **3** (cause of) excited interest **~al** *adj* **1** wonderful **2** causing excited interest or shock **~ally** *adv*

sensationalism *n* the intentional producing of excitement or shock, esp. by books, magazines, etc., of low quality

sense *n* **1** intended meaning **2** good and esp. practical understanding and judgment **3** any of the five natural powers of sight, hearing, feeling, tasting, and smelling **4** power to understand and judge a particular thing: *a poor sense of direction* **5** feeling, esp. one that is hard to describe **6 make sense** : **a** have a clear meaning **b** be a wise course of action **7 make sense (out) of** understand ♦ *vt* feel in the mind **senses** *pl n* powers of (reasonable) thinking **~less** *adj* **1** showing a lack of meaning, thought, or purpose **2** unconscious

sense of occasion *n* **1** natural feeling that tells one how one should behave at a particular social event **2** suitable feeling produced in someone by an important event

sense organ *n* eye, nose, tongue, ear, etc.

sensibility also **sensibilities** *pl n* delicate feeling about style or what is correct, esp. in art or behaviour

sensible *adj* **1** having or showing good sense; reasonable **2 sensible of** *fml* recognizing; conscious of **–bly** *adv*

sensitive *adj* **1** quick to feel or show the effect of something **2** easily offended **3** showing delicate feelings or judgment: *a sensitive performance* **4** knowing or understanding the feelings and opinions of others **5** (of an apparatus) measuring exactly **6** needing to be dealt with carefully so as not to cause trouble or offence **~ly** *adv* **–tivity** *n*

sensitize, -tise *vt* make sensitive

sensor *n* apparatus for discovering the presence of something, such as heat or sound

sensory *adj fml* of or by the bodily senses

sensual *adj* **1** of bodily feelings **2** interested in or suggesting physical, esp. sexual, pleasure **~ity** *n*

sensuous *adj* **1** giving pleasure to the senses **2** sensual (2) **~ly** *adv* **~ness** *n*

sent *past t. and p. of* send

sentence *n* **1** group of words forming a

complete statement, command, question, etc. **2** (order given by a judge which fixes) a punishment for a criminal found guilty in court ♦ *vt* (of a judge) give a punishment to
sententious /sen'tenshəs/ *adj fml* full of supposedly wise moral remarks **~ly** *adv* **~ness** *n*
sentient /'senshənt/ *adj fml* having feelings and consciousness
sentiment *n* **1** tender feelings of pity, love, sadness, etc., or imaginative remembrance of the past **2** *fml* thought or judgment caused by a feeling **~al** *adj* **1** caused by sentiment **2** showing too much sentiment, esp. of a weak or unreal kind **~ally** *adv* **~ality** *n* **sentiments** *pl n* opinion
sentinel *n lit* guard; sentry
sentry *n* soldier guarding a building, entrance, etc.
sepal *n* small leaf underneath a flower
separable *adj* that can be separated **-bly** *adv*
separate *v* **1** *vi/t* move, set, keep, or break apart **2** *vi* stop living together as husband and wife **-ation** *n* **1** separating or being separated **2** (time of) being or living apart ♦ *adj* **1** different **2** not shared **3** apart **~ly** *adv*
separatism *n* belief that a particular political or religious group should be separate, not part of a larger whole **-ist** *n*
sepia *n* reddish-brown colour
sepoy *n* Indian soldier in a British regiment
sepsis *n* septicaemia
September *n* the 9th month of the year
septet *n* (music for) seven musicians
septic *adj* infected with bacteria
septicaemia, *AmE* **-cemia** /ˌsepti'seemyə/ *n* dangerous infection spread through the body in the blood
septic tank *n* large container in which sewage is broken up and changed by bacteria
septuagenarian *n* person 70-79 years old
septum *n* **-ta** dividing wall or membrane in the body
sepulchre, *AmE* **-er** /'sep(ə)lkə/ *n lit* burial place **-chral** *adj fml or lit* like or suitable for a grave **-chrally** *adv*
sequel *n* **1** something that follows, esp. as a result **2** film, book, etc., which continues where an earlier one ended
sequence *n* **1** group following each other in order **2** order in which things follow each other **3** scene in a film
sequential *adj* arranged in or following in sequence **~ly** *adv*
sequestered *adj lit* quiet and hidden
sequestrate *vt* seize (property) by legal order until claims on it are settled **-ation** *n* **-ator** *n*
sequin *n* small round shiny piece sewn on a garment for decoration
sequoia /si'kwoyə/ *n* extremely tall coniferous Californian tree
seraglio /se'rahli·oh/ *n* **-os** harem
seraphic *adj* like an angel, esp. in beauty or purity **~ally** *adv*
Serbo-Croat *n* Slavonic language used in Yugoslavia
sere *adj lit* dry, withered
serenade *n* piece of music played or sung to a woman by a lover ♦ *vt* sing or play a serenade to
serendipity *n* ability to make useful discoveries by chance **-tous** *adj*
serene *adj* completely calm and peaceful **~ly** *adv* **serenity** *n*
serf *n* slave-like farm worker in former times **~dom** *n* state or fact of being a serf
serge *n* strong woollen cloth
sergeant *n* **1** soldier in charge of others, but below the officers **2** policeman of middle rank
sergeant major *n* soldier just above a sergeant in rank
serial *adj* of, happening in or arranged in a series ♦ *n* written or broadcast story appearing in parts at fixed times **~ize, ~ise** *vt* print or broadcast as a serial
serial number *n* number marked on something to show which one it is in a series
series *n* **series** group of the same or

similar things coming one after another or in order
serif *n* short fine line coming at an angle from the top or bottom of a letter
serious *adj* **1** causing worry and needing attention **2** not cheerful or funny **3** needing or having great skill or thought **~ly** *adv* **~ness** *n*
sermon *n* talk given by a priest as part of a church service
serpent *n lit* snake
serpentine *adj* like a snake, esp. coiling or winding ♦ *n* green mottled stone
serrated *adj* having (an edge with) a row of V-shapes like teeth
serried *adj* **serried ranks** *lit* large numbers of people or things close together
serum *n* **serums** *or* **sera** liquid containing disease-fighting substances, put into a sick person's blood
serval *n* African wild cat
servant *n* person paid to do personal services for someone, esp. in their home
serve *v* **1** *vi/t* do work (for); give service (to) **2** *vt* provide with something necessary or useful: *The pipeline serves the whole town.* **3** *vt* offer (food, a meal, etc.) for eating **4** *vt* attend to (a customer in a shop) **5** *vt* spend (a period of time), esp. in prison **6** *vi/t fml* be good enough or suitable for (a purpose) **7** *vi/t* (esp. in tennis) begin play by hitting (the ball) to one's opponent **8** *vt law* deliver (a summons) **9 serve someone right** be suitable punishment ♦ *n* act or manner of serving in tennis **~r** *n* **1** something used in serving food **2** player who serves in tennis
service *n* **1** act or work done for someone **2** attention to guests in a hotel, restaurant, etc., or to customers in a shop **3** (operation of) an organization doing useful work: *the postal service* **4** (duty in) the army, navy, etc. **5** religious ceremony **6** examination of a machine to keep it in good condition **7** serve **8** set of dishes, cups, etc. ♦ *vt* repair or put in good condition ♦ *adj* for the use of people working in a place, rather than the public
serviceable *adj* fit for (long or hard) use; useful
service charge *n* amount added to a bill to pay for a particular service
service flat *n* rented flat where certain services, e.g. cleaning, are provided
serviceman *n* **-men** male member of the army, navy, etc.
service station *n* garage (2)
servicewoman *n* **-men** female member of the army, navy, etc.
serviette *n* napkin
servile *adj derog* behaving like a slave **~ly** *adv* **-vility** *n*
serving *n* amount of food for one person
servitor *n arch.* male servant
servitude *n lit* state of being a slave or one who is forced to obey another
servomechanism *n* lightly powered controlling and correcting device within a more powerful machine
sesame *n* Asian plant producing small edible seeds
sesquipedalian /ˌseskwipəˈdaylyən/ *adj fml or humorous* using or being very long words
session *n* **1** formal meeting or group of meetings of esp. a parliament or court **2** period of time used for a particular purpose
sestet *n* verse or poem of six lines
set[1] *v* **set,** *pres. p.* **-tt- 1** *vt* put (to stay) in the stated place **2** *vt* fix; establish: *set a date for the wedding* **3** *vt* put into the correct condition for use: *set the table* **4** *vt* cause to be: *set a prisoner free* **5** *vt* give (a piece of work) for someone to do **6** *vt* put the action of (a film, story, etc.) in the stated place and time **7** *vi/t* (cause to) become solid **8** *vi* (of the sun, moon, etc.) go below the horizon **9** *vt* write or provide music for (a poem or other words to be sung) **10** *vt* put (a broken bone) into a fixed position to mend **11** *vt* arrange (hair) when wet to be in a particular style when dry **12** *vt* arrange for printing **set about** *phr vt* **1** begin **2** attack **set back** *phr vt* **1** place at esp. the stated distance behind

something **2** delay **3** cost (a large amount) **set in** *phr vi* (of bad weather, disease, etc.) begin (and continue) **set off** *phr v* **1** *vi* begin a journey **2** *vt* cause to explode **3** *vt* cause (sudden activity) **4** *vt* make (one thing) look better by putting it near something different **set on** *phr vt* (cause to) attack **set out** *phr v* **1** *vt* arrange or spread out in order **2** *vi* begin a journey **3** *vt* begin with a particular purpose or goal **set to** *phr vi* begin eagerly or determinedly **set up** *phr vt* **1** put into position **2** prepare (a machine, instrument, etc.) for use **3** establish or arrange (an organization, plan, etc.) **4** provide with what is necessary or useful ♦ *adj* **1** fixed; prescribed: *set books/hours* **2** determined: *set on going* **3** unmoving; rigid: *a set smile* **4** at a fixed price: *a set dinner* **5** *infml* ready

set² *n* **1** group forming a whole: *a set of gardening tools* **2** television or radio receiving apparatus **3 a** scenery and props representing the place of action in a stage play **b** place where a film is acted **4** group of games in a tennis match **5** group of people of a particular social type

setback *n* something that delays or prevents successful progress

set piece *n* something carried out using a well-known formal pattern or plan

setsquare *n* three-sided right-angled plate for drawing or testing angles

sett, set *n* burrow of a badger

settee *n* long soft seat with a back, for more than one person

setter *n* long-haired dog used by hunters

setting *n* **1** the going down (of the moon, sun, etc.) **2** way or position in which an instrument is prepared for use **3 a** set of surroundings **b** time and place where the action of a book, film, etc., happens

settle *v* **1** *vi* start to live in a place **2** *vi/t* (place so as to) stay or be comfortable **3** *vi/t* come or bring to rest, esp. from above **4** *vi/t* make or become quiet, calm, etc. **5** *vt* decide on firmly; fix **6** *vt* provide people to live in (a place) **7** *vt* pay (a bill) **settle down** *phr vi* **1** give one's serious attention e.g. to a job **2** establish a home and live a quiet life **3** become used to a way of life, job, etc. **settle for** *phr vt* accept (something less than hoped for) **settle in** *phr vi/t* (help to) get used to a new home, job, etc. **settle on** *phr vt* decide or agree on; choose **settle up** *phr vi* pay what is owed ♦ *n* long wooden seat with a high back **~d** *adj* **~r** *n* member of a new population

settlement *n* **1** movement of a population into a new place to live there **2** newly-built small village in an area with few people **3** agreement or decision ending an argument **4** payment of money claimed **5** formal gift or giving of money

set-to *n* short fight or quarrel

set-up *n* arrangement; organization

seven *determiner, n, pron* 7 **~th** *determiner, adv, n, pron* 7th

seventeen *determiner, n, pron* 17 **~th** *determiner, adv, n, pron* 17th

seventh heaven *n* complete happiness

seventy *determiner, n, pron* 70 **–tieth** *determiner, adv, n, pron* 70th

seventy-eight *n* record played at 78 revolutions a minute

seven-year itch *n* dissatisfaction after seven years of marriage

sever *vt fml* **1** divide in two, esp. by cutting **2** break off; terminate **~ance** *n*

several *determiner, pron* more than a few but not very many; some ♦ *adj fml* separate

severally *adv fml* separately

severance pay *n* money paid by a company to a worker dismissed through no fault of his or her own

severe *adj* **1** causing serious harm, pain, or worry **2** not kind or gentle **3** completely plain and without decoration **~ly** *adv* **severity** *n*

sew *vi/t* **sewed, sewn** fasten (esp. cloth) with thread **sew up** *phr vt* **1** close or repair by sewing **2** settle satisfactorily

sewage *n* waste material, esp. excrement, carried in sewers
sewer *n* large underground pipe for carrying away sewage and water, esp. in a city
sewerage *n* system of removing waste material through sewers
sex *n* **1** condition of being male or female **2** set of all male or female people **3** (activity connected with) sexual intercourse ♦ *vt* find out whether (an animal) is male or female
sexagenarian *n* person between 60 and 69 years old
sex appeal *n* power of being sexually attractive to other people
-sexed *suffix* having the stated amount of sexual desire: *over-sexed*
sexism *n* (unfair treatment coming from) the belief that one sex is better, cleverer, etc., than the other **–ist** *adj, n*
sex object *n* person regarded exclusively for their sex appeal
sexology *n* study of sexual behaviour
sex organ *n* part of the body used in producing children
sexpot *n infml* sexy woman
sextant *n* instrument for measuring angles between stars, to find out where one is
sextet *n* (music for) six musicians
sexton *n* someone who takes care of a church building
sextuplet *n* any of six children born together
sexual *adj* of or connected with sex **~ly** *adv* **~ity** *n* interest in, the expression of, or the ability to take part in sexual activity
sexual intercourse *n* bodily act between two people in which the sex organs are brought together
sexy *adj* sexually exciting **–ily** *adv* **–iness** *n*
SF *abbrev. for:* science fiction
sforzando /sfawtˈsandoh/ *n, adj, adv* **-os** *or* **-di** (musical note) played with sudden loudness
sh, shh *interj* (used for demanding silence)
shabby *adj* **1** untidy, uncared-for, and worn-out **2** unfair and ungenerous **–bily** *adv* **–biness** *n*
shack *n* small roughly built house or hut **shack up** *phr vi infml* live together without being married
shackle *n* metal band for fastening the arms or legs ♦ *vt* fasten (as if) with shackles
shad *n* **shad** type of herring
shade *n* **1** slight darkness, made esp. by blocking of direct sunlight **2** something which provides shade or reduces light: *a lampshade* **3** degree or variety of colour **4** slight difference: *shades of meaning* **5** slight amount **6** *lit* ghost **7** **put in the shade** cause to seem much less important by comparison ♦ *v* **1** *vt* shelter from direct light **2** *vt* represent shadow on (an object in a picture) **3** *vi* change gradually **shady** *adj* **1** in or producing shade **2** probably dishonest
shades *pl n* **1** *infml* sunglasses **2** **shades of** this reminds me of
shadow *n* **1** shade (1) **2** dark shape made on a surface by something between it and direct light **3** dark area: *shadows under her eyes* **4** slightest amount **5** form from which the real substance has gone ♦ *adj* (in Britain) of the party opposing the government in parliament ♦ *vt* follow and watch closely, esp. secretly **~y** *adj* **1** hard to see or know about clearly **2** full of shade
shadow-box *vi* fight with an imaginary opponent **~ing** *n*
shaft *n* **1** thin rod forming the body of a weapon or tool, such as a spear or axe **2** bar which turns to pass power through a machine **3** long passage going down **4** either of two poles that an animal is fastened between to pull a vehicle **5** beam (of light) **6** something shot like an arrow: *shafts of wit* ♦ *vt AmE sl* treat unfairly and very severely
shag¹ *n* rough strong tobacco
shag² *vt* **-gg-** *BrE taboo sl* have sex with
shag³ *n* bird like a cormorant
shagged out *adj BrE sl* very tired

shaggy *adj* being or covered with long uneven untidy hair **–giness** *n*
shaggy-dog story *n* long joke with a purposely pointless ending
shagpile *n* long soft pile on a carpet
shah *n* sovereign of Iran
shake *v* **shook**, **shaken 1** *vi/t* move up and down and from side to side with quick short movements **2** *vi/t* hold (someone's right hand) and move it up and down, to show esp. greeting or agreement **3** *vt* move (one's head) from side to side to answer 'no' **4** trouble; upset **5** *vi* (of a voice) tremble **shake off** *phr vt* get rid of; escape from **shake up** *phr vt* **1** make big changes in (an organization), esp. to improve it **2** mix by shaking ♦ *n* **1** act of shaking **2** *infml* moment **shaky** *adj* shaking; unsteady **shakily** *adv*
shakedown *n infml* **1** last test operation of a new ship or aircraft **2** *AmE* act of getting money dishonestly **3** place prepared as a bed
shaker *n* **1** utensil used to sprinkle or mix by shaking **2** *cap.* member of an American sect living a simple, celibate, communal life
shakes *pl n infml* nervous shaking of the body from disease, fear, etc.
Shakespearean, **–ian** *adj* of William Shakespeare (1564-1616), English dramatist
shake-up *n* rearrangement of an organization
shale *n* soft rock which splits naturally
shall *v aux neg. short form* **shan't** (used with **I** and **we**) **1** (expresses the future tense) **2** (used in questions or offers)
shallot *n* small mild onion
shallow *adj* **1** not deep **2** lacking deep or serious thinking **shallows** *pl n* shallow area in a river, lake, etc.
shalom *interj* (Jewish greeting and farewell)
shalt *v* **thou shalt** *arch.* you shall
sham *n* **1** something that is not what it appears or is said to be **2** falseness; pretence ♦ *adj* not real ♦ *vi/t* **-mm-** put on a false appearance (of)
shaman *n* priest with magic powers
shamateur *n derog* one who officially plays sport for no money but in fact receives payment
shamble *vi* walk awkwardly, dragging the feet
shambles *pl n* (place or scene of) great disorder
shambolic *adj BrE infml* completely disordered or confused
shame *n* **1** painful feeling caused by knowledge of guilt, inability, or failure **2** ability to feel this **3** loss of honour **4** something one is sorry about **5 put to shame** show to be less good by comparison ♦ *vt* **1** bring dishonour to **2** cause to feel shame **~ful** *adj* which one ought to feel ashamed of **~fully** *adv* **~fulness** *n* **~less** *adj* **1** not feeling suitably ashamed **2** done without shame **~lessly** *adv* **~lessness** *n*
shamefaced *adj* showing suitable shame **~ly** *adv*
shammy *n* chamois (2)
shampoo *n* **-poos** liquid soap for washing the hair ♦ *vt* **-pooed**, **-pooing** wash with shampoo
shamrock *n* plant with three leaves on each stem that is the national emblem of Ireland
shandy *n* beer mixed with esp. lemonade
shanghai *vt* trick or force into doing something unwillingly
Shangri-La *n* distant beautiful imaginary place where everything is pleasant
shank *n* smooth end of a screw or drill
shanks's pony *n humorous* walking as a means of getting somewhere
shan't *v short for:* shall not
shantung *n* silk cloth with a slightly rough surface
shanty[1] *n* small roughly built house
shanty[2] *n* song sung by working sailors
shantytown *n* (part of) a town where poor people live in shanties
shape *n* **1** outer form of something **2** general character or nature of something **3** (proper) condition, health, arrangement, etc. **4 take shape** begin to be

or look like the finished form ♦ *v* **1** *vt* give a particular shape to **2** *vi* develop in the stated way **shape up** *phr vi* **1** develop well or in the stated way **2** begin to perform more effectively, behave better, etc. **~less** *adj* **~lessness** *n* **~ly** *adj* (of a person) having an attractive shape

shard *n* broken piece of a bowl, cup, etc.

share *n* **1** part belonging to, owed to, or done by a particular person **2** part of the ownership of a business company, offered for sale to the public ♦ *v* **1** *vi/t* have, use, pay, etc., with others or among a group **2** *vt* divide and give out in shares

sharecropper *n* (esp. in the US) farmer who pays part of his rent in produce

shareholder *n* owner of company shares

share-out *n* act of giving out shares of something

sharia, sheria *n* system of law followed by Muslims

shark *n* **1 shark** *or* **sharks** large dangerous fish with sharp teeth **2** *infml* person clever at getting money from others dishonestly

sharkskin *n* **1** (leather from) the skin of a shark **2** smooth, stiff, strong cloth

sharp *adj* **1** having or being a thin cutting edge or fine point **2** not rounded **3** causing a sensation like that of cutting, pricking, biting, or stinging: *a sharp taste* **4** quick and strong: *a sharp blow* **5** sudden: *a sharp turn* **6** clear in shape or detail **7** quick and sensitive in thinking, seeing, etc. **8** angry **9** (in music) above the right note ♦ *adv* **1** exactly at the stated time **2** suddenly **3** above the right note ♦ *n* (in music) sharp note **~ly** *adv* **~en** *vi/t* become or make sharp or sharper **~ener** *n* **~ness** *n*

sharp end *n infml* part of a job, organization, etc., where the most severe problems are experienced

sharper, sharp *n* cheat

sharp practice *n* dishonest but not quite illegal activity

sharpshooter *n* person skilled in shooting

shat *past t. and p. of* shit

shatter *v* **1** *vi/t* break suddenly into very small pieces **2** *vt* shock very much **3** *vt infml* tire very much

shave *v* **1** *vi/t* cut off (a beard or face hair) with a razor or shaver **2** *vt* cut hair from (a part of the body) **3** *vt* cut off (very thin pieces) from (a surface) **4** *vt* come close to or touch in passing ♦ *n* act of shaving **~r** *n* electric shaving tool **shaving** *n* very thin piece cut off from a surface

shaving cream *n* soapy paste put on the face to make shaving easier

shawl *n* large piece of cloth worn over a woman's head or shoulders or wrapped round the body

she *pron* (used for the female subject of a sentence) ♦ *n* female: *a she-goat*

sheaf *n* **sheaves 1** bunch of grain plants tied together **2** many things held or tied together

shear *v* **sheared, sheared** *or* **shorn 1** *vt* cut off wool from (a sheep) **2** *vi/t* break under a sideways or twisting force **3 be shorn of** have (something) completely removed from one **shears** *pl n* large cutting tool like scissors

sheath *n* **sheaths 1** closefitting case for a blade **2** condom

sheathe *vt* put away in a sheath

shebang *n* **the whole shebang** *infml* everything

shebeen *n* (Irish) unlicensed bar

she'd *short for:* **1** she would **2** she had

shed[1] *n* lightly built single-floored (wooden) building

shed[2] *vt* **shed,** *pres. p.* **-dd- 1** cause to flow out **2** get rid of (outer skin, leaves, hair, etc.) naturally **3** get rid of (something not wanted or needed) **4** (of a vehicle) drop (a load of goods) by accident **5 shed blood** cause wounding or esp. killing **6 shed light on** help to explain

sheen *n* shiny surface

sheep *n* **sheep** grass-eating animal farmed for its wool and meat **~ish** *adj* uncomfortable because one knows one

has done something wrong or foolish **~ishly** *adv* **~ishness** *n*
sheepdip *n* (chemical used in) a bath for sheep, to destroy parasites
sheepdog *n* dog trained to control sheep
sheepskin *n* skin of a sheep made into leather, esp. with the wool still on
sheer[1] *adj* **1** pure; nothing but: *sheer luck* **2** very steep **3** (of cloth) very thin ♦ *adv* straight up or down
sheer[2] *vi* change direction quickly
sheet *n* **1** large four-sided piece of cloth used on a bed **2** broad regularly shaped piece of a thin or flat material **3** broad stretch of something: *a sheet of ice*
sheet anchor *n* dependable person or thing; mainstay
sheeting *n* (material for making) sheets
sheet lightning *n* lightning in broad diffused form
sheet music *n* music printed on single sheets
sheikh /shayk, sheek/ *n* Arab chief or prince **~dom** *n*
sheila *n AustrE infml* young woman
shekel *n* unit of money in Israel
shekels *pl n sl* money
shelf *n* **shelves 1** flat (narrow) board fixed against a wall or in a frame, for putting things on **2** narrow surface of rock underwater **3 on the shelf** not likely to marry, esp. because one is too old
shelf-life *n* time something can be kept before it starts to deteriorate
shell *n* **1** hard outer covering of a nut, egg, fruit, or certain types of animal **2** outer surface or frame of something **3** explosive for firing from a large gun **4 come out of one's shell** begin to be friendly or interested in others ♦ *vt* **1** remove from a shell or pod **2** fire shells at **shell out** *phr vi/t infml* pay
she'll *short for:* she will
shellac *n* natural resin used as a varnish
shellacking *n AmE infml* severe defeat
shellfish *n* **-fish** soft-bodied water animal with a shell (e.g. an oyster or lobster)
shellshock *n* illness of the mind, esp. in soldiers caused by the experience of war **~ed** *adj*
shelter *n* **1** building or enclosure giving protection **2** protection, esp. from bad weather ♦ *v* **1** *vt* give shelter to **2** *vi* take shelter
shelve *v* **1** *vt* put aside until a later time **2** *vi* slope gradually
shelves *pl. of* shelf
shelving *n* shelves
shemozzle *n infml* fuss, to-do
shenanigans *pl n infml* **1** rather dishonest practices **2** mischief
shepherd *n* person who takes care of sheep ♦ *vt* lead or guide like sheep
shepherdess *n* female shepherd
shepherd's pie *n* dish of minced meat with a topping of potato
sherbet *n* sweet powder, often added to water
sherd *n* shard
sheriff *n* **1** elected law officer in a local area in the US **2** royally appointed chief officer in an English county
Sherpa *n* member of a Tibetan people skilled in mountain-climbing
sherry *n* pale or dark brown strong wine (originally) from Spain
she's *short for:* **1** she is **2** she has
Shetland pony *n* very small breed of pony
shew *vi/t* **shewed, shewn** *arch.* show
shibboleth *n* **1** word used to test which party, class, etc., a person belongs to **2** once-important custom or phrase which no longer has much meaning
shickered *adj AustrE & NZE infml* drunk
shield *n* **1** something carried as a protection from being hit **2** representation of this, used for a coat of arms, badge, etc. **3** protective cover ♦ *vt* protect
shift *v* **1** *vi/t* move from one place to another **2** *vt* get rid of; remove **3 shift for oneself** take care of oneself ♦ *n* **1** change in position or direction **2** (period worked by) a group of workers which takes turns with others **3** loose

fitting simple dress **~less** *adj* lazy and lacking in purpose **~y** *adj* looking dishonest; not to be trusted **~ily** *adv* **~iness** *n*

shift key *n* key on a typewriter or other keyboard pressed to print a capital letter

shift stick *n AmE for* gear lever

Shiite *n* Muslim of a sect who are followers of Ali, son-in-law of Muhammad

shillelagh /shi'layli/ *n* Irish cudgel

shilling *n* former British coin worth 12 old pence ($\frac{1}{20}$ of £1)

shilly-shally *vi* waste time instead of taking action

shimmer *vi* shine with a soft trembling light

shin *n* the part of the leg below the knee ♦ *vi* **-nn-** climb using the hands and legs, esp. quickly and easily

shindig *n infml* noisy party

shine *v* **shone 1** *vi/t* (cause to) give off light **2** *vt* (*past t. and p.* **shined**) polish **3** *vi* be clearly excellent ♦ *n* **1** brightness **2** act of polishing **3 take a shine to** start to like **shiny** *adj* bright

shingle[1] *n* stones on a seashore **-gly** *adj*

shingle[2] *n* **1** roof tile, esp. of wood **2** woman's short haircut ♦ *vt* **1** cover with tiles **2** cut in a shingle

shingles *n* disease producing painful red spots, esp. round the waist

shinny *vi AmE* shin

Shinto also **Shintoism** *n* ancient religion of Japan

ship *n* **1** large boat **2** large aircraft or space vehicle **3 when one's ship comes in/home** when one becomes rich ♦ *vt* **-pp- 1** send by ship **2** send over a large distance by road, air, or rail **~per** *n* dealer who ships goods **~ping** *n* ships as a group

-ship *suffix* (*in nouns*) **1** condition of having or being the stated thing: *partnership* **2** the stated skill: *scholarship*

shipboard *n* **on shipboard** on a ship

shipmate *n* fellow sailor on the same ship

shipment *n* **1** load of goods sent by sea, road, rail, or air **2** sending, carrying, and delivering goods

shipshape *adj* clean and neat

shipwreck *n* destruction of a ship, e.g. by hitting rocks or by sinking ♦ *vt* **1** cause to suffer shipwreck **2** ruin

shipyard *n* place where ships are built or repaired

shire *n* **1** *arch.* county **2** large carthorse

shires *pl n* areas of England away from the cities

shirk *vi/t* avoid (unpleasant work or responsibility) **~er** *n*

shirring *n* decorative gathering in cloth

shirt *n* cloth garment for the upper body with sleeves and usu. a collar

shirtsleeves *n* **in (one's) shirtsleeves** wearing nothing over one's shirt

shirtwaister *n* dress with a bodice like a shirt

shirty *adj infml* angry

shish kebab *n* kebab cooked on skewers

shit *n taboo* **1** solid waste from the bowels **2** something of no value: *I don't give a shit.* **3** worthless or unpleasant person ♦ *vi* **-tt-** *taboo* pass solid waste from the bowels ♦ *interj taboo* (expressing anger or annoyance) **~ty** *adj taboo sl* unpleasant

shiver[1] *vi* shake, esp. from cold or fear ♦ *n* feeling of shivering **~y** *adj*

shiver[2] *vi/t* shatter ♦ *n* splinter

shoal[1] *n* dangerous bank of sand near the surface of water

shoal[2] *n* large group of fish swimming together

shock[1] *n* **1** (state or feeling caused by) an unexpected and usu. very unpleasant event **2** violent force from a hard blow, crash, or explosion, or from electricity ♦ *vt* cause unpleasant or angry surprise to ♦ *adj* very surprising: *shock tactics* **~ing** *adj* **1** very offensive, wrong, or upsetting **2** very bad: *I've got a shocking cold.* **~ingly** *adv*

shock[2] *n* thick mass (of hair)

shock absorber *n* apparatus fitted to a vehicle to lessen the effect of violent movement

shock-headed *adj* having thick bushy hair

shock troops *pl n* specially trained assault troops

shod *past t. and p. of* shoe

shoddy *adj* **1** cheaply and badly done **2** ungenerous; dishonourable **-dily** *adv* **-diness** *n*

shoe *n* **1** covering worn on the foot **2 in someone's shoes** in someone's position: *I'd hate to be in your shoes.* ♦ *vt* **shod** fix a horseshoe on

shoehorn *n* device used to ease a shoe over the heel

shoelace *n* thin cord for fastening a shoe

shoestring *n* **on a shoestring** with a very small amount of money

shogun *n* military governor in Japan before 1867

shone *past t. and p. of* shine

shoo *interj* (used for driving away esp. birds and animals) ♦ *vt* drive away (as if) by saying 'shoo'

shook *past t. of* shake

shoot *v* **shot 1** *vi* fire a weapon **2** *vt* (of a person or weapon) send out (e.g. bullets) with force **3** *vt* hit, wound, or kill e.g. with a bullet **4** *vi* move very quickly or suddenly: *The car shot past us.* **5** *vi/t* make (a photograph or film) (of) **6** *vi* kick or throw a ball to make a point in a game **7** *vt AmE* play (a game of pool) **8 shoot one's mouth off** talk foolishly or indiscreetly **9 shoot the bull/the breeze** *AmE infml* have an informal not very serious conversation **shoot down** *phr vt* **1** bring down (a flying aircraft) by shooting **2** reject (an idea) **shoot up** *phr v* **1** *vi* go upwards, increase, or grow quickly **2** *vt infml* damage or wound by shooting **3** *vi/t sl* inject (a drug) directly into a vein ♦ *n* **1** new growth from a plant **2** occasion for shooting, esp. of animals

shooting gallery *n* covered range with targets for shooting practice

shooting star *n* meteor

shooting stick *n* stick with a spike and a handle which unfolds to make a seat

shoot-out *n* battle between gunfighters

shop *n* **1** *BrE* building or room where goods are sold **2** subjects connected with one's work: *Let's not talk shop.* ♦ *v* **-pp- 1** *vi* visit shops to buy things **2** *vt BrE infml* tell the police about (a criminal) **shop around** *phr vt* compare prices or values in different shops before buying **~per** *n* **~ping** *n* goods bought when visiting shops

shop assistant *n BrE* person who serves customers in a shop

shop floor *n* area, esp. in a factory, where the ordinary workers work

shopkeeper *n esp. BrE* person in charge of a small shop

shoplift *vi* steal from a shop **~er** *n*

shopsoiled *adj* slightly damaged or dirty from being kept in a shop for a long time

shop steward *n* trade union officer representing members in a place of work

shore *n* **1** land along the edge of a sea, lake, etc. **2 on shore** on land; away from one's ship

shore up *phr vt* support (something in danger of falling) with props

shorn *past p. of* shear

short *adj* **1** measuring a small or smaller than average amount in distance, length, or height **2** lasting only a little time, or less time than usual or expected **3** a shorter (and often more usual) way of saying: *The word 'pub' is short for 'public house'.* **4** not having or providing what is needed: *I'm short of money.* **5** rudely impatient **6** (of pastry) rich in fat and easily broken **7 short of: a** not quite reaching **b** except for **8 short on** without very much or enough (of): *He's a nice fellow but short on brains.* ♦ *adv* **1** suddenly: *He stopped short.* **2 fall short (of)** be less than (good) enough (for) **3 go short (of)** be without enough (of) **4 run short (of)** : **a** not have enough left **b** become less than enough ♦ *n* **1** drink of strong alcohol, such as whisky **2** short film shown before the main film at a cinema **3** short circuit **4**

for short as a shorter way of saying it **5** **in short** all I mean is; to put it into as few words as possible
shortage *n* amount lacking; not enough
shortbread *n* sweet buttery biscuit
short-change *vt* **1** give back less than enough money to a buyer **2** fail to reward fairly
short circuit *n* faulty electrical connection where the current flows the wrong way and usu. puts the power supply out of operation **short-circuit** *vi/t* (cause to) have a short circuit
shortcoming *n* fault; failing
short cut *n* quicker more direct way
shorten *vi/t* make or become shorter
shortening *n* edible fat (e.g. butter or lard) added to pastry
shortfall *n* deficit
shorthand *n* system of special signs for fast writing
shorthanded *adj* without enough workers or helpers
shorthand typist *n* person who takes down words in shorthand and then types them out
short-haul *adj* (of an aircraft flight) covering a fairly short distance
Shorthorn *n* type of English cattle
short-list *n BrE* list of the best ones chosen from an original long list ♦ *vt BrE* put on a short list
short-lived *adj* lasting only a short time
shortly *adv* **1** soon **2** impatiently **3** in a few words
short order *n AmE* order for food that can be quickly cooked **short-order** *adj*
short-range *adj* covering a short distance or time
shorts *pl n* **1** short trousers **2** *esp. AmE* short underpants
short shrift *n* unfairly quick or unsympathetic treatment
shortsighted *adj* **1** unable to see distant things clearly **2** not considering what may happen in the future **~ly** *adv* **~ness** *n*
short-term, short term *adj, n* (concerning) a short period of time; (in or for) the near future: *short-term planning*
short wave *n* radio broadcasting on waves of less than 60 metres
shot *v* **1** *past t. and p. of* shoot **2 be/get shot of** *sl* get rid of ♦ *n* **1** (sound of) shooting a weapon **2** hit or kick (of a ball in sport) **3** person who shoots with the stated skill **4** attempt: *I'll have a shot at it.* **5** metal balls for shooting from shotguns or cannons **6 a** photograph **b** single part of a film made by one camera without interruption **7** injection: *a shot of penicillin* **8** sending up of a spacecraft or rocket: *a moon shot* **9** a small drink (esp. of whisky) all swallowed at once **10 a shot in the arm** something which acts to bring back a better, more active condition **11 a shot in the dark** a wild guess unsupported by arguments
shotgun *n* gun fired from the shoulder, usu. having two barrels, used esp. to kill birds
shotgun wedding *n* wedding that has to take place, esp. because the woman is pregnant
shot put *n* competition in sport to throw a heavy metal ball as far as possible **shot-putter** *n* **shot-putting** *n*
should *v aux* **1 a** ought to **b** will probably **2** (used after **that** in certain expressions of feeling): *It's odd that you should mention him.* **3** (used instead of **shall** in conditional sentences with **I** and **we** as the subject and a past tense verb): *I should be surprised if he came.* **4** (to express humour or surprise): *As I left the house, who should I meet but my old friend Sam.* **5 I should** (when giving advice) you ought to: *I should go (if I were you).* **6 I should have thought** *esp. BrE* (shows surprise): *I should have thought you'd know the answer.*
shoulder *n* **1 a** the part of the body at each side of the neck where the arms are connected **b** part of a garment which covers this part of the body **2** part where something widens slopingly: *the shoulder of a bottle* **3 shoulder to shoulder: a** side by side **b** together; with the same intentions ♦ *vt* accept

(e.g. a heavy responsibility)

shoulder blade *n* either of two flat bones in the upper back

shouldn't *short for:* should not

shout *vi/t* speak or say very loudly **shout down** *phr vt* prevent a speaker being heard by shouting ♦ *n* loud cry or call

shove *vi/t* **1** push, esp. roughly or carelessly **2** *infml* move oneself: *Shove over and let me sit down.* ♦ *n* strong push

shove-halfpenny *n* game in which players push coins or discs towards scoring areas on a flat board

shovel *n* long-handled tool with a broad blade for lifting loose material ♦ *vi/t* **-ll-**, (*AmE* **-l-**) move or work (as if) with a shovel

show *v* **showed, shown 1** *vt* allow or cause to be seen: *Show me your ticket.* **2** *vi* be able to be seen: *The stain won't show.* **3** *vt* go with and guide or direct: *May I show you to your seat?* **4** *vt* explain, esp. by actions: *Show me how to do it.* **5** *vt* make clear; prove: *This piece of work shows what you can do when you try.* **6** *vt* cause to be felt in one's actions: *They showed their enemies no mercy.* **7** *vi sl* show up (2) **show off** *phr v* **1** *vi derog* behave so as to try to get attention and admiration **2** *vt* show proudly or to the best effect **show up** *phr v* **1** *vt* make clear the (esp. unpleasant) truth about **2** *vi* arrive; be present ♦ *n* **1** performance, esp. in a theatre or on television or radio **2** collection of things for the public to look at: *a flower show* **3** showing of some quality: *a show of temper* **4** outward appearance: *a show of interest* **5** splendid(-seeming) appearance or ceremony **6** effort; act of trying: *They've put up a very good show this year.* **~y** *adj* (too) colourful, bright, or obtrusive

show business *n* job of people who work in television, films, or the theatre

showcase *n* a set of shelves enclosed in glass on which objects are placed for display

showdown *n* settlement of a quarrel in an open direct way

shower *n* **1** short-lasting fall of rain (or snow) **2** fall or sudden rush of many small things: *a shower of sparks* **3** (apparatus for) washing the body by standing under running water ♦ *v* **1** *vi* fall in showers **2** *vt* scatter or cover in showers **3** *vi* wash in a shower **~y** *adj* with showers of rain

showgirl *n* girl who sings or dances in a musical

showing *n* **1** performance: *a poor showing* **2** act of putting on view

show jumping *n* competition for riding horses over fences

showman *n* **-men 1** person whose business is producing public entertainments **2** person who is good at gaining public attention **~ship** *n*

shown *past p. of* show

show-off *n derog* person who shows off

showpiece *n* fine example for exhibition

showroom *n* room where samples of goods for sale are displayed

shrank *past t. of* shrink

shrapnel *n* metal scattered from an exploding bomb

shred *n* **1** small narrow piece torn or roughly cut off **2** slightest bit: *not a shred of evidence* ♦ *vt* **-dd-** cut or tear into shreds

shrew *n* **1** very small mouselike animal **2** bad-tempered scolding woman **~ish** *adj*

shrewd *adj* **1** showing good practical judgment **2** likely to be right: *a shrewd estimate* **~ly** *adv* **~ness** *n*

shriek *vi/t, n* (cry out with) a wild high cry

shrift *n arch.* **1** confession **2** forgiveness

shrike *n* bird that feeds on insects

shrill *adj* (of a sound) high and (painfully) sharp ♦ *vi/t* utter (with) a high sharp sound **shrilly** *adv* **~ness** *n*

shrimp *n* small 10-legged sea creature

shrine *n* **1** holy place, where one worships **2** box containing the remains of a holy person's body

shrink[1] *v* **shrank, shrunk 1** *vi/t* (cause to) become smaller **2** *vi* move back and away **shrink from** *phr vt* avoid, esp. from fear **~age** *n* loss in size
shrink[2] *n infml* psychoanalyst or psychiatrist
shrinking violet *n* shy person
shrive *vt* **shrived, shrove,** *past p.* **shriven** *arch.* (of a priest) to hear confession and pronounce forgiveness
shrivel *vi/t* **-ll-** (*AmE* **-l-**) (cause to) become smaller by drying and wrinkling
shroud *n* **1** cloth for covering a dead body **2** something that covers and hides ♦ *vt* cover and hide
Shrove Tuesday *n* Tuesday before Lent
shrub *n* low bush
shrubbery *n* mass or group of shrubs
shrug *vi/t* **-gg-** raise (one's shoulders), esp. showing doubt or lack of interest **shrug off** *phr vt* treat as unimportant or easily dealt with ♦ *n* act of shrugging
shrunk *past p. of* shrink
shrunken *adj* having been shrunk
shuck *n* husk or pod ♦ *vt esp. AmE* remove husks or pods from **shuck off** *phr vt* cast aside
shucks *interj AmE infml* (used to express disappointment)
shudder *vi* shake uncontrollably for a moment ♦ *n* act of shuddering
shuffle *v* **1** *vi/t* mix up (playing cards) so as to produce a chance order **2** *vi* walk by dragging one's feet slowly along ♦ *n* **1** act of shuffling cards **2** slow dragging walk
shuffleboard *n* game in which wooden discs are pushed by cues
shufti *n infml* look
shun *vt* **-nn-** avoid with determination
shunt *vt* **1** *esp. BrE* move (a train) from one track to another **2** move around or away: *Smith has been shunted to a smaller office.* ♦ *n* **1** conductor which forms a parallel path in an electrical circuit **2** surgical device which diverts the flow of blood
shush *interj* (used for demanding silence)
shut *v* **shut,** *pres. p.* **-tt- 1** *vi/t* put into a covered or folded position; close: *Shut the door.* **2** *vt* keep or hold by closing in: *He shut himself in his room.* **3** *vi/t* stop operating: *The shops shut at 5.30.* **shut down** *phr vi/t* (cause to) stop operation, esp. for a long time or forever **shut off** *phr vi/t* **1** stop in flow or operation, esp. by turning a handle or pressing a button **2** keep separate or away **shut up** *phr v* **1** *vi/t* (cause to) stop talking **2** *vt* keep enclosed
shutdown *n* cessation or suspension of an activity
shut-eye *n infml* sleep
shutter *n* **1** part of a camera which opens to let light fall on the film **2** movable cover for a window ♦ *vt* close (as if) with shutters
shuttle *n* **1** (vehicle used on) a regular short journey: *a shuttle service* **2** reusable spacecraft **3** thread-carrier in weaving ♦ *v* **1** *vt* transport by a shuttle **2** *vi* move rapidly back and forth
shuttlecock *n* light feathered object struck in badminton
shuttle diplomacy *n* international talks carried out by a negotiator who travels between the countries concerned
shy[1] *adj* **1** nervous in the company of others **2** (of animals) unwilling to come near people ♦ *vi* (esp. of a horse) make a sudden (frightened) movement **shy away from** *phr vt* avoid something unpleasant **~ly** *adv* **~ness** *n*
shy[2] *vi/t* throw with a quick movement ♦ *n* throw
shyster *n AmE infml* dishonest person, esp. a lawyer
SI *abbrev. for:* Système International d'Unités; a decimal system of units for measuring length, weight, time, sound, temperature, light, and substance
Siamese *pl n, adj* (people) of Thailand
Siamese cat also **Siamese** *n* slender cat with pale body and darker ears, paws, tail, and face
Siamese twin *n* either of two people with their bodies joined from birth
sibilant *adj, n* (making or being) a sound

like *s* or *sh*

sibling *n* brother or sister

sibyl *n* woman with the gift of prophecy

sic *adv* intentionally so (used after a printed word to show that it is a deliberate oddity or a deliberately reproduced mistake)

sick *adj* **1** ill **2** throwing or about to throw food up out of the stomach **3** feeling annoyance, dislike, and loss of patience: *I'm sick of your complaints.* **4** unnaturally or unhealthily cruel: *a sick joke* **~ness** *n* **1** illness **2** feeling sick

sickbay *n* room with beds for sick people

sicken *v* **1** *vt* cause to feel sick **2** *vi* become ill **~ing** *adj* extremely displeasing or unpleasant **~ingly** *adv*

sickie *n AustrE infml* day's sick leave

sickle *n* small tool with a curved blade for cutting long grass ♦ *adj* sickle-shaped

sick leave *n* absence from work because of illness

sickle-cell anaemia *n* hereditary anaemia in which red blood cells are malformed

sickly *adj* **1** weak and unhealthy **2** unhealthily pale **3** causing a sick feeling

sick pay *n* money paid to an employee on sick leave

side *n* **1** surface that is not the top, bottom, front, or back **2** edge; border: *A square has four sides.* **3** either of the two surfaces of a thin flat object **4** part in relation to a central line: *I live on the other side of town.* **5** place or area next to something: *On one side of the window was a mirror.* **6** part or quality to be considered: *Try to look at both sides of the question.* **7** (group holding) a position in a quarrel, war, etc.: *I'm on your side.* **8** sports team **9** part of a line of a family that is related to a particular person **10 on the side** as a (sometimes dishonest) additional activity: *She does some teaching on the side.* ♦ *vi* support the stated side in an argument: *She sided with me.*

sidearm *n* weapon worn at the side

sideboard *n* long, wide, low cupboard for crockery, glasses, and cutlery

sideboards, *AmE* **sideburns** *pl n* hair on the sides of a man's face

sidecar *n* small carriage fastened to the side of a motorcycle

side effect *n* effect in addition to the intended one

side issue *n* question or subject apart from the main one

sidekick *n infml* a (less important) helper or companion

sidelight *n* **1** small lamp at the side of a vehicle **2** piece of additional (not very important) information

sideline *n* **1** activity in addition to one's regular job **2** line marking the limit of play on a sports field

sidelong *adj* directed sideways: *a sidelong glance*

sidereal /sieˈdiəri·əl/ *adj tech* of or calculated by the stars

sidesaddle *adv, n* (on) a woman's saddle on which one sits sideways

sideshow *n* separate small show at a fair or circus

sideslip *vi* slip sideways **sideslip** *n*

sidesman *n* person who helps the churchwarden during a service

sidesplitting *adj* very funny; causing uncontrollable laughter

sidestep *vi/t* **-pp- 1** step aside to avoid (esp. a blow) **2** avoid (an unwelcome question, problem, etc.)

sidestroke *n* swimming stroke done while lying on one's side

sideswipe *n* incidental attacking remark ♦ *vt* hit on the side while passing

sidetrack *vt* cause to leave one subject or activity and follow another (less important) one

sidewalk *n AmE* pavement

sidewards, *AmE* **sideward** *adv* towards one side

sideways *adv* **1** with one side (not the back or front) forward or up **2** towards one side

siding *n* piece of railway track where carriages are parked
sidle *vi* move sideways **sidle up** *phr vi* walk secretively or nervously up (to someone)
siege *n* operation by an army surrounding a city or fortified place to force the people inside to surrender
sienna *n* brownish yellow or reddish brown pigment
sierra *n* range of mountains
siesta *n* short sleep after the midday meal
sieve *n* tool with a net or holes for letting liquid or small objects through ♦ *vt* put through or separate with a sieve
sift *v* **1** *vt* put (something non-liquid) through a sieve **2** *vi/t* examine (things in a mass or group) closely: *sifting the evidence*
sifter *n* caster (2)
sigh *vi* let out a deep breath slowly and with a sound, usu. expressing sadness, satisfaction, or tiredness ♦ *n* act or sound of sighing
sight *n* **1** power of seeing **2** the seeing of something: *I caught sight of her.* **3** something seen **4** range of what can be seen: *The train came into sight.* **5** something worth seeing: *the sights of London* **6** part of an instrument or weapon which guides the eye in aiming **7** something which looks very bad or laughable **8** *infml* a lot: *She earns a sight more than I do.* **9 a sight for sore eyes** a person or thing that one is glad to see **10 at first sight** at the first time of seeing or considering **11 at/on sight** as soon as seen or shown **12 in sight: a** in view **b** near ♦ *vt* see for the first time **~ed** *adj* able to see **~ing** *n* case of someone or something being sighted: *several sightings of rare birds* **~less** *adj* blind **~ly** *adj* attractive
sight-read *vi/t* play or sing (written music) at first sight **~er** *n* **~ing** *n*
sightseeing *n* visiting places of interest **–seer** *n*
sign *n* **1** mark which represents a known meaning: + *is the plus sign.* **2** movement of the body intended to express a meaning **3** notice giving information **4** something that shows the presence or coming of something else: *There are signs that the economy may be improving.* **5** also **star sign** any of the 12 divisions of the zodiac ♦ *vi/t* **1** write (one's name) on (a written paper), esp. officially or to show that one is the writer **2** signal **3** sign up **sign away** *phr vt* give up formally by signing a paper **sign on** *phr vi/t* **1** (cause to) join a working force by signing a paper **2** state officially that one is unemployed **sign up** *phr vi/t* (cause to) sign an agreement to take part in something or take a job **~er** *n*
signal¹ *n* **1** sound or action which warns, commands, or gives a message: *a danger signal* **2** action which causes another to happen **3** apparatus by a railway track to direct train drivers **4** message sent by radio or television waves ♦ *vi* **-ll-** (*AmE* **-l-**) give a signal
signal² *adj* remarkable **~ly** *adv*
signal box *n* small building near a railway from which signals and points are controlled
signalize, –ise *vt fml* distinguish
signalman, *n* **-men** someone who works railway signals
signatory /ˈsɪgnət(ə)ri/ *n fml* signer of an agreement, esp. among nations
signature *n* person's name written by himself or herself
signature tune *n* short piece of music used regularly to begin and end a particular radio or TV programme
signet *n* seal¹ (1)
significant *adj* **1** of noticeable importance or effect **2** having a special meaning, indirectly expressed **~ly** *adv* **–cance** *n*
signify *v fml* **1** *vt* mean **2** *vi/t* make known (esp. an opinion) by an action **3** *vi* matter **–fier** *n* **–fication** *n*
sign language *n* system of hand gestures used for communication (e.g. by the deaf)
Signor *n* (title for an Italian man)

Signora *n* (title of an Italian woman)
Signorita *n* (title of an Italian unmarried woman or girl)
signpost *n* sign showing directions and distances ♦ *vt esp. BrE* provide with signposts to guide the driver
Sikh *n, adj* (follower) of a monotheistic Indian religion that developed from Hinduism in the 16th century **~ism** *n*
silage *n* plants preserved as winter cattle food
silence *n* **1** (period of) absence of sound **2** not speaking or making a noise **3** failure to mention a particular thing ♦ *vt* cause or force to be silent **silencer** *n* apparatus for reducing noise
silent *adj* **1** free from noise **2** not speaking **3** failing or refusing to express an opinion, etc. **4** (of a letter) not pronounced **~ly** *adv*
silhouette /ˌsilooh'et/ *n* dark shape seen against a light background ♦ *vt* cause to appear as a silhouette
silica *n* silicon compound occurring in sand and many rocks
silicon *n* simple non-metallic substance found commonly in natural compounds
silicon chip *n* chip in a computer or other electronic machinery
silicone *n* organic silicon compound used esp. in lubricants and insulating materials
silicosis *n* lung disease caused by breathing silica dust
silk *n* (smooth cloth from) fine thread produced by silkworms **~en** *adj* **1** silky **2** made of silk **~y** *adj* soft, smooth, and shiny
silkworm *n* caterpillar which produces silk
sill *n* shelflike part at the bottom of a window
silly *adj* not serious or sensible; foolish **–liness** *n*
silly season *n infml* period in the summer when there is not much news so newspapers print silly stories about unimportant things
silo *n* **1** round tower-like enclosure for storing silage **2** underground missile-firing base
silt *n* loose mud brought by a river or current **silt up** *phr vi/t* fill or become filled with silt
silvan *adj* sylvan
silver *n* **1** soft whitish precious metal **2** spoons, forks, dishes, etc., made of silver **3** silver (-coloured) coins **4** silver medal ♦ *adj* **1** made of silver **2** of the colour of silver ♦ *vt* cover with silver **~y** *adj* **1** like silver in shine and colour **2** having a pleasant metallic sound
silver birch *n* common birch with white bark
silverfish *n* **-fish** *or* **-fishes** small silver-coloured wingless insect
silver paper *n* paper with a shiny metallic coating
silverside *n* cut of beef from the leg, often salted
silversmith *n* craftsman who works with silver
silver wedding *n* 25th anniversary of a wedding
simian *adj, n* (of or like) a monkey or ape
similar *adj* almost but not exactly the same; alike **~ly** *adv* **~ity** *n* **1** quality of being similar **2** way in which things are similar
simile /'simili/ *n* expression which describes one thing by comparing it with another (as in *as white as snow*)
similitude *n fml* likeness
simmer *vi/t* cook gently in (nearly) boiling liquid **simmer down** *phr vi* become calmer
simper *vi* smile in a silly unnatural way
simple *adj* **1** without decoration; plain **2** easy **3** consisting of only one thing or part **4** (of something non-physical) pure: *the simple truth* **5** easily tricked; foolish ♦ *n arch.* herb with medicinal use **–ply** *adv* **1** in a simple way **2** just; only: *I simply don't know.* **3** really; absolutely: *a simply gorgeous day*
simple-minded *adj* **1** foolish **2** simple and unthinking in mind **~ly** *adv*

simple-mindedness *n*
simpleton *n* weak-minded trusting person
simplicity *n* quality of being simple
simplify *vt* make simpler **–fication** *n*
simplistic *adj derog* treating difficult matters as if they were simple **~ally** *adv*
simulacrum *n* **–crums** *or* **–cra** *fml* likeness; representation
simulate *vt* give the appearance or effect of **–lation** *n*
simultaneous *adj* happening or done at the same moment **~ly** *adv* **~ness, -neity** *n*
sin *n* **1** offence against God or a religious law **2** *infml* something that should not be done ♦ *vi* **-nn-** do wrong **~ful** *adj* wicked **~fully** *adv* **~ner** *n*
since *adv* **1** at a time between then and now: *She left in 1979, and I haven't seen her since.* **2** from then until now: *He came here 2 years ago and has lived here ever since.* **3** ago: *I've long since forgotten his name.* ♦ *prep* from (a point in past time) until now: *I haven't seen her since 1979.* ♦ *conj* **1 a** after the past time when: *I haven't seen her since she left.* **b** continuously from the time when: *We've been friends since we met at school.* **2** as: *Since you can't answer, I'll ask someone else.*
sincere *adj* free from deceit or falseness; honest and true **~ly** *adv* **–cerity** *n*
sine *n* (in trigonometry) the fraction that is calculated for an acute angle by dividing the side opposite it in a right-angled triangle by the hypotenuse
sinecure /ˈsinikyooə/ *n* paid job with few or no duties
sine die /ˌsieni ˈdee·ay/ *adv tech* without fixing a date (e.g. for the next meeting)
sine qua non /ˌsini kway ˈnon/ *n* essential thing
sinew *n* strong cord connecting a muscle to a bone **~y** *adj*
sing *v* **sang, sung 1** *vi/t* produce (music) with the voice **2** *vi* make or be filled with a ringing sound: *It made my ears sing.* **~er** *n*
singe *vt* burn slightly
Singhalese *n, adj* Sinhalese
single *adj* **1** being (the) only one: *a single sheet of paper* **2** considered by itself; separate: *He understands every single word I say.* **3** unmarried **4** for the use of only one person: *a single bed* **5** *BrE* (of a ticket) for a journey to a place but not back **single out** *phr vt* choose from a group for special attention ♦ *n* **1** *BrE* a single ticket **2** record with only one short song on each side **–gly** *adv* one by one; not in a group
single-breasted *adj* (of a coat or jacket) with one central row of buttons
single file *adv, n* (in) a line (e.g. of people) moving one behind another
single-handed *adj* without help from others **~ly** *adv*
single-minded *adj* having one clear aim or purpose **~ly** *adv* **~ness** *n*
singles *n* **singles** *n* (tennis) match between two players
singlet *n* vest or sleeveless shirt
singleton *n* something on its own, esp. the only card of its suit in a hand
singsong *n* **1** repeated rising and falling of the voice in speaking **2** *BrE* informal gathering for singing songs
singular *adj* **1** (of a word) representing only one thing **2** *fml* unusually great ♦ *n* singular word or form **~ly** *adv fml* particularly
Sinhalese *adj, n* (of) the larger group of inhabitants of Sri Lanka
sinister *adj* **1** threatening or leading to evil **2** (esp. in heraldry) on the left
sink *v* **sank, sunk 1** *vi/t* (cause to) go down below a surface, out of sight, or to the bottom (of water) **2** *vi* get smaller **3** *vi* fall from lack of strength: *He sank into a chair.* **4** *vi* lose confidence or hope: *My heart sank.* **5** *vt* make by digging: *sink a well* **6** *vt* put (money, labour, etc.) into **sink in** *phr vi* become fully and properly understood ♦ *n* **1** large kitchen basin for washing **2** sewer **3** place where water collects
sinker *n* weight for sinking a fishing

line

sinking feeling *n infml* uncomfortable feeling in stomach caused by fear or helplessness

sinking fund *n* fund set up and added to for paying off a debt in full

Sino- *prefix* **1** Chinese: *Sinophile* **2** Chinese and: *Sino-Soviet*

sinology *n* study of Chinese language, history and culture **–gist** *n*

sinuous *adj* full of curves; winding **~ly** *adv*

sinus *n* any of the air-filled spaces in the bones behind the nose

sip *vi/t* **-pp-** drink with very small mouthfuls ♦ *n* very small amount drunk

siphon *n* **1** tube for removing liquid by natural pressure **2** bottle for holding and forcing out a gas-filled drink ♦ *vt* remove with a siphon

sir *n* **1** (used respectfully when speaking to an older man or one of higher rank) **2** (used at the beginning of a formal letter): *Dear Sir, ...* **3** (*cap.*) British rank of honour for a man

sire *n* **1** horse's male parent **2** *lit* (used when speaking to a king) ♦ *vt* (esp. of a horse) be the father of

siren *n* **1** apparatus for making a loud long warning sound **2** dangerous beautiful woman

sirloin *n* beef cut from the best part of the lower back

sirocco *n* **-os** hot wind of the Mediterranean

sirrah *n arch.* (disrespectful way of addressing a man)

sisal *n* (tropical plant whose leaves yield) a strong white fibre used in making rope

sissy *n* girlish or cowardly boy ♦ *adj* like a sissy

sister *n* **1** female relative with the same parents **2** *BrE* nurse in charge of a hospital ward **3** female member of a religious group **4** female member of the same group (used esp. by supporters of the women's movement) ♦ *adj* belonging to the same group: *our sister organization* **~hood** *n* **1** being (like) sisters **2** society of women leading a religious life **~ly** *adj* like a sister

sister-in-law *n* **sisters-in-law** sister of one's husband or wife; one's brother's wife

sit *v* **sat,** *present p.* **-tt- 1** *vi* rest on a seat or on the ground with the upper body upright **2** *vi/t* (cause to) take a seat **3** *vi* (of an official body) have one or more meetings **4** *vt BrE* take (a written examination) **5** *vi* (take up a position to) be painted or photographed **6 be sitting pretty** be in a very good position **7 sit tight** keep in the same position; not move **sit back** *phr vi* rest and take no active part **sit in** *phr vi* take another's regular place, e.g. in a meeting **sit in on** *phr vi* attend without taking an active part **sit on** *phr vt* **1** be a member of (a committee, etc.) **2** delay taking action on **sit up** *phr v* **1** *vi/t* (cause or help to) rise to a sitting position from a lying one **2** *vi* sit properly upright in a chair **3** *vi* stay up late; not go to bed **4** *vi* show sudden interest, surprise, or fear: *Her speech really made them sit up and take notice.*

sitar *n* Indian lute with a long neck

sitcom *n* situation comedy

site *n* place where a particular thing happened or is done ♦ *vt* put or esp. build in a particular position

sit-in *n* method of protest in which a group of people enter a public place, stop its usual services, and refuse to leave

sitter *n* **1** person who sits for a painter or photographer **2** baby-sitter

sitting *n* **1** serving of a meal for a number of people at one time **2** act of having one's picture made **3** meeting of an official body

sitting duck *n* one easy to attack or cheat

sitting room *n esp. BrE* living room

situate *vt fml* put in a particular place or position

situated *adj* **1** in the stated place or position **2** in the stated situation: *How are you situated for money?*

situation *n* **1** set of conditions, facts, and/or events **2** *fml* position with regard to surroundings **3** *fml* job

situation comedy *n* humorous television or radio show typically having a number of standard characters who appear in different stories every week

six *determiner, n, pron* **1** 6 **2 at sixes and sevens** in disorder **~th** *determiner, adv, n, pron* 6th

six-pack *n* set of six bottles or cans of drink

six-shooter *n* revolver holding six bullets

sixteen *determiner, n, pron* 16 **~th** *determiner, adv, n, pron* 16th

sixth sense *n* ability to know things without using any of the five ordinary senses

sixty *determiner, n, pron* 60 **-tieth** *determiner, adv, n, pron* 60th

size[1] *n* **1** (degree of) bigness or smallness **2** bigness: *A town of some size.* **3** standard measurement: *These shoes are size 9.* **size up** *phr vt* form an opinion or judgment about

size[2] *n* gluey substance used to make things stiffer or less porous **size** *vt*

sizeable *adj* quite large

sizzle *vi* make a sound like food cooking in hot fat

sjambok /ˈshambok/ *vt, n* **-kk-** *SAfrE* (beat with) a heavy leather whip

skate[1] *n* **1** blade fixed to a shoe for moving along on ice **2** roller skate ♦ *vi* move on skates **skate over/around** *phr vt* avoid treating seriously **skater** *n*

skate[2] *n* large fish used as food

skateboard *n* short board with two small wheels at each end for standing on and riding

skedaddle *vi infml* run away

skein /skayn/ *n* **1** loosely coiled length of yarn or thread **2** flock of wildfowl in flight

skeleton *n* **1** structure consisting of all the bones in the body **2** structure on which more is built or added **3 skeleton in the cupboard** secret of which a person or family is ashamed ♦ *adj* enough simply to keep an operation going: *a skeleton staff* **-tal** *adj*

skeleton key *n* key that opens many different locks

skeptic *n AmE* sceptic

sketch *n* **1** simple quickly made drawing **2** short description **3** short humorous scene ♦ *vi/t* draw a sketch (of) **~y** *adj* not thorough or complete **~ily** *adv* **~iness** *n*

skew *vt* cause to be not straight or exact ♦ *adj* oblique or distorted

skewbald *n, adj* (animal) with spots and patches of white and another colour

skewer *n* long pin put through meat for cooking **skewer** *vt*

skew-whiff *adj infml* askew

ski *n* **skis** long thin piece of wood, metal, or plastic fixed to boots for travelling on snow ♦ *vi* **skied,** *present p.* **skiing** travel on skis **~er** *n*

skibob *n* bicycle-like vehicle on skis **~ber** *n* **~bing** *n*

skid *vi* **-dd-** (of a vehicle or wheel) slip sideways out of control ♦ *n* act of skidding

skid row *n esp. AmE* district frequented by down-and-outs

skiff *n* light rowing or sailing boat

skiffle *n* jazz or folk music played by a group using some improvised instruments

skilful, also *AmE* **skillful** *adj* having or showing skill **~ly** *adv*

ski lift *n* conveyor for taking people up or down a mountain slope, which has bars or seats hanging at intervals from a power-driven endless overhead cable

skill *n* special ability to do something well **~ed** *adj* having or needing skill: *a skilled job*

skillet *n esp. AmE* frying pan

skim *v* **-mm- 1** *vt* remove from the surface of a liquid **2** *vi/t* read quickly to get the main ideas **3** *vi/t* (cause to) move quickly (nearly) touching (a surface) ♦ *n* thin layer ♦ *adj* having the cream removed by skimming

skimp *vi/t* spend, provide, or use less (of) than is needed **~y** *adj* not enough

skin *n* **1** natural outer covering of the body **2** skin of an animal for use as fur or leather **3** natural outer covering of some fruits and vegetables: *banana skins* **4** the solid surface that forms over some liquids **5 by the skin of one's teeth** only just ♦ *vt* **-nn-** remove the skin from **~ny** *adj* very thin
skin-deep *adj* on the surface only
skin-dive *vi* swim underwater without heavy breathing apparatus **skin diver** *n*
skin flick *n infml* pornographic film
skinflint *n* someone who dislikes giving or spending money
skinhead *n* (esp. in Britain) young person with very short hair, esp. one of a group who behaves violently
skint *adj BrE infml* having no money
skin-tight *adj* (of clothes) fitting tightly against the body
skip[1] *v* **-pp- 1** *vi* move in a light dancing way **2** *vi/t* leave out (something in order); not deal with (the next thing) **3** *vi* move in no fixed order **4** *vi* jump over a rope passed repeatedly beneath one's feet **5** *vi/t* leave hastily and secretly: *The thieves have skipped the country.* **6** *vt* fail to attend or take part in (an activity) ♦ *n* light quick stepping and jumping movement
skip[2] *n BrE* large metal container for carrying away unwanted things
skipper *n* captain of a ship or sports team ♦ *vt* act as captain; lead
skirl *vi, n* (make) the sound of bagpipes
skirmish *n* short military fight, not as big as a battle
skirt *n* woman's outer garment that hangs from the waist ♦ *vi/t* **1** be or go round the outside (of) **2** avoid (a difficult subject)
skirting board *n* board fixed along the base of an inside wall
skit *n* short acted scene making fun of something
skitter *vi* skip or glide lightly
skittish *adj* (esp. of a horse) easily excited and frightened **~ly** *adv* **~ness** *n*
skittle *n* bottle-shaped object used in a game (**skittles**) where a player tries to knock down a set of them with a ball
skive *vi infml* avoid work **skiver** *n*
skivvy *vi, n derog* (do work appropriate for) a low-paid female servant
skua *n* large North Atlantic seabird
skulduggery, skull- *n infml* devious behaviour
skulk *vi* hide or move about slowly and secretly, through fear or shame or for some evil purpose
skull *n* head bone, enclosing the brain
skullcap *n* closely-fitting brimless cap
skunk *n* **1** small N American animal which gives out a bad-smelling liquid when attacked **2** *infml* nasty person
sky *n* space above the Earth, where clouds and the sun, moon, and stars appear
skydiving *n* sport of falling by parachute
sky-high *adj, adv* at or to a very high level
skyjack *vt* hijack (an aircraft)
skylark *n* meadow lark that sings while hovering ♦ *vi* lark about
skylight *n* window in a roof
skyline *n* shape or view of esp. city buildings against the sky
skyrocket *vi* increase suddenly and steeply
skyscraper *n* very tall city building
slab *n* thick flat usu. four-sided piece: *a stone slab*
slack[1] *adj* **1** not pulled tight **2** not careful or quick **3** not firm; weak: *slack discipline* **4** not busy ♦ *n* part (e.g. of a rope) which hangs loose ♦ *vi* **1** be lazy **2** reduce in speed or effort **slacks** *pl n* informal trousers **~en** *vi/t* make or become slack **~ness** *n*
slack[2] *n* very small pieces of coal
slack water *n* period at the turn of the tide
slag *n* **1** waste material left when metal is separated from its rock **2** *BrE sl* worthless or immoral woman **slag off** *phr vt* **-gg-** *BrE sl* make extremely unfavourable remarks about
slain *past p. of* slay

slake *vt lit* satisfy (thirst) with a drink

slalom *n* ski race down a very winding course

slam *v* **-mm- 1** *vi/t* shut loudly and forcefully **2** *vt* push or put hurriedly and forcefully: *She slammed on the brakes.* **3** *vt* attack with words ♦ *n* noise of a door being slammed

slander *n* (act of) saying something false and damaging about someone ♦ *vt* harm by making a false statement **~ous** *adj*

slang *n* very informal language that includes new and sometimes not polite words and meanings and is often used among particular groups of people, and not usu. in serious speech or writing ♦ *vt BrE* attack with rude angry words **~y** *adj*

slant *v* **1** *vi/t* (cause to) be at an angle **2** *vt usu. derog* express in a way favourable to a particular opinion ♦ *n* **1** slanting direction or position **2** particular way of looking at or expressing facts or a situation

slap *n* **1** hit with the flat hand ♦ *vt* **-pp- 1** give a slap to **2** place quickly, roughly, or carelessly ♦ *adv* also **slap-bang** directly; right: *slap in the middle of lunch*

slapdash *adj* careless

slaphappy *adj* careless

slapstick *n* humorous acting with fast violent action and simple jokes

slap-up *adj BrE* excellent and in large quantities: *a slap-up meal*

slash *v* **1** *vi/t* cut with long sweeping violent strokes **2** *vt* reduce very greatly ♦ *n* **1** long sweeping cut or blow **2** straight cut making an opening in a garment

slat *n* thin narrow strip, esp. of wood or metal **~ted** *adj*

slate[1] *n* **1** dark grey easily splittable rock **2** piece of this used in rows for covering roofs **3** small board of this, used for writing on **4 on the slate** on credit ♦ *vt esp. AmE* designate: *slated for public office*

slate[2] *vt BrE* attack in words

slattern *n* untidy woman

slaughter *vt* **1** kill (many people) cruelly or wrongly **2** kill (an animal) for food **3** *infml* defeat severely in a game ♦ *n* slaughtering

slaughterhouse *n* building where animals are killed for food

slave *n* **1** person who is owned by (and works for) another **2** person completely in the control of: *a slave to drink* ♦ *vi* work hard with little rest

slave driver *n* person who makes you work very hard

slaver[1] *n* ship or person that carries or sells slaves **~y** *n* **1** system of having slaves **2** condition of being a slave

slaver[2] *vi* **1** let saliva run out of the mouth **2** be unpleasantly eager or excited

Slavic also **Slavonic** *adj* (characteristic) of the Slavs

slavish *adj* **1** showing complete obedience to and willingness to work for others **2** copied too exactly, without originality **~ly** *adv* **~ness** *n*

slay *vt esp. lit* **slew, slain** kill

SLD *abbrev. for:* Social and Liberal Democrats

sleazy *adj* dirty, poor-looking, and suggesting immorality **–ziness** *n*

sled *vi, n* **-dd-** sledge

sledge *vi, n* (travel on) a vehicle for sliding along snow on two metal blades

sledgehammer *n* heavy long-handled hammer

sleek *adj* **1** (of hair or fur) smooth and shining **2** stylish and without unnecessary decoration ♦ *vt* smooth **~ly** *adv* **~ness** *n*

sleep *n* **1** natural unconscious resting state **2** act or period of sleeping **3 go to sleep: a** begin to sleep **b** (of an arm, leg, etc.) become numb, or feel pins and needles **4 put to sleep** kill (a suffering animal) mercifully ♦ *vi* **slept 1** rest in sleep **2** provide beds or places for sleep (for a number of people): *The house sleeps 6.* **sleep around** *phr vi derog* have sex with a lot of different people **sleep in** *phr vi* sleep late in the morning

sleep off *phr vt* get rid of (a feeling or effect) by sleeping **sleep on** *phr vt* delay deciding on (a matter) until next day **sleep together** *phr vi* (of two people) have sex **sleep with** *phr vt* have sex with **~er** *n* **1** sleeping person **2** *esp. BrE* heavy piece of wood, metal, etc., supporting a railway track **3** train with beds **4** *esp. AmE* book, play, or record that has a delayed or unexpected success **~y** *adj* **1** tired **2** inactive or slow-moving **~ily** *adv* **~iness** *n*

sleeping bag *n* large cloth bag for sleeping in

sleeping car *n* railway carriage with beds for passengers

sleeping partner *n* business partner who does no active work in the business

sleeping pill *n* pill which helps a person to sleep

sleeping sickness *n* serious African disease which causes great lethargy

sleepless *adj* **1** not providing sleep: *a sleepless night* **2** unable to sleep **~ly** *adv* **~ness** *n*

sleepwalker *n* person who walks about while asleep **-ing** *n*

sleepyhead *n* sleepy person

sleet *n* partly frozen rain ♦ *vi* (of sleet) fall

sleeve *n* **1** part of a garment for covering (part of) an arm **2** *esp. BrE* stiff envelope for keeping a record in **3 up one's sleeve** kept secret for use at the right time

sleigh *n* large (horse-drawn) sledge

sleight of hand /sliet/ *n* **1** skill and quickness of the hands in doing tricks **2** clever deception

slender *adj* **1** gracefully or pleasingly thin **2** small and hardly enough: *slender resources*

slept *past t. and p. of* sleep

sleuth *n* detective **sleuth** *vi*

slew¹ *past t. of* slay

slew² *vi/t* turn or swing violently

slew³ *n esp. AmE infml* large amount

slice *n* **1** thin flat piece cut off: *a slice of bread* **2** kitchen tool with a broad blade for serving food **3** portion ♦ *v* **1** *vt* cut into slices **2** *vi/t* hit (a ball) so that it moves away from a straight course

slick *adj* **1** smooth and slippery **2** skilful and effective, so as to seem easy **3** clever and able to persuade, but perhaps not honest ♦ *n* area of oil esp. floating on the sea **~ly** *adv*

slicker *n* **1** *infml* a well-dressed, self-confident, but probably untrustworthy person: *a city slicker* **2** *AmE* raincoat

slide *v* **slid 1** *vi/t* go or send smoothly across a surface **2** *vi* move quietly and unnoticed **3 let something slide** let a situation or condition continue, esp. getting worse, without taking action ♦ *n* **1** slipping movement **2** fall: *a slide in living standards* **3** apparatus for sliding down **4** piece of film through which light is passed to show a picture on a surface **5** small piece of thin glass to put an object on for seeing under a microscope

slide rule *n* ruler with a middle part that slides along, for calculating numbers

sliding scale *n* system of pay, taxes, etc., calculated by rates which may vary according to changing conditions

slight *adj* **1** small in degree: *a slight improvement* **2** thin and delicate **3 in the slightest** at all ♦ *vt* treat disrespectfully or rudely **~ing** *adj* insulting ♦ *n* insult **~ly** *adv* **1** a little: *slightly better* **2** thinly and delicately: *He's very slightly built.* **~ness** *n*

slim *adj* **-mm- 1** attractively thin **2** (of probability) very small ♦ *vi* **-mm-** try to make oneself thinner **~ly** *adv* **~mer** *n*

slime *n* unpleasant thick sticky liquid

slimy *adj* **1** unpleasantly slippery **2** *derog* trying to please in order to gain advantage for oneself **-mily** *adv* **-miness** *n*

sling *vt* **slung 1** throw roughly or with effort **2** hang **3 sling one's hook** *BrE sl* go away **4 sling mud at** say unfair and damaging things about (esp. a political opponent) ♦ *n* **1** piece of cloth hanging from the neck to support a damaged arm **2** strap used to hurl a stone

slingshot *n esp. AmE* catapult

slink *vi* **slunk** move quietly and secretly, as if in fear or shame

slip[1] *v* **-pp- 1** *vi* slide out of place unexpectedly or by accident **2** *vi/t* move or put smoothly or unnoticed **3** *vi/t* put on or take off (a garment) quickly **4** *vi* get worse or lower: *slipping standards* **5** *vi* make a mistake **6** *vt* escape from: *It slipped my mind.* **7** give secretly: *I slipped the waiter some money.* **8 let slip: a** fail to take (a chance) **b** make known accidentally ♦ *n* **1** small mistake **2** woman's undergarment like a skirt or loose dress **3** young, slender person: *a slip of a girl* **4** slipway **5 give someone the slip** escape from someone

slip[2] *n* **1** small or narrow piece of paper **2** cutting from a plant

slip[3] *n* thin mixture of clay and water, used in pottery

slipknot *n* **1** knot that slips along a rope (e.g. to form a noose) **2** knot that comes undone with one pull

slip-on *n, adj* (shoe) that slips on and off easily

slippage *n* (amount of) slipping

slipped disc *n* painful displacement of one of the discs of cartilage between the vertebrae

slipper *n* light soft shoe worn indoors

slippery *adj* **1** very smooth or wet, so one cannot easily hold or move on it **2** not to be trusted

slip road *n BrE* road for driving onto or off a motorway

slipshod *adj* carelessly done

slipstream *n* **1** area of low air pressure behind a fast-moving vehicle **2** stream of air driven backwards by an aircraft engine

slip-up *n* usu. slight mistake

slipway *n* sloping track for moving ships into or out of water

slit *n* long narrow cut or opening ♦ *vt* **slit**; *present p.* **-tt-** make a slit in

slither *vi* **1** move smoothly and twistingly **2** slide unsteadily

sliver *n* small thin piece cut or broken off

slivovitz *n* plum brandy

slob *n* rude, dirty, lazy, or carelessly dressed person

slobber *vi* **1** let saliva dribble from the mouth **2** express emotion very sentimentally

sloe *n* (small dark fruit of) the blackthorn

slog *vi* **-gg-** *BrE* move or work with much effort ♦ *n* something needing much effort

slogan *n* short phrase expressing a political or advertising message

sloop *n* small sailing ship

slop *vi/t* **-pp-** go or cause (a liquid) to go over the side of a container: *You're slopping paint everywhere!* **slop about/around** *phr vi infml* **1** move about in a lazy purposeless way **2** play in or move about in anything wet or dirty ♦ *n* **1** food waste, esp. for feeding animals **2** *derog* tasteless liquid food

slop basin *n* small bowl into which dregs from tea or coffee cups can be emptied at table

slope *vi* lie neither completely upright nor completely flat **slope off** *phr vt BrE* go away secretly esp. to avoid work ♦ *n* **1** piece of sloping ground **2** degree of sloping

sloppy *adj* **1** (of clothes) loose, informal and careless **2** not careful or thorough enough **3** silly in showing feelings **–pily** *adv* **–piness** *n*

slosh *v* **1** *vi/t* move or cause (liquid) to move about roughly and noisily, making waves **2** *vt BrE infml* hit **~ed** *adj infml* drunk

slot *n* **1** long straight narrow hole **2** place or position in a list, system, or organization ♦ *vi/t* **-tt- 1** (be) put into a slot **2** fit into a slot

sloth /slohth/ *n* **1** *esp. lit* laziness **2** slow-moving animal of S America **~ful** *adj* lazy **~fully** *adv* **~fulness** *n*

slot machine *n* **1** *BrE* vending machine **2** *AmE* one-armed bandit

slouch *vi* walk, stand, or sit in a tired-looking round-shouldered way ♦ *n* lazy, useless person

slouch hat *n* soft hat with a wide brim

slough *n lit* **1** bog **2** bad condition that is hard to get free from

slough off *phr vt* **1** (esp. of a snake) throw off (dead outer skin) **2** *esp. lit* get rid of as something worn out or unwanted

slovenly /ˈsluvnli/ *adj* **1** untidy **2** very carelessly done **–liness** *n* **sloven** *n* untidy person

slow *adj* **1** having less than a usual speed; not fast **2** taking a long time: *a slow job* **3** (of a clock) showing a time that is earlier than the right time **4** not quick in understanding **5** not active: *Business is slow.* ♦ *vi/t* make or become slower ♦ *adv* slowly: *slow-moving traffic* **~ly** *adv* **~ness** *n*

slowcoach *n BrE infml* slow-acting person

slowdown *n* **1** lessening of speed or activity **2** *AmE* go-slow

slowworm *n* snake-like lizard without legs

sludge *n* thick soft mud

slug¹ *n* small soft limbless creature, like a snail with no shell

slug² *vt* **-gg-** *esp. AmE* hit hard

slug³ *n esp. AmE* **1** bullet **2** *infml* amount of strong alcoholic drink taken at one swallow

sluggard *n* lazy person

sluggish *adj* not very active or quick **~ly** *adv* **~ness** *n*

sluice *n* passage for controlling the flow of water ♦ *vt* wash with a large flow of water

slum *n* city area of bad living conditions and old unrepaired buildings ♦ *vi* **1** amuse oneself by visiting a place on a much lower social level: *go slumming* **2** **slum it** live very cheaply **~my** *adj*

slumber *vi, n lit* sleep

slump *vi* **1** drop down suddenly and heavily **2** decrease suddenly ♦ *n* **1** sudden decrease, esp. in business **2** time of seriously bad business conditions and high unemployment

slung *past t. and p. of* sling

slunk *past t. and p. of* slink

slur¹ *vt* **-rr-** **1** pronounce unclearly **2** run (musical notes) together ♦ *n* running together of musical notes

slur² *vt* **-rr-** make unfair damaging remarks about **slur** *n*

slurp *vt* drink noisily **slurp** *n*

slurry *n* mixture of water and insoluble matter (e.g. mud)

slush *n* **1** partly melted snow **2** silly love stories **~y** *adj*

slush fund *n* money secretly kept for dishonest payments

slut *n* **1** sexually immoral woman **2** untidy, lazy woman **~tish** *adj* **~tishly** *adv* **~tishness** *n*

sly *adj* **1** secretly deceitful or tricky **2** playfully unkind: *a sly joke* **3 on the sly** secretly **~ly** *adv* **~ness** *n*

smack¹ *vt* **1** hit with the flat hand **2** open and close (one's lips) noisily in eagerness to eat ♦ *n* blow with the open hand ♦ *adv* exactly; right: *smack in the middle*

smack² *n* flavour **smack of** *phr vt* have a taste or suggestion of

smack³ *n* small sailing boat used in fishing

small *adj* **1** of less than usual size, amount, or importance **2** young: *small children* **3** doing only a limited amount of business: *small shopkeepers* **4** slight: *small hope of success* **5 feel small** feel ashamed or humble ♦ *n* narrow middle part (of the back) **~ness** *n*

small arms *pl n* guns made to be carried in one or both hands for firing

small beer *n infml* person or thing of little importance

small change *n* coins of low value

small fortune *n* very large amount of money

small fry *n* young or unimportant person

smallholding *n BrE* small farm

small hours *pl n* after midnight

small-minded *adj* having narrow or ungenerous views **~ly** *adv* **~ness** *n*

smallpox *n* serious infectious disease which leaves marks on the skin

small print *n* something deliberately made obscure in an agreement or contract
small screen *n* television
small talk *n* light conversation on non-serious subjects
small-time *adj* limited in activity, ability, or profits
smarmy *adj BrE* unpleasantly and falsely polite
smart *adj* **1** quick or forceful: *a smart blow on the head* **2** *esp. BrE* neat and stylish **3** *esp. AmE* clever **4** fashionable ♦ *vi, n* (cause or feel) a stinging pain **~ly** *adv* **~ness** *n*
smart aleck *n* annoying person who pretends to know everyting
smarten up *phr vi/t* improve in appearance
smash *v* **1** *vi/t* break into pieces violently **2** *vi/t* throw, drive, or hit forcefully **3** *vt* put an end to: *The police have smashed the drugs ring.* **4** *vt* hit (the ball) with a hard stroke ♦ *n* **1** (sound of) a violent breaking **2** hard downward, attacking shot, as in tennis **3** very successful new play or film: *a smash hit* **4** smash-up **~ing** *adj esp. BrE* very fine; wonderful **~er** *n esp. BrE* very attractive person
smash-and-grab *n, adj* (robbery) committed by breaking a shop window and snatching goods on display
smash-up *n* serious road or railway accident
smattering *n* limited knowledge: *a smattering of German*
smear *vt* **1** spread (a sticky or oily substance) untidily across (a surface) **2** make unproved charges against (someone) in order to produce unfavourable public opinion ♦ *n* **1** mark made by smearing **2** unfair unproved charge against someone: *a smear campaign*
smear test *n* medical test on material from the cervix, esp. for discovering cancer
smell *v* **smelled** *or* **smelt 1** *vi* have or use the sense of the nose **2** *vt* notice (as if) by this sense: *I think I smell gas!* **3** *vi* have a particular smell: *The bread smells stale.* **4** *vi* have a bad smell **5 smell a rat** guess that something wrong or dishonest is happening ♦ *n* **1** power of using the nose to discover the presence of gases in the air **2** quality that has an effect on the nose: *a flower with a sweet smell* **3** bad smell **~y** *adj* bad-smelling
smelt[1] *vt* melt (ore) for removing the metal
smelt[2] *n* small fish like a trout
smidgin *n infml* small amount
smile *n* pleased or amused expression in which the mouth is turned up at the ends ♦ *vi* make a smile **smilingly** *adv*
smirch *vt* **1** stain **2** bring disgrace on **smirch** *n*
smirk *vi, n* (make) a silly self-satisfied smile
smite *vt* **smote, smitten** *lit* strike hard
smith *n* maker of metal things: *a silversmith*
smithereens *n* **(in)to smithereens** into extremely small bits
smithy *n* blacksmith's workshop
smitten *past p. of* smite ♦ *adj* suddenly in love
smock *n* long loose shirtlike garment with a yoke ♦ *vt* ornament with smocking
smocking *n* gathered cloth held in place by embroidery
smog *n* thick dark unpleasant mist in cities
smoke *n* **1** usu. white, grey, or black gas produced by burning **2** act of smoking tobacco ♦ *v* **1** *vi/t* suck in smoke from (a cigarette, cigar, or pipe) **2** *vi* give off smoke: *smoking chimneys* **3** *vt* preserve (fish or meat) with smoke **smoke out** *phr vt* fill a place with smoke to force (a person or animal) to come out from hiding **smoker** *n* person who smokes **smoky** *adj* **1** filled with smoke **2** tasting of or looking like smoke **smoking** *n* practice or habit of smoking e.g. cigarettes
smokescreen *n* **1** cloud of smoke produced to hide something **2** some-

thing that hides one's real intentions

smokestack *n* **1** tall chimney of a factory or ship **2** *AmE* funnel (2)

smokestack industry *n esp. AmE* the branch of industry that produces cars, ships, steel, etc.

smolder *v AmE* smoulder

smooch *vi* kiss and hold lovingly **~er** *n* **~y** *adj*

smooth *adj* **1** having an even surface; not rough **2** (of a liquid mixture) without lumps **3** even in movement, without sudden changes: *a smooth flight* **4** (too) pleasant or polite ♦ *vt* make smooth(er) **smooth over** *phr vt* make (difficulties) seem small or unimportant **~ly** *adv* **~ness** *n*

smorgasbord *n* buffet with a variety of Swedish dishes

smote *past t. of* smite

smother *vt* **1** cover thickly or in large numbers **2** die or kill from lack of air **3** keep from developing or happening: *smother a yawn*

smoulder *vi* **1** burn slowly with (almost) no flame **2** have or be violent but unexpressed feelings

smudge *n* dirty mark with unclear edges ♦ *vi/t* make or become dirty with a smudge

smug *adj* **-gg-** too pleased with oneself **~ly** *adv* **~ness** *n*

smuggle *vt* take in or out secretly or illegally **-gler** *n* **-gling** *n* taking goods to another country illegally

smut *n* **1** small piece of dirt **2** morally offensive talk **~ty** *adj* rude

snack *n* amount of food smaller than a meal ♦ *vi AmE* eat a snack

snaffle *n* jointed bit for a bridle

snafu *vt, n* (bring into) a state of total confusion **snafu** *adj*

snag *n* **1** hidden or unexpected difficulty **2** rough or sharp projecting part ♦ *vt* **-gg-** catch on a snag

snail *n* small slow-moving soft-bodied limbless reptile with a shell on its back

snake *n* **1** long thin limbless reptile, often with a poisonous bite **2** deceitful person **3 a snake in the grass** a false friend ♦ *vi* move twistingly

snake charmer *n* person who controls snakes by playing music

snap *v* **-pp- 1** *vi/t* close the jaws quickly (on) **2** *vi/t* break suddenly and sharply **3** *vi/t* move with a sharp sound: *The lid snapped shut.* **4** *vi* speak quickly and angrily **5** *vt infml* to photograph **6 snap out of it** free oneself quickly from a bad state of mind **snap up** *phr vt* take or buy quickly and eagerly ♦ *n* **1** act or sound of snapping **2** informal photograph **3** card game ♦ *adj* done without warning or long consideration: *snap judgments* ♦ *interj* (used to show that two things are identical) **~py** *adj* **1** stylish; fashionable **2** hasty; quick

snapdragon *n* garden plant with bright double-lipped flowers

snapper *n* fish found in warm seas

snapshot *n* snap (2)

snare *n* **1** trap for small animals **2** deceiving situation ♦ *vt* catch in a snare

snare drum *n* small drum with strings that produce a rattling sound

snarl[1] *vi* **1** (of an animal) make a low angry sound **2** speak angrily ♦ *n* act or sound of snarling

snarl[2] *n* tangle **snarl up** *phr vt* entangle

snarl-up *n* confused state, esp. of traffic

snatch *vi/t* take (something) quickly and often violently or wrongfully ♦ *n* **1** act of snatching **2** short incomplete part: *snatches of conversation* **~er** *n*

snazzy *adj infml* stylishly good-looking or attractive **-zily** *adv*

sneak *vi/t* **snuck** *AmE* go or take quietly and secretly ♦ *n BrE derog sl* schoolchild who gives information about the wrongdoings of others **~er** *n AmE* plimsoll **~ing** *adj* **1** secret: *a sneaking admiration* **2** not proved but probably right: *a sneaking suspicion* **~y** *adj* acting or done secretly or deceitfully

sneak preview *n* a chance to see something new, esp. a film, before anyone else has done so

sneak thief *n* thief who steals small

things without burglary or violence
sneer *vi* express contempt, esp. with an unpleasant curling smile ♦ *n* sneering look or remark
sneeze *vi, n* (have) a sudden uncontrolled burst of air from the nose
snick *vt* **1** cut slightly **2** hit (a cricket ball) with the edge of a bat
snicker *vi* snigger
snide *adj* indirectly but unpleasantly expressing a low opinion **~ly** *adv* **~ness** *n*
sniff *v* **1** *vi* breathe in loudly, esp. in short repeated actions **2** *vi/t* do this to discover a smell (in or on) **3** *vt* take (a harmful drug) through the nose **sniff at** *phr vt* dislike or refuse proudly **sniff out** *phr vt* discover or find out (as if) by smelling ♦ *n* act or sound of sniffing **~er** *n*
sniffle *vi* sniff repeatedly ♦ *n* mild cold
snifter *n infml* small drink of spirits
snigger *vi* laugh quietly or secretly in a disrespectful way **snigger** *n*
snip *vt* **-pp-** cut with quick short strokes, esp. with scissors ♦ *n* **1** act of snipping **2** *BrE* bargain
snipe *n* game bird with a long thin beak ♦ *vi* **1** shoot from a hidden position **2** make an unpleasant indirect attack in words **sniper** *n*
snippet *n* small bit: *a snippet of information*
snitch *v infml* **1** *vi* inform (on someone) **2** pilfer
snivel *vi* **-ll-** (*AmE* **-l-**) act or speak in a weak complaining crying way
snob *n* person who pays too much attention to social class, and dislikes people of a lower class **~bery** *n* behaviour of snobs **~bish** *adj* **~bishly** *adv*
snog *vi* **-gg-** *BrE infml* hold and kiss each other **snog** *n*
snood *n* **1** net to hold long hair at the back **2** woollen tube worn loosely over the head
snook *n* gesture with thumb to nose
snooker *n* **1** game in which a player hits balls into holes round a table **2** position of the balls in snooker which prevents a successful shot ♦ *vt* **1** prevent from making a successful shot in snooker **2** *infml* defeat (someone, a plan, etc.)
snoop *vi* pry into other people's affairs **~er** *n*
snooty *adj infml* proudly rude **-ily** *adv* **-iness** *n*
snooze *vi, n* (have) a short sleep
snore *vi* breathe noisily while asleep ♦ *n* act or sound of snoring
snorkel *n* breathing tube for underwater swimmers ♦ *vi* swim with a snorkel
snort **1** *vi* make a rough noise by forcing air down the nose, often in impatience or anger **2** *vt* sniff (3) ♦ *n* act or sound of snorting
snot *n sl* nasal mucus
snotty-nosed *adj* (esp. of a young person) trying to act as if one is important; rude
snout *n* animal's long nose
snow *n* frozen rain that falls in flakes ♦ *vi* (of snow) fall **snow in/up** *phr vt* prevent from travelling by a heavy fall of snow **snow under** *phr vt* overwhelm: *snowed under with work* **~y** *adj*
snowball *n* ball of pressed snow, as thrown by children ♦ *vi* increase faster and faster
snowdrift *n* deep mass of snow piled up by the wind
snowdrop *n* plant of early spring with a small white flower
snowman *n* **-men** /-men/ figure of a person made out of snow
snowplough, *AmE* **-plow** *n* apparatus or vehicle for clearing away snow
snow shoe *n* light oval disc attached to shoes for walking on snow
snowstorm *n* very heavy fall of snow
Snr *BrE abbrev. for:* Senior
snub[1] *vt* **-bb-** treat (someone) rudely, esp. by paying no attention to them ♦ *n* act of snubbing
snub[2] *adj* (of a nose) short and flat
snuck *AmE past t. and p. of* sneak
snuff[1] *n* powdery tobacco for breathing into the nose

snuff² *vt* put out (a candle) by pressing the burning part **snuff out** *phr vt* put a sudden end to

snuffle *v* **1** *vi* sniffle **2** *vi/t* talk or say through the nose

snug *adj* **-gg- 1** giving warmth, comfort, protection, etc. **2** (of clothes) fitting closely and comfortably ♦ *n* small room in a pub

snuggle *vi* settle into a warm comfortable position

so *adv* **1** to such a (great) degree: *It was so dark I couldn't see.* **2** (used instead of repeating something): *He hopes he'll win and I hope so too.* **3** also: *He hopes he'll win and so do I.* **4** very: *We're so glad you could come!* **5** in this way **6** yes; it is true: *'There's a fly in your soup.' 'So there is!'* **7** *fml* therefore **8 and so on/forth** and other things of that kind **9 or so** more or less: *It'll only cost 15p or so.* **10 so as to** : **a** in order to **b** in such a way as to **11 so long!** *infml* goodbye **12 so many/much: a** a certain number/amount: *a charge of so much a day* **b** an amount equal to: *These books are just so much waste paper!* ♦ *conj* **1** with the result that: *It was dark, so I couldn't see.* **2** therefore: *He had a headache, so he went to bed.* **3** with the purpose (that): *I gave him an apple so (that) he wouldn't go hungry.* **4** (used at the beginning of a sentence) **a** (with weak meaning): *So here we are again.* **b** (to express discovery): *So that's how they did it!* **5 so what**? why is that important?; why should I care? ♦ *adj* **1** true: *Is that really so?* **2 just so** arranged exactly and tidily

soak *vi/t* **1** (cause to) remain in liquid, becoming completely wet **2** (of liquid) enter (a solid) through the surface **soak up** *phr vt* draw in (a liquid) through a surface ♦ *n* **1** (act of) soaking **2** *infml* drunkard **~ed** *adj* thoroughly wet, esp. from rain **~ing** *adv, adj* very (wet)

so-and-so *n* **1** one not named **2** unpleasant or annoying person

soap *n* **1** usu. solid substance used with water for cleaning esp. the body **2** *infml* soap opera **~y** *adj*

soapbox *n* **on one's soapbox** stating one's opinions loudly and forcefully

soap opera *n* continuing television or radio story about the daily life and troubles of the same set of characters

soapstone *n* soft grey-green or brown stone

soar *vi* **1** (of a bird) fly high without moving the wings **2** rise steeply: *Prices soared.*

sob *vi* **-bb-** cry while making short bursts of sound breathing in ♦ *n* act or sound of sobbing

sober *adj* **1** not drunk **2** *fml* thoughtful, serious, or solemn; not silly ♦ *vi/t* make or become thoughtful: *a sobering thought* **sober up** *phr vi/t* (cause to) recover from being drunk **~ly** *adv*

sobriety /sə'brie·əti/ *n* being sober

sobriquet /'sohbri,kay/ *n fml* nickname

sob story *n* story intended to make the hearer or reader cry, feel pity, or feel sorry

so-called *adj* (undeservedly but) commonly described in the stated way

soccer *n BrE* football played with a round ball

sociable *adj* fond of being with others; friendly **–bly** *adv* **–bility** *n*

social *adj* **1** of human society or its organization **2** living together by nature **3** based on rank in society: *social class* **4** for or spent in time or activities with friends (rather than work): *an active social life* **~ly** *adv*

social climber *n derog* person who tries to get accepted into a higher social class

social democracy *n* political theory that favours gradual and democratic adoption of socialism

socialism *n* political system aiming at establishing a society in which everyone is equal **–ist** *adj, n*

socialite *n* person who goes to many fashionable parties

socialize, -ise *v* **1** *vi* spend time with others in a friendly way **2** *vt* fit or train for life in society **3** *vt* adapt in accordance with social needs or socialist principles: *socialised medicine* **~r** *n* **-zation** *n*

social science *n* study of people in society, including sociology and economics

social security *n* government money paid to the unemployed, old, sick, and others in need

social services *pl n esp. BrE* (local) government services to help people, such as education and health care

social work *n* work done to help those in difficulty or trouble **~er** *n*

society *n* **1** everyone considered as a whole: *Society has a right to expect obedience to the law.* **2** group of people who share laws and organization: *modern Western society* **3** organization of people with similar aims or interests: *She joined the university film society.* **4** fashionable people **5** being with other people **-tal** *adj* of society

socioeconomic *adj* based on a combination of social and economic conditions

sociology *n* study of society and group behaviour **-ogical** *adj* **-ogist** *n*

sock[1] *n* **1** cloth covering for the foot **2** **pull one's socks up** *BrE* try to improve

sock[2] *vt sl* strike hard ♦ *n* forceful blow

socket *n* hole into which something fits

sod[1] *n* (piece of) earth with grass and roots growing in it

sod[2] *n BrE sl* person or thing that causes a lot of trouble and difficulty

soda *n* **1** soda water **2** sodium

soda fountain *n AmE* place in a shop at which soft drinks and ice cream are served

soda water *n* gas-filled water esp. for mixing with other drinks

sodden *adj* very wet

sodium *n* silver-white metal found naturally only in compounds

sodium bicarbonate *n* white weakly alkaline salt used in baking powder and digestive medicines

sodomite *n* person who practises sodomy

sodomy *n fml or law* any of various sexual acts, esp. anal sex between males

Sod's law *n sl* natural tendency for things to go wrong

sofa *n* comfortable seat for two or three people

soft *adj* **1** not hard or stiff **2** smooth to the touch **3** quiet **4** restful and pleasant: *soft colours* **5** with little force; gentle: *a soft breeze* **6** easy: *a soft job* **7** too kind **8** not in good physical condition **9** dealing with ideas not facts: *one of the soft sciences like psychology* **10** not of the worst or most harmful kind: *Cannabis is a soft drug.* **11** (of a drink) containing no alcohol and usu. sweet and served cold **12** (in English pronunciation) **a** (of the letter *c*) having the sound /s/ and not /k/ **b** (of the letter *g*) having the sound /dʒ/ and not /g/ **13** (of water) free from minerals that stop soap forming lather easily **14** *infml* foolish: *He's soft in the head.* **~ly** *adv* **~ness** *n*

softball *n* game similar to baseball

soft-boiled *adj* (of an egg) boiled not long enough for the yolk to become solid

soft copy *n* information stored in a computer's memory or shown on a screen, rather than in printed form

soften *vi/t* (cause to) become soft(er) or more gentle **soften up** *phr vt* break down opposition of (someone) **~er** *n*

softhearted *adj* easily made to act kindly or feel sorry for someone **~ly** *adv* **~ness** *n*

softie *n* softy

soft landing *n* landing made by a spacecraft without suffering any damage

soft option *n* course of action which will give one less trouble

soft palate *n* soft back part of the palate

soft-pedal *vt* make (a subject, fact, etc.) seem unimportant

soft sell *n* selling by gentle persuading

soft soap *n* saying nice things about people, esp. as a means of persuading

soft-soap *vt* use soft soap on

soft-spoken *adj* having a mild or gentle voice
soft spot *n* fondness
soft touch *n infml* someone from whom it is easy to get what one wants because they are kind or easily deceived
software *n* set of programs that control a computer
softwood *n* cheap easily-cut wood from trees such as pine and fir
softy *n* weak or sentimental person
soggy *adj* completely (and unpleasantly) wet **–giness** *n*
soigné /ˈswahnyay/ *adj* elegant
soil[1] *n* top covering of the earth in which plants grow; ground
soil[2] *vt fml* make dirty
soiree /ˈswahray/ *n* evening party, often including an artistic performance
sojourn /ˈsojən/ *vi lit* live for a time in a place **sojourn** *n* **~er** *n*
solace *n* (something that gives) comfort for someone full of grief or anxiety ♦ *vt* **1** give comfort to **2** relieve
solar *adj* of or from the sun
solar cell *n* apparatus for producing electric power from sunlight
solarium *n* **-ia** *or* **-iums** glass-walled room for sitting in the sunshine
solar panel *n* number of solar cells working together
solar plexus *n* **1** system of nerves between the stomach and the backbone **2** *infml* stomach
solar system *n* sun and the planets going round it
sold *past t. and p. of* sell
solder *n* easily-meltable metal used for joining metal surfaces ♦ *vt* join with solder
soldering iron *n* heated tool for melting and applying solder
soldier *n* member of an army **soldier on** *phr vi* continue working steadily in spite of difficulties
soldier of fortune *n* mercenary
soldiery *n lit* body of soldiers
sole[1] *n* bottom surface of the foot or of a shoe
sole[2] *n* flat fish often used for food
sole[3] *adj* **1** only **2** unshared: *sole responsibility* **~ly** *adv* only
solecism /ˈsoliˌsiz(ə)m/ *n* doing something wrong, esp. in grammar or social behaviour
solemn *adj* **1** without humour or lightness; serious **2** (of a promise) made sincerely **3** of the most formal kind **~ly** *adv* **~ness** *n* **~ity** *n* **1** solemness **2** formal act proper for a grand event
solemnize, -ise *vt* perform (esp. a marriage) with formal ceremony **–ization** *n*
sol-fa *n* system of names given to different musical notes
solicit *v* **1** *vt fml* ask for **2** *vi esp. law* advertise oneself as a prostitute
solicitor *n* (esp. in England) lawyer who advises people, prepares contracts, etc.
solicitous *adj fml* helpful and kind **~ly** *adv* **~ness** *n*
solicitude *n* solicitousness
solid *adj* **1** not liquid or gas **2** not hollow **3** firm and well made **4** that may be depended on **5** not mixed with any other (metal): *a watch of solid gold* **6** having length, width and height ♦ *n* solid object or substance **~ly** *adv* **~ity** *n* quality or state of being solid
solidarity *n* loyalty within a group
solidify *vi/t* (cause to) become solid or hard **–fication** *n*
solid-state *adj* **1** having electrical parts, esp. transistors, that run without heating or moving parts **2** (of physics) relating to the structure of solid material
solidus *n* (in punctuation) an oblique stroke
soliloquy /səˈliləkwi/ *n* speech made by an actor alone on stage
solipsism *n* theory that only the self exists or can be known **–ist** *n* **–istic** *adj*
solitaire *n* **1** *AmE for* patience (2) **2** (piece of jewellery having) a single jewel, esp. a diamond
solitary *adj* **1** (fond of being) alone **2** in a lonely place **3** single **–rily** *adv* **–riness** *n*

solitude *n* state of being alone

solo *n* **solos** something done by one person alone, esp. a piece of music for one performer ♦ *adj, adv* **1** without a companion or esp. instructor **2** as or being a musical solo **~ist** *n* performer of a musical solo

solstice *n* time of the longest and shortest days of the year

soluble *adj* **1** that can be dissolved **2** solvable **–bility** *n*

solution *n* **1** answer to a problem or question **2** liquid with a solid mixed into it

solve *vt* find an answer to or explanation of **solvable** *adj*

solvent *adj* not in debt ♦ *n* liquid that can turn solids into liquids **–vency** *n*

solvent abuse *n* glue-sniffing

somatic *adj* of or affecting the body

sombre, *AmE* **-ber** *adj* sadly serious or dark **~ly** *adv* **~ness** *n*

sombrero *n* **-os** high-crowned, wide-brimmed hat

some *determiner* **1** a certain number or amount of **2** an unknown or unstated: *She went to work for some computer firm or other.* **3** quite a large number or amount of: *The fire lasted for some time.* **4** *infml* no kind of: *Some friend you are!* **5** a fine or important: *That was some speech you made!* ♦ *pron* **1** an amount or number of the stated thing(s) **2** certain ones but not all ♦ *adv* **1** about (the stated number): *Some 50 people came.* **2** *AmE* rather; a little: *'Are you feeling better?' 'Some, I guess.'*

-some *suffix* **1** (in adjectives) causing: *troublesome* **2** (in nouns) group of the stated number: *foursome*

somebody *pron* someone ♦ *n* a person of some importance: *He thinks he's really somebody.*

somehow *adv* **1** in some way not yet known or stated **2** for some reason: *Somehow I don't believe her.*

someone *pron* a person (but not a particular or known one)

someplace *adv AmE* somewhere

somersault *n* rolling jump in which the feet go over the head and then land on the ground **somersault** *vi*

something *pron* **1** some unstated or unknown thing **2** better than nothing: *At least we've got the car, that's something.* **3 something of a(n)** rather a(n); a fairly good

sometime *adv* at some uncertain or unstated time ♦ *adj fml* former

sometimes *adv* on some occasions but not all

somewhat *adv* a little; rather

somewhere *adv* **1** (at or to) some place **2 get somewhere** begin to succeed

somnambulist *n* sleepwalker **–lant** *adj*

somnolent *adj* **1** drowsy **2** causing sleep **~ly** *adv* **–ence** *n*

son *n* **1** someone's male child **2** (used by an older man to a much younger man or boy): *What's your name, son?*

sonar *n* apparatus for finding underwater objects with sound waves

sonata *n* usu. three- or four-part piece of music for one or two instruments

son et lumière *n* performance using light and sound to give a dramatic account of a place's history

song *n* **1** short piece of music with words for singing **2** act or art of singing **3** music-like sound of birds **4 for a song** very cheaply

song and dance *n infml* unnecessary or unwelcome fuss

songbird *n* perching bird that utters musical sounds

songster *n* **1** singer **2** singing bird

song thrush *n* common European thrush

sonic *adj* of or concerning the speed of sound or sound

sonic boom also **sonic bang** *n* explosive sound produced by the shock wave from an aircraft which is travelling faster than the speed of sound

son-in-law *n* **sons-in-law** *or* **son-in-laws** daughter's husband

sonnet *n* 14-line poem

sonny *n* (used in speaking to a young boy)

son-of-a-bitch *n* **sons-of-bitches, son-**

of-a-bitches *taboo* someone strongly disliked
sonorous /ˈsonərəs/ *adj* having a pleasantly full loud sound **~ly** *adv* **-rity** *n*
soon *adv* **1** within a short time **2** quickly; early: *How soon can you finish it?* **3** willingly: *I'd sooner stay here.*
soot *n* black powder produced by burning **~y** *adj* **~iness** *n*
soothe *vt* **1** make less angry or excited **2** make less painful **soothingly** *adv*
soothsayer *n lit* person who tells the future
sop *n* something offered to gain someone's favour or stop them complaining
sop up *phr vt* **-pp-** take up (liquid) into something solid
sophism /ˈsofiz(ə)m/ *n* **1** sophistry **2** correct-sounding but false argument
sophist *n* person who practises sophistry
sophisticate *n* sophisticated person
sophisticated *adj* **1** experienced in and understanding the ways of society **2** highly developed **-tion** *n*
sophistry /ˈsofistri/ *n* use of false deceptive arguments
sophomore *n* student in the second year of a US college course
soporific *n, adj* (something) causing sleep
sopping *adv, adj* very (wet)
soppy *adj BrE* **1** foolish **2** too full of expressions of tender feelings **-pily** *adv* **-piness** *n*
soprano *n* **-nos 1** (someone, esp. a woman, with) the highest human singing voice **2** instrument which plays notes in the highest range
sorbet *n* dish of ice with a usu. fruit taste
sorcery *n* doing of magic with the help of evil spirits **sorcerer** *n* **sorceress** *n*
sordid *adj* **1** completely lacking fine or noble qualities; low **2** dirty and badly cared for **~ly** *adv* **~ness** *n*
sore *adj* **1** painful, esp. from a wound or hard use **2** likely to cause offence: *Don't joke about his weight: it's a sore point with him.* **3** *AmE* angry ♦ *n* painful usu. infected place on the body ♦ *adv lit* sorely **~ly** *adv fml* very much **~ness** *n*
sorghum *n* cereal grown in tropical areas
sorority *n* society of American female students
sorrel[1] *n* plant with sour-tasting leaves
sorrel[2] *n* **1** orange-brown colour **2** sorrel-coloured animal
sorrow *n* sadness; grief ♦ *vi* grieve **~ful** *adj* **~fully** *adv* **~fulness** *n*
sorry *adj* **1** feeling sadness, pity, or sympathy **2** ashamed of or unhappy about an action **3** causing pity mixed with disapproval: *You look a sorry sight.* ♦ *interj* **1** (used for excusing oneself or expressing polite refusal, disagreement, etc.) **2** (used for asking someone to repeat something one has not heard)
sort *n* **1** group all sharing certain qualities; kind **2** person: *She's not such a bad sort.* **3 of sorts** of a poor or doubtful kind **4 out of sorts** feeling unwell or annoyed **5 sort of** *infml* rather ♦ *vi/t* put (things) in order **sort out** *phr vt* **1** separate from a mass or group **2** *BrE* deal with
sortie *n* **1** short trip into an unfamiliar place **2** short attack by an army
sort-out *n* act of tidying up
SOS *n* urgent message for help
so-so *adj, adv* neither very bad(ly) nor very good/well
sot *n* drunkard
sotto voce /ˌsotoh ˈvohchi/ *adv fml* quietly
sou *n* coin of small value
soubriquet /ˈsoohbriˌkay/ *n* sobriquet
soufflé *n* light fluffy baked dish of eggs and flour
sought *past t. and p. of* seek
sought-after *adj esp. BrE* wanted because of rarity or high quality
soul *n* **1** part of a person that is not the body and is thought not to die **2** person: *Not a soul was there.* **3** perfect example: *Your secret is safe with him; he's the soul*

of discretion. **4** most active part or influence: *She's the life and soul of any party.* **5** attractive quality of sincerity: *The performance lacks soul.* **6** soul music

soul brother *n* (used by young black people) a black man

soul-destroying *adj* (esp. of a job) very uninteresting

soulful *adj* expressing deep feeling **~ly** *adv* **~ness** *n*

soulless *adj* having no warm or attractive qualities **~ly** *adv* **~ness** *n*

soul music *n* type of popular music usu. performed by black singers

soul-searching *n* deep examination of one's mind and conscience

soul sister *n* (used by young black people) a black woman

sound[1] *n* **1** what is or may be heard **2** idea produced by something read or heard: *From the sound of it, I'd say the matter was serious.* ♦ *v* **1** *vi* seem when heard: *His explanation sounded suspicious.* **2** *vi/t* (cause to) make a sound: *Sound the trumpets.* **3** *vt* signal by making sounds: *Sound the alarm.* **4** *vt* pronounce **5** *vt* measure the depth of (water) using a weighted line **sound off** *phr vi* express an opinion freely and forcefully **sound out** *phr vt* try to find out the opinion or intention of

sound[2] *adj* **1** not damaged or diseased **2** showing good sense or judgment: *sound advice* **3** thorough **4** (of sleep) deep and untroubled **5 as sound as a bell** in perfect condition ♦ *adv* deeply **~ly** *adv* **~ness** *n*

sound[3] *n* **1** long broad inlet of sea **2** long passage of water connecting two larger bodies

sound barrier *n* point at which an aircraft reaches the speed of sound

sound effects *pl n* sounds produced to give the effect of natural sounds in a radio or TV broadcast or film

sounding board *n* means used for testing thoughts, opinions, etc.

soundings *pl n* **1** measurements made by sounding water **2** carefully quiet or secret enquiries

soundproof *adj* that sound cannot get through or into ♦ *vt* make soundproof

soundtrack *n* recorded music from a film

soup *n* **1** liquid cooked food often containing pieces of meat or vegetables **2 in the soup** in trouble

soupçon /ˈsooh(p)son/ *n* little bit; dash

soup kitchen *n* place giving out free basic meals to people in need

soup up *vt* make more powerful

sour *adj* **1** acid-tasting: *sour green apples* **2** tasting bad because of chemical action by bacteria: *sour milk* **3** bad-tempered; unfriendly **4 go/turn sour** go wrong ♦ *vi/t* (cause to) become sour **~ly** *adv* **~ness** *n*

source *n* where something comes from; cause

sour grapes *n* pretending to dislike what one really desires, because it is unobtainable

sourpuss *n* complaining humourless person

souse *vt* **1** drench **2** pickle **soused** *adj infml* drunk

south *n* **1** the direction which is on the right of a person facing the rising sun **2 a** the part of a country which is further south than the rest **b** the southeastern states of the US ♦ *adj* **1** in the south **2** (of wind) from the south ♦ *adv* towards the south **~ward** *adj, adv*

southeast *n, adj, adv* (direction) halfway between south and east **~ern** *adj*

southerly *adj* south

southern *adj* of the south part of the world or of a country **~er** *n* person who lives in or comes from the southern part of a country

southpaw *n* left-handed person, esp. a boxer

southwest *n, adj, adv* (direction) halfway between south and west **~ern** *adj*

souvenir *n* object kept as a reminder of an event, journey, place, etc.

sou'wester *n* waterproof hat

sovereign *n* **1** ruler **2** former British

gold coin worth £1 ♦ *adj* (of a country) independent and self-governing **~ty** *n* **1** complete freedom and power to act or govern **2** quality of being a sovereign state
soviet *n* elected council in a communist country
Soviet *adj* of the USSR or its people
sow[1] *vi/t* **sowed, sown** *or* **sowed** plant (seeds) on (a piece of ground) **~er** *n*
sow[2] *n* female pig
soy, soya *n* soya beans
soya bean, soybean *n* bean of an Asian plant which produces oil
soy sauce *n* dark brown sauce made from fermented soya beans
sozzled *adj BrE infml* drunk
spa *n* (health resort with) a spring of mineral water
space *n* **1** something measurable in length, width, or depth; room: *There's not enough space in the cupboard for all my clothes.* **2** quantity or bit of this: *looking for a parking space* **3** region beyond the Earth's atmosphere **4** limitless area that surrounds all objects **5** period of time: *within the space of a few years* ♦ *vt* place apart; arrange with spaces between
space-age *adj* very modern
spacecraft *n* vehicle able to travel beyond the Earth's atmosphere
spaced out *adj infml* dazed or stupefied (as if) by drugs
spaceman *n infml* astronaut
spaceship *n* (esp. in stories) spacecraft for carrying people
space shuttle *n* vehicle for carrying people and supplies between the Earth and a space station
space station *n* large spacecraft intended to stay above the Earth and act as a base e.g. for scientific tests
spacesuit *n* pressurized garment worn in space
space walk *n* trip outside a spacecraft made by an astronaut
spacious *adj* having a lot of room **~ly** *adv* **~ness** *n*
spade[1] *n* broad-bladed tool for digging
spade[2] *n* playing card with one or more figures shaped like black printed leaves on it
spadework *n* hard preparatory work
spaghetti *n* pasta in the form of long thin strings
spake *old use, past tense of* speak
span[1] *past t. of* spin
span[2] *n* **1** length between two limits, esp. of time: *over a span of 3 years* **2** length of time over which something continues: *concentration span* **3** (part of) a bridge, arch, etc., between supports **4** distance from the end of the thumb to the little finger in a spread hand ♦ *vt* **-nn- 1** form an arch or bridge over **2** include in space or time
spangle *n* small shiny piece sewn on for decoration ♦ *vt* decorate with spangles
Spaniard *n* Spanish person
spaniel *n* dog with long ears and long wavy hair
Spanish *n, adj* (people) of Spain
spank *vt* slap (esp. a child) for punishment, esp. on the buttocks **spank** *n*
spanking *adj* brisk ♦ *adv* completely
spanner *n BrE* **1** metal tool with jaws or a hollow end, for turning nuts or bolts **2** **a spanner in the works** a cause of confusion to a plan or operation
spar[1] *vi* **-rr- 1** practise boxing **2** fight with words
spar[2] *n* pole supporting a ship's ropes or sails
spare *vt* **1** give up (something that is not needed) **2** keep from using, spending, etc.: *No expense was spared.* **3** not give (something unpleasant): *Spare me the gory details.* **4** *esp. lit* not punish or harm ♦ *adj* **1** kept for use if needed: *a spare tyre* **2** free: *spare time* **3** rather thin **4 go spare** *BrE infml* be very angry ♦ *n BrE* spare part
spare part *n* machine part to take the place of one that is damaged
spare part surgery *n infml* replacement of diseased organs by donated organs
spareribs *pl n* (dish of) pig's ribs with their meat
spark *n* **1** small bit of burning material

flying through the air **2** electric flash passing across a space **3** very small but important bit: *not a spark of humour* ♦ *vi* **1** produce a spark **2** lead to (esp. something unpleasant) **3** *esp. AmE* encourage **spark off** *phr vt* cause (esp. something violent or unpleasant)

sparkle *vi* **1** shine in small flashes **2** show life and brightness ♦ *n* act or quality of sparkling **–kling** *adj* **1** full of life and brightness **2** (of wine) effervescent

sparkler *n* **1** hand-held firework **2** *sl* diamond

spark plug, also *BrE* **sparking plug** *n* part inside an engine that makes a spark to light the petrol and start the engine

sparrow *n* very common small brownish bird

sparse *adj* scattered; not crowded **~ly** *adv* **~ness** *n*

spartan *adj* simple, severe, and without attention to comfort

spasm *n* **1** sudden uncontrolled tightening of muscles **2** sudden short period of uncontrolled activity: *spasms of coughing*

spasmodic *adj* happening irregularly or non-continuously **~ally** *adv*

spastic *n, adj* (person) suffering from a disease in which some parts of the body will not move

spat[1] *past t. and p. of* spit

spat[2] *n* cloth covering for the instep and ankle

spat[3] *n infml* short quarrel

spate *n esp. BrE* **1** flood **2** large number or amount coming together at the same time

spatial *adj fml* of or in space **~ly** *adv*

spatter *vi/t* scatter (drops of liquid) or be scattered on (a surface)

spatula *n* (kitchen) tool with a wide flat blade for spreading, mixing, etc.

spawn *n* eggs of water animals like fishes and frogs ♦ *vi* **1** produce spawn **2** produce esp. in large numbers

spay *vt* remove the ovaries of (a female animal)

speak *v* **spoke, spoken 1** *vi* say things; talk **2** *vi* express thoughts, ideas, etc., in some other way than this: *Actions speak louder than words.* **3** *vt* say; express: *Is he speaking the truth?* **4** *vt* be able to talk in (a language) **5** *vi* make a speech **6** *vi* mean in the stated way what is said: *personally speaking, I agree* **7 so to speak** as one might say **8 to speak of** worth mentioning **speak for** *phr vt* express the thoughts, opinions, etc., of **speak out** *phr vi* speak boldly, freely and plainly **speak up** *phr vi* **1** speak more loudly **2** speak out **~er** *n* **1** person making a speech **2** person who speaks a language **3** loudspeaker

-speak *suffix* jargon used in the stated activity: *computerspeak*

speakeasy *n* (esp. in the US in the 1920s and 1930s) place for the illegal sale and drinking of alcohol

spear *n* weapon consisting of a sharp-pointed pole ♦ *vt* push or throw a spear into

spearhead *n* forceful beginner and/or leader of an attack or course of action ♦ *vt* lead forcefully

spearmint *n* common mint plant with a fresh taste

spec *n* **on spec** *BrE* as a risk

special *adj* **1** of a particular kind; not ordinary **2** particularly great or fine: *a special occasion* ♦ *n* **1** something not of the regular kind **2** *AmE infml* an advertised reduced price in a shop **~ly** *adv* **1** for one particular purpose **2** unusually

Special Branch *n* department of the British police force concerned with action against the state

specialist *n* **1** person with skill or interest in a particular subject **2** doctor who specializes in a particular sort of illness

speciality, *AmE usu.* **specialty** *n* **1** person's particular field of work or study **2** finest product

specialize, **-ise** *vi* limit one's study, business, etc., to one particular area **–ization** *n*

special license *n law* marriage license permitting marriage without banns or at a time or place not usually allowed
special pleading *n* argument that ignores unfavourable aspects of a case
specie /ˈspeeshi/ *n* money in coin
species *n* **-cies** group of similar types of animal or plant
specific *adj* **1** detailed and exact: *specific instructions* **2** particular; fixed or named: *a specific tool for each job* **~ally** *adv*
specification *n* **1** detailed plan or set of descriptions or directions **2** act of specifying
specific gravity *n* density of a substance compared with that of water
specifics *pl n* particulars
specify *vt* state exactly
specimen *n* **1** single typical thing or example **2** piece or amount of something to be examined: *The doctor needs a specimen of your blood.*
specious /ˈspeesh(y)əs/ *adj* seeming correct but in fact false **~ly** *adv* **~ness** *n*
speck *n* very small piece or spot
speckle *vt, n* (mark with) any of a number of small irregular marks
spectacle *n* **1** unusual sight, esp. something grand and fine **2** object of laughing, disrespect, or pity **spectacles** *pl n* glasses
spectacular *adj* unusually interesting and grand ♦ *n* spectacular entertainment **~ly** *adv*
spectator *n* person watching an event or sport
spectre, *AmE* **-ter** *n lit* ghost **-tral** *adj*
spectrum *n* **-tra 1** set of bands of different colours into which light may be separated by a prism **2** broad and continuous range: *both ends of the political spectrum*
speculate *vi* **1** make guesses **2** buy things to sell later in the hope of profit **-lator** *n* **-lative** *adj* **-lation** *n*
speculum *n* mirror
sped *past t. and p. of* speed
speech *n* **1** act, power, or way of speaking **2** set of words spoken formally to a group of listeners **~less** *adj* unable to speak because of strong feeling **~lessly** *adv*
speechify *vi* speak pompously
speech synthesizer *n* computer system that can produce sounds similar to human speech
speed *n* **1** rate of movement: *a speed of 2000 kilometres an hour* **2** quickness of movement or action: *travelling at speed* **3** *sl* amphetamine ♦ *v* **speeded** *or* **sped 1** *vi/t* go or take quickly **2** *vi* drive illegally fast **speed up** *phr vi/t* (cause to) go faster **~y** *adj* fast **~ily** *adv* **~iness** *n*
speedometer *n* instrument showing how fast a vehicle is going
speed trap *n* place where police observe the speed of cars
speedway *n* sport of racing motorcycles on a closed track
speedwell *n* small plant with blue flowers
speleology /ˌspeeliˈoləji/ *n* scientific study of caves **-gist** *n*
spell[1] *v* **spelt,** *esp. AmE* **spelled 1** *vi* form words (correctly) from letters **2** *vt* name in order the letters of (a word) **3** *vt* (of letters) form (a word): *B-O-O-K spells 'book'.* **4** *vt* have as an effect: *His disapproval spells defeat for our plan.* **spell out** *phr vt* explain in the clearest possible way **~er** *n* **~ing** *n* way a word is spelt
spell[2] *n* **1** unbroken period of time: *spells of sunshine* **2** quickly passing attack of illness: *a dizzy spell* ♦ *vt* take the place of
spell[3] *n* (words producing) a condition produced by magical power
spellbind *vt* hold the complete attention of
spend *vt* **spent 1** pay (money) for goods or services **2** pass or use (time) **~er** *n*
spent *adj* **1** already used; no longer for use **2** worn out
spendthrift *n* person who wastes money
sperm *n* **sperm** *or* **sperms** male sex cell which unites with the female egg to produce new life

spermaceti /ˌspuhməˈseeti, -ˈseti/ *n* waxy solid obtained from the oil of whales
spermatozoon *n* **-oa** sperm
spermicide *n* substance that kills sperm **–idal** *adj*
sperm whale *n* large toothed whale with a huge blunt head
spew *vi/t* (cause to) come out in a rush or flood
sphagnum /ˈsfagnəm/ *n* moss that grows in bogs
sphere *n* **1** ball-shaped mass **2** area or range of existence, meaning, action, etc.: *this country's sphere of influence* **spherical** *adj* ball-shaped **spherically** *adv*
spheroid *n* shape very like a sphere **~al** *adj*
sphincter *n* muscular ring that contracts or closes a body opening
sphinx *n* **1** ancient Egyptian image of a lion with a human head **2** person who behaves or speaks in a mysterious way
spic, spick *AmE derog taboo* Spanish-speaking American
spice *n* **1** vegetable product used for giving taste to food **2** (additional) interest or excitement ♦ *vt* add spice to **spicy** *adj* **1** containing (much) spice **2** slightly improper or rude
spick-and-span *adj* completely clean and tidy
spider *n* small eight-legged creature, of which many types make webs to catch insects **~y** *adj* long and thin like a spider's legs
spiel /s(h)peel/ *n infml* talk intended to persuade or impress
spigot *n* **1** small plug used in a cask **2** part of a tap, esp. on a barrel, that controls flow
spike *n* **1** pointed piece, esp. of metal **2** metal point fixed to the bottom of a (sports) shoe **3** group of grains or flowers on top of a stem ♦ *vt* **1** drive a spike into **2** add a strong alcoholic drink to (a weak or non-alcoholic one) **3** stop (esp. an article in a newspaper) from being printed or spread **4 spike someone's guns** take away an opponent's power **spiky** *adj*
spill[1] *vi/t* **spilt,** *esp. AmE* **spilled 1** (cause to) pour out accidentally and be lost **2 spill the beans** *infml* tell a secret too soon or to the wrong person ♦ *n* fall from a horse or vehicle
spill[2] *n* thin twist of paper or piece of wood
spin *v* **span** *or* **spun,** *past p.* **spun;** *pres. p.* **-nn- 1** *vi/t* turn round and round fast **2** *vi/t* make (thread) by twisting (cotton, wool, etc.) **3** *vt* produce in thread-like form: *a spider spinning a web* ♦ *n* **1** act of spinning **2** fast turning movement **3** short trip for pleasure **4** a steep drop: *The news sent prices into a spin.* **5 in a (flat) spin** in a confused state of mind **spin out** *phr vt* cause to last long enough or too long **~ner** *n*
spina bifida *n* defect of the spine which leaves part of the spinal cord unprotected
spinach *n* vegetable with large soft leaves
spinal *adj* of the backbone
spinal cord *n* thick cord of important nerves enclosed in the spine
spindle *n* **1** machine part round which something turns **2** pointed rod onto which thread is twisted **–dly** *adj* long, thin, and weak-looking
spindle tree *n* small tree with bright berries
spine *n* **1** row of bones down the centre of the back **2** stiff pointed part of an animal or plant **3** side of a book along which the pages are fastened **~less** *adj* weak and cowardly **~lessly** *adv* **~lessness** *n* **spiny** *adj* prickly
spine-chilling *adj* very frightening
spinet *n* small harpsichord
spinnaker *n* large sail for racing
spinney *n* small wood
spinning jenny *n* early factory machine for spinning several threads at once
spinning wheel *n* small domestic machine for spinning thread
spin-off *n* (useful) indirect product of a process

spinster *n* unmarried woman
spiral *n, adj* **1** (curve) winding round and round a central line or away from a central point **2** process of continuous upward or downward change ♦ *vi* **-ll-** (*AmE* **-l-**) move in a spiral
spire *n* tall thin pointed roof of a church tower
spirit *n* **1** person's mind or soul **2** being without a body, such as a ghost **3** quality of lively determination or brave effort: *a girl with spirit* **4** person of the stated kind of temper: *a free spirit* **5** central quality or force: *the spirit of the law* **6** attitude: *Please take my remarks in the spirit in which they were intended.* **7** strong alcoholic drink **8 in spirit** in one's thoughts ♦ *vt* take secretly or mysteriously **spirits** *pl n* state of one's mind: *in high spirits* **~ed** *adj* lively **~edly** *adv* **~less** *adj* depressed **~lessly** *adv* **~lessness** *n*
spirit level *n* device containing a bubble in a tube of liquid, used to indicate whether a surface is level
spiritual *adj* **1** of the spirit rather than the body **2** religious ♦ *n* religious song originally sung by US blacks **~ly** *adv*
spiritualism *n* belief that the dead communicate with the living **-ist** *n*
spirituality *n* attachment to religious values
spit[1] *v* **spat;** *pres. p.* **-tt- 1** *vi/t* throw out (liquid or other contents) from the mouth with force **2** *vt* say with effort or anger **3** *vi* rain very lightly ♦ *n* saliva
spit[2] *n* **1** thin rod on which meat is cooked over a fire **2** small usu. sandy point of land running out into a stretch of water ♦ *vt* impale
spit and polish *n* great esp. military attention to a clean and shiny appearance
spite *n* **1** desire to annoy or harm **2 in spite of** taking no notice of: *They continued, in spite of my warning.* ♦ *vt* annoy or harm intentionally **~ful** *adj*
spitfire *n* quick-tempered person
spitting image *n* exact likeness
spittle *n* saliva
spittoon *n* receptacle for spit
spiv *n* man who makes money by sharp practice or petty fraud
splash *v* **1** *vi/t* **a** (cause to) fall or move about in drops or waves, esp. wildly or noisily **b** throw a liquid against (something): *He splashed his face with cold water.* **2** *vt* report as if very important, esp. in a newspaper **3** *vi/t BrE* spend freely: *I splashed out and bought a new dress.* **splash down** *phr vi* (esp. of a spacecraft) land in the sea ♦ *n* **1** (sound or mark made by) splashing **2** forceful effect: *make a splash in society*
splashdown *n* landing in the sea (esp. of a spacecraft)
splashy *adj esp. AmE* big, bright, and very noticeable
splatter *vi/t* splash in small drops
splay *vi/t* spread out or become larger at one end
splayfooted *adj* having very flat spread-out feet
spleen *n* **1** organ that controls the quality of the body's blood supply **2** bad temper
splendid *adj* **1** grand in appearance or style **2** very fine; excellent **~ly** *adv*
splendiferous *adj infml* splendid **~ly** *adv* **~ness** *n*
splendour, *AmE* **-dor** *n* excellent or grand beauty
splenetic *adj* bad-tempered **~ally** *adv*
splice *vt* **1** fasten end to end to make one continuous length **2** *BrE infml* join in marriage ♦ *n* join made by splicing
splint *n* flat piece for keeping a broken bone in place
splinter *n* small sharp piece, esp. of wood, broken off ♦ *vi/t* break into splinters
splinter group *n* group of people that has separated from a larger body
split *v* **split;** *pres. p.* **-tt- 1** *vi/t* divide along a length, esp. by a blow or tear **2** *vi/t* divide into separate parts **3** *vt* share **4** *vi/t* separate into opposing groups or parties **5 split hairs** concern oneself with small unimportant differences ♦ *n* cut, break, or division made by split-

ting **~ting** *adj* (of a headache) very bad
split-level *adj* (of a building) with floors on different levels within one storey
split pea *n* dried pea separated into its two natural halves
split personality *n* set of two very different ways of behaving present in one person
splits *n* movement in which a person's legs are spread wide and touch the floor along their whole length
split second *n* very short moment
splodge, splotch *n* large irregular mark or smear **splodge, splotch** *vt* **splodgy, splotchy** *adj*
splosh *vi* make a loud splash
splurge *vi/t* spend more than one can usu. afford
splutter *vi* **1** talk quickly, as if confused **2** make a wet spitting noise **splutter** *n*
spoil *v* **spoiled** *or* **spoilt 1** *vt* destroy the value, worth, or pleasure of; ruin **2** *vt* treat very or too well: *Go on, spoil yourself, have another cake.* **3** *vi* decay **spoil for** *phr vt* **1** be very eager for **2 be spoilt for choice** find it difficult to decide or choose **spoils** *pl n lit* things taken without payment
spoilage *n* loss by being spoiled
spoilsport *n* person who ruins others' fun
spoke[1] *past t. of* speak
spoke[2] *n* any of the bars connecting the outer ring of a wheel to the centre
spoken *past p. of* speak
spoken for *adj infml* closely connected with a person of the opposite sex
spokesperson *n* person (a **spokesman** or **spokeswoman**) chosen to speak officially for a group
spoliation /ˌspohliˈaysh(ə)n/ *n* act of plundering or damaging
sponge *n* **1** simple sea creature with a rubber-like body **2** piece of this or plastic like it, which can suck up water and is used for washing ♦ *v* **1** *vt* clean with a sponge **2** *vi derog* get things from people free by taking advantage of their generosity **~r** *n* person who sponges on others **spongy** *adj* not firm
sponge bag *n* small waterproof bag to hold washing things
sponge cake *n* light cake made from eggs, sugar, and flour
sponsor *n* **1** company or person giving money to help others to do something **2** person who takes responsibility for a person or thing ♦ *vt* act as a sponsor for: *a concert sponsored by American Express* **~ship** *n*
spontaneous *adj* happening naturally, without planning or another's suggestion **~ly** *adv* **-taneity** *n*
spoof *n* funny untrue copy or description ♦ *vt* make or perform a spoof of
spook *vt esp. AmE* cause (esp. an animal) to be suddenly afraid ♦ *n infml* ghost
spooky *adj* causing fear in a strange way **–ily** *adv*
spool *n* cylinder onto which things are wound
spoon *n* kitchen tool consisting of a small bowl with a handle, used esp. for eating ♦ *vt* take up with a spoon
spoonerism *n* expression in which the initial sounds of two words have changed places (e.g. *tasted worm* for *wasted term*)
spoon-feed *vt* **1** feed with a spoon **2** teach (people) in very easy lessons
spoor *n* tracks or droppings of a wild animal
sporadic *adj* happening irregularly **~ally** *adv*
spore *n* very small cell that acts like a seed: *a mushroom's spores*
sporran *n* fur pouch worn with the kilt in Highland dress
sport *n* **1** activity needing physical effort and skill and usu. done as a competition according to rules **2** friendly or kind person ♦ *vt* wear or show publicly: *sporting a brand new coat* **sports** *pl n BrE* athletics competition **~ing** *adj* **1** fair and generous **2** (fond) of outdoor sports **~ingly** *adv* **~y** *adj BrE infml* good at and/or fond of sport **~s** *adj* suitable for sport **~ive** *adj* playful **~ively** *adv* **~iveness** *n*

sports car *n* low fast car

sportsman *n* **-men** person who plays sport(s) **~ship** *n* fairness to one's opponent, esp. in sport

sportswoman *n* **-women** woman who plays sport(s)

spot *n* **1** usu. round part different from the main surface: *a blue dress with white spots* **2** small diseased mark on the skin **3** place: *a beautiful spot for a picnic* **4** small or limited part of something: *one of the brighter spots in the news* **5** *BrE* small amount: *a spot of bother* **6** *infml* difficult situation **7** spotlight **8 on the spot: a** at once **b** at the place of the action **c** in a position of having to make the right action or answer: *The question really put me on the spot.* ♦ *vt* **-tt- 1** see; recognize **2** mark with spots **3** *AmE* allow as an advantage in a game **~less** *adj* completely clean **~lessly** *adv* **~ter** *n* person who looks for the stated thing: *a train spotter* **~ty** *adj* **1** having spots on the face **2** *AmE* with some parts less good than others

spot check *n* examination of a few chosen by chance to represent all **spot-check** *vt*

spotlight *n* **1** (light from) a large lamp with a directable beam **2** public attention ♦ *vt* direct attention to

spouse *n fml or law* husband or wife

spout *n* **1** opening from which liquid comes out: *the spout of a teapot* **2** forceful (rising) stream of liquid **3** *BrE infml* **up the spout: a** ruined **b** pregnant ♦ *v* **1** *vi/t* come or throw out in a forceful stream **2** *vt derog* pour out in a stream of words

sprain *vt* damage (a joint in the body) by sudden twisting **sprain** *n*

sprang *past t. of* spring

sprat *n* young herring

sprawl *vi/t* spread out awkwardly or ungracefully ♦ *n* sprawling position or area

spray *vi/t* send or come out in a stream of small drops (onto) ♦ *n* **1** water blown in very small drops **2** liquid to be sprayed out from a container under pressure: *hair spray* **3** small branch with its leaves and flowers

spread *v* **spread 1** *vi/t* (cause to) become longer, broader, wider, etc. **2** *vi/t* (cause to) have an effect or influence or become known over a wider area: *The news soon spread.* **3** *vi* cover a large area or period **4** *vt* put over (a surface): *Spread butter on the bread.* ♦ *n* **1** act or action of spreading **2** soft food for spreading on bread: *cheese spread* **3** large or grand meal

spread-eagle *vt* put into a position with arms and legs spread wide

spreadsheet *n* type of computer program that allows figures (e.g. about sales, taxes, and profits) to be shown in groups on a screen so that quick calculations can be made

spree *n* period of much wild fun, spending, drinking, etc.

sprig *n* small end of a stem with leaves ♦ *vt* decorate with a design of sprigs

sprightly *adj* cheerful and active **-liness** *n*

spring *v* **sprang, sprung 1** *vi* move quickly and suddenly as if by jumping: *The soldiers sprang to attention.* **2** *vi/t* open or close with a spring *to spring a trap* **3** *vt* produce (as) (a surprise): *She sprang the news on us.* **4 spring a leak** (of a ship, container, etc.) begin to let liquid through a hole, etc. **spring from** *phr vt* have as its origin **spring up** *phr vi* come into existence suddenly ♦ *n* **1** season between winter and summer **2** length of wound metal that comes up again after being pressed down **3** place where water comes naturally from the ground **4** elastic quality **5** act of springing **~y** *adj* elastic

springboard *n* **1** flexible board off which people who dive jump **2** strong starting point

springbok *n* Southern African gazelle

spring-clean *vi/t* clean (a house) thoroughly **spring-clean** *n*

springer spaniel *n* spaniel used for finding game

spring onion *n* small, mild flavoured onion eaten in salads
spring roll *n* Chinese filled pancake
spring tide *n* very high tide occurring at new and full moon
sprinkle *vt* scatter (small drops or bits) on or over (a surface) **-kler** *n* apparatus for sprinkling drops of water
sprint *vi* run very fast **sprint** *n* **~er** *n*
sprite *n* fairy
sprocket *n* (tooth on) a wheel with a toothed edge for engaging a chain
sprout *vi/t* send or come out as new growth ♦ *n* **1** new growth on a plant **2** brussels sprout
spruce[1] *adj* neat and clean **spruce up** *phr vt* make (esp. oneself) spruce **~ly** *adv* **~ness** *n*
spruce[2] *n* tree of northern countries with short needle-shaped leaves
sprung *past p. of* spring
spry *adj* (esp. of older people) active **~ly** *adv* **~ness** *n*
spud *n* **1** *infml* potato **2** small spade
spume *n* foam
spun *past t. and p. of* spin
spunk *n* **1** *infml* courage **2** *sl* semen
spur *n* **1** sharp object fitted to a rider's boot, used to make a horse go faster **2** event or influence leading to action **3** length of high ground coming out from a mountain range **4 on the spur of the moment** without preparation or planning ♦ *vt* **-rr-** urge or encourage forcefully
spurge *n* bushy plant with milky juice
spurious /ˈspyooəri·əs/ *adj* **1** based on incorrect reasoning **2** pretended; false **~ly** *adv* **~ness** *n*
spurn *vt* refuse or send away with angry pride
spurt *vi/t* **1** make a spurt **2** (cause to) flow out suddenly or violently ♦ *n* **1** sudden short increase of effort or speed **2** spurting of liquid or gas
sputnik *n* (Russian) satellite
sputter *vi* make repeated soft explosive sounds
sputum *n* mucus and saliva that is coughed up
spy *n* **1** person employed to find out secret information **2** person who watches secretly ♦ *v* **1** *vi* watch or search secretly **2** *vt* catch sight of
spyglass *n* small telescope
sq *abbrev. for:* square
squab *n* **1** fledgling pigeon **2** thick cushion for a seat
squabble *vi, n* (have) a quarrel about unimportant things
squad *n* group of people working as a team
squadron *n* large group of **a** soldiers with tanks **b** warships **c** aircraft in the airforce
squalid *adj* **1** very dirty and unpleasant **2** of low moral standards **~ly** *adv* **~ness** *n*
squall *n* sudden strong wind **~y** *adj*
squalor *n* squalid conditions
squander *vt* spend foolishly and wastefully
square[1] *n* **1** shape with four straight equal sides forming four right angles **2** broad open area with buildings round it in a town **3** result of multiplying a number by itself ♦ *adj* **1** being a square **2** of an area equal to a square with sides of the stated length: *1 square metre* **3** forming (nearly) a right angle: *a square jaw* **4** fair; honest: *a square deal* **5** equal in points: *The teams are all square.* **6** having paid and settled what is owed ♦ *v* **1** *vt* put into a square shape **2** *vt* divide into squares **3** *vt* multiply by itself: *2 squared is 4.* **4** *vi/t* (cause to) fit a particular explanation or standard **5** *vt* cause (totals of points or games won) to be equal **6** *vt* pay or pay for **7** *vt* pay or settle dishonestly: *There are government officers who will have to be squared.* **square up** *phr vi* settle a bill ♦ *adv* squarely **~ly** *adv* directly: *He looked her squarely in the eye.*
square dance *n* dance for four couples who face each other in a square
square meal *n infml* good satisfying meal
square one *n* the starting point
square rig *n* rig in which the main sails

are square and set across the ship **square-rigged** *adj* **square-rigger** *n*

square root *n* number which when squared equals a particular number: *2 is the square root of 4.*

squash[1] *v* **1** *vt* flatten; crush **2** *vi/t* push or fit into a small space **3** *vt* force into silence or inactivity ♦ *n* **1** act or sound of squashing **2** game played in a four-walled court with rackets and a small ball **3** *BrE* sweet fruit drink. **~y** *adj* soft and easy to squash

squash[2] *n esp. AmE* any of a group of vegetables with hard skins, including marrows and pumpkins

squat *vi* **-tt- 1** sit with the legs drawn up under the body **2** live in an empty building without permission ♦ *adj* ungracefully short or low and thick **~ter** *n* person who squats in a building

squaw *n* North American Indian woman

squawk *vi* **1** (of a bird) make a loud rough cry **2** complain loudly **squawk** *n*

squeak *vi, n* (make) a short very high quiet sound **~y** *adj*

squeal *n* a long very high cry ♦ *vi* **1** make a squeal **2** *sl* give secret information about one's criminal friends to the police **~er** *n*

squeamish *adj* easily shocked or upset by unpleasant things **~ly** *adv* **~ness** *n*

squeegee *n* tool with a flexible rubber blade, for spreading and removing liquid

squeeze *v* **1** *vt* press firmly (together), esp. from opposite sides **2** *vt* get or force out (as if) by pressure: *squeeze the juice from an orange* **3** *vi/t* fit or go by forcing or crowding: *She squeezed through the narrow opening.* **4** *vt* cause many difficulties to: *Higher lending rates are squeezing small businesses.* ♦ *n* **1** act of squeezing **2** difficult situation caused by high costs or not enough supplies

squelch *vi, n* (make) the sound of soft mud being pressed **~y** *adj*

squib *n* small firework

squid *n* **squid** *or* **squids** sea creature with ten arms at the end of its long body

squidgy *adj BrE infml* pastelike; soft and wet

squiffy *adj infml* slightly drunk

squiggle *n* short wavy or twisting line

squint *vi* **1** look with almost closed eyes **2** have a squint ♦ *n* **1** condition in which the eyes look in different directions **2** act of squinting

squire *n* main landowner in an English village or country area

squirearchy, squirarchy *n* class of country landowners **–archical** *adj*

squirm *vi* twist the body about, esp. from discomfort, shame, or nervousness

squirrel *n* small furry tree-climbing animal

squirt *vi/t, n* (force or be forced out in) a thin stream

Sr *abbrev. for:* Senior

SS[1] *abbrev. for:* steamship

SS[2] *n* Schutzstaffel; Hitler's bodyguard and special police force

ssh *interj* (used for asking for less noise)

St *abbrev. for:* **1** Street **2** Saint

-st *suffix* -est

stab *vi/t* **-bb-** strike forcefully (into) with a pointed weapon ♦ *n* **1** act of stabbing **2** try: *I'll have a stab at it.* **3 a stab in the back** an attack from someone supposed to be a friend **~bing** *adj* (of pain) sharp and sudden **~bing** *n*

stable[1] *adj* not easily moved, upset, or changed **–bilize -bilise** *vi/t* **–bilizer, -biliser** *n* **–bility** *n*

stable[2] *n* **1** building where horses are kept **2** group of things with one owner ♦ *vt* keep in a stable

stable lad *n* groom in a racing stable

stabling *n* room in a stable

staccato *adj, adv* played with very short notes

stack *n* **1** neat pile: *a stack of dishes* **2** large pile of hay or straw stored outdoors **3** also **stacks** *pl* large amount ♦ *vt* make into a neat pile (on)

stadium *n* **-diums** *or* **-dia** large building

containing a sports field and seats for spectators

staff *n* **1** the workers in a place **2 staves** long thick stick or pole **3** stave (1) ♦ *vt* provide workers for

stag *n* **1** fully grown male deer **2** *BrE* person who buys shares in a new company hoping to sell them quickly at a profit ♦ *adj* for men only: *a stag party*

stage *n* **1** raised floor on which plays are performed **2** centre of action or attention: *on the centre of the political stage* **3** state reached at a particular time in a course of events: *The project was cancelled at an early stage.* **4** part of a journey or long race **5** any of the separate driving parts of a rocket ♦ *vt* **1** perform or arrange for public show **2** cause to happen, esp. for public effect

stagecoach *n* (in former times) horse-drawn carriage providing a regular passenger service

stage door *n* entrance to a theatre used by the people working there

stage fright *n* nervousness felt at performing in front of an audience

stage-manage *vt* arrange for public effect, so that a desired result will happen as if naturally **~ment** *n*

stage manager *n* person in charge of a theatre stage

stagestruck *adj* in love with the theatre and esp. wishing to be an actor

stage whisper *n* loud whisper intended to be heard by everyone

stagey *adj* stagy

stagflation *n* condition of economic inflation combined with industrial stagnation

stagger *v* **1** *vi/t* walk unsteadily, almost falling **2** *vt* shock greatly **3** *vt* arrange so as to happen at different times ♦ *n* unsteady movement, as if about to fall

staging *n* **1** production of a play **2** scaffolding

staging post *n* place where regular stops are made on long journeys

stagnant *adj* **1** (esp. of water) not flowing or moving, and often bad-smelling **2** not developing or growing **-nate** *vi* cease to develop **-nation** *n*

stagy *adj* artificial

staid *adj* serious and dull by habit **~ly** *adv* **~ness** *n*

stain *vi/t* discolour in a way that is hard to repair ♦ *n* **1** stained place or spot **2** mark of guilt or shame

stained glass *n* coloured glass for making patterns in windows

stainless steel *n* steel that does not rust

stair *n* step in a set of stairs **stairs** *pl n* number of steps for going up or down, esp. indoors: *a flight of stairs*

staircase *n* set of stairs with its supports and side parts

stake *n* **1** pointed post for driving into the ground **2** share in a project, esp. investment **3** money risked on the result of something **4** post to which a person was tied for being killed, esp. by burning **5 at stake** at risk ♦ *vt* **1** risk the loss of (something) on a result **2 stake a claim** state that something should belong to one **stake out** *vt* keep secret watch on (a place)

stakeout *n* surveillance of an area or person

stalactite *n* sharp point of rock hanging from a cave roof

stalagmite *n* sharp point of rock standing on a cave floor

stale *adj* **1** no longer fresh **2** no longer interesting or new **~ ness** *n*

stalemate *n* **1** (in chess) position in which neither player can win **2** situation in which neither side in a quarrel can get an advantage

stalk[1] *n* thin plant part with one or more leaves, fruits, or flowers on it

stalk[2] *v* **1** *vt* hunt by following closely and secretly **2** *vi* walk stiffly or proudly

stall[1] *n* **1** *BrE* small open-fronted shop or other selling place in a market **2** indoor enclosure for an animal **stalls** *pl n BrE* seats on the main level of a theatre or cinema

stall[2] *vi/t* **1** (cause to) stop because there is not enough speed or engine power **2** delay ♦ *n* act of stalling

stallholder *n* person who rents and runs

a market stall
stallion *n* male horse kept for breeding
stalwart *adj, n* strong and dependable (person) **~ly** *adv* **~ness** *n*
stamen *n* male pollen-producing part of a flower
stamina *n* strength to keep going
stammer *vi/t* speak or say with pauses and repeated sounds ♦ *n* habit of stammering
stamp *v* **1** *vi/t* put (the feet) down hard **2** *vt* mark by pressing: *The title was stamped in gold on the book.* **3** *vt* stick a stamp onto **stamp out** *phr vt* put an end to ♦ *n* **1** small piece of paper for sticking onto e.g. a letter to be posted **2** tool for pressing or printing onto a surface: *a date-stamp* **3** mark made by this **4** act of stamping the foot
stampede *n* **1** sudden rush of frightened animals **2** sudden mass movement ♦ *vi/t* (cause to) go in a stampede or unreasonable rush
stamping ground *n* a favourite very familiar place
stance *n* **1** way of standing **2** way of thinking; attitude
stanch *vt AmE* staunch
stanchion *n* strong upright supporting bar
stand *v* **stood 1** *vi* support oneself on one's feet in an upright position **2** *vi* rise to a position of doing this: *They stood (up) when he came in.* **3** *vi* be in height: *He stands 5 feet 10 inches.* **4** *vi/t* (cause to) rest in a position, esp. upright or on a base: *The clock stood on the shelf.* **5** *vi* be in a particular state of affairs: *How do things stand at the moment?* **6** *vi* be in a position (to gain or lose): *He stands to win a fortune if he comes top.* **7** *vt* like; bear: *I can't stand whisky.* **8** *vi* remain true or in force: *My offer still stands.* **9** *vt* pay the cost of (something) for (someone else): *He stood them a wonderful meal.* **10** *vi BrE* compete for an office in an election: *standing for Parliament* **11 stand a chance/hope** have a chance/hope **12 stand on one's own two feet** be able to do without help from others **13 stand to reason** be clear to all sensible people **stand by** *phr v* **1** *vt* remain loyal to **2** *vt* keep (a promise, agreement, etc.) **3** *vi* be present or near **4** *vi* remain inactive when action is needed **5** *vi* wait in readiness **stand down** *phr vi* **1** yield one's position or chance of election **2** leave the witness box in court **stand for** *phr vt* **1** represent; mean: *The B in his name stands for Brian.* **2** have as a principle **3** accept without complaining **stand in** *phr vi* take the place of the usual person for a time **stand out** *phr vi* **1** have an easily-seen shape, colour, etc. **2** be clearly the best **stand up** *phr vt* **1** remain in good condition in spite of: *Will it stand up to continuous use?* **2** be accepted as true: *The charges will never stand up in court.* **3** fail to meet (someone, esp. of the oposite sex) as arranged **stand up for** *phr vt* defend; support ♦ *n* **1** place for selling or showing things **2** piece of furniture for putting things on: *a hatstand* **3** open-fronted building for watchers at a sports ground **4** raised stage: *the judge's stand* **5** strong defensive effort **6** *AmE* witness box
standard *n* **1** level of quality that is considered proper or acceptable **2** something fixed as a rule for measuring weight, value, etc. **3** ceremonial flag ♦ *adj* of the usual kind; ordinary **~ize** *vt* make all the same in accordance with a single standard **–ization** *n*
standard-bearer *n* **1** person who carries a standard **2** leader
standard lamp *n BrE* lamp on a tall base which stands on the floor
standard of living *n* degree of wealth and comfort in everyday life that a person, group, or country has
standby *n* **1** one kept ready for use **2 on standby: a** ready for action **b** able to travel, esp. in a plane, only if there is a seat no one else wants
stand-in *n* person who takes the place or job of someone else for a time

standing *n* **1** rank, esp. based on experience or respect **2** continuance: *a friend of long standing* ♦ *adj* continuing in use or force: *a standing invitation*

standing order *n BrE* order to a bank to pay a fixed amount to someone at fixed periods

standoff *n AmE* tie; deadlock

standoffish *adj* rather unfriendly **~ly** *adv* **~ness** *n*

standpipe *n* pipe directly connected to a water main

standpoint *n* point of view

standstill *n* condition of no movement; stop

stand-up *adj* **1** done or used by people standing up: *a stand-up meal* **2** concerned with telling jokes to an audience: *a stand-up comedian*

stank *past t. of* stink

stanza *n* division of a poem

staphylococcus /ˌstafiloh'kokəs/ *n* **-ci** bacterium that causes infection of wounds

staple¹ *n* piece of wire put through sheets of paper and bent to fasten them together ♦ *vt* fasten with staples **stapler** *n*

staple² *adj* used all the time; usual; ordinary ♦ *n* main product: *a staple among British products*

star *n* **1** very large mass of burning gas in space, seen as a small bright spot in the night sky **2** figure with five or more points, used as a sign of something: *a five star hotel* **3** heavenly body regarded as determining one's fate: *born under an unlucky star* **4** famous performer: *a film star* ♦ *v* **-rr- 1** *vi/t* appear or have as a main performer: *a film starring Charlie Chaplin* **2** *vt* mark with stars **~ry** *adj* filled with stars

starboard *n* right side of a ship or aircraft

starch *n* **1** white tasteless substance that is an important part of foods such as grain and potatoes **2** cloth-stiffening substance *vt* stiffen with starch **~y** *adj* **1** full of, or like, starch **2** stiffly correct and formal **-ily** *adv*

star chamber *n derog* secretive and powerful court

star-crossed *adj lit* ill-fated

stardom *n* state of being a famous performer

stardust *n* air of romance or magic

stare *vi* look for a long time with great attention ♦ *n* long steady look

starfish *n* flat sea animal with five arms forming a star shape

stargazer *n* **1** *infml* astronomer or astrologer **2** impractical dreamer **~ing** *n*

stark *adj* **1** hard, bare, or severe in appearance **2** complete: *stark terror* ♦ *adv* completely: *stark naked* **~ly** *adv* **~ness** *n*

starkers *adj infml* naked

starlet *n* young actress hoping to become famous

starling *n* common greenish-black European bird

starry-eyed *adj* full of unreasonable hopes

Stars and Stripes *n* the flag of the US

star-studded *adj* filled with famous performers

start *v* **1** *vi/t* begin **2** *vi/t* (cause to) come into existence: *How did the trouble start?* **3** *vi/t* (cause to) begin operation: *The car won't start.* **4** *vi* begin a journey **5** *vi* make a sudden sharp movement, esp. from surprise ♦ *n* **1** beginning of activity **2** first part or moments **3** place of starting **4** amount by which one is ahead of another **5** sudden sharp movement **~er** *n* **1** competitor in a race or match at the start **2** person who gives the signal for a race to begin **3** instrument for starting a machine **4** first part of a meal **5 for starters** first of all

starting gate *n* gate that opens to start a race

startle *vt* give a sudden slight shock to

starve *vi/t* **1** (cause to) suffer from great hunger **2** (cause to) not have enough: *starved of affection* **starvation** *n*

starveling *n* very thin person or animal

star wars *n infml* SDI

stash *vt infml* store secretly; hide **stash** *n*

state *n* **1** particular way of being; condition: *the current state of our economy* **2** *infml esp. BrE* very nervous, anxious condition: *Don't get in(to) such a state.* **3** government or political organization of a country: *industry controlled by the state* **4** nation; country **5** self-governing area within a nation: *the states of the US* **6** official grandness and ceremony ♦ *vt* say or mention, esp. formally or in advance **~less** *adj* belonging to no country **~lessness** *n* **~ly** *adj* **1** formal; ceremonious **2** grand in style or size **~liness** *n*

statecraft *n* skill of a statesman

State Department *n* the American government department which deals with foreign affairs

stately home *n* large country house of historical interest

statement *n* **1** (formal) written or spoken declaration **2** list showing money paid and received

state-of-the-art *adj* using the most modern methods or materials

stateroom *n* passenger's private room on a ship

States *infml* the US

stateside *adj, adv* of, in, or to the US

statesman *n* **-men** respected political or government leader **~ship** *n*

static *adj* **1** not moving or changing **2** of or being electricity that collects on the surface of objects ♦ *n* electrical noise spoiling radio or television signals **~ally** *adv*

statics *n* science dealing with the forces that produce equilibrium among solid bodies

station *n* **1 a** (building at) a place where the stated public vehicles regularly stop: *a bus station* **b** *esp. BrE* place like this where trains regularly stop **2** building for the stated service or activity: *a polling station* **3** broadcasting company or apparatus **4** one's position in life; social rank: *She married beneath her station.* ♦ *vt* put (esp. a person) into a certain place for esp. military duty

stationary *adj* not moving

stationer *n* seller of stationery

stationery *n* materials (esp. paper) for writing and typing

station house *n AmE* police station

stationmaster *n* person in charge of a railway station

station wagon *n AmE* estate car

statistics *pl n* **1** numbers which represent facts or measurements **2** science that deals with and explains these **–tical** *adj* **–tically** *adv* **statistician** *n* person who works with statistics

statuary *adj, n* (of or suitable for) statues

statue *n* (large) stone or metal likeness of a person, animal, etc.

statuesque *adj* like a statue in formal still beauty

statuette *n* small statue that goes on a table or shelf

stature *n* **1** degree to which someone is regarded as important or admirable **2** person's height

status *n* **1** rank or condition in relation to others **2** high social position **3** state of affairs at a particular time

status quo *n* existing state of affairs

statute *n* law

statute book *n* body of enacted law

statute law *n* written enacted law

statutory /ˈstatyoot(ə)ri/ *adj* fixed or controlled by law

staunch[1] *adj* dependably loyal; firm **~ly** *adv* **~ness** *n*

staunch[2] *vt* stop the flow of (blood)

stave *n* **1** set of five lines on which music is written **2** thin strip of wood **stave in** *phr vt* break **stave off** *phr vt* keep away: *just enough food to stave off hunger*

staves *pl of* staff (2)

stay[1] *vi* **1** remain in a place rather than leave **2** continue to be; remain: *trying to stay healthy* **3** live in a place for a while: *staying at a hotel* **4 stay put** not move **5 stay the course** last or continue for the whole length of **stay on** *phr vt* remain after the usual leaving time ♦ *n* **1** period of living in a place **2** *law* stopping or delay: *a stay of execution*

stay[2] *n* strong wire or rope that supports a mast

staying power *n* stamina

stays *pl n* old-fashioned corset

St Bernard *n* large strong Swiss dog used in mountain rescue

std *abbrev. for:* standard

STD *n* subscriber trunk dialling; system enabling direct dialling of long-distance telephone calls

stead *n* **in someone's stead** *fml* instead of someone

steadfast *adj* **1** firmly loyal **2** not moving or movable **~ly** *adv* **~ness** *n*

steady *adj* **1** firm; not shaking: *a steady hand* **2** not varying wildly; regular: *a steady speed* **3** not likely to change: *a steady job* **4** dependable ♦ *vi/t* make or become steady **–ily** *adv* **–iness** *n*

steak *n* flat piece of meat, esp. beef or fish

steak tartare *n* minced steak eaten raw

steal *v* **stole, stolen 1** *vi/t* take (what belongs to someone else) without permission **2** *vi* move secretly or quietly **3** *vt* take secretly or improperly: *stealing a look at someone* **4 steal the show** get all the attention and praise expected by someone else ♦ *n infml, esp. AmE* something for sale very cheaply

stealth *n* acting quietly and secretly or unseen **~y** *adj* **~ily** *adv*

steam *n* **1** water gas produced by boiling **2** power produced by steam under pressure: *a steam engine* **3 under one's/its own steam** by one's/its own power or effort ♦ *v* **1** *vi* give off steam **2** *vi* travel by steam power **3** *vt* cook with steam **4** *vt* use steam on: *He steamed the letter open.* **steam up** *phr vi/t* **1** cover or become covered with a mist of cooling water **2** *infml* make angry or excited **~er** *n* **1** ship driven by steam power **2** container for cooking food with steam **~y** *adj* **1** of or containing steam **2** *infml* erotic

steamed-up *adj infml* excited and angry

steamroller *n* vehicle with heavy metal rollers for flattening new road surfaces ♦ *vt* force in spite of all opposition: *He was steamrollered into signing the agreement.*

steamship *n* a large non-naval ship driven by steam power

steed *n lit* horse

steel *n* hard strong metal made from iron ♦ *vt* make (esp. oneself) unfeeling or determined **~y** *adj* like steel in colour or hardness **~iness** *n*

steel band *n* West Indian band playing drums cut from metal oil barrels

steel wool *n* fine steel fibres bunched together, used for scouring

steep[1] *adj* **1** rising or falling at a large angle **2** (esp. of a price) too high **~ly** *adv* **~ness** *n*

steep[2] *vt* **1** keep in liquid **2 steeped in** thoroughly filled or familiar with

steeple *n* high pointed church tower

steeplechase *n* long race with fences to jump over **~r** *n* **–sing** *n*

steeplejack *n* person who repairs towers and tall chimneys

steer[1] *vt* **1** direct the course of (esp. a boat or road vehicle) **2 steer clear (of)** keep away (from); avoid

steer[2] *n* young castrated male animal of the cattle family

steerage *n* part of a passenger ship for those with the cheapest tickets

steering wheel *n* wheel turned to make a vehicle go left or right

stein /s(h)tien/ *n* **1** earthenware beer mug **2** *AmE* tankard

stellar *adj* of the stars

stem[1] *n* **1** part of a plant on which leaves or smaller branches grow **2** narrow upright support: *the stem of a wineglass* **stem from** *phr vt* result from

stem[2] *vt* **-mm-** stop (the flow of)

stench *n* very strong bad smell

stencil *n* **1** sheet of stiff material with patterns or letters cut in it **2** mark made by putting paint or ink through the holes in this onto a surface ♦ *vt* **-ll-** (*AmE* **-l-**) make (a copy of) with a stencil

Sten gun *n* lightweight submachine gun
stenographer *n* shorthand typist
stentorian /sten'tawri·ən/ *adj fml* (of the voice) very loud
step *n* **1** act of moving by raising one foot and bringing it down somewhere else **2** the sound this makes **3** short distance: *It's just a step away from here.* **4** flat edge on which the foot is placed for going up or down **5** act, esp. in a set of actions, which should produce a certain result: *We must take steps to improve matters.* **6** movement of the feet in dancing **7 in/out of step: a** moving/not moving the feet at the same time as others in marching **b** in/not in accordance or agreement with others **8 step by step** gradually ♦ *vi* **-pp- 1** go by putting one foot usu. in front of the other **2** tread **3 step on it!** go faster **4 step out of line** act differently from others or from what is expected **step down/aside** *phr vi* leave one's job or position **step in** *phr vi* intervene **step up** *phr vt* increase
step- *prefix* related through a parent who has remarried
stepladder *n* folding two-part ladder joined at the top
steppes *pl n* large treeless area in Russia and parts of Asia
stepping-stone *n* **1** any of a row of large stones for walking across a stream on **2** way of improvement or getting ahead
stereo *adj* using a system of sound recording in which the sound comes from two different places ♦ *n* **-os 1** stereo record player **2** stereo sound
stereophonic *adj* stereo
stereoscopic *adj* seen or seeing in three dimensions
stereotype *n usu. derog* fixed set of ideas about what a particular type of person or thing is like ♦ *vt derog* treat as an example of a fixed general type **-typical** *adj* **-typically** *adv*
sterile *adj* **1** which cannot produce young **2** free from all (harmful) bacteria, etc. **3** lacking new ideas **4** (of land) not producing crops **-ility** *n* **-ilize, -ilise** *vt* make sterile **-ilization, -ilisation** *n*
sterling *n* British money ♦ *adj* **1** (esp. of silver) of standard value **2** of the highest standard, esp. in being loyal and brave
stern[1] *n* severe and serious **~ly** *adv* **~ness** *n*
stern[2] *n* back part of a ship
sternum *n* **-nums** *or* **-na** vertical bone at the front of the chest
steroid *n* chemical that has a strong effect on the workings of the body
stertorous /'stuhtərəs/ *adj* making a harsh snoring or gasping sound **~ly** *adv*
stethoscope *n* tube with which doctors can listen to people's heartbeats
stetson *n* hat with a wide brim worn by US cowboys
stevedore /'steevədaw/ *n* docker
stew *vi/t* cook slowly and gently in liquid ♦ *n* **1** dish of stewed meat and vegetables **2** confused anxious state of mind
steward *n* **1** person who serves passengers e.g. on a ship or plane **2** person in charge of a public meeting or event **steward** *vi/t*
stewardess *n* female steward
stick[1] *n* **1** small thin piece of wood **2** thin wooden or metal rod used e.g. for support while walking or in a game **3** thin rod of any material: *a stick of chalk/celery*
stick[2] *v* **stuck 1** *vt* push: *She stuck her fork into the meat.* **2** *vi/t* fasten or be fastened with glue or a similar substance **3** *vi/t* (cause to) become fixed in position: *He got his finger stuck in the hole.* **4** *vt infml* put: *Stick your coat down over there.* **5** *vt esp. BrE* like; bear **6** *vt BrE sl* keep (something unwanted by the speaker) **stick around** *phr vi* not go away **stick by** *phr vt* continue to support **stick out** *phr v* **1** *vi/t* (cause to) come out beyond a surface: *Her ears stick out.* **2** *vt* continue to the end of (something difficult) **3 stick one's neck out** *infml* take a risk **stick to** *phr vt* **1**

refuse to leave or change: *stick to one's decision* **2 stick to one's guns** *infml* continue on a course of action in spite of attacks **stick up for** *phr vt* defend (someone) by words or actions **~er** *n* **1** label with a message or picture, which can be stuck to things **2** *infml* determined person

sticking plaster *n* plaster (2)

stick-in-the-mud *n* person who will not change or accept new things

stickleback *n* small freshwater fish

stickler *n* person who demands the stated quality: *a stickler for punctuality*

stickpin *n* decorative pin

sticks *n infml* a country area far from modern life

stick-up *n infml* robbery carried out by threatening with a gun

sticky *adj* **1** like or covered with glue or a similar substance **2** difficult; awkward: *a sticky situation* **-iness** *n*

stiff *adj* **1** not easily bent or changed in shape **2** formal; not friendly **3** strong, esp. in alcohol **4** difficult; severe: *stiff competition* ♦ *adv* extremely: *I was scared stiff.* ♦ *n sl* dead body **~ly** *adv* **~en** *vi/t* make or become stiff **~ness** *n*

stiff-necked *adj* proudly obstinate

stiff upper lip *n* ability to accept unpleasant events without appearing upset

stifle *v* **1** *vi/t* (cause to) be unable to breathe properly **2** *vt* keep from happening: *stifling a yawn*

stigma *n* mark of shame **~tize** *vt* describe very disapprovingly

stigmata *pl n* (marks like) the nail marks on Christ's body

stile *n* arrangement of steps for climbing over a fence or wall

stiletto *n* **-tos** small thin dagger

stiletto heel *n BrE* high thin heel of a woman's shoe

still¹ *adv* **1** (even) up to this/that moment: *He's still here.* **2** in spite of that: *It's raining. Still, we must go out.* **3** even: *a still greater problem* **4** yet: *He gave still another reason.* ♦ *adj* **1** not moving **2** without wind **3** silent; calm **4** (of a drink) not containing gas ♦ *vi/t* make or become calm ♦ *n* photograph of a scene from a (cinema) film **~ness** *n*

still² *n* apparatus for making alcohol

stillbirth *n* child born dead

stillborn *adj* born dead

still life *n* **still lifes** painting of objects, esp. flowers and fruit

stilt *n* either of a pair of poles for walking around on high above the ground

stilted *adj* very formal and unnatural

Stilton *n* strong-tasting cheese with grey-blue marks

stimulate *vt* **1** cause to become more active or grow faster **2** *fml* excite (the body or mind) **-lant** *n* **1** drug which gives one more power to be active **2** stimulus **-lation** *n*

stimulus *n* **-li** something that causes activity

sting *vi/t* **stung 1** have, use, or prick with a sting **2** (cause to) feel sharp pain ♦ *n* **1** pain-producing organ used by certain insects and plants for attack or protection **2** wound caused by this **3** sharp pain

sting ray *n* fish of the ray family with a long tail and sharp spines on its back

stingy *adj infml* ungenerous; mean **-gily** *adv* **-giness** *n*

stink *vi* **stank, stunk 1** give off a strong bad smell **2** *infml* be very unpleasant or bad: *Your plan stinks.* ♦ *n* strong bad smell

stint *n* limited or fixed amount, esp. of shared work ♦ *vt* give too small an amount (of)

stipend /ˈstiepend/ *n* priest's wages

stipendiary /stieˈpendyəri/ *adj* receiving regular payment for professional services **stipendiary** *n*

stipple *vt* draw or paint (on) with dots or small strokes **stipple** *n* **-pling** *n*

stipulate *vt* state as a necessary condition **-lation** *n*

stir *v* **-rr- 1** *vt* move around and mix (esp. liquid) with e.g. a spoon **2** *vi/t* make or cause a slight movement (in): *She stirred in her sleep.* **3** *vt* excite: *a stir-*

ring tale of adventure **4** *vi infml* cause trouble between others **stir up** *phr vt* cause (trouble) ♦ *n* **1** act of stirring **2** (public) excitement
stirrup *n* D-shaped metal piece for a horse-rider's foot to go in
stirrup cup *n* farewell drink
stirrup pump *n* small hand pump held in place by the foot
stitch *n* **1** amount of thread put with a needle through cloth or through skin to close a wound **2** single turn of the wool round the needle in knitting **3** sharp pain in the side caused by running **4** *infml* clothes: *He hadn't got a stitch on.* **5 in stitches** laughing helplessly ♦ *vi/t* sew
stoat *n* European weasel
stock *n* **1** supply: *a large stock of food* **2** (supply of) goods for sale: *Have you any blue shirts in stock?* **3** money lent to a government or company: *stocks and shares* **4** liquid made from meat, bones, or vegetables, used in cooking **5** farm animals, esp. cattle **6** a family line, of the stated sort: *She comes from farming stock.* **7 take stock (of)** consider a situation carefully so as to make a decision ♦ *vt* keep supplies of ♦ *adj* commonly used, esp. without much meaning: *stock excuses*
stockade *n* strong defensive fence **stockade** *vt*
stockbroker *n* someone who buys and sells stocks and shares for others
stock car *n* ordinary car adapted for racing
stock exchange *n* place where stocks and shares are bought and sold
stockinet, -ette *n* soft stretchy fabric used esp. for bandages
stocking *n* close-fitting garment for a woman's foot and leg
stocking-filler *n* small inexpensive Christmas present
stock-in-trade *n* things habitually used: *A pleasant manner is part of a politician's stock-in-trade.*
stockist *n BrE* one who keeps particular goods for sale
stockman *n* **-men** man who looks after farm animals
stock market *n* stock exchange
stockpile *n* large store for future use ♦ *vt* make a stockpile of
stocks *pl n* wooden frame in which criminals were fastened in former times
stock-still *adv* not moving at all
stocktaking *n* making a list of goods held in a business
stocky *adj* thick, short, and strong **-ily** *adv* **-iness** *n*
stockyard *n* yard in which farm animals are kept before sale, slaughter, or shipping
stodge *n* unpleasantly heavy and uninteresting food **stodgy** *adj* **1** like stodge **2** uninteresting and difficult
stoic *n* person who remains calm and uncomplaining **~al** *adj* patient when suffering, like a stoic **~ally** *adv* **~ism** *n* stoical behaviour
stoke *vt* fill (an enclosed fire) with fuel **stoker** *n* person who fills and tends a furnace, esp. on a ship
stokehold *n* part of a steamship containing the boilers and furnaces
stol *adj* short takeoff and landing; (of an aircraft) able to operate from a short runway
stole[1] *past t. of* steal
stole[2] *n* long piece of material worn over the shoulders
stolen *past p. of* steal
stolid *adj* showing no excitement when strong feelings might be expected **~ly** *adv* **~ity** *n*
stomach *n* **1** baglike organ in the body where food is digested **2** front part of the body below the chest **3** desire; liking: *He's got no stomach for a fight.* ♦ *vt* accept without displeasure; bear
stomach pump *n* apparatus for drawing the contents out of the stomach
stomp *vi* walk heavily
stone *n* **1** fairly large piece of rock **2** rock **3** (*pl* **stone** *or* **stones**) a measure of weight equal to 14 pounds or 6.35 kilograms **4** single hard seed of certain

fruits **5** piece of hard material formed in an organ of the body ♦ *vt* **1** throw stones at **2** take the stone out of (a fruit) **stoned** *adj infml* **1** under the influence of drugs **2** very drunk **stony** *adj* **1** containing or covered with stones **2** cruel **stonily** *adv*

Stone Age *n* earliest known time in human history, when stone tools were used

stonemason *n* person who cuts stone for building

stone's throw *n* short distance

stonewall *vi esp. BrE* behave obstructively **~er** *n*

stoneware *n* strong ceramic ware made from clay containing flint

stonework *n* parts of a building made of stone

stony broke *adj BrE infml* having no money at all

stood *past t. and p. of* stand

stooge *n* person who habitually does what another wants

stool *n* seat without back or arm supports

stoolpigeon *n infml* person who helps the police to trap another

stoop *vt* **1** bend the upper body forwards and down **2** stand like this habitually **stoop to** *phr vt* lower one's standards by doing (something) ♦ *n* habitual stooping position

stop *v* **-pp- 1** *vi/t* (cause to) no longer be moving or operating **2** *vi/t* (cause to) end: *The rain has stopped.* **3** *vt* prevent **4** *vi* pause **5** *vi esp. BrE* remain; stay: *stopping at a fine hotel* **6** *vt* block: *The pipe's stopped up.* **7** *vt* stop from being given or paid: *stop a cheque* **stop off** *phr vi* make a short visit to a place while making a journey elsewhere **stop over** *phr vi* make a short stay before continuing a journey ♦ *n* **1** act of stopping or the state of being stopped **2** bus stop **3** (switch operating) a set of pipes on an organ **4 pull all the stops out** do everything possible to complete an action **~per** *n* object for closing a bottle

stopcock *n* tap for controlling the flow of water in a pipe

stopgap *n* something that fills a need for a time

stopover *n* short stay between parts of a journey

stoppage *n* **1** stopping, esp. of work **2** amount taken away from one's pay **3** blocked state

stop press *n* late news put into a paper

stopwatch *n* watch that can be started and stopped to measure periods exactly

storage *n* (price paid for) storing

store *vt* **1** make and keep a supply of for future use **2** keep in a special place while not in use ♦ *n* **1** supply for future use **2** place for keeping things **3** large shop **4** *esp. AmE* shop **5 in store: a** being stored **b** about to happen: *There's trouble in store.* **6 set . . . store by** feel to be of (the stated amount of) importance **stores** *pl n* (building or room containing) military or naval goods and food

storey, *AmE* **-ry** *n* floor or level in a building

storied *adj lit* celebrated in stories or history

stork *n* large bird with a long beak, neck, and legs

storm *n* **1** rough weather condition with rain and strong wind **2** sudden violent show of feeling: *a storm of protest* **3 take by storm: a** conquer by a sudden violent attack **b** win great approval from (those who watch a performance) ♦ *v* **1** *vt* attack (a place) with sudden violence **2** *vi* go angrily **~y** *adj*

storm trooper *n* member of the Nazi party militia

stormy petrel *n* small black and white seabird

story *n* **1** account of events, real or imagined **2** news article **3** lie: *Have you been telling stories again?* **4** *AmE* storey

storybook *adj* as perfectly happy as in a fairy story for children

story line *n* events in a film, book, or play

stoup *n* **1** large drinking vessel **2** basin

for holy water in a church
stout *adj* **1** rather fat **2** brave and determined **3** strong and thick ♦ *n* strong dark beer **~ly** *adv* **~ness** *n*
stouthearted *adj lit* brave **~ly** *adv*
stove *n* enclosed apparatus that can be heated for cooking or to provide warmth
stow *vt* put away or store, esp. on a ship **stow away** *phr vi* hide on a ship or plane in order to make a free journey
stowage *n* (space for) stowing
stowaway *n* person who stows away
straddle *vt* **1** have one's legs on either side of **2** be or fall on either side of (something), rather than in the middle
strafe *vt* attack with gunfire from an aircraft
straggle *vi* move, grow, or spread untidily **–gler** *n* one who is behind a main group **–gly** *adj* growing or lying untidily
straight *adj* **1** not bent or curved **2** level or upright **3** neat; tidy **4** honest, open, and truthful **5** (of the face) with a serious expression **6** (of alcohol) without added water **7** correct: *set the record straight* **8** *sl* heterosexual ♦ *n* straight part, esp. on a race track ♦ *adv* **1** in a straight line **2** directly (and without delay): *Get straight to the point.* **3** clearly: *I can't think straight.* **4 go straight** leave a life of crime **~ness** *n*
straight and narrow *n* honest life
straightaway *adv* at once
straightedge *n* tool with a straight edge for testing the flatness of surfaces
straighten *vt* (cause to) become straight, level, or tidy **straighten out** *phr vt* remove the confusions or difficulties in: *straighten out one's business affairs* **straighten up** *phr vi* get up from a bent position
straightforward *adj* **1** honest and open, without hidden meanings **2** simple **~ly** *adv* **~ness** *n*
straight up *adv BrE infml* honestly (used in questions and answers)
strain¹ *v* **1** *vt* damage (a body part) through too much effort or pressure **2** *vi* make (too) great efforts **3** *vt* separate (a liquid and solid) by pouring through esp. a strainer **4** *vt* force beyond acceptable or believable limits: *straining the truth* ♦ *n* **1** (force causing) the condition of being tightly stretched **2** troubling influence **3** damage caused by straining a body part **~ed** *adj* **1** not natural in behaviour; unfriendly **2** tired or nervous **~er** *n* instrument with a net for straining things
strain² *n* **1** breed or type of plant or animal **2** *lit* tune
strait also **straits** *pl* — *n* narrow water passage between two areas of land **straits** *pl n* difficult situation: *in dire straits*
straitened *adj* difficult because lacking money
straitjacket *n* **1** garment for a violently mad person that prevents arm movement **2** something preventing free development
straitlaced *adj* having severe, rather old-fashioned ideas about morals
strand¹ *n* single thin thread
strand² shore
stranded *adj* in a helpless position, unable to get away
strange *adj* **1** unusual; surprising **2** unfamiliar **~ly** *adv* **~ness** *n*
stranger *n* **1** unfamiliar person **2** person in an unfamiliar place
strangle *vt* **1** kill by pressing the throat to stop breathing **2** stop the proper development of **–gler** *n* **–gulation** *n*
stranglehold *n* strong control which prevents action
strap *n* strong narrow band used as a fastening or support ♦ *vt* **-pp-** fasten with straps
straphanging *n infml* **1** holding on to a strap or handle for support while standing in a bus or train **2** commuting **~ger** *n*
strapping *adj* big and strong
strata *pl of* stratum
stratagem *n* trick or plan for deceiving or gaining an advantage
strategic *adj* **1** part of a plan, esp. in war

2 right for a purpose **~ally** *adv*
strategist *n* person skilled in (military) planning
strategy *n* **1** skilful (military) planning **2** particular plan for winning success
stratify *vt* arrange in separate levels or strata **–fication** *n*
stratosphere *n* outer air surrounding the Earth, starting at about 10 kilometres above the Earth
stratum *n* **-ta 1** band of a particular rock **2** part of something thought of as divided into different levels
straw *n* **1** dried stems of grain plants, such as wheat **2** single such stem **3** thin tube for sucking up liquid
strawberry *n* (plant with) a small red juicy fruit
strawberry mark *n* red birthmark
straw poll *n* unofficial examination of opinions before an election, to see what the result is likely to be
stray *vi* wander away ♦ *n* animal lost from its home ♦ *adj* **1** wandering; lost **2** single; not in a group
streak *n* **1** thin line or band, different from what surrounds it **2** bad quality of character: *a stubborn streak* **3** period marked by a particular quality: *a lucky streak* ♦ *v* **1** *vi* move very fast **2** *vt* cover with streaks **~y** *adj* marked with streaks **~er** *n* person who runs naked through a public place
stream *n* **1** small river **2** something flowing: *a stream of traffic* **3** group of pupils of similar ability **4 on stream** in(to) production ♦ *v* **1** *vi* flow strongly **2** *vi* move in a continuous flowing mass **3** *vi* float in the air **4** *vt esp. BrE* group in streams **~er** *n* long narrow piece of paper for throwing
streamline *vt* **1** give a smooth shape which moves easily through water or air **2** make more simple and effective **–lined** *adj*
street *n* **1** road in a town **2 streets ahead** much better **3 up/down one's street** in one's area of interest
streetcar *n AmE* tram
street-credibility also *infml* **street-cred** *n* popular acceptance among young esp. working-class people
streetwalker *n* prostitute
streetwise *adj infml* clever enough to succeed and live well in the hard world of the city streets
strength *n* **1** (degree of) being strong **2** way in which something is good or effective: *the strengths and weaknesses of the plan* **3** force measured in numbers: *The police are at full strength.* **4 on the strength of** persuaded or influenced by **~en** *vi/t* become or make strong or stronger
strenuous *adj* **1** needing great effort **2** showing great activity: *a strenuous denial* **~ly** *adv* **~ness** *n*
streptococcus *n* **-ci** bacterium causing infections esp. in the throat **–cal** *adj*
streptomycin /ˌstreptəˈmiesin/ *n* strong drug that kills bacteria
stress *n* **1** (worry resulting from) pressure caused by difficulties **2** force of weight caused by pressure **3** sense of special importance **4** degree of force put on a part of a word when spoken, or on a note in music: *In 'under' the main stress is on 'un'.* ♦ *vt* **1** mention strongly **2** put stress on (part of a word)
stretch *v* **1** *vi/t* (cause to) become wider or longer **2** *vi* spread out: *The forest stretched for miles.* **3** *vi* be elastic **4** *vi* straighten one's limbs to full length: *stretch out your arms* **5** *vt* allow to go beyond exact limits: *stretch a rule* **6 stretch one's legs** have a walk esp. after sitting for a long time ♦ *n* **1** act of stretching **2** elasticity **3** long area of land or water **4** continuous period: *14 hours at a stretch* **5 at full stretch** using all one's powers **~y** *adj* elastic
stretcher *n* covered frame for carrying a sick person
strew *vt* **strewed, strewn** *or* **strewed** *esp. lit* **1** scatter **2** lie scattered over
strewth *interj BrE sl* (used to express surprise and annoyance)
striated /strieˈaytid/ *adj* striped
striation *n* **1** stripe **2** arrangement of stripes

stricken *adj* showing the effect of trouble or illness: *grief-stricken*

strict *adj* **1** severe in making people behave properly **2 a** exact: *strict instructions* **b** complete: *in strict secrecy* **~ly** *adv* **~ness** *n*

stricture *n* **1** expression of blame **2** limit

stride *vi* **strode, stridden** walk with long steps ♦ *n* **1** long step **2 make strides** improve or do well **3 take something in one's stride** deal with a difficult situation easily

strident *adj* with a hard sharp sound or voice **~ly** *adv* **–dency** *n*

strides *pl n AustrE infml* trousers

stridulate *vi* (of insects) make noise by rubbing parts of the body together **–ation** *n*

strife *n* trouble and quarrelling between people

strike *v* **struck 1** *vt* hit sharply **2** *vt* make a (sudden) attack **3** *vt* harm suddenly: *They were struck down with illness.* **4** *vt* light (a match) **5** *vi/t* **a** make known (the time), esp. by the hitting of a bell **b** (of time) be made known in this way **6** *vi* stop working because of disagreement **7** *vt* find; meet: *strike oil* **8** *vt* have a particular effect on: *Her behaviour struck me as odd.* **9** *vt* come suddenly to mind **10** *vt* produce (a coin or similar object) **11** *vt* make (an agreement): *strike a bargain* **12 strike a chord** remind someone of something **13 strike a note of** express (a need for): *The book strikes a warning note.* **14 strike camp** take down tents when leaving a camping place **15 strike it rich** find sudden wealth **strike off** *phr vt* remove (someone or their name) from (an official list) **strike out** *phr vi* **1** go purposefully in the stated direction **2 strike out on one's own** take up an independent life **3** cross out **strike up** *phr vt* **1** begin playing or singing **2** start to make (a friendship) ♦ *n* **1** act or time of striking: *The workers are on strike.* **2** attack, esp. by aircraft **3** success in finding esp. a mineral in the earth: *an oil strike*

strikebound *adj* subject to a strike

strikebreaker *n* worker hired to do a striker's job **–king** *n* action taken to break up a strike

striker *n* **1** worker on strike **2** attacking player in football

striking *adj* very noticeable, esp. because beautiful or unusual **~ly** *adv*

striking distance *n* **within striking distance** very close (to)

Strine *n infml* Australian English

string *n* **1** thin cord **2** thin cord or wire stretched across a musical instrument to give sound **3** set of objects on a thread: *a string of pearls* **4** set of things or events following each other closely: *a whole string of complaints* **5 no strings attached** (esp. of an agreement) with no limiting conditions **6 two strings to one's bow** more than one interest or ability **strings** *pl n* all the (players of) violins, cellos, etc., in an orchestra ♦ *vt* **strung 1** put strings on (a musical instrument or racket **2** put with others onto a thread **3 highly strung** (of a person) very sensitive and easily excited **4 strung up** very excited, nervous, or worried **string along** *phr v* **1** *vt* encourage the hopes of deceitfully **2** *vi* go (with someone else) for a time, esp. for convenience **string out** *phr vt* spread out in a line **string up** *phr vt* **1** hang high **2** kill by hanging **~y** *adj* **1** (of food) full of unwanted threadlike parts **2** unpleasantly thin, so that the muscles show

string bean *n AmE* runner bean

stringent *adj* (esp. of rules or limits) severe **~ly** *adv* **–ency** *n*

strip *v* **-pp- 1** *vt* remove (the covering or parts of) **2** *vi/t* undress, usu. completely **3** *vt* remove the parts of (esp. an engine) **strip of** *phr vt* take away (something of value) from ♦ *n* **1** narrow piece **2** clothes of a particular colour worn by a team in soccer **~per** *n* **1** striptease performer **2** tool or liquid for removing things: *paint stripper*

strip cartoon *n BrE* comic strip

stripe *n* **1** different-coloured band **2**

usu. V-shaped sign worn on a uniform to show rank **striped** *adj* **stripy** *adj*

strip lighting *n* lighting provided by long fluorescent tubes

stripling *n lit* young man

strip mining *n* open-cast mining

striptease *n* removal of clothes by a person, performed as a show

strive *vi* **strove** *or* **strived, striven** *or* **strived** make a great effort

strobe light, strobe *n* light which goes on and off very quickly

stroboscope *n* instrument giving very short glimpses of a moving object

strode *past t. of* stride

stroke *vt* pass the hand over gently ♦ *n* **1** hit, esp. with a weapon **2** act of stroking **3** line made by a single movement of a pen or brush **4** act of hitting a ball **5** (movement repeated in) a method of swimming **6** sudden bursting of a blood vessel in the brain **7** unexpected piece (of luck) **8** sound of a clock striking **9 at a stroke** with one direct action

stroll *vi, n* (take) a slow walk for pleasure **~er** *n* **1** person who strolls or is strolling **2 a** *BrE* light foldable pushchair **b** *AmE* pushchair

strolling *adj* travelling from place to place

strong *adj* **1** having great power **2** not easily becoming broken, changed, destroyed, or ill **3** having a powerful effect on the mind or senses: *a strong smell* **4** (of a drink or drug) having a lot of the substance which gives taste or produces effects: *This coffee's too strong.* **5** having the stated number of members: *a club 50 strong* **6 strong on: a** good at doing **b** eager and active in dealing with **~ly** *adv*

strongbox *n* firm lockable box for keeping valuable things in

stronghold *n* **1** fort **2** place where a particular activity is common

strong language *n* swearing; curses

strong point *n* something one is good at

strong room *n* special lockable room esp. in a bank where valuable things are kept

strontium *n* soft metal, of which a harmful form (**strontium 90**) is given off by atomic explosions

strop *n* leather strap for sharpening razors

strophe *n* group of lines in a poem **-phic** *adj*

stroppy *adj BrE infml* tending to quarrel or disobey **-pily** *adv*

strove *past t. of* strive

struck *past t. and p. of* strike

structure *n* **1** way in which parts are formed into a whole **2** something constructed or organized ♦ *vt* arrange so that each part is properly related to others **-tural** *adj* **-turally** *adv*

strudel *n* thin pastry rolled round a fruit filling

struggle *vi* **1** make violent movements, esp. in fighting **2** make a great effort ♦ *n* hard fight or effort

strum *vi/t* **-mm-** play carelessly or informally on (esp. a guitar, banjo, or piano)

strumpet *n arch.* prostitute

strung *past t. and p. of* string

strut¹ *n* supporting rod in a structure

strut² *vi* **-tt-** walk proudly

strychnine /ˈstrikneen/ *n* poisonous drug

stub *n* **1** short left-over part of esp. a cigarette or pencil **2** small piece left in a book after tearing out a cheque or ticket ♦ *vt* **-bb-** hit (one's toe) against something **stub out** *phr vt* put out (a cigarette) by pressing **~by** *adj* short and thick: *stubby fingers*

stubble *n* **1** short growth of beard **2** remains of cut wheat **-bly** *adj*

stubborn *adj* **1** having a strong will; (unreasonably) determined **2** difficult to use, move, or change **~ly** *adv* **~ness** *n*

stucco *n* plaster stuck (decoratively) onto walls

stuck *past t. and p. of* stick ♦ *adj* **1** unable to go further because of difficulties **2 stuck with** having to do or have, esp. unwillingly **3 get stuck in** *infml* begin forcefully

stuck-up *adj infml* too proud in manner
stud[1] *n* **1** removable button-like fastener, esp. for collars **2** large-headed nail ♦ *vt* **-dd-** cover (as if) with studs
stud[2] *n* **1** number of horses kept for breeding **2** *taboo* man who has sex a lot and thinks he is very good at it
studbook *n* record of pedigrees, esp. of horses
student *n* **1** person studying at a college or university **2** person with a stated interest: *a student of life*
studio *n* **1** place where films, recordings, or broadcasts are made **2** workroom for a painter or photographer
studious *adj* **1** fond of studying **2** careful **~ly** *adv* **~ness** *n*
study *n* **1** also **studies** *pl* act of studying **2** thorough enquiry into a particular subject, esp. including a piece of writing on it **3** workroom; office **4** drawing or painting of a detail: *a study of a flower* **5** piece of music for practice ♦ *v* **1** *vi/t* spend time in learning **2** *vt* examine carefully **studied** *adj* carefully considered: *a studied remark* **studiedly** *adv*
stuff *n* **1** matter; material **2** one's possessions or the things needed to do something ♦ *vt* **1** fill **2** push so as to be inside **3** put stuffing inside **4** fill the skin of (a dead animal) to make it look real **5** cause (oneself) to eat as much as possible **6 get stuffed!** *sl* (an expression of dislike, esp. for what someone has said) **stuff up** *phr vt* block **~ing** *n* **1** filling material **2** cut-up food put inside a fowl before cooking
stuffed shirt *n* dull person who thinks himself important
stuffy *adj* **1** (having air) that is not fresh **2** *derog* formal and old-fashioned **–ily** *adv* **–iness** *n*
stultify *vt* make (someone's) mind dull **–fication** *n*
stumble *vi* **1** catch one's foot on something and start to fall **2** stop and/or make mistakes in speaking **stumble across/on/upon** *phr vt* meet or find by chance
stumbling block *n* something preventing action or development
stump[1] *n* **1** base of a cut-down tree **2** useless end of something long that has been worn down or cut off **3** any of the three sticks at which the ball is aimed in cricket ♦ *v* **1** *vt* leave (someone) unable to reply **2** *vi* walk heavily or awkwardly **~y** *adj* short and thick in body
stun *vt* **-nn-** **1** make unconscious **2** shock greatly **3** delight **~ning** *adj* very attractive **~ningly** *adv* **~ner** *n* attractive person
stung *past t. and p. of* sting
stunk *past p. of* stink
stunt[1] *n* **1** dangerous act of skill **2** attention-getting action: *publicity stunts*
stunt[2] *vt* prevent full growth (of)
stunt man *n* person who does stunts esp. in films
stunt woman *n* woman who does stunts
stupefy *vt* **1** surprise (and annoy) extremely **2** make unable to think **–faction** *n*
stupendous *adj* surprisingly great or good **~ly** *adv* **~ness** *n*
stupid *adj* foolish **~ly** *adj* **~ity** *n*
stupor *n* nearly unconscious unthinking state
sturdy *adj* **1** strong and firm **2** determined **–dily** *adv* **–diness** *n*
sturgeon *n* large edible fish
stutter *vi/t* speak or say with difficulty in pronouncing esp. the first consonant of words ♦ *n* habit of stuttering
sty[1], **stye** *n* infected place on the eyelid
sty[2] *n* pigsty
Stygian /ˈstiji·ən/ *adj* unpleasantly dark
style *n* **1** (typical) manner of doing something **2** fashion, esp. in clothes **3** high quality of social behaviour or appearance **4** type or sort **5 in style** in a grand way ♦ *vt* **1** design **2** give (a title) to: *He styles himself 'Lord'.* **stylish** *adj* fashionable and good-looking **stylishly** *adv* **stylist** *n* **1** person who invents styles or fashions **2** person with a (good) style of writing **stylize** *vt* present in a simplified style rather than naturally **stylistic** *adj* of style

stylus *n* **-luses** *or* **-li** needle-like instrument in a record player that picks up sound signals from a record
stymie *vt infml* thwart
styptic *n, adj* (substance) which stops bleeding
Styrofoam *n AmE tdmk for* polystyrene
suave /swahv/ *adj* with smooth (but perhaps insincere) good manners **~ly** *adv* **~ness** *n*
sub *n infml* **1** submarine **2** substitute **3** *BrE* amount of money paid to someone from their wages before the usual day of payment ♦ *vt* **-bb-** subedit
sub- *prefix* **1** under; below: *subzero* **2** smaller part of: *subcategory* **3** less than; worse than: *subhuman* **4** next in rank below: *sublieutenant*
subaltern /ˈsubəlt(ə)n/ *n BrE* army officer of lower rank than a captain
subaqua *adj* of or for underwater sports
subatomic *adj* smaller than an atom
subconscious *adj, n* (present at) a hidden level of the mind, not consciously known about **~ly** *adv* **~ness** *n*
subcontinent *n* large mass of land smaller than a continent, esp. India
subcontract *vt* hire someone else to do (work which one has agreed to do) **~or** *n* person or firm that has had work subcontracted to it
subculture *n* (customs of) a particular group within a society
subcutaneous /subkyoohˈtaynyəs/ *adj med* beneath the skin
subdivide *vt* divide into even smaller parts **-division** *n*
subdue *vt* **1** gain control of **2** make gentler **-dued** *adj* **1** of low brightness or sound **2** unusually quiet in behaviour
subedit *vt* look at and put right (material to be printed) **~or** *n*
subheading also **subhead** *n* title of part of a piece of writing
subhuman *adj* of less than human qualities
subject *n* **1** thing being dealt with, represented, or considered: *the subject of the painting* **2** branch of knowledge being studied **3** word that comes before a main verb and represents the person or thing that performs the action of the verb or about which something is stated **4** member of a state: *British subjects* ♦ *adj* **1** tending; likely: *He's subject to ill health.* **2** not independent: *a subject race* **3 subject to** depending on: *subject to your approval* ♦ *vt* defeat and control **subject to** *phr vt* cause to experience or suffer **~ion** *n* **1** act of subjecting **2** state of being severely controlled by others
subjective *adj* **1** influenced by personal feelings (and perhaps unfair) **2** existing only inside the mind; not real **~ly** *adv* **-tivity** *n*
subjoin *vt fml* add at the end
sub judice /subˈjoohdisi/ *adj* now being considered in a court of law, and therefore not allowed to be publicly mentioned
subjugate *vt* defeat and make obedient **-gation** *n*
subjunctive *adj, n* (of) a verb form expressing doubt, wishes, or unreality: *In 'if I were you' the verb 'were' is in the subjunctive.*
sublease *vt* sublet ♦ *n* contract of subletting
sublet *vt* **-let,** *pres. p.* **-tt-** rent (property rented from someone) to someone else
sublimate *vt* replace (natural urges, esp. sexual) with socially acceptable activities **-mation** *n*
sublime *adj* **1** very noble or wonderful **2** *infml* complete and usu. careless or unknowing **~ly** *adv* **-limity** *n*
subliminal *adj* at a level which the ordinary senses are not conscious of **~ly** *adv*
submachine gun *n* light machinegun
submarine *n* (war)ship which can stay under water ♦ *adj* under or in the sea
submariner *n* one of the crew of a submarine
submerge *vi/t* **1** (cause to) go under the surface of water **2** cover or completely hide **-mersion** *n* act of submerging or state of being submerged

–**mergence** *n*

submersible *n, adj* (boat) which can go under water

submit *v* **-tt- 1** *vi* admit defeat **2** *vt* offer for consideration **3** *vt esp. law* suggest –**mission** *n* **1** submitting **2** opinion **3** obedience **4** *law* request; suggestion –**missive** *adj* too obedient –**missively** *adv* –**missiveness** *n*

subnormal *adj* below average

suborbital *adj* of less than one orbit

subordinate *adj* less important ♦ *n* someone of lower rank ♦ *vt* put in a subordinate position –**ation** *n*

suborn /sə'bawn/ *vt law* persuade to do wrong, esp. tell lies in court

subplot *n* second, less important plot in a play or novel

subpoena /sə(b)'peenə/ *n* written order to attend a court of law **subpoena** *vt*

subscribe *vi* pay regularly, esp. to receive a magazine **subscribe to** *phr vt* agree with; approve of –**scriber** *n*

subscription *n* **1** act of subscribing (to) **2** amount paid regularly, esp. to belong to a society or receive a magazine

subsequent *adj* coming afterwards or next ~**ly** *adv*

subservient *adj* too willing to obey ~**ly** *adv* –**ence** *n*

subset *n* set that is part of a larger set

subside *vi* **1** return to its usual level; become less **2** (of land or a building) sink down **subsidence** *n*

subsidiary *adj* connected with but less important than the main one ♦ *n* subsidiary company

subsidy *n* money paid, esp. by government, to make prices lower or encourage an activity –**dize** *vt* give a subsidy to (someone) for (something): *subsidized school meals*

subsist *vi* remain alive ~**ence** *n* **1** ability to live, esp. on little money or food **2** state of living with little money or food

subsoil *n* layer of material between surface soil and rock

subsonic *adj* (flying) at less than the speed of sound

substance *n* **1** material; type of matter: *a sticky substance* **2** truth: *There is no substance in these rumours.* **3** real meaning, without the unimportant details **4** wealth **5** importance, esp. in relation to real life: *There was no real substance in the speech.*

substantial *adj* **1** solid; strongly made **2** satisfactorily large: *a substantial meal* **3** noticeably large (and important): *substantial changes* **4** concerning the main part **5** wealthy ~**ly** *adv* **1** in all important ways: *They are substantially the same.* **2** quite a lot

substantiate *vt* prove the truth of –**ation** *n*

substantive *adj* having reality, actuality, or importance

substation *n* place where electricity from a generating station is transformed for distribution

substitute *n* one taking the place of another ♦ *v* **1** *vt* put in place of another **2** *vi* act or be used instead –**tution** *n*

substratum *n* –**ta** level or foundation lying beneath another

substructure *n* foundation

subsume *vt fml* include

subsume *vt fml* include as part of a group –**sumption** *n*

subtenant *n* person to whom property is sublet

subtend *vt* (in geometry) have opposite

subterfuge *n* deceiving or slightly dishonest trick(s)

subterranean *adj* underground

subtitle *n* secondary or explanatory title –**ed** *adj*

subtitles *pl n* translation printed over a foreign film

subtle *adj* **1** hardly noticeable: *subtle differences* **2** clever in arrangement: *a subtle plan* **3** very clever in noticing and understanding –**tly** *adv* –**tlety** *n*

subtotal *n* total which is part of a larger total

subtract *vt* take (a number or amount) from a larger one ~**ion** *n*

subtropical *adj* of or suited to an area near the tropics

suburb *n* outer residential area of a town **~an** *adj*
suburbia *n* (life and ways of people who live in) suburbs
subvention *n fml* financial support
subvert *vt* try to destroy the power and influence of **–versive** *adj* trying to destroy established ideas or defeat those in power **–versively** *adv* **–versiveness** *n* **–version** *n*
subway *n* **1** path under a road or railway **2** *AmE* underground railway
succeed *v* **1** *vi* do what one has been trying to do **2** *vi* do well, esp. in gaining position or popularity **3** *vt* follow after **4** *vi/t* be the next to take a rank or position (after): *Hammond succeeded Jones as champion.*
success *n* **1** degree of succeeding; good result **2** person or thing that succeeds **~ful** *adj* **~fully** *adv*
succession *n* **1** following one after the other: *in quick succession* **2** many following each other closely: *a succession of visitors* **3** succeeding to a position
successive *adj* following each other closely in time **~ly** *adv*
successor *n* person who takes an office or position formerly held by another
succinct /sək'singkt/ *adj* clearly expressed in few words **~ly** *adv* **~ness** *n*
succour, *AmE* **-cor** *vt, n lit* help
succubus *n* **-bi** demon in female form who has sexual intercourse with sleeping men
succulent *adj* **1** juicy and tasty **2** (of a plant) having thick leaves or stems that hold liquid ♦ *n* succulent plant **~ly** *adv* **–lence** *n*
succumb *vi* stop opposing
such *predeterminer, determiner* **1** of that kind: *I dislike such people.* **2** to so great a degree: *He's such a kind man.* **3** so great; so good, bad or unusual: *He wrote to her every day, such was his love for her.* ♦ *pron* **1 any/no/some such** any/no/some (person or thing) like that: *No such person exists.* **2 as such** properly so named
such and such *predeterminer infml* a certain (time, amount, etc.) not named
suchlike *adj, pron* (things) of that kind
suck *v* **1** *vi/t* draw (liquid) in with the muscles of the mouth **2** *vt* hold (something) in one's mouth and move one's tongue against it: *sucking one's thumb* **3** *vt* draw powerfully: *The current sucked them under.* **suck** *n*
sucker *n* **1** person or thing that sucks **2** flat piece which sticks to a surface by suction **3 a** easily cheated person **b** someone who likes the stated thing very much: *a sucker for ice cream* **4** long shoot from the roots or base of a plant
suckle *vi/t* feed with milk from the breast
suckling *n arch.* child or young animal still fed on its mother's milk
sucrose *n tech* common form of sugar
suction *n* drawing away air or liquid, esp. to lower the air pressure between two objects and make them stick to each other
sudden *adj* happening unexpectedly and quickly **~ly** *adv* **~ness** *n*
suds *pl n* mass of soapy bubbles
sue *vi/t* bring a legal claim (against)
suede *n* soft leather with a rough surface
suet *n* hard fat used in cooking
suffer *v* **1** *vi* experience pain or difficulty **2** *vt* experience (something unpleasant) **3** *vt* accept without dislike: *He doesn't suffer fools gladly.* **4** *vi* grow worse: *His work has suffered since his illness.* **~ing** *n*
sufferance *n* **on sufferance** with permission, though not welcomed
suffice *vi/t* be enough (for)
sufficient *adj* enough **~ly** *adv* **–ciency** *n*
suffix *n* group of letters or sounds added at the end of a word (as in kind*ness*, quick*ly*)
suffocate *vi/t* (cause to) die because of lack of air **–cation** *n*
suffragan *adj* (of a bishop) assisting or subordinate to a bishop of higher rank

suffragan *n*
suffrage *n* right to vote in national elections
suffragette *n* woman seeking the right to vote by militant tactics
suffuse *vt* spread all through **-fusion** *n*
sugar *n* sweet white or brown plant substance used in food and drinks ♦ *vt* put sugar in **~y** *adj* **1** containing or tasting of sugar **2** insincerely pleasant
sugarcane *n* tall tropical plant from whose stems sugar is obtained
sugar daddy *n infml* older man who provides a young woman with money and presents in return for sex and companionship
suggest *vt* **1** state as an idea for consideration **2** give signs (of): *The latest figures suggest that business is improving.* **~ive** *adj* **1** (perhaps) showing thoughts of sex **2** which leads the mind into a particular way of thinking **~ively** *adv* **~ible** *adj* easily influenced **~ion** *n* act of suggesting or something suggested
suicide *n* **1** killing oneself **2** person who does this **3** action that destroys one's position **-cidal** *adj* **1** likely or wishing to kill oneself **2** likely to lead to death or destruction
suit *n* **1** short coat with trousers or skirt of the same material **2** garment for a special purpose: *a bathing suit* **3** any of the four sets of playing cards ♦ *vt* **1** be convenient for; satisfy **2** match or look good on (someone): *That hairstyle doesn't suit you.* **3 be suited (to/for)** be suitable **4 suit oneself** do what one likes
suitable *adj* fit or right for a purpose **-bly** *adv* **-bility** *n*
suitcase *n* case for carrying clothes and possessions when travelling
suite *n* **1** set of matching furniture **2** set of hotel rooms **3** piece of music made up of several parts
suiting *n* material for making men's suits
suitor *n lit* man wishing to marry a particular woman
sulk *vi* be silently bad-tempered **~y** *adj* **~ily** *adv* **~iness** *n*
sullen *adj* showing silent dislike, bad temper, or lack of interest **~ly** *adv* **~ness** *n*
sully *vt lit* spoil
sulpha drug also **sulphonamide** *n* drug used against disease-causing bacteria
sulphate, *AmE* **-fate** *n* salt formed from sulphuric acid
sulphide *n* compound of sulphur with another element
sulphur, *AmE* **-fur** *n* substance found esp. as a light yellow powder **~ous** *adj*
sulphuric acid *n* powerful acid
Sultan *n* Muslim ruler
sultana *n* **1** small dried grape **2** (*often cap.*) wife, mother, or daughter of a sultan
sultanate *n* (country under) the rule of a sultan
sultry *adj* **1** (of weather) hot, airless, and uncomfortable **2** causing or showing strong sexual desire **-trily** *adv* **-triness** *n*
sum *n* **1** total produced when numbers are added together **2** amount (of money) **3** simple calculation **sum up** *phr v* **-mm- 1** *vi/t* summarize **2** *vt* consider and form a judgment of
summary *n* short account giving the main points ♦ *adj* **1** short **2** done at once without attention to formalities: *summary dismissal* **-rize** *vt* make a summary of
summation *n* **1** summary **2** total
summer *n* hot season between spring and autumn **~y** *adj* like or suitable for summer
summerhouse *n* small building in a garden, to sit in in summer
summer school *n* course of teaching given in a university or college during the summer vacation
summit *n* **1** highest point **2** top of a mountain **3** meeting between heads of government
summon *vt* order officially to come
summon up *phr vt* get (a quality in oneself) ready for use

summons *n, vt* order to appear in a court of law
sump *n* part of an engine holding the oil supply
sumptuary *adj* concerned with expenditure
sumptuous *adj* expensive and grand **~ly** *adv* **~ness** *n*
sum total *n* the whole, esp. when less than expected or needed
sun *n* **1** star round which the Earth moves **2** sun's light and heat: *sitting in the sun* **3** star round which planets may turn ♦ *vt* **-nn-** place (oneself) in sunlight **~ny** *adj* **1** having bright sunlight **2** cheerful
sunbathe *vi* sit or lie in strong sunlight **–bather** *n*
sunbeam *n* a beam of sunlight
sunbed *n* couch under a sunlamp
sunbelt *n* southern and southwestern parts of the US
sunburn *n* sore skin caused by too much strong sunlight **–burnt, ~ed** *adj*
sundae *n* ice cream dish with fruit and nuts
Sunday *n* the 7th day of the week, between Saturday and Monday
sunder *vt lit* separate
sundial *n* apparatus producing a shadow which shows the time
sundown *n* sunset
sundries *pl n* small and unimportant articles
sundry *adj* **1** various **2 all and sundry** all types of people; everybody
sunflower *n* tall plant with large yellow flower and edible seeds
sung *past p. of* sing
sunglasses *pl n* glasses with dark lenses for protection from sunlight
sunk *past p. of* sink
sunken *adj* **1** that has (been) sunk **2** below the surrounding level: *a sunken garden*
sunlamp *n* ultraviolet lamp for browning the skin
sunlight *n* light from the sun
sunlit *adj* brightly lit by the sun
Sunni *adj, n* (of) a follower of the main branch of the Muslim religion
sunrise *n* time when the sun appears after the night
sunrise industry *n* industry such as electronics or the making of computers, that is taking the place of older industries
sunroof *n* **1** flat roof where people can sunbathe **2** part of a car roof that can be moved back
sunset *n* time when the sun disappears as night begins
sunshade *n* sort of umbrella for protection from the sun
sunshine *n* strong sunlight
sunspot *n* dark cooler area on the sun's surface
sunstroke *n* illness caused by too much strong sunlight
suntan *n* brownness of the skin caused by being in strong sunlight
suntrap *n* sheltered place that gets a lot of sunshine
super *adj* wonderful; extremely good
super- *prefix* greater or more than: *superhuman/supertanker*
superannuated *adj* **1** too old for work **2** old-fashioned **–ion** *n* pension
superb *adj* excellent; wonderful **~ly** *adv*
supercharge *vi/t* **1** increase the power of (an engine) with a supercharger **2** fill with power or emotion **~r** *n* apparatus for producing more power from an engine by injection of air
supercilious /ˌsoohpəˈsili·əs/ *adj derog* (as if) thinking that others are of little importance **~ly** *adv* **~ness** *n*
superconductor *n* metal which at very low temperatures allows electricity to pass freely **–tivity** *n*
superego *n* **-os** (in Freudian psychology) the conscience
superficial *adj* **1** on the surface; not deep **2** not thorough or complete **~ly** *adv* **~ity** *n*
superfluous /s(y)oohˈpuhfloo·əs/ *adj* more than is necessary; not needed **~ly** *adv* **–fluity** *n*
supergrass *n BrE* person, esp. a crimi-

nal, who supplies the police with a lot of information about the activities of criminals

superhuman *adj* (as if) beyond or better than human powers

superhuman *adj* beyond normal human powers

superimpose *vt* put (something) over something else, esp. so that both can be (partly) seen **–position** *n*

superintend *vt* be in charge of and direct **~ent** *n* **1** person in charge **2** British police officer of middle rank

superior *adj* **1** of higher rank **2** better **3** of high quality **4** *derog* (as if) thinking oneself better than others ♦ *n* person of higher rank **~ity** *n*

superlative *adj* **1** *grammar* expressing 'most' **2** extremely good ♦ *n grammar* superlative form of an adjective or adverb

superman *n* **–men** man of very great ability or strength

supermarket *n* large food shop where one serves oneself

supernatural *adj* of or caused by the power of spirits, gods, and magic **~ly** *adv*

supernova *n* very bright exploding star

supernumerary *n, adj* (person or thing) added to the usual or necessary number

superpower *n* very powerful nation

supersede *vt* take the place of

supersonic *adj* (flying) faster than the speed of sound

superstar *n* very famous performer

superstition *n* (unreasonable) belief based on old ideas about luck or magic **–tious** *adj* **–tiously** *adv*

superstructure *n* upper structure built on a base

supervene *vi infml* happen so as to cause an interruption

supervise *vt* watch (people or work) to make sure things are done properly **–visor** *n* **–visory** *adj* **–vision** *n*

superwoman *n* **–men** woman of very great ability or strength

supine *adj* **1** lying on one's back **2** lazy and ineffectual **~ly** *adv*

supper *n* evening meal

supplant *vt* take the place of

supple *adj* bending easily and gracefully **–ply** *adv* **~ness** *n*

supplement *n* **1** additional amount to supply what is needed **2** additional separate part e.g. of a newspaper or magazine ♦ *vt* make additions to **~ary** *adj* additional

supplementary benefit *n* (in Britain) government money given to those with not enough to live on

suppliant *n, adj* (a person) begging or praying

supplicate *vi/t* beg (God or a powerful person) for help **–cation** *n* **–cant** *n*

supply *vt* **1** provide (something) **2** provide things to (someone) for use ♦ *n* **1** amount for use: *a supply of food* **2** (system for) supplying: *the supply of electricity* **3 in short supply** scarce **–plier** *n* **supplies** *pl n* things necessary for daily life, esp. food

supply and demand *n* balance between the amount of goods for sale and the amount that people actually want to buy

support *vt* **1** bear the weight of, esp. so as to prevent from falling **2** approve of and encourage **3** be loyal to: *supporting the local football team* **4** provide money for (someone) to live on **5** strengthen (e.g. an idea or opinion) ♦ *n* **1** state of being supported **2** something that supports **3** active approval and encouragement **4** money to live on **~er** *n* person who supports a particular activity, team, or principle **~ive** *adj* providing encouragement, help, etc. **~able** *adj* tolerable

supporting part also **supporting role** *n* small part in a play or film

suppose *vt* **1** consider to be probable: *As she's not here, I suppose she must have gone home.* **2 be supposed to: a** ought to; should **b** be generally considered to be ♦ *conj* **1** (used for making a suggestion): *Suppose we wait a while.* **2** what would/will happen if **~dly** *adv* as is believed; as it appears **–posing** *conj* suppose

supposition *n* **1** act of supposing or guessing **2** guess

suppository /səˈpozət(ə)ri/ *n* piece of meltable medicine placed in the rectum or vagina

suppress *vt* **1** bring to an end by force **2** prevent from being shown or made public: *suppressing her anger* **~ion** *n*

suppressor *n* **1** person or thing that suppresses **2** device to prevent electrical interference

suppurate /ˈsupyooˌrayt/ *vi* discharge pus **–ation** *n*

supranational *adj* going beyond national boundaries or interests **~ ism** *n* **~ist** *n*

supremacist *n* person who believes in the supremacy of a particular group

supreme *adj* **1** highest in degree **2** most powerful **~ly** *adv* extremely **supremacy** *n*

supremo *n* **-mos** *infml* powerful person

surcharge *n* (demand for) an additional payment ♦ *vt* make (someone) pay a surcharge

surd *n tech* quantity which cannot be shown in whole numbers

sure *adj* **1** having no doubt **2** certain (to happen) **3** confident (of having): *I've never felt surer of success.* **4 be sure to** don't forget to **5 make sure: a** find out (if something is really true) **b** take action (so that something will certainly happen) **6 sure of oneself** certain that one's actions are right ♦ *adv* **1** certainly **2 for sure** certainly so **3 sure enough** as was expected **~ly** *adv* **1** I believe, hope, or expect: *Surely you haven't forgotten?* **2** safely **~ness** *n*

surefire *adj* certain to succeed

surefooted *adj* able to walk, climb, etc., in difficult places without falling

surety /ˈshooəriti/ *n* **1** person who takes responsibility for the behaviour of another **2** money given to make sure that a person will appear in court

surf *n* white air-filled waves breaking on a shore ♦ *vi* ride as a sport over breaking waves near the shore, on a surfboard **~ing** *n* sport of surfing **~er** *n* person who goes surfing

surface *n* **1** outer part of an object **2** top of liquid **3** what is easily seen, not the main (hidden) part ♦ *adj* **1** superficial: *surface friendliness* ♦ *vi* come up to the surface of water

surface mail *n* post carried by land or sea

surface-to-air *adj* (of a weapon) fired from the earth towards aircraft

surfboard *n* board for riding on surf

surfeit /ˈsuhfit/ *n* too large an amount ♦ *vt* satiate

surge *n* **1** sudden powerful forward movement **2** sudden increase of strong feeling ♦ *vi* **1** move forwards like powerful waves **2** (of a feeling) arise powerfully

surgeon *n* doctor who does surgery

surgery *n* **1** performing of medical operations **2** *BrE* place where or time when a doctor or dentist treats patients **3** *BrE* period of time when people can consult e.g. a member of parliament or lawyer

surgical *adj* **1** of or used for surgery **2** (of a garment) worn as treatment for a particular physical condition **~ly** *adv*

surly *adj* bad-tempered and bad-mannered **surliness** *n*

surmise *vt* suppose; guess **surmise** *n*

surmount *vt* **1** succeed in dealing with (a difficulty) **2** be on top of

surname *n* person's family name

surpass *vt* go beyond, esp. be better than **~ing** *adj lit* extremely

surplice *n* long white outer garment worn by priests in church

surplus *n, adj* (amount) additional to what is needed or used

surprise *n* **1** (feeling caused by) an unexpected event **2 take by surprise** come on (someone) unprepared ♦ *vt* **1** cause surprise to **2** find, catch, or attack when unprepared

surprising *adj* unusual; causing surprise **~ly** *adv*

surreal *adj* having a strange dreamlike

unreal quality **~ism** *n* modern art or literature that treats subjects in a surreal way **~ist** *n* (artist or writer) concerned with surrealism

surrender *v* **1** *vi/t* give up or give in to the power (esp. of an enemy); admit defeat **2** *vt* give up possession of ♦ *n* act of surrendering

surreptitious /ˌsurəpˈtishəs/ *adj* done secretly, esp. for dishonest reasons **~ly** *adv* **~ness** *n*

surrey *n* light horse-drawn carriage

surrogate *n, adj* (person or thing) acting or used in place of another

surround *vt* be or go all around on every side ♦ *n* (decorative) edge or border **~ing** *adj* around and nearby **~ings** *pl n* place and conditions of life

surveillance /suhˈvayləns/ *n* close watch kept on someone or something

survey *vt* **1** look at or examine as a whole **2** examine the condition of (a building) **3** measure (land) ♦ *n* **1** act of surveying: *a survey of a house* **2** general description **~or** *n* person whose job is to survey buildings or land

survive *vi/t* continue to live or exist (after), esp. after coming close to death: *She survived the accident.* **–vival** *n* **1** act of surviving **2** something which has survived from an earlier time **–vivor** *n*

susceptible *adj* **1** easily influenced (by) **2** likely to suffer (from) **–bility** *n*

sushi *n* Japanese dish of rice and raw fish

suspect *vt* **1** believe to be so; think likely: *I suspected he was ill but didn't like to ask him.* **2** believe to be guilty ♦ *n* person suspected of guilt ♦ *adj* of uncertain truth, quality, or legality

suspend *vt* **1** hang from above **2** hold still in liquid or air **3** make inactive for a time: *The meeting was suspended while the lights were repaired.* **4** prevent from taking part for a time, esp. for breaking rules **~er** *n* fastener for holding up a woman's stockings **~ers** *pl n AmE* braces for trousers

suspense *n* state of uncertainty causing anxiety or pleasant excitement

suspension *n* **1** act of suspending or fact of being suspended **2** apparatus fixed to a vehicle's wheels to lessen the effect of rough roads

suspension bridge *n* bridge hung from strong steel ropes fixed to towers

suspicion *n* **1 a** a case of suspecting or being suspected: *under suspicion of murder* **b** lack of trust: *treat someone with suspicion* **2 a** a feeling of suspecting: *I have a suspicion you're right.* **b** belief about someone's guilt: *They have their suspicions.* **3** slight amount **–cious** *adj* **1** suspecting guilt or wrongdoing **2** making one suspicious: *suspicious behaviour* **–ciously** *adv*

suss *vt BrE sl* discover the fact that **suss out** *phr vt BrE sl* quietly or secretly find out details about

sustain *vt* **1** keep strong **2** keep in existence over a long period **3** suffer: *The car sustained severe damage.* **4** hold up (the weight of)

sustenance *n* food or its ability to keep people strong and healthy

suttee *n* Hindu custom of a widow being cremated on her husband's funeral pyre

suture *n* (stitch or thread used in) surgical sewing **suture** *vt*

suzerain *n* **1** feudal lord **2** state that controls the foreign affairs of another state

svelte *adj* slender

swab *n* piece of material that can take up liquid, esp. used medically ♦ *vt* **-bb-** clean (a wound) with a swab

swaddle *vt* wrap (a baby) tightly in narrow strips of cloth

swag *n* **1** *infml* goods obtained in a robbery **2** *AustrE* pack of personal belongings

swagger *vi* walk or behave (too) confidently or proudly **swagger** *n*

swagman *n AustrE* tramp

swain *n lit* **1** peasant **2** lover or suitor

swallow[1] *v* **1** *vi/t* move (the contents of the mouth) down the throat **2** *vt* accept patiently or with too easy belief: *It was an obvious lie, but he swallowed it.* **3** *vt* not show or express: *swallow one's* *pride* **swallow up** *phr vt* take in and cause to disappear ♦ *n* act of swallowing or amount swallowed

swallow² *n* small bird with a double-pointed tail

swam *past t. of* swim

swami *n* Hindu religious teacher

swamp *n* (area of) soft wet land ♦ *vt* **1** fill with water **2** overload **~y** *adj* wet like a swamp

swan *n* **1** large white long-necked water bird **2** act of swanning ♦ *vi* **-nn-** *infml* go or travel aimlessly for pleasure

swank *vi, n infml* (act or speak too proudly, making) false or too great claims **~y** *adj infml* very fashionable or expensive

swansong *n* one's last performance or piece of artistic work

swap *vi/t* **-pp-** exchange (goods or positions) so that each person gets what they want ♦ *n* **1** exchange **2** something (to be) exchanged

sward *n lit* piece of grassy land

swarf *n* small bits of e.g. metal thrown off by a cutting or grinding tool

swarm *n* large moving mass of insects ♦ *vi* move in a crowd or mass **swarm with** *phr vt* be full of (a moving crowd)

swarthy *adj* having fairly dark skin

swashbuckling *adj* full of showy adventures and sword fighting

swastika *n* cross with the arms bent at right angles used as a Nazi symbol

swat *vt* **-tt-** hit (an insect), esp. so as to kill it **~ter** *n*

swatch *n* sample of cloth

swath, swathe *n* grass cut or space cleared by a scythe or mowing machine

swathe in *phr vt* wrap round in (cloth)

sway *v* **1** *vi/t* swing from side to side **2** *vt* influence, esp. so as to change opinion ♦ *n* **1** swaying movement **2** *lit* influence

swear *v* **swore, sworn 1** *vi* curse **2** *vi/t* make a solemn promise or statement, esp. by taking an oath: *She swore to tell the truth.* **3** cause to take an oath **swear by** *phr vt* have confidence in (something) **swear in** *phr vt* **1** cause (a witness) to take the oath in court **2** cause to make a promise of responsible action, etc.: *The elected President was sworn in.*

sweat *n* **1** body liquid that comes out through the skin **2** anxious state **3** *infml* hard work **4 no sweat** *infml* (used for saying that something will not cause any difficulty) ♦ *vi* **1** produce sweat **2** be very anxious or nervously impatient **3 sweat blood** *infml* work unusually hard **~y** *adj* **1** covered in or smelly with sweat **2** unpleasantly hot

sweatband *n* band of material worn to absorb sweat

sweated labour *n* long hours of work for little money

sweater *n* (woollen) garment for the upper body, usu. without fastenings

sweatshirt *n* loose cotton garment for the upper body

sweatshop *n* place producing goods by sweated labour

swede *n* large round yellow root vegetable

Swede *n* person from Sweden

Swedish *adj* of Sweden

sweep *v* **swept 1** *vt* clean or remove by brushing **2** *vi/t* move (over) or carry quickly and powerfully: *A wave of panic swept over her.*|*We were swept along by the crowd.* **3** *vi* lie in a curve across land **4** *vt* win completely and easily, as in elections **5** *vi* (of a person) move in a proud, firm manner **6 sweep someone off their feet** fill someone with sudden love or excitement **7 sweep something under the carpet,** *AmE* **under the rug** keep (something bad or shocking) secret **sweep aside** *phr vt* refuse to pay any attention to ♦ *n* **1** act of sweeping **2** long curved line or area of country **3** person who cleans chimneys **4** sweepstake **~er** *n* **~ing** *adj* **1** including many or most things: *sweeping changes* **2** too general: *a sweeping statement*

sweepstake *n* form of risking money, esp. on a horserace, in which the winner gets all the losers' money

sweet *adj* **1** tasting like sugar **2** pleasing to the senses: *sweet music* **3** charming; lovable: *What a sweet little boy!* ♦ *n BrE* **1** small piece of food made with sugar or chocolate **2** dessert **~en** *vt* **1** make sweeter **2** *infml* bribe **~ly** *adv* **~ness** *n*

sweetbread *n* sheep's or cow's pancreas used as food

sweetbrier *n* wild rose with fragrant leaves

sweet corn *n* corn[1] (2)

sweetener *n* **1** substance used instead of sugar to make food or drink taste sweet **2** *infml* bribe

sweetheart *n lit* person whom one loves

sweetmeat *n arch.* sweet or food rich in sugar

sweet pea *n* climbing plant with sweet-smelling flowers

sweet potato *n* tropical yellow root vegetable

sweet talk *n infml* insincere talk intended to please or persuade **sweet-talk** *vt*

sweet tooth *n* liking for sweet and sugary things

sweet william *n* garden plant with small, bright flowers

swell *vi/t* **swelled, swollen** *or* **swelled 1** increase gradually to beyond the usual or original size **2** fill or be filled, giving a full round shape ♦ *n* rolling up-and-down movement of the surface of the sea ♦ *adj AmE* excellent **~ing** *n* **1** act of swelling **2** swollen place on the body

swelter *vi* experience the effects of unpleasantly great heat

swept *past t. and p. of* sweep

swept-back *adj* having the front edge pointing backwards at an angle from the main part

swerve *vi, n* (make) a sudden change of direction

swift *adj* quick ♦ *n* small brown fast-flying bird like a swallow **~ly** *adv* **~ness** *n*

swig *vt* **-gg-** *infml* drink, esp. in large mouthfuls **swig** *n*

swill *vt* **1** wash with large streams of water **2** *infml* drink, esp. in large amounts ♦ *n* partly liquid pig food

swim *v* **swam, swum** *present p.* **-mm- 1** *vi* move through water using the limbs or fins **2** *vt* cross by doing this **3** *vi* be full of or surrounded with liquid **4** *vi* seem to spin round and round: *My head was swimming.* **5 swim with the tide** follow the behaviour of other people around one ♦ *n* **1** act of swimming **2 in the swim** knowing about and concerned in what is going on in modern life **~mer** *n*

swimming bath *n BrE* public swimming pool

swimming costume *n* close-fitting garment for swimming

swimming pool *n* large usu. outdoor container filled with water and used for swimming

swindle *vt* cheat, esp. so as to get money ♦ *n* act of swindling **swindler** *n*

swine *n* **swine 1** *fml or lit* pig **2** *sl* unpleasant person **–nish** *adj* unpleasant

swing *v* **swung 1** *vi/t* move backwards and forwards or round and round from a fixed point: *Soldiers swing their arms as they march.* **2** *vi/t* move in a smooth curve: *The door swung shut.* **3** *vi* turn quickly **4** *vi* start smoothly and rapidly: *We're ready to swing into action.* **5** *vi infml* be hanged to death, as a punishment ♦ *n* **1** act of swinging **2** children's swinging seat fixed from above by ropes or chains **3** noticeable change: *a big swing in public opinion* **4** jazz music of the 1930s and 1940s with a strong regular active beat **5 go with a swing** happen successfully **6 in full swing** having reached a very active stage

swingeing *adj esp. BrE* very severe

swinging *adj* lively and up-to-date

swipe *vt* **1** hit hard **2** *infml* steal ♦ *n* sweeping blow

swirl *vi/t* move with twisting turns ♦ *n* twisting mass

swish[1] *vi/t* move through the air with a sharp whistling noise ♦ *n* act of swishing

swish[2] *adj infml* fashionable and expensive

Swiss *adj* of Switzerland

Swiss roll *n* roll of sponge cake spread with jam

switch *n* **1** apparatus for stopping or starting an electric current **2** sudden complete change ♦ *vi/t* change or exchange **switch off/on** *phr vt* turn (an electric light or apparatus) off/on with a switch **switch over** *phr vi* **1** change completely **2** change from one radio or television channel to another

switchback *n esp. BrE* roller coaster

switchblade *n AmE* flickknife

switchboard *n* place where telephone lines in a large building are connected

swivel *vi/t* **-ll-** (*AmE* **-l** -) turn round (as if) on a central point

swiz, swizz *n BrE infml* something that makes one feel cheated or disappointed

swizzle stick *n* rod for mixing drinks

swollen *past. p. of* swell

swoon *vi lit* **1** experience deep joy or desire **2** faint

swoop *vi* come down sharply, esp. to attack **swoop** *n* swooping action

swop *v, n* swap

sword *n* weapon with a long sharp metal blade and a handle

swordfish *n* large fish with a long pointed upper jaw

swordplay *n* action or skill of fighting with swords

swordsman *n* **-men** (skilled) fighter with a sword **~ship** *n*

swordstick *n* walking stick in which a sword is concealed

swore *past t. of* swear

sworn *past p. of* swear

swot *vi* **-tt-** *BrE infml* study hard, esp. to get good examination results ♦ *n derog* person who swots

swum *past p. of* swim

swung *past t. and p. of* swing

sybaritic /ˌsibəˈritik/ *adj* being or liking great and expensive comfort and physical pleasures

sycamore *n* tree with five-pointed leaves and winged fruit

sycophant /ˈsikəˌfant/ *n* person who praises people insincerely to gain personal advantage **~ic** *adj* **~ically** *adv* **–phancy** *n*

syllable *n* part of a word containing a single vowel sound **–labic** *adj*

syllabus *n* arrangement of subjects for study over a period of time

syllogism /ˈsiləˌjiz(ə)m/ *n* arrangement of two statements which must lead to a third

sylphlike *adj* (of a woman) gracefully thin

sylvan *adj lit* of or in the woods

symbiosis *n* condition in which two living things depend on each other for existence **–otic** *adj*

symbol *n* something that represents something else: *The dove is the symbol of peace.* **~ism** *n* use of symbols **~ize** *vt* represent by or as a symbol **~ic** *adj* representing **~ically** *adv*

symmetry *n* **1** exact likeness in size and shape between opposite sides **2** effect of pleasing balance **–trical** *adj* **–trically** *adv*

sympathy *n* **1** sensitivity to and pity for others' suffering **2** agreement or understanding: *I am in sympathy with their aims.* **–thize** *vt* feel or show sympathy **sympathies** *pl n* feelings of support or loyalty **–thetic** *adj* feeling or showing sympathy **–thetically** *adv*

symphony *n* usu. four-part piece of music for an orchestra **–nic** *adj*

symposium *n* **-iums** *or* **-ia** meeting to talk about a subject of study

symptom *n* **1** outward sign of a disease **2** outward sign of inner change, new feelings; etc. **~atic** *adj* being a symptom

synagogue *n* building where Jews worship

synchromesh *n* part of the gears of a car which allows them to change smoothly

synchronize, -nise /ˈsingkrəˌniez/ *vt* **1** cause to happen at the same time or speed **2** cause (e.g watches) to show the same time **–nization** *n*

syncopate *vt* change (the beat of music) by giving force to the beats that are usu. less forceful **–pation** *n*

syncope /ˈsingkəpi/ *n* loss of consciousness in fainting

syndicate *n* group of people or companies combined for usu. business purposes ♦ *vt* sell (written work or pictures) to many different newspapers or magazines

syndrome *n* **1** set of medical symptoms which represent an illness **2** any pattern of qualities or happenings typical of a general condition

synod *n* meeting of church members to decide ecclesiastical matters

synonym *n* word with the same meaning as another **~ous** *adj*

synopsis *n* summary

syntax *n* way in which words are ordered and connected in sentences **–tactic** *adj*

synthesis *n* **-ses 1** combining of separate things or ideas into a complete whole **2** something made by synthesis **–size** *vt* make by synthesis, esp. make (something similar to a natural product) by combining chemicals **–sizer** *n* electrical instrument, like a piano, that can produce many sorts of different sounds, used esp. in popular music

synthetic *adj* artificial **~ally** *adv*

syphilis *n* very serious venereal disease

syphon *n, vt* siphon

syringe *n* (medical) instrument with a hollow tube for sucking in and pushing out liquid, esp. through a needle ♦ *vt* clean with a syringe

syrup *n* sweet liquid, esp. sugar and water

system *n* **1** group of related parts which work together forming a whole: *the postal system* **2** ordered set of ideas, methods, or ways of working: *the American system of government* **3** the body, thought of as a set of working parts: *Travelling always upsets my system.* **4** orderly methods **5** society seen as something which uses and limits individuals: *to fight the system* **~atic** *adj* based on orderly methods and careful organization; thorough **~atically** *adv*

systemic /si'steemik/ *adj* affecting the whole of an organism

systems analyst *n* someone who studies (esp. business) activities and uses computers to plan better ways of carrying them out

T

T, t the 20th letter of the English alphabet

ta *interj BrE sl* thank you

tab *n* **1** small piece of e.g. paper, cloth, or metal, fixed to something **2 keep tabs on** watch closely

Tabasco also **Tabasco sauce** *n tdmk for* very hot sauce

tabby *n* cat with dark and light bands of fur

tabernacle *n* container for religious objects

table *n* **1** piece of furniture with a flat top on upright legs **2** set of figures arranged in rows across and down a page ♦ *vt* **1** *BrE* put forward for consideration e.g. by a committee, **2** *AmE* leave until a later date for consideration

tableau *n* **~s** *or* **-eaux** scene on stage shown by a group of people who do not move or speak

table d'hôte *n* complete meal at a fixed price

tableland *n* large area of high flat land

tablespoon *n* large spoon for serving food

tablet *n* **1** small solid piece of medicine **2** small block (of soap) **3** flat piece of stone or metal with words on it

table tennis *n* indoor game in which a small ball is hit across a net on a table

tabloid *n* newspaper with small pages and many pictures

taboo *n* **-boos** strong social or religious custom forbidding something ♦ *adj* strongly forbidden by social custom

tabor /ˈtaybə/ *n* small drum

tabulate *vt* arrange as a table **–lar** *adj* **–lation** *n*

tachograph *n* apparatus for recording the speed of a vehicle and the distance it has travelled

tachometer *n* instrument for measuring speed

tacit *adj* accepted or understood without being openly expressed: *tacit approval* **~ly** *adv*

taciturn /ˈtasiˌtuhn/ *adj* tending to speak very little **~ity** *n*

tack *n* **1** small nail **2** sailing ship's direction **3** long loose stitch ♦ *v* **1** *vt* fasten with tacks **2** *vi* change the course of a sailing ship

tackle *n* **1** act of stopping or taking the ball away from an opponent in sport **2** apparatus used in certain sports: *fishing tackle* **3** (system of) ropes and wheels for heavy pulling and lifting ♦ *v* **1** *vt* take action in order to deal with **2** *vt* speak to fearlessly so as to deal with a problem **3** *vi/t* stop or rob with a tackle in sport

tacky *adj* **1** sticky **2** of low quality **–iness** *n*

taco *n* **-os** Mexican flat bread with filling

tact *n* skill of speaking or acting without offending people **~ful** *adj* **~fully** *adv* **~less** *adj* **~lessly** *adv* **~lessness** *n*

tactic *n* plan or method for gaining a desired result **tactics** *pl n* art of arranging and moving military forces in battle **tactical** *adj* **1** of tactics **2** done to get a desired result in the end: *a tactical retreat* **tactician** *n* person skilled in tactics

tactile *adj* of or able to be felt by the sense of touch

tadpole *n* small creature that grows into a frog or toad

taffeta *n* stiff shiny cloth

taffy *n AmE* toffee

Taffy *n derog* Welshman

tag *n* **1** small piece of paper or material fixed to something and bearing information **2** game in which one child chases the others until he/she touches one of them ♦ *vt* **-gg- 1** fasten a tag to **2** provide with a name or nickname **tag along** *phr vi* go with someone by following closely behind **tag on** *phr vt* add

tagliatelle /ˌtalyəˈteli/ *n* pasta made in flat strips

tail *n* **1** long movable part at the back of a creature's body **2** last or back part (of something long): *the tail of an aircraft* **3** person employed to follow someone ♦ *vt* follow (someone) closely, esp. without their knowledge **tail away/off** *phr vi* lessen gradually **tails** *pl n* **1** side of a coin without a ruler's head on it **2** tailcoat

tailback *n* line of traffic stretching back from where its flow has been halted

tailboard *n* movable board at the back of a cart or lorry

tailcoat *n* man's coat with a long back divided into two below the waist

tailgate *n* **1** tailboard **2** door at the back of a hatchback car ♦ *vi/t AmE* drive closely behind (a vehicle)

tailor *n* person who makes outer garments for men ♦ *vt* fit to a particular need **~-made** *adj* exactly right for a particular need or person

tailspin *n* uncontrolled spinning fall of a plane

tailwind *n* wind coming from behind

taint *vt, n* (spoil with) a small amount of decay, infection, or bad influence

take *v* **took, taken 1** *vt* move from one place to another: *Take the chair into the garden.* **2** *vt* remove without permission: *Someone's taken my pen.* **3** *vt* subtract: *What do you get if you take 5 from 12?* **4** *vt* get possession of; seize: *Rebels have taken the airport.* **5** *vt* get by performing an action: *He took notes.* **6** *vt* start to hold: *She took my arm.* **7** *vt* use for travel: *I take the train to work.* **8** *vt* be willing to accept: *Will you take a cheque?* **9** *vt* accept as true or worthy of attention: *Take my advice.* **10** *vt* be able to contain: *The bus takes 55 passengers.* **11** *vt* be able to accept; bear: *I can't take* *his rudeness.* **12** *vt* need: *The journey takes two hours.* **13** *vt* do; perform: *He took a walk.* **14** *vt* put into the body: *take some medicine* **15** *vt* make by photography **16** *vt* have (a feeling): *take offence* **17** *vi* have the intended effect; work: *Did the vaccination take?* **18** *vt* attract; delight: *The little house took my fancy.* **19** *vt* understand: *I take it you know each other.* **20 be taken ill** become (suddenly) ill **21 take it easy** *infml* relax **22 take one's time: a** use as much time as is necessary **b** use too much time **take aback** *phr vt* surprise and confuse **take after** *phr vt* look or behave like (an older relative) **take apart** *phr vt sl* harm a place or person **take back** *phr vt* **1** admit that (what one said) was wrong **2** cause to remember a former period in one's life: *That takes me back!* **take in** *phr vt* **1** reduce the size of (a garment) **2** provide lodgings for **3** include **4** understand fully **5** deceive **take off** *phr v* **1** *vi* (of a plane, etc.) rise into the air to begin a flight **2** *vi infml* leave without warning: *One day he just took off.* **3** *vt* mimic **4** *vt* have as a holiday from work: *I took Tuesday off.* **take on** *phr vt* **1** start to employ **2** begin to have (a quality or appearance) **3** start to quarrel or fight with **4** accept (e.g. work or responsibility) **take out** *phr vt* **1** go somewhere with (someone) as a social activity **2** obtain officially: *take out insurance* **3 take someone out of himself** amuse or interest someone so that their worries are forgotten **4 take it out of someone** use all the strength of someone **take out on** *phr vt* express (one's feelings) by making (someone) suffer: *He tends to take things out on his wife.* **take over** *phr vi/t* gain control of and responsibility for (something) **take to** *phr vt* **1** like, esp. at once **2** begin as a practice or habit: *He took to drink.* **3** go to for rest or escape **take up** *phr vt* **1** begin to interest oneself in: *I've taken up the guitar.* **2** complain, ask, or take further action about: *I'll take the matter up with my lawyer.* **3** fill or use (space or time), esp. undesirably **4** accept (someone's) offer: *I'll take you up on that.* **5** continue (a story) **take up with** *phr vt* **1** become friendly with **2** be very interested in: *She's very taken up with her work.* ♦ *n* **1** filming of a scene **2** takings

takeaway *n BrE* (meal from) a restaurant that sells food to eat elsewhere

take-home pay *n* salary or wages remaining after tax and other payments have been deducted

takeoff *n* **1** rising of a plane from the ground **2** amusing mimicry

takeout *n AmE* takeaway

takeover *n* act of gaining control of esp. a business company

taker *n infml* person willing to accept an offer

takeup *n* rate at which something offered is accepted

takings *pl n* money received, esp. by a shop

talcum powder also **talc** *n* crushed mineral put on the body to dry it or make it smell nice

tale *n* **1** story **2** false story; lie

talent *n* (people with) special natural ability or skill **~ed** *adj*

talisman *n* **-mans** object with magic protective powers

talk *v* **1** *vi* speak: *Can the baby talk yet?* **2** *vi* give information by speaking, usu. unwillingly: *We have ways of making you talk.* **3** *vi* gossip **4** *vt* speak about: *It's time to talk business.* **talk down to** *phr vt* speak to (someone) condescendingly **talk into/out of** *phr vt* persuade (someone) to do/not to do (something) **talk over** *phr vt* speak about thoroughly and seriously **talk round** *phr vt* persuade (someone) to change their mind ♦ *n* **1** conversation **2** informal lecture **3** way of talking: *baby talk* **4** subject much talked about: *Her sudden marriage is the talk of the street.* **5** empty or meaningless speech **talks** *pl n* formal exchange of opinions **~er** *n*

talkative *adj* liking to talk a lot **~ness** *n*

talking point *n* subject of conversation or argument
talking-to *n* angry talk in order to blame or criticize
tall *adj* **1** of greater than average height **2** of the stated height from top to bottom: *He is 6 feet tall.*
tallboy *n* tall chest of drawers
tall order *n* something unreasonably difficult to do
tallow *n* hard animal fat used for candles
tall story *n* story that is difficult to believe
tally *n* recorded total ♦ *vi* be exactly equal; match
Talmud *n* written body of Jewish law and tradition
talon *n* sharp powerful claw of a hunting bird
tamarind *n* (acid fruit of) a tropical tree
tamarisk *n* shrub with fine narrow leaves
tambour *n* **1** small drum **2** round frame to hold cloth for embroidery
tambourine *n* drumlike musical instrument with small metal plates round the edge
tame *adj* **1** not fierce or wild **2** dull; unexciting ♦ *vt* make (an animal) tame **~ly** *adv* **~ness** *n* **tamer** *n*
Tamil *n* (person speaking) a language of south India and Sri Lanka
tamp *vt* force down by a series of light blows
tamper with *phr vt* touch or change without permission, esp. causing damage
tampon *n* cylinder of cotton put into a woman's vagina to absorb blood during menstruation
tan[1] *v* **-nn- 1** *vt* change (animal skin) into leather by treating with tannin **2** *vi/t* turn brown, esp. by sunlight ♦ *n* **1** brown skin colour from sunlight **2** yellowish brown colour
tan[2] *abbrev. for:* tangent (2)
tandem *n* **1** bicycle for two riders **2 in tandem** with both working closely together
tandoori *n* (meat cooked by) an Indian method of cooking in a big clay pot
tang *n* strong sharp taste or smell **~y** *adj*
tangent *n* **1** straight line touching the edge of a curve **2** (in trigonometry) the fraction that is calculated for an angle by dividing the side opposite it in a right-angled triangle by the side next to it **3 go/fly off at a tangent** change suddenly to a different course of action or thought **~ial** *adj*
tangerine *n* sort of small orange
tangible *adj* **1** clear and certain; real: *tangible proof* **2** touchable **–bly** *adv*
tangle *vi/t* (cause to) become a confused mass of twisted threads ♦ *n* confused mass or state
tango *n* **-gos** South American dance ♦ *vi* dance the tango
tank *n* **1** large liquid or gas container **2** enclosed armoured military vehicle
tankard *n* large usu. metal beer mug
tanker *n* ship or road vehicle carrying large quantities of liquid or gas
tanner *n BrE infml* coin worth six old pence
tannic acid *n* tannin
tannin *n* reddish acid found in parts of certain plants
Tannoy *n BrE tdmk for* system of loudspeakers for public information
tantalize, -ise *vt* cause to desire something even more strongly by keeping it just out of reach
tantalus *n* case in which bottles or decanters can be locked, without being hidden
tantamount *adj* having the same effect (as): *Her answer is tantamount to a refusal.*
tantrum *n* sudden uncontrolled attack of angry bad temper
Taoism /ˈtowiz(ə)m/ *n* religion developed in ancient China based on the idea of an underlying universal harmony
tap[1] **1** turnable apparatus for controlling the flow of liquid from a pipe or barrel **2 on tap** ready for use when needed

♦ *vt*-**pp**- **1** use or draw from: *tapping our reserves of oil* **2** listen secretly by making an illegal connection to (a telephone)

tap[2] *vi/t, n* -**pp**- (strike with) a light short blow

tap dance *n* dance in which one strikes the floor loudly with special shoes

tape *n* **1** (long piece of) narrow material **2** (long piece of) narrow plastic magnetic material on which sounds or pictures are recorded ♦ *vt* **1** record on tape **2** fasten or tie with tape **3 have something taped** *infml* understand something thoroughly or have learnt how to deal with it

tape deck *n* apparatus in a tape recorder that winds the tape and makes contact with it for playing or recording

tape measure *n* narrow band of cloth or bendable metal used for measuring

taper *vi/t* make or become gradually narrower towards one end ♦ *n* thin candle

tape recorder *n* electrical apparatus for recording and playing sound with magnetic tape

tapestry *n* (piece of) cloth with pictures or patterns woven into it

tapeworm *n* long flat worm which is a parasite of the intestine

tapioca *n* granules made from a starchy root, used esp. in making sweet dishes

tapir /ˈtaypə/ *n* **-ir** *or* **irs** piglike animal of tropical America and Southeast Asia

tappet *n* machine part that transmits motion

tap root *n* main root of a plant, which grows straight down

tar *n* black meltable substance used for making roads and preserving wood ♦ *vt* -**rr**- **1** cover with tar **2 tarred with the same brush** having the same faults

taramasalata *n* Greek appetizer made of fish roe

tarantella *n* (music for) a fast Italian dance

tarantula *n* large poisonous spider

tardy *adj* **1** slow in acting or happening **2** *AmE* late **–dily** *adv* **–diness** *n*

tare[1] *n* **1** weight of wrapping material for goods **2** weight of an empty goods vehicle

tare[2] *n* **1** *lit* weed **2** type of vetch

target *n* **1** something aimed at in shooting practice **2** place, thing, or person at which an attack is directed **3** total or object which one tries to reach: *a production target of 500 cars a week* ♦ *vt* cause to be a target

tariff *n* **1** tax on goods coming into a country **2** *fml* list of prices in a hotel or restaurant

tarmac *n* **1** tar and small stones for making road surfaces **2** area where aircraft take off and land

tarn *n* small mountain lake

tarnish *vi/t* make or become discoloured or less bright

tarot /ˈtaroh/ *n* set of 22 special cards used for telling the future

tarpaulin *n* (sheet or cover of) heavy waterproof cloth

tarragon *n* pungent herb

tarry *vi lit* stay in a place for a while

tart[1] *adj* bitter **~ness** *n*

tart[2] **1** pastry container holding fruit or jam **2** *derog* sexually immoral or provocative woman **tart up** *phr vt infml derog* dress up, esp. cheaply or gaudily **~y** *adj*

tartan *n* (woollen cloth with) a pattern of bands crossing each other, esp. representing a particular Scottish clan

tartar[1] *n* **1** chalklike substance that forms on teeth **2** acid derived from the juice of grapes

tartar[2] *n infml* fierce person with a violent temper

tartaric acid *n* acid of plant origin used in food and medicines

tartar sauce, tartare sauce *n* mayonnaise with chopped pickles and olives

task *n* **1** piece of (hard) work (to be) done **2 take someone to task** speak severely to someone for a fault or failure

task force *n* military or police group set up for a special purpose

taskmaster *n* someone who makes

people work very hard
tassel *n* tied bunch of threads hung decoratively
taste *n* **1** quality by which a food or drink is recognized in the mouth: *Sugar has a sweet taste.* **2** sense which recognizes food or drink as sweet, salty, etc. **3** ability to make (good) judgments about beauty or style **4** personal liking: *She has expensive tastes in clothes.* ♦ *v* **1** *vt* experience or test the taste of **2** *vi* have a particular taste: *These oranges taste nice.* **3** *vt lit* experience: *having tasted freedom* **~ful** *adj* showing good taste in style **~less** *adj* **1** not tasting of anything **2** showing bad taste in style **tasty** *adj* pleasant-tasting
taste bud *n* group of cells on the tongue used in tasting
tat *n BrE sl* something of very low quality
ta-ta *interj esp. BrE* goodbye
tatters *n* **in tatters: a** (of clothes) old and torn **b** ruined **-tered** *adj* (dressed in clothes that are) in tatters
tattle *vi* gossip
tattoo[1] *n* **-toos** pattern made by tattooing ♦ *vt* make (a pattern) on the skin (of) by pricking with a needle and inserting coloured dyes **~ist** *n*
tattoo[2] *n* **-toos 1** outdoor military show with music **2** fast beating of drums
tatty *adj sl, esp. BrE* untidy or in bad condition **-tily** *adv*
taught *past t. and p. of* teach
taunt *vt* try to upset with unkind remarks or ridicule ♦ *n* taunting remark
taut *adj* stretched tight **~ly** *adv* **~ness** *n* **~en** *vi/t*
tautology /taw'toləji/ *n* unnecessary repeating of the same idea in different words **-gical, -gous** *adj*
tavern *n lit* pub
tawdry *adj* cheaply showy; showing bad taste **-driness** *n*
tawny *adj* brownish yellow
tax *n* money which must be paid to the government ♦ *vt* **1** make (someone) pay a tax **2** charge a tax on: *Cigarettes are heavily taxed.* **3** push to the limits of what one can bear: *Such stupid questions tax my patience.* **~able** *adj* that can be taxed **~ing** *adj* needing great effort **~ation** *n* (money raised by) taxing
tax-deductible *adj* that may legally be subtracted from one's total income before it is taxed
tax haven *n* country with low rates of tax
taxi *n* car with a driver which can be hired ♦ *vi* (of an aircraft) move along the ground before taking off or after landing
taxidermy *n* stuffing the skins of dead animals so that they look real **-mist** *n*
taxi rank *n* place where taxis wait to be hired
taxonomy *n* system or process of classification, esp. of plants or animals according to their natural relationships
tax shelter *n* strategy which enables one legally to avoid paying tax
TB *abbrev. for:* tuberculosis
T-bone, T-bone steak *n* thick beef steak containing a T-shaped bone
tea *n* **1** (drink made by pouring boiling water onto) the dried cut-up leaves of an Asian bush **2** drink made like tea from the stated leaves: *mint tea* **3** (esp. in Britain) small afternoon meal
teabag *n* small paper bag full of tea leaves
tea cake *n* round currant bun eaten toasted with butter
teach *v* **taught 1** *vi/t* give knowledge or skill of (something) to (someone): *He taught me French.* **2** *vt* show (someone) the bad results of doing something: *I'll teach you to be rude to me!* **~er** *n* person who teaches, esp. as a job **~ing** *n* **1** job of a teacher **2** also **teachings** *pl* moral beliefs taught by someone of historical importance: *the teachings of Christ*
tea chest *n* large square box in which tea is packed for export
teach-in *n* organized exchange of opinions about a subject of interest

tea garden *n* **1** tea plantation **2** restaurant where refreshments are served outdoors
teak *n* hard yellowish brown wood from Asia, used for furniture
teal *n* small wild duck
team *n* **1** group of people who work or esp. play together: *a football team* **2** two or more animals pulling the same vehicle **team up** *phr vi* work together for a shared purpose
teamster *n AmE* truck driver
teamwork *n* (effective) combined effort
teapot *n* container in which tea is made and served
tear[1] *v* **tore, torn 1** *vt* pull apart by force, esp. so as to leave irregular edges **2** *vi* become torn **3** *vt* remove with sudden force: *He tore off his clothes.* **4** *vi* rush excitedly **5 be torn between** be unable to decide between **tear down** *phr vt* pull down; destroy **tear up** *phr vt* destroy completely by tearing ♦ *n* hole made by tearing
tear[2] *n* **1** drop of salty liquid that flows from the eye, esp. because of sadness **2 in tears** crying **~ful** *adj* **~fully** *adv* **~fulness** *n*
tearaway *n BrE* noisy, sometimes violent young person
tear gas *n* gas that stings the eyes
tearjerker *n* very sad book or film
tease *v* **1** *vi/t* make jokes (about) or laugh (at) unkindly or playfully **2** *vt* annoy on purpose **3** *vt* separate the threads in (e.g. wool) ♦ *n* someone fond of teasing **teaser** *n* difficult question
teasel, teazel, teazle *n* **1** (dried head of) a tall plant with prickly leaves and flowers **2** wire brush for raising the nap on woollen cloth
teaspoon *n* small spoon
teat *n* **1** rubber object through which a baby sucks liquid from a bottle **2** animal's nipple
tea towel *n* cloth for drying washed crockery and cutlery
tech *n* technical college
technical *adj* **1** concerned with scientific or industrial subjects or skills **2** needing special knowledge in order to be understood: *His arguments are rather too technical for me.* **3** according to an (unreasonably) exact interpretation of the rules **~ly** *adv*
technical college *n* (esp. in Britain) college teaching practical subjects
technicality *n* small (esp. unimportant) detail or rule
technician *n* highly skilled scientific or industrial worker
technique *n* method of doing an activity that needs skill
technocrat *n often derog* scientist or technician in charge of an organization
technology *n* practical science, esp. as used in industrial production **-gist** *n* **-gical** *adj*
teddy bear also **teddy** *n* toy bear
teddy boy also **ted** *n* (in Britain in the 1950s) a young man who followed a fashion which included dress imitating the style of the early 1900s
tedious *adj* long and uninteresting **~ly** *adv* **~ness** *n*
tedium *n* state of being tedious
tee *n* small object on which a golf ball is placed to be hit **tee off** *phr vi* drive the ball from a tee **tee up** *phr vi/t* place (the ball) on a tee
teem *vi* (of rain) fall very heavily **teem with** *phr vt* have (a type of creature) present in great numbers
teenager *n* person of between 13 and 19 years old **teenage** *adj*
teens *pl n* period of being a teenager
teenybopper *n* young girl who follows the latest trends in fashion and pop music
teeny weeny *adj infml* extremely small
teepee *n* tepee
tee shirt *n* T-shirt
teeter *vi* stand or move unsteadily
teeter-totter *n AmE* seesaw
teeth *pl of* tooth
teethe *vi* (of a baby) grow teeth
teething troubles *pl n* problems in the early stages of using something
teetotal *adj* drinking no alcohol **~ler** *n*
Teflon *n tdmk for* artificial substance to

which things will not stick, used esp. on kitchen pans

tele- *prefix* **1** at or over a long distance: *telepathy* **2** by or for television: *telerecording*

telecast *n* broadcast on television

telecommunications *pl n* sending and receiving of messages over a distance, esp. by means of radio and telephone

telegram *n* message sent by telegraph

telegraph *n* method of sending messages along wire by electric signals ♦ *vt* send by telegraph **~ic** *adj* **~y** *n* **~er, ~ist** *n*

telegraphese *n* style of writing using the fewest words possible

telegraph pole *n* pole for supporting telephone wires

telekinesis /ˌteliki'neesis/ *n* moving of solid objects by the power of the mind

telemarketing also **teleselling** *n* selling by telephone

telemetry *n* collection of information by an instrument (a **telemeter**) that takes measurements and transmits the results by radio

teleology *n* a belief that all things are designed to fulfil a purpose **~gical** *adj*

telepathy *n* sending of messages directly from one mind to another **–thic** *adj* **–thically** *adv*

telephone *n* (apparatus for) the sending and receiving of sounds over long distances by electric means ♦ *vi/t* (try to) speak (to) by telephone

telephonist *n* person whose job is to make telephone connections

telephoto lens *n* special lens used for photographing very distant objects

teleprinter also **teletypewriter** *n* machine with a keyboard and a printer for sending and receiving telex messages

Teleprompter *n tdmk for* device that unrolls a script line by line in front of a person appearing on television

telescope *n* tube with a special lens or mirror for magnifying very distant objects ♦ *vi/t* shorten, esp. **a** by one part sliding over another **b** by crushing **–scopic** *adj* **1** of or related to a telescope **2** that telescopes

teletext *n* system of broadcasting written information (e.g. news) on television

televise *vt* broadcast on television

television *n* (apparatus for receiving) the broadcasting of pictures and sounds by electric waves

telex *n* **1** method of sending written messages round the world by telephone and satellite **2** message sent by telex ♦ *vt* send by telex

tell *v* **told 1** *vt* make (something) known to (someone) in words **2** *vt* warn; advise: *I told you it wouldn't work.* **3** *vt* order: *I told him to do it.* **4** *vi/t* find out; know: *How can you tell which button to press?* **5 all told** when all have been counted **tell against** *phr vt* count in judgment against **tell off** *phr vt* speak severely to (someone who has done something wrong) **tell on** *phr vt* **1** have a bad effect on **2** *infml* (used esp. by children) inform against (someone)

teller *n* **1** bank clerk **2** person who counts votes

telling *adj* sharply effective: *a telling argument*

telltale *adj* being a small sign that shows something

telly *n sl* television

temerity /tə'merəti/ *n* foolish confidence; rashness

temp *n infml* secretary employed for a short time ♦ *vi infml, esp. BrE* work as a temp

temper *n* **1** state of mind **2** angry or impatient state of mind ♦ *vt* **1** harden (esp. metal) by special treatment **2** make less severe: *justice tempered with mercy*

tempera *n* method of painting using pigments mixed with a thick liquid (e.g. egg yolk and water)

temperament *n* person's character esp. with regard to being calm or excitable **~al** *adj* **1** having or showing frequent changes of temper **2** caused by temperament **~ally** *adv*

temperance *n* **1** being temperate **2** complete avoidance of alcohol

temperate *adj* **1** (of an area's weather) neither very hot nor very cold **2** avoiding too much of anything

temperature *n* **1** degree of heat or coldness **2** bodily temperature higher than the correct one; fever

tempest *n lit* violent storm

tempestuous *adj* full of wildness or anger **~ly** *adv* **~ness** *n*

template *n* shape used as a guide for cutting something hard

temple¹ *n* building where people worship a god or gods, esp. in the Hindu and Buddhist religions

temple² *n* flattish area on each side of the forehead

tempo *n* **-pos 1** rate of movement or activity **2** speed of music

temporal *adj* **1** of practical rather than religious affairs **2** of time

temporary *adj* lasting for only a limited time **–rily** *adv*

temporize, -ise *vi* **1** delay or hedge in negotiations to gain time **2** conform to current pressures for a time

tempt *vt* (try to) persuade (someone) to do something wrong **~ation** *n* **1** act of tempting **2** something that tempts, esp. by being very attractive **~ing** *adj* very attractive **~er** *n*

ten *determiner, n, pron* 10

tenable *adj* **1** (of a point of view) that can be reasonably supported or held **2** (of a job) that can be held for the stated period

tenacious /tə'nayshəs/ *adj* bravely firm **~ly** *adv* **–city** *n*

tenant *n* person who pays rent for the use of a building or land **–ancy** *n* **1** length of time a person is a tenant **2** use of a place as a tenant

tenantry *n* group of tenants, esp. of farm land

tench *n* **tench** *or* **tenches** European freshwater fish

tend¹ *vt* be likely

tend² *vt* take care of

tendency *n* **1** likelihood of often happening or behaving in a particular way **2** special liking and natural skill: *She has artistic tendencies.*

tendentious /ten'denshəs/ *adj* (in discussion) unfairly leaving out other points of view **~ly** *adv* **~ness** *n*

tender¹ *adj* **1** not difficult to bite through **2** needing careful handling; delicate **3** sore **4** gentle, kind, and loving **~ly** *adv* **~ness** *n*

tender² *v* **1** *vt* present for acceptance: *She tendered her resignation.* **2** *vt* offer in payment of debt **3** *vi* make a tender ♦ *n* statement of the price one would charge

tender³ *n* coal- or water-carrying railway vehicle

tenderfoot *n* **–feet** *or* **–foots** inexperienced beginner

tenderhearted *adj* easily made to feel love, pity, or sorrow **~ly** *adv*

tenderize, -ise *vt* make (meat) tender by special preparation

tenderloin *n* back fillet of pork or beef

tendon *n* strong cord connecting a muscle to a bone

tendril *n* thin curling stem by which a plant holds on to things

tenement *n* large building divided into flats, esp. in a poor city area

tenet *n* principle; belief

tenner *n BrE sl* £10

tennis *n* game played by hitting a ball over a net with a racket

tennis elbow *n* pain and inflammation of the elbow, caused by strain

tenor *n* **1** (man with) the highest natural man's singing voice **2** instrument with the same range of notes as this: *a tenor saxophone* **3** general meaning (of something written or spoken)

tenpin *n* any of the ten bottle-shaped objects to be knocked over with a ball in **tenpin bowling**

tense¹ *adj* **1** stretched tight **2** nervously anxious ♦ *vi/t* (cause to) become tense **~ly** *adv* **~ness** *n*

tense² *n* form of a verb showing time and continuity of action: *the future tense*

tensile *adj* of tension (1) **–ility** *n*
tension *n* **1** degree to which something is (able to be) stretched **2** nervous anxiety **3** anxious, untrusting, and possibly dangerous relationship: *racial tensions in the inner city* **4** *tech* electric power: *high-tension cables*
tent *n* cloth shelter supported usu. by poles and ropes, used esp. by campers
tentacle *n* long snakelike boneless limb of certain creatures
tentative *adj* **1** not firmly arranged or fixed: *a tentative agreement* **2** not firm in making statements or decisions **~ly** *adv*
tenterhooks *n* **on tenterhooks** anxiously waiting
tenth *determiner, adv, n, pron* 10th
tenuous *adj* slight **~ly** *adv* **~ness** *n*
tenure *n* **1** act, right, or period of holding a job or land **2** right to keep one's job, esp. as a university teacher
tepee *n* tent used by North American Indians
tepid *adj* only slightly warm
tequila /təˈkeelə/ *n* strong alcoholic drink made in Mexico
tercentenary also **tercentennial** *n* 300th anniversary
term *n* **1** division of the school or university year: *the summer term* **2** fixed period: *a 4-year term as president* **3** word or expression, esp. as used in a particular activity: *'Tort' is a legal term* ♦ *vt* name; call; describe as **~ly** *adj*
termagant *n, adj* (woman who is) noisy and quarrelsome
terminal *adj* of or being an illness that will cause death ♦ *n* **1** main building for passengers or goods at an airport or port **2** apparatus for giving instructions to and getting information from a computer **3** place for electrical connections: *the terminals of a battery* **~ly** *adv*
terminate *vi/t fml* (cause to) come to an end **–nation** *n*
terminology *n* (use of) particular terms: *legal terminology* **–logical** *adj*
terminus *n* **-ni** *or* **-nuses** stop or station at the end of a bus or railway line
termite *n* antlike insect that feeds on wood
terms *pl n* **1** conditions of an agreement or contract **2** conditions of sale **3 come to terms** reach an agreement **4 come to terms with** accept (something unwelcome) **5 on good/bad/friendly terms** having a good, bad, etc., relationship
tern *n* small white sea bird
terpsichorean *adj fml* of dancing
terrace *n* **1** level area cut from a slope **2** flat area next to a building **3** steps on which watchers stand in football grounds **4** row of joined houses ♦ *vt* form into terraces (1)
terraced house *n BrE* house which is part of a terrace
terracotta *n* (articles of) reddish brown baked clay
terra firma *n* dry land; solid ground
terrain *n* (area of) land of the stated sort
terrapin *n* **-pin** *or* **-pins** small freshwater turtle
terrarium *n* **-ria** *or* **-riums** closed container for rearing animals or growing plants
terrestrial *adj* of the Earth or land, as opposed to space or the sea
terrible *adj* **1** extremely severe: *a terrible accident* **2** extremely bad or unpleasant: *a terrible meal* **–bly** *adv* **1** extremely severely or badly **2** extremely: *terribly sorry*
terrier *n* type of small active dog
terrific *adj* **1** excellent **2** very great **~ally** *adv* extremely
terrify *vt* frighten extremely
territory *n* **1** (area of) land, esp. as ruled by one government: *This island is French territory.* **2** area belonging to (and defended by) a particular person, animal, or group **3** area for which one person or group is responsible **–rial** *adj* **1** of or being land or territory **2** (of animals) showing a tendency to guard one's own territory
terror *n* extreme fear
terrorism *n* use of violence for political purposes **-ist** *n*
terrorize, –ise *vt* fill with terror by

threats or acts of violence
terrycloth also **terry** *n* thick cotton cloth with uncut loops on both sides, used for making towels
terse *adj* using few words, often to show anger **~ly** *adv* **~ness** *n*
tertiary /ˈtuhshəri/ *adj* third in order
Terylene *n tdmk for* synthetic polyester fibre
TESOL *n* teaching English to speakers of other languages
tessellated *adj* made of small tiles
test *n* **1** set of questions or tasks to measure someone's knowledge or skill **2** short medical examination: *an eye test* **3** use of something to see how well it works: *nuclear weapon tests* **4 put to the test** find out the qualities of (something) by use ♦ *vt* **1** study or examine with a test **2** provide difficult conditions for: *a testing time for the country* **3** search by means of tests: *The company is testing for oil.*
testament *n* **1** *fml* will[2] (4) **2** (*cap.*) either of the two main parts of the Bible: *the Old Testament* **~ary** *adj* of or according to a will
testate *adj* having made a will **-tor** *n* person who has made a will
test case *n* legal case which sets a new precedent
testicle *n* either of the two round sperm-producing organs in male animals
testify *vi/t* **1** make a solemn statement of truth **2** show (something) clearly; prove
testimonial *n* **1** formal written statement of someone's character and ability **2** something given or done to show respect or thanks
testimony *n* formal statement of facts, esp. in a court of law
testis *n* **-tes** testicle
test match *n* international cricket or rugby match
testosterone *n* male hormone governing production of secondary male characteristics
test tube *n* small glass tube, closed at one end, used in scientific tests
test-tube baby *n* baby conceived by artificial insemination, esp. when egg and sperm are joined outside the mother's body
testy *adj* bad-tempered **-tily** *adv*
tetanus *n* serious disease, caused by infection of a cut, which causes the muscles to stiffen
tetchy *adj* sensitive in a bad-tempered way **-chily** *adv* **-chiness** *n*
tête-à-tête *n* private conversation between two people
tether *n* rope to which an animal is tied ♦ *vt* fasten with a tether
Teutonic *adj* **1** of or being the ancient German people **2** German
text *n* **1** main body of printed words in a book **2** exact original words e.g. of a speech **3** textbook: *a set text* **4** sentence from the Bible used by a priest in a sermon **~ual** *adj*
textbook *n* standard book used for studying a particular subject, esp. in schools ♦ *adj* **1** ideal: *textbook journalism* **2** typical
textile *n* woven material
texture *n* quality of roughness or smoothness, coarseness or fineness, of a surface or substance
-th *suffix* (makes adjectives from numbers): *seventh*
thalidomide *n* drug no longer used because it caused unborn babies to develop wrongly
than *conj, prep* **1** (used in comparing things): *This is bigger than that.* **2** when; as soon as: *No sooner had we started to eat than the doorbell rang.*
thane *n* **1** minor landholder in Anglo-Saxon England **2** Scottish feudal lord
thank *vt* express one's gratefulness to
thanks *pl n* **1** (words expressing) gratefulness **2 thanks to** because of **~ful** *adj* **1** glad **2** grateful **~fully** *adv* **~less** *adj* not likely to be rewarded with thanks or success
thanks *interj* thank you
thanksgiving *n* **1** (an) expression of gratefulness, esp. to God **2** (*cap.*) holiday in the US

thank you *interj* (used for politely expressing thanks or acceptance)

that *determiner, pron* **those 1** (being) the person, thing, or idea which is understood or has just been mentioned or shown **2 that's that** that is the end of the matter ♦ *conj* **1** (used for introducing clauses): *She said that she couldn't come.* **2** (used as a relative pronoun) which/who(m): *This is the book that I bought.* ♦ *adv* to such a degree; so: *It wasn't that difficult.*

thatch *vt, n* (make or cover with) a roof covering of straw **~er** *n*

thaw *v* **1** *vi/t* change from a solid frozen state to being liquid or soft **2** *vi* become friendlier or less formal ♦ *n* **1** period when ice and snow melt **2** increase in friendliness

the *definite article, determiner* (used for referring to a particular thing) ♦ *adv* **1** (used in comparisons, to show that two things happen together): *The more he eats, the fatter he gets.* **2** (in comparisons to show that someone or something is better, worse, etc., than before): *She looks (all) the better for two weeks holiday in Spain.*

theatre, *AmE* usu. **-ter** *n* **1** building where plays are performed **2** the work of people involved with plays: *He's in the theatre.* **3** large room where public talks are given **4** room where medical operations are done **5** area of activity in a war **-atrical** *adj* **1** of the theatre **2** too showy; not natural **-atrically** *adv* **-atricality** *n*

theatregoer *n* person who goes regularly to theatres

thee *pron lit* (*object form of* **thou**) you

theft *n* stealing

thegn *n* thane

their *determiner* of them: *their house*

theirs *pron* of them; their one(s): *It's theirs.*

theism /ˈthee,iz(ə)m/ *n* belief in the existence of one god **-ist** *n* **-istic** *adj*

them *pron* (*object form of* **they**): *I want those books; give them to me.*

theme *n* **1** subject of a talk, work of art, or piece of writing **2** repeated idea, image, or tune in writing or music

theme park *n* enclosed outdoor area containing amusements which are all based on a single subject (e.g. space travel)

themselves *pron* **1** (*reflexive form of* **they**): *They saw themselves on television.* **2** (*strong form of* **they**): *They built it themselves.* **3 (all) by themselves**: **a** alone **b** without help **4 to themselves** not shared

then *adv* **1** at that time: *I was happier then.* **2** next; afterwards.... *and then we went home.* **3** in that case; as a result: *Have you done your homework? Then you can watch television.* **4** besides; also

thence *adv fml* from that place

thenceforth also **thenceforward** *adv fml* from that time on

theo- also **the-** *prefix* concerning God or gods: *theology*

theocracy *n* government by divine guidance **-atic** *adj*

theodolite *n* instrument for measuring angles in surveying

theology *n* study of religious ideas and beliefs **-ologian** *n* **-ological** *adj*

theorem *n* mathematical statement that can be proved by reasoning

theoretician *n* person who develops or studies the theory of a subject; theorist

theory *n* **1** statement intended to explain a fact or event **2** general principles and methods as opposed to practice **-rize, -rise** *vi* form a theory **-retical** *adj* existing in or based on theory, not practice or fact **-retically** *adv* **-rist** *n*

therapeutic /therəˈpyoohtik/ *adj* **1** for the treating or curing of disease **2** having a good effect on one's health or state of mind: *I find swimming very therapeutic.* **-tics** *pl n* branch of medicine concerned with the cure of disease

therapy *n* treatment of illnesses of the body or mind **-pist** *n*

there *adv* **1** at or to that place: *He lives*

over there. **2** (used for drawing attention to someone or something): *There goes John.* **3 all there** healthy in mind **4 there and then** at that exact place and time **5 there you are: a** here is what you wanted **b** I told you so ♦ *interj* (used for comforting someone or expressing victory, satisfaction, etc.): *There, there. Stop crying.* ♦ *pron* (used for showing that something or someone exists or happens, usu. as the subject of **be, seem**, or **appear**): *There's someone at the door to see you.*

thereabouts *adv* near that place, time, number, etc.

thereafter *adv* after that

thereby *adv* by doing or saying that

therefore *adv* for that reason; as a result

thereof *adv fml* of or belonging to it

thereupon *adv* **1** about that matter **2** without delay

therm *n* (measurement of heat equal to) 100 000 British thermal units

thermal *adj* of, using, producing, or caused by heat ♦ *n* rising current of warm air

thermion /ˈthuhm,i·ən/ *n* electron emitted by an incandescent substance **~ic** *adj* **~ics** *pl n* science dealing with thermions

thermodynamics *n* scientific study of heat and its power in driving machines

thermometer *n* instrument for measuring temperature

thermonuclear *adj* nuclear (1)

thermoplastic *adj* capable of softening whenever heated and setting when cooled **thermoplastic** *n*

thermos *n tdmk for* flask (3)

thermosetting *adj* becoming permanently rigid after heating and shaping

thermostat *n* apparatus for keeping e.g. a machine or room at an even temperature

thesaurus *n* dictionary with words grouped according to similarities in meaning

these *pl. of* this

thesis *n* **-ses 1** long piece of writing on a particular subject, done to gain a higher university degree **2** opinion or statement supported by reasoned arguments

thespian *adj, n* (of drama or) an actor

thew *n* **1** muscle **2** strength

they *pron* (used as the subject of a sentence) **1** those people, animals, or things **2** people in general: *They say prices are going to rise.* **3** (used to avoid saying **he** or **she**): *If anyone knows, they should tell me.*

they'd *short for:* **1** they had **2** they would

they'll *short for:* they will

they're *short for:* they are

they've *short for:* they have

thick *adj* **1** having a large or the stated distance between opposite surfaces **2** (of liquid) not flowing easily **3** difficult to see through: *thick mist* **4** full of; covered with: *furniture thick with dust* **5** with many objects set close together: *a thick forest* **6** *BrE sl* stupid ♦ *adv* **1** thickly **2 thick and fast** quickly and in large numbers ♦ *n* **1** part, place, etc., of greatest activity **2 through thick and thin** through both good and bad times **~ly** *adv* **~en** *vi/t* make or become thicker **~ness** *n* **1** being thick **2** layer

thicket *n* thick growth of bushes and small trees

thickhead *n infml* stupid person **~ed** *adj*

thickset *adj* having a broad strong body

thick-skinned *adj* not easily offended

thief *n* **thieves** person who steals

thieve *vi* steal

thigh *n* top part of the human leg

thimble *n* small cap put over the end of the finger when sewing

thin *adj* **-nn- 1** having a small distance between opposite surfaces **2** not fat **3** (of a liquid) flowing (too) easily; weak **4** with few objects widely separated: *a thin audience* **5** easy to see through: *thin mist* **6** lacking force or strength: *a thin excuse* **7 thin end of the wedge** something which seems unimportant but will open the way for more serious things of a similar kind ♦ *adv* thinly ♦ *vi/t* make or become thinner **~ly** *adv* **~ness** *n* **~ner** *n* liquid (e.g. turpentine) used to thin paint

thin air *n infml* state of not being seen or not existing

thine *determiner* thy ♦ *pron lit* (*possessive form of* **thou**) yours

thing *n* **1** unnamed or unnameable object: *What do you use this thing for?* **2** remark, idea, or subject: *What a nasty thing to say!* **3** act; activity: *the first thing we have to do* **4** event: *A funny thing happened today.* **5** that which is necessary or desirable: *Cold beer's just the thing on a hot day.* **6** the fashion or custom: *the latest thing in shoes* **7** *sl* activity satisfying to one personally: *Tennis isn't really my thing.* **8 have a thing about** have a strong like or dislike for **9 make a thing of** give too much importance to **10 the thing is** what we must consider is **things** *pl n* **1** general state of affairs; situation **2** one's personal possessions: *Pack your things in your suitcase.*

think *v* **thought 1** *vi* use the mind to make judgments **2** *vt* have as an opinion; believe: *Do you think it will rain?* **3** *vt* understand; imagine: *I can't think why you did it.* **4** *vt* have as a plan: *I think I'll go swimming tomorrow.* **5 think aloud** to speak one's thoughts as they come **think about** *phr vt* consider seriously before making a decision **think of** *phr vt* **1** form a possible plan for **2** have as an opinion about: *what do you think of that?* **3** take into account: *But think of the cost!* **4** remember **5 not think much of** have a low opinion of **6 think better of** decide against **think out/through** *phr vt* consider carefully and in detail **think over** *phr vt* consider seriously **think up** *phr vt* invent (esp. an idea) ♦ *n* act of thinking **~er** *n*

thinking *n* opinion: *What's the government's thinking on this?* ♦ *adj* thoughtful; able to think clearly

think tank *n* committee of experts formed to evolve new ideas

thin-skinned *adj* easily offended

third *determiner, adv, n, pron* 3rd

third degree *n* hard questioning and rough treatment

third party *n* **1** person other than the two main people concerned **2** person other than the holder protected by an insurance agreement

third person *n* form of verb or pronoun used to indicate a person or thing that is being spoken about

third-rate *adj* of very low quality

Third World *n* the countries of the world which are industrially less well-developed

thirst *n* **1** desire for drink **2** lack of drink: *I'm dying of thirst* **3** strong desire: *the thirst for knowledge* **~y** *adj* feeling or causing thirst **~ily** *adv*

thirteen *determiner, n, pron* 13 **~th** *determiner, adv, n, pron* 13th

thirty *determiner, n, pron* 30 **–tieth** *determiner, adv, n, pron* 30th

this *determiner, pron* **these 1** (one) going to be mentioned, to happen: *I'll come this morning.* **2** (one) near or nearer in place, time, thought, etc.: *Give me these, not those.* **3** *infml* a certain: *There were these two men standing there…* ♦ *adv* to this degree: *It was this big.*

thistle *n* plant with prickly leaves and usu. purple flowers

thistledown *n* fluffy hairs from the seed head of a thistle

thither *adv* to or towards that place

thong *n* narrow length of leather used esp. for fastening

thorax *n med* part of the body between the neck and the abdomen

thorn *n* **1** sharp growth on a plant **2 thorn in one's flesh** continual cause of annoyance **~y** *adj* **1** prickly **2** difficult to deal with

thorough *adj* **1** complete in every way **2** careful about details **~ly** *adv* **~ness** *n*

thoroughbred *n, adj* (animal, esp. a horse) from parents of one very good breed

thoroughfare *n* large public road

thoroughgoing *adj* very thorough;

complete
those *pl of* that
thou *pron lit* (used of a single person) you
though *conj, adv* **1** in spite of the fact (that): *Though it's hard work, I enjoy it.* **2** but: *I'll try, though I don't think I can.* **3 as though** as if
thought *past t. and p. of* think ♦ *n* **1** something thought; idea, etc. **2** thinking **3** serious consideration **4** intention: *I had no thought of causing any trouble.* **5** attention; regard: *acting with no thought to her own safety* **~ful** *adj* **1** thinking deeply **2** paying attention to the wishes of others **~fully** *adv* **~less** *adj* showing a selfish or careless lack of thought **~lessly** *adv* **~lessness** *n*
thousand *determiner, n, pron* **thousand** *or* **thousands** 1000 **~th** *determiner, adv, n, pron* 1000th
thrall *n lit* slavery
thrash *v* **1** *vt* beat (as if) with a whip or stick **2** *vt* defeat thoroughly **3** *vi* move wildly or violently **thrash out** *phr vt* find an answer (to) by much talk and consideration
thread *n* **1** very fine cord made by spinning e.g. cotton or silk **2** line of reasoning connecting the parts of an argument or story **3** raised line that winds round the outside of a screw ♦ *vt* **1** put thread through the hole in (a needle) **2** put (a film or tape) in place on an apparatus **3** put (things) together on a thread **4 thread one's way through** go carefully through (e.g. crowds)
threadbare *adj* (of cloth) very worn
threat *n* **1** expression of an intention to harm or punish someone **2** something or someone regarded as a possible danger
threaten *v* **1** *vt* make a threat (against): *They threatened to blow up the plane.* **2** *vt* give warning of (something bad): *The sky threatened rain.* **3** *vi* (of something bad) seem likely: *Danger threatens.*
three *determiner, n, pron* 3
three-D *n* three-dimensional form or appearance
three-dimensional *adj* having length, depth, and height
three-legged race *n* race run by pairs of competitors with their inside legs tied together
three-line whip *n* order from a political party telling its MPs to attend a debate and vote in a specified way
three-quarter *adj* consisting of three fourths of the whole
threequarter, threequarter back *n* player in rugby between half back and fullback
three R's *pl n* reading, writing, and arithmetic, considered as forming the base of children's education
threnody *n* song of lament
thresh *vt* separate the grain from (e.g. corn) by beating
threshold *n* **1** point of beginning: *scientists on the threshold of a research breakthrough* **2** piece of stone or wood across the bottom of a doorway
threw *past t. of* throw
thrice *adv lit* three times
thrift *n* not spending too much money **~y** *adj* **~ily** *adv* **~less** *adj* wasteful with money
thrill *n* (something producing) a sudden strong feeling of excitement, fear, etc. ♦ *vi/t* (cause to) feel a thrill **~er** *n* book or film telling a very exciting (crime) story
thrive *vi* **thrived** *or* **throve, thrived** develop well and be healthy, strong, or successful
throat *n* **1** passage from the mouth down inside the body **2** front of the neck
throaty *adj* hoarse **–tily** *adv*
throb *vi* **-bb-** (of a machine, the action of the heart, etc.) beat heavily and regularly ♦ *n* throbbing
throes *pl n* **1** *lit* sudden violent pains, esp. caused by dying **2 in the throes of** struggling with (some difficulty)
thrombosis *n* **-ses** formation of a blood clot in a blood vessel **–botic** *adj*
throne *n* ceremonial seat of a king or queen

throng *n* large crowd ♦ *vi/t* go as or fill with a throng
throstle *n* thrush[1]
throttle *vt* seize (someone) by the throat to stop them breathing ♦ *n* valve controlling the flow of petrol into an engine
through *prep, adv* **1** in at one side (of) and out at the other: *Water flows through this pipe.* **2** from beginning to end (of): *I read through the letter.* ♦ *prep* **1** by means of; because of: *The war was lost through bad organization.* **2** *AmE* up to and including: *Wednesday through Saturday* ♦ *adv* **1** so as to be connected by telephone **2 through and through** completely ♦ *adj* **1** finished; done: *Are you through yet?* **2** having no further relationship: *I'm through with him!* **3** allowing a continuous journey: *a through train*
throughout *prep, adv* in, to, through, or during every part (of)
throughput *n* amount of work or materials dealt with in a particular time
throughway , thruway *n AmE* very wide road for high-speed traffic
throw *v* **threw, thrown 1** *vi/t* send (something) through the air with a sudden movement of the arm **2** *vt* move or put forcefully or quickly: *The two fighters threw themselves at each other* **3** *vt* cause to fall to the ground: *Her horse threw her.* **4** *vt* direct: *I think I can throw some light on the mystery.* **5** *vt* operate (a switch) **6** *vt* shape from wet clay when making pottery **7** *vt* make one's voice appear to come from somewhere other than one's mouth **8** *vt infml* arrange (a party) **9** *vt* confuse; shock: *Her reply really threw me.* **10 throw a fit** have a sudden uncontrolled attack of anger **11 throw oneself on/upon** put complete trust in **12 throw one's weight about** give orders to others, because one thinks one is important **throw away** *phr vt* **1** get rid of **2** waste (an opportunity) **throw in** *phr vt* **1** supply additionally without increasing the price **2 throw in the sponge/towel** admit defeat **throw off** *phr vt* **1** recover from **2** escape from **throw open** *phr vt* allow people to enter **throw out** *phr vt* **1** get rid of **2** refuse to accept **throw over** *phr vt* end a relationship with **throw together** *phr vt* build or make hastily **throw up** *phr v* **1** *vt* stop doing (esp. a job) **2** *vt* bring to notice: *The investigation has thrown up some interesting facts.* **3** *vi sl* vomit ♦ *n* **1** act of throwing **2** distance thrown **~er** *n*
throwaway *adj* **1** spoken casually: *throwaway lines* **2** disposable: *throwaway cutlery*
throwback *n* (example of) a return to something in the past
thrum *vi/t* **-mm-** play (e.g. a stringed instrument) idly
thrush[1] *n* common singing bird with a spotted breast
thrush[2] *n* infectious disease of the mouth, throat, and vagina
thrust *vi/t* **thrust** push forcefully and suddenly ♦ *n* **1** act of thrusting **2** forward-moving power of an engine **3** (main) meaning
thud *vi, n* **-dd-** (make) the dull sound of something heavy falling
thug *n* violent criminal
thumb *n* **1** short thick finger set apart from the other four **2 all thumbs** *infml* very awkward with the hands **3 thumb one's nose at** *infml* make fun of **4 thumbs up/down** an expression of approval/disapproval **5 under someone's thumb** *infml* under the control of someone ♦ *vt* **thumb a lift** ask passing motorists for a ride by signalling with one's thumb **thumb through** *phr vi/t* look through (a book) quickly
thumbnail *n* nail of the thumb ♦ *adj* small or short: *a thumbnail description*
thumbscrew *n* instrument for crushing the thumbs to cause great pain
thumbtack *n AmE* drawing pin
thump *v* **1** *vt* hit hard **2** *vi* make a repeated dull sound: *My heart thumped.* ♦ *n* (sound of) a heavy blow

thumping *adj infml* very (big)
thunder *n* loud explosive noise that follows lightning ♦ *v* **1** *vi* produce thunder **2** *vi* produce or go with a loud noise **3** *vt* shout loudly **~ous** *adj* very loud **~ously** *adv* **~y** *adj*
thunderbolt *n* **1** thunder and lightning together **2** event causing great shock
thunderclap *n* a single loud crash of thunder
thunderstruck *adj* shocked
Thursday *n* the 4th day of the week
thus *adv fml* **1** in this way **2** with this result **3 thus far** up until now
thwack *n, v* whack
thwart *vt* prevent from happening or succeeding ♦ *n* seat across a boat
thy *determiner lit (possessive form of* **thou**) your
thyme *n* small herb used in cooking
thyroid *n* gland in the neck that controls growth and activity
tiara *n* piece of jewellery like a small crown
tibia *n* **-iae** *or* **-ias** *med* chief bone in the shin
tic *n* sudden unconscious movement of the muscles
tick[1] *n* **1** short repeated sound of a watch or clock **2** mark showing esp. correctness **3** *sl, esp. BrE* moment ♦ *v* **1** *vi* (of a watch or clock) make a tick **2** *vt* mark with a tick **3 make (someone) tick** *infml* motivate (someone) **tick off** *phr vt infml* speak sharply to **tick over** *phr vi* continue working at slow steady rate
tick[2] *n* very small blood-sucking arachnid
tick[3] *n* **on tick** *infml* on credit
ticker tape *n* paper tape on which a telegraphic machine prints information
ticket *n* **1** piece of paper or card showing that payment for a service has been made **2** piece of card showing e.g. the price and size of goods **3** printed notice of an offence against the traffic laws **4** *infml* exactly the thing needed: *This hammer is just the ticket.* ♦ *vt* put a ticket on
ticking *n* strong cloth used for mattress and pillow covers
tickle *v* **1** *vt* touch (someone's body) lightly to produce laughter or nervous excitement **2** *vi* give or feel a prickly sensation **3** *vt* delight or amuse ♦ *n* (act or feel of) tickling **-lish** *adj* **1** sensitive to being tickled **2** (of a problem or situation) rather difficult
tick-tack-toe *n AmE* noughts and crosses
tidal wave *n* very large dangerous ocean wave
tiddler *n BrE* very small fish
tiddly *adj BrE infml* slightly drunk
tiddlywinks *n* game of flicking small plastic discs into a cup
tide[1] *n* **1** regular rise and fall of the sea **2** current caused by this **3** feeling or tendency that moves or changes like the tide: *the tide of public opinion* **tide over** *phr vt* help (someone) through (a difficult period) **tidal** *adj*
tidemark *infml* mark round the inside of an empty bath showing the level to which it was filled
tideway *n* (current in) a channel in which the tide runs
tidings *pl n lit* news
tidy *adj* **1** neat **2** *infml* fairly large: *a tidy income* ♦ *vi/t* make (things) tidy **tidily** *adv* **tidiness** *n*
tie *n* **1** band of cloth worn round the neck **2** string or wire used for fastening something **3** something that unites: *the ties of friendship* **4** something that limits one's freedom **5** result in which each competitor gains an equal score ♦ *v* **tied;** *pres. p.* **tying 1** *vt* fasten by knotting **2** *vt* make (a knot or bow) **3** *vi/t* finish (a match or competition) with a tie **tie down** *phr vt* **1** limit the freedom of **2** force to be exact **tie in** *phr vi* have a close connection **tie up** *phr vt* **1** limit free use of (money or property) **2** connect **3 tied up** very busy
tie-breaker also **tiebreak** *n* method of selecting a winner from contestants with tied scores
tied cottage *n* house owned by an em-

ployer and rented to a worker, the tenancy depending on the job

tied house *n* pub owned or rented by a brewery and selling its products

tie-dye *vt* tie (cloth or yarn) before dyeing, so that parts are protected from the dye

tie-in *n* product that is connected in some way with an event, e.g. a TV show

tiepin *n* decorative clip for holding a tie in place

tier *n* **1** any of a number of rising rows of esp. seats **2** level of organization

tie-up *n* connection

tiff *n* slight quarrel

tiffin *n* light meal at midday or mid-morning

tiger *n* **1** large Asian wild cat that has yellowish fur with black bands **2** fierce or brave person

tiger lily *n* Asian lily with orange flowers

tight *adj* **1** firmly fixed in place; closely fastened **2** fully stretched **3** fitting (too) closely; leaving no free room or time: *a tight schedule* **4** difficult to obtain: *Money is tight just now.* **5** marked by close competition: *a tight finish* **6** *sl* ungenerous with money **7** *sl* drunk **8 in a tight corner/spot** in a difficult position ♦ *adv* tightly **~ly** *adv* **~en** *vi/t* make or become tighter **~ness** *n*

tights *pl n* very close fitting garment covering the legs and lower body

tight-fisted *adj infml* very ungenerous, esp. with money **~ness** *n*

tight-lipped *adj* **1** having the lips pressed together **2** not saying anything

tightrope *n* rope tightly stretched high above the ground, on which someone walks

tigress *n* female tiger

tike *n* tyke

tilde /ˈtildə/ *n* accent ~ put over the letter *n* in Spanish

tile *n* **1** thin shaped piece of baked clay or other material used for covering roofs, walls, or floors **2 (out) on the tiles** enjoying oneself wildly ♦ *vt* cover with tiles

till[1] *prep, conj* until

till[2] *n* drawer where money is kept in a shop

till[3] *vt lit* cultivate (the ground)

tillage *n arch.* cultivation of land

tiller *n* long handle for turning a boat's rudder

tilt *v* **1** *vi/t* (cause to) slope (as if) by raising one end **2** *vi* fight with a lance ♦ *n* **1** slope **2** combat with lances **3 (at) full tilt** at full speed

timber *n* **1** wood for building **2** growing trees **3** wooden beam, esp. in a ship ♦ *vt* cover or support with timbers

timberline *n* treeline

timbre /ˈtambrə/ *n* tone of a voice or instrument

timbrel *n* small hand drum or tambourine

time *n* **1** continuous measurable quantity from the past, through the present, and into the future **2** period: *It happened a long time ago.* **3** period in which an action is completed, esp. in a race: *Her time was just under four minutes.* **4** particular point stated in hours, minutes and seconds: *The time is 4 o'clock.* **5** particular point in the year or day **6** occasion: *I've been here several times.* **7** experience connected with a period or occasion: *We had a great time at the party.* **8** period in history: *in ancient times* **9** point when something should happen: *The plane arrived on time.* **10** rate of speed of a piece of music **11 behind the times** old-fashioned **12** *sl* **do time** go to prison **13 take one's time** not hurry **14 the time of one's life** a very enjoyable experience ♦ *vt* **1** arrange the time at which (something) happens **2** measure the time taken by or for **3** (in sport) make (a shot) at exactly the right moment **~less** *adj* **1** unending **2** not changed by time **~lessness** *n* **~ly** *adj* happening at just the right time: *a timely warning* **~liness** *n* **timer** *n* person or machine that measures or records time

time-and-motion *adj* concerning the measurement and study of the effectiveness of work methods

time bomb *n* **1** bomb set to explode at a particular time **2** situation likely to become very dangerous

time capsule *n* strong, sealed container filled with objects and documents intended to give an impression of the time when it was closed to people who open it many years later

time exposure *n* (photograph taken by) exposure of film to the light for more than a second

time-honoured *adj* sanctioned by tradition

time immemorial *n lit* long ago in the past

timekeeper *n* person who records the time esp. taken by competitors in a race, or worked by employees

time lag *n* period of time between two closely connected events

time-lapse *adj* (of a system of filming) using a series of still shots taken at intervals and then run together, to give a speeded-up impression of a slow process

time limit *n* period of time in which something must be done

timepiece *n arch. or tech* clock or watch

times *n* (used to show an amount that is calculated by multiplying something the stated number of times): *Their house is at least 3 times the size of ours.* ♦ *prep* multiplied by: *3 times 3 is 9.*

timeserver *n derog* person who acts so as to please those in power at the time **–ving** *adj, n*

time-sharing *n* **1** use of one main computer by many people in different places **2** several people buying or renting a house (esp. for holidays), each using it for short periods each year **time-share** *adj*

time signature *n* mark, esp. two numbers, to show the number and length of beats in a bar of music

time switch *n* electrical switch linked to a clock, that is set to start an operation at a certain time

timetable *n* **1** list of the travelling times of public transport **2** (list of) the times of classes in a school, etc. ♦ *vt* **1** to plan for a future time: *The meeting was timetabled for tomorrow.* **2** arrange according to a timetable

timeworn *adj* **1** worn or damaged by time **2** very old

time zone *n* region of the Earth using one standard time

timid *adj* fearful; lacking courage **~ly** *adv* **~ity** *n*

timing *n* choosing the exact moment for doing something to get the best effect

timorous /ˈtim(ə)rəs/ *adj* fearful **~ly** *adv* **~ness** *n*

timpani *pl n* set of kettledrums in an orchestra **–ist** *n*

tin *n* **1** soft whitish metal **2** *BrE* small closed metal container in which food is preserved ♦ *vt* **-nn-** pack (food) in tins **~ny** *adj* **1** of or like tin **2** having a thin metallic sound

tincture *n* medical substance mixed with alcohol

tinder *n* material that burns easily, used esp. for lighting fires

tinderbox *n* **1** box holding the things needed for lighting a fire, before the invention of matches **2** potentially dangerous situation

tine *n* pointed part of a fork or antler

tinfoil *n* very thin bendable sheet of shiny metal

tinge *vt* give a small amount of colour to: *black hair tinged with grey* ♦ *n* small amount

tingle *vi, n* (feel) a slight, not unpleasant, stinging sensation

tin god *n infml* person who esteems himself, or is esteemed by others, more highly than is reasonable

tin hat *n infml* metal helmet worn by soldiers

tinker *vi* work without a definite plan or useful results, making small changes, esp. when trying to repair or improve something ♦ *n* **1** act of tinkering **2** travelling mender of pots and pans

tinkle *vi* make light metallic sounds ♦ *n* **1** tinkling sound **2** *BrE sl* telephone

call
tinnitus /tiˈnietəs/ *n* ringing sound produced by a disorder of hearing
tin opener *n BrE* tool for opening tins
Tin Pan Alley *n* writers, players, and producers of popular music
tinplate *n* thin sheets of iron or steel covered by tin
tin-pot *adj* worthless and unimportant, but perhaps thinking oneself to be important
tinsel *n* **1** threads of shiny material used for (Christmas) decorations **2** something showy that is really cheap and worthless
tint *n* pale or delicate shade of a colour ♦ *vt* give a tint to
tintack *n* small nail
tintinnabulation *n* ringing of bells
tiny *adj* extremely small
-tion *suffix* (in nouns) -ion
tip[1] *n* **1** (pointed) end of something **2** part stuck on the end: *cigarettes with tips* **3 on the tip of one's tongue** not quite able to be remembered ♦ *vt* **-pp-** put a tip on: *tipped cigarettes*
tip[2] *v* **-pp- 1** *vt BrE* pour **2** *vi/t* (cause to) fall over **3** *vi/t* (cause to) lean at an angle ♦ *n esp. BrE* **1** place where unwanted waste is left **2** *infml* extremely untidy dirty place
tip[3] *n* small amount of money given to someone who does a service ♦ *vi/t* **-pp-** give a tip (to)
tip[4] *n* helpful piece of advice ♦ *vt* **-pp-** suggest as likely to succeed **tip off** *phr vt* give a warning or piece of secret information to
tip-off *n* warning or information
tipple *n infml* alcoholic drink ♦ *vi/t* drink alcohol, esp. habitually **~r** *n*
tipster *n* person who gives advice about the likely winner of horse and dog races
tipsy *adj infml* slightly drunk **-sily** *adv*
tiptoe *n* **on tiptoe** on one's toes with the rest of the foot raised ♦ *vi* walk on tiptoe
tip-top *adj infml* excellent
tirade *n* long, angry speech
tire[1] *vi/t* (cause to) become tired **~less** *adj* never getting tired **~some** *adj* **1** annoying **2** uninteresting **~somely** *adv* **~someness** *n*
tire[2] *n AmE* tyre
tired *adj* **1** needing rest or sleep **2** no longer interested: *I'm tired of doing this.* **3** showing lack of imagination or new thought: *tired ideas* **~ly** *adv* **~ness** *n*
tiro *n* tyro
tissue *n* **1** the material animals and plants are made of; cells: *lung tissue* **2** thin light paper, esp. for wrapping **3** paper handkerchief **4** something formed as if by weaving threads together: *a tissue of lies*
tit[1] *n* small bird of various sorts
tit[2] *n sl* woman's breast
titan /ˈtiet(ə)n/ *n* person of great ability
titanic *adj* very great in degree: *a titanic struggle*
titanium *n* light strong metal used in compounds
titbit *n* small piece of particularly nice food
titchy *adj infml* very small
titfer *n sl* hat
tit for tat *n* something unpleasant given in return for something unpleasant one has suffered
tithe *n* tax paid to the church in former times
titillate *vt* excite, esp. sexually **-lation** *n*
titivate *vi/t* make smart
title *n* **1** name of a book, play, painting, etc. **2** word such as 'Lord', 'President', or 'Doctor' used before someone's name to show rank, office, or profession **3** legal right to ownership **4** position of unbeaten winner: *the world heavyweight boxing title* **titled** *adj* having a noble title, such as 'Lord'
titmouse *n* tit[1]
titter *vi* laugh quietly in a nervous or silly way **titter** *n*
tittle *n* very small part
tittle-tattle *n* gossip
titty *n* tit[2]

titular /ˈtityoolə/ *adj* holding a title but not having any real power: *a titular head of state*
tizzy *n* *infml* state of excited worried confusion
T-junction *n* place where two roads meet in the shape of a T
TNT *n* powerful explosive
to *prep* **1** in a direction towards: *the road to London* **2 a** (used before a verb to show it is the infinitive): *I want to go.* **b** used in place of infinitive: *We didn't want to come but we had to.* **3** in order to: *I came by car to save time.* **4** so as to be in: *I was sent to prison.* **5** touching: *Stick the paper to the wall.* **6** for the attention or possession of: *I gave it to her.* **7** in connection with: *the answer to a question* **8** (of time) before: *It's 10 to 4.* **9** per: *30 miles to the gallon* ♦ *adv* **1** so as to be shut: *Pull the door to.* **2** into consciousness: *She came to.*
toad *n* animal like a large frog
toad in the hole *n* sausages baked in batter
toadstool *n* (uneatable) fungus
toady *vi* be too nice to someone of higher rank, esp. for personal advantage ♦ *n* person who toadies
to and fro *adv* forwards and backwards or from side to side
toast *n* **1** bread made brown by heating **2** act of ceremonial drinking to show respect or express good wishes: *They drank a toast to their guest.* ♦ *vt* **1** make brown by heating **2** warm thoroughly **3** drink a toast to **~er** *n* electrical apparatus for making toast
toastmaster *n* person who introduces toasts and speakers at a formal dinner
tobacco *n* dried leaves of a certain plant prepared esp. for smoking in cigarettes, cigars or pipes **~nist** *n* seller of tobacco, cigarettes, etc.
toboggan *n* long board for carrying people over snow **toboggan** *vi*
toby jug *n* small jug or mug shaped like a person, usu. a stout man in a three-cornered hat
toccata *n* piece of music in a free style, esp. for organ, harpsichord, or piano
tocsin *n* (bell rung as) a warning signal
tod *n* **1** fox **2 on one's tod** *sl* alone
today *adv, n* **1** (on) this day **2** (at) this present time
toddle *vi* **1** walk, esp. with short unsteady steps **2** *infml* walk; go **–dler** *n* child who has just learnt to walk
toddy *n* drink of whisky and hot water
to-do *n infml* **to-dos** state of excited confusion or annoyance
toe *n* **1** any of the five small movable parts at the end of the foot **2** part of a shoe or sock covering these **3 on one's toes** fully ready for action ♦ *vt* **1** touch with the toes **2 toe the line** act obediently
toe cap *n* strengthened toe of a shoe
toehold *n* place for putting the end of the foot when climbing
toff *n infml* upper-class person
toffee *n* (piece of) a hard brown confectionery made from sugar and butter
toffee-nosed *adj sl* snobbish
toga *n* loose outer garment worn in ancient Rome
together *adv* **1** in or into a single group, body, or place **2** with each other **3** at the same time **4** in agreement; combined **5 together with** in addition to ♦ *adj infml* **1** (of a person) very much in control of life **2 get it together** have things under control **~ness** *n* friendliness
toggle *n* bar-shaped wooden button
togs *pl n infml* clothes
tog up/out *phr vt infml* dress in fine clothes
toil *n lit* hard work ♦ *vi lit* work or move with great effort
toilet *n* **1** (room containing) a seatlike apparatus for receiving and taking away the body's waste matter **2** *fml* act of washing and dressing oneself
toilet paper *n* paper for cleaning oneself after passing waste matter from the body
toiletries *pl n* things used in washing, making oneself tidy, etc.
toilet roll *n* rolled-up length of toilet

paper
toilet water *n* weak form of perfume
toils *pl n* something in which one becomes firmly trapped
token *n* **1** outward sign: *They wore black as a token of mourning.* **2** card which can be exchanged for goods: *a book token* ♦ *adj* **1** being a small part representing something greater **2** *derog* done so as to seem acceptable: *a token effort*
tokenism *n derog* practising just enough positive discrimination to give a good impression
told *past t. and p. of* tell
tolerate *vt* **1** permit (something one disagrees with) **2** suffer (someone or something) without complaining **–rable** *adj* fairly good; not too bad **–rably** *adv* fairly **–rance** *n* **1** ability to suffer pain, hardship, etc., without being harmed or damaged: *a low tolerance to cold* **2** allowing people to behave in a way one disagrees with, without getting annoyed **3** toleration (1) **–rant** *adj* showing or practising tolerance **–rantly** *adv* **–ration** *n* **1** allowing opinions and customs different from one's own to be freely held or practised **2** tolerance (2)
toll[1] *n* **1** tax paid for using a road or bridge **2** bad effect: *The death toll in the accident was 9.*
toll[2] *vi/t* ring (a bell) or be rung slowly and repeatedly
tomahawk *n* North American Indian axe
tomato *n* **-toes** soft red fruit eaten raw or cooked as a vegetable
tomb *n* (large decorative cover for) a grave
tombola *n* lottery in which tickets are picked from a box
tomboy *n* spirited young girl who enjoys rough and noisy activities
tomcat *n* male cat
tome *n lit or humorous* large heavy book
tomfoolery *n* foolish behaviour
tommy gun *n* light machine gun
tomorrow *adv* on the day following today ♦ *n* **1** day after today **2** future
tom-tom *n* long narrow drum played with the hands
ton *n* **1** a measure of weight equal to 1.016 tonnes **2** also **tons** *pl* a very large amount **tons** *adv sl* very much
tonality *n* **1** tonal quality **2** (organization of music according to) a musical key
tone *n* **1** quality of sound, esp. of a musical instrument or the voice **2** variety or shade of a colour **3** general quality or nature **4** proper firmness of bodily organs and muscles **tone down** *phr vt* reduce in force **tone in** *phr vi/t* (cause to) match **tone up** *phr vt* make stronger, brighter, or more effective **tonal** *adj*
tone-deaf *adj* unable to tell the difference between musical notes
tone poem *n* piece of music written to give an impression of a scene, person, or idea
tongs *pl n* two movable arms joined at one end, for holding and lifting things
tongue *n* **1** movable organ in the mouth used in talking, tasting, licking, etc. **2** object like this in shape or purpose: *tongues of flame* **3** language **4 hold one's tongue** remain silent **5 (with) tongue in cheek** insincerely
tongue-tied *adj* unable to speak freely, esp. because of nervousness
tongue twister *n* word or phrase difficult to say
tonic *n* **1** something, esp. a medicine, that increases health or strength **2** tonic water **3** first note of a musical scale ♦ *adj* **1** of or based on the musical tonic **2** healthy and strengthening
tonic water *n* sort of gassy water usu. mixed with strong alcoholic drink
tonight *adv, n* (during) the night of today
tonnage *n* **1** amount of goods a ship can carry, expressed in tons **2** ships, esp. those that carry goods
tonne *n* a measure of weight equal to 1000 kilograms

tonsil *n* either of two small organs at the back of the throat
tonsillitis *n* painful soreness of the tonsils
tonsorial *adj humorous* of a barber or his work
tonsure /ˈtonshə/ *n* **1** rite of shaving the top of the head of a new priest or monk **2** shaved part of a priest's or monk's head **tonsure** *vt*
too *adv* **1** to a greater degree than is necessary or good: *You're driving too fast.* **2** also: *I've been to Australia, and to New Zealand too.* **3 only too** very
took *past t. of* take
tool *n* hand-held instrument, such as an axe or hammer
toot *vt* make a short warning sound with (a horn) **toot** *n*
tooth *n* **teeth 1** small bony object growing in the mouth, used for biting **2** any of the pointed parts standing out e.g. from a comb or saw **3** ability to produce an effect: *The present law has no teeth.* **4 tooth and nail** very violently **5 get one's teeth into** do (a job) very actively and purposefully **6 in the teeth of** against and in spite of: *in the teeth of fierce opposition* **7 set someone's teeth on edge** give someone an unpleasant sensation (like those) caused by certain acid tastes or high sounds **~less** *adj* **~y** *adj*
toothbrush *n* small brush for cleaning one's teeth
toothpaste *n* paste for cleaning one's teeth
toothpick *n* short thin pointed stick for removing food from the teeth
toothsome *adj* tasty
tootle *v infml* **1** *vi/t* play (a wind instrument) in a quiet, rambling way **2** *vi* drive in a leisurely way
top[1] *n* **1** the highest or upper part: *the top of a tree* **2** the best or most important part or place: *at the top of the class* **3** cover: *bottle tops* **4 at the top of (one's) voice** as loudly as possible **5 get on top of** *infml* be too much for: *This work is getting on top of me.* **6 on top of: a** able to deal with **b** in addition to **7 on top of the world** *infml* very happy **8 over the top** *infml, esp. BrE* more than is reasonable, sensible, or proper ♦ *adj* highest: *at top speed* ♦ *vt* **-pp- 1** be higher, better, or more than: *Our profits have topped £1 million.* **2** form a top for: *a cake topped with cream* **3 top the bill** be chief actor or actress in a play **top off** *phr vt esp. AmE* complete successfully by a last action **top up** *phr vt* fill (a partly empty container) with liquid **~less** *adj* leaving the breasts bare
top[2] *n* child's toy that spins round
topaz *n* (precious stone cut from) a yellowish mineral
top brass *pl n sl* officers of high rank in the armed forces
top dog *n* person in the most advantageous or powerful position
topdressing *n* coating (e.g. of fertilizer) spread over land but not dug in
topee, topi *n* hard hat for protecting the head in tropical sunshine
top-flight *adj infml* of high position or quality
top hat *n* man's formal tall usu. black or grey hat
top-heavy *adj* too heavy at the top
topiary *n* art of cutting trees and bushes into decorative shapes
topic *n* subject e.g. for conversation or writing
topical *adj* of or being a subject of present interest **~ly** *adv* **–lity** *n*
topknot *n* **1** hair bunched or coiled on top of the head **2** bunch or knot (e.g. of ribbons) worn on top of the head
top-notch *adj* being one of the best
topography /toˈpogrəfi/ *n* (science of describing) the shape and height of land **–phical** *adj*
topper *n infml* top hat
topping *n* something put on top, esp. a garnish on food
topple *vi/t* (cause to) become unsteady and fall down
top-secret *adj* that must be kept extremely secret
topsoil *n* upper, fertile level of soil, in

which most plants have their roots
topspin *n* turning movement given to a ball to make it spin through the air
topsy-turvy *adj, adv* in complete disorder and confusion
tor *n* high rocky hill
torch *n* **1** *BrE* small electric light carried in the hand **2** mass of burning material carried by hand to give light **3** *AmE* blowlamp
tore *past t. of* tear
toreador *n* bullfighter
torment *n* very great suffering ♦ *vt* cause torment to **~or** *n*
torn *past p. of* tear
tornado *n* **-does** *or* **-dos** very violent wind that spins at great speed
torpedo *n* **-does** long narrow motor-driven explosive apparatus fired through the sea to destroy ships ♦ *vt* attack or destroy (as if) with a torpedo
torpid *adj derog* inactive; slow **~ly** *adv* **~ity** *n*
torpor *n derog* inactivity
torque[1] /tawk/ *n* twisted metal collar
torque[2] *n* force that produces rotation
torrent *n* violently rushing stream of water **-rential** *adj*
torrid *adj* **1** (esp. of weather) very hot **2** full of strong feelings and uncontrolled activity, esp. sexual: *a torrid love affair*
torsion *n* **1** act of twisting or turning **2** state of being twisted or turned **3** force that brings a solid back into shape after twisting
torso *n* **-sos** human body without the head and limbs
tort *n law* wrongful but not criminal act
tortilla *n* Mexican flat bread
tortoise *n* slow-moving land animal with a hard shell
tortoiseshell *n* material from a tortoise's or turtle's shell, brown with yellowish marks ♦ *adj* mottled black, brown and yellow
tortuous /ˈtawtyoo·əs/ *adj* **1** twisted; winding **2** not direct in speech, thought or action **~ly** *adv* **~ness** *n*
torture *vt* cause great pain or suffering to ♦ *n* **1** act of torturing **2** severe pain or suffering **-turer** *n*
Tory *n, adj* (member) of the Conservative Party **~ism** *n*
toss *v* **1** *vt* throw **2** *vi/t* (cause to) move about rapidly and pointlessly: *He tossed and turned all night.* **3** *vt* move or lift (part of the body) rapidly: *She tossed her head.* **4** *vt* mix lightly: *toss a salad* **5** *vi/t* throw (a coin) to decide something according to which side lands upwards: *Let's toss for it.* ♦ *n* **1** act of tossing **2** *BrE sl* the least amount: *I couldn't give a toss.*
toss-up *n* even chance; uncertainty
tot *n* **1** very small child **2** small amount of a strong alcoholic drink
total *adj* complete; whole ♦ *n* **1** complete amount **2 in total** when all have been added up ♦ *vt* **-ll-** (*AmE* **-l-**) be when added up: *His debts totalled £9000.* **~ly** *adv* completely **~ity** *n* completeness
totalitarian *adj* of or based on a centrally controlled system of government that does not allow any political opposition **~ism** *n*
totalizator *n* machine for registering bets and calculating winnings
tote[1] *vt infml, esp. AmE* carry, esp. with difficulty
tote[2] *abbrev. for* totalizator
totem *n* person or thing used as sign or symbol of an organization or society
totter *vi* move or walk unsteadily, as if about to fall
tot up *phr vt* add up
toucan *n* tropical bird with a very large beak
touch *v* **1** *vi/t* be separated (from) by no space at all: *Their hands touched.* **2** *vi/t* feel or make connection (with), esp. with the hands: *The model is fragile, don't touch (it).* **3** *vt* eat or drink: *I never touch alcohol.* **4** *vt* compare with: *Nothing can touch a cold drink on a hot day!* **5** *vt* cause to feel pity, sympathy, etc.: *a touching story* **6 touch wood** touch something made of wood to keep away bad luck **touch down** *phr vi* (of a plane or spacecraft) land **touch off** *phr vt* cause (a violent event) to start **touch**

on/upon *phr vt* talk about shortly
touch up *phr vt* **1** improve with small additions **2** *sl* touch a person in a sexually improper way ♦ *n* **1** sense of feeling **2** way something feels: *the silky touch of her skin* **3** act of touching **4** connection, esp. so as to receive information: *He's gone to Australia, but we keep in touch by letter.* **5** particular way of doing things: *a woman's touch* **6** small details: *putting the finishing touches to the plan* **7** special ability: *I'm losing my touch.* **8** slight attack of an illness: *a touch of flu* **9** slight amount: *It needs a touch more salt.* **10** (in football) area outside the field of play **~ed** *adj* **1** grateful **2** slightly mad **~y** *adj* easily offended or annoyed **~ily** *adv* **~iness** *n*

touch-and-go *adj* of uncertain result; risky

touchdown *n* landing of a plane or spacecraft

touché /ˈtooshay/ *interj* (used to acknowledge a hit in fencing or the success of an argument or witty remark against oneself)

touchline *n* line along each of the longer sides of a football field

touch paper *n* fuse of slow-burning paper on a firework

touchstone *n lit* something used as a test or standard

touch-type *vi* type without looking at the keyboard

tough *adj* **1** not easily weakened or broken **2** difficult to cut or eat: *tough meat* **3** difficult: *a tough job* **4** not kind, severe: *a tough new law against drunken driving* **5** unfortunate: *tough luck* **~ly** *adv* **~en** *vi/t* make or become tougher **~ness** *n*

toupee /ˈtoohˌpay/ *n* small wig worn by a man

tour *n* **1** act of travelling round a country or walking round e.g. a building looking at interesting things **2** period of duty in a job, esp. abroad **3** journey to take part in e.g. performances or sports matches ♦ *vi/t* visit as a tourist **~ism** *n* **1** travelling for pleasure, esp. on one's holidays **2** the business of providing holidays for tourists **~ist** *n* **1** person travelling for pleasure **2** sportsman on tour

tour de force *n* show of great skill

tournament *n* **1** competition **2** (in former times) competition of fighting skill

tourney /ˈtooəni/ *vi, n arch.* (take part in) a tournament

tourniquet /ˈtooəniˌkay/ *n* something twisted tightly round a limb to stop bleeding from a wound

tousle *vt* make (hair) untidy

tout *vt derog* try to persuade people to buy (one's goods or services) ♦ *n BrE derog* person who offers tickets e.g. for the theatre, at very high prices

tow *vt* pull (esp. a vehicle) with a rope or chain ♦ *n* **1** act of towing **2 in tow** following closely behind **3 on tow** being towed

towards, toward *prep* **1** in the direction of **2** just before in time: *We arrived towards noon.* **3** in relation to: *What are their feelings towards us?* **4** for the purpose of: *Each week we save £5 towards our holiday.*

towel *n* piece of cloth or paper for drying things ♦ *vt* **-ll-** (*AmE* **-l-**) rub or dry with a towel

towelling, *AmE* **toweling** *n* thickish cloth, used for making esp. towels

tower *n* **1** tall (part of a) building **2** tall metal framework for signalling or broadcasting ♦ *vi* be very tall **~ing** *adj* very great: *a towering rage*

tower block *n esp. BrE* tall block of flats or offices

tower of strength *n* person who can be depended on for help or support

town *n* **1** large group of houses and other buildings where people live and work **2** all the people who live in such a place **3** the business or shopping centre of a town **4** the chief city in an area **5** (life in) towns and cities in general **6 go to town** act or behave freely or wildly **7 (out) on the town** enjoying oneself, esp. at night

town clerk *n* (until 1974) the chief official of a British town

town crier *n* person employed to make announcements to the people of a town

town hall *n* public building for a town's local government

township *n* (in South Africa) a place where black citizens live

townspeople *n* **1** people of a particular town **2** people (**townsmen** and **townswomen**) who live in towns

towpath *n* path along the bank of a canal or river

toxaemia /tok'seemyə/ *n* condition in which the blood contains poisons

toxic *adj* poisonous **~ity** *n*

toxicology *n* study of poisons and poisoning

toxin *n* poison produced in plants and animals

toy *n* **1** object for children to play with **2** small breed of dog **toy with** *phr vt* **1** consider (an idea) not very seriously **2** play with or handle purposelessly

trace¹ *vt* **1** find, esp. by following a course **2** copy lines or the shape of something using transparent paper ♦ *n* **1** mark or sign showing the former presence of someone or something: *She had vanished without trace.* **2** small amount of something: *traces of poison in his blood*

trace² *n* rope, chain, etc., fastening a cart or carriage to the animal pulling it

trace element *n* chemical element present in plants and animals in minute quantities, and necessary to healthy development

tracer *n* **1** bullet that leaves a trail of smoke or fire **2** substance used to trace the course of a chemical or biological process

tracery *n* patterns with decorative branching and crossing lines

trachea /trə'kee·ə/ *n* windpipe

trachoma *n med* contagious eye disease

track *n* **1** marks left by a person, animal, or vehicle that has passed before **2** narrow (rough) path or road **3** railway line **4** course for racing **5** piece of music on a record or tape **6 in one's tracks** *infml* where one is; suddenly **7 keep/lose track of** keep/fail to keep oneself informed about **8 makes tracks** leave, esp. in a hurry ♦ *vt* follow the track of **track down** *phr vt* find by hunting or searching **~er** *n*

track record *n* degree to which someone or something has performed well or badly up to now

tracksuit *n* loose-fitting suit worn by people when training for sport

tract¹ *n* **1** wide stretch of land **2** system of related organs in an animal: *the digestive tract*

tract² *n* short article on a religious or moral subject

tractable *adj* easily controlled or governed **-bly** *adv* **-bility** *n*

traction *n* **1** type of pulling power: *steam traction* **2** force that prevents a wheel from slipping **3** medical treatment with a pulling apparatus used to cure a broken bone or similar injury

traction engine *n* large steam- or diesel-powered vehicle used to pull heavy loads

tractor *n* motor vehicle for pulling farm machinery

trad, trad jazz *n* style of jazz developed in the 1920s

trade *n* **1** business of buying, selling, or exchanging goods, esp. between countries **2** particular business: *the wine trade* **3** job, esp. needing skill with the hands: *the printer's trade* **4** stated amount of business: *doing a good trade* ♦ *v* **1** *vi* buy and sell goods **2** *vt* exchange: *I traded my radio for a typewriter.* **trade in** *phr vt* give in part payment for something new: *I traded my old car in.* **trade off** *phr vt* balance (one situation or quality) against another, with the aim of producing an acceptable or desirable result **trade on** *phr vt* take unfair advantage of

trademark *n* **1** sign or word put on a product to show who made it **2** thing by which a person or thing may habitually be recognised

trade name *n* name given by a producer to a particular product
trade off *n* balance between two (opposing) situations or qualities
tradesman *n* **-men 1** shopkeeper **2** worker or seller who comes to people's homes
trade union *n* workers' organization to represent their interests and deal with employers **~ism** *n* **~ist** *n*
trade wind *n* wind blowing almost continually towards the equator
tradition *n* **1** opinion, custom, or principle passed down from the past to the present **2** (passing down of) such customs **~al** *adj* **~ally** *adv*
traditionalism *n* great respect for tradition **-ist** *n*
traduce *vt* slander
traffic *n* **1** (movement of) vehicles, planes, or ships **2** trade, esp. in illegal things **3** business done in carrying passengers or goods ♦ *v* **-ck-** **traffic in** *phr vt* trade in (esp. illegal things) **~ker** *n*
traffic lights *pl n* set of coloured lights for controlling road traffic
traffic warden *n BrE* official who controls the parking of vehicles on streets
tragedian /trəˈjeediən/ *n* actor or writer of tragedy
tragedienne *n* actress of tragedy
tragedy *n* **1** terrible, unhappy, or unfortunate event **2** serious play that ends sadly **3** these plays considered as a group
tragic *adj* **1** of or related to tragedy **2** very sad, unfortunate, etc. **~ally** *adv*
tragicomedy *n* (type of) play or story combining tragic and amusing parts
trail *n* **1** track or smell followed by a hunter **2** path across rough country **3** stream of e.g. dust or smoke behind something moving ♦ *v* **1** *vi/t* drag or be dragged along behind **2** *vt* track **3** *vi* (of a plant) grow along a surface **~er** *n* **1** vehicle pulled by another **2** excerpts of a new film shown to advertise it
train[1] *n* **1** line of railway carriages pulled by an engine **2** set of related things one after another: *train of thought* **3** part of a long garment that spreads over the ground behind the wearer **4** long line of moving people, animals or vehicles
train[2] *v* **1** *vi/t* give or be given instruction, practice, or exercise **2** *vt* aim (a gun) **3** *vt* direct the growth of (a plant) **~ee** *n* person being trained **~er** *n* **1** person who trains **2** shoe used for sports **~ing** *n* **1** practical instruction **2** **in/out of training** in/not in a healthy condition for a sport
traipse *vi* walk tiredly
trait /trayt, tray/ *n* particular quality of someone or something
traitor *n* someone disloyal, esp. to their country **-rous** *adj*
trajectory *n* curved path of an object fired or thrown through the air
tram *n* usu. electric bus that runs on metal lines set in the road
trammels *pl n* something that limits free activity **trammel** *vt*
tramp *vi* **1** walk heavily **2** walk steadily, esp. over a long distance ♦ *n* **1** *esp. BrE* wandering person with no home or job who begs for food or money **2** long walk **3** sound of heavy walking
trample *vi/t* step (on) heavily; crush under the feet
trampoline *n* frame with springy material on which people jump up and down
tramp steamer *n* ship that takes goods irregularly to various ports
trance *n* sleeplike condition of the mind
tranny *n infml* transistor (2)
tranquil *adj* pleasantly calm, quiet, or free from worry **~lize,** *AmE* **~ize** *vt* make calm (esp. with tranquillizers) **~lizer,** *AmE* **~izer** *n* drug for reducing anxiety and making people calm **~lity,** *AmE* **~ity** *n* calmness
trans- *prefix* across: *transatlantic*
transact *vt* do and complete (a piece of business) **~ion** *n* **1** act of transacting **2** piece of business **transactions** *pl n* records of meetings of a society

transatlantic *adj* connecting or concerning countries on both sides of the Atlantic ocean

transcend *vt* go beyond (a limit or something within limits) **~ent** *adj* going far beyond ordinary limits **~ence** *n*

transcendental /ˌtransenˈdentl/ *adj* going beyond human knowledge, understanding and experience **~ism** *n* **~ist** *n*

transcribe *vt* **1** write an exact copy of **2** write down (something said) **3** arrange (a piece of music) for instrument or voice other than the original

transcript *n* exact written or printed copy **~ion** *n* **1** act or process of transcribing **2** transcript

transept *n* part of a cross-shaped church at right angles to the nave

transfer *v* **-rr- 1** *vi/t* move from one place, job, etc., to another **2** *vt* give ownership of property to another person **3** *vi* move from one vehicle to another ♦ *n* **1** act or process of transferring **2** something transferred **3** *esp. BrE* picture for sticking or printing onto a surface **~ence** *n* **~able** *adj*

transfigure *vt* change so as to be more glorious **–ration** *n*

transfix *vt* make unable to move or think e.g. because of terror

transform *vt* change completely **~er** *n* apparatus for changing electrical force, esp. to a different voltage **~ation** *n*

transfusion *n* act of putting one person's blood into another's body

transgress *v* **1** *vt* go beyond (a proper or legal limit) **2** *vi* do wrong **~or** *n* **~ion** *n*

transient *adj* lasting or staying for only a short time **-ence** *n* **~ly** *adv*

transistor *n* **1** small apparatus for controlling the flow of electric current **2** small radio with transistors **~ize, ~ise** *vt* provide with transistors

transit *n* going or moving of people or goods from one place to another

transition *n* (act of) changing from one state to another **~al** *adj*

transitive *adj* (of a verb) that must have an object or a phrase acting like an object

transitory /ˈtransit(ə)ri/ *adj* transient **–rily** *adv* **–riness** *n*

translate *vi/t* change (speech or writing) into a different language **–lator** *n* **–lation** *n*

transliterate *vt* write in a different alphabet **–ation** *n*

translucent /tranzˈloohs(ə)nt/ *adj* allowing light to pass through (although not transparent) **–cence, -cency** *n*

transmigration *n* passing of the soul after death into another body

transmit *v* **-tt- 1** *vi/t* broadcast: *transmit a radio distress signal* **2** *vt* pass to another person: *transmit a disease* **3** *vt* allow to pass through itself: *Water transmits sound* **~ter** *n* broadcasting apparatus **–mission** *n* **1** act of transmitting **2** television or radio broadcast **3** parts of a vehicle that carry power to the wheels

transmogrify *vt* transform usu. with grotesque or humorous effect **–fication**

transmute *vt* change into something completely different (and better) **–mutation** *n*

transom *n* transverse piece of a frame, e.g. of a door or window

transparent *adj* **1** that can be seen through **2** easily understood **3** obvious: *a transparent lie* **~ly** *adv* **–ency** *n* **1** quality of being transparent **2** slide (4)

transpire *v* **1** *vi* become known **2** *vi* happen **3** *vi/t* give off (a gas or liquid) through pores

transplant *vt* **1** move (a plant) from one place and plant it in another **2** move (an organ, piece of skin, hair, etc.) from one part of the body to another, or one person to another ♦ *n* **1** something transplanted **2** act or operation of transplanting an organ: *a heart transplant* **~ation** *n*

transponder *n* radio or radar apparatus that sends out a signal in response to a signal it receives

transport *vt* carry from one place to another ♦ *n* **1** *esp. AmE* also **transportation** (means or system of) transporting: *London's public transport includes buses and trains.* **2 in a transport/in transports of** *lit* filled with (joy or delight) **~er** *n* long vehicle on which several cars can be carried

transpose *vt* **1** change the order or position of (two or more things) **2** to change the key of a piece of music **–position** *n*

transputer *n* extremely powerful computer microchip

transubstantiation *n* belief that in the Mass the sacramental bread and wine become the body and blood of Christ

transverse *adj* lying or placed across: *a transverse beam* **~ly** *adv*

transvestite *n* person who likes to wear the clothes of the opposite sex **–tism** *n*

trap *n* **1** apparatus for catching and holding an animal **2** plan for deceiving (and catching) a person: *The police set a trap to catch the thief.* **3** two-wheeled horse-drawn vehicle **4** *sl* mouth: *Keep your trap shut!* **5** *AmE* bunker (3) ♦ *vt* **-pp- 1** place or hold firmly with no hope of escape **2** trick; deceive **3** catch (an animal) in a trap **~per** *n*

trapdoor *n* small door in a roof or floor

trapeze *n* short bar hung high above the ground used by acrobats to swing on

trapezium, *AmE* **trapezoid** *n* **-iums, -ia** quadrilateral in which only one pair of sides is parallel

trapezoid, *AmE* **trapezium** *n* quadrilateral in which no sides are parallel **~al** *adj*

trappings *pl n* articles of dress or decoration, esp. as an outward sign of rank

Trappist *n, adj* (member) of a Roman Catholic religious order noted for its vow of silence

trap-shooting *n* sport of shooting at clay discs fired into the air by a powerful spring

trash *n* **1** something of extremely low quality or value **2** *AmE* rubbish (1) **~y** *adj*

trashcan *n AmE* dustbin

trauma *n* damage to the mind caused by a shock or terrible experience **~tic** *adj* deeply and unforgettably shocking **~tize, -ise** *vt*

travail *n arch.* **1** hard and painful work **2** labour (3) **travail** *vi*

travel *v* **-ll-** (*AmE* **-l-**) **1** *vi/t* make a journey (through) **2** *vt* cover (the stated distance) on a journey **3** *vi* go, pass, or move: *At what speed does light travel?* ♦ *n* travelling: *foreign travel* **~led,** *AmE* **~ed** *adj* experienced in travel: *a much travelled writer* **~ler,** *AmE* **~er 1** person on a journey **2** travelling salesman

travels *pl n* journeys, esp. abroad

travel agent *n* someone who makes people's travel arrangements

traveller's cheque *n* cheque that can be exchanged abroad for foreign currency

travelogue, *AmE also* **-og** *n* film or talk describing foreign travel

traverse *vt* pass across, over, or through ♦ *n* sideways movement across a rock face

travesty *n* something that completely misrepresents the nature of the real thing: *The trial was a travesty of justice.*

trawl *vi/t, n* (fish with) a large net drawn along the sea bottom **~er** *n* boat that uses a trawl

tray *n* flat piece e.g. of plastic or metal for carrying things, esp. food

treachery *n* **1** disloyalty or deceit **2** disloyal or deceitful act **–rous** *adj* **1** very disloyal or deceitful **2** full of hidden dangers: *treacherous currents* **–rously** *adv*

treacle *n BrE* thick dark liquid made from sugar **–ly** *adj*

tread *v* **trod, trodden 1** *vi* put one's foot when walking; step: *Don't tread on the flowers!* **2** *vt* walk along: *tread a path* **3** *vt* press firmly with the feet **4 tread water** keep upright in water by moving the legs ♦ *n* **1** act, way, or sound of walking **2** pattern of raised lines on a tyre **3** part of a stair on which the foot is placed

treadle *n* apparatus worked by the feet to drive a machine ♦ *vi* operate a treadle

treadmill *n* something providing repeated uninteresting work

treason *n* disloyalty to one's country, esp. by helping its enemies **~able** *adj law* of or being treason **~ous** *adj*

treasure *n* **1** wealth esp. in gold or jewels **2** very valuable object or person ♦ *vt* keep or regard as precious: *treasured memories*

treasurer *n* person in charge of an organization's money

treasure trove *n* something valuable found in the ground and claimed by no one

treasury *n* government department that controls and spends public money

treat *vt* **1** act or behave towards: *He treated his horses very cruelly.* **2** deal with or handle: *Treat the glass carefully.* **3** try to cure medically **4** put through a chemical or industrial action: *metal treated against rust* **5** pay for (someone's) food, drink, or entertainment ♦ *n* **1** something that gives great pleasure, esp. when unexpected **2** act of treating someone: *The meal's my treat, so put away your money.* **~ment** *n* **1** act or way of treating someone or something **2** substance or method for treating someone or something

treatise *n* serious book on a particular subject

treaty *n* formally signed agreement between countries

treble[1] *predeterminer* three times as much or as many as ♦ *vi/t* make or become three times as great

treble[2] *n* **1** boy with a high singing voice **2** upper half of the whole range of musical notes

tree *n* **1** tall long-living plant with a wooden trunk or stem **2** treelike bush: *a rose tree* **~less** *adj*

tree fern *n* large tropical fern with a woody stem

tree line *n* height or latitude beyond which trees will not grow

trefoil /ˈtrefoyl, ˈtree-/ *n* **1** clover or a similar plant with leaves of three leaflets **2** clover-leaf shape

trek *vi, n* **-kk-** (make) a long hard journey, esp. on foot

trellis *n* light upright wooden framework on which plants are grown

tremble *vi* **1** shake uncontrollably **2** be very worried: *I tremble to think what may happen.* **tremble** *n*

tremendous *adj* **1** very great in amount or degree **2** wonderful: *What a tremendous party!* **~ly** *adv*

tremolo *n* rapid reiteration of a note or alternate notes to produce a tremulous effect

tremor *n* shaking movement

tremulous *adj* slightly shaking **~ly** *adv* **~ness** *n*

trench *n* long narrow hole cut in the ground, esp. as a protection for soldiers

trenchant *adj* (of language) forceful and effective **~ly** *adv* **–ncy** *n*

trench coat *n* belted raincoat

trencher *n* wooden plate

trencherman *n* hearty eater

trend *n* **1** general direction or course of development **2** popular fashion **~y** *adj infml* very fashionable

trendsetter *n* person who starts or popularizes the latest fashion **–ting** *adj*

trepan *vt med* cut a round piece from (the skull) as part of a medical operation

trephine *vt* trepan ♦ *n* instrument for trepanning

trepidation *n* anxiety

trespass *vi* go onto privately owned land without permission **trespass on** *phr vt* use too much ♦ *n* **1** *lit* sin **2** (act of) trespassing **~er** *n*

tresses *pl n lit* woman's long hair

trestle *n* wooden beam with a pair of spreading legs, used esp. for supporting a table (**trestle table**)

trews *pl n* trousers

tri- *prefix* three: *trilingual*

triad *n* **1** group of three **2** *(often cap.)*

Chinese criminal secret society

trial *n* **1** (act of) hearing and judging a person or case in a court of law: *He's on trial for murder.* **2** (act of) testing to find out if something is good: *We gave her the job for a trial period.* **3** cause of worry or trouble **4 stand trial** be tried in court **5 trial and error** trying several methods and learning from one's mistakes

trial run *n* testing of something new to see if it works properly

triangle *n* figure or shape with three straight sides and three angles **–gular** *adj*

triangulation *n* method of working out a position or distance by calculations from a triangle

triathlon *n* athletic contest involving running, swimming, and cycling **–lete** *n* competitor in a triathlon

tribe *n* people of the same race, beliefs, and language living together under the leadership of a chief **tribal** *adj*

tribulation *n* trial (3)

tribunal *n* sort of court that deals with particular matters: *an industrial relations tribunal*

tributary *n* river that flows into a larger river **tributary** *adj*

tribute *n* **1** something said or given to show respect or admiration **2** payment by a nation to another that is stronger

trice *n* **in a trice** very quickly

triceps *n* **–ceps** *or* **–cepses** large muscle along the back of the upper arm

trichology /triˈkoləji/ *n* study of problems of hair growth **–gist** *n*

trick *n* **1** clever act or plan to deceive or cheat someone **2** something done to make someone look stupid: *children playing tricks on their teacher* **3** amusing or confusing skilful act: *card tricks* **4** quick or clever way to do something **5** cards played or won in a single part of a card game **6 do the trick** fulfil one's purpose ♦ *vt* deceive ♦ *adj* full of hidden difficulties: *a trick question* **~ery** *n* use of deceiving tricks **~y** *adj* **1** difficult to deal with: *a tricky problem* **2** (of a person or actions) clever and deceitful

trickle *vi* flow in drops or a thin stream ♦ *n* thin slow flow

trick-or-treat *vi* (of children) go to people's houses on Hallowe'en and ask for treats under threat of playing tricks on people who refuse

trickster *n* deceiver; cheater

tricolour, *AmE* **-or** *n* three-coloured flag, esp. the national flag of France

tricycle *n* three-wheeled bicycle

trident *n* forklike weapon with three points

tried *past t. and p. of* try

triennial *adj* happening every three years

trier *n* person who always tries hard

trifle *n* **1** (esp. in Britain) sweet dish made of cake set in jelly with fruit, cream, etc. **2** something of little value or importance **3 a trifle** rather: *You were a trifle rude* **trifle with** *phr vt* treat without seriousness or respect **–fling** *adj* of little value or importance

trigger *n* piece pulled with the finger to fire a gun ♦ *vt* start (esp. a number of things that happen one after the other)

trigger-happy *adj* too eager to use violent methods

trigonometry *n* mathematics dealing with the relationship between the sides and angles of triangles

trilateral *adj* having three sides

trilby *n esp. BrE* man's soft hat with a brim

trill *vi/t, n* (sing, play, or pronounce with) a rapidly vibrating sound

trillion *n* **-on** *or* **-ons 1** one million million **2** *infml* very many

trilobite *n* small prehistoric sea creature

trilogy *n* group of three related books, plays, etc.

trim *vt* **-mm- 1** make neat by cutting **2** decorate, esp. round the edges **3** move (sails) into the correct position for sailing well ♦ *n* **1** act of cutting **2 in (good) trim** proper condition ♦ *adj* **-mm-** pleasingly neat **~ming** *n* decoration or

useful addition
trimaran *n* small sailing boat with three hulls
trinitrotoluene *n* TNT
Trinity *n* (in the Christian religion) the union of the three forms of God (the Father, Son, and Holy Spirit) as one God
trinket *n* small decorative object of low value
trio *n* **-os 1** group of three **2** piece of music for three performers
trip *v* **-pp- 1** *vi/t* (cause to) catch the foot and lose balance **2** *vi/t* (cause to) make a mistake: *He tried to trip me up with awkward questions.* **3** *vi lit* move or dance with quick light steps ♦ *n* **1** short journey, esp. for pleasure **2** act of tripping **3** *sl* period under the influence of a mind-changing drug **~per** *n esp. BrE* person on a pleasure trip
tripartite *adj* involving three parties: *tripartite treaty*
tripe *n* **1** wall of a cow's stomach used as food **2** *sl* worthless talk or writing
triple *adj* having three parts or members ♦ *vi/t* increase to three times the amount or number
triple jump *n* athletic event involving a hop, a step, and a jump
triplet *n* any of three children born together
triplex *adj* having three parts
triplicate *n* **in triplicate** in three copies, one of which is the original
tripod *n* three-legged support, esp. for a camera
tripos *n* examinations for the BA degree at Cambridge University
triptych /ˈtripˌtik/ *n* picture with three folding parts
tripwire *n* stretched wire that sets off e.g. a trap or explosive if touched
trireme *n* galley with three banks of oars
trisect *vt tech* divide into three esp. equal parts
trite *adj* (of a remark) common and uninteresting **~ly** *adv* **~ness** *n*
triumph *n* (joy or satisfaction caused by) a complete victory or success ♦ *vi* be victorious **~al** *adj* of or marking a triumph **~ant** *adj* (joyful because one is) victorious **~antly** *adv*
triumvirate *n* group of three, esp. three people in power
trivalent *adj tech* having a valency of three
trivet *n* **1** stand for holding a pot over a fire **2** metal stand for a hot dish on a table
trivia *pl n* trivial things
trivial *adj* **1** of little worth or importance **2** ordinary **~ize, -ise** *vt* **–ality** *n*
trod *past t. of* tread
trodden *past p. of* tread
troglodyte /ˈtrogləddiet/ *n* person who lives in a cave **–dytic** *adj*
troika *n* **1** Russian carriage drawn by three horses **2** group of three people working together
Trojan horse *n* something or someone that attacks or weakens something secretly from within
troll[1] *n* dwarf or giant of Scandinavian folk tales
troll[2] *vi/t* **1** sing cheerfully **2** fish (in or for) with a line pulled behind a boat
trolley *n* **1** small cart, esp. pushed by hand **2** *esp. BrE* small table on wheels, for serving food and drink **3** trolleybus
trolleybus *n* bus driven by electricity from wires above it
trollop *n* slut
trombone *n* brass musical instrument with a long sliding tube **–nist** *n*
troop *n* **1** (moving) group of people or animals **2** group of soldiers esp. on horses ♦ *vi* move in a group **troops** *pl n* soldiers
trooper *n* **1** soldier in a cavalry or armoured unit **2** *AmE* and *AustrE* policeman
trope *n* figure of speech
trophy *n* **1** prize for winning a competition or test of skill **2** something kept as a reminder of success
tropic *n* line round the world at $23^1/_2°$ north (**the tropic of Cancer**) and south

(**the tropic of Capricorn**) of the equator **tropics** *pl n* hot area between these lines **~al 1** *adj* of the tropics **2** very hot: *tropical weather*
tropism *n* response of an organism to a stimulus such as light
trot *n* **1** horse's movement, slower than a canter **2** slow run **3 on the trot: a** one after another: *She won three races on the trot.* **b** continuously active ♦ *vi* **-tt-** move at the speed of a trot **trot out** *phr vt* repeat in an uninteresting unchanged way: *trotting out the same old excuses*
troth *n arch.* one's pledged word; betrothal
Trotskyist *also* **Trotskyite, Trot** *derog n, adj* (person) following the Communist principles of Leon Trotsky, including belief in a world-wide, working-class revolutionary movement
trotter *n* pig's foot
troubadour *n* travelling singer and poet of former times
trouble *n* **1** (cause of) difficulty, worry, or annoyance: *I didn't have any trouble doing it; it was easy.* **2** state of being blamed: *He's always getting into trouble with the police.* **3** inconvenience or more than usual work or effort: *I took a lot of trouble to get it right.* **4** political or social disorder **5** failure to work properly: *heart trouble* ♦ *v* **1** *vi/t* worry **2** *vt* cause inconvenience to **3** *vi* make an effort **~some** *adj* annoying
troublemaker *n* person who causes trouble
troubleshooter *n* person who finds and removes causes of trouble in machines or organizations
trough *n* **1** long container for animal's food **2** long hollow area between waves **3** area of low air pressure
trounce *vt* defeat completely
troupe *n* company of entertainers
trouper *n* experienced performer
trousers *pl n* two-legged outer garment covering the body from the waist downwards **trouser** *adj*
trousseau *n* **-seaux** *or* **-seaus** clothes and other personal articles of a woman getting married
trout *n* **trout** *or* **trouts** river (or sea) fish used for food
trowel *n* **1** flat-bladed tool for spreading e.g. cement **2** garden tool like a small spade
troy weight *n* system of weights used for gold and jewels
truant *n* **1** pupil who stays away from school without permission **2 play truant** be a truant **–ancy** *n*
truce *n* agreement for the stopping of fighting
truck[1] *n* **1** large motor vehicle for carrying goods **2** *BrE* open railway goods vehicle ♦ *vt AmE* carry by truck **~er** *n AmE* truck driver
truck[2] *n* **have no truck with** avoid any connection with
truck farm *n AmE* market garden
truckle bed *n* low bed that fits under a higher bed
truckle to *phr vi* be subservient to
truculent *adj* willing or eager to quarrel or fight **~ly** *adv* **–lence** *n*
trudge *vi* walk slowly and with effort ♦ *n* long tiring walk
true *adj* **1** in accordance with fact or reality **2** real: *true love* **3** faithful; loyal **4** exact: *a true likeness* ♦ *n* **out of true** not having correct shape or balance
truly *adv* **1** in accordance with the truth **2** really: *a truly wonderful experience* **3** sincerely: *truly sorry*
true-blue *adj* completely loyal
true-life *adj* based on fact
truelove *n lit* sweetheart
truffle *n* underground fungus highly regarded as food
trug *n* wooden gardening basket
truism *n* statement that is clearly true
trump *n* **1** card of a suit chosen to be of higher rank than other suits in a game **2 turn/come up trumps** do the right or needed thing, esp. unexpectedly at the last moment ♦ *vt* beat by playing a trump **trump up** *phr vt* invent (a false charge or reason)
trump card *n* something that gives a

clear and unquestionable advantage

trumpery *adj* **1** worthless **2** tawdry **trumpery** *n*

trumpet *n* high-sounding brass musical instrument consisting of a long usu. winding tube ♦ *v* **1** *vi* (of an elephant) make a loud sound **2** *vt* declare or shout loudly **~er** *n* trumpet player

truncate *vt* shorten (as if) by cutting off the top or end **–ation** *n*

truncheon *n* short thick stick used as a weapon by a policeman

trundle *vi/t* move heavily or awkwardly on wheels

trunk *n* **1** main stem of a tree **2** large box in which things are packed for travelling **3** elephant's long nose **4** body without the head or limbs **5** *AmE* boot[1] (2) **trunks** *pl n* men's shorts for swimming

trunk call *n BrE* a telephone call made over a long distance

trunk line *n* major route of communication, esp. main railway or telephone line between large towns

trunk road *n* main road for long-distance travel

truss *vt* **1** tie up firmly and roughly **2** tie (a bird's) wings and legs in place for cooking ♦ *n* **1** medical supporting belt worn by someone with a hernia **2** framework of beams built to support e.g. a roof or bridge

trust[1] *n* **1** firm belief in the honesty, goodness, worth, etc., of someone or something **2** (arrangement for) the holding and controlling of money for someone else: *a charitable trust* **3** responsibility: *employed in a position of trust* **4 take on trust** accept without proof ♦ *vt* **1** believe in the honesty and worth of, esp. without proof **2** allow someone to do or have something: *Can he be trusted with a gun?* **3** depend on **4** hope, esp. confidently: *I trust you enjoyed yourself.* **trust in** *phr vt fml* have faith in **~ful**; also **~ing** *adj* (too) ready to trust others **~fully, ~ingly** *adv* **~y** *adj lit* dependable

trustee *n* **1** person in charge of a financial trust **2** member of a group controlling the affairs of e.g. a company or college

trusteeship *n* **1** position of a trustee **2** government of an area by a country or countries appointed by the United Nations **3** also **trust territory** area under this form of government

trust fund *n* money controlled by a trust

trustworthy *adj* dependable **–thily** *adv* **–thiness** *n*

truth *n* **1** that which is true: *Are you telling the truth?* **2** quality of being true: *I doubted the truth of what he said.* **3** true fact **~ful** *adj* **1** (of a statement) true **2** habitually telling the truth **~fully** *adv* **~fulness** *n*

try *v* **1** *vi/t* make an attempt: *I tried to persuade him, but failed.* **2** *vt* test by use and experience: *Have you tried this new soap?* **3** *vt* examine in a court of law: *He was tried for murder.* **4** *vt* cause to suffer, esp. with small annoyances: *Her constant questions try my patience.* **5** *vt* attempt to open (a door, window, etc.) **try on** *phr vt* **1** put on (a garment, etc.) to see if it fits or looks well **2** *infml* behave badly to see if it will be tolerated: *Take no notice, he's just trying it on.* **try out** *phr vt* test by use or experience ♦ *n* **1** attempt **2** winning of points in rugby by pressing the ball to the ground behind the opponents' line **tried** *adj* known to be good from experience

try-on *n infml* attempt at deception

tryout *n infml* test performance

tryst *n arch.* (arrangement for) a lovers' meeting

tsar *n* (until 1917) male ruler of Russia

tsarina /zahˈreenə/ *n* (until 1917) **1** female ruler of Russia **2** wife of the tsar

tsetse fly /ˈtetsi/ *n* African fly that causes sleeping sickness

T-shirt *n* light informal collarless garment for the upper body

T-square *n* ruler shaped like a T

tub *n* **1** round container for washing, packing, or storing **2** bath

tuba *n* large brass musical instrument

that produces low notes
tubby *adj infml* rather fat
tube *n* **1** hollow round pipe **2** small soft metal or plastic container for e.g. paint or paste which you get out by pressing **3** pipe in the body: *the bronchial tubes* **4** *BrE* the underground **tubing** *n* tubes **tubular** *adj* in the form of tubes
tuber *n* fleshy underground stem, such as a potato
tuberculosis *n* serious infectious disease that attacks esp. the lungs **tubercular** *adj*
tub-thumper *n infml* public speaker with an emotional style
TUC *n* Trades Union Congress; the association of British trade unions
tuck *vt* **1** put (the edge of) into a tight place for neatness, protection, etc. **2** put into a private or almost hidden place: *a house tucked away among the trees* **tuck in** *phr vi* eat eagerly **tuck up** *phr vt* make (esp. a child) comfortable in bed by pulling the sheets tight ♦ *n* **1** narrow flat fold of material sewn into a garment **2** *BrE* sweets, cakes, etc., as eaten by schoolchildren: *a tuck shop*
tucker[1] *AustrE* and *NZE infml* food
tucker[2] *vt AmE* tire greatly
-tude *suffix* -itude: *disquietude*
Tuesday *n* the 2nd day of the week
tuft *n* small bunch
tug *vi/t* **-gg-** pull hard ♦ *n* **1** sudden strong pull **2** also **tugboat** small boat used for pulling and guiding ships in narrow places
tug-of-love *n BrE infml* situation in which a child's parent tries to get the child back from someone else, such as the child's other parent
tug-of-war *n* sport in which two teams pull against each other on a rope
tuition *n* teaching; instruction
tulip *n* garden plant with large colourful cup-shaped flowers
tulip tree *n* tree with large tulip-shaped flowers
tulle /t(y)oohl/ *n* soft silky net
tumble *vi* **1** fall suddenly and helplessly, esp. rolling over **2** *infml* understand
tumble down *phr vi* collapse ♦ *n* fall
tumbledown *adj* nearly in ruins
tumble drier *n* machine for drying clothes by spinning them in a heated drum
tumbler *n* **1** large drinking glass **2** part in a lock that is moved by the turning key **3** acrobat
tumbleweed *n* North American desert plant that breaks from its roots in autumn and is blown by the wind
tumbrel, -bril *n* simple farm cart, esp. one used to carry prisoners to execution in the French Revolution
tumescent /tyooh'mes(ə)nt/ *adj* swollen or swelling **–cence** *n*
tumid *adj* swollen
tummy *n infml* stomach
tumour, *AmE* **-mor** *n* mass of quickly growing diseased cells in the body
tumult *n* confused noise and excitement **~uous** *adj* noisy
tumulus /'tyoohmyooləs/ *n* mound raised over a grave
tuna *n* **tuna** *or* **tunas** large sea fish used for food
tundra *n* treeless plain on the edge of the arctic regions
tune *n* **1** (pleasing) pattern of musical notes **2 in/out of tune: a** at/not at the correct musical level **b** in/not in agreement or sympathy **3 to the tune of** to the amount of ♦ *vt* **1** set (a musical instrument) to the correct musical level **2** put (an engine) in good working order **tune in** *phr vi* turn on a radio, esp. so as to listen to a particular radio station **~ful** *adj* having a pleasant tune **~fully** *adv* **tuner** *n* person who tunes musical instruments
tungsten *n* hard metal used esp. in making steel
tunic *n* **1** loose usu. belted garment which reaches to the knees **2** short coat forming part of a uniform
tuning fork *n* two-pronged metal instrument that gives a fixed note when struck
tunnel *n* usu. man-made underground passage ♦ *vi/t* **-ll-** (*AmE* **-l-**) make a

tunnel (under or through)

tunnel vision *n* **1** defect of sight in which a person can only see straight ahead **2** tendency to consider only one part of a question, without even trying to examine others

tunny *n* tuna

turban *n* **1** Asian head covering made by winding cloth round the head **2** woman's small high-fitting hat

turbid *adj* **1** (of a liquid) not clear; muddy **2** confused **~ly** *adv* **~ity, ~ness** *n*

turbine *n* motor in which liquid or gas drives a wheel to produce circular movement

turbocharger also **turbo** *n* device that compresses the air-petrol mixture in an internal combustion engine to make it more powerful

turbojet *n* (aircraft) engine that forces out a stream of gases behind itself

turbulent *adj* violent and disorderly or irregular **–lence** *n* **1** being turbulent **2** turbulent air movements **~ly** *adv*

turd *n taboo* **1** piece of excrement **2** *sl* offensive person

tureen *n* large deep dish for serving soup from

turf *n* **1** grass surface **2** *pl* **turves** piece of this **3** horseracing ♦ *vt* cover with turf **turf out** *phr vt sl, esp. BrE* throw out; get rid of

turf accountant *n* bookmaker

turgid *adj* (of language or style) too solemn and self-important **~ly** *adv* **~ness, ~ity** *n*

Turk *n* inhabitant of Turkey

turkey *n* **1** bird rather like a large chicken, used for food **2** *AmE sl* play in theatre which does not succeed **3** *sl, esp. AmE* stupid person **4 talk turkey** *infml, esp. AmE* speak seriously and plainly esp. about business

Turkish *n, adj* (language) of Turkey

Turkish bath *n* health treatment in which one sits in a very hot steamy room

Turkish delight *n* jelly-like sweet

turmeric *n* deep yellow spice from the root of a tropical plant

turmoil *n* state of confusion and trouble

turn *v* **1** *vi/t* move round a central point: *The wheels turned.* **2** *vi/t* move so that a different side faces upwards or outwards: *She turned the pages.* **3** *vi* change direction **4** *vt* go round: *The car turned the corner.* **5** *vi* look round: *She turned to wave.* **6** *vt* aim; point: *They turned their hoses on the burning building.* **7** *vi/t* (cause to) become: *His hair has turned grey.* **8** *vi* go sour: *The milk's turned.* **9** *vt* pass: *She's turned 40.* **10 turn a phrase** say a clever thing neatly **11 turn one's hand to** begin to practise (a skill) **12 turn one's head** make one too proud **13 turn one's stomach** make one feel sick **turn away** *phr vt* **1** refuse to let in **2** refuse to help **turn down** *phr vt* **1** refuse **2** reduce the force of (something) by using controls: *Can you turn that radio down?* **turn in** *phr v* **1** *vt* no longer continue **2** *vi* go to bed **3** *vt* deliver to the police **4** *vt* give back; return **5** *esp. AmE* hand in; deliver: *He's turned in some very poor work lately.* **turn off** *phr vt* **1** stop the flow or operation of **2** *sl* cause to lose interest, often sexually **turn on** *phr vt* **1** cause to flow or operate **2** depend on **3** attack suddenly and without warning **4** *sl* excite or interest strongly, often sexually **5** *sl* (cause to) take an illegal drug, esp. for the first time **turn out** *phr v* **1** *vt* stop the operation of (a light) **2** *vt* drive out; send away **3** *vi* come out or gather (as if) for a meeting or public event **4** *vt* produce: *The factory turns out 100 cars a day.* **5** *vt* empty (a cupboard, pocket, etc.) **6** happen to be in the end: *The party turned out a success.* **7** *vt* dress: *an elegantly turned-out woman* **turn over** *phr vt* **1** think about; consider **2** deliver to the police **3** (of an engine) to run at the lowest speed **4** do business **turn over to** *phr vt* give control of (something) to **turn up** *phr v* **1** *vi* be found **2** *vi* arrive **3** *vt* find **4** *vt* shorten (a garment) by folding up the bottom **5** *vi* happen **6 turn up one's nose (at some-**

thing or someone) suggest by one's behaviour that (something or someone) is not good enough for one ♦ *n* **1** act of turning (something) **2** change of direction **3** rightful chance or duty to do something: *It's my turn to speak.* **4** development: *She's taken a turn for the worse.* **5** point of change in time: *at the turn of the century* **6** attack of illness: *He had one of his funny turns.* **7** shock **8** short stage performance **9 a good turn** a useful or helpful action **10 on the turn: a** about to turn or change **b** *infml* (of milk) about to go sour **11 out of turn** unsuitably: *I hope I haven't spoken out of turn.* **12 to a turn** (of food) cooked perfectly **~ing** *n* place where one road branches off from another

turnabout *n* reversal of direction

turncoat *n* disloyal person

turning point *n* point at which a very important change happens

turnip *n* plant with a large round yellowish root used as a vegetable

turnkey *n* jailer ♦ *adj* built and handed over ready for operation

turn-off *n* **1** smaller road branching off from a main road **2** *infml* something that causes one to feel dislike or lose interest, esp. sexually

turn-on *n infml* something that excites or interests one strongly, esp. sexually

turnout *n* **1** number of people who attend **2** occasion on which one disposes of all unwanted things **3** *AmE* wide place in a narrow road

turnover *n* **1** rate at which a particular kind of goods is sold **2** amount of business done **3** number of workers hired to fill the places of those who leave **4** small pie: *apple turnover*

turnpike *n* road which drivers have to pay to use

turnround also **turnaround** *n* **1** (time taken for) receiving and dealing with something (e.g. a loaded ship or plane) and sending it back **2** reversal of a trend

turnstile *n* small gate that turns round, set in an entrance to admit people one at a time

turntable *n* **1** round spinning surface on which a record is placed to be played **2** machine including such a round surface

turn-up *n* **1** *BrE* turned-up bottom of a trouser leg **2** also **turn-up for the book(s)** unexpected and surprising event

turpentine *n* thin oil used esp. for cleaning off unwanted paint

turpitude *n fml* shameful wickedness

turquoise /ˈtuhkwoyz/ *n* (piece of) a precious greenish-blue mineral ♦ *adj* turquoise-coloured

turret *n* **1** small tower at the corner of a building **2** turning structure e.g. on a warship or plane that contains a gun

turtle *n* **1** four-legged (sea) animal with a hard horny shell **2 turn turtle** (of a ship) turn over

turtle dove *n* small wild pigeon

turtleneck *n* (garment with) a high close-fitting neck

turves *pl. of* turf (2)

tusk *n* very long pointed tooth, usu. one of a pair: *an elephant's tusks*

tussle *vi infml* fight roughly without weapons ♦ *n* rough struggle or fight

tussock *n* tuft of grass or reeds

tut *interj* (shows annoyance or disapproval)

tutelage /ˈtyoohtilij/ *n* **1** guardianship **2** instruction **-lary** *adj*

tutor *n* **1** private teacher **2** (in British colleges) teacher who guides a student's studies ♦ *vt* teach **~ial** *n* short period of instruction given by a college tutor

tutti-frutti *n* ice cream containing small pieces of mixed fruit

tutu *n* short stiff skirt worn by women ballet dancers

tuxedo /tukˈseedoh/ also *infml* **tux** *n* **-dos** *AmE* dinner jacket

TV *n* television

twaddle *n infml* nonsense

twain *n lit* (set of) two

twang *n* **1** quick ringing sound **2** sound of human speech (as if) produced partly through the nose ♦ *vi/t* (cause to) make a twang

twat *n taboo* **1** vagina **2** foolish person

tweak *vt* seize, pull, and twist: *He tweaked her ear.* **tweak** *n*

twee *adj* too dainty or sentimental

tweed *n* coarse woollen cloth **tweeds** *pl n* (suit of) tweed clothes

tweedy *adj* **1** like or made of tweed **2** (upper class and) fond of outdoor activities

tweet *vi, n* (make) the short weak high noise of a small bird

tweeter *n* loudspeaker that gives out high sounds

tweezers *pl n* small two-part jointed tool for handling very small objects

twelfth *determiner, adv, n, pron* 12th

twelve *determiner, n, pron* 12

twenty *determiner, n, pron* 20 **-tieth** *determiner, adv, n, pron* 20th

twerp *n BrE sl* fool

twice *predeterminer, adv* **1** two times

twiddle *vi/t* turn (something) round with one's fingers, usu. purposelessly

twig[1] *n* small thin stem on a tree or bush

twig[2] *vi* **-gg-** *BrE sl* to understand

twilight *n* (faint light at) the time when day is about to become night **-lit** *adj*

twill *n* strong woven cotton cloth

twin *n* either of two people born to the same mother at the same time

twin bed *n* either of two beds in a room for two people

twine *n* strong string ♦ *vi/t* twist; wind

twinge *n* sudden sharp pain

twinkle *vi* **1** shine with an unsteady light: *The stars twinkled.* **2** (of the eyes) be bright with cheerfulness or amusement ♦ *n* **1** twinkling light **2** brightness in the eye

twirl *vi/t* **1** spin **2** curl ♦ *n* sudden quick spin or circular movement

twist *v* **1** *vi/t* bend or turn so as to change shape: *She twisted the wire into the shape of a star.* **2** *vt* wind: *Twist the wires together.* **3** *vi* move windingly **4** *vt* turn: *She twisted her head round.* **5** *vt* hurt (a joint or limb) by turning it sharply **6** *vt derog* change the true meaning of **7 twist someone's arm** persuade someone forcefully or threateningly **8 twist someone round one's little finger** be able to get someone to do what one wants ♦ *n* **1** act of twisting **2** bend **3** unexpected development: *a strange twist of fate* **~er** *n* **1** dishonest cheating person **2** *AmE infml* tornado

twit *n BrE sl* fool

twitch *vi/t* move with a twitch: *His eyelid twitched.* ♦ *n* repeated short sudden unconscious muscle movement **~y** *adj* nervous; anxious

twitcher *n* keen bird-watcher

twitter *vi, n* **1** (of a bird) (make) short high rapid sounds **2 all of a twitter** (of people) in a very excited state

twixt *prep lit* between

two *determiner, n, pron* **1** (the number) 2 **2 in two** in two parts **3 one or two** a few

two-bit *adj AmE* petty; small-time

twofaced *adj* deceitful; insincere

two-handed *adj* **1** used with both hands **2** needing two people

twopence also **tuppence** *n* (coin worth) two pence

twopenny also **tuppenny** *adj* **1** costing two pence **2** also **twopenny-halfpenny** *infml* of very little value

two-piece *n, adj* (a suit or costume) consisting of two matching parts

twosome *n* group of two people or things

two-step *n* (music for) a ballroom dance

two-time *vt* be unfaithful to (a girlfriend or boyfriend)

two-way *adj* moving or allowing movement in both directions

-ty *suffix* -ity: *cruelty*

tycoon *n* rich powerful businessman

tying *pres. p. of* tie

tyke *n* **1** mongrel dog **2** *infml* child **3** *infml* person from Yorkshire

tympanum *n* **1** eardrum **2** space within an arch and above a lintel

type *n* **1** sort; kind; example of a group or class: *She's just that type of person.* **2** small blocks with raised letters on them, used in printing **3** printed letters: *italic type* ♦ *vi/t* write with a typewriter or word processor

typecast *vt* **-cast** repeatedly give (an actor) the same kind of part

typeface *n* size and style of printed letters

typescript *n* typewritten copy of something

typeset *vt* **typeset**, *pres. p.* **-tt-** set in type for printing **~ter** *n* **~ting** *n*

typewriter *n* machine that prints letters by means of finger-operated keys

typhoid *n* infectious disease causing fever and often death, produced by bacteria in food or drink

typhoon *n* very violent tropical storm

typhus *n* infectious disease that causes fever, severe headaches, and red spots on the body

typical *adj* showing the usual or main qualities of a particular sort of thing **~ly** *adv* **~ness, ~ity** *n*

typify *vt* be a typical mark, sign, or example of

typist *n* secretary employed mainly for typing letters

typography *n* **1** preparing matter for printing **2** arrangement and appearance of printed matter **–phic** *adj*

tyrannize, -nise *vt* use power over (a person or country) with unjust cruelty

tyranny *n* use of cruel or unjust ruling power **–ical** *adj*

tyrant *n* cruel unjust ruler

tyre *n BrE* thick band of rubber round the outside edge of a wheel

tyro *n* beginner

tzar *n* tsar

tzarina *n* tsarina

U

U, u the 21st letter of the English alphabet

ubiquitous /yoohˈbikwitəs/ *n adj* happening or existing everywhere **–quity** *n*

U-boat *n* German submarine of the Second World War

udder *n* large, hanging milk-producing organ of a female animal, e.g. a cow

UFO *n* **UFO's** *or* **UFOs** strange object in the sky, thought of as a spacecraft from another world

ugh *interj* (expresses extreme dislike)

ugly *adj* **1** unpleasant to see **2** very unpleasant or threatening: *in an ugly mood* **ugliness** *n*

ugly duckling *n* person less attractive than others in early life but becoming attractive later

UHF *abbrev. for:* ultrahigh frequency

UK *n* the United Kingdom

ukase /yoohˈkayz/ *n* edict

ukulele /ˌyoohkəˈlayli/ *n* sort of small guitar

ulcer *n* sore place where the skin is broken **~ate** *vi* turn into or become covered with ulcers **~ous** *adj*

ullage *n* amount of space left in a container of liquid, e.g. a wine bottle

ulterior *adj* deliberately concealed: *an ulterior motive*

ultimate *adj* being or happening after all others: *our ultimate destination* **~ly** *adv* in the end

ultimatum *n* **-tums** *or* **-ta** statement of conditions to be met, not open to argument

ultra- *prefix* very, esp. excessively: *ultramodern*

ultrahigh frequency *n* (sending out of

radio waves at) an extremely high rate (over 300 000 000 hertz)
ultramarine *adj* very bright blue
ultrasonic *adj* (of a sound wave) beyond the range of human hearing
ultraviolet *adj* (of light) beyond the purple end of the range of colours that can be seen by humans
umber *adj, n* (of) a dark or yellowish brown
umbilical cord *n* tube of flesh which joins an unborn creature to its mother
umbrage *n* **take umbrage** be offended
umbrella *n* **1** folding cloth-covered frame for keeping rain off the head **2** protecting power or influence **3** anything which covers or includes a wide range of different parts
umlaut /ˈoomlowt/ *n* sign (¨) placed over a German vowel to show how it is pronounced
umpire *n* judge in charge of certain games, such as cricket and tennis ♦ *vi/t* act as an umpire (for)
umpteen *determiner, pron infml* a large number (of) **~th** *n, determiner*
un- *prefix* **1** *(adjectives and adverbs)* not: *uncomfortable* **2** *(verbs)* make or do the opposite of: *untie*
unabated *adj* without losing force
unable *adj* not able
unaccountable *adj* hard to explain; surprising **-bly** *adv*
unaccustomed *adj* **1** not used (to) **2** unusual
unadopted *adj* (of a road) not maintained by the local council
unadulterated *adj* pure
unadvised *adj* not sensible
unaffected *adj* **1** not influenced or changed **2** sincere **~ly** *adv*
un-American *adj* not consistent with US customs or principles
unanimous *adj* with everyone agreeing: *a unanimous decision* **~ly** *adv* **-nimity** *n*
unanswerable *adj* that cannot be answered or argued against
unapproachable *adj* aloof
unarmed *adj* without weapons
unassuming *adj* quiet and unwilling to make claims about one's good qualities
unattached *adj* **1** not connected **2** not married or engaged
unattended *adj* alone, with no one present or in charge
unavailing *adj* having no effect **~ly** *adv*
unawares *adv* unexpectedly or without warning
unbalance *vt* make slightly mad
unbar *vt* **1** remove a locking bar from **2** open
unbearable *adj* too bad to be endured
unbeknown *adv* without the stated person knowing: *Unbeknown to me, he had left.*
unbelief *n* lack of belief in matters of religious faith – **-liever** *n* **-lieving** *adj* sceptical **-lievable** *adj* difficult to believe **-lievably** *adv*
unbend *v* **-bent 1** *vi/t* straighten **2** *vi* behave more informally
unbending *adj* unwilling to change; unfriendly
unbidden *adj* uninvited
unbind *vt* loosen the fastenings of
unblushing *adj* unashamed
unborn *adj* not yet born
unbosom *vt lit* **unbosom oneself** tell one's secret troubles and worries
unbounded *adj* limitless
unbowed *adj esp. lit* not defeated
unbridled *adj* not controlled, and esp. too active or violent
unburden *vt* free (oneself or one's mind) by talking about a secret trouble
uncalled-for *adj* not deserved, necessary, or right
uncanny *adj* not natural or usual; mysterious **-nily** *adv*
unceremonious *adj* **1** informal **2** rudely quick **~ly** *adv*
uncertain *adj* **1** doubtful **2** undecided or unable to decide **3** likely to change: *uncertain weather* **~ly** *adv* **~ty** *n*
uncharitable *adj* severe in judging others **-bly** *adv* **~ness** *n*
uncharted *adj esp. lit* (of a place) not well known enough for maps to be made

unchristian *adj* not in the spirit of Christianity
uncle *n* brother of one's father or mother, or husband of one's aunt
unclean *adj* not (religiously) pure
Uncle Sam *n infml* the US
Uncle Tom *n derog* black person who is very friendly or respectful to white people
uncomfortable *adj* **1** not comfortable **2** embarrassed **–bly** *adv*
uncommitted *adj* not having agreed to support a particular group or programme
uncommonly *adv* very
uncompromising *adj* (bravely) unchangeable in one's opinions or actions **~ly** *adv*
unconcerned *adj* **1** not worried **2** not interested or taking part **~ly** *adv* **~ness** *n*
unconditional *adj* not limited by any conditions **~ly** *adv*
unconscionable /unˈkonsh(ə)nəbl/ *adj fml* unreasonable in degree or amount **–bly** *adv*
unconscious *adj* **1** having lost consciousness **2** not intentional **~ly** *adv* **~ness** *n*
unconsidered *adj* **1** not carefully thought out **2** unimportant
uncountable *adj* that cannot be counted: *'Furniture' is an uncountable noun – you can't say 'two furnitures'.*
uncouple *vt* separate **a** from a couple **b** by undoing a coupling
uncouth *adj* rough and bad-mannered **~ly** *adv* **~ness** *n*
uncover *vt* **1** remove a covering from **2** find out (something unknown or kept secret)
uncritical *adj* not exercising judgment **~ly** *adv*
uncrowned king *n* person considered the best in a particular activity
unction *n* anointing
unctuous *adj* full of unpleasantly insincere kindness or interest **~ly** *adv* **~ness** *n*
uncut *adj* not cut, esp. **a** (of a jewel) not shaped by cutting **b** (of a film or story) not shortened or expurgated
undaunted *adj* not at all discouraged or frightened **~ly** *adv*
undeceive *vt* inform (a mistaken person) of the truth
undecided *adj* not yet having (been) decided; in doubt **~ly** *adv* **~ness** *n*
undeniable *adj* clear and certain **–bly** *adv*
under *prep* **1** below; covered by **2** less than: *under £5* **3** working for; controlled by: *Spain under Franco.* **4** (expresses various states or relationships): *under threat of dismissal|under the impression* **5** in the state or act of: *under discussion/contract* **6 under age** too young in law, esp. for drinking alcohol, driving a car, etc. **7 under cover (of)** hidden (by): *They escaped under cover of darkness.* ♦ *adv* **1** in or to a lower place **2** less: *children of 9 or under*
under- *prefix* **1** too little: *underexposed* **2** below: *undersea*
underachieve *vi* perform less well than one could **–er** *n*
underact *vi/t* act (a part) with restraint, or without enough force
underarm *adj, adv* (in sport) with the hand below the shoulder
underbelly *n esp. lit* weak or undefended part of a place or plan
underbrush *n esp. AmE* undergrowth
undercarriage *n* aircraft's wheels and wheel supports
undercharge *vi/t* take too small an amount of money from (someone)
underclothes *pl n* underwear
undercoat *n* covering of paint that goes under the main covering
undercover *adj* acting or done secretly, esp. as a spy
undercurrent *n* **1** hidden current of water beneath the surface **2** hidden tendency: *an undercurrent of discontent*
undercut *vt* **-cut**; *pres. p.* **-tt-** sell things more cheaply than (a competitor)
underdeveloped country *n* country that

needs to develop its industries and improve living conditions
underdog *n* one always treated badly by others or expected to lose in a competition
underdone *adj* not completely cooked
underestimate *v* **1** *vi/t* guess too low a value (for) **2** *vt* have too low an opinion of ♦ *n* estimate which is too small **–ation** *n*
underfed *adj* having not enough food
underfelt *n* thick felt underlay
underfoot *adv* beneath the feet
undergo *vt* **-went, -gone** experience (esp. something unpleasant or difficult)
undergraduate *n* person doing a university course for a first degree
underground *adj* **1** below the Earth's surface **2** secret; representing a political view not acceptable to the government ♦ *n* **1** (*often cap.*) underground railway system **2** secret group fighting or opposing the rulers of a country ♦ *adv* **go underground** hide from political view for a time
undergrowth *n* bushes and low plants growing around trees
underhand also **underhanded** *adj* (secretly) dishonest ♦ *adj, adv* underarm
underlay *n* material laid under a carpet
underlie *vt* **-lay, -lain** be a hidden cause or meaning of
underline *vt* **1** draw a line under **2** give additional force to, so as to show importance
underling *n* person of low rank
undermanned *adj* (of a factory, etc.) having too few workers
undermentioned *adj* referred to at a later point
undermine *vt* **1** weaken or destroy gradually: *Criticism undermines his confidence.* **2** wear away the earth beneath
underneath *prep, adv* under; below
undernourished *adj* not well enough fed for good health and development
underpants *pl n* underclothes for the lower part of the body
underpass *n* path or road under another road or railway
underpin *vt* **-nn-** strengthen or support (an argument)
underplay *vt* **1** underact **2** play down the importance of something
underprivileged *adj* poor and living in bad social conditions
underrate *vt* give too low an opinion of
underscore *vt* underline
undersecretary *n* (in Britain) high-ranking government official who advises ministers
undersell *vt* **1** sell goods at a lower price than **2** put too low a value on
undersexed *adj* having unusually little sexual desire
underside *n* lower side or surface
undersigned *n* whose signature is beneath the writing: *We, the undersigned...*
undersized *also* **undersize** *adj* smaller than is usual
understaffed *adj* undermanned
understand *v* **-stood 1** *vi/t* know or find the meaning (of) **2** *vt* know or feel closely the nature of **3** *vt* take or judge (as the meaning) **4** *vt* have been informed: *I understand you wish to join.* **5** *vt* add (something unexpressed) in the mind to make a meaning complete **~able** *adj* **1** that can be understood **2** reasonable **~ably** *adv* **~ing** *n* **1** brain power; ability to understand **2** private informal agreement **3** sympathy **~ing** *adj* sympathetic
understate *vt* express less strongly than one could or should **~ment** *n*
understudy *n* actor able to take over from another in a particular part if necessary ♦ *vt* be an understudy for
undertake *vt* **-took, -taken 1** take up or accept (work or a position) **2** promise **–taking** *n* **1** piece of work; job **2** promise
undertaker *n* funeral arranger **–ing** *n*
under-the-counter *adj* secret, esp. illegal
undertone *n* **1** low voice **2** hidden meaning or feeling
undertow *n* undercurrent flowing in a

different direction to the surface current
underwater *adj, adv* (used, done, or lying) below the surface of a stretch of water
underwear *n* clothes worn next to the body under other clothes
underweight *adj* weighing less than is expected or usual
underwent *past t. of* undergo
underworld *n* **1** criminals considered as a social group **2** home of the dead in ancient Greek stories
underwrite *vt* **-wrote, -written** support, esp. with money **–writer** *n* person who makes insurance contracts
undesirable *adj* not wanted; unpleasant ♦ *n* someone regarded as immoral, criminal, or socially unacceptable **–bility** *n*
undeveloped *adj* (usu. of a place) not having industry, mining, building, etc.
undies *pl n infml* (women's) underwear
undivided *adj* complete
undo *vt* **-did, -done 1** unfasten (something tied or wrapped) **2** remove the effects of: *The fire undid months of hard work.* **~ing** *n* cause of someone's ruin or failure
undoubted *adj* known for certain to be (so) **~ly** *adv*
undreamed-of *also* **undreamt-of** *adj* unimagined
undress *v* **1** *vi* take one's clothes off **2** *vt* take (someone's) clothes off ♦ *n fml* lack of clothes **~ed** *adj* wearing no clothes
undue *adj* too much; unsuitable **unduly** *adv*
undulate *vi* rise and fall like waves **–lation** *n*
undying *adj lit* which will never end
unearth *vt* **1** dig up **2** discover
unearthly *adj* **1** very strange and unnatural **2** *infml* (of time) very inconvenient
uneasy *adj* worried; anxious **–ily** *adv* **–iness** *n*
uneconomic also **uneconomical** *adj* not producing profit; wasteful
unedifying *adj* unpleasant or offensive to the moral sense
unemployed *adj* not having a job ♦ *pl n* people without jobs
unemployment *n* **1** condition of lacking a job **2** lack of jobs for numbers of people in society
unenviable *adj* not to be wished for, esp. because of difficulty
unequal *adj* **1** not of equal size **2** not balanced or fair **3** inadequate **~ly** *adv*
unequalled, *AmE* **-qualed** *adj* the greatest possible
unequivocal /ˌuniˈkwivəkl/ *adj* totally clear in meaning **~ly** *adv*
unerring *adj* without making a mistake **~ly** *adv*
UNESCO *n* United Nations Educational, Scientific, and Cultural Organization
uneven *adj* **1** not smooth, straight, or regular **2** odd (2) **3** varying in quality: *uneven work* **~ly** *adv* **~ness** *n*
unexceptionable *adj* satisfactory **–bly** *adv*
unexpurgated /unˈekspuhˌgaytid/ *adj* (of a book, play, etc.) with nothing that is considered improper taken out; complete
unfailing *adj* continuous **~ly** *adv*
unfair *adj* not just or reasonable **~ly** *adv*
unfaithful *adj* having sex with someone other than one's regular partner **~ly** *adv* **~ness** *n*
unfaltering *adj* firm; unhesitating **~ly** *adv*
unfathomable *adj* that one cannot understand; mysterious
unfavourable, *AmE* **-vorable** *adj* **1** expressing disapproval **2** opposite to what is needed or wanted **-bly** *adv*
unfeeling *adj* not sympathetic **~ly** *adv* **~ness** *n*
unfettered *adj* free from control
unfit *adj* **1** not in good health **2** not having the right qualities or skills
unflagging *adj* tireless
unflappable *adj* always calm, esp. in difficult situations
unflinching *adj* fearless **~ly** *adv*

unfold *v* **1** *vt* open from a folded position **2** *vi/t* (cause to) become clear: *as the story unfolded*
unforgettable *adj* too strong in effect to be forgotten **-bly** *adv*
unfortunate *adj* **1** that makes one sorry **2** unlucky **3** slightly rude **~ly** *adv*
unfounded *adj* not supported by facts
unfrequented *adj* not often visited
unfrock *vt* dismiss (a priest)
unfurl *vt* unroll and open (e.g. a flag or sail)
ungainly *adj* not graceful; awkward **-liness** *n*
ungodly *adj* **1** not religious **2** *infml* unearthly (2)
ungovernable *adj* not controllable
ungrateful *adj* **1** not grateful **2** *lit* (of work) giving no reward or result **~ly** *adv* **~ness** *n*
unguarded *adj* unwisely careless, esp. in speech **~ly** *adv* **~ness** *n*
unguent /ˈung·gwənt/ *n* ointment
unhand *vt lit* stop holding or touching: *Unhand me, sir!*
unhappy *adj* **1** sad **2** not satisfied **3** not appropriate **4** unlucky **-pily** *adv* **-piness** *n*
unhealthy *adj* **1** not in good health **2** showing or likely to cause bad health **3** unnatural (2) **-thily** *adv* **-lness** *n*
unheard-of *adj* very unusual
unhinge *vt* make mad
unholy *adj* terrible; unreasonable: *an unholy row*
unholy alliance *n* grouping of people or esp. organizations that are usu. separate or opposed but have come together for a bad purpose
unhorse *vt lit* cause to fall from a horse
uni- *prefix* one; single; mono-: *unicellular*
UNICEF *n* United Nations International Children's Fund
unicorn *n* imaginary horselike animal with a single horn
uniform *n* sort of clothes worn by all members of a group ♦ adj the same all over; regular **~ly** *adv* **~ed** *adj* **~ity** *n*
unify *vt* bring together so as to be a single whole or all the same **-fication** *n*
unilateral *adj* done by only one group: *unilateral disarmament* **~ly** *adv*
unimpeachable *adj fml* that cannot be doubted or questioned **-bly** *adv*
uninhibited *adj* acting spontaneously without worrying about what others might think **~ly** *adv* **~ness** *n*
uninitiated *pl n* people who are not among those who have special knowledge or experience
uninterested *adj* not interested
union *n* **1** club or society, esp. a trade union **2** group of states: *the Soviet Union* **3** joining **4** *lit* (unity in) marriage
unionize, -ise *vi/t* (cause to) become a member of a trade union **-ization** *n*
Union Jack *n* British flag
unique *adj* **1** being the only one of its type **2** unusual **3** better than any other **~ly** *adv* **~ness** *n*
unisex *adj* of one type for both male and female
unison *n* **1** being together in taking action **2** everyone singing or playing the same note
unit *n* **1** group within a larger organization: *the hospital's X-ray unit* **2** amount forming a standard of measurement: *The pound is a unit of currency.* **3** whole number less than 10 **4** something, e.g. a piece of furniture, which can be fitted with others of the same type
unite *v* **1** *vt* join **2** *vi* become one **3** *vi* act together for a purpose
United Kingdom *n* England, Scotland, Wales, and Northern Ireland
unit trust *n* company through which one can buy shares in various companies
unity *n* being united or in agreement
universe *n* everything which exists in all space **-versal** *adj* among or for everyone or in every place: *universal agreement* **-versally** *adv* **-versality** *n*
university *n* **1** place of education at the highest level, where degrees are given **2** members of this place
unkempt *adj* (esp. of hair) untidy
unkind *adj* not kind; cruel or thought-

less **~ly** *adv* **~ness** *n*

unknown quantity *n* **1** person or thing whose qualities and abilities are not yet known **2** (in mathematics) a number represented by the letter x

unlearn *vt* forget by a deliberate effort

unleash *vt* allow (feelings or forces) to act with full force

unleavened /un'lev(ə)nd/ *adj* made without yeast

unless *conj* except if: *Don't come unless I ask you to.*

unlettered *adj* **1** not well educated **2** illiterate

unlike *prep* **1** different from **2** not characteristic of ♦ *adj* different

unlikely *adj* **1** not expected; improbable **2** not likely to happen or be true **–lihood** *n*

unload *v* **1** *vt* remove (a load) from (something) **2** *vi/t* remove bullets from (a gun) or film from (a camera) **3** *vt* get rid of

unloose *vt* set free

unloosen *vt* loosen

unmask *vt* show the hidden truth about

unmentionable *adj* too shocking to be spoken about

unmindful *adj* forgetting or not considering

unmitigated *adj* in every way (bad): *an unmitigated disaster*

unnatural *adj* **1** unusual **2** against ordinary good ways of behaving: *unnatural sexual practices* **~ly** *adv*

unnerve *vt* take away (someone's) confidence or courage

unnumbered *adj* **1** without an identifying number **2** innumerable

unobtrusive *adj* not (too) noticeable **~ly** *adv*

unorthodox *adj* not following usual beliefs or methods **~ly** *adv* **~y** *n*

unpack *vi/t* remove (possessions) from (a container)

unpalatable *adj* unpleasant and difficult for the mind to accept

unparalleled *adj* unequalled

unpick *vt* take out (the stitches) from (something)

unplaced *adj* not one of the first three in a race or competition

unpleasant *adj* **1** not enjoyable **2** unkind **~ly** *adv*

unprecedented *adj* never having happened before **~ly** *adv*

unpretentious *adj* not attempting to seem important **~ly** *adv* **~ness** *n*

unprincipled *adj* without moral values; unscrupulous

unprintable *adj* too offensive to express

unqualified *adj* **1** not limited **2** not having suitable knowledge or experience

unquestionable *adj* which cannot be doubted; certain **–bly** *adv*

unravel *vt* **-ll-** (*AmE* **-l-**) **1** *vi/t* become or cause (threads) to become separated or unwoven **2** *vt* make clear (a mystery)

unreal *adj* seeming imaginary or unlike reality **~ity** *n*

unremitting *adj* (of something difficult) never stopping **~ly** *adv*

unrequited *adj* not given in return

unrest *n* troubled or dissatisfied confusion, often with fighting

unrivalled, *AmE* **-valed** *adj* better than any other

unroll *vi/t* open from a rolled condition

unruly *adj* **1** behaving wildly: *unruly children* **2** hard to keep in place: *unruly hair*

unsaddle *vt* **1** remove a saddle from **2** unseat

unsavoury, *AmE* **-vory** *adj* unpleasant or unacceptable in moral values

unscathed *adj* not harmed

unscramble *vt* put (a scrambled message) into order

unscrew *vt* **1** remove the screws from **2** undo by twisting

unscripted *adj* without previous planning; not based on a script

unscrupulous *adj* not caring about honesty and fairness **~ly** *adv* **~ness** *n*

unseasonable *adj* unusual for the time of year, esp. bad **-bly** *adv*

unseat *vt* **1** remove from a position of power **2** (of a horse) throw off (a rider)

unseemly *adj* not proper or suitable (in

behaviour)

unsettle *vt* make more anxious or dissatisfied **–tled** *adj* (of weather or a political situation) likely to get worse

unsightly *adj* ugly

unskilled *adj* **1** not trained **2** not needing skill

unsociable *adj* not enjoying social activity; reserved

unsocial *adj* unsuitable for combining with family and social life: *working unsocial hours*

unsound *adj* **1** not healthy or strong **2** not based on valid reasoning

unspeakable *adj* terrible **–bly** *adv*

unstinting *adj* very generous

unstop *vt* remove an obstruction or stopper from

unstring *vt* **1** remove or loosen the strings of (e.g. a musical instrument) **2** upset the stability of (a person)

unstuck *adj* **1** not fastened **2 come unstuck** go wrong; be unsuccessful

unstudied *adj* natural

unsung *adj lit* not famous though deserving to be

unswerving *adj* firm **~ly** *adv*

untapped *adj* not yet put to use

untenable *adj* impossible to defend

unthinkable *adj* that cannot be considered or accepted; impossible

untie *vt* **1** undo (a knot) **2** unfasten by undoing knots

until *prep, conj* **1** up to (the time that): *Don't start until he arrives.* **2** as far as: *We stayed on the train until London.*

untimely *adj* **1** premature **2** not appropriate

unto *prep lit* to

untold *adj* very great

untouchable *adj* **1** that cannot or may not be touched **2** that cannot be reached **3** of the lowest Hindu caste ♦ *n* person of the lowest caste

untoward *adj* unexpected and undesirable

untrammelled, *AmE* **-meled** *adj* allowed to act or develop with complete freedom

untruth *n* lie

unused *adj* **1** not used up **2** not accustomed

unusual *adj* **1** not common **2** interesting because different from others **~ly** *adv* **1** very **2** in an unusual way

unutterable *adj* **1** terrible **2** complete: *an unutterable fool* **~bly** *adv*

unvarnished *adj* without additional description

unveil *vt* **1** remove a covering from **2** show publicly for the first time

unversed *adj* not experienced or informed

unvoiced *adj* not expressed in words

unwaged *adj euph* unemployed

unwarranted *adj* (done) without good reason

unwell *adj* (slightly) ill

unwieldy *adj* awkward to move, handle, or use

unwind *v* **-wound 1** *vi/t* undo (something wound) or become undone **2** *vi* become calmer and free of care

unwitting *adj* not knowing or intended: *their unwitting accomplice* **~ly** *adv*

unwritten rule *n* usual custom not officially stated

up *adv* **1** to or at a higher level **2** (shows increase): *Profits are up.* **3** to the north: *driving up to Scotland* **4** out of bed: *We stayed up late.* **5** so as to be completely finished: *Eat up your vegetables.* **6** into small pieces: *She tore it up.* **7** on top: *right side up* **8 up against** having to face (something difficult) **9 up and down: a** higher and lower: *jumping up and down* **b** backwards and forwards: *walking up and down* **10 up to: a** towards and as far as: *He walked up to me and asked my name.* **b** until: *up to now* **c** good, well, or clever enough for: *He's not up to the job.* **d** the duty or responsibility of: *I'll leave it up to you.* **e** doing (something bad): *What are you up to?* ♦ *prep* **1** to or at a higher level on: *walking up the stairs* **2** to or at the top or far end of: *They live just up the road.* ♦ *adj* **1** directed up: *the up escalator* **2** (of a road) being repaired **3 be up** be happening; be the matter **4 be well up**

in/on know a lot about **5 up and about** out of bed (again) and able to walk **6 up for: a** intended or being considered for **b** on trial for ♦ *vt* **-pp-** increase
up-and-coming *adj* new and likely to succeed
up-and-up *n* **on the up-and-up** improving; succeeding
upbeat *adj infml* cheerful
upbraid *vt* scold
upbringing *n* (way of) training and caring for a child
upcoming *adj* about to happen
update *vt* **1** make more modern **2** supply with the latest information **update** *n*
upend *vt* stand upside down
upfront *adj* very direct and open
upgrade *vt* give a more important position to
upheaval *n* great change and confusion, with much activity
upheld *past t. and p. of* uphold
uphill *adj, adv* **1** up a slope **2** difficult: *an uphill task*
uphold *vt* **-held 1** prevent from being weakened or taken away **2** declare (a decision) to be right **~er** *n*
upholster *vt* cover and fill (a seat) **~er** *n* **~y** *n* material covering and filling a seat
upkeep *n* (cost of) keeping something repaired and in order
upland *n* higher land in an area **upland** *adj*
uplift *vt* encourage cheerful or holy feelings in **uplift** *n*
up-market *adj* being or using goods produced to meet the demand of the higher social groups
upon *prep fml* on[1] (1,2,3)
upper *adj* at or nearer the top: *the upper arm* ♦ *n* **1** top part of a shoe **2 on one's uppers** *infml* very poor
upper case *adj, n* capital (letters)
upper class *n* highest social class, esp. with noble titles **upper-class** *adj*
upper hand *n* control
uppermost *adv* in the highest or strongest position
uppity also **uppish** *adj* putting on airs
upright *adj* **1** exactly straight up; not bent or leaning **2** completely honest ♦ *n* upright supporting beam
uprising *n* rebellion
uproar *n* confused noisy activity, esp. shouting **~ious** *adj* very noisy, esp. with laughter **~iously** *adv* **~iousness** *n*
uproot *vt* **1** tear (a plant) from the earth **2** remove from a home or settled habits
ups and downs *pl n* good and bad periods
upset *vt* **-set;** *pres. p.* **-tt- 1** turn over, esp. accidentally, causing confusion or scattering **2** cause to be worried, sad, or angry **3** make slightly ill ♦ *n* **1** slight illness: *a stomach upset* **2** unexpected result
upshot *n* result in the end
upside down *adj* **1** with the top turned to the bottom **2** in disorder
upstage *adv, adj* at the rear of a stage ♦ *adj* haughty ♦ *vt* take attention away from (someone) for oneself
upstairs *adv, adj* on or to a higher floor
upstanding *adj* **1** tall and strong **2** honest **~ness** *n*
upstart *n* someone who has risen too suddenly or unexpectedly to a high position
upstream *adv, adj* moving against the current of a river
upsurge *n* sudden rise
upswing *n* improvement
uptake *n* **1** ability to understand: *He's rather slow on the uptake.* **2** rate at which something is absorbed or accepted
uptight *adj infml* anxious and nervous
up-to-date *adj* **1** modern **2** including or having all the latest information
uptown *adj, adv AmE* to or in the residential areas of a city
upturn *n* a favourable change
upward *adj* going up **upwards** *adv* more than
upwardly-mobile *adj* able or wishing to move into a higher social class and become more wealthy

uranium *n* radioactive metal used in producing atomic power
Uranus *n* the planet 7th in order from the sun
urban *adj* of towns
urbane *adj* smoothly polite **~ly** *adv* **–banity** *n*
urbanize, -ise *vt* make like (people living in) a city **–ization** *n*
urchin *n* small dirty untidy child
-ure *suffix* act or result of doing the stated thing: *closure*
urge *vt* **1** try strongly to persuade: *He urged me to reconsider.* **2** drive forwards: *He urged the horses onwards with a whip.* ♦ *n* strong desire or need
urgent *adj* that must be dealt with at once **~ly** *adv* **urgency** *n*
uric *adj* of or found in urine
urinal /yoo(ə)ˈrienl/ *n* container or building for (men) urinating
urine *n* liquid waste passed from the body **urinary** *adj* **urinate** *vi* pass urine from the body **urination** *n*
urn *n* **1** large metal container for serving tea or coffee **2** container for the ashes of a burnt dead body
us *pron* (*object form of* **we**)
US *abbrev. for:* **1** also **USA** the United States (of America) **2** of the United States: *the US navy*
usage *n* **1** way of using a language: *a book on English usage* **2** (type or degree of) use
use *n* **1** using or being used **2** ability or right to use something: *He lost the use of his legs.* **3** purpose: *A machine with many uses.* **4** advantage; usefulness: *It's no use complaining.* **5 in use** being used **6 make use of** use **7 of use** useful ♦ *v* **1** *vt* employ for a purpose; put to use: *Oil can be used as a fuel.* **2** *vt* finish; consume **3** *vt* take unfair advantage of **4** *vi* (used in the past tense for showing what always or regularly happened): *I used to go there every week, but I no longer do.* **use up** *phr vt* finish completely **~ful** *adj* that fulfils a need well **~fully** *adv* **~fulness** *n* **~less** *adj* **1** not useful **2** unable to do anything properly **~lessly** *adv* **usable** *adj* **used** *adj* that has already had an owner: *used cars* **user** *n*
used to *adj* no longer finding (something) strange or annoying because it has become familiar
user-friendly *adj* easy to use or understand **–liness** *n*
usher *n* someone who shows people to their seats in a public place ♦ *vt* bring by showing the way
usherette *n* female usher in a cinema
USSR *abbrev. for:* Union of Soviet Socialist Republics; the Soviet Union; Russia
usual *adj* in accordance with what happens most of the time **~ly** *adv* in most cases; generally
usurp /yoohˈsuhp/ *vt* steal (someone else's power or position) **~er** *n*
usury /ˈyoohzyəri/ *n* lending money to be paid back at an unfairly high rate of interest **–rer** *n*
utensil *n* object with a particular use, esp. a tool or container
uterus *n med* womb **–rine** *adj*
utilitarian *adj* **1** made to be useful rather than decorative **2** believing in utilitarianism
utilitarianism *n* belief that the best actions are those giving the greatest happiness to the greatest number
utility *n* **1** degree of usefulness **2** public service, such as water supplies
utilize, -ise *vt* use[2] (1) **–ization, -isation** *n*
utmost *adj* very great: *done with (the) utmost care* ♦ *n* the most that can be done: *I did my utmost to prevent it.*
utopia *n* perfect society **-pian** *adj* impractically trying to bring social perfection
utter[1] *adj* (esp. of something bad) complete: *utter nonsense* **~ly** *adv*
utter[2] *vt* make (a sound) or produce (words) **~ance** *n* **1** speaking **2** something said
uttermost *adj* utmost
U-turn *n* **1** turning movement in a vehicle which takes one back in the direc-

tion one came from **2** complete change, resulting in the opposite of what has gone before

uvula /ˈyoohvyoolə/ *n* small piece of flesh hanging down at the top of the throat

uxorious /ukˈsawri·əs/ *adj* very fond of one's wife **~ly** *adv* **~ness** *n*

V

V, v the 22nd letter of the English alphabet

v *abbrev. for:* **1** verb **2** versus **3** very

vacancy *n* unfilled place, such as a job or hotel room

vacant *adj* **1** empty **2** (of a job) having no worker to do it **3** showing lack of interest or serious thought **~ly** *adv*

vacate *vt* cease to use or live in: *Kindly vacate your seats.*

vacation *n* **1 a** *esp. AmE* holiday **b** *esp. BrE* time when universities are closed **2** vacating ♦ *vi esp. AmE* have a holiday

vaccine *n* substance put into the body to protect it against disease **–cinate** *vt* put vaccine into **–cination** *n*

vacillate *vi* keep changing one's mind **–lation** *n*

vacuous *adj* **1** showing foolishness: *a vacuous grin* **2** with no purpose or meaning **~ly** *adv* **–uity** *n*

vacuum *n* space completely without air or other gas ♦ *vt* clean with a vacuum cleaner

vacuum cleaner *n* electric apparatus for sucking up dirt

vacuum flask *n* flask (3)

vacuum-packed *adj* wrapped in plastic with all air removed

vacuum pump *n* pump for removing air or gas from an enclosed space

vagabond *n lit* person who lives a wandering life

vagary /ˈvaygəri/ *n* chance event that has an effect on one

vagina *n* passage from the outer female sex organs to the womb

vagrant *n law* person with no home who wanders around and usu. begs **vagrancy** *n* being a vagrant

vague *adj* **1** not clearly seen, described, or understood **2** unable to express oneself clearly **~ly** *adv* **~ness** *n*

vain *adj* **1** admiring oneself too much **2** unsuccessful; unimportant: *a vain attempt* **3 in vain** unsuccessfully **~ly** *adv*

vainglorious *adj* boastful **~ly** *adv* **~ness** *n*

valance *n* drapery hung as a border esp. along the edge of a bed or shelf

vale *n* (in poetry and place-names) broad low valley

valediction *n lit* (act of) saying goodbye **–tory** *adj* used in valediction

valency /ˈvaylənsi/ *n* measure of the power of atoms to form compounds

valentine *n* (card sent to) a lover chosen on **Saint Valentine's Day** (February 14th)

valerian *n* plant with medicinal qualities

valet *n* **1** man's personal male servant **2** hotel servant who cleans and presses clothes

valetudinarian /ˌvaliˌtyoohdiˈneəri·ən/ *n* hypochondriac

valiant *adj esp. lit* very brave **~ly** *adv* **1** very bravely **2** very hard: *He tried valiantly to pass the exam.*

valid *adj* **1** (of a reason or argument) firmly based and acceptable **2** that can legally be used: *a ticket valid for 3 months* **~ly** *adv* **~ate** *vt* make valid **~ity** *n*

valise *n* small travelling bag

Valium *n tdmk for* diazepam; a tranquillizing drug

valley *n* land between two lines of hills or mountains

valour, *AmE* **-or** *n esp. lit* great bravery **–orous** *adj* **–orously** *adv*

valuable *adj* **1** worth a lot of money **2** very useful ♦ *n* something valuable
valuation *n* **1** calculating how much something is worth **2** value decided on
value *n* **1** usefulness or importance, esp. compared with other things **2** worth in esp. money: *goods to the value of £500* **3** worth compared with the amount paid: *a restaurant offering the best value in town* ♦ *vt* **1** calculate the value of **2** consider to be of great worth
values *pl n* standards or principles **~less** *adj* **–uer** *n*
value-added tax *n* VAT
value judgment *n* judgment about the quality of something, based on opinion rather than facts
valve *n* **1** part inside a pipe which opens and shuts to control the flow of liquid or gas through it **2** closed airless glass tube for controlling a flow of electricity
valvular *adj* like or of a valve
vamoose *vi AmE sl* depart quickly
vamp[1] *vi, n* (play) an improvised accompaniment
vamp[2] *n* seductive and exploiting woman
vampire *n* imaginary evil creature that sucks people's blood
vampire bat *n* large bat which sucks blood
van[1] *n* covered road vehicle or railway carriage for carrying esp. goods
van[2] *n* **in the van** taking a leading part
vanadium *n* metallic element used in alloys
vandal *n* person who destroys beautiful or useful things **~ism** *n* needless damage to esp. public buildings **~ize** *vt* destroy or damage intentionally
vane *n* bladelike turning part of a machine
vanguard *n* **1** leading part of some kind of advancement in human affairs: *scientists in the vanguard of medical research* **2** front of a marching army
vanilla *n* strong-smelling plant substance used in food
vanish *vi* **1** disappear **2** cease to exist
vanity *n* **1** being too proud of oneself **2** quality of being without lasting value
vanquish *vt esp. lit* defeat completely
vantagepoint *n* **1** good position from which to see **2** point of view
vapid *adj* dull **~ly** *adv* **~ness, ~ity** *n*
vapour, *AmE* **-por** *n* gaslike form of a liquid, such as mist or steam **vaporize** *vi/t* change into vapour **vaporous** *adj*
vapours *pl n arch. or humorous* feeling of shock or faintness
variable *adj* that changes or can be changed; not fixed or steady ♦ *n* variable amount **–bly** *adv*
variance *n* **at variance (with)** not in agreement (with)
variant *n, adj* (form) that is different and can be used instead: *variant spellings*
variation *n* **1** (example or degree of) varying **2** any of a set of pieces of music based on a single tune
varicose veins *pl n* swollen blood tubes, esp. in the legs
varied *adj* **1** various (1) **2** (always) changing
variegated *adj* marked irregularly with different colours **–gation** *n*
variety *n* **1** not being always the same: *a job lacking variety* **2** group containing different sorts of the same thing: *a wide variety of colours* **3** sort: *a new variety of wheat* **4** entertainment with many short performances
variform *adj tech* existing in various forms
various *adj* **1** different from each other **2** several **~ly** *adv*
varlet *n arch.* wicked or worthless person
varmint *n AmE* troublesome person, esp. a boy
varnish *n* liquid that gives a hard shiny surface to esp. wooden articles ♦ *vt* cover with varnish **varnish over** *phr vt* cover up (something unpleasant)
varsity *adj, n* (of) a university
vary *v* **1** *vi* be different (from each other): *Houses vary in size.* **2** *vi/t* change, esp. continually: *varying one's work methods*

vascular *adj* of or containing veins
vase *n* deep decorative pot for esp. flowers
vasectomy *n* operation for cutting the sperm-carrying tubes in a man
Vaseline *n tdmk for* petroleum jelly
vassal *n* person of low social rank in the Middle Ages
vast *adj* extremely large **~ly** *adv*
vat *n* large liquid container for industrial use
VAT *n* value-added tax; tax added to the price of an article
Vatican *n* (palace in Rome which is) the centre of government of the Roman Catholic Church
vaudeville /ˈvawdəˌvil/ *n AmE* variety (4)
vault[1] *n* **1** thick-walled room for storing valuable things **2** underground room, esp. for storage or for dead bodies **3** arched roof
vault[2] *vi* jump using the hands or a pole to gain more height ♦ *n* act of vaulting **~er** *n*
vaunt *vt esp. lit* boast about
VC *n* Victoria Cross; award for bravery in battle
VCR *n* video cassette recorder; video (2)
VD *n* venereal disease
VDU *n* visual display unit; apparatus with a screen which shows information, esp. from a computer or word processor
've *short for:* have
veal *n* meat from a calf
vector 1 (in science) a quantity which has direction and size and can be represented by an arrow of a length related to its size **2** insect which carries a disease **3** course of an aircraft
veer *vi* change direction
veg *n BrE infml* vegetables
vegan *n* vegetarian who does not eat any animal produce, including dairy produce
vegetable *n* **1** plant grown for food to be eaten with the main part of a meal **2** human being who exists but has little or no power of thought
vegetarian *n* person who eats no meat ♦ *adj* **1** of or related to vegetarians **2** made up only of vegetables
vegetate *vi* lead a dull inactive life
vegetation *n* plants
vehement /ˈvee·əmənt/ *adj* forceful **~ly** *adv* **–mence** *n*
vehicle *n* **1** something, esp. with wheels, in or on which people or goods are carried **2** means of expressing or showing something
vehicular /veeˈikyooləl/ *adj* of or designed for vehicles
veil *n* **1** covering for a woman's face **2** something that covers and hides: *a veil of mist* **3 take the veil** (of a woman) become a nun ♦ *vt* cover (as if) with a veil: *veiled in secrecy* **~ed** *adj* expressed indirectly: *veiled threats*
vein *n* **1** tube carrying blood back to the heart **2** thin line running through a leaf or insect's wing **3** metal-containing crack in rock **4** small but noticeable amount: *a vein of cruelty* **5** state of mind: *in a sad vein*
Velcro *n tdmk for* fabric fastener
veld *n* high flat grassland of South Africa
vellum *n* fine parchment
velocipede *n* early type of bicycle
velocity *n* speed
velour /vəˈlooə/ also **velours** *n* heavy material with a velvety surface
velvet *n* cloth with a soft furry surface on one side only **~y** *adj* soft like velvet
velveteen *n* fabric made in imitation of velvet
venal *adj* acting or done to gain unfair reward or personal advantage
vend *vi/t* sell
vendetta *n* feud
vending machine *n* machine into which one puts money to obtain small articles
vendor *n* seller, esp. of a house or land
veneer *n* **1** thin covering of wood on an article **2** false outer appearance: *a veneer of respectability* ♦ *vt* cover with a veneer
venerable *adj* deserving respect or honour because of great age

venerate *vt* treat (someone or something old) with great respect or honour **-ration** *n*

venereal disease *n* disease passed on by sexual activity

venetian blind *n* window covering with long flat bars that can be turned to let in or shut out light

vengeance *n* **1** revenge **2 with a vengeance** *infml* very greatly

vengeful *adj esp. lit* fiercely wishing to take vengeance **~ly** *adv* **~ness** *n*

venial *adj* (of a mistake or fault) not very serious, and therefore forgivable

venison *n* deer meat

venom *n* **1** liquid poison produced by certain animals **2** great anger or hatred **~ous** *adj* **~ously** *adv* **~ness** *n*

venous *adj tech* **1** of the veins **2** (of blood) in the veins

vent *n* **1** opening or pipe by which gas, smoke, etc., escape **2 give vent to** express freely: *giving vent to his anger*

vent on *phr vt* express by making (someone or something) suffer: *venting her fury on the cat*

ventilate *vt* let or bring fresh air into **-lator** *n* **1** apparatus for ventilating **2** apparatus for pumping air into and out of the lungs of someone who cannot breathe properly **-lation** *n*

ventricle *n* chamber in the bottom of the heart that pumps blood out into the body

ventriloquist *n* someone who can make their voice seem to come from someone or somewhere else, **-quism** *n*

venture *v* **1** *vi* risk going **2** *vt* dare to say ♦ *n* (new and risky) course of action

venture capital *n* money lent to start up a new business company, esp. a risky one **~ist** *n*

venturesome *adj lit or AmE* ready to take risks

venue *n* place arranged for something to happen

Venus *n* the planet 2nd in order from the sun

veracious /vəˈrayshəs/ *adj* truthful **~ly** *adv*

veracity /vəˈrasəti/ *n* truthfulness

veranda , -dah *n* open area with a floor and roof beside a house

verb *n* word or group of words that is used in describing an action, experience, or state, such as *wrote* in *she wrote a letter*, or *put on* in *he put on his coat*

verbal *adj* **1** spoken, not written **2** of words and their use **3** of a verb **~ly** *adv* in spoken words

verbalize, -ise *vi/t* express (something) in words

verbal noun *n* noun describing an action, formed by adding *-ing* to the verb

verbatim /vuhˈbaytim/ *adv, adj* repeating the actual words exactly

verbiage /ˈvuhbi·ij/ *n* too many unnecessary words

verbose *adj* using too many words **~ly** *adv* **-bosity** *n*

verdant *adj lit* green with growing plants **-ancy** *n*

verdict *n* **1** decision made by a jury at the end of a trial about whether the prisoner is guilty **2** judgment; opinion

verdigris /ˈvuhdigris/ *n* green or bluish deposit formed on copper or brass

verdure *n lit* (greenness of) growing plants

verge *n* **1** edge, esp. of a path or road **2 on the verge of** nearly; about to **verge on** *phr vt* be near to: *dark grey, verging on black*

verger *n* person who looks after the inside of a church

verify *vt* make certain that (something) is true **-fiable** *adj* **-fication** *n*

verily *adv arch.* truly

verisimilitude /ˌverisiˈmilityoohd/ *n fml* quality of seeming to be true

veritable *adj* (used to give force to an expression) real **-bly** *adv*

verity *n* truth

verkrampte *n SAfrE* person with very conservative views

vermicelli /ˌvuhmiˈcheli/ *n* pasta in the form of very thin strings

vermiculite *n* very light mica used in

insulation
vermilion *adj* bright reddish orange
vermin *pl n* **1** insects and small animals that do damage **2** people who are a trouble to society **~ous** *adj*
vermouth *n* drink made from wine with aromatic herbs added
vernacular *adj, n* (in or being) the language spoken in a particular place
vernal *adj* of spring
verruca *n* **-as** or **-ae** wart, usu. formed on the sole of the foot
versatile *adj* that can do many different things or has many uses **–tility** *n*
verse *n* **1** writing in the form of poetry, esp. with rhymes **2** single division of a poem **3** short numbered group of sentences in the Bible or other holy book
versed *adj* experienced; skilled: *thoroughly versed in the arts of diplomacy*
versification *n* composition of verse
version *n* **1** form of something that is slightly different from others of the same sort: *This dress is a cheaper version of the one we saw in the other shop.* **2** one person's account of an event: *The 2 eyewitnesses gave different versions of the accident.*
verso *n* **–sos** *tech* left-hand page of a book
versus *prep* in competition with; against
vertebra *n* **-brae** small bone in the backbone
vertebrate *n* animal with a backbone
vertex *n* **–texes** or **–tices** **1** angle opposite the base of a triangle **2** meeting point of the two lines of an angle **3** highest point
vertical *adj* forming a 90° angle with the ground or bottom; upright **~ly** *adv*
vertiginous /vuhˈtijinəs/ *adj* causing or suffering from vertigo
vertigo *n* unpleasant feeling of unsteadiness at great heights
verve *n* forcefulness and eager enjoyment
very *adv* **1** to a great degree: *a very exciting book* **2** in the greatest possible degree: *I did my very best to help.* ♦ *adj* (used for giving force to an expression) actual: *He died in that very bed.*
vespers *n* church service in the evening
vessel *n* **1** ship or large boat **2** (round) container, esp. for liquids **3** tube that carries liquid through a body or plant
vest *n* **1** *BrE* undergarment for the upper body **2** *AmE* waistcoat
vestal virgin *n* unmarried female temple servant in ancient Rome
vested interest *n* a personal reason for doing something, because one gains advantage from it
vestibule *n* **1** room or passage through which larger rooms are reached **2** *AmE* enclosed passage at each end of a railway carriage which connects it with the next carriage
vestige *n* **1** (small) remaining part: *the last vestiges of royal power* **2** slightest bit: *not a vestige of truth* **–gial** *adj*
vest in, vest with *phr vt fml* give the legal right to possess or use (power, property, etc.) to (someone)
vestment *n* (priest's) ceremonial garment
vestry *n* room in a church for esp. changing into vestments
vet *n* animal doctor ♦ *vt* **-tt-** examine carefully for correctness, past record, etc.
vetch *n* beanlike climbing plant
veteran *n, adj* **1** (person) with long service or (former) experience, esp. as a soldier **2** (thing) that has grown old with long use
veterinary *adj* of the medical care of animals: *veterinary surgeon*
veto *vt* **vetoed,** *pres. p.* **vetoing** officially refuse to allow ♦ *n* **vetoes** (act of) vetoing
vex *vt* displease; trouble **~ation** *n*
vexatious *adj* vexing **~ly** *adv* **~ness** *n*
vexed question *n* matter that causes fierce argument and is difficult to decide
VHF *abbrev. for:* very high frequency
via *prep* travelling through
viable *adj* able to succeed in actual use:

an economically viable plan **–bility** *n*
viaduct *n* high bridge across a valley
vial *n* phial
viands *n pl lit* food
vibes *pl n infml* **1** vibraphone **2** vibrations; atmosphere
vibrant *adj* **1** powerful and exciting **2** (of colour or light) bright and strong **~ly** *adv* **vibrancy** *n*
vibraphone *n* musical instrument with metal bars set in a frame
vibrate *vi/t* (cause to) move with a slight continuous shake **vibration** *n*
vibrato *n* **–tos** slight tremulous effect given to musical sound
vibrator *n* vibrating electrical device used in massage
vicar *n* priest in charge of a parish
vicarage *n* vicar's house
vicarious /vieˈkeəri·əs, vi-/ *adj* experienced indirectly, e.g. by watching or reading **~ly** *adv*
vice- *prefix* next in rank below: *vice-president*
vice¹ *n* **1** (kind of) evil behaviour or living **2 a** fault of character: *Laziness is his one vice.* **b** bad habit: *Smoking is my only vice.*
vice² *BrE n* tool with metal jaws for holding things firmly
vice-chancellor *n* (in Britain) head of a university
vicereine /ˈviesˌrayn/ *n* **1** wife of a viceroy **2** woman viceroy
viceroy *n* person ruling as a representative of a king or queen
vice versa *adv* the opposite way around
vicinity *n* area nearby
vicious *adj* **1** showing an unpleasant desire to hurt: *a vicious kick* **2** dangerous: *a vicious-looking knife* **~ly** *adv* **~ness** *n*
vicious circle *n* situation in which unpleasant causes and effects lead back to the original starting point
vicissitudes /viˈsisityoohdz/ *pl n* changes, esp. from good to bad, that have an effect on one
victim *n* one who suffers as the result of something **~ize, -ise** *vt* cause to suffer unfairly **~ization** *n*
victor *n* winner
Victorian *adj* **1** of the time when Queen Victoria ruled Britain (1837-1901) **2** very respectable (esp. in matters of sex)
victoria plum *n* sweet red plum
victory *n* winning **–torious** *adj* **1** that has won: *the victorious team* **2** showing victory: *a victorious shout*
victualler, *AmE* also **–ler** *n* provider of food, esp. to soldiers
victuals *pl n* food
vicuna /viˈkyoonə/ *n* (wool from) an animal related to the llama
video *adj* for (recording and) showing pictures on television ♦ *n* **-os 1** videotape recording **2** machine for making and showing these ♦ *vt* **videoed;** *pres. p.* **videoing** videotape
video- *prefix* of, for, or using recorded pictures
videodisc *n* disc for video recording
video nasty *n infml* video film including scenes of extremely unpleasant violence
videorecorder *n* video (2)
videotape *n* band of magnetic material on which moving pictures are recorded ♦ *vt* record on videotape
vie *vi* **vied,** *pres. p.* **vying** compete
view *n* **1** what one can see **2** opinion: *In my view, he's a fool.* **3 in view of** taking into consideration: *In view of the unusual circumstances, we'll cancel it.* **4 on view** being shown to the public **5 with a view to** with the intention of ♦ *vt* **1** consider; regard: *I view the matter very seriously.* **2** examine by looking **3** watch television **~er** *n* person watching television
viewfinder *n* apparatus on a camera showing a small picture of what is to be photographed
viewpoint *n* point of view
vigil *n* act of staying (awake and) watchful for some purpose
vigilance *n* watchful care **-lant** *adj* always prepared for possible danger **–lantly** *adv*
vigilance committee *n AmE* group of

vigilantes
vigilante /ˌvijiˈlanti/ *n sometimes derog* person who tries by unofficial means to punish crime
vignette /viˈnyet/ *n* short effective written description
vigour, *AmE* **-or** n active strength or force **-orous** *adj* **-orously** *adv*
Viking *n* Scandinavian attacker (and settler) in northern and western Europe from the 8th to the 10th centuries
vile *adj* **1** low, shameful, and worthless: *a vile slander* **2** extremely unpleasant: *vile food* **~ly** *adv*
vilify *vt* say unfairly bad things about **-fication** *n*
villa *n* **1** house in a holiday area, esp. to let **2** large ancient Roman country house
village *n* collection of houses in a country area, smaller than a town **villager** *n* person who lives in a village
villain *n* **1** (esp. in stories) bad person **2** *BrE infml* criminal **~ous** *adj* threatening great harm; evil
villein *n* medieval peasant
vim *n* energy and enthusiasm
vinaigrette /ˌvinəˈgret/ *n* mixture of oil and vinegar put on salads
vindicate *vt* **1** free from blame **2** prove (something that was in doubt) to be right **-cation** *n*
vindictive *adj* wishing to harm someone who has harmed you **~ly** *adv* **~ness** *n*
vine *n* climbing plant, esp. one that produces grapes
vinegar *n* acid-tasting liquid used in preparing food **~y** *adj*
vineyard *n* piece of land with vines for making wine
vinous *adj* of, like, or caused by wine
vintage *n* particular year in which a wine is made ♦ *adj* **1** of the best quality **2** *BrE* (of a car) made between 1919 and 1930
vintner *n* wine merchant
vinyl *n* firm bendable plastic
viol *n* early stringed musical instrument
viola[1] *n* musical instrument like a large violin
viola[2] *n* small pansy
violate *vt* **1** act against (something solemnly promised or officially agreed): *violate a treaty* **2** come violently into (and spoil) **3** have sex (with a woman) by force **-lation** *n*
violent *adj* using, showing or produced by great damaging force **~ly** *adv* **-lence** *n* **1** extreme (and damaging) force **2** use of force to hurt people
violet *n* small plant with sweet-smelling purple flowers
violin *n* small four-stringed wooden musical instrument played by drawing a bow across the strings **~ist** *n*
violincello *n* cello
VIP *n* person of great influence or fame
viper *n* small poisonous snake
virago /viˈrahgoh/ *n* **-oes** or **-os** **1** loud angry woman **2** *arch.* woman of great strength and courage
virgin *n* person who has not had sex ♦ *adj* unused; unspoiled **~ity** *n* state of being a virgin
virginals *pl n* small harpsichord
virginia creeper *n* climbing plant with leaves that are bright red in autumn
virile *adj* having the strong and forceful qualities expected of a man, esp. in matters of sex **-ility** *n*
virology *n* branch of science that deals with viruses
virtual *adj* almost or unofficially the stated thing **~ly** *adv* almost; very nearly
virtue *n* **1** condition of being morally good **2** morally good quality, such as truthfulness or loyalty **3** advantage: *The plan's great virtue is its simplicity.* **4 by virtue of** as a result of; by means of **-tuous** *adj* morally good **-tuously** *adv* **-tuousness** *n*
virtuoso *n* **-si** extremely skilled (musical) performer **-osity** *n* virtuoso's skill
virulent *adj* **1** (of a poison or disease) very powerful and dangerous **2** full of bitter hatred: *virulent abuse* **~ly** *adv* **-lence** *n*

virus *n* extremely small living thing that causes infectious disease **viral** *adj*
visa *n* official mark put on a passport to allow someone to enter or leave a particular country
visage *n lit* face
vis-à-vis /ˌvee zah ˈvee/ *prep fml* with regard to
viscera /ˈvisərə/ *pl n* internal organs of the body **–al** *adj*
viscount /ˈviekownt/ *n* British nobleman between an earl and a baron in rank
viscountess *n* the wife of a viscount, or a woman of the rank of viscount in her own right
viscous /ˈviskəs/ also **viscid** *adj* (of a liquid) thick and sticky **–cosity** *n*
vise *n AmE* vice²
visible *adj* **1** that can be seen **2** noticeable **–bly** *adv* noticeably **–bility** *n* **1** clearness with which things can be seen over a particular distance **2** ability to give a clear view
vision *n* **1** ability to see **2** wise understanding of the future **3** picture in the mind **4** something supposedly seen when in a sleeplike state or as a religious experience
visionary *adj* **1** having vision regarding the future **2** grand but impractical ♦ *n* visionary person
visit *v* **1** *vi/t* go to and spend time in (a place) or with (a person) **2** *vt* go to (a place) to make an official examination **3** *vi AmE* stay **visit on** *phr vt* direct (anger, etc.) against **visit with** *phr vt AmE* talk socially with ♦ *n* act or time of visiting **~or** *n*
visitation *n* **1** official visit **2** act of God
visor *n* face or eye protector on a hat or helmet
vista *n* view stretching away into the distance
visual *adj* **1** of or done by seeing **2** having an effect on the sense of sight: *the visual arts* **~ly** *adv* **~ize** *vt* imagine, esp. as if by seeing
vital *adj* **1** extremely necessary or important **2** necessary to stay alive **3** full of life and force **~ly** *adv* in the highest possible degree
vitality *n* **1** cheerful forceful quality **2** ability to remain alive or effective
vital statistics *pl n* measurements round a woman's chest, waist, and hips
vitamin *n* chemical substance found in certain foods and important for growth and good health
vitiate *vt* weaken
viticulture *n* (science of) the cultivation of vines
vitreous *adj* glassy
vitrify *vi/t* (cause to) become glass or like glass
vitriol *n* **1** extremely powerful acid **2** cruel wounding quality of speech and writing **~ic** *adj* fiercely cruel in speech or judgment
vituperative /viˈtyoohpərətiv/ *adj* full of angry disapproval **~ly** *adv* **–ation** *n*
vivacious *adj* (esp. of a woman) full of life and fun **~ly** *adv* **–city** *n*
viva voce *also* **viva** *n* spoken examination
vivid *adj* **1** (of light or colour) bright and strong **2** producing sharp clear pictures in the mind: *a vivid description* **~ly** *adv* **~ness** *n*
viviparous /viˈvipərəs/ *adj* producing babies, rather than eggs
vivisection *n* performing of operations on animals to test medical treatments or new products
vixen *n* female fox
viz *abbrev. for:* videlicet; that is to say
vizier *n* Muslim chief minister
V-neck *n* V-shaped neck opening of a dress or shirt
vocabulary *n* **1** words known, learnt, or used: *a child's limited vocabulary* **2** short list of words with their meanings
vocal *adj* **1** of or produced by the voice: *vocal music* **2** expressing one's opinion loudly **~ly** *adv* **~ist** *n* singer **~ize** *vi/t*
vocal cords *pl n* muscles in the throat that produce sounds when air passes through them
vocation *n* **1** particular fitness or ability for a worthy kind of work **2** job, esp.

one which you do because you have a vocation **~al** *adj* of or for a job: *vocational training*

vociferate *vi* shout, esp. angrily **–ation** *n*

vociferous /voh'sif(ə)rəs/ *adj* expressing oneself forcefully or noisily **~ly** *adv*

vodka *n* strong colourless Russian alcoholic drink

vogue *n* popular fashion ♦ *adj* popular at present: *vogue words*

voice *n* **1** sound(s) produced in speaking or singing **2** ability to produce such sounds: *She's lost her voice.* **3** right to express oneself: *I have no voice in the decision.* ♦ *vt* express in words, esp. forcefully: *voicing their opinions*

voice-over *n* voice of an unseen person on a film or television show

void *n* empty space ♦ *adj law* having no value or effect ♦ *vt* make void

voile /voyl/ *n* fine thin material

volatile *adj* **1** quickly changing, esp. easily becoming angry or dangerous **2** (of a liquid) easily changing into gas **–tility** *n*

vol-au-vent *n* small pastry case filled with meat or vegetables

volcano *n* **-noes** *or* **-nos** mountain which sometimes throws out hot gases and melted rock **–canic** *adj* **1** of a volcano **2** violently forceful

vole *n* small mouse-like animal

volition *n* **of one's own volition** *fml* because one wishes to, not because one is told to by someone else

volley *n* **1** many shots fired together **2** kicking or hitting of a ball before it has hit the ground ♦ *v* **1** *vi* (of guns) be fired together **2** *vi/t* hit or kick (as) a volley

volleyball *n* team game played by hitting a large ball across a net with the hands

volt *n* unit of electrical force **~age** *n* electrical force measured in volts

volte-face *n* sudden change of policy

voluble *adj* talking a lot **–bly** *adv* **–bility** *n*

volume *n* **1** (degree of) loudness of sound **2** size of something measured by multiplying its length by its height by its width **3** any of a set of books **4** amount: *the increasing volume of passenger traffic*

voluminous *adj* **1** filling or containing a lot of space **2** producing or containing (too) much writing **~ly** *adv* **~ness, -inosity** *n*

voluntary *adj* acting or done willingly, without being forced **–arily** *adv*

volunteer *n* person who has volunteered ♦ *v* **1** *vi/t* offer to do something without payment or reward, or without being forced **2** *vt* tell without being asked: *He volunteered a statement to the police.*

voluptuary *n* enthusiast for physical pleasure

voluptuous *adj* **1** suggesting or expressing sexual pleasure **2** giving a fine delight to the senses **~ly** *adv* **~ness** *n*

vomit *vi* throw up (the contents of the stomach) through the mouth ♦ *n* swallowed food thrown back up through the mouth

voodoo *n* set of magical religious practices in esp. Haiti

voracious *adj* eating or wanting a lot of food **~ly** *adv* **–city** *n*

vortex *n* **-texes** *or* **-tices** **1** powerful circular moving mass of water or wind **2** *lit* situation that makes one powerless: *sucked into the vortex of war*

votary *n* regular worshipper or admirer

vote *v* **1** *vi* express one's choice officially, esp. by marking a piece of paper or raising one's hand **2** *vt* agree, by a vote, to provide (something) **3** *vt infml* agree as the general opinion: *I vote we leave now.* ♦ *n* **1** (choice or decision made by) voting **2** number of such choices made by or for a particular person or group: *an increase in the Liberal vote* **3** right to vote in political elections **voter** *n*

votive *adj* done or given to fulfil a religious vow

voucher *n* **1** *BrE* ticket usable instead of money **2** official paper given to prove that money has been paid

vouch for *phr vt* state one's firm belief in the good qualities of, based on experience
vouchsafe *vt lit* give, say, or do as a favour
vow *vt, n* (make) a solemn promise or declaration of intention
vowel *n* speech sound made without closing the air passage in the mouth or throat: *A, e, i, o and u are vowels.*
voyage *n* long journey by ship ♦ *vi lit* make a voyage **–ager** *n*
voyeur *n* person who gets sexual excitement by (secretly) watching others have sex **~ism** *n*
vs *AmE abbrev. for:* versus
vulcanize, -ise *vt* strengthen (rubber) by chemical treatment
vulgar *adj* **1** very rude or bad-mannered **2** showing bad judgment in matters of beauty or style **~ly** *adv* **~ity** *n* **~ize** *vt*
vulgar fraction *n* fraction expressed as a number above and a number below a line
Vulgate *n* Latin translation of the Bible authorized by the Roman Catholic church
vulnerable *adj* **1** easy to attack **2** (of a person) easily harmed; sensitive **–bility** *n*
vulpine *adj* of or like a fox
vulture *n* **1** large tropical bird which feeds on dead animals **2** person who has no mercy and who uses people
vulva *n* **-as** or **-ae** female genitals
vying *pres. p. of* vie

W

W , w the 23rd letter of the English alphabet
W *abbrev. for:* **1** west(ern) **2** watt

wacky *adj esp. AmE* silly **–iness** *n*
wad *n* **1** many thin things pressed or folded thickly together **2** small thick soft mass
wadding *n* soft material used esp. for packing or in medicine
waddle *vi* walk like a duck
wade *vi/t* walk through (water) **~r** *n* **1** bird that wades to find its food **2** high rubber boot for wading **wade into** *phr vt* begin (to attack) forcefully and with determination **wade through** *phr vt* do or complete (something long or dull) with an effort
wadge *n BrE infml* wad (1)
wadi /ˈwodi/ *n* dry river bed in the desert
wafer *n* **1** thin crisp biscuit **2** thin round piece of special bread used in the Communion ceremony
wafer-thin *adj* extremely thin
waffle[1] *n* light sweet cake marked with raised squares
waffle[2] *vi BrE infml* talk or write meaninglessly and at great length **waffle** *n*
waft *vi/t* move lightly (as if) on wind or waves
wag[1] *vi/t* **-gg-** shake (esp. a body part) from side to side **wag** *n*
wag[2] *n infml* amusing man **~gish** *adj* like a wag; humorous
wage *vt* carry on (a war)
wage freeze *n* attempt, esp. by government, to keep pay from rising
wager *n, vi/t* bet
wages *pl n* also **wage** payment for work done
waggle *vi/t* move quickly from side to side
wagon also *BrE* **waggon** *n* **1** strong usu. horse-drawn goods vehicle **2** *BrE* railway goods vehicle **3** *esp. AmE* trolley **4 on the wagon** *infml* no longer drinking alcohol
wagon-lit /ˌvagonh ˈlee/ *n* sleeping carriage on a (continental) train
wagon train *n* travelling column of wagons
wagtail *n* small bird with a long

wagging tail

waif *n esp. lit* uncared-for or homeless child or animal

wail *vi, n* (make) a long cry (as if) in grief or pain

wainscot /ˈwaynskət/ *n* skirting board

waist *n* **1** narrow part of the human body below the chest **2** narrow part of a garment or apparatus

waistband *n* strengthened part of trousers, a skirt, etc., that fastens round the waist

waistcoat *n esp. BrE* garment without arms worn under a jacket

waistline *n* (length or height of) an imaginary line round the waist

wait *v* **1** *vi* do nothing in the expectation of something happening **2** *vt* not act until: *wait one's turn* **3** *vi* remain unspoken, unheard, etc. **4 wait and see** delay an action or decision until the future becomes clearer **5 wait at table** serve meals, esp. as a regular job **wait on** *phr vt* **1** serve food to, esp. in a restaurant **2 wait on someone hand and foot** serve someone very humbly ♦ *n* act or period of waiting **~er** *n* someone who serves food to people **~ress** *n* female waiter

waiting game *n* tactic of being patient

waiting list *n* list of people who will be dealt with later

waiting room *n* room at a station, doctor's office, etc., where people wait

waive *vt fml* state that (a rule, claim, etc.) is no longer in effect **~r** *n* written statement waiving a right, claim, etc.

wake[1] *vi/t* **woke** *or* **waked, woken** *or* **waked** (cause to) stop sleeping **~ful** *adj* sleepless **~fulness** *n* **waking** *adj* of the time when one is awake: *all my waking hours*

wake[2] *n* **1** track left by a ship **2 in the wake of** as a result of

wake[3] *n* gathering to grieve over a dead person

waken *vi/t* wake

walk *v* **1** *vi* move slowly on foot so that at least one foot is always touching the ground **2** *vt* walk along: *walk the streets* **3** *vt* go with on foot: *I'll walk you to the bus stop.* **4** *vt* take (an animal) for a walk ♦ *n* **1** (short) journey on foot **2** way of walking **3** place, path, or course for walking **walk into** *phr vt* **1** get caught by (something) through carelessness **2** get (a job) very easily **walk off/away with** *phr vt* **1** steal and take away **2** win easily **walk out** *phr vi* **1** leave suddenly and disapprovingly **2** go on strike **walk out on** *phr vt* leave suddenly **walk over** *phr vt* treat badly **~er** *n*

walkabout *n* **1** period of wandering by an Australian aborigine **2** walk among crowds by a public figure

walkie-talkie *n* portable radio for talking as well as listening

walking papers *pl n AmE* marching orders

walking stick *n* stick for support while walking

Walkman *n tdmk for* personal stereo

walk of life *n* position in society, esp. one's job

walk-on *n* small usu. non-speaking part in a play

walkout *n* **1** action of disapprovingly leaving a meeting, organization, etc. **2** industrial strike

walkover *n* easy victory

walkway *n* passage or platform for walking

wall *n* **1** upright surface, esp. of brick or stone, for enclosing something **2** side of a room or building **3** enclosing or inside surface: *the walls of a blood vessel* **4 go to the wall** (esp. in business) be ruined **6 go up the wall** *infml* get very angry **wall off** *phr vt* separate with a wall **wall up** *phr vt* close or enclose with a wall **~ed** *adj* surrounded with a wall

wallaby *n* animal like a small kangaroo

wallah *n Ind E* worker; operative

wallbars *pl n* bars attached to a wall for exercising

wallet *n* small flat case for documents and paper money

walleyed *adj arch.* squinting outwards

wallflower *n* **1** garden plant with sweet-smelling flowers **2** person who gets left out of social activity

Walloon *n* French-speaker from Belgium

wallop *vt, n infml* (hit with) a powerful blow

wallow *vi* move, roll, or lie about happily in deep mud, water, etc.

wallpaper *n* decorative paper (for) covering the walls of a room ♦ *vt* cover the walls of (a room) with wallpaper

Wall Street *n* centre of the American business and money world, in New York

wall-to-wall *adj* **1** covering the whole floor **2** annoyingly present everywhere

wally *n BrE infml* fool

walnut *n* **1** edible brain-shaped nut **2** wood from its tree, used for furniture

walrus *n* **-ruses** *or* **-rus** large sea animal with two very long downward-pointing teeth

waltz *vi, n* (do) a rather slow dance for a man and a woman

wampum /ˈwampəm/ *n* beads used by N American Indians for money or ornament

wan *adj esp. lit* weak and tired

wand *n* stick used by someone doing magic tricks

wander *v* **1** *vi/t* move about without a fixed course or purpose **2** *vi* be or become confused and unable to make or follow ordinary conversation **~er** *n* **~ings** *pl n* long travels

wanderlust *n* strong desire to travel to faraway places

wane *vi* get gradually smaller ♦ *n* **on the wane** becoming smaller or weaker

wangle *vt infml* get by a trick

wank *vi BrE taboo sl* masturbate **~er** *n BrE taboo sl* fool

want *vit* **1** have a strong desire for **2** wish the presence of **3** wish to find; hunt: *wanted by the police* **4** *infml* need: *The house wants painting.* **want for** *phr vt fml* lack ♦ *n* **1** lack **2** severe lack of things necessary for life **~ing** *adj fml* **1** lacking **2** not good enough

wanton *adj fml* **1** (of something bad) having no just cause **2** (esp. of a woman) sexually improper

wapiti /ˈwopiti/ *n* large N American deer

war *n* **1** (example or period of) armed fighting between nations **2 in the wars** *infml* having been hurt or damaged **~ring** *adj* fighting (each other)

warble *vi* (esp. of a bird) sing with a continuous varied note **~r** *n* any of various songbirds

war clouds *pl n lit* signs that a war is getting likelier

war crime *n* illegal act done while fighting a war

ward *n* **1** large room in a hospital **2** political division of a city **3** person legally protected by another

-ward, -wards *suffix* in the stated direction

warden *n* person in charge of a place or people

warder *n BrE* prison guard

ward off *phr vt* keep away (something bad)

wardrobe *n* **1** large cupboard for clothes **2** person's collection of clothes

wardroom *n* officers' room in a warship

ware *n* articles or goods, esp. as made from the stated material: *tinware*

warehouse *pl n* large building for storing things

wares *pl n esp. lit* things for sale

warfare *n* war

warfarin /ˈwawfərin/ *n* chemical used for poisoning rats and mice

war game *n* pretended battle to test military plans

warhead *n* explosive front end of a missile

warhorse *n* **1** powerful horse used in war **2** person or thing of long experience or use

warlike *adj* fierce; liking to fight

warlock *n* male witch

warlord *n* supreme military leader

warm *adj* **1** having enough heat or pleasant heat **2** able to keep one warm: *warm clothes* **3** showing strong good feelings: *a warm welcome* **4** seeming cheerful or friendly: *warm colours* ♦ *vi/t* make or become warm **warm to** *phr vt* **1** begin to like **2** become interested in **warm up** *phr vi/t* prepare for action or performance by exercise or operation in advance **~ly** *adv*

warm-blooded *adj* maintaining a constant and fairly high body temperature, whether the surroundings are hot or cold **~ness** *n*

warmhearted *adj* generous **~ly** *adv* **~ness** *n*

warming pan *n* pan filled with coals to warm a bed

warmonger *n derog* person who wants war

warmth *n* being warm

warn *v* **1** *vi/t* tell of something bad that may happen, or of how to prevent it **2** *vt* give knowledge of some future need or action **~ing** *n* **1** telling in advance **2** something that warns

warp *vi/t* turn or twist out of shape ♦ *n* **1** warped place **2** threads running along the length of cloth

warpath *n* **on the warpath** angry and looking for someone to fight or punish

warrant *n* **1** official document allowing something **2** *fml* proper reason for action ♦ *vt* **1** cause to seem right or reasonable **2** promise (that something is so)

warrant officer *n* one just below an officer in rank (e.g. a sergeant-major)

warranty *n* written guarantee

warren *n* **1** area where rabbits live **2** place where one can easily get lost

warrior *n lit* soldier

warship *n* naval ship used for war

wart *n* small hard swelling on the skin

warthog *n* large African wild pig

wartime *n* period during which a war is going on

wary *adj* careful; looking out for danger **-ily** *adv*

was *1st and 3rd person sing. past t. of* be

wash *v* **1** *vt* clean with liquid **2** *vi* wash oneself **3** *vt* carry by the force of moving water: *crops washed away by the floods* **4** *vi/t esp. lit* flow (against or over) continually **5** *vi* be (easily) believed: *His story won't wash.* **6 wash one's dirty linen (in public)** make public unpleasant subjects which ought to be kept private **7 wash one's hands of** refuse to have anything more to do with or to accept responsibility for ♦ *n* **1** act of washing **2** things to be washed **3** movement of water caused by a passing boat **wash down** *phr vt* **1** clean with a lot of water **2** swallow with the help of liquid **wash out** *phr vt* destroy or prevent by the action of water, esp. rain **wash up** *phr v* **1** *vi BrE* wash dishes, knives, etc., after a meal **2** *vt* (of the sea) bring in to the shore **3** *vi AmE* wash (2) **~able** *adj* **~ing** *n* clothes that are to be or have just been washed

washbasin *AmE* **washbowl** *n* fixed basin for washing the hands and face

washboard *n* board of corrugated metal for scrubbing clothes on

washcloth *n AmE* facecloth

washed-out *adj* **1** faded **2** very tired

washed-up *adj infml* with no further possibilities of success

washer *n* **1** ring of metal, plastic, etc., for making a joint tight under a screw, between two pipes, etc. **2** person or machine that washes

washerwoman *n* **-men** (in former times) woman who washed other people's clothes

washing machine *n* machine for washing clothes

washing-up *n BrE* dishes, knives, etc., (to be) washed after a meal

washout *n* failure

washroom *n AmE* toilet (1)

washstand *n* stand holding a basin and jug for washing

wasn't *short for:* was not

wasp *n* black and yellow beelike insect **~ish** *adj* sharply bad-tempered and cruel **~ishness** *n*

WASP, Wasp *n esp. AmE* White Anglo-Saxon Protestant; an American whose family was originally from N. Europe

wassail /ˈwosayl/ *vi arch.* **1** carouse **2** go carol-singing
wastage *n* **1** wasteful loss **2** reduction in numbers
waste *n* **1** loss through wrong use or less than full use **2** used or unwanted matter **3** wide empty lonely stretch of water or land ♦ *vt* **1** use wrongly or not at all **2** *fml* make (the body) extremely thin ♦ *adj* **1** (of ground) empty and unused **2** got rid of as used or useless **~ful** *adj* tending to waste things **~fully** *adv*
wasteland *n* barren or ugly area of land
wastepaper basket also *esp. AmE* **wastebasket** *n* small container for throwing away unwanted things
waster *n derog* extravagant person
wastrel /ˈwaystrəl/ *n arch.* waster
watch *v* **1** *vi/t* look (at) attentively **2** *vt* be careful about **3 watch it!** be careful **4 watch one's step** act with great care ♦ *n* **1** small clock worn esp. on the wrist **2** act of watching **3** period of duty on a ship **watch for** *phr vt* look for; expect and wait for **watch out** *phr vi* take care **watch out for** *phr vt* **1** keep looking for **2** be careful of **watch over** *phr vt* guard and protect; take care of **~er** *n* **~ful** *adj* careful to notice things **~fully** *adv* **~fulness** *n*
watchdog *n* **1** dog kept to guard property **2** person or group that tries to prevent loss, waste, or undesirable practices
watchman *n* **-men** guard, esp. of a building
watchword *n* word or phrase expressing a guiding principle
water *n* **1** liquid found as rain, in the sea, etc., and commonly drunk **2 hold water** be true or reasonable **3 make/pass water** *euph* urinate ♦ *v* **1** *vt* pour water on (a plant or area) **2** *vt* supply (esp. animals) with water **3** *vi* (of the mouth or eyes) form or let out watery liquid **water down** *phr vt* **1** weaken by adding water **2** reduce the force of **waters** *pl n* **1** sea near or round a country **2** water of the stated river, lake, etc. **~y** *adj* **1** containing too much water **2** very pale
water bed *n* bed with a water-filled mattress
water biscuit *n* crisp unsweetened biscuit
water buffalo *n* Asian buffalo which is often domesticated
water butt *n* barrel for collecting rain-water
water cannon *n* apparatus for shooting out a powerful stream of water, esp. for controlling crowds
water closet *n* WC
watercolour *n* **1** paint mixed with water rather than oil **2** picture painted with this
watercourse *n* (channel for) a stream of water
watercress *n* water plant with leaves used as food
watered silk *n* silk with a shiny, wave-like pattern
waterfall *n* very steep fall of water, esp. in a river
waterfowl *n* **-fowl** or **-fowls** swimming bird
waterfront *n* land along a stretch of water, esp. in a port
waterhole *n* pool where animals come to drink
water ice *n* sorbet
watering can *n* container for pouring water onto garden plants
watering hole *n* **1** waterhole **2** *infml* pub or similar drinking place
watering place *n* **1** waterhole **2** spa
water jump *n* stretch of water to be jumped over in a race
water level *n* height to which a mass of water has risen or sunk
water lily *n* water plant with large round floating leaves
waterline *n* level reached by water up the side of a ship
waterlogged *adj* **1** (of ground) very wet **2** (of a boat) full of water
Waterloo *n* (deserved) defeat after a time of unusual success
watermark *n* **1** partly transparent mark

in paper **2** mark that shows a level reached

water meadow *n* meadow near a river, which is often flooded

watermelon *n* large round green fruit with juicy red flesh

watermill *n* mill driven by moving water

water pistol *n* toy gun which shoots water

water polo *n* game played by two teams of swimmers with a ball

waterpower *n* power from moving water to drive machines

waterproof *adj, n* (an outer garment) which does not allow water, esp. rain, through ♦ *vt* make waterproof

water rat *also* **water vole** *n* large vole that can swim and lives in river banks

watershed *n* point of very important change

waterside *n* edge of a river, lake, etc.

water skiing *n* sport of being pulled across water on skis **–skier** *n*

water softener *n* machine or chemical used to remove unwanted minerals from water

waterspout *n* tornado that draws up a column of water from the sea

water supply *n* flow of water provided for a building or area, and system of lakes, pipes, etc., that provides it

water table *n* level below which water can be found in the ground

watertight *adj* **1** which water cannot pass through **2** allowing or having no mistakes or possibility of doubt: *a watertight plan*

waterway *n* stretch of water which ships travel along

waterwheel *n* wheel which is turned by moving water, esp. to give power to machines

water wings *pl n* air-filled float to support a swimmer

waterworks **1** place from which a public water supply is provided **2** *infml* urinary system **3** *infml derog* fit of crying

watt *n* measure of electrical power

wattle *n* thin sticks woven over poles to form a fence or wall

wave *v* **1** *vi/t* move (one's hand or something in it) as a signal **2** *vi* move gently from side to side in the air **3** *vi/t* (cause to) curve regularly: *waved hair* **wave aside** *phr vt* push aside (a suggestion, objection, etc.) without giving attention to it ♦ *n* **1** raised moving area of water, esp. on the sea **2** movement of the hand in waving **3** feeling, way of behaving, etc., that suddenly starts and increases: *a crime wave* **4** form in which light, sound, etc., move: *radio waves* **5** evenly curved part of the hair **wavy** *adj* having regular curves

wave band *n* band of sound waves of similar lengths, used for radio broadcasting

wavelength *n* **1** distance between two radio waves **2** radio signal sent out on radio waves that are a particular distance apart **3** level of understanding between two people

waver *vi* be uncertain or unsteady in direction or decision

wax[1] *n* solid meltable fatty or oily substance ♦ *vt* put wax on, esp. as a polish **~y** *adj*

wax[2] *vi* **1** (esp. of the moon) get gradually larger **2** *lit* (of a person) become: *wax eloquent*

waxworks *n* **-works** (place with) models of people made in wax

way *n* **1** road, path, etc., to follow in order to reach a place **2** direction: *He went that way.* **3** distance: *a long way from home* **4** method: *Do it this way.* **5** manner: *the cruel way in which he treats his animals* **6** single part of a whole; detail; point: *In many ways I agree.* **7 by the way** (used to introduce a new subject in speech) **8 by way of: a** by going through **b** as a sort of: *a few sandwiches by way of lunch* **9 get one's own way** do or get what one wants in spite of others **10 give way (to): a** admit defeat in an argument or fight **b** break **c** become less useful or important than **d** allow oneself to show (esp. a feeling) **e**

allow other traffic to go first **11 go out of the/one's way (to do)** take the trouble (to do); make a special effort **12 have a way with one** have an attractive quality which persuades others **13 out of/in the way (of)** (not) blocking space for forward movement **14 make one's way** go **15 make way for** allow to pass or develop freely **16 no way** *infml* no **17 out of the way** unusual or not commonly known **18 under way** moving forwards ♦ *adv* far: *That's way outside my area.* **ways** *pl n* customs; habits

waybill *n* document showing details of goods or passengers being carried

wayfarer *n lit* traveller

waylay *vt* **-laid**, **-lain** *or* **-laid 1** attack (a traveller) **2** find or stop (someone) to speak to them

way-out *adj infml* strange; unusual

-ways *suffix* -wise (1)

wayside *n* side of the road or path

wayward *adj* **1** difficult to guide or control **2** not well aimed **~ly** *adv* **~ness** *n*

WC *n* toilet (1)

we *pron* (*used as the subject of a sentence*) **1** the people speaking; oneself and one or more others **2** *fml* (used by a king or queen) I

weak *adj* **1** having little power **2** easily becoming broken, changed, destroyed, or ill **3** having little taste: *weak tea* **4** unable to control people **5** not reaching a good standard: *His maths is rather weak.* **~ly** *adv* **~en** *vi/t* (cause to) become weaker **~ness** *n* **1** fact or state of being weak **2** part that spoils the rest **3** fault in character **4** strong liking: *a weakness for chocolate*

weak-kneed *adj* cowardly

weakling *n derog* weak person

weal *n* mark on the skin where one has been hit

wealth *n* **1** (large amount of) money and possessions **2** *fml* large number **~y** *adj* rich

wean *vt* gradually give (a baby) solid food instead of milk **wean from** *phr vt* gradually persuade to give up

weapon *n* something to fight with, such as a gun or sword **~ry** *n* weapons

wear *v* **wore**, **worn 1** *vt* have (esp. clothes) on the body **2** *vt* have (a particular expression) on the face **3** *vi/t* (cause to) show the effects of continued use, rubbing, etc. **4** *vi* last in the stated condition: *an old person who has worn well* **5** *vt infml* find acceptable **wear down** *phr vt* weaken **wear off** *phr vi* (of a feeling, effect, etc.) become gradually less **wear on** *phr vi* pass slowly in time **wear out** *phr v* **1** *vi/t* (cause to) be reduced to nothing or a useless state by use **2** *vt* tire greatly ♦ *n* **1** clothes of the stated sort: *evening wear* **2** damage from use **3** quality of lasting in use

wear and tear *n* damage from use

wearisome *adj* tiring and boring or annoying **~ly** *adv* **~ness** *n*

weary *adj* very tired ♦ *vi/t* (cause to) become weary **–ily** *adv* **–iness** *n*

weasel *n* small fierce furry animal **weasel out** *phr vi AmE infml* escape a duty by clever dishonest means

weasel word *n derog* word used for avoiding a direct statement

weather *n* **1** particular condition of wind, sunshine, rain, snow, etc. **2 under the weather** slightly ill ♦ *v* **1** *vt* pass safely through (a storm or difficulty) **2** *vi/t* change from the effects of air, rain, etc.

weather-beaten *adj* marked or damaged by the wind, sun, etc.

weatherboard *n* board used in constructing outside walls

weathercock *n* weather vane topped by a figure, esp. a cock

weather eye *n* constant watchfulness

weather forecast *n* description of weather conditions as they are expected to be

weatherman *n* **-men** person who describes likely future weather conditions, esp. on television or radio

weatherproof *adj* able to keep out wind and rain ♦ *vt* make weatherproof

weather ship *n* ship at sea which reports on weather conditions

weather station *n* place for monitoring weather conditions

weather vane *n* small apparatus that is blown round to show the direction of the wind

weave *v* **wove, woven 1** *vi/t* form threads into (material) by drawing them singly under and over a set of longer threads **2** *vt* twist; wind: *a bird's nest woven from straws* **3** (*past t. and p.* **weaved**) *vi* move twistingly ♦ *n* style or pattern of woven material **~r** *n*

web *n* net of thin threads made by a spider **~bed** *adj* having skin between the toes, to help in swimming

webbing *n* strong woven bands used for belts, supports, etc.

web-footed *adj* having webbed feet

wed *vi/t* **wedded** *or* **wed** *esp. lit* marry

we'd *short for:* **1** we had **2** we would

wedding *n* marriage ceremony

wedding breakfast *n* celebratory meal after a marriage

wedding ring *n* ring worn to show that one is married

wedge *n* **1** V-shaped piece of wood, metal, etc., for keeping something in place or splitting something **2** V-shaped piece ♦ *vt* fix firmly (as if) with a wedge

Wedgwood *n tdmk for* fine china, esp. blue and white

wedlock *n lit* **1** being married **2 out of wedlock** of unmarried parents

Wednesday *n* the 3rd day of the week

wee[1] *adj* very small

wee[2] *vi infml* urinate ♦ *n* act of urinating

weed *n* **1** unwanted wild plant **2** physically weak person ♦ *vi/t* remove weeds from (a garden) **weed out** *phr vt* get rid of (less good ones) **~y** *adj* physically weak

weedkiller *n* substance for killing weeds

week *n* **1** period of seven days, usu. thought of as starting on Monday and ending on Sunday **2** period worked during a week

weekday *n* day other than Saturday or Sunday

weekend *n* Saturday and Sunday, esp. when considered a holiday

weekly *adj, adv* (happening) every week or once a week ♦ *n* magazine or newspaper which appears once a week

ween *vt arch.* imagine, suppose

weeny *adj infml* extremely small

weep *vi* **wept** *fml or lit* cry **~ing** *adj* (of a tree) with branches hanging down

weevil *n* small insect which eats (and spoils) grain, seeds, etc.

wee-wee *vi, n infml* wee[2]

weft *n* threads running across cloth

weigh *v* **1** *vt* find the weight of **2** *vi* have the stated weight **3** *vt* consider or compare carefully **4** *vt* raise (an anchor) **weigh down** *phr vt* make heavy with a load **weigh in** *phr vi* join in a fight or argument **weigh on** *phr vt* worry **weigh up** *phr vt* form an opinion about, esp. by balancing opposing arguments

weighbridge *n* machine for weighing vehicles and their loads

weight *n* **1** (measured) heaviness of something **2** something heavy **3** piece of metal of known heaviness, used for weighing things **4** value; importance: *attach weight to something* **5** (something that causes) a feeling of anxiety ♦ *vt* **1** make heavy, esp. by fastening weights **2** include conditions in (something) that give a (dis)advantage **~less** *adj* **~y** *adj* **1** heavy **2** *fml* important and serious

weight lifting also **weight training** *n* sport of lifting heavy weights **-ter** *n*

weightwatcher *n* person dieting to lose weight

weir *n* wall-like structure across a river controlling its flow

weird *adj* **1** strange; unusual **2** unusual and not sensible or acceptable **~ly** *adv* **~ness** *n*

weirdo *n* **-os** *sl* strange person

welch *vi* welsh

welcome *interj* (a greeting to someone who has arrived) ♦ *vt* **1** greet (someone newly arrived), esp. with friendliness **2** wish to have; like ♦ *adj* **1** acceptable

and wanted **2** allowed freely (to have): *I've plenty of cigarettes; you're welcome to one.* ♦ *n* greeting
weld *vt* join (metal) by melting **~er** *n*
welfare *n* **1** comfort, health, and happiness; wellbeing **2** help with living conditions, social problems, etc.
welfare state *n* (country with) a system of social help for poor, sick, etc., people
welkin *n lit* sky
we'll *short for:* **1** we will **2** we shall
well[1] *adv* **better, best 1** in a good way **2** thoroughly: *well beaten* **3** much; quite: *well within the time* **4** suitably; properly: *I couldn't very well refuse.* **5 as well: a** also **b** with as good a result **6 as well as** in addition to **7 well and truly** completely **8 well out of** lucky enough to be free from (an affair) ♦ *adj* **better, best 1** in good health **2** in an acceptable state ♦ *interj* **1** (expresses surprise) **2** (introduces an expression of surprise, doubt, etc.)
well[2] *n* **1** place where water can be taken from underground **2** oil well **3** deep narrow space inside a building, for stairs or a lift ♦ *vi* flow
well-adjusted *adj* (of a person) fitting in well with society
well-advised *adj* sensible
well-appointed *adj* excellently equipped
wellbeing *n* personal and physical comfort, esp. good health and happiness
well-bred *adj* having or showing high social rank, with good manners
well-connected *adj* knowing or esp. related to people of high social rank or influence
well-disposed *adj* friendly; sympathetic
well-done *adj* thoroughly cooked
well-found *adj* well-appointed
well-founded *adj* based on sound evidence or reasoning
well-groomed *adj* neat and clean
well-grounded *adj* **1** fully instructed **2** well-founded
well-heeled *adj infml* rich
well-hung *adj sl* having a large penis
wellie *n BrE infml* wellington
well-informed *adj* knowing a lot about several subjects or parts of a particular subject
wellington *n esp. BrE* rubber boot for keeping the foot and lower leg dry
well-intentioned *adj* acting in the hope of good results, though often failing
well-known *adj* known by many people; famous
well-lined *adj infml* **1** full of money **2** (of the stomach) full of food
well-meaning *adj* well-intentioned
well-meant *adj* based on good intentions
well-nigh *adv* almost
well-off *adj* **1** rich **2** lucky
well-oiled *adj infml* drunk
well-preserved *adj* (of someone or something old) still in good condition
well-read *adj* having read many books and got a lot of information
well-rounded *adj* **1** having a pleasantly rounded shape **2** having or including a wide range of experience
well-spoken *adj* having a socially acceptable way of speaking
wellspring *n* source of constant supply
well-thought-of *adj* liked and respected
well-timed *adj* said or done at the most suitable time
well-to-do *adj* rich
well-tried *adj* often used and found reliable
well-turned *adj* **1** well shaped **2** well expressed
well-wisher *n* person who wishes another to succeed, have good luck, etc.
well-worn *adj* (of a phrase) overused
welsh *vi derog* avoid payment
Welsh *n adj* (inhabitant) of Wales
Welsh rabbit *n* cheese on toast
welt *n* strip between a shoe sole and upper
welter *n* large confused mixture
welterweight *n* boxer of middle weight
wench *n lit* young woman
wend *v* **wend one's way: a** travel (slowly) **b** leave
Wendy house *n BrE* toy house for

children to play in

went *past t. of* go

wept *past t. and p. of* weep

were *past t. of* be

we're *short for:* we are

werewolf /ˈweəˌwoolf/ *n* (in stories) person who sometimes turns into a wolf

west *n* **1** (*often cap.*) direction towards which the sun sets **2** (*cap.*) western Europe and the US ♦ *adj* **1** in the west **2** (of wind) from the west ♦ *adv* **1** towards the west **2 go west** *infml*: **a** die **b** be damaged or broken **~ward** *adj, adv*

West End *n* western part of central London, where shops, theatres, etc. are

westerly *adj* west

western *adj* of the west part of the world or of a country ♦ *n* story about life in the middle of the US in the past, with cowboys and gunfights **~er** *n* someone who lives in or comes from western Europe or the US

westernize, -ise *vt* cause to have or copy the customs typical of America and Europe **–ization** *n*

West Indian *n, adj* (inhabitant) of the West Indies

wet *adj* **-tt- 1** covered with or being liquid **2** rainy **3** *BrE* weak in character and unable to get things done **4 wet through** completely covered in or with liquid ♦ *n* **1** rainy weather **2** *BrE infml* moderate person in the British Conservative Party ♦ *vt* **wet** *or* **wetted**; *pres. p.* **-tt-** make wet **~ness** *n*

wet blanket *n* person who discourages others or prevents them from enjoying themselves

wet dream *n* sexually exciting dream resulting in a male orgasm

wet-nurse *vt* treat with too much care

wet suit *n* rubber garment for keeping the body warm in sea sports

we've *short for:* we have

whack *vt* hit with a noisy blow ♦ *n* **1** (noise of) a hard blow **2** *BrE infml* (fair) share **~ed** *adj BrE infml* very tired **~ing** *adj, adv infml* (very) big

whale *n* **1** extremely large fishlike animal **2 a whale of a time** a very enjoyable time **~r** *n* **a** person who hunts whales **b** ship from which whales are hunted **whaling** *n* hunting whales

whalebone *n* horny material obtained from whales

wham *n* (sound of) a hard blow

wharf /wawf/ *n* **wharfs** *or* **wharves** place where ships are tied up to unload and load goods

what *predeterminer, determiner, pron* **1** (used in questions about an unknown thing or person) **2** the thing(s) that: *Tell me what to do.* **3** (shows surprise): *What a strange hat!* ♦ *adv* **1 to what extent:** *What do you care?* **2 what with** (used for introducing the cause of something, esp. something bad)

whatever *determiner, pron* **1** no matter what **2** anything: *Eat whatever you like* **3** (shows surprise) what: *Whatever is it?* ♦ *adj* at all: *no money whatever*

whatnot *n infml* anything (else)

wheat *n* (plant producing) grain from which flour is made

wheatgerm *n* vitamin-rich part of the wheat kernel separated in milling

wheatmeal *n* brown wheat flour

wheedle *vi/t* try to persuade (someone) by pleasant but insincere words

wheel *n* **1** circular frame which turns to allow vehicles to move, to work machinery, etc. **2** curving movement in marching **3** steering wheel of a car or ship **4 wheels within wheels** hidden influences having effects on surface behaviour ♦ *v* **1** *vt* move (a wheeled object) with the hands **2** *vi* turn round suddenly **3** *vi* (of birds) fly round in circles **4 wheel and deal** *vi infml* make deals, esp. in business or politics, in a skilful and perhaps dishonest way **~ed** *adj* having wheels

wheelbarrow *n* small one-wheeled cart pushed by hand

wheelbase *n* distance between a vehicle's front and back wheels

wheelchair *n* wheeled chair for someone who cannot walk

wheeler-dealer *n* someone skilled at doing clever (but perhaps not always honest) deals, esp. in business or politics

wheelhouse *n* small cabin from which a ship is steered

wheelie *n* act of riding a bicycle on its back wheel

wheelwright *n* maker of wooden wheels

wheeze *vi* make a noisy whistling sound in breathing ♦ *n* **1** wheezing sound **2** *infml* joke or clever trick **wheezy** *adj*

whelk *n* type of shellfish

whelp *n esp. lit derog* young animal, esp. a dog

when *adv, conj* **1** at what time; at the time that **2** considering that; although: *Why did you do it when I told you not to?*

whence *adv, conj lit* from where

whenever *adv, conj* **1** at whatever time **2** every time

where *adv, conj* at or to what place; at or to the place that

whereabouts *adv* where in general (not exactly) ♦ *n* place where a person or thing is

whereas *conj* (shows an opposite) but

whereby *adj fml* by means of which

wherefore *adv, conj lit* why

whereupon *conj* without delay after and because of which; and then

wherever *adv* **1** to or at whatever place **2** (shows surprise) where

wherewithal *n* enough money

wherry *n* **1** long light rowing boat **2** large light barge or fishing boat

whet *vt* **-tt- whet someone's appetite** make someone wish for more

whether *conj* if ... or not

whey *n* watery part of milk

which *determiner, pron* **1** (used in questions, when a choice is to be made) **2** (shows what thing is meant): *This is the book which I told you about.* **3** (adds information): *The train, which only takes an hour, is quicker than the bus.*

whichever *determiner, pron* **1** only (one) of the set that: *Take whichever seat you like.* **2** no matter which

whiff *n* **1** brief smell of something

Whig *n* member of a former British political party supporting parliament against the crown

while *n* length of time ♦ *conj* **1** during the time that **2** although **3** whereas **4** and what is more **while away** *phr vt* pass (time) in a pleasantly lazy way

whilst *conj* while

whim *n* sudden (often unreasonable) idea or wish

whimper *vi* make small weak trembling cries **whimper** *n*

whimsy *n* strange humour **–sical** *adj* fanciful; with strange ideas **~sically** *adv*

whine *vi* **1** make a high sad sound **2** complain (too much) in an unnecessarily sad voice **whine** *n*

whinge *vi derog* complain, esp. of unfair treatment

whinny *vi* make a soft neighing sound

whip *n* **1** long piece of esp. rope or leather on a handle, used for hitting animals or people sharply **2** *esp. BrE* (person who gives) an order to a member of Parliament to attend and vote ♦ *v* **-pp- 1** *vt* hit with a whip **2** *vi/t* move quickly: *He whipped out his gun.* **3** *vt* beat (esp. cream or eggs) until stiff **4** *vt infml* defeat **5** *vt BrE infml* steal **whip up** *phr vt* **1** cause (feelings) to become stronger, **2** make quickly **~ping** *n* beating as a punishment

whipcord *n* **1** thin tough cord **2** ribbed cotton or woollen cloth

whip hand *n* control

whiplash *n* **1** blow from a whip **2** sudden violent movement of the head and neck, as in a car accident, causing injury

whippersnapper *n* presumptuous young person

whippet *n* small greyhound

whipping boy *n* person who (unfairly) gets the blame and/or punishment

whippoorwill /ˈwipəˌwil/ *n* N American woodland bird

whip-round *n esp. BrE* collection of money within a group

whirl *vi/t* move round and round very fast ♦ *n* **1** act of whirling **2** very fast (confused) movement or activity **3 give something a whirl** *infml* try something **4 in a whirl** confused

whirligig *n* something that spirals or continuously whirls

whirlpool *n* fast circular current of water

whirlwind *n* tall tube of air moving dangerously at high speed ♦ *adj* happening very quickly or suddenly

whirlybird *n infml* helicopter

whirr *vi, n* (make) the regular sound of something turning and beating against the air

whisk *vt* **1** remove, either by quick light brushing or by taking suddenly **2** beat (esp. eggs), esp. with a whisk ♦ *n* small hand-held apparatus for beating eggs, cream, etc.

whisker *n* long stiff hair near an animal's mouth **whiskers** *pl n* hair on the sides of a man's face

whiskey *n* Irish or US whisky

whisky *n* strong alcoholic drink made from grain, esp. in Scotland

whisper *v* **1** *vi/t* speak or say very quietly **2** *vt* suggest or pass (information) secretly ♦ *n* **1** very quiet voice **2** rumour

whist *n* card game for four players

whistle *n* **1** simple (musical) instrument played by blowing **2** high sound made by air blowing through a narrow opening ♦ *v* **1** *vi* make a high sound esp. by blowing through the lips **2** *vt* produce (a tune) by doing this

whistle-stop *adj* stopping briefly at many places

whit *n fml* small amount

Whit *n* Whitsun

white *adj* **1** of the colour of snow and milk **2** pale **3** of a pale-skinned race **4** (of coffee) with milk or cream ♦ *n* **1** white colour **2** pale-skinned person **3** part of an egg surrounding the yolk **whiten** *vi/t* (cause to) become white(r)

white ant *n* termite

whitebait *n* small fish used as food

white blood cell also **white corpuscle** *n* blood cell that fights infection

white-collar *adj* of or being office workers, indoor workers, etc.

white dwarf *n* hot, dense star near the end of its life

white elephant *n* useless article

white flag *n* sign of surrender

Whitehall *n* (street in London containing many of the offices of) the British government

white heat *n* temperature at which metal turns white

white hope *n* person who is expected to bring great success

white-hot *adj* extremely hot

White House *n* official Washington home of the US president

white knight *n* person or organization that puts money into a business company to save it from being taken over by another company

white lie *n* harmless lie

white meat *n* light-coloured meat, e.g. from poultry

white noise *n* jumble of sound of identical intensity

whiteout *n* obscuring of visibility in polar regions

white paper *n* Government report, usu. outlining policy

white slave *n* woman abducted to be a prostitute

white spirit *n* solvent made from petroleum

white-tie *adj* (of parties and other social occasions) at which the men wear white bow ties and tails

whitewash *n* **1** white liquid for covering walls **2** *derog* attempt to hide something wrong **3** complete defeat ♦ *vt* **1** cover with whitewash **2** make (what is bad) seem good

whither *adv lit* to which place

whiting *n* sea fish used as food

whitlow *n* inflammation around a fingernail or toenail

Whitsun *n* (period around) the 7th Sunday after Easter

whittle *vt* **1** cut thin pieces off (wood) **2**

reduce

whizz, whiz *vi* **-zz-** move very fast (and noisily) ♦ *n* **1** whizzing sound **2** *infml* someone who is very fast, clever, or skilled in the stated activity

whizz kid *n* person who makes quick successes in life

who *pron (used esp. as the subject of a sentence)* **1** what person? **2** (shows what person is meant): *the people who live in that house* **3** (adds information about a person): *This is my father, who lives in Glasgow.*

whoa *interj* (call to a horse to stop)

whodunit,, **whodunnit** *n* story, film, etc., about a crime mystery

whoever *pron* **1** anyone at all **2** no matter who: *Whoever it is, I don't want to see them.* **3** (shows surprise) who

whole *adj* all; complete ♦ *n* **1** complete amount, thing, etc. **2 on the whole** generally; mostly **wholly** *adv*

wholefood *n* food in a simple natural form

whole-hearted *adj* with all one's ability, interest, etc.; full **~ly** *adv*

whole hog *n infml* farthest limit

wholemeal *adj* (made from flour) without the grain-covering removed

whole number *n* integer

wholesale *adj, adv* **1** sold in large quantities to shopkeepers (rather than directly to customers) **2** *usu. derog* very great or complete: *wholesale slaughter* **-saler** *n* seller of goods wholesale

wholesome *adj* **1** good for the body or health **2** having a good moral effect **~ly** *adv* **~ness** *n*

whom *pron fml* (object form of **who**)

whoop *vi* **1** make a loud cry, as of joy **2 whoop it up** *infml* enjoy oneself a lot ♦ *n* a loud shout of joy

whoopee *interj* (cry of joy) ♦ *n* **make whoopee** enjoy oneself a lot

whooping cough *n* (children's) disease with attacks of serious coughing and difficult breathing

whoops *interj* (said when one has made a mistake)

whoosh *vi, n* (move quickly with) a rushing sound

whopper *n infml* **1** big thing **2** big lie **-ping** *adj, adv* very (big)

whore *n lit or derog* prostitute

whorl *n* shape of a line curving outwards from a centre

whose *determiner, pron* of whom

why *adv, conj* **1** for what reason? **2** the reason for which **3 why not** (used in suggestions): *Why not sell it?* ♦ *n* **the whys and wherefores (of)** reasons and explanations (for)

WI *abbrev. for*: **1** West Indies **2** Women's Institute

wick *n* **1** burning thread in a candle or lamp **2 get on someone's wick** *BrE infml* annoy someone

wicked *adj* **1** morally bad; evil **2** playfully bad **~ly** *adv* **~ness** *n*

wickerwork *n* (objects made from) woven canes, sticks, etc. ♦ *adj* also **wicker** made of wickerwork: *wicker baskets*

wicket *n* **1** set of three stumps at which the ball is aimed in cricket **2** stretch of grass on which cricket is played

wicketkeeper *n* fielder who stands behind the wicket to catch the ball

wide *adj* **1** large from side to side **2** covering a large range: *wide experience* ♦ *adv* **1** completely (open or awake) **2** (in sport) away from the correct or central point **3 wide of the mark** not suitable, correct, etc., at all **~ly** *adv* over a wide range **widen** *vi/t* make or become wider

wide boy *n BrE infml* cleverly dishonest person, esp. a businessman

wide-eyed *adj* **1** with eyes very fully open **2** accepting or admiring things too easily

widespread *adj* existing or happening in many places

widgeon *n* freshwater duck

widow *n* woman whose husband has died

widower *n* man whose wife has died

width *n* size from side to side

wield *vt* have and/or use (power,

influence, etc.)
wife *n* **wives** woman to whom a man is married
wig *n* covering of false hair for the head
wigging *n infml* scolding
wiggle *vi/t* move with quick small movements
wight *n arch.* person
wigwam *n* a North American Indian tent
wild *adj* **1 a** living in natural conditions, not changed by human beings: *wild animals* **b** (of people) not civilized **2** uncontrollably violent **3** showing very strong feelings, esp. of anger **4** showing lack of thought or control: *a wild guess* **5** *infml* having a very eager liking ♦ *n* natural areas full of animals and plants, with few people **~ly** *adv* **~ness** *n*
wild boar *n* large European wild pig
wildcat strike *n* sudden unofficial strike
wildebeest /ˈwildəˌbeest, ˈvil-/ *n* **-beest** large African antelope
wilderness *n* **1** unchanging stretch of land with no sign of human presence **2** **into the wilderness** (sent) out of political life, esp. for doing wrong
wildfire *n* **like wildfire** very quickly
wildfowl *pl n* (water) birds shot for sport
wild-goose chase *n* useless search for something that cannot be found
wildlife *n* animals living in natural conditions
wiles *pl n* tricks; deceitful persuading
wilful, *AmE* **willful** *adj* **1** doing what one wants in spite of other people **2** (of something bad) done on purpose **~ly** *adv* **~ness** *n*
will *v aux 3rd person sing.* **will,** *pres. t. negative short form* **won't 1** (expresses the future tense) **2** be willing to **3** (shows what always happens): *Oil will float on water.* **4** (shows what is possible): *This car will hold five people.*
will² *n* **1** power of the mind to make decisions and act in accordance with them **2** what someone wishes or intends: *against one's will* **3** stated feelings towards someone: *ill will.* **4** official statement of the way someone wants their property to be shared out after they die **5** **at will** as one wishes **6** **with a will** enthusiastically ♦ *vt* **1** make or intend to happen, esp. by the power of the mind **2** bequeath to someone in a will
willies *pl n infml* fit of nervousness
willing *adj* **1** ready; not refusing: *willing to help* **2** done or given gladly: *willing help* **3** eager: *a willing helper* **~ly** *adv* **~ness** *n*
will-'o-the-wisp *n* **1** ignis fatuus **2** elusive goal, person, etc.
willow *n* tree which grows near water, with long thin branches **~y** *adj* pleasantly thin and graceful
willow pattern *n* oriental story-telling design on china
willpower *n* strength of mind
willy-nilly *adv* regardless of whether it is wanted, or not
wilt *v* **1** *vi/t* become or cause (a plant) to become less fresh and start to die **2** *vi* (of a person) become tired and weaker
wily *adj* clever, esp. at getting what one wants **wiliness** *n*
wimp *n* weak or useless person, esp. a man **~ish** *adj* **~ishly** *adv*
wimple *n* cloth worn over the head and neck by medieval women and some nuns
win *v* **won,** *pres. p.* **-nn- 1** *vi/t* beat one's opponent(s) (in): *win a race* **2** *vt* be given as the result of success: *win £100* **3** *vt* gain: *trying to win his friendship* **win over** *phr vt* gain the support of by persuading ♦ *n* (esp. in sport) victory; success **~ner** *n* **~ning** *adj* very pleasing or attractive **~nings** *pl n* money won
wince *vi* move back suddenly (as if) from something unpleasant, often twisting the face
winceyette *n* soft light cotton fabric
winch *n* apparatus that turns to pull up heavy objects ♦ *vt* pull up with a winch
wind¹ *n* **1** strongly moving air **2** breath or breathing **3** *esp. BrE* (condition of having) gas in the stomach **4** **get wind of**

hear about, esp. accidentally or unofficially **5 put/get the wind up** *infml* make/become afraid or anxious **6 (something) in the wind** (something, esp. that is secret or not generally known) about to happen/being done **7 take the wind out of someone's sails** *infml* take away someone's confidence or advantage, esp. by saying or doing something unexpected ♦ *vt* make breathless **~y** *adj* with a lot of wind

wind² *v* **wound 1** *vt* turn round and round **2** *vi* go twistingly: *a winding path* **3** *vt* tighten the working parts of by turning: *wind a clock* **4** *vt* move by turning a handle: *Wind down the car window.* **wind down** *phr v* **1** *vi* rest until calmer, after work or excitement **2** *vt* bring to an end gradually **wind up** *phr v* **1** *vt* bring to an end **2** *vi* get into the stated unwanted situation in the end **3** *vt* annoy or deceive (someone) playfully

windbag *n* person who talks too much

windbreak *n* something giving shelter from the wind

windcheater *n esp. BrE* anorak

windchill *n* cooling of the air due to wind

windfall *n* **1** fruit blown down off a tree **2** unexpected lucky gift

wind instrument *n* musical instrument played by blowing air through it

windjammer *n* large fast sailing boat

windlass *n* machine for hoisting or hauling

windmill *n* building with a corn-crushing machine driven by large sails turned by the wind

window *n* (glass-filled) opening in the wall of a building, in a car, etc., to let in light and air

window box *n* box of earth for growing plants outside a window

window dressing *n* **1** art of arranging goods in shop windows **2** *usu. derog* something additional intended to attract people but hiding the true purpose

windowpane *n* one whole piece of glass in a window

window-shop *vi* **-pp-** look at goods in shop windows without necessarily intending to buy

windpipe *n* air passage from the throat to the lungs

windscreen, *AmE* **windshield** *n* piece of transparent material across the front of a vehicle, for the driver to look through

windscreen wiper *n* movable arm which clears rain from the windscreen of a car

wind-sock *n* open cloth tube to indicate wind direction

windsurfing *n* sport of riding on sailboards **-er** *n*

windswept *adj* **1** open to continual strong wind **2** as if blown into an untidy state

wind tunnel *n* enclosed place through which air is forced at fixed speeds to test aircraft

windward *n, adj, adv* (direction) against or facing the wind

wine *n* alcoholic drink made from grapes ♦ *vi/t* **wine and dine** have or give a meal and wine

wing *n* **1** limb used by a bird, insect, etc., for flying **2** part standing out from a plane which supports it in flight **3** part standing out from the side: *the west wing of the palace* **4** *BrE* side part of a car that covers the wheels **5** (in sport) far left or right of the field **6** group with different opinions or purposes from the main organization: *the left wing of the Labour Party* **7 take wing** fly (away) **8 under someone's wing** being protected, helped, etc., by someone ♦ *v* **1** *vi* fly (as if) on wings **2** *vt* wound slightly **wings** *pl n* **1** sides of a stage, where an actor is hidden from view **2 in the wings** hidden and waiting for action **~ed** *adj* having wings **~er** *n* **1** player on the wings of a sportsfield **2** person on the stated political wing

winge *vi* whinge

wingnut *n* metal nut with projecting parts to help in turning it

wingspan also **wingspread** *n* distance

from the end of one wing to the end of the other when both are stretched out

wink *vi/t* **1** close and open (an eye) quickly **2** flash or cause (a light) to flash on and off **wink at** *phr vt* pretend not to notice (something bad) ♦ *n* **1** winking of the eye **2** even a short period of sleep

winkle *n* small shellfish **winkle out** *phr vt esp. BrE* get or remove with difficulty

winnow *vt* remove (unwanted parts) from (grain) by a current of air

wino *n* **-os** *infml* person addicted to drinking alcohol

winsome /ˈwins(ə)m/ *adj lit* attractive **~ly** *adv* **~ness** *n*

winter *n* cold season between autumn and spring ♦ *vi* spend the winter **-try** *adj*

winter sports *pl n* sports done on snow or ice

wipe *vt* rub (a surface or object) to remove (dirt, liquid, etc.) **wipe out** *phr vt* destroy or remove all of **wipe up** *phr vt* remove with a cloth ♦ *n* act of wiping **~r** *n*

wire *n* **1** (piece of) thin threadlike metal **2** *AmE* telegram ♦ *vt* **1** connect up wires in (esp. an electrical system) **2** fasten with wire(s) **3** *AmE* send a telegram to **wiring** *n* system of (electric) wires **wiry** *adj* rather thin, with strong muscles

wireless *n* radio

wire-tapping *n* listening secretly to other people's telephone conversations with an electrical connection

wisdom *n* quality of being wise

wisdom tooth *n* large late-growing back tooth

wise *adj* **1** sensible **2** having long experience and much knowledge **3 none the wiser** knowing no more, after being told **wise up** *phr vi/t AmE* (cause to) learn or become conscious of the true situation **~ly** *adv*

-wise *suffix* **1** in the stated way or direction **2** with regard to: *businesswise*

wiseacre /ˈwiezaykə/ *n arch.* smart aleck

wisecrack *vi, n* (make) a clever joke

wise guy *n infml* person who claims to know how things are done

wish 1 *vt* want (something impossible) **2** *vi* want and try to cause something (as if) by magic **3** *vt* hope that (someone) will have (something), esp. expressed as a greeting **4** *vt fml* want ♦ *n* **1** feeling of wanting something **2** thing wished for **3** attempt to make a wanted thing happen (as if) by magic

wishbone *n* V-shaped chicken bone pulled apart before making a wish

wishful thinking *n* false belief that something is true or will happen simply because one wishes it

wishy-washy *adj* without determination or clear aims and principles

wisp *n* small twisted bunch **~y** *adj*

wisteria /wiˈstiəri·ə/ *n* climbing plant with blue flowers

wistful *adj* sad because of unfulfilled hopes or thoughts of the past **~ly** *adv* **~ness** *n*

wit[1] *n* **1** ability to say clever amusing things **2** witty person **3** also **wits** *pl.* power of thought; cleverness **4 at one's wits end** too worried by difficulties to know what to do next **5 have/keep one's wits about one** be ready to act quickly and sensibly **~ty** *adj* cleverly amusing **~tily** *adv*

wit[2] *v* **to wit** *lit or law* that is (to say)

witch *n* woman with magic powers

witchcraft *n* performing of magic

witchdoctor *n* man who cures people by magic

witch-hunt *n* search for people with disliked political views, in order to remove them from power

with *prep* **1** in the presence or company of **2** having: *a book with a green cover* **3** by means of; using **4** in support of **5** against: *competing with foreign companies* **6** with regard to; in the case of: *in love with someone* **7** at the same time and rate as: *improving with age* **8** in spite of **9** because of: *trembling with fear* **10 with it** giving proper attention to what is going on **11 with me/you**

following my/your argument **12 with that** at once after that; then

withdraw *v* **-drew, -drawn 1** *vt* take away or back **2** *vi/t* move away or back **3** *vi/t* (cause to) not take part: *She withdrew from the election.* **~al** *n* (act of) withdrawing **~n** *adj* quiet and not interested in other people

withdrawal symptoms *pl n* painful or unpleasant effects which are the result of breaking or stopping a habit, esp. the taking of a drug

wither *vi/t* (cause to) become dry, shrivelled, pale, and lifeless **~ing** *adj* sharply severe **~ingly** *adv*

withers *pl n* part of a horse between the shoulders

withhold *vt* **-held** refuse to give

within *adv, prep* **1** not more than **2** inside

without *prep, adv* not having; lacking

withstand *vt* **-stood** not be defeated or damaged by

witless *adj* foolish

witness *n* **1** person who saw something happen **2** person who gives information to a court of law **3** person who watches another sign a document, and then signs it as proof of having seen them ♦ *vt* **1** be present at and see **2** watch or sign (a document) as a witness **3** be a sign or proof of

witness box, *AmE* **witness stand** *n* enclosed area where witnesses stand in a court

witter *vi BrE infml derog* chatter, esp. complainingly

witticism *n* clever amusing remark

wives *pl of* wife

wizard *n* **1** (in stories) old man with magical powers **2** extremely skilful person **~ry** *n*

wizened *adj* (as if) dried up, with lines on the skin

WO *abbrev. for:* warrant officer

woad *n* ancient blue dye

wobble *vi/t* move unsteadily from side to side **wobble** *n* **–bly** *adj* wobbling

woe *n fml or lit* **1** great sorrow **2** a trouble **~ful** *adj* **1** *esp. lit* very sad **2** (of something bad) very great **~fully** *adv*

woebegone *adj* very miserable

wok *n* deep round Chinese cooking pan

woke *past t. of* wake

woken *past p. of* wake

wold *n* open hilly area

wolf *n* **wolves 1** fierce wild animal of the dog family **2** man who seeks women for sex only **3 wolf in sheep's clothing** person who seems harmless but is hiding evil intentions ♦ *vt* eat quickly in large amounts

wolfhound *n* large dog, originally for hunting wolves

wolf whistle *n* whistle of admiration for an attractive woman

wolverine /ˈwoolvəreen/ *n* carnivorous mammal of northern forests

woman *n* **women 1** adult female person **2 woman of the world** experienced woman who knows how people behave **~hood** *n* quality or time of being a woman **~ly** *adj* having good qualities suitable to a woman

womanize, -ise *vi* (of a man) habitually pay attention to many women for sexual purposes **~r** *n*

womb *n* round organ inside female mammals in which their young develop

wombat *n* small bearlike Australian animal

women's movement *n* (all the women who join in making) a united effort to improve the social and political position of women

won *past t. and p. of* win

wonder *n* **1** feeling of strangeness, surprise, and usu. admiration **2** wonderful or surprising thing **3 do/work wonders** bring unexpectedly good results **4 (it's) no/little/small wonder** it is not surprising; naturally ♦ *vi/t* **1** express a wish to know, in words or silently **2** be surprised: *It's not to be wondered at that she's angry.* ♦ *adj* unusually good or effective **~ful** *adj* unusually good; causing pleasure or admiration **~fully** *adv* **~ment** *n* wonder (1)

wonderland *n* magical or wonderful

place

wondrous *adj lit* wonderful **~ly** *adv* **~ness** *n*

wonky *adj BrE infml* **1** unsteady and likely to break or fail **2** not in a straight line

wont *adj fml* likely (to) ♦ *n fml* what the stated person usually does **~ed** *adj fml* customary

won't *short for:* will not

woo *vt* **1** *lit* try to make (a woman) love and marry one **2** try to gain the support of

wood *n* **1** substance of which trees are made **2** also **woods** *pl* place where trees grow, smaller than a forest **3 out of the wood** *BrE* free from danger, difficulty, etc. **~ed** *adj* covered with trees **~en** *adj* **1** made of wood **2** stiff; unbending **~y** *adj* of or like wood

woodcock *n* game bird with a long thin beak

woodcut *n* wooden block with a design cut on it, to be printed from

wooden spoon *n BrE* imaginary prize for finishing last in a competition

woodland also **woodlands** *pl. n* wooded country

woodlouse *n* **-lice** small many-legged creature that can roll itself into a ball

woodpecker *n* bird with a long beak that makes holes in trees

woodwind *n* (players of) wind instruments made of wood (e.g. clarinets)

woodwork *n* **1** *esp. BrE* skill of making wooden objects **2** parts of a house that are made of wood

woodworm *n* damaged condition of wood caused by the young of certain beetles, which make holes

woof[1] *n, interj* sound made by a dog

woof[2] *n* weft

woofer *n* loudspeaker that gives out deep sounds

wool *n* **1** soft thick hair of sheep **2** thick thread made from this **~len,** *AmE* **~en** *adj* made of wool **~ly** *adj* **1** of or like wool 2 (of thoughts) not clear in the mind ♦ *n* woollen garment

woolgathering *n* thinking of other things instead of what one should be paying attention to

woozy *adj infml* having an unsteady feeling in the head **-iness** *n*

Worcester sauce /ˈwʊstə/ *n* sharp-tasting savoury sauce

word *n* **1** (written representation of) one or more sounds which can be spoken to represent an idea, object, etc. **2** short conversation: *I'd like a word with you.* **3** message or piece of news: *send word* **4** promise: *I give you my word.* **5 by word of mouth** by speaking and not by writing **6 have words (with)** argue angrily (with) **7 (not) in so many words** (not) directly expressed in those words but only suggested **8 put words in(to) someone's mouth: a** tell someone what to say **b** claim falsely that someone has said a particular thing **9 take someone's word for it** accept what someone says as correct **10 word for word** in exactly the same words ♦ *vt* express in words **~ing** *n* words in which something is expressed **~y** *adj* using or containing more words than necessary

word-perfect *adj* repeating or remembering every word correctly

word processor *n* small computer for esp. ordinary office work

wore *past t. of* wear

work *n* **1** activity done to produce something or gain a result rather than for amusement **2** job; business **3** something made or done by someone: *The murder was the work of a madman.* **4** object produced by painting, writing, etc. **5 have one's work cut out** have something difficult to do, esp. in the time allowed ♦ *v* **1** *vi* do an activity which uses effort, esp. as one's job **2** *vi* (of a machine, plan, etc.) operate (properly) **3** *vt* make (a machine or person) do work **4** *vt* make (one's way) by work or effort **5** *vi/t* make or become by small movements: *This little screw has worked loose.* **6** *vt* produce (an effect): *work wonders* **7 work to rule** obey the rules of one's work so exactly that one causes inconvenience to others, as a form of industrial action **work off** *phr vt* get rid of by work or effort **work out** *phr v* **1** *vt* calculate (the answer to) **2** *vi* have a result; develop **3** *vt* plan; decide **4** *vi* reach the stated amount by being calculated **5** *vi* exercise **work up** *phr vt* **1** make excited, anxious, etc. **2** cause oneself to have: *work up some enthusiasm* **3** develop steadily **~able** *adj* which can be put into effect; usable **~er** *n* **1** person who works **2** member of the working class

workaday *adj* ordinary and/or dull

workaholic *n* person who likes to work too hard

workbench *n* (table with) a hard surface for working on with tools

workbook *n* school book with questions and exercises

work coat *n AmE* overall (1)

workforce *n* all the workers in a factory or in industry generally

workhorse *n* **1** person who does most of the (dull) work **2** useful machine, vehicle, etc., for performing continuous jobs

workhouse *n* (in former times) place where unemployed people lived

working *adj* **1** used for work: *working clothes* **2** (of time) spent in work **3** useful as a basis for further development

working class *n* social class of people who work with their hands **working-class** *adj*

working knowledge *n* enough practical knowledge to do something

working order *n* state of working well, with no trouble

working party *n* committee which examines and reports on a particular matter

workings *pl n* **1** way something works or acts **2** parts of a mine which have been dug out

workload *n* amount of work that a person or machine is expected to do in a particular period of time

workman *n* **-men** man who works with his hands, esp. in a particular skill or trade **~like** *adj* showing the qualities of a good workman **~ship** *n* (signs of) skill in making things

workout *n* period of physical exercise

works *n* **works 1** *pl* moving parts of a machine **2** factory **3 give someone the works** *sl* **a** give someone everything **b** attack someone violently

workshop *n* **1** room where heavy repairs and jobs on machines are done **2** period of group activity and study

work-shy *adj* not liking work and trying to avoid it

worktop *n* flat surface in a kitchen for preparing food

work-to-rule *n* act of working strictly to rules as a form of industrial action

world *n* **1** the Earth **2** group of living things: *the animal world* **3** a particular area of human activity: *the world of football* **4** people generally **5** human life and its affairs: *the ways of the world* **6** planet **7** large number or amount: *This medicine did me the world of good.* **8 for all the world like/as if** exactly like/as if **9 (have) the best of both worlds** (have) the advantage which each choice offers, without having to choose between them **10 in the world** (in a question expressing surprise): *Where in the world have you been?* **11 out of this world** unusually good; wonderful **12 worlds apart** completely different **~ly** *adj* **1** material **2** too much concerned with human society, rather than religious things **~liness** *n*

world-beater *n* person or thing thought able to compete successfully with anyone/anything in the world

world-class *adj* among the best in the world

world-famous *adj* known all over the world

worldly-wise *adj* having a sophisticated knowledge of the way people behave

world power *n* nation with very great power and influence

world view *n* philosophy of life

world-weary *adj* tired of life **–riness** *n*

worldwide *adj, adv* in or over all the

world
worm *n* **1** small thin creature with no bones or limbs **2** worthless, cowardly, etc., person ♦ *vt* move by twisting or effort **worm out** *phr vt* obtain gradually by questioning
worm's-eye view *n* view from a humble position
wormwood *n* plant that produces a bitter oil
worn *past p. of* wear
worn-out *adj* **1** no longer usable **2** very tired
worrisome *adj* **1** causing worry **2** inclined to worry **~ly** *adv*
worry *v* **1** *vi/t* (cause to) be anxious **2** *vt* (esp. of a dog) chase and bite (an animal) ♦ *n* (person or thing that causes) anxiety **–ried** *adj* anxious **~ing** *adj*
worrywart /ˈwuriˌwawt/ *n AmE infml* person who worries a lot about unimportant things
worse *adj* **1** (*comparative of* bad) of lower quality; more bad **2** more ill (than before) **3 none the worse (for)** not harmed (by) **4 the worse for wear** harmed by use over a period ♦ *adv* in a worse way or to a worse degree ♦ *n* something worse **worsen** *vi/t* (cause to) become worse
worship *n* (showing of) strong (religious) feelings of love, respect, and admiration ♦ *vi/t* **-pp-** (*AmE* **-p-**) show worship (to) **~per,** *AmE* **~er** *n* **~ful** *adj* **~fully** *adv*
worst *adj* (*superlative of* bad) of lowest quality; most bad ♦ *n* **1** worst thing or part **2 at (the) worst** if the worst happens **3 get the worst of** suffer most from **4 if the worst comes to the worst** if there is no better way ♦ *adv* (*superlative of* badly) most badly
worsted /ˈwoostid/ *n* wool cloth
wort /wuht/ *n* malt liquid from which beer is made
worth *prep* **1** of the stated value **2** deserving: *not worth seeing* **3 for all one is worth** with all possible effort **4 for what it's worth** though I'm not sure it's of any value **5 worth it** useful; worthwhile **6 worth one's salt** worthy of respect or of being so called **7 worth one's/someone's while** worthwhile to one/someone ♦ *n* value **~less** *adj* **1** of no value **2** (of a person) of bad character **~lessness** *n*
worthwhile *adj* with a good enough result to deserve the trouble taken
worthy *adj* **1** deserving respect or serious attention **2** deserving: *worthy of admiration* **3** good but not very exciting or interesting **–thily** *adv* **–thiness** *n*
-worthy *suffix* **1** fit or safe for **2** deserving of
would *v aux* **1** (past of will) **2** (shows what is likely or possible): *What would you do if you won a million pounds?* **3** (shows what always happened): *We would meet for a drink after work.* **4 would better** *AmE* had better
would-be *adj* which one wants or intends to be, but isn't: *a would-be musician*
wouldn't *short for:* would not
wound[1] *n* damaged place on the body, esp. caused by a weapon ♦ *vt* cause a wound to
wound[2] *past t. and p. of* wind[2]
wound-up *adj* anxiously excited
wove *past t. of* weave
woven *past p. of* weave
wow *interj infml* (expresses surprise and admiration) ♦ *n sl* a great success ♦ *vt sl* cause surprise and admiration in someone
wowzer *n AustrE sl* killjoy
WPC *abbrev. for:* woman police constable
wpm *abbrev. for:* words per minute
wrack *n* **1** remains of something destroyed **2** type of seaweed
wraith /rayth/ *n lit* ghost
wrangle *vi, n* (take part in) an angry or noisy quarrel **~r** *n*
wrap *vt* **-pp-** cover in material folded over **wrap up** *phr v* **1** *vi* wear warm clothes **2** *vt* complete (a business deal, meeting, etc.) **3 wrapped up in** giving

complete attention to ♦ *n* **1** *esp. AmE* garment for covering a woman's shoulders **2 under wraps** secret **~per** *n* loose paper cover **~ping** *n* material for folding round and covering something

wrasse /ras/ *n* spiny fish of warm seas

wrath *n fml or lit* strong fierce anger **~ful** *adj* **~fully** *adv*

wreak /reek/ *vt esp. lit* perform or bring about (something violent or unpleasant)

wreath *n* usu. circular arrangement of flowers or leaves **a** given at a funeral **b** placed on the head as a sign of honour

wreathe *vt esp. lit* circle round and cover completely

wreck *n* **1** sunken or destroyed ship **2** something in a very bad condition **3** *fml* ruin; destruction **4** person whose health is destroyed ♦ *vt* destroy **~age** *n* broken parts of a destroyed thing

wren *n* very small brown European bird

wrench *vt* **1** pull hard with a twist **2** twist and damage (a joint of the body) ♦ *n* **1** act of or damage caused by wrenching **2** separation that causes mental suffering **3** spanner

wrest *vt* **1** pull (away) violently **2** *esp. lit* obtain with difficulty

wrestle 1 *vi/t* fight by trying to hold or throw one's opponent **2** *vi* struggle **~r** *n* person who wrestles as a sport

wretch *n* **1** unfortunate person **2** annoying person

wretched *adj* **1** very unhappy **2** of a bad type which makes one unhappy: *a wretched headache* **3** annoying **~ly** *adv* **~ness** *n*

wriggle *vi/t* move from side to side **wriggle out of** *phr vt* escape (a difficulty) by clever tricks ♦ *n* wriggling movement

wring *vt* **wrung 1** twist or press (wet clothes) to remove (water) **2** twist (the neck) hard, causing death **3** press (esp. one's hands) together hard **4** obtain by severe or cruel methods **5 wringing wet** very wet **~er** *n* machine for wringing clothes

wrinkle *n* **1** small line or fold, esp. on the skin owing to age **2** *infml* useful suggestion or trick ♦ *vi/t* (cause to) form wrinkles **-kly** *adj*

wrist *n* joint between the hand and the arm

wristwatch *n* watch with a band for fastening round the wrist

writ *n* official legal document telling someone (not) to do a particular thing

write *v* **wrote, written 1** *vi/t* make (marks representing letters or words) with a tool, esp. a pen or pencil **2** *vt* think of and record, esp. on paper: *write a report* **3** *vt* complete by writing words: *write a cheque* **4** *vi/t* produce and send (a letter) **5 written on/all over** clearly showing because of the expression on **6 writ large** *lit* on a larger or grander scale **write down** *phr vt* record (esp. what has been said) in writing **write off** *phr vt* **1** accept as lost or useless or as a failure **2** remove (esp. a debt) from the record **write out** *phr vt* write in full **write up** *phr vt* write (again) in a complete and useful form **~r** *n* **writing** *n* **1** handwriting **2** written work or form: *Put it down in writing.* **3** activity of writing books, articles, etc. **writings** *pl n* written works

write-off *n* something completely ruined and unrepairable

write-up *n* written report giving a judgment

writhe *vi* twist the body (as if) in great pain

written *past p. of* write

wrong *adj* **1** not correct **2** morally bad **3** not in a proper or healthy state **4** not suitable: *the wrong time to visit* ♦ *adv* **1** wrongly **2 go wrong: a** stop working properly **b** make a mistake **c** end badly ♦ *n* **1** morally bad behaviour **2** *fml* unjust or bad action **3 in the wrong** mistaken or deserving blame ♦ *vt* be unfair to or cause to suffer **~ful** *adj* unjust or illegal **~fully** *adv*

wrongdoing *n* (example of) bad or illegal behaviour **-doer** *n*

wrong-foot *vt* put at a disadvantage by a sudden change of approach
wrongheaded *adj* stubbornly mistaken **~ly** *adv* **~ness** *n*
wrote *past t. of* write
wrought *adj lit* made
wrought iron *n* iron shaped into a useful, pleasing form
wrung *past t. and p. of* wring
wry *adj* showing a mixture of amusement and dislike, disappointment, etc. **~ly** *adv* **~ness** *n*

X, x the 24th letter of the English alphabet
xenon *n* rare gas
xenophobia /ˌzenəˈfohbi·ə/ *n* unreasonable fear and dislike of foreigners **-bic** *adj*
xerox *vt, n* (make) a photographic copy on an electric copying machine
Xmas *n infml* Christmas
X-ray *n* **1** powerful unseen beam which can pass through solid things, used esp. for photographing conditions inside the body **2** photograph taken with this **3** medical examination with this **x-ray** *vt* photograph, examine, or treat with X-rays
xylem /ˈzieləm/ *n* tissue that forms the woody part of plants
xylophone *n* musical instrument with many small wooden bars hit with a hammer

Y

Y, y the 25th letter of the English alphabet
-y *suffix* **1** (in adjectives) of; like; having: *glassy|noisy* **2** (makes nouns more informal): *granny* **3** (in nouns) -ity: *jealousy*
yacht *n* **1** light sailing boat used esp. for racing **2** large motor-driven pleasure boat **~ing** *n* sailing in a yacht
yachtsman *n* **-men** sailor in a yacht
yak[1] *n* long-haired cow of central Asia
yak[2] *vi* **-kk-** *derog* talk continuously about unimportant things
yam *n* tropical plant with a root eaten as a vegetable
yang *n* masculine active principle in Chinese philosophy
yank *vi/t* pull suddenly and sharply **yank** *n*
Yank *n BrE derog* American person
Yankee *n* **1** American person **2** *AmE* inhabitant of the northeastern US **Yankee** *adj*
yap *vi* **-pp-** *derog* **1** (of a dog) bark continuously **2** talk noisily about unimportant things **yap** *n*
yard[1] *n* a measure of length equal to 3 feet or 9.144 metres
yard[2] *n* **1** (partly) enclosed area next to a building **2** area enclosed for the stated activity or business: *a coalyard*
yardarm *n* either end of a long pole that supports a sail
yardstick *n* standard of measurement or comparison
yarn *n* **1** long continuous thread used esp. in making cloth **2** story
yarrow *n* plant with flat heads made up of small white flowers
yashmak *n* cloth worn across the face

by Muslim women

yaw *vi* (of a ship or aircraft) turn to the side out of the proper course

yawl *n* **1** sailing boat with two masts **2** small boat carried on a ship

yawn *vi* **1** open the mouth wide and breathe deeply, esp. from tiredness **2** be(come) wide open: *a yawning chasm* ♦ *n* **1** act of yawning **2** *infml* something dull

yaws *n* tropical disease producing sores

yd *abbrev. for:* yard(s)[1]

ye *pron lit* (used of more than one person) you

yea *adv lit* yes

yeah *adv infml* yes

year *n* **1** period of 365 (or 366) days, or 12 months, esp. as measured from January 1st to December 31st **2** period of about a year in the life of an organization: *the school year* **~ly** *adj, adv* (happening) every year or once a year

year dot *n BrE infml* a very long time ago

yearling *n* animal between one and two years old

yearlong *adj* lasting a whole year

yearn *vi esp. lit* have a strong (sad) desire **~ing** *n esp. lit* strong desire

yeast *n* form of very small plant with a chemical action used for producing alcohol in making wine and beer and for making bread light and soft **~y** *adj*

yell *vi/t, n* shout

yellow *adj* **1** of the colour of gold **2** *infml* cowardly ♦ *vi/t* (cause to) become yellow **~ish** *adj*

yellow fever *n* serious tropical disease

Yellow Pages *pl n* book with telephone numbers of businesses

yelp *vi, n* (make) a sharp high cry, esp. of pain

yen[1] *n* **yen** unit of Japanese money

yen[2] *n* strong desire

yeoman *n* **-men** *BrE, esp. lit* farmer who owns and works his own land

yeoman of the guard *n* member of a military corps who act as attendants of the sovereign and as warders of the Tower of London

yes *adv* **1** (used for accepting or agreeing) **2** (used for replying)

yes-man *n* **-men** *derog* someone who always agrees with their leader or employer

yesterday *adv, n* (on) the day before today

yesteryear *n esp. lit* the recent past

yet *adv* **1** up until this time: *He hasn't arrived yet.* **2** in future, and in spite of how things seem now: *We may yet win.* **3** even: *a yet bigger problem* **4** still: *I have yet to be told:* **5 as yet** yet (1) ♦ *conj* but even so: *strange yet true*

yeti *n* large hairy manlike animal said to live in the Himalaya mountains

yew *n* tree with small dark leaves and red berries

Y-fronts *pl n BrE* type of men's underpants

Yiddish *n* language spoken by Jews from eastern Europe

yield *v* **1** *vt* produce: *a tree which yields a large crop* **2** *vt* give up control of: *yield a position of advantage* **3** *vi* admit defeat ♦ *n* amount produced: *a high yield of fruit* **~ing** *adj* **1** not stiff or fixed **2** (too) easily persuaded

yin *n* female inactive principle in Chinese philosophy

yippee *interj* (shout of delight or success)

yob also **yobbo** *n* **-bos** *BrE infml* rude or troublesome young man

yodel *vi/t* **-ll-** (*AmE* **-l-**) sing with many changes between the natural voice and a very high voice

yoga *n* Hindu system of control of the mind and body, often including special exercises

yoghurt *n* milk that has thickened and turned slightly acid through the action of certain bacteria

yogi *n* person who practises (and teaches) yoga

yoke *n* **1** bar joining two animals for pulling a vehicle or heavy load **2** frame across someone's shoulders for carrying two equal loads **3** *lit* controlling power: *the hated yoke of their con-*

querors **4** part of garment from which the rest hangs ♦ *vt* join (as if) with a yoke
yokel *n* simple or foolish country person
yolk *n* yellow part of an egg
yonder *adj, adv esp. lit* that; over there
yonks *n BrE infml* very long time
yore *n lit* very long time ago
Yorkshire pudding *n* baked batter pudding served with beef
you *pron* (used as subject or object) **1** person or people being spoken to: *I love you.* **2** anyone; one: *You can't trust such people.* **3** (used for addressing someone, esp. angrily): *You fool!*
you'd *short for:* **1** you had **2** you would
you'll *short for:* **1** you will **2** you shall
young *adj* in an early stage of life or development ♦ *pl n* **1** young people generally **2** young animals
youngster *n* young person
your *determiner* of you: *your house*
you're *short for:* you are
yours *pron* **1** of you; your one(s) **2** (used at the end of a letter): *Yours sincerely, Janet Smith.* **3 yours truly: a** (polite phrase written at the end of a letter) **b** *infml* I; me; myself
yourself *pron* **-selves 1** (reflexive form of **you**): *Don't hurt yourself.* **2** (*strong form of* **you**): *Did you make it yourself?* **3 (all) by yourself: a** alone **b** without help **4 to yourself** not shared
youth *n* **1** period of being young **2** *often derog* young person, esp. male **3** young people as a group: *the youth of today* **~ful** *adj* (seeming) young **~fully** *adv* **~fulness** *n*
you've *short for:* you have
yowl *vi, n* (make) the loud long cry of a cat or dog in distress
yo-yo *n* **-yos** toy made of a thick grooved disc that runs up and down a string
yucca *n* tall plant with white flowers
yucky *adj infml* extremely unpleasant
Yugoslav *n* inhabitant of Yugoslavia
yule *n lit* Christmas
yuppie, yuppy *n* young person in a professional job with a high income, esp. one who enjoys spending money and having a fashionable way of life

Z

Z, z the 26th and last letter of the English alphabet
zany *adj* amusingly foolish
zap *v* **-pp-** *infml* **1** *vt* attack and/or destroy **2** *vi/t* move quickly and forcefully **~py** *adj* full of life and force
zeal *n fml* eagerness **~ous** *adj* eager; keen **~ously** *adv* **~ousness** *n*
zealot /ˈzelət/ *n* someone who is (too) eager in their beliefs
zebra *n* **-bra** *or* **-bras** horselike African animal with broad black and white stripes
zebra crossing *n* (in Britain) set of black and white lines across a road where people have a right to walk across
zebu *n* ox with a large fleshy lump over the shoulders
Zen *adj, n* (of) a Japanese Buddhist sect that seeks truth through meditation
zenith *n* highest or greatest point of development or success
zephyr /ˈzefə/ *n lit* soft west wind
zeppelin *n* large airship
zero *n* **-ros** *or* **-roes 1** (sign representing) the number 0 **2** point between + and - on a scale: *The temperature was below zero.* **2** nothing: *zero growth* **zero in on** *phr vt* **1** aim a weapon directly at **2** aim one's attention directly towards
zero hour *n* time at which something important is to begin
zest *n* **1** pleasantly exciting quality: *The danger adds zest to the affair.* **2** eagerness: *a zest for life* **3** outer skin of an orange or lemon **~ful** *adj* **~fully** *adv*

zigzag *vi n* **-gg-** (go in) a line shaped like a row of z's
zillion *determiner, n, pron infml* extremely large number
zinc *n* bluish-white metal
Zionism *n* political movement to establish and develop an independent state of Israel for the Jews **–ist** *adj, n*
zip *n* **1** fastener with two sets of teeth and a sliding piece that joins the edges of an opening by drawing the teeth together **2** liveliness ♦ *v* **-pp- 1** *vt* fasten with a zip **2** *vi/t* move very quickly and forcefully **~per** *n AmE* zip (1)
zip code *n AmE* postcode
zither *n* flat musical instrument played by pulling sharply at its strings
zits *pl n sl* spots on the skin
zodiac *n* imaginary belt in space along which the sun, moon, and nearest planets seem to travel, divided into 12 equal parts used in astrology
zombie *n* **1** *derog* someone who moves or acts very slowly or lifelessly **2** dead person made to move by magic
zone *n* area marked off from others by particular qualities or activities: *a danger zone* ♦ *vt* give a particular purpose to (an area): *a part of town zoned for industrial development* **zonal** *adj*
zonked *adj infml* extremely tired
zoo *n* **zoos** park where many types of wild animal are kept for show
zoology *n* scientific study of animals *adj* **–gist** *n* **-gical** *adj*
zoom *vi* **1** go quickly with a loud noise **2** (of a cinema camera) move quickly between a distant and a close view **3** increase suddenly and greatly
zoom lens *n* curved lens which a camera can zoom in and out while keeping the picture clear
Zoroastrian *n, adj* (follower) of **Zoroastrianism**, the religion founded in the 6th century by Zoroaster in Persia
zucchini /zooh'keeni/ *n* **-ni** *or* **-nis** *AmE* courgette
Zulu *n* member of one of the native peoples of South Africa **Zulu** *adj*

LANGUAGE NOTES

Grammar

People who grow up speaking English as their first language know a great deal about the grammar of the language. They know, for example, that in English you say 'I gave the cat some fish' and not 'I the cat gave fish some' or 'I giving the cat fish yesterday'. However, many people do not know the grammatical terms that are used to describe words and the way they go together in sentences. The following sections explain some of the main terms.

Parts of speech (sometimes called 'word classes')
Nouns: words which mean things (**table, animal, nation**), substances (**sugar, beer**), states of mind (**happiness, despair**), abstract states and abstract terms generally (**hunger, thing, credit, marketing, popularity, privatization**).
She kicked the **ball** into the next **field**
Eat up your **dinner**
It gives me great **pleasure** to open this **fete**

Words in this dictionary which are nouns are followed by the abbreviation **'n'**.

Verbs: words which show that an action is happening or being done (**hit, fall, boil, cut put, do**), words which show what people are doing, saying or feeling (**ask, consider, want, laugh, see**), words which go together with other verbs to show when something has happened or is happening (**have, be**).
I'll just **wash** the dishes.
Can you **give** me your address?
'Oh no!', he **said**.
She **has written** all the software

Adjectives: words which explain more about a noun, i.e. a thing, person or state (**hard, cheerful, exact, essential, blue, German**). Adjectives usually come in two places in the sentence in English – before a noun or after the verb 'to be'.
It's an **easy** job (tells you more about the job)
You're a **cruel** person (tells you more about the person)
They are **green** balloons OR
The balloons are **green** (tells you more about the balloons)
He's a **sexy French** actor (tells you more about the actor)

Words in this dictionary which are adjectives are followed by the abbreviation 'adj'.

Adverbs: words which explain more about a verb (**funnily, guiltily, positively, forwards**), or which explain more about an adjective or another adverb (**extremely, very**). Adverbs often show how something has happened or is happening.

He grinned **cheekily**
It collapsed **loudly**
It runs **backwards**
She could reach the top shelf **fairly easily**
I could go **further** and say it more **angrily**

Another kind of adverb shows the speaker's attitude to what is being said in the rest of the sentence (**unfortunately, obviously**).

Fortunately, it's raining so we can't go
Surely, I explained all that before

A third kind of adverb shows the link that the speaker is making between what he or she is about to say and what he or she has just said (**therefore, however**). These adverbs are rather like the second type of conjunction which is explained in the next section. The difference is that with these adverbs you can put a conjunction like 'and' immediately before the adverb.

The temperature cools and **therefore** the liquid expands
Rising interest rates leads to rising mortgage payments which in turn contributes to rising inflation. **Thus** we see a spiralling upward pressure.

Words in this dictionary which are adverbs are followed by the abbreviation 'adv'.

Conjunctions: words which link two or more sentences or two parts of the sentence which are the same type, for example two nouns or two phrases or clauses (**and, or**).

Bangers **and** mash
Merry Christmas **and** a Happy New Year
He hasn't decided whether to go by train **or** by car
Are you going by bicycle **or** will you walk?
She was going to fix it yesterday **but** she didn't have the right tools

Another kind of conjunction links two clauses together in the sentence (**although, because, if**). With this kind of conjunction, one part of the sentence is a main clause (it could be a sentence by itself).

It was a very interesting programme **though** it was a bit long
She won't go to sleep **unless** you read her a story first
He fell **because** he had twisted his ankle

Words in this dictionary which are conjunctions are followed by the abbreviation 'conj'.

Prepositions: words which link (usually) nouns to another part of the sentence. They can often be used to show where something is (**in, on, over**) or when it happens (**at, by**). A preposition cannot be used without introducing a noun phrase (**in** the box, **on** the table) or sometimes a verb ending in -ing or a part of the sentence beginning with 'what', 'which', 'where', 'when', 'who', 'whom', 'whose', 'how'. Some prepositions are made up of more than one word but they are still considered as a single preposition (**apart from, in spite of**).

They ran **down** the hill
Will you be back **by** nine?
She lives **on** Milsom Street **by** the old bakery **at** number 432
I saw it **in front of** the television
By asking now you'll save problems later
At what time shall we meet?
What time shall we meet **at**?

Words in this dictionary which are prepositions are followed by the abbreviation 'prep'.

Pronouns: words which stand in for a particular person or thing which the speaker uses when he or she doesn't want to mention them by name again (**he, she, they, ours**). Pronouns are also the words for the speaker himself or herself (**himself, myself**) and for a collection of people or things that the speaker does not want to or can't name individually (**anyone, everything**).

Hamish came round yesterday. **He** said **he** would drop by again later
I agree with **you**
Someone will have to take **it** to **her**
It's not **yours**, **it**'s **theirs**
Will **you** give **it** to **them yourself**?

Words in this dictionary which are pronouns are followed by the abbreviation 'pron'.

Articles: the two articles are **a**, which is called the indefinite article, and **the**, which is called the definite article.

I gave her **a** big hug
The casserole is in **the** oven

Determiners: words which come before nouns, like articles do, but which give a bit more information about the noun such as how many of the things there are (**several, some**), which one the thing is (**this, that**) or whose the thing is (**hers, mine**). This last type of determiner is sometimes called a possessive. **The** and **a** are also determiners but the term 'article' is more specific.

He hit the bull's eye **every** time
I haven't got **any** money
I can lend you **my** shirt if you like
It's **this** book I meant, not **that** one

Interjections: words which are used on their own to show strong emotion such as astonishment, outrage or pain. They are always written with an exclamation mark after them (**Holy Smoke!, Ouch!, Whoopee!**)

Words in this dictionary which are interjections are followed by 'interj'.

More about nouns

The plural of a noun is the form that is used when the noun refers to more than one of a thing (**bats, elephants, videos**). Nouns which refer to things that there can be one of or several of like this are called **count nouns**. Some count nouns have irregular plurals which are not made by just adding 's' (**feet, knives, mice**). Irregular plural endings are shown in the dictionary.

Some nouns do not have a plural form and cannot be counted, either because they are abstract (**love, despair**) or because they are thought of as a mass of stuff (**flour, milk**) or because they are general (**furniture, information**). These nouns are either called **uncount nouns** or **mass nouns**.

Some nouns are names (**Jack, Thames, Budapest**) and these are called **proper nouns**. All the other nouns, whether count or uncount, can also be referred to collectively as **common nouns** to distinguish them from proper nouns.

More about verbs

The simplest kinds of sentence are made up of a noun followed by a verb, or a noun followed by a verb followed by another noun (I laughed. She bored me). If we say that the verb shows an action being performed, then the first noun in these sentences is the person doing the action and the second noun is the person the action is being done to. The person (or thing) that does the action is called the subject and the person (or thing) that the action is done to is called the object.

In 'he died' **he** is the subject
In 'she hit the dog' **she** is the **subject** and **the dog** is the **object**

Some verbs are not used with an object. When a person dies, they don't die something, they just die. If a verb is used without an object it is called **intransitive**. Die is an intransitive verb. Some verbs are used with an object. People do not just hit, they hit things (or other people). If the verb is used with an object it is called **transitive**. Hit is a transitive verb.

Transitive verbs are shown as 'vt' in this dictionary, intransitive verbs are shown as 'vi' and verbs which are both are shown as 'vi/t'.

Some verbs can be used with two objects (**give, make, offer**).

I **made** him a whisky sour
She **lent** Bob that book
Read them a story

You can change the sentences round and put a preposition before the first object which is called the **indirect object**. The object which is not used after a preposition is called the **direct object**

I **made** a whisky sour for him
She **lent** that book to Bob
Read a story to them

The **indirect objects** are **him, Bob,** and **them**. The **direct objects** are **whisky sour, book** and **story**.

All the transitive verb examples given so far are in the **active** voice, with the subject performing the action of the verb on or towards the object. The sentences can also be changed around with the same meaning to be in the passive voice. In the passive voice the thing on which the action is performed goes in the subject position, the main verb comes after a form of the verb 'to be' and the person or thing that does the performing comes after the verb.

Active:
I **changed** the tyre
Joanna **bought** the more expensive videos
A professional **will strip** the table

Passive:
The tyre **was changed by** me
The more expensive videos **were bought by** Joanna
The table **will be stripped by** a professional

The verb **'be'** and some verbs (**seem, feel**) are usually followed by an adjective or adjective phrase (group of words that go together in the position of an adjective). The adjective that comes after these verbs is called a **complement**. It is sometimes possible to have a noun or noun phrase after this type of verb but it is still called a complement and not an object.

I am very happy to meet you (**very happy** is the complement)
He **looks** rather sad (**rather sad** is the complement)
I **feel** sick (**sick** is the complement)
I **feel** a new woman (**a new woman** is the complement)

Verbs in a sentence are sometimes made up of more than one word (we **are going**, he **has eaten** it, **did** he **go**?, she **might like** it). The extra parts of the verb (**are, has, did, might**) are called **auxiliary** verbs. When used as auxiliaries, 'have' (has, had, etc) and 'be' (is, are, being, etc) are mainly used to form **tenses** (show when things happened). 'Be' is also used in the passive voice, as explained above.

You **have** already eaten three doughnuts
I **was** hoping you'd call
I **have been** walking round London all day
I'**ve** suggested that before
I **was** knocked over by a pushchair

'Do', when used as an auxiliary, is used in negatives, questions and to give emphasis.

I wish you **did**n't snore
Did you remember the sugar?
You **do** go on a bit sometimes!

Another kind of auxiliary (**can, could, shall, should, may, might, will, would, must, ought to**) is used with a verb to show, for example, whether something is possible, whether it is allowed, whether it will happen in the future and so on. These words are sometimes called **modal auxiliaries**.

I **could** do it if I tried
Will you be on the phone long?
He says he **might** have left it on the table
Passengers for the 3:05 to Glasgow **should** change to platform 3
I was hoping you'**d** call

Verbs which are auxiliaries or modal auxiliaries are shown in this dictionary as 'v aux'

Spelling Table

To find a word that you have heard but not seen.

Sound	Example	Some other spellings	Letters
Consonants			
b	back	rubber	bb
c	(see k)		
ch	cheer	match	tch
		nature	t(u)
		question	t(i)
		cello	c
		Czech	cz
d	day	ladder	dd
		could	ld
f	few	physics	ph
		cough	gh
		coffee	ff
		half	lf
g	girl	bigger	gg
		ghost	gh
		vague	gue
		guard	gu
h	hot	who	wh
j	jump	edge	dg
		age	g
		soldier	di
		exaggerate	gg
		gradual	du
k	key	cool	c
		school	ch
		lock	ck
		tobacco	cc
		saccharine	cch
l	led	ball	ll
		battle	le
m	sum	bomb	mb
		hammer	mm
		autumn	mn
		calm	lm
		phlegm	gm
n	sun	know	kn
		gnaw	gn
		funny	nn
		pneumonia	pn
p	pen	happen	pp
		shepherd	ph
r	red	marry	rr
		wriggle	wr
		rhubarb	rh
		diarrhoea	rrh
s	soon	psychology	ps
		city	c
		nice	ce
		scene	sc
		mess	ss
		scissors	sc
		sword	sw
sh	fish	ocean	c
		sure	s
		machine	ch
		station	t(i)
		tissue	ss
		fascism	sc
		fuschia	sch
		conscious	sc
		passion	ss
		tension	s(i)
		politician	c(i)

Sound	Example	Some other spellings	Letters
		schedule	sch
zh	pleasure	vision	s(i)
		usual	s(u)
		seizure	z(u)
t	tea	Thomas	th
		doubt	bt
		fright	ght
		butter	tt
		pterodactyl	pt
v	view	of	f
		Stephen	ph
w	wet	when	wh
x	box	except	xc
		sticks	cks
		forks	ks
		accident	cc
z	zero	was	s
		scissors	ss
		xylophone	x
		dazzle	zz
Vowels			
a	bad	plaid	ai
ah	father	heart	ea
		half	al
		laugh	au
		clerk	er
		Shah	ah
or	ball	caught	au
		board	oa
		draw	aw
		four	our
		floor	oor
		port	or
		George	eor

Sound	Example	Some other spellings	Letters
eh	make	pay	ay
		steak	ea
		vein	ei
		weigh	eigh
		reign	eig
		straight	aigh
		prey	ey
		gauge	au
		train	ai
		café	é
		matinée	ée
		Gaelic	ae
e	bed	said	ai
		bread	ea
		guest	(g)ue
		bury	u
		leopard	eo
		leisure	ei
		friend	ie
ee	sheep	field	ei
		ceiling	ei
		police	i
		team	ea
		key	ey
		people	eo
		scene	e
		Quay	ay
iə	here	appear	ear
		idea	ea
		fierce	ier
		beer	eer
		souvenir	ir
		sphere	ere
		theory	eor
e	there	hair	air

Sound	Example	Some other spellings	Letters
		bare	are
		their	eir
		prayer	ayer
		scarce	ar
		aeroplane	aer
		mayor	ayor
i	ship	women	e
		valley	ey
		mountain	ai
		foreign	eig
		sieve	ie
ie	bite	eye	eye
		pie	ie
		buy	uy
		try	y
		dye	ye
		sigh	igh
		height	eigh
uh	bird	fern	er
		worm	or
		earn	ear
		journal	our
		Guernsey	uer
		conoisseur	eur
o	pot	cough	ou
		laurel	au
		John	oh
oh	note	soap	oa
		soul	ou
		grow	ow
		toe	oe
		brooch	oo
		beau	eau
		mauve	au
		though	ough

Sound	Example	Some other spellings	Letters
		folk	ol
		sew	ew
ooh	boot	group	ou
		flew	ew
		blue	ue
		fruit	ui
		through	ough
		rheumatism	eu
aw	poor	tour	our
		sure	ure
ow	now	plough	ough
		ounce	ou
oy	boy	poison	oi
u	cut	blood	oo
		young	ou
		does	oe
oo	wood	wolf	ol
		could	oul
		put	u

Mathematics

Numbers

Powers

Four squared $= 4^2 = 4 \times 4 = 16$
Two cubed $= 2^3 = 2 \times 2 \times 2 = 8$
Three to the power of four $= 3^4 = 3 \times 3 \times 3 \times 3 = 81$

Roots

A root is an inverse of a power
$\sqrt{}$ stands for 'square root'
$\sqrt[3]{}$ stands for 'cube root'
$\sqrt[5]{}$ stands for 'fifth root'
$\sqrt{9} = 3$ because $3^2 = 9$
$\sqrt[3]{8} = 2$ because $2^3 = 8$

Percentages

A percentage is a fraction in which the denominator is 100.

$$25\% = \frac{25}{100}$$

The upper number in a fraction is called the 'numerator'; the lower number is called the 'denominator':

$\frac{2}{3}$ numerator / denominator

To find 12 as a percentage of 72 use the formula:

$$\frac{12}{72} = \frac{?}{100}$$

To find 7% of £1.62 use the formula:

$$\frac{7}{100} \times 1.62 = ?$$

Geometry

Basic shapes – 2 dimensional (plane)

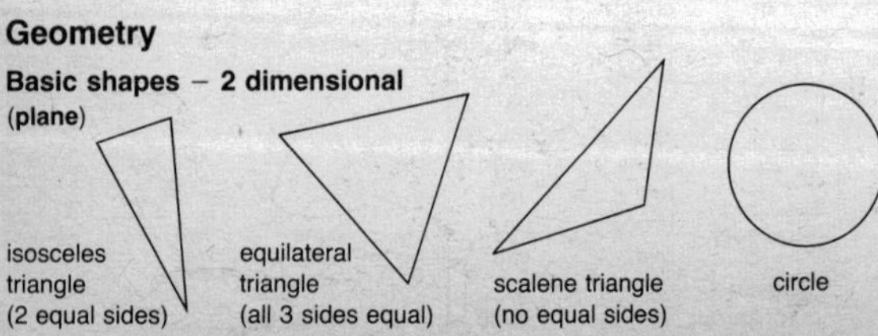

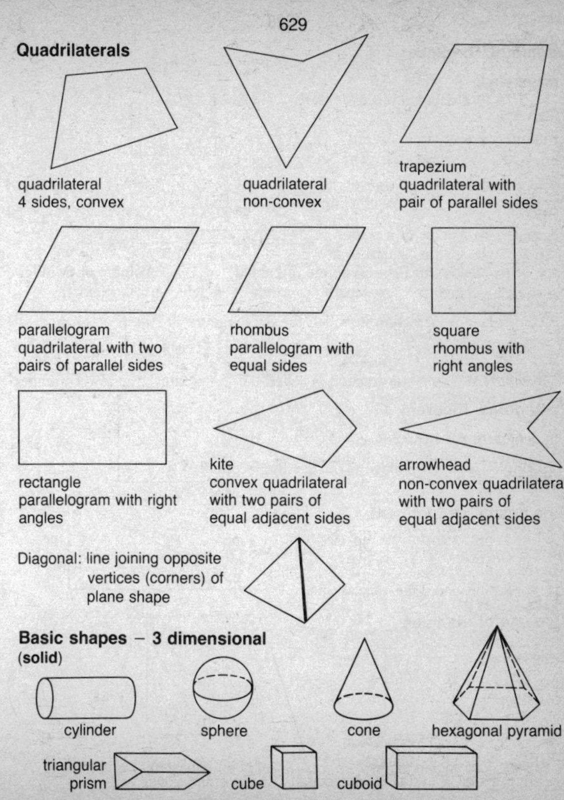
Quadrilaterals
quadrilateral
4 sides, convex
quadrilateral
non-convex
trapezium
quadrilateral with
pair of parallel sides
parallelogram
quadrilateral with two
pairs of parallel sides
rhombus
parallelogram with
equal sides
square
rhombus with
right angles
rectangle
parallelogram with right
angles
kite
convex quadrilateral
with two pairs of
equal adjacent sides
arrowhead
non-convex quadrilateral
with two pairs of
equal adjacent sides
Diagonal: line joining opposite
vertices (corners) of
plane shape
Basic shapes – 3 dimensional
(solid)
cylinder
sphere
cone
hexagonal pyramid
triangular
prism
cube
cuboid

Geometric formulae

Area of circle $= \pi r^2$
$\pi = 3.14$ to 2 decimal places.

Circumference of circle $= \pi d$
$= 2\pi r$

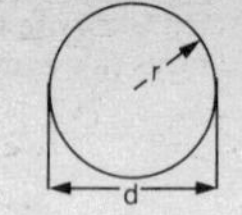

Area of triangle $= \frac{1}{2}$ base $\times$ height

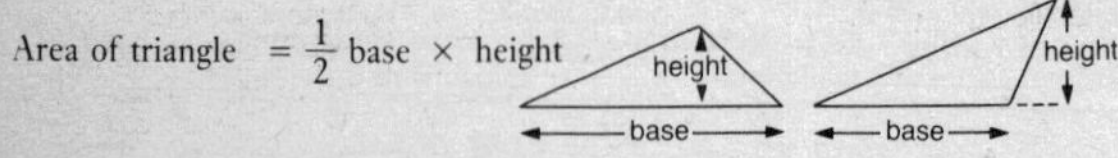

Area of parallelogram
= base × height

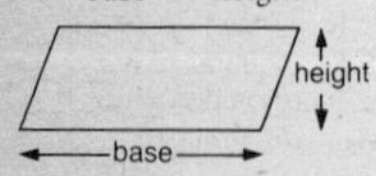

Volume of cuboid
= length × width × height

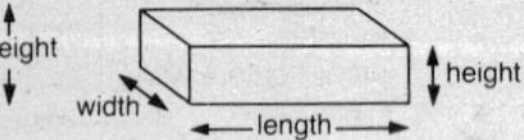

Volume of cylinder
$= \pi r^2 h$

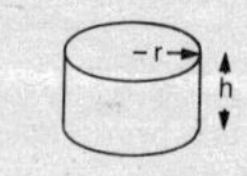

Pythagoras' theorem

The length of the hypotenuse =
the square root of the sum of the squares
of the other two sides

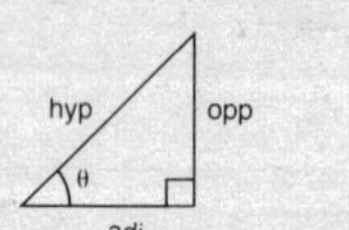

Sine cosine and tangent

$\sin\theta = \frac{opp}{hyp}$ $\cos\theta = \frac{adj}{hyp}$ $\tan\theta = \frac{opp}{adj}$

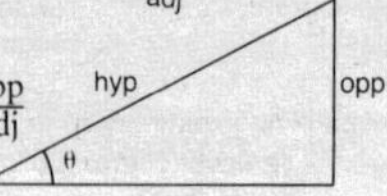

NB: Sin is pronounced the same as sine.

Two useful triangles

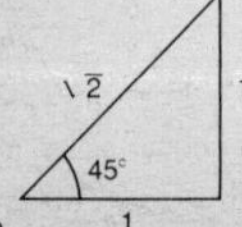

half square
(isosceles right angled triangle)

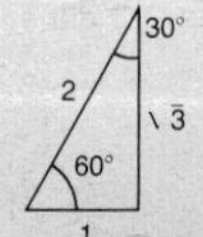

half of an equilateral triangle

so $\sin 45° = \frac{1}{\sqrt{2}}$, $\cos 60° = \frac{1}{2}$

Bearing

The angle measured clockwise from North to an object, stated with three digits (for example 272°, 015°).

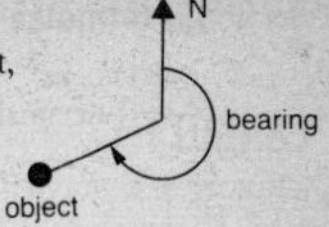

Statistics

A pie chart shows the proportion of a whole group or population.

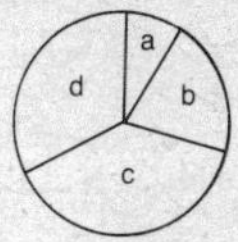

A bar chart shows the actual number of things with different characteristics.

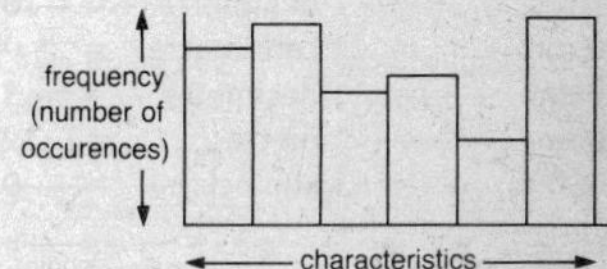

Averages

Series of numbers 1 3 2 3 4 0 8

The arithmetic mean is

$$\frac{\text{total of numbers}}{\text{number of numbers}} = \frac{1 + 3 + 2 + 3 + 4 + 0 + 8}{7} = \frac{21}{7} = 3$$

The mode is the number that appears most frequently.

Number	No. of times it appears
0	1
1	1
2	1
3	2
4	1
8	1

mode = 3

The median is the number that divides the data into equal halves after it has been put into increasing/decreasing order.

0 1 2 3 3 4 8

↑ median = 3

Weights and measures

Length

		1 inch	=	25.4 mm
12 inches	=	1 foot	=	0.305 m
3 feet	=	1 yard	=	0.914 m
1760 yards	=	1 mile	=	1.61 km
		1 millimetre	=	0.039 in
10 mm	=	1 centimetre	=	0.394 in
10 cm	=	1 decimetre	=	3.937 in
10 dm	=	1 metre	=	39.37 in
1000 m	=	1 kilometre	=	0.6214 mile

1 light year = 9.46070×10^{15} metres = 5.87848×10^{12} miles
1 Astronomical Unit = 1.496×10^{11} metres
1 parsec = 3.0857×10^{16} metres = 3.2616 light years

1 digit	=	1.9 cm	=	¾ in
1 hand	=	10 cm	=	4 in
1 palm (length)	=	20 cm approx	=	8 in
(breadth)	=	10 cm approx	=	4 in
1 span	=	23 cm approx	=	9 in
1 cubit	=	46 cm approx	=	18 in
1 pace	=	75 cm approx	=	30 in
1 link	=	20.1 cm	=	7 11/12 in
1 ell	=	1.14 m	=	45 in
1 fathom	=	1.83 m	=	6 ft
1 rod, pole, or perch	=	5.03 m	=	5½ yd
1 chain	=	20.1 m	=	22 yd
1 furlong	=	201 m	=	220 yd
1 league (variable)	=	5 km	=	3 mi

Area

		1 square inch	=	6.452 cm^2
144 sq in	=	1 square foot	=	9.29 dm^2
9 sq ft	=	1 square yard	=	0.836 m^2
4840 sq yd	=	1 acre	=	4046.86 m^2
			=	0.4047 ha
640 acres	=	1 square mile	=	258.99 ha
			=	2.59 km^2
		1 sq centimetre	=	0.155 in^2
100 cm^2	=	1 sq metre	=	1.196 yd^2
100 m^2	=	1 are	=	119.6 yd^2
100 ares	=	1 hectare	=	2.471 acres
100 ha	=	1 sq kilometre	=	0.387 mi^2

Cubic measure

		1 cubic inch	=	16.4 cm^3
1728 cu in	=	1 cubic foot	=	0.283 m^3
27 cu ft	=	1 cubic yard	=	0.765 m^3
		1 cu centimetre	=	0.061 in^3
1000 cu cm	=	1 cu decimetre	=	0.035 ft^3
1000 cu dm	=	1 cu metre	=	1.308 yd^3

Capacity measure

		1 fluid ounce	=	28.4 ml
5 fl oz	=	1 gill	=	0.142 l
4 gill	=	1 pint	=	0.568 l
2 pt	=	1 quart	=	1.136 l
4 qt	=	1 gallon	=	4.546 l
		1 millilitre	=	0.002 pt
10 ml	=	1 centilitre	=	0.018 pt
10 cl	=	1 decilitre	=	0.176 pt
10 dl	=	1 litre	=	1.76 pt
1000 l	=	1 kilolitre	=	220 gall

Weight

		1 grain	=	64.8 mg
		1 dram	=	1.772 g
16 drams	=	1 ounce	=	28.35 g
14 pounds	=	1 stone	=	6.35 kg
2 stones	=	1 quarter	=	12.7 kg
4 quarters	=	1 hundredweight	=	50.8 kg
20 cwt	=	1 (long) ton	=	1.016 tonnes
		1 milligram	=	0.015 grain
10 mg	=	1 centigram	=	0.154 grain
10 cg	=	1 decigram	=	1.543 grains
10 dg	=	1 gram	=	15.43 grains
			=	0.035 oz
1000 g	=	1 kilogram	=	2.205 lb
100 kg	=	1 tonne (metric ton)	=	0.984 (long) ton
1 slug	=	14.5939 kg	=	32.174 lb

Approximate metric/imperial conversions

1 inch ≃ 25 mm
1 foot ≃ 30 cm
8 km ≃ 5 miles
1 metre ≃ 39 inches
100 g ≃ ¼ lb
450g ≃ 1 lb
1 kg ≃ 2.2 lb
50 kg ≃ 1 cwt
1 tonne ≃ 1 ton